ASHEVILLE-BUNCOMBE TECHNICAL INSTITUTE

NORTH CAROLINA
STATE BOARD OF EDUCATION
DEPT. OF COMMUNITY COLLEGES
LIBRARIES

Discarded
Date FEB 1 6 2022

D1307321

ASHEVILLE-BUNCOMBE TECHNICAL INSTITUTE

NORTH CAROLINA
STATE BOARD OF EDUCATION
DEPT. OF COMMUNITY COLLEGES
LIBRARIES

The ENCYCLOPEDIA of EDUCATION

LEE C. DEIGHTON, *editor-in-chief*

VOLUME 9

THE MACMILLAN COMPANY & THE FREE PRESS

Copyright © Crowell-Collier Educational Corporation 1971

All rights reserved. No part of this book
may be reproduced or transmitted in any form
or by any means, electronic or mechanical,
including photocopying, recording, or by any
information storage and retrieval system,
without permission in writing from Crowell-
Collier Educational Corporation.

Library of Congress Catalogue Card Number 70–133143

Manufactured in the United States of America

THE
ENCYCLOPEDIA
OF
EDUCATION

T

(continued)

TEACHER EMPLOYMENT, FINANCIAL ASPECTS

2. COLLECTIVE NEGOTIATIONS

Formal relationships between local teacher groups and boards of education—called either professional negotiations or collective bargaining—became increasingly commonplace in U.S. public education during the 1960's. By 1970 more than half of the nation's nearly 2 million public elementary and secondary school teachers were working under some form of written agreement between a board of education and a teacher organization. More significantly, over 400,000 teachers were covered by more than 900 comprehensive signed contracts with boards which contained salary schedules, grievance procedures, and clauses covering a wide variety of working conditions and professional matters (*Negotiation Research Digest* 1970, 3, no. 5:13–16).

The nation's two predominant teacher organizations—the American Federation of Teachers and the National Education Association—are flourishing. Despite the loss of some teaching and administrative members during the 1960's, the NEA still has great strength in all areas of the country outside the largest cities; more than 1.6 million (80 percent) of the nation's teachers are enrolled either in the NEA itself or in its important state and local affiliates (National Education Association 1969). In 1970 the AFT had over 200,000 members, largely in the major cities of the country—New York, Philadelphia, Detroit, Boston, Cleveland, Chicago, Baltimore, and Washington, D.C.—where the union holds exclusive representation rights (*American Teacher* 1970, no. 1:3).

Despite the nearly universal but frequently unenforceable strike ban for public employees, growing teacher militancy is evident in strike actions, which have increased precipitously as negotiating activities have spread across the country. During the 1967–1968 school year, for instance, there were 114 work stoppages by teachers, which accounted for one-third of the total number of teacher strikes and 80 percent of the man-days of instruction lost through strikes since 1940.

Legal background. In 1960, Wisconsin was the only state which had specific legislation mandating negotiations between local teacher groups and boards of education. By early 1970, 21 states had laws requiring—according to the dictates of the statute—that boards of education or their representatives discuss, negotiate, or "meet and confer," if a teacher organization so requested. In an additional four states, laws relating to interaction between teachers and boards were permissive in that they provided that a board might or might not, at its discretion, recognize and negotiate with an organization representing the district's teachers.

State laws allowing for formal bargaining in the schools differ widely on several crucial questions. One question concerns the composition of the bargaining unit; for instance, are principals and others who have supervisory responsibilities to be included in the same negotiating unit as rank-and-file teachers? Also, definitions of the scope of subjects to be dealt with in negotiations range from "salaries and related economic policies" to "any mutually agreed upon matters." The procedures to be followed in the event of a negotiating impasse also vary among the states. Although combinations of mediation and fact-finding are most common, some states provide for binding arbitration of negotiating disputes which do not involve the expenditure of money.

In 1970 those states with negotiating laws prohibited strikes by public employees, with three important exceptions: Hawaii, Pennsylvania, and Vermont.

Although a state's passage of a statute mandating negotiations tends to stimulate bargaining and the adoption of negotiation agreements, much collective bargaining with teachers occurs on a de facto basis in states which as yet have no relevant legislation.

Teacher militancy. During the 1960's teacher militancy became a new fact of life in public education and resulted in the adoption of increasingly formal bargaining relationships between school boards and teachers. There are, of course, many factors which are responsible for this development.

Most important has been the teachers' desire for more money and benefits. Teachers want more money for themselves and more money for public education generally; the latter cause is frequently shared by boards of education. Teachers have repeatedly seen that collective power exercised through negotiations and militancy generally pays off in the short run, at least, in terms of large salary increases and more community support for education.

The percentage of men in the teaching force, who are frequently committed to a lifetime career, is increasing, and teachers of both sexes are better trained and prepared than ever before. Also, the turnover among public school teachers is decreasing. As a result, the teaching ranks are in a sense becoming more professionalized, and teachers at least appear to desire a larger voice in determining exactly how and under what conditions they will teach.

Teachers in many school systems feel the need for a voice in restructuring what they view as the essentially paternalistic, anachronistic, and bureaucratic web of rules and policies which control their work. As do blue-collar employees in the private sector, many teachers also desire a way of protesting allegedly arbitrary or discriminatory applications of rules and policies.

Legislation granting organizing and bargaining rights to public school teachers is clearly both a cause and effect of teacher militancy. Quite important also has been the intense rivalry in many cities and states between the NEA and the AFT; this conflict was spurred on during the early 1960's by AFL-CIO support of the AFT, one manifestation of the desire of the larger labor movement to organize white-collar workers in general.

Significant, too, in the genesis of the teacher bargaining movement have been the monumental problems of large city school systems; dissatisfaction of teachers in the large cities seems greater than in small-town, rural, or suburban systems. Although there were numerous formal bargaining relationships between boards and teacher organizations scattered across the country prior to 1960, the negotiations movement in the schools clearly received its most profound impetus from the spectacular organizing and negotiating efforts, accompanied by effective displays of collective power, of the United Federation of Teachers in New York City (the largest local of the AFT, AFL-CIO) in the early 1960's. The federation's successes in New York spurred the NEA and its affiliates in many localities to become increasingly concerned with negotiations and "teacher power," and in many instances the association began behaving like a union. This process, once begun, was self-sustaining.

Finally, the mid-twentieth century seems to be "an age of political activism, in which collective action, demonstrations, and thrusts for power are both fashionable and effective (Wynn 1967, p. 4). The new teacher militancy has clearly derived considerable support and nourishment from this broad cultural context.

The money issue. Money has been the primary issue in negotiations with teachers, and salary disputes have been the major cause of strikes, sanctions, and other overt and dramatic manifestations of collective teacher power. In districts which are engaged in formal bargaining and where teachers have threatened to exercise collective power or have in fact gone on strike, teachers have received more money, at least over the short run, on both the salary schedule and in the form of fringe benefits than they would have without formal negotiations (Perry & Wildman 1970; Rehmus & Wilner 1968).

In the average district, the additional money for increased salaries and fringe benefits has come primarily from three sources. In the initial years of bargaining under strike or strike-threat conditions, local communities and, in the case of large cities, state legislatures have often provided the additional amounts necessary to satisfy demands made at the bargaining table and to keep teachers on the job. In some states, negotiations have forced school districts either to liquidate reserves and surpluses or to go into debt to meet the demands of teachers. And in some instances, more money for higher salaries and fringe benefits has simply been taken from other categories of the school budget and reallocated to teacher remuneration. During negotiations teachers may suggest that their salaries, for instance, should have priority over funds allocated for textbooks, building maintenance, adult education, and the hiring of additional teachers.

However, although bargaining in many school districts has been responsible for giving teachers monetary gains considerably in excess of those which would have been forthcoming without bargaining, several factors indicate that the rate of increase in teacher salaries in "hard bargaining" districts may well diminish in the foreseeable future. Other public employees are also organizing, negotiating, and demanding from their city halls or state legislatures their "fair share" of the tax dollar. As a result of this phenomenon and of taxpayer resistance, municipal officials and taxpayers in general may stiffen their opposition to the pressure of teachers and their organizations for ever larger school budgets, which make up a constantly increasing proportion of total state and local expenditures. Moreover, liquidating surpluses or establishing a debt position does not constitute a viable long-run source for continual increase of teacher salaries. And opportunities which may exist in the early years of bargaining for the reallocation of funds within the school budget to increase teacher salaries and fringe benefits tend to diminish rapidly in succeeding negotiations.

Working conditions. Collective negotiations in education have had a significant impact on many of the rules and regulations governing the teacher's daily work life. The length of the school year, although frequently controlled by law, has been reduced to the legal minimum through negotiations in numerous districts. Similarly, in some systems bargaining has resulted in a shortening of the school day; some contracts even specify the precise number of hours a teacher is expected to be in the school and on duty. Gains made in these areas by teacher organizations have been largely at the expense of slack time in the schedule in systems which are well above maximums set by law or above the average for districts in a given area.

In some schools, teachers have successfully bargained for reductions in both the number of classes teachers have per day or per week and the number of preparation periods for which each teacher may be responsible in a given semester or school year. In other instances, negotiations have gained for teachers duty-free lunch periods and additional preparation and planning periods in both elementary and high schools. In some systems in which teachers have gained additional nonteaching time, administrators and teachers have come into conflict over the use of unassigned time or preparation periods.

Teachers have effectively used the power generated by collective bargaining to control or curtail work required outside the regularly scheduled teaching day and have gained extra compensation for overtime and extracurricular activities. After-school meetings may be limited by contract in terms of both duration and frequency; in some contracts time for parent-teacher conferences has been provided within the regular teaching schedule.

The success of negotiating teachers either in gaining extra pay or compensatory free time for extra work loads and extracontractual duties or in ensuring the equalized rotation of such additional chores has forced a tightening of schedule-making procedures in some districts and has had a significant impact on the discretion and flexibility which can be exercised by the local school principal. In many systems, a major accomplishment, from the classroom teacher's point of view, has been the relief gained from not having to perform clerical and nonteaching chores such as milk and book distribution, money collection, scoring standardized tests, register-keeping, and supervision of playgrounds, cafeterias, sidewalks, corridors, or buses.

Assignment and programming, traditionally significant areas for the exercise of discretion by the local school administrator, have received much attention in school bargaining. Frequently, the thrust of teacher efforts has been to ensure administrator objectivity in making assignments by insisting on at least a modified use of the seniority concept or on the rotation of choice positions.

Many boards, however, have insisted on retaining a large degree of discretion and flexibility for those responsible for assignment and programming in recognition of the number of variables involved and the high degree of imprecision necessarily associated with the process.

Boards, increasingly acknowledging the inevitability of bargaining over class size, have, in many cases, found to be groundless their fears that negotiating on such a crucial basic policy issue might result in significant compromises. Many of the class-size clauses appearing in teacher collective agreements simply institutionalize existing practices. Outside the large city school systems, where the impact of class-size clauses can be considerable, the major effect of including class-size provisions in the contract and of making them subject to the grievance procedure has been to force school administrations to make shifts ensuring that district-wide averages become maximums for each teacher. Many teacher contracts now specify that summer school or night school assignments be made according to seniority, rotated among faculty members, or offered first to teachers who have not previously taught summer or night school; some contracts also guarantee that teachers within the system will be offered opportunities for extra teaching assignments before persons outside the system are hired.

The content of a teacher's official file has received much attention in school bargaining because of its implications for personnel decisions within the system and because of the impact it might have on a teacher's efforts to seek a job elsewhere. Many negotiated agreements provide teachers with the right to examine their files upon request and, in some instances, the right to make a formal written rebuttal to any derogatory material therein.

Also of considerable significance are the increasing demands, made by teachers and frequently stoutly resisted by boards, for so-called due-process protections through grievance procedures and arbitration for discipline, dismissal, demotion, or removal from extra-increment positions of both tenure and nontenure teachers. Teachers argue that "just cause," "objective evaluation," and other due-process standards enforceable through grievance and arbitration procedures are necessary to protect them from arbitrary and discriminatory actions by school authorities. Boards argue, however, that the protections already granted under tenure laws and court-enforceable standards of fairness are both considerable and quite sufficient.

Negotiations on working conditions have to an extent substituted centralized, bargaining-table decision-making for decentralized decision-making previously exercised most often by the local school principal. Principals have lost discretion in the process and, in a number of districts, are actually undertaking organization themselves as a means of securing a stronger voice in decision-making if not of checking and reversing the centralizing trend itself. However, although the impact of the negotiated agreement on the local school principal and other administrators is often considerable, school administrations seem to have maintained and protected what they perceive to be a necessary minimum both of discretion and of flexibility.

Policy and professional questions. School boards entering into negotiations often express fear that formal bargaining will deprive the community of control over its schools and destroy opportunities for creative administrative leadership. Moreover, teacher organizations proudly assert that increased control over basic district policy and a strong voice in professional matters are primary goals of the negotiations movement in education.

It is difficult if not impossible to distinguish clearly between issues of educational policy and salaries and working conditions. For instance, the salary schedule and teacher benefits are generally accepted as bargainable, and negotiations in these areas do not intrude unduly on a board's policy prerogatives. However, if raising teachers' salaries as a result of bargaining forces a budget reallocation of sums set aside, for instance, for textbooks or for hiring additional professional personnel, a decision on school district policy is clearly involved. Examples of the difficulty of distinguishing between policy and working conditions can be cited endlessly. Similarly, no satisfactory distinction can be made between policy matters and many so-called professional issues. For instance, basic decisions concerning many aspects of curriculum, methodology, or textbook selection are clearly both policy questions for the board and professional concerns of the teachers.

Although teachers have traditionally, through one medium or another, exercised influence over numerous policy and professional questions and continue to do so, in few cases have negotiations actually forced a significant shift in basic school district policy on an unwilling board, and few boards have been blocked from initiating action or change solely by teacher power. However, collective negotiations in education is a relatively new phenomenon. It must be recognized that the potential clearly exists for power generated by negotiations to bring about significant changes or shifts in the distribution of authority among boards, administrators, and teacher organizations with respect to policy and professional matters.

Although specific substantive issues which might be considered in the policy or professional realm have rarely become the focal point of conflict at the bargaining table, dramatic exceptions exist. In the fall of 1967, for instance, a key teacher demand in New York City (resisted by the board and partially the cause of New York's teacher strike in the fall of 1967) was for the extension to more inner-city schools of the expensive More Effective Schools program. Also, in the fall and early winter of 1968, teachers in New York struck three times in the struggle over decentralization and community control during an escalation of a basic conflict which far transcended the normal negotiating process.

Although bargaining and conflict between boards and teachers over specific clauses and tangible issues involving policy or professional matters may be relatively rare, bargaining is being used to establish procedures and structures for interaction and thus to assure teachers a voice in so-called policy and professional questions outside and independent of the process of negotiations over the collective agreement. For instance, a number of contracts have provided for committees to be established for a wide variety of research, deliberative, and decision-making purposes embracing such subjects as curriculum, methodology, textbook selection, promotion to the principalship, screening and recommendation of candidates for openings at any level in the system (including the superintendency), methods of achieving pupil and teacher integration in the system, and pupil discipline. Sometimes the establishment of committees for such purposes has constituted a dramatic departure from past practice. In other cases, the actual results of the innovative contract clause may be anything but impressive.

One author has predicted that a system of adversary, conflict-oriented bargaining over salaries and a narrowly defined range of working conditions may evolve in the public schools, coupled with a parallel structure modeled on university departmental committees and faculty senates to provide for teacher participation and involvement in professional and policy matters (Griffiths 1966).

The dynamics of school negotiations. Collective bargaining is, at least in some school districts, a power relationship and a process of accommodation essentially through compromise and concession-making on matters over which there is conflict between the teacher organization and the board.

With the advent of bargaining in the schools, teacher organizations have frequently become political institutions which, like unions in private industry, must have something to deliver to their membership. And school boards and administrations often "play the bargaining game," much as management does in private industry. The administration finds it necessary to at least make it appear that the teachers were successful in getting more in negotiations than they would have in the absence of bargaining and collective pressure. The school board allows the teacher organization to have a function at the bargaining table so that organizational leadership will not be threatened, so that teacher-group expectations will be reasonably fulfilled, and so that strikes or serious impasses will be avoided.

The high expectations developed by teachers during organizing campaigns, the desire of the teacher organization to gain everything at once, and the determination of the school board and the administration neither to relinquish their prerogatives too readily nor to create dangerous precedents for the future all seem to cause some hostility and conflict during initial contract bargaining in many school districts.

In the schools, as elsewhere, the realignment of power relationships and organizational structures which accompanies the advent of bargaining brings with it a preoccupation with procedure and a large measure of uncertainty on the part of the management about the roles to be played in the new bargaining process by top administrative personnel and board members. In a majority of bargaining relationships, the superintendent bears the responsibility for conducting the relationship on the board side; increasingly, the superintendent is finding that he must assume responsibility for negotiations if he wishes to maintain the desired degree of control over the administration of his system, even though he may not actually conduct face-to-face bargaining sessions. Also, as bargaining relationships mature, board members seem to find negotiating too time-consuming and are glad to delegate the chore to the district superintendent or to the staff.

Future trends. Collective negotiations in the schools have been compatible with the educational enterprise. The single salary schedule was traditional long before negotiations became commonplace. Before the negotiations movement, there was also a lack of objective, widely acceptable standards by which to judge teacher performance and, thus, an absence of teacher accountability and merit pay differentials. Seniority and other objective standards for the movement and placement of teachers were widely used. All these factors virtually ensured the easy transfer of private-sector collective bargaining principles and practices to the field of public school teaching.

After less than a decade of bargaining in education, its accomplishments were already considerable and its potential to contribute positively to the public educational enterprise seemed great. However, many questions remain to be answered in the future.

The problem of making collective bargaining effective and meaningful in the absence of the compulsions for settlement engendered by the right to strike is wholly unresolved both in the schools and in other areas of public employee bargaining. If teachers and other groups of public employees continue to strike successfully, the states may find it desirable and necessary to centralize decision-making on salaries and other important aspects of the employment relationship. The purposes of such centralization would be, first, to achieve a parity within education among all districts of all sizes within a given state and, second, to achieve a parity among teachers and other employees within the government service. The result would be statewide and perhaps, ultimately, nationwide salary schedules. Such centralization would considerably diminish the role and significance of the present local board of education and local teacher group. More important, however, relatively uniform nationwide or statewide salary schedules could make it difficult or impossible to experiment with innovations which many claim are badly needed in the present pay and employment practices of the schools.

Aside from the question of the inevitability of statewide salary bargaining, it may be asked whether collective bargaining, far from revolutionizing education, may in fact result in an affirmation or freezing of the status quo. There are good reasons to believe that collective bargaining, which tends to look with suspicion on individual advantage because of the internal political dynamics of employee organizations, may make it difficult to depart from or modify significantly the uniform single salary schedule concept—which dictates, for example, that mathematics or science teachers in relatively short supply must be paid the same as, say, social studies teachers in relatively plentiful supply. Similarly, school districts may well discover that a well-entrenched system of collective negotiations makes it difficult to experiment with the systems analysis approach to differentiated staffing, input-output measurement of teacher performance, and differential pay plans based on merit.

The impact of collective bargaining on the decentralization of some of the larger educational bureaucracies in the nation's major cities remains uncertain. It is clear, however, that in many cities decentralization plans that grant significant autonomy to local school districts or to individual schools on subjects previously covered uniformly in citywide contracts will undoubtedly meet powerful resistance from teacher organizations at the bargaining table. It is also possible that, with growing surpluses in the teacher labor market, teacher organizations will resist, through collective negotiations, the adoption of any new automated instructional methodology which may potentially reduce the demand for classroom teachers.

With significant tangible accomplishments already effected as a result of collective negotiations in education, boards, administrators, teachers, and the public all must ensure that bargaining in the schools continues to play a dynamic and adaptable role in helping meet the future public education needs of the United States.

BIBLIOGRAPHY

American Teacher. Published ten times a year by the American Federation of Teachers.
BLUM, ALBERT A., ed. 1969 *Teacher Unions and Associations: A Comparative Study.* Urbana, University of Illinois Press.

CARLTON, PATRICK W., AND HAROLD I. GOODWIN, eds. 1969 *The Collective Dilemma: Negotiations in Education.* Worthington, Ohio, Charles A. Jones.

CORWIN, RONALD G. 1965 "Militant Professionalism, Initiative, and Compliance in Public Education." *Sociology of Education*, 38, no. 4:310–330.

DOHERTY, ROBERT E., AND WALTER E. OBERER 1967 *Teachers, School Boards, and Collective Bargaining: A Changing of the Guard.* Ithaca, New York State School of Industrial and Labor Relations.

Educators Negotiating Service. Published semimonthly by the Educational Service Bureau, Inc.

ELAM, STANLEY M., MYRON LIEBERMAN, AND MICHAEL H. MOSKOW, eds. 1967 *Readings on Collective Negotiations in Public Education.* Chicago, Rand McNally.

Government Employee Relations Report. Published weekly by the Bureau of National Affairs, Inc.

GRIFFITHS, DANIEL E. 1966 "Board-Superintendent-Teacher Relations: Viable Alternatives to the Status Quo." Frank W. Lutz and Joseph J. Azzarelli, eds., *Struggle for Power in Education.* New York, Center for Applied Research in Education. Pages 96–110.

HANSLOWE, KURT L. 1967 *The Emerging Law of Labor Relations in Public Employment.* Ithaca, New York State School of Industrial and Labor Relations.

ISR Journal. Published periodically by the Institute for Staff Relations and Governance at New York University.

LIEBERMAN, MYRON, AND MICHAEL H. MOSKOW 1966 *Collective Negotiations for Teachers: An Approach to School Administration.* Chicago, Rand McNally.

NATIONAL EDUCATION ASSOCIATION 1969 *NEA Handbook for Local, State and National Associations, 1969–1970.* Washington, D.C., The Association.

Negotiation Research Digest. Published ten times a year by the National Education Association, Research Division.

PERRY, CHARLES R., AND WESLEY A. WILDMAN 1970 *The Impact of Negotiations in Public Education: The Evidence From the Schools.* Worthington, Ohio, Charles A. Jones.

REHMUS, CHARLES M., AND EVAN WILNER 1968 *The Economic Results of Teacher Bargaining: Michigan's First Two Years.* Research papers in industrial relations and human resources, no. 6. Detroit, Michigan Institute of Labor and Industrial Relations.

SHILS, EDWARD B., AND C. TAYLOR WHITTIER 1968 *Teachers, Administrators, and Collective Bargaining.* New York, Thomas Y. Crowell.

SOMERS, GERALD G., ed. 1969 "Impasse Resolution, the Community, and Bargaining in the Public Sector." *Proceedings of the Twenty-first Annual Meeting.* Madison, Wis., Industrial Relations Research Association. Pages 31–69.

STINNETT, T. M., JACK H. KLEINMANN, AND MARTHA L. WARE 1968 *Professional Negotiation in Public Education.* New York, Macmillan.

"Symposium: Labor Relations in the Public Sector" 1969 *Michigan Law Review*, 67, no. 5:entire issue.

TAYLOR, GEORGE W. 1966 "The Public Interest in Collective Negotiations in Education." *Phi Delta Kappan*, 48, no. 1:16–32.

WILDMAN, WESLEY A. 1971 "Teachers and Collective Negotiations." Albert A. Blum, ed., *White Collar Workers.* New York, Random House.

WILDMAN, WESLEY A., AND CHARLES R. PERRY 1966 "Group Conflict and School Organization." *Phi Delta Kappan*, 47, no. 1:244–251.

WILDMAN, WESLEY A., ROBERT K. BURNS, AND CHARLES R. PERRY 1969 *Collective Action by Public School*

Teachers: Final Report. 4 vols. Washington, D.C., ERIC Clearinghouse on Teacher Education.

WYNN, D. RICHARD 1967 *Policies of Educational Negotiation: Problems and Issues.* Tri-State Area School Study Council Research Monograph. University of Pittsburgh.

WESLEY A. WILDMAN

3. RETIREMENT PLANS

Retirement systems for teachers are established to attract and retain teachers of high ability, to enhance teacher morale, and to retire with dignity and financial security those teachers whose usefulness has diminished because of age or disability. All 50 states, Puerto Rico, the District of Columbia, and several cities have retirement systems for teachers. However, teachers who belong to a city system usually are not members of a state system, although provisions exist for intrastate reciprocity. Teachers are required to belong to the appropriate system in their state.

In 36 states and Puerto Rico, the state retirement system includes such certified personnel as teachers, principals, administrators, and, in some instances, other school employees such as clerks. In the remaining 14 states, the state retirement system includes other public employees in addition to school employees. City retirement systems are usually limited to certified school personnel.

Financing methods. Retirement benefits are financed from three sources: contributions by the members, contributions by the state or city, and return on investments.

Member contributions. All retirement systems except Delaware's are jointly contributory; that is, teachers and the state contribute to the system. Teachers' contributions are usually a flat percentage of their gross salary, although in a few systems contributions are made on only part of the gross salary. In a few other systems, teachers' contribution rates may vary with age, sex, and date of entry into the retirement plan.

Government contributions. Public financing is of three types: pay-as-you-go (or cash disbursement) plans, partial reserve plans, and fully funded plans. In a pay-as-you-go system, the public's share of the cost is appropriated each year in the amount needed for those living on retirement benefits. In a partial reserve system, public funds are appropriated when a member retires and are sufficient to finance the future benefits due that member. In a fully funded (or reserve) system, public money is appropriated each year in an amount actuarially determined to be sufficient (when added to past and future appropriations and teacher contributions with interest) to accumulate the funds necessary to pay the future benefits due each member.

Investments.   Over $15 billion is invested by retirement systems for teachers; this makes retirement big business. Since the late 1950's, particularly, there has been a trend toward liberalizing investment provisions in retirement laws. Formerly, many systems were limited to investment in government bonds and prohibited from investing in equities. Today, some systems are limited to investments specifically set out in the law; others are permitted to invest a certain percentage of funds in common stock.

Investments and the return on investments are extremely important for retirement systems. Thus, fully funded plans are recommended because they have more funds available for investment. The more funds there are to invest during the teacher's active career, the greater the returns. Obviously, a substantial investment return can be used to increase benefits and keep down costs financed from the other sources. A high return on investments, however, cannot be the primary goal of investment policy of a retirement system. Since the purpose of a system is to provide benefits for its members far into the future, retirement systems must make prudent, long-term, low-risk investments. Most systems employ investment counselors to advise boards of trustees on investments. However, with few exceptions, it is the responsibility of the boards to set investment policy and to approve investments within the requirements set out in the retirement law.

Benefits.   There are three types of benefits usually paid by retirement systems: service retirement allowances, disability retirement allowances, and death and survivor benefits. Most systems permit a retiring member to select one of several options for the payment of his retirement allowance; for example, he may wish to provide survivor benefits for his dependents.

Service retirement allowances.   Service retirement allowance provisions state that when a member has reached a specified age or has served a specified number of years, or has met whatever qualifications for retirement are set out in the law, he shall be eligible for an allowance based on both his own accumulated contributions and

on state or city appropriations. Most systems have provisions for early retirement with the benefit actuarially reduced. In a fully funded system, the funds in the system are sufficient to pay his benefit when he meets retirement qualifications.

The allowance may be of the money-purchase type or the fixed-benefit type. A money-purchase benefit is calculated to be that allowance equal to the actuarial equivalent of the member's accumulated contributions plus the appropriations on his behalf from public funds. Under a money-doubled plan the accumulated contributions of the member are matched by an equal amount from public funds.

The fixed-benefit type is an allowance calculated by a formula involving a percentage of the final average salary multiplied by the number of years of service. Final average salary is usually defined as the average salary paid in the last five or ten years before retirement or the average of the highest salaries paid in any five years while the teacher was a member of the system.

Most systems now use some type of fixed-benefit formula because an adequate fixed-benefit formula tends to provide greater benefits for teachers than a money-purchase formula. Since the fixed benefit is based on final average salary, the allowance will likely be related to the highest salary paid during a teacher's career. The benefits under a money-purchase plan, however, are based on contributions made over the span of the teacher's career; obviously, the earlier contributions will be less since the salary was lower. Nevertheless, since both formulas are tied to salary, low salaries for teachers will result in correspondingly low benefits. Adequate salaries are required in order to produce adequate retirement benefits.

Disability retirement allowances.   Disability retirement allowances usually apply to permanent disability only, since other plans provide coverage for temporary disability. Disability retirement is available to those people who have been members of retirement systems for a specified period of time, usually five or ten years.

Usually a medical board must certify that the member is no longer physically or mentally capable of continuing in public school teaching; after retirement on disability, periodic physical examinations are generally required. Frequently the law provides that a person retired on disability may not earn more in future employment than the difference between the retirement allowance and the salary earned prior to retirement.

Disability benefits may be of the money-purchase type or the fixed-benefit type. Under a money-doubled benefit, the contributions accumulated up to the time the member becomes disabled are matched by the state or city, and the allowance calculated on this total will be the actuarial equivalent of that amount, payable in equal sums for the life of the retiring member. In plans providing a fixed benefit for service retirement, disability benefits are usually a specified percentage of the allowance which would have been payable had the member continued in service until he met the qualifications for service retirement. For many years, an adequate retirement benefit for a career teacher was considered to be about 50 percent of the final average salary. Although most knowledgeable persons in the field would now recommend 75 to 80 percent as an adequate retirement benefit, few retirement systems presently provide this amount, and a few do not even provide 50 percent.

Death and survivor benefits. If a member dies before retirement, his contributions, usually including interest, are paid to his estate or to a named beneficiary. No part of the public appropriation on his behalf is paid to his estate or his beneficiary. However, death benefits are paid by many systems. These benefits are in addition to or in lieu of the refund of the member's own contributions with interest and may be paid in a lump sum or in monthly disbursements to named beneficiaries or to unnamed dependent children and his widow.

Postretirement increases. Like all people living on a fixed income during periods of inflation, retired teachers find that their allowances do not purchase today what they once did. As a result, several legislatures each year have found it necessary to increase the benefits of those already retired. These increases take several forms, including across-the-board payments of a flat amount, percentage increases, increases in minimum benefits, and increases to those who retired prior to a certain date. Often these increases are related to increases in the cost of living.

Such increases are stopgaps at best and force groups of active and retired teachers to request legislative increases every few years. In addition,

if the legislation is not properly drawn, it may face challenges as an unconstitutional payment of public funds for past services. Several methods have been used to avoid this kind of challenge; for example, retired teachers in one state agreed to be available for substitute-teaching duty in return for increases in retirement benefits. In another state, retired teachers contributed additional amounts to the system, thus creating a new contract on which to base increases.

To avoid these problems, a few systems have provided a program for automatic increases. A variable annuity plan was begun in 1958 by the Wisconsin Teachers Retirement System, one of the first teacher systems to establish such a plan. Most variable annuity plans provide that a member may elect to have part of his funds invested in common stock; thus, at retirement he will have accumulations in both the fixed and variable portions of the system. The fixed portion provides a set annuity based on the formula. The variable portion is evaluated annually and the annuity is increased or decreased for the succeeding fiscal year. Three factors determine the amount of increase or decrease: interest and dividend income, capital gain or loss based on the market value of securities, and mortality experience among annuitants. Usually, common stocks increase in value during periods when the cost of living increases. Therefore, the purpose of a variable annuity plan based upon common stock investments is to provide increases in retirement benefits during such periods, thus lessening the need to seek increases in retirement benefits from the legislature. And the retirant will know he can rely on the fixed portion of his benefit, although the variable portion may fluctuate.

In addition to Wisconsin, the retirement systems of Minnesota, Oregon, New York City, and Milwaukee have variable annuity plans. In the past few years, more systems have adopted automatic increase plans related to the Consumer Price Index than have adopted variable plans.

The Public School Teachers' Pension and Retirement Fund of Chicago attacked the problem in another way. Members contribute 0.5 percent of their salary annually in addition to their regular contribution rates. The retirement allowance is then automatically increased 1.5 percent each year beginning at either the anniversary date of the allowance or at age 60, whichever is earlier.

Also, the Maine State Retirement System provides cost-of-living increases in allowances for retired people at the same percentage received by active employees in general salary adjustments. Teacher retirement systems with automatic increase plans are still a small minority. Therefore, providing retirement benefits that remain adequate after a few years is still a major problem.

Teacher mobility. Perhaps teachers face no problem so great (except for inadequate benefits) as that of loss of benefits when they move from one state to another during the course of their careers. It was once thought that the problem could be solved by reciprocity; that is, either the teacher's present retirement system would transfer funds accumulated on his behalf to his new system, or the new system would assume the liabilities for services rendered in another state. Reciprocity was to be accomplished by having all systems agree to use one of these methods and to adopt similar provisions. However, experience has shown that neither of these methods has worked. In addition to the expense involved (which would be great in those states to which migration of teachers is large), many states view the retirement system as a device to attract and retain good teachers and therefore are reluctant to adopt a system of reciprocity, which enables teachers to move from state to state.

As a result, two other methods have been used to solve the problem. One method provides some kind of credit for out-of-state teaching service. Of course, those states which must recruit a large number of out-of-state teachers are most likely to provide such credit. Even these states, however, place limits on the amount of out-of-state credit available, primarily because of the cost factor.

At the present time, vested and deferred benefits present the most feasible solution. Under this method, benefits vest after a certain number of years of service, although payment is deferred until normal retirement age. A teacher who moves from the system in which his benefits have vested to teach in another state does not withdraw his contributions; instead, at retirement, he receives a benefit not only from the system of which he is a member at retirement but also from any system in which his benefits have vested for earlier years of service. This method will work only if all systems provide early vesting and if teachers do not withdraw their contributions when they move. Despite the fact that the National Education

Association and its National Council on Teacher Retirement have long urged vesting after five years of service or less, few states have complied. The most common period for vesting is after ten or 15 years of service, with some systems making no provision at all. The pressure to solve this problem increases as the mobility of teachers increases. In response to this pressure, legislation has been introduced in Congress. If such legislation is enacted, both federal and state funds would be available to provide retirement benefits for mobile teachers.

Social Security coverage. Until 1950 teachers were not eligible for coverage by the federal Social Security Act of 1935. Today about two-thirds of the teachers in the United States are covered by Social Security as well as by a retirement system. The Social Security Act provided that teachers and other public employees who were members of retirement systems could vote to determine whether they would be covered by Social Security. If a majority of members of a public retirement system voted for coverage, all present and future members of the system would then be covered. In certain states named in the federal law, those voting for coverage were covered, those against were not; all future members would be covered, regardless of how the majority voted.

In some states, Social Security coverage was adopted in addition to the existing retirement plan—this is called full supplementation. In other states the existing retirement plan was amended at the time Social Security coverage was adopted; however, both plans are operated separately. There are many variations in the ways Social Security coverage is coordinated with retirement systems.

BIBLIOGRAPHY

ADVISORY COMMISSION ON INTERGOVERNMENTAL RELATIONS 1963 *Transferability of Public Employee Retirement Credits Among Units of Government.* Washington, D.C., Government Printing Office.

KLEINMANN, JACK H. 1962 "Retirement." *Fringe Benefits for Public School Personnel: A Comparative Study of Principles and Practices in Education, Government, and Private Employment.* New York, Teachers College Press. Pages 87–120.

KRAFT, LEONARD E. 1966 "Teachers Must Leave Retirement Benefits Behind." National Education Association, *Journal,* 55, no. 2:50.

LILLYWHITE, RAY L., AND MARTHA L. WARE 1966 "Retirement Benefits and Teacher Mobility." National Education Association, *Journal,* 55, no. 4:15–16.

NATIONAL EDUCATION ASSOCIATION. OFFICE OF TEACHER RETIREMENT 1969 *Teacher Retirement System Summaries.*

Washington, D.C., National Council on Teacher Retirement.

NOLTE, M. CHESTER, AND JOHN P. LINN 1963 "Tenure and Retirement of Teachers." *School Law for Teachers.* Danville, Ill., Interstate. Pages 111–136.

Proceedings of the National Education Association, National Council on Teacher Retirement. Washington, D.C., The Association. Published annually.

REMMLEIN, MADALINE K., AND MARTHA L. WARE, eds. 1970 "Retirement and Social Security Benefits." *School Law.* 3rd ed. Danville, Ill., Interstate. Pages 177–201.

The Yearbook of School Law. Danville, Ill., Interstate. Published annually.

MARTHA L. WARE

TEACHER EMPLOYMENT, LEGAL ASPECTS

1. NEGOTIATIONS	Reynolds C. Seitz
2. EMPLOYMENT IN SCHOOLS	Frieda S. Shapiro
3. EMPLOYMENT PROCESS	Martha L. Ware
4. SEPARATION AND DEMOTION	James Everette DeVaughn

1. NEGOTIATIONS

Since the passage in 1935 of the Wagner Act, which created the National Labor Relations Board (NLRB), millions of workers in the private sector of employment have been given the right to organize and to bargain or negotiate collectively with their employers regarding wages, hours, and other terms and conditions of employment. Today this right is widely exercised in the field of private employment. The opportunity for public employees to negotiate with their employers was not frequently demanded until after World War II, when public employees, including teachers, began to press for the right. Year by year the pressure has been increasing greatly for the right to join organizations, including unions, and through such organizations to negotiate on wages, hours, and other conditions of employment.

Realistically, the hurdle erected at one time by some courts and legislative bodies to prevent public employees from joining employee organizations no longer exists. Today it seems certain that the First Amendment, through its protection of freedom to assemble, ensures the right to join an employee organization.

A logical approach to a discussion of the legal aspects of teacher negotiations requires an understanding of the term "negotiations." If the term carried only a connotation that teachers, through their representatives, could present certain requests to a school board or its representatives and both sets of representatives could discuss these requests as completely and for as long a time as the school board permitted, then there would be no need for this article. The law cannot prohibit any individual or group from making a request of an employer, even if the employer is a public employer. The law cannot keep the public employer from discussing the matter presented if he elects to do so. There is nothing new about representatives of teachers and school boards carrying on talks prompted by requests from teachers. Indeed, in certain school districts this has been going on ever since the formation of the district.

However, if the term "negotiations" signifies a procedure which takes away from a school board the sole discretion as to whether to discuss with teachers their requests and how much time to make available for such talks and imposes upon the board certain responsibilities by way of responses, it is necessary to determine the legality of such imposition. Certainly, if the imposed procedure deprives the school board of the ultimate authority to fix conditions of work, it can validly be argued that there is an illegal infringement upon the legislative power of the school board.

Good faith bargaining. Negotiations are imposed upon school boards by statutes. A number of state statutes of this type have appeared since the late 1950's. Instead of using the word "negotiations," these statutes have used such expressions as "collective bargaining," "professional negotiations," and "professional bargaining." However, if a statute clearly intends to require that a certain fundamental technique be used by the parties at any negotiating session, the phrase "good faith" will usually precede the phrase "negotiation," "professional bargaining," "collective bargaining," or "professional negotiations." The statute will require the parties to negotiate in good faith, and it is this phrase which carries the legal connotation of the actual negotiating technique required. If the phrase "good faith" is omitted, there is no sure enunciation of rules of procedure. If the good faith directive is included, the legislature has shown an intent that negotiating procedure conform to the dictates of many NLRB, federal court, and U.S. Supreme Court decisions which define good faith in collective bargaining or negotiations.

Although the decisions interpret the National Labor Relations Act as it applies in industry, there is no logical reason why the concept of the technique of good faith negotiations in the public employee field should be interpreted any differently. At least it seems certain that no state court will require any more by way of negotiations than do the NLRB and the federal courts.

The concept of what is dictated by the requirement of good faith is not changed because the phrase, instead of being followed by the mere word "negotiations," is followed by such terms as "collective bargaining," "professional negotiations," or "professional bargaining." All the terms are synonymous as far as suggesting a procedure; it is the expression "good faith" which dictates the technique to be used.

In order to evaluate the position that courts have taken in respect to the allegation that a statute requiring good faith negotiations is invalid since it constitutes an infringement on the legislative power of the school board, it is important to appreciate the techniques which the courts have said are dictated by the concept of negotiations in good faith (Seitz 1969; 1966a; 1966b; 1964).

It was decided early that good faith negotiating does not permit the employer to come to the bargaining table and assume the position that he will listen attentively to all proposals and if he hears anything to which he can agree, he will so indicate. A party cannot enter negotiations with the announcement, "We don't want to waste time, so we will tell you in advance that we will never sign any contract which does not contain the terms which we will now name." For example, a school board could not open with such a proposal attached to a condition that the contract must contain a clause giving sole control over class load and size to the board. The technique is not good faith bargaining, since it constitutes a take-it-or-leave-it approach. Such an approach indicates to the other party that it cannot have any agreement unless it consents to the inclusion of a significant term in the contract about which the proposer will not bargain.

Change the facts somewhat. Assume that a teacher representative has demanded a binding arbitration clause in connection with grievance settlement procedure. Assume the representative of the school board agrees but replies, "We will tell you now that we will reserve sole control over class load and size." This, unlike the previous example, does not violate good faith negotiations, since it does not constitute a take-it-or-leave-it approach. It is simply a counterproposal, a response to an employee demand for an arbitration clause. Firmness on one or more issues when the whole record reveals no intent to dodge the obligation to bargain in good faith is no violation of the requirement—the employer does not have to make concessions to every demand. This is specifically stated in some statutes, but logic leads to the same conclusion.

Although a proposal in the form of some concession is not required as an answer to every demand, the other party must declare what it is or is not willing to do and offer supporting reasons. There may be danger, however, if a party makes all of its counterproposals final too early in negotiations. This may be the import of the General Electric case decided by the NLRB in 1964 (150 NLRB No. 36) and reviewed by the second circuit in 1969 (418 F. 2d 736).

There is no doubt at all that an employer can in due course, after good faith bargaining, put forth his final offer.

An important question is whether a board or a court can find absence of good faith if the agreement which the employer is willing to sign reveals that the employer has failed to concede anything substantial. When such facts exist, the board has found bad faith, in spite of the National Labor Relations Act, which specifically states, in Section 8(c), that the "obligation (to bargain collectively) does not compel either party to agree to a proposal or require the making of a concession." The board could not believe that good faith bargaining would not by its very nature produce some concession of substance. The Federal Court of Appeals for the Fifth Circuit overruled the board (*White* v. *NLRB*, 225 F. 2d 564). It stressed that the employer had not refused to bargain, that it had explained its position and given reasons therefor. The court felt that it could not undertake to determine good faith under a standard as to whether it thought the terms of a labor agreement were wise. However, the court did not hold that under no possible circumstances could the mere content of various proposals and counterproposals be sufficient evidence of a want of good faith. The court stressed: "We can conceive of one party to such bargaining procedure suggesting proposals of such a nature or type or couched in such objectionable language that they would be calculated to disrupt any serious negotiations."

Since the board and the courts are not bound by the decision in areas other than the fifth circuit, the way is open in some jurisdictions for a determination that since the employer failed to concede anything substantial, there is evidence of bad faith. However, it is certain that the board and the courts are not going to find lack of good faith just because they feel that the terms of a contract were not wise.

Good faith bargaining does not require fruitless marathon sessions—it recognizes that there will come a point when the parties arrive at an impasse. If an impasse does develop, certain acts, such as unilateral action on the part of an employer, can violate the dictate of good faith negotiation. If an employer grants benefits that have never been discussed at the bargaining table, he violates the good faith requirement. However, the Court of Appeals for the Fifth Circuit differed with the NLRB and found no violation if after an impasse the employer granted something which had been discussed during negotiations and which the employer had indicated he would grant (*NLRB v. Intracoastal Terminal, Inc.*, 286 F. 2d 954).

The unilateral granting of a benefit before an impasse in respect to a topic being discussed at the negotiating table is a circumvention of the duty to bargain and is held to be as bad as a flat refusal (*NLRB v. Katz*, 369 U.S. 736).

Problems can arise as to what bargaining is required during the term of a contract if one is negotiated. Industry has solved this by introducing a zipper clause into the contract. This type of clause states that the parties have bargained with respect to every aspect of rates of pay, hours of employment, and other conditions of employment; that the total results of their bargaining are embodied in the contract; and that omission of any reference to any aspect of these subjects is intended to be a waiver of the right to bargain with respect to it during the term of the contract.

Good faith bargaining demands a realistic interchange of reasons, information, and data. Parties are not expected to bargain in the dark.

Subject matter. No discussion of the philosophy of good faith collective negotiations can avoid dealing with the matter of what subjects must be bargained about. The U.S. Supreme Court has handed down a decision in this matter

(*NLRB v. Wooster Division of Borg-Warner Corp.*, 356 U.S. 342). The Court divided the subjects into those which are illegal and cannot be bargained about, those which are mandatory and must be bargained about, and those which are voluntary and can be bargained about. The Court was construing the phrase in the National Labor Relations Act which requires bargaining on wages, hours, and other terms and conditions of employment.

The concept that some subject matter is illegal is very important in the area of public employment. This idea recognizes that bargaining often collides with existing statutes and cannot disregard such statutes.

In industry the trend of court decisions has been to constantly expand the area of mandatory negotiations. However, it is still recognized that there are some fundamental management rights which need not be negotiated. Justice Potter Stewart, in his concurring opinion in the decision in which the Supreme Court best explained why it supports the legality of collective bargaining (*Fibreboard Paper Products Corp.* v. *NLRB*, 379 U.S. 203), took special pains to set forth some examples. One illustration is the right to determine the scope of the enterprise. Stewart admitted that decisions in this field would have some relationship to conditions of employment, but he asserted that they lie at the "core of entrepreneurial control" and, therefore, the employer does not have to bargain about them.

Similar decisions will be made in the field of public employer-employee bargaining. Many state courts will probably follow the trend of the federal courts in working with fact situations in the industrial field and bringing more and more subjects within the area of mandatory negotiations. The struggle will be in the area of the right of teachers to bargain for a role in the employment, promotion, and transfer process. Another field for debate will be the right to bargain about choice of textbooks, curriculum, and other aspects of the instructional program. Since teachers are trained professionals, it is entirely probable that administrative boards and courts can be influenced to feel that decisions relative to the instructional program should be treated as falling within a concept such as conditions of employment. Indeed, a similar argument may succeed in respect to permitting teachers to bargain for a role in connection with hiring and promotion.

Since the question of board right is likely to be somewhat uncertain, it is predictable that some states will specify the right by statute in a more precise way than the mere use of the general direction that negotiations are to concern the issues of wages, hours, and other terms and conditions of employment.

Such matters as class loads, breaks, discipline of students, extracurricular duties, and rest room facilities fall within the concept of conditions of employment and are mandatory subjects of negotiations.

The contour which has been given to the meaning of the term "collective negotiations" in the preceding paragraphs has induced many state courts and is certain to induce more such judicial bodies to conclude that the requirement does not force a public employer to capitulate. A technique has been delineated, but a school board is not forced to give in to demands. Therefore, many state courts have found that the school board has not improperly delegated its legislative power. Other state courts are certain to adopt this philosophy. Presently, however, this is not the universal trend. Some courts still continue to talk of the requirement of collective bargaining as illegal by reason of causing a public employer to surrender its legislative power. As recently as 1967, a dictum by the chief justice of the Wisconsin supreme court indicated adherence to such philosophy (*Joint School District No. 8, City of Madison* v. *Wisconsin Employment Relations Board,* 154 N.W. 2d 78). The attitude seems wrong, since collective negotiations does not impose capitulation upon the public employer.

The U.S. Supreme Court has made clear that even though the requirement of collective negotiations does not force capitulation to demands, it has a very significant value. The Court recognized that there is no certainty that agreement will come out of collective negotiations but stated that agreement is likely to be the result, with ensuing harmony in employment relations (*Fibreboard Paper Products Corp.* v. *NLRB,* 379 U.S. 203).

The statute which gives public employees the right to join organizations and engage in collective negotiations with their employers will frequently contain provisions of the following type: the setting up of an administrative board to determine appropriate units and to supervise elections by secret ballot to ascertain what organization represents the teachers; the dictate that bargaining be on an exclusive basis with the representative elected; the order that when agreement is reached, it should be reduced to written contract form; the directive that if an impasse is reached in negotiations, a mediator should be called in to try to settle the dispute, and if he fails, a fact finder will be appointed who will be empowered to make recommendations; and the permission that disputes concerning the interpretation of a negotiated contract can be settled by binding arbitration.

The statute can specifically make it an unfair practice to interfere with the rights of public employees to organize. It can also specifically label as unfair a refusal of either party to negotiate in good faith and, if necessary, can impose certain penalties.

Many administrative boards and courts have had no difficulty in finding all such provisions valid. Provisions for bargaining on an exclusive basis are protected against the charge that public employees must be given the constitutional right to present their position to their employer by the provision in the statute that any individual employee or minority group shall have the right to present grievances to the employer. This gives the employer an opportunity to evaluate the position of the individual or the minority but does not require bargaining.

The provision for binding arbitration has been validated by a number of courts. In answer to the charge that the board has surrendered its legislative power, the courts distinguish between arbitration designed to interpret a dispute arising under a negotiated contract and arbitration that might attempt to empower an outsider to write the terms of a contract if an impasse in negotiations arises. The courts see in the agreement to settle a dispute arising under a contract something which should be encouraged as less expensive than a suit in court and as a technique calculated to mitigate the temptation to stop work by way of protest.

The whole area of collective negotiations in public employment is so new that it is still possible to find jurisdictions that erect hurdles by finding many of the statutory provisions set forth above illegal. As time goes on, it seems reasonable to predict that more and more of the hurdles will disappear. Indeed, if the states continue to erect the hurdles, it seems quite possible that the federal government could, under the doctrine of a recent U.S. Supreme Court holding (*Maryland* v. *Wirtz,* 88 S. Ct. 2017), step in and regulate.

Absence of statutes. Brief comment is required on the status of the right of teachers to negotiate if no state statute gives them protection. Although more and more statutes are coming into being, the majority of states still have not passed such legislation. If there is no statute, the trend is that the states will find no illegality if the parties voluntarily decide to bargain and eventually negotiate a contract. It should be remembered, however, that if a statute does not decree good faith collective negotiations, no technique is outlined, and the employer is not obligated to follow the rules.

The trend is to give a statutory right to engage in good faith collective bargaining. There is nothing inherent in the technique of good faith collective negotiations which militates against producing a climate that will ensure better education for children. Good faith negotiations require not merely formal but real recognition by both parties that bargaining is a shared process in which each party has a right to play an active role. Each party balances what is desired against known costs of unresolved disagreement. These costs on the one side may be such things as loss of competent employees and the fostering of a general low morale and on the other side the loss of community support if unreasonable demands are made.

The U.S. Supreme Court feels the chances are good that issues will be reasonably resolved. It is this philosophy which is inducing more and more state courts to uphold the validity of teacher collective negotiations.

BIBLIOGRAPHY

SEITZ, REYNOLDS C. 1964 "Rights of Public School Teachers to Engage in Collective Bargaining and Other Concerted Activities." L. O. Garber, ed., *1963 Yearbook of School Law.* Danville, Ill., Interstate. Pages 204–222.

SEITZ, REYNOLDS C. 1966a "Legal Aspects of Public School Teacher Negotiating and Participating in Concerted Activities." *Marquette Law Review,* 49, no. 3:487–511.

SEITZ, REYNOLDS C. 1966b "Public Employee Negotiating and School Board Authority." Arthur A. Rezny, ed., *Legal Problems of School Boards.* Cincinnati, Anderson. Pages 113–150.

SEITZ, REYNOLDS C. 1969 "School Board Authority and the Right of Public School Teachers to Negotiate—A Legal Analysis." *Vanderbilt Law Review,* 22:239 ff.

REYNOLDS C. SEITZ

2. EMPLOYMENT IN SCHOOLS

How much teachers are to be paid, how their salaries are to be structured, and under what conditions they are to work are determined by the employing school boards, subject to constitutional and statutory provisions. However, in school systems throughout the United States the traditional pattern of unilateral decision-making by school boards in these matters has given way in recent years to the collective negotiation process that has dramatically altered the employment relations between school boards and teachers.

Agreements reached on salaries, fringe benefits, and conditions of work as a result of collective negotiation between school boards and the representatives of recognized teacher organizations include many issues not specifically covered by statutes. Collective negotiation also has created machinery for the settlement of grievances and has given teachers a voice in the formulation of educational policy, developments that are bound to affect future court decisions.

Salaries. While local school boards are empowered to determine the salaries of teachers and administrators, their general authority may be limited by one or more of several types of statutes. Among these are laws in some states that require the school boards to adopt salary schedules but do not otherwise impose salary levels. In about 30 states local school boards must observe statutory minimum-salary requirements in establishing salaries for classroom teachers and other professional personnel whose positions are covered under the minimum-salary laws (National Education Association . . . 1968). The purpose of these laws is to improve salary standards by setting a floor below which school boards may not go in paying teachers, but these laws in no way prohibit the payment of higher salaries than those prescribed legislatively. Although compliance with the law is mandatory in most minimum-salary states, a few states give local school boards the option of conforming to the statutory salary requirements or forgoing state aid.

Although state minimum-salary laws vary greatly, the structure of minimum-salary requirements can take one of three forms. Most states have a mandated minimum-salary schedule that recognizes both preparation and experience, but a few provide a single minimum salary for all teachers or two or more flat minimum amounts based on educational preparation only.

Other strictures governing school boards include specific statutes in a number of states prohibiting unequal pay for men and women teachers of like training, experience, and position and barring discrimination on the basis of sex, marital status, race, or religion. There are also provisions in state teacher-tenure laws that prevent reduction in salary of a teacher below the level of the preceding year unless the reduction is part of a uniform plan affecting the entire school district. In Kentucky, where this provision exists, the court ruled in 1953 that a reduction in the salaries of all principals but not of other professional staff members was invalid (*Greenup County Board of Education* v. *Harper*, 256 S.W. 2d 37).

National studies of teacher compensation show that teachers' salaries vary according to academic preparation, experience, position, extra duties, supervisory responsibilities, and other relevant criteria. On many occasions over the years teachers have challenged the salary actions of school boards through lawsuits. The challenges have included questions with respect to different rates of pay for various positions, grades, or classes of professional school employees, increases or reductions in salary, and withholding of increments in salary.

Generally, courts will not interfere with the discretionary authority of school boards to determine salaries of teachers unless this discretion has been abused by arbitrary, discriminatory, or unreasonable action or unless a statute or a constitutional provision has been violated.

In judging the validity or legality of a school-board salary determination, the court asks whether the decision is "reasonable." Where reasonableness has been demonstrated, school-board salary policy has been sustained. For example, courts have upheld differential salary schedules for high school teachers as properly based on higher educational requirements (*Schoening* v. *Board of Education of City of New York*, 8 Misc. 2d 1957, 169 N.Y.S. 2d 711: [1957] affirmed 7 A.D. 2d 1015, 185 N.Y.S. 2d 232); salary increases for teachers who elected to comply with a salary schedule provision and earned additional educational credits (and salary reductions for those who did not), on the grounds that completing a course of study in one summer out of four has a reasonable relationship to the teacher's ability to discharge his professional duties (*Rible* v. *Hughes*, 24 Cal. App. 2d 437, 150 P. 2d 455 [1944]); the withholding of a salary increment from a teacher with a master's degree and life certificate for failure to comply with a local school board's professional growth requirement (*Richards* v. *Board of Education of Township*

High School District N. 201, 21 Ill. 2d 104, 171 N.E. 2d 37 [1960]); and the denial of salary increments for unfavorable performance (*Kopera* v. *Board of Education of Town of West Orange, Essex County*, 60 N.J. Super. 288, 158 A. 2d 842 [1960]). On the other hand, although it was recognized by the school board, a union security clause that required union membership by teachers as a condition for receiving salary increases was held to be illegal and void as to tenure teachers, on the ground that the school board had no authority or power to discriminate between the salaries of union and nonunion teachers (*Benson* v. *School District No. 1 of Silver Bow County*, 136 Mont. 77, 344 P. 2d 117 [1959]).

Although salary distinctions could rest on personal characteristics besides training, experience, and competency, the law is clear that salary differences based solely on race are prohibited under the Fourteenth Amendment of the Constitution (*Alston* v. *School District of Norfolk*, 112 F. 2d 992 [4th Cir. 1940]; cert. denied, 311 U.S. 693 [1940]). Differences in teachers' pay based on sex have not as yet been adjudicated as a federal constitutional question. However, the legality of a school board practice of paying men teachers more than women teachers was challenged under a statute requiring equal pay for equal work. In this instance, the court upheld a higher salary for a male teacher by distinguishing between the duties of a female supervisor of arithmetic and those of a male supervisor of manual training (*Murphy* v. *School Committee of Lawrence*, 321 Mass. 478, 73 N.E. 2d 835 [1947]). But another court under a similar equal pay statute required a school board to pay the same salary to men and women teachers of physical education, reasoning that there was no difference in their work other than that the men taught boys and the women taught girls (*Chambers* v. *Davis et al.*, 131 Cal. App. 500, 22 P. 2d 27 [1933]).

Extracurricular duties. Teachers often render services outside regular classroom instruction and after the close of the regular school day. These services range from supervising student newspapers and acting as advisers to student clubs to coaching school plays and intramural and interscholastic athletic teams. May a school board require a teacher to perform these extra duties? Must the duties be specified in the employment contract, and is the teacher entitled to extra pay?

Judicial precedents uphold the right of a

school board to assign extra duties without extra pay to teachers where the extra duties are related to the school program, even when the employment contract is silent on the performance of nonteaching duties. However, the extra assignment must be reasonable. For some courts this means that the activities must be educationally justifiable, professional, related to the teacher's interests and capabilities, in the area of instruction in which the teacher is licensed or employed, not a burden in time and amount, and equitably distributed among the teaching staff (*Parrish* v. *Moss*, 200 Misc. 375, 106 N.Y.S. 2d 577; affirmed, 279 A.D. 608, 107 N.Y.S. 2d 580 [1951]).

A somewhat broader view was adopted by a California court which made no distinction as to whether the assigned extra duties were within or outside the teacher's regular duties. This court ruled that a reasonable number of extra assignments impartially made to each male faculty member to supervise students and protect their welfare at school-sponsored athletic games outside school hours were within the scope of the teacher's employment, even though not mentioned in the employment contract (*McGrath* v. *Burkhard*, 131 Cal. App. 2d 367, 280 P. 2d 864 [1955]). In harmony with this view, another court held that while a school board could assign a teacher to extracurricular activities related to the school program, its statutory authority was exceeded when it assigned a teacher to supervise a private bowling club activity found to be recreational and unrelated to the school program (*Pease* v. *Millcreek Township School District*, 412 Pa. 378, 195 A. 2d 104 [1963]).

Leaves of absence. In many states, specific statutory provisions determine the type and amount of leaves of absence for public school teachers and the conditions under which they are available. In the absence of specific provisions, the general authority given to school boards to grant leaves of absence to teachers, or the broad power conferred on school boards to maintain and operate the schools, provides the legal basis for adopting short-term and long-term leave policies for a variety of reasons.

The leaves of absence most commonly the subject of statutory law are for sickness, including absence for family illness or bereavement; sabbaticals; exchange teaching inside and outside the United States; professional study; and military duty, jury duty, and other civic duties. As

with most other state school laws, the substance of leaves of absence provisions for teachers varies considerably from state to state.

In all but a dozen states sick leave is covered by statute or by state board of education regulations (National Education Association . . . 1969*a*). Mandatory statewide statutory provisions for fully paid sick leave prevail in about 30 states, which prescribe the number of paid sick-leave days that must be allowed in a school year and the amount of unused sick leave that may be accumulated. School boards in some states are authorized to exceed the statutory requirements. A growing number of state sick-leave laws allow the transfer of accumulated unused sick leave when a teacher moves from one school system to another within the state.

School boards also may be authorized (and in a few states required) to grant long-term leaves of absence to teachers for physical or mental disability. School boards have the power to place teachers on involuntary leave without pay for extended periods in case of sickness or disability or for reasons such as becoming a candidate for public office.

Sabbatical leave for professional study, research, travel, or health restoration is specifically provided by statute in two-fifths of the states. The practice of granting sabbatical leaves to teachers exists in states without express statutes relating to this type of leave (National Education Association . . . 1969*b*). However, an express statute clarifies the power of school boards, which would otherwise hesitate to adopt sabbatical leave programs without enabling legislation. Whether the sabbatical leave is a matter of right or a matter of privilege depends on the language of the statute. Usually, the laws authorize rather than require school boards to grant sabbaticals to teachers. But whether mandatory or permissive, these laws usually specify the number of leaves the school system may grant in any one year, the eligibility requirements for the sabbatical, the length of leave allowed, the level of salary, and the conditions to be met by the teacher during and on completion of his leave. Other typical provisions protect the teacher's rights of tenure, retirement, salary increments, and other benefits while he is on sabbatical.

Although questions about leaves of absence come before the courts, sick-leave pay is rarely the subject of court action. However, as recent decisions show, compliance with school-board rules or statutory provisions on sick leave are essential if the teacher is to be paid during the period of absence (*Garber* v. *Board of Education of City of New York*, 50 Misc. 2d 711, 271 N.Y.S. 329 [1966]; *Yankum* v. *City of Boston*, 348 Mass. 92, 202 N.E. 2d 253 [1964]).

More frequently litigated are questions of legal rights relative to sabbatical leave, including the pertinent question of whether the teacher has the right to a sabbatical. In the case of one teacher who was eligible for a sabbatical under the existing statutes but was twice refused the leave on the grounds of a teacher shortage, the court ruled that the school board had no authority to deny the teacher the sabbatical leave without evidence that the board had tried and failed to find a substitute (*State ex rel. Scoggins* v. *Vernon Parish School Board*, 44 So. 2d 385 [La. 1950]).

As for the teacher's rights after sabbatical leave is granted, a California court ruled that the assignment of a returning tenure teacher to a different grade in a different school was in compliance with a sabbatical-leave statute which provided that at the expiration of a leave of absence, unless a school employee otherwise agrees, he shall be reinstated to the position held at the time the leave was granted. According to the court, this provision did not entitle the teacher to be reassigned to his former position. The school board acted properly as long as the teacher was reinstated in an assignment within the scope of the teaching certificate he held at the time the sabbatical leave began (*Adelt* v. *Richmond School District*, 250 Cal. App. 2d 149, 58 Cal. Rptr. 151 [1967]; hearing denied, Cal. Sup. Ct. [1967]). Another court decided that a school board can recover salary paid to a teacher during a sabbatical leave when the teacher fails to live up his agreement either to return to service in the school system for a full year after the expiration of the leave or to return the salary he received while on leave (*Central School District No. 2 of the Town of Oyster Bay, Nassau County* v. *Cohen*, 302 N.Y.S. 2d 398 [1969]).

Maternity leave is seldom the subject of specific legislative enactment. Few states have statutory provisions on this subject; in only three states must maternity leaves of absence be given. In practice, however, school boards throughout the country have exercised their discretionary authority and adopted maternity-leave policies. Teachers are expected to comply with school-board rules and regulations governing maternity leave, provided the time the school board requires the teacher to remain away from school both before and after childbirth is reasonable (*State ex rel. Sepulvado* v. *Rapids Parish School Board*, 236 La. 482, 108 So. 2d 96 [1959]). Violation of reasonable maternity-leave rules may be grounds for dismissal (*Board of School Directors of Ambridge Borough School District, Beaver County* v. *Snyder*, 346 Pa. 103, 29 A. 2d 34 [1942]).

There is judicial authority that absence from school because of pregnancy may be the basis for dismissal of a tenure teacher. Some courts have reasoned that although it is not specified in the tenure statute as a cause of dismissal, pregnancy constitutes incompetency or neglect to teach (*Appeal of School District of City of Bethlehem*, 151 Pa. Super. 522, 30 A. 2d 726 [1943]; *West Mahanoy Tp. School Board*, 1 So. 2d 344 [La. 1941]). In another case, where a tenure law listed the specific causes for dismissal and where absence from duty owing to pregnancy was not enumerated, a school-board resolution requiring expectant mothers to give up their teaching positions permanently was ruled unreasonable and arbitrary (*State ex rel. Penny* v. *Rapides Parish School Board*, 1 So. 2d 344 [La. 1941]). And a New York court upheld a determination of the state commissioner of education that, as a matter of public policy, probationary teachers are entitled to maternity leaves of absence under the long-established principles recognized and applied to tenure teachers (*Board of Education of City School District of the City of Poughkeepsie* v. *Allen*, 30 A.D. 2d 742, 291 N.Y.S. 2d 243 [1968]).

Political and personal restrictions.   Since 1952, the concept that public employment is a privilege subject to whatever conditions the public employer sees fit to impose has been rejected by the U.S. Supreme Court in a series of decisions on constitutional guarantees of freedom of speech and association under the First Amendment.

This concept was expressly rejected by the Court first in *Wieman* v. *Updegraff* (344 U.S. 183 [1952]), then in *Shelton* v. *Tucker* (364 U.S. 479, 487, [1960]), where the Court stated: "The vigilant protection of constitutional freedoms is nowhere more vital than in the community of American schools." More recently, in *Keyishian* v. *Board of Regents* (385 U.S. 589, 605–606 [1967]) and *Pickering* v. *Board of Education of Township High School District 205, Will County, Illinois* (391 U.S. 565, 568 [1968]) the Court reiterated its rejection of the theory that public employment may be denied altogether or be subject to any conditions, regardless of how unreasonable. The Pickering decision continued:

At the same time it cannot be gainsaid that the State has interests as an employer in regulating the speech of its employees that differ significantly from those it possesses in connection with regulation of speech of the citizenry in general. The problem in any case is to arrive at a balance between the interests of the teacher, as a citizen, in commenting upon matters of public concern and the interest of the state, as an employer, in promoting the efficiency of the public services it performs through its employees.

It. is in the context of these Supreme Court pronouncements that restrictions on outside political and personal activities of teachers should be viewed.

Like other Americans, public school teachers meet citizenship responsibilities through active political participation in government affairs. As private citizens, teachers exercise rights to vote, to work for the support of or opposition to matters on the ballot (which may include school-related issues), to be active in a political party, and to campaign for candidates for public office. In many instances, teachers exercise the right to seek, campaign for, and serve in elective public office. Nevertheless, questions do arise about the extent to which teachers may be restricted by provisions in state constitutions and statutes or by local school-board rules from engaging in partisan and nonpartisan political activities.

Few laws specifically impede or prevent teachers from taking part in political affairs at the national, state, or local level (National Education Association . . . 1961). However, two types of relevant statutes are found in a number of states. The first type, concerned with solicitation, covers public employees and is designed to protect the integrity of the civil service. It is both restrictive and protective: on the one hand, it prohibits public employees from soliciting either funds or services for political purposes; on the other hand, it protects them from similar solicitation. In some states these provisions are of a form that does or could apply to public school teachers. The second type is a specific statute that ensures

teachers the right to engage in political activities after school hours, away from school premises; and in a manner that does not interfere with the performance of school duties.

In addition, some state constitutions prohibit dual office holding. In general, teachers are regarded as public employees and not as public officers. This suggests that the dual office-holding restrictions may be inapplicable to teachers. Ultimately, judicial interpretation of the constitutional language would determine if this is so, should the issue arise for teachers in a state with such restrictions.

One state, Oregon, amended its constitutional provisions against dual office holding so that persons employed by the state board of higher education and members of any school board could, at the same time, hold seats in the state legislature (Article XV, Sec. 8). This amendment superseded a court ruling that a teacher could not retain his position in the public schools while he was a member of the legislature (*Monaghan* v. *School District No. 1, Clackamus County*, 211 Ore. 360, 315 P. 797 [1957]). A court in Alaska construed the state constitutional provision that no legislator may hold another office or position of profit in the state to mean that a legislator could not hold a position as teacher or superintendent in the state-operated school district. Expressly left open by this court was the question of whether this constitutional provision also precluded legislators from being employed as teachers by political subdivisions of the state, the local school districts (*Begich* v. *Jefferson*, 441 P. 2d 27 [1968]). In another case, a Texas court ruled that a city councilman who was also a teacher at a state-supported college (and who was paid in both capacities with tax-derived funds) was an employee in his teaching position and not an officer holding two civil service offices of emolument in violation of state constitutional prohibitions (*Tilley* v. *Rogers*, 405 S.W. 2d 220 [1966]).

The right of a teacher to continue in and be paid for his teaching employment after his election to public office was settled in New Jersey by the adoption of a statute providing that a teacher-legislator is entitled to time off from his school duties, without loss of pay, while attending sessions of the legislature or hearings or meetings of legislative committees (*New Jersey Statutes Annotated*, Title 18 A, sec. 18 A: 6–8.2). Similarly, California provides by statute that a permanent certificated teacher who is elected to the legislature shall be granted a leave of absence by the school board; during the leave he may be employed in the school district for less than full-time service for such salary, terms, and conditions as may be mutually agreed upon (*West's California Annotated Education Code*, sec. 13552.5).

On the question of school salary payments to a teacher-legislator, the Oklahoma court ruled that teachers are not disqualified from serving in the public schools during their elected term of office in the state legislature but may be paid for teaching services only with locally raised funds; payment under any teaching contract may not be made from state funds appropriated to the school district during the teacher's incumbency as a legislator, for this would violate the conflict-of-interest provisions in the state constitution governing members of the legislature (*State ex rel. Settles* v. *Board of Education of Independent School District No. D-38 of McCurtain County, Oklahoma*, 389 P. 2d 356 [1964]).

Apart from statutory or constitutional provisions, school-board rules may sometimes place conditions on the political activities of teachers. The validity of a school-board rule requiring teachers who become candidates for public office to take an involuntary leave of absence without pay during their candidacy and (if elected) during their time in office was challenged in court and upheld as a valid and reasonable exercise of the board's power (*School City of East Chicago* v. *Sigler*, 219 Ind. 9, 36 N.E. 2d 760 [1941]; *Chatham* v. *Johnson*, 195 So. 2d 62 [Miss. 1967]). On the other hand, a school-board requirement that a teacher take involuntary leave during his candidacy for political office in Indiana was clarified by a 1965 statute declaring that a teacher may not be dismissed, suspended, or required to take a mandatory leave unless there is evidence that his activity while a candidate has impaired the effectiveness of his school service and has interfered with the carrying out of his contractual obligations as a teacher (*Burns Indiana Statutes Annotated* [Supp.] Title 28, sec. 28–4338).

As to other political activities of teachers, judicial decisions indicate that courts are not likely to uphold a local school board in the dismissal, suspension, or nonappointment of teachers active in politics when their involvement does not detract from their efficiency, is not conducted during school hours, and does not violate state statutes (*Adams* v. *State ex rel. Sutton*, 69 So. 2d 309 [Fla. 1954]; *Goldsmith* v. *Board of Education of Sacramento City High School District*, 66 Cal. App. 157, 225 Pac. 783 [1924]).

A school board's prohibition of all political activities by teachers except voting and the board's denial of reemployment to a teacher at least partly because of his political activities in the face of this policy were ruled unreasonable, arbitrary, and discriminatory violations of the rights of the teacher under the First and Fourteenth amendments. The court held that the complete ban on the rights of teachers to express political opinions and to engage in political activities deprived them of their First Amendment rights of free speech (*Montgomery* v. *White*, U.S. District Court, Eastern District, Texas, Civil Action No. 4933 [October 24, 1969]).

Under limited circumstances, teachers may even carry on activities of a political nature on school premises, according to the California supreme court. This court held that in the absence of evidence of a clear and substantial threat to order and efficiency in the schools, a school board may not prohibit the circulation for signatures by and to teachers on off-duty time on school premises of a petition concerned with financing of public education and addressed to public officials (*Los Angeles Teachers Union, Local 1021, American Federation of Teachers* v. *Los Angeles City Board of Education*, Cal. App. 2d, 78 Cal. Rptr. 723 [1969]).

Under a series of court decisions in the late 1960's, personal outside activities of teachers (other than politics) involving the assertion of rights within the ambit of the First Amendment may not be the basis for dismissal or refusal to reemploy when the activities do not interfere with the efficiency of the schools. Even in states without teacher-tenure laws, courts have ruled illegal the discharge or failure to renew the contracts of competent teachers for no other reason than participation on their own time in community activities on behalf of Negro civil rights, including demonstrating, picketing, and distributing handbills (*Johnson* v. *Branch*, 364 F. 2d 177 [4th Cir. 1966]; cert. denied, 385 U.S. 1003 [1967]; *Rackley* v. *School District No. 5, Orangeburg County, S.C.*, 258 F. Supp. 676 [D.S.C. 1966]).

In another case, involving an outside but school-related activity, it was held that the dismissal of probationary teachers solely on the ground of membership in a teachers' union would be unjustified since the right of freedom of association under the First Amendment confers the right to form and join a labor union (*McLaughlin* v. *Tilendis*, 398 F. 2d 287 [7th Cir. 1968]).

In 1968 the right of a teacher to speak out critically as a private citizen on issues of public importance relative to school matters without fear of retaliatory dismissal came before the Supreme Court of the United States in *Pickering* v. *Board of Education of Township High School District 205, Will County, Illinois* (391 U.S. 563). In this case a tenured teacher was dismissed after a hearing because of a letter he wrote to a local newspaper. The letter, partially erroneous, was critical of the way the school board handled proposals to raise school revenues and distributed financial resources between the educational and the athletic programs. The letter also charged the school superintendent with attempting to prevent teachers in the school district from opposing or criticizing a proposed bond issue. The school board determined that the publication of the letter was "detrimental to the efficient operation and administration of the schools of the district." The dismissal of the teacher was upheld in the state courts but was reversed by the U.S. Supreme Court.

In reaching its decision, the Court said that the interests of the teacher as a citizen in making public comments on matters of public concern must be balanced against the state's interest as an employer in promoting the efficiency of public services it performs through its employees. The Supreme Court did not find, after independent examination of the record, that the teacher's public statements in any way impeded the teacher's proper performance of his daily classroom duties or interfered with the regular operation of the schools generally. In such circumstances, the Court concluded that "the interest of the school administration in limiting teachers' opportunities to contribute to public debate is not significantly greater than its interest in limiting a similar contribution by any member of the general public." In this case, since "the fact of employment is only tangentially and insubstantially involved in the subject matter of the public communication made by the teacher," the teacher was to be regarded as a member of the general public. The Supreme Court held that under the circumstances, without proof of false statements knowingly and recklessly made by the teacher, the school board could not discharge the teacher for exercising his right to speak on issues of public importance.

The Pickering decision and the other recent decisions mentioned indicate the measure of protection afforded teachers against school-board restrictions imposed on outside activities.

BIBLIOGRAPHY

NATIONAL EDUCATION ASSOCIATION. RESEARCH DIVISION 1961 *Statutory Provisions and Judicial Decisions Relating to Political Activities of Public-School Teachers.* Research Memo 1961–32. Washington, D.C., The Association.

NATIONAL EDUCATION ASSOCIATION. RESEARCH DIVISION 1968 *State Minimum-Salary Laws for Teachers, 1968–1969.* Research Report 1968-R15. Washington, D.C., The Association.

NATIONAL EDUCATION ASSOCIATION. RESEARCH DIVISION 1969a *School Law Summaries: Leaves of Absence.* Washington, D.C., The Association.

NATIONAL EDUCATION ASSOCIATION. RESEARCH DIVISION 1969b *Leaves of Absence Provisions for Teachers, 1968–69.* Washington, D.C., The Association.

FRIEDA S. SHAPIRO

3. EMPLOYMENT PROCESS

A teacher must meet two sets of standards in order to be employed—those for a state certificate and those of the local school board for which he wants to work. A teaching certificate indicates that the holder has met the state's legal requirements to follow the teaching profession. However, it does not mean that the holder will obtain a teaching position.

Certification requirements. Every state, the District of Columbia, and Puerto Rico require that a person have a certificate in order to teach in the public schools. A certificate is the legal evidence of competence and the authorization to receive payment from public funds for teaching.

Certification authority is typically vested in the state board of education; however, in about seven states this authority is retained by the legislature. In most states minimum certification requirements are set by statute, and the state board has authority to set additional standards. Statutory requirements may pertain to the applicant's age, citizenship, health, loyalty, and educational background. In 1970, 28 states, the District of Columbia, and Puerto Rico required that an applicant either be a citizen of the United States or file a declaration of intent to become a citizen. In ten states a certificate cannot be issued unless the teacher has already been hired for a specific job. At least 43 states require that an applicant without teaching experience be recommended by the college he attended and that an applicant with experience be recommended by the school board employing him. Although 17 states do not have them, minimum age requirements are common. In 29 states age 18 is the minimum, and a few states have set a minimum age of 19 or 20.

Several states still have special course requirements—that is, a requirement which can be met only by taking the course in an institution of higher education within the state. The trend is away from such requirements, and even in those states which still have them, administrative flexibility is practiced in applying them.

Loyalty provisions. In 1970 about 21 of the state certification laws required the applicant for a teacher's certificate to sign some form of oath of allegiance or loyalty to the state and federal governments. In many other states loyalty requirements were contained in other statutes which affected teachers. Through the years such laws have been challenged as unconstitutional in the state and federal courts, and the U.S. Supreme Court has considered this issue several times. Some statutes which provide for penalizing a teacher who belongs to "subversive organizations" have been declared unconstitutional because they are vague and "overbroad." In one case the Court held that if scienter is lacking—that is, if the teacher does not know the organization to which he belongs is considered subversive—punitive action cannot be taken against the teacher (*Keyishian* v. *Board of Regents of the University of the State of New York*, 385 U.S. 589 [1967]). The Court has ruled that a teacher can be penalized for membership in a subversive organization only if it is his "specific intent" to further the illegal aims of that organization (*Wieman et al.* v. *Updegraff et al.*, 344 U.S. 183 [1952]). However, the Court has affirmed without opinion a state court ruling that an affirmative oath—that is, one in which the teacher swears to uphold the state and federal constitutions and to be a dedicated teacher—is constitutional (*Elfbrandt* v. *Russel et al.*, 384 U.S. 11 [1966]).

On the basis of the Supreme Court and the state court opinions on loyalty statutes, it seems clear that those which are negative—those which require a teacher to promise not to do something—and those which involve membership in sub-

versive organizations must meet rigid tests for constitutionality. However, statutes requiring a teacher to take an affirmative oath—to swear to uphold state and federal constitutions—will be received more favorably by courts.

Other legal issues. The question which most often reaches the courts regarding certification is whether or not an individual who meets all of the state's qualifications may demand that the appropriate certificate be issued to him. In general, the courts have held that the issuing agency has discretion in determining whether an applicant has met all of the requirements for a certificate; however, once the determination has been made that the applicant does meet these requirements, the certificate may not be withheld.

Another type of case which frequently reaches the courts arises when a board of education contracts with a teacher who does not hold a valid certificate. It is clear that in all states a teacher who is to be employed must hold a valid, appropriate certificate from the state in which he seeks employment. However, state laws differ as to whether he must already hold the certificate in order to enter into a valid contract. In some states the teacher must have a valid certificate at the time he and the board contract for his services. In some states his teaching contract will be valid, even if it is signed before he has a certificate, if he receives the certificate before he actually begins to teach. (As previously noted, ten states require the prospective teacher to show evidence of employment before the certificate will be issued.) In other states the teacher's contract will be valid if he receives his certificate before he receives any of his salary. The issue in the court cases is whether the contract between the board and the teacher is void. If the teacher is not certificated at the time required by the laws of the state in which he seeks employment, the courts will declare his contract void and therefore unenforceable, although the teacher may recover salary for any service he may have rendered.

Certification statutes and regulations do specify grounds for revocation of a teacher's certificate, but revocation may occur only after a hearing. If the certificate is suspended or revoked, the teacher may not be employed or continue to be employed.

Types of certificates. T. M. Stinnett, in his *Manual on Certification Requirements for School*

Personnel in the United States (1970), has classified the various types of teacher's certificates issued according to the length of time for which they are valid, the level of preparation required for their issuance, and the types of teaching positions they authorize. Stinnett's manual is the best source of such information as requirements for state certification and regulations governing renewal of certificates. The manual also includes an analysis of trends in certification laws.

Interstate reciprocity. The increasing mobility of qualified teachers is making more severe the problem of state certification laws interfering with a teacher's continuing his career in a state other than the one in which he began teaching. The problem is not new; as early as the 1890's attempts were made to devise plans for exchange of certificates between states. Since then various methods have been used to solve the problem, among them regional compacts and acceptance by a state of graduates of institutions accredited by the National Council for Accreditation of Teacher Education.

A recent effort which offers some hope of success is the work of the Interstate Certification Project, sponsored by the New York State Department of Education, Division of Teacher Education and Certification. The project has developed a model statute and a model teacher's contract. The statute includes a provision permitting a state which enacts it to contract with another state which also has enacted such a law to establish the conditions under which each state will accept certified teachers from the other.

Governance of the profession. The teaching profession has long sought to govern itself. At the present time, in most states standards for certification are set by state statutes and by state boards of education, whose members are not teachers.

In many states, however, professional standards boards and professional practices commissions, composed of members of the teaching profession, advise the government agencies which establish and enforce certification requirements. Standards boards review certification requirements and procedures and make recommendations for change to the official body charged with issuing certificates. These boards may also hear and make recommendations as to the disposition of cases in which individual exceptions are sought from existing requirements. Practices commissions rec-

ommend competency and ethical standards to the official agency charged with determining whether or not teachers should be reprimanded or have their licenses suspended or revoked. The commissions typically are authorized to hold hearings in such cases and to advise the official agency on the disposition of each case.

In one state, Oregon, one board has been established to advise on both certification requirements and professional practices. In addition, several of the state statutes establishing practices commissions seem to authorize them to make recommendations on certification standards as well as on professional practice standards.

Employer's requirements. The fact that a teacher has met the requirements for and holds a valid certificate does not mean that he will be employed; a local board of education may impose additional requirements. For example, a teacher may need only a bachelor's degree for certification, but a board may require a master's degree of those who teach English in its high schools.

Some local school districts require all applicants for teaching positions to take examinations and be placed on eligibility lists, from which appointments are made. Court cases arising under this procedure often involve such questions as whether the test was proper, whether the applicant was ranked properly on the eligibility list, and whether appointments were made from the list in the order in which the applicants' names appeared or at least from among applicants near the top of the list.

In most states the school board must hire the teacher. In only a few may the superintendent employ. In the absence of a statute specifically permitting the superintendent to hire, the board may not be bound by his employment contract with a teacher.

Boards of education must follow the procedure for employment mandated by state law. In some states statutes require that the superintendent recommend and the board hire. In a few states the board may not refuse without just cause to employ teachers recommended by the superintendent. The board must meet formally as a body when it agrees to employ a teacher. Several states have laws against nepotism, which boards must obey. Typically, the statute prohibits employment of teachers who are related in some way to those who employ them, such as school board members.

Employment contracts.   When the teacher and the board of education have agreed that the teacher will be employed, a contract is signed. Like virtually all other contract agreements, the employment contract must have five elements to be valid.

First, the contract must be between competent parties—that is, the parties entering into the contract must have the legal capacity to do so. If state law requires that an individual have a certificate before entering into an employment contract, a teacher who does not hold a certificate does not have the legal capacity to make a valid employment contract. Similarly, if it is required that the board of education employ teachers, a superintendent does not have the legal capacity to contract with a teacher.

Second, the contract must be based on mutual assent. There must be a definite offer and an unqualified acceptance of that offer. Whether such an offer and acceptance exist has been the subject of much litigation. A board of education may withdraw its offer at any time prior to the teacher's acceptance. In addition, for a valid contract to exist, the teacher must accept the terms of the contract as offered. If he accepts subject to certain changes in the terms, he really is rejecting the board's offer and making a counteroffer, and no contract results unless the board accepts fully the terms of this counteroffer. If the teacher does decide to fully accept the offer, this acceptance must be communicated to the board. In most states the contract of employment must be in writing. However, cases have reached the courts in which boards of education have employed qualified teachers on the basis of oral contracts even though a requirement that the contract be written existed; the courts have held that in such circumstances a teacher may recover compensation for services rendered if the board had knowledge that the teacher was working.

The third element of a valid contract is that it be sufficiently definite to be enforceable. If the language or the terms of the contract are so ambiguous that a court cannot ascertain the intent of the parties, the contract will not be enforced. Courts have declared unenforceable a contract which promised to pay a higher salary (the contract did not state the amount) to a superintendent if funds were available because the amount of the salary was not certain prior to the performance of the contract (*Morris* v. *Rob-*

ertson, 198 So. 290 [Miss. 1940]). It is a principle of contract law (the parol evidence rule) that, in interpreting written contracts which appear to be complete, courts will not hear testimony as to oral agreements made prior to or at the time of signing of the written contract which add to or detract from the written contract. If a term in the written contract is ambiguous, testimony may be accepted to determine what the parties meant. However, if no such evidence can be presented and if the contract is ambiguous, a court will not enforce the agreement.

The fourth requirement of a valid contract is that it provide for consideration. Each party must receive something of value (for example, money or the services of the teacher) in exchange for what he gives up or does. It has been held that an employment contract which did not state the wages to be paid the teacher could not be enforced because of lack of consideration (*Cleavenger* v. *Board of Education of Barbour County et al.*, 170 S.E. 901 [W.Va. 1933]).

The fifth requirement of a valid contract is that it conform to state law and public policy. This element is seldom a problem in teachers' contracts. However, a contract between a board member and his own board of education will be considered against public policy and thus be unenforceable.

Void and voidable contracts.   Some contracts which are not valid at the time they are entered into may be ratified and thus made as enforceable as if they had been valid initially. A board may ratify a contract which it had the power to make (for example, an otherwise valid contract between a teacher and a superintendent in a state in which only a board of education may hire). Such contracts are voidable—that is, the board may void them by not ratifying. A board may ratify by taking formal action or by accepting the services of the teacher as if he were performing under a valid contract. If a voidable contract is ratified, it is ratified as a whole, and all of its terms become enforceable.

Void contracts, as opposed to voidable ones, cannot be ratified, even by formal board action. For example, if, contrary to state law, a teacher does not have a valid certificate when the board employs him, the contract is void, and the board may not ratify it because it had no authority to make the contract in the first place.

Master contracts. In many school districts negotiations between teachers' organizations and school boards result in master contracts which cover all the teachers in the district. Most of these contracts are authorized by state statutes regulating collective bargaining. The contents of the contracts are negotiated for the teachers by representatives of the teacher organization, and enforcement is the responsibility of the organization on behalf of the teachers covered by the contract.

Teachers subsequently employed are subject to the master contract and may not individually contract with the board. In some states statutes may require the issuance of individual contracts even when there is a master contract. In such cases the terms of the individual contracts must conform to those of the master contract.

Some master contracts contain agency shop or financial responsibility provisions. These provisions require all teachers, within a certain time after beginning employment, either to join the organization which negotiated the contract or pay the organization a sum of money, usually the amount of its annual dues, to defray the costs of negotiating and enforcing the contract.

Agency shop clauses have been challenged in the courts and were upheld in Michigan, although in other states older cases indicate that they would not be upheld. Whether such clauses are upheld in future cases will probably depend in large part upon the provisions of the statute under which master contracts are negotiated.

BIBLIOGRAPHY

Bryson, Joseph E. 1963 *Legality of Loyalty Oath and Non-oath Requirements for Public School Teachers.* Boone, N.C., Miller.

"Loyalty Oaths" 1968 *Yale Law Journal,* 77:739–766.

New York (State). Department of Education, Division of Teacher Education and Certification 1968 *Interstate Certification Project.* Albany, N.Y., The Department.

Remmlein, Madaline K., and Martha L. Ware, eds. 1970 *School Law.* 3rd ed. See Chapter 1, "Certification and Appointment," and Chapter 3, "Loyalty Requirements." Danville, Ill., Interstate.

Stinnett, T. M. 1969 "Teacher Certification." Robert L. Ebel, ed., *Encyclopedia of Educational Research.* 4th ed. New York, Macmillan. Pages 1410–1414.

Stinnett, T. M. 1970 *A Manual on Certification Requirements for School Personnel in the United States.* Washington, D.C., National Commission on Teacher Education and Professional Standards in cooperation with the National Education Association.

MARTHA L. WARE

4. SEPARATION AND DEMOTION

The legality of separations or demotions of professional personnel in education rests upon the observance of rights available to the released or demoted individual under the U.S. Constitution, federal statutes, state constitutions, state statutes (provided provisions in these documents do not conflict with the U.S. or state constitutions or federal laws), provisions of legal contracts, and the common law. A study of violations of substantive and procedural due process rights in separation or demotion of professional personnel in education revealed that from January 1946 to June 1963, 47 percent of the subsequently litigated actions by local public boards of education and by boards of regents were reversed by state or federal appellate courts on due process grounds (DeVaughn 1964).

Some due process violations occurred through failure of local boards to observe the following individual rights guaranteed under the U.S. Constitution: the First Amendment right of free speech and the right peaceably to assemble and petition; the Fifth Amendment rights not "to be a witness against [oneself], nor be deprived of life, liberty, or property, without due process of law"—rights which have been declared applicable not only in criminal proceedings but in hearings of any nature (Corwin 1948; Griswold 1955); and the Sixth Amendment guaranties of procedural due process, now also pertinent to all hearings in civil as well as criminal cases. The Fourteenth Amendment made these rights applicable in state (as well as federal) actions and added the guaranty that no state can deny any of its citizens the equal protection of the laws.

These constitutional provisions have been widely invoked in the mid-twentieth century to restrain local public school boards and boards of regents in separations or demotions of professional personnel. Recently, the First Amendment and Fifth Amendment guaranties have been invoked to protect the rights of Negro teachers who were separated in consolidations of schools or school systems or who, because of civil rights activities, were dismissed during the contract period or failed to have contracts renewed. Procedural due process violations have accounted for many reversals of local board action—for example, for deficiency or absence of specific charges, lack of hearing, or failure to provide due process guaranteed by law.

One may generalize that, except for the federal constitutional requirements, the statutes of the states govern the legality of separations of professional personnel and for the most part protect the tenure rights of teachers. However, local board rules not in conflict with federal or state constitutional provisions and statutes have the force of law and influence the employment status of the individual teacher or administrator. In addition, legal contracts whose provisions are not in conflict with constitutional or statutory provisions or with rules and regulations of state or local boards of education can determine the legal bases for either the separation or demotion of professional personnel.

Definitions. Several types of employment contracts are in use. Some terms used to refer to these contracts or used within them are commonly defined as follows: An annual contract is an employment contract for one year under which notice of the school board's intention not to renew is not required. A continuing contract is an employment contract for one year which is covered by a statutory requirement to provide notice on or before a given date of intention not to renew. In the absence of such notice, the contract is automatically renewable for the subsequent year. A statement of causes for nonrenewal may or may not be required by statute. Probation is an employment status under annual contracts for a specified number of years. Usually, any notice of election not to renew or not to grant permanent status must be given on or before a given date. Whether such nonelection must be supported by charges depends upon applicable statutory provisions. Tenure is a permanent, continuing employment status. Separation or demotion of tenured employees may legally occur only after written notice of specific statutory charges is given and a hearing is held during which the employee has the rights to have counsel, to subpoena witnesses and documents, to have testimony given under oath or affirmation, to hear and cross-examine opposing witnesses, to have a decision rendered on the preponderance of evidence on each specific charge, and to have a transcript of the proceedings made for possible use on appeal. Termination is the separation of an employee at the end of the contract period by nonrenewal of the contract. Dismissal is the separa-

tion during the contract year of a teacher working under an annual contract or a continuing contract or of a probationary teacher in a tenure system or the separation at any time of a tenured teacher.

Tenure systems vary in the degree to which they protect the employment rights of the individual probationary teacher. In some jurisdictions written notice of separation and specific charges must be given to the teacher a certain number of days before the effective date of the separation. In other states, notice a certain number of days in advance without a statement of cause is sufficient. In still other jurisdictions the statutes require that notice and a statement of specific charges be given from one to three months in advance and that the employee have such time to remove the alleged deficiencies. Tenure statutes require full due process in dismissals of tenured employees, the burden of proof resting on the school board.

Violations of substantive due process. Teachers have been dismissed by local boards for exercising the Fifth Amendment right not to testify against themselves before the House Un-American Activities Committee or a similar group. In some cases the mere refusal to testify was used as a cause for dismissal (*Slochower* v. *Board of Higher Education, City of New York*, 350 U.S. 551 [1956]; *Laba* v. *Newark Board of Education*, 23 N.J. 364, 129 Atl. 2d 273 [1957]; *Lowenstein* v. *Newark Board of Education*, 33 N.J. 277, 163 Atl. 2d 156 [1960]; *Lowenstein* v. *Newark Board of Education*, 35 N.J. 94, 171 Atl. 2d 265 [1961]; *Mass* v. *Superior Court*, 17 Cal. Rptr. 549, 304 Pac. 2d 1015 [1956]; *Mass* v. *Board of Education of San Francisco Unified School District*, 39 Cal. Rptr. 739, 394 Pac. 2d 579 [1964]). In other cases the refusal led to dismissal for "incompetency" or deficiency in "civic responsibility, judgment, appreciation and ideals" (*Board of Education* v. *Intille et al.*, 401 Pa. 1, 163 Atl. 2d 420 [1960]; *Board of Public Education, School District of Philadelphia* v. *Watson*, 401 Pa. 62, 163 Atl. 2d 60 [1960]). In reviewing such cases on appeal, the courts have ruled that the local boards denied constitutional guaranties and have ordered that the teachers be reinstated.

A teacher in New Hampshire refused under the First Amendment to answer questions relating to the content of a lecture he gave at the University of New Hampshire and to reveal his association with the Progressive Party (although he denied at the outset that he was ever a member of the Communist Party or any front organization). The teacher was jailed for contempt by a state superior court, and the highest court of the state affirmed the decision of the superior court under the doctrine that the state may abridge personal constitutional freedoms to protect itself against subversion. The U.S. Supreme Court reversed the state court decision and affirmed the individual rights of the teacher in the following words: "We conclude that the record in this case does not sustain the power of the State to compel the disclosures that the witness refused to make" (*Sweezy* v. *New Hampshire*, 354 U.S. 234 at 235 [1957]). The Court added: "We do not now conceive of any circumstance wherein a state interest would justify infringement of rights in these fields" (*ibid.* at 251).

In New York, Rosenberg, a dismissed probationary teacher, challenged the constitutionality of the New York statute providing for dismissal of probationary teachers without a hearing and alleged that the reason for the board action was his exercise of the First Amendment right of free speech in making public speeches against the Vietnam war. A federal district court upheld the constitutionality of the state statute but retained the case for hearing on the free speech issue (*Rosenberg* v. *Allen*, 258 F. Supp. 511 [1966]).

Recently, First Amendment rights have been affirmed in cases arising in school systems using annual contracts. In South Carolina a Negro teacher with ten years of experience and an excellent record was not given a contract for the 1964–1965 school year and was given no reasons for the termination; her principal had recommended that her contract be renewed. It was widely known that the teacher had been involved in civil rights activities, including picketing stores practicing segregation. After hearing the case, a federal district court directed employment and damages, reasoning that under South Carolina statutes the school board had discretionary power to decline to renew the contract of any teacher but that the exercise of such power could not be arbitrary, capricious, or discriminatory. The court concluded that the teacher's inference that the reason for her termination was her participation in civil rights activities was the only inference

possible and that nonrenewal of the contract violated the First and Fourteenth amendments (*Williams* v. *Sumter School District No. 2*, 255 F. Supp. 397 [1966]).

Rackley, another Negro teacher in South Carolina, had been active in local civil rights activities and had been arrested for trespassing after being charged with disturbing the business of a hospital and distributing handbills urging action against segregation. Despite an excellent classroom record, she was dismissed after warning on October 7, 1963, on charges of breaking the law. A federal district court directed reinstatement and payment of salary for the remainder of the 1963–1964 school year, concluding that the teacher was dismissed without good and sufficient cause and that the board's action was based upon the teacher's exercise of rights protected under the First and Fourteenth amendments and therefore constituted discriminatory exercise of the board's powers. The court stated that its ruling was necessary so as not to "curtail, impinge or infringe upon freedom of political expression or association, or any other constitutionally protected right" (*Rackley* v. *School District No. 5, Orangeburg County, South Carolina*, 258 F. Supp. 676 at 677 [1966]).

A Negro teacher in North Carolina had an exemplary record for 12 years but failed to have her contract renewed, allegedly because of charges of being tardy at an athletic contest, arriving a few minutes late to school (but being present before the starting time for her class), creating a fire hazard by failing to keep cabinets clean, and failing to stand in the door of her room during class change. The teacher filed action in federal court and alleged that she was not reemployed because of a disagreement with her principal about her civil rights activities. Evidence was introduced that the tensions did not affect her classroom effectiveness. The U.S. Court of Appeals for the Fourth Circuit found that the only reasonable inference as to the cause of the termination was the school board's objection to the teacher's civil rights activities. The inferred cause was unconstitutional, and reemployment was directed (*Johnson* v. *Branch*, 364 F. 2d 177 at 182 [1966]).

A now leading case on First Amendment rights of teachers is that of *Pickering* v. *Board of Education of Township High School District 205* (391 U.S. 563 [1968]). A teacher wrote a letter to the local newspaper in which he criticized the school board and school administrators for their allocation of funds between athletics and regular school programs, their attempts to curb criticism of the teachers, and their failure properly to inform the public of facts.

The board dismissed the teacher after a full hearing on charges of disloyalty, disruption of discipline, creation of disharmony and conflict within the professional staff, interference with the orderly operations of the school system, and publication of statements, some of them false, which impugned the "motives, integrity, truthfulness, [and] responsibility" of both the board members and the school administrators and damaged their professional reputations. Reversing the Illinois supreme court's affirmation of the dismissal, the U.S. Supreme Court reasoned that the letter stated a position on an issue of vital public concern by a member of the teaching staff, which should be most knowledgeable on such an issue. The Court discounted the charges of disloyalty and disruption of discipline and control. It noted that no evidence was presented in the trial court to support the charge of disruption, controversy, and conflict and significantly observed that the teacher's critical statements were in no way directed toward any person with whom he would normally be in contact during his daily work. The Court also noted that the letter was published after the public defeat of a proposed tax increase and that the letter was received with apathy and disbelief.

There were, admittedly, unintentionally false statements of fact in the letter, but the Court did not see this as fatal to the appellant, particularly since the board could have corrected the facts by a letter to the same paper or by other means. There was no evidence that the teacher's daily effectiveness in the classroom was diminished or that publication of the letter interfered with the operations of the school. The Court concluded that "absent proof of false statements knowingly or recklessly made by him, a teacher's exercise of his right to speak on issues of public importance may not furnish the basis for his dismissal from public employment" (391 U.S. 563 at 574).

In Virginia, upon consolidation of Negro and white schools, seven Negro teachers were notified of release through nonrenewal of their annual contracts. When new teachers were employed to fill vacancies, the seven released teachers instituted suit, alleging discrimination because of race in violation of the Fourteenth Amendment. No evaluative records were kept in the district which would have permitted valid comparisons between the released teachers and white teachers in the system or applicants for teaching positions. Evidence introduced indicated that, previously, in consolidations of white schools, surplus teachers were retained and placed in other vacancies. The Fourth Circuit Court of Appeals directed that the teachers be reemployed to fill vacancies for which they were qualified by certificate and experience without comparison to white teachers in the system or to new applicants (*Franklin* v. *County School Board of Giles County*, 360 F. 2d 325 [1966]).

A similar case was adjudicated in Arkansas by the U.S. Court of Appeals for the Eighth Circuit. The court directed that the teachers' names be placed on a preferential hiring list and that money damages be determined on an individual basis (*Smith* v. *Board of Education of Morrilton School District No. 32*, 365 F. 2d 770 [1966]).

Several cases in 1967 and 1968 foreshadowed the holdings by the Fifth Circuit Court of Appeals in *Singleton* v. *Jackson Municipal Separate School District* (419 F. 2d 1211 [1970]) and in multiple joined cases from Alabama, Florida, Georgia, Louisiana, Mississippi, North Carolina, and Texas, which firmly established specific due process guidelines required in reduction, consolidation, and integration of staff. In many cases federal courts found discrimination against Negro professionals.

One of the leading cases, decided in 1967, was *Wall* v. *Stanly County Board of Education* (259 F. Supp. 238, 378 F. 2d 275). Mrs. Audry Wall, a Negro, had taught for 13 years, largely in Stanly County. She held a master's degree. She was recommended by her principal for the 1965–1966 school year in an annual contract situation. The board approved her contract contingent only upon the allocation of a teaching position in her school. The board had adopted a freedom-of-choice integration plan, which caused a decrease in allocations from the state. In effect, however, there was an increase in allocations in white schools and a decrease in allocations in Negro schools. The court noted that the board controlled all teaching spaces —yet it was considering teaching spaces in Negro schools separately from teaching spaces in white schools, where an additional 50 applicants were employed. Positions had been allocated by the state board without regard to race or schools. The U.S. Court of Appeals for the Fourth Circuit said,

"The premise of such a proposition is that Mrs. Wall was not employed as a teacher in the Stanly County School System but was employed *as a Negro teacher in a Negro school.* Such a premise is unlawful. It is repugnant to the Fourteenth Amendment" (378 F. 2d 275 at 277).

Mrs. Wall had secured a position elsewhere for 1965–1966. The appeals court awarded damages to include salary differences and moving costs; directed that if she were employed in Stanly County for 1967–1968, the cost of moving back would be considered; and directed the district court to order the board to put Mrs. Wall, if she wished, on the roster of teacher applicants for 1967–1968 and to require that she be considered objectively in comparison with all teachers. The appeals court further directed that the board consider Mrs. Wall's 12 years of service.

If Wall were then denied employment, the district court was to require a full report of the reasons for denial and was to scrutinize that report to ensure that the school board had acted in good faith and without regard to race. The burden was placed upon the board to justify its conduct by clear and convincing evidence.

A North Carolina board of education was directed to reexamine its practices in all areas of faculty and staff employment—hiring, assignment, retention and dismissal, in-service training programs, and teachers' meetings—in *Tell et al.* v. *Pitt County Board of Education* (272 F. Supp. 703 [1967]). The court listed nonracial criteria to be used—educational background and qualifications, including graduate degrees obtained; specialized training in given fields; experience in teaching generally and in subjects for which there were openings; performance on employment application tests; personality, age, general appearance, and attitudes; reputation; and recommendations and references. The court stated: "If any testing is required, all applicants for the position in question must take the test(s)" (272 F. Supp. 703 at 708).

The above criteria were to be applied in reaching decisions to retain, promote, or dismiss. The principal's recommendation would be primary, provided the principal's appraisal was made with a racially unbiased eye.

The court prescribed the following conditions of fairness in an annual contract system: "Fundamental fairness requires that a teacher be notified of charges against him or her and that he or she be given an opportunity to respond and the knowledge of and right to demand a hearing before final action is taken in cases of dismissal" (272 F. Supp. 703 at 710).

In another case a high school's staff needs were reduced by four teachers when freedom-of-choice was implemented in 1965–1966, three weeks after school started. Two of the four were finally dismissed as not needed. The court strongly pointed out violations of due process under the Fourteenth Amendment. All nontenured teachers in the system were considered as new applicants. In determining dismissals consideration was given primarily to the grades involved. The court said the school system had failed to establish objective standards: ". . . [T]hey designed a pattern which could only result in discrimination against Negro teachers" (*Rolfe* v. *County Board of Education of Lincoln County, Tennessee*, 282 F. Supp. 192 [1966], 391 F. 2d 77 at 109 [1968]). These teachers were compared only with other Negro teachers, a process the court found so restrictive that it resulted in discrimination. Objective standards to compare all teachers were required, the court said, standards which could have included personality, reputation, physical defects, manner of speech, love of children, ability to cooperate, disciplinary ability, general appraisal, philosophy, general appearance, attitude, optimism, age-group interests, sense of humor, and parent-student reactions. Mandatory injunction was granted to the two dismissed defendants; the school board was ordered to reinstate them in their most recent positions and in the same salary range. The injunction was to continue unless the court modified its order, and the school system was required to submit within 90 days a set of objective standards for approval of the district court.

In a Louisiana school district four Negro probationary teachers were not given renewal contracts when formerly segregated staffs and student bodies were integrated, requiring reduction of staff. Finally, two probationary Negro teachers were released, and they brought suit demanding reinstatement. The superintendent had offered them placement at a one-room school for grades 1–8 located 60 miles out of town. They were told to take this assignment or else. But instead of taking the assignment, they chose to enter suit. One of the teachers had only one noted deficiency in his service, resulting from his not accepting responsibility for students during a trip; the teacher was never confronted with this deficiency. The federal district court found that the two teachers were compared only with teachers at their own school and not with all teachers in the system. The court said that the teachers' probationary status should be only one of the criteria used to decide contract renewal and that the teachers should be compared with all teachers in the school system. The court found discrimination and ordered reinstatement (*Williams* v. *Kimbrough*, 295 F. Supp. 578 [1969]).

Another case involved the separation of ten Negro teachers after a school reorganization. The ten teachers were dismissed after they were compared—on the basis of their records, degrees, fields or grade levels, experience, and performance the previous year—with white teachers in the system and with applicants in their fields or grade levels. The U.S. Court of Appeals for the Fourth Circuit found that comparing teachers having satisfactory service with new applicants was a denial of due process when the same was not done in the case of white teachers. The court invoked the Wall case and ordered damages and new contracts for certain of the ten teachers on the basis of the court's own analysis of qualifications and needs (*North Carolina Teachers Association* v. *Asheboro City Board of Education*, 393 F. 2d 736 [1968]).

A federal district court in Georgia issued a decision to the effect that when one or more Negro teachers were displaced in desegregation, no staff vacancy in the system could be filled by recruitment from outside unless no proposed displaced teacher was qualified by objective standards (*Graves* v. *Walton County Board of Education*, 300 F. Supp. 188, aff. 410 F. 2d 1153 [1968]).

In 1969 a federal district court in Arkansas held that those in charge of a school system may not constitutionally discriminate against Negro school administrators and teachers on the basis of race. Upon integration of staff, evaluation of the Negro professional in comparison with others in his field or fields must be conducted, and the better qualified professionals must be retained and the less qualified ones released. In the case before the court the principal was reinstated by the court despite board dissatisfaction with his administration of the school. In the same case, a Negro teacher who was terminated, although a white teacher with the same subject qualification but with less experience was retained, was also reinstated. The court found the termination racially discriminatory and unconstitutional (*McBeth* v. *Board of Education of DeVall's Bluff School District No. 1, Ark.*, 300 F. Supp. 1270 [1969]).

In 1970 the Fifth Circuit Court of Appeals held that all personnel being dismissed as a result of integration must be selected on the basis of objective and reasonable nondiscriminatory standards from among all staff members of the school district. Prior to a reduction, the school board must develop or require the development of nonracial objective criteria to be used in selecting staff members to be dismissed or demoted, and these criteria must be available for public inspection and must be retained by the school district (*Singleton* v. *Jackson Municipal Separate School District*, 419 F. 2d 1211 [1970]). "Demotion" was defined in the above case as an assignment in which a staff member receives less pay or less responsibility than in his former position; an assignment which requires a lesser degree of skill than the previous position; or an assignment in which the staff member is asked to teach a subject or grade other than one for which he is certified or in which he has had substantial experience within a reasonably current period. (See *Singleton* v. *Jackson Municipal Separate School District*, 419 F. 2d 1211 [1970], the key case widely cited, and the cases joined in that decision.)

Procedural deficiencies. A number of terminations and dismissals have been reversed by the courts because deficiencies in the procedures used by the school board to release the employee violated the employee's rights. Deficiencies which have led to reversal include failing to provide an adequate hearing, failing to notify the employee of the specific charges to be brought against him in a hearing, or failing to give him warning of the deficiencies in his professional performance.

Warning and professional assistance. Increasingly, when deficiencies in a teacher's performance are correctable and do not lead to harm which cannot be undone, statutes are requiring educational administrators and school boards to give warning of such deficiencies and to provide professional assistance to help the teacher overcome his weaknesses. The laws covering school personnel in the cities of St. Louis, Mo., and Kansas City, Kan., and in the states of California, Florida, Illinois, Louisiana, Michigan, New Jersey, New Mexico, and Pennsylvania contain provisions requiring notice of and time for correction of deficiencies; in some cases evidence of professional assistance to the teacher to help him reach a satisfactory level of performance must be presented for a separation to be upheld. For example, Lewing, a teacher in Louisiana, was charged with repeated tardiness (among other things). She testified that she did not know that she had been tardy except for one time when her baby was ill. The superintendent and the principal admitted that they had not discussed the tardiness with the teacher and thus had given her no warning that they considered her performance deficient. The supreme court of Louisiana stated: "We believe that plaintiff should have been specifically warned by her superiors and given an opportunity to correct her tardiness. Based on lack of notice and warning to plaintiff, we find that the School Board acted arbitrarily in its decision" (*Lewing* v. *De Soto Parish School Board*, 238 La. 43 at 56, 113 So. 2d 462 at 466 [1959]).

Notice of specific charges. Written notice to a teacher of the specific charges to be brought against him is required in tenure systems, and even in nontenure systems statutes usually require that notice and a reasonable time (often ten days) to answer charges and to request a hearing be provided in cases of dismissal during a contract year. Further time is required for preparation of a defense against the proposed action after the hearing date is set. In one case in which a tenured teacher received notice of charges in December after having been denied a teaching assignment in September (*Morman* v. *Board of Education, Richmond County*, 218 Ga. 48, 126 S.E. 2d 217 [1962]) and in another in which new charges and specifications were added without prior notice at the hearing for a tenured principal (*Johns* v. *Jefferson Davis Parish School Board*, 154 So. 2d 581 [1963]), the actions of the local school boards were reversed.

In separate cases the terminations of two teachers in different school districts were reversed by the supreme court of Alabama because the teachers were given notice before the statutory date of the intention of the boards to consider reelection or nonelection after the statutory date (*Board of Education of Randolph County* v. *State*, 256 Ala. 107, 53 So. 2d 371 [1951]; *Whittington* v. *Barbour County Board of Education*, 250 Ala. 692, 36 So. 2d 83 [1948]).

A summary demotion (without reasons) of a principal and assistant principal of a high school to lower paying positions constituted dismissals and violated rights under Tennessee's teacher tenure statute (*Blair* v. *Mayo*, 450 S.W. 2d 582 [1970]). The injunction granted by the chancery court of Cannon County was affirmed.

Four teachers at the University of Wisconsin were suspended by the university's president; no charges and specifications were presented to them. The teachers filed suit pleading for a temporary restraining order and the lifting of suspension. Their plea was granted on the grounds that First and Fourteenth amendment procedural due process requirements of notice of charges and specifications had not been met. The court attached a proviso allowing the president to suspend the teachers if due process was provided (*Lafferty* v. *Carter*, 310 F. Supp. 465 [1970]).

Hearing proceedings. Deficiencies in hearing proceedings were present in about one-half of the cases in which decisions of public boards of education or boards of regents were reversed. Although the dismissal of Slochower, a tenured college professor in New York, was fatal because of the infringement of the substantive Fifth Amendment right not to bear witness against oneself, the U.S. Supreme Court also noted the serious procedural deficiency in the summary dismissal of this professor without the hearing required by statute (*Slochower* v. *Board of Higher Education, City of New York*, 350 U.S. 551 [1956]).

A tenured teacher in Indiana reported for her hearing at the appointed time and place, waited 30 minutes for a quorum of the board to be present, and then waited an additional hour and ten minutes while the board, without explanation, did not go into session. The teacher and her attorney then left, and 15 minutes later the board went into session and dismissed the teacher. The supreme court of Indiana reinstated the teacher (*State ex rel. Thurston* v. *School District, City of Anderson et al.*, 236 Ind. 649, 142 N.E. 2d 914 [1957]).

A Pennsylvania case involved two principals who were summoned before their school board to show cause why they should not be demoted; charges and evidence were not presented by the board. The court held that, since the burden of proof in such cases rests with the board, the action of the board did not in fact constitute a hearing on charges and specifications (*Tassone et al.* v. *Redstone Township School District*, 408 Pa. 290, 183 Atl. 2d 536 [1962]).

Deficiencies in hearing proceedings were fatal in cases in which evidence to support charges against a tenured teacher related to the teacher's probationary period (*Roller* v. *Young*, 147 Ohio St. 13, 67 N.E. 2d 710 [1946]) and in which evidence to support dismissal of an individual holding tenure as a teacher in adult education related to alleged deficiencies as a teacher of agriculture (*Hebert* v. *Lafayette Parish School Board*, 146 So. 2d 848 [1962]).

Admission by the school board of hearsay evidence against the objection of the defense attorney was one reason for the reinstatement of a teacher by an Illinois court of appeals. Another reason for the teacher's reinstatement was the refusal of the board, at 11:15 P.M., to continue the hearing even though all of the defense witnesses had not been heard (*Lusk* v. *Community Consolidated School District No. 95*, 20 Ill. App. 2d 252, 155 N.E. 2d 650 [1959]).

In another case, Rehberg was charged with improper conduct toward girls in his class. He notified the board he would have many witnesses at his hearing. The hearing was conducted in a small room, which was filled by board witnesses when the teacher's witnesses appeared at the appointed time. The teacher's witnesses were then kept waiting outside until a late hour. The dismissal action of the board was reversed by the supreme court of Michigan, which affirmed the ruling of the Michigan Tenure Hearing Commission, partially because of unequal treatment of witnesses (*Rehberg* v. *Ecorse School District*, 345 Mich. 731, 77 N.W. 2d 131 [1956]).

The right to cross-examine opposing witnesses is a fundamental procedural right. When Forman, an Arizona teacher, was denied this right at his dismissal hearing, the Arizona supreme court took the unusual step of issuing a writ calling for the certified record of the proceedings of the local board, and an examination of this record led the court to overturn the board's decision (*Forman* v. *Creighton School District No. 14*, 87 Ariz. 329, 351 Pac. 2d 165 [1960]). Similarly, the decision of a board to dismiss Steele was reversed by the supreme court of Alabama because, at the dismissal hearing, the superintendent of schools testified in support of the dismissal but refused, with board approval, to answer questions during cross-examination designed to show bias against

Steele because of union leadership (*State* v. *Board of Education of Fairfield*, 252 Ala. 254, 40 So. 2d 689 [1949]).

Boards are expected to base their findings on fact and their conclusions on the preponderance of evidence on each specific charge. Failure to do so has led to reversal of board decisions in many instances—for example, *Midway School District* v. *Griffeath* (29 Cal. 2d 13, 172 Pac. 2d 857 [1946]); *Board of Education of Choctaw County et al.* v. *Kennedy* (256 Ala. 478, 55 So. 2d 511 [1951]); *Board of Trustees of Lassen Union High School District* v. *Owens* (23 Cal. Rptr. 710 [1962]); *Compton* v. *School Directors of District No. 14* (8 Ill. App. 2d 243, 131 N.E. 2d 544 [1955]); *Chandler* v. *East St. Louis School District 189* (35 Ill. App. 2d 317, 182 N.E. 2d 774 [1962]); *School District No. 13, Saguache County* v. *Mort* (115 Colo. 571, 176 Pac. 2d 984 [1947]); *Lusk* v. *Community Consolidated School District No. 95* (20 Ill. App. 2d 252, 155 N.E. 2d 650 [1959]); and *Rehberg* v. *Ecorse School District* (345 Mich. 731, 77 N.W. 2d 131 [1956]).

Possible bias on the part of board members participating in dismissal hearings has caused courts to reverse dismissals in many cases. In one case a board member conducted an investigation of a business manager; to a third party called the employee a "thief"; brought all nine charges upon which dismissal was based; made statements during the hearing but refused, with board approval and over the objection of the defense attorney, to testify under oath; and then cast the deciding vote to dismiss. A New Jersey court reversed the board action on the ground of bias and directed a hearing under the New Jersey Tenure Employees Hearing Act of 1960 (*Hoek* v. *Board of Education of Asbury Park*, 75 N.J. Super. 182, 182 Atl. 2d 577 [1962]).

When board members are charged at dismissal hearings with affidavits of bias, the board should act on the charges by majority vote, those charged with bias abstaining, and culpable members should disqualify themselves to avoid reversal or remand of the board decision (*State ex rel. Allen* v. *Board of Public Instruction of Broward County, Florida*, 214 So. 2d 7 [1968]).

In a case decided in March 1970, a federal district court in Wisconsin found violations of constitutional due process in the nonelection of two probationary teachers even though the Wisconsin tenure statutes clearly provide for nonrenewal of probationary teachers' contracts without a statement of cause. In this case there was a very confused fact situation, which led the court to hold that Fourteenth Amendment rights were involved. The teachers were notified of the intent not to employ them and were given a softened statement of reasons by the superintendent. There was a conference scheduled between the board and the teachers, but no counsel for the teachers was present, and the superintendent and his staff left when the teachers arrived. The conference purported to be a hearing, but without charges and specifications, without proceedings to prove any charges, and without the right of the teachers to respond. There was evidence that the board had acted on the basis of a different charge from the one presented to the teachers by the superintendent. In consideration of the confused fact situation and of the great professional harm that could result to the two teachers, the court invoked rights beyond the state statutes. Relying on the Fourteenth Amendment, the court found violations of constitutional due process and said the teachers had a right to a hearing to prove arbitrariness. The reasoning of the court seems clear —if charges are communicated, they must be sufficiently clear and specific to allow defense; if a hearing is held, it must provide full procedural due process, the parties having knowledge of the causes considered both by the individual bringing charges and by the members of the quasi-judicial body making the decision, and those charged having an opportunity to respond under due process guaranties (*Gouge* v. *Joint School District No. 1,* 310 F. Supp. 984 [1970]).

It is understood that this case is not on appeal. If it were to be affirmed by a circuit court of appeals or by the U.S. Supreme Court, the decision would have a deep impact on the tenure status of local government employees—in effect, giving these employees automatic tenure even in nontenure jurisdictions.

In another case, testimony of the secretary of the board indicated that the members had decided prior to the hearing of the case to dismiss the teacher. One of the reasons for which the Colorado supreme court reversed the dismissal was prejudgment (*School District No. 13, Saguache County* v. *Mort,* 115 Colo. 571, 176 Pac. 2d 984 [1947]).

Shockley, a tenured principal, was charged with insubordination. During the hearing, he alleged bias against him by the board because of his efforts to enroll his daughter in an all-white school, and he requested permission to prove bias. He was allowed the requested opportunity, but later he was interrupted and prevented from concluding his presentation of evidence. The Delaware supreme court remanded the case for a rehearing on the charge of bias (*Board of Education, Laurel District* v. *Shockley,* 52 Dela. 237, 149 Atl. 2d 331, 155 Atl. 2d 323 [1959]).

In one case a dismissal was reversed because of evidence of bias on the part of two board members who indicated they were basing their votes to dismiss on grounds not related to the charges; the vote to dismiss was five to four (*Lowenstein* v. *Newark Board of Education,* 35 N.J. 94, 171 Atl. 2d 265 [1961]).

Indirection. A teacher who had not reached the mandatory retirement age was told that the system had no place for him and was given pension claim forms to fill out. The supreme court of New Mexico ruled that the teacher had been removed by indirection rather than by hearing on charges (*Sanchez* v. *Board of Education, Town of Belen,* 68 N.M. 440, 362 Pac. 2d 979 [1961]). Final disposition of the case could not take place at the time because the teacher's application for retirement was in process. In subsequent litigation the same court held that the teacher was not properly dismissed when an unsatisfactory evaluation form signed by his principal and a supervisor had been used as charges and specifications (*Belen Municipal Board of Education* v. *Sanchez,* 75 N.M. 386, 405 Pac. 2d 229 [1965]).

In another case a high school principal, after a squabble over administration of his school, was transferred to the position of director of guidance and supervisor of adult education, a position which required him to work on a 12-month basis at the same salary. A Louisiana court of appeals held that, in fact, the administrator was demoted not transferred, since he was certified as a principal and would have to study to become qualified for the new position. The court ruled that because the demotion was not accompanied by a hearing on specific charges as required by statute, the administrator had to be reinstated in his old position. The court established a guideline by stating that it would consider a lowering of professional standing to be a demotion (*Aswell* v. *Jackson Parish School Board,* 176 So. 2d 741 [1965]).

A similar case arose in Tennessee, the principal being transferred to another school and given a lower salary. The Tennessee supreme court affirmed the trial court's decision granting the principal the salary differential (*State* v. *Rasnake*, 352 S.W. 2d 427 [1961]).

A board of education in Massachusetts dismissed a teacher for wearing a beard. The board had never published a policy on this matter prior to the teacher's receipt of a letter from his superintendent stating that the wishes of the board were that teachers not have beards while performing their professional duties. The teacher was not given specific direction as to what was expected of him or as to what alternatives were available to him. A federal district court ordered the teacher reinstated (*Lucia* v. *Duggan*, 303 F. Supp. 1122 [1969]).

Recommendations. The following recommendations for school boards on dealing with separations or demotions of professional personnel were summarized in a doctoral project report by De-Vaughn (1964):

(1) A board's policy on dismissal for "remediable" deficiency should include providing notice of specific deficiencies, which should be alleged only after and on the basis of sufficient observations. The notice should include dates, instances, and supporting records.

(2) Policy on dismissal for "remediable" deficiency should provide for reasonable time after notice is given for correction of alleged deficiencies before charges are preferred.

(3) Prior to preferment of charges for incompetency, a complete evaluation should be conducted, including frequent observations (in which supervisory personnel participate). The observations must be of sufficient length to establish facts, specific incidents, and examples, with times and dates. Deficiencies should be pointed out in conference, with follow-up by letter summarizing understandings and stating conditions for continuing employment.

(4) A detailed preliminary investigation should be prescribed policy. The investigation should be conducted by a designated professional staff member, in coordination with legal counsel, for the following spe-

cific purposes: (a) to establish probable cause by unbiased examination of all evidence and (b) to establish evidence through examination of witnesses and documents fixing specific acts or incidents of neglect, with dates, times, and places.

(5) Witnesses on both sides of the issues should be examined, and assurances that reprisals will not be made should be given to witnesses opposing separation.

(6) Administrators and boards of education should determine the extent of job security or tenure intended by the statutes, and such statutes should be studied with the purpose of seeking through legislative delegations clarity in the following minimum provisions: (a) valid causes for separation, (b) differences, if any, between probationary provisions and tenure provisions, and (c) length of probationary period, conditions of termination for probationary personnel, and conditions of dismissal for both probationary and tenure personnel.

(7) Policy should specify the following as minimum requirements in charges and specifications: (a) that charges be based on statutory or constitutional cause, (b) that charges be particularized as to specific acts or incidents of neglect, with times, dates, and places of occurrence, and (c) that charges and specifications be added, deleted, or altered only through notification to the employee at least ten days before the hearing.

(8) When a board gives notice of suspension, reassignment, or dismissal, it should observe the following procedure: (a) notice should be given in writing with ten days allowed for answer by the teacher; (b) charges and specifications should accompany the notice and be considered a part of such notice; (c) charges and specifications should comply with the particulars contained in recommendation seven; (d) the teacher should be given notice of his rights under statutes and/or board rules; and (e) communications of notice should be sent by registered mail or by messenger, so that there is proof of delivery.

(9) Administrators and boards of education should draft and seek passage of legislation designed to provide all professional em-

ployees the following minimum due process guaranties in dismissal hearings: (a) the right to have a public hearing (at the option of the teacher upon written request after notice and charges), (b) the right of a teacher to present testimony in his own behalf and the opportunity to have witnesses and documents subpoenaed, (c) the right of counsel, (d) the right to hear opposing testimony and to challenge witnesses and cross-examine them on testimony offered, (e) the right to have depositions from witnesses legally unable to answer subpoenas, (f) the right to inspect documents used in evidence, (g) the right to have testimony given under oath or affirmation, (h) the right to have testimony recorded and to have a copy of the record of the proceedings in time to allow preparation of an appeal, and (i) the right to have elements of pleading and evidence challenged and ruled upon by the presiding member of the board. (If such guaranties are not already included in statutes or subsequently added to them, the guaranties should be written into board policy and administrative regulations to protect both the individual concerned and the board.)

(10) Policy should require that the following be minimum standards of conduct for board members when performing their quasi-judicial role: (a) their findings should be based on the preponderance of evidence by charge and specification, and they should avoid basing judgment on nonrelated considerations; (b) if a board member is involved in an investigation, he should govern his conduct in such a way that he is not subject to a charge of bias, and if he is challenged with good cause, he should withdraw from the quasi-judicial role; (c) members should exercise care in making statements which might indicate prejudgment, and both judgments and statements should be based on findings arrived at in a full hearing at an official meeting; (d) members should avoid assuming the role of prosecutor in hearings; (e) boards should be careful to seek full evidence on both sides of issues or at least to give the opposing effort a full hearing; and (f) hearings should be conducted with formality to

guarantee the full rights of the individual under charges as outlined in recommendation nine.

(11) To avoid indirection, policy should prescribe full proceedings as listed in previous recommendations. When separation is deemed advisable and when negotiations, voluntary retirement, or transfer do not offer promise of success, the board should take direct action to prefer charges and to follow the recommended procedures.

Summary. This article has attempted to indicate, by illustrative cases rather than by an exhaustive list, the standards set by courts of law to govern separations or demotions of teachers and administrators in both tenure and nontenure situations. The cases demonstrate the obligation of administrators and boards of education to observe with care the constitutional rights of individual employees, the proscriptions and prescriptions of federal and state statutes, and the rules and regulations of state and local boards of education and boards of regents.

One may well expect to see further litigation, both with and without racial overtones, involving teachers' individual rights of free speech and peaceful protest. Transfers or reassignments designed to achieve staff integration may well bring additional litigation. Although due process guidelines to be observed in staff reductions were clearly established in the Singleton case, school boards continue to fail to heed them. The extent of teachers' individual freedoms relative to dress or modes of grooming may also become a central issue for the courts.

It would be hazardous to guess the limitations and freedoms which may become legal standards, but, in general, in the jurisprudence of the United States stereotyped conformity in thought, speech, and dress has not been fostered. Opinions of attorneys general on doubtful questions—that is, questions which have not been litigated or questions on which there is lack of agreement in the decisions—may be helpful as guides to administrators, boards of education, and boards of regents. If a decision on a specific matter is urgently needed, the safe way to establish guidance is to initiate litigation to determine the required standard.

In the area of procedural standards, strict observance of statutes and board rules and regulations not in conflict with those statutes is advisable. If statutes are outmoded, ambiguous, or too fragmentary or silent as to procedure, local legislative delegations are available to make the school code meet required expectations and serve the purposes of sound educational policy and practice.

The possible effects of formal documents adopted in professional negotiations on the legal aspects of separation of professional employees also cannot be precisely determined. This is a subject of particular concern when formal agreements are reached on employment status and the applicable statutes either have not set limits on substantive areas to be negotiated and standards for representation or are so silent or fragmentary that they provide little guidance as to valid causes for separation and adequate procedures for separation.

Given the facts that from 1946 to 1963, 47 percent of the subsequently litigated decisions by school boards to separate or demote teachers were reversed by the courts on due process grounds and that the tempo of cultural change in the United States has increased markedly since 1963, it is likely that school boards and administrators can be properly guided on legal questions in personnel administration only by employing or retaining a lawyer knowledgeable in the field and by utilizing legal research tools. This seems to be the only course of action open to school boards and educational administrators, since ignorance of the law is not an accepted excuse for violating it.

BIBLIOGRAPHY

CORWIN, EDWARD S. 1948 *The Constitution and What It Means Today.* 10th ed. Princeton, N.J., Princeton University Press.

DAVIS, FREDERICK 1961 "Enforcing Academic Tenure: Reflections and Suggestions." *Wisconsin Law Review,* 1961, no. 2:200–220.

DEVAUGHN, JAMES EVERETTE 1964 "Administrative Error in Separation or Reassignment of Professional Personnel in Education: An Analysis of Violations of Due Process as Revealed in Decisions of State and Federal Appellate Courts During the Period January 1946–June 1963, With Implications and Guidelines for Policy and Practice." Doctor of education project report. New York, Teachers College.

EDWARDS, NEWTON 1955 *The Courts and the Public Schools: The Legal Basis of School Organization and Administration.* Rev. ed. University of Chicago Press.

GARBER, LEE O., AND E. EDMUND REUTTER, JR. 1969 *Yearbook of School Law.* Danville, Ill., Interstate.

GELLHORN, WALTER 1960 *American Rights: The Constitution in Action.* New York, Macmillan.

GELLHORN, WALTER, AND CLARK BYSE 1954 *Administrative Law: Cases and Comments.* Brooklyn, N.Y., Foundation Press.

GRANT, JAMES A. CLIFFORD 1960 *Our Common Law Constitution.* Boston University Press.

GRISWOLD, ERWIN N. 1955 *The 5th Amendment Today: Three Speeches.* Cambridge, Mass., Harvard University Press.

HAMILTON, ROBERT ROLLA, AND E. EDMUND REUTTER, JR. 1958 *Legal Aspects of School Board Operation.* New York, Teachers College Press.

HARVARD UNIVERSITY. LAW SCHOOL 1956 *Government Under Law.* Edited by Arthur E. Sutherland. Cambridge, Mass., Harvard University Press.

KELLY, ALFRED H., AND WINFRED A. HARBINSON 1955 *The American Constitution: Its Origins and Development.* Rev. ed. New York, Norton.

MASON, ALPHEUS T., AND WILLIAM M. BEANEY 1959 *The Supreme Court in a Free Society.* Englewood Cliffs, N.J., Prentice-Hall.

MCGEHEE, LUCIUS P. 1906 *Due Process of Law Under the Federal Constitution.* Northport, N.Y., Thompson.

MOTT, RODNEY L. 1926 *Due Process of Law.* Indianapolis, Ind., Bobbs-Merrill.

NATIONAL EDUCATION ASSOCIATION. RESEARCH DIVISION 1960 *School Law Summaries.* Washington, D.C., The Association.

REMMLEIN, MADALINE K., AND MARTHA L. WARE, eds. 1970 *School Law.* 3rd ed. Danville, Ill., Interstate.

SCHWARTZ, BERNARD 1955 *American Constitutional Law.* Cambridge University Press.

SPURLOCK, CLARK 1955 *Education and the Supreme Court.* Urbana, University of Illinois Press.

Teachers Day in Court. Published annually by the Research Division of the National Education Association.

JAMES EVERETTE DEVAUGHN

TEACHER MILITANCY

Public school teachers are no longer the docile handmaidens of education. At varying rates and with varying degrees of intensity in communities throughout the United States, teachers have been mobilized and have begun to wage battle to advance their interests. Higher salaries, better working conditions, and improvements in education command their attention as never before. Teacher participation in educational policy-making is increasing, and more and more local school districts are beginning to provide for collective negotiations of one sort or another (Lieberman & Moskow 1966; Steffensen 1964; Stinnett et al. 1966).

The National Education Association (NEA) and the American Federation of Teachers (AFT) and their state and local affiliates are the organizational channels for the contemporary teachers' movement. To achieve their objectives these groups use tactics which range from campaigns in school board or municipal elections, criticism of educational authorities, picketing, packing public meetings of boards of education, and encouraging teachers to refuse to participate in extracurricular activities to work slowdowns, professional holidays, strikes, mass resignations, the withholding of salary agreements, and recommendations that no new teachers accept assignments in uncooperative state or local school systems (Moskow 1966).

It is impossible to calculate all instances of aggressive behavior by teacher groups in recent years, but conflict is on the rise. According to the U.S. Bureau of Labor Statistics, during the two decades from 1940 to 1959, 86 work stoppages involving 23,000 people occurred. In the brief span of six years, from 1960 to 1966, as many as 51 stoppages involving over 81,000 people were conducted by teacher groups throughout the nation. In the 1967–1968 school year about 92,000 teachers withheld their services in 32 work stoppages called by AFT affiliates alone. There can be little doubt that teacher quiescence is giving way to teacher militancy.

Militant motivations. The aggressive activities of teachers and their organizations tend to crowd other aspects of their lives from public view. A strike in New York City, mass resignations in Florida, and the imposition of sanctions in Oklahoma are events that command public notice. As a result, popular conceptions of the new teacher militancy all stress behavioral features—aggressive activity, hard conflict, open warfare. Many people refer to the phenomenon, but only a few have attempted conceptual or operational definitions of it. In a study of militant professionalism among high school teachers in Ohio and Michigan, Corwin (1965) used two indexes of militancy: the incidence of conflict and the disposition of teachers toward taking initiative in professional matters. In a study of teacher unionization in New York City and Perth Amboy, N.J., Cole (1969) employed an index combining attitudes and behavior with regard to strikes because he considered both to be significant parts of a teacher's support for a militant group.

To explore and understand the concept of militancy, it is helpful to consider attitudes and behavior separately—that is, how teachers perceive and evaluate the educational world, on the one hand, and what they actually do, on the other. Participation, power, and combat all characterize the contemporary teachers' movement.

Each one can be conceived of as a motivational dimension of militancy. Participation reflects the goal, power the strategic, and combat the tactical orientations of teachers.

The goal orientation takes into account teachers' desires for participation in deciding the roles their organizations should play in determining policies on salaries, personnel, curriculum, the organization of the school system, and other educational matters. What is important, as far as participation is concerned, is less the desire for change in the substance of policy and more the desire for change in the procedures by which substantive policies are decided by school authorities. In terms of participatory goals, teachers may want either a decisive or consultive role. The former means that educational-policy decisions would hinge upon the approval of teacher groups; the latter requires that the opinions of teacher groups be taken into account but not considered in any sense binding. The strategic orientation concerns the power of teacher organizations and of other major participants in educational policy-making. Teachers may or may not feel it necessary either to increase the power of their own organization or to diminish the power of other policy-makers. The tactical orientation, which most resembles popular notions, concerns a teacher's readiness to be actively militant. Some teachers are more inclined than others to combativeness and conflict and more willing than others to act forcefully and take risks.

Conceptually, goals, strategies, and tactics should be viewed as distinctive motivational components, although empirically they tend to fit together. Some teachers may desire to participate on equal footing with school authorities and still not be disposed to employ aggressive methods to achieve such a goal. Others may be combative but willing to fight only for specific benefits while accepting a consultive role in other educational decisions.

Participation, power, and combat are major elements in the current doctrines of the NEA and AFT, but participation is perhaps the most significant, particularly in terms of the future of teacher organizations. The more ambitious the participatory objectives, the greater the impetus a group will have to forcefully challenge the distribution of educational power. Both national organizations increasingly advocate teacher participation in educational policy-making. The right to exercise professional judgment, to play a part in selecting teaching materials and planning the curriculum, to have some say on class size and nonteaching assignments, and to be given a major voice in determining salaries and related welfare benefits are all being claimed by the two national organizations (Lieberman & Moskow 1966; Stinnett et al. 1966). The NEA and the AFT also agree on the need for organizational power at national, state, and local levels. NEA doctrine advocates group power by means of professional negotiation; AFT doctrine calls for collective bargaining (Steffensen 1964).

The attainment of power and participation may depend upon persuasion or pressure. Both the NEA and AFT naturally espouse collective action, but they disagree about the inevitability of conflict. The many differences in purpose, resources, structures, and philosophies between the two organizations cause them to operate differently: the union relies chiefly on force, the association on persuasion (West 1967). The NEA stresses consensus, rejecting the idea that conflict between teachers and school authorities is a normal state of affairs. The AFT stresses disagreement, believing that many of the major differences which divide teachers and their employers can be settled only by combat (Doherty & Oberer 1967; Wildman & Perry 1966).

Despite the increasing militancy of the NEA, doctrinal and motivational differences still persist between the two national organizations. One study surveyed 185 teacher leaders in nine organizations of five large cities and found sharp contrasts in orientations. Those heading AFT locals were considerably more likely than those heading NEA affiliates to advocate a decisive participatory voice, prescribe greater power for their own groups and less for other participants, and express combativeness and a willingness to take forceful action (Rosenthal 1969).

Determinants of militancy. Militant attitudes and behavior can be explained in a variety of ways. Some militancy can be attributed to the characteristics of individuals—including their teaching and nonteaching statuses—and some can be attributed to the forces in the general political atmosphere and in the local settings in which public education is conducted.

Surveys have demonstrated the relationship of various teacher characteristics to militancy. Sex and militancy have been found highly correlated.

Males are more likely than females to join teachers' unions and to be militantly predisposed for two reasons. First, men are generally more aggressive than women, since societal expectations encourage males to be dominant and power oriented and females to be receptive and submissive. Second, more men than women regard teaching as a lifetime career and have greater need of the benefits, particularly of the pecuniary sort, which militancy promises to bring. It has also been said that men are less able than their female colleagues to economically stand meager salaries or to psychologically endure low status (Lowe 1965; Rosenthal 1969).

Age and teaching experience are also related to militancy. Younger teachers and those with only a few years of teaching experience are more militant than older and more experienced ones. Younger teachers have had less time to accommodate themselves to the status quo and have had proportionately greater exposure to the currents of militancy in the nation. By contrast, older teachers who are on maximum salary and nearing retirement can gain less and risk more by committing themselves to a militant movement. Often they began teaching at a time when jobs were scarce and are therefore likely to be more security-minded than their younger colleagues (Cole 1968).

Teaching levels, estimates of educational conditions, and job conceptions matter as well. Secondary school teachers are more inclined to militancy than elementary ones; teachers who are dissatisfied with conditions in a school system are more predisposed than those who are comparatively contented (Rosenthal 1969); and those who are "professionally" oriented also are more militant than those who are "bureaucratically" oriented (Corwin 1965).

In Cole's examination of teachers' support for the United Federation of Teachers (UFT), the New York City affiliate of the AFT, not only sex and age but also religion, political affiliation, and class of origin were shown to be relevant determinants of militancy. He found that Jewish religious affiliation, Democratic Party allegiance, and lower-class origins create militant predispositions. He explained that these statuses caused prior socialization in attitudes so that teachers were predisposed to respond positively when the UFT called its strikes in order to improve salaries and working conditions. He concluded that a major cause of the union's success in the late 1950's and early 1960's was due to the change in the composition of the city's teaching staff. Most of the people entering the system in the first three decades of the twentieth century were Christians. The majority entering since then have been Jewish. The percentage of male teachers rose from 11 percent in 1920 to 20 percent in 1960, and the number of young teachers in the system also increased significantly. Thus, the UFT was provided with a larger potential base of leaders, activists, members, and supporters (Cole 1968).

A number of investigators have emphasized changes in the structure and organization of education as explanations of militancy. Some have attributed militancy to the increasing professionalization of teaching, which inevitably challenges traditional control of schools by laymen and their administrative representatives (Corwin 1967). Others have argued that the trend toward bigger school systems and larger schools results in a loss of identity by teachers; increasing bureaucratization, further centralization of decision-making, and a widening gap between classroom teachers and school executives encourage militant feelings by the rank and file (Bridges 1964). According to still others, recent trends in administration which encourage participation by the rank and file have whetted the appetites of teachers and caused their expectations to rise. As one observer noted, ". . . democratic administration of any enterprise may actually hasten the process of organization and power accumulation" (Wildman 1964).

Teacher attitudes also are viewed as a product of the times. Several NEA officials maintain, for example, that teachers are swept up in the movement by people throughout the world who are committed to the end of colonialism and paternalism (Stinnett et al. 1966). Changing attitudes are also believed to be an outgrowth of regulations governing public employment—such as President John F. Kennedy's executive order in 1962 and the host of state and local regulations which permit government employees to organize unions. As a result, government and municipal workers—including not only teachers but also policemen, firemen, sanitation men, transit workers, postal employees, and social service workers—have started to organize, to insist on a voice in making agency policies in areas of interest to them, and to challenge employers through protests, demonstrations, and strikes.

In one combination or another, the above factors and trends go far in explaining the heightened militancy of teachers. But another essential and even more proximate cause is the heated organizational rivalry between the NEA and AFT and their local affiliates. Specifically, the major impetus of group competition and teacher militancy was the rapid ascendancy of the United Federation of Teachers. By winning their two strikes, in 1960 and 1962, the New York City union probably set a pattern of teacher militancy for decades to come.

Militant behavior. Contemporary teacher militancy is a group phenomenon, and therefore it is useful to conceive of militant behavior as organizational behavior. A satisfactory explanation of organizational behavior requires more than the examination of individual or organizational motivation. Militant motivation may be necessary for militant action, but it is not sufficient. Depending on the circumstances, even the most militantly oriented may move cautiously rather than precipitously, diplomatically rather than combatively; and even the least militantly oriented may be forced to take extreme measures.

Opportunities—conditions and situations that facilitate or impede forceful action by teacher groups—must exist if attitudes are to be translated into behavior. Although teachers who are militantly inclined will interpret situations and conditions differently from those who are acquiescent, opportunities are not entirely dependent on perceptions. Whether opportunities for organizational action exist depends on a number of conditions operative in local educational environments—such as the styles of the political community, the conduct of educational administrators, and the dispositions of teachers in the school system.

To a considerable extent, environmental forces shape opportunities for group action. To some extent, statutes and regulations enacted by state and local governments determine the opportunities for more and less militantly motivated groups (Wollett 1967). Important, too, are local political cultures and patterns of community politics. Some community patterns encourage consensus and agreement, whereas others encourage competition and contention. Teacher groups, among others, are influenced by the integrative or conflictive elements in a community. The community characterized by a high degree of integration impedes militant teacher action. Here, although people clash over who runs things, how public affairs are conducted, and who gets what, the dominating features are cultural homogeneity, widely shared attachments, and complementary interests. The community characterized by a high degree of disintegration facilitates militant teacher action. Here, although certain fundamental agreements exist, cultural heterogeneity, conflicting attachments, and competing interests are more pervasive (Rosenthal 1969).

Directly relevant to group opportunities are the attitudes and practices of those traditionally considered to be educational authorities, particularly school board members, superintendents, and school administrators. Some authorities who adamantly oppose any change in the rules of the game, especially participation by teachers in policy-making, tend to feed and sustain group militancy and provoke group action. Authorities who either respond to teacher demands in benevolent fashion or skillfully practice techniques of diversion and delay tend to restrain teacher organizations from aggressive action (Corwin 1965; Rosenthal 1969).

More important than outside influences are the attitudes within a community of teachers and the kinds of opportunities they present to their leaders, who must decide whether or not to act. Organizational programs and tactics are greatly influenced by the views of teachers who are being recruited as members or as supporters in a contest for representation, by the feelings of group members, by group activists who compete with the incumbent leadership, and by the competition stemming from rival organizations. All of these are shaped partly by the attitudes and practices of the traditional educational authorities.

Leaders pay careful attention to recruitment in an effort to enlarge membership because a large membership provides a major base of group strength. The larger a group, the greater its wealth, since income derives mainly from per capita dues. Financial security, in turn, makes it possible to maintain a full-time leadership and a professional staff, propagandize the membership and increase cohesion, finance public relations campaigns aimed at outsiders, and risk whatever financial penalties are incurred by illegal action. Furthermore, numbers are impressive to educational, municipal, and state officials—the people whom teacher organizations try hard to impress.

The more members there are, the more widespread the involvement in organizational activities and campaigns and the greater a group's political muscle.

In their quest for membership, leaders of many groups are careful not to sponsor actions that might deter potential joiners or alienate present members. As a rule, the attitudes of rank-and-file teachers in a school system act as a restraint on militant behavior. Although surveys of nationwide samples of classroom teachers show that almost nine in ten support some type of group action and that half believe strikes are justified under extreme circumstances, such as low salaries, most teachers remain essentially conservative. Certainly, leaders perceive them this way (Cole 1968; Rosenthal 1969). Proportionately few teachers, including organization members, can be relied on to share the more militant motivations of group leaders. The teachers who join an organization because they are expected to, because they are requested to by school administrators, or because they want the fringe benefits which accompany membership (Moskow 1967) are unlikely to bring much conviction or fervor to an affiliation they regard as nominal. They are usually apathetic and uninvolved. Those who join because they think they can increase their power and advance their individual and collective interests through organizational membership (Zeigler 1966) potentially possess the qualities that can be converted by organizational leadership into militant activism, but such members are not necessarily predisposed to forceful action. Whether they are depends upon their attitudes toward the educational establishment: the more predisposed express resentment, the less predisposed exhibit deference and loyalty toward school authorities (Rosenthal 1969).

A countervailing force to teacher conservatism which impels a group to militant action is competition either from within an organization or from a local rival. Frequently, competition between rival teacher groups engenders increased militancy in both. Ordinarily a union pushes an association toward aggressive activity, and soon each is attempting to outdo the other. Internal competition works in the same way. For example, a group's leadership is often challenged by a more militant faction. Then, despite the relative conservatism of the rank and file, incumbents move more strenuously against the educational establishment in order to solidify their support and to preserve their leadership positions (*ibid.*).

Consequences of teacher militancy. There is increasing evidence that militant behavior by teacher groups has had an impact on organizational growth, the distribution of power within school systems, and teacher participation in the resolution of educational policy issues.

When teachers are discontented with a school system, militant group behavior leads to increases in organizational support, membership, and the chance of representational recognition by traditional educational authorities. Winning benefits is important, but a hard-hitting campaign designed to achieve them can be advantageous in itself. It has been shown that the drive by the teachers' union in Boston to win sick-leave benefits and duty-free lunch periods and the 1962 strike by the UFT in New York City resulted in large gains in group membership. As a consequence of the 1962 strike, for instance, the appeal of the UFT was notably enhanced. The way the strike itself was run, and not the benefits which accompanied its settlement, had a major impact on the organization's growth. Its mobilizing effects were tremendous and lasting (Rosenthal 1966).

Militant behavior has also begun to change the distribution of power in education. Individual teachers acting alone have always been far from powerless because of the high professional autonomy and low visibility of classroom activities. But they can increase their power by acting in concert with their colleagues and by establishing formal frameworks of professional negotiation or collective bargaining (Wildman 1964). They have made considerable progress in recent years: The main question is no longer whether school authorities will negotiate with their personnel but rather is how the authorities will negotiate and on what kinds of matters.

The increasing power of teacher groups has put the educational establishment in the United States on the defensive. The American Association of School Administrators has pledged to resist any effort to displace the superintendent and his authority in matters affecting the interest and welfare of school personnel (Stinnett et al. 1966). The National School Boards Association is equally anxious to protect the authority of its constituent groups (Webb 1967).

The defensiveness and fears of the managers of public education are justified. One union official commented: "Power is never given to anyone. Power is taken, and it is taken from someone. Teachers, as one of society's powerless groups, are now starting to take power from supervisors and school boards. This is causing and will continue to cause a realignment of power relationships" (Shanker 1966, p. 23). Other union leaders believe that the time has passed for school boards and administrators to run the schools without significant teacher involvement.

Relationships are changing at the state level, where traditional educational alliances between teacher associations, school board associations, and administrator groups are becoming difficult to maintain (Usdan 1968). Altered distributions of power are also evident at the local level, particularly in large cities where teacher groups have been most militant; the authority of superintendents, school boards, and school principals has been diminished (Cronin 1967). In contrast, the educational power of municipal officials may be increasing. As a rule, mayors have tried to remain aloof from school politics. Now more of them are intervening to settle disputes between teacher organizations and school boards. Apparently, militant tactics prod mayors into exercising new and greater influence over salary issues and consequently over budgetary policies for the school system. In New York City, which is an exceptional case, the UFT president summed up the situation: ". . . there is no real function for the Board of Education. . . . The city administration is calling the shots on all important matters, not only budgetary but in such areas as community involvement" ("A Talk With Albert Shanker" 1968, p. 256). In large cities, militancy by teacher groups may also give rise to militancy by neighborhood groups of Negro parents. In New York City the prolonged teacher strike of 1967 aroused discontent in the ghetto communities and helped stimulate the development of Negro-parent power to counterbalance white-teacher power.

Teachers have increased their own influence, but their influence continues to be less than that of mayors, school boards, and superintendents. The participation and effects of teacher organizations have been greatest in areas in which personal and material rewards for constituents are sought. Efforts have been concentrated in winning higher salaries and related economic benefits, and substantial gains have been made.

Also, much energy has been devoted to seeking changes that would lighten the workload of teachers—duty-free lunch periods, special personnel and aides, increased preparation time, reduction in the number of instructional periods, relief from nonteaching and clerical duties, and limitations on class size—and although accomplishments in this area are fewer than economic gains, they are still substantial. In addition, teacher organizations have tried to prevent school authorities from moving in directions believed to be inimical to the interests of organization constituents. The organizations have achieved considerable success by acting defensively, as veto groups, to prevent the lengthening of the school day and year or the imposition of involuntary assignment systems.

The participation and effects of teacher organizations generally have been minimal on issues where rewards for teachers are more abstract and impersonal and less immediate—such as improvements in the quality of the teaching force, in the education of the underprivileged, in curricular offerings, or in the ways in which schools are organized and administered.

Tactics. There are three major patterns of organizational militancy and influence. Nonmilitant organizations acquiesce, content to accept decisions made for them and benefits offered to them. Organizations which are militantly motivated but restricted by limited opportunities play the role of reminders and suggesters. By means of personal diplomacy or skillful persuasion, they exert some influence on choices made by educational authorities. Many groups follow these two patterns.

The third pattern is that of militant organizations which pursue their motivational inclinations, take advantage of opportunities, and exploit their resources in order to play a participatory role. By means of pressure—prodding, bargaining, demonstrating, and striking—they convince school authorities of the educational merits and political wisdom of their solutions for school problems. The UFT is perhaps the prototype of this pattern. Not only has it sought and attained higher economic benefits and improved working conditions, but it has also attempted, with some success, to design and establish innovations in education, such as the More Effective Schools program. Real differences have separated the UFT and educational authorities. Allowing for extreme positions taken for purposes of bargaining, the two sides have repeatedly stood far apart. Yet, a good number of disputes have been resolved more to the satisfaction of the union than to that of their opponents.

Conclusions. It is still too early to tell whether teacher groups will accomplish reform. By demanding higher salaries, they have helped reshape the allocation of resources to public education. By demanding a larger role in decision-making, they have helped to reshape the distribution of power within public education. Although they have made progress recently, their power is less than overwhelming. Their impact is limited, if no longer negligible. With few local exceptions, teacher groups are no match for the established governors of education; they still do not hold a commanding position or control educational policy. However, militancy is transforming the educational scene. Although teachers have traditionally held marginal roles in policy-making, the organizations which are most militant seem to be able to successfully participate in and influence educational policy decisions. It is probable that power by teacher groups can only be achieved through conflict. If this is true, then more militant behavior means greater organizational influence. At the present time and in the immediate future, militant behavior appears to be the path leading to greater organizational power and increased organizational participation in educational policy-making.

BIBLIOGRAPHY

"A Talk With Albert Shanker" 1968 *Phi Delta Kappan*, 49, no. 5:255–256.

BRIDGES, EDWIN M. 1964 "Teacher Participation in Decision Making." *Administrator's Notebook*, 12, no. 19.

COLE, STEPHEN 1968 "The Unionization of Teachers: Determinants of Rank-and-File Support." *Sociology of Education*, 41, no. 1:66–87.

COLE, STEPHEN 1969 *The Unionization of Teachers: A Case Study of the U.F.T.* New York, Praeger.

CORWIN, RONALD G. 1965 "Militant Professionalism, Initiative and Compliance in Public Education." *Sociology of Education*, 38, no. 4:310–331.

CORWIN, RONALD G. 1967 "Professional Persons in Public Organizations." Stanley M. Elam et al., eds., *Readings on Collective Negotiations in Public Education.* Chicago, Rand McNally. Pages 47–67.

CRONIN, JOSEPH H. 1967 "School Boards and Principals—Before and After Negotiations." *Phi Delta Kappan*, 49, no. 3:123–127.

DOHERTY, ROBERT E., AND WALTER E. OBERER 1967 *Teachers, School Boards, and Collective Bargaining: A Changing of the Guard.* Ithaca, N.Y., New York State School of Industrial and Labor Relations, Cornell University.

Lieberman, Myron, and Michael H. Moskow 1966 *Collective Negotiations for Teachers: An Approach to School Administration.* Chicago, Rand McNally.

Lowe, William T. 1965 "Who Joins Which Teachers' Group?" *Teachers College Record,* 66, no. 7:614–619.

Moskow, Michael H. 1966 *Teachers and Unions: The Applicability of Collective Bargaining to Public Education.* Philadelphia, Industrial Research Unit, Wharton School of Finance and Commerce, University of Pennsylvania.

Moskow, Michael H. 1967 "Teacher Organizations: An Analysis of the Issues." Stanley M. Elam et al., eds., *Readings on Collective Negotiations in Public Education.* Chicago, Rand McNally. Pages 234–247.

Rosenthal, Alan 1966 "The Strength of Teacher Organizations: Factors Influencing Membership in Two Large Cities." *Sociology of Education,* 39, no. 1:359–380.

Rosenthal, Alan 1967 "Administrator-Teacher Relations: Harmony or Conflict?" *Public Administration Review,* 27, no. 2:154–161.

Rosenthal, Alan 1969 *Pedagogues and Power: Teacher Groups in School Politics.* Syracuse, N.Y., Syracuse University Press.

Shanker, Albert 1966 "Teacher-Supervisory Relationships: A Symposium." *Changing Education,* 1, no. 1:17–23.

Steffensen, James P. 1964 *Teachers Negotiate With Their School Boards.* Washington, D.C., U.S. Office of Education.

Stinnett, T. M., et al. 1966 *Professional Negotiation in Public Education.* New York, Macmillan.

Usdan, Michael D. 1968 "New York State's Educational Conference Board: A Coalition in Transition." *Phi Delta Kappan,* 49, no. 6:328–331.

Webb, Harold 1967 "The National School Boards Association and Collective Negotiations." Stanley M. Elam et al., eds., *Readings on Collective Negotiations in Public Education.* Chicago, Rand McNally. Pages 196–202.

West, Allan M. 1967 "The NEA and Collective Negotiations." Stanley M. Elam et al., eds., *Readings on Collective Negotiations in Public Education.* Chicago, Rand McNally. Pages 147–161.

Wildman, Wesley A. 1964 "Implications of Teacher Bargaining for School Administration." *Phi Delta Kappan,* 46, no. 4:152–158.

Wildman, Wesley A., and Charles R. Perry 1966 "Group Conflict and School Organization." *Phi Delta Kappan,* 47, no. 5:244–251.

Winick, Charles 1963 "When Teachers Strike." *Teachers College Record,* 64, no. 7:593–604.

Wollett, Donald H. 1967 "The Importance of State Legislation." Stanley M. Elam et al., eds., *Readings on Collective Negotiations in Public Education.* Chicago, Rand McNally. Pages 94–102.

Zeigler, Harmon 1966 *The Political World of the High School Teacher.* Eugene, Center for the Advanced Study of Educational Administration, University of Oregon.

Alan Rosenthal

TEACHER PROFILE

Reliable and valid studies of the characteristics of the public school teacher were relatively rare until the 1960's. Generally speaking, until that time most studies of teachers' characteristics did not apply to teachers in urban settings, let alone to teachers of nations other than the United States. As noted by sociologists Brookover and Gottlieb, most such studies "[were] based exclusively on investigations conducted in small homogeneous, semi-rural communities with conditions not comparable to those prevailing in large metropolitan areas" (1964, p. 309). These limitations are especially significant because of the rapidity with which the United States has changed from a rural society to a highly complex industrial society, with an ever-increasing demand for highly trained teachers. The difficulty in accurately depicting teachers is further compounded by the fact that studies only a few years or a few months old have been followed by major events which may have modified the character of teaching across the country.

Among the forces that have made a dramatic impact upon the character of teaching are attempts to give teachers enlightened perspectives toward children from poor families and to extend successful teaching to the entire spectrum of American social classes; changes in civil rights laws and fair employment practices; pressures to recruit a larger number of black Americans for teaching and educational administration; the increasing militancy of teachers in determining procedures for recruitment, dismissal for inappropriate classroom conduct, and reimbursement; waves of G.I. Bill students who are entering the field of education; and numbers of individuals who are teaching perhaps to avoid military service. With the limitations caused by these new forces in mind, information which was obtained from the few national studies available is presented here.

The most comprehensive of the available studies were conducted by the National Education Association (1967a; 1968b; 1970), the U.S. Office of Education (Coleman et al. 1966), and Herriott and St. John (1966).

These studies provide the basis for describing the social profile of the approximately 2 million elementary and secondary teachers in the United States. Where information is available, the differences and similarities between elementary and secondary teachers, between teachers in large and small school systems, and between rural and urban teachers will be described. Several sociological implications will also be indicated.

As of 1970, the most recent general study of teachers was an NEA survey (1968c), which provides the basic statistical profile of the American teacher. In the spring of 1967 the average public school teacher was 39 years old; had taught for 12 years, eight of which were in the same school system; and reported an average salary of $6,789. (According to the Office of Education's National Center for Educational Statistics, the projected average salary for 1970 was $8,475.) The elementary school teacher taught an average of 28 pupils in 1967, and the secondary school teacher taught an average of five class periods with 26.4 pupils per class. All but 6.1 percent of the teachers had a four-year degree, and 25.7 percent held a master's degree or doctorate.

Teaching, of course, is not a totally homogeneous profession; thus, there are important differences within the profile. In 1969, 43 percent of male teachers, for example, had advanced degrees, whereas only 21 percent of female teachers had such degrees (National Education Association . . . 1970). Male teachers are also likely to earn more money than female teachers. Secondary school teachers seem to be more mobile than elementary teachers. Some of the major dimensions of the teacher profile include current economic status, social class background, race, parental education, amount and type of teacher training, size of school, and participation in community activities.

Economic status. According to NEA estimates, the average income for public school teachers in the United States in 1969 was $8,840 for secondary teachers and $8,320 for elementary teachers. This difference in salary between elementary and secondary teachers can in part be attributed to differences in the salaries paid to male and female teachers. The mean salary of secondary male teachers was $9,160, whereas female secondary teachers received a mean salary of $8,670. The average salary for female elementary teachers was approximately $400 less than that of their male counterparts (National Education Association . . . 1970). Education may also play a role since males generally have higher educational levels than females. In general, male teachers are younger, better educated, and higher paid than female teachers.

Since average salary indications can sometimes be misleading, it is important to look at the percentage of teachers included in smaller salary brackets. It is estimated that in 1969–1970 (Na-

tional Education Association . . . 1970) about 2.9 percent of all public school teachers were paid less than $5,500; 13 percent, from $5,500 to $6,499; 18.7 percent, from $6,500 to $7,499; 20.5 percent, from $7,500 to $8,499; 16.1 percent, from $8,500 to $9,499; 21.1 percent, from $9,500 to $11,499; and 7.8 percent, $11,500 and over. Thus, about 29 percent of all public school teachers earned over $9,500 in 1969–1970, and about 15 percent earned less than $6,500.

The size of the school district is another important factor affecting salary. In large school systems 91.7 percent of the teachers earned salaries of over $7,000, whereas in small school systems only 76.4 percent earned such salaries. This may be due to the tendency for small school systems to employ a larger proportion of teachers under 25 years of age. It is also quite possible that differences in the salary levels of small and large school systems may not be so great when local cost of living is considered.

Other important considerations in assessing the economic position of teachers are the maximum scheduled salaries for classroom teachers and the proportion of teachers who supplement their incomes by working at other jobs. For teachers with a master's degree or less, the average maximum salary which could be earned in 1967 was $8,890; in 1965 the average maximum was $7,956; and in 1963 the average maximum salary which could be earned was $7,297. (These gains are significantly higher than parallel cost of living increases in the same time period.) Whether this trend in increasing maximum salaries will continue remains to be seen. In 1966–1967, approximately the same proportion of teachers, 8.7 percent, supplemented their teaching incomes as ten years earlier, 7.7 percent (National Education Association . . . 1968b). Hence, it appears that higher income levels have not affected the extent to which some teachers seek to supplement their incomes with second jobs. The small increase probably reflects the increase in males in the profession.

Social origins. Under the broad topic of social origins, three major variables will be reviewed: socioeconomic status, race, and educational level of parents.

Socioeconomic status (SES). In 1911, 52 percent of the teachers in the United States came from farm families (Coffman 1911), and only about 22 percent appear to have come from urban middle-class backgrounds. This situation, of course, changed dramatically in the following half century. In the 1930's studies indicated that a large but declining proportion of teachers still came from farm backgrounds but that increasing percentages were coming from town or urban middle classes. There was also considerable evidence that teachers in the East were being recruited from the upper middle class, whereas in the West and Midwest teachers came from the lower middle class (Warner et al. 1944).

Three substantial nationwide studies during the 1960's bring the picture up to date. Data presented by Herriott and St. John (1966) indicate that among teachers in urban schools, the number actually reared on farms declined to 13.7 percent, although the number raised in rural or small communities (having a population of less than 10,000) was still a disproportionately large 38 percent. Only 45.2 percent of the teachers came from cities of over 50,000. It should be re-emphasized, however, that these are data from urban schools alone. For the same urban schools, 47.2 percent of the teachers had fathers in white-collar occupations, and 36.8 percent had fathers who were blue-collar workers (Herriott & St. John 1966). These data are not broken down by region of the country, but they are broken down by the SES of school taught in. Even in the economically poor inner-city schools (many of them ghetto schools), 35 percent of the teachers were from rural or small-town backgrounds and 45 percent were from the white-collar class.

From a slightly different perspective, Werts (1966) did a study of future teachers who graduated from college in June 1961. Werts reaffirmed the overrepresentation of children of farmers in the ranks of teachers. Werts also confirmed the belief of numerous early commentators by revealing the relatively low socioeconomic status of the parents of future teachers compared to other college graduates. Of the four broad SES categories into which the subjects were divided, Werts found that the group composed of children of farmers, manual laborers, semiskilled workers, and clerical workers was substantially overrepresented in the future teacher population. However, it should be pointed out that if teaching has lower status than other occupations selected by college graduates, teaching still has high status

relative to the population as a whole and is indeed a route of upward mobility. However, the number of poor blacks, especially poor black males, entering education is still very small.

Werts' study went beyond the simple SES level of classification and indicated the overselection or underselection of teaching by children whose parents represent most major occupational groups. Among male college graduates, those whose parents were businessmen, salesmen, and teachers were overrepresented among the future teachers, whereas those whose parents were engineers, physicians, and college professors were underrepresented. The same is true of women graduates except that none of the higher SES occupations are overrepresented.

Race. Excellent data on the subject of racial origins of teachers are available from the report entitled *Equality of Educational Opportunity,* better known as the Coleman Report (Coleman et al. 1966). The report is one of the most recent and sophisticated national studies, and all comments on race of teachers can be taken directly from the published tables of the report. (Some of the findings are not commented upon in the main report itself, however.)

It is perhaps surprising to note that on an overall national level, teaching is probably the most perfectly integrated occupation. The national teacher ratios of 88 percent white to 11 percent Negro to 1 percent other nonwhite fit almost exactly the national census figures of 1960. The overall percentage of nonwhite teachers is very close to what it would be if teacher status were randomly assigned.

Unfortunately, these figures obscure more than they reveal. Percentages vary drastically from rural to urban sections of the country and from region to region, with considerable social implications. In the rural North the teacher is likely to be white regardless of the race of his pupils. In the rural South the teacher is quite likely to be the color of his pupils. A disproportionate share of the black teachers in the United States are from the segregated rural southern schools.

A racial analysis of teachers in metropolitan areas is less clear-cut. Although there is still a large proportion of black teachers in the southern schools, the regional differences are considerable. In 1965, 11 percent of all secondary teachers in the urban Northeast were nonwhite, but the comparable figure was only 3 percent for the Midwest, and a sizable 28 percent for the Southwest (probably reflecting a combination of segregated schools in Texas and Oklahoma, Indian schools, and a scattering of Mexican-American schools). The pattern is roughly similar for urban elementary schools.

The data concerning the degree of racial segregation of teachers are complex (although on the whole indicating overwhelming segregation) and are not of direct concern here except to note that the number of white children taught by nonwhite teachers is microscopically small. On the other hand, nonwhite students are much more likely to have white instructors, especially in the Northeast, where 80 percent of the teachers were white, and in the West, where 82 percent of the teachers were white. In short, the racial origins of teachers of black and white pupils are not the same.

In spite of the massive body of evidence indicating the extent of segregation in American education (among both pupils and teachers), there are few studies of how attitudes toward students and the teaching profession differ between white and nonwhite teachers. One study found that black teachers saw black students more favorably and with more individualized characteristics than did white teachers and that black teachers were more highly satisfied with the teaching situation (Brookover & Gottlieb 1964). However, that study was unable to use controls for several important background characteristics, and therefore it is unclear whether the results are mainly related to race. Future studies could well be directed toward understanding what the raw statistics regarding teachers' race mean in terms of behavior, attitudes, and so forth.

Parental education.   Another index of social origins is parental education. Again using the Coleman Report as a source, several highly predictable findings emerge. One is that the educational level of the parents of both nonwhite teachers and rural teachers is low. But within the context of this major finding several unexpected findings emerge.

For example, mothers of teachers generally have higher educational attainment than fathers. This somewhat surprising difference is persistent across region, race, and degree of urbanization, except for the metropolitan Northeast, where

the fathers' educational level is higher than that of the mothers. On a national basis, neither fathers' nor mothers' education averages 12 years (presumably high school education). Age is certainly a factor here (parents of younger teachers usually have more education). Nonetheless, in most areas of the United States the parents of the typical teacher did not graduate from high school. However, if one parent did graduate from high school, it seems more likely to have been the teacher's mother. These findings probably imply more clearly the exact kind of middle-class family in which the present generation of teachers originates than do findings related to fathers' occupations or family income.

Some other differences regarding parental education involve race and region. The differences between black and white educational levels is greatest in the South, where, for example, the education of the parents of rural black elementary teachers averages no more than grade school level. Yet outside the South, the difference in parental education between white and black teachers is quite small. In the urban West there are no differences between the parental education levels of white and black teachers.

The South provides further surprises in that, although the rural South shows very low parental education levels, in the urban South parents of white teachers have higher educational levels than the national average. Black teachers' educational levels are not far from the national average, and, interestingly, the mothers of black secondary school teachers had an educational level equal to the overall national average. The average difference in mothers' education and fathers' education for black teachers is an unparalleled one full year.

Teachers' preparation.   In 1931 it is estimated that only about one-third of America's teachers had four-year degrees. By 1956 the figure had risen to about three-fourths (National Education Association . . . 1968a). By 1966, however, in urban schools 97 percent of the teachers in cities with a population of over 50,000 had degrees (Herriott & St. John 1966). A more precise distinction among these urban teachers indicates that 67 percent had only bachelor's degrees, 28 percent had master's degrees, and 2 percent had doctoral degrees.

The Coleman Report finds similar percentages of persons holding degrees among metropolitan teachers (95 percent), with smaller percentages among nonwhite (91 percent), southern (85 percent), and rural (74 percent) teachers. These data are from 1965. The typical figure, however, is a college degree for all areas, regions, or racial groups. A later NEA national survey (1970) indicates that 5 percent of teachers did not have degrees in 1969–1970.

Coleman feels, however, that verbal facility is perhaps a better indicator than a degree of general educational and intellectual preparation. The Coleman Report provides some interesting comparisons of the verbal facility of various teacher populations. In rural areas the verbal facility of elementary teachers, for example, is a full two points (on a 28-point scale) below that of urban teachers. Likewise, the difference in verbal facility betwen white and black teachers averages about 2.5 points across all regions.

Somewhat surprisingly, there were no consistent differences between urban and rural secondary teachers, and in the North and West rural teachers tended to have higher verbal facility scores than urban teachers (despite lower average education). Nor were there any significant differences between the average verbal facility of elementary teachers (22.8) and that of secondary teachers (22.9).

The figures regarding the preparation of teachers are encouraging. Teachers without degrees seem to be rapidly disappearing, and there is an increasing proportion of teachers who hold advanced degrees. Although the formal education of teachers has increased, there is little or no systematic knowledge pertaining to the actual preparation of teachers. The information provided by a simplistic measure of verbal facility in the Coleman Report seems to indicate that the picture of teacher capability is not as homogeneous or as predictable as the levels of formal education might indicate.

In 1965 approximately 61 percent of all elementary teachers had a degree in education, 16 percent had a degree in some academic field, 12 percent were undetermined, and 11 percent lacked any college degree (Coleman et al. 1966). These proportions were nearly identical for white and nonwhite teachers; however, considerable differences appeared between metropolitan and nonmetropolitan teachers. Metropolitan teachers had an increased number of degrees in all categories, thus leaving a small number of teachers

(5 percent) without degrees. The ratio between education degrees and academic degrees, however, remained essentially unchanged. In the nonmetropolitan areas it becomes more difficult to generalize because of a wide variation among regions. In terms of a major in education the range runs from 70 percent for nonwhite, rural, southern teachers to 40 percent for nonwhite, rural, southwestern teachers. The range is probably a result primarily of the rigidities of the segregated teachers college in the old South and the relative absence of the normal school in the newer university systems of the Southwest. Apparently the impact of this difference is especially important for the nonwhite teachers in that both extremes are found in nonwhite groups.

In all, roughly 50 percent of all American teachers employed in 1965 attended a normal school or teachers college, and 39 percent attended institutions where no graduate work was offered. As of 1965, virtually all American secondary school teachers had college degrees, but a sizable minority of these degrees (33 percent) were in elementary education, and 25 percent of all secondary school teachers attended a teachers college or normal school.

Size of school system. Data from the NEA (1967a) indicate that a large proportion of American teachers continued to teach in medium to small school districts. Roughly 43 percent of all teachers taught in districts ranging from 3,000 to 25,000 in enrollment. And a surprisingly large proportion (32.6 percent) taught in districts of under 3,000 in enrollment. The remaining teachers taught in large metropolitan school districts of over 25,000 in enrollment.

In large school districts (those having an enrollment of over 25,000) 27.7 percent of the teachers had graduate degrees, whereas 22.9 percent of the teachers in small districts (those having an enrollment of less than 25,000) had graduate degrees. The stability of teachers in small districts has been much greater than that of teachers in large districts: 87 percent of teachers in small districts have taught in no more than two school systems, whereas the comparable figure for teachers in large districts is 43.6 percent. This stability is inversely related to average salary: the median salary of teachers in large districts was $7,135, whereas the median salary of teachers in small districts was $6,624.

This difference in salary was beyond what could be accounted for by the differences in education.

Community participation. According to several reports, teachers are more active politically than the general public is. According to Blau (1964), over 89 percent of all public school teachers voted in the 1960 election, whereas only 69 percent of the total eligible population went to the polls. Blau's study indicates that 12 percent of all teachers have contributed to a political party, that 9 percent have served as party workers, and that 2.8 out of every 100 teachers have been candidates for public office. In each case, these percentages are more than double those applicable to the population as a whole. Thus, doubt is cast on two earlier sociological analyses of the teacher's role (Waller 1932; Getzels & Guba 1955), which report that teachers are not granted full status as political persons. The Getzels and Guba study focuses on the questionable right of teachers to participate in radical political or religious activities. Furthermore, the fact that teachers participate in legitimate mainstream politics does not invalidate the contention that in many communities teachers are not to espouse radical causes or belong to unusual religious sects. (A number of teachers have lost their jobs because of their opposition out of school to the Vietnam war.)

Blau (1964) reports that slightly more secondary teachers than elementary teachers participate in politics. Also, although a slightly smaller proportion of teachers in small districts voted or gave money to a political party in contrast to teachers from large districts, a slightly larger proportion of teachers from small districts served as party workers and were candidates for public office.

Another study (National Education Association 1967a), reporting more generally on teachers as citizens, gives some general figures for teachers' participation in the community. The NEA study indicates that in 1966, 22 percent of teachers were members of political parties and that 85.5 percent were members of a church or synagogue. The study reports the same figure as Blau (2.8 percent) for the percentage of teachers who have been candidates for elective office.

The NEA study interestingly reports a sharply declining rate of participation on the part of teachers in community organizations during the 1960's. There was a sharp decline in political party membership—from 30.8 percent in 1961 to 22 percent in 1966—and a similarly large decrease in memberships in fraternal or auxiliary groups—from 32.6 percent to 19.3 percent during the same period. Smaller drops were reported in church membership (one percentage point) and in participation in youth groups (21.2 percent to 19.7 percent). This apparent decline in activity is difficult to interpret: whether it is due to the increasing professionalism of teaching (leading to less local identification) or whether it reflects a growing alienation of teachers from the local community is hard to say. Since the same report indicates a small increase in teacher mobility, it seems likely that there is decreasing identification with the community on the part of teachers.

In one area, however, there is an unambiguous increase in teachers' participation, and this is in the area of professional or labor organizations. Between 1960 and 1965 membership in the NEA (and its affiliates) increased in every region, state, and major city, with the exception of New York. Membership in the American Federation of Teachers and related organizations also increased in many states and cities. The general implication is that teachers' activities in the community seem to have shifted slightly from local and general political concerns to national and professional activities.

BIBLIOGRAPHY

BLAU, PETER M. 1964 *Exchange and Power in Social Life.* New York, Wiley.

BROOKOVER, WILBUR B., AND DAVID GOTTLIEB 1964 *A Sociology of Education.* 2nd ed. New York, American Book.

COFFMAN, LOTUS D. 1911 *The Social Composition of the Teaching Population.* New York, Teachers College Press.

COLEMAN, JAMES S., et al. 1966 *Equality of Educational Opportunity.* Washington, D.C., Government Printing Office.

GETZELS, JACOB WARREN, AND E. GUBA 1955 "The Structure of Roles and Role Conflict in the Teaching Situation." *Journal of Educational Sociology,* 29, no. 1:30–40.

HERRIOTT, ROBERT E., AND NANCY H. ST. JOHN 1966 *Social Class and the Urban School: The Impact of Pupil Background on Teachers and Principals.* With a foreword by Neal Gross. New York, Wiley.

NATIONAL EDUCATION ASSOCIATION 1967a "Estimated Enrollments: Teachers and Administrators." *NEA Research Bulletin,* 45, no. 2:63.

NATIONAL EDUCATION ASSOCIATION 1967b *The American Public School Teacher: 1965–66.* Washington, D.C., The Association.

NATIONAL EDUCATION ASSOCIATION 1968a *Estimates of School Statistics.* Washington, D.C., The Association.

NATIONAL EDUCATION ASSOCIATION. COMMITTEE ON EDUCATIONAL FINANCE 1968b *Financial Status of the Public Schools.* Washington, D.C., The Association.

NATIONAL EDUCATION ASSOCIATION. COMMITTEE ON EDUCATIONAL FINANCE 1968c "Profile of the Public School

Classroom Teacher." *Financial Status of the Public Schools, 1968*. Washington, D.C., The Association. Page 21.

NATIONAL EDUCATION ASSOCIATION. RESEARCH DIVISION 1970 *NEA Research Bulletin*, 48, no. 2:entire issue.

WALLER, W. 1932 *The Sociology of Teaching*. New York, Russell. Also published in 1939 by Wiley.

WARNER, WILLIAM LLOYD, ROBERT J. HAVIGHURST, AND MARTIN B. LOEB 1944 *Who Shall Be Educated? The Challenge of Unequal Opportunities*. New York, Harper.

WERTS, C. E. 1966 "Social Class and Initial Career Choice of College Freshmen." *Sociology of Education*, 39, no. 1:74–85.

WILLIAM S. BENNETT, JR., and

EDSEL L. ERICKSON

TEACHER-STUDENT INTERACTION, HIGHER EDUCATION

1. FACULTY VIEWPOINT   Robert C. Wilson and Gerry G. Gaff

2. STUDENT VIEWPOINT   Wagner Thielens, Jr.

1. FACULTY VIEWPOINT

The nature and quality of faculty-student interaction on college campuses is determined in large part by the roles played by the professors.

Historically there have been several significant changes in the status and activities of college professors. Knapp observed that "the college professor in America has been asked to perform three quite disparate functions: first, the reconnaissance of the frontiers of human knowledge; second, the imparting of 'information'; and third, the inculcation of values and the development of character" (1962, p. 292). Although all three functions have always been present, Knapp suggested that the relative emphasis on each of these aspects has changed from one historical period to another. For example, from the time the church-related colonial colleges were founded until the latter part of the nineteenth century, professors emphasized the religious and moral function of developing students' character. Later, stimulated by the Morrill Act of 1862, the growth of state universities, and the expansion of scientific disciplines, professors acquired more technical competence in their fields of specialization and strengthened their informational function. This function predominated until after World War II, when with massive support from the federal government the research function increased in importance among faculty concerns.

Academic revolution. Focusing on the period after World War II, Jencks and Riesman (1968) concluded that there has been an academic revolution. As faculty members were supported in their research by external funds and guided by standards of competence defined by their academic disciplines, they gained power within their institutions. Several observers have declared that professors have used this power to advance their own professional interests, that is, to reduce their teaching loads, conduct more research, and teach graduate students.

By the end of the 1960's the prevailing notion was that faculties had lost interest in teaching students (especially undergraduates), abandoned their character formation function as more and more universities refused to stand in *loco parentis*, and concentrated their energies on professionally rewarding research and the associated lucrative consulting activities. This notion was articulated by politicians ("Get the professors back in the classroom, where they belong"), echoed by citizens (whose financial support to public and private schools lagged), reinforced by the mass media (Fischer 1965; Hechinger 1969), sloganized by student activists ("Don't trust anyone over 30"), and apparently confirmed by the widespread student turmoil. Although the evidence for this prevailing view was considerable, it is noteworthy that none of these analyses were based upon data systematically obtained from faculty members themselves.

Research. The research literature on professors has certain limitations. First, relatively few empirical studies have been conducted on faculty members. Much of the literature consists of assertions, accusations, and assumptions which lack substantiation and which abound in sweeping generalizations. Second, of those empirical studies which have been conducted, relatively few have derived data directly from faculty members themselves. Most current knowledge about faculty is based on reports by students concerning their perceptions of teachers or their reactions to teachers' efforts. Third, of those studies which have solicited information directly from faculty members, few involve more than one institution. Most findings in these studies are narrow in focus, local in interest, and limited in generalizability. Fourth, of those studies which have obtained information from faculty in more than one institution, very few have examined faculty interaction with students in more than a peripheral way.

Major topics of investigation have been career patterns (Caplow & McGee 1958; Gustad 1960; Brown 1967; Eckert & Stecklein 1961); academic freedom (Lazarsfeld & Thielens 1958); professional orientation and interests (Gouldner 1957–1958; Medsker 1960; Clark 1966); institutional goals (Gross & Grambsch 1968); and attitudes about educational innovations (Evans & Leppmann 1967; Martin 1969).

To be sure, there has been some research on faculty-student interaction from the faculty perspective, but the research literature in this area is quite restricted. Only two major studies—those of single institutions—have focused upon faculty-student relations from the point of view of faculty members. Zelda Gamson (1966) interviewed professors at a small, nonresidential, experimental college on the campus of a large state university and reported that natural scientists and social scientists held very different educational attitudes. The natural scientists held a utilitarian orientation in that they emphasized cognitive development of students, thought faculty should maintain their distance from students, and were unconcerned about developing student commitment to the new college. The social scientists adopted a normative orientation in that they thought faculty should help students to develop personally as well as intellectually, develop close egalitarian relationships with students, and encourage student commitment to the experimental college. In a subsequent paper, Gamson (1967) further reported that natural scientists emphasized performance—that is, they favored uniform standards for grading, had little informal interaction with students, and expressed an equal degree of concern for all students. Social scientists emphasized personalism—that is, they used individualized standards for grading, had much informal interaction with students, and associated with a select group of students.

Vreeland and Bidwell (1966) interviewed a large random sample of faculty members at an eastern university with a large and distinguished undergraduate program. They classified departments according to whether faculty members held technical goals of helping students acquire the skills and methods of a field and career, moral goals of helping students acquire a broad outlook and a sense of the value dimensions of a field or career, or mixed goals, a combination of the other two kinds. Departments classified by this

scheme did not fall neatly into the formal categories of natural science, humanities, or social science. Furthermore, they found that faculty members in departments having moral goals tended to have more interest in undergraduate teaching and more interaction with students both in and out of class.

A few other studies have been peripherally concerned with faculty-student relations. Gross and Grambsch (1968) studied the goal structure of 68 major universities. They provided faculty members and administrators (whose responses were similar) with a list of 47 possible institutional goals and asked them to indicate how important each should be. The goal of emphasizing undergraduate instruction was in 44th place on both the perceived and preferred lists. The authors concluded about goals related to students:

> According to our respondents, goals related to students receive relatively little emphasis at American universities today, the one exception being that of training students for scholarship, research, and creative endeavor. But there is some feeling, apparently, that universities should pay more attention to educating the student. The goals of cultivating the student's intellect and developing his objectivity rank high on the list of preferred goals. . . . But it is felt that too much attention is paid to preparing students for useful careers, facilitating upward mobility, and providing a full round of student activities. (Gross & Grambsch 1968, p. 109)

The questionnaire developed by Gross and Grambsch was shortened, revised, and administered to faculty, administrators, and students in 14 small private liberal arts colleges participating in the Danforth Foundation's Institute for College Development. There a very different picture emerged (Zimmerman 1969). A number of student-related goals were reported by faculty members to actually be among the most important goals of their schools, and that was the way the faculty members wanted it. They thought, however, that the goals of preparing students for useful careers and providing for student activities were over-emphasized, while the goals of developing students' objectivity and cultivating students' intellect were underemphasized. From these two studies it would seem that the nature of faculty-student interaction would vary considerably on these two types of campuses.

Martin studied institutional character in eight

colleges and universities. He theorized that academic life is increasingly dominated by a value configuration which he called the conventional standard of excellence. For the faculty member this involves such factors as getting a degree from a prestigious university, teaching in a specialized area of his discipline, conducting research, and maintaining a position in his national professional association. Two corollaries of this emergence of professionalism are that professors hold a high value on cognitive rationality and that "students have been limited to a formal, even tutelary, relationship with faculty . . ." (1969, p. 229). Martin found evidence to support these ideas, although they gained less support in the new and smaller schools in his sample than from the older and larger schools.

Findings of survey. To learn more about the characteristics of faculty teaching practices, out-of-class contacts with students, satisfactions, and related matters, Wilson and Gaff conducted a multicollege survey of faculty members in 1968. Six diverse colleges were selected: one campus of a large state university, a large state college, a medium-sized public junior college, a medium-sized private suburban university, a small liberal arts college, and a small Protestant denominational college. In the four smaller schools the entire faculty was surveyed, but in the two larger schools a random sample of about 400 was selected. A total of 1,085 questionnaires were returned, for a gross response rate of 70 percent. The remainder of this article will focus on a few of the findings which are relevant to understanding teacher-student interaction as perceived by faculty members themselves.

Teaching. First, faculty members were asked about the major sources of satisfaction in their personal and professional lives. When presented with a list of alternatives, about nine out of ten checked "teaching." Furthermore, over 90 percent said effectiveness as a teacher should be either a quite important or very important criterion in decisions pertaining to promotion and salary matters at their school; to these 90 percent this criterion was far more important than any of the other criteria, which included research and scholarly activity.

According to these data, a far greater proportion of professors are committed to teaching than the prevailing notion implies. But what kind of teaching? In this connection it is important to ask whether their conception of teaching extends beyond the classroom to include out-of-class meetings with students.

Out-of-class contacts. Faculty members were asked how many times during the two weeks before the survey they had met with students outside of class for at least ten to 15 minutes to talk. As illustrated in Table 1, 95 percent said they had talked with students in their role as instructor about intellectual or academic issues; 40 percent said they did this five or more times. Ninety-three percent said they advised students about their academic program, 81 percent said they served as career advisers, and 74 percent indicated that they had seen students simply as friends. They reported less time spent discussing campus issues or helping students resolve disturbing personal problems. Although there is considerable variation between the types of out-of-class relations with students, it is apparent that most faculty members establish and maintain contact with students in a variety of capacities. Furthermore, some of these relationships (such as friendship) go well beyond what is nominally expected of a faculty member.

There is a great deal of variation in the practices of individual faculty members. This is understandable, since most professors are relatively free to define their relationships with students outside of class—to decide whether, when, and on what terms to meet with students. It is therefore relevant to ask a further question. Which faculty members have a great deal of contact with students and which have little contact? In order to answer this question, the answers of each respondent to the above six alternatives were added together to give an index of total amount of reported contact with students. On the basis of

Table 1. Percentage of faculty reporting out-of-class contacts with students*

ROLE CAPACITIES	NUMBER OF CONTACTS			
	None	1–2	3–4	5 or more
Instructor	5	24	31	40
Educational adviser	7	21	26	45
Career adviser	19	45	21	15
Friend	26	34	22	18
Counselor	46	41	9	5
Campus citizen	48	38	10	4

* Percentages do not add up to 100 because of rounding

the distribution of these scores, the entire sample was divided into three groups: a high-contact group with an approximate median of 21 contacts in the two-week period, a moderate-contact group with a median of 15 contacts, and a low-contact group with a median of seven contacts. By comparing their answers to other items on the questionnaire, one can learn about how these three groups are similar or different on a number of related variables.

First, there are a few variables which, somewhat surprisingly, do not differentiate the three groups. Despite all of the talk during the 1960's about a generation gap and about the inability of youth to trust professors over 30, there were no significant differences between the groups in either age or rank. That is, faculty who were younger or in lower ranks did not report having more contact with students than their older or higher ranking colleagues. Also, the research orientation of professors was not related to the amount of contact they had with students. That is, there were an equal number of each group who thought research should be important for faculty members at their school, who thought that research and scholarly activity should be important in decisions pertaining to promotion and salary matters, and who had delivered papers, written articles, or authored books.

Contrary to some earlier formulations (Gouldner 1957–1958) which suggest that faculty members who are oriented to cosmopolitan matters such as research and professional guilds are not interested in local matters such as teaching and meeting students, these data indicate that a research orientation is not associated with reduced student contact. Nor is area of academic specialization associated with the amount of interaction between faculty and students. Contrary to the findings of Gamson (1966; 1967), approximately the same proportions of professors in the humanities, natural sciences, social sciences, and professional fields have much and little contact with students.

Educational philosophy. What *is* related to the amount of contact with students is a professor's educational philosophy. More of the high-contact group than of the other groups agreed that "students learn class material best if a teacher takes a personal interest in them." For these high-contact persons, out-of-class contact with students is a way of helping them to learn the classroom content. In addition, significantly

more of the high-contact group agreed with these two statements: "The emotional and personal development of a student should be as important to a teacher as his intellectual development" and "A college education ought to change students' values as well as develop their minds." Those who have much contact with students apparently do so in an effort to influence them in areas outside their intellects. Conversely, part of the reason why some faculty have little contact with students is because they are less likely to think that such interaction aids student learning and because they are less interested in affecting the student in noncognitive areas.

Not only do the groups have different educational philosophies; they also go about their classroom teaching differently. Persons in the high-contact group use a more student-centered teaching style. That is, they more often said they did such things as explaining why they conducted classes as they did; inviting students to make class plans or policy; encouraging everyone to get actively involved in the discussion; and inviting student criticism of their ideas.

Behind these practices are a number of attitudinal characteristics. More of the high-contact group thought teachers should relate to students as their intellectual equals, adapt class assignments to the needs and interests of each student, and evaluate a student's classroom performance in relation to his capacities. In contrast, more of the low-contact group were in favor of teachers' assuming the role of a knowledgeable authority, making uniform class assignments, and using generalized standards of achievement. In short, the virtues of egalitarianism, individualism, and relative achievement were more highly valued by the high-contact group, while the virtues of authority, uniformity, and standardized achievement were more highly valued by the low-contact group.

It is likely that these attitudes are expressed in a variety of ways in the classroom—for example, in the degree to which teachers adopt student-centered teaching practices. The teacher's attitudes are doubtless perceived by students, who probably seek out-of-class contact with those teachers who hold more favorable attitudes toward students.

It is usually up to students to carry a classroom relationship further by approaching a professor outside of class, but professors can and do indicate their receptivity to student contact by their classroom behavior. In this fashion, each group of professors sets in motion a series of self-fulfilling prophecies. For example, those who think students learn class material best if teachers take a personal interest in them probably maintain a number of personal contacts with students and, by virtue of these contacts, learn how their personal interest shapes students' achievements. On the other hand, those who think a personal interest is less important probably develop few close out-of-class relationships and are not in a position to acquire evidence which will contradict their beliefs. Thus each set of attitudes shapes behavior and events so that they provide experiential confirmation of those different views.

There were other factors related to the degree of teacher-student contact. Significantly more in the high-contact group said that teaching was a major source of satisfaction in their lives, perceived that they enjoyed a better reputation as a teacher among students, and reported greater satisfaction with the stimulation they received from students. It appears that close interaction with students is associated with a number of intrinsic gratifications which have traditionally been regarded as among the major rewards of the teaching profession.

However, more of the high-contact group also indicated that they were dissatisfied with the amount of pressure in their work. Meeting with students and helping them to develop their minds and their personalities is time-consuming and even fatiguing work. Furthermore, a larger proportion of the faculty with a high degree of student contact thought teaching effectiveness should be more important in pay and promotion decisions at their schools. Apparently these persons who have elected to have much contact with students feel that they are not adequately compensated for this added burden.

This feeling seems not to be limited to the large research-oriented university; each of the six different types of schools apparently has the same problem of recognizing and rewarding the contribution of faculty members who carry their commitment to teaching to out-of-class interaction with students. Although the psychic satisfactions of working closely with students may be great, teachers—even committed ones—would like to see their efforts recognized in a tangible way by the formal reward structure of the school.

The method of surveying faculty members themselves thus yields different evidence and different interpretations of faculty-student interaction than do other methods. The evidence here is that most faculty members are committed to teaching, believe informal out-of-class contacts with faculty are an important part of a student's education, and maintain a variety of relationships with students out of class. Of course, there is a range of variation on these matters, and those faculty who have more contact differ from their colleagues who have less contact in a variety of ways: in their educational philosophies, classroom teaching practices, theories of teaching and learning, gratification derived from teaching, and views of the formal reward structure. It is these variables, and not age, rank, research orientation, or area of specialization, which are associated with the amount of interaction faculty have with students.

BIBLIOGRAPHY

BROWN, DAVID G. 1967 *The Mobile Professors.* Washington, D.C., American Council on Education.

CAPLOW, THEODORE, AND REECE J. McGEE 1958 *The Academic Marketplace.* New York, Basic Books.

CLARK, BURTON R. 1966 "Organizational Adaptation to Professionals." Howard M. Vollmer and Donald Mills, eds., *Professionalization.* Englewood Cliffs, N.J., Prentice-Hall. Pages 282–291.

ECKERT, RUTH E., AND JOHN E. STECKLEIN 1961 *Job Motivation and Satisfactions of College Teachers: A Study of Faculty Members in Minnesota Colleges.* Cooperative Research Monograph No. 7. Washington, D.C., Government Printing Office.

EVANS, RICHARD I., AND PETER K. LEPPMANN 1967 *Resistance to Innovation in Higher Education.* With a foreword by Nevitt Sanford. San Francisco, Jossey-Bass.

FISCHER, JOHN 1965 "The Editor's Easy Chair: Is There a Teacher on the Faculty?" *Harper's,* 230, no. 1377:18–28.

GAMSON, ZELDA F. 1966 "Utilitarian and Normative Orientation Toward Education." *Sociology of Education,* 39, no. 1:46–73.

GAMSON, ZELDA F. 1967 "Performance and Personalism in Student-Faculty Relations." *Sociology of Education,* 40, no. 4:279–301.

GOULDNER, ALVIN W. 1957–1958 "Cosmopolitans and Locals: Toward an Analysis of Latent Social Roles." Parts 1 and 2. *Administrative Science Quarterly,* 2, no. 3:281–306; 2, no. 4:444–480.

GROSS, EDWARD, AND PAUL V. GRAMBSCH 1968 *University Goals and Academic Power.* Washington, D.C., American Council on Education.

GUSTAD, JOHN W. 1960 *The Career Decisions of College Teachers: A Report of Research in the Southern Region.* With the assistance of Bernard G. Berenson and Phil Welsh. SREB Monograph Series No. 2. Atlanta, Southern Regional Educational Board.

HECHINGER, FRED 1969 "Student Targets: Professors Are Next." *Change,* 1, no. 1:36–40.

JENCKS, CHRISTOPHER, AND DAVID RIESMAN 1968 *The Academic Revolution.* Garden City, N.Y., Doubleday.

KNAPP, ROBERT 1962 "Changing Functions of the College Professor." Nevitt Sanford, ed., *The American College: A Psychological and Social Interpretation of the Higher Learning.* New York, Wiley. Pages 290–311.

LAZARSFELD, PAUL F., AND WAGNER T. THIELENS 1958 *The Academic Mind: Social Scientists in a Time of Crisis.* Glencoe, Ill., Free Press.

MARTIN, WARREN B. 1969 *Conformity: Standards and Change in Higher Education.* San Francisco, Jossey-Bass.

MEDSKER, LELAND L. 1960 *The Junior College: Progress and Prospect.* New York, McGraw-Hill.

VREELAND, REBECCA S., AND CHARLES E. BIDWELL 1966 "Classifying University Departments: An Approach to the Analysis of Their Effects Upon Undergraduates' Values and Attitudes." *Sociology of Education*, 39, no. 3:237–254.

ZIMMERMAN, W. DAVID 1969 "A Report: College Goals and Governance." *Danforth News and Notes*, 5:1–9.

ROBERT C. WILSON and JERRY G. GAFF

2. STUDENT VIEWPOINT

College and university teaching is a little understood and possibly quite ineffectual craft. Despite the centuries of campus encounters between professors and their students, no sizable fund of wisdom and experience has accumulated to guide these meetings. We lack both established knowledge of the processes through which instructors teach and students learn and sophisticated skills that put this knowledge to effective work in the classroom. A college teacher must either rely on his instincts, imitate his own teachers, put faith in a textbook or a "method," or adapt the precepts of practitioner-client encounters in other callings to his classrooms. The outcome of these rough-hewn efforts is uncertain. Even granting that students' papers and examinations reflect what they have learned, an instructor can only guess how much of this learning he transmitted to them directly, in the classroom or outside, and how much was acquired from the course's reading list or other sources.

An accumulation of reliable evidence is required to find out if college instruction is effective, to ensure that innovations are also improvements, and to move forward toward the funded knowledge and trained skills of a teaching profession. The approach should be one of neutral empirical inquiry, which does not offer persuasive speculations on how the classroom must surely operate, or write prescriptions for how it ought to, but tries simply to find out how it actually works. As a promising beginning, there is a sizable body of research on the college classroom. On most campuses, a substantial share of the intended teaching and learning is presumed to take place in the classroom in extended communication between an instructor and his students. This article reports some representative findings on this in-structional process and the research procedures that have produced them. The examples are drawn almost entirely from research on undergraduate education in the United States. Numerous studies have been made of the classroom in secondary schools and in graduate and professional schools, but these will not be discussed, since the educational processes they depict may prove to differ importantly from their undergraduate counterparts.

Normative standards.   When an instructor and a group of students enter a classroom to start an undergraduate course, what takes place has already been considerably determined. Much of this prior shaping is provided by normative standards. So ubiquitous and firmly established as to be easily overlooked, they enter the classroom as rules, informal mores, and shared values and beliefs. Well-fixed rules give basic structuring to contemporary higher education: the primary educational arena is to be a classroom; teacher and students are to meet there for 50 minutes at specified times; there will be a seminar, a lecture course, a weekly problem session, office hours, a term paper, a final examination. Other standards, the largely unwritten but often powerful campus mores, further establish proper procedure. Lacognata (1964; 1966) has sketched their patterns on three campuses. The three student bodies and the one faculty studied were all in clear agreement, for example, that students should not depend on constant pushing from the teacher to learn and that students should feel free to interrupt the instructor for relevant questions. The consensus differed from campus to campus, however, on such matters as basing assignments on ability and defining the student as subordinate to the teacher in the classroom.

Much educational attention has been devoted to the problem of finding the best classroom structure for effective communication between a teacher and his students. Over many years, the question has most frequently been framed in polarized terms, of lecture versus dialogue. Should the instructor lecture to a largely nonspeaking student audience, or should he and his students speak back and forth in a "discussion"? The difference has seemed sufficiently profound to lead some educational authorities to assume substantial differences in learning processes and often to conclude that one of the forms is intrinsically more effective as education.

Normatively, research makes clear, the lecture does not receive wholehearted approval. Of the three campuses surveyed by Lacognata, only one tended to favor the "straight lecture" method over "discussion-type" classes. Among one group of Stanford students, less than a third preferred lectures (Giddan et al. 1968). A finding by Bowers (1964) suggests not only a general tendency toward disrespect for lecturing but more concrete consequences. When 5,400 students at 99 American colleges were asked about the prevalence of student dishonesty in the previous semester, half again as many of those in lecture courses reported instances of cheating on tests as in seminar and discussion courses.

Most undergraduates in a psychology course at Rhode Island College felt emphatically that as part of an ideal teacher-student relationship, student participation is necessary (Very 1968). Yet other evidence suggests that for students the ideal classroom is primarily a lecture hall. In studies on a number of campuses, student portraits of the ideal professor turn out to focus on abilities that make a model speaker: mastery of subject, good organization, clarity of presentation, a choice of materials that will interest students and satisfy their needs, enthusiasm for his topic, and so on. When Gadzella (1968) asked a group of undergraduates at Western Washington State College to describe an ideal teacher in their own language, and then asked others for possible additions, the resulting set of 25 characteristics included only two that explicitly involve an instructor's skills in classroom dialogue. When the list was submitted to the student body, less than a third considered it central for a good instructor to "respect differences of opinion and accept constructive criticism," and even fewer selected the second trait. In contrast, three-quarters cited the instructor's knowledge of his topic. These findings may indicate only that students have not yet formed solidified expectations which spell out how an instructor should conduct an ideal classroom dialogue. Students may require participation and yet have little sense of how a teacher should best provide for it.

The student portrait of the ideal professor is relatively consistent from campus to campus. Thorough subject knowledge is the trait most widely sought. It was ranked first among 35 traits considered at Oregon State in the late 1920's (Clinton 1930), and in 1965 it was still the most

salient of the 25 abilities to the Washington undergraduates just mentioned. Other student bodies have almost uniformly placed subject mastery at or near the top (Bousfield 1940; Riley et al. 1950; Quick & Wolfe 1965; Lehmann 1966; Pogue 1967). Other highly regarded qualities are the teacher's capacity to convey information and ideas clearly, his ability to organize his presentation well, and his enthusiasm for his topic. Although educational writers sometimes assert that the college teacher must in particular be warm, or protective and supportive, these qualities are in little actual demand among undergraduates. At the University of Oregon, for instance, less than 5 percent of the students thought it crucial that an ideal professor should "like college youth and be interested in them as individuals" (Quick & Wolfe 1965).

As students acquire college experience and a sense of mastering their course work, the lecture-centered image of the model undergraduate instructor may undergo modification. Spaights (1967) found that one group of freshmen at Ohio State, having earned above-average grades the first semester, were by the second semester already complaining more than their classmates about overemphasis on the lecture method and under-participation in planning courses. A majority of 84 percent thought faculty members should offer closer student contacts, as compared to 33 percent of the lower-ranking freshmen. Pressure for more active association with teachers, in class and out, can evidently stem directly from successful absorption of those teachers' lectures and can also find quick expression in the students' sense of what is fitting.

In setting their standards for superior teaching, students also take into consideration that different subjects may require different teaching skills. At Brooklyn College the student body believed that a teacher of the arts should above all have expert subject knowledge (Riley et al. 1950). But for a social science instructor they valued such mastery less than his ability to encourage thought, his systematic organization of materials, and his tolerance of student disagreement.

Other shaping forces. The relationships that develop when teacher and students meet will also be affected by other existing forces. The instructor's actual behavior will be filtered through the preconceptions of his campus reputation, through a variety of congruences between himself and his students, and through the habits and biases of student personality structure.

If a student has heard that Professor Jones is amusing, or boring, or brilliant, he is likely to emerge from the professor's lecture feeling that it was amusing or boring or brilliant. According to an established principle of social psychology, an individual's preconceptions strongly determine what he will select to perceive, and his selections tend to confirm his preconceptions. In a study by Kelley (1949), a temporary teacher was presented to students in three separate classes, using a biography sheet as a plausible device to inform half of each class that the instructor was "rather cold" and the other half that he was "very warm." In the identical 20-minute class session, those introduced to the instructor as warm found him significantly more considerate, informal, humane, humorous, and mature than did those introduced to him as cold.

A college teacher may have even less control over the ways he is like or unlike his students, yet these congruences can affect their relationship considerably. If a teacher uses the same language as his students, his images and slang expressions will be understood and the scope of his vocabulary will not be beyond theirs. In a similar vein, communication will often be better if teacher and student share values that are relevant to the topic at hand. In a course on child psychology, for example, if both teacher and student believe that permissiveness to children is best (Bills 1952) or agree in an introductory psychology course that "people with a firm moral code are better adjusted" (Runkel 1956), the student will be better disposed and more receptive to the teacher than if they have opposing beliefs. It also seems likely that compatible cognitive processes, with inductive thinker speaking to inductive hearer or deductive to deductive, should be helpful.

The same instructor can be quite differently perceived according to the nature of the student's personality and his history of personal relationships. At a private college in the Midwest, male undergraduates with a nurturant inclination—generous, affectionate, quick to offer help—tended to see their instructors as able in their subject, good at stimulating intellectual curiosity, and lacking in personal peculiarities; their less generous fellow men saw the same faculty members as less competent and wholesome (Rezler 1965). Ofchus and Gnagey (1963) describe how sopho-

more women in a course on child development at Illinois State University perceived their teacher. Typically, a girl who reported that her father or mother was highly critical of her behavior described the class instructor as less willing to permit student disagreement with his opinions than did a girl whose parents were less critical. Evidently these students had transferred their experiences with parents as authority figures directly onto the new authority figure in the classroom.

A student's academic record also is likely to be intricately involved in his perceptions of his teachers. The able student, presumably, hears what his teacher is saying more accurately than the poor student, but the matter does not end there. Already in their second semester, Spaights' freshmen at Ohio State University saw two quite different faculties: 94 percent of those with below-average first-term records considered their professors impersonal, aloof, and indifferent; only 17 percent of those with higher grades agreed. The faculty was dictatorial and authoritarian to 79 percent of the weaker students but only to 25 percent of the more able; it lacked enthusiasm to 71 and 32 percent, respectively. These student judgments may have been in part an overreaction to their first strong taste of the undergraduate pecking order—the faculty had, in fact, treated the two groups quite differently on their examinations. Yet the contrasting imagery of teachers is striking.

Classroom methods of instruction. If prior influences do much to shape classroom processes, what has research found to describe the actualities of these processes and their educational outcomes? Studies have approached the undergraduate classroom, mainly, in three quite different ways.

One of these deals with methods of classroom instruction and their results. The term "method" is often used to describe instruction in which much of the teacher's behavior (and often that of his students) is guided by a set of prescriptions or traditions concerning educational techniques and practices. Research has studied the outcome of numerous methods, characteristically by comparing two undergraduate classes in which the same course is taught by different methods, one of them experimental. Other possible differences are minimized by having the same instructor teach matched or randomly divided student groups.

In general, the results have not encouraged either wider use of the experimental methods or closer research scrutiny of particular classroom processes. Dubin and Taveggia (1968) collected 91 comparative studies that appeared in the literature between 1924 and 1965. Among comparisons of any two methods, they found that the number in which the average final examination scores or improvement scores favored one method closely matched the number which favored the other. This was true for broad comparisons, for example, between lecture methods and discussion methods or between face-to-face instruction and independent study methods, and for more specific comparisons, for example, between discussion and lecture plus discussion or between lecture and supervised independent study. These authors provide particularly strong evidence for a conclusion that, indeed, others had also reached earlier (McKeachie 1963; Wallen & Travers 1963): Since the examination results obtained by any one teaching method are on average no different from those obtained by any other, no single method has any *inherent* advantage or disadvantage for those aspects of education that are measured by course examinations.

The long-standing debate over the merits of lecture and dialogue has led to innumerable efforts to match the two procedures against each other and to frequent publication of the results. Dubin and Taveggia located 45 studies in which a lecture and a discussion method were compared in a total of 88 separate pairs of classes. The result was typical: in 45 of the 88 comparisons the average examination or improvement scores favored the lecture class, and in 43 the discussion class.

The failure of novel teaching methods to produce expected improvements in learning suggests that the educational theories on which the new methods were based do not correspond any better than do the old methods to the actualities of teaching and learning behavior. One study has indicated that both may often be wide of the mark. A group of teachers at the University of Chicago once concluded that the lecture requires mainly passive thinking from the student and provides few opportunities for analytic and problem-solving thought. They decided to switch from lectures to discussion sessions in which students would take extensive part in an attack on problems. Tape recordings of entire classroom hours devoted to both types of instruction revealed, to their astonishment, that the instructors continued

to do most of the talking in the discussion sessions (Bloom 1953; 1954). Students' thoughts during the lectures and discussions were also recorded after the class sessions. Of these, a large proportion turned out to be unrelated to the academic topic under consideration—36 percent in the lectures and 45 percent in the discussions. In both types of class, somewhat more than a tenth of the thought had a passive character, with students simply listening and recording ideas. They remained alike in their sporadic but recurring attempts to apply and utilize the day's ideas. Although the process was not anticipated, they were also alike in devoting substantial energies to making evaluations: about a fifth of all student thought went into judgments on the relevance, adequacy, and correctness of current proceedings. During discussion sessions, the students did engage more actively in problem-solving; such inward efforts to answer a question, solve a problem, or relate a specific point to an abstraction occupied one-twelfth of their classroom attention but were virtually nonexistent among the lecture students. At the same time, the discussions stimulated considerably less effort at comprehension than the lectures; perhaps because students recognized much that was familiar in listening to their peers, they less frequently tried to find their own illustrations of a point under consideration and less often experienced a sense of new insight. The discussion methods also had the unplanned effect of remolding the students' irrelevant thought. In lectures a student's stray musings were largely devoted to tangential associations with words and phrases used by the instructor and to daydreams about the world outside of class. In discussions they more often dwelt on the student himself and his classmates, perhaps to compare performance or abilities.

Outside the classroom, students are likely to give discussion sessions more credit than lectures for stimulating their minds and their sense of academic duty. They assert that discussion keeps them in general more active mentally (Brinkley 1952) and helps in particular to stimulate independent thinking (Jenkins 1951; Eglash 1954). They feel prepared to assume more of the responsibility for learning (Patton 1955). And though discussion students can expect no special benefits on course examinations, a number of studies indicate that they may be more adept at using the knowledge they have acquired—for instance, in recognizing examples of course concepts and in applying course principles to new problems (Barnard 1942; Dawson 1956; Cameron 1966).

When grades are not at stake and students are taking a less active part in determining the course's outcome, differences in the impact of lecture and discussion methods may have a better chance to appear. Furthermore, the similar examination results of two methods can misleadingly conceal an array of compensatory differences: the lecture students may learn for themselves what the discussion students acquire in class, and vice versa.

In any case, the assembled research does not show that all lectures and all discussions produce identical examination results. Some student groups in a lecture course earned considerably better marks than the paired discussion class, and some did better in the discussion than the lecture. Perhaps the winning lectures and discussions had distinctive traits that did not appear in other versions of these methods.

Traits. The second empirical approach to the undergraduate classroom, research on particular traits, could thus prove useful to illuminate how teaching methods work. Undoubtedly, furthermore, in a large majority of the classrooms the instructor does not adhere to a method. Here too, particular traits—of the teacher, the student, the student class, and their mutual environment—may prove to have crucial importance.

An example will illustrate both the possibility and the prevalent dearth of research. It is generally assumed that the instructor's knowledge of his subject makes an obvious and crucial contribution to his students' learning. Characteristically, however, research has yet to obtain measures of college instructors' level of expert knowledge, verify that students recognize differences in knowledge among their instructors, and then relate such measures to student accomplishment and change. But there are suggestive pieces of evidence. In a normal-school course on child development, sophomore women who considered their instructor highly competent adopted more of his value stance toward children and child education than did others who found him less competent (Ofchus & Gnagey 1963). Thistlethwaite (1960) asked a nationwide cohort of Merit Scholarship winners to describe the instructor who had most influenced their desire to learn. Two of the four key characteristics reflected the teacher's extensive knowledge of his discipline: he frequently pointed out unresolved problems on which research is needed, and he placed high priority on helping the student obtain broad familiarity with knowledge and ideas in his field. Brief speeches on economic, social, and political issues, though not presented by their instructor, have repeatedly been found more effective in changing the opinions of an undergraduate audience if the speaker is regarded as an expert (Hovland et al. 1953). Taken together, these studies consistently intimate that the scope of a professor's knowledge has definite influence, not only on his students' own acquisition of knowledge but also on their motivations and values.

How can students, themselves deficient in expert knowledge, judge how knowledgeable their teachers are? Speech studies suggest that a number of classroom factors shape these perceptions. Undergraduates considered a speaker more expert and more informed when they heard him present a fluent exposition than when they heard the same speech with frequent pauses and repetition of phrases (McCroskey & Mehrley 1969); evidently interruptions can make the same materials hard to absorb. If the presentation was well organized, the students also attributed more expertise to the speaker than if he offered the same sentences in a random sequence. This linkage has been made in the college classroom: when 2,000 students at Oklahoma A & M rated 55 instructors, the teachers judged outstanding in scholarship were also those considered strongest in organization of their courses (Coffman 1954). Undoubtedly, good organization puts materials into clear relationship and sharp focus. Both fluency and sound organization, in addition, may help psychologically to convince students that an instructor has authority.

Further, if undergraduates like a speaker, they are reluctant to deny his expertise (Hovland et al. 1953). Rather alarmingly, too, they have been found to gauge a speaker's knowledgeability by the frequency with which he cites his own professional work, though they remain unaffected by the references to other authorities (Ostermeier 1967).

For these studies, students were explicitly asked to make judgments, and to make them individually after a short hearing in an experimental setting. Whether perceptions of instructor expertise develop in similar fashion when spontaneously formed in the natural setting of the classroom will require special research. Still, perceived expertise has emerged in experiments as woven not only from a core of knowledge but potentially also from diverse other threads, of organization and friendliness and of frequent reference to a man's own work and infrequent reference to others'. Perhaps an ability such as expertise can neither exist nor be perceived without other qualities and abilities to give it delineation. Among the 55 Oklahoma instructors, the same teachers rated strong in scholarship by their classes were also those most often found outstanding for clear expression, enthusiasm for their subject, and organization of their courses—traits linked earlier as the four most central abilities of the ideal professor. The discovery of such natural and functional bonds is one aim of research on teaching styles, to be considered shortly.

It may prove true that, in similar fashion, important classroom attributes are in general each complexly linked to an array of shaping traits. Turning to the student, a further illustration is the amount of talk an undergraduate contributes to a class.

The traits that have been provisionally linked by research to student participation in class discussion form a lengthy list. Several are traits of the instructor. Although warmth is not required to make a college teacher ideal, it can help his students to talk in class. This was the view of almost all Stanford undergraduates in a course that put discussion at a premium (Giddan et al. 1968). When a substitute teacher was introduced as very warm, other students not only saw different qualities in him than classmates told he was quite cold, they also took considerably greater part in the discussion he led (Kelley 1949). An instructor's iconoclastic values may appeal to students; a majority in the Stanford survey said they could talk more freely in classes of instructors who raise questions about traditional beliefs and attitudes. Some students will talk more if the instructor is grading their comment (13 percent at Stanford), but many others will talk less (55 percent). Critical evaluation of a student comment can stimulate him to defend his position (70 percent), but it can also cause him to clam up (30 percent). The qualities students desire in an ideal teacher, we would guess, may often make for ideal listening. A teacher's broad knowledge might excite students into comment but also awe them into silent awareness of their limitations. Half of the Stanford students were more impelled to speak if an instructor said something they found illogical or uninformed than if his presentation were strong. A teacher's clarity of expression and firm organization of material could have a similarly ambivalent effect. But his enthusiasm for his topic, perhaps, demands less hard work and discipline for its achievement by students and should be more directly infectious.

Student traits that affect participation in dialogue are also numerous. The variety of student motivations has already been intimated. They speak because they feel friendly toward the warm instructor, or share another's iconoclasm; they hope to disprove the instructor, to improve their grades, to enjoy expressing a thought, and to forget grades. Students who talk differ from their classmates in a number of other ways. Student ability has consistently been linked to talking, in the studies at Stanford (Korn & Black 1962; Thoresen 1966) and elsewhere (Smith & Dunbar 1951). Talkers are likely to have done better on the verbal part of the Scholastic Aptitude Test, though not on the mathematics part, and to have a higher college grade average. At Stanford, those who volunteered most often to speak in the history of Western civilization course that was studied were usually majoring in humanities or social science; their silent classmates were often in natural science and less conversant with the topic.

Personality inventories depict talkers as more self-confident, self-seeking, active, and competitive than their classmates. Their self-assertion, however, is channeled by qualities that are usually incompatible in personality studies: they are also more cooperative, appreciative, respectful, and gentle, and so can direct their assertiveness into responsive contributions. As guiding values, they more often prize intellectual and cognitive activity. They are better informed, more critical, more imaginative and insightful.

The talkers take greater part at home in discussion of ideas and public events. Speaking during a course's class sessions is an expression of a strong involvement with the course and with education: those who speak study more intensively for the course, think and read on their own about the issues raised, talk about them more with other students, and feel more that the course has helped their powers of analysis. They remember extra reading in high school and an active role in high school classrooms.

In some cases the classroom trait that induces a student to speak is not a trait of the instructor, or of the student, but a favorable pairing of the two. Sharing the instructor's values was helpful to nearly half the Stanford undergraduates, who said they talked more freely if the teacher held philosophical or political views resembling their own. A sense of comparable standing could also matter. In some departments at a distinguished eastern university, the faculty viewed students as intelligent, well-read, and often able to challenge their instructors; they treated students as capable junior colleagues and typically had frequent conversations with them (Vreeland & Bidwell 1966). In other departments students were seen as beginners learning the basic facts and thus unable to address a teacher on his own level. Half of the Stanford undergraduates could speak more freely in class if they were on a first-name basis with the teacher. Other similarities—in age, sex, intelligence, ethnic origin, or processes of thought—may help students talk to instructors.

The interacting traits may be complementary, with one individual supplying what the other lacks. McKeachie (1961) found that under instructors considered very warm by their classes, students with a special need for positive feeling in personal relationships earned more high grades than low, while the reverse was true of their more emotionally insulated classmates. But under teachers rated low in providing warmth, the students who needed little of it had the majority of high marks.

Traits of the entire student group in a classroom, such as its size, its average level and range of ability, its competitiveness and seriousness, may also matter. The physical arrangement of the class must be considered. In one study, students talked more when seated around a seminar table than in a room with seats in straight rows (Sommer 1967). Some Stanford students talk more if they are not sitting too close to the instructor.

There is no reason to assume that any of these traits will have a distinctive effect on the course of class dialogue regardless of other influences. Thus, research finds that able students tend to do more of the talking. In one of the Stanford studies, ability and talk were clearly linked in small classes, but in larger classes, perhaps as both names and talents grew less visible, the tie began to disappear.

If talkers differ in so many ways from their classmates, do they also benefit from their participation? In the Chicago study the nonparticipants were doing as much relevant thinking as participants. For example, when an instructor asked a direct question, the students in the room would begin to think about the answer whether they spoke or not (Schulz 1951). The Stanford talkers and the Chicago talkers (Stern et al. 1956) both earned better grades, but both groups were also initially more able, and the Stanford grade was partly based on class participation. Smith and Dunbar (1951) compared pairs of frequent and infrequent talkers who were closely matched in ability. The participants gained slightly more in their capacity to apply course materials and also improved somewhat more on seven of eight other measures of intellectual achievement. But we cannot be sure whether their class participation was an intrinsic stimulus to learning or simply a willingness to talk when asked. Furthermore, in other instances participants have not received better marks than their classmates (Deignan 1955; Johnson & Smith 1953; Parlett 1968).

Classroom styles. Classroom styles, in the third empirical approach, are natural combinations of traits of the instructor, his students, and their environment. Ideally, a research study to investigate styles and their importance in undergraduate education would go through a number of steps. First, since little is established about the workings of the college classroom, information about a broad array of traits depicting the participants and their environs, on the assumption that any might well have relevance, would be collected from a large and representative number of classrooms. The techniques of factor analysis and multivariate analysis would then be used to sift this body of information for answers to several questions: Are there patterns linking certain traits into recurring classroom styles? Are these styles, or some of them, important in determining various educational outcomes? Are particular traits in a style especially responsible for its overall outcome? Can some traits be indigenous to varied styles and have differing impact depending on their context? A sizable number of studies have been addressed to the first question, and several to the second, but few to the remainder.

Potentially, each of the numerous traits or aspects of a classroom situation might have its own separate contribution to make, with a sheerly cumulative end result. But research studies have invariably found that traits do tend to cluster into styles, and ordinarily only a small number of styles (Coffman 1954; Gibb 1955; Solomon 1966).

An excellent study by Solomon, Bezdek, and Rosenberg (1963) of 24 evening courses in introductory American government and their instructors is representative. The research obtained 169 separate measures on a broad range of classroom traits, using four independent measuring instruments: a student questionnaire completed just before the end of the course; ratings made independently by two teams of observers, based on a searching examination of the variables in a college classroom; a content analysis of the tape recordings also obtained by the observers; and the teacher's own questionnaire describing his course objectives and classroom satisfactions. Eight factors were found, showing that there were eight statistically separable groupings of teacher and student behavior. Each was a distinctive style composed of interlinked traits, which described in substantial part the teacher-student relationships existing in a number of the 24 classrooms. These classrooms coincided only haphazardly with those in which any other style was found.

One teaching style in the Solomon study was both unusually successful and unenthusiastically received. At its core was a procedure in which the instructor asked pointed questions and then praised the responding students without offering or indicating most of the right answers. Possessing an especially sound grasp of his subject, the instructor was clear in his commitment to political science and came to class well-prepared and enthusiastic about his topic. His manner was intense; he spoke rapidly and paced about, gesturing frequently. His speech was clear, avoiding both unnecessarily technical terms and oversimplifications. Yet he did not stress well-organized presentation or extensive transmission of content. For his goal, as he said, was not primarily to broaden his students' factual knowledge or understanding of principles, or to improve their analytical abilities, but to help them acquire a greater degree of self-awareness and to change some of their basic attitudes and values.

It was to these ends, undoubtedly, that he concentrated attention not only on the verbal exchange he prompted but also on the nonverbal qualities of his relationship with students. With confidence he offered frequent good-humored remarks, encouraged laughter, and made clear that

he liked and accepted his students. He was on the alert for small signs, noticing restless movement or a spell of unusual quiet. In such ways the room was kept smoothly under firm but unstated control.

In this easy, disciplined atmosphere, the instructor posed his questions. Particularly often he asked for interpretations, but frequently also for facts. If he kept the initiative by asking questions, he made sure he was not so forceful as to cause discomfort or anxiety in his listeners.

In answering questions, his students were not likely to try their ideas out loud or to express opinions. They were hesitant, in fact, to produce the interpretations he requested and confined their speech to the factual more than in the other classrooms observed. The instructor listened carefully and then responded thoughtfully; in the observers' opinion, he showed genuine respect for his students' capabilities and real interest in their views. His reply, evidently by design, typically did not indicate whether a student's answer was right or wrong. It offered general approval, perhaps applauding the student's manner of expression or thanking him for presenting a particular point of view. If a student answer was clearly wrong, he would indicate the error but also remark that "your underlying assumption is widely held," or the like. Again he attempted to shelter students from discomfort or embarrassment. But he did not always try to shelter them from intellectual discomfort, at least not by giving them the resolutions to his questions or by accommodating to their views in his own remarks.

At the end of the semester the results of this teaching style were objectively excellent. Student improvement on a test of factual knowledge about American government was well above the already substantial average for the other classes. And while the typical class did not improve on a test of concept comprehension, involving the ability to generalize and to apply principles, this teaching style produced a definite gain. Yet the students felt that they had learned slightly less factual information and gained somewhat less in general understanding than did other classes. Their overall evaluation of the instructor was also slightly below the average. They were substantially more interested than most in doing further reading in political science, although not in taking further courses. Thus they reacted as though the questions raised in class were still unanswered in their minds. They disliked this tantalizing and unfinished state of affairs and did not realize that they had been led to think productively about unresolved problems and, perhaps out of frustrated curiosity, to acquire an abundance of facts.

The empirical delineation of this style illustrates a prime virtue of research, the discovery of the unrecognized. Here is a teaching style little resembling either the established classroom styles of campus folklore or the experimental methods drawn from contemporary theory. Yet one study has shown that it exists and has much value; it may turn out to exist, and matter, in many classrooms.

Some of the other styles found among the classrooms in the Solomon study will sound more familiar: the laissez-faire instructor who asks broad questions to start lengthy undirected student discussions, the warm friend, the authoritarian lecturer, the flamboyant dramatizer, the needler, the comment crowner who rewards each student statement with a long and eloquent elaboration of its merits. Often the patterned elements of two or even more styles appeared markedly in the same classroom.

Factor analysis can establish only that the ingredient traits of a particular style all tend to be found together. Yet as noted earlier, such correlations of classroom traits may prove to reflect the patterns of influence that are shaping the classroom. In our description of the question-asking instructor's style, just above, we deliberately used language that implies a greater flow of causal influence in the linkages between its traits than the research procedure warrants. For example, we suggested that the instructor's desire to develop student self-awareness contributed to his unusual alertness to the subtle qualities of classroom interaction, that the alertness helped to create the strong but indirect control, that the control was exemplified in a pointed approach to asking questions, and so on. The research established only that the desire, alertness, control, and questioning all tended to be found together in the same classrooms. If our step turns out to be rightly taken, the classroom style begins to emerge as a crucial educational entity. For if such mutually shaping linkages of traits do occur, styles may prove to be the basic qualities which give life and unity to a college classroom, and key forces affecting the learning that ensues.

BIBLIOGRAPHY

BARNARD, J. DARRELL 1942 "The Lecture-Demonstration Versus the Problem-solving Method of Teaching a College Science Course." *Science Education*, 26, no. 2:121–132.

BILLS, ROBERT E. 1952 "The Effect of a Value on Learning." *Journal of Personality*, 21, no. 2:217–222.

BLOOM, B. S. 1953 "Thought Processes in Lectures and Discussions." *Journal of General Education*, 7, no. 3:160–169.

BLOOM, B. S. 1954 "The Thought Process of Students in Discussion." Sidney J. French, ed., *Accent on Teaching*. New York, Harper. Pages 23–46.

BOUSFIELD, W. A. 1940 "Educational Research and Statistics: Students' Ratings of Qualities Considered Desirable in College Professors." *School and Society*, 51, no. 1313: 253–256.

BOWERS, WILLIAM J. 1964 *Student Dishonesty and Its Control in College.* Cooperative Research Project No. 1672. New York, Bureau of Applied Social Research, Columbia University.

BRINKLEY, S. G. 1952 "Mental Activity in College Classes: Student Estimate of Relative Value of Ten Learning Situations." *Journal of Experimental Education*, 20, no. 4:373–378.

CAMERON, HOWARD K. 1966 "The Effectiveness of Feedback in Teaching Principles of Educational Psychology." *Journal of Experimental Education*, 34, no, 3:53–56.

CLINTON, R. J. 1930 "Qualities College Students Desire in College Instructors." *School and Society*, 32, no. 830:702.

COFFMAN, WILLIAM E. 1954 "Determining Students' Concepts of Effective Teaching From Their Ratings of Instructors." *Journal of Educational Psychology*, 45, no. 5:277–286.

DAWSON, MURRAY D. 1956 "Lectures Versus Problem-solving in Teaching Elementary Soil Science." *Science Education*, 40, no. 5:395–404.

DEIGNAN, FRANCIS J. 1955 "A Comparison of the Effectiveness of Two Group Discussion Methods." Ed.D. dissertation. Boston University School of Education.

DUBIN, ROBERT, AND THOMAS C. TAVEGGIA 1968 *The Teaching-Learning Paradox: A Comparative Analysis of College Teaching Methods.* Eugene, Center for the Advanced Study of Educational Administration, University of Oregon.

EGLASH, ALBERT 1954 "A Group-discussion Method of Teaching Psychology." *Journal of Educational Psychology*, 45, no. 5:257–267.

GADZELLA, BERNADETTE M. 1968 "College Students' Views and Ratings of an Ideal Professor." *College and University*, 44, no. 1:89–96.

GIBB, CECIL A. 1955 "Classroom Behavior of the College Teacher." *Educational and Psychological Measurement*, 15, no. 3:254–263.

GIDDAN, NORMAN S., et al. 1968 "A Scale to Measure Teacher-Student Interaction." *Journal of Experimental Education*, 36, no. 3:52–58.

HOVLAND, CARL IVER, IRVING L. JANIS, AND HAROLD H. KELLEY 1953 *Communication and Persuasion: Psychological Studies of Opinion Change.* New Haven, Conn., Yale University Press.

JENKINS, RUSSELL L. 1951 "The Relative Effectiveness of Two Methods of Teaching Written and Spoken English (Communication)." Ed.D. dissertation. East Lansing. Michigan State College.

JOHNSON, DONALD M., AND HENRY CLAY SMITH 1953 "Democratic Leadership in the College Classroom." *Psychological Monographs*, 67, no. 11:1–20.

KELLEY, HAROLD H. 1949 "The Effects of Expectations Upon First Impressions of Persons." *American Psychologist*, 4, no. 7:252.

KORN, HAROLD A., AND JOHN D. BLACK 1962 "Factors Influencing Student Participation in Classroom Discussion." Stanford Counseling Center Research Report. Stanford, Calif., Stanford University.

LACOGNATA, A. A. 1964 "University Extension Faculty and Student Role Expectations: An Empirical Analysis." *Journal of Experimental Education*, 33, no. 2:107–120.

LACOGNATA, A. A. 1966 "A Comparative Analysis of Private and State College Student Academic Expectations." *Journal of Educational Research*, 60, no. 1:32–34.

LEHMANN, IRVIN J. 1966 "The College Faculty as Perceived by Graduates and Non-graduates." *Journal of Educational Measurement*, 3, no. 2:169–173.

MCCROSKEY, JAMES C., AND R. SAMUEL MEHRLEY 1969 "The Effects of Disorganization and Nonfluency on Attitude Change and Source Credibility." *Speech Monographs*, 36, no. 1:13–21.

MCKEACHIE, WILBERT J. 1961 "Motivation, Teaching Methods, and College Learning." Marshall Jones, ed., *Nebraska Symposium on Motivation*. Lincoln, University of Nebraska Press. Pages 111–143.

MCKEACHIE, WILBERT J. 1963 "Research on Teaching at the College and University Level." N. L. Gage, ed., *Handbook of Research on Teaching*. Chicago, Rand McNally. Pages 1118–1172.

OFCHUS, LEON T., AND WILLIAM J. GNAGEY 1963 "Factors Related to the Shift of Professional Attitudes of Students in Teacher Education." *Journal of Educational Psychology*, 54, no. 3:149–153.

OSTERMEIER, TERRY H. 1967 "Effects of Type and Frequency of Reference Upon Perceived Source Credibility and Attitude Change." *Speech Monographs*, 34, no. 2:137–144.

PARLETT, MALCOLM 1968 "Physics Students: Bound or Free?" *Commission on College Physics Newsletter*, no. 18, December 1968, pp. 3–6.

PATTON, JOSEPH ALEXANDER 1955 "A Study of the Effects of Student Acceptance of Responsibility and Motivation on Course Behavior." Ph.D. dissertation. Ann Arbor, University of Michigan.

POGUE, F. G., JR. 1967 "Students' Ratings of the Ideal Teacher." *Improving College and University Teaching*, 15, no. 2:133–136.

QUICK, ALAN F., AND ARNOLD D. WOLFE 1965 "The Ideal Professor." *Improving College and University Teaching*, 13, no. 3:133–134.

REZLER, AGNES G. 1965 "The Influence of Needs Upon the Student's Perception of His Instructor." *Journal of Educational Research*, 58, no. 6:282–286.

RILEY, JOHN W., JR., BRYCE F. RYAN, AND MARCIA LIFSHITZ 1950 *The Student Looks at His Teacher*. New Brunswick, N.J., Rutgers University Press.

RUNKEL, PHILIP J. 1956 "Cognitive Similarity in Facilitating Communication." *Sociometry*, 19, no. 3:178–191.

SCHULZ, STELLA BEIL 1951 "A Study of Relationships Between Overt Verbal Behavior in the Classroom and Conscious Mental Processes of the Students." Ph.D. dissertation. University of Chicago.

SMITH, HENRY CLAY, AND DONALD S. DUNBAR 1951 "The Personality and Achievement of the Classroom Participant." *Journal of Educational Psychology*, 42, no. 2:65–84.

SOLOMON, DANIEL 1966 "Teacher Behavior Dimensions, Course Characteristics, and Student Evaluations of Teachers." *American Educational Research Journal*, 3, no. 1:35–47.

SOLOMON, DANIEL, WILLIAM E. BEZDEK, AND LARRY ROSENBERG 1963 *Teaching Styles and Learning*. Brookline, Mass., Center for the Study of Liberal Education for Adults.

SOMMER, ROBERT 1967 "Classroom Ecology." *Journal of Applied Behavioral Science*, 3, no. 4:489–503.

SPAIGHTS, ERNEST 1967 "Students Appraise Teachers' Methods and Attitudes." *Improving College and University Teaching*, 15, no. 1:15–17.

STERN, GEORGE G., MORRIS I. STEIN, AND BENJAMIN S. BLOOM 1956 *Methods in Personality Assessment*. Glencoe, Ill., Free Press.

THISTLETHWAITE, DONALD L. 1960 "College Press and Changes in Study Plans of Talented Students." *Journal of Educational Psychology*, 51, no. 4:222–234.

THORESEN, CARL E. 1966 "Oral Non-participation in College Students: A Study of Characteristics." *American Educational Research Journal*, 3, no. 3:198–210.

VERY, PHILIP S. 1968 "Real and Ideal Characteristics of the Teacher-Student Relationship." *Perceptual and Motor Skills*, 27, no. 3, part 1:880–882.

VREELAND, REBECCA S., AND CHARLES E. BIDWELL 1966 "Classifying University Departments: An Approach to the Analysis of Their Effects Upon Undergraduates' Values and Attitudes." *Sociology of Education*, 39, no. 3:237–254.

WALLEN, NORMAN E., AND ROBERT M. W. TRAVERS 1963 "Analysis and Investigation of Teaching Methods." N. L. Gage, ed., *Handbook of Research on Teaching*. Chicago, Rand McNally. Pages 448–505.

WAGNER THIELENS, JR.

TEACHERS, EDUCATION OF

1. OVERVIEW

Teacher education programs have been the focus of much disagreement and debate, a reflection of the state of continuing uncertainty as to the nature, function, and goals of the schools themselves and as to the ways in which and by whom the schools are to be initiated, administered, and controlled. Central to this debate is the teacher, with the burden of accountability falling increasingly on the programs, institutions, and professionals that train teachers.

The 1940's through the 1960's saw a progressive intensification of debate on teacher education by both professionals and laymen. The result was less agreement on and less uniformity of organization, processes, goals, and controls than ever before. On the other hand, there were distinct signs of the emergence of programs seeking to forge patterns of teacher education that would be dynamically oriented to the imperatives of a changing school serving a changing society. It may be argued, therefore, that the diversity of teacher education patterns is not so much an indication of indecisiveness as it is a sign of dynamic change and the willingness to experiment with alternatives.

The appraisal of any program of education must begin with a consideration of the program's goals. Since a program of teacher education seeks to prepare teachers, it must ultimately be judged by the degree to which it develops the competencies that are needed for the successful functioning of a teacher. Although this may seem an obvious principle, the identification and evaluation of teacher competencies is subject to much controversy, with each view having its own distinctive implications for the nature of teacher education.

Nature of the teaching function. Teaching is a social function, its aim being to guide desirable growth in others. It involves a social relationship, the interaction of teacher and pupil. A school is an organized community of learners and teachers, ordered to facilitate their communication. The social function of teaching can be analyzed from a variety of points of view, all interrelated but each with its own implications for determining teacher competencies and in turn with implications for the ordering of teacher education.

Goals. The pedagogic goal influences the teaching method. Such goals as student appraisal and stimulation, presentation of new knowledge, development of student skills, drill in recently acquired competencies, and review of knowledge all affect the type of teacher and student activity required. The arts of questioning, describing, and demonstrating are used in various ways by the teacher to stimulate such student activities as listening, observing, reading, answering, discussing, reporting, and writing. The teacher's task is to use the proper combination of methods to achieve the desired pedagogic goal. For example, the question-answer method of the formal recitation is essentially a device for student appraisal, whereas the lecture method is essentially a means of imparting information.

Both of these methods can go far beyond their primary goals: the recitation by developing the student's ability to analyze, appraise, generalize, and recall; the lecture by inspiring, demonstrating, and clarifying, particularly if the lecturer is responsive to student questions. In both methods, the teacher is dominant, and he initiates and controls the lines of communication. Discussion, on the other hand, is essentially a method whereby the teacher seeks to achieve an interplay of minds on a common problem for the purpose of developing in each student the powers of communication, persuasion, and reasoning. The role of the teacher in this type of learning situation is quite different from that in the recitation or the lecture. His function here is to guide without overtly dominating: to act as a resource when needed, to moderate strong differences of opinion, and to stimulate interest when attention wanes.

The competencies required of the teacher in achieving these and other pedagogic goals necessitate the use of a wide variety of teaching methods, knowledge of their applications and limitations, and the ability to evaluate their results in each situation. Standard examinations and supervisory directives must be known and mastered, and the range of teacher choice among these varying methods (significantly wide in even the most prescriptive school situations) must be determined and proper teaching plans made and applied. The teacher must be able to recognize the consequences of his goal-centered teaching behavior and be a versatile and effective master of the means at his disposal.

Skills and subject matter. Another way of analyzing the teaching function is to consider the nature of the skills and the subject matter to be acquired by the student. For example, learning a second language presents methodological implications for teaching quite distinct from learning a laboratory science. Oral language requires the habitual, almost immediate translation of thought into speech. The understanding of written language requires a similar habitual, immediate translation of the seen language into thought. Both require a methodology that progressively moves from analysis through exercise to habit formation. If the learning is to be of a second language, the process becomes infinitely more complicated, involving the ultimate goal of reducing the dominant role of the primary language and developing the ability to think in the second language. With habit formation as a goal, the methods most appropriate are largely drill centered, involving much use of repetition and imitation.

In contrast, the method of science is analytical and experimental. In its concern for understanding and manipulating the physical world, it involves preeminently the discipline of discovery. The student of science must therefore be provided with the opportunity to participate in the method of science through observation, manipulation, and actual experimentation. Therefore, the teaching-learning method of the science laboratory is quite different from that of the language laboratory, largely because of the nature of the disciplines and the skills themselves.

Similar distinctive teaching-learning imperatives can be derived from the nature of all the disciplines and skills characteristic of a school curriculum. For example, the requirements of poetry, music, and art are different from those of history, economics, and mathematics. The former rely more on the development of aesthetic experience, the latter more on the development of intellectual power.

The teacher competencies associated with the nature of the subject matter transcend the basic knowledge of the subject itself. To be sure, one must know a language before one can begin to think about teaching it, and one must know chemistry before guiding the student in an open-ended laboratory experiment. However, it does not necessarily follow that one knows how to teach French as a second language merely because one is a native French speaker or knows how to teach reading because one knows how to read.

A second level of competencies, therefore, is to know the ways a discipline or skill is best learned —that is, the characteristics inherent in each discipline that are pedagogical determinants. These competencies are enhanced by both the depth and the breadth of the teacher's understanding of his own and other fields. The greater the teacher's range of knowledge and interests, the greater his ability to make curricular choices that will enrich his teaching, to keep motivation high, to take advantage of current developments in his field, and to differentiate his teaching in accord with the talents, interests, and needs of his students.

The student. A student's various developmental stages present differences in such critical factors as attention span, relation to peers and adults, motivations, interest, habits, experience, learning skills, and personality needs, all of which inevitably affect the teaching function. At each stage, the range of individual differences may also be significant. These may include differences in intelligence, interests, levels of maturity, personality, home environments, and social relations.

On the other hand, a certain age group organized according to homogeneity in scholastic ability, for example, presents its own unique teaching requirements; a coeducational group presents different conditions from one composed of either boys or girls only; and youngsters from middle-class families have significantly different requirements than do those from lower socioeconomic groups. The life-styles characteristic of the homes and neighborhoods in which the children are reared also exert an influence. The social dynamics of any given classroom community—friendships, enmities, and the degree and kind of communication among individuals—all may affect the direction and organization of learning activity.

Each group and each individual within a group thus present unique social conditions that inevitably affect the organization and conduct of instruction and that require distinctive teacher competencies. Knowledge of the students provides the most important foundation for effective teaching. The more knowledge of each student a teacher has, the better will be his basis for dealing effectively with the student.

A particularly subtle but necessary skill of the teacher is to recognize the nature and needs of a student as revealed through his behavior. The shy, withdrawn pupil who participates minimally or not at all in activities of the class, the aggressive extrovert who seeks to dominate, the attention-seeker, the defier, the absentminded daydreamer —all present the teacher with the challenges of discovering the underlying causes of that behavior, of capitalizing on traits that enhance learning, and of modifying or neutralizing traits that inhibit learning. Particularly crucial is that the teacher recognize symptoms of emotional disturbance and, when necessary, recommend professional care.

Since teaching is essentially a social function, the classroom teacher must understand and be skilled in guiding the dynamics of group behavior, particularly as they affect the progress of individual learning. The teacher must also be skilled in ways of organizing and directing the activity of large and small groups to ensure maximum individual participation. All these skills require an acute sensitivity to the actions, motivations, and feeling of others.

The teacher.   Opponents of teacher education programs that stress professional training beyond mastery of subject matter are fond of maintaining that teachers are born, not made. Yet, rarely do such critics attempt to identify the qualities needed to make a teacher—whether developed by training or there by inheritance. Inescapably, however, the nature of the educative process is shaped in considerable measure by the kind of person the teacher is, particularly in his relationships with his students and colleagues.

Although there is no single prototype by which all teachers can be judged, it is possible to designate certain personal characteristics that are favorable and certain that are adverse to effective teacher functioning. A teacher, performing in a position of leadership and guidance, is expected to be able to establish an empathic working relationship with students based on mutual acceptance of one another's roles. Central to the establishment of this relationship is the teacher's personal satisfaction in his life with students. For example, a teacher who feels uncomfortable, unhappy, resentful, inadequate, or fearful in the company of students will almost certainly engender negative reactions on the part of his students. Teachers need not be revered by their pupils, but they must be accepted as mentors. Their counsel should be received with a sufficient degree of willing acceptance and even occasional enthusiasm, rather than with reluctance, apathy, or defiance. Thus, the effective teacher likes his work, is contented in the company of his students, and is an accepted, even liked, leader in the learning community.

The acceptable range of positive characteristics for a teacher is wide, both in kind and degree. Some teachers are at their best in supporting roles, as when guiding small-group discussions or stimulating individual creative activity; others work best as performers in large-group teaching situations. Differences in teaching style may, of course, reflect the requirements of the type of learning activity, the subject under consideration, the skill to be developed, and the developmental level and social dynamics of the student group; in every

case, however, the teaching style is a product of the teacher's own experience, training, and personal qualities.

Associated with these factors of teacher personality and teaching style are a wide variety of competencies. Central to them all is the teacher's skill in self-appraisal, in getting to know himself as others see him, and in being able to predict the consequences of his actions on the behavior and feelings of others. This is probably the most complex and difficult of competencies to develop and perhaps the one most neglected in teacher development programs of the past. It is a psychologically demanding process, one that involves self-analysis not only of strengths but also of shortcomings, not only of positive feelings and motivations but also of prejudices and personal inadequacies. Yet, no process is more necessary to the development of a teacher because in no profession is the personal nature of the practitioner more crucial than in teaching. Because students are exposed to the influence of teachers for a major portion of their growing years, the kind of a person a teacher is, how he is viewed by students, and how he affects them are important factors in students' character development.

Professional environment.   The professional environment—for example, facilities, equipment, class size, class schedules, lighting, and ventilation —all influence teaching. Whether the seats are fixed or movable; whether the class size is 15, 30, 45, or 60; whether the period of instruction is 40 minutes, 80 minutes, or all day; whether the teacher is responsible for one group of 30 all the time or for five groups of 30 on a shared basis with others; whether the teacher has at his call instructional aids, such as projectors, cameras, and tape recorders; whether his students at the end of the semester are the same as those he had at the beginning (in inner-city schools there may be as much as a 100 percent turnover in any given group each semester); whether there are resources such as parks, museums, libraries, and factories available in the community; and the extent to which the teacher's environment is supportive and the extent to which it is hostile—all of these factors influence and, in many cases, determine the character of the teaching function. There is no standard environment for teaching and learning, but the proper manipulation and adaptation of the physical environment to desired ends is imperative.

The human environment is also a factor to be considered. Each school has characteristics of its own created by the relationships among teachers, supervisors, parents, and the community. Some of these relationships are positive—for example, the sympathetic guidance provided by a supervisor to a beginning teacher, the provision by a parent group of supplementary human and material resources for the teacher, and the sharing of experiences and resources by groups of teachers. Others may be negative—for example, the punitive actions of a superior, the apathy or hostility of a community, and the lack of cooperation among teachers.

Teachers must develop both adaptive and creative skills in utilizing the physical environment and resources for teaching. They must be able to make the best use of whatever is available, seek to counteract those elements that inhibit learning, and adapt to educational use all possible resources from inside and outside the school. As a professional, the teacher must also develop his role as a participating member of an academic community composed of both peers and superiors. The same situation holds true, although in different ways, in the development of his relationships with parents, community groups, and government agencies and officials. Finally, the best teachers will exercise leadership in their profession, become active in professional councils, and seek continuing improvement in educational quality through such professional activity.

Foundational and instrumental approaches. In teacher education programs, the amount of attention and importance accorded to student-centered and learning-centered competencies, as opposed to those that are largely subject-matter centered, is greater the lower the age level of the students to be taught; the reverse is true the older the age level of the students to be taught. Thus, training for early childhood teachers is predominantly child-learning centered, and training for college teaching (if indeed it can be considered that such training exists) is predominantly subject-matter centered, with secondary school teacher training occupying an uneasy middle ground between the two extremes.

It is useful, however, to consider the possibilities of translating the outcomes in teacher competencies into learning activities. Because the end of teacher education is the adequate functioning of the teacher in the classroom, all elements of teacher education must be judged in these terms. The primary function of teacher education is, therefore, the education of teachers, not education for its own sake, although the best of programs so motivated may indeed prove to have validity beyond their professional function.

There are two basic functional categories of learning activities in teacher education—the foundational and the instrumental. Teacher education programs do not necessarily fall into one or the other of these categories but rather exist on a continuum, with the two descriptive categories at opposite ends and with most of the programs embodying both in varying degrees.

In regard to knowledge of students, the foundational approach deals with such broad topics as the developmental characteristics of childhood and adolescence, the dynamics of individual and group behavior, and the nature of learning; the instrumental approach deals with the characteristics and behavior of individual students and groups of students in terms of the implications for teaching. Each approach may use the method of the other but for different purposes. The foundational approach uses the study of a particular child for the purpose of inducing and illustrating generalizations about the characteristics of all children. The instrumental approach uses generalizations about children for deductive purposes, to better understand the characteristics of a particular child. Thus, the former seeks knowledge and understanding largely for its own sake; the latter seeks to find the operational implication of knowledge. One emphasizes understanding the theory; the other, understanding of and ultimately skill in the applications of theory.

In regard to subject-matter competence, the foundational approach builds a background of knowledge of the discipline itself. Although the instrumental approach considers the teaching material for each discipline at the various levels, the goal is to build skill in making curricular choices from the vast material available and skill in organizing teaching units of subject matter. In this approach, the treatment of subject matter is in terms of the specific group of students for whom it is being planned, as in an in-service curriculum workshop for teachers. In the foundational approach, the treatment of subject matter is undertaken for its own sake, not necessarily with a view toward teaching it to others.

In regard to the teaching environment, study

of the school as both a reflection and an instrument of society would be largely foundational, but study of a specific social neighborhood and its influence on the functioning of the school would tend to be instrumental. In regard to the individual's own development as a teacher, such outcomes as appraisal of the teacher as a person and as he functions in a classroom situation are almost entirely instrumental in nature, although foundational knowledge of the nature of personality, motivations, and the dynamics of the classroom is useful.

Both the foundational and the instrumental approaches have their place in the curriculum of teacher education. One is not necessarily more important or more pervasive than the other, except that the ultimate aim of teacher education is, after all, essentially instrumental—the development of a teacher who can function effectively in the classroom.

Patterns.   Every recognized program of teacher education embodies in some form a combination of the foundational and instrumental approaches to training. However, the curricular and organizational patterns vary from one program to another in several major respects: first, the emphasis given to the foundational approach versus the instrumental approach (with programs for early childhood and elementary school teachers generally being weighted more in favor of the instrumental approach and programs for secondary school teachers weighted more in favor of the foundational approach); second, the institutional sponsorship of programs (varying from single-purpose teachers colleges to multipurpose institutions with incorporated schools or departments of teacher education); third, the relationship of professional study to general higher education (either being integrated or with professional study following regular academic study); fourth, the length of time beyond high school required to complete a program of teacher education leading to permanent certification as a teacher (once two years but now usually four or five years).

Although content may differ, most teacher education programs share certain common elements. For example, the requirements of a program leading to an academic degree are generally accepted as part of the program for teachers and include the usual distribution of requirements in the freshman and sophomore years. In addition, secondary education programs require concentration in the subject or subjects to be taught, and early childhood education programs require, if not a major, then some additional work in a broad spectrum of liberal arts courses.

Most programs also require foundational studies in philosophy, psychology, and sociology. These subjects are considered necessary for an understanding of the place and function of the school in modern society, of the development of children and adolescents, and of learning and teaching processes. Programs may also require instrumental studies in methodology and in the adaptation of content to teaching.

In the area of professional practice and experience, a wide variety of activities are generally required. These include not only observations of children, teachers, and classroom procedures but also supervised student teaching as well as paid part-time internships. These internships have a wide range of emphases and are placed at varying points in the curriculum, some in conjunction with and some separate from professional courses. These elements are present in most programs, but their relative extent, their importance, and their placement in a sequence of education may vary considerably.

Issues.   The conflicts in teacher education have centered primarily on the content, organization, and control of the issues in teacher education rather than on basic ideals and philosophies.

Balancing content.   The long-standing conflicts between the proponents of the liberal arts and the proponents of professional education studies in teacher education represent one of the less admirable chapters in the history of higher education. These conflicts all too often have been waged at an emotional level far out of keeping with the supposedly judicious atmosphere prevailing at a university.

With the gradual transformation of single-purpose teachers colleges into comprehensive institutions embodying strengthened liberal arts programs, however, and with liberal arts colleges increasingly incorporating teacher education programs in their curricula, the confrontation of the liberal arts professor with his educationist colleague has become increasingly frequent and indeed necessary. At its worst, this confrontation is an emotionally charged trading of accusations of anti-intellectualism and of academic blindness and irrelevance. At its best, it is a sincere attempt to marshal all the human resources of an institution, of whatever discipline and academic background, in a cooperative effort to build collectively planned and executed programs for the education of teachers. James B. Conant (1963) points out that blame for disputes may be ascribed to both sides, and he calls for the development of mutual understanding and cooperative effort.

Representative of efforts to achieve cooperation are the activities of the National Commission on Teacher Education and Professional Standards, which sponsors conferences and publications at both national and state levels involving liberal arts proponents and educationists, as well as school administrators, teachers, school board members, and even students. The American Association of Colleges for Teacher Education, the dominant voluntary organization of all higher institutions engaged in teacher education in the United States, includes among its voting membership not only an administrator from each institution but a representative from the liberal arts faculty as well.

Certification. The requirements for licensing and certification are the major determinants of the nature of teacher-training programs. These requirements are the statutory responsibility of official state bodies, and specifications may range from generalized, permissive, competency-centered requirements to detailed prescriptions for courses. From the point of view of a university engaged in teacher education, the less prescriptive the certification requirements, the greater the possibility of institutional self-determination regarding the curriculum. From the point of view of public authorities charged with upholding professional standards, the establishment of specific requirements at least establishes a common professional background necessary to maintain minimum levels of preparation.

Prescriptive certification requirements have been under attack from many quarters, both from within and from without the universities. Criticism has been particularly strong among those who argue for greater university autonomy in programming and among those who see in the prescriptions a plot by the educational establishment to maintain the status quo (Koerner 1963).

That these criticisms are bearing fruit is shown by a gradual liberalization of certification requirements in many states. This liberalization has taken several forms. Under the approved-program approach, a teacher education institution submits its program for approval by the certi-

fication agency, which encourages the institution to experiment with new ideas and programs without necessarily being restricted by existing state requirements. Once the program is approved, the graduates of the program are automatically certified.

Another practice is to express requirements in terms of competencies rather than of number of credits completed. This practice is often followed in conjunction with the approved-program approach and emphasizes such competencies as a reading, writing, and speaking knowledge of a foreign language. Certification of achievement is left up to the discretion of the university or is determined by means of an independently administered examination. Thus, the candidate and the university are provided with methods of determining the achievement of required competencies other than having completed a certain number of credits in specified courses. This practice, too, gives a great deal of latitude to the institution as well as to the candidate.

The lack of national standards for teacher education prompted the creation of a professional accreditation organization, the National Council for Accreditation of Teacher Education (NCATE), which, in conjunction with regional higher education accrediting associations and using similar procedures and principles, was expected to provide a national yardstick for teacher education. Since its inception in 1952, however, the NCATE has led a troubled existence, and its continuance as an effective standard-setting agency is in jeopardy in spite of a generally favorable review of its operation sponsored by the American Council on Education (Mayor & Swartz 1965).

The trend toward liberalizing and generalizing certification requirements has continued into the 1970's, with the result that differences in training programs are encouraged. Whether with the weakening of professional accreditation machinery sufficient safeguards for evaluation and review will be developed remains to be seen.

Teacher preparation. Since teachers must be prepared to work in an institutional setting, the nature of that setting must be taken into account in the training program; that is, the program must be relevant to the professional situation in which the teacher will find himself. On the other hand, the training institution is expected to be at the forefront of progress in teaching, transmitting the latest and best in theory and practice. The necessity of finding the proper balance between the realistic (the way things happen to be) and the normative (the way things should be) is probably the most difficult problem faced by any teacher education program.

Preoccupation with this problem has led to many significant changes in both the organization and content of training programs. Most of these changes have been aimed at bringing the training institution and the schools into working relationships that would provide colleges with realistic laboratories for observation and practice and schools with the services of experts and scholars. These relationships vary considerably in scope and organization. In its most formally developed form, the university assumes direct responsibility for running a school (in the same way that a medical school runs a teaching hospital). At one time such schools were predominantly campus or model schools, removed from the realistic setting of a school serving a neighborhood and therefore subject to the criticism of being different from the situation in which most new teachers would find themselves. In recent years, however, universities have been entering into close working partnerships with public neighborhood schools. These partnerships have ranged from the university assuming actual control of the entire operation to casual arrangements for observation and student teaching. It is becoming increasingly evident that partnerships between schools and colleges in teacher-training programs will have to become increasingly formalized if both the realistic and normative functions of training are to be realized. In any case, the traffic of professors to the schools, and of teachers to the universities, for purposes of mutual enrichment of each other's programs is becoming increasingly heavy.

Continuing education.   Even the best of pre-service teacher education programs can do no more than produce a beginning teacher. The transformation of the beginner into the competent professional and the continuing need for that teacher to keep abreast of changing needs and resources have expanded teacher education programs far beyond the level of basic preservice preparation. The trend in permanent teacher certification requirements is toward an additional year of university preparation beyond the baccalaureate, and school systems are increasingly providing lures of higher salaries for professional study even beyond the first graduate year. Variations in content and form of in-service education

programs are even more extensive than those at the preservice level, and all the issues relating to such questions as content relevance, control, and liberal versus professional training pertain to in-service education with even greater urgency than to preservice training. There is, however, agreement as to the need for continuing education, and the decades ahead will inevitably see a lengthening of the time required for teacher education, particularly at the in-service and continuing education levels.

The unprecedented growth and change in all fields of human knowledge and the rapidly changing social scene, particularly in the cities, have created imperatives for teacher education almost at the emergency level. The 1950's and 1960's saw the development, largely federally financed, of teacher institutes, particularly in the fields of science and mathematics, and developments in the study of disadvantaged children and youth. These institutes, operating on a full-time intensive basis during the summer months, were attended by thousands of teachers on an in-service basis. It seems inevitable that a training practice begun on an emergency basis will be incorporated into ongoing programs of continuing education for teachers.

Professional training.   The most common pattern of teacher education incorporates professional education, culminating in student teaching, into a baccalaureate degree program, with much of the professional studies being taken in the junior and senior years. This training is then followed by graduate in-service programs of various kinds, leading to permanent teacher certification or to positions in school administration, guidance, or other educational specialities.

An entirely different pattern builds upon a liberal arts undergraduate degree, with little or no professional content. All basic professional preparation, including an internship, is concentrated in a program leading to a master of arts in teaching (MAT) degree. This type of program was pioneered by such prestige institutions as Harvard University and has been widely heralded as a more viable approach to teacher education than the prevailing pattern.

Proponents of the MAT approach claim that it provides a richer liberal arts base, since there is no diversion of credits from academic to professional studies in the baccalaureate program, and that its concentration on professional preparation with an internship as the core provides a more realistic and intensive preparation for teaching. Proponents of the prevailing pattern believe that it provides greater opportunity to screen candidates for teaching by affording a more gradual and longer introduction to professional studies, that the juxtaposition of liberal and professional studies provides greater possibilities for their mutual support, and that the chronic teacher shortage requires the earlier entrance into the profession that the undergraduate preservice program affords.

Whatever the merits of the two modes of organization, MAT programs have managed to prepare only a very small fraction of the teachers needed. Many of the larger institutions offer both types of programs, with the MAT program largely reserved for graduates of liberal arts colleges that do not have professional teacher education programs and for college graduates who have made a belated choice of teaching as a career.

Sources of information. The American Association of Colleges for Teacher Education publishes a yearbook annually. The yearbooks report the proceedings of the annual meetings of the association and describe current trends and issues as discussed by leaders in the field.

The annual yearbooks published by the Association for Student Teaching, on a different theme each year, are primary sources of information about current developments in teacher education. Each issue contains an annotated bibliography on all phases of teacher education.

The National Commission on Teacher Education and Professional Standards issues annual conference reports. The conferences and the reports are notable for the joint participation by professional educators, liberal arts professors, schoolteachers and administrators, and interested laymen. The reports contain discussions of many of the most significant new developments and experiments in teacher education.

The most influential professional journal in the field is the *Journal of Teacher Education*, published quarterly by the National Commission on Teacher Education and Professional Standards. In its pages can be found reports and discussions representing many different points of view on current issues and trends in teacher education.

BIBLIOGRAPHY

ALLEN, PAUL M., et al. 1970 *Teacher Self-appraisal: A Way of Looking Over Your Own Shoulder.* Worthington, Ohio, Charles A. Jones.

AMERICAN ASSOCIATION OF COLLEGES FOR TEACHER EDUCATION 1969 *Recommended Standards for Teacher Education.* Washington, D.C., The Association.

BLEWETT, EVELYN J., ed. 1969 *Elementary Teacher Training Models.* OE-58033. Washington, D.C., Government Printing Office.

BORROWMAN, MERLE L., ed. 1965 *Teacher Education in America: A Documentary History.* New York, Teachers College Press.

CONANT, JAMES B. 1963 *The Education of American Teachers.* New York, McGraw-Hill.

COTTRELL, DONALD P. 1970 *National Policy for the Improvement of the Quality of Teacher Education.* Washington, D.C., American Association of Colleges for Teacher Education.

GOSDEN, P. H. J. H., comp. 1969 *How They Were Taught: An Anthology of Contemporary Accounts of Learning and Teaching In England, 1800–1950.* New York, Barnes & Noble.

KOERNER, JAMES D. 1963 *The Miseducation of American Teachers.* Boston, Houghton Mifflin.

LINDLEY, J. STILES, et al. 1960 *Teacher Education in the United States.* New York, Ronald Press.

MAYOR, JOHN R., AND WILLIS G. SWARTZ 1965 *Accreditation in Teacher Education: Its Influence on Higher Education.* Washington, D.C., National Commission on Accrediting.

POSTMAN, NEIL, AND CHARLES WEINGARTNER 1969 *Teaching as a Subversive Activity.* New York, Delacorte.

ROGERS, VINCENT R., ed. 1970 *Teaching in the British Primary School.* New York, Macmillan.

HERBERT SCHUELER

2. HISTORY

Formal, highly self-conscious efforts to create a profession of teaching, with the elaborate artifacts of formal training, credentials, organization, and internal propaganda, began in Western Europe in the seventeenth century and accelerated rapidly in conjunction with the growth of nationalistic systems of universal state-supported schooling in the early nineteenth century. Formal training for the professions of statesmanship, scholarship, and the priesthood had emerged long before, and novices in these older professions had been educated and trained in literature and techniques later to be appropriated by those attempting to professionalize the teaching of children and youth. But in the United States as a whole in 1830, in regions of the United States as late as 1920, and in the minds of many Americans as late as 1940, a moderately schooled older sister or mother, working in a homelike environment, functioned in what was considered an adequate manner as a teacher of children.

The formal history of American teacher education and professionalization is conventionally a story of one triumphal march from Samuel R. Hall's Concord, Vt., normal school in 1823 to the modern National Education Association and the great graduate schools of education. This version of history is misleading.

The advocates of professionalization achieved considerable success in securing favorable licensure legislation and remarkable success in propagandizing among those who became stalwarts in organizations affiliated with the NEA. Yet, in the minds of many Americans the older sisters or the scholars whose professional model harked back to an earlier era—men who knew their subject matter although they were not professionally trained as teachers—were often considered superior to professional teachers as defined by the dominant group. In 1940 independent primary and secondary schools largely ignored the requirements of professional certification, and even public schools often bypassed them by arranging temporary or emergency certification of people they wished to hire.

Although this historical treatment covers only the period up to 1940, current events suggest either that earlier triumphs were not so complete as conventionally described or else that in recent decades there has occurred a reversal of earlier trends. In the late 1960's the movement for community control of the schools and for the development of career ladder plans which would staff schools with community residents who shared the ethnic and economic values of students reflected a continuing belief that familial-like tutelage is critically important. At the same time, the new curriculum and new technology movements disclosed a lack of confidence in the professional teacher as defined and prepared by formal teacher education programs and as identified by major professional organizations, such as the NEA and its affiliates. On the collegiate level, the scholar whose professional identity is defined by his discipline—for example, the ministry, history, or physics—still dominates the teaching function, as he has throughout American history. Before 1940 there was no serious movement to develop a profession of college teaching as such, and sporadic movements in this direction have been largely abortive since that time.

Beginnings of professionalization. The drive to professionalize primary and secondary teachers was begun in the northeastern United States in the first half of the nineteenth century. Its leading exponents were such people as James G. Carter, Horace Mann, Henry Barnard, and Calvin Stowe. As a group these men were largely trained for the law and the ministry, and although several are well known as educational statesmen, few ever spent any considerable amount of time as actual teachers. Their concern as ministers and statesmen was to ensure an orderly society by creating a stable, conservative corps of dedicated and self-effacing people who would, in turn, inculcate habits of obedience, loyalty, morality, and economic efficiency in the young. The dominant instrument adopted to create the teaching profession was an American version of the Prussian normal school. Its American exponents, sometimes hard pressed by charges of un-Americanism, were quick to assert that the American normal school served a republican rather than a monarchical political system. Nevertheless, one suspects they would have been less than candid had they not admitted some sympathy for the Prussian monarch Frederick William IV, who charged in 1848 that he had trusted the normal school graduates to prepare loyal citizens and that they had instead produced a revolution.

Implicit in the campaigns for a system of universal publicly controlled schooling was the assumption that the primary group—the family and the face-to-face community—could no longer be relied upon to maintain orderly and efficient social action through familial tutelage, private schooling, apprenticeship, and communal ritual. Later in the nineteenth century, John Dewey, Francis W. Parker, and others would explicitly define the ideal school as a simplified and purified home and community, and they would talk about the teacher's maternal, paternal, and community leadership roles. These models had undergirded the earlier movements.

Some of the parameters for a profession of teaching were reasonably well defined, at least in negative terms, as early as James G. Carter's *Essays on Popular Education* (1827): a profession needs a specially designed preparatory institution to ensure singleness of purpose for students and teachers; it must develop a body of theoretical knowledge and practical skills relevant to its function; and it should function under the watchful eye of the state to ensure that incompetence is minimized and dedication to public ends maintained.

The necessity for internal propaganda—literature specifically directed at the profession and designed both to instruct and to inspire identification with the profession—was also quickly, if not consciously, recognized. William Russell launched his *American Journal of Education* in 1826, and the *American Annals of Education and Instruction* was begun by William C. Woodbridge in 1830. Horace Mann's *Common-School Journal* was launched in 1835, and Henry Barnard's *Connecticut Common School Journal* began the following year. Between 1830 and 1850 the *Lectures and Proceedings of the American Institute of Instruction* carried the most significant discussions of educational, including pedagogical, issues in America. For hard information about education, teachers and schoolmen were largely indebted to Henry Barnard's *American Journal of Education* (1855–1881) until he and his successors as United States commissioners of education developed the information-gathering and information-disseminating resources of the U.S. Bureau of Education in the second half of the nineteenth century.

Those who called the profession of teaching into existence were primarily ministers and/or statesmen rather than professional teachers. The journals, the teacher-preparation institutions, the organizations, and certain individuals themselves reflected during the nineteenth century an ambivalence between the function of educational statesmanship and the functions of pedagogy. A crudely accurate generalization is that all tended throughout the century to move from statesmanship to pedagogical professionalism. Paul Mattingly, in his perceptive "Professional Strategies and New England Educators, 1825–1860" (1968), clearly illustrated this trend with respect to such individuals as Bronson Alcott and Samuel Read Hill, such organizations as the American Institute of Instruction, and such institutions as the lyceum and the teachers' institute.

Mattingly, citing Henry Barnard, asserted that the first of what was to become a flood of conventions and organizations dedicated to the expansion of public education and the professionalization of teaching occurred in Brooklyn in the spring of 1826. Its sponsor was the Reverend Samuel May; among his associates were William Russell and Thomas Gallaudet, indefatigable exponents of teacher-training institutions. May, who ventured into teaching as a part-time job and as a minor ministry, eventually organized a lyceum in Brooklyn for the in-service training of teachers. The more extensive American lyceum movement developed by Josiah Holbrook carried considerable responsibility for teacher training for several decades, until it was succeeded by the more sharply focused teachers' institutes.

Associated with Holbrook and the American lyceum through the School Agents Society was Samuel Read Hall, founder of what is usually considered the first normal school, a private one in Connecticut in 1823. After the failure of the private venture, Hall had gone on to direct a teachers' seminary in conjunction with Phillips Andover Academy in 1830. This teachers' seminary, or teachers' department, was but one of many attached to academies and colleges in the second and third decades of the nineteenth century. The proponents of the state normal schools were to call them failures, and many of them did collapse.

However, the reported collapse of teacher preparation in academic secondary schools and colleges is something of a distortion. As public high schools emerged, either as separate foundations or as the gradual upward extension of the common school, the practice of maintaining a teachers' class in the upper years continued. There are no clear data on how extensive this form of teacher education was; perhaps historians have neglected those agencies because commitment to the professional view made it important to concentrate on the approved types of institutions—the normal schools and universities. Nevertheless, it is clear that Edward A. Sheldon began to expound Pestalozzian pedagogy to a teachers' class in the Oswego, N.Y., high school before that class was upgraded to state normal school status. It is also clear that such urban agencies as Chicago Teachers College and Harris Teachers College in St. Louis emerged from the efforts of city school administrators to prepare their own teachers in the context of existing academic secondary schools.

Rise of normal schools. From the standpoint of what came to be the dominant professional ideology, the decisions of Charles Brooks, Horace Mann, Henry Barnard, Calvin Stowe, and others to choose the single-purpose, publicly controlled normal school as the most promising profession-building agency was decisive. In their thinking the Prussian experience was conclusive. Brooks has been impressed by Victor Cousin's *Report on Prussian Instruction* (1833), had corresponded with the author, and had visited Prussia in 1833 and 1834. On his return, Brooks campaigned tirelessly for the establishment in Massachusetts of a Prussian-model normal school; he held 13 conventions dedicated to this cause in Massachusetts alone during a single 12-month period, 1836–1837. Largely as a result of his efforts, the first state normal school was established in 1838 at Lexington. Calvin Stowe, from Ohio, was similarly inspired by Cousin and by a Prussian visit; Mann and Barnard followed their paths.

In the nineteenth century it was unrealistic to assume that a majority of common-school teachers could be prepared in the relatively few struggling normal schools provided by the state, even though such schools proliferated widely after 1860. However, the common school reformers hoped that these normal schools would set the professional standards. The successors to Mann and Barnard as chief state school officers thus usually secured legislation providing for statewide, virtually automatic licensure of graduates from the public normal schools and later teachers colleges. However, in most states local and county school committees or superintendents could give only local and short-term certificates to teachers in their districts. The implication was clear—those who had mastered the instruction and imbibed the inspiration offered in the public normal schools provided the model.

In the early decades the theoretical or ideological components of the normal school curriculum were derived from the standard works on moral and mental philosophy, works which themselves largely reflected secularized Protestant presuppositions with a dash of Anglo-American philosophic realism. The pedagogical values were those of order and a thorough mastery of fact and basic mathematical and English language skills. This isolation of normal school students from other kinds of mature students was deemed necessary to ensure dedication to teaching as a calling and, one suspects, to prevent the emergence of skepticism or cynicism about the prevailing social order. Either through role-playing in the normal school classes or increasingly through demonstration classes or primary schools attached to the normal schools, prospective teachers were given opportunities to observe the master teacher at work and gradually to assume direct responsibility for practice teaching.

This basic Prussian–New England model normal school persisted throughout the nineteenth century, with three somewhat significant changes. Two new pedagogical systems, the Pestalozzian

and the Herbartian, emerged in the 1870's and 1890's respectively, and particularly in the frontier states, a mildly camouflaged attempt to provide general secondary and collegiate education for students whose destiny was other than teaching emerged.

From the beginning the common and normal school movements included certain broad Pestalozzian strains. Among these were the ideas that by making the school a miniature ideal community general social reform would be encouraged and that the child normally developed from mastery of the sensed concrete to the emergence of higher cognitive processes, or faculties, as the language of the time preferred. However, in the early 1860's a highly formalized pedagogy based on English as well as Swiss Pestalozzian models was developed and promoted by Edward Sheldon in Oswego. Object teaching, as this pedagogy came to be identified, swept the normal schools for a decade or so. Although it later lost prominence as a system of instruction, it left educational theory and practice greatly predisposed to value concrete and direct experience and to think rigorously in terms of precise unit planning.

The Herbartian movement which succeeded object teaching as the dominant pedagogical method in the 1890's was, in both Europe and the United States, a part of the same intellectual tradition. Herbart had taken the intuitive insights of Rousseau and Pestalozzi and developed them into a more intellectually respectable version of cosmic philosophy based on hypothetical-deductive models. In the United States the fountainhead of Herbartian pedagogy was Illinois Normal University, one of the normal schools with the most mature students and one which early broke from the artisan orientation of the New England models.

The dramatic, if brief, success of the Herbartian movement was partly a function of the development of the American university in the final decades of the nineteenth century. These were the years in which the new social sciences, again based initially on German models, emerged. The new psychology of William James and G. Stanley Hall, the new philosophy of Charles S. Peirce, William James, and John Dewey, the new political economy of Richard T. Ely, the new history of Herbert B. Adams, and the new sociology of Lester Frank Ward and Albion Small were all institutionally oriented, and all directed attention to formal schooling. These disciplines were developed in research-oriented universities, and they attracted theoretically oriented minds. Herbartianism was more appealing to such men than the cookbook pedagogy of the Pestalozzians, although it quickly lost favor as philosophic empiricism replaced idealism. Even such philosophical idealists as Josiah Royce and William T. Harris quickly came to prefer Kant to Herbart.

For a brief period, essentially the decade of the 1890's, the scientific study of education was an acceptable, even prestigious, enterprise for scholars in the new social science departments of private universities like Chicago, Clark, and Johns Hopkins and in such state universities as Michigan and Wisconsin. Scholars and administrators from these universities joined the debates in the meetings and committees of the NEA and encouraged the development of university schools of education.

However, once the schools of education were established, scholars from other social science and philosophical departments tended to withdraw or to be driven from the study of educational institutions and practices as such. In several of the great national universities—for example, Johns Hopkins, Chicago, Clark, and later Stanford—the dominant professional methods continued to be those of the scholar. At other places—for example, Harvard, Teachers College at Columbia, and the state universities of Michigan, Wisconsin, and California—sharp divisions occurred between those who perceived themselves as professional scholars and those who took pride in being professional schoolmen. In most of the state universities, some of whose schools of education antedated the emergence of the new research-oriented universities, the professionalism was that of the schoolmen from the beginning; the professors of education were largely recruited from among the successful practitioners.

NEA—its affiliates and opponents. Those who initially set about to create a profession of teachers were not themselves practicing educators, although some became such. The professionalizing institutions they established—for example, the American Institute of Instruction, the lyceums and institutes, and the normal schools—quite expectedly came, in time, under the control of those who by disposition, training, and experience did perceive themselves as professional teachers. However, the more powerful thrust for professionalism came from organizations initially controlled by

the teachers. When the new university scholars joined the debates of the NEA, they encountered a group of people who had already established a strong sense of professional identity.

Roughly from 1885 to 1905 the professional scholars from the universities were highly active in the NEA and were members of such of its crucial committees as the Committee of Ten. Their participation and later withdrawal probably in part resulted from the fact that these were the eras in which sharp definitions were being made of the function of each type of school—elementary, secondary, and collegiate—in a more tightly articulated system. But it is also true that the traditions of the NEA—those of professional schoolmen—and the traditions of the new university—those of the professional scholar—were different.

Organizations of practicing primary and secondary school teachers go back at least as far as 1794, when the Society of Associated Teachers of New York City was established. In 1845 statewide organizations were formed in Rhode Island, New York, and Massachusetts. By 1856, 12 more state associations were under way. Leaders of the Massachusetts and New York associations, Daniel B. Hager and Thomas W. Valentine, respectively, initiated the organization of the National Teachers Association in 1857. This association was, in turn, parent to the National Educational Association in 1870. The name of the organization took its present form in 1908, when the word "Educational" was changed to "Education."

The primary function of the NEA was clearly set forth in the first sentence of the still unchanged preamble to its constitution: "To elevate the character and advance the interests of the profession of teaching and to promote the cause of public education in the United States. . . ." Within five years of its founding, the association began to assert its role as guardian of pedagogical orthodoxy, a crucial function in any established profession. Discussion from the floor of the 1864 national meeting included damning criticism of Sheldon's *Object Teaching*. In response, the association provided a demonstration of Sheldon's methods and established a committee to investigate and report to the 1865 convention on the desirability of the Oswego procedures.

Shortly after the formation of the National Teachers Association, the American Normal School Association, whose first convention in 1859 was given over to defining the science of education, was established. Six years later, in 1865, an earlier organization of state and local school administrators was re-formed into the National Association of School Administrators, an organization with potential power to control the directions in which the profession of teaching might move. In 1870 these two organizations were combined with the National Teachers Association, thus encouraging the development of a unified profession.

The practice of incorporating any potentially competing professional agency has been consistent enough to be considered a settled policy of the NEA. Thus, when in 1925 the American Association of Teachers Colleges (AATC) began to talk of national standards and accreditation procedures for teacher education, it too became affiliated with the NEA, replacing the old normal school department. The AATC, which originated in 1902 as the North Central Council of State Normal School Presidents, became in 1948 the American Association of Colleges for Teacher Education (AACTE). Since accreditation procedures have been historically tied to state certification for teachers, the AACTE joined with other NEA affiliates, including organizations of chief state school officers, in the establishment of the National Council for Accreditation of Teacher Education.

Other groups with a potentially crucial role in establishing the characteristic behavior of the teaching profession were also linked to the NEA. Thus, among educational researchers the National Society for the Study of Education originated under the wing of the NEA as the National Herbart Society for the Scientific Study of Education in 1895, and the American Education Research Association, founded in 1915, became a department of the NEA in 1930. The Educational Policies Commission, which has sought to involve distinguished laymen in the study of major policy issues, was formed by the NEA and its affiliated Department of Superintendence in 1935.

So far as organizations involving large numbers of practicing teachers are concerned, only the American Federation of Teachers remained outside the control or major influence of the NEA. After its formation in major urban centers, primarily Chicago, Gary, and New York, in 1916, the AFT provided an option to the dominant view of the profession of teaching. Although no less concerned than the NEA with power to control the preparation, admission to practice, internal disci-

pline, and conditions of employment of teachers, the AFT sharply attacked the assumption of common interest between classroom teachers and other educational workers perceived by the AFT as management. It also sharply disagreed about the degree of militancy appropriate to teachers in the pursuit of better working conditions.

More basic than these tactical issues separating those who supported the NEA from those choosing the AFT was a difference in the historical tradition with which each group identified itself. At least until the 1940's, the concept of profession institutionalized in the NEA, in the schools of education, and in the processes of certification and employment was derived from such apostles of good order, nonviolence, gentlemanly social behavior, and pious suffering in the good cause as Henry Barnard and Horace Mann. Of the old professions, the NEA model was that of the ministry, although professional rhetoricians preferred to cite that of medicine. Under this model a good school and a good school system were familial, with a wise, firm, but loving father at its head.

The AFT, on the other hand, grew up under the sponsorship of organized labor. Its historical heroes were in the early workingmen's parties, and its more recent heroes were Samuel Gompers and the militant John Dewey, as opposed to the gentle John Dewey of the NEA. Up until 1940 one could get a poetically accurate view of the attitudes of these two groups if one viewed the exponents of the AFT generally as sons of urban industrial workers and the NEA exponents as sons and daughters of small town polite society members and pious farmers.

Emergence of teachers and states colleges. When the state of Massachusetts established its first public normal school in 1839, the modern distinctions between elementary school, secondary school, and collegiate institution had not yet emerged; there was, in fact, no system of education. Although prestigious colleges did demand literacy in the vernacular and at least some mastery of the classical languages and basic mathematics, even they were still enrolling students with little or no prior formal school attendance. Less distinguished institutions—variously called academies, seminaries, institutes, English high schools, and colleges—were offering instruction which ranged from basic literacy to natural history and moral philosophy as taught at places like Harvard. Therefore, terms like secondary and collegiate education are misleading when applied to such institutions as the early normal schools. With respect to maturity and amount of previous schooling, the girls who entered the first normal-school class at Lexington, Mass., were quite like the young men entering academies at the same time. If they had had a year or so of tutoring in the classical languages, they would have also been comparable to those entering many so-called colleges.

The normal schools along the Atlantic seaboard did try to limit their academic curricula to a rigorous review of subject matter actually covered in the common, primary schools. Geometry, for example, was eschewed, although it had become a staple of academies. Although normal school principals often expanded the curriculum into what would become secondary school and collegiate subject matter, the controlling boards often resisted these moves even as late as 1890. A marked exception to the rule was the New York State Normal School at Albany, which had been established to prepare secondary school teachers and which therefore acquired collegiate characteristics early.

In the frontier states, on the other hand, the normal schools provided scarcely concealed general academic education almost from the beginning. Although constrained to advertise themselves as teacher-training institutions, their recruitment publicity consistently argued that the young man or woman who graduated from their extended courses, even if he left the profession of teaching, would find himself in possession of a diploma from a first-rate "people's college," a term widely used by the academies and seminaries. Moreover, these same normal schools early developed courses for prospective teachers who had already had some high school or academy experience. Thus, from its beginning in 1852 the Michigan State Normal School at Ypsilanti provided a curriculum whose academic content was considerably broader and more advanced than that to be retaught in the primary schools. There were efforts to restrict this tendency, but by 1881 the legal right of that institution to prepare secondary school teachers was established, and it had become possible for students to study most of what was being offered in many American colleges. Other midwestern schools—for example, Illinois Normal University and Indiana State Normal School at Terre Haute —were comparable.

If one defines a college as an institution whose work presupposes the completion of a secondary school program, the normal schools, even in the New England states, were moving toward collegiate status by the time of the Civil War. Many normal schools provided multiple "courses," a term which in the nineteenth century meant what curricula or programs mean in the twentieth. It was not uncommon to have one-year, two-year, or three-year curricula; and short courses running from a few weeks up to six months were occasionally offered for those who could not afford the extended course or whose previous academic preparation in secondary schools or colleges made all but the strictly professional instruction offered by normal schools unnecessary. As early as 1860 some normal schools were instructing some collegiate students; as late as 1920 some offered courses for students who held no secondary school diploma. Therefore, the shift from normal school to teachers college was partly a shift in the proportions of different kinds of students involved.

The change in title from "state normal school" to "state teachers college" generally reflected the development of a four-year program based on prior completion of a high school program and rewarded by the receipt of a baccalaureate degree. In some cases it also implied that secondary school teachers as well as elementary school teachers were being prepared by the institution. This transition occurred largely between 1910 and 1940, with the peak decade being the 1920's.

By 1930, when the teachers college movement was at its peak, the curriculum of the primary school itself had become much more complex than it had been in the heyday of the normal school. Starting in the 1880's, first nature study and then science education had crept into the curriculum; to a significant extent under the influence of the Herbartians, the social studies had become a major element by the beginning of the twentieth century. Moreover, the new pedagogy of the progressive era demanded a teacher who was expected to select her own materials rather than follow a closely prescribed course of study and who was theoretically capable of following a student's emerging intellectual interest into its more advanced and systematic ramifications. Elementary and secondary school teachers did need more advanced scientific and social scientific knowlege than had their nineteenth-century predecessors. Moreover, by 1930 university research in the disciplines related to education had produced a large corpus of theoretical, scientific, and technical literature which, even if not taught directly as part of teacher preparation, presupposed some understanding of social scientific and philosophic concepts.

One suspects that the primary motives in upgrading the normal schools concerned professional stature and prestige. Real wages, and certainly job security, had increased substantially throughout the nineteenth century as a result of certification and the accompanying public assumption that special training and expertise were useful attributes of teachers. Prior to 1839 a few distinguished grammar school teachers were held in fairly high repute as learned men of the community. At the same time, it was a rare young man who dedicated himself to a lifelong career of teaching, especially on the primary school level. The norm for men was to take a brief turn at teaching while on the way through college or apprenticeship to more lucrative and influential positions in law, the ministry, commerce, or politics. A century later these careers were still often more lucrative and somewhat more prestigious, but no longer did one feel apologetic for accepting a teaching career in the public schools. For males, at least, the new profession of school administration opened up opportunities for substantial salaries and public influence.

Yet, the status of a particular vocation, especially one tied to formal schooling, is partly a function of the education of its practitioners in relation to that of other occupations. In 1840 a person with some kind of professional schooling beyond the common school was a member of a fairly small educational elite in many communities; by 1890 one had to have advanced somewhat beyond the secondary school level to maintain a similar relative position. By 1940 some postsecondary education was available to a substantial portion of the population. The graduates of the new teachers colleges, with their baccalaureate degrees, probably ranked little higher, if at all, in the educational hierarchies of their local communities than had the graduates of the nineteenth-century normal school. By 1940, if teaching was to be considered among the learned professions, the baccalaureate was essential. Although throughout history there had been much talk of upgrading the profession, on relative grounds the teacher educators were doing little more than holding their own. Therefore, one could have predicted that in states like California, with a relatively high proportion of college graduates,

campaigns would begin to require a fifth year of formal collegiate-level education for teachers. This, of course, is what occurred.

Teacher education in universities and colleges. Beginning with the seventeenth century, the Latin grammar schools had been clearly viewed as pre-collegiate institutions and as secondary schools in the European sense, which distinguished classical language schools from primary schools concentrating on the development of literacy in the vernacular languages. In the nineteenth century the American academies and the English high schools went through a period when they were considered people's colleges—that is, alternatives to the college. By the mid-nineteenth century most of these had found a place between the primary vernacular school and the college. Throughout the nineteenth century teachers for all three of these types of secondary schools tended to be men with some collegiate education. With the previously mentioned exceptions of the midwestern normal schools and Albany State Normal School, the dominant assumption throughout the century was that the college and university were responsible for preparing secondary school teachers. It was also assumed that no professional training as such was required, which meant that the secondary school teachers perceived their profession as that of scholars rather than of teachers as defined in the normal school culture.

From the beginning a number of the new midwestern state universities maintained a normal department which brought ill-prepared students up to the nominal university entry level and assisted in the preparation of teachers for the common schools. In connection with these normal departments, universities, beginning perhaps with Iowa in 1873, began to hire professors of pedagogy. At the same time, on the national level there was growing agitation for the pedagogical training of secondary school teachers and for the entry of universities and colleges into the business of professional teacher education.

In 1879 the University of Michigan appointed William H. Payne to a chair in the "science and art of teaching," and out of his efforts grew what may be considered the first full-fledged department of education. Michigan was concerned with the preparation of secondary school teachers, but its faculty viewed secondary school teaching as an entry into the profession of school administration. In fact, in a number of urban centers the secondary school teacher was likely to have supervisory duties over the primary schools in his area. Therefore, he was more likely to be a policymaker and an educational statesman. The training program, as it developed at Michigan and later in other university departments of education as they emerged, was more theoretically oriented than was that of the normal schools. However, the tendency to emphasize the theoretical, not historical, foundations of pedagogy was not simply a function of the universities' concern with the preparation of educational leaders. By 1890, when the movement for university teacher education was in full swing, the new social sciences were rapidly emerging from their historical roots in mental and moral philosophy. Questions of human development and learning and of education as social policy were intriguing to many university professors, and the university professors of education were more likely to court the approval of their immediate colleagues than that of the schoolmen.

Nevertheless, there was at last one argument given by such pioneers as William H. Payne which would later bear increasing weight in teacherscollege circles. It was the argument that at least educational leaders should be educated in company with their age-peers destined for other positions of social leadership. By 1940 the isolation of prospective teachers from other highly educated people, which had been considered an advantage to the founders of the normal school movement, was increasingly seen as disadvantageous, partly because the teachers colleges themselves remained relatively low-status institutions and partly because in increasingly complex debates about public school policies and practices, school people were more comfortable if they had shared a common collegiate culture with their opponents and allies. Horace Mann had wanted his teachers to be special kinds of people; teachers and teacher educators of the 1940's found it painful to be too sharply set apart from other college educated people. The trend to convert teachers colleges into multipurpose state colleges, which was well under way in the 1940's, was thus understandable.

BIBLIOGRAPHY

AMERICAN COUNCIL ON EDUCATION 1946 *The Improvement of Teacher Education: A Final Report by the Commission on Teacher Education.* Washington, D.C., The Council.

AMERICAN FEDERATION OF TEACHERS. COMMITTEE ON EDUCATIONAL RECONSTRUCTION 1955 *Organizing the Teaching Profession: The Story of the American Federation of Teachers.* Glencoe, Ill., Free Press.

BORROWMAN, MERLE L. 1956 *The Liberal and Technical in Teacher Education: A Historical Survey of American Thought.* New York, Teachers College, Bureau of Publications.

BORROWMAN, MERLE L., ed. 1965 *Teacher Education in America: A Documentary History.* New York, Teachers College Press.

CARTER, JAMES G. 1827 *Essays on Popular Education.* Boston, Bowles and Dearborn.

COUSIN, VICTOR 1833 *Rapport sur l'état de l'instruction publique en Prusse.* Paris, F. G. Leurault. An English version was published in 1835 by Wiley and Long under the title *Report on Prussian Instruction.*

ELSBREE, WILLARD S. 1939 *The American Teacher: Evolution of a Profession.* New York, American Book.

History of Education in Michigan 1965–1969 3 vols. Vol. 1: *Education in the Wilderness,* by Floyd R. Dain. Vol. 2: *The Michigan Search for Educational Standards,* by Charles R. Starring and James O. Knauss. Vol. 3: *Schools of an Urban Society,* by Donald W. Disbrow. Lansing, Michigan Historical Commission.

LEARNED, WILLIAM S., et al. 1920 *The Professional Preparation of Teachers for American Public Schools.* Bulletin No. 14. New York, Carnegie Foundation for the Advancement of Teaching.

MAGNUM, VERNON 1928 *The American Normal School, Its Rise and Development in Massachusetts.* Baltimore, Warwick and York.

MATTINGLY, PAUL 1968 "Professional Strategies and New England Educators, 1825–1860." Ph.D. thesis. Madison, University of Wisconsin.

MONROE, WALTER S. 1952 *Teacher-Learning Theory and Teacher Evaluation, 1890 to 1950.* Urbana, University of Illinois Press.

NATIONAL EDUCATION ASSOCIATION 1889 *The Report of the Chicago Committee.* Proceedings. Chicago, The Association.

National Survey of the Education of Teachers 1922 Bulletin 1922, No. 10, Vol. 6. Washington, D.C., Government Printing Office.

NORTON, ARTHUR O. 1926 *The First Normal School in America: The Journals of Cyrus Peirce and Mary Swift.* Cambridge, Mass., Harvard University Press.

PANGBURN, JESSIE M. 1932 *The Evolution of the American Teachers College.* New York, Teachers College.

STOWE, CALVIN E. 1839 *Common Schools and Teachers' Seminaries.* Boston, Marsh, Copen, Lyon, and Webb.

WESLEY, EDGAR B. 1957 *N.E.A., The First Hundred Years: The Building of the Teaching Profession.* New York, Harper.

MERLE L. BORROWMAN

3. IN-SERVICE TRAINING

In-service education is designed to promote the continuous development of the teacher after he enters the teaching profession by providing planned and systematic instruction within an educational setting. The need for further study is directly related to the ability of a teacher to perform his teaching tasks. The more the nature of his role changes, the more frequently the teacher must receive in-service education. An experienced teacher may need such added training because of a change in his assignment (for example, a change from independent to team teaching, a move to a new location, or the introduction to the curriculum of new subject matter or techniques, such as the new math) or a radical change in the socioeconomic and/or ethnic composition of the school population. In-service courses may also help a beginning teacher in applying theory learned in college programs to actual classroom situations.

Sources of training. At least three groups—colleges and universities, local school systems, and teachers themselves—are vital in determining the quantity and quality of in-service programs. Colleges and universities have traditionally assumed the responsibility for providing preservice and degree programs. Today, critics agree that institutional responsibility cannot terminate with the awarding of a degree. Teachers continually face new and challenging situations which require different or improved competence, and teacher-training institutions possess the materials, facilities, and expertise best designed to assist the teacher in keeping abreast of changing demands and maintaining his performance.

Local school systems, which are charged with the responsibility of providing and evaluating educational programs, should be in a position to identify problems and provide in-service training to remedy any weaknesses. If an evaluation calls for certain objectives, then the school system should provide the materials, skilled guidance, technical knowledge, or new concepts or techniques necessary to achieve those objectives.

When a school system hires a teacher, it purchases certain professional skills; in the process of selection it should make clear precisely the competence expected of teachers and staff, and then provide the means to ensure continued development and skilled performance.

The problems or situations which dictate the need for in-service training arise in the classroom or in the local setting. The solutions, when possible, should be sought from within the same setting to guarantee a comprehensive examination of the problems and their related forces. Most problems are not unique to a given school or to a single staff member but affect many teachers in the system. For example, since approximately 50 percent of all teachers leave the field within their first five years of service, one may reasonably

ask how well they have been served by in-service training and whether beginners leave the profession *because* their needs are not met by in-service programs during the crucial first years.

Within the local school system, teachers are closest to the teaching-learning (classroom) situation and are in the best position to identify areas of need and to assist in program development. Because they are one of the most powerful forces for determining change and improvement, teachers must be the ones to execute changes if any notable results are to be realized from in-service programs. Since those who help plan and implement a program are the ones likely to derive the most benefit from it, teachers must be involved in developing their own in-service programs.

Although colleges and universities, local school systems, and teachers should be involved in identifying the needs for in-service and implementing the remedial programs, none can accomplish the job alone. They must work together and bring their respective strengths to bear to provide effective in-service programs.

Characteristics of programs. As yet there are no national or regional associations or standards committees to ensure the quality or quantity of in-service programs other than those directly related to college degree programs or to state certification. Nevertheless, there are certain commonly accepted procedures for planning and implementing effective local programs.

In-service courses should evolve from the carefully identified needs of staff members, either in a single school or throughout the school district. Objectives should be clearly stated, and appropriate accompanying instructional activities should be selected. In-service programs should be flexible, continually responsive to the teacher's changing needs and dvelopment, and dedicated to clarifying the practical applications of theory, so that the teacher's classroom may become a laboratory for testing ideas and methods suggested in the course.

Participation in in-service programs should be voluntary unless deemed essential by the school system. But in-service programs should be directly related to the assignment of the teacher. No particular advantage accrues to the teacher or to the school system when in-service experiences are unrelated to the teacher's role. The course offered should be of such intrinsic value and relevance that teachers will feel impelled to participate. Of course, the nature of the in-service program and the frequency of participation should depend upon a teacher's ability, performance, and years of service.

Types of in-service education. Generally, in-service training can be obtained in college credit courses offered as part of a degree program; in courses conducted by school system personnel with or without the assistance of industries and universities; and in workshops, lecture series, travel, experimentation, and individualized study sponsored by colleges, universities, or local school systems and their subdivisions.

In-service problems. One problem common to preservice and in-service programs results from the impact of rapid changes in society: such courses may lag behind current needs. Too often, colleges or universities cannot afford to institute new programs or to noticeably change existing programs until there is a well-established need by a sufficiently large number of school systems. Moreover, since it may take several years for these institutions to incorporate new programs and to provide special services, often the local school system's needs are not met by preservice. Also, within a local school system the need for change usually exceeds the means available for realizing changes in school programs; in some cases, by the time appropriate methods are developed, the need has shifted.

The high cost of providing adequate in-service training is another problem. Releasing staff during the school day requires employing additional staff members to supervise students. Moreover, besides the expense of more instructors, travel facilities, and materials, the implementation of the new program that results from an effective in-service course increases costs considerably. Another problem is selecting competent personnel to direct and teach in a specific program. Many complications can arise in the attempt to coordinate the large numbers of people needed to ensure that the persons affected by a decision will have a voice in it.

Trends. Curriculum reform in elementary and secondary education, which was accelerated by the entry of the United States into the space race, generated many in-service courses designed to improve the teacher's command of subject matter. To develop the instructor's ability to present the new math, science, and social studies, in-service training was primarily concerned with the teacher's cognitive development. In recent years the dramatic sociological and ideological conflicts which have arisen in American society, while requiring emphasis on the cognitive domain, have also demanded programs dealing with the teacher's affective development. Research has shown that the personal characteristics of a teacher —his expectations (Rosenthal & Jacobson 1968), sources of satisfaction (Wayson 1966), and receptivity to change (Bridges & Reynolds 1968)—are of great significance to his success in the classroom, sometimes even more important than his intellectual competence and professional skill. Some critics have described the educational innovations of the 1960's as merely a major manipulation of some rather minor variables (Frymier 1968). True change in instruction, these critics say, will come only as teachers develop greater sensitivity to the psychological and sociological variables that affect learning (Fantini & Weinstein 1968).

In-service programs should be concerned with the teacher's humanistic development, his behavioral skills, the organizational setting in which he performs, and his role in expanding school-university relationships. Although the attitudes and standards that teachers set for their students are likely to be related to the students' attitudes and aspirations (Rosenthal & Jacobson 1968) and although the effective performance of such tasks is in large measure dependent upon the teacher's own personality (Dandes 1966), little has been done by colleges of education in preservice courses or by school systems during in-service training to help the teacher understand his own nature, motives, and behavior. Future in-service programs should provide more opportunities for teachers to explore their attitudes, values, and beliefs through small-group counseling, sensitivity training, and individual guidance. They should also provide teachers who are newly assigned to slum areas with a systematic, controlled exposure to the subculture of the inner city, so that these beginners will view inner-city behavior patterns not as pathological but as social adjustments to existing conditions. Thus, the teachers' "culture shock" may be reduced and their attitude made more positive and conducive to establishing a healthful teaching-learning environment.

The growing realization of the uniqueness of each teacher and his intentions has led to a number of research projects emphasizing the need for multiple criteria to measure adequate classroom performance (Strom & Galloway 1967). Attempts are being made to develop individualized in-service programs that recognize alternative paths to improving teacher competence and that allow participants to progress at differing rates. The flexibility and adaptability offered by such an approach should free school systems from exclusive reliance on traditional in-service "courses."

While there is a considerable body of research on the learning process, until recently comparatively little attention was given to the process of teaching. Many educators believe that the scientific study of teaching through the use of systems for analyzing classroom behavior is a promising development (Flanders 1965; Amidon & Hunter 1966). Methods for helping teachers analyze verbal interaction in the classroom and assess the effectiveness of classroom management techniques on student misbehavior are being utilized in some urban in-service programs and may be adopted by others (Gump & Kounin 1957; Kounin & Gump 1958; Kounin et al. 1966).

Once the teacher has identified the behavior patterns in his classroom, he must acquire a variety of teaching styles which permit him to vary his pedagogical approach as his needs change (Hodges & Joyce 1966); some aids to developing these skills are microteaching, simulation, videotaping, and time-lapse photography (Allen 1966).

It is becoming increasingly evident that a teacher's behavior cannot be divorced from the organizational context in which he performs (Argyris 1961), for organizational variables operate in such a way as to give individual schools distinguishing personalities or climates (Halpin & Croft 1963; Feldvebel 1964) that influence the teacher's attitudes and values (Flizak 1968). The validity of the concept that a teacher's experience and flexibility are inversely related may depend upon the nature of the teacher's experience and the characteristics or climate of the school in which it is gained (Bridges & Reynolds 1968). For example, a teacher with many years of experience in a school where innovation is encouraged may be much more flexible than a second-year or third-year teacher in a school which tries to operate a "tight ship."

In-service planners must be sensitive to variations in the climate of a school in developing their programs. A workshop to introduce team teaching into a school with an authoritarian structure and a low value placed on experimentation should differ considerably from one planned for a school with an open structure and high value placed on innovation.

There is a growing awareness that if teacher education is to be effective there must be a closer relationship between preservice and in-service training (Rivilin 1966). One way in which this objective is being fulfilled is by employing a "clinical professor," a master classroom teacher who holds a joint appointment in the school system and the university. He divides his time between classroom teaching and clinical supervision of college students enrolled in the education program. His chief function is to aid the student in the practical application of his teacher-training courses (Hazard et al. 1967).

Another promising innovation in the expanding school-university relationship is the development of work-study programs designed to provide education majors with an early exposure to the classroom setting. Instead of waiting until their senior year to teach, for the first three years of the program students attend the university for three quarters and are employed by the school system during the fourth. College courses on educational psychology or curriculum planning may be scheduled evenings during the work experience, and every attempt is made to see that concepts and techniques learned are properly applied.

BIBLIOGRAPHY

ALLEN, DWIGHT W. 1966 "A New Design for Teacher Education: The Teacher Intern Program at Stanford University." *Journal of Teacher Education*, 17, no. 3:296–301.

ALLEN, DWIGHT W., AND RICHARD M. KRASNO 1968 "New Perspectives in Teacher Preparation." *National Elementary Principal*, 47, no. 6:36–42.

AMIDON, EDMUND, AND ELIZABETH HUNTER 1966 "Direct Experience in Teacher Education. Innovation and Experimentation." *Journal of Teacher Education*, 17, no. 3:282–289.

ARGYRIS, CHRIS 1961 "Organizational Leadership." Luigi Petrullo and Bernard M. Bass, eds., *Leadership and Interpersonal Behavior*. New York, Holt. Pages 326–354.

BRIDGES, EDWIN M., AND LARRY B. REYNOLDS 1968 "Teacher Receptivity to Change." *Administrator's Notebook*, 16, no. 6:entire issue.

BROADBENT, FRANK W. 1967 "Simulating Problems of Beginning Teachers." *Elementary School Journal*, 68, no. 1:39–43.

BURLEIGH, JUDITH C., AND HAROLD W. PETERSON 1967 "Videotapes in Teacher Education." *Elementary School Journal*, 68, no. 1:35–38.

DANDES, HERBERT M. 1966 "Psychological Health and Teaching Effectiveness." *Journal of Teacher Education*, 17, no. 3:301–306.

FANTINI, MARIO D., AND GERALD WEINSTEIN 1968 *The Disadvantaged: Challenge to Education*. New York, Harper.

FELDVEBEL, ALEXANDER M. 1964 "Organizational Climate, Social Class, and Educational Output." *Administrator's Notebook*, 12, no. 8:entire issue.

FLANDERS, NED A. 1965 *Teacher Influence, Pupil Attitudes, and Achievement.* Washington, D.C., U.S. Office of Education.

FLIZAK, CHRISTOPHER W. 1968 "Organizational Structure and Teacher Role-Orientation." *Administrator's Notebook*, 17, no. 2:entire issue.

FRYMIER, JACK R. 1968 "Teachers: Not Will But Can They Change?" *SEC Newsletter*, 2, no. 6:1–4.

GUMP, PAUL V., AND JACOB S. KOUNIN 1957 "Effects of Teachers' Methods of Controlling Misconduct Upon Kindergarten Children." *American Psychologist*, 12:396 ff.

HALLER, EMIL J. 1967 "On Moving to Smaller Rooms." *Administrator's Notebook*, 15, no. 6:entire issue.

HALPIN, ANDREW W., AND DON B. CROFT 1963 "The Organizational Climate of Schools." *Administrator's Notebook*, 11, no. 7:entire issue.

HAZARD, WILLIAM R., B. J. CHANDLER, AND LINDLEY J. STILES 1967 "The Tutorial and Clinical Program for Teacher Education." *Journal of Teacher Education*, 18, no. 3:269–276.

HODGES, RICHARD E., AND BRUCE R. JOYCE 1966 "Instructional Flexibility Training." *Journal of Teacher Education*, 17, no. 4:409–416.

KOUNIN, JACOB S., AND PAUL V. GUMP 1958 "The Ripple Effect in Discipline." *Elementary School Journal*, 62:158–162.

KOUNIN, JACOB S., WALLACE V. FRIESEN, AND A. EVANGELINE NORTON 1966 "Managing Emotionally Disturbed Children in Regular Classrooms." *Journal of Educational Psychology*, 57, no. 1:1–13.

RIVILIN, HARRY 1966 "A New Pattern for Urban Teacher Education." *Journal of Teacher Education*, 17, no. 2:177–184.

ROSENTHAL, ROBERT, AND LENORE JACOBSON 1968 *Pygmalion in the Classroom: Teacher Expectation and Pupils' Intellectual Development.* New York, Holt.

STROM, ROBERT, AND CHARLES GALLOWAY 1967 "Becoming a Better Teacher." *Journal of Teacher Education*, 18, no. 3:285–292.

WAYSON, WILLIAM W. 1966 "Source of Teacher Satisfaction in Slum Schools." *Administrator's Notebook*, 14, no. 9:entire issue.

JOHN W. LETSON

4. LABORATORY EXPERIENCE

In 1948 a committee of the American Association of Teachers Colleges (now the American Association of Colleges for Teacher Education) advanced the idea of professional laboratory experience for education students and provided this definition: ". . . all those contacts with children, youth, and adults (through observation, participation, and teaching) which make a direct contribution to understanding of individuals and their guidance in the teaching-learning process" (American Association of Teachers . . . 1948, p. 4). The definition implied sharp criticism of programs of professional education then current, which seemed to be based on the notion that a prospective teacher should pursue a course of didactic study in the college classroom and then prove that he understood the theory by teaching under supervision in a campus laboratory school. Although some programs provided a limited opportunity to observe master teachers and to make case studies of individual pupils, a majority of programs included only one laboratory experience, a concentrated period of practice teaching lasting one to three hours per day for several weeks, usually in the final year of teacher preparation. Practice teaching was considered a testing ground, an opportunity for the student teacher to show his competence (American Association of Colleges . . . 1956; Borrowman 1965; Conant 1963; Stiles 1960). The committee's delineation of laboratory experience and its recommendations with respect to practice called for major revisions in programs of teacher education, revisions that took account of available knowledge about learning and human development and about the complexities of schools, pupils, and teaching.

During the decade following the committee's report, professional educators took seriously the challenge of providing more laboratory experience in preservice teacher-education programs. A range and variety of direct contacts with pupils, teachers, materials, schools, and communities became a component of most professional programs. Full-time student teaching in representative schools became one of a sequence of laboratory experiences spread over the entire professional preparation of teachers. Although efforts were made to improve the quality of the laboratory and the student's experience, the most noticeable revision was an increase in the amount of time allocated to laboratory experience. Even so, the emphasis on direct experience as a means for studying the conditions surrounding teaching and for testing ideas in practice was an improvement in teacher education.

Just as the 1950's were a period when agreement on the need for laboratory experience was consolidated and the time devoted to such experience was increased in most teacher-education programs, the 1960's were a period of significant advancement with regard to the nature and quality of the direct experience. Description of professional laboratory experience in teacher education began to focus, not on the mechanical matters of quantity and scheduling, but on the quality of the laboratory and the activities carried on within it.

A laboratory is generally a place where scientific study is carried on. The central purpose of persons working in a laboratory is to discover new knowledge, to verify knowledge already available, or to test knowledge by applying it to practical problems and conditions. In teacher education, a laboratory is a place for systematic study of teaching—a place where a student may discover what teaching is and how the many and diverse variables in a complex teaching-learning environment interact with one another. It is a place where a prospective teacher may test his knowledge of teaching and verify or modify his understanding of that knowledge. But for the teacher in training, a laboratory serves a purpose beyond that generally ascribed to laboratories in the pure sciences. The student of teaching is concerned about his own behavior and how he may respond to and influence factors in the environment. Therefore, to him a laboratory is also a place where he may act as a teacher, analyze the consequences of his action, and plan ways of modifying his behavior and testing their effects. In short, in addition to serving as a center for the discovery and verification of knowledge relevant to teaching generally, the teacher-education laboratory is a place where the student may study his own specific behavior as a basis for improving it.

Several kinds of laboratories are used to serve both these purposes in the education of teachers. Although regular schools and centers in them—classrooms, clinics, libraries, and so on—serve most frequently as laboratories, other kinds are also widely employed. A university may set up special centers, where representative types of school programs are carried on. Often a laboratory simulates designated conditions of teaching and learning, so that specific behaviors may be studied outside the complexities of a typical classroom.

A school board, a curriculum committee, a parents' association, a community council, a team of counselors, a teachers' organization, or any other group that has a relationship to teaching may serve as a laboratory. Similarly, a playground, a lunchroom, a principal's office, or a corner drugstore may be a place where a future teacher studies matters relevant to his activities in the classroom and school.

Location, activities carried on, persons involved, sponsoring agent—these are not the criteria for determining what is a laboratory in teacher education. Rather, a laboratory for the prospective teacher is any setting where he engages in systematic study of human beings in action that contributes to his understanding of teaching and his ability to perform with increasing excellence as a teacher.

Laboratories and the prospective teacher's activities in them can be comprehended more fully by placing them in the context of certain related developments in education. Especially important for teacher-education laboratories are focus on the study of education by specialists in many fields, with emphasis on systematic study of teaching behavior; utilization of technology in the classroom and laboratory; innovations in staffing schools and classrooms; and individualization in the art and style of teaching.

Research on education.   A notable number of psychologists, sociologists, social psychologists, anthropolgists, and other social scientists are applying their scholarship to the study of education and schooling (Denton 1967). Growing numbers of subject-matter specialists have developed interest in and concern for the teaching of their specialty in elementary and secondary schools (Borrowman 1965; Conant 1963; Mayor & Swartz 1965). Professors of education, who in the past too often became more and more removed from the reality of the classroom with each year in teacher education, are now entering schools and using them as laboratories for continuing scholarly work (American Association of Colleges . . . 1968a; Elam 1967; Keppel 1966; Smith 1962). Practitioners in schools—teachers, supervisors, administrators, and other specialists—as mature professional scholars, are frequently engaged in analytical study of their practice (Schaefer 1967), and all of these specialists use some type of laboratory for their study.

The expansion of the study of education by scholars in many fields has made a significant impact on programs of laboratory experience for future teachers. First and perhaps most important, it has demonstrated the value of a laboratory as a center for inquiry, a place where scholars identify questions, test hypotheses, and discover relationships. Second, specialists carrying on study of educational practice may be, and often are, college teachers. These specialists usually involve their students in their research, either indirectly, by utilizing it as substance for study by the students, or directly, by inviting the students to join them in their inquiries. Consequently, a student teacher may have laboratory experience very early in his training program and continuing throughout, as a result of his professor's study of education. Third, the laboratory in which the education student later conducts his own study of teaching and relevant matters is likely to be the same laboratory in which specialists are engaged in study, and they can make available to him ideas, methods, materials, and conditions to facilitate his own inquiries and offer him guidance.

Until recently there was little direct study of teaching, either by scholars in education or by students in training. Former investigations of teaching actually focused, for the most part, on teacher characteristics and teacher effectiveness. Only in limited ways did researchers examine teacher behavior. It is clear, however, that teacher behavior can be defined and described, that such behavior can be studied in its own right, and that direct study of teaching can yield important findings (Gage 1963; Simon 1967).

The contributions of recent research on teaching to teacher education cannot be overemphasized. A most important influence has been the subsequent reexamination of the organizing structure of professional education programs. A traditional four-year program includes some or all of the following courses, often in the order listed: introduction to education; psychological foundations of education (learning theory and developmental psychology); sociological foundations of education (school and society); general principles (teaching in the secondary school, teaching in the elementary school); special methods (teaching social studies in the secondary school, science in the elementary school); practice teaching; history and/ or philosophy of education.

When students have opportunity to observe in schools in connection with the above courses, their attention is generally focused on pupils, materials, procedures, climate, and physical environment. Often students have no opportunity to get into schools or other laboratories for firsthand study until they begin practice teaching in their senior year. The important observation about this typical program is that it does not involve the student in direct study of teaching; rather it engages his attention in everything surrounding and influencing teaching and seldom causes him to examine teaching behavior directly. When he

moves into practice teaching, emphasis continues to be placed on general planning for teaching, discipline in the classroom, materials of instruction, and study of individual pupils.

The inadequacy of this approach has been brought into bold relief by scholars' inquiries into the meaning which their current research has for the professional education program. Out of these inquiries have emerged proposals for the restructuring of the program, based on the premise that the study of teaching should be the central core around which professional preparation should be organized. (For one illustration of such a proposal, see the American Association of Colleges for Teacher Education's *A Proposal for the Revision of the Pre-service Professional Component of a Program of Teacher Education*, 1964; its follow-up report, *Conceptual Models in Teacher Education* 1967, and its *Professional Teacher Education*, 1968b.) These proposals call for a centering on the study of teaching, beginning with a definition and examination of teaching behavior and including an investigation of knowledge relevant to teaching and an analysis by the student of his own teaching behavior.

Another significant contribution is made by research focuses, tools, and methods, which can be adopted or adapted to the study of teaching by prospective teachers. For example, it is known that the kinds of questions asked by a teacher bear a close relationship to the level of thinking involved in pupils' responses. An important focus of the study of verbal teaching behavior, therefore, is questioning. Several researchers have produced instruments and methods for analyzing questioning behavior and its relation to the cognitive processes of pupils (Bellack 1966; Sanders 1966). The teacher-in-training not only acquires the knowledge accruing from research but uses the methods and tools of research for analyzing teaching behavior, both his own and that of others.

New ideas about the materials and settings appropriate for the study of teaching have also been contributed by research in this field. Whereas formerly it was common, in studying teaching, to make use of one kind of material in one setting—actual teaching in a classroom—research has shown that films, videotapes, audiotapes, and typescripts can be effectively employed (Allen 1966; Keach 1966; Simon 1967). It has also become clear that much teaching behavior can be practiced and analyzed in settings that simulate part or all of a classroom and that important kinds of learning by teachers-in-training can result from teaching one pupil or a small group of pupils.

When these contributions of research (and others that are emerging) are taken fully into account, the focus of the student's laboratory experience is on the study of teaching. This is the focus that gives meaning to the many activities he carries on.

Technology. The availability of new electronic devices has also brought about major transformations in programs of laboratory experience. One of the most important activities of the student in a laboratory is the observing, recording, and analyzing of behavior—pupil behavior, teacher behavior, and the interaction of pupils and teachers. However, outcomes derived from observation are minimal if the focus is vague, if there is a lack of objectivity in recording, and if techniques of analysis are superficial. As indicated earlier, current developments in research on teaching provide precise focuses for observing and analyzing behavior. Technology provides the means for objective recording and immediate feedback for analysis (American Association of Colleges . . . 1964; Kallenback 1966; Schueler 1967; Skinner 1968).

Important stages in the student's discovery and testing of his own ways of dealing with teaching situations, formerly almost exclusively left until practice teaching, have been introduced in simulated settings earlier in the professional program. Videotape, for example, makes possible microteaching and other systems of feedback, analysis, and retrial.

Students can make many kinds of observations by means of closed-circuit television. Observation by television does not provide the same experience as being on the spot in the classroom, and some observation in person is still considered essential, but a well-directed television camera makes available certain kinds of situations that could not otherwise be observed. If the television system provides for intercommunication (and many do), what is seen on the screen can simultaneously be discussed by students, college teacher, and other participants.

The tools and methods of current research and the utilization of technology combine to make accessible to students a new range of significant learning opportunities. When such opportunities are well used, students' need for time in the classroom as a laboratory is decreased, and their readiness to engage in high-quality experiences when they are in classrooms is increased.

Staffing schools and classrooms. In many ways teachers work as members of teams: teams of peers, who plan and conduct programs for large groups of pupils; teams of workers with differentiated functions and status, who combine efforts to assist pupils in a single classroom; teams of specialists, who join in research (Davis 1966; Joyce & Harootunian 1967). New patterns in staffing schools and classrooms are having positive effect on laboratory experience for teachers-in-training. For one thing, the importance of teamwork is being highlighted. Attention is being given to analysis of its properties and to deliberate development of behaviors needed in team situations. As is true of teaching, much can be learned about team behavior by observation and study of others, but in the final analysis one must test one's own capacities and skills in a real team situation. Because this is so, one important experience for the student in the laboratory is the assuming of responsibility as a team member and the analysis of his own behavior in order to improve it.

New staffing patterns make available to the student a range of differentiated roles into which he can move in accordance with his readiness. For example, early in his program he may move into the classroom as an aide to the regular teacher; later he may become a teaching assistant; and still later he may assume the teaching role. It is important for a student teacher to be confronted with the need to make decisions and to feel responsible for the consequences of his decisions. When differentiated functions are performed by team members and the responsibilities assigned to each member are made clear, a preservice student gains satisfaction and reward from feeling that what he does makes a difference—that he is important.

Individualization in the laboratory. What is hoped for as the outcome of a teacher-education program is a teacher who finds satisfying self-expression in his individual, personal style of encounter with others in the teaching act. With such a goal in mind, persons responsible for laboratories and the student's experience in them allow a wide latitude for creativity, independence, and differences in pace and style of learning. The rigid course-credit-term pattern in higher education creates many problems in this regard. However, with a range of laboratories of various types available and with diversified activities going on in them, the chances for individual expression are greater. Also, where focus in the laboratory is on inquiry rather than on imitation, the student is free to ask questions that are important to him and to seek answers in ways consistent with his personal style. This is one of the earmarks of a high-quality professional laboratory (Combs 1965; Massialas & Zivin 1967).

School-university partnership. Student teaching continues to be the major laboratory experience in preservice teacher education programs. Formerly a narrowly circumscribed experience in a campus school under the direction of a master teacher, student teaching has become a more comprehensive, off-campus experience, in which the student is guided by appropriate school and university personnel. Similar involvement of a wider range of persons and of community schools has become characteristic of all laboratory experience (American Association of Colleges . . . 1968a; Bennie 1966).

This wider involvement of schools and personnel has precipitated developments which are especially advantageous to laboratories and activities in them. For example, increasing numbers of school personnel—teachers, supervisors, principals, etc.—are involved in preservice preparation of teachers. Literally thousands of teachers every year have in their classrooms students who are preparing to teach. As school personnel assume more responsibility for the induction of new members to the profession, their interest in and concern about the quality of teacher preparation increase. Their influence on future teachers is known to be tremendous. College and university personnel recognize the contribution made by practitioners in the schools; school personnel are cognizant of the important role played by higher education.

The increased involvement of persons in both the schools and the universities has brought about a partnership between them which promises significant contributions to both university and school programs. The fact that more university professors are spending more time in the schools is having beneficial effect on university programs by reason of the feedback of reality into courses and seminars. Placing greater responsibility for the education of teachers on school personnel is stimulating classroom teachers to engage in advanced study at universities and prepare themselves for discharging their new role of teacher educator, a role formerly assumed only by university personnel.

Teacher education does not cease with graduation from a college or university program and certification to teach. It is a career-long process. The gap between preservice and in-service education of teachers is rapidly being closed as universities work in schools and as schools become an integral part of university programs of teacher education.

The school is expected to be a center for inquiry not only for pupils but also for teachers (Schaefer 1967; Jackson 1968). For the teacher, his classroom, his school, and his community are laboratories in which he continues to carry on his search for better answers to questions about teaching and learning. Laboratory experience in his university program is the foundation for the development of the attitudes and the competencies that will sustain his scholarship as a professional practitioner. This is the ultimate goal of laboratory activities, and the degree to which a teacher continues to engage in inquiry is a measure of the success of a program of laboratory experience.

BIBLIOGRAPHY

ALLEN, DWIGHT W. 1966 "A New Design for Teacher Education: The Teacher Intern Program at Stanford University." *Journal of Teacher Education*, 17, no. 3:296–301.

AMERICAN ASSOCIATION OF COLLEGES FOR TEACHER EDUCATION 1956 *Teacher Education for a Free People.* Edited by Donald Peery Cottrell. Oneonta, N.Y., The Association.

AMERICAN ASSOCIATION OF COLLEGES FOR TEACHER EDUCATION 1960 *Television in Teacher Education.* Edited by Edwin P. Adkins. Washington, D.C., The Association.

AMERICAN ASSOCIATION OF COLLEGES FOR TEACHER EDUCATION 1967 *Conceptual Models in Teacher Education: An Approach to Teaching and Learning.* Edited by John R. Vedvin. Washington, D.C., The Association.

AMERICAN ASSOCIATION OF COLLEGES FOR TEACHER EDUCATION 1968a *Partnership in Teacher Education.* Edited by E. Brooks Smith et al. Washington, D.C., The Association.

AMERICAN ASSOCIATION OF COLLEGES FOR TEACHER EDUCATION 1968b *Professional Teacher Education.* Washington, D.C., The Association

AMERICAN ASSOCIATION OF COLLEGES FOR TEACHER EDUCATION. TEACHER EDUCATION AND MEDIA PROJECT 1964 *A Proposal for the Revision of the Pre-service Professional Component of a Program of Teacher Education.* Prepared by Herbert F. La Grone, director. Washington, D.C., The Association.

AMERICAN ASSOCIATION OF TEACHERS COLLEGES. COMMITTEE ON STANDARDS AND SURVEYS 1948 *School and Community Laboratory Experiences in Teacher Education.* By the

Subcommittee of the Standards and Surveys Committee of the American Association of Teachers Colleges, John G. Flowers, chairman. Oneonta, N.Y., The Association.

BELLACK, ARNO, et al. 1966 *The Language of the Classroom.* New York, Teachers College Press.

BENNIE, WILLIAM A. 1966 *Cooperation for Better Student Teaching.* Minneapolis, Burgess.

BORROWMAN, MERLE L., ed. 1965 *Teacher Education in America: A Documentary History.* New York, Teachers College Press.

COMBS, ARTHUR WRIGHT 1965 *The Professional Education of Teachers: A Perceptual View of Teacher Preparation.* Boston, Allyn & Bacon.

CONANT, JAMES B. 1963 *The Education of American Teachers.* New York, McGraw-Hill.

DAVIS, HAROLD S. 1966 *How to Organize an Effective Team Teaching Program.* Englewood Cliffs, N.J., Prentice-Hall.

DENTON, DAVID E. 1967 "A Call for a Society of Educologists." *School and Society,* 95:82–83.

ELAM, STANLEY, ed. 1967 *Improving Teacher Education in the United States.* A report of a symposium sponsored jointly by Phi Delta Kappa International and the Stanford University Chapter of Phi Delta Kappa. Bloomington, Ind., Phi Delta Kappa.

GAGE, NATHANIEL LEES, ed. 1963 *Handbook of Research on Teaching.* A project of the American Educational Research Association. Chicago, Rand McNally.

JACKSON, PHILIP WESLEY 1968 *Life in Classrooms.* New York, Holt.

JOYCE, BRUCE R., AND BERJ HAROOTUNIAN 1967 *The Structure of Teaching.* Chicago, Science Research Associates.

KALLENBACK, W. W. 1966 "Microteaching as a Teaching Methodology." Paper presented at the Conference on Instructional Methods and Teacher Behavior. Berkeley, Laboratory for Educational Research and Development, University of California.

KEACH, EVERETT THOMPSON 1966 *Elementary School Teaching: A Casebook.* New York, Wiley.

KEPPEL, FRANCIS 1966 *The Necessary Revolution in American Education.* New York, Harper.

MASSIALAS, BYRON GEORGE, AND JACK ZIVIN 1967 *Creative Encounters in the Classroom: Teaching and Learning Through Discovery.* New York, Wiley.

MAYOR, JOHN R., AND WILLIS G. SWARTZ 1965 *Accreditation in Teacher Education: Its Influence on Higher Education.* Washington, D.C., National Commission on Accrediting.

NATIONAL EDUCATION ASSOCIATION. NATIONAL COMMISSION ON TEACHER EDUCATION AND PROFESSIONAL STANDARDS 1961 *New Horizons for the Teaching Profession.* A report of the Task Force on New Horizons in Teacher Education and Professional Standards. Edited by Margaret Lindsey. Washington, D.C., The Association.

SANDERS, NORRIS M. 1966 *Classroom Questions: What Kinds?* New York, Harper.

SCHAEFER, ROBERT JOSEPH 1967 *The School as a Center of Inquiry.* The John Dewey Society Lectureship Series, No. 9. New York, Harper.

SCHUELER, HERBERT 1967 *Teacher Education and the New Media.* A study carried out by Hunter College, City of New York. Washington, D.C., American Association of Colleges for Teacher Education.

SIMON, ANITA, ed. 1967 *Mirrors of Behavior.* 6 vols. Philadelphia, Research for Better Schools, Inc., and Center for the Study of Teaching, Temple University.

SKINNER, B. F. 1968 *The Technology of Teaching.* New York, Appleton.

SMITH, ELMER REID, ed. 1962 *Teacher Education: A Reappraisal.* Report of a conference sponsored by the Fund for the Advancement of Education. New York, Harper.

STILES, LINDLEY JOSEPH, et al. 1960 *Teacher Education in the United States.* New York, Ronald Press.

MARGARET LINDSEY

TEACHERS INSURANCE AND ANNUITY ASSOCIATION

The Teachers Insurance and Annuity Association is a limited eligibility, nonprofit service organization that provides a cooperative pooling of staff benefits for colleges, universities, independent schools, and other nonprofit and tax-exempt educational and scientific institutions. TIAA annuity and insurance plans help staff members of such institutions meet the financial needs of serious illness, old age, and death.

The Carnegie Foundation for the Advancement of Teaching, working with a special commission established to develop a comprehensive benefit system for employees in higher education, established TIAA in 1918 as a special-purpose, nonprofit life insurance company under New York state laws. The new organization took over the work begun a decade earlier by the foundation, which Andrew Carnegie had endowed to provide "retiring allowances" and other benefits for college professors and their families. The College Retirement Equities Fund, which provided the world's first variable annuity to help staff members' retirement incomes keep pace with rising living costs, was established in 1952 as a companion company to TIAA and has the same nonprofit status and the same limited eligibility as TIAA.

Program. The association's major service is the fully funded and fully vested retirement program, covering a quarter of a million staff members in 2,200 participating institutions. Within the general framework of the program, each institution establishes the provisions of its retirement plan—eligibility to participate, level of annuity contributions, retirement age, and so forth—in the form of a board resolution. The individually owned annuities, issued by TIAA and CREF to participating staff members, provide the contractual basis for the accumulation and payment of retirement benefits.

The level of annuity contributions and the degree of sharing between the institution and the staff member range from plans where the college and the participant each contribute 5 percent of salary to plans where the college contributes 15 percent or more of salary and the participant contributes nothing. The generally accepted goal is to provide a disposable (after-tax) retirement income equal to about two-thirds of preretirement disposable income. All of the contributions are fully and immediately vested in the individual, so that he owns all benefits as he earns them and they are his for life whether he stays at one institution or moves among several during his career. If he dies before retirement, all accumulated benefits pass to his family or estate.

The participant may elect to have the total monthly contributions applied to his TIAA annuity or to have from 25 to 75 percent applied to his CREF annuity. The portion applied to the TIAA annuity is invested in bonds and mortgages and accumulates at compound interest over the years to provide a guaranteed, fixed-dollar annuity income that does not change in amount from year to year during retirement, except as dividends are added. The portion applied to CREF is invested in a diversified portfolio of common stocks, and at retirement the participant's accumulated share in this fund becomes the basis for his lifetime variable annuity income, which increases as the values of the common stocks rise and decreases as they fall. The combined program provides a retirement income that is more responsive to economic change than a fixed-dollar annuity alone and is less volatile than a variable annuity alone.

Other benefit plans. TIAA provides group insurance plans especially designed to meet the needs of colleges and universities and their staff members. The plans include group life, major medical, and long-term total disability insurance. In addition, there are individual life insurance plans, which educators purchase from the association directly by mail. TIAA maintains a counseling staff to correspond with participants in regard to questions about retirement income, Social Security benefits, taxes, family protection, and other related matters.

Research. TIAA also serves as a central clearinghouse for higher education on current trends and developments in benefit planning as well as in other elements of academic employment. This continuing program of research into the needs of the profession has led to the development of several new types of benefits and to the publication of books, bulletins, and articles on pension planning, Social Security, taxes, insurance needs, and the like. Other research, supported by foundation grants, has been carried out by TIAA in association with various educational organizations. This includes studies of financing the college education of faculty children, of loan funds for college students, of retirement and insurance benefits for faculty serving in educational or consulting posts abroad, of faculty benefits other than insurance and annuities (such as housing mortgage loans, health services, and leaves of absence), and of the salaries and benefits earned by college administrative officers.

THOMAS C. EDWARDS

TEAM TEACHING

Team teaching is any form of teaching in which two or more teachers regularly and purposefully share responsibility for the planning, presentation, and evaluation of lessons prepared for the same group of students. Although there are almost as many variations as there are teams, all team teaching is based on the premise that teachers can accomplish more working together than working alone. When team teaching is properly conducted, it provides a balanced program of large-group instruction, small-group discussion, and independent study.

Types of teams. Despite the many variations, only two major types of teaching teams have evolved: hierarchic and synergetic.

The structure of a hierarchic teaching team may be likened to a pyramid, with the team leader at the apex, master teachers just below, and regular teachers at the base. A major purpose of this type of team is to provide teachers with a means of professional advancement without having to leave the classroom. However, many teachers feel the establishment of superior levels tends to diminish the importance of the regular teacher's role. Therefore, even where hierarchic teams are first established, they often give way to a more synergetic approach.

Synergetic teaching teams are formed through the cooperation of two or more teachers working together as professional equals. The master teacher concept is repudiated, and the instructional leadership rotates according to interest or need. One member may assume the leadership for a single lesson or unit of work and relinquish it for the next. The stress is on working with, not for, colleagues.

Although synergetic teams sometimes select permanent leaders for administrative purposes, the leader generally does not receive extra pay or privileges for accepting the assignment. In some schools, department chairmen have become members of synergetic teams and wear two hats. Administratively, they carry the burden of extra duties; instructionally, they function as regular members of teams and share leadership with teammates during various units of work.

Synergetic teams vary in their approaches, from limited cooperation to complete association. For this reason, these teams are sometimes referred to as cooperative or associative teams, the distinction based upon the degree of partnership achieved by the participants.

History. Many studies have recognized the value of team teaching and have recommended its widespread use. The most noted of these studies and those that gave early impetus to improving staff utilization practices were done by the National Association of Secondary School Principals and by the National Education Association.

Although variations of team teaching have been employed for years, the term "team teaching" is relatively new, having first appeared in the *Educational Index* for June 1957. The popularity of teaching teams, as well as the expression itself, can be traced directly to the formation in May 1956 of the NASSP Commission on the Experimental Study of the Utilization of the Staff in the Secondary School and to the yeoman effort of its director, Dr. J. Lloyd Trump. This commission, aided by the Ford Foundation and the Fund for the Advancement of Education, encouraged a series of experiments determined to discover new and more effective means of staff utilization. Among these experiments the most successful was popularly called team teaching.

Team teaching has undergone a steady, rapid growth. An indication of how quickly the idea caught on may be seen in an NEA poll of 1,400 elementary and secondary school principals for the period 1955–1965: in 1955, 5 percent of the elementary and secondary school principals had instituted teaching teams in their schools; by 1960 the percentage had reached 15 percent in the elementary schools and 12 percent in the secondary schools; and by 1965 the percentage was 30 per-

cent in the elementary schools and 31 percent in the secondary schools.

Undoubtedly the popularity of team teaching was greatly enhanced by the NEA's Project for the Improvement of the Instructional Program of the Public Schools. In 1959 a 14-member national committee composed of classroom teachers, public school administrators, and university professors was charged with the following task: "Make thoughtful and creative recommendations to serve as a guide to the profession and the public in their combined efforts to study and improve the quality of the instructional program in the schools." After three years of study, the official project report recommended experimentation, innovation, flexible grouping, flexible space, and team teaching.

Team planning. Team teachers recognize that pupils learn from teachers, by themselves, and from each other. In examining these three processes, team teachers have found a basic way to plan lessons. They study the curriculum, develop objectives, determine essential ideas to be taught, and then answer three questions:

(1) What can students learn best from explanations by others?
(2) What can students learn by themselves?
(3) What can students learn by interaction between themselves and their teachers?

The answer to the first question suggests large-group instruction; to the second, independent study; and to the third, small-group discussion.

Large-group instruction. Typical teachers in conventional classes spend an undue portion of time talking. Most fail to realize they are delivering unprepared, unillustrated, low-quality lectures. According to the NASSP, secondary school teachers spend an average of 46 percent of their time engaged in activities that could be done more efficiently in large groups.

Seeking answers to problems of class size, researchers have conducted hundreds of studies in the past 20 years. A survey of the literature reveals that reduction of class size makes little difference when methods remain unchanged. Thus, the idea that a group of 30 is best for all teaching situations is no longer accepted in all quarters. It is recognized that pupils can hear a speech, see a film, listen to an orchestra, or watch a television broadcast in groups of varying size, some of which may be quite large. It also is recognized that large-group instruction uses the abilities of outstanding teachers more fully. A teacher conserves time and energy by giving one presentation to five groups of 30 students simultaneously instead of making five presentations to one group at a time. Hours saved may be utilized in preparation of background material and for rehearsals and planning.

Many teachers feel that a vital part of large-group instruction is the opportunity it affords youngsters to learn how to listen, to take notes, and to behave. Surprisingly, experience has shown that disciplinary problems tend to disappear in the large group. Team teachers feel this is due to the presence of more than one teacher in the room. While one is concentrating on the presentation, another takes care of attendance, tardiness, deportment, and other details.

Properly used, large-group instruction is excellent for basic orientation, motivation, and enrichment. It can be employed to present many ideas in a short period of time. It ensures an orderly and coherent presentation, in contrast to the digressions normally found in the traditional classroom. A large-group presentation may be profitably used to prepare students for demonstrations, independent study, or small-group discussion. It may be used to encourage attention, to teach note taking and outlining, to arouse curiosity, to stimulate inquiry, and to develop imagination and creativity.

Independent study. Educators have long maintained that the ultimate goal in education is to make each person a thinking, lifelong learner. Those who really believe each child should become increasingly responsible for his own education as he grows older must focus their attention in that direction. Boys and girls cannot learn independent study habits in school unless they are given appropriate time and space.

There is no longer any question about the need for independent study. The only question is whether administrators should urge teachers to use it wisely as part of a planned program or allow them to continue to treat study as something which takes place only in a study hall or at home. The introduction of independent study in the regular program is an extension of democracy. It recognizes that every student is an individual and encourages each to progress to the limit of his ability.

To be effective, independent study must be a part of, not apart from, the regular program.

It should be conducted in an instructional media center (IMC) where books, tapes, films, and records are readily available; where the librarian can provide direction when needed; and where the teacher is free to meet with individuals who have moved beyond conventional goals or with those in need of remedial help.

Properly conducted, independent study will help pupils gradually grow in self-correction, self-analysis, and self-direction.

Small-group discussion. Small-group discussion tests the effectiveness of any team-teaching program. If students have been properly motivated to look, listen, read, and think, they will welcome the opportunity to express their ideas.

Discussion in small groups improves interpersonal relations among students, promotes problem solving, and develops more effective communication skills. Small-group discussion is essential if students are to be closely involved in the free exchange of ideas. The student learns respect for another's point of view. He learns that his own ideas must be presented for review in the court of public opinion. He not only acquires pertinent information but also participates in a process which tends to stretch and strengthen his mind. Although each student has complete freedom to express his thoughts, he soon learns not all talk is good talk—that lack of preparation, ignorance of facts, or irrational remarks will affect his status in the group. On the other hand, the recognition accorded a worthwhile contribution encourages everyone to do his best.

Small-group discussion does not mean an oral quiz conducted by a teacher in the traditional class of 30. Evidence in the field of group dynamics, backed up by experience in hundreds of schools, has shown that effective interaction can take place only in groups smaller than 15. Since informality is vital to interaction, the group should be seated around a conference table or at desks arranged in a circle. Sitting in rows, staring at the backs of necks, is usually not conducive to discussion.

Team teachers often remark that discussion groups become so interesting it is all they can do to refrain from participating. Naturally, in the teacher's role as a consultant and adviser, he may have to clarify issues and correct erroneous information, but even this function should gradually diminish as pupils gain proficiency. In time the teacher should find himself more of an observer and counselor. His is the job of providing educational problems and learning experiences. From the small group he will obtain insights that should lead to improved large-group presentations and even more effective independent study. In the small group the teacher can begin to evaluate the effectiveness of his own teaching.

Obviously, small-group methods vary from subject to subject and grade to grade. At the primary level small groups may meet for remedial work or for enrichment. One group may be composed of those needing help with modern mathematics or reading; another may contain those working together on clay models or on a puppet show. Whether groups are homogeneously or heterogeneously formed depends entirely on the purpose. The achievement range may be narrowed for remedial work and widened for interest groups. The same is true in the upper grades. Groups should be flexible and based upon need.

Teachers who accept the challenge are able to capitalize on the tremendous advantages offered by the small group. They learn what pupils are really thinking. They find out who is reading and what is retained. They discover which ideas stimulate and which stupefy. They find new ways to bring out the introvert and to control the extrovert. They note those who think before speaking and those who speak before thinking. Small-group discussion gives teachers the opportunity to know students as never before and provides a wealth of material for individual conferences.

Facilities and equipment. Although some buildings severely handicap the development of teams, new uses for old facilities often may be found. For large-group instruction many teams use an auditorium, little theater, multipurpose room, cafeteria, band room, choral room, study hall, or school lobby. Others, finding no suitable space, have removed walls between rooms.

Space and equipment for small-group discussion pose no problem. Classrooms, library conference rooms, and cafeterias all have proven excellent. The single requirement is that students be able to engage in face-to-face discussion. Although it is advantageous to work with only one small group at a time, many teachers have found they can easily supervise two groups within the same or adjoining rooms. This, of course, depends upon the rapport established between teacher and pupils.

Space for independent study is usually difficult to locate. Libraries in secondary schools often are inadequate and in elementary schools frequently are nonexistent. To fill this educational gap, schools converting to team teaching usually develop IMC's designed for independent study. Such centers encourage pupils to explore many sources and to use a variety of materials. Cartridge-loading 8mm. film projectors can be operated by the smallest child. Hand viewers for filmstrips are enjoyed by children of every age. Tape recorders, placed on tables with several sets of earphones, provide inexpensive, functional listening stations. Pupils at each level use the library key, develop bibliographies, and use all types of material—written, visual, and auditory.

Schools having television facilities employ videotapes for independent study, as well as large-group instruction. Different programs are fed into the IMC for use by students engaged in makeup or review sessions.

In addition to space for reading, looking, and listening, a good IMC has areas for discussion and for preparation of visual aids. With the increasing use of the overhead projector, transparencies are indispensable for the modern instructor. In many schools pupils are encouraged to use such visual aids in their own classroom reports.

Teaching machines and programmed learning materials, found in many IMC's, can be advantageous. The program never loses patience. It gives immediate reinforcement when the student is correct and provides instant correction when he is wrong. Students master the materials at their own rate and seem to enjoy doing so. Programmed learning also permits individualization of instruction. For example, after correcting a set of themes, an English teacher may assign different phases of programmed materials to each student requiring remedial help. One may have to study clauses and phrases, another punctuation, a third verbs and adverbs, and so on. All are not required to listen to a lesson needed by only a few. Teachers also use programmed learning for enrichment or advanced study. In some schools students take complete programmed courses in subjects for which no qualified instructors are available.

To meet the challenge of tomorrow, modern educators realize teachers and pupils need access to a wide range of materials. They recognize space must be provided for study, viewing, listening, and discussing. No longer satisfied with embalming the past, they are creating an atmosphere which encourages exploration and discovery.

Supervising the team.   A successful team-teaching program depends more on people than upon the purse, more on faculties than upon facilities. One may find dormant programs in schools designed for team teaching and dynamic programs in archaic buildings. Invariably, administrative leadership and careful planning are the keys to success. As educational reports repeatedly state, reform must be instituted by administrators.

Those seeking change realize that team teaching offers the advantage of introducing change through internal rather than external forces. Many traditional teachers fight change; most team teachers welcome it. In contrast to conventional teachers who see each technological advance as a potential threat, team teachers use new media to enrich and enhance their instruction. They find television an asset, not a burden; programmed learning a boon, not a bane; audiovisual aids a help, not a hindrance.

However, the principal must be wary of success. Once teachers are secure, they may lapse into a comfortable routine and fall far short of their potential. Both praise and constructive criticism do much to improve team operations. For example, because large-group instruction is similar to traditional classroom teaching, there is a tendency to overemphasize this method. Presentations may get too long, particularly in the secondary school. Lectures should normally be held to 30 minutes or less, and time should always be allowed for questions immediately after the summary. The principal should be careful to see that large-group instruction is not used more than 30 or 40 percent of the time.

Because teachers tend to dominate discussion, principals should frequently check the small groups. If teachers are talking too much, they need more in-service training. All staff members, whether in teams or not, should be familiar with group dynamics techniques, inductive teaching, and the discovery method.

Independent study also must be observed. Indolent or inconsiderate teachers may use the library or IMC as a dumping ground. Much of the value is lost if teachers are not available to help pupils. This phase of team teaching gives the teacher an opportunity to work with a single student or with a few. By giving individual attention, the teacher can encourage the discouraged and spur the inspired.

Challenge of a new role. Team teaching is not easy. It means moving from a self-centered role to one of shared responsibility. It means that leadership and "followership" are both important. It requires the use of professional judgment about group size and group composition; discussion and evaluation of methods of instruction; and new uses of space, time, and equipment.

Objective observers sometimes say team teaching is simply organized "good" teaching. This is quite true. Team teachers do many of the things any good teacher should do but is physically incapable of doing. Teachers working alone may face 30 or more students for every activity. They can try to work with a few, but they cannot ignore the others who clamor for attention. When teachers work together, class size may be varied. Whether a teacher works with one or several, he can concentrate on what he is doing because the remaining students are in the hands of capable colleagues. This opportunity for flexible grouping and individualization of instruction is one of the greatest advantages of team teaching.

Pupil evaluation. Team teaching has been a headache to evaluators. Traditionally they have compared experimental groups to control groups and reported change. When they try the same procedure with team teaching, the measuring sticks seldom work—there are too many variables. Once teachers change methods, unproductive procedures are discarded or modified. This makes the evaluation task increasingly more difficult. In the end, the evaluator usually resorts to standardized tests and compares pupils solely on that basis. Such reports, by the hundreds, invariably say the same thing: "Team students did as well as or better than those in the traditional program." In a way, this is surprising. Standardized tests, based on recall, should favor pupils taught in conventional classes.

While the evaluators anxiously try to answer the question "Do students in a team program learn more?," team teachers are concerned with the natural response "Learn more of what?" Objective tests fail to consider the skills that team teachers stress. Listening habits, note taking, large-group behavior, self-expression, and the new 3 R's—reason, research, and responsibility—are left to subjective evaluation. Objective measures of the true value of team teaching must await the development of improved testing procedures.

Education is not cheap. Although team teaching originally was considered a means for saving money, this proved to be a fallacy. Money does not guarantee good education, but good education does cost money. Schools developing a team-teaching program often spend more for summer workshops and in-service education; for consultant service and travel expenses; for clerical help and teacher aides; for audiovisual equipment and instructional materials. Some spend to remodel rooms for large-group instruction and to develop IMC's. As independent study skills improve, library circulation increases, and more is spent for books. Even in new schools designed for team teaching, money saved on construction is usually plowed back to provide better equipment.

Although many skillful principals have managed to develop successful team-teaching programs without spending more, few maintain they have done so for less.

Why team teach? Today schools adopt team teaching for other than monetary reasons. Most state three purposes:

(1) To improve staff utilization;
(2) To improve use of facilities and equipment; and
(3) To improve instruction.

Improvements in staff utilization are readily apparent. Team teaching recognizes and encourages individual differences in teachers, as well as in students; emphasizes flexibility and variation; and shuns repetition and duplication. Savings in time and effort are reinvested in the individual child. Extra effort is expended on planning and preparation. Talents are blended; weaknesses are minimized. Teachers assume a variety of roles and teach in their areas of interest and strength.

Attempts to equip every room with a large collection of books, tapes, filmstrips, and records are doomed before they begin. If everything the teacher might use were placed in his classroom, schools would need unlimited funds or rubber walls. Common sense dictates a more economical use of public funds. When centers are established for large-group instruction and independent study, a limited amount of equipment serves a large number of teachers and pupils. When teachers move out of their self-contained rooms and share materials as well as ideas, there are plenty of each to go around.

The most important subject in any school is the child. This makes improvement of instruction a major goal. Although team teaching does not cure poor teachers, it does give them a chance to be observed, critiqued, and improved. Working

alone, many teachers have retired not with 40 years of experience but with one year of experience repeated 40 times. Working in teams, teachers have an opportunity for 40 years of professional growth.

BIBLIOGRAPHY

BAIR, MEDILL, AND RICHARD G. WOODWARD 1964 *Team Teaching in Action*. Boston, Houghton Mifflin.

BEGGS, DAVID W. III 1964 *Decatur-Lakeview High School: A Practical Application of the Trump Plan*. Englewood Cliffs, N.J., Prentice-Hall.

BEGGS, DAVID W. III, ed. 1964 *Team Teaching: Bold New Venture*. Indianapolis, Ind., Unified College Press.

BUSH, ROBERT N., AND DWIGHT W. ALLEN 1964 *A New Design for High School Education*. New York, McGraw-Hill.

DAVIS, HAROLD S. 1966 *How to Organize an Effective Team Teaching Program*. Englewood Cliffs, N.J., Prentice-Hall.

DAVIS, HAROLD S., comp. 1967 *Team Teaching Bibliography*. Cleveland, Ohio, The Educational Research Council of America.

EDUCATIONAL FACILITIES LABORATORIES 1960 *Profiles of Significant Schools: Schools for Team Teaching*. New York, The Laboratories.

EDUCATIONAL FACILITIES LABORATORIES 1965 *Profiles of Significant Schools: Schools Without Walls*. New York, The Laboratories.

EDUCATIONAL FACILITIES LABORATORIES 1966 *Profiles of Significant Schools: Middle Schools*. New York, The Laboratories.

FORD FOUNDATION 1960 *Time, Talent and Teachers*. New York, The Foundation.

GOODLAD, JOHN I., AND ROBERT H. ANDERSON 1963 *The Nongraded Elementary School*. Rev. ed. New York, Harcourt.

LOBB, M. DELBERT 1964 *Practical Aspects of Team Teaching*. San Francisco, Calif., Fearon.

National Association of Secondary-School Principals, *Bulletin*. January editions for 1958–1962 inclusive.

NATIONAL EDUCATION ASSOCIATION 1964 *Schools for the 60s*. New York, McGraw-Hill.

POLOS, NICHOLAS C. 1965 *The Dynamics of Team Teaching*. Dubuque, Iowa, W. C. Brown.

SHAPLIN, JUDSON T., AND HENRY F. OLDS, JR., eds. 1964 *Team Teaching*. New York, Harper.

TRUMP, J. LLOYD, AND DORSEY BAYNHAM 1961 *Focus on Change: Guide to Better Schools*. A report prepared for the National Association of Secondary-School Principals, Commission on the Experimental Study of the Utilization of the Staff in the Secondary School. Chicago, Rand McNally.

HAROLD S. DAVIS

TECHNICAL EDUCATION

The development of scientific research and the large-scale application of science in engineering and the related physical sciences—such as medicine and health, agriculture, forestry, and the marine and oceanographic sciences—have required special assistants, known as technicians, to work as the liaison between the professional director and the skilled and unskilled workmen. As the professional's job becomes primarily administrative and managerial, the specially trained technicians or technical assistants become first-line supervisors, special assistants, or specialized teammates. A technician serves as the knowledgeable worker who can be the professional's assistant and delegate; can do the routine testing and technical-information gathering; and can perform specialized services under professional direction.

The training of assistants has always been a way to extend the effectiveness of artists, scientists, or other professionals. When the task becomes too big for one professional to accomplish himself, he must delegate parts of it to assistants. Helpers may learn what they need to know in on-the-job training by observing and practicing under the tutelage of the professional. When the technical preparation required of the assistant is too complicated to be efficiently accomplished in on-the-job training, the basic principles underlying the professional field of work and some related skills must be taught formally before the trainee is capable of being an effective technical assistant.

Kinds of technicians. There are many kinds of technicians, just as there are many kinds of professional scientists and engineers. Various descriptive names are given to the different kinds of technicians, but almost all may be classified as physical science and related engineering technicians, biological science technicians, agriculture technicians, or technicians in the combined physical and biological sciences.

Physical science and related engineering technicians include aeronautical and aerospace technicians, architectural and building construction technicians, civil (highway and structural) technicians, chemical technicians, electrical and electronics technicians, electromechanical technicians, instrumentation technicians, mechanical design or production (including earth sciences) technicians, nuclear technicians, oceanographic (physical) technicians, printing (including photography and graphic arts) technicians, and radiological (physical) technicians.

The biological sciences use technicians for health and related technologies, dental hygiene and dental laboratories, occupational and rehabilitation therapy, physical therapy, medical laboratories, radiological (including X-ray) apparatus, and nursing (associate's degree).

Technicians are useful in such agricultural areas as livestock production (cattle, sheep, swine, and horses); dairy production; poultry; diversified farm production; farm crop production (field crops, forage, vineyards, and intensive vegetable culture); ornamental horticulture (nursery, floriculture, turf management, arboriculture, landscape development); grain, feed, seed, and farm supply services; forestry; conservation, recreation, and wildlife; and soil science, reclamation, and conservation.

Technicians are found in the combined physical and biological science technologies, which include agricultural equipment (farm machines and mechanization systems); dairy product processing; food processing (canning, drying, freezing, and freeze drying); biomedical mechanisms; oceanographic sciences (fishing, aquiculture, mariculture, and other biological specialities); sanitation and environmental control (water and waste water, solid waste, atmosphere); and scientific data-processing.

The foregoing kinds of technicians are generally known to the public. However, it is important to recognize that there is a whole new spectrum of specialized, nonbaccalaureate technicians who support and assist professionals of all kinds. For example, the occupational equivalent of the technician is required in the financial and administrative management sector of business; in marketing, transporting, and servicing industrial products; and in law enforcement. Nondegree specialists are emerging as assistants in libraries, in the social services, and in the child care and guidance and recreational fields.

Manpower needs. Unemployment resulting from job elimination and shortages of skilled manpower in technical fields could be alleviated if more people were prepared to be and were employed as technicians.

In the United States, programs to educate electrical, electronic, mechanical, civil, architectural and building, chemical, metallurgical, instrumentation, and data-processing technicians produce from 60,000 to 75,000 technicians a year (U.S. Department of Labor 1966). This is only half the required number. To meet the demands for more and better health services, many thousands of practical nurses, dental hygienists, and other specialized hospital, medical, and dental laboratory technicians are also needed.

Educational programs are not well developed for the new kinds of technicians, although the demand for them is great. Needed as new technicians, according to the U.S. Office of Education (USOE), are approximately 50,000 biomedical hospital equipment technicians, 100,000 electromechanical technicians, 100,000 agricultural production and service technicians, 10,000 communications and telemetry technicians, 10,000 computerized drafting technicians, 30,000 electronic computer service technicians, 15,000 numerically controlled machine tool technicians, 20,000 water pollution control technicians, and 5,000 chemical manufacturing process control technicians. Oceanographic, radiological, nuclear, electrooptical, urban planning, police science, fire protection, and air pollution technicians are also needed, but relatively few or virtually none are being trained.

The figures given are conservative. For example, at a meeting with USOE officials, representatives of the office machine and computer industry estimated that 150,000 additional electronic computer service personnel would be needed by the 1970's (five times the figure given above).

There is a growing need for agricultural production and related technicians. In 1964 the average age of the owners of the farm production facilities in the United States was over 51 (U.S. Department of Commerce . . . 1967). This means that about half of them will be nominally or actually retired by 1980. Probably more than 100,000 farmers will retire each year.

Because of the technological advances in agricultural production, new farmers will need the equivalent of a technician's education to be economically effective. In addition to new farmers, thousands of specialized agricultural service personnel—including specialists in processing, fertilizers, pesticides, herbicides, fungicides, and farm supplies—will be needed each year (Brooking & Hunsicker 1966).

Job opportunities. The modern and highly trained technician usually starts to work for someone else in his chosen field, but with experience and additional study he may establish his own business. For example, an enterprising, skilled technician may produce special components for modern machinery, instruments, and electronic gear, or he may manufacture farm, forest, or ocean products; also, he may provide special services to industrial, agricultural, forest, ocean, or health service establishments. Technicians usually work for others in such areas as research, design, and development; production; or marketing and servicing. With experience they may advance to supervisory or managerial positions of great responsibility.

Research, design, and development technicians. Technicians who work in the area of research, design, and development of new products usually work closely with engineers or scientists. They help design, develop, and experimentally refine new machinery, products, techniques, or services.

Design technicians help engineers and scientists make the basic studies required to build a new machine, help make the routine design of the machine's components, make routine stress analyses and determinations of strength of materials, assist in getting the components made and in assembling them into the final unit, and test the first model of the machine. They also assist the engineers in making any necessary modifications in the machine to make it do the specified job. Most of their work is done in laboratories or design departments.

Industrial production technicians. Industrial production technicians assist production specialists or scientists in the efficient production of such things as machinery, goods, food, and fibers.

The industrial production technician—sometimes called production technician or industrial technician—primarily supports the production managers who mass produce the completed experimental machine. He must sometimes redesign parts for more efficient production; specify and set up machinery, fixtures, and quality control devices to be used to produce all parts; and assemble and finish the machines. An understanding of flow of materials, use of time-and-motion study methods, plant layout, production methodology, statistical methods, and quality control techniques are necessary for this job.

Marketing and servicing technicians. Technicians in the field of marketing and servicing must help market as broadly as possible, deliver, and service manufactured products. Technical knowledge of the products and an understanding of their scientific principles are required.

Preparatory programs. Organized programs to educate technicians began in the United States about 1900, when a few private technical institutes and still fewer public institutions began to provide special, postsecondary education for technicians who would work with mechanical, electrical, civil, and industrial production engineers.

The curricula, as intensive and rigorous as those for professional engineers, were only about half as long (usually two academic years). Applied mechanical and basic sciences were studied in greater depth than in baccalaureate programs.

Because of the success of these early programs, graduates of high-quality two-year postsecondary programs for engineering and physical science technicians became among the most sought after specialized personnel in the United States. Today such technicians usually start their employment after graduation at pay equal to or greater than graduates of baccalaureate programs other than engineering and physical science programs.

Because a technician functions between the professional and the skilled worker, he must have both theoretical and practical knowledge. The professional is educated primarily to understand and work with theory; the skilled worker has a minimum of theoretical knowledge but has the skill to do practical tasks; and the technician has less theoretical knowledge than the professional and less practiced skill than the skilled worker but is able to understand and perform, to a limited extent, the work of both.

The objective of preparatory programs for technicians is to provide a competency broad enough to allow the graduate to choose between a variety of related work opportunities, called clusters. A graduate electronics technician, for example, is able to choose among jobs in research, production, and sales and services, or he may even start his own small business. He is qualified to work in such varied fields as aerospace, communications, aeronautics, and biomedical equipment. This capability to undertake diverse employment makes the well-qualified technician attractive to a large variety of potential employers.

Students in technician programs must gain an understanding of the principles of science and mathematics underlying the chosen field of study; must learn to use the procedures, materials, devices, techniques, equipment, and processes of the scientific field easily and competently; and must develop the ability to communicate with the professionals with or for whom they will work.

Programs for educating technicians are characterized by intensive classroom and laboratory learning. About 50 percent of classroom and laboratory work is devoted to the study of applied science and the technical specialty. A planned sequence of courses emphasizes scientific principles and provides practice with scientific equipment. Mathematics is taught early in the technical program. The prospective technician also practices communication skills and reporting and takes elementary courses in economics, organizations, and human relations.

USOE sample program. A person enrolled in a two-year, postsecondary course for training as an instrumentation technician would be required to follow a rigorous four-semester program requiring school, laboratory, and outside study. Each semester lasts for 16 weeks.

In the first semester a student's courses would include: physics for instrumentation, requiring three hours a week of classroom instruction, four hours a week of laboratory work, and six hours a week of outside study; mathematics, requiring five hours a week of class study and ten hours of outside study; mechanical measuring principles, requiring three hours a week of classwork and six hours a week each of laboratory study and outside study; communication skills, requiring three hours a week of class study and six hours of outside study; and instrument shop practice in the laboratory, requiring four hours a week of laboratory work. In all, 56 hours of work are demanded of the student in the first-semester curriculum.

The second-semester curriculum is equally difficult. Courses in physics for instrumentation, mathematics, electrical circuits (AC and DC), and technical reporting are required. The physics for instrumentation course is a continuation of the first-semester course and requires the same amount of time; the mathematics course is also a continuation of the first-semester course, but the time required is reduced to four hours of class study and eight hours of outside work; the courses in electrical circuits and technical reporting each require three hours of classwork, six hours of laboratory work, and six hours of outside study. The hours of work demanded of the second-semester student total 55.

Between the first and second years of the program, students have the option of going to summer school to further their knowledge. Students can take courses to meet the special requirements of the state or institution in which they are planning to work and may also take a course in chemistry for instrumentation.

More advanced studies are undertaken during the second year of the program. In the third semester, students are required to have three class hours, six laboratory hours, and six outside study hours of electrical measuring principles; three class hours, six laboratory hours, and six study hours of electronics; three class hours, four laboratory hours, and six outside study hours of control principles and telemetry; three laboratory hours of calibration and standardization; and three class hours and six outside study hours of general and industrial economics. The total hours spent on course work during the third semester is 55.

The fourth semester also demands 55 hours of study. Control systems analysis requires four hours each of class and laboratory work and eight hours of outside study; electronics for instrumentation requires three hours each of class and laboratory work and six hours of outside study; computer principles and systems requires three hours of classwork, two of laboratory work, and six of outside study; instrumentation projects requires one hour of classwork and six hours of laboratory work; and industrial organization and institutions requires three hours of classwork and six of outside work.

Technician and professional curricula. The basic difference or contrast between a two-year technical program and the first two years of a professional program—such as an engineering program—is that in the first two years of the mechanical technology program 47 percent of the course work is devoted to the field of specialization, whereas in the first two years of the mechanical engineering program only 6 percent is specialized. The engineering curriculum devotes 68 percent of its time to providing extensive study in mathematics and science, whereas the technical curriculum devotes 27 percent of the two-year period to these disciplines. However, in the technical curriculum about 12 percent of the technical course work is devoted to mathematical analysis and to applications of the physical sciences, compared to only about 3 percent in the engineering program. The remaining time in both programs is devoted to general education courses (U.S. Office of Education 1965a).

Schools. Although employers and hospitals offer both training and retraining programs, employers have found it difficult to make on-the-job training programs effective; there is an increasing need for technicians to have language, scientific, and mathematical skills not often taught in on-the-job training programs. Formal class and laboratory instruction best fulfill these requirements. The armed forces also provide technical training programs, but a study reporting 1963 data showed that these programs were a minor factor in preparing civilian technicians (U.S. Department of Labor 1966).

State reports to the USOE indicate that throughout the United States over 300 public postsecondary institutions offer programs in agricultural technology. There are 800 to 900 known public and private, nonprofit, postsecondary institutions offering training programs for technicians in the physical sciences and related engineering fields, and about the same number offering training in the health occupations. Health training programs are usually run in cooperation with clinics or hospitals to provide clinical experience for the students. No complete inventory is available of the capabilities or total training capacity of private institutions which specialize in educating engineering technicians or specialized health service personnel.

Technician programs have been offered in both public and private technical institutes, or technical colleges, for many years. Divisions of some four-year colleges and universities offer programs for technicians, and many high schools offer programs directed toward the preparation of technicians for work or for further technical study. The greatest growth in technician education, however, has been in public community colleges, technical institutes, and area technical and vocational schools. Many institutions have also developed part-time and evening programs in technical education.

To determine whether the applicant is qualified for postsecondary programs, schools usually employ tests of ability, interest, and aptitude, and most schools require a personal interview so both student and school may assess the student's potential.

Usually the prerequisites for entry include graduation from high school or its equivalent. Three standard secondary units of English are required; the student should be able to demonstrate capability in reading, writing, and oral communication. Two standard secondary units of mathematics, including algebra and plane geometry or their equivalents, are requisites for acceptance. Intermediate algebra and trigonometry are desirable (and may be required) for many programs in physical science and related engineering technologies. In addition, at least one standard secondary unit of science with laboratory is needed. Physics is considered the most desirable science course, and chemistry the next, for the physical science and related engineering technologies. Chemistry usually is the preferred science requisite, with physics or biology the second choice, for those interested in the health and agricultural technologies.

Pretechnical, postsecondary programs. It is becoming increasingly evident that the future of many technical programs and, indeed, the capability to satisfy the needs of the United States for highly skilled technicians will depend upon the development of postsecondary programs which qualify promising youths who have the desire but lack the scholastic preparation to enter high-quality technician programs.

Recruitment of qualified students is a major problem in the development of technician education programs. The academic requirements for entering a high-quality technician program are practically the same as for entering baccalaureate programs in science or engineering, and there are not enough qualified high school graduates entering any of these programs.

Analysis of available statistics showed that for every student who entered a baccalaureate program there were perhaps three or four who applied for admittance and were rejected, who did not apply at all because they did not want a four-year baccalaureate program, or who believed they could not complete one. Nearly half the students who entered college programs directed toward a baccalaureate degree did not complete the program or receive the degree.

An increasing number of technical institutions provide one-year programs to give remedial instruction to promising but underprepared students. The programs are variously called student development, opportunity, or pretechnical programs, according to the institution.

More than 20 years of experience with these programs has shown that if students lack the equivalent of both a full year of high school mathematics and a year of physics or chemistry (with laboratory), two semesters of these subjects usually qualify them to enter high-quality technical programs and give them a good chance of successful completion. During the academic year, they usually also strengthen their reading and study skills

and take at least one specialized laboratory course which does not require an extensive mathematical or scientific background.

The most successful of these programs try to enroll more than 100 students each fall semester. A pretechnical program with fewer students is economically unfeasible, seldom has adequate staff and facilities, and does not provide enough additional, qualified students to fill classes in the school's technician programs.

Facilities. Technician programs must have adequate facilities that are attractive and functionally efficient. The head of the technical or occupational division of the program and his staff should be responsible for recommending to the administrative head of the institution the purchase of necessary facilities and should supervise the installation of the laboratories and equipment.

By using portable equipment and modular construction, which ensures flexible use of building spaces, economical adjustments in the program can easily be made. Lecture-demonstration rooms and classrooms should be equipped with up-to-date teaching aids and demonstration equipment. Adequately furnished, lighted, and equipped office and study space should be provided for all staff members. For instructors who teach science or laboratory courses, spacious and well-equipped work and preparation areas are essential.

Laboratory equipment for technician programs must be of high quality, since the objectives and strength of the programs lie in providing intensive training in a wide variety of laboratory situations. In equipping a laboratory, a thorough study should be made of all the simulation, demonstration, and teaching systems available. An increasing number of manufacturers have developed preassembled equipment systems for the laboratory.

It is essential that the demonstration or simulation equipment used to teach specific principles is real apparatus, typical of that used on the job. It is not enough to demonstrate the principle clearly; the student must see and understand the principle as applied with the standard apparatus used in the technology, and he must learn how to use the apparatus.

Most facilities and equipment for technician programs must be purchased. However, it is sometimes advantageous to lease or rent some kinds of apparatus or equipment. Electronic data-processing equipment is often leased because the purchase of a computer system is very expensive and because rapid technological changes soon make parts of the system obsolete. Various kinds of agricultural equipment may also be rented or leased for much less than purchase cost.

Laboratory facilities and training provisions for the health technologies require special planning, with the assistance of professional practitioners. Science laboratories, classrooms, and technical specialty facilities—such as facilities equipped like doctors' or dentists' offices—are used to teach the basic principles of the health technologies. Often community facilities, such as hospitals, must be used to provide the clinical and training experiences essential to such programs.

Some programs, particularly in the agricultural field, require extensive and highly specialized laboratories: nursery areas and greenhouses for ornamental horticulture, barns and feeding and milking facilities for dairy production technology, a farm area for crop production or agricultural equipment technologies, or a timber area for forest technology. These facilities serve most satisfactorily when owned, but leasing arrangements may be feasible in some cases.

After any technician program gets under way and all the required equipment has been purchased, it is still necessary to provide an annual equipment and supply budget. These funds are required to replace or repair equipment, restock expendable items, and purchase new equipment required by technological change. Substantially more than the annual allowance may be required if new types of special equipment are needed to keep the program up-to-date. No technical education program can attain its objectives with an obsolete laboratory.

Faculty. A highly trained, experienced, technically competent, and enthusiastic staff—including the department heads, teaching staff, coordinators, counselors, librarians, and all who assist them in the instructional process—is one of the most important factors in the success of any program to educate technicians.

Qualifications. To be effective, faculty members of technical programs must have interests and capabilities which transcend their areas of specialization. Total instructional staff coordination is necessary to provide an orderly, interrelated, relevant, timely, and interesting curriculum for the students. In order to attain maximum reinforcement of all concepts and principles

taught, instructors should relate their subject to the other courses in the curriculum.

The library is an extension of every classroom and laboratory. Librarians should have a science and technical background and a professional library science education. In addition, some formal preparation in the teaching field and some experience in a technical library would be useful.

Instructors in the technical specialty courses must have a comprehensive understanding of the scientific principles underlying each aspect of their subjects. They must be able to use all of the appropriate equipment and techniques and to perform the required special services with the confidence of a skilled technician. The attainment of professional or equivalent preparation in the subject specialty is required. Usually the instructional staff acquire their subject-specialty preparation in professional schools.

Recent experience has shown that graduates of high-quality technician education programs who have acquired suitable employment experience and who have continued their technical education to professional level (baccalaureate degree or beyond) often become excellent teachers in programs for technicians. Persons with this background are likely to understand the objectives and unique instructional requirements of technical education and often bring to the program enthusiasm and an appreciation of the values of technical education that are essential to the success of the program. Teachers with this background may become increasingly important because of the trend in most programs for educating professional physical scientists, engineers, and applied biological scientists toward teaching more theory and giving less laboratory experience. This usually does not prepare the recently graduated professional to be either educationally or psychologically capable of teaching technicians; he has not learned and practiced the skills, procedures, and special techniques required of technicians.

All members of the teaching staff should have employment experience involving extensive practice of the skills and competencies they are to teach. The employment experience should have been long enough—usually from three to five years—for the teachers to have developed the skills, judgment, and mature capabilities expected of technicians.

Duties and teaching loads. The most successful technician programs are usually taught by full-time instructors. Considering the time and money required to get a new program started—four or five years and usually hundreds of thousands of dollars—and the time required to develop a closely coordinated teaching team, it is understandable that a staff composed largely of part-time teachers cannot bring the real leadership, permanent interest, and maximum effectiveness to a program that is expected of a teacher who is an experienced, full-time employee. High-quality instruction cannot be obtained through the extensive use of part-time teachers from local industries or from institutions whose objectives are either to teach professionals or to provide vocational training involving specialized crafts and skills but little scientific theory.

A minimum of two, and usually three, full-time faculty members is required to teach the technical specialty courses to 25 to 40 students in a typical technology program. Students can be taught in one lecture group but may have to be divided into two sections of 12 to 20 for laboratory work. One of the full-time instructors is usually recognized as the head of the program. He must be technically competent in all phases of the technology, able to plan and equip the facilities, capable of developing and initiating the details of the curriculum, able to provide leadership in student selection and graduate placement, and able to coordinate departmental teaching efforts.

In addition to the staff which teaches the technical specialty courses, faculty members must be provided to teach communication skills, technical reporting, mathematics, basic science, and general courses in the curriculum. Off-campus staff teaching and supervising clinical, medical, or other laboratory technologies in cooperative programs must be professionally and technically competent, able to cope with school and clinic officials and with employers, and able to exercise a high degree of independent judgment as teachers and representatives of the school.

Teaching loads for the faculty should be defined and followed. A work load of 15, and not more than 20, contact hours each week should constitute a full teaching load for instructors in technician programs, since the teachers need ample time to assist students, develop courses, plan effective laboratory experiments, and improve instructional techniques.

Professional development. Technological development in the various technical fields is rapid and certain to continue. Teachers must keep their knowledge of scientific and pedagogical theory and practice up-to-date.

Year-round employment permits time for study and development of new programs or improvements in existing ones; it also facilitates the operation of summer programs. Frequent visits to the places where students are or will be employed can help the teaching staff evaluate program performance and help keep the staff aware of the technological changes in the field.

Encouragement of instructional staff self-development is increasingly being provided by released-time and financial assistance for attendance at professional and technical society meetings, special teacher-training institutes, and special courses.

Sabbatical leaves or other grants of time should be provided for the instructional staff and particularly for the teachers of the technical specialty courses, who must keep up-to-date in the skills and special competencies expected of technicians in their field. Employment experience to update teachers is very desirable but sometimes not easy to arrange. However, active membership in technical societies and intimate acquaintance with active advisory committees frequently provide channels for short-term (three months to one year) employment. Periodic return to formal study to renew competencies in the fundamental principles that underlie each particular field is of equal importance.

Serving as consultants in their fields of specialization also motivates instructional staff members to broaden their horizons, keep up-to-date, retain and improve their technical competencies, and make themselves more interesting and effective instructors.

Federal legislation. The U.S. government grants financial assistance to help establish new technical education programs, to encourage the expansion of already established programs, and to help train teachers.

NDEA Title VIII. The need to educate technicians was first recognized by the U.S. government with the passage of Title VIII of the National Defense Education Act of 1958. Under this act the U.S. Office of Education was directed by Congress to grant matching funds to the states to train the highly skilled technicians needed for national defense.

Under the act, $47.5 million was granted to the states through 1963, starting with $3.75 million in 1959 and increasing to $15 million in 1963. The programs aided by the act grew from about 260 schools enrolling 48,500 students in 1959 to about 880 schools enrolling over 220,000 students in 1964. More than half the enrollees were employed adults improving their technical competence in special courses. State and local dollars spent exceeded $2 for each federal dollar (U.S. Office of Education . . . 1965*b*).

Vocational Education Act of 1963. The Vocational Education Act of 1963, which continued the provisions of Title VIII of the National Defense Education Act of 1958, the George-Barden Act, and the Smith-Hughes Act, provided substantially increased funds to meet the vocational and technical education needs of many people of all ages in all communities.

For the first time, funds were provided for the construction of facilities as well as for teacher salaries, libraries, laboratories and equipment, and other materials and services for vocational and technical programs. The 1963 act required equal matching of federal funds with state and/or local funds. Funds granted to states were administered by the state boards for vocational education. The act removed the restrictions limiting the use of funds for technicians "necessary to national defense" so technicians of all kinds could be educated.

Federal funds appropriated under the act through fiscal 1969 were in excess of $1.17 billion, averaging a little over $260 million a year from 1967 to 1969. State and local funds spent exceeded $2 for each federal dollar.

Title I of the Vocational Education Act granted appropriations for basic vocational and technical education programs; for programs for the disadvantaged and the handicapped; for grants to colleges, universities, and public agencies conducting research and experimental, developmental, or pilot projects in vocational and technical education; for construction and operation of residential vocational schools for youths between the ages of 15 and 21; for facilities for residential vocational education schools; for work-study programs and part-time work programs for full-time students; and for curriculum development and the training of personnel in curriculum development.

Title I also created the 21-member National Advisory Council on Vocational Education appointed by the president and including 14 representatives from postsecondary and adult vocational education programs and seven representatives from the general public. The council advises the U.S. commissioner of education on regulations and conduct and distributes results of evaluations of programs. Funds are authorized for the cost of this service. The act also requires states to establish advisory councils with responsibilities similar to the national council's. Federal funds are provided for the cost of their services.

Major revisions were made in the Vocational Education Act of 1963 by the Vocational Education Amendments of 1968 (P.L. 90–576). The amendments authorized about double the funds —over $3 billion for 1969–1972—for the regular vocational and technical education programs. Several special features and authorizations were added to the original act to make vocational and technical education more accessible to the general public.

Total authorizations for all titles—including both regular and special programs—were $542.1 million for fiscal 1969, $857.65 million for fiscal 1970, $870.15 million for fiscal 1971, and $910.15 million for fiscal 1972. Authorizations for regular vocational education programs were established at $565 million for fiscal 1973 and for each year thereafter. Additional money was provided for certain other administrative costs and dissemination activities, if they became necessary. Funds may be used by the U.S. commissioner of education and by state boards to make grants to or contracts with local education agencies for planning, developing, and operating exemplary occupational programs. The new authorizations were in addition to $28.8 million authorized for vocational education under the Smith-Hughes Act of 1917.

Higher Education Facilities Act of 1963. Congress authorized $1.2 billion for construction of facilities for public and nonprofit private colleges in the Higher Education Facilities Act of 1963. Of these funds, 22 percent were earmarked for construction of facilities for community colleges and technical institutes. Such institutions were made eligible for federal funds amounting to 40 percent of the state expenditure, whereas other higher education institutions qualifying under the act were entitled to federal shares up to 33.3 percent, indicating the importance which Congress attached to programs for technical education.

Because the act encouraged more institutions to offer postsecondary technician programs, information from the USOE has shown that both the number and variety of programs have grown, the quality of the programs has generally improved, and student enrollments have increased.

Higher Education Act of 1965. Title I of the Higher Education Act of 1965 authorized $25 million for fiscal 1969 and $35 million for fiscal 1970 to enable the commissioner to give stipends to vocational education personnel to attend institutions of higher education with approved vocational leadership development programs. A cost allowance payment to the institution of up to $3,500 per year was included.

The act also authorized the commissioner to make grants to state boards to pay the cost of programs for training or retraining vocational and technical education personnel.

BIBLIOGRAPHY

BAYLISS, SYLVIA J., ed. 1970 *Career Opportunities for Technicians and Specialists: Community Service and Related Specialists.* Chicago, J. G. Ferguson.

BROOKING, WALTER J., ed. 1969 *Career Opportunities for Technicians and Specialists: Engineering Technicians.* Chicago, J. G. Ferguson.

BROOKING, WALTER J., AND H. N. HUNSICKER 1966 *More Skilled Agricultural Technicians Are Needed. Agricultural Education,* 38, no. 12, June 1966.

FERRIS STATE COLLEGE 1967 *Michigan Technicians Need Study.* Big Rapids, Mich., The College.

KINSINGER, ROBERT E., ed. 1970 *Career Opportunities for Technicians and Specialists: Health Technicians.* Chicago, J. G. Ferguson.

NEW YORK (STATE). UNIVERSITY 1968 *Agricultural and Technical College at Cobbleskill Catalog, 1968-1969.* Cobbleskill, The College.

PEARCE, C. A. 1964 *Technical Manpower in New York State.* Special Bulletin No. 239. Vols. IA, IB, and II. Albany, Division of Research and Statistics, New York State Department of Labor.

PRAKKEN, LAWRENCE W. 1969 *Technician Education Yearbook 1969–1970.* Ann Arbor, Mich., Prakken Publications.

RONEY, MAURICE W. 1964 "An Analysis of the Interrelationship of Mathematics, Science, and Subject Matter in Selected Technical Institute Curricula." Ed.D. dissertation. College Park, University of Maryland.

SIDNEY, HOWARD, ed. 1969 *Career Opportunities for Technicians and Specialists: Agricultural, Forestry, Oceanographic Technicians.* Chicago, J. G. Ferguson.

U.S. DEPARTMENT OF COMMERCE. BUREAU OF THE CENSUS 1967 *U.S. Census of Agriculture, 1964.* Washington, D.C., Government Printing Office.

U.S. DEPARTMENT OF LABOR 1966 *Technician Manpower: Requirements, Resources, and Training Needs.* Bulletin No. 1512. Washington, D.C., Government Printing Office.

U.S. DEPARTMENT OF LABOR 1967 *Manpower Report of the President and a Report on Manpower Requirements, Resources, Utilization, and Training.* Washington, D.C., Government Printing Office.

U.S. OFFICE OF EDUCATION. DIVISION OF VOCATIONAL AND TECHNICAL EDUCATION 1964 *Chemical Technology—A Suggested 2-year Post High School Curriculum.* OE-80031. Washington, D.C., Government Printing Office.

U.S. OFFICE OF EDUCATION 1965a *Occupational Criteria and Preparatory Curriculum Patterns in Technical Education.* OE-80015. Washington, D.C., Government Printing Office.

U.S. OFFICE OF EDUCATION. DIVISION OF VOCATIONAL AND TECHNICAL EDUCATION 1965b *Progress in Technical Vocational Education Programs Under Title III of the George-Barden Act. Fiscal Years 1959–1964.* Washington, D.C., Government Printing Office.

U.S. OFFICE OF EDUCATION. DIVISION OF VOCATIONAL AND TECHNICAL EDUCATION 1965c *Scientific and Technical Societies Pertinent to the Education of Technicians.* OE-80037. Washington, D.C., Government Printing Office.

U.S. OFFICE OF EDUCATION. DIVISION OF VOCATIONAL AND TECHNICAL EDUCATION 1966 *Electronic Technology—A Suggested 2-year Post High School Curriculum.* Rev. ed. OE-80009A. Washington, D.C., Government Printing Office.

U.S. OFFICE OF EDUCATION. DIVISION OF VOCATIONAL AND TECHNICAL EDUCATION 1966 *Instrumentation and Automatic Control—Suggested Techniques for Determining Courses of Study in Vocational and Technical Education Programs.* OE-80043. Washington, D.C., Government Printing Office.

U.S. OFFICE OF EDUCATION. DIVISION OF VOCATIONAL AND TECHNICAL EDUCATION 1966 *Instrumentation Technology —A Suggested 2-year Post High School Curriculum.* OE-80033. Washington, D.C., Government Printing Office.

U.S. OFFICE OF EDUCATION. DIVISION OF VOCATIONAL AND TECHNICAL EDUCATION 1967 *Pretechnical Post High School Programs, Suggested Guide.* Prepared by Walter J. Brooking, assisted by Alexander Ducat. OE-80049. Technical Education Program Series, 12. Washington, D.C., Government Printing Office.

U.S. OFFICE OF EDUCATION. DIVISION OF VOCATIONAL AND TECHNICAL EDUCATION 1968 *Criteria for Technician Education, A Suggested Guide.* OE-80056. Washington, D.C., Government Printing Office.

U.S. OFFICE OF EDUCATION. DIVISION OF VOCATIONAL AND TECHNICAL EDUCATION 1968 *Forest Technology, A Suggested 2-year Post High School Curriculum.* OE-80054. Washington, D.C,, Government Printing Office.

WIGGS, GARLAND D., ed. 1970 *Career Opportunities for Technicians and Specialists: Marketing, Business, and Office Specialists.* Chicago, J. G. Ferguson.

WALTER J. BROOKING

TECHNICIANS, TRAINING OF

1. ENGINEERING TECHNICIANS   H. Russell Beatty

2. INDUSTRIAL TECHNICIANS   John K. Wolfe

3. SCIENCE TECHNICANS   William G. Torpey

1. ENGINEERING TECHNICIANS

The technician is the liaison man between the engineer and the skilled workman. He conveys the engineer's concepts and creations to the craftsman through instructions which he draws, writes, or states. When he draws the instructions, he is a draftsman or designer. When he writes the instructions, he is a production planner, manufacturing methods man, or specifications writer. When he delivers his instructions orally, he is a supervisor. Sometimes he is employed as a serviceman on complex equipment such as jet aircraft, computers, or automated production lines, where he is called upon to use his technical knowledge in diagnosing the faulty operation of the machine and to use his manual skill in correcting the difficulty. Quite often his services are required to sell products when the customer requires a technical explanation of the advantages of the product before he will buy it.

The engineer, the technician, and the craftsman work together in the engineering field as a team. The engineer develops new technology, the technician instructs the craftsman in the proper use of the technology, and the craftsman utilizes the technology in manufacturing the product. The special talents of each are needed by a company if it is to operate efficiently.

Each of the three major categories of workers on the engineering team—craftsman, technician, and engineer—may be further subdivided. The technician category may be divided into three subcategories: industrial technician, engineering technician, and engineering technologist. There are no sharp dividing lines between the functions performed by workers in each of these subcategories. The technician's field of specialization is called engineering technology or industrial technology.

Table 1 indicates the usual preparation for the various places on the engineering team.

The industrial technician. The industrial technician is trained primarily in the manufacturing or construction processes. He receives a background in drafting and design, planning and estimating, and the science related to his technical specialty.

Area vocational schools offer industrial technology programs as a two-year postsecondary extension of vocational high school courses. A number of community colleges also offer courses of this type.

Colleges of education are beginning to offer four-year programs in industrial technology as adjuncts to their programs for training industrial arts teachers. Students usually receive the degree of bachelor of industrial technology upon graduation. Students enrolled in these courses generally receive the equivalent of two full years of liberal arts education along with the two full years of technical education. There appears to be a growing demand for industrial technicians with a broad background of this type.

Engineering technicians and technologists. Educational programs in engineering technology are generally two years in length, although some require three years, and recently there has been a trend to establish some four-year programs leading to a bachelor of technology degree. Many different kinds of colleges are involved in engineering technology education. There are the two-year techni-

Table 1. Preparation for occupations in the engineering field

OCCUPATION	EDUCATION	TRAINING
Skilled craftsman	High school equivalent—with algebra and trigonometry	Apprenticeship: four years' trade training under journeyman or equivalent
Industrial technician	High school equivalent plus two years' postsecondary schooling—with algebra, trigonometry, and four semester hours of physical science	One year on-the-job or equivalent trade training
Engineering technician	High school plus two years' postsecondary schooling—with elementary calculus and eight semester hours of physical science	Six months' trade training or equivalent
Engineering technologist	High school plus four years' college-level schooling—with differential and integral calculus and 12 semester hours of physical science	Six months' trade training or equivalent
Bachelor's level engineer	High school plus four years' college-level schooling—with differential equations, three semester hours of advanced mathematics, and 16 semester hours of physical science	No trade training
Master's level engineer	High school plus five years' college-level schooling—with differential equations, six semester hours of advanced mathematics, and 20 semester hours of physical science	No trade training

cal institutes or colleges which specialize in engineering technology education. There are many junior or community colleges which offer engineering technology education as one of several curricula. There are a number of senior colleges and universities that offer engineering technology education as well as engineering education. The appropriate associate degree is generally awarded to graduates from the two-year and three-year curricula, and the baccalaureate degree is awarded to graduates from the four-year curricula.

A typical two-year engineering technology program requires the student to earn between 60 and 80 semester hours of credit before graduation. The mathematics sequence of nine to 12 semester hours includes algebra, trigonometry, and calculus. The physical science sequence of six to eight credit hours is generally in physics but might include chemistry or biology, depending upon the technical specialty. Fifteen semester hours of nontechnical courses are usually included, consisting of English composition and study in such fields as literature, history, sociology, and economics. The balance of the curriculum is devoted to technical courses, some designed to develop technical skills such as drafting, but most designed to provide the engineering science and technology background essential for competence as an engineering technician in a particular technical specialty.

The four-year engineering technology program is too new to have any clearly defined pattern of subject matter. Most of the programs offered have merely added a number of liberal arts and business administration courses to the two-year engineering technology base in an attempt to broaden the curriculum rather than to give it more technological depth. An increase in the number of technological courses is likely, because engineering technologists require more extensive technical preparation, as well as a broader liberal arts education, than do engineering technicians.

Unlike most engineering students, most engineering technology students are less interested in the mathematical theory underlying engineering practice than they are in the application of the theory to the solution of technical problems. Technology students are frequently weaker in verbal ability than the average college student, although they are generally stronger in mathematical ability. The typical engineering technology student scores about 500 on mathematical

aptitude and about 425 on verbal aptitude on the Scholastic Aptitude Tests of the College Entrance Examination Board.

Colleges offering engineering technology programs usually accept only those students who are well prepared for engineering technology studies and have completed a college preparatory program that includes four years of English, two years of algebra, one year of plane geometry, and one year of physics or chemistry. Such colleges generally accept students who earn "C" grades, whereas engineering colleges generally require "A" or "B" grades. Most students enrolling in engineering technology courses graduated from high school in the second quarter or upper half of the third quarter of their class. They are frequently students who aspired to become engineers but did not earn grades that would warrant their admission to engineering colleges.

Engineering technology education is more specialized than engineering education. The choice of the technical specialty generally must be made by the student prior to enrolling in the technical college. There are a wide variety of choices available, and new ones are evolving each year. Among the curricula that have been accredited by the Engineers' Council for Professional Development in one or more institutions of higher education in the United States are aeronautical engineering technology, architectural engineering technology, civil engineering technology, electrical engineering technology, electronic engineering technology, mechanical engineering technology, metallurgical engineering technology, and nuclear engineering technology.

The rapidity with which changes in technology are occurring in industry today makes it imperative that engineering technology educators do everything possible to keep their programs current with present technological practice. The recent developments in the electronics field, with semiconductors replacing tubes and the subsequent introduction of integrated circuits, illustrates the rapidity with which changes are taking place.

Employment of engineering technicians. The engineering technician can speak the language of the engineer and has some of the skills of the craftsman. Logically, then, he is in an extremely good position to interpret the scientific concepts and technical ideas of the engineer to the craftsman so that products may be manufactured efficiently. Most engineers have neither the skill nor the desire to work at the drafting board. The actual layout and detailing of machinery are therefore left to the engineering technician. Wherever there is a need to employ engineers, there is also a need to employ engineering technicians. A minimum of one engineering technician is needed for every engineer employed if the division of labor between professional and semi-professional workers is to result in the best utilization of the special abilities of both. Frequently, two or three engineering technicians are needed for each engineer.

A great variety of occupations is open to the engineering technician. He supervises skilled workers in the production or construction of such engineering projects as buildings, roads, machines, missiles, electronic apparatus, and transportation equipment. He interprets the engineer's ideas so that the projects may proceed economically. He is frequently employed in the research laboratory to build the experimental models needed by the scientist or engineer. He often works in manufacturing as a methods man, a production planner, a tool designer, a plant layout man, or a production supervisor. Sometimes his talents are used in a manufacturing plant's engineering department to supervise maintenance or the installation of new machinery. Engineering technicians with extrovert personalities frequently become members of a technical sales staff.

The engineering technician works in the business machine maintenance field. Today's complex electronic computers and data processing equipment require maintenance men with more engineering knowledge than is needed by the mechanics who repair such equipment as typewriters and adding machines. In the early days of the electronic computer, the manufacturers found that their maintenance mechanics were not able to provide adequate maintenance service, and in desperation they recruited engineering college graduates to provide this service. The turnover was very high because professional engineers soon became dissatisfied with this type of work. The solution was found in the employment of engineering technicians. However, the supply of such graduates from the colleges has not been adequate to fill the needs of the electronic computer manufacturers, and many of the manufacturers have set up educational programs of their own to satisfy the demand. Lately, special electromechanical technology programs have been established in a number of colleges with the support of the electronic computer industry.

The aircraft maintenance field is another rapidly expanding market for engineering technology graduates. The large modern jet aircraft requires the employment of well-educated engineering technicians to ensure that the maintenance service is of high quality.

Well-qualified engineering technicians are also needed to give maintenance service to customers who are purchasing highly automated machinery for the production of chemicals, drugs, foods, and similar goods. Frequently an investment of millions of dollars is made in one of these production lines. Downtime is very costly, and every effort is made to minimize it. No longer can the ordinary mechanic be expected to understand the intricate functioning of electronic controls, hydraulic and pneumatic devices, and numerous other complex mechanisms. Technicians must receive special education for maintenance engineering work in programs that are intermediate between those designed for the skilled craftsman and those designed for the professional engineer.

Many engineering technicians work in the electrical power industry in power plant operating positions. With the recent developments in nuclear reactors, atomic plants have become competitive with fossil fuel plants, and it is estimated that close to 5,000 engineering technicians will be required as reactor operators by 1975. The electrical power industry has discovered that many of their technical positions in the areas of operation and planning can be filled adequately by engineering technicians.

The construction field employs large numbers of engineering technicians. Some of them work on the design of buildings and other structures in the office of an architect or engineer. Many work as estimators, materials takeoff men, construction planners, and supervisors. A considerable number become building materials salesmen. Some become licensed builders and set up their own building contractor's businesses.

Many engineering technicians are self-employed as owners of technical businesses. Some are in manufacturing, and others are in construction. Some operate instrument service shops, and others are in boat or machinery maintenance work. Because their education is oriented toward practical applications, many engineering technicians have opportunities to establish small businesses that often expand into very profitable enterprises.

Opportunities for large numbers of engineering technicians are also opening up in the fields of urban renewal and conservation, particularly the control of air and water pollution.

Employment of engineering technologists. The development of the four-year program to produce engineering technologists is relatively new, and very little factual information about employment opportunities for engineering technologists is available. When a shortage of engineers becomes particularly acute, industry employs engineering technologists to fill many vacant engineering jobs, especially those which are applications-oriented rather than research-oriented. The engineering technologist is more broadly educated than the engineering technician and can fill positions in industry, especially in sales and supervision, where his kind of education best meets the needs of the employer.

Engineering educators and industry seem to be moving toward a prerequisite of five years of engineering education for qualification as a professional engineer. Many tasks, however, can be performed adequately by persons with less than five years of engineering education, but the jobs require a greater technical preparation than an engineering technician possesses. Part of the gap between the master's level engineer and the engineering technician may be filled by bachelor's level engineers who are not accepted by a graduate school. Such persons will need a reorientation from theory to applications before they can serve effectively, and industry may provide this reorientation through an internship program. However, industry will also be interested in the graduate of the four-year engineering technology program, who already has an applications orientation.

Accreditation. Engineering technology programs at both the associate and baccalaureate levels are accredited by the Engineers' Council for Professional Development, which also accredits engineering curricula. Accreditation applies to individual curricula and not to the institution as a whole. Before a college may apply for professional accreditation by the ECPD, it must obtain accreditation as an institution from one of the regional accrediting associations, such as the New England Association of Colleges and Secondary Schools or the Middle States Association of Colleges and Secondary Schools.

Professional society activities. There is a close relationship between the engineer and the engineering technicians who support his work. Because of this, the professional engineering societies have a strong interest in the education and development of engineering technicians. The Engineers' Council for Professional Development, in addition to accrediting engineering technology curricula, has also provided for engineering technician representation on its guidance committee. This committee provides high school guidance directors with information and assembly programs with speakers so that high school students will know more about career possibilities in the entire engineering field. The Junior Engineering Technical Society, an organization for high school students who are interested in engineering as a career, also provides guidance information on both engineering and engineering technology. The American Society for Engineering Education has created a Technical Institute Administrative Council as one of its major divisions, with the chairman of the council serving as a vice-president and member of the board of directors of the society. The National Society of Professional Engineers has an Engineering Technicians Committee which provided leadership in establishing the Institute for the Certification of Engineering Technicians in 1960. ICET certifies engineering technicians as junior engineering technicians, engineering technicians, or senior engineering technicians. The NSPE Engineering Technicians Committee also helped to establish the American Society of Certified Engineering Technicians in 1964. The Engineering Manpower Commission, affiliated with the Engineers Joint Council, conducts supply and demand studies and salary studies for engineers and engineering technicians.

BIBLIOGRAPHY

AMERICAN SOCIETY FOR ENGINEERING EDUCATION 1962 *Characteristics of Excellence in Engineering Technology Education: Final Report of the Evaluation of Technical Institute Education.* Urbana, Ill., The Society.

BEATTY, H. RUSSELL 1967 "Careers in Engineering Technology." *JETS Journal,* 14, no. 7:4–15.

BEATTY, H. RUSSELL 1968 "The Development of Technical Education." *Journal of Engineering Education,* 58, no. 9:1063–1065.

Curricula Leading to Degrees in Engineering Technology in the United States. New York, Engineers' Council for Professional Development. Published annually.

"Education of the Engineering Technician" 1966 *Journal of Engineering Education*, 57, no. 3:entire issue.

ENGINEERING MANPOWER COMMISSION 1966 *Salaries of Engineering Technicians*. New York, The Commission.

HENNINGER, GEORGE ROSS 1959 *The Technical Institute in America*. New York, McGraw-Hill.

Technician Manpower: Requirements, Resources, and Training Needs. Bureau of Labor Statistics, U.S. Department of Labor, Bulletin 1512, 1966. Washington, D.C., Government Printing Office.

The Engineering Technician 1968 New York, McGraw-Hill.

H. RUSSELL BEATTY

2. INDUSTRIAL TECHNICIANS

Industrial technicians assist industrial engineers and scientists in almost every phase of their work, often performing some of the tasks that would otherwise take the time of these more highly trained technical personnel. Technical education for industry should prepare the student both to communicate with his co-workers through talks and reports and to continue the learning process throughout his working career.

Areas of specialization. Most technicians are oriented toward a specific area, such as electronics, electrical engineering, mechanics, chemistry, or automation. The work of the technician is often directed toward a specific area within a particular industrial field. The work may also be concerned with a specific function within the industrial organization. The functions are often categorized as research and development, manufacturing, quality control, installation and maintenance, and technical marketing and sales.

Technicians in research and development assist professional engineers and scientists in conducting experiments by setting up calibrating instruments, operating other sensitive instruments, and conducting specific tests. They develop skills on the job. Research technicians also help design, fabricate, and assemble experimental and testing equipment. Some do drafting and design work and make extensive calculations.

Technicians in manufacturing are involved with quality control, inspection, testing and operation of intricate machines, plant layout, and time-study methods.

Technicians who work in installation and maintenance are involved in assembling equipment at the factory, shipping the equipment, and setting it up at the customer location. The same technician often has both installation and service functions, since detailed knowledge of the product is needed to both install and repair. Often a satisfied customer will approach the installation or service technician for new orders or plant expansion. In this role the technician becomes a salesman for his company's products.

In civil engineering, technicians with a knowledge of surveying and drafting measure the characteristics of construction sites, determine land boundaries, and analyze soil samples, collecting information for plots, maps, and surveys. These technicians also work with geologists, meteorologists, and environmental scientists.

School and college training programs. Technicians for industry are trained in a variety of educational institutions, both private and tax-supported. Two-year technical institutes and community colleges provide an excellent source for industrial technicians. Applicants to such two-year institutions should have a minimum of a 2.00 or "C" secondary school average and should have completed at least two years of high school mathematics and one year of a science (other than biology or a general survey). Those who wish to be draftsmen often need some secondary school training in graphics.

Recently some four-year colleges have initiated four-year programs in engineering technology in recognition of the increased complexity of the work expected of the industrial technician. Applicants to colleges with four-year technical programs should have nearly a 3.00 or "B" secondary school average and should have had more mathematics and science courses than applicants for a two-year program. The number of four-year programs will continue to increase as the U.S. economy increases in technical complexity.

It is often possible for a skilled worker to acquire the skills needed to become a technician by attending the extension division of an engineering college on a part-time basis. Most areas of technology require the student to devote approximately one-half of his course time to his field. The other half is divided among basic courses in mathematics, science, and liberal arts. The program differs from many four-year college programs in that laboratory work is emphasized, so that students rapidly become familiar with equipment and techniques used in industry.

Extension programs are proving useful in some two-year and four-year colleges. An employed technician may elect to return part-time to improve his knowledge of theory through study programs. Admission to an extension program is usually somewhat more flexible than is required for initial full-time study. Criteria for acceptance to extension status may be based more on motivation and aptitude than on academic preparation. A longer period of study is required when extension courses are pursued, but both degrees and final status are fully comparable when viewed by the industrial employer.

Industrial training programs. In many employment areas sufficient numbers of trained technicians are not available to meet industrial needs. Junior and community colleges furnish graduates to nearby industries in generally sufficient numbers, but employers outside these localities often can meet their specialized needs only through their own training programs. Industrial training programs have also been found necessary for some highly specialized technical jobs for which school and college programs are not readily available. A large percentage of industrial technicians are trained within the industrial complex. Until recently, for example, industry provided its own education for operation, control, and repair of numerical control equipment for the operation of large machine tools. Many companies operate training schools which accept students on a broad basis; that is, the graduate may accept employment with a company other than the one supporting the school. Trainees taken on by industry as candidates for these programs may be skilled technical workers, nontechnical workers, or new high school graduates.

Industrial technician training programs include both extensive on-the-job training and academic education. Instructors may be from industrial or academic institutions. The academic portion of the education may be accomplished in a variety of ways, usually in cooperation with a local school or college. Occasionally correspondence schools are helpful. Increasing emphasis will probably be placed on closed-circuit television, as equipment and expertise increase in this field. The duration of industrial training programs varies widely.

It is very difficult to estimate the numbers involved in these specialized programs, since new specialties are often unclassified until the training is completed. The government training program, under the Manpower Development and Training Act of 1962 (with subsequent modifications), has provided basic training for technicians in occu-

pations for which shortages exist in particular localities.

Military training programs. Technicians who were trained while serving in the armed forces have become more important in providing for industrial manpower needs. Many engineering and physical science technicians now obtain their training in the military. It has been estimated that in recent years between 5 and 10 percent of the total number of electronics technicians have had their primary training in the armed forces. In many instances trainees enter the civilian technical market without additional preparation, although military training may have to be supplemented later with background theory courses.

The number of technicians trained in the armed forces is far greater than the number known to enter industrial employment, and it is possible that with the cooperation of both industry and the military, improved counseling at the time of military discharge could influence many more of these highly trained technicians to take similar positions in the civilian economy. Government agencies at state and federal levels can often assist in the job matching process.

Job placement. Administrators at technical schools often arrange interviews between students and interested industrial employers. It is possible to have arrangements made through friends, technical societies, or in response to occasional newspaper ads. Faculty members are often asked by industrial employers to recommend suitable students for particular openings. Interested high school graduates can also contact local companies for information on training programs.

Career development. Work as an industrial technician develops aptitudes and skills which often open up new areas for personal growth. It is possible to go on to management and to teaching, a field in which there is presently a serious shortage and in which employment opportunities are quite good. Some technicians may return to school for further study in preparation for careers in the fields of space, laser electronics, and the like. After several years in industry, many technicians started their own businesses.

BIBLIOGRAPHY

ARNOLD, W. M. 1969 *Career Opportunities for Technicians and Specialists.* Chicago, Ill., J. G. Ferguson.
BENT, RALPH D. 1965 "Employers Evaluate Training Programs for Technicians in the Electronics and Aerospace Industries." *Technical Education News,* 24, no. 3:1–2.

BODEAU, A. C. 1964 "What Abilities Do Technicians in Industry Need? Mechanical Aptitude, Manual Skills, Technical Knowledge." *Technical Education News*, 24, no. 1:1–3.

Industrial Arts and Vocational Education: The Shop Teachers' Professional Magazine. Published monthly, September–June.

IRWIN, D. E. 1963 "GE User Specialized Education of Engineering Technicians." *Technical Education News*, 23, no. 2:7–8.

Journal of Engineering Education. Published ten times a year by the American Society for Engineering Education.

NATIONAL SOCIETY OF PROFESSIONAL ENGINEERS 1962 *The Certification of Engineering Technicians.* New York, The Society.

"Technical Assistants in Physics in the U.S." 1963 *Physics Today*, 16, no. 3:48–54.

Technical Education News. Published three times a year.

Technician Education Yearbook 1965–66. Ann Arbor, Michigan, Prabskin.

U.S. OFFICE OF EDUCATION 1958 *Vocational-Technical Education for American Industry.* Prepared by Lynn A. Emerson. Circular 530. Washington, D.C., Government Printing Office.

WERTHEIMER, MICHAEL D. 1964 *Employment of Scientific and Technical Personnel in Industry.* BLS Bulletin 1418. Washington, D.C., Government Printing Office.

JOHN K. WOLFE

3. SCIENCE TECHNICIANS

A science technician is one whose education and experience qualify him to work as an aide to a scientist or engineer in the fields of science or technology. The technician has sufficient theoretical knowledge and craft skills to enable him to understand and work with the professional scientist and the skilled craftsman.

The training of a science technician is directly related to the duties he will perform. According to the Commission on Science Education of the American Association for the Advancement of Science, the duties of a scientist may be divided into 14 processes: observing, classifying, measuring, communicating, inferring, predicting, using space-time relationships, using number relationships, interpreting data, controlling variables, making operational definitions, formulating hypotheses, experimenting, and formulating models. As an aide, a science technician assists a scientist in at least six of these processes: observing, measuring, communicating, using space-time relationships, using number relationships, and controlling variables. In addition, the science technician performs other nonprofessional tasks such as setting up and calibrating instruments. Prior to 1960, formal education for science technicians was offered primarily by technical institutes. However,

the availability of federal financial support for technical education—such as the authorizations of the National Defense Education Act of 1958, the Vocational Educational Act of 1963, and the 1968 amendments to the 1963 act—has considerably increased the number and types of educational institutions offering education for technicians; the largest increase has been in junior and community colleges. There has also been a growing amount of curriculum experimentation. Diverse curricula exist in both accredited and nonaccredited programs and institutions.

Types of programs. An individual may become a science technician by learning the necessary skills in on-the-job training while working as a craftsman, by participating in a specialized program sponsored by the military, or by supplementing an incomplete college background in science or engineering with on-the-job training. The usual method of training is on-the-job training under the supervision of a scientist, engineer, or senior technician, although a few employers have formal training programs for science technicians.

The choice of assignments for the technician trainee and the methods used by a supervisor to impart on-the-job training are highly individualized and follow no consistent pattern. A close, cooperative association between trainee and supervisor is essential to the success of on-the-job training. The length of time required to train science technicians through on-the-job training depends on the trainee's education, his science or engineering background, and his previous work experience.

An individual may pursue a formal postsecondary education program designed to train persons to be science technicians. Postsecondary education for science technicians is usually offered in technical institutes, junior and community colleges, area vocational schools, and divisions of four-year colleges and universities. A two-year science technician program which leads to an associate's degree in science or engineering technology is generally considered the most effective way for an individual to become fully qualified as a science technician.

Cooperative education—that is, a program of planned and coordinated classroom-laboratory study and employment experience—is offered in some educational institutions. Under proper supervision a cooperative education program has certain advantages over the traditional program. A cooperative education program affords closely supervised practice for the student in his chosen occupation in an actual work environment and provides an opportunity for the student to use modern equipment often not available at an educational institution. The curriculum in cooperative education programs tends to be up-to-date because of the close relationship between educational institutions and employers.

The student works for an employer for two or three terms out of a total period of two or three calendar years. The break points in the cooperative program—that is, when the student goes to an employer for work—are correlated with particular phases of academic study. Agreements are made between the educational institution and the employer about the basic conditions of work—such as salary, job title, and extent of supervision. Students become part of the total work force of the organization, but supervisors from the academic institution visit and counsel them while they are on the job. While they are working, students are assigned only a minimal amount of schoolwork. An evaluation of the student's work is recorded by the educational institution as a counseling aid.

Both professional scientists and science technicians participate in continuing education programs to strengthen their backgrounds and to keep them up-to-date in their specialties. Continuing education programs in the form of short courses, workshops, seminars, and formal courses are given either in the plant or at an educational institution. The curriculum is usually geared to impart understanding and skills for a particular need and subject area.

Curriculum content. Technology programs are usually composed of courses which fall into four categories: basic sciences, mathematics, technical specialty, and general education (U.S. Office of Education 1968a).

Basic science courses are usually taken early in the two-year program in order to provide a background for the specialized courses studied later in the program. Science courses are generally applications oriented and include fundamental and applied physics; chemistry; and light, heat, sound, and solid-state and nuclear physics. Some biological sciences are required of trainees specializing in a field such as water and wastewater technology. Topics in biological science include studies of microstructure, circulation, and photosynthesis.

The required mathematics courses develop the student's ability to understand and apply basic mathematical principles, concepts, and techniques. The minimum essentials required are algebra and trigonometry. In some curricula, analytic geometry, calculus, and differential equations are needed.

Science or technical specialty courses usually compose about 50 percent of the curriculum. They stress the application of basic scientific principles to the specialized methods and procedures which will constitute the student's primary work in his chosen field. Such courses provide the special knowledge and skills required. Late in the program, the student is often required to undertake a special project which will demonstrate his competence in his specialty. The project may be part of a specialty course or be a course in itself.

General education courses consist of communications and social studies courses. Communications courses attempt to improve skills in grammar, spelling, composition, reading, and comprehension and in representing concepts and data graphically. These courses use materials that relate to technical subject matter. The objective of the social studies courses is to develop an understanding of social organizations and interpersonal relationships. Courses include elementary economics, industrial organization, social psychology, and duties and responsibilities of citizenship.

According to a survey of 25 postsecondary institutions, the range of required credit hours for two-year technology programs varied from a minimum of 62 to a maximum of 80 (U.S. Office of Education 1962). The credit hour requirements determined by this survey closely approximate the current requirements.

Sample postsecondary program. Although curricula for two-year postsecondary programs vary, typical curricula have been prepared for guidance and as aids to evaluation. An example of such a curriculum is a suggested program in metallurgical technology prepared by the U.S. Office of Education (1968b).

In the first semester mathematics, physics (heat and optics), general chemistry, communication skills, and an introduction to metallurgy are the required courses. The total amount of time required for classwork, laboratory work, and outside study in the first semester is 56 hours.

The second-semester courses include mathematics, physics (electricity and mechanics), analytical chemistry, foundry, technical reporting, and technical drawing and graphic representation. The total hours of work demanded of the second-semester student are 55.

The third-semester student studies physical metallurgy and metallography, properties of material, refractories and furnaces, and general and industrial economics. The total time required in this semester is 53 hours.

The fourth semester of study also requires 53 hours of work and includes courses in process metallurgy, nondescriptive inspection, control instrumentation, and industrial organization and institutions.

Sample associate's degree program. A basic pattern for most technology programs leading to an associate's degree has been widely followed since its development by the American Society for Engineering Education (1962). This program has been used as a standard especially by educational institutions seeking academic accreditation by the Engineers' Council for Professional Development.

The society proposed that a minimum of 60 credit hours of courses be required for an associate's degree. The courses should include nine credit hours of mathematics, six credit hours of physical sciences, six credit hours of technical skills, 24 credit hours of technical specialties, six credit hours of communications, six credit hours of humanities and social studies courses, and three credit hours of such other courses as management and human relations. In an ideal program, however, the society suggested that 12 credit hours of mathematics and 33 credit hours of technical specialty courses be required. The total credit hours required would then be 72.

Comparing specialized and general programs. If a certain training program for science technicians is designed to qualify an individual for employment in one of a cluster of highly specialized related jobs, the curriculum is more specific than it is in programs designed to train an individual in one of a wide range of jobs in a broad field of science.

Sample specialized program. A typical program having a very specialized curriculum is a program that trains science technicians to work in pollution control areas. Programs in pollution control technology train individuals to deal with problems related to the control of liquid, gaseous, and solid wastes. Science technicians usually work in waste water and water treatment plants, in government pollution control agencies, in industrial firms, and in related organizations.

The major duties of air pollution control technicians, water treatment technicians, waste and sewage system technicians, and solid waste disposal technicians are basically similar. An air pollution technician, for example, collects air samples for routine monitoring, for special studies, and for ensuring compliance with regulations; installs, services, maintains, and repairs equipment and facilities; prepares reports of special studies; and keeps records of activities. The other pollution control technicians perform similar duties related to their specialties.

A two-year program leading to an associate's degree in pollution control offered by Purdue University in 1969 included the following courses: an introduction to pollution control, general chemistry, college algebra and trigonometry, engineering calculations, elementary surveying, and English composition in the first semester; an introduction to microbiology, physics (mechanics and heat), drafting fundamentals, land surveying and subdivision, and an introduction to sociology in the second semester; sanitary chemistry and biology, water supply operations, hydraulics and drainage, physics (electricity, sound, and light), and principles of speech in the third semester; and air pollution control, solid waste disposal, wastewater treatment, specifications, contracts, and estimating, technical report writing, and an elective in the fourth semester.

Sample general program. An approach to training individuals for a wide range of jobs in a broad field of science was developed in 1968 by the American Institute of Biological Sciences (AIBS) for the education of biotechnicians. The approach stressed four basic areas of concentration: preparing, communicating, observing, and measuring. These basic areas were then divided into steps to make learning easier.

The AIBS suggested that about 50 percent of a program's time be devoted to preparation. The trainees should learn construction practices, the use of tools, and how to build, repair, and maintain laboratory and field apparatus. Arithmetic and simple algebra should be taught. The trainees should learn to diagnose failures and logic errors in systems and to synthesize systems from parts. Instruction in calibration should enable students to produce reliable error curves and to predict failures. In addition, they should learn to adopt a policy of preventive maintenance—that is, to keep apparatus and facilities in operating and low-error condition.

About 20 percent of the time should be spent in improving the trainee's communication skills. Practice in vocabulary, spelling, writing, and grammar should be given. The students must also learn how to operate a computer.

According to the AIBS, about 15 percent of the time should be devoted to developing observation skills. The trainee must be taught to recognize the relative importance of various aspects of experimental systems, to make error-free observations under various conditions, and to learn darkroom techniques—such as developing film and making slides and prints.

The AIBS suggested that about 15 percent of the time be spent concentrating on teaching the trainee the techniques and methods of measuring commonly encountered variables, what to do with data, and how to recognize and control error and uncertainty.

Role of industry. Industry is helping to expand science technician education. Employers are donating surplus equipment and products for use as teaching aids, developing literature to enrich curricula, and providing summer employment opportunities for students and faculty in technical education programs. An increasing number of employers are participating in cooperative education programs for science technician education.

The existence of corporate-related education programs like those at the RCA Institute and the General Motors Institute and the spread of contract technician programs sponsored by such companies as Bell and Howell and International Telephone and Telegraph illustrate action by industry which could be extended to embrace the training of science technicians. The competition afforded by corporate education programs is a healthy influence on other technician education programs.

Goals and challenges. The goal of educators concerned with science technician education is to provide high-quality education which will lead to gainful employment. This objective requires periodic examination and possible revision of the content of the training program. The challenge to educators is to ensure that the graduates

of technical education programs are well prepared for performing job duties. If they are not, employers might establish their own education programs for science technicians.

Educators responsible for the development of curricula for science technicians must consider many issues in order to devise programs that suit the needs of trainees and that will provide the best and most thorough education.

It must be decided if there is a common core of understanding which every science technician needs to have. If there is one, educators must decide whether to concentrate on this core and to leave the teaching of the details of specific jobs to employers in on-the-job training. The merits of cooperative programs must be defined, and it must be decided if some topics are better taught before the student is employed on a rotation schedule and if there are other topics which are better taught after the student has had some employment experience. Curriculum planners must compare night-school programs with day-school programs for science technicians to ensure compatibility. Ways to modify entrance requirements for science technology programs without sacrificing quality in the programs must be found in order to permit the entrance into such programs of many disadvantaged but potentially capable youth.

Action has been taken to find out what science technicians should be taught and what teaching methods are most successful in science technician programs. An increasing amount of research, often federally funded, is being done on various phases of the curriculum. The goal of this research is to find new methods and techniques which will increase program effectiveness. Greater effort is being made in the United States to identify future needs for science technicians. These needs are being translated into future training requirements, helped, in part, by making a longer period of time available for planning purposes. Additional useful guides for curriculum development are being written. These guides and the availability of consultant help assist in the establishment of more meaningful curricula.

BIBLIOGRAPHY

AMERICAN SOCIETY FOR ENGINEERING EDUCATION 1962 *Characteristics of Excellence in Engineering Technology Education: Final Report of the Evaluation of Technical Institute Education.* Urbana, Ill., The Society.

U.S. OFFICE OF EDUCATION 1962 *Occupational Criteria and Preparatory Curriculum Patterns in Technical Education*

Programs. OE-55011. Vocational Division Bulletin 296. Washington, D.C., Government Printing Office.

U.S. OFFICE OF EDUCATION 1968a *Criteria for Technician Education.* OE-80056. Washington, D.C., Government Printing Office.

U.S. OFFICE OF EDUCATION 1968b *Metallurgical Technology—A Suggested 2-year Post High School Curriculum.* Prepared by Walter J. Brooking. OE-81012. Washington, D.C., Government Printing Office.

WILLIAM G. TORPEY

TECHNOLOGICAL CHANGE AND EDUCATION

Technological advances during the past 200 years in the United States and other parts of the industrialized world have radically changed the way the labor force has been utilized and have transformed education and training for work. Up to the last half of the eighteenth century, virtually the entire population was engaged in farming or handicraft work, using tools and methods that were little different from those of ancient times. In the slowly changing preindustrial era, illiteracy and a lack of schooling were no great handicaps to the worker who learned his trade through apprenticeship and whose status usually remained fixed throughout his lifetime.

The growth of the factory system, the greater division of labor, and the transfer of tasks involving manual skills to machines resulted inevitably in obsolescence of the apprenticeship system of industrial training. The stress in the machine age, as Thorstein Veblen once noted, instead of being on detailed mastery of a craft, "falls rather more decidedly on general intelligence and information" (1914, p. 307). Preparation for work could be acquired more effectively in the school classroom · than through the workday routine of industry.

Mass production further simplified the skills factory workers needed. Jobs were designed as machine-paced, repetitive routines which the man on the assembly line could perform with a minimum of training. This highly productive technology also brought about a new division of labor. The scientific-management movement prescribed the transfer of all initiative and control from the worker on the job to industrial engineers and a new managerial hierarchy. The continuous flow of production depended on a technical staff for planning and coordinating complex operations and on an army of white-collar workers to serve in offices and stores.

Projected trends in technology indicate that there will be greater requirements for manpower with specialized educational qualifications and a diminished demand for those qualified only for heavy physical and repetitive tasks. The expansion of the electronics, aerospace, instrument, and other science-based industries, the institutionalization of research and development, and the rapid growth of medical, educational, recreational, business, and governmental services are new forces gradually reshaping the manpower structure of the economy.

The concept of a postindustrial society has been propounded to describe the emerging stage of technological development in which possession of scientific knowledge becomes increasingly a strategic route to economic success (Bell 1968). Technological change is deliberately fostered, and knowledge workers—scientists, engineers, teachers, doctors, technicians, and other professionally trained workers—become the most rapidly growing group in the work force.

Because modern society is making an increasingly heavy investment in education, there has been a correspondingly strong interest in efforts to anticipate technological trends and their possible manpower effects. The slower pace of the past allowed a gradual adjustment to emerging developments, but in an age of rapid change, forecasts are necessary to speed up the adjustment process. Projections of future occupational requirements based on well-grounded possibilities could provide educators with a foundation for designing curricula, counseling students, and preparing teachers (Siegel 1967).

Broad technological developments can be forecast about a decade ahead and examined and assessed in a general way for their educational implications, although it should be recognized that such forecasting remains a difficult and imprecise art. New equipment, new processes, and new materials form a web of increasing complexity, with changes in one field reinforcing changes in others. How fast such changes will take place will depend on the state of the economy, the incentive to invest, the attitudes of consumers, and many other economic, social, and political forces too complex to anticipate with any certainty.

Revolution in farm production. The transformation of farming in the United States from a way of family living to a science-based, capital-intensive agribusiness has been one of the most radical changes since the mid-1930's. No one invention or discovery but advances in many fields and the widespread dissemination of new and old technology increased farm productivity fivefold between 1935 and 1968. Farm output doubled, but farm employment was reduced by nearly 75 percent. Many millions left rural areas and crowded into urban centers.

The agricultural revolution is likely to continue at a rapid pace. Greater use of specialized labor-saving machinery; controlled application of fertilizers, insecticides, weed killers, and other chemical aids; use of biological agents to eliminate pests; and adoption of discoveries in plant and animal genetics will be important means of increasing productivity. These advances stem from the combined research efforts of scientists at land-grant colleges with those at associated experimental stations, the U.S. Department of Agriculture, and large commercial processors and machinery producers.

Prospective advances depend increasingly on cooperation among specialists from different scientific disciplines. Controlled-environment facilities for starting and growing crops, for example, require teams of plant physiologists, horticulturists, and agronomists to determine the best combination of temperature and moisture for optimum plant growth (U.S. Department of Agriculture 1968). Another far-reaching development, the mechanization of fruit and vegetable harvesting, involves the collaboration of engineers who design harvesting machinery with plant breeders and geneticists who tailor plants, such as tomatoes, to withstand mechanized handling.

Technological innovation in agriculture will create problems of adjustment as well as opportunities for improving human welfare. For example, the provision of new protein-rich foods to children of poor families could reduce the incidence of learning disabilities that result from malnutrition; but a practical system of distribution must first be organized. Also, greater productivity resulting from mechanization of fruit and vegetable harvesting will involve reemployment and relocation of many thousands of displaced migratory workers whose lack of education poorly equips them for jobs in urban labor markets.

Automatic production in industry. Mechanization replaced human muscle with mechanical power and substituted the rigid precision of the machine for the varying control that the eye exerts on the craftsman's hand. Current trends replace the human monitor of these mechanical processes with a system of servomechanisms, that is, devices that direct rather than supply power and are activated by the result of the production process itself. Instruments for sensing and measuring temperature, pressure, and chemical composition—many of which come from scientific research laboratories—report on what is happening; servomechanisms alter the rate or direction of the process to bring it back to the desired path without human intervention. This type of automatic control is usually what engineers mean by automation.

Automatic control is advancing most rapidly in process industries, such as the power, petroleum refining, steel, chemical, and cement industries. Production processes, such as those in oxygen furnaces or catalytic crackers, which are too fast or too sensitive to disturbance for human control, are regulated by computer process controls. These systems rapidly and automatically perform complex computations based on vast quantities of operational data supplied by instruments and feed back the results to set the control devices automatically.

New concepts of control in metalworking are expanding the areas of production which can be automated. Numerical control of machine tools and other equipment involves electronic devices which guide tools with a minimum of operator assistance. A great advantage of numerically controlled tools is that they can be quickly changed from one small job to another, whereas earlier types of automatic production equipment were suitable only for mass production. The amount of operator time is reduced, but a worker in a new job category—parts programmer—is required to prepare the control instructions, and electronic maintenance workers are needed to service the complex circuitry.

The factory of the future will employ fewer workers in handling materials or in supervising the step-by-step operation of machinery. Conveyors will move work from one station to the next in a continuous flow. Flexible robots—programmed mechanisms which perform like human arms in the handling of objects—will replace laborers in loading and unloading parts on fast-operating machinery. An important direction in machinery design is the trend toward integration of a number of hitherto separate steps into a cycle of operations which can be done by one large machine with little, if any, human monitoring. Many jobs on the assembly line will be eliminated by machines which can assemble parts into products, especially where the parts have been redesigned to simplify machine handling. Entire departments will be controlled from remote locations, the worker using television for surveillance.

Computerization of information processing. The invention of the computer and its subsequent uses have already been ranked with the printing press, the steam engine, and the telephone as revolutionary breakthroughs in the development of technology. The computer affords an opportunity to substitute automatic machinery for human judgment in making elementary decisions in a great variety of activities. It becomes practicable to acquire, process, and store information on a scale and at a speed far beyond the possibilities of previous methods. Like mechanical energy and materials, computerized information has become an indispensable input of modern industry.

Spectacular improvements in computers since their invention in 1947 have been made as a result of the remarkable progress in the miniaturization of electronic circuitry. Each new advance, from the transistor to microelectronics and the latest large-scale integrated circuitry, has expanded by 1,000 times or more the capacity of a single computer, without increasing its physical size. By 1980 computers may have speeds of one-billionth of a second per operation and memory capacities at least ten times larger than 1970 models.

In the future it is expected that efforts will be made to use the enormous capacity of computers more efficiently by reducing steps requiring human intervention between the data and the machine. Machines for directly "reading" printing and even handwriting and devices for interpreting the human voice will eliminate the preparatory steps still done by clerks. Computer time-sharing will permit many users at different sites to communicate with a central computer concurrently, as in a telephone system.

Computers were first adopted commercially in 1951; over 60,000 computers were in use in 1970, and more than 100,000 were expected to be in use by the mid-1970's. Since the first computers were applied in the large-scale paper-work factories of insurance companies, banks, and government agencies, computers have been extended to the accounting, marketing, production, and engineering offices of most large corporations, and to hospital record rooms and large central libraries.

City officials are taking advantage of computer technology to cope with the increasingly complex problems of urban planning, law enforcement, traffic control, and school administration. A computer service industry for programming, storing, and retrieving information is being formed. Although many opportunities for applying computer technology in business and government are constantly being discovered, future progress will depend on the availability of trained managers, systems analysts, and programmers—the people who design the software necessary to operate the system.

The computer's phenomenal capability to correlate masses of data affords scientists the means to study with greater accuracy the workings of complex dynamic systems, such as the economy, an atomic reactor, or high-speed aircraft. The development of this capability, according to one eminent scientist, "is one of the most significant intellectual advances of our time" (Wiesner 1965, p. 35). This type of simulation or experimentation with a mathematical model of an actual system "makes possible engineering designs which at best could only have been achieved by laborious and costly trial and error methods and in many instances probably not successfully completed at all." Computers have been especially valuable tools to scientists engaged in research on high-energy physics, space, geophysics, crystallography, and weather control. The most far-reaching results of the computer may be the new knowledge, inventions, and industries which may stem from research that could not be undertaken by any other means.

Improvements in communications. Man's ability to overcome barriers of distance and time in transmitting and receiving information is being greatly enlarged by new inventions and refinements of existing systems. Communication engineers are striving to reproduce the sights and sounds of any event, whether a sports contest or a landing on the moon, as faithfully as possible. The result is the global village in which crises, ideas, news, and fashions are transmitted quickly from continent to continent.

"Through communication satellites, laser beams, and ultraminiaturization," according to David Sarnoff, "it will be possible by the end of the century to communicate with anyone, anywhere, at any time, by voice, sight, or written message" (1964). For many businessmen this extended system, with two-way color picture-phones, high fidelity telephones, and color facsimile transmission, could provide an electronic substitute for long-distance travel. With voice, data, and visual transmission to overseas points becoming as reliable and as rapid as domestic systems, business can operate on a global scale with greater facility and efficiency.

New electronic devices will expand the technical potential of television and radio broadcasting for family entertainment but will not necessarily improve the educational value or diversity of the presentations. Videotape recordings could provide visual playbacks of outstanding stage performances just as audiotapes can for concerts. Among other electronic innovations already technically feasible are a system of FM broadcasting that allows listeners to respond to questions posed by the broadcaster; a one-way facsimile system that provides the television viewer with a permanent record of a broadcast; and four-channel sound over FM radio.

The spread of electronic means of communication is becoming an educational force that could profoundly change the world outlook of many people. According to Kenneth E. Boulding, a leading economist, "the network of electronic communication is inevitably producing a world superculture, and the relations between this superculture and the more traditional national and regional cultures of the past remains the great question mark of the next fifty years" (Boulding 1967–1969, p. 209).

Progress in transportation. Technological advances in transportation during the 1970's will greatly facilitate worldwide travel and even extraterrestrial expeditions. Little improvement, however, is expected in reducing commuting time to work. Novel systems of urban mass transportation, such as moving belts, small automated cars, and monorails, are projected, although costly and extensive replanning of cities might be necessary.

Several new types of aircraft are scheduled to be put into service in the 1970's. The jumbo jet is expanding the industry's capacity to handle the rapidly increasing demand for overseas travel. Although the sonic boom may prevent 1,000 mile per hour flights by supersonic aircraft over the continental United States, high-speed transoceanic travel could bring remote areas in the South Pacific within six hours flying time and open up new regions to economic development and mass

tourism. Short flights between urban centers could also be speeded up by the more flexible aircraft, such as vertical takeoff and landing, vertical and short takeoff and landing, and short takeoff and landing airplanes. As air travel expands, complementary changes in size of airports and automation of air traffic control, baggage handling, and many other services are being planned.

In the competition for traffic, railroads are likely to continue to lose ground to buses, trucks, private cars, and pipelines, as well as to airlines. Railroads are increasing their productivity with improved diesel engines, automated traffic control, and computerized ticket sales, but the future of passenger train service may depend more on reorganization of its financial base. More freight trains will operate in conjunction with the more flexible trucking industry by means of piggybacking or containerized freight, which greatly reduces the need for labor to transfer heavy goods.

Water transportation is undergoing similar modernization. New ships are being automated to reduce manpower requirements; high-speed hydrofoils are operating on rivers; supertankers for oil, ore, and grain are being launched, some for use in arctic waters; and container ships which reduce longshoring manpower requirements are being put into service. Oceanographic research may eventually open up vast areas to mining and fish farming.

Advances in medical technology. New developments stemming from research and clinical practice are likely to change the number of and training for many jobs in the health field. Some changes, like the use of measles vaccine, tend to reduce the demand for scarce medical personnel, whereas new methods of disease detection and new types of patient-care facilities are likely to expand requirements. With rising standards for acceptable health care and the increasing availability of insurance, the explosive rise in the demand for medical personnel is expected to continue in the 1970's.

Electronics is being applied increasingly to diagnosis and patient monitoring. Mass physical examinations, with a score of automated laboratory tests, could be given to everyone at low cost if sufficient manpower and funds were available to institute the programs. In the clinical laboratory various types of automated devices are being introduced for routine blood and urine analyses. X-ray images can be transmitted by wire from rural hospitals to expert diagnosticians in urban centers; and total monitoring systems in the operating room and the intensive care unit measure changes in critical body functions. Technicians will be able to work more quickly and accurately, but more highly trained staffs will be required (U.S. Department of Labor 1967).

Spectacular advances in cardiac surgery, kidney and heart transplants, and the use of artificial organs place heavy responsibilities of patient choice on the medical profession. On the frontiers are the possibilities of developing techniques of genetic treatment and engineering and of finding ways to control cerebral processes and human behavior. Biomedical experimentation raises so many ethical questions that many scientists propose extensive public discussion to clarify their rights and duties.

New techniques in building and urbanism. As urban population continues to expand, there is mounting concern about the lack of adequate housing and the declining quality of city life. New methods of industrialized building and new concepts of environmental design will need to be considered to realize the national goal of decent homes for all.

Industrialized house building emphasizes prefabrication of components, such as doors and walls or complete rooms, which are fitted together at the site with a minimum of skilled labor. The mobile home is an example of a completely factory-built unit that might even be stacked for urban multifamily housing. Prefabrication saves skilled labor through greater mechanization and specialization, with carpenters and painters affected more than electricians and plumbers.

The use of conventional methods, however, is likely to persist because of building codes and consumer preferences. Construction craftsmen in the future will use more powered tools, a greater variety of plastics, and larger materials-handling equipment. The flow of work will be planned more systematically by computerized methods such as the program evaluation and review technique (PERT) and the critical path method (CPM).

Urban planners will be increasingly concerned with rebuilding the central cores of large cities. By the year 2000 half the population of the United States, according to Kahn and Wiener (1967), will be concentrated in three gigantic megalopolises: Boswash, extending from Boston to Washington; Chipitts, from Chicago to Pittsburgh; and Sansan, from San Francisco to San Diego. Some planners believe that entirely new cities must be built to accommodate the burgeoning population in a livable environment.

Expansion of the energy supply. The search for new sources and methods of producing energy continues in many directions. A growing and weathly population dependent on automobiles and home appliances and an increasingly automated industry require ever larger supplies of all forms of energy.

The use of low-cost nuclear power is expected to eventually eliminate the possibility of a power shortage caused by limited supplies of fossil fuels and water power. Since nuclear plants must be built on a large scale for economical operation, planners envisage clusters of energy-consuming activities built around giant thermonuclear plants at sites near the sea—in Texas or California, for example. These "nuplexes" would use low-cost power to desalinate seawater for drinking and irrigation, produce fertilizers, process minerals from the sea, and warm the ocean for recreation and fishing. Conceivably, nuclear power could create opportunities for the development of areas long considered barren and depressed (Revelle 1965).

Conventional and exotic nonnuclear sources are also being explored. More oil will be sought from offshore wells, arctic fields, and oil shale deposits in western states. Geothermal sites are being developed for their steam. Fuel cells, magneto-hydro-dynamic (MHD) power, and thermionic and solar energy are attractive sources of electricity because they eliminate the need for large and costly turbogenerators.

New forms of energy will also be used in factory production. While today's manufacturing is still largely based on the application of mechanical energy, workers in the future will need to know how to use electrochemical, ultrasonic, laser optical, electromagnetic, and electronic modes in metalworking. These forms provide the worker with precise control of minute quantities of intense power and afford a means of measuring to closer tolerances.

New materials. The development of new materials is an important and growing feature of technological advance. Materials engineering, which incorporates concepts of molecular engineering, is becoming a recognized specialty. Some new materials satisfy previously unmet needs or even generate new uses, expanding demand and employment. Others are essentially substitutes for existing products and therefore adversely affect long-established industries.

Synthetic materials developed by chemical engineers compete with steel, glass, leather, wood, and paper. As the flow of new man-made materials continues, competition among synthetics as well as with natural materials is likely to be more intense.

Composite materials—which are made by combining metals, ceramics, glass, and polymers into materials with unique properties—may cause far-reaching changes in engineering and construction. Their lightness, stiffness, and strength are highly useful in supersonic flight and underseas exploration. Eventually their use in building construction may eliminate heavy masonry and facilitate building along more varied and aesthetic lines (Kelly 1967).

Improving environmental quality. New directions for technological change are appearing as a result of concern about the deteriorating quality of the environment. Historically, the possibility of contamination by technological improvements was never taken into account in the push for greater output and efficiency. Today, it may be necessary to assess proposed technological changes from an ecological point of view and to estimate possible expense to the community as well as to industry in determining their full cost. These additional considerations may result in deferring some changes and slowing the pace of technological advance.

Environmental quality is being increasingly harmed by the vast amounts of waste materials of mass production and consumption which have long been dumped, with little restraint, into the earth, air, and water. Automobiles, aircraft, and factories emit fumes and gases which pollute the atmosphere. Bodies of water have been seriously contaminated not only by sewage and oil spills but also by pesticides, detergents, and fertilizers and the heat generated by power plants. Discarded cans, bottles, and cars litter the highways and the countryside.

With greater expectations about standards of living, there has been growing interest in conservation efforts that feature changes in technology. For example, the development of practical electric, gas turbine, and steam-powered automo-

biles would result in a reduction of pollutants from gasoline combustion engines. Smokeless atomic power plants and methods of recycling solid wastes promise improved environmental conditions. More funds are being channeled into research on simpler and more effective techniques of contraception. In the long run, learning to live as if the earth were a spaceship with limited resources of space, air, water, and land will become an essential part of everyone's education.

Implications for education. Greater productivity as a result of technological progress could provide opportunities for enlarging the resources allocated to schools—subject to competition with research, defense, and other sectors of the economy —for their share of the nation's greater output. It could also afford a larger percent of the population the opportunity to remain out of the labor force to pursue studies for avocational and vocational purposes. The most profound effects on education will come from changes in occupational requirements which will necessitate constant reassessment of the ways people are being prepared for work.

Projections of the occupational structure of the 1980 U.S. labor force indicate that the most rapid growth will be among white-collar occupations. Table 1 depicts changes among major groups. Professional and technical workers are expected to be the fastest-growing occupational group. Clerical and service workers are also expected to increase rapidly. Sales workers and managers are projected to increase but at slower rates. Blue-collar jobs, as a group, will also increase at a slower rate. Nonfarm laborers will decline, along with farm workers. Although the fastest-growing groups are those employing people with the highest educational levels, modern technology will continue to depend on the vast majority of people with average education and abilities to do routine jobs in industry, the trades, and services (U.S. Department of Labor 1970b).

There is considerable evidence that technological advances in the foreseeable future will involve industrial job changes along the following lines: continued reduction in the number of manual material-handling laborers; relatively fewer machine operators performing repetitive manual tasks; more machine and instrument monitors with functions demanding a sense of responsibility, alertness, and ability to understand the whole production process; more maintenance workers

Table 1. Employment by major occupational group
(in thousands)

OCCUPATIONAL GROUP	1968 EMPLOYMENT		PROJECTED 1980 REQUIREMENTS		CHANGE 1968–1980	
	Number	Percent	Number	Percent	Number	Percent
White-collar workers	35,551	46.8	48,300	50.8	12,749	35.9
Professional and technical	10,325	13.6	15,500	16.3	5,175	50.1
Managers, officials, and proprietors	7,776	10.2	9,500	10.0	1,724	22.2
Clerical workers	12,803	16.9	17,300	18.2	4,497	35.1
Sales workers	4,647	6.1	6,000	6.3	1,353	29.1
Blue-collar workers	27,525	36.3	31,100	32.7	3,575	13.0
Craftsmen and foremen	10,015	13.2	12,200	12.8	2,185	21.8
Operatives	13,955	18.4	15,400	16.2	1,445	10.4
Nonfarm laborers	3,555	4.7	3,500	3.7	−55	−1.5
Service workers	9,381	12.4	13,100	13.8	3,719	39.6
Farm workers	3,464	4.6	2,600	2.7	−864	−33.2
Total	75,920	100.0	95,100	100.0	19,180	25.0

Source: U.S. Department of Labor 1970b.

with skill to quickly diagnose breakdowns in complex electronic equipment; and more technical workers with a grasp of mathematics, science, systems analysis, and programming. There will be less stress on manual dexterity and traditional know-how and more on knowledge, precision, and perceptual aptitudes. The broad-gauged specialist will be in demand. All jobs will probably be subject to more frequent changes as the pace of technological change continues to be rapid. The average worker, therefore, will need to be retrained for several different, but probably related, jobs during his working life.

The trend in manpower requirements suggests a need for improvements at all levels of the educational system. Obviously, functional illiteracy is a crushing handicap in finding work in a technological society. Greater efficiency in teaching basic reading, writing, and arithmetic skills, therefore, becomes a prime goal of school systems. According to a noted educator, "we must educate for a person happily versatile, receptive to and comfortable with change. This calls for increased emphasis on cultivated general intelligence, abstraction, and basic academic skills, as opposed to performance skills" (Rogers 1965, p. 331).

Basic knowledge and skills in mathematics, science, language, and social studies, acquired in a general high school, are increasingly regarded as essential, even for those who do not plan to go to college. Such skills are usable in the great variety of situations the individual encounters in his role as an employee, citizen, or consumer in an era of rapid change, widespread affluence, and worldwide travel and communication. For most students, vocational training would be deferred until after high school; for others, some combination of general and vocational education is considered essential for greater adaptability.

The establishment of a nationwide system of free public education through two years of post-secondary school was recommended by the National Commission on Technology, Automation, and Economic Progress (1966) as a means of facilitating adjustment to change. Training in trade, technical, and business occupations at the skilled-worker level would be provided at area vocational-technical schools. Community colleges would provide liberal education as well as technical and paraprofessional training. Such schools train computer programmers; medical, instrumentation, and electronic technicians; and other types of subprofessionals who will be increasingly required to supplement the limited supply of doctors, engineers, and scientists.

Meeting the rising long-term demand for scientific and technical manpower involves complex problems of finding resources to finance university growth; at the same time, efforts to ensure opportunities for all qualified applicants, regardless of income, must be pursued. New interdisciplinary fields, such as urban engineering, geochemistry, and bionics, are being recognized, and training in computer technology is being incorporated into preparation for virtually all technical fields. Some universities are trying to avoid training an oversupply of specialists by concentrating on teaching fundamentals of science, rather than on training students in engineering practices likely to become obsolete. Finally, educators advocate humanistic and social studies for engineers so that they as prime agents of change will be able to appreciate more fully the interaction between human values and attitudes and the progress of technology (Soderberg 1967).

The prospect of multiple careers for individuals as the pace of technological change quickens is already creating interest in providing opportunities for continuing education throughout the worker's lifetime. The principle is recognized in cases of technological change, in which employers provide on-the-job or formal retraining as part of the total cost of the change. Some employers also sponsor formal educational programs to assist their employees to keep abreast of technical advances and to upgrade their skills. The introduction of the metric system in American industry, for example, may require the reeducation of millions of employees. A few unions try to ensure the employability of their members by maintaining extensive training programs on the latest technology—for example, the International Typographical Union's school for training typesetters on the latest electronic equipment. The federal government, under the Manpower Development and Training Act of 1962, assists unemployed workers to retrain themselves for available jobs. The availability of learning opportunities at any age could, over the long run, finally diminish resistance to change and hasten the diffusion of new technology with a minimum of hardship.

BIBLIOGRAPHY

AYRES, ROBERT U. 1969 *Technological Forecasting and Long Range Planning*. New York, McGraw-Hill.

BELL, DANIEL 1968 "The Measurement of Knowledge and Technology." Eleanor H. Sheldon and Wilbert E. Moore, eds., *Indicators of Social Change*. New York, Russell Sage Foundation. Pages 145–246.

BOULDING, KENNETH E. 1967–1969 "Expecting the Unexpected." Edgar L. Morphet and Charles O. Ryan, eds., *Prospective Changes in Society by 1980: Designing Education for the Future*. New York, Citation Press. Pages 199–213.

CALDER, NIGEL, ed. 1965 *The World in 1984*. 2 vols. Baltimore, Penguin.

CHASE, STUART 1969 *The Most Probable World*. Baltimore, Penguin.

DRUCKER, PETER F. 1969 *Age of Discontinuity: Guidelines to Our Changing Society*. New York, Harper.

"Education and Automation—The Coming World of Work and Leisure" 1964 National Association of Secondary-School Principals, *Bulletin*, 48, no. 295:entire issue.

EWALD, WILLIAM R., JR., ed. 1968 *Environment and Change: The Next Fifty Years*. Bloomington, Indiana University Press.

FIELD, ROGER K. 1969 "Tomorrow's Communications Start With Today's Designs." *Electronics*, 42, no. 24:73–103.

FORBES, ROBERT J. 1968 *Conquest of Nature: Technology and Its Consequences*. New York, Praeger.

FOREIGN POLICY ASSOCIATION, eds. 1968 *Toward the Year 2018*. New York, Cowles Education Corporation.

GINZBERG, ELI, ed. 1964 *Technology and Social Change*. New York, Columbia University Press.

GREENBERGER, MARTIN, ed. 1962 *Computers and the World of the Future*. Cambridge, Mass., MIT Press.

GUNN, JAMES E., ed. 1966 *Man and the Future*. Lawrence, University Press of Kansas.

"Information" 1966 *Scientific American*, 215, no. 3:entire issue.

KAHN, HERMAN, AND ANTHONY J. WIENER 1967 *The Year 2000*. New York, Macmillan.

KELLY, ANTHONY 1967 "The Nature of Composite Materials." *Scientific American*, 217, no. 3:160–176.

KRANZBERG, MELVIN, AND CARROLL W. PURSELL, JR., eds. 1967 *Technology in Western Civilization*. Vol. 2: *Technology in the Twentieth Century*. New York, Oxford University Press.

"Materials" 1967 *Scientific American*, 217, no. 3:entire issue.

MORPHET, EDGAR L., AND CHARLES O. RYAN, eds. 1967–1969 *Prospective Changes in Society by 1980: Designing Education for the Future*. New York, Citation Press.

MUELLER, EVA, et al. 1969 *Technological Advance in an Expanding Economy: Its Impact on a Cross Section of the Labor Force*. Ann Arbor, Survey Research Center, Institute for Social Research, University of Michigan.

NATIONAL ACADEMY OF SCIENCES 1967 *Applied Science and Technological Progress*. A Report to the Committee on Science and Astronautics, U.S. House of Representatives. Washington, D.C., Government Printing Office.

NATIONAL COMMISSION ON TECHNOLOGY, AUTOMATION, AND ECONOMIC PROGRESS 1966 *Technology and the American Economy*. 6 vols. Washington, D.C., Government Printing Office.

ORGANIZATION FOR ECONOMIC COOPERATION AND DEVELOPMENT 1965 *Requirements of Automated Jobs*. Final Report and Supplement, North American Joint Conference, Washington, D.C., December 8–10, 1964. International Seminars 1963–1964. Paris, The Organization.

PREHODA, ROBERT W. 1967 *Designing the Future: The Role of Technological Forecasting*. Philadelphia, Chilton.

REVELLE, ROGER 1965 "A Long View From the Beach." Nigel Calder, ed., *The World in 1984*. Vol. 1. Baltimore, Penguin. Pages 106–114.

ROGERS, VIRGIL M. 1965 "Implications of Automation for Education." Organization for Economic Cooperation and Development, *Requirements of Automated Jobs*. Final Report and Supplement, North American Joint Conference, Washington, D.C., December 8–10, 1964. International Seminars 1963–1964. Paris, The Organization. Pages 329–337.

SARNOFF, DAVID 1964 "By the End of the Twentieth Century." *Fortune*, 69, no. 5:116–119.

SCOTT, ELLIS L., AND ROGER W. BOLZ, eds. 1969 *Automation and Society*. Athens, Ga., Center for the Study of Automation and Society.

SIEGEL, IRVING H., ed. 1967 *Manpower Tomorrow: Prospects and Priorities.* New York, Augustus M. Kelley.

SIMON, HERBERT 1965 *The Shape of Automation for Men and Management.* New York, Harper.

SODERBERG, C. RICHARD 1967 "A Note on Engineering Education." National Academy of Sciences, *Applied Science and Technological Progress.* A Report to the Committee on Science and Astronautics, U.S. House of Representatives. Washington, D.C., Government Printing Office. Pages 399–413.

SPORN, PHILIP 1963 *Energy: Its Production, Conversion and Use in the Service of Man.* New York, Pergamon.

STEIBER, JACK, ed. 1966 *Employment Problems of Automation and Advanced Technology: An International Perspective.* New York, St. Martin's.

"The Biosphere" 1970 *Scientific American,* 223, no. 3: entire issue.

U.S. DEPARTMENT OF AGRICULTURE 1968 *Science for Better Living: Yearbook of Agriculture.* Washington, D.C., Government Printing Office.

U.S. DEPARTMENT OF LABOR 1966 *Technological Trends in Major American Industries.* Bureau of Labor Statistics Bulletin No. 1474. Washington, D.C., Government Printing Office.

U.S. DEPARTMENT OF LABOR 1967 *Technology and Manpower in the Health Service Industry, 1965–75.* Manpower Administration Research Bulletin No. 14. Washington, D.C., Government Printing Office.

U.S. DEPARTMENT OF LABOR 1970a *Outlook for Computer Process Control.* Bureau of Labor Statistics Bulletin No. 1658. Washington, D.C., Government Printing Office.

U.S. DEPARTMENT OF LABOR 1970b *The U.S. Economy in 1980: A Summary of BLS Projections.* Bureau of Labor Statistics Bulletin No. 1673. Washington, D.C., Government Printing Office.

VEBLEN, THORSTEIN (1914) 1964 *The Instinct of Workmanship, and the State of the Industrial Arts.* New York, Norton.

WALKER, CHARLES R., ed. 1968 *Technology, Industry and Man: The Age of Acceleration.* New York, McGraw-Hill.

WIESNER, JEROME B. 1965 *Where Science and Politics Meet.* New York, McGraw-Hill.

EDGAR WEINBERG

TECHNOLOGY IN EDUCATION

The technology of education can be defined as the purposeful utilization, in combination or separately, of objects, techniques, devices, events, and relationships to increase the effectiveness of the educational process. The technology of education has value only to the extent that it actively assists learners in obtaining knowledge and skills. Educational technology is fundamentally aimed at improving the efficiency of educational systems by increasing the rate, depth, precision, and value of the learning which takes place. In a general way, technology has been employed in all educational systems and is not to be confused with mechanical devices.

Within the context of society, educational technology must consider which combinations from the immense accumulation of skills and knowledge should be learned by the new generations to prepare them for adult participation. The process of selection raises the question of criteria. What are the best guidelines and principles to use in selecting content, learning methods, and equipment?

Beyond selection, there is the problem of allocating and arranging subject matter, methods, and equipment. A specific problem arises as to the relevance of materials and methods to the immediate and long-range needs, interests, and values of the learners.

Equipment. In equipment design, priority should be given to ensuring that learners participate in a learning environment which is as compatible as possible with the way human beings learn. Equipment should be designed to adapt to the requirements of the learner and to fit into the learning process of the classroom. As things now stand, most equipment does not meet these specifications. Learning materials still must be fitted to existing equipment not specifically designed to increase the efficiency of learning.

Whether any particular device is functionally more efficient than any other will depend primarily upon whether the device is compatible with the dynamics of the learning process, the prior experience of the learner with the body of materials to be presented, and the learner's physical, attitudinal, and motivational preconditioning for use of hardware, software, and the particular response modes of the equipment.

In this connection, then, a piece of hardware or software placed in an educational context may have a lower functional efficiency as a learning tool than the teacher-textbook-lecture-examination pattern. The test of the value of a new technique for education is not whether learning occurs. Learning is always occurring. The test is whether the new technique improves the learning rate and depth of understanding as compared with existing approaches.

Computer-based methods have come increasingly into the technology of education through computer-assisted instruction. Computerized storage and retrieval of defense and medical information are commonplace, and these methods could be readily adapted for curriculum planning, but little has been done in this area.

Educational technology is still largely a classroom supplement. Teachers now have access to film projectors, filmstrips, slide projectors, and tape recorders and can tune in on educational television hookups for special broadcasts. There is also a good deal of programmed instructional material available. Teaching machines may ultimately prove more effective in a specific learning situation than texts or printed programs, since they offer greater control over the contingencies involved in learning. Systems for learning language which employ programmed texts and recording-playback devices are not uncommon at the college level and have been used in some high schools. More exotic devices incorporating computer storage, a typewriter response mode, film presentation, and an audio-input and record system have received attention. The programmed text and teaching machine, the language laboratory, the responsive environment, and computer-assisted instruction are all largely focused on individual instruction. The classroom in which such devices are used becomes a number of discrete capsules in which individual learners interact with machines or programmed texts. Although the individualized learning capsule simplifies the programming problem considerably, it also excises perhaps the major source of classroom motivation to respond—namely, obtaining, maintaining, and improving one's status position within the classroom as a society. Motivation springing from group participation is absent in the capsulized classroom. When the classroom is carefully structured as a society in which the individual learner is rewarded for participation, motivation is simplified.

The teacher normally supplements his verbal output with such materials as textbooks, blackboards, maps, panels, posters, feltboards, and slide and overhead projectors. Essentially these devices are limited to the presentation of immobile two-dimensional forms. The two-dimensional surface provides a convenience for illustrating relatively simple static, spatial, and temporal relationships.

The printed word, on the blackboard or in a text, is still the most powerful and persuasive device available for conveying information. Textbooks, however, lack certain crucial learning ingredients. They are limited by the scope of the text, the vocabulary of the learner, the level of learner involvement, the lack of a feedback system, the incompatibility with an active response requirement, and the lack of a means for evalu-

ation of performance. Textbooks are economical and efficient informational devices but are not organized to ensure a learning product. The programmed text is designed to supply the learning ingredients missing from the conventional textbook. Software programs have not yet distinguished themselves by their quality, but their fundamental advantages over conventional textbooks should make them increasingly acceptable.

The printed word will be both pervasive and prepotent in whatever form the new technology takes. Textbooks will always remain a major force in any educational technology because of their portability, low cost, and ready availability, but other types of meaning carriers will also find use in well-articulated learning systems.

Dynamic two-dimensional devices. Films, television, filmstrips, and sequences of slides have value for indicating mobile three-dimensional relationships in a two-dimensional space. The use of closed-circuit television for instruction in surgery is one particularly dramatic use of such dynamic images. However, films and television are not usually educationally productive, since they lack provisions for learner response and their presentation sequences are often dictated by entertainment rather than learning considerations; none of these devices provides a method of recording responses, a related feedback system, or a method of evaluating learning.

The use of such dynamic two-dimensional devices is generally based on the unsupportable assumption that education takes place in an atmosphere of passive viewing or listening. Most educational films do not require the learner to make responses, the prime prerequisite for any system of learning. Learning is an active process in which the learner expends energy to achieve a higher level of performance; learning can be said to have occurred only when goals can be reached more often, more quickly, and with less energy than before.

Audio systems. The long-standing tradition of voice delivery by a teacher accounts in some part for the current popularity of various mechanical-electronic voice-reproducing devices in the classroom. Phonograph reproduction is little used in education except to reproduce music because of the technical complexities and costs involved in making recordings for classroom instruction. Reel-tape and cassette recorders, however, are useful to the teacher for reducing the drudgery involved in repeating a presentation to a succession of classes. These devices have become rather common in language learning, since they permit learners to perform language exercises individually. Used for this purpose, audiotapes promote increased learner response and provide both feedback and self-evaluation. However, when tapes are used in lieu of live lecturers, they minimize exchange between learners and lecturer, reducing social interaction, feedback, and evaluation.

The teaching machine. The teaching machine is a two-dimensional device, with or without an audio component, which controls the input of information to the learner and sharply defines the responses required. It provides some means by which the learner can compare his response with a desired response. As program carriers, teaching machines have a number of advantages over programmed texts. Machines can control the amount of information presented to the learner at any one time, focusing the learner's attention and limiting confusion. Also, they prevent the learner from looking ahead for the required response rather than thinking his way through to it. In addition, teaching machines may be linked to computers to permit ongoing evaluation and to adjust the program to the learner's level of performance.

There are, however, several barriers to the use of machines in the classroom. First, there is some apprehension in the teaching profession that teaching machines will produce unemployment, since several educational technologists initially suggested that the machines would permit learners to function more effectively in the absence of teachers than in their presence. Second, a teaching machine is no more effective than the programs it carries, and there have been many programs of dubious quality. Third, the process of creating machine programs is expensive, and they are available for only a small portion of the curriculum. Until an adequate reservoir of proved programs for teaching machines becomes available, teaching machines will be largely utilized in such specialized areas as home study, in the military, and in industry, where limited programs can be employed profitably.

Teaching machines have been successfully used in instructional programs. The use of machines in combination with teachers represents a middle ground in educational technology between the conventional classroom and more sophisticated systems. It seems reasonable to expect that, as cost per student declines, proved machine programs become available, and teachers come to consider instructional machines as supportive rather than threatening, teaching machines will emerge as common learning tools in the typical classroom.

Three-dimensional devices. Where the learning task involves terminology, relationships, and functions of a complex and important object, three-dimensional constructions have several advantages. A static three-dimensional device may be a simple mock-up representing an object itself, such as an enlarged plastic replica of a flower or an engine, cut out and mapped to indicate names along with morphological structures and functions.

Dynamic three-dimensional devices are sometimes necessary to demonstrate such interactions and relationships as the flow of blood through the body, piston action and fuel flow in an engine, and changes in cloud structure and related weather. Three-dimensional devices are most useful when they can be assembled and disassembled. If the learner can piece together the object—for example, by assembling a circuit, constructing a specimen plant, or assembling a plastic skeleton —the effectiveness of the device is increased. Since such devices are usually expensive and difficult to produce, they should be employed primarily to teach vital materials at the core of the curriculum.

The three-dimensional operational response. Much daily modern performance involves the development of operational skills, such as driving, flying a plane, typing, and using a slide rule. Techniques for drafting a blueprint, operating a lathe, and drawing or painting involve combinations of operational sequences. Skills in manipulating equipment in such areas as chemistry, physics, botany, zoology, medicine, and dentistry are largely operational also. When the learning task involves ordering learner responses into a required sequence of activity, the task is operational. A Link trainer, for example, is an operational ground trainer in which the student pilot attempts to "fly" by manipulating controls based on instrument readings, airway maps, voice procedures, radio and radar reflection, and light blinkers. The pilot performs action sequences in response to signals, many of which occur concurrently. He must continually select, interpret, and reject information correctly to reach his goal. The trainer ensures that ground performance is preparation for responding to predictable combinations of signals which occur in the air. The three-dimensional operational concept has now been successfully adapted to driver training courses in many high schools.

Selection. The selection of a device to facilitate learning involves three steps: First, the definition of the learning task; second, the identification and isolation of the learning objective; and third, the selection of the learning materials, devices, and evaluation techniques necessary to ensure achievement of the learning objective.

Learning tasks may occur at one or more of the following seven levels:

(1) terminology—dates, names, and classifications;

(2) mapping spatial locations in two and three dimensions, temporal relationships, and morphology;

(3) operational tasks—responses to simple signals and readings in absolutely defined sequence;

(4) functional system relationships—dynamic interactions and processes which result in complex patterns;

(5) functional-operational relationships—complex tasks which involve an analysis of complex interactions;

(6) abstractions and generalizations—tasks involving organizing complex situations into simple expressions, applying criteria to complex data to provide a basis for increased precision in making decisions, and reducing complex data to statistical or symbolic form;

(7) theory and assumptions—tasks at the highest level of conceptual functioning, in which hypotheses are developed from theory and tested and the results are then analyzed to improve theory.

In the development of driving skills, for example, the learning task occurs at levels 1, 2, and 3. At level 1 the learner must master terms such as *brake, steering wheel, hood,* and *headlights* and must learn to interpret road signs and street signs. At the next two levels the learner must deal with relationships such as safe driving as related to locations of crosswalks, fire hydrants, and parking distances, safe distance and speed as related to weather conditions, and so on. At level 3 the learner must master sequences like that required to ignite the engine.

For any learning task, levels 1 and 2 require some device which permits the presentation of both language and key spatial relationships. Both levels could be satisfied by means of a two-dimensional surface suited to the presentation of materials in printed form; a chalkboard combined with a lecture by a teacher and a text would satisfy the requirements for both levels. However, a programmed text or teaching machine which would satisfy both levels fully while ensuring a high rate of student response, feedback, and ongoing performance evaluation could be used more effectively. Level 3 demands a learning device which helps to develop psychomotor skills, such as those involved in shifting gears, using brakes, and safely adapting the movement of a car to road conditions.

Learning at level 4 would involve such functional relations as consequences for engine heat as related to friction, water volume and water flow, lubrication, type of fuel, engine speed, type of alloys and metals used, and so on. Such interactional effects cumulating among functional components are central to level 4. Level 5 would relate the functional interactions of level 4 to the method of operation. The effect of high or low speed operation on the incidence of malfunction between functional components would be learned at level 5.

The development of conceptual skills at levels 6 and 7 would be required where the learning objectives demand a knowledge of the principles and laws of physics (including hydraulics, gases, inertia factors, properties of metals and other materials, and so on). Level 7 would be used where such laws and principles were utilized at a research or developmental level. Learning at these higher levels is still accomplished through textbooks, journal articles, communication between the lecturer and student, and, of course, life experiences.

Learner response. A vital function of any technical device or method of education is to ensure a high rate of appropriate responses, or positive affect shifts, at appropriate times to develop the desired skills. A corollary to this point is that (all other things being equal) the greater the affective investment by the learner in producing his response, the greater his gratification when the response succeeds. A piece of educational equipment or a procedure designed to involve the learner in completing an equation, a map, or an anatomical drawing is therefore more effective than one which merely requires him to press a button to indicate which one of several preselected options is most acceptable. The very energy invested for a meaningful completion is an important consideration in the perceived gratification of success or the felt frustration of failure. The feedback to the learner response should be meaningful and related to the problem or item presented. Buzzers, lights, and other signals, although useful, fail to supply the learner with either the correct response or methods of overcoming error. Similarly, a test with scores marked wrong or right and with no other information to the learner similarly fails to provide either the correct responses or the methods of achieving them.

The educational technologist who organizes learning systems is primarily concerned with maintaining the learning value of adequate responses by ensuring that the learner sees his success as an achievement. This perception arises not only from the learning materials, which may or may not be viewed as important to the learner per se, but even more from the learner's personal values, interests, and needs and from the degree to which these are involved in the total learning context. An effective educational system is one through which, regardless of his learning history and the learning goals with which he began, the learner develops the skills required and is motivated to the learning system's objectives. A high frequency of response has been shown repeatedly to be insufficient to improve learning performance when the learner does not know the results of his efforts. On the other hand, when the learner makes a high level of response investment within a well-sequenced learning system which provides meaningful feedback, response frequency largely determines the rate at which learning takes place. Thus, high rates of response are trivial or even counterproductive in the absence of other key factors in learning, but when these factors are present, a high response rate increases the efficiency of the learning system.

Criteria of evaluation. Once a system has been designed and put into operation, it is evaluated both as a whole and as a set of components. The primary evaluation concerns the degree to which the system contributes to the achievement of its own learning objectives. This evaluation may be performed in absolute terms. Suppose, for

example, that the objectives are to develop a ninth-grade reading level, a command of pre-algebraic arithmetic, an ability to plan and present a project, and a given level of written communication skills. Measuring devices can be constructed to determine, by directly evaluating performance, the degree to which these objectives have been attained. A representative sample of students can be selected and their scores analyzed in terms of the system objectives.

In addition, measures can be taken of such key subcomponents as error rate, learner reactions to meaningfulness and relevance, and the mean and variance of the response rate. Once all the information has been collected, weaknesses of the learning system can be revealed. Decisions can then be made concerning system modification. Such decisions might result in changes in system objectives and could provoke modifications in various system relationships.

In addition to evaluations within a single system, a cross-system evaluation should be made to compare the relative effectiveness of different systems designed to obtain similar objectives.

Finally, we must evaluate a system's product. A college system for training engineers should evaluate graduates to determine whether they possess the necessary engineering skills to perform effectively on the job, adapt flexibly to differing job conditions, maintain sufficient task involvement to meet job output goals, are socially effective with subordinates, peers, and supervisors, and possess sufficient language skills to precisely interpret what is required and to communicate their own plans and requirements effectively.

Suitable instruments to measure the product of learning systems must be provided when the system produces graduates. These data, reflecting postsystem performance and adaptation, could then be combined with the within-system information to provide criteria for modifications as well as new system objectives. In a complex, evolving society, educational technology must also evolve to conform to and support changes in the technology of the society as a whole.

Relevance. The basic function of educational technology is to maintain relevance in the educational process; technologists have made progress in this direction. It is possible, for example, to organize a learning environment (the classroom, school, or job development center) as a miniature social system which produces the responses required in the postscholastic environment. We may design the learning system in such a way that learners must interact socially in order to achieve preestablished learning goals (as, for example, in the Lincoln, Neb., Job Corps). A life-simulator classroom system has been experimentally developed for preschool children at the Micro-Social Learning Center in Vineland, N.J. These life-simulators or microsocial learning systems may be organized so as to tie role and status in the classroom learning society to levels of mastery. Mastery at a high level entitles the learner to a high status role with increased responsibility for the learning of others, including evaluation of their progress.

Educational technologists have modified the design of the learning space to permit learners to progress through a carefully structured series of positions as they develop prespecified output skills. As learners move from position to position, their responsibilities and functions expand; they can perceive that increasing responsibility, opportunity, and freedom are tightly linked to level of attainment. The teacher and aides make sure that the flow of the learning system is smooth and that learners always have sufficient information to function effectively at their positions in the system.

Efficiency. The major problem facing educational technology is that of developing methods of fairly evaluating the variety of educational approaches. For example, it might be important to decide if the new math is superior or inferior to other methods of teaching mathematics at the same level. For the same content, the question may be whether programmed instruction in a textbook is superior to conventional teaching or superior to the same course presented by computer-assisted instruction.

The following six criteria have been selected to illustrate one means of evaluating the effectiveness of different systems: (1) the number of learners in a learning group of mean size; (2) the mean learner gain on a standard test such as the Scholastic Aptitude Test, the Metropolitan Achievement Test, or the Wechsler Intelligence Scale for Children; (3) the time in units of 100 hours of method use; (4) the cost of the learning system (excluding innovative or experimental costs) over a fixed time period; (5) the gain per 100 hours of time applied per student; and (6) the proportion of learners who attained the objective of the learning system. (The approach, of course, would vary with different evaluation problems.)

The system of evaluation should measure the degree to which the method assists learners. It should include time required, objective test scores, costs, and the degree to which students are aided in attaining their life goals. In addition, the analyses should be designed to permit comparisons between alternative methods and offer evidence as to how the system could be improved.

Ideal system. It is possible to conceptualize an ideal educational system in which the classroom performance has learning objectives relevant to students' lives. The learners would have a high rate of response, since they would interact with each other to transmit information, to provide feedback, and to develop social skills. The hardware-software mix of the classroom would be developed specifically to ensure the fulfillment of program objectives. The teacher in this environment would plan and coordinate all phases of learner activity to ensure learner progress and mastery. Teaching machines might be employed to reduce costs and provide support for the teacher. More sophisticated methods involving the use of computers might be used to provide added flexibility, ongoing evaluation of learner performance, and greater adaptability to individual differences.

A strategy must be developed to correct the learner's initial weaknesses and to move him through the learning sequence at an efficient rate. Hardware and software teaching methods and the classroom ecology as a whole must be modified to achieve optimum depth, extent, and precision of learning at all stages of the learning system. On completion of each substage, the learner should have established all skills required for entry into the next level.

Analysis of entry skills required at succeeding levels will determine the skills required upon completion of any particular stage in the learning system. Thus, nursery school learning requirements will be dictated by kindergarten entry requirements. High school learning objectives are determined by college performance or job-training requirements. College performance objectives in turn are dictated by requirements in the various fields in which graduates must participate.

No arrangements of methods, materials, and techniques should be regarded as a fixed learning system. Learner reactions to the learning system are vital and should be obtained routinely as part of the system evaluation. Both major and minor system objectives should be evaluated to determine the level of learner involvement. Extensive learner criticisms should be used as signals for reexamination of the materials to determine if they are obsolete or if the problem is merely one of emphasis or method of presentation.

The central problem is to devise an educational system which is organic to our own epoch. Modern U.S. society requires that each individual be equipped with immensely greater personal resources and capabilities than ever before. An effective technology of education is a necessity if the young are to be prepared adequately for the flux of adult experience. Technology is not to be confused with equipment; equipment in itself offers no panacea. Any given piece of equipment must be selected or rejected on the basis of its contribution to readying the learner for effective adult life performance. The problem is, in short, a total systems problem.

To fully justify itself, a new educational technology must solve problems which have resisted the conventional system. In short, a technology of education justifies itself only to the extent that it provides an evolving education for an evolving society. Its power is demonstrated by the extent to which it contributes to overcoming pauperized learning histories, emotional disturbance, and physical and intellectual handicaps.

BIBLIOGRAPHY

ANDERSON, RICHARD C. 1967 "Educational Psychology." *Annual Review of Psychology*, 18:129–164.

AUSUBEL, DAVID P. 1963 *The Psychology of Meaningful Verbal Learning*. New York, Grune.

BRUNER, JEROME S., JACQUELINE J. GOODNOW, AND GEORGE A. AUSTIN 1967 *A Study of Thinking*. New York, Science Editions.

DEESE, JAMES, AND STEWART H. HULSE 1967 *The Psychology of Learning*. 3rd ed. New York, McGraw-Hill.

ESTES, WILLIAM K. 1960 "Learning." Chester W. Harris, ed., *Encyclopedia of Educational Research*. 3rd ed. New York, Macmillan. Pages 752–768.

GAGNÉ, ROBERT M. 1965 *The Conditions of Learning*. New York, Holt.

GLASER, ROBERT 1964 "Implications of Training Research for Education." *Theories of Learning and Instruction*. Sixty-third Yearbook of the National Society for the Study of Education, Part 1. University of Chicago Press. Pages 153–181.

GLASER, ROBERT 1966 "The Design of Instruction." *The Changing American School*. Sixty-fifth Yearbook of the National Society for the Study of Education, Part 2. University of Chicago Press. Pages 215–242.

GOLDIAMOND, ISRAEL 1966 "Perception, Language, and Conceptualization Rules." Benjamin Kleinmuntz, ed., *Problem Solving: Research, Method and Theory*. New York, Wiley. Pages 183–224.

HILGARD, ERNEST R., AND GORDON H. BOWER 1966 *Theories of Learning*. 3rd ed. New York, Appleton.

HULL, CLARK L. 1943 *Principles of Behavior: An Introduction to Behavior Theory*. New York, Appleton.

KELLER, FRED S., AND WILLIAM N. SCHOENFELD 1950 *Principles of Psychology*. New York, Appleton.

MELTON, ARTHUR W. 1941 "Learning." Walter S. Monroe, ed., *Encyclopedia of Educational Research*. 1st ed. New York, Macmillan. Pages 668–690.

MILLER, ROBERT B. 1962 "Analysis and Specification of Behavior for Training." Robert Glaser, ed., *Training Research and Education*. University of Pittsburgh Press.

OSGOOD, CHARLES E., et al. 1957 *The Measurement of Meaning*. Urbana, University of Illinois Press.

ROTHKOPF, ERNST Z. 1965 "Some Theoretical and Experimental Approaches to Problems in Written Instruction." John D. Krumboltz, ed., *Learning and the Educational Process*. Chicago, Rand McNally. Pages 193–221.

SKINNER, B. F. 1938 *The Behavior of Organisms: An Experimental Analysis*. New York, Appleton.

THORNDIKE, EDWARD L. 1914 *Educational Psychology*. Vol. 2: *The Psychology of Learning*. New York, Teachers College Press.

WOOLMAN, MYRON 1965–1966 "Cultural Asynchrony and Contingency in Learning Disorders." Jerome Hellmuth, ed., *Learning Disorders*. Vol. 1. Seattle, Wash., Special Child Publications of the Seattle Seguin School, Inc. Pages 123–169.

MYRON WOOLMAN

TELEVISION, INSTRUCTIONAL

The term "instructional television" refers to the use of the television medium in any of its various technical forms to present information, ideas, and experiences in any subject area and at any level as some portion of an organized educational program. The methods and practices of instructional television are rapidly evolving in the wake of changing educational philosophies and newly developing communications alternatives.

Uses. The uses of instructional television in an organized educational program are varied but have been described in the following categories: total teaching, supplementary, enrichment, and remedial. If television is used for total teaching, all major content and basic concepts are presented by television. In supplementary use, television programs present material carefully correlated with the principal course material but not otherwise ordinarily provided. For enrichment, television is used to present material considered desirable in subject areas other than the principal course of study. In its remedial aspect, television is used to present materials for makeup work or concentrated emphasis in narrow subject areas.

Television has been used most often in a supplementary fashion, followed in order by enrichment and remedial uses. Initially television was seldom considered or used as a total teaching means. This situation is changing.

Experience has indicated that instructional television is most effectively used as an integral part of the overall educational program. Depending upon how extensively television is used, it may affect the full range of educational concerns, such as staffing, curriculum, administration, budgeting, and space allocation. It has proven wise to start modestly with a broad range of applications. As is the case with many other instructional tools, the administrators, curriculum specialists, and teachers who are expected to work with instructional television must first be given the opportunity to understand it.

Extensive studies have been made regarding the conditions and effects of the use of instructional television. In general, studies about the instructional use of television have focused a great deal of attention on the teaching and learning process and have revealed how relatively little is known about learning. Approximately 20 years of investigations have shown that generally students taught by television do as well as or better than students taught by conventional means (Kumata 1956; Carpenter & Greenhill 1958; Reid & MacLennan 1967). Instructional television has been successfully used to teach almost any subject at any grade level. Instructional television has proven to be more effective when classroom activities are related to the television presentations. Such factors as television screen size, color, and the size of the viewing group (all viewers must have an adequate view of the screen) have yet to be positively correlated with the effectiveness of instructional television in teaching and learning. A constructive attitude on the part of teachers, administrators, parents, and students is essential to the effectiveness of instructional television.

Instructional television is used over a period of time to provide the teacher and student with materials related in some fashion to an organized educational program. These materials are most often in the form of lessons and are related to each other in a lesson-series. Instructional television presentations for viewers ranging from the elementary grades to postgraduate and professional levels use lesson-series which either are specifically created locally or are acquired from other sources through purchase, rental, exchange, or borrowing. In every case care should be taken to be certain that instructional television lesson-series meet specifically determined curriculum needs.

Materials. Certain benefits can be achieved from the specific creation or production of instructional television materials. Specifically created materials can be made directly responsive to locally determined curriculum design and content. The local creation of materials presents a ready means of involving educational administrators and staff, curriculum specialists, and teachers in instructional television. Under certain circumstances creating materials locally may be less expensive than purchasing or leasing educationally equivalent materials. The creation of local materials provides an opportunity to obtain unique and unusual local resources which are not readily available and to maintain archives of them.

Certain benefits, however, can be obtained from instructional television materials that are not produced locally. Materials offered by reputable producers and distributors have usually been tested and validated in several educational programs. Such materials represent an easy and convenient means of introducing new content and techniques and other innovations into curricula and procedures already established. When the need for the material is immediate and the future use of the material may be relatively limited, acquired materials may be less expensive than educationally equivalent material created locally. The acquisition of instructional television materials created by others is a way to obtain ready access to unique or unusual demonstrations, interviews, experiences, and resources not otherwise locally available.

Most typically a combination of locally created materials and materials acquired from national and regional instructional television libraries are used. In recent years there has been an increasing trend to acquire carefully designed and created materials from national and regional libraries instead of creating materials locally. Educational agencies and participating individuals are becoming more sophisticated in their requirements for and uses of instructional television materials, and local resources are often not adequate to meet these requirements. National and regional libraries are making available a wider range of materials of better quality from year to year.

Libraries. The National Instructional Television Center in Bloomington, Ind., is typical of the national instructional television libraries. It serves schools, colleges, and continuing education through the rental of lesson-series covering a wide variety of subjects. Lesson-series are distributed on videotape and film for use in educational programs utilizing various kinds of instructional television technical facilities. Interested educational agencies may obtain preview lessons and sample teacher and student materials. Regional offices are operated throughout the United States. A newsletter is distributed, and brochures for each lesson-series offered describe the subject, grade level, content, participants, and rental costs. Other national instructional television libraries are the Great Plains National Instructional Television Library in Lincoln, Neb.; MPATI, Inc., at Purdue University in Lafayette, Ind.; and Western Video Industries ITV in Los Angeles. Among the many additional sources for instructional television materials are educational television broadcast stations, educational agencies which have created their own materials, government agencies, and motion picture film distributors.

Broadcast. One of the most notable ways in which instructional television may be used in an organized educational program is instructional television broadcasting—that is, the presentation of instructional materials in the form of a lesson-series or a telecourse by either a commercial or a noncommercial (educational) VHF or UHF television broadcast station. Telecourses are broadcast for students ranging from kindergarten through college as part of their in-school work. Broadcast television is also used by individuals in an educational program for credit or certification in an independent viewing situation such as at home. Broadcast television is also used by groups on the job or in a similar vocational or professional context. The advantage of conducting instructional television by means of broadcast is that large numbers of students over an extensive geographic area may be reached simultaneously.

Broadcasting over educational television stations during the daytime hours is the principal means of providing instructional television services to children throughout the United States in the kindergarten through sixth grade levels as part of their in-school work. Reasons given by the schools for using instructional television in their educational programs are to improve instruction, to extend the curriculum, to accommodate increased enrollment, to alleviate a teacher shortage, and to reduce cost.

Regional authority. A regional instructional television broadcast authority is an organization of schools which wishes to use an instructional television service provided by a television broadcast station. Generally, no single school can afford to support its own television broadcast station. Even though some individual schools do establish a television broadcast station, the costs of the in-school broadcast service are usually apportioned among neighboring schools that receive the station and that wish to use the service. The regional instructional television broadcast authority seeks to serve the broadest possible curriculum needs of its member schools in content and grade-level areas that have been agreed upon. Generally, the authority is an entity separate from the broadcast station and is controlled and operated by the member schools. Through the authority the schools determine the ways in which their curriculum needs will be met, either by creating their own instructional television materials or by acquiring materials from outside sources.

Production. The procedure usually followed by a school or a regional instructional television authority for the development and creation of a television presentation begins with an assessment of needs by superintendents, administrators, supervisors, teachers, and students. After a specific subject topic is identified, one or more working meetings are held involving the curriculum consultants, the instructional television teacher, appropriate resource persons, and the instructional television coordinator and the television production staff to identify production objectives, an outline of events, and needed resources.

The instructional television teacher acts as the production leader and utilizes the services of the persons mentioned above to develop the television production script, the production setting, and the study guide for use by the teachers and students in the classroom. Reviewing committees make suggestions and give final approval. The planned instructional television presentation is rehearsed and then produced. After the production is completed, the instructional television teacher takes major responsibility for completing the classroom study guide. After the presentation is broadcast and used in the classroom, its effectiveness is determined from tests, letters, reaction sheets, and similar means. Based upon available information, an evaluation of the presentation is made by administrators, curriculum specialists, teachers, and students. Corrections are made as required. The process begins again for the next presentation.

Advantages and disadvantages. Although the broadcasting of instructional television presentations for in-school use has been most successful on the kindergarten through sixth grade levels, it has had relatively little success as an in-school service for grades 7 through 12 or on college levels. Scheduling of school classes to use the television broadcast presentations has been identified as the principal difficulty. Generally, students at the seventh grade level and higher have a great variety of individualized schedules organized on a departmental basis. An instructional television service based upon the use of a television broadcast station has difficulty arranging a broadcast schedule to reach students in the higher grades at an appropriate time with specified subject matter for in-school use. The broadcast of some television presentations, in an effort to meet the needs of the secondary student, is frequently repeated throughout the day. Another approach has been to reschedule presentations by developing the technical means to videotape broadcasted materials at the participating schools and then play back the videotape at times convenient for students' use.

A further impediment to the use of broadcast instructional television presentations by students at higher grades is of a curricular nature. The vast majority of instructional television materials offered are designed and created for the teacher who is a generalist rather than a subject specialist. The instructional television materials from national and regional sources are almost uniformly offered in the form of a subject-centered lesson-series devoted to one particular subject out of the many that the classroom teachers are responsible for teaching. To the teacher whose responsibilities require expertise in a great many areas, instructional television materials in the form of

subject-centered lesson-series are a blessing. The instructional television teacher who is a specialist relieves the classroom teacher of the responsibility of a particular expertise and in addition permits the generalist to spend time on other content matters. When the student moves to higher grade levels, where the teaching responsibilities as a whole or in part are conducted by subject specialists, an instructional television service plays a different role. Teachers who are subject specialists generally have a greater need for segmented materials than for subject-centered lesson-series. This is particularly true at the college and university levels. Most sources and distributors of recorded materials for instructional television have generally made available only subject-centered lesson-series. Instructional materials in lesson-series configurations presented on television have been popular at secondary and college levels where either the materials have been created by the educational agency for its own administration and use or the materials have been acquired from other sources for total teaching purposes. Only in recent years have sources of distributed materials begun to make available materials which appeal more to the specialist.

One way in which educational philosophies and practices are changing is that students at all educational levels are being addressed as individuals having specific educational needs. Individually prescribed instruction, performance contracting, and educational accountability programs are examples of efforts to design meaningful educational experiences for each student by enlisting the aid of specialized materials and specialized teaching staff. Schools are changing the form, content, and operation of their curriculum. Some schools are becoming departmentalized even in the second and third grades.

The services provided by instructional television must adapt to such changes in organized educational programs. The unique ability of television broadcasting to provide for wide geographic dissemination of broadly agreed upon materials to predetermined grade levels was at first a boon to schools but is now of decreasing value. Instructional television must now begin to solve problems other than those of scheduling and providing for content conformity.

Closed-circuit. School levels from kindergarten through sixth grade are beginning to adopt alternatives to broadcasting for the conduct of instructional television presentations. These alternatives lie in the use of a variety of smaller-scale television dissemination methods which are termed closed-circuit.

Closed-circuit television refers to the origination, distribution, and display of television presentations to specifically identified and controlled reception points. Closed-circuit television permits viewing only with television receivers or monitor display devices which are specially connected or equipped. Broadcast television, or open circuit, permits anyone with a standard home television receiver and an antenna to view the broadcast presentation. Generally speaking, as many separate closed-circuit television systems as desired may be operated independently of each other in any given area. Only a limited number of broadcast television stations may be operated in any given area because of the inherent limitations of the radio frequency transmission spectrum. A closed-circuit television system is a special-purpose, private television communications system. It may be as small as a visual public address system operating within only a single room and designed to give close-up views to persons in the rear rows. Alternately, a closed-circuit television system may reach viewers around the world. The only limits to the use of a closed-circuit television system are the extent of needs and available resources.

A closed-circuit television system uses technical facilities that are identical or similar to those used by a television broadcast facility. When a closed-circuit television system is designed to undertake and accomplish objectives which are almost identical to those performed by a television broadcast station, then the space, staffing, facilities, and budgetary requirements of the closed-circuit television system become almost indistinguishable from the requirements of a television broadcast station in many respects. Very often, however, in closed-circuit television an organized educational program can use instructional television techniques involving resources of a lesser magnitude than those involved in a television broadcast station. As the objectives become well understood and carefully defined, the technical and related facilities of a closed-circuit, special-purpose television communications system can be more specifically designed to attain these objectives than would be the case of a television broadcast facility. In fact, closed-circuit instructional tele-

vision may prove more effective and economical than broadcast television.

The essential difference between broadcast and closed-circuit television lies in the wide range of dissemination, or distribution, alternatives offered by closed-circuit. Broadcast television uses as its only distribution method the transmission of picture and sound signals through the air by wireless means. When the audience to be reached lies over a large geographic area and the essential requirement is to reach this audience by the most efficient means possible, then distribution by broadcast television would appear prima facie to be the best alternative. But when the audience to be reached by television is more narrowly defined geographically or may be reached more economically by means other than television broadcast, then some form of closed-circuit television would appear to be the best alternative. Intended viewers may be reached by closed-circuit means such as cable, low-power microwave, and 2,500 mHz/ITFS (Instructional Television Fixed Service) wireless transmissions, or simply through the distribution of recorded videotape or film to be played back or projected at the point of use.

The use of closed-circuit television has great appeal to organized educational programs, since the content, method of presentation, and time of presentation may be specifically designed and controlled to best meet the educational and schedule needs of the intended viewers. Some instructional closed-circuit systems are designed to permit the viewer to exercise initiative in content selection and time scheduling. Such systems are known variously as dial access or random access retrieval systems. The instructional materials are assembled in a collection which takes the form of a library of audiotapes, videotapes, and films. The closed-circuit system provides the interconnecting links for the transmission of sound, picture, and control signals between each particular user's location and the central collection of materials. Random access retrieval systems are most popular at secondary and higher education levels, where the curriculum is organized by subjects and the maturity of the students permits the responsibilities of self-study.

The leading educational television broadcast stations are starting to devote more of their daytime broadcast hours to educational programs for preschool and business and industry audiences. Such programs have the same concerns for the individualization of instruction as do kindergarten through college programs but are not easily adapted to such alternatives as closed-circuit instructional television. In the offing are cable television distribution systems and television cassette, or cartridge, devices for the individual viewer in preschool, business and industry, and professional and continuing education programs.

Adult education. Instructional television has had various uses for adults. Continuing education programs of a nonprofessional nature at nonresident colleges and universities are organized for the most part on a small class, face-to-face basis. Since there is not the year-to-year continuity in faculty and student body as is the case with programs at colleges and universities where students are matriculating residents, the conditions do not arise for the development of any sort of significant ongoing instructional television service. The factors of available faculty, available meeting space, and student enrollment in the case of adult education have appeared self-adjusting on a class-by-class basis and have not required resorting to more effective methods made possible by the use of instructional television techniques. In situations where the administration of an organized adult education program has sought to maximize its total overall enrollment, instructional television broadcast techniques have been used with some notable success. One such example is that of the Chicago City College, a junior college which has established a special staff and curriculum for its two-year TV College. This is conducted by means of television broadcast for students at home and leads to an associate of arts degree. This instructional television broadcast program is financially supported by a central budgetary allocation.

The more prevalent trend in adult education is that each discernible class unit be almost self-supporting. It is difficult to establish the concentration of resources necessary to initiate the use of instructional television as undertaken by Chicago City College. There are regular efforts, however, to use instructional broadcast television techniques for generalized adult education. The successful maintenance of these efforts depends upon central financial support. This can take the form of donated public service time of commercial television or of a public relations or public service undertaking by a college or university for its surrounding community. Although by nature of its openness television broadcast is capable, on the one hand, of providing a large viewing audience, on the other hand, it has rarely been a successful means of providing the necessary revenue from individual student registrations.

The adult education programs which more successfully use instructional television techniques lie in the area of professional and specialized education in medicine, law, engineering, and science. These programs have been designed to appeal to the professional need on the part of concerned individuals to maintain a continuous self-education program. In these cases the adult students will financially support the use of television either individually or through their professional associations. In some cases long-term government or foundation support has played an important role. When broadcast television techniques have been used, some highly selective strategies have been employed to reach only the target viewers. For example, the television sound and picture have been scrambled in such a manner that a special decoding device made available only to the participants must be used in order to view the broadcasts. This technique has been most often used in continuing medical education. Another approach has been to transmit unscheduled broadcasts for which the time and content are known only to those who are properly registered.

However, in recent years the pace of closed-circuit technology has developed to the point where closed-circuit instructional television techniques have been increasingly used instead of broadcast techniques. The Federal Communications Commission has looked with decreasing favor on the use of television broadcast frequencies for the transmission of material whose content is of relatively narrow interest. The commission has in fact authorized a low-power 2,500 mHz/ITFS to provide the kind of special purpose communication desired over modestly sized geographic areas for educational programs which had previously used conventional television broadcast stations.

A wide range of closed-circuit television distribution techniques have been used to provide service for medical, legal, scientific, and engineering educational programs. Combinations of cable and microwave links have been used to interconnect statewide, regional, and nationwide points.

A number of states have appropriated funds to establish closed-circuit systems devoted, among other things, to servicing organized educational programs using instructional television techniques for professional level education as well as kindergarten through college education. In a number of locations in the United States, industries which rely heavily upon professional scientific and engineering skills have pooled their resources to organize specific educational programs based upon closed-circuit television techniques. The lectures and demonstrations of the teaching personnel are transmitted as they are given by means of cable, microwave, and 2,500 mHz/ITFS links as well as by means of recorded videotape to the scientific and engineering personnel who remain at their industrial, research, and laboratory locations. In a number of cases participation in these educational programs may lead to credit toward a degree.

A rapidly growing area in which instructional television is being used is in business and industry. Broadcast television techniques are used on a cooperative basis by companies in a given geographic area as a means of pooling their financial resources to acquire and disseminate needed instructional and training materials covering such topics as management, supervisory, and clerical skills. Presentations are organized on a lesson-series basis and are most often viewed on the job during released-time periods. Business and industry use closed-circuit television facilities and techniques for many applications beyond that of instructional—that is, organized educational—television. Such uses include administrative communication, briefings, sales training, product information, surveillance, and data collection. Educational agencies and institutions are beginning to emulate the practices of business and industry by applying their instructional television facilities and resources to broader communication uses.

BIBLIOGRAPHY

CARPENTER, C. R., AND L. P. GREENHILL 1958 *An Investigation of Closed-circuit Television for Teaching University Courses.* University Park, Pennsylvania State University.

CHU, GODWIN C., AND WILBUR SCHRAMM 1967 *Learning From Television: What the Research Says.* Stanford, Calif., Institute for Communications Research.

GORDON, GEORGE N. 1970 *Classroom Television.* New York, Hastings House, Communication Arts Books.

GRIFFITH, BARTON L., AND DONALD W. MACLENNAN, eds. 1964 *Improvement of Teaching by Television.* Columbia, University of Missouri Press.

KUMATA, HIDEYA 1956 *An Inventory of Instructional Television Research.* Ann Arbor, Mich., Educational Television and Radio Center.

MURPHY, JUDITH, AND RONALD GROSS 1966 *Learning by Television.* New York, Fund for the Advancement of Education.

REID, J. C., AND DONALD W. MACLENNAN 1967 *Research in Instructional Television and Film.* Washington, D.C., U.S. Office of Education.

SIEPMANN, CHARLES A. 1958 *TV and Our School Crisis.* New York, Dodd, Mead.

U.S. HOUSE OF REPRESENTATIVES. COMMITTEE ON EDUCATION AND LABOR 1970 *To Improve Learning. A Report to the President and the Congress by the Commission on Instructional Technology.* Washington, D.C., Government Printing Office.

KEN WINSLOW

TENNESSEE VALLEY AUTHORITY, EDUCATION PROGRAMS

The Tennessee Valley Authority, a federal government corporation headed by a three-member board of directors, was created by act of Congress on May 18, 1933. Its directors are appointed by the president and are subject to confirmation by the Senate. Its purpose is to conduct a unified program of resource conservation, development, and use to increase the economic development of the seven-state Tennessee Valley region and also to advance its national defense capabilities. This includes improvement of navigability and control of flood waters in the Tennessee River and its tributaries, generation of electric power, and advancement of agriculture, forestry, and industrial opportunities. It also includes programs of education for the public and training programs for TVA employees.

The TVA controls the system of dams that harnesses the Tennessee River and its tributaries; electrical power is generated in both hydro and fuel plants. The dams contribute to regulation of the lower Ohio and Mississippi rivers. Lakes created by the dams provide outdoor recreation opportunities. The system maintains a continuous 9-foot-draft channel for navigation on the full 650 miles of the Tennessee main stream, from Paducah, Ky., to Knoxville, Tenn. At Muscle Shoals, Ala., near Wilson Dam, the authority operates the National Fertilizer Development Center.

Much of the TVA's progress in developing natural and human resources is traceable to programs of education, training, and demonstration. From the beginning the TVA has had educational involvements with its employees, the people of the

Tennessee Valley, private industry, institutions, and government.

Professional and administrative training. The TVA uses a variety of training methods for developing the abilities of white-collar employees and managerial staff.

Formal training programs are used to reinforce continuous informal training, to accelerate training processes, or to provide specific skills. Examples of formal training include rotation training for engineers, office training for secretarial and clerical employees, courses related to electronic data-processing, and supervisory management training.

By assigning employees to take formal training outside the TVA, the agency benefits from the facilities of other agencies, educational institutions, and private industries. Examples of such benefits include participation of managerial personnel in conferences for federal executives, graduate training in urban and regional planning, and training in the design and operation of nuclear reactors.

The TVA encourages its employees and managerial staff to undertake self-development activities through independent study for which leave or altered work schedules may be arranged, through voluntary educational classes after work hours, through provisions for attendance at professional meetings, and through similar educational opportunities.

TVA employee-training programs have contributed to the reputation the authority has for efficiency, probity, and accomplishment. Today these programs and their managers have the benefit of nearly four decades of experience, and they have profited from union cooperation from the outset. Other organizations, domestic and foreign, have visited the TVA to learn how the authority operates and have been given plans and instructional material.

Programs for students. Several cooperative student-training programs are available to undergraduate college students of the Tennessee Valley region. Among these are programs for cooperative students in technology and science, in engineering, and in business administration. The technological program includes students from technical and vocational institutes and from colleges and universities having two-year certificate or associate degree programs. The engineering and business

administration programs are limited to students enrolled in colleges and universities. Each of the participating institutions must have established an ongoing cooperative program or be willing to establish one.

A college student in a TVA cooperative student-training program alternates between academic study and TVA employment. Two students are assigned to one billet; one works while the other goes to school. The student must both meet the academic standards of his school and perform satisfactorily on the job. Rates of pay for TVA student employment are based on the relative difficulty of the work performed and the responsibility borne.

The TVA has cooperative programs with a number of southeastern colleges and universities. Engineering schools of the following institutions participate in the engineering program: Agricultural and Technical College of North Carolina, North Carolina State University, Auburn University, Georgia Institute of Technology, Mississippi State University, Southern University and Agricultural and Mechanical College, Tennessee Agricultural and Industrial State University, Tennessee Technological University, Tuskegee Institute, Virginia Polytechnic Institute, and also the universities of Alabama, Florida, Kentucky, South Florida, Tennessee, and Louisville.

In order to provide practical experience as a supplement to academic course work, the TVA offers paid internships to a small number of college undergraduate and graduate students. The interns carry out work assignments (usually during the summer months) which would otherwise be done by the TVA's union staff members. The assignments are intended to have educational value for the students as well as to help the TVA get its work done. The student interns are selected by faculty members or committees at their colleges.

The Southern Regional Training Program in Public Administration, a graduate program in which the University of Alabama, the University of Kentucky, and the University of Tennessee cooperate, was founded with TVA assistance in 1944. The TVA and other federal, state, and municipal agencies offer paid summer internships to the graduate students who receive fellowships in the program. The goal of the program is to increase the number of well-trained young administrators available for public service in the southern states and to use the strongest public administration resources of each of the cooperating universities in doing so.

When schools and colleges or their students ask for assistance in their academic programs, the TVA offers a wide variety of aids. This assistance ranges from sending printed materials to students who are writing term papers or themes on resource development to arranging for graduate students to carry out research projects as part of the requirements for advanced degrees. Whole classes frequently visit the agency's construction projects and research laboratories. Schools borrow TVA documentary and technical films. Occasionally, educational institutions collaborate with the TVA in developing special institutes or workshops.

Educating the public. The TVA is concerned with education in many ways which involve and affect the general public. In its early days the agency built and operated model schools and established library services for its workers and their families. The new services were then made available to other residents of the counties as well; eventually the schools and libraries were taken over by the valley states and counties. The TVA now plays a role in a variety of economic and educational opportunity programs for the disadvantaged of the region. In July 1967 the TVA added an educational relations specialist to its Knoxville staff. In addition to helping to develop internal training programs, he also has duties pertaining to the education of the public including: coordinating the TVA's major educational activities to achieve the optimum results in terms of economic and social advancement; advising the TVA's various offices and operating divisions on educational resource factors pertinent to their particular programs; representing the TVA in relationships with local, state, and federal agencies and with educational institutions; working through local organizations, such as the Tributary Area Development associations, on projects to best utilize local educational resources and to upgrade the educational and skill levels of the local citizens; identifying educational projects significant to regional development for which federal funds are available; and advising and assisting in their procurement. The public education program is an endeavor which attempts to keep faith with the congressional mandate that the Tennessee Valley Authority would be something more than a producer of electricity.

Fertilizer demonstration program. The beginnings of the fertilizer demonstration program date back to World War I, when German submarines threatened the U.S. supply of munitions nitrates from Chile. Under the National Defense Act of 1916, President Woodrow Wilson authorized the construction of two synthetic nitrate plants at Muscle Shoals, Ala., along a treacherous stretch of the Tennessee River. A large dam and a steam electric plant to supply the great amounts of power needed to operate the nitrate plants were also authorized. The National Defense Act provided that these facilities should be available for the production of fertilizers during peacetime.

But the war ended before any nitrates had been produced; the construction of Wilson Dam was not completed until 1925, and there was controversy for years over the proper use of the facilities. The Tennessee Valley Act of 1933 settled the matter: The facilities were transferred to the TVA to provide a national center for improving fertilizer materials and use.

One of the TVA's first public educational programs, started in 1935, was the fertilizer farm test-demonstration program. It is based on the idea that seeing is believing. Farmers sign up with the TVA, through the extension services of the land-grant colleges, to use new fertilizers. In the process of learning to use them and of following farming recommendations of the county agent, the farmer demonstrates to his neighbors what modern fertilizers and farming methods will do. Over the years the results have been remarkable—significantly changing agriculture in the Southeast. The program eventually became national in scope, spreading to farmers in over 40 states.

A second program—distributor demonstration, in which commercial fertilizer producers and distributors participate—hastened the spread of new fertilizer knowledge and made improved fertilizers widely available to farmers. The TVA regularly holds major demonstrations at Muscle Shoals to show its latest developments in fertilizer technology to industry. The one in 1968 was attended by representatives of 160 industrial organizations from 35 states and from 51 firms in 24 foreign countries.

In 1965 the Agency for International Development (AID) signed an agreement with the TVA for the education and training of fertilizer technicians and executives from developing countries. In October 1968, AID reported that over 100 participants from 16 countries had been trained in the three-year period.

Instruction in electrical applications. Instruction in the application of electrical power to household, farm, and industrial needs is carried out principally through the Rural Electrification Administration Cooperatives and the municipal electric systems which buy and distribute TVA power. The TVA is a wholesale power supplier for 160 local electric systems—108 municipalities, 50 cooperatives, and two small privately owned utility companies—serving 2 million customers. The TVA's Electrical Demonstration Branch works with these distributors in publicizing electricity's uses through booklets and studies.

Other educational programs are frequently offered by the TVA. An example is Design for Living Electrically, a two-day conference primarily for home economists, given annually in Huntsville, Ala. The program is well attended by educators from the area's colleges and universities and by industry representatives. Electrical development personnel of the 160 local electric systems attend training programs conducted by the TVA in Chattanooga, Tenn.

These efforts implement the specific section of the TVA act requiring that power be sold so as to promote the widest possible use of electricity and to assist in the region's development.

Forestry education. In cooperation with state and other agencies, the TVA conducts research and development programs in forestry, in fish and wildlife management, in watershed protection, in health services related to its operations, and in economic development of tributary areas through citizen associations. The results of its research and development are passed on in the form of educational and training programs, in cooperation with the other agencies.

Forestry education is a particularly productive TVA program. The preamble to the TVA act states that the authority should "provide for reforestation and the proper use of marginal lands in the Tennessee Valley." A forestry division was one of the first offices established by the TVA. In the early 1930's, 10 percent of the region's 14 million acres of forest burned every year (by the early 1970's it was less than .5 percent). The prevalent attitude was that fires were a natural

phenomenon and control impractical. This attitude justified the further belief that trees were made for short-term exploitation. Enlisting local cooperation, the TVA set up hundreds of meetings in schoolhouses to show fire prevention movies and to give talks on the value of conservation. County superintendents of schools, teachers, students, newspaper editors, ministers, and influential citizens cooperated in one way or another and in varying degrees. Over the years, conservation caught on; seedling trees helped prevent land erosion, sawmills became more efficient, wood industries were born and grew, and new paper mills were built.

Because of education, people in the valley are giving more attention than before to management for watershed protection, outdoor recreation, and maximum timber production. Today the valley states operate several forestry trade schools, and TVA employees are lent as instructors.

Tributary Area Development Program. Education is a key part of the TVA's Tributary Area Development Program. In this program the TVA is working with special development organizations in 15 subregions of the Tennessee Valley on projects in industrial and agricultural development, river control, recreation, education, and job-skill training.

The TVA is assisting two rural counties in the Sequatchie Valley in east Tennessee with a pioneering plan for multicounty high school consolidation, vocational training, and overall educational improvement. The need for adult education was demonstrated in the Lower Hiwassee Valley of east Tennessee when 137 adults returned to school to work toward high school certificates. Some 260 unemployed and uneducated adults were successfully taught reading, writing, arithmetic, and basic job skills in a pilot project in three tributary areas. A specially designed mobile home has been turned into a programmed adult learning laboratory in the Bear Creek area of northwest Alabama.

Land Between the Lakes. One of the most recent of the TVA's educational programs is the Land Between the Lakes demonstration in outdoor recreation and conservation. The Land Between the Lakes is a long, narrow strip of land with 300 miles of shoreland situated between the Tennessee and Cumberland rivers just before they empty into the Ohio in southwest Kentucky. It once supported an iron-producing industry, but this declined in the late nineteenth century and the land became sparsely settled and untended. The TVA's Kentucky Dam made a lake out of the Tennessee River on the west side of the strip in 1944, and the U.S. Army Corps of Engineers' Barkley Dam did the same out of the Cumberland River on the east side in 1965. The Land Between the Lakes is undergoing TVA development, with emphasis on outdoor recreation, wildlife preservation, and conservation education—in other words, multiple-use land and water management. In addition to hundreds of campsites, boat ramps, swimming areas, playgrounds, and hiking trails, the Land Between the Lakes has a conservation education center, where conservation is brought into focus for visitors and students. A feature of this is a youth station, which has dormitory buildings, a dining facility, and teaching space. School groups can stay here for up to two weeks studying conservation and examining the natural, historical, and cultural environment. This outdoor laboratory provides direct learning experience in conservation, and it provides opportunities for bringing conservation into the total school curriculum. Information on the youth station can be obtained from Land Between the Lakes Headquarters, TVA, Golden Pond, Ky.

Employee training programs. The TVA's employee training programs provide a bonus benefit to the region. Many employees who have received training in fields ranging from power plant operation to fertilizer production move to other jobs in the valley. The overall level of job skills for the region's labor force consequently shows a gain.

The TVA's education and training programs for its employees receive support from labor organizations. The authority's employee-relationship policy, formulated in 1935 by the first board of directors, identified education and training as a desirable area for union and management cooperation, and this idea has been written into subsequent collective bargaining agreements. Joint training committees carry out the programs.

In 1937 apprenticeship was established as the means of becoming a journeyman in the TVA. Apprentices are trained as airplane mechanics, asbestos workers, blacksmiths, boiler makers, bricklayers, carpenters, cement masons, electricians, equipment mechanics, gas and diesel mechanics, grade and paving equipment operators, structural iron workers, construction and maintenance linemen, machinists, millwrights, office-appliance re-

pairmen, operating engineers, painters, plumbers, sheetmetal workers, steamfitters, substation electricians, and so on.

A specific example of the joint administration of TVA employee training is the training of operators for hydro and steam plants and substations. In 1935 the TVA found that it would have to train men to operate turbines, boilers, generators, and substations. Until 1937 a TVA management committee trained the operators. Then the TVA and the International Brotherhood of Electrical Workers named a joint committee to plan and conduct the program. By 1970 about 1,200 trainees had completed this program. The program has continued and now includes training in the operation of nuclear power plants. The TVA has found ways of shortening the training by months and years. Classroom instruction and actual work experience are the two elements of the program, with the latter receiving more emphasis in terms of hours of learning.

BIBLIOGRAPHY

CLAPP, GORDON R. 1955 *The TVA: An Approach to the Development of a Region.* University of Chicago Press.

DARWIN, WILLIAM N., AND ALBERT K. THURMOND 1951 "Good Management: Key to Successful Sawmilling." *Southern Lumberman,* 182:62–64.

FREDRIKSEN, C. W., AND HELMAR MARTINSON 1955 "Helping Supervisors Train Themselves in Human Relations." *Personnel,* 31, no. 4:323–334.

LILIENTHAL, DAVID E. 1964 *The Journals of David E. Lilienthal.* Vol. 1: *The TVA Years, 1939–1945.* New York, Harper.

MASSEY, JOHN E. 1965 "Labor-Management Cooperation in TVA." *Public Personnel Review,* 26:130–134.

MITCHELL, JAMES P. 1960 "Labor-Management Cooperation in TVA." *Power Magazine,* 104, no. 1:199–201.

SEIGWORTH, KENNETH J. 1968 "Forestry Plus . . . in the Tennessee Valley." *Journal of Forestry,* 66:324–328.

TENNESSEE VALLEY AUTHORITY. NATIONAL FERTILIZER DEVELOPMENT CENTER 1968 *Annual Report.* Muscle Shoals, Ala., The Authority.

"TVA Helps AID's Fertilizer Program." 1968 *War on Hunger,* 11:6–7.

WILLIAM STURDEVANT

TENURE, ACADEMIC

See COLLEGE TEACHING: TENURE IN COLLEGES AND UNIVERSITIES.

TEST INFORMATION, SOURCES OF

In the twentieth century, testing in its many forms has come to occupy a sizable place in the American educational scene. According to one estimate, the number of ability tests given each year in the United States is now in excess of the total population (Goslin 1963), and this estimate does not include a constantly growing variety of personality tests, interest inventories, research instruments, and other special purpose measures.

The proliferation of tests began in the late nineteenth century (Chauncey & Dobbin 1963). By 1946 new tests and new editions of old tests were being produced at the rate of about a thousand every five or six years (Hildreth 1946), and there is no reason to believe that since then the production rate has diminished. As a consequence, the total accumulation of test titles in and out of print has increasingly tended to overwhelm the potential test user with the all but impossible problem of locating the particular testing instruments best suited to his purposes.

Early bibliographies. Attempts to alleviate the difficulty of locating suitable tests began in 1910 with Whipple's first edition of the *Manual of Mental and Physical Tests;* this was updated and expanded to two volumes five years later (Whipple 1914–1915). From 1911 to 1920, Freeman published a series of articles on tests in the *Psychological Bulletin.* During the 1920's further efforts along the same line were made to keep various segments of the test-using public in touch with the increasing number of instruments coming on the market (Freyd 1927; Froemming 1927), but the bibliographical coverage in these was considerably less than total and was usually limited to tests of special types.

The first comprehensive bibliography of objective tests of all types was produced by Hildreth in the early 1930's (Hildreth 1933). Entitled *A Bibliography of Mental Tests and Rating Scales,* it contained over 3,000 entries in four functional categories: intelligence and mental processes; educational and scholastic aptitude and achievement; personality tests and rating scales; and vocational aptitude, skills, and achievement. To be included, an instrument had to be objective either in whole or in part, capable of use by persons other than the test author himself, and either available from a publisher or adequately described in a professional journal. Hildreth cautioned the reader that her listing was otherwise nonselective and observed that some of the items included were out of date or of such inferior quality that they should probably not have been published at all. In addition to the title of the test, its authorship, source, and date of publication, each entry showed the age range of the population for whom the test was intended and gave occasional references to studies in which it had been used. The majority of the tests included originated in England, France, or Germany, with a few from other countries. Hildreth published an updated edition of her bibliography in 1939 and a supplement to this second edition in 1946.

The intent and principal value of Hildreth's work is that it provides a reasonably complete cataloging of tests from 1879 to 1945. Her bibliographies are a rich source of information for tracing the origin and development of tests in many different areas and for identifying varying trends and emphases in the period covered. By design, however, they do not contain any evaluation of the tests listed nor any data on their validity, reliability, and norms.

In 1939 and 1940, Wang published *An Annotated Bibliography of Mental Tests and Scales.* This two-volume compendium, containing 3,575 entries, furnished, in addition to some reference data, a brief description of the content of each test with currently available information on its validity, reliability, and norms. Tests were classified according to function. The first volume was organized in three general sections: measurement of mental capacity, measurement of personality and character, and measurement of vocational aptitude and abilities. The second volume dealt with measures of educational achievement. Wang limited his coverage to tests in the English language, but within that limitation he listed all the tests he could find, including those that were obsolete and out of print. The special value of his annotated bibliography lay in the thumbnail sketches of the measures he itemized and his brief discussions of their technical characteristics and standardization, if any. However, like Hildreth, he scrupulously avoided passing judgment on the quality of the tests described.

"Mental Measurements Yearbooks." The need for some method of providing the test consumer with an assessment of test quality based on sound technical criteria became apparent to a number of people in the 1920's (Ruch 1925; Kelley 1927). Ruch suggested that, in the interest of protecting the public, an impartial fact-finding organization should be established to evaluate the claims of test authors and publishers by conducting comparative studies of the usefulness and statistical properties of tests then currently available. The nearest approach to such a bureau of standards has been the monumental series of six *Mental Measurements Yearbooks* (MMY's) published by Buros (1938; 1941; 1949; 1953; 1959; 1965).

Shortly before he published the first MMY, Buros had compiled and published three bibliographies covering the tests that had appeared from 1933 to 1936 (1935; 1936; 1937). Their 850 entries were intended to supplement those in Hildreth's 1933 publication. In the last of these early bibliographies Buros also included a list of 291 books dealing with educational and psychological measurement and research and 600 reviews of these books excerpted from 82 journals.

What was new and significant about the 1938 MMY was that it contained specially solicited reviews of many of the tests listed. These reviews were prepared by recognized authorities in the fields covered by the tests. In some instances, the original test reviews were supplemented by others reprinted from professional journals. Two other features of the 1938 MMY were carried over from the 1936 bibliography: a section on recently published mental measurements books, with reviews drawn from the professional literature; and a similar section on recently published research and statistical books. Two other sections gave a listing of regional testing program reports and a directory of the publishers of tests and of journals and books having to do with measurement and research. The general pattern established in the 1938 MMY was maintained with only minor variations in the following editions. The objective throughout was to provide an up-to-date and comprehensive source of information about available tests and materials related to testing.

The MMY's are cumulative. Each one attempts to cover all tests and relevant books and articles published in English-speaking countries since the publication of the preceding yearbook. By means of an elaborate system of cross-references, the latest volume at any point in the series provides the reader with a key to items in the earlier volumes. As a consequence, the series as a whole constitutes the most nearly exhaustive single source of information about tests and measurements that exists anywhere in the world. The first two editions, for instance, contain 1,684 test entries; the third MMY, 705; the fourth, 830; the fifth, 957; and the sixth, 1,219.

Furthermore, accompanying each entry is a list of references to all known published and unpublished materials on the construction, validity, use, and limitations of that specific test. These reference lists are sometimes of extraordinary length. In the series as a whole, for example, there are over 700 references to studies involving the Stanford-Binet intelligence scale and about 3,000 references to studies of the Rorschach.

The classification scheme used to accommodate this mass of material has varied somewhat with succeeding editions of the yearbooks, but it appears to have settled down to one having 15 major categories: achievement batteries, business education, character and personality, English, fine arts, foreign languages, intelligence, mathematics, miscellaneous, multi-aptitude batteries, reading, science, sensorimotor, social studies, and vocations. Subcategories include such headings as agriculture, bookkeeping, etiquette, manual dexterity, music, physics, Russian, and vision.

From the outset, the distinctive feature of the MMY's was the inclusion of the critical reviews of current tests. The editor hoped that such reviews would not only give the test consumer helpful information for evaluating the test publishers' products but also force the publishers themselves to put fewer and better tests on the market and to provide, concurrently with publication, accurate and detailed information on the technical qualities and limitations of their tests. In short, the purpose was to raise professional standards in both the production and use of tests. To this end, each reviewer was encouraged to be frankly critical of the test assigned to him; to point out inadequacies and ambiguities in the publisher's statements concerning its construction, validity, and appropriate use; to give a succinct appraisal of the test by comparing its merits with those of competing tests; and to express all such observations in language that could be understood by lay test users (Buros 1965).

The magnitude of this undertaking is evident in the fact that the grand total of test reviews in all six volumes comes to 3,638. Reviewers were usually college teachers in education and psychology, specialists in test construction and research, or college instructors in pertinent subject fields. Professional cooperation was extensive: nearly 400 reviewers contributed an average of two reviews apiece to the sixth MMY. To provide a degree of balance in the appraisals, Buros tried to have each test reviewed from two or more differing perspectives.

Although the reviews inevitably reflect the

biases of their authors, the majority are carefully and professionally analytical. The editor's request that the reviewers be frankly critical has been usually well heeded, with the result that the MMY's have come increasingly to serve as a kind of technical conscience for the test publishing business. The MMY series has achieved broad acceptance by test-makers, specialists, and test users as an indispensable standard reference (Langmuir 1960; Dyer 1968). It has become, in effect, an instrument through which conscientious professionals in testing periodically speak to the educational public as well as to each other.

One of the principal objectives of the MMY's has been to provide up-to-date information on tests available. However, because of the large number of tests which are developed each year and the very considerable task of assembling and organizing the reviews and reference data pertaining to them, this objective has been only partially achieved. The irregular intervals between publication of successive volumes of the compendium produce a time lag. In an effort to remedy this situation Buros brought out, in the period between the fifth and sixth MMY's, a listing of tests in print (Buros 1961) and a reprinting in full of two publications on test standards: *The Technical Recommendations for Psychological Tests and Diagnostic Techniques*, which had appeared in a 1954 special issue of the *Psychological Bulletin*, and *Technical Recommendations for Achievement Tests*, which had been published by the American Educational Research Association in 1955. These two were superseded in 1966 by a single document, *Standards for Educational and Psychological Tests and Manuals*.

After the publication of the sixth MMY, Buros produced another interim supplement, *Reading Tests and Reviews* (1968); three future supplements are expected to cover personality, intelligence, and the vocations. *Reading Tests and Reviews* contains, in addition to a list of the tests that had appeared since the sixth MMY, a complete reprinting of the reading sections in all six yearbooks, including the critical reviews.

Other bibliographic references. In addition to the MMY's, there are several other sources of information about new tests and new information about old tests. Test publishers' annual catalogs are the primary source for listings of tests coming on the market. The catalogs generally give brief descriptions of the tests offered, the purposes for which they are intended, and the types of interpretive data and accessory materials that are available with the tests. The catalogs, indispensable to those wanting to be informed about tests available for purchase, do not, however, provide any dependable information on how well the tests described fulfill the purposes for which they were designed. Such information must be initially sought in the publishers' test manuals and then adjusted wherever possible on the basis of data produced by independent investigators.

Another source of information about currently available tests is the bimonthly *Test Collection Bulletin*, published by Educational Testing Service (ETS). The bulletin reports new acquisitions to the ETS test collection—a complete file of all standardized tests published in the United States and in many other countries. The bulletin also contains listings of experimental tests, of publishers' catalogs, of descriptive materials on scoring services and systems, of test reviews, and of reference volumes on testing.

Educational Testing Service also publishes reports addressed to special groups of test users. One of these reports, a listing of college level achievement tests, gives the name and source not only of the tests of commercial publishers but also of those tests used by the American College Testing Program, the College Entrance Examination Board, and the College Proficiency Examination Program run by the New York state education department. A similar report is oriented toward the testing needs of junior colleges, and a third describes the tests and operational details of all statewide testing programs in the United States and its territorial possessions.

Although bibliographies are the starting point for locating tests for possible use in schools and colleges, they do not provide sufficient information for determining whether a given test is in fact capable of yielding usable results for a particular purpose. The large accumulation of studies and reviews in the professional literature suggests that most new tests and many of the old familiar ones fall seriously short of producers' claims and educators' expectations. Access to this technical information, however, is difficult for most test users, since the information is widely scattered through many books and periodicals and is ordinarily embedded in concepts and terminology unfamiliar to the great majority of educators.

Probably the most effective attack on the first part of this problem, opening up the technical literature on testing, is to be found in the *Review of Educational Research.* In 1932 and 1933 this journal devoted three entire issues to educational and psychological testing (Freeman 1932; Baker 1932; Stenquist 1933). The journal has continued the practice at three-year intervals. These issues of the review have three significant features: they are prepared by experts, each of whom is assigned a chapter covering the area of testing in which he has special knowledge; each chapter provides a running summary of all the test development and research known to have been done during the preceding three-year period; and each provides, as nearly as possible, an exhaustive list of references to current articles on the subject.

There are three journals that focus principally on one or another aspect of research in educational and psychological measurement. The oldest, *Psychometrika*, is primarily concerned with studies in psychometric theory and methodology. Although it assumes a degree of mathematical sophistication that puts its contents beyond the reach of most persons concerned with the practical aspects of testing, many of the theoretical problems with which it deals are nevertheless basic to the long-run improvement of measurement. The next oldest journal in the field is *Educational and Psychological Measurement*. It carries articles reporting on various types of problems in measurement, analyzing research in the development of tests, and describing testing programs. Two especially relevant features are its reviews of books on measurement and related matters and a section containing reports of studies of the validity of specific tests. The youngest periodical specializing in educational measurement per se is the *Journal of Educational Measurement*, which, in addition to reporting studies on various technical and practical aspects of educational testing, frequently includes reviews of new tests.

Another recently established journal, the *American Educational Research Journal*, devotes considerable attention to test research as well as other matters and frequently reports on new test developments. It also contains, from time to time, critical reviews of newly published tests. A number of specialized journals—such as the *Journal of Consulting Psychology*, the *English Journal, College and University*, and the *Journal of Speech and Hearing Disorders*—occasionally carry reviews of tests related to their fields or articles pertaining to the use of such tests. The articles and reviews in most of these periodicals are indexed in the *Education Index*, a monthly publication that provides a cumulative subject index to a selected list of educational periodicals, proceedings, and yearbooks. "Tests and scales," one of the general subject headings, is subdivided into sections listing articles on such topics as construction, criteria, criticism, and reviews of tests. Finally, an indispensable source of up-to-date summary information on books and articles related to testing is to be found in *Psychological Abstracts*, a monthly publication that provides "nonevaluative summaries of the world's literature in psychology and related disciplines."

To find his way to a working understanding of this wealth of material, the test user has available any number of texts that explain the fundamental principles of educational and psychological measurement, the general scope of the tests available, their possibilities, and the pitfalls to be avoided in their application and interpretation (Anastasi 1968; Cronbach 1960; Davis 1964).

BIBLIOGRAPHY

AMERICAN PSYCHOLOGICAL ASSOCIATION 1966 *Standards for Educational and Psychological Tests and Manuals.* Prepared by a joint committee of the American Psychological Association, the American Educational Research Association, and the National Council on Measurements in Education. Washington, D.C., The Association.

ANASTASI, ANNE 1968 *Psychological Testing.* 3rd ed. New York, Macmillan.

BAKER, HARRY J., et al., eds. 1932 "Tests of Intelligence and Aptitude." *Review of Educational Research,* 2, no. 4:entire issue.

BUROS, OSCAR K., ed. 1935 *Educational, Psychological, and Personality Tests of 1933 and 1934.* New Brunswick, N.J., School of Education, Rutgers University.

BUROS, OSCAR K., ed. 1936 *Educational, Psychological, and Personality Tests of 1933, 1934, and 1935.* New Brunswick, N.J., School of Education, Rutgers University.

BUROS, OSCAR K., ed. 1937 *Educational, Psychological, and Personality Tests of 1936.* New Brunswick, N.J., School of Education, Rutgers University.

BUROS, OSCAR K., ed. 1938 *The 1938 Mental Measurements Yearbook of the School of Education, Rutgers University.* New Brunswick, N.J., Rutgers University Press.

BUROS, OSCAR K., ed. 1941 *The Nineteen Forty Mental Measurements Yearbook.* Highland Park, N.J., Gryphon Press.

BUROS, OSCAR K., ed. 1949 *The Third Mental Measurements Yearbook.* New Brunswick, N.J., Rutgers University Press.

BUROS, OSCAR K., ed. 1953 *The Fourth Mental Measurements Yearbook.* Highland Park, N.J., Gryphon Press.

BUROS, OSCAR K., ed. 1959 *The Fifth Mental Measurements Yearbook.* Highland Park, N.J., Gryphon Press.

BUROS, OSCAR K., ed. 1961 *Tests in Print.* Highland Park, N.J., Gryphon Press.

BUROS, OSCAR K., ed. 1965 *The Sixth Mental Measurements Yearbook.* Highland Park, N.J., Gryphon Press.

Buros, Oscar K., ed. 1968 *Reading Tests and Reviews*. Highland Park, N.J., Gryphon Press.

Chauncey, Henry, and John E. Dobbin 1963 *Testing: Its Place in Education Today*. New York, Harper.

Cronbach, Lee J. 1960 *Essentials of Psychological Testing*. 2nd ed. New York, Harper.

Davis, Frederick B. 1964 *Educational Measurements and Their Interpretation*. Belmont, Calif., Wadsworth.

Dyer, Henry S. 1968 "Review of *The Sixth Mental Measurements Yearbook*." *American Educational Research Journal*, 5, no. 1:109–113.

Educational Testing Service 1968 *State Testing Programs: A Survey of Functions, Tests, Materials, and Services*. Princeton, N.J., The Service.

Freeman, Frank N., ed. 1932 "Character Tests and Their Applications Through 1930." *Review of Educational Research*, 2, no. 3:185–270.

Freyd, Max 1927 "Selection of Typists and Stenographers: Information on Available Tests." *Journal of Personnel Research*, 5, no. 10:490–510.

Froemming, A. H. 1927 "Bibliography of Character Tests and Measurements." *Journal of Educational Research*, 16, no. 3:223–226.

Goslin, David A. 1963 *The Search for Ability*. New York, Russell Sage Foundation.

Hildreth, Gertrude H., ed. 1933 *A Bibliography of Mental Tests and Rating Scales*. 2nd ed. New York, Psychological Corp.

Hildreth, Gertrude H., ed. 1939 *A Bibliography of Mental Tests and Rating Scales*. 2nd ed. New York, Psychological Corp.

Hildreth, Gertrude H., ed. 1946 *A Bibliography of Mental Tests and Rating Scales, 1945 Supplement*. New York, Psychological Corp.

Kelley, Truman L. 1927 *Interpretation of Educational Measurements*. Yonkers, N.Y., World Book.

Langmuir, Charles R. 1960 "Buros' Magna Opera." *Contemporary Psychology*, 5:387–390.

Ruch, G. M. 1925 "Minimum Essentials of Reporting Data on Standard Tests." *Journal of Educational Research*, 12, no. 5:349–358.

Stenquist, John L., et al., eds. 1933 "Educational Tests and Their Uses." *Review of Educational Research*, 3, no. 1:entire issue.

Wang, Charles K. A., ed. 1939–1940 *An Annotated Bibliography of Mental Tests and Scales*. 2 vols. Peiping, China, Catholic University Press.

Whipple, Guy M. 1914–1915 *Manual of Mental and Physical Tests*. 2nd ed. 2 vols. Baltimore, Warwick and York.

Henry S. Dyer

TEST RELIABILITY

Test reliability is the consistency with which a test measures whatever it measures. Test reliability is expressed mathematically in terms of variance errors of measurement and reliability coefficients.

Variability within an individual. Several examples of variability within individuals will help to introduce the concept of true score, the concept of error of measurement, and the basic model of classical test theory.

Measurement of height. When we repeatedly measure an individual or object, we do not expect to get exactly the same figure each time. This is clearly seen when one measures the height of a particular child several times. Though presumably the child has a certain true height, small differences in the obtained height score will occur, even when he is measured several times independently by the same measurer with the same measuring instrument at short intervals of time. The boy will slouch a bit more one time than another, stand a little differently on the measuring spot, and so on; his measurer will have a slightly different angle of viewing the markings, a slightly different part of the boy's head on which to rest the measuring bar, and so on.

Variations from one height measure to another will tend to be greater, of course, when different measurers are used for the successive measurements, when the measurements are taken at different times of the day or week, when different measuring instruments are used, and when the boy's clothing is not standardized. (For example, he might wear street shoes one time, tennis shoes another, and no shoes the third time.) Each added variation tends to increase the variation of the boy's height scores, even though his true height has not changed. If we measure him over a long enough time, however, his true height itself may change also, thereby introducing a systematic effect into the measurement series to supplement the random changes from one measurement to another.

Besides the concept of a true height for the boy, one might use the concept of a perfectly correct ruler with which to measure his height, like the criterion meterstick kept by the National Bureau of Standards to ensure standardization of measurement of linear distance in the metric scale. Each manufacturer of rulers has a criterion ruler or its equivalent, from which the rulers he produces vary randomly in length within the limits of the quality control standards he maintains. The length of the criterion used by one manufacturer may differ from that used by another, thus leading to systematic (rather than random) differences in rulers from various factories. In measurement, such systematic errors are much more objectionable than are random errors, unless the latter are large. For example, if a man weighs himself on a scale that is systematically 3 percent too low and does not know this, he regularly underestimates his actual weight. If, however, a second scale varies randomly considerably above and below his actual weight but is correct on the average, he might prefer the consistently underweighing scale to the unbiased but inconsistent one. In some cases a little bias may be better than a great deal of random error, particularly when the extent of bias (−3 percent in the above example) is known and can therefore be compensated for.

Measurement of height involves interchangeable units. If one could cut up a yardstick or meterstick into its inches or centimeters without losing any sawdust, he could reassemble it any way he pleased without bothering about the original position of the units. What was initially the first inch could become the last. A person who is 69 inches tall is also 68, 67, . . . , 1 inch tall, a fortiori. The 69 is just a convenient marker that makes it unnecessary to add up the units. If the labeling numbers were not in order, one would have to count the number of units.

This interchangeability is a nice property of physical measurement that psychological measurement usually lacks. For example, if an examinee marks the 69th item of a vocabulary test correctly, we do not know that he marked all the preceding 68 items correctly, even if they were arranged in ascending order of difficulty for a previously tested group of persons like him. Quite probably he made at least one clerical error or did not know one or more of the generally easier items, so that his score is less than 69. The units of the vocabulary test—that is, its items —are not interchangeable, whereas the units of a height "test" or of a weight "test" are. Therefore, for psychological tests composed of distinct units such as items, the internal consistency of the test becomes important, whereas the concept of internal consistency is not applicable to the measurement of height or weight, because such tests are by definition perfectly consistent internally. The "total scores" on a height test contain errors of measurement, but the individual items do not.

Measurement of vocabulary. One may draw a sample of words from some source such as a dictionary and create a test with them. The same test could be administered repeatedly to an examinee without intervening instruction, but his scores probably would not fluctuate much because the words that he did not know at one time he probably would not know at another. For these reasons (memory carry-over and lack of independence of the items from form to form) the test-retest procedure is seldom used by specialists.

One might draw from a dictionary successive random samples of, say, 50 words each and use each such sample to devise a randomly parallel form of the vocabulary test. Then an examinee's score would vary from form to form for a number of reasons: fluctuations in motivation and recall, luck in guessing, idiosyncrasies of the examinee's experience which make a word that is difficult for most other examinees easy for him, unequal difficulties of the items in one form as compared to another, and so on.

The usual solution is to stratify the pool of items by content and difficulty and then to construct forms that are matched with each other on content and difficulty. This eliminates much of the variation in difficulty from form to form. If such forms meet certain rather stringent requirements, they are called parallel forms.

Boredom and fatigue can affect the form-to-form variability for a particular examinee; therefore, rarely are more than two or three forms administered to the same examinee during a short period of time. Using so few forms does not permit a good assessment of his between-form variability, however, so (as we shall see later) it is usually assessed indirectly and approximately.

A number of other influences affect an examinee's score on a test. Some of these are the physiological and psychological condition of the test taker (headache, quarrel with girl friend, and so on), the quality of instructions and management of the testing session, heat, lighting, noise, and speededness of the test. (A test is speeded if not enough time is allowed for the examinee to reveal the full extent of his knowledge of the tested material.)

Earlier we noted that the units of the vocabulary test are not identical stimuli. This is true in two senses. They are usually unequally difficult, and even those that are equally difficult are not strictly interchangeable, because they are not equally difficult for all examinees. For instance, for all boys who are at least 60 inches tall, the 58th inch is sure to be "answered correctly," whereas for all boys who score 60 on a certain vocabulary test, there is no assurance that they all answered item 58 correctly.

Despite this, we usually consider that scores from a well-devised vocabulary test form an "interval" scale such that the difference between scores of, say, 38 and 44 is considered to have the same meaning as the difference between scores of

52 and 58—that is, six points at one place on the score continuum is assumed to be comparable to six points at another place.

However, a zero score on a certain vocabulary test does not usually indicate zero knowledge of vocabulary, because quite likely the test was prepared by eliminating those items too difficult or too easy for anyone in the group to be tested. The person who answers nothing correctly on this test could score above zero on an easier vocabulary test. Most psychological tests have no true zero point for the ability or other characteristic being measured and therefore are not ratio scales. One cannot show that John is twice as intelligent as Bill, but of course it is sensible to say that John weighs twice as much as Bill or is twice as tall. This is seen readily when one ponders the incorrect statement that, on the Fahrenheit scale (where 0 is 32° below freezing), 64° is twice as warm as 32°. Scientists do have an absolute scale of temperature (Kelvin), on which ratio statements are meaningful.

As with height, measures of vocabulary over a considerable interval of time tend to be affected by growth or decline in vocabulary knowledge; this tendency constitutes a nonrandom source of variation.

Measurement of creativity. Can one measure "creativity"? First, it is necessary to operationalize that glamorous term. Yes, one can devise a test in which the examinee is asked to name all the uses he can think of for a brick. One can say, "Write down all the words you can think of in two minutes that rhyme with 'moon.'" Or one can say, "Write down all the words you can think of in one minute that begin with the letters *ba*." These are three examples of the many different ways in which fluency, originality, and other qualities can be assessed by "divergent-thinking" instructions. Of course, the various tasks are not strictly equivalent psychologically. An examinee may be appreciably better at one than at another.

What is the effective length of a given creativity test? Presumably, it is the population of possible responses—uses of a brick, words that rhyme with "moon," words that start with *ba*, and so on. These are more implicit than is the number of words comprised in a vocabulary test, where convergent thinking (giving the one possible correct answer) is measured, but they are no less real.

Some "creative" acts may be more variable within an individual from time to time than are others. Also, fluency and originality may fluctuate more than, for example, vocabulary knowledge or height.

Faking. One cannot score higher on a vocabulary test than his knowledge and good luck permit. A boy cannot, for example, choose to fake a perfect score on a 100-item vocabulary-knowledge test when his "true" knowledge is 50. (Of course, if he has more knowledge than the scorer, he can give an answer he knows the scorer considers correct even though he knows that another answer which the scorer would mark incorrect is actually right.) On certain types of psychological inventories, however, one has the choice of responding to each item as he "really believes" or as he suspects will be considered desirable. Personality tests, interest inventories, and the like are such devices. The question "Do you like spinach?" freely permits an answer of either yes or no, though for the tester's purpose one response may prove to be better than another. Contrast that question with "What is the meaning of the word "hirsute"? A person who does not know what the word means cannot put down the correct response just to please the examiner. He can fake ignorance by pretending not to know the meaning of the word when he actually does, but he cannot fake knowledge and pretend to know it when he does not.

Items that permit faking "good" allow certain response sets, including social desirability bias, to operate. Also, responses to such items will usually be much more a function of the situation and the instructions than will responses to an ability test. This makes for greater consistency in some cases and greater variability in others. Items that can be faked require special analyses that a number of personality psychologists have proposed.

The concept of true score. If a single individual could be measured an infinite number of times with parallel forms of the same test, the arithmetic mean of his obtained scores would be his true score. For height, this would require an infinite number of measurements of his height, independently made under identical specified conditions. For vocabulary knowledge, it would mean administering the population of items to him in a virtually infinite number of forms of the vocabulary test, each containing the same number of items. This definition is hypothetical but is still quite useful despite its metaphysical overtones.

The concept of error of measurement. The difference between an examinee's obtained score on a particular form of a test and his true score is called his error of measurement. Errors of measurement for an examinee are conceived of as fluctuating randomly around his true score. The mean error of measurement is zero for each examinee.

The basic model of classical test theory. The obtained score of an examinee on a particular form of a test equals his true score plus his error of measurement on that form. This statement is the basic model of classical test theory, which dates from the pioneer work of Charles Spearman (1904). An examinee's obtained score varies randomly from form to form or occasion to occasion, and so does his error of measurement. An examinee's true score is a constant over all forms or occasions.

If an examinee's obtained scores change systematically (rather than randomly) over time, errors of measurement will have a nonrandom trend that at least partially invalidates the simple model above.

Because a particular examinee's true score is a constant (that is, the same for any form of the test), his true score covaries zero with his errors of measurement. One cannot predict his errors of measurement from his true score or predict his true score from his errors of measurement.

An examinee's obtained scores on the various forms of the test covary perfectly with his errors of measurement, since the former vary only because the latter do. The variance of an examinee's obtained scores equals the variance of his errors of measurement. ("Variance," in statistics, is a measure of how different from each other a group of numbers, such as an individual's obtained scores, are.)

The variance of the errors of measurement of a particular examinee is a measure of the consistency of measurement for that person. This variance may differ from examinee to examinee, as when John wears variable-height heels whereas Bill does not, so that from one time to another height measures vary more for John than for Bill.

In many applications, errors of measurement for a given examinee are assumed to be distributed normally—that is, in the shape of the so-called normal curve—around that examinee's true score.

Variability between individuals. Though the within-individual model discussed above is the basis for classical test-score theory, in practice one usually has one or two obtained scores for each of a number of different examinees rather than a large number of obtained scores for a single examinee. Thus, between-individual variability constitutes much of the content of reliability determinations.

The persons-by-items set of data. The most common set of data for study consists of the scores of a group of examinees on a group of items. Each examinee has answered exactly the same items as every other examinee, so one has a persons-by-items matrix of item scores. These data can be analyzed in several ways. One can study variation among item scores for one person, variation among persons for a single item, variation among persons for the sum of item scores (that is, variation among the total scores of the persons), and so on.

Of great importance is the correlation of the scores on item 1 with the scores on item 2, on item 1 with item 3, and so on. The average intercorrelation of the items is a rather good estimate of the randomly-parallel-form reliability coefficient of the typical item in the population of items sampled. If a form contains I items, and if their mean intercorrelation is $\bar{r}$, then the reliability coefficient, r, of the examinees' total scores on the form can be estimated as

$$(1) \qquad r = \frac{I\bar{r}}{1 + (I - 1)\bar{r}}$$

where $\bar{r}$ can vary from $-1/(I - 1)$ to 1; r can, in principle, vary from 0 to 1. This is a one-form measure of the internal consistency (that is, the homogeneity) of the items. It is quite closely related to the Kuder-Richardson Formula 20, Hoyt, and α coefficients, which involve a slightly different coefficient of correlation (intraclass) rather than the mean interclass $\bar{r}$.

For the persons-by-items matrix of item scores, the variance error of measurement is a function of the variance of the item scores minus the variation of the item means and minus the variance of the person means.

Extension of the classical model. Using the simple, basic model of classical test theory, obtained score = true score + error of measurement, one finds that the variance of the obtained scores of a group of examinees equals the variance of their true scores plus the variance of their errors of measurement (one error of measurement per examinee). The proportion of the obtained-score variance due to true scores plus the proportion due to errors of measurement equals 1, or 100 percent. Therefore, the proportion of obtained-score variance due to true scores equals 1 minus the proportion due to errors of measurement.

The variance of errors of measurement equals the product of the variance of obtained scores and the proportion of total variance not due to true scores.

The above relationships are shown better by mathematical symbols than by words. Let X stand for obtained score, T for true score, and E for error of measurement. Let σ^2 represent a variance of measures for the population of examinees. Then the following relationships hold:

$$(2) \qquad X = T + E$$

the basic model of classical test-score theory;

$$(3) \qquad \sigma_X^2 = \sigma_T^2 + \sigma_E^2$$

the variance of sum of noncovarying T and E;

$$(4) \qquad \frac{\sigma_T^2}{\sigma_X^2} + \frac{\sigma_E^2}{\sigma_X^2} = 1$$

proportion of variance due to T and to E sums to unity;

$$(5) \qquad \frac{\sigma_T^2}{\sigma_X^2} = 1 - \frac{\sigma_E^2}{\sigma_X^2}$$

proportion of variance due to T is unit complement of proportion due to E;

$$(6) \qquad \sigma_E^2 = \sigma_X^2 \left(1 - \frac{\sigma_T^2}{\sigma_X^2}\right)$$

the variance error of measurement for a randomly chosen examinee. The quantity σ_E^2 is the average of the individual examinees' variance errors of measurement.

A few other symbols will facilitate further discussion. Let σ_{XT} represent the covariance of obtained scores with true scores for the population of examinees. Let ρ_{XT} represent the population coefficient of correlation of obtained scores with true scores. Then

$$(7) \qquad \sigma_{XT} = \sigma_T^2$$

the covariance of X with T is the variance of T.

$$(8) \qquad \rho_{XT} = \frac{\sigma_T}{\sigma_X}$$

the correlation of X with T is the ratio of the standard deviation of T to the standard deviation of X.

$$(9) \qquad \rho_{XT}^2 = \frac{\sigma_T^2}{\sigma_X^2}$$

the squared correlation of X with T is the proportion of the obtained-score variance that is true-score variance. This is defined to be the one-form reliability coefficient.

$$(10) \qquad \sigma_E^2 = \sigma_{(X-T)}^2 = \sigma_X^2(1 - \rho_{XT}^2)$$

variance error of measurement. Formula (10) is equivalent to formula (6).

$$(11) \qquad \sigma_{XE} = \sigma_E^2$$

covariance of obtained scores with the errors of measurement they contain is the variance error of measurement, which cannot be negative.

$$(12) \qquad \rho_{XE} = \frac{\sigma_E}{\sigma_X} = \sqrt{1 - \rho_{XT}^2}$$

the correlation of obtained scores with the errors of measurement they contain is the proportion of the standard deviation of obtained scores that is error standard deviation or the square root of the unit complement of the one-form reliability coefficient. It cannot be negative. This is the mathematical basis for the statistical phenomenon known as regression to the mean due to errors of measurement. Large obtained scores tend to contain large (positive) errors of measurement, and small obtained scores tend to contain small (that is, large negative) errors of measurement. For the next examining, on a parallel form of the test, the expected error of measurement for any examinee is zero, so high scores from the first form will tend to drop and low scores to rise.

$$(13) \qquad \hat{T}_p = \mu_X + \rho_{TX}^2(X_p - \mu_X)$$

where $\hat{T}_p$ is the estimated true score of the pth person, μ_X is the population mean of the obtained (or of the true) scores, and X_p is the obtained score (X) of the pth person ($p = 1, 2, \ldots, \infty$). Thus, the estimated true score is a regressed obtained score, regressed $(1 - \rho_{TX}^2)$th of the way to the group mean. For example, if the reliability coefficient of the group is 0.80, each obtained score is moved 20 percent closer to the group mean.

$$(14) \qquad \sigma_{(T-\hat{T})}^2 = \sigma_T^2(1 - \rho_{TX}^2) = \rho_{TX}^2\sigma_X^2(1 - \rho_{TX}^2)$$
$$= \rho_{TX}^2\sigma_E^2$$

the variance error of estimate for estimating T from X is the product of the reliability coefficient and the variance error of measurement. This variance error of estimate is almost always less than the variance error of measurement shown in formulas (6) and (10).

$$(15) \qquad \sigma^2_{\{T-[\mu_T+\rho^2_{TX}(T-\mu_T)]\}} = \rho^4_{TX}\sigma^2_E$$

variance error of measurement for $\hat{T}$, which is almost always smaller than the variance error of estimate in formula (14). The expression in square brackets is the true score analogous to the obtained score $\hat{T}$.

$$(16) \qquad \sigma^2_{(\hat{X}-\hat{T})} = \frac{\sigma^2_E}{P}$$

the variance error of measurement of the mean of P obtained scores, $\bar{X}$, is one-Pth of the variance error of measurement of a single obtained score, X.

Kuder-Richardson Formula 20. All of the above formulas are expressed in terms of parameters—that is, of values for an infinite number of examinees. Therefore, they are conceptual formulas, rather than computational ones. To do actual computations, one substitutes statistics for parameters: s^2 in place of σ^2, r^2_{XT} in place of ρ^2_{XT}. Computing s^2_X by means of a computationally convenient version of the following definitional formula is straightforward:

$$(17) \qquad s^2_X = \frac{\sum\limits_{p=1}^{P}(X_p - \bar{X})^2}{P}$$

where P persons (examinees) have been tested, and X_p is the obtained score of the pth examinee. But how does one estimate ρ^2_{XT}? Earlier in this article an approximate procedure involving the mean item intercorrelation was mentioned (see formula 1). There are two seemingly different but algebraically equivalent ways to get a slightly better result more easily.

Two special cases of these, published by G. Frederic Kuder and Marion W. Richardson (1937), are suitable only when the items of the test are scored 1 if marked correctly and 0 otherwise. One of these is the well-known Kuder-Richardson Formula 20:

$$(18) \quad KR20 = \frac{I}{I-1}\left[1 - \frac{\sum\limits_{i=1}^{I}\frac{R_i}{P}\left(1 - \frac{R_i}{P}\right)}{s^2_X}\right]$$

where I is the number of items, P is the number of persons tested, R_i is the number of persons who answered the ith item correctly, and s^2_X is the variance of the obtained scores of the P persons tested. The value of KR20 can vary from as low as 0 to as high as almost 1. It can reach 1 only if all items are of exactly the same difficulty—that is, only if $R_1 = R_2 = \ldots = R_I$; however, the negative bias due to varying item difficulties is usually not great. More influential is the heterogeneity of the group tested. As s^2_X increases, KR20 tends to increase also. This is true for all reliability coefficients, because the basic formula for the reliability coefficient can be expressed as

$$(19) \qquad \rho^2_{XT} = 1 - \frac{\sigma^2_E}{\sigma^2_X}$$

The value of σ^2_E for a particular test tends to change little from group to group, whereas σ^2_X is heavily dependent on the dispersion of the X's. For example, one would expect a reading test to have a higher reliability coefficient for grades 7 to 9 than for grade 8 alone, because the variance of obtained scores in the three grades will undoubtedly be considerably greater than the variance of obtained scores in just one of those grades, whereas the variance error of measurement for a given examinee will be the same, whether we consider all three grades or only one.

If one can find in the manual for a test an estimated variance error of measurement, s^2_E, that seems reasonably appropriate for the group one has tested (for example, based on the same sex, on one form only, and on roughly the same grade and ability level), it is easy to compute a reliability coefficient by substituting in the formula

$$(20) \qquad r^2_{XT} = 1 - \frac{s^2_E}{s^2_X}$$

the s^2_E from the manual and the s^2_X computed for the particular group one has tested. For instance, if the manual lists s^2_E as being 25 and s^2_X is computed to be 100, the reliability coefficient is .75. Beware the test manual that reports extremely high reliability coefficients—for example, .95 for a 50-item test—unless you are convinced that the group on which the coefficient is based is not highly heterogeneous compared with yours. For instance, by including the scores of both mentally retarded fifth-grade girls and engineering seniors, one could exhibit impressively high reliability for a spatial-relations test that has low reliability for typical tenth-graders.

The value of KR20 will tend to be high, even if the mean item intercorrelation is low, provided that the test consists of a large number of items. For example, if the mean item intercorrelation is .13, the reliability coefficient of a 60-item test will be approximately $60(.13)/[1 + (60 - 1).13] = .90$. This is approximately the result for the mathematical part of the Scholastic Aptitude Test at a typical national administration. For a less heterogeneous group than that large national sample, the mean item intercorrelation would be less than .13, and hence the one-form reliability coefficient would be less than .90.

One-form reliability coefficients are inappropriate for speeded tests, because they tend to be spuriously high for them. A speeded test is one on which an appreciable number of examinees could have scored higher had they been allowed more time. A pure-speed test is one on which everyone would make a perfect score (aside from careless marking) if he had enough time. A pure-power test is one on which nobody would raise his score except in chance fashion no matter how much more time he were given. The items on most power tests are arranged in ascending order of difficulty, with the easier items coming first, so that the examinee runs out of knowledge or ability before he runs out of time. Thus, the mere fact that most persons were unable in the time allowed to mark every item does not in itself indicate that the test has an appreciable speed component, but the fact that virtually everyone did indeed have time to mark the last items on the test means that it is not speeded. The only straightforward way to estimate the reliability coefficient of a speeded test is to administer two separately timed forms of it. These may be comparable half-forms *a* and *b*, in which case the reliability coefficient is estimated to be

$$(21) \qquad r_X = \frac{2r_{ab}}{1 + r_{ab}}$$

Kuder-Richardson Formula 21. If instead of using the difficulty of each item separately, as in KR20 (formula 18), one computes a single overall average item difficulty, $(R_1 + R_2 + \ldots + R_I)/PI = \bar{X}/I$, which for simplicity we shall call D, the simpler Kuder-Richardson Formula 21 results:

$$(22) \qquad KR21 = \frac{I}{I-1}\left[1 - \frac{ID(1-D)}{s_X^2}\right]$$
$$= \frac{1}{I-1}\left[I - \frac{\bar{X}(I-\bar{X})}{s_X^2}\right]$$

The KR20 coefficient will usually be larger than KR21 and sometimes a great deal larger. It can-

not be smaller. When item difficulties do not vary, $KR20 = KR21$. Besides being a computationally shortcut lower bound to KR20, KR21 has special properties of its own for certain situations (Webster 1960). However, Cureton (1966) warns that KR21 should be used "as a short formula for estimating the reliabilities of . . . any tests where nonfunctional items have not been eliminated in advance by item analysis."

Hoyt's ANOVA coefficient. In 1941, Cyril Hoyt derived a general formula for a one-form internal-consistency reliability coefficient. KR20 proved to be a special case of Hoyt's coefficient, applicable when the right response to each item was scored 1 and all other responses to the item were scored 0. Hoyt worked from a persons-by-items matrix of item scores and utilized the analysis of variance (ANOVA):

$$(23) \qquad r_H = \frac{MS_{persons} - MS_{(persons \times items)}}{MS_{persons}}$$
$$= 1 - \frac{MS_{(persons \times items)}}{MS_{persons}}$$

where MS is an analysis-of-variance mean square. One can think of $(I)MS_{(persons \times items)}$ as the variance error of measurement, $(I)MS_{persons}$ as the variance of obtained scores, and $I[MS_{persons} - MS_{(persons \times items)}]$ as the variance of true scores. The value of r_H tends to vary from 0 to 1.

Cronbach's alpha coefficient. Lee J. Cronbach (1951) proposed an algebraically equivalent but seemingly different version of r_H that closely resembles the formula for KR20, which is a special case of it:

$$(24) \qquad r_C = \frac{I}{I-1}\left(1 - \frac{\sum_{i=1}^{I} s_i^2}{s_X^2}\right)$$

where s_i^2 is the variance of the scores for the ith item. Because $r_H = r_C$, one can take his choice of computational procedures—analysis of variance or variance of items and of obtained scores.

Stepped-up split-half reliability coefficient. Before the Kuder-Richardson internal-consistency formulas were offered in 1937, the usual way to obtain a one-form reliability coefficient was to split a test longitudinally into two presumably parallel halves (say *a* and *b*) by, for example, putting all the odd-numbered items into one form and all the even-numbered items into the other. This was done after the form had been administered to the examinees with a single time limit. Then for each examinee a score on half *a* and a score on half *b* were obtained. These half-test scores were correlated to yield r_{ab}, an estimate of the reliability coefficient of a test half as long as the full form. To estimate the split-half reliability coefficient of the whole test the following formula was used:

$$(21) \qquad r_X = \frac{2r_{ab}}{1 + r_{ab}}$$

The value of r_C is approximately the average of all possible r_X's for a given set of items. (There are 126 ways to split-half a ten-item test.) If a test consists of heterogeneous items, however, it will be better to split-halve it than to compute r_H, r_C, or KR20, unless the test can be divided into homogeneous subsets of items for each of which $MS_{(persons \times items)}$ can be computed separately. Then the formula becomes

$$(25) \quad r_H = \\ 1 - \frac{I_1 MS_{(p \times i)_1} + I_2 MS_{(p \times i)_2} + \cdots + I_S MS_{(p \times i)_S}}{MS_{persons}}$$

where there are S subsets and I_s items in the *s*th subset. The principle is that items within each homogeneous subset will intercorrelate better than they will correlate with items in other subsets, thus causing r_H determined by separate computation of the error variance for each subtest to exceed r_H for the items as a whole. This type of procedure is used, for example, for the Scholastic Aptitude Test, where two separately timed sections of items contribute to the verbal score and two other sections to the mathematical score.

Spearman-Brown prophecy formula. If a test composed of I items has a one-form reliability coefficient of ρ_{XT}^2, what will be the reliability coefficient of a test composed of nI such items? It will be estimated to be

$$(26) \qquad \rho_{X_n T_n}^2 = \frac{n\rho_{XT}^2}{1 + (n-1)\rho_{XT}^2}$$

This is the Spearman-Brown prophecy, or step-up, formula. We have already used it four times above. Another illustration may help. If a certain test has a one-form reliability coefficient of .25, how reliable will a comparable test three times as long probably be? Using formula (26), we obtain $3(.25)/[+ (3-1).25] = .50$. By tripling the length of the test, we have doubled its reliability coefficient.

Of course, we are assuming not only that the added items intercorrelate as well with each other and with the original items as the original items intercorrelated but also that fatigue, boredom, warming-up influences, and so on equally characterize the shorter and the longer tests. In practice, the Spearman-Brown formula tends to give useful estimates.

Correcting for attenuation. True scores on one test correlate better with true scores on another test than obtained scores on the two tests correlate. Let X represent obtained scores on one test and Y represent obtained scores on the other. Then

$$(27) \qquad \rho_{T_X T_Y} = \frac{\rho_{XY}}{\rho_{T_X X}\rho_{T_Y Y}}$$

where T_X stands for true scores on test X and T_Y stands for true scores on test Y. The denominator of the ratio is the product of the positive square roots of two reliability coefficients. It cannot exceed 1 and will equal 1 only when both tests are perfectly reliable. Otherwise, it will be less than 1 and therefore inflate the obtained correlation coefficient, ρ_{XY}, to make the resulting figure larger. This is the correction for attenuation in ρ_{XY}—that is, for the lessening as compared with the correlation of true scores—caused by errors of measurement in obtained scores from test X and test Y. Perhaps this can be seen better when the formula is reoriented as

$$(28) \qquad \rho_{XY} = \rho_{T_X T_Y}(\rho_{T_X X}\rho_{T_Y Y})$$

because the less-than-unity expression in parentheses reduces $\rho_{T_X T_Y}$ to yield ρ_{XY}.

A numerical illustration follows. Let the obtained scores on a vocabulary and a word-meaning test correlate .70. If the one-form reliability coefficient of obtained scores on the vocabulary test for the group on which the .70 was obtained is .81 and for the word-meaning test is .64, the coefficient of correlation corrected for attenuation is $.70/(.90)(.80) = .97$; it seems that the two tests are measuring nearly the same thing. If we had error-free measures of both X and Y, we would expect them to correlate .97 rather than the .70 that the actual fallible measures do correlate.

When predicting criterial scores Y from predictor scores X, one may wish to correct for attenuation due to X but not Y, because X may be improvable, whereas Y may not be. The correlation between the scores on an academic aptitude test (X) and college grades (Y) illustrates this situation. It may be practicable to increase the reliability coefficient of the scores by lengthening the test but quite difficult to increase the reliability coefficient of the college grades.

Sometimes it may be impracticable to improve the reliability coefficient of either variable (such as high school grades correlated with college grades), and yet for theoretical reasons it may be interesting to study the underlying true-score relationship.

The concept of comparable forms. Thus far we have considered mostly the characteristics of a single form of the test, except that for speeded tests or ones with heterogeneous items two forms were suggested. More generally, classical test theory makes much use of the concept of parallel forms of the test. The simple model is

$$(29) \qquad X_{pf} = T_p + E_{pf}$$

and

$$(30) \qquad X_{pf'} = T_p + E_{pf'}$$

where X_{pf} is the obtained score of the pth person on the fth form and $X_{pf'}$ is the obtained score of that same person on the different form of the same test. The person's true score is considered identical from one form to the other. Errors of measurement on the two forms are assumed to covary zero with each other and with the true scores. The variance error of measurement for form f is assumed to be the same as the variance error of measurement for form f'. Therefore, because the variance of true scores must be identical for the two forms, the variance of obtained scores for form f is the same as that for form f'.

Two-form reliability coefficients. From the above model one can derive the formula for the correlation of obtained scores on the two forms for an infinite number of persons. It is

$$(31) \qquad \rho_{X_f X_{f'}} = \frac{\sigma_T^2}{\sigma_X^2}$$

so from prior work with one form (see formula 9) we note that

$$(32) \qquad \rho_{X_f X_{f'}} = \rho_{XT}^2$$

This means that one can estimate the one-form reliability coefficient from the correlation of scores on two strictly parallel forms. The two forms must be administered with such little time interval between them and under such conditions that the examinees' true scores do not change differentially from one form to the next. No harm is done if each examinee's true score changes by the same amount as any other examinee's, as when because of practice effects each examinee earns two true-score points more on form f' than on the prior form f.

This restriction, that there must be no differential instability of true scores if the two-form correlation is to be used to estimate ρ_{XT}^2, is highly important. Most two-form correlations are coefficients of equivalence and stability, whereas split-half r's, KR20, r_H, and r_C are coefficients of equivalence only—equivalence of the two halves administered essentially simultaneously or equivalence of the items of which the form is composed. An appreciable time interval is likely to lower $r_{X_f X_{f'}}$; over long time periods it may drop greatly. How much it drops under particular conditions must be determined empirically rather than theoretically, however.

Also, the magnitude of $r_{X_f X_{f'}}$ will depend on how similar forms f and f' actually are. In practice, they may be far from interchangeable. One can estimate the extent to which they are parallel by studying the description of the way in which they were generated and by trying them out. Because differences in means do not directly affect the magnitude of correlation coefficients, it is less important for determining reliability coefficients that the two forms be equally difficult than that they have parallel content.

In practice, one may want merely to know how closely the actual scores on form f and form f' correlate over an appreciable period of time instead of trying to use $r_{X_f X_{f'}}$ to estimate r_H, r_C, or a stepped-up split-half r.

Five types of comparable forms. There are five chief types of comparable forms. The type closest to the concept of parallel forms is obtained by matching items from one form to the other on relevant characteristics such as content and difficulty.

Sometimes one form is reused at a later time with the same examinees, so that the "comparable" forms are in fact identical physically, though perhaps not psychologically. Sameness of content and memory carry-over from one occasion to the other will probably cause correlated errors of measurement that make the computed reliability coefficient (of stability only, not of equivalence) higher than if independent forms were used.

Some of the carry-over can probably be reduced by randomizing the order of the options of the items and perhaps the order of the items themselves the second time.

Frederic M. Lord has proposed that items be sampled randomly to yield randomly parallel forms of the test (Lord & Novick 1968). That method is beyond the scope of this article, but it should be noted that the resulting forms will vary in difficulty randomly rather than having a fixed true-score mean from form to form.

We have already considered the fourth method, which is split-halving the items of a single form, yielding two sets of scores which can be used to determine a coefficient of equivalence.

The fifth procedure involves use of the analysis of variance to estimate variance components for the standardization sample that can be employed flexibly in various field situations. This procedure was developed by Lee J. Cronbach, Goldine C. Gleser, and Nageswari Rajaratnam (see Cronbach et al. 1971).

Variance errors of measurement from differences. When one has two half-test scores for each examinee, what is the appropriate test-theory model? A simple but effective one is

$$(33) \qquad X_{pa} = T_{pa} + E_{pa}$$

and

$$(34) \qquad X_{pb} = (T_{pa} + c) + E_{pb}$$

where X_{pa} is the obtained score of the pth person on half a and c is a constant (the same for all persons). From this model comes a formula for the standard error of measurement of the X_{pf}'s— that is, of the obtained scores on the whole form. It is simply the variance of the difference between the half-scores, the $(X_{pa} - X_{pb})$'s:

$$(35) \qquad \sigma^2_{(X_a-X_b)} = \sigma^2_{[(E_a-E_b)-c]} = \sigma^2_{(E_a-E_b)}$$
$$= \sigma^2_{(E_a+E_b)} = \sigma^2_E$$

because the errors of measurement on the two half-tests are assumed to covary zero, and the variance of the difference between two uncorrelated variables is equal to the variance of their sum.

This result is close to that which would be secured by the conventional formula

$$(36) \qquad \sigma^2_E = \sigma^2_X\left(1 - \frac{2\rho_{ab}}{1+\rho_{ab}}\right)$$

even though this latter formula involves the assumption that $\sigma^2_a = \sigma^2_b$.

The variance error of measurement of scores from parallel forms can be computed simply as $\sigma^2_{(x_f - x_{f'})}/2$. This is the variance error of measurement of either form f or form f'. The variance error of measurement for $(X_{pf} + X_{pf'})$ is $\sigma^2_{(x_f - x_{f'})} = \sigma^2_{E_f} + \sigma^2_{E_{f'}}$. Alternatively but equivalently for the variance error of measurement of either form,

$$(37) \qquad \sigma^2_E = \frac{\sigma^2_{x_f} + \sigma^2_{x_{f'}}}{2}(1 - \rho_{x_f x_{f'}})$$

Here the variances of obtained scores on the two forms are averaged, even though in the model they are assumed to be identical. This averaging is especially useful in actual practice, where sampling fluctuations virtually guarantee that $s^2_{x_f}$ and $s^2_{x_{f'}}$ will not be identical.

Use of reliability measures. One wants the variance error of measurement of a test to be as small as possible so that the true score of an examinee can be inferred closely from his obtained score. Also, one wants the variance error of measurement of a test to be small relative to the variance of obtained scores so that differences between true scores of examinees can be discriminated closely. If one is to get reliable information from test scores, the signal-to-noise ratio must be high. Variance of true scores corresponds to the signal, and variance of errors of measurement represents the noise. The former should be as large as possible relative to the latter. When the ratio is 1, the reliability coefficient for the test scores is 0. As the ratio approaches infinity, the reliability coefficient approaches 1.

If one chooses an examinee at random and affixes to his obtained score plus and minus one times the positive square root of the variance error of measurement (that is, $X_{pf} \pm s_E$), there are 68 chances in 100 that the examinee's one and only true score, T_p, falls within that interval. For example, if his obtained score is 54 and the standard error of measurement, s_E, is 4, there are 68 chances in 100 that his true score is not lower than 50 or higher than 58. More precisely, if we had 100 X_p's for one examinee and the corresponding 100 s_E's and formed 100 such intervals, 68 of them would "capture" his true score; 32 would not.

Note again that you do not need to know the

test's reliability coefficient itself in order to make statements about within-individual variation of obtained scores. You do need it, however, in order to see how well the test differentiates among the examinees. The reliability coefficient itself is the percent of the obtained-score variance that is true-score variance. The higher this coefficient, right up to 1, the more finely you can discriminate among the examinees. A coefficient high enough for one purpose may not be sufficiently high for another. Recall also that the mean of a group fluctuates less because of errors of measurement than does a single obtained score. Reliability high enough to differentiate groups reliably may not be high enough to use in estimating whether one examinee's true score is higher than another examinee's.

It has not been possible to discuss all important aspects of reliability theory and practice, nor have proofs and derivations been offered. The interested reader, will find ample discussions, proofs, and derivations listed in the bibliography.

BIBLIOGRAPHY

AMERICAN PSYCHOLOGICAL ASSOCIATION 1966 *Standards for Educational and Psychological Tests and Manuals*. Washington, D.C., The Association.

CAMPBELL, DONALD T., AND JULIAN C. STANLEY 1966 *Experimental and Quasi-experimental Designs for Research*. Chicago, Rand McNally.

CRONBACH, LEE J. 1951 "Coefficient Alpha and the Internal Structure of Tests." *Psychometrika*, 16, no. 3:297–334.

CRONBACH, LEE J., et al. 1971 *The Reliability of Behavorial Measurements*. New York, Wiley.

CURETON, EDWARD E. 1966 "Kuder-Richardson Reliabilities of Classroom Tests." *Educational and Psychological Measurement*, 26, spring issue:13–14.

DAVIS, FREDERICK B. 1964 *Educational Measurements and Their Interpretation*. Belmont, Calif., Wadsworth.

DuBOIS, PHILIP H. 1970 "Varieties of Psychological Test Homogeneity." *American Psychologist*, 25, no. 6:532–536.

FISKE, DONALD W. 1966 "Some Hypotheses Concerning Test Adequacy." *Educational and Psychological Measurement*, 26, no. 1:69–88.

GULLIKSEN, HAROLD O. 1950 *Theory of Mental Tests*. New York, Wiley.

HORST, PAUL 1966 *Psychological Measurement and Prediction*. Belmont, Calif., Wadsworth.

HOYT, CYRIL 1941 "Test Reliability Estimated by Analysis of Variance." *Psychometrika*, 6:153–160.

KUDER, G. FREDERIC, AND MARION W. RICHARDSON 1937 "The Theory of the Estimation of Test Reliability." *Psychometrika*, 2:151–160.

LORD, FREDERIC M., AND MELVIN R. NOVICK 1968 *Statistical Theories of Mental Test Scores*. With contributions by Allan Birnbaum. Reading, Mass., Addison-Wesley.

NORMAN, WARREN T. 1967 "On Estimating Psychological Relationships: Social Desirability and Self-report." *Psychological Bulletin*, 67, no. 4:273–293.

NUNNALLY, JUM C. 1967 *Psychometric Theory*. New York, McGraw-Hill.

SPEARMAN, CHARLES 1904 "The Proof and Measurement of Association Between Two Things." *American Journal of Psychology*, 15:72–101.

STANLEY, JULIAN C. 1964 *Measurement in Today's Schools*. 4th ed. Englewood Cliffs, N.J., Prentice-Hall.

STANLEY, JULIAN C. 1970 "Definition of True Score Appropriate for Estimated True Scores." *Educational and Psychological Measurement*, 30, no. 3:525–531.

STANLEY, JULIAN C. 1970 "Reliability." Robert L. Thorndike, ed., *Educational Measurement*. 2nd ed. Washington, D.C., American Council on Education. Pages 356–442.

WEBSTER, HAROLD 1960 "A Generalization of Kuder-Richardson Reliability Formula 21." *Educational and Psychological Measurement*, 20, no. 1:131–138.

JULIAN C. STANLEY

TEST SCORES AND NORMS

The process of standardizing an objective test involves one or more formal administrations of the test, precisely as it is intended to be given in practice, in order to provide supplementary information to aid in the use of the test scores. These administrations are designed to yield data which may form the basis for establishing a scale system for the test; they may be used to derive a set of norms or interpretive data; and, for tests that are made available in more than one form, they may be used to determine a set of equivalency tables which will allow the conversion of scores on the different forms of the test to a common scale. This article will devote a section to each of these three aspects of the process of test standardization. A fourth section will deal with the problem of comparable scores on tests of dissimilar psychological functions.

Scaling. Unlike the more common scales of physical measurement—for example, the scales of height, weight, and temperature—which have acquired meaning through continued use and familiarity, the raw score scales of educational and psychological tests have no interpretable meaning of their own. For this reason, among others, the scores that are ordinarily reported for tests are seldom reported in terms of the raw score scales but rather in terms of derived scales, some of which have been defined and constructed to have special normative meaning and, in that particular sense, to be self-interpreting scales. The IQ scale, the grade equivalent scale, and McCall's T-Scale (1939), for example, are typical of those that have normative meaning.

There are additional reasons for using systems of derived score scales for standardized tests in preference to the original raw score scales (Angoff 1962). First, the raw score scale, representing as it does merely a count of the number of items answered correctly (frequently minus a correction for haphazard guessing), is no more than an ordinal scale. As such, the raw score scale only ranks individuals with respect to their performance on the test but, unlike the fundamental physical scales of height and weight, yields neither equally spaced units (except in the purely arbitrary sense of equal increments of items answered correctly) nor a meaningful absolute zero. An interval scale, at least, is required if score differences in different regions of the scale are to be compared meaningfully. In order to make comparisons of this sort possible, raw score scales are often converted to derived scales in which the unit separations between scores are in some defined sense equal. The Flanagan scaled score system (1939; 1951) and Gardner's K-Scores (1947) are derived scales of this type.

Second, derived score scales are used when more than one form of a test is available and the forms are to be used interchangeably. In such instances the scores on the forms are frequently equated in order to adjust for form-to-form differences in raw score characteristics and are expressed on a derived scale which is clearly different from the raw score scale and is used as a referent for all test forms. The scale for the admissions tests of the College Entrance Examination Board is one of a number of such types of scales (Wilks 1961).

Third, for the sake of convenience in handling test score data, it is frequently desirable to convert raw scores to scales with preassigned values in round numbers that are easy to recall and easy to use. The stanine scale (Flanagan 1948; 1951) is one of many such scales. In fact, the derived scales for nearly all published tests are defined with this characteristic in mind.

Some of the derived scales for educational and psychological tests are distributive in the sense that they are based on the distribution of the scores of a group of individuals. Occasionally that group is a normative group—that is, a group that has been randomly selected from an explicitly defined population whose characteristics give interpretive meaning to the scores. (A scale so derived is normative in the statistical sense—that is, in the sense of describing performance as it exists. Other scales may be normative in the clinical or standard-setting sense—that is, in the sense of describing performance as it should be.) Thus, although some scales are distributive and normative, other scales are distributive but nonnormative, since the groups on which they are based do not necessarily have normative or interpretive value. An example is the scale for the College Board tests, based on the performance of the self-selected group of examinees who assembled to take the Scholastic Aptitude Test in April 1941 for admission to college. Finally, there are nonnormative scales that are also nondistributive as just defined, scales like the type developed by Tucker (1951; 1953), Rasch (1960), and others, which are invariant with respect to the group on which data were collected for their determination.

Percentage mastery scale.   There are a number of different derived scales in existence. One such scale is the percentage mastery scale, on which the scores are taken to represent an absolute kind of judgment that the student has mastered some percentage of the subject matter under consideration. Thus, a score of 78 percent, for example, is taken to imply that since the examinee has answered 78 percent of the test successfully, he has therefore mastered 78 percent of the material covered by the test. An additional feature of the scale is that certain specified percentage values are taken to indicate "passing" or "honors" performance. Although the percentage mastery scale is still widely used, especially by classroom teachers, it is generally thought to be one of the poorest ways to express test performance, principally because it implies an absolute type of evaluation which is not only illusory but also untenable; in addition, it disregards the difficulty of the test items, which will naturally vary from test to test.

Unadjusted linear transformation.   A frequently used scale is the unadjusted linear transformation (standard scores), apparently first described by Hull (1922), in which the obtained mean and standard deviation for a group of examinees (ω) are transformed to a scale with arbitrary preassigned values for the mean and standard deviation. The formula for making this transformation is given in the equation

$$(1) \qquad \frac{C - M_{s_{\omega}}}{s_{c_{\omega}}} = \frac{X - M_{x_{\omega}}}{s_{x_{\omega}}}$$

where X and C refer, respectively, to raw and scaled scores. When rearranged, the equation may be expressed in the form, $C = AX + B$, a linear equation which permits the conversion of raw scores to scaled scores. In this equation, A (the slope) $= s_{c\omega}/s_{x\omega}$, and B (the intercept—that is, the value of C when $X = 0$) $= M_{c\omega} - AM_{x\omega}$. The quantities $M_{c\omega}$ and $s_{c\omega}$ are the arbitrarily chosen values for the scaled score mean and standard deviation. Since the conversion from raw to scaled scores is linear, utilizing only the first two moments (that is, the mean and the standard deviation), it simply relocates the mean to the desired value and changes the size of the units to yield the desired standard deviation. It does not, however, exert any effect on the shape of the distribution.

Percentile derived linear scale. Another type of linear transformation is the percentile derived linear scale. This scale is defined simply by specifying, for example, that a particular percentage of individuals in a specially chosen group will pass and that some other particular percentage will receive honors. The scores corresponding to these percentages are found in the distribution of raw scores and transformed respectively to a pair of preassigned scaled scores, as in the equations

$$(2) \quad C_p = AX_p + B \quad \text{and} \quad C_h = AX_h + B$$

where p and h refer, respectively, to pass and honors, X_p and X_h are the observed raw scores, and C_p and C_h are the preassigned scaled scores. The values of A and B (the slope and intercept, respectively, of the conversion equation) are found by solving the simultaneous equations (2), and the conversion line is extrapolated over the entire raw score range. (It should be noted that the passing and honors scores, X_p and X_h, could have been assigned in a normative-clinical fashion, instead of in the normative-statistical fashion described, as a result of the arbitrary decision of one or more standard-setters who would simply choose the levels of raw score, X_p and X_h, that in their judgment merited the passing and honors scaled scores, C_p and C_h.)

Percentile rank scale. Perhaps the most familiar scale for reporting test scores is the percentile rank scale, which gives the percentage of individuals in a particular group scoring below the midpoint of each score or score interval. The precise percentile rank is obtained by totaling the frequencies for all the scores below the particular score, adding half the frequencies at the score, and dividing by the total number of cases. Percentile

ranks are essentially self-interpreting scale values and are used for making (statistical) normative evaluations of an individual's performance. Distributions of percentile ranks for the groups on whom the ranks are based are necessarily rectangular. The percentile rank scale itself is clearly ordinal, and, according to most points of view, its units are unequal since they represent equal proportions of a group, not equal intervals on a scale of ability.

Normalized scales. One type of transformation which is often made with the purpose of giving raw scores a more fundamental meaning is the transformation to a normalized scale. The reasoning is that since the raw score scale or a linear transformation of it is dependent on the characteristics of the particular items chosen for the test, it is therefore advisable to transform the scale to some other system of units that would be independent of these characteristics and, in the sense of a particular operational definition, equally spaced. The transformation to a normalized scale is chosen on the assumption that mental ability is fundamentally normally distributed for an unselected population and that equal segments on the base line of such a normal curve would mark off equal units of mental ability. The procedure followed in deriving such a scale makes use of a standard table of the normal curve and results in a systematic differential expansion and contraction of the units in various regions of the raw score scale in order to transform the distribution of raw scores to a normal shape. A summary of the procedural steps is as follows: The test is administered to a random sample of a defined population. Percentile ranks are computed, plotted, and smoothed. Smoothed percentile ranks are read off the graph, converted to normal deviates (by referring to a table of the normal curve), and further converted to a scale with an arbitrarily defined mean ($M_{c\omega}$) and standard deviation ($s_{c\omega}$) by means of the equation

$$(3) \quad C_n = s_{c\omega}z_n + M_{c\omega}$$

where z_n is the normal deviate and C_n is the normalized scale value.

A well-known normalized scale is the stanine scale (Flanagan 1948; 1951), which was first used in the Air Force Aviation Psychology Program during World War II. The stanine scale is a single-digit scale extending from 1 to 9 (it derives its name from "standard nine") with preassigned percentages derived from a table of the normal curve and falling in each of nine score categories as follows: score 9, 4 percent; score 8, 7 percent; score 7, 12 percent; score 6, 17 percent; score 5, 20 percent; score 4, 17 percent; score 3, 12 percent; score 2, 7 percent; and score 1, 4 percent—yielding a distribution with a mean of 5 and standard deviation of about 2.

Another system of scaled scores based on the normal curve transformation, one which has important theoretical and practical value, is Flanagan's scaled score system (Flanagan 1939; 1951), which attempts to normalize the distributions of several partially overlapping groups simultaneously. A variant of this system is one provided by Gardner's K-Scores (1947), which follows the model of the Flanagan system in many respects but assumes the more general Pearson Type III curve instead of the normal curve (which is a Pearson Type III curve with zero skewness).

IQ scale. Originally defined as the ratio ($\times$ 100) of mental age to chronological age, the IQ (intelligence quotient) scale (Terman & Merrill 1937) is intended to convey the meaning of test performance in terms of normal expectations for a child of a given age and is principally used at those ages where the function measured increases rapidly with age. The method of producing the scale of mental age units is as follows: (1) Representative samples of children at all ages are given the intelligence test. (2) The mean or median test score of the children at each age interval (essentially the regression of score on age) is plotted against the midpoint of the age interval. (3) A smooth curve is drawn through the points. (4) The age corresponding to each level of performance is read off the curve and is thus defined as the mental age for that level of performance. The mental age is, therefore, the chronological age for which a given test performance is average.

The primary value of the IQ scale lies in its apparent simplicity and in its built-in comparability from one age to the next (IQ constancy), which holds if the sampling is adequate and comparable across ages, if the growth pattern in the items is comparable from one child to the next, and if the dispersion of scores is the same at every age.

The disadvantages of the IQ scale are quite serious, however. For example: (1) Since the correlation of age and test score is imperfect, there are necessarily two quite different regressions, the regression of score on age and the regression of age on score, yielding two possibly quite different

definitions of mental age, not one. As a result, the definition of mental age is not a unique one. (2) The mental age is dependent on the amount of dispersion about the regression line. However, no account of this dispersion is taken in the determination of the mental age. (3) A mental age is meaningful only if there is an age for which the given test performance is average. Therefore, mental ages (and IQ's) are not meaningful for superior children in mid-adolescence—where performance on IQ tests appears to level off—and beyond. (4) The mental age notion implies that a six-year-old with a mental age of nine years has the mental equipment of a nine-year-old. This may be true but only in a highly restricted sense.

The popularity of the IQ scale has led to the development of other such indexes, such as the educational quotient (EQ), which is the ratio of "educational age" to chronological age, and even the achievement quotient (AQ), which is the ratio of the EQ to the IQ. The AQ is often used to represent overachievement and underachievement in terms of the ratio of actual achievement to potential ability. However, there is considerable doubt that the AQ is as meaningful as it has been represented to be. Flanagan (1951) has presented an excellent review of the problems inherent in the AQ that severely limit its usefulness.

Because of the observed variation in the standard deviation of ratio IQ's at different ages, an IQ for an individual can easily shift about from one age to the next, and not necessarily because of any change in his relative intelligence level. In order to eliminate this type of fluctuation, the IQ's that are commonly used today are deviation IQ's rather than ratio IQ's. Deviation IQ's are essentially standard scores, resulting from a conversion system which yields a mean of 100 and usually a standard deviation of 16 at each age level. (An exception is the Wechsler Intelligence Scale for Children [Seashore et al. 1950], which uses a standard deviation of 15.) In the standardization of some tests that yield IQ's, the shape of the distribution of scores at each age level has been altered to yield normalized scores.

Grade equivalents. Another scale, similar in most of the important respects to the mental age scale, is the scale of grade equivalents. Grade equivalents are derived very much like mental ages, differing principally in the fact that test performance is plotted against grade rather than age. Unlike the mental age scale, which is more appropriate to tests of general intellectual ability, grade equivalent scales are ordinarily developed for achievement tests in specific subject-matter areas. The disadvantages of grade equivalent scales parallel most of the disadvantages of the mental age scales. The disadvantages are more pronounced and serious in the case of grade equivalents, however, for several reasons. First, the grade equivalent values vary greatly, depending on the nature of the particular subject matter tested and also depending on the grade level at which the subject is introduced in the school and the manner in which it is pursued through the grades. Second, the grade equivalent is affected by the particular customs of promotion and retardation in the schools, customs which vary widely from one locality to another and from one time to another. Third, the grade equivalent has little meaning in any subject-matter area in which the teaching is closely tied to grade level and in which the student has no opportunity to learn material beyond his grade level. But these difficulties and problems are not the only ones inherent in the grade equivalent. Flanagan (1951) and Angoff (1971a) provide a fuller discussion of these issues.

Nonnormative scales. Some recognition has been given to the view that the normative type of scale is not necessarily the most useful (Angoff 1962; Lindquist 1953; Tucker 1953). Although (the argument goes) this scale does give immediate normative meaning, as it is intended to do, the norms on which it is based can become obsolete with the passage of time and can thereby cause the scale itself to become obsolete. Nonnormative scales, however, not being dependent on norms, can be retained indefinitely. Moreover, the commitment of a normative scale to a particular norms group is unnecessarily restrictive since that group may not always be the appropriate group to use. Finally, it is argued, the real meaning that is typically a part of a scale of measurement is not necessarily the one that is incorporated into the scale but is one that develops with familiarity and use over the course of time. Familiarity and use are made possible, in the case of a test for which there are two or more forms available, by rigorous form-to-form equating and by the provision of supplementary normative data which are revised and altered as conditions warrant.

Many of the scales for psychological tests in use today are nonnormative-distributive in the sense defined earlier in this article, but there are some nonnormative scales that are also nondistributive. One of them is the Guttman scale (1950), which was originally developed for opinion and attitude measurement. A perfect scale of ability in the Guttman sense is one in which an individual who passes an item of given difficulty will pass any other item of lesser difficulty; similarly, an individual who fails an item of given difficulty will fail any other item of greater difficulty. Thus, knowledge of a person's score on a test that forms a Guttman scale permits perfect reproduction of his actual responses. In that sense the Guttman model is completely deterministic. However, this characteristic is not likely to be realized in practice for ability-test data because of the large errors of measurement or, in another sense, because of the low interitem correlations. An alternative approach has been suggested in the models of a number of investigators (Birnbaum 1968; Lawley 1943; Lazarsfeld 1950; Lord 1952a; 1952b; Rasch 1960; Tucker 1951; 1953) in which the probability of the subject's giving a particular response is completely determined by his ability, the difficulty of the item, and its discriminating power.

A nonnormative (in the statistical sense) linear conversion to scaled scores may be established by arbitrary decision or by agreement among judges, as described earlier in connection with the percentile derived linear scale. Another type of nonnormative scale, which is useful when there are multiple forms of the test, may be derived directly from the scores of the test itself simply by renaming any two raw score values with corresponding arbitrary scaled score designations. The relationship between the pair of raw scores and the pair of scaled scores automatically defines the linear conversion from all possible raw scores to the derived scale. The details of the method are quite simple. One scaled score number, C_1, is arbitrarily assigned to some raw score value, say zero, and another scaled score number, C_2, is arbitrarily assigned to another raw score value, say the maximum possible score on the test. The foregoing two relationships define a pair of simultaneous equations,

$$(4) \quad C_1 = AX_1 + B \quad \text{and} \quad C_2 = AX_2 + B$$

which, when solved, define the slope $A = (C_2 - C_1)/(X_2 - X_1)$ and the intercept $B = C_1 - AX_1$ (or $B = C_2 - AX_2$). In the case of this scale, as with all others, later forms of the test perpetuate the scale simply as a result of having been equated to the initial referent form—form X.

Norms. Test norms are usually presented in the form of percentile rank distributions, based on the performance of well-defined groups of people whose characteristics are presumably known to the test user. Norms are useful principally for interpreting the scores of individuals and for acquiring a familiarity with the test. They also help the user to develop an understanding of the characteristic differences in the subgroups of the general population. In a manner of speaking, the percentile rank may be regarded as an evaluation of performance (in the statistical sense) as distinct from the score, which represents the measurement of performance—although, as has been pointed out in the preceding section, normative evaluations are sometimes incorporated directly in the scale of scores. Because an individual has membership in more than one group, it is frequently desirable to develop norms on a number of different populations, each of which will very likely yield a different percentile rank for a given level of performance.

Types of norms.   National norms, appropriate to the educational or age level (or levels) for which the test is intended, are the most general and possibly the most commonly used type of norms. One of the problems in defining the national norms group arises from the large number, variety, and complexity of the characteristics of students, as well as of the characteristics of schools and communities that are correlated with or relevant to test scores. Moreover, because of this vast heterogeneity, the national norms group is not always thought to be ideally suited for making the kinds of decisions for which test scores are often needed. For these reasons, when the categories are sufficiently distinct and meaningful, differentiated norms are prepared separately by category of the relevant variables—for example, by sex, educational level, region, type of school, type of community, and type of student body.

In many instances the most useful kinds of norms are the local norms, collected by the test user himself and based on students enrolled in his own institution. Such norms have the advantage of representing a homogeneous group that is familiar to the test user and is characterized by the effects of the particular local conditions and practices in the context of which the test scores will be used.

Since norms are useful to the extent that the reference group is known and meaningful to the user, a valid case can be made for norms that are based not on a random sample of some defined population but on all the students of a special, handpicked, well-known population segment—for example, all freshmen in several similar colleges or all ninth-grade students in New York, Philadelphia, and Chicago. These "special-study" norms capitalize on the familiarity of these groups to the test user and are helpful both in answering specific questions he may have and in the formation of specific decisions. Occasionally a college will want to compare the distribution of its students' scores with those of other colleges which it regards as its competitors for the same applicant pool. Distributions of this kind are not ordinarily made available by the test publisher. Sometimes these institutions manage to exchange their data individually and directly. Sometimes the test publisher can make available to the test user who requests it a set of "user-selected" norms—a combined distribution for the students enrolled at certain institutions specified by the user. It would be expected that the publisher would specify some minimum number of institutions for such a norms group and would also specify the manner in which the students must be selected to represent each institution.

Differentiated norms are multiple sets of norms that are prepared separately by category on a second variable or set of variables in combination —for example, age, grade, or socioeconomic status (ordered variables) or sex, geographical region, type of school support, or type of community (unordered variables). Age or grade norms are a common type of differentiated norms. They make use of the relationship between test performance and age or grade, as is done with age and grade equivalents, but they avoid some of the hidden problems of interpreting the equivalents—the variation in dispersion from age to age (and from grade to grade) and the variation in dispersion from test to test for individuals at the same age or grade level. These problems are avoided by recognizing the inherent dispersion among individuals and capitalizing on it in interpreting scores, as is typically done in the preparation of norms. Some of the problems with grade norms still remain, however, in interpreting the scores of achievement tests. These problems have to do with the fact that test performance is highly dependent on changing subject-matter emphasis in the curriculum and, in a more subtle way, on changing policies and practices regarding promotion and the consequent changes in the distribution of ages for children in the same grade. In order to standardize the distribution of age within grade, some test constructors have suggested the development of modal age norms—that is, grade norms for children of approximately the same age.

Differentiated norms may be regarded as bivariate norms, in which the independent variable is the variable on which the differentiation has been made. Generally, these norms are distributions of test scores for different categories on the independent variable. Under some circumstances, however, it is preferable for the norms to be presented as distributions of scores on the independent variable for categories of test score. Probably the best example of this latter type of norm is the expectancy table, which gives percentile rank distributions on the criterion variable (say, grade-point average in college) for each of a number of categories of test score. The expectancy table itself is worked out directly from the scatterplot of test score versus criterion. The figures of the expectancy table give the likelihood, for an individual who has earned a score of X on the test, of earning a criterion score of Y or better. There are other such bivariate norms. Ebel (1962) suggested that the test score X of an individual be interpreted in terms of his likelihood of earning a score of Y or better on a short test of parallel content and difficulty which has been made available to the test user for examination and study.

The test score of an individual can also be made meaningful by describing the likelihood of his performing tasks of known difficulty satisfactorily (for example, by saying, on the basis of data collected for the purpose of score interpretation, that a person who earns a score of X on the French test is highly likely to be able to read a French newspaper with comprehension) or by estimating the likelihood that he would later earn quality ratings such as outstanding, excellent, good, fair, or poor (or high honors, honors, pass, or fail) on some criterion performance. In all these types of score interpretation the bivariate plot of score versus rating is a necessary part of the process. The value of referring the test scores to these ratings lies in the assumption that the ratings are familiar and meaningful to the user and reasonably reliable.

Although the norms that test publishers have customarily made available are norms based on the performance of individuals for use in the evaluation of individuals, publishers have increasingly, and for very good reason, made available distributions of school means for use in the evaluation of the mean performance of groups of individuals. Since distributions of means are much less dispersed than distributions of individual scores, the former are not useful for the evaluation of the performance of individuals.

Sampling. One of the principal sources of error in norms arises from the problems of drawing a sample from the norms population to use in representing the norms. Unlike the error of measurement in a mean, for example, which tends to vanish as a function of the size of the sample for which an evaluation is sought, the error in norms tends to vanish as a function of the size of the norms sample itself. Once the norms are determined, the error, which may be considered random at the time of sample selection (if the sampling has been done appropriately), now remains in the norms in the form of a bias and is transmitted to all evaluations of the score equally, whether it is an individual's score or the mean score for many individuals. In addition to the usual and expected errors of sampling which can be assessed only if the sampling is truly random, there are other errors of sampling that cannot be assessed and which will very likely cause a bias in the norms (Cornell 1960). Samples that are subject to such errors include (1) a conveniently available sample, (2) a sample which is thought to be "typical," (3) a sample selected on the basis of "expert" opinion, (4) a sample with a high proportion of nonparticipation (almost inevitable in norms development), (5) a sample based on an outdated or otherwise inadequate list of the target population, and (6) a "quota" sample, in which the choice of the particular school within the general framework of the sampling plan is not automatic but deliberate and conscious.

There are various methods of selecting samples, which are most often used not singly but in combination. The simplest is the unrestricted (or simple random) method, which essentially calls for throwing all individuals into a common pool and selecting a sample of specified size from the pool, preferably with the aid of a table of random numbers. A modification of this procedure is the stratified-random process, in which the total population is first divided into homogeneous categories (or strata) on the basis of one or more variables that are correlated with test score (for example, age, sex, or socioeconomic status). The sample is then formed by drawing the individuals at random from each stratum. This procedure ensures that each stratum will be appropriately and proportionately represented in the sample. A third type is the systematic or spaced sample, in which the list of individuals in the population is divided into as many blocks as desired for the sample size (the number of blocks = the number of individuals in the sample), and every nth individual is selected (where n = the number of individuals in each block), starting with a randomly selected individual in the first block. A preferred method, especially if the population list has been prepared in some systematic order (for example, alphabetically), is to draw each individual at random from his block.

The foregoing procedures may be used either in drawing samples of individuals from populations of individuals or in drawing samples of schools from populations of schools. Very seldom, however, are norms samples selected with the individual as the sampling unit. Usually the school is selected as the primary unit of sampling for norms, and all the students or a random sample of all the students in each school are selected for the norms. This kind of successive sampling is called two-stage sampling. The procedure can, of course, be extended to multistage sampling. It is important to recognize that the sampling error of norms in which "natural groups," or clusters, of individuals have been selected is necessarily different from, and generally larger than, sampling error associated with simple random sampling of individuals. This is because communities, schools, classrooms, and so on generally represent homogeneous clusters whose means are more dispersed than the means of random samples of the same size in which the individual is the unit of sampling. Generally speaking, for an overall sample of a given size, the more reliable norms are those based on a large number of clusters and on a small number of individuals from each cluster, rather than the reverse.

Equating. When two or more forms of a test are available for interchangeable use, it is generally considered necessary, in order to adjust for differences in level and range of difficulty, to equate the forms—that is, to convert the system of units on one form to the system of units on the other form so that the scores earned on the two forms will be directly equivalent after conversion. What is under consideration here is the conversion be-

tween two measures of the same function in the sense of a conversion from inches to centimeters, pounds to grams, Fahrenheit to centigrade, and so on. Given this sense in which the concept of equating is used, the conversion will be unique, except for random error, and independent of the particular data used to derive the conversion. Similarly, the conversion will be applicable to all individuals for whom the measures are appropriate. A generally accepted operational definition of equating is as follows: Two scores, one on form X and the other on form Y (where X and Y are parallel in function and equally reliable), are equivalent if their corresponding percentile ranks in any group are equal. The procedure following from this definition is one that adjusts the scale of scores of form X (say) to yield the same distribution in all respects as exists for form Y. If the distributions are dissimilar in shape, then this general (equipercentile) definition will result in a curvilinear conversion from the raw score scale of one form to the scale of the other form. The curvilinearity reflects a systematic expansion and contraction in different regions of the raw score scale of one form in order to cause its distribution to conform to the shape of the distribution of the other form. If, however, the two distributions already have the same shape, then the conversion will approximate a straight line. In such instances a linear definition of equating may be useful, by which one explicitly asserts that the first two moments of the two distributions (the means and standard deviations), but none beyond the second, are respectively equal. That is, the mean and standard deviation of raw scores on one form are simply redefined as equivalent, respectively, to the mean and standard deviation of scores on the other form. Paralleling the equipercentile definition of equating, the linear definition of equating specifies that two scores, one on form X and the other on form Y, are equivalent if their corresponding standard-score deviates in any group are equal. In statistical notation, this is to say that

$$(5) \qquad z_y = z_x \qquad \text{or} \qquad \frac{Y - M_y}{s_y} = \frac{X - M_x}{s_x}$$

Equation (5) is a linear equation, more conveniently expressed in the form $Y = AX + B$, where A (the slope of the line) $= s_y/s_x$ and B (the intercept) $= M_y - AM_x$.

A number of different methods of equating,

appropriate for different types of data and described in some detail by Angoff (1971a), are available. In this article three major types of methods will be presented. Within each type both the linear and the curvilinear (equipercentile) counterparts will be described.

One form administered to each group. A large, heterogeneous group of examinees is chosen and divided into two random halves, one half (α) taking form X, the other half (β) taking form Y (Lord 1950).

For the linear method of equating, it is assumed that the two groups are strictly equivalent. Under this assumption the mean and standard deviation on form X are redefined to be equal, respectively, to the mean and standard deviation on form Y. More specifically, with the means and standard deviations in hand—on form X for group α and on form Y for group β—equation (5) is applied to the data, with the appropriate group-identifying subscripts for X and Y, to yield the conversion equation, $Y = AX + B$.

For the curvilinear method of equating, it is similarly assumed that the two groups are strictly equivalent. The percentiles (that is, the scores attaching to particular percentile ranks) on form X are redefined as equivalent, under this assumption, to the corresponding percentiles (that is, those attaching to the same percentile ranks) on form Y. The details of the procedure may be described as follows: Two distributions are formed, one on form X for group α and another on form Y for group β. Percentile ranks are computed on each distribution for each of about 30 score intervals and the ogives are plotted and smoothed. Corresponding percentiles for each of about 30 percentile ranks are read from the two smoothed ogives and plotted, one against the other. This plot is then smoothed and extrapolated to the end points on each form and used to record the conversion from form X to form Y and vice versa.

Both forms administered to each group. A large group of examinees is chosen and divided into two random halves, one half (α) taking the forms in the order X–Y, the other half (β) taking the forms in the order Y–X. The basic assumption in this method is that the practice effect, in standard-score units, of form Y on form X performance is the same as the practice effect of form X on form Y performance and that the practice effect is independent of score level (Lord 1950).

For the linear method of equating, the average of the means and the average of the standard deviations (more precisely, the square root of the average of the variances) on form X are redefined to be equal, respectively, to the average of the means and standard deviations on form Y. Otherwise stated, the data from this administration are used to find a linear equation of the form, $Y = AX + B$, where

$$(6) \qquad A = \sqrt{\frac{s_{y_\alpha}^2 + s_{y_\beta}^2}{s_{x_\alpha}^2 + s_{x_\beta}^2}}$$

and

$$(7) \qquad B = \tfrac{1}{2}(M_{y_\alpha} + M_{y_\beta}) - \tfrac{A}{2}(M_{x_\alpha} + M_{x_\beta})$$

An approximate curvilinear analogue of this method calls for combining the data on form X and also on form Y for the two half groups and applying the equipercentile (curvilinear) method described in the case where one form is administered to each group.

One form and a common equating test administered to each group. One form is administered to each of two groups, and a common equating test is administered to both groups (Angoff 1961; Gulliksen 1950; Lord 1955a).

If one form is administered to each group, then inevitably there will be differences in the mean levels and dispersions of the two groups (α and β) used for equating. In order to adjust for these differences, an additional (equating) test, form U, equivalent in function and in difficulty to forms X and Y (but perhaps shorter), is administered to both groups. The differences between groups α and β, as observed in their performance on form U, are then used as a basis for adjusting the observed statistics on forms X and Y. Form U may be a separately timed test distinct from X and Y or a set of common items interspersed throughout X and Y. In any case, it should be administered in precisely the same way to both groups. That is to say, the form U items should insofar as possible be equally subject to contextual and ordinal effects for both groups and equally subject to the effects of speededness, motivation, practice, boredom, or fatigue. The assumption basic to this method is that the regression of form X on form U is the same for the combined group ($\alpha + \beta$) as for group α; also that the regression of form Y on form U is the same for the combined group as for group β. (The same equating procedure may be derived by assuming, as does Lord [1955a], that the α and β groups are randomly drawn from the same population.)

For the linear method of equating, estimates of mean and variance are made on both forms X and Y for the combined group of examinees (t) taking form U ($t = \alpha + \beta$). As before, the (estimated) mean and standard deviation on form X are redefined to be equal, respectively, to the (estimated) mean and standard deviation on form Y. The equations for these estimations are given in equations (8) through (11), followed by a brief description of the use of the estimated statistics in the formation of the conversion equation.

$$(8) \qquad \hat{M}_{x_t} = M_{x_\alpha} + b_{xu_\alpha}(M_{u_t} - M_{u_\alpha})$$

$$(9) \qquad \hat{M}_{y_t} = M_{y_\beta} + b_{yu_\beta}(M_{u_t} - M_{u_\beta})$$

$$(10) \qquad \hat{s}_{x_t}^2 = s_{x_\alpha}^2 + b_{xu_\alpha}^2(s_{u_t}^2 - s_{u_\alpha}^2)$$

$$(11) \qquad \hat{s}_{y_t}^2 = s_{y_\beta}^2 + b_{yu_\beta}^2(s_{u_t}^2 - s_{u_\beta}^2)$$

In these equations $b_{xu} = r_{xu}(s_x/s_u)$ and $b_{yu} = r_{yu}(s_y/s_u)$. The estimates $\hat{M}_{x_t}$, $\hat{M}_{y_t}$, $\hat{s}_{x_t}^2$, and $\hat{s}_{y_t}^2$, are applied to form the conversion equation $Y = AX + B$, where $A = \hat{s}_{y_t}/\hat{s}_{x_t}$ and $B = \hat{M}_{y_t} - A\hat{M}_{x_t}$.

A curvilinear analogue of this method (suggested to the author by Frederic M. Lord) is one which estimates the frequencies in the distributions of scores on forms X and Y for the combined group—group t. Using these estimated distributions, the form X and form Y scores are equated by means of the equipercentile method described above. A brief summary of the steps in the procedure follows: (1) Combine the two distributions of form U to form one distribution for group t. (2) Working with the scatterplot of U versus X (U on the horizontal axis, X on the vertical axis), multiply, for each interval of score (i) on form U, the ratio of frequencies f_{i_t}/f_{i_α} by each of the cell frequencies in the column for score U_i. When this is completed for the columns of all values of U_i, there will be a new scatterplot of U versus X estimated for group t. (3) Sum the new frequencies in the cells across the values of U. These summed frequencies now represent the estimated distribution on form X for group t. The next steps in the process are to repeat steps (1), (2), and (3) for the scatterplot of U versus Y for group β. With these two estimated distributions in hand, one for group t on form X and the other for group t on form Y, the two forms, form X and form Y, may be equated by the equipercentile method.

Uses of various methods. The three designs described above are appropriate in different types of situations. The second is the most demanding since it requires the administration of both forms to all examinees. It is also the most reliable. The third is next in order of the time demands it imposes on the student (depending, of course, on the length of form U), but of the three procedures it offers the greatest degree of flexibility and variety, since form U can be conceived of and used in a number of ways. The simplest of the three procedures is the first, but it is also the least precise. However, because of its simplicity it is probably the least susceptible to clerical and administrative errors. For the same reason it may ease the task of attracting larger groups of examinees for the equating administration; the use of larger groups for equating will, of course, tend to enhance the precision of the equating.

There are a number of other methods of equating available in addition to those described here, some of them variations of the equating-test method described in this article, some based on other conceptions of the use of an equating test, and still others that make use of item data rather than score data (Angoff 1971a).

For some tests the forms are available at a number of different levels of difficulty. Such test forms are usually equated, or "articulated," by means of one of the three methods described here or by a variant of one of these methods. Although these articulated test systems are highly useful, especially for tracking individual and group progress, a principal and often expressed concern is that the psychological function measured—especially when the function is highly dependent on the curriculum—may change from level to level, with the result that the notion of a single reference scale for all forms may tend to lose its meaning. Problems attendant on the use of conversion systems for tests that do not measure the same psychological function are discussed in the following section.

Comparable scores. Unlike the problem of equivalent scores, which is restricted to the equating of test forms that measure the same psychological function, the problem of comparable scores may be thought of simply as the problem of "equating" tests of different psychological functions (Angoff 1966). Although score equivalence for parallel forms, when defined on the basis of one group of examinees, will be equally applicable to any group of examinees, comparability across nonparallel tests can be depended on to hold only with other groups that are drawn from the same population as the group on whom the comparability was first established. Thus, comparability between two tests is defined only with respect to a particular group (or population) of examinees. In addition, it is defined only with respect to a particular sense of comparability or a particular method of deriving it.

The logic of the distinction between equivalent and comparable scores may be illustrated when, for example, we ask if person A is "larger" than person B. If both persons are measured in the same way and with the same type of instrument, say an extended ruler, then the comparison is meaningful without qualification, even though one ruler is laid off in feet and inches and the other is laid off in centimeters. However, if different dimensions are under consideration, say height for person A and weight for person B, then the comparison of size for these two persons is meaningful only in a particular sense, for example, with reference to a group or population which is defined for this purpose as "standard."

Although the notion of comparability has some serious restrictions, it is particularly useful (in fact, necessary) when, for example, we wish to compare and rank the general level of scholarship of students who have taken different combinations of courses in college. If the terms of the comparability have been appropriately defined, then such a ranking may be appropriate. However, all too often the comparability is not properly defined and is open to serious question.

Although the logic of comparable scores is different from the logic of equivalent scores, the procedures for deriving comparable scores are similar, often identical, to the procedures for deriving equivalent scores. Very likely the most defensible procedure for deriving comparable scores is that described for the case where one form is administered to each group. To derive comparable scores, tests (*not* test forms) X and Y are administered to random halves of a group drawn, also at random, from a defined population. However, with some reservations the common-equating-test method and perhaps others are also appropriate. One example of the application of the common-equating-test method to such a problem may be found in the case of the Achievement Tests of the College Board, whose scales are ad-

justed to reflect the abilities (as measured by the College Board Scholastic Aptitude Test) of the students who choose to take them. The basic reference group for defining this comparability is the group on which the scale for the Scholastic Aptitude Test is defined.

If the methods of equating parallel tests are adapted to the problem of comparable scores on nonparallel tests, then two sets of criteria must be applied for evaluating the appropriateness of the comparability—one relating to the equating of tests of the same function and one relating to the "equating" of tests of different function. In the former instance there are at least three sources of error: (1) in the reliability of the measuring instruments themselves, (2) in the design of the equating experiment and the method of treating the data, and (3) in the choice of samples used to establish the conversion. In the latter instance —that is, in the problem of comparability—those same sources of error are applicable, and two other sources of error are applicable as well, relating to: (4) the degree to which the tests for which comparable scores are sought are similar in function and (5) the degree to which the group on whom the table of comparable scores is based is appropriate, when the type of individual for whom the table is to be used is considered. With these criteria in mind it would then be necessary to consider the purpose for which the table is to be used and the nature of the decisions that would be based on it in order to evaluate the degree of error that could be tolerated before a table of comparable scores is used.

BIBLIOGRAPHY

ANGOFF, WILLIAM H. 1960 "Measurement and Scaling." Chester W. Harris, ed., *Encyclopedia of Educational Research.* 3rd ed. New York, Macmillan. Pages 807–817.

ANGOFF, WILLIAM H. 1961 "Basic Equations in Scaling and Equating." Samuel S. Wilks, ed., *Scaling and Equating College Board Tests.* Princeton, N.J., Educational Testing Service. Pages 120–129.

ANGOFF, WILLIAM H. 1962 "Scales With Nonmeaningful Origins and Units of Measurement." *Educational and Psychological Measurement,* 22, no. 1:27–34.

ANGOFF, WILLIAM H. 1966 "Can Useful General-purpose Equivalency Tables Be Prepared for Different College Admissions Tests?" Invitational Conference on Testing Problems, 1966, *Testing Problems in Perspective.* Edited by Anne Anastasi. Washington, D.C., American Council on Education. Pages 251–264.

ANGOFF, WILLIAM H. 1971a "Scales, Norms, and Equivalent Scores." Robert L. Thorndike, ed., *Educational Measurement.* Washington, D.C., American Council on Education. Pages 508–600.

ANGOFF, WILLIAM H., ed. 1971*b* *The College Board Admissions Testing Program*. New York, College Entrance Examination Board.

AUSTRALIAN COUNCIL FOR EDUCATIONAL RESEARCH 1951 *A Statistical Theory of Objective Test Scores*. By John A. Keats. Hawthorn, Victoria, The Council.

BIRNBAUM, ALLAN 1968 "Some Latent Trait Models and Their Use in Inferring an Examinee's Ability." Frederic M. Lord and Melvin R. Novick, *Statistical Theories of Mental Test Scores*. Reading, Mass., Addison-Wesley. Pages 397–479.

CORNELL, FRANCIS G. 1960 "Sampling Methods." Chester W. Harris, ed., *Encyclopedia of Educational Research*. 3rd ed. New York, Macmillan. Pages 1181–1183.

EBEL, ROBERT L. 1962 "Content Standard Test Scores." *Educational and Psychological Measurement*, 22, no. 1:15–25.

FAN, CHUNG-TEN 1957 "On the Applications of the Method of Absolute Scaling." *Psychometrika*, 22:175–183.

FLANAGAN, JOHN C. 1939 *The Cooperative Achievement Tests*. A bulletin reporting the basic principles and procedures used in the development of their system of scaled scores. New York, Cooperative Test Service, American Council on Education.

FLANAGAN, JOHN C., ed. 1948 *The Aviation Psychology Program in the Army Air Forces*. Report No. 1. Washington, D.C., Government Printing Office.

FLANAGAN, JOHN C. 1951 "Units, Scores, and Norms." Everet F. Lindquist, ed., *Educational Measurement*. Washington, D.C., American Council on Education. Pages 695–763.

FLANAGAN, JOHN C. 1962 "Symposium: Standard Scores for Aptitude and Achievement Tests." *Educational and Psychological Measurement*, 22, no. 1:35–39.

GARDNER, ERIC F. 1947 "Determination of Units of Measurement Which Are Consistent With Inter and Intra Grade Differences in Ability." Ed.D. dissertation. Cambridge, Mass., Harvard University.

GARDNER, ERIC F. 1962 "Normative Standard Scores." *Educational and Psychological Measurement*, 22, no. 1:7–14.

GULLIKSEN, HAROLD 1950 *Theory of Mental Tests*. New York, Wiley.

GUTTMAN, LOUIS 1950 "The Basis for Scalogram Analysis." Samuel A. Stouffer et al., *Studies in Social Psychology in World War II*. Vol. 4: *Measurement and Prediction*. Princeton, N.J., Princeton University Press. Pages 60–90.

HULL, CLARK L. 1922 "The Conversion of Test Scores Into Series Which Shall Have Any Assigned Mean and Degree of Dispersion." *Journal of Applied Psychology*, 6, no. 3:298–300.

KISH, LESLIE 1965 *Survey Sampling*. New York, Wiley.

LAWLEY, D. N. 1943 "On Problems Connected With Item Selection and Test Construction." *Proceedings of the Royal Society of Edinburgh*, 61–A, part 3:273–287.

LAZARSFELD, PAUL F. 1950 Chapters 10 and 11. Samuel A. Stouffer et al., *Studies in Social Psychology in World War II*. Vol. 4: *Measurement and Prediction*. Princeton, N.J., Princeton University Press. Pages 362–472.

LEVINE, RICHARD S. 1955 "Equating the Score Scales of Alternate Forms Administered to Samples of Different Ability." Research Bulletin RB 55–23. Unpublished paper. Princeton, N.J., Educational Testing Service.

LINDQUIST, E. F. 1930 "Factors Determining Reliability of Test Norms." *Journal of Educational Psychology*, 21, no. 7:512–520.

LINDQUIST, E. F. 1940 "Sampling in Educational Research." *Journal of Educational Psychology*, 31, no. 8:561–574.

LINDQUIST, E. F. 1953 "Selecting Appropriate Score Scales for Tests." Invitational Conference on Testing Problems, 1952, *Proceedings*. Princeton, N.J., Educational Testing Service. Pages 34–40.

LINDQUIST, E. F. 1966 "Norms by Schools." Invitational Conference on Testing Problems, 1966, *Testing Problems in Perspective*. Edited by Anne Anastasi. Washington, D.C., American Council on Education. Pages 269–271.

LORD, FREDERIC M. 1950 "Notes on Comparable Scales for Test Scores." Research Memorandum RM 50–48. Unpublished paper. Princeton, N.J., Educational Testing Service.

LORD, FREDERIC M. 1952*a* *A Theory of Test Scores*. Psychometric Monograph No. 7. Richmond, Va., William Byrd Press.

LORD, FREDERIC M. 1952*b* "The Scale Proposed for the Academic Ability Test." Research Memorandum RM 52–3. Unpublished paper. Princeton, N.J., Educational Testing Service.

LORD, FREDERIC M. 1955*a* "Equating Test Scores—A Maximum Likelihood Solution." *Psychometrika*, 20, no. 3:193–200.

LORD, FREDERIC M. 1955*b* "The Standard Error of Norms and the Standard Error of Measurement." Research Memorandum RM 55–16. Unpublished paper. Princeton, N.J., Educational Testing Service.

LORD, FREDERIC M. 1959 "Test Norms and Sampling Theory." *Journal of Experimental Education*, 27, no. 4:247–263.

LORD, FREDERIC M. 1962 "Estimating Norms by Item-sampling." *Educational and Psychological Measurement*, 22:259–267.

McCALL, WILLIAM A. 1939 *Measurement*. New York, Macmillan.

RASCH, GEORG 1960 *Probabilistic Models for Some Intelligence and Attainment Tests*. Studies in Mathematical Psychology, 1. Copenhagen, Danish Institute for Educational Research.

SCHRADER, WILLIAM B. 1960 "Norms." Chester W. Harris, ed., *Encyclopedia of Educational Research*. 3rd ed. New York, Macmillan. Pages 922–927.

SCHULTZ, MARGARET K., AND WILLIAM H. ANGOFF 1956 "The Development of New Scales for the Aptitude and Advanced Tests of the Graduate Record Examinations." *Journal of Educational Psychology*, 47, no. 5:285–294.

SEASHORE, HAROLD, ALEXANDER WESMAN, AND JEROME DOPPELT 1950 "The Standardization of the Wechsler Intelligence Scale for Children." *Journal of Consulting Psychology*, 14:99–110.

STEVENS, S. S. 1951 "Mathematics, Measurements, and Psychophysics." *Handbook of Experimental Psychology*. New York, Wiley. Pages 1–49.

SWINEFORD, FRANCES, AND CHUNG-TEN FAN 1957 "A Method of Score Conversion Through Item Statistics." *Psychometrika*, 22, no. 2:185–188.

TERMAN, LEWIS M., AND MAUD A. MERRILL 1937 *Measuring Intelligence*. Boston, Houghton Mifflin.

THURSTONE, L. L. 1925 "A Method of Scaling Psychological and Educational Tests." *Journal of Educational Psychology*, 16, no. 7:433–451.

THURSTONE, L. L. 1926 "The Mental Age Concept." *Psychological Review*, 33:268–278.

TUCKER, LEDYARD R 1951 "Academic Ability Test." Research Memorandum RM 51–17. Unpublished paper. Princeton, N.J., Educational Testing Service.

TUCKER, LEDYARD R 1953 "Scales Minimizing the Importance of Reference Groups." Invitational Conference on Testing Problems, 1952, *Proceedings*. Princeton, N.J., Educational Testing Service. Pages 22–28.

VOTAW, DAVID F., JR. 1948 "Testing Compound Symmetry in a Normal Multivariate Distribution." *Annals of Mathematical Statistics*, 19:447–473.

WILKS, SAMUEL S., ed. 1961 *Scaling and Equating College Board Tests*. Princeton, N.J., Educational Testing Service.

WRIGHT, B. D. 1968 "Sample-free Test Calibration and Person Measurement." Invitational Conference on Testing Problems, 1967, *Proceedings*. Princeton, N.J., Educational Testing Service. Pages 85–101.

WILLIAM H. ANGOFF

TEST VALIDITY

Validity is the principal consideration in the use of a test. Any test, whether produced by an educational psychologist for a publishing company or by a teacher in his classroom, is valid for some purposes and invalid for others. For example, a test which is supposed to measure arithmetic reasoning may be an adequate predictor of subsequent school success, but it may depend so much on reading that it tells little about reasoning ability. If every educator analyzed every test critically, fewer educational decisions would be made on the basis of inadequate information.

Validation is the process of studying the accuracy of predictions and inferences made from scores or of descriptive and explanatory interpretations of scores; in this process several types of information are integrated. The logic of test validation is similar to that used in validation of a scientific theory. The same principles which apply to the validation of educational tests apply, though with certain changes of emphasis, to the validation of psychological tests, observations of behavior in the classroom, ratings by judges of teachers and students, scores on questionnaires, and scores based on interviews.

If a test is to serve as a predictor, predictions from the test score have to be checked against some later observation (criterion). The criterion may be the final grade in a course, salary ten years after graduation, score on an achievement test in mathematics, or the school principal's rating of a teacher. Where the aim of testing is to predict such a criterion, the usefulness of the test can be judged simply by how well it predicts this criterion in a tryout situation.

Strictly speaking, one does not validate a test; rather, one evaluates a certain kind of interpretation of data derived from a specified procedure. A particular test is published for users who have many different purposes. An achievement test in mathematics may be used to select students for admission to a certain college and to assist students in selecting academic majors, in choosing the courses they will take the following semester, or in deciding on tentative career plans. Each use requires a different interpretation, and each interpretation has its own degree of validity. Hence, there is no such thing as "the" validity of a test. No test is valid for all purposes, in all situations, or for all groups of students. The College Entrance Examination Board Scholastic Aptitude Test (SAT) does not predict equally well in all colleges, and its mathematics and verbal subscores have different predictive value for different curricula within the same college. Furthermore, even if this test is proved to have validity for predicting college marks, it does not necessarily have validity for predicting professional success.

Every validity study provides information about the usefulness of a test when it is administered using certain procedures. For published tests, procedures are specified in detail: a time limit, the instructions to be read to the group, rules for scoring, and so forth. Appraisal techniques such as interviews or ratings are much less controlled; different raters acquire their information in different settings and take different things into account. Validity data collected when one procedure is used do not apply when the procedure is altered. For example, suppose that the graders of an essay test stress grammatical structure in the validation study. If, in some later application, teachers give most weight to logic, the marks the teachers assign do not have the same meaning as those in the validity study; hence, the evidence from that study does not apply.

Broadly speaking, tests are used in two ways: to arrive at decisions and to arrive at descriptions. Those who use tests to help them make decisions include admissions officers, officials who assign pupils to remedial treatments, and those who certify students as having completed a training program. Students themselves utilize tests in making decisions—such as the selection of a college major. Tests are also used to formulate descriptions—summary statements used in diverse ways by teachers, counselors, and students. If a test is used as the basis for a decision, the test report includes a specific recommendation; if it is used to arrive at a description, the information is stored until it is needed to reach a recommendation about a specific question. In scientific research, tests describe effects that bear on the soundness of theories.

Terminology. In analyzing tests several different kinds of validity must be considered. There are three main aspects of validity for descriptive purposes: content validity, educational significance, and construct validity. In validity for decision-making the two basic considerations are validity for selection and validity for placement. For each kind of interpretation a different kind of evidence regarding validity is pertinent.

In order to clarify the terminology of test validation, it is useful to consider the questions a high school principal might wish to answer with the aid of a mathematics test given at the end of a first course in algebra (grade 9). One of the first questions he might ask is "Have these students mastered the kinds of problems covered in the algebra course?" This is a descriptive question and cannot be answered unless the test has content validity for the course. Content validity means that test items represent the pertinent body of content or range of tasks. The test user must inspect each item for pertinence and compare the distribution of content to that in the domain. The adequacy of the procedure for item selection should also be reviewed.

Another question which might arise is "Which of the subskills—such as factoring and adding signed numbers—are still troublesome for these students and should be taught more thoroughly in the future?" This question is also descriptive, at a different level of detail.

A third important question is "Have the students gotten what they should from the algebra course?" This question is concerned with whether the test covers all the outcomes of educational significance. This is a descriptive question but much broader than the previous ones; it is the question of a statesman rather than of a quality-control inspector.

The principal might also ask "Have these students developed mathematical intuition?" This proposed descriptive interpretation involves a construct and requires construct validation—a process which involves consolidated interpretation of evidence as to what psychological qualities a test measures. The pertinent question in this type of validation is "Are descriptions based on the test truthful in their implications?" Judgment must be used to compare, in revealing circumstances, the achievement of high and low scorers.

Another question which might occur is "Which students should be encouraged to take second-year algebra?" This is a selection decision; it rests essentially on the assumption that the test forecasts achievement in the second course. The kind of study required is often referred to as predictive validation. In this type of validation it is necessary to determine whether selected students are better in criterion performance than students chosen randomly from the group which meets the basic requirements for admission to the program. Judgment on the part of each user of the test is necessary to examine the suitability of the criterion and to decide whether the situation in which he is using the test is similar to the situation in which validation was carried out.

It is also possible that the principal might ask "Which pupils should be placed in an accelerated section of mathematics next year and which in a slow section?" This is a decision about placement. Again, the predictive power of the test is critical, but the issue is the expected difference in achievement of each pupil under the two kinds of instruction; the term "differential validation" applies to such a study. Validation for placement involves asking whether students assigned to different instructional groups learn more than students treated uniformly. In this type of validation, as in validation for selection, the test user must exercise judgment in examining the suitability of the criterion and in deciding whether the new situation is similar to the situation in which the test was originally validated.

Further amplification of the terminology of test validation is provided by assuming that the principal is considering a (somewhat implausible) test whose items are of three types:

(1) What value of x satisfies the equation
$x + 3 = 8$?

    (a) 2
    (b) 3
    (c) 4
    (d) 5
    (e) 6

(2) Solve the equation $y^2 - 2y - 3 = 0$.

    (a) 0, 1
    (b) −1, 3
    (c) 1, −3
    (d) 2, 4
    (e) 3, −5

(3) Who was the third president of the United States?

    (a) Lincoln

    (b) Jefferson

    (c) Taft

    (d) Washington

    (e) Adams

A person judging the content validity of this test would surely point out that many types of problems in first-year algebra are missing from the test—graphs, word problems, and so forth. Further, items like the third question are extraneous on an algebra test.

In regard to educational significance, questions (1) and (2) are important, but an educator should also be concerned with many other types of problems normally considered in a first course in algebra, as well as the pupil's liking for mathematics, his confidence in attempting mathematical work, and other variables. From this point of view, the test is not invalid so much as incomplete.

In an analysis of construct validity, inspection shows that the test does not bear on what is usually called intuition. If the matter were disputed, one could apply the test to both more and less intuitive students (as determined by individual testing and observation) and look for a score difference.

Determining the predictive validity for success in second-year algebra requires a study in which the scores of pupils in a tryout group at the end of the ninth grade are compared with their later achievement in second-year algebra. A follow-up study is also required to determine validity for assignment of pupils to accelerated or slow mathematics classes. Some pupils with a particular score on the test (82 percent, for example) should be observed in an accelerated section and others in a slow section to determine which treatment is more beneficial for these pupils.

Validity for description. A test is used to describe a student whenever a teacher or administrator makes such statements as: "John can read very well."/"Sheila is mentally retarded."/"Sally can solve calculus problems."/"Don is interested in science." Similar descriptive statements are made about groups, especially in evaluation of instructional programs. In validating a descriptive interpretation the important question to be asked is "How true are the implications of the description?"

Content validity and educational significance. Content validity refers to the degree to which the test measures the specified educational objectives; educational significance is determined by asking whether the test covers the important objectives, which may or may not be specified. Both considerations are important, and they are essentially the same in character.

Content validity has to do with task requirements and observable behavior; inferences about internal processes which are unobservable are relegated to the domain of construct validity. If a test is content-valid, this means that competent judges agree that the test items represent the universe of tasks the test purports to measure.

To judge an achievement test, the objectives of the instruction—the range of tasks the student is to learn to perform or the habits he is to develop—must be stated. Test items are judged against this set of specifications. One researcher has defined a representative sample of test items as "one that *re-presents* the universe—that is, one that duplicates or reproduces the essential characteristics of the universe in their proper proportion and balance" (Lennon 1956, p. 301).

Statements of objectives must be clear and concrete to be useful in judging a test. The objective for students in a French course may be not simply to master the language but perhaps to understand conversation on everyday topics. A test of vocabulary or grammatical usage would be of limited validity for measuring the ability to understand conversation. A content-valid test for this objective would probably take the form of a recording of a conversation by a native speaker of French; the student would be required to listen to the recording and then answer questions about the content. The teacher must guard against too much similarity between the recorded conversation and his instruction, since a student's comprehension of what his own teacher says is not the same as comprehension of French conversation generally.

In judging content validity one must consider what responses are called for as well as what topics are dealt with. For example, in a U.S. Navy gunnery school a written verbal test proved to be much less related to practical performance than a pictorial test which tested the same type of information as the written verbal test except that the questions were asked by means of pictures supplemented by words (Ninth Naval District Headquarters . . . 1945). Another example is a test of ability to alphabetize which required file clerks to select from a list of five names presented in haphazard order the name which would appear third after alphabetization. This test was completely unrelated to speed in inserting a fifth name into a list of four names already alphabetized, which is probably closer to the actual on-the-job task (Mosier 1947).

It is also true that the same content, written differently, may measure different things: test items may call for much or little reading ability, fine or coarse discrimination, recall or reasoning, and so on. A test item that has content validity presents no irrelevant difficulty. That is, if a student fails the item, it should be solely because he has not learned the content the item is intended to test. To put it differently, every item ought to be as easy as it can be made, without altering the central content. If content validity is desired, tricky questions, vague questions, and wordy questions should be ruled out. In most school subjects, time pressure also interferes with content validity.

Another important aspect of the content validity of an objective test is the manner in which the test is scored. It is obvious that competent judges should agree with the scoring key of an objective test. A less obvious point is that the scoring method implicitly weights the importance of the objectives measured by the test. For instance, an objective very important to the test user may be measured by only one or two items, while an objective the user considers less important may be measured by three or more items. If the reported test score consists of the count of items correct, this score may mask a deficiency the test user wants to detect.

Content validity has nothing to do with statistical aspects of the test. In particular, one does not seek test items that are highly intercorrelated since choosing items for homogeneity tends to impair the coverage of the intended content. The correlation of the test items with a criterion is also irrelevant to content validity.

It is important to realize that a content interpretation may be valid for one purpose or one setting and invalid for another. For example, if a certain published test measures objectives unlike those of a particular curriculum, it would be invalid to use the test results to judge the competence of teachers using that curriculum. The test may, however, cast light on the ability of this curriculum to develop a competence that some educators consider important. For example, a certain instructional program may not ask students to develop the ability to solve quadratic equations by graphing. If a test which includes items of this kind indicates that the students are not developing this ability incidentally, educators who are considering the program for adoption are warned of the omission.

Educational objectives change from place to place and from time to time. A test appropriate in helping to evaluate a course or a pupil in one school district is inappropriate in a district where the objectives are different. In only a few skill subjects are objectives essentially uniform, and the advent of the new math and audiolingual language teaching shows that objectives of even the most traditional subjects can be redefined. Thus, the content considered important when a test is developed may become outdated.

Test titles sometimes cause trouble even when the content of the test is educationally significant. Parents, counselors, and teachers may read meanings into the title of a test that are unjustified. A so-called intelligence test does not measure the inherited characteristics of an individual, but many people think it does. A test of "scientific thinking" may be a test of information, of willingness to give back to the teacher the words he has stated, or even of a preference for responding "uncertain" rather than "certain" to controversial statements. Test interpreters have to go beneath the title to consider precisely what a tests calls for. A test is not defined by its title but by the tasks included by the test and the rules used to select the items. The test manual should state warranted interpretations of the test and the evidence supporting these interpretations.

The data collected to evaluate the progress of students in a course should adequately assess the outcomes which the school considers important. If a single test does not measure some objectives that are important to the school district, then supplementary data must be collected on these other objectives. A single test or a single type of test rarely covers all the important outcomes. When evaluation is confined to a test of one objective, it is likely that teachers will come to stress that one objective and that students will concentrate on that kind of learning. For example, testing solely on grammar can set back the development of creative writing. When "achievement" standards are stressed, character development is likely to receive less attention and emphasis than academic achievement. Because it is not practical to test every outcome in depth, any testing program lacks full validity, no matter how good the tests are for their limited purposes. Test data alone are an inadequate base for some major conclusions about the educational program.

For purposes of evaluation it may be appropriate to include a test on an objective not emphasized in the course or program pupils have taken. It would be unjust to mark pupils on such a test, but the attitude or ability data gained from such a test enriches the evaluation of the course. This illustrates the point that a test can be valid for some purposes and invalid for others. If it is found that the attitude or ability not emphasized is developing normally, there is no need for concern. But if the class does badly on the test, and the ability or attitude is desirable, the instruction should probably be changed.

Construct validity. Construct validity is concerned with the psychological qualities contributing to a test score. The concept of construct validation was developed originally in connection with personality tests; its roots are in the philosophy of science (Hempel 1966).

There are three major procedures in construct validation: correlation, experimentation, and logical analysis. A correlation procedure compares students high on a particular test with students low on the same test or some other test or observation. For example, if a test is to assess artistic creativity, it would be expected that high school seniors who have had four years of experience in producing original paintings would score higher on the test than seniors who have not produced original paintings. As a different example, if galvanic skin response (GSR) and the Manifest Anxiety Scale (MAS) are both hypothesized to indicate level of anxiety, a high correlation between GSR scores and MAS scores would be expected. But if a theoretical distinction is made between the typical level of trait anxiety—as measured by the MAS—and the level of state anxiety at the time of the test—as measured by the GSR at this moment—only a rather low correlation would confirm the theory. Similarly, if a so-called creativity test correlates highly with a well-known test of reasoning ability, this may mean that the creativity test measures nothing but garden-variety reasoning.

A high correlation between two tests does not prove, however, that the tests measure the same construct. An arithmetic reasoning measure could correlate highly with a measure of mathematical intuition because students who have best learned one skill rank equally high in the other. The evidence that distinguishable attributes are being measured by the two tests might be provided by the scores of students from another school where instruction emphasizes one skill and not the other. If one wished to clarify the nature of intuition, one might even design special instruction to prove that intuition can be increased without improving arithmetic reasoning. Construct validation investigates whether different indicators of the same construct converge so that they imply the same conclusion about the persons being tested and whether indicators of distinct constructs give distinguishable results (Campbell & Fiske 1959).

One way of examining convergence and distinctiveness of indicators is factor analysis. This statistical technique summarizes intercorrelations among variables. Factor analysis is treacherous, however, since different types of analyses can lead to different conclusions about the same data (Cronbach 1970).

Experimentation, the second important means of construct validation, involves making some change in the subjects' experience prior to the test or in the testing procedure. For instance, the previous example introduced an experiment by suggesting that special instruction be designed to prove that intuition can be increased without improving arithmetic reasoning. Experimentation could also be used in the validation of a reading comprehension test. Theoretically, a reading comprehension test should not depend very much on speed. In order to determine whether scores on a particular test are affected by the amount of time allotted for the test, one could ask students to change to a colored pencil at the end of the normal time limit and then continue for an additional period of five to ten minutes. If the ranking of students based on comprehension scores for the regular period differs substantially from the ranking for the longer period, the test depends on speed more than it should.

The third method of construct validation is logical analysis. For example, careful study of a reading comprehension test might lead to the hypothesis that the items favor students with a high interest in science. This hypothesis could be tested by comparing the test scores with those on a second test that was not science-oriented.

Every time an educator asks the question "Yes, but what does the test *really* measure?" he is asking for information about construct validity. For instance, a test entitled reading comprehension might stimulate an educator to ask such questions as: How much does speed of reading enter into the scores? Do the reading paragraphs have special appeal to students with special interests? Does the test measure comprehension at levels higher than mere recall or word recognition? Does the score depend heavily on vocabulary size? Does the test favor students who use a particular test-taking strategy—such as first reading the questions and then reading the paragraph?

Construct validation of a personality or attitude test might require evidence on such questions as: How easily can a student fake his answers? How do high scorers differ from low scorers in different situations? In a sense, construct validation is concerned with internal processes that produce a high score—such as ego strength, motivations, and critical thinking. Construct validators investigate hypotheses about the processes taking place within an individual in order to explain his performance. Such processes cannot be observed directly, but controlled observations of behavior can evaluate the reasonableness of the hypotheses.

Statements about construct validity may use various statistics to support interpretations of the test, but there is no mathematical index of construct validity. Construct validation is an integrative interpretation of evidence. The argument for the construct validity of the Stanford-Binet scale as a measure of general intelligence, for example, would require a summary of 60 years of research on adults and schoolchildren with this test or other procedures relevant to the construct in countries all over the world.

A construct is a category created in order to organize experience into general statements having the form of laws. A construct interpretation of a test may name a trait (such as motivation to achieve) or describe a kind of situation (such as fine manual work). A theory may be defined as a set of statements from which predictions about events are derived; it is a kind of map, perhaps sketchy, of a region of knowledge. A theory should put into perspective what is already known and give the scientist a hint of what is yet to be dis-

covered. A worthwhile theory should lead to the formulation of hypotheses, provoke experiments, and suggest predictions in a wide variety of situations. The hypotheses generated by the theory should be testable in the sense that the scientist knows what observations would confirm the hypotheses and how to achieve these observations. The theory language may contain terms that refer to unobservable events; such concepts become empirically meaningful to the extent that they account for observable phenomena.

The meaning of a proposition is established by the conditions under which the proposition is confirmed by a group of scientists. The physicist Bridgman argued at one time that "the concept is synonymous with the corresponding set of operations" (1927, p. 5), though he later softened this rule that one concept equals one operation (1945). The original strict statement was carried into psychological research and even into educational measurement by some influential writers. Skinner, for example, wrote that "we must explicate an operational definition for every term unless we are willing to adopt the vague usage of the vernacular" (1945, p. 270).

However, this insistence upon operational definitions would force thinking into a rigid mold and force the abandonment of many useful concepts. In developing the idea of construct validation, Cronbach and Meehl (1955) joined the philosophers of science who dissent from a strict operationalism in which every term is defined by one, and only one, set of operations. When there are many response variables, they argued, it is mandatory to subsume them under constructs, since otherwise there must be a separate set of laws for every measure of outcome. Content validation is operationalist in conception; there is a defined universe of pertinent tasks. But a content-valid measure (of paragraph reading, for example) can be fully interpreted only in terms of mental processes that are inferred rather than defined.

Observations are connected with constructs, and constructs with other constructs, by sentences that make explicit the inferences of the scientist. Thus, an interlocking network of sentences constitutes a theory. Cronbach and Meehl explain that "scientifically speaking, to 'make clear what something *is*' means to set forth the laws in which it occurs" (*ibid.*, p. 290). These laws are inferred from accumulated data and are intended not merely to summarize the data but also to unify and, hence, to explain the data. To be operationally meaningful, a statement must (at least in principle) be confirmable—that is, the network must tie it to observables. It is extremely difficult to validate a theory. The most that can be said is that the hypotheses produced by a certain theory are consistent with facts, and it is always possible that these same facts would agree also with other theories.

A construct ought to have diverse properties, capable of being indicated or observed in several distinct ways. The more such indicators there are, the richer the network and the more useful the construct. The vagueness inherent in the use of a construct can be reduced by expanding the network of laws surrounding the construct.

A construct cannot be reduced to observables since it contains "surplus meaning." This surplus meaning contains the potential for future scientific development and is "an indispensable part of theory for those who are concerned with the progress of scientific knowledge" (Caws 1965, p. 58).

In examining the validity of a network or a specific statement, negative evidence must be taken seriously. Negative evidence can mean that the indicator does not reflect the construct, that the construct needs to be revised, or that the investigation is unsound.

Strictly speaking, a theory can never be verified or proved; this is true also of a construct interpretation proposed for a test. One could never complete every possible check on a theory. Every theoretical statement is tentative—tenable rather than true. Sometimes experimentation indicates that a construct is incorrect; for example, experimentation has disproved the formerly held theory that a substance called ether fills the upper regions of space. A construct can be considered a kind of temporary scaffolding in theory construction. The justification of a construct is strengthened when the construct predicts more and more diverse observations. The evidence must be made public so that other scientists may criticize and offer alternative interpretations. Nonpublic evidence which refers to something "observed by the writer in many clinical cases" is worthless as evidence because refutation of the researcher's report is impossible (Cronbach & Meehl 1955).

Concern for achievement. Concern for achievement, a construct of considerable interest to educators, provides a useful example of construct validation. The measurement of achievement motivation is difficult since actual achievement is influenced by such factors as ability, knowledge, and the desire for social approval. Thus, a person might achieve without having a particular urge to overcome obstacles or control situations.

A hint toward the study of motives was given by Freud, who searched in dreams and free associations for clues to unconscious motives. "The interpretation of dreams," he said, "is the royal road to a knowledge of the unconscious activities of the mind" (1899, p. 608). Fantasy production is less constrained than other behavior by the limits of reality or by abilities.

One study measured the achievement motive in college males by administering a series of paper-and-pencil tests and then presenting a series of pictures from the Thematic Apperception Test (TAT) and asking the students to write a story about each picture within a five-minute time period (McClelland et al. 1953). Stories written by men who had been told that the tests would indicate intelligence and leadership capabilities referred to "standards of excellence" and to "doing well" more often than stories written by other subjects under neutral directions. A scoring key was then established for the stories so that persons tested subsequently received a total test score that supposedly would indicate their concern for achievement. This test has been used for studies on such factors as the effect of parental expectation on the child's concern for achievement (Rosen & D'Andrade 1959; Atkinson & Feather 1966; Smith 1969).

Game situations were devised to test the evolving theory of concern for achievement. It was supposed, for example, that strong concern for achievement implied a tendency to prefer medium-level risks. In a ringtoss game, subjects were asked to select a distance in the range of 1 to 15 feet from which they would throw a ring at a peg; in this way the subject could adjust the distance according to his estimation of his probability of success. A gambling preference game was devised in which subjects chose high-, medium-, or low-risk preferences in a poker-dice game. A third sign of risk-taking behavior was how long a student worked on a three-hour examination.

Anxiety was measured by a questionnaire, and concern for achievement was measured by the picture-stories of the TAT and another test which required completion of stories on achievement themes. The hypothesis that anxiety and concern for achievement are distinct constructs was confirmed by low correlations of the questionnaire with the other two tests.

The theory held that high achievement motivation implies readiness to seek an opportunity to succeed, while anxiety implies desire to avoid failure. More specific hypotheses were that subjects with high concern for achievement and low anxiety would select an intermediate distance in the ringtoss game, would persist in the three-hour examination, and would prefer risks of about .50 in the poker-dice game, while subjects with low concern for achievement and high anxiety would prefer extreme distances in the ringtoss game (either very close to the peg or very far away from the peg), would leave the three-hour examination early, and would prefer extreme odds in the poker-dice game. The theoretical network thus linked three test indicators and three situational indicators by means of three constructs.

All the hypotheses were supported except that students with test scores indicating high achievement motivation and low anxiety did not choose intermediate risks in the poker-dice game. Consequently, the investigators modified the network to say that concern for achievement is influential only when the subject's efforts can improve his chance for success. A later study by Raynor and Smith (1966) supported this interpretation.

This summary of a fragment of the research and theory of achievement relies heavily on the review by Atkinson and Feather. Other psychologists might suggest alternative networks or cite studies that challenge part of the theory. Acceptable construct interpretation of a test must rest on the concurrence of persons who have studied the available data carefully and who have agreed on the interpretation.

Validity for decision-making. Tests are used in making many kinds of decisions. Colleges select entering freshmen on the basis of their verbal and mathematical test scores on the College Entrance Examination Board tests. Placement test scores may be used to place students at the proper level in a sequence of courses in a foreign language. In an individualized system of instruction, placement tests may be used to select the instructional unit a student should work on next. In all these cases the assumption is that the test has some predictive value which is useful in selecting the right course of action.

It is helpful to distinguish selection from placement. In selection, a fraction of an applicant group is admitted, and the institution has no further concern with the persons rejected. In placement, each student is assigned to one of several treatments; no one is rejected. Choices among curricula and choices among remedial procedures are examples of placement, or classification.

Validity for selection. For selection, tests should be correlated with later outcomes; the higher the correlation, the better. A college may want to select applicants likely to make good grades; if so, it will seek a test that predicts grade average. To learn whether a proposed test gives valid information for such a purpose, the ideal procedure is to administer the test to a group of applicants who meet the basic requirements for participation in the program and admit all of them (or a random sample), without inspecting their test scores. After a meaningful time period information on outcome—that is, the criterion information—may be collected. The investigator may tabulate criterion scores against predictor scores to learn the proportion of good records among applicants who had high, low, or intermediate predictor scores. This procedure shows what distribution of records will be obtained if future applicants below a certain score level are rejected.

It is often impractical to admit the full range of applicants in order to get representative data. A validity study can be carried out within a group that has been selected, but only hazardous extrapolation allows prediction of the probable performance of students similar to those who were eliminated from the sample.

The test-criterion relation is often summarized in a validity coefficient. This index reaches 1.00 if prediction is perfect and drops to .00 if outcomes have no correspondence to predictions. Multiple correlation procedures assign weights to several predictor tests and evaluate their combined predictive power. Typically, grade records or aptitude tests predict subsequent academic performance or performance in vocational training with coefficients in the range 0.40 to 0.70. Prediction of job success is generally poorer than this, but, even so, selection based on tests has an economic payoff.

It is advisable to analyze the value of the predictor for distinctive subgroups of applicants. An employer ought to check validity separately for males and females, blacks and whites, high school graduates and high school dropouts, and so forth. The ability of the test to predict the criterion may vary from subgroup to subgroup. It is not profitable, however, to make analyses for very small groups; about 40 persons is a minimum size, and several hundred are needed to establish any complicated weighting formula.

Validity of a test differs from place to place. If curricula and instructional methods of two institutions differ, the test that predicts for one institution may not predict for the other. The ability range of the applicant group and the level of competition within the school also influence a test's predictive ability. The validity coefficient will be lower in a selected group than in an unselected group. Thus, a test useful in selecting entering freshmen at a prestigious university may not be useful in predicting differences among the accepted freshmen on some subsequent criterion, simply because these freshmen are similar in ability. It should also be noted that a predictor that validly forecasts marks in English that rest on usage and punctuation may have little power to predict what level of creative writing skill the student will reach; a test valid for one criterion may be invalid for another.

The correlation of a test with a criterion may change over time, for a variety of reasons. For example, a verbal reasoning test may predict college marks better in one decade than another because of changes in the ability range of students or in the curricula they select. As another example, in the Strong Vocational Interest Blank, which attempts to predict what careers will satisfy a student, a key identifying aviator interests was made in the late 1930's. But the aviator of that day was a lone daredevil; today he is a junior executive, hemmed in by routines, regulations, and responsibilities. The original scoring key predicted satisfaction in doing what aviators did in the 1930's. To use that key to tell today's student that he will enjoy being an aviator because his interests are like those of aviators is unjustified, so long as there is no evidence supporting the current validity of the key.

A sound criterion is essential in validating a predictor. Ordinarily the person who uses the test for selection is interested in several kinds of outcome and might find various kinds of criterion information significant. Commonly used criteria are achievement tests, job-proficiency

tests, judgments (including marks), and career data. For example, an achievement test in reading at the end of the year may be used as criterion for a reading-readiness test; a rating of teacher interns may be used to validate selection rules; career information (such as which persons completed training or which stayed in the occupation) may be used to validate predictions made in guidance.

The person reading a published validation study should critically consider whether the criterion reflects the outcomes he values. Too often, a study relies on whatever criterion is easy to obtain, neglecting other criteria of equal educational importance. In particular, validation studies too often emphasize proficiency and knowledge and neglect to obtain evidence on motivational outcomes of instruction. The college student who develops a mature outlook on life is surely a better "product" than the knowledge-packed student who does not develop such an outlook. Admission rules should use the student with a mature outlook on life as a model. They will not do this if tests are checked only on their ability to predict marks. Validation studies of occupational tests tend to concentrate on end-of-training criteria; however, performance on the job would be a more significant criterion. Success in training too often depends more on verbal ability than does success in work. Moreover, what predicts success in the short run may not be the best long-range predictor. Long-term follow-up studies are highly important wherever practicable.

The benefit of using a test varies according to the importance of the decision, the cost of testing, and the proportion of applicants selected. If almost every applicant is accepted for an educational treatment (for example, if a junior college intends to admit nearly every high school graduate who applies), expensive admission tests cannot be justified. On the other hand, when only a small fraction of the applicants can be accepted, tests are usually beneficial. Sometimes a test that predicts an important outcome with a coefficient of .30 is more useful than another test that predicts a less important outcome with a coefficient of .60. Costly procedures having considerable validity are usually justified, and so are inexpensive procedures of modest validity. Obviously, the more uses to which a test result can be put, the greater the utility of the test. The question of how large a validity correlation should be in order for a test to be useful has no simple answer. High validity should be sought to improve decisions that can be reversed only at great cost, if at all. An inexpensive test with moderate validity can be useful, however, when the cost of mistaken decisions is modest.

All that has been said implies that an administrator who wishes to use tests for selection can use published validity studies only as a preliminary indication as to which tests may be relevant. A published validity coefficient indicates, for example, how well a test predicted the performance of engineering students in a certain time and place; results in another engineering school may be better or worse. The same is true for validity of employment tests; no matter how good the published reports on a test for stenographers are, the employer who uses the test ought to accumulate records of his own workers to check its effectiveness in his office.

Validity for placement. Tests are also used to make placement decisions. For example, ninth graders may be assigned to general mathematics, regular algebra, or an enriched algebra course on the basis of their marks in eighth-grade mathematics. Placement decisions are valid if the pupils accomplish more in mathematics than they would have if assigned in some other manner. The greater the accomplishment, the more valid the placement.

Validation of placement procedures is much like that of selection. Pupils in the score range where either treatment may plausibly be considered are divided at random between the alternative courses. Specifically, the group of students having grades of B+ in arithmetic might be randomly divided between the enriched and the regular algebra course to learn how they fare in each. In due time, criterion information is collected. Validation of placement procedures presents a difficult logical problem because the two courses deal with different things and the criterion test must apply to both. The decision-maker must judge whether a score of 75 percent on a test over the enriched program is a better or worse outcome than a score of 90 percent over the content of the regular course. A measure is valid for placement if students who score high on it do better in the more difficult instructional program than in the less difficult one, and students who score low on the measure achieve their best outcome in the less difficult program. There are serious practical

difficulties in carrying out such validation studies, and therefore the desired information is not often available for tests recommended for use in placement.

Use of validation studies. The information on test validity that the publisher of a test is expected to present to aid critical analysis is outlined in standards prepared by professional organizations (*Standards for Educational and Psychological Tests* 1966). The test user can profit from careful study of the test manual and critical reviews in *The Sixth Mental Measurements Yearbook* (Buros 1965) and earlier volumes. An article entitled "Test Validation" by Cronbach (1970) provides a detailed discussion of how validity studies are carried out.

In the final analysis, the responsibility for use of a test rests with the person who interprets the test for his unique purposes. However well a test is validated, it can be misused. The user who understands the research on validation will be careful not to place more faith in the test than it deserves and will not ask it to do what it cannot do.

Every validation study adds to the understanding of what a test means and how it relates to classroom events. The accumulation of studies helps to generate a theory of individual differences among students. This accumulating understanding provides the foundation for designing new educational situations and new measuring instruments. Since these new situations and instruments need to be validated, the process of investigation never ends.

BIBLIOGRAPHY

ATKINSON, JOHN W., AND NORMAN T. FEATHER, eds. 1966 *A Theory of Achievement Motivation.* New York, Wiley.

BRIDGMAN, PERCY W. (1927) 1946 *The Logic of Modern Physics.* New York, Macmillan.

BRIDGMAN, PERCY W. 1945 "Some General Principles of Operational Analysis." *Psychological Review,* 52:246–249.

BUROS, OSCAR KRISEN 1965 *The Sixth Mental Measurements Yearbook.* Highland Park, N.J., Gryphon Press.

CAMPBELL, DONALD T., AND DONALD W. FISKE 1959 "Convergent and Discriminant Validation by the Multitrait-Multimethod Matrix." *Psychological Bulletin,* 56, no. 2:81–105.

CAWS, PETER 1965 *The Philosophy of Science: A Systematic Account.* Princeton, N.J., Van Nostrand.

CRONBACH, LEE J. 1970 "Test Validation." R. L. Thorndike, ed., *Educational Measurement.* Washington, D.C., American Council on Education.

CRONBACH, LEE J., AND PAUL E. MEEHL 1955 "Construct Validity in Psychological Tests." *Psychological Bulletin,* 52, no. 4:281–302.

Freud, Sigmund (1899) 1961 *Interpretation of Dreams.* New York, Wiley.

Hempel, Carl G. 1966 *Philosophy of Natural Science.* Englewood Cliffs, N.J., Prentice-Hall.

Lennon, Roger T. 1956 "Assumptions Underlying the Use of Content Validity." *Educational and Psychological Measurement,* 16, no. 3:294–304.

McClelland, D. C., et al. 1953 *The Achievement Motive.* New York, Appleton.

Mosier, Charles I. 1947 "A Critical Examination of the Concepts of Face Validity." *Educational and Psychological Measurement,* 7, no. 2:191–205.

Ninth Naval District Headquarters. Training Aids Section 1945 "A Comparative Study of Verbalized and Projected Pictorial Tests in Gunnery." Great Lakes, Ill., Unpublished.

Raynor, Joel O., and Charles P. Smith 1966 "Achievement-related Motives and Risk-taking in Games of Skill and Chance." *Journal of Personality,* 34, no. 2:176–198.

Rosen, B. C., and R. D'Andrade 1959 "The Psychosocial Origins of Achievement Motivation." *Sociometry,* 22, no. 3:185–218.

Skinner, B. F. 1945 "The Operational Analysis of Psychological Terms." *Psychological Review,* 52, no. 5:270–277.

Smith, Charles P., ed. 1969 *Achievement-related Motives in Children.* New York, Russell Sage Foundation.

Standards for Educational and Psychological Tests 1966 Washington, D.C., American Psychological Association.

Lee J. Cronbach and Thomas J. Quirk

TESTING AND ASSESSMENT PROGRAMS, NATIONAL

Education has traditionally had two purposes: to develop literacy and to prepare the elite for their occupational and social roles. The progress of a nation in developing literacy was usually appraised in terms of the percentage of its children enrolled in the elementary school, the percentage finishing the program, and the percentage of adults who had completed various years of schooling. It was not thought to require prolonged schooling or education of high quality to attain literacy; hence, these indexes of educational exposure were deemed adequate to judge the extent of a nation's success in reaching the goal of universal education.

Teachers and other school staff members have always known that the attainment of literacy is not guaranteed by an individual's having attended school. They have observed their students and have used various tests and examinations as a basis for giving grades and for identifying the learning problems of individual students. However, these devices were not used to judge the educational level of a community, state, or nation, nor were they constructed to serve such a function.

History of educational assessments. In most countries, secondary and higher education has traditionally been available to only a small fraction of youth because it was commonly believed that only a few had the capability of benefiting from it. Since those seeking secondary and higher education for themselves or their children far outnumbered the available educational openings, educational testing and examining programs became preoccupied with attempts to rank students from highest to lowest or to separate the good students from the poor ones. The tests and other devices used by the state or the educational institutions were constructed to measure individual differences among the students and not to assess the extent to which they had learned what the schools attempted to teach. The tests could indicate that John made a higher score than James but did not attempt to assess systematically and comprehensively what had been learned by both of them.

In the United States during World War I, induction officers noted wide variations in the apparent levels of education among recruits from different states. It was for this reason that Leonard Porter Ayres, director of education and statistics of the Russell Sage Foundation, developed educational indexes for each state, but these were based on factors that reflected what was put into the schools and did not furnish an appraisal of what students had learned. These indexes included such data as the proportion of the school-age population actually in school, the average expenditures per pupil, and the average number of school grades completed by adults. Indexes like these were used in some states to arouse people to improve their relative educational position—for example, by increasing school expenditures, by requiring more education for teachers, and by raising the age of compulsory education—but they furnished no dependable evidence about the educational results of schooling within the states.

At the end of World War II, another wave of interest developed in interstate educational comparisons as a result of the differences among the states in the percentage of rejections by the Selective Service. Studies were made of the relative standing of states in terms of the percentage of Selective Service rejections and the percentage selected for officer training, but these comparisons were not a satisfactory basis for a national assessment. Those young people examined by the

Selective Service and by the military classification officers were not a representative sample of all youth in the states. Tests given at induction centers attempt to identify persons whose general literacy is below that of the average fifth-grader rather than assessing the range of educational achievements of American youth. Similarly, the tests used in the selection for Officer Candidate School focus on the level of achievement of the highest quarter of graduating high school seniors and are not intended to cover the range of what youth learn in school. None of these appraisals elicit the kind of information that would be afforded by a national assessment of educational achievement.

The great interest in national assessment programs that developed in the United States in the 1960's arose from the public's increasing recognition that effective education is essential for the constructive participation of all youth in modern industrial society. As the importance of education gained wider public appreciation, the need for dependable information about its adequacy became apparent. Teachers, administrators, school boards, legislators, community leaders, and the general public need information about educational progress to make wise decisions about the further development of education. Facts about the numbers of schools, teachers, and pupils and figures on the money expended were available, but sound and adequate information about the educational results was never obtained until the inception of a comprehensive national assessment program.

Project Talent. Until 1960 no nation had made a direct attempt to assess the educational achievement of its people. Project Talent provided the first comprehensive data regarding the achievement of a national sample of American high school students. This study was not instituted to assess the educational attainments of the nation but rather to appraise the differential abilities of high school students and to trace their later educational and occupational experiences; the study thus sought to learn the extent to which a student's abilities acquired through the school years were being developed through postsecondary education and utilized in occupations related to his educational experiences. The initial stage in this project was the formulation and administration of a two-day battery of aptitude and achievement tests which included a detailed inventory of the student's background, characteristics, and plans. This battery was taken by 440,000 students in 1,353 secondary schools throughout the United States in March of 1960. The plan called for follow-up information to be obtained from these students—one year, four years, ten years, and 20 years after their high school graduation.

Project Talent is not a comprehensive national assessment because the youth involved were only those in high school at that time and did not include those who had dropped out or were in other institutions. Furthermore, the tests used did not attempt to survey all of the important school objectives, seeking only to appraise what the average students, not the most advanced or the least advanced, had learned.

Nevertheless, the results may be helpful to those concerned with the improvement of education. The project reported on the student's ability to read and understand the writings of ten standard literary authors and the contents of ten popular American magazines. The study found that 60 percent of the ninth-grade students and 85 percent of the 12th-grade students could read and understand the writings of Louisa May Alcott. The corresponding figures for the writings of Rudyard Kipling were 17 percent for the ninth-graders and 44 percent for the 12th-graders; for Joseph Conrad's writings the figures were 12 percent and 35 percent, respectively. The writings of the most difficult author among the ten, Thomas Mann, were understood by fewer than 1 percent of the ninth-graders and only 4 percent of the 12th-graders.

It was also reported that 75 percent of the ninth-graders and 92 percent of the 12th-graders comprehended the contents of movie magazines. However, passages from the *Reader's Digest* were understood by only 18 percent of the ninth-graders and 45 percent of the 12th-graders. Passages from *Time* were understood by fewer students; only 7 percent of the ninth-grade students and 25 percent of the 12th-graders comprehended them.

Project Talent also reported on the occupational plans of the high school students. Only 19 percent of the boys who had indicated in the tenth grade that they were planning one of 30 occupations as a career reported the same plans three years later. For the boys indicating their career plans in grade 12, only 31 percent reported the same plans one year later.

The reports of Project Talent include a wide variety of data that provide at least indirect evidence of the educational achievements of a large sample of high school students.

National Assessment of Educational Progress. The Committee on Assessing the Progress of Education was formed to provide a source of comprehensive, censuslike data on educational progress. Established in 1964 by the Carnegie Corporation of New York and supported in part by the Fund for the Advancement of Education, the committee devoted four years to the preparation of the first assessment, which was conducted in 1969–1970. The ten areas selected for assessment were reading, writing (written expression), science, mathematics, social studies, citizenship, vocational education, literature, art, and music. Other areas were expected to be included later.

The first assessment surveyed three subjects— science, citizenship, and writing—to begin a five-year cycle of assessment testing. In 1970–1971 reading and literature were assessed, and in the following three years the assessment of the remaining five subjects was scheduled to be conducted. In 1974–1975 the five-year cycle was expected to begin again. This cycling approach makes it possible to have a continuing staff instead of reassembling a new staff every three years.

In searching for suitable instruments for appraising the educational achievements of children, youth, and adults, the achievement tests commonly used in American schools were examined and determined to be unsatisfactory for the national assessment. Achievement tests contain a very large proportion of items that are near the 50 percent level of difficulty because they were constructed to measure individual differences among pupils, to appraise what the average student knows, and to establish reliable average scores for grades or schools. Such tests are not adequate because a national assessment is as much concerned with what almost every child has learned as with what the average child has learned. Commonly used achievement tests are also inadequate for the assessment project in the respect that they concentrate on items of fact and on simple skills. They fail to give sufficient attention to such important areas as complex problem-solving, interest in reading, and the habits of civic participation.

Program development. To develop assessment exercises for all of the ten areas, four organiza-

tions with wide experience in test construction were employed. They were first asked to submit educational objectives for the areas to be assessed—objectives that would serve as the basis for developing the actual assessment exercises. Scholars, teachers, and curriculum specialists in each field formulated statements of the objectives which reflected the contributions of that particular field and which were being seriously undertaken by the schools. For each of the major objectives, prototype exercises were constructed, which, in the opinion of scholars and teachers, gave students an opportunity to demonstrate that they had learned what the objective implied. These objectives and prototype exercises were reviewed by eleven independent lay panels, who judged each objective as defined by the prototype items in terms of its importance for people today and its desirability to the judges regarding its inclusion into their own children's education. This procedure was designed to ensure that every objective was considered important by scholars, was accepted as an educational task by the school, and, in addition, was deemed desirable by leading lay citizens.

From three to 12 objectives were formulated and approved for each subject area. For instance, the fifth objective for social studies is to instill in the student a reasoned commitment to the values that sustain a free society. The objective is subdivided into four levels of sophistication—one for each age level. In this case, for example, at age nine the student should demonstrate respect for the views and feelings of other people and be able to tell why this respect is desirable; at age 13 he should uphold freedom of speech, the press, religion, and assembly and be able to give a reason why he does; at age 17 he should indicate belief in the rule of law and be able to justify his belief; as an adult he should believe in open opportunity for advancement and be able to justify his belief.

After the objectives were reviewed and approved, the contractors constructed for each of the four age groups a large and representative sample of exercises to measure the attainment of each objective. The exercises had to meet three specific criteria: (1) each exercise had to reflect accurately one of the objectives; (2) each exercise had to be sufficiently clear to the individual taking the test and had to quickly communicate information to laymen about a student's knowledge or performance; and (3) the exercises had to sample knowledge and skills at three levels of difficulty—one-third of the exercises representing those things that practically all examinees can do, one-third those things that an average number can do, and one-third those things that only the ablest can do—thereby providing a picture of what is learned by the total range of students. The new exercises constructed for the assessment use individual interviews, samples of written work and art and music products, and performance tests for appraising such abilities and skills as those developed through vocational education. The resulting information from the first round of the assessment when compared to that obtained in later assessments can thus serve as a basis for measuring progress.

The following ten examples indicate the variety of assessment exercises developed:

(1) On this calendar, draw a ring around the date which is two weeks after December 8. (Mathematics, age nine)

(2) Show on this picture of a clock face where the hands will be at 9:30. (Mathematics, age nine)

(3) The noonday temperatures in a town in New Jersey were recorded for one week. The temperature the first day was 30°F, the second day it was 25°, the third day it was 30°, the fourth day it was 31°, the fifth day it was 23°, the sixth day it was 32°, and the seventh day it was 29°. What season of the year was this most likely to have been? (Science, age nine)

(4) We are going to have a Parent-Teacher Association meeting in our school on Monday evening at 7 P.M. Will you write a little note inviting your parents to attend? (Writing, age nine)

(5) The examiner says, "I am going to play a little tune. When it is finished, will you hum the tune for me?" (Music, age nine)

(6) The examiner says, "I am going to play a song you have often heard." After the song has been played, the examiner asks, "Can you tell me the name of the song?" (Music, age nine)

(7) The examiner says, "Can you sing or play a musical instrument? Sing or play something for me." (Music, age nine)

(8) Here are four pictures. Do some of them seem alike to you? Which ones? (Art, age nine)

(9) Here is an article which tells you how to make a paper hat. Here is the material. See if you can make a hat. (Reading, age 13)

(10) Name as many planets in our solar system as you can. (Science, age 13)

Exercises for 17-year-olds and young adults are similar in purpose to the exercises for children but correspond to the greater maturity and development expected of these older groups. In appraising the acquisition of occupational skills among 17-year-olds, much more equipment is involved.

Assessed groups. A national assessment of educational progress will not be very meaningful unless it can identify specific problems relating to groups of individuals. Current concern regarding the educational crisis in the large cities and the plight of disadvantaged children, for instance, indicate the importance of gathering data by community type and socioeconomic status. Questions are also frequently raised concerning differences in educational achievement in the various geographic regions. The particular populations that need to be treated separately may change in the future, but age, sex, socioeconomic status, geographic location, and community size and type will probably be significant for some time. Hence, the initial national assessment was based upon representative samples for each of 768 populations defined by the following subdivisions: four geographic regions, four age groups (young people aged nine, 13, and 17 and adults between 26 and 35), both sexes, two socioeconomic levels, race (Negro, white, and other), and community size (large cities, small cities, suburban fringe, and rural small town).

The assessment included nine-year-olds, who are expected to have achieved some of the goals of primary education; 13-year-olds, who have normally made substantial progress in attaining the goals of elementary education; and 17-year-olds, the majority of whom are still in high school. After that age a major fraction is no longer in school. Adults are also surveyed because they represent the chief factor in determining the educational level of a community and because they are the final products of the common schools. However, because of the changes in school curricula and school attendance since the mid-1930's, adults over 35 represent the products of a very differently oriented educational program. Many adults under 26 are still in professional schools.

Administration procedure. A comprehensive assessment of three subjects was obviously impractical as it would have required so many exercises that one person would need at least eight hours to complete all of them. A greater number of exercises was included than could be asked of an individual because the assessment was concerned with the response of a group rather than the response of an individual. Thus, 12 persons, dividing the exercises equally among them, could take all of the exercises together in 40 minutes. As a result of this procedure, 240,000 persons furnished 20,000 responses to each of the assessment exercises without giving more than 40 minutes of their time, therefore involving little or no inconvenience to individuals or to schools.

Results. As the assessment for each age group is completed, the results are recorded and analyzed. Reports are then prepared and released to the public. These reports publish a sample of the exercises themselves to give the reader a clear idea of what is being assessed and also present the percentages of examinees who answered each exercise correctly and, when it is considered important, an indication of frequently given incorrect responses. For the sample of 13-year-old boys of relatively high socioeconomic status from large cities of the Northeast, it might be found, for example, that 86 percent comprehended the plain sense of a simple newspaper paragraph, 89 percent devoted two hours or more each week to voluntary reading, and 39 percent demonstrated one or more employable skills. Because the data are reported only in terms of large groups of individuals located within the four major geographic regions, comparisons are avoided between individuals, schools, and school systems. Because the exercises themselves are included in the report, the significance of the responses can be understood by interested laymen.

The national assessment shows promise of furnishing the American public with comprehensive and dependable data about the educational progress and problems of important groups within the nation.

RALPH W. TYLER

TESTING AND THE PROTECTION OF PRIVACY

Any person who takes a test reveals something about himself which he may or may not want to reveal. The schoolchild who takes an achievement test discloses information to the teacher about the degree to which he has profited from classroom instruction. The college applicant who takes a scholastic aptitude test reveals to college admissions officers information about his capabilities for college work. The job applicant who takes a battery of tests provides his prospective employer with information about his capabilities for employment.

The student or applicant usually has no option about participating in such testing programs. He has recourse only if it can be demonstrated that the tests are used to discriminate against him on some basis irrelevant to his achievement or potential. For example, an employer cannot use intelligence tests as obstacles to the employment of persons on the basis of race, although he can use them to increase the general quality of his labor force. Questions about use of spare time, preferred activities, family relations, annoyances, interest in owning property, or reflections on one's childhood might seem quite unrelated to likely success in school or employment. Yet often the responses to such questions will clarify the factors preventing an individual from achieving to the limit of his abilities or the factors leading to satisfaction or dissatisfaction in a given line of work.

Providing information about one's personal characteristics often leads to conflict between society's desire to learn enough about each individual so that he can be helped to find his appropriate place in the culture and society's desire to protect the individual from unwarranted intrusions into his private life.

Uses of testing. The use of tests is integral to all programs of education. Their proper employment can ensure the matching of educational programs with the state of students' knowledge and their motivation. By assessing the degree of success attained, tests aid in the modification of instruction as it progresses. Appropriate measures of achievement, ability, and attitudes are needed to determine the amount of learning acquired by each student and to decide on the nature of later programs.

Tests vary in form: they may be oral or written; they may require "short answers," as in multiple-choice examinations, or "long answers," as in essay examinations; they may ask for items of knowledge or require performance of a particular task.

Tests used are generally classified into three main categories: achievement tests; tests to predict achievement, usually called aptitude or ability tests; and tests of noncognitive factors, such as personality tests, interest tests, and tests of attitudes or values.

Ordinarily, achievement tests relate directly to the content and objectives of the educational program, so that scores on such tests indicate clearly the degree to which the objectives were attained. However, testing in educational settings may include many measures that are not strictly evaluations of achievement but refer instead to the motivations, values, personality characteristics, prior experiences, likes, dislikes, opinions, or attitudes of students. In these it is not only the item content which is different; the purposes for which the tests are given are also different. It is known that many nonintellectual factors may impede or facilitate learning. Information about such factors can provide cues for individualizing instruction or assigning areas of study, or it can indicate the absence of adequate motivation to learn.

Standards of privacy. At the same time that there has been a growing use of tests, there has been in recent years a growing awareness of and interest in the issue of privacy. Views about the nature of privacy and its value in a society have become more sophisticated. The need of the individual to reserve for himself and his intimates certain features of his own private life has gradually been recognized as an important aspect of personality. If privacy is nonexistent the individual is seriously diminished, the quality of life is impaired, and important aspects of personality development associated with selective and appropriate revelation of one's self to intimate acquaintances are lost.

An analysis of the meaning of privacy is provided in the report of the Panel on Privacy and Behavioral Research sponsored by the U.S. Office of Science and Technology. Privacy was defined in the report as:

> . . . the right of the individual to decide for himself how much he will share with others his thoughts, his feelings, and the facts of his personal life. It is a right that is essential to insure dignity and freedom of self-determination. . . . Privacy is the right to live one's life in one's own way, to formulate and hold one's own beliefs, and to express thoughts and share feelings without fear of observation or publicity beyond that which one seeks or acquiesces in. (1967, pp. 2, 8)

Privacy is defined not only in terms of the right of the individual to reveal or to withhold items of information about himself but also terms of his ability to maintain control over the dissemination of information that he has provided for a specific purpose so that it may not be used for any other.

This definition provides a basis for standards of good practice in the use of tests and test scores and in the choice of items for use in tests other than achievement examinations. Applying these principles would require that each person tested should freely and willingly consent to answer the questions asked. He should be free—in fact, encouraged—to disregard those questions which he does not wish to answer because they relate to aspects of his person, personal life, or background that he chooses not to reveal. Scores of tests should be used only for the purposes to which the participant has agreed. The scores should be safeguarded to ensure that they not be seen or used by persons other than those committed to the implicit contract with the person tested.

Points of conflict. In practice, testing standards are much debated. A great deal of public attention has been directed to specific items in tests and questionnaires. Publicity has centered mainly on personality tests and, of this group, primarily on the Minnesota Multiphasic Personality Inventory (MMPI). Although the MMPI was developed to improve the quality of psychiatric classification, its scores provide much useful information on persons who function satisfactorily, if not quite perfectly, that it has become widely used for many purposes. Because of the original intent, the MMPI includes some questionable items. Respondents are asked to mark as "true" or "false" items like these:

> There is something wrong with my sex organs.
> I dream about things that are best kept to myself.
> Sometimes I feel as though there is a tight band around my head.
> I believe in the second coming of Christ.
> I feel sure there is only one true religion.
> Christ performed miracles.
> I love my mother.
> Children should be taught all the main facts about sex.

Obviously, items of this kind are irrelevant or inappropriate when such a test is used with children or prospective employees. Widespread criticism of the MMPI has resulted.

However, emphasis on such questions avoids

the main issue. Privacy is invaded when a person is led to reveal something of himself that he did not intend to reveal. If the subject taking the MMPI desires to omit any question, he may do so. This will not trouble the examiner, because he is prepared for that possibility. The examiner does not look at the responses to particular items on a test. Instead, he uses a scoring system which summarizes all responses. Items concerning sexual behavior, attitudes toward parents, and belief in God can be left blank or can be removed from inventories with only slight impact on the scoring schemes. What is critical is that the scoring schemes of personality tests of this sort provide information about the characteristics of the individual in a way that is not obviously related to items to which he responded. The score provides data on personal matters such as attitudes, beliefs, and emotional problems and disorders that the individual may not have realized he was revealing.

Clearly, personality tests can be used without concern in those settings where the examiner and the subject have a confidential relationship, as in counseling. When it is clearly evident to the subject that the use of a test is to his own advantage, the issue of privacy does not arise. But in many settings, such a demonstration of intent would be difficult, if not impossible. For example, the propriety of using personality tests is questionable in preemployment test batteries and in screening for assignment to certain sensitive jobs.

Protection of privacy. Thus, it is clear that current testing practices in schools, government, and industry often fail to meet ideal standards of privacy. Moreover, these standards frequently fail to provide adequate guidance in testing situations where the subject cannot know in advance what he may reveal about himself. When a subject agrees to be tested, his consent should be informed consent. Consent cannot be given in the absence of adequate knowledge about what one is consenting to. If a particular examination reveals dimensions of the individual's personality which the individual himself did not know existed, then consent has little meaning.

The individual who takes part in any examination process initiates a relationship of confidence with the examiner and thereby places a heavy burden on that person. Assurances must be given that the purposes of the testing are honestly described, that the results will be used in the manner specified in the consenting relationship, and

that no improper disclosure of findings will be made to persons not involved in the agreement. This trusting relationship also places a substantial responsibility upon the sponsoring institution to guarantee that the terms of the agreement are observed. Prudence suggests that the agreement be made explicit.

Sometimes agreements are made that cannot be enforced. A public school teacher, for example, cannot give assurance to her pupils that the parents will not see the test scores, since in some states public officials are required to reveal test scores to parents. Usually no confidential relationship exists in a teaching setting, so that court orders may be obtained to require the examiner to make available a test score. Sometimes data are filed in computers, where many persons have access to the results. To ensure that only agreements are made that can be kept, institutions will find it increasingly necessary to develop explicit codes of conduct for the collection and use of data.

Professional associations, such as the American Psychological Association, have improved their codes of ethics in recent years to require greater attention to issues of privacy. These associations provide guides for conduct and sanctions against members who ignore them. These sanctions are effective against established professional workers who value membership in their professional societies but have little effect on marginal operators and often fail to affect institutional practice. Many colleges and universities have had to develop written codes to define the way in which records, including test scores, are to be obtained, filed, and controlled.

The development of large computers and increasingly efficient retrieval techniques make it possible to accumulate information from a wide variety of sources and then to consolidate it to provide a rather complete dossier on an individual. As data banks in the government and in the private sector multiply, the need to ensure the confidentiality of items stored in computers is critical. It may be possible to develop procedures and write statutes to maintain this confidentiality and to ensure that unwarranted revelation does not occur.

However, there is always the risk that the collection and storage in computers of many items of information may occur under one set of regulations but that the need for the data will become so impelling that another set of regulations will be drawn up to permit usage contrary to that originally intended. If, for example, information on race, religious status, or political activities were collected with assurances of restricted use under one political administration, a later administration might change the rules, citing the existence of a clear and present danger. Any assurances of confidentiality must include this possibility.

Privacy versus needs of society. There are qualities valued more highly than privacy by society. The public interest is sometimes of foremost concern. The public interest is attacked when an unstable individual hijacks a jet aircraft, when an undetected psychopath assassinates an important national leader, or when the emotional status of a student makes him incapable of normal progress or causes him to disrupt the classroom. Thus, it becomes clear that in order to maintain an orderly society, the need to know about human characteristics is sometimes as important as, or even more important than, the privacy of each individual.

This issue is amply displayed when we study the effects of a disastrous home environment on the development of children. If to protect privacy we require consent or a trusting relationship, we certainly would need the consent of the persons who have legal custody of the children, the parents. Parents who are seriously deficient in meeting their obligations in rearing children, are brutal in their treatment of them, or are raising them in a home in which there is a great deal of disorder or antisocial activity are not likely to consent to being studied. Clearly, there are many instances in which it is useful for society to learn a great deal about individuals where their consent will not readily be given.

Who should decide whether the right of privacy is more important than the knowledge to be gained? Surely it is not the parents in the illustration given above, nor is it the investigator who expresses interest in the data, for he is far too committed to his own research program to be objective. The United States Public Health Service established in 1966 a set of procedures for the review of the propriety of all studies it supports involving human subjects. The required procedures involve a group of competent and impartial judges. Such review groups may approve studies even when privacy is invaded or informed consent is not obtained, if the requirements of the research study and the need to know fully justify the action.

The widespread attention to tests as invaders of the privacy of individuals has stimulated leaders in psychological testing to review their practices in order to ensure that the principles on which they operate are correct and to make explicit the procedures under which testing occurs. This review is essential if socially desirable uses of testing are to be increased and abuses are to be reduced. It is hoped that extensive discussions of these issues will also aid the development of a more mature concept of the nature and values of privacy in all aspects of society.

BIBLIOGRAPHY

U.S. OFFICE OF SCIENCE AND TECHNOLOGY 1967 *Privacy and Behavioral Research.* Report of the Panel on Privacy and Behavioral Research. Washington, D.C., Government Printing Office.

KENNETH E. CLARK

TESTING PROGRAMS, STATEWIDE

Although state testing programs have been prominently featured in educational literature only since the 1960's, they have a long history. In 1865, New York State administered its first Regents examinations (Tinkelman 1966). Several other state programs had their beginnings in the 1920's, when new forms of achievement examinations—objective tests—were developed for and introduced in the schools. The development of intelligence and scholastic aptitude tests during this time gave further impetus to state programs where these tests were used in addition to, or instead of, achievement tests.

Development. By the mid-1930's, state testing programs were of interest and concern to educators and measurement specialists. In 1937 representatives of 15 state programs and nonprofit testing agencies met, under the leadership of the American Council on Education's Committee on Measurement and Guidance, to discuss common problems (Atkins 1938). With the exception of the World War II years, this group has met annually. Invitations to the Conference of Directors of State Testing Programs have been limited to those responsible for or involved in the conduct of state testing programs. The number of participants at the conference has increased over the years—48 representatives from 26 states, Puerto

Rico, and Washington, D.C., attended the 1968 annual conference.

President Dwight D. Eisenhower called attention in 1957 to state testing programs when he indcated the need for nationwide testing of high school students and a system of incentives for qualified students to pursue scientific or professional careers. The subsequent passage of the National Defense Education Act of 1958 (NDEA) not only encouraged but gave financial support to testing, guidance, and scholarship programs. A few years earlier, a survey had indicated that 26 states, or 54 percent, had testing programs (Traxler 1954). A later survey revealed that 42 states, or 84 percent, were then offering a total of 74 programs (Educational Testing Service 1968). More than one program was reported by 18 states, with one state reporting as many as eight programs.

Types of programs. State departments of education conduct statewide testing in 26, or 62 percent, of the states which have such programs; responsibility is shared with state colleges or universities in nine states, or 21 percent. In seven states, or 17 percent, the program is the responsibility of a state college or university (Educational Testing Service 1968).

In all but five states, or 12 percent, participation in the state program is voluntary. Among the most precise laws requiring schools to administer a state testing program was that passed by the 1968 session of the California legislature. Beginning with the 1969–1970 school year, schools were required to administer tests of basic skills, intelligence, and physical performance. Basic skills are defined as reading, spelling, basic mathematics, and grammar. This testing is done in the last elementary grade—grade 6 or grade 8—and in grade 12. Testing in the content courses, such as literature, history, advanced mathematics, and science, is also required. The tests are selected by the state board of education.

Substantial numbers of schools participate in the testing programs offered by their states. The data on the extent to which schools participate in voluntary state programs, however, are not available in any consistent form. Some states report their participation in terms of the number of students tested; these figures range from about 8,000 to 1.75 million. The lower numbers generally indicate programs that are limited to selected groups of students. Other schools report in terms

of the percentage of students, schools, or districts participating in programs; this ranges from 73 percent to 96 percent (Educational Testing Service 1968).

Tests and services available to schools participating in voluntary state programs vary considerably. While some programs offer only specified batteries, others permit schools to select instruments from an extensive list of offerings. In addition to providing tests, 24 states, or 57 percent of those with testing programs, also provide both scoring and reporting services, and 19 states, or 45 percent, also provide special score interpretation materials and services. Professional workshops and in-service training programs are offered by 11 states, or 26 percent; other services designed to aid schools in the administration and scoring of tests and the interpretation of test results are offered by about an equal number of states.

The Iowa testing programs are illustrative of programs where a single specified battery is offered. The Iowa Tests of Basic Skills are available for grades 3 through 9; the Iowa Tests of Educational Development are recommended for the secondary grades. Scoring, reporting, and consulting services are provided for these instruments. Summary reports of test results as well as reports on research findings on these tests are prepared to aid in the interpretation of results.

The Michigan state program, on the other hand, suggests tests and programs which schools might administer but urges that local conditions be considered in their selection and use. Consulting services are available to aid schools in the planning of testing programs and the interpretation and use of results. Scoring and reporting services are offered for a wide variety of published tests. An annual conference sponsored by the Michigan School Testing Service provides an opportunity for school personnel to hear presentations by prominent measurement specialists and to discuss current problems and issues in testing. Relevant publications are also made available to participating schools.

All but four states use nationally standardized instruments available from test publishers. Intelligence or scholastic aptitude tests and measures of achievement—batteries and tests in individual subjects—are among those most often included in state programs. Of the 42 states that have programs, 36, or 86 percent, provide measures of achievement and 30, or 71 percent, use intelligence and achievement tests of some kind. In order that schools may compare the performance of their students with that of students in other schools in the state, 18 states, or 43 percent of the states that use nationally standardized tests, prepare local norms.

Although nationally standardized tests are favored, ten states, or 24 percent, construct their own instruments or have an outside agency develop tests which measure the extent to which their specific educational objectives have been achieved. These instruments either are the sole offerings in the program or are used in combination with nationally standardized tests. Typically, such instruments are constructed by committees of teachers; if they are developed by outside agencies, those in the state who are best able to define the instructional and measurement objectives of their schools specify the content.

New York is perhaps the state most active in developing its own instruments. Eight programs are conducted for a variety of purposes. For six of these, committees of teachers or the Bureau of Elementary and Secondary Educational Testing of the State Department of Education develop the measures which are used in the programs. For example, in the New York College Proficiency Examination Program—which provides adults who have not completed their high school education with an opportunity to demonstrate educational growth and maturity and thereby receive a New York State high school diploma—examination specifications for 28 subject areas are drawn up. College faculty committees construct many of the questions. Most of these examinations are three hours in length. They vary in format and may include multiple-choice, short-answer, and essay questions.

For the well-known New York State Regents examinations, 50 new examinations are prepared annually by committees of classroom teachers who are actively engaged in teaching the subjects. The examinations are pretested on students in high school classes, edited, and reviewed independently by other classroom teachers and a committee of principals and superintendents. For the actual examinations, the students' papers are scored locally by teachers under the supervision of the principal, who establishes and maintains proper rating standards. The state education department provides uniform answer keys and rating guides and arranges for a review of a representative sam-

pling of all papers by a staff of trained, experienced teachers.

Grades 7–9 and 10–12 are the levels for which most states provide testing services. In 20 states, or 48 percent, however, there is a program for at least one elementary grade and one secondary grade. Thirteen states, or 31 percent, test students at four levels—K–3, 4–6, 7–9, and 10–12—in the elementary and secondary schools.

Purposes. The purposes for which state testing programs are conducted vary considerably. Programs which are designed to select students for scholarships and other awards or to establish high school and college equivalency tend to have only one major objective. Almost all other programs, however, have multiple objectives. The Minnesota Statewide College Testing Program, for example, has as its major objective the guidance of high school students into appropriate colleges or vocations. The Minnesota Scholastic Aptitude Test and a questionnaire on postsecondary plans, school activities, and socioeconomic background are administered to high school juniors. The results of the testing, as well as the student's high school grade average, are reported to the colleges as an aid to counselors in the guidance and placement of students.

Although the primary objective of the Minnesota program is to provide information for use in student guidance, the program also aims to furnish educators with a continuous inventory of talents in the state, provide information to further the science of predicting human behavior, and improve the education of young people. To accomplish these objectives, test and questionnaire data are reported to high schools to aid in counseling seniors, and all Minnesota colleges receive rosters for use in their admissions processes. A continuous research program provides interpretive data which are useful in high school guidance and college admissions; the program also contributes to knowledge about the prediction of academic success.

If testing programs were characterized by a single objective, they might be said to demonstrate a concern for the development of the individual student's talents to their fullest. The most frequently cited purpose is guidance—educational and vocational planning. Assessment of the academic progress of students is also among the major objectives of many programs. College admissions, placement and grouping of students, the identification of special problems and talents, and the awarding of scholarships are less common objectives, but they also relate to the student's present status and future development.

A second purpose of a number of state programs is to evaluate the effectiveness of educational programs. Here an effort is made to provide an instructional program which will enable the student to develop his maximum potential. These state testing programs are designed to evaluate to what extent this goal has been achieved. The 12th-grade program conducted in Florida is an example of a program that seeks to aid schools in student guidance and curriculum evaluation. The instruments used in this program are a standardized aptitude test and a battery of achievement tests developed by an outside agency on the basis of specifications set by representatives from Florida's schools and colleges. Interpretive data for individual guidance and for evaluation of the extent to which schools have achieved their educational objectives are supplied to the schools.

According to Horst, there are four requirements for a good state testing program:

First, functional requirements or objectives to be achieved by the programs; second, administrative requirements, which consider some of the practical problems or conditions to be satisfied; third, interpretational facilities which must be available if the program is to be successful; and finally, certain technical requirements which an adequate program must satisfy. (1963, p. 394)

Occasionally states considering initiating a testing program have inquired about blueprints that designate specifically named instruments for use at specific grade levels. Unless the state first considers its own educational objectives and measurement needs, the adoption of this kind of blueprint could lead to the establishment of a program quite unsuitable for its schools. Serious consideration of the requirements discussed by Horst should aid in the development of a good testing program—that is, a program which serves the educational measurement needs of the schools in the state.

BIBLIOGRAPHY

ATKINS, J. K. 1938 "The 1937 Educational Conference: A Review." *Educational Record*, 19, supp. no. 11:5–18.
EDUCATIONAL TESTING SERVICE 1968 *State Testing Programs: A Survey of Functions, Tests, Materials, and Services.* Princeton, N.J., The Service.
HORST, PAUL 1963 "The Statewide Testing Program." *Personnel and Guidance Journal*, 41, no. 5:394–402.
TINKELMAN, SHERMAN N. 1966 "Regents Examinations in New York State After 100 Years." *Proceedings of the 1965 Invitational Conference on Testing Problems.* Princeton, N.J., Educational Testing Service. Pages 85–94.
TRAXLER, ARTHUR E. 1954 "The Status of Statewide Testing Programs." *1954 Achievement Testing Program in Independent Schools and Supplementary Studies.* Educational Records Bulletin No. 63. New York, Educational Records Bureau. Pages 86–92.

ANNA DRAGOSITZ

TESTING, PROJECTIVE TECHNIQUES

Projective techniques are those tests and psychological procedures specifically designed to evoke from the subject responses that involve projection of his inner thoughts, his fantasies and wishes, and his perceptions of himself and the world around him. The stimulus is deliberately ambiguous, permitting a wide range of possible responses.

Suppose, for example, a person is presented with an amorphous, meaningless stimulus like an inkblot and is asked to use his imagination and describe what he sees. He may choose to ignore most of the stimulus, selecting only a small part as the basis for his response; or he may strive to include the whole inkblot in a single concept. The color, form, or shading of the inkblot may be the basis for his association. He may see only one or two simple things, or he may have a number of associations which he tries to weave together as one complex response. The number and variety of possibilities are almost endless. Whatever his response, the task requires that he impose some degree of structure and meaning upon what is admittedly only an inkblot. In so doing, he projects his fantasies, ideas, and perceptions upon the stimulus, revealing some aspects of his private inner world and personality.

Generally speaking, the subject is unaware of what he can reveal about himself in his responses. Analysis and interpretation of the test protocol—the written record of the session—are highly complex procedures usually requiring special training and experience. Although quantitative scores can be derived from most tests which use projective techniques, many clinicians prefer to analyze the subtle qualitative aspects of the subject's responses, applying principles drawn from depth psychology.

After Frank (1948) introduced the term "projective method" in 1939, a large number of techniques were developed that were designed to encourage the subject to reveal important aspects of his personality by the way in which he perceives, organizes, adapts, or relates to ambiguous, potentially affect-laden stimuli that are presented to him in a standardized manner. Only a few such techniques have survived as important methods in personality assessment.

While there are many ways to classify projective techniques, the most common basis for categorization is the kind of response the technique elicits from the subject. Nearly all projective techniques can be classified in one of five categories: (1) association techniques—tests like the Rorschach or the word-association tests, where the subject tells what comes to mind as he looks at or listens to the stimulus; (2) construction techniques—tests like the Thematic Apperception Test, in which the subject, using a picture as a stimulus, is asked to tell a story; (3) completion techniques—tests like the sentence-completion method, in which the subject is given a specific incomplete sentence stem (for example, "My mother——") and is asked to add his own ending; (4) choice or ordering techniques—tests like the Szondi Test or the picture-arrangement test, where the subject chooses the stimulus he likes best or arranges a series of pictures in a sequence to tell a story; and (5) expressive techniques—cathartic methods involving doll play, painting, psychodrama, or other activities which may stimulate emotional reactions.

Rorschach technique and derivatives. The best-known projective technique is the Rorschach, which consists of ten inkblots—five chromatic and five black-and-white (Rorschach 1921). The subject is given one card at a time and is encouraged to tell what he sees in the inkblot while the examiner records his reaction time, his verbal response, and any other behavior that might later prove to be diagnostically significant. After completing the ten cards, the subject goes back over his responses, answering the examiner's questions concerning the location, determinants, and content of each percept reported. A typical protocol will contain from eight to 80 responses, depending upon the productivity of the subject.

The two most common systems for scoring the formal aspects of a Rorschach protocol are those developed by Beck (1949) and Klopfer and his associates (1954). Both systems are refinements of Rorschach's original method, in which he stressed the importance of analyzing a person's mode of perception—whether the inkblot was interpreted

by the subject as a whole or in part; whether the form, color, or shading of the inkblot was primarily responsible for evoking the response; and whether the person reported a static, lifeless percept or one imbued with life and action (the movement score).

Most clinicians who employ the Rorschach for psychodiagnostic purposes use a global, or holistic, approach emphasizing qualitative aspects of the analysis rather than quantitative scores. Working from a psychoanalytic or dynamic point of view, the skilled clinical examiner focuses upon the interpersonal context in which the projective technique is applied. In other words, the technique provides a standardized, semistructured, ambiguous stimulus for evoking associations and behavior as part of a depth interview in which the roles, expectancies, biases, fears, and wishes of both examiner and subject must be carefully analyzed and interpreted (Schafer 1954).

Although thousands of articles have been published on the Rorschach in professional journals, the scientific yield of such studies has been very low. The Rorschach method has been criticized severely for failure to provide an objective scoring system that is free of arbitrary conventions and that shows high interscorer agreement, for lack of satisfactory internal consistency, for failure to provide cogent evidence of clinical validity, and for lack of predictive validity with respect to outcome of treatment or later behavior. Much of the controversy over the Rorschach arises from failure to distinguish between the Rorschach as a projective technique in the hands of a skilled clinician and the Rorschach as a psychometric device that yields scores having relevance for personality assessment.

Dissatisfaction with the Rorschach led to the development of several derivatives, the most extensive of which is the Holtzman Inkblot Technique (HIT). Consisting of two parallel forms, each containing 45 carefully matched inkblots and two identical warm-up blots, the HIT can be administered individually or in group form using colored slides projected on a screen (Holtzman et al. 1961; Swartz & Holtzman 1963). An adaptation of the group method can be scored objectively by a computer (Gorham 1967). Unlike the Rorschach, for which the subject can give as many or as few responses as he wishes for each card, the HIT involves only one response for each card, thereby overcoming one of the more serious psychometric weaknesses of the Rorschach. High interscorer reliability and internal consistency have been found for 22 standardized inkblot scores covering the location, determinants, content, and other features of responses often analyzed in the Rorschach. Extensive normative tables are reported for a wide range of populations to aid in interpretation. As in the Rorschach, depth analysis of qualitative features in a protocol can also be undertaken by an experienced clinician.

Thematic Apperception Test and derivatives. The Thematic Apperception Test (TAT) consists of 31 black-and-white pictures which suggest various events that are fairly common in the experience or fantasies of most persons; pictures depict such scenes as a boy looking at a violin, a man looking out a window, a woman lying down on a couch with a man standing by, and a man bending over a figure on a bed. Usually 20 or fewer cards are actually used in any given situation, since the cards vary in appropriateness as to age and sex. The pictures are presented to the subject one at a time, and he is asked to make up a story about each, with a plot and an outcome. The examiner records the story, making note of any side remarks and behavior that may be significant in assessing the subject's personality (Murray et al. 1938). Occasionally, with articulate subjects, slides are projected on a screen to permit group administration, and each participating individual is asked to write out his own response.

Interpretation typically involves a card-by-card detailed analysis of the story content and takes into consideration the subject's identification with the "hero" figure. The examiner will try to note subtle signs of hostility, guilt, conflict, or anxiety in the subject, his imaginative capacity, defense mechanisms, strivings, needs, and hopes, his preoccupations and misperceptions, and such formal characteristics as the subject's style, organization, response time, and verbosity. The validity of a clinical interpretation is based on the assumption that the subject projects his own inner personality upon the picture as he tells his story. Consistently repeated themes are especially noted as evidence of strong trends within the individual, particularly when a theme is used for pictures where ordinarily it would not be evoked.

The TAT is more refractory to quantitative analysis than the HIT largely because of the difficulties encountered in coding and scoring narrative material. More progress has been made in the quantitative analysis of stimulus-response characteristics in the TAT than in the analysis of more meaningful personality characteristics of the subjects themselves. Nevertheless, some attempts to measure the needs of individuals as they interact with the press of environments—by the analysis of motives expressed in fantasy productions on the TAT—have proved to be significant. A comprehensive review of various systems for analysis of TAT protocols has been made by Murstein (1963).

Soon after the publication and fairly widespread adoption of the TAT, a large number of other storytelling techniques appeared, most developed for the purpose of special research. Among the more durable and better known of these derivations are Bellak's Children's Apperception Test, Symonds' Picture-Story Test, the Michigan Picture Test, Shneidman's Make-A-Picture Story Test, Van Lennep's Four Picture Test, Twitchell-Allen's Three-Dimensional Apperception Test, and Blum's Blacky Pictures Test. The Blacky Pictures Test is of special interest because the 12 cartoon drawings chronicling the events in the life of a small dog named Blacky are tailored to fit psychoanalytic theory.

Completion methods. In the Rorschach the subject is given a great deal of freedom to respond in almost any way he chooses. The TAT is more restrictive because the pictures are rather highly structured and definite. The sentence-completion and word-association methods are still more confining: the subject is limited to a single association or sentence completion for each stimulus. The direct linkage of stimulus and response and the short, discrete nature of each item in most of the completion methods make it possible to compile a large number of items in one protocol. While qualitative analysis may still be undertaken using a clinical approach, more objective scoring systems are often employed.

In the word-association test the examiner reads the stimulus word aloud and the subject responds immediately with the first word that comes to mind as an association. Both the reaction time and the content of the word are analyzed. Special word lists have been compiled by different investigators, often with normative data on major populations. The study of associative thought under controlled conditions can provide information about personal dynamics, mental complexes, and defense systems.

The sentence-completion test consists of a large number of incomplete sentence stems, such as "My fears——" or "The people I like best ——," printed as items in a test booklet. The subject is urged to complete each sentence by writing out a response in his own words. Afterward, the responses are classified and scored by the examiner.

Other projective methods. In some projective techniques a subject chooses stimuli from among several presented or places stimuli in a preferred sequence. Such sorting tasks can be considered projective techniques only when the methods have enough latitude to allow the subject to project his own thoughts or feelings into the response. Such methods are only occasionally used for the study of personality since they do not ordinarily evoke data sufficiently rich for clinical interpretation.

More commonly used are several of the expressive techniques, such as the various methods of doll play, painting, and drawing. Techniques involving doll play and puppetry are applicable to both personality assessment and therapy, especially when used by a skilled clinician with young children, for whom these media are particularly appropriate. A wide variety of drawing techniques have been successfully employed in personality assessment, the most common of which are the Draw-A-Person Test and the House-Tree-Person Test. Important aspects of the subject's self-image and his perception of others are often revealed by such techniques.

Evaluative importance. Led by the Rorschach and the TAT, projective techniques have become firmly established since 1945 as an essential part of the clinician's battery of psychodiagnostic procedures. Nevertheless, the methods have proved difficult to objectify and validate—partly because suitable criteria for validation are difficult to obtain and partly because the global approach preferred by the experienced clinician is refractory to scientific analysis.

While it may be true that significant aspects of inner personality are sometimes revealed by certain projective techniques, it is another matter to find the key to a valid interpretation of the test results. Even the best of projective test protocols reflects but a small fragment of the total personality and contains innumerable possibilities for misinterpretation. For this reason, the wise clinician uses a variety of different assessment techniques that tap different levels of personality functioning and tries to arrive at an overall interpretation based on as much information as possible.

BIBLIOGRAPHY

ABT, LAWRENCE E., AND LEOPOLD BELLAK, eds. 1950 *Projective Psychology*. New York, Knopf.

ANDERSON, HAROLD H., AND GLADYS L. ANDERSON, eds. 1951 *An Introduction to Projective Techniques and Other Devices for Understanding the Dynamics of Human Behavior*. New York, Prentice-Hall.

BECK, SAMUEL J. 1949 *Rorschach's Test*. Vol. 1: *Basic Processes*. 2nd ed., rev. New York, Grune.

FRANK, LAWRENCE K. 1948 *Projective Methods*. Springfield, Ill., Thomas.

GORHAM, DONALD R. 1967 "Validity and Reliability Studies of a Computer-based Scoring System for Inkblot Responses." *Journal of Consulting Psychology*, 31, no. 1:65–70.

HOLTZMAN, WAYNE H., et al. 1961 *Inkblot Perception and Personality*. Austin, University of Texas Press.

KLOPFER, BRUNO, et al. 1954 *Developments in the Rorschach Technique*. Vol. 1: *Technique and Theory*. Yonkers, N.Y., World Book.

LINDZEY, GARDNER 1961 *Projective Techniques and Cross-cultural Research*. New York, Appleton.

MURRAY, HENRY A., et al. 1938 *Explorations in Personality*. New York, Oxford University Press.

MURSTEIN, BERNARD I. 1963 *Theory and Research in Projective Techniques*. New York, Wiley.

RABIN, A. I., ed. 1968 *Projective Techniques in Personality Assessment*. New York, Springer.

RORSCHACH, HERMANN (1921) 1942 *Psychodiagnostics*. Translated from the German by P. Lemkau and B. Kronenburg. Bern, Huber.

SCHAFER, ROY 1954 *Psychoanalytic Interpretation in Rorschach Testing*. New York, Grune.

SWARTZ, JON D., AND WAYNE H. HOLTZMAN 1963 "Group Method of Administration for the Holtzman Inkblot Technique." *Journal of Clinical Psychology*, 19, no. 4:433–441.

ZUBIN, JOSEPH, LEONARD D. ERON, AND FLORENCE SCHUMER 1965 *An Experimental Approach to Projective Techniques*. New York, Wiley.

WAYNE H. HOLTZMAN

TESTING SITUATION

A psychological test is administered by an examiner, trained in the theory and practical aspects of test construction, to a subject, who by his presence agrees to answer the questions and complete the required procedures. The examiner assumes that if the subject is cooperative, the examination will determine his true psychological status and that the decisions made as a result of the test will be based on objective, scientific procedures. Sometimes a test subject has little choice as to whether he will take a test. A prospective employer may require testing as a condition for employment, or a judge or school principal may order a test given. But if a subject volunteers to take a test, he assumes that it will be as impartial as an X ray.

Both parties in the psychological testing situation, therefore, have made assumptions about the validity of the enterprise they have agreed to undertake. What are these assumptions, and what evidence is there to support them?

The examiner. First, the subject assumes that the examiner is detached, impartial, totally objective, and professional in his orientation. The role of the examiner can be likened to that of the baseball umpire: the job has to be done, and its performance should proceed independently of the needs, expectations, previous history, and prejudices of the official.

The evidence on this point does not lend much encouragement to the belief that the examiner is a totally objective, unbiased observer. In one experiment, people pretending to be genuine subjects for an intelligence test were trained to act either warm, friendly, and interested toward the examiner or cold, unfriendly, and aloof. It was found that warm subjects were given more help by the examiner and more generous scoring on their responses than cold subjects (Masling 1959).

In an experiment of similar design, examiners who administered and scored a projective test made more favorable interpretations of the warm subjects' responses than of those given by the cold subjects. Where the responses were essentially identical, the warm subjects were described in the case report as healthy and psychologically intact; whereas the cold subjects were seen as showing many signs of neurosis and failure to cope adequately with impulses (Masling 1957).

Even the choice of which psychological tests to use may be determined in part by nonprofessional considerations. Having a female client look at and respond to sexual stimuli may satisfy voyeuristic needs of a male examiner (Schafer 1954). Masling and Harris investigated the files of a university clinic for evidence of sex bias in the administration of the Thematic Apperception Test. They found that four of the cards used in the test, those portraying either sexual or romantic themes, were not administered equally to all clinic clients. Male examiners showed these four cards much more frequently to female clients than did they to male clients, while the female examiners made no such distinction. The interaction between male examiners and female clients produced many more Rorschach responses than the male examiner–male client situations; again, female examiners showed no sexual bias (Harris & Masling 1969; Masling & Harris 1969).

These results are in exact agreement with those reported by Rosenthal (1967). In his investigation of the influence of sex in the psychological experiment, he found that male experimenters (or examiners) showed more interest in and awareness of female subjects (or clients) than male subjects, while female experimenters remained neutral. Thus, sexual interaction influences both experiments and test administration when the psychologist is male and the subject is female.

The examiner is instructed, exhorted, and expected to render his professional services in an unbiased manner, and he may attempt to do so; but his sexuality, his background, and his values may unwittingly be expressed in his work. Most psychologists are either born into the middle class or have achieved that status through their own efforts. They tend to view lower-class values negatively. Haase (1956) investigated the influence of class bias in the interpretation of projective test responses by having 75 psychologists rate Rorschach responses with regard to a number of dimensions. The subjects were described as coming from either the lower class or the middle class. The results showed a distinct class bias operating against the lower-class subjects. Whereas the lower-class subjects were described as having character disorders, the middle-class subjects were said to be normal or neurotic.

These studies document what is already known about "objective" judgments: there can be no truly depersonalized, totally unbiased judgments from a living, predicting, experiencing human being, no matter what his training or commitment. There can only be more or less objective behavior. The psychological examiner is betrayed by his humanness, and his professional judgment frequently will show evidence of subjective bias.

Testing conditions. The second assumption is that the subject's test performance will result solely from his responses to the test items and will be independent of the testing situation. There is abundant evidence on this issue (Masling 1960; 1966), all suggesting that this assumption is even less tenable than the first.

A number of studies have demonstrated that subjects tend to give different projective test responses to different examiners (Baughman 1951; Meyer & Partipilo 1961). Thus, the assigning of Examiner A to administer a projective test to a subject automatically ensures a somewhat different test record than would have been obtained with Examiner B. Something about each examiner produces test responses peculiar to him. This special quality may be the examiner's personality (Hammer & Piotrowski 1953; Turner & Coleman 1962), his skin color (Sattler 1966; Pasamanick & Knobloch 1955), or an aspect of his physical appearance, such as a mustache, which stimulates differential responding by the subject (Yagoda & Wolfson 1964).

Such external circumstances as the decorations in the testing room (Rabin et al. 1954) and the sight of a stack of test cards yet to be administered (Epstein et al. 1962) have exerted some influence on the subjects' projective test responses. When the vast amount of experimental data in this area is considered, it is apparent that the subject responds not only to the test items but to many other aspects of the testing situation as well. It is hoped that he responds primarily to the test stimuli, but there is no reason to expect him not to be influenced by everything connected with the test—the examiner's sex, race, and personality, the room, the setting, and anything else which the subject associates with the test.

A third assumption is that the act of observing psychological behavior does not alter the behavior itself. In physics Heisenberg's uncertainty principle, stating that the measuring of the velocity of a particle affects the location of that particle, has long been accepted. Psychology, however, has not yet seriously considered the issue of whether the assessment of a response changes what the psychologist is interested in measuring. The assumption has generally been made (it is perhaps a very naïve assumption) that every subject will be motivated by a desire to give the examiner his best efforts. In order to ensure that the subject tries hard, the examiner is urged in the course of his training to establish rapport, a condition that is supposed to lull the subject into a state of trust, so that he will feel no pain from the testing and no threat from the psychologist.

For many subjects, being tested is so common-place an event that responses may be secured without trauma or suspicion. In this category are those middle-class children who attend the best urban or suburban schools and who are tested, timed, rehearsed, and observed as frequently and carefully as a Thoroughbred is checked before a big race. These children speak the same language as the examiner, share his desire for achievement, and understand the importance of the stopwatch and verbatim recording of responses. They have little to fear from him, since he is an ally.

Others in our culture, however, may find psychological testing unique or threatening, or both. Anyone referred for testing by the order of a court, school principal, or employment office can be expected to be somewhat suspicious of the motives and methods of the examiner and the purposes of the test; the "wrong" answer may be held against him, and the consequences may be disastrous. For a nonvoluntary subject to trust the beneficence of the examiner and the validity of the test is as unrealistic as the lamb trusting the wolf and probably occurs as infrequently. When the subject sees the examiner as working for the benefit of someone else—the court, the school, the boss—he can be expected to be wary, to say as little as possible, and then to say only what he thinks is desired. A subject may see blood, violence, and assorted sexual objects in the Rorschach inkblots, but if he wishes to be hired as a computer salesman or to obtain early parole, he may say, "This reminds me of a bat."

The subject's personality influences testing in a complex manner. Highly anxious subjects do better on some tests and worse on others than less anxious subjects. Every teacher has had students who claim to know the material thoroughly but who freeze under the pressure of the testing situation. Unfortunately, the teacher can evaluate only what the pupil is able to perform in public and does not ordinarily have access to the knowledge the child might be able to demonstrate in the safety and comfort of his own room.

There is considerable evidence that some pupils are severely penalized by their inability to perform under the stress of an examination (Sarason 1960; 1966). Others perform better under competitive conditions. Apparently, requiring a demonstration of knowledge under the usual conditions of testing—the emphasis on the importance of the test, the time limits on responding, the furious writing of others in the room, the serious consequences of low scores—will improve the performance of some subjects and limit that of others. The final score will combine in some unspecified manner both intellectual and personality variables.

College aptitude tests and classroom tests yield scores for each subject's performance, but these numbers reflect factors beyond "simple" intellectual variables. Decisions are made on the basis of these scores, so that some pupils are passed, some failed, some accepted for college, some rejected. Unfortunately, it is impossible to unravel the separate components and determine the exact contribution each of these factors makes to the final score. However, there is good reason to believe that the biblical adage applies to test evaluation: "For to him who has will more be given; and from him who has not, even what he has will be taken away" (Mark 4:25).

In addition to nonvoluntary subjects and highly anxious subjects, there are those who feel sufficiently estranged from the values implicit in testing to be genuinely unable or unwilling to comply with the test demands. Some adult males feel foolish and uncomfortable in fulfilling Thematic Apperception Test instructions to describe how the characters in the pictures feel; these men describe in detail the physical stimuli of the pictures, but to make up stories about pictures, to supply the feelings of imaginary people, is babyish and unacceptable. Similarly, the Draw-A-Person test is frequently seen by adults as childish and demeaning.

For subjects who have been out of school for years, an intelligence test may seem to be another example of a classroom test, and they resent being treated as pupils. Verbatim recording of test responses frightens some subjects who may wonder for what purpose the psychologist's notes will be used; for them verbatim recordings are associated with police and court business, and the safest course of action to follow under those circumstances is to trust no one and say nothing. That ordinary implement of an achievement-oriented society, the stopwatch, may well impair the performance of subjects who for cultural reasons have never felt any great need to rush about quickly and complete projects with mindless haste.

Test validity. The final assumption about the use of tests is that the test score will bear either a logical or empirical relationship to some external criterion. The test is given because of the belief that the subject's score will either describe his present performance (a classroom examination) or predict future performance (college entrance tests).

However, there is a growing realization that the traditional testing situation and traditional test items result in serious underestimation of the ability and talent of Negro subjects. Evidence reveals that Negroes perform far better on the job than their test scores predicted. For example, Stalnaker (1948) found that southern Negro high school students could compete successfully at good universities, even though their test scores were lower than those of many whites. Clark and Plotkin (1963) reported that in the sample of Negro college students they observed, most scored below the national norm on the college aptitude tests but were above the norm in remaining in college.

Since test scores of Negroes are poor predictors of performance, and the error in prediction generally slights their potential ability, we can assume that the caste- and class-oriented testing situation and test items combine to produce assessment procedures grossly inappropriate for this group of subjects. While most of the recent research has concentrated on the Negro, it is likely that the abilities of other minority groups—such as Puerto Ricans, Mexican Americans, American Indians, and Appalachian whites—are also underestimated by inappropriate testing procedures.

The psychological test is ordinarily used as a tool of a society heavily committed to competition, achievement, success, and evaluation. The tests are devised by middle-class whites, and the test norms are ordinarily based on the scores of cooperative white subjects who are readily accessible for testing purposes. They are usually administered by middle-class whites to middle-class subjects. Under these circumstances psychological tests have been of considerable benefit. However, when other groups of subjects are compelled to achieve particular scores on tests in order to be accepted for employment or college, serious inequities may result.

Summary. This discussion has outlined very briefly some of the assumptions made in the use of tests and some of the evidence regarding these assumptions. Because the discussion has focused on the extent to which the usual testing situation reduces the descriptive and predictive ability of tests, the reader might be tempted to conclude that all tests under all circumstances are inaccurate and inappropriate assessment devices. To do this would be to mistake the worm in the apple for the whole apple.

Tests have been of great use in evaluation, counseling, and placement of people in positions where they can work most effectively and with greatest satisfaction. But there are limitations to the usefulness of tests, just as there are limitations to any single solution for complex problems. There are sufficient weaknesses in any test and sufficient flaws in both the examiner and testing situation to avoid treating a test score as a concrete, immutable fact. Uncritical acceptance of a test result is not justified by either testing theory or testing research and may well result in unwise decisions about the test subject.

BIBLIOGRAPHY

BAUGHMAN, EMMETT E. 1951 "Rorschach Scores as a Function of Examiner Differences." *Journal of Projective Techniques*, 15, no. 2:243–249.

CLARK, KENNETH B., AND LAWRENCE PLOTKIN 1963 *The Negro Student at Integrated Colleges.* New York, National Scholarship Service and Fund for Negro Students.

EPSTEIN, SEYMOUR, ELIZABETH LUNDBORG, AND BERT KAPLAN 1962 "Allocation of Energy and Rorschach Responsivity." *Journal of Clinical Psychology*, 18, no. 2:236–238.

HAASE, WILLIAM 1956 "Rorschach Diagnosis, Socio-economic Class, and Examiner Bias." Ph.D. dissertation. New York University.

HAMMER, EMANUEL F., AND ZYGMUND A. PIOTROWSKI 1953 "Hostility as a Factor in the Clinician's Personality as It Affects His Interpretation of Projective Drawings." *Journal of Projective Techniques*, 17, no. 2:210–216.

HARRIS, S., AND JOSEPH MASLING 1969 "Examiner Sex, Subject Sex and Rorschach Productivity." *Journal of Consulting and Clinical Psychology*, 33.

KATZ, IRWIN, S. OLIVER ROBERTS, AND JAMES M. ROBINSON 1962 "Effects of Task Difficulty, Race of Administrator, and Instructions on Digit-Symbol Performance of Negroes." *Journal of Personality and Social Psychology*, 2, no. 1:53–59.

MASLING, JOSEPH 1957 "The Effects of Warm and Cold Interaction on the Interpretation of a Projective Protocol." *Journal of Projective Techniques*, 21, no. 4:377–383.

MASLING, JOSEPH 1959 "The Effects of Warm and Cold Interaction on the Administration and Scoring of an Intelligence Test." *Journal of Consulting Psychology*, 23, no. 4:336–341.

MASLING, JOSEPH 1960 "The Influence of Situational and Interpersonal Variables in Projective Testing." *Psychological Bulletin*, 57, no. 1:65–85.

MASLING, JOSEPH 1966 "Role-related Behavior of the Subject and Psychologist and Its Effects Upon Psychological Data." David Levine, ed., *Nebraska Symposium on Motivation.* Lincoln, University of Nebraska Press. Pages 67–103.

MASLING, JOSEPH, AND S. HARRIS 1969 "Sexual Aspects of TAT Administration." *Journal of Consulting and Clinical Psychology*, 33:166–169.

MEYER, M. L., AND MICHAEL A. PARTIPILO 1961 "Examiner Personality as an Influence on the Rorschach Test." *Psychological Reports*, 9:221–222.

PASAMANICK, BENJAMIN, AND HILDA KNOBLOCH 1955 "Early Language Behavior in Negro Children and the Testing of Intelligence." *Journal of Abnormal and Social Psychology*, 50, no. 3:401–402.

RABIN, ALBERT, WILLIAM NELSON, AND MARGARET CLARK 1954 "Rorschach Content as a Function of Perceptual Experience and Sex of the Examiner." *Journal of Clinical Psychology*, 10, no. 2:188–190.

ROSENTHAL, ROBERT 1967 "Covert Communication in the Psychological Experiment." *Psychological Bulletin*, 67, no. 5:356–367.

SARASON, IRWIN G. 1960 "Empirical Findings and Theoretical Problems in the Use of Anxiety Scales." *Psychological Bulletin*, 57, no. 5:403–415.

SARASON, IRWIN G. 1966 *Personality: An Objective Approach.* New York, Wiley.

SATTLER, JEROME 1966 "Statistical Reanalysis of Canady's 'The Effect of "Rapport" on the IQ: A New Approach to the Problem of Racial Psychology.' " *Psychological Reports*, 19, no. 3:1203–1206.

SCHAFER, ROY 1954 *Psychoanalytic Interpretation in Rorschach Testing: Theory and Application.* New York, Grune.

STALNAKER, JOHN M. 1948 "Identification of the Best Southern Negro High School Seniors." *Scientific Monthly*, 67, no. 3:237–239.

TURNER, GEORGE C., AND JAMES COLEMAN 1962 "Examiner Influence on Thematic Apperception Test Responses." *Journal of Projective Techniques*, 26, no. 4:478–486.

YAGODA, GERALD, AND WILLIAM WOLFSON 1964 "Examiner Influence on Projective Test Responses." *Journal of Clinical Psychology*, 20, no. 3:389.

JOSEPH M. MASLING

TESTING SPECIAL GROUPS

1. INDUSTRY

Personnel tests have become widely used in U.S. industry since the end of World War II, largely because industry has recognized that many of an applicant's qualifying characteristics cannot be accurately evaluated in an interview. Although an interview is still always used, many employers give more weight to an applicant's test scores than to the subjective judgment of an interviewer.

One basic purpose for which personnel tests are used in industry is the selection and placement of employees. Even in a very tight labor market, when almost every applicant is being hired for some job, personnel tests are often very helpful in placing new employees on jobs at which their chances of success are greater than if they had been placed randomly or according to the judgment of an interviewer.

Most industries try to promote men from within the company rather than go outside it to find men suitable for higher level jobs. Also, many U.S. companies are forced to promote employees according to the terms of their agreements with unions. Although unions normally want all promotions to be based solely on seniority, many are willing to permit the most qualified men to be promoted if it can be shown that they are the most capable. Personnel tests are often used, therefore, to show which men have or do not have the necessary capacity for a higher level job.

Personnel tests are also used in an effort to reduce turnover. Hiring and training new employees is expensive; for example, it has been estimated that the average cost of hiring and training an unskilled shop employee is at least $150. Since it is not unusual for a department which averages 1,000 employees to have a turnover rate of 36 percent, such a department would spend $54,000 a year on hiring and training employees. Personnel tests have often enabled a company to reduce turnover significantly and thus to realize appreciable monetary savings.

In addition, modern industry is in a constant state of flux. As new processes are instituted, employees must be transferred to different jobs. However, an employee's performance on one job is not always a good indication of how he would do on a different one. If tests have been established for many of the jobs in a plant, an employee's scores on such tests can furnish a reasonably valid basis for his transfer to a different job.

Selecting and validating tests. Before any test is used, it should itself be tested. In other words, the employer should ascertain that persons who score high on the test are more satisfactory employees than those who score low. However, he must first decide who are his more satisfactory employees. This, in turn, can only be achieved by selecting a criterion of job success.

Criteria of job success fall into four broad categories. The criterion of production includes how much each employee produces and the qual-

ity of his work. Second, personnel data, such as absenteeism, accidents, and turnover, can be considered. Subjective judgments, such as a rating of each employee's job performance by his immediate supervisor, is a third criterion. Fourth, job samples, which show how well an employee performs on a work sample similar or identical to his regular job, may be used.

The choice of one or more criteria for job success is a task that management must accomplish before a validation study for a test can be conducted. After the decision about criteria has been made, the validation of the test is usually accomplished in one of two standard ways (Tiffin & McCormick 1965).

The present-employee method, which establishes a test's concurrent validity, consists of administering the test to a group of employees who had been hired by other employment methods and are now at work on the same or similar jobs. The employees are asked to take the test in order to help the personnel department establish the validity of the test as a future employment instrument; they are assured that their test scores will have no bearing, either at that time or in the future, on their jobs or later promotion within the company. At least 90 percent of a company's employees are usually quite willing to take the test once this assurance has been given by the management.

After the test has been administered, the personnel department obtains an independent rating of job success (according to the preestablished criterion) for each employee in the group and then determines the test's concurrent validity— that is, the relationship between test scores and job success.

When using the follow-up method, which determines predictive validity, the test is given to all new employees when they are hired. However, the tests are not immediately scored; they are simply filed for future research. After the new employees have been on their jobs long enough to be rated on their performance, the personnel department obtains a rating of job success for each of the new employees and determines the test's predictive validity—that is, the relationship between test scores obtained at the time of hiring and subsequent job success.

Testing skills and competence. Many companies have had great success in using tests that have first passed the validation procedure. The tests that have most often been found to be valid are intelligence tests, mechanical aptitude tests, dexterity tests, tests for jobs in skilled trades, and visual skills tests.

Intelligence. Tests of mental ability, or intelligence tests, have been more widely used than any other kind of test. If the job in question calls for what is commonly thought of as mental alertness, good judgment, or a quick mind, an intelligence test can usually identify employees or applicants who will be successful on the job.

For example, a paper company which was considering the use of personnel tests asked all its supervisors to rate the clerks under them as A (good) or B (not as good). All 86 clerks working in the mill were then given the Tiffin and Lawshe Adaptability Test, a 15-minute test of mental ability. Of the clerks who had received test scores ranking them in the top fifth of all clerks tested, 75 percent had been rated A. Only 36 percent of those ranking in the bottom fifth had been rated A. Therefore, although there was a marked relation between test scores and job success, the test did not predict job success with 100 percent accuracy (Tiffin & Lawshe 1943).

Many validation studies of personnel tests give results similar to these. Although a prospective employee who receives a high score on such a test is more likely to succeed than a low scorer, there are always exceptions. No test measures everything required on a job. Even if an employee scored high on a test found to be valid for his job, he may lack some critical trait not covered by the test and thus perform poorly. Moreover, an employee who scored quite low on the test may still be satisfactory if he is willing to work very hard or has an abundance of other characteristics which tend to compensate for his relative lack of ability.

Mechanical aptitude. Many shops require a certain amount of mechanical knack, or mechanical aptitude, although they do not require very much mental ability.

For example, a group of maintenance men in a refrigerator plant were rated by the plant manager in overall job performance. These men were then given the Purdue Mechanical Adaptability Test, a 15-minute test dealing with many different kinds of mechanisms, such as automobile storage batteries, doorbells, and soldering irons. Among the men who made scores ranking in the top fifth

on the test, 94 percent had been rated above average in job performance. Among men scoring in the lowest fifth on the test, only 25 percent had been rated above average on the job (Lawshe, Semanek, & Tiffin 1946).

Dexterity. Many routine assembly jobs in industry require neither considerable mental ability nor very much mechanical aptitude. Such jobs often require little more than good finger, wrist, or forearm dexterity.

A dexterity test involving the fingers, wrist, and forearm was administered to 111 women when they were hired to work as inspector-packers in a pharmaceutical plant. The women were hired without regard to the scores they made on the test; the test data were used only as part of a follow-up study. After the women had been on the job for several months, a cutback in production made it necessary to lay off all 111 women. Before each woman was dismissed, however, her foreman noted whether he would like to have her rehired when production picked up. The criterion of job success was thus very simple: the foreman either did or did not want the woman back.

The dexterity test was proved valid in that the foremen were willing to rehire 64 percent of the women whose test scores were between 42 and 50 (and who thus ranked in the top fifth on the test) when they were initially hired and 54 percent of the women who had scored 41 (and were thus in the second fifth). Only 30 percent of the women who scored in the lowest fifth were wanted back. In putting the results of this study to use, the company later hired only persons who scored 41 or above (Lawshe & Balma 1966).

Trade information. It is quite easy to determine how well a person can type, take shorthand, or operate a comptometer by administering a test which requires the use of the skill in question. There are several very good tests of this sort available. It might be equally simple to determine whether a man can operate a machine tool, such as an engine lathe, by trying him out on one. But in the case of a machine tool, if the man happens to be somewhat unqualified, he might not only ruin the machine but also injure himself. Industry cannot afford to risk either of these events, especially because of its liability for an applicant's injuries.

Employment departments, therefore, never let the applicant actually show whether he can operate a machine tool. Fortunately, several paper-

and-pencil trade information tests have been developed that clearly show whether an applicant for a job in a skilled trade has the necessary qualifications.

The Purdue Trade Information Test in Engine Lathe Operation, for example, contains 74 questions dealing with an engine lathe, the answers to which should be known to tradesmen in the field. To validate this test, it was administered to 30 journeymen machinists and 30 vocational school students who had had at least one year of shop instruction with machine tools. The students were not complete novices, nor had they had the training and experience of journeymen in the trade. All of the men in the top fifth and 93 percent of those in the second fifth of those tested were journeymen. Not one person ranking in the lowest fifth, however, was a journeyman (Cochran 1955).

Visual skills. Most companies administer a visual acuity test primarily to protect themselves from unjustified claims for compensation. This vision test is given by a medical department, and the score becomes a part of the new employee's record. The tests given by the medical department for this purpose is a test for distance visual acuity, because the compensation laws in every state give primary consideration to distance visual acuity in awarding compensation claims.

Research has shown, however, that certain other visual skills are of much greater importance than distance visual acuity to production on many, if not most, industrial jobs. A battery of visual skills tests developed to measure these other visual skills can be administered with the Orthorater, an instrument developed by Bausch and Lomb, Inc. Among the visual skills measurable with this instrument is near-point visual acuity.

The effect of near-point visual acuity on certain kinds of job performance was proved in the case of 51 seamers in a hosiery plant. The criterion of job success used in the study was the number of hose seamed in one workweek, or in other words, the actual production of each worker. When a test of near-point visual acuity was administered by means of the Orthorater, 90 percent of the workers who scored in the top fifth were above average in production, and only 10 percent scoring in the lowest fifth were above-average seamers.

Although the measurement of visual skills with a screening instrument such as the Orthorater is

done by the personnel department in order to place new employees, it is always done in close cooperation with the medical department or company physician. Applicants or present employees whose visual skills are not adequate for the job for which they are under consideration are referred to a professional doctor, either an ophthalmologist or an optometrist. At least 90 percent of these people can quickly have their visual skills brought up to a suitable level through professional eye care.

Testing personality. Many companies have observed for years that personality characteristics cause an employee to fail on the job as often as, or more often than, does lack of capacity, skills, or technical competence. Therefore, many psychologists have made serious efforts to develop valid personality tests. Unfortunately, these efforts have met with only very limited success. The basic reason for their failure seems to be that personality tests are not tests at all; they are questionnaires (Thurstone 1955).

Questionnaires, often mistakenly called tests, can be and often are answered by a job applicant or candidate for promotion in just the way that will make him appear to be the kind of man the employer is seeking. For example, no one would say that he has ever walked across the street to avoid meeting someone if he is seeking a job as a salesman. The fact that personality questionnaires can be readily faked has been shown in numerous studies (Bass 1957; Longstaff 1948; Longstaff & Jurgensen 1953; Rusmore 1956; Dicken 1959; Tiffin & McCormick 1965).

Real tests cannot be faked in this way. A person taking a mental test cannot fake the test by solving more problems in the time allotted than he can solve. He can miss problems, if he wants to, and thus fake the test by making himself appear to be less bright. But he cannot make himself seem brighter than he actually is. Although some of the more recent efforts to develop personality questionnaires that are really tests and cannot be faked have shown slight promise, the field of personnel testing still seems to be a long way from this goal.

Summary. Personnel tests are widely used in industry. They validly measure many characteristics that cannot be identified during a personal interview. Tests must be validated for the jobs in question. When this has been done, an employer knows exactly how they will work for his company. Industry recognizes, however, that even valid tests are not perfect. Occasionally, test results lead to the hiring of unsatisfactory employees and to the rejecting of applicants who, if hired, would have been quite satisfactory. Nevertheless, if the tests have been validated, the chances of employing satisfactory employees through the use of tests are far greater than the chances of getting good employees when tests are not used. However, personality "tests" are not tests at all. They are questionnaires and, therefore, have very little validity as employee selection devices.

BIBLIOGRAPHY

Bass, Bernard M. 1957 "Faking by Sales Applicants of a Forced Choice Personality Inventory." *Journal of Applied Psychology*, 41, no. 6:403–404.

Cochran, Robert 1955 "A Trade Information Test in Engine Lathe Operation." M.S. thesis. Lafayette, Ind., Purdue University.

Dicken, Charles F. 1959 "Simulated Patterns on the Edwards Personal Preference Schedule." *Journal of Applied Psychology*, 43, no. 6:372–378.

Lawshe, C. H., and Michael J. Balma 1966 *Principles of Personnel Testing*. 2nd ed. New York, McGraw-Hill.

Lawshe, C. H., Irene Semanek, and Joseph Tiffin 1946 "The Purdue Mechanical Adaptability Test." *Journal of Applied Psychology*, 30, no. 5:442–453.

Longstaff, Howard P. 1948 "Fakability of the Strong Interest Blank and the Kuder Personal Preference Record." *Journal of Applied Psychology*, 32, no. 4:360–369.

Longstaff, Howard P., and C. E. Jurgensen 1953 "Fakability of the Jurgensen Classification Inventory." *Journal of Applied Psychology*, 37, no. 2:86–89.

Rusmore, Jay T. 1956 "Fakability of the Gordon Personal Profile." *Journal of Applied Psychology*, 40, no. 3:175–177.

Thurstone, L. L. 1955 "The Criterion Problem in Personality Research." *Educational and Psychological Measurement*, 15, no. 4:353–361.

Tiffin, Joseph, and C. H. Lawshe 1943 "The Adaptability Test: A Fifteen Minute Mental Alertness Test for Use in Personnel Allocation." *Journal of Applied Psychology*, 27, no. 2:152–163.

Tiffin, Joseph, and Ernest J. McCormick 1965 *Industrial Psychology*. 5th ed. Englewood Cliffs, N.J., Prentice-Hall.

Whyte, William H., Jr. 1957 *The Organization Man*. New York, Simon and Schuster.

Joseph Tiffin

2. THE CULTURALLY DISADVANTAGED

The term "disadvantaged" is used here to refer to both social and cultural deficiencies. It is not identical with "minority group," since in any minority group there may be some individuals who have also attained bicultural middle-class status and who suffer little if any disadvantage relative to the majority culture. Conversely, some disadvantaged individuals may be of the same ethnic and religious backgrounds as the majority of the population and yet live in pockets of poverty and in cultural isolation. Many of the disadvantaged groups in the United States today are found among Negroes, white people in such impoverished areas as Appalachia, Spanish-speaking people, American Indians, and recent immigrants.

The children of these families are disadvantaged in not having had the usual middle-class opportunities in home, neighborhood, and school environments which encourage the use and development of those characteristics that middle-class-oriented schools recognize and reward. Studies of these children show a considerable number of purportedly significant characteristics, but the lists are not uniform or consistent. Nonetheless, in contrast to the middle-class child, it may be hypothesized that the lower-class child will be less verbal, less self-confident, more fearful of strangers, less motivated in the areas of scholastic and academic achievement, less competitive in intellectual matters, more easily antagonized, less conforming to middle-class norms of behavior and conduct, more apt to be bilingual, less exposed to intellectually stimulating materials at home, less exposed to a variety of recreational outlets, less knowledgeable about the world outside his immediate neighborhood, and more likely to attend inferior schools (Deutsch et al. 1964).

These characteristics account for many of the difficulties in the use of standardized tests with disadvantaged children. Even the best of these tests may fail to uncover the true capacity for development of most underprivileged children. The difficulties in using standardized tests with these children are of three kinds: reliability of differentiations within the subgroups of the disadvantaged; predictive validity; and validity of test interpretation.

Reliability of differentiations. Reliability is the likelihood of achieving consistent measures of the same child with the same or an equivalent test at different times. The reliability of a test is stated as a reliability coefficient, which is a statistic expressing the relationship between two sets of scores. It is the custom for test publishers to describe in the test manuals the composition of the group upon which their statements of reliability are based. But the manuals currently available do not report reliability data for specific disadvantaged groups. There are several factors which suggest that most published reliability coefficients are not relevant to these groups. The most important of these factors is the spread of scores.

Spread of scores. In general, standardized tests show a wide spread of scores for the sample groups upon which the reliability of the tests is based. The greater the spread, the higher the reliability coefficient. Therefore, a group with a substantially and characteristically narrow range of scores presents a problem of differentiation within the group. When a test whose reliability is based upon a wide spread of scores is used with a homogeneous group of children, its actual reliability is lower than the reported reliability coefficient would lead one to expect.

There is substantial evidence that disadvantaged children have a smaller spread of scores than children from middle-income families. This restricted range of scores tends to lower the reliability of the tests in differentiating between any two or more individuals within a disadvantaged group. The problem is not one of comparing different socioeconomic groups but of identifying individual differences within the group.

There is a growing conviction that most of the published educational and psychological tests are unreliable for the purpose of differentiating between disadvantaged children. Most of this evidence is indirect; that is, it is based upon studies of social class and socioeconomic differences rather than upon test performance per se.

Interfering characteristics. The characteristics of underprivileged children noted above undoubtedly affect test taking and test performance. In particular, these characteristics tend to interfere with consistency of performance from test to retest, even when these tests are administered by the same examiner. Consistency is further impaired when different examiners are involved. For example, a Negro ghetto child typically has little contact with white adults except as remote figures (teachers, policemen, relief investigators, truant officers) likely to produce harm or discomfort. To such a child, a white examiner might seem so threatening as to inhibit his responses or to narrow them to monosyllabic replies which do not reflect his real knowledge. A retest by a black examiner might conceivably elicit fuller responses and produce a higher although inconsistent score. Sarason and his associates (1960) demonstrated that test scores are affected by examiner variables, such as age, sex, race, and professional and socioeconomic status, and by such factors as the examiner's aggressiveness, responsiveness, and personal warmth.

Another example involves the fact that disadvantaged children are often convinced that success in school will make little difference later in securing jobs and higher income. While the parents of these children may believe that education is important for upward mobility, they do not put much faith in the schools their children attend. With this background, their children will tend to reject anything associated with their schools. In taking tests, their aim is to finish quickly and to escape the constraints of the testing situation. Their test performance may involve more guessing, skipping, and random response than will the performance of children who accept the test as a normal and important part of schooling. If retested under more positive circumstances, the disadvantaged children might have markedly higher scores.

Local norms. The test responses of disadvantaged children, deriving from their experiences and attitudes, account for the narrow range of their test scores and for their test-retest unreliability. When the national norms of standardized tests do not provide sufficient differentiation at the lower end of the scale, locally established norms are useful.

It is often desirable to compare the performance of the disadvantaged child with that of the advantaged child. On other occasions it is desirable and necessary to compare his performance with that of other disadvantaged children in order to determine his relative deprivation or to compare one test performance with another. Local norms are a means of meeting these objectives, as long as testing is conducted under uniform and facilitating conditions.

Responsible use of tests with disadvantaged children requires thoughtful consideration of the group to be tested and of the expected use to be made of the test scores. It is not enough to consider the reliability coefficient of a test; the size and composition of the norm samples must also be taken into account. It is essential to determine whether the standard error of measurement varies at different score levels and whether the evidence of reliability is relevant to the group with which the test is to be used. The reliability and differentiability of test results are affected by cultural differences, and disadvantaged children are often handicapped by preconditions and response patterns which do not belong in the testing situation.

Predictive validity. The second area of difficulty in using standardized tests with the disadvantaged is the use of test scores as predictors. Three kinds of factors may reduce the predictive validity of a test: test-related factors, complexity of criteria, and the effects of intervening events. These factors have some effect on the predictive validity of tests with all groups, but their impact on the disadvantaged is substantially greater than on the advantaged.

If test scores were being used only to state an individual's standing relative to a particular norm group, it would not be important to consider his social and cultural disadvantage relative to that same group. There is nothing necessarily invidious in reporting a disadvantaged child's IQ and percentile rank on the national norms of an intelligence test. Difficulties arise because interpretations and explanations are made of these scores, and long-range predictions may be based upon them.

Test-related factors. The validity of a test is the degree to which it measures what it is supposed to measure. Validity is determined by checking test results against some external standard, called a criterion. Thus, if a test is designed to predict the probable success of students in future college work, the standard, or criterion, would be the actual record of the students in college. Certain factors in the testing situation may impair the predictive validity of a test. These are factors that relate only to the test itself and do not appear in the criterion; that is, they disturb test scores but do not interfere with criterion performance. They include test-taking skill, degree of anxiety, level of motivation, degree of novelty in the test itself, and rapport between examiner and examinee.

Some of these factors may not work to the detriment of the disadvantaged. Test anxiety, for example, is more prevalent and disruptive in middle-income groups (Sarason et al. 1960). But most of the test-related factors that limit validity are prejudicial to the disadvantaged. Dreger and Miller (1960) reported the problems of white examiners testing Negro children; Klineberg (1935) noted the effect upon American Indian children of taking timed tests; and Haggard (1954) described the frustration of disadvantaged children facing test procedures for the first time.

Standardized interest and personality inventories are especially vulnerable when normative interpretation of a disadvantaged person's responses is attempted. It is difficult for someone to be interested in something that he knows nothing about, and if satisfactions and rewards for a pursuit are missing, if family, neighborhood, and peer group express no support for an activity, a child is not likely to express an interest in it. Enriched experience for disadvantaged children might substantially change their responses to an interest inventory. Similarly, items on personality inventories pertaining to such factors as home or social adjustment, social customs, and religious beliefs may produce responses to which national norms are inappropriate. Local norms which permit measurement of the disadvantaged individual against his own group would be more useful.

Once again, predictive validity is the heart of the matter. The employer, the counselor, and the teacher must take background factors into account in making decisions as to probable future behavior of disadvantaged persons.

Complexity of criteria. The criteria against which test scores are measured usually concern adjustment or achievement, in which a great many factors are involved. The criterion behavior is much more complex than the behavior sampled by the tests. School grades are a common criterion, but school grades are the results of motivation, classroom behavior, rapport with the teacher, peer influence, and study habits, as well as intelligence and academic skill. A scholastic aptitude test does not and cannot measure these contributing factors, and to this extent its validity is impaired. In considering the scholastic aptitude of disadvantaged persons, it is advisable to take into account their background, personality, and motivation, since these factors may produce different learning results in the disadvantaged than a scholastic aptitude test score would lead one to expect.

In order to meet the need for impartiality and objectivity, the administrators of state or national scholarships use test scores for screening and cutoff points. This procedure handicaps the disadvantaged, since they tend not to do well on ability and achievement tests. Some alternative procedures are needed to provide opportunities for the disadvantaged student. These procedures should be based on more individualized evaluation of the student's qualifications.

DeHaan and Kough (1956) reported the following among the characteristics of superior and talented students: they learn rapidly, although not necessarily those lessons assigned in school; they reason soundly, think clearly, recognize relationships, comprehend meanings, and may or may not come to conclusions expected by the teacher; they are able to influence others to work toward desirable or undesirable goals. It is reasonable to suppose that these characteristics would appear in superior disadvantaged students, but such characteristics are not measured by aptitude tests and are revealed only by observation.

Intervening events. If the interval between a test and a criterial assessment is a long one, a variety of intervening changes may occur to reduce the predictive validity of the test. Test scores have a tyrannical rigidity which does not take into account change factors affecting later assessment either favorably or adversely. Such factors as illness, a change of teachers, a shift in level of aspiration, remedial training, emotional crisis, and growth spurts or retrogression in abilities will alter the predictive validity of a test.

Relative to advantaged groups or to the general population, disadvantaged children show a decline in academic aptitude and achievement over a period of time. This decline may be the effect of continuing lack of opportunity and consequent decreased interest in the academic school program. These continuing factors are cumulative, and as intervening events they impair the predictive validity of tests unless they are taken into account. If, for example, it were known in advance that a student or a group would face either undesirable environmental influences or improved circumstances (perhaps special guidance and training), some estimate of the effects of these changes could be used along with test results, and the validity of the tests would be improved.

This kind of expectation obviously cannot be built into a standardized test or test manual. It can be derived only from local sources. "In this connection, it should be recognized that attempts to appraise human 'potential' without defining the milieu in which it will be given an opportunity to materialize are as futile as attempts to specify the horsepower of an engine without knowing how it will be energized" (Deutsch et al. 1964, p. 137).

Cultural unfairness. Educational tests have been criticized as being unfair to disadvantaged groups because the test items are bound to a culture to which the disadvantaged do not have access. The tests, in effect, differentiate culturally advantaged and culturally disadvantaged children. Where educational attainment is measured, this differentiation is a necessity of the situation because factors related to educational success are molded by the culture. Differences in educational attainment deriving from social inequity rather than native ability may be considered culturally and socially unfair. The predictive validity of a test depends upon the degree to which it accurately reflects this unfairness. The tests themselves are not invalid because they do so. Improvement of educational opportunity may remove or lessen differences in attainment, and if it has this effect, the tests with predictive validity will reflect the change. Change is required in the criterion rather than in the test.

This is not to say that test bias is impossible. If a test shows greater differences between advantaged and disadvantaged than occur in the criterion, it may properly be called a biased test. If a test calls for a performance particularly difficult for the disadvantaged but one that is unrelated to academic achievement, it is biased. The test would disclose cultural disadvantage but would be unrelated to the criterion and hence of no value in predicting the student's future academic achievement.

Aptitude and ability tests, as distinguished from achievement tests, have strong criterion validity for some purposes, but they do not reflect the true capacity for development in disadvantaged children. In measuring factors of academic success, they must measure abilities that have been shaped by the culture. In addition, the test content, the mode of response, and the motivation for responding depend upon the cultural context in which the child has lived. Efforts have been made to produce culture-fair or culture-free tests, but the results of these tests have been low in predictive validity. These tests have reduced the dependency upon formal education and upon speed of response, but they have not been successful in identifying capacities obscured by the commonly used academic aptitude and achievement tests.

Standardized tests, despite their cultural bias, are useful means for assessing traits of disadvantaged children. Many children score relatively higher on achievement tests than in classroom grades, the latter often being affected by success or failure in social or interpersonal behavior. For these children, the standardized tests buffer the adverse subjective evaluations of teachers from different backgrounds in which nonconforming behavior is penalized.

Validity of test interpretation. The third general area of difficulty in using standardized tests with disadvantaged children is not a factor of the tests themselves but of those who employ them. Interpretation of the results of psychological and educational tests requires the competence of a trained professional. The importance of professional interpretation is most obvious when test results are made the basis of decisions affecting the child's entire future.

Failure to take into account the background and characteristics of disadvantaged groups has led to three significant errors in interpretation of test results.

Deviation error. The first error in test interpretation is the deviation error, which is the tendency to regard responses differing from those of the cultural majority as indications of maladjustment or personality difficulty. Such deviating responses may, in fact, indicate complete adjustment to the values of the disadvantaged group of which the examinee is a member. To avoid the deviation error, it is essential to take into account the examinee's circumstances and the range of his experience. To a prospective employer, as to a school guidance counselor, what should matter is not the specific responses but the likelihood that maladjustment may lead to disruptive or otherwise unsatisfactory behavior.

> A performance IQ that is high in relation to the individual's verbal IQ on the Wechsler scales *may* signify psychopathic tendencies, but it also may signify a poverty of educational experience. Perceiving drunken males beating up women on the Thematic Apperception Test may imply a projection of idiosyncratic fantasy or wish, but it may also imply a background of rather realistic observation and experience common to some minority group children. (Deutsch et al. 1964, p. 140)

For children in certain situations, test responses that indicate a low degree of motivation or a self-image that is oversubmissive may realistically reflect their life conditions. Were these children to give responses more typical of the general population, they might well be regarded as subgroup deviants. Thus, whether test responses reflect

secondary defenses against anxiety or are the direct result of a socialization process has immense diagnostic import and makes knowledge of the individual's social and cultural background crucial to the interpretation of test results (Deutsch et al. 1964).

Simple determinant error. The simple determinant error is the assumption that test content involves only a single pure trait, process, or factor unaffected by the testing situation or the conditions of the group being tested. In fact, a test with a particular group may measure factors other than the one it was designed to measure. Anastasi (1968) notes that a test which is designed to measure the effects of instruction in such areas as mechanics or mathematics may be unduly influenced by the ability to understand verbal directions or by the speed of performing simple, routine tasks. Thus, a test of arithmetic skill may be measuring the ability to read and to follow directions.

Similarly, a test may measure motivation as well as the trait purportedly being measured. The motivation of middle-class groups to do well on tests is strong enough to ensure that responses reflect the differences that the test was intended to measure. In other groups, however, where success with tests is not valued highly, the effort expended in test taking varies with the individual. Even for a particular child among the disadvantaged, motivation may vary with the test situation and the kinds of materials involved. The result is a confusing variance in test scores.

Other factors affect test results, creating further problems of interpretation. For example, the way in which a question is asked must be taken into account. A child may be able to identify a figure (discrimination) but not be able to name it (vocabulary) or reproduce it (motor skill). It therefore makes a difference which of these tasks he is asked to perform. According to Anastasi (1968), test performance may also be affected by the response sets with which subjects approach the test. That is, the nature of the instructions and the form in which test items are expressed may set the examinee to respond in a particular way. Among the response sets that affect test performance are the tendency to agree with positively stated items, the willingness to risk guessing, and the tendency to answer "true" rather than "false" when the answer to a true-false item is not known. In short, test scores are usually multiply determined rather than determined by one factor only.

Incomplete content coverage. An inadequate or circumscribed sampling of an area results in impairment of the content validity of a test. This factor is of particular interest in the area of intelligence. "In a broad sense, most intelligence test items tap abilities involving language and symbol systems, although opportunities for developing these abilities vary considerably from one social group to another" (Deutsch et al. 1964, p. 142). A child coming from a family or community which sets little store by language skills, uses vague rather than specific language and employs severely limited linguistic structures will score relatively low on an intelligence test. Yet the meaning of this score differs greatly from the meaning of a higher score achieved by a child coming from a family or neighborhood where language skills are highly valued and developed. The cultural and social background of the disadvantaged must be taken into account in test-score interpretation not only to avoid under-evaluating test performance but in some cases to avoid overevaluating performance.

The social and religious practices of some groups also foster the development of specialized skills and vocabulary. To the degree that there is an overlap of a subgroup value system and performances required in a test, the test results will be spuriously high. This is simply a special case of the general rule that intelligence-test results are determined by cultural opportunities. The hazard in interpretation is the assumption that the test scores of the disadvantaged child measure for all time his capacity to learn.

New directions. The difficulties in testing disadvantaged groups do not lead to the conclusion that tests are without value. Tests are powerful tools for diagnosis and evaluation; but they are only tools, and they must be used thoughtfully. The test scores of disadvantaged children have a different meaning from numerically identical scores of advantaged children because the disadvantaged child is handicapped in so many ways. The educator's task is to discover what lies behind these scores and to undertake remedial measures to overcome the handicaps.

There are several possible means of reducing the difficulties in testing the disadvantaged. A program might be devised for measuring separate skills first, with a gradual increase in the use of more complex items that involve several skills. Items and tests can be developed to minimize factors irrelevant to the criterion and to maximize those that are critically relevant. These tests should be considered as an integral part of teaching and training, a means of continuously measuring learning capabilities. Finally, more use can be made of everyday behavior as evidence of competence to mediate the interpretations of standardized test results, especially when children are being considered for special aid programs or when academic prediction is not the major objective.

BIBLIOGRAPHY

ANASTASI, ANNE 1968 *Psychological Testing.* 3rd ed. New York, Macmillan.

DeHAAN, ROBERT F., AND JACK KOUGH 1956 *Teacher's Guidance Handbook.* Vol. 1: *Identifying Students With Special Needs.* Secondary school ed. Chicago, Science Research Associates.

DEUTSCH, MARTIN, et al. 1964 "Guidelines for Testing Minority Group Children." *Journal of Social Issues,* 20, no. 2:127–145.

DREGER, RALPH MASON, AND KENT MILLER 1960 "Comparative Psychological Studies of Negroes and Whites in the United States." *Psychological Bulletin,* 57, no. 5:361–402.

GUILFORD, JOY PAUL 1954 *Psychometric Methods.* 2nd ed. New York, McGraw-Hill.

HAGGARD, ERNEST A. 1954 "Social Status and Intelligence: An Experimental Study of Certain Cultural Determinants of Measured Intelligence." *Genetic Psychological Monographs,* 49, second half:141–186.

KLINEBERG, OTTO 1935 *Race Differences.* New York, Harper.

SARASON, SEYMOUR K., et al. 1960 *Anxiety in Elementary School Children.* New York, Wiley.

JOSHUA A. FISHMAN

3. THE ARMED FORCES

Personnel tests are used to ensure that an individual assigned to a job can be expected to perform that job acceptably. He may not be able to do the job better than anyone else, nor is the job necessarily the one he can do best. In an organization the size of the U.S. military establishment, jobs to be filled and individuals whose highest abilities would be required in the job hardly ever match exactly. However, through new computerized techniques and the development of mathematical theory, methods are becoming available for assigning men to jobs which will put to use their highest abilities.

Scientific management in the U.S. military began with the development of mental tests. The Army Alpha and Army Beta tests of World War I and the Army General Classification Test (AGCT) of World War II, designed to measure overall ability, were used initially as aids in categorizing men for training and jobs. The Armed Forces Qualification Test (AFQT), which was developed and administered after the World War II period, also measures overall ability, although four part scores—vocabulary, arithmetic reasoning, use of tools, and spatial relations—can also be computed. The AFQT has been used primarily to determine mental qualifications of potential enlistees and Selective Service registrants.

Mass testing in World War I. On the day the United States entered World War I, a group of members of the American Psychological Association called a special session to consider what they might do in support of the nation's military effort. One result of this meeting was the development of the Army Alpha Test (for literates) and the Army Beta Test (for illiterates). Adapted from early group tests devised by Arthur S. Otis, the Alpha and Beta tests were objective and reliably valid paper-and-pencil tests, which could be .applied rapidly and economically on a large scale. Tests and other evaluative techniques were used to identify the mentally incompetent, to classify men in broad groups according to mental capabilities, and to assist in selecting potential officers and personnel for special assignments. Psychologists assisted in evaluating neuropsychiatric patients at military hospitals and in developing ways to assess and stimulate combat effectiveness and morale.

Psychological testing in World War II. In the 1920's the services resumed pre-World War I procedures, with what was in effect an apprenticeship system of selection and assignment. Yet, in industry and education advances were made in aptitude testing, vocational guidance, personnel evaluation, and management. When efforts of psychologists were marshaled in support of U.S. defense efforts in 1939, the compelling needs of the armed services governed activities.

The fundamental job was mass evaluation to classify recruits for training and job assignment. Of all the services, the army, confronted with problems associated with the immediate induction and organization of vast numbers of men, had the greatest need for mass procedures. The adjutant general of the army and advisory psychologists decided on the construction of a new classification test with emphasis on assessing

"trainability." By 1940 the Army General Classification Test was ready; by the end of the war it had been administered in its various forms to over 9 million men.

Early postwar years. In the early postwar years, military psychology was sharpening its measurement tools and applying them to help the military establishment adjust to peacetime status and reduced numbers. The human factors research organizations associated with the defense effort did not abandon their activities in the military sphere, as they had done after World War I; rather, they accepted, and even sought to anticipate, the personnel and manpower resource problems of military management.

Screening procedures. The Armed Forces Qualification Test (AFQT), introduced in 1950, was developed jointly by the services, with the Personnel Research Section of the army (now the Behavior and Systems Research Laboratory) having primary responsibility. The AFQT was the first psychological test designated by Congress for a specific purpose—to determine mental acceptability for military service—with a mandatory qualifying score. It was also the first screening test used by all the services—the earliest AFQT forms replaced a variety of screening tests and scoring systems that had been used by the several services. Four successive pairs of alternate forms have since been introduced. Use of one test by the army, navy, air force, and marine corps made it possible to develop an equitable policy of distribution of mental ability among the services.

The concept of a common screening test for all the services was based on the principle that the same basic abilities were required by all the services for initial enlistment or induction. The AFQT contains 100 questions—25 each on vocabulary, arithmetic reasoning, understanding of tool usage, and spatial relations. Scores are converted to percentile scores based on the scores of the troops in World War II. The AFQT is a good predictor of performance in training for military jobs.

While a single test is now used in all armed forces entrance and examining stations, the screening practices of the several services are by no means uniform. Unlike the other services, the army uses the Selective Service System to meet the portion of its requirement for enlisted personnel which it does not meet through voluntary enlistment. An average over several years shows approximately 45 percent inductees and 55 percent volunteers.

Army screening procedures. Mental screening for induction into the army is accomplished mainly by the AFQT. For volunteers, a preliminary estimate of acceptability is obtained by use of the Enlistment Screening Test. Selective Service registrants whose scores are in the 31st percentile or higher on the AFQT (meaning they did better than at least 30 percent of those tested) are considered acceptable; those who score below the tenth percentile are rejected. Congressional legislation in 1958 authorized the army to apply supplementary screening for more specific aptitudes to the men who score between the tenth and 30th percentile. The Army Qualification Battery (AQB-1) was introduced in 1961 as a means of determining whether men of relatively low mental ability could meet the army's differential aptitude requirements. The AQB is also used to determine the eligibility of applicants who want to take a specific training program.

The present AQB consists of the four subtests of the AFQT (in short form) and additional short aptitude tests: clerical speed, mechanical aptitude, automotive information, electrical information, the classification inventory, and the general information test, which measures interests.

The supplementary screening reflects the results of army research studies. Men with scores on specific aptitudes equivalent to the 31st percentile have tended to be able to pass a related training program and perform acceptably on the job. Men with low general aptitude are required to have two specific aptitude scores at or above the 31st percentile.

Navy screening program. The navy usually depends on voluntary enlistments. A short general test given at recruiting stations indicates whether an applicant is likely to meet navy standards. The AFQT is the primary mental screening test. The Basic Test Battery, administered at the beginning of boot training, provides information on which to base assignment to job-training programs. The navy accepts as few applicants as possible who score below the 31st percentile on the AFQT. In recent years the navy has provided its recruiters with a set of short classification-type tests to determine whether applicants who are considered for enlistment meet special training requirements.

Although the marine corps is under the Department of the Navy, its problems tend to be more like those of the army. As a result, the marine corps screening program for those who enlist uses the AFQT and the army's AQB in a manner similar to the army's screening of applicants for enlistment.

Air force screening program. Like the navy, the air force usually obtains personnel through voluntary enlistment. In contrast to the screening and classification procedures of the other services, the air force projects position requirements and then enlists personnel with the specific aptitudes to fill these requirements. Recruiting stations are notified of these requirements periodically. With these quotas and established qualifying scores, recruiters arrange for testing sessions and then select applicants who qualify. Aptitude qualifications are in effect determined before the applicant is sent to an examining station to take the AFQT. The test battery, called the Airman Qualifying Examination (AQE), provides the primary information for classification. Qualitative requirements are high, and only borderline cases are screened on the basis of the AFQT, which is used with a relatively low cutting score.

The AQE provides scores in four aptitude areas —general, electronics, administrative, and mechanical. A percentile scale similar to that used with the AFQT is computed.

Classification batteries. All the services recognize the need to assess the abilities of personnel with greater precision than can be achieved in a general screening process. The differences among the three chief services in mission, job structure, and administrative approach require several programs by which servicemen and servicewomen are assigned to training and jobs.

Army. To classify a soldier adequately for job training and to assign him in accordance with total manpower requirements, the army has to know not only the general capability of the man but also his individual pattern of aptitudes— what jobs he can do best, how many outstanding aptitudes he has, and how he compares with others in each aptitude. Measures of the individual's aptitudes are derived from his scores on tests of the Army Classification Battery, administered during initial processing. The aptitude measures, or aptitude area scores, are composites of test scores, each composite representing a combination of aptitudes required in a particular set of jobs which make up an occupational area.

The aptitude area system corresponds essentially to the job classification structure, in which occupational areas are defined by those jobs having similar aptitude requirements. A given score in the appropriate aptitude area is prerequisite to assignment in a given occupational area.

The army adopted the aptitude area system of classification, often called differential classification, in 1949. After a long period of development, including the use of criteria based on actual combat performance, the combat aptitude areas were introduced in 1955. On both the individual tests and the aptitude composites, scores are expressed in terms of army standard scores. (The standard score is a useful method of stating how much above or below the average a score is. For the army, the average score is 100.)

The object of differential classification is to train enlisted personnel so that the available talent will yield the highest total of effective performance in army jobs, according to the test scores which should indicate how well a man will perform.

Navy. The navy classification tests are used in various combinations to assign recruits to training in about 60 naval ratings, or occupational fields. The test combinations, which in effect form aptitude composites, are used to predict performance in the service schools. The combinations, however, have never been formally designated, as have those of the other services. The score is translated into the navy standard score, with a mean of 50 and standard deviation of 10. Not all recruits take all the tests of the battery. The electronics technician selection test, the sonar pitch memory test, the radio code test, and the foreign language aptitude test are administered to personnel who score above the mean on a combination of the general classification test and the arithmetic test.

Air force. In 1958 the air force instituted preenlistment aptitude testing and centralized classification testing. The Airman Qualifying Examination became, in 1959, the sole basis for both screening and classifying enlistees. The current Airman Qualifying Examination–62 consists of ten tests which, in various combinations, yield four composites or aptitude indexes, which are expressed in terms of a 20-point percentile scale ranging from a minimum score of 1 to a maximum of 95 (with a mean of 47.5 and a standard deviation of 28.8).

Changing nature of testing programs. The testing programs of all the services are subject to change. Most change in tests is gradual: long-term refinement of form and content, exploration of new theory and methodology, adjustment to technological progress with consequent restructuring of jobs and training curricula. More rapid change must take place when qualifying standards are abruptly lowered to take in a larger segment of the available input.

Computerized techniques for processing psychological data have enabled the military to make better use of testing and have speeded the progress being made toward optimal assignment of all personnel. For example, at the time the aptitude area system was devised for the army, each composite was purposely limited to from two to four test scores in order to make computation feasible at field statistical centers. When revised aptitude areas were introduced in 1955, composites were limited to two tests in order to simplify computation and make results more speedily available to classification officers. More recent experimentation has demonstrated that more effective prediction is achieved when all the test scores are taken into account. With advanced computerized techniques, data from the total battery can contribute classification information.

Special selection programs. In some jobs, proficiency is the skilled performance of specific operations. In others, the elements contributing to proficiency are much less tangible—ability to work with others, courage and resourcefulness in combat, skill in communicating ideas, and quality of leadership. These elements are considered in selection for such special assignments as combat leadership, officer training, paratrooper service, and the army's Special Forces.

The military services have arrived at essentially parallel methods for selecting individuals either for direct commissioning as officers or for training to be commissioned or noncommissioned officers. Measures of arithmetic reasoning and of verbal and spatial skills are standard for prediction of success in officer training. The air force uses additional sensitive measures of spatial skills in its aircrew selection.

Aptitude tests are less effective in determining interpersonal and leadership skills important to both commissioned and noncommissioned officers. Here, noncognitive measures are relied upon primarily. Biographical inventories, attitude and preference scales, experience and activities inventories, and temperament and personality tests are used in various programs. On the basis of extended tryout, these devices seem suitable for use in the selection of leaders. Such measures seem to test what a man will do rather than what he can do. The most useful measure of how a would-be officer or a noncommissioned officer will perform appears to be an average of ratings of the individual made by his colleagues, provided the group has been together long enough for members to know something about one another. As short a period as five days produces stable ratings in some groups. The army has moved most decisively in the rigorous evaluation of peer-rating procedures and in their incorporation in selection procedures for special assignments. All three services have found that peer ratings collected during training help predict later officer performance as measured by official ratings obtained periodically. All three branches have had difficulty in developing paper-and-pencil personality tests that are useful for this purpose.

Role of tests. A calculated risk is involved when personnel decisions are made on the basis of tests. Tests are reliable, but they are not perfectly reliable. A few points difference in scores does not always mean a real difference between the individuals receiving the scores. Yet, when a minimum qualifying score is set, it is recognized and used throughout the service as the dividing line between those who are acceptable for service or for a given assignment and those who are not. Admittedly, some of the men accepted would, if retested, fall below the minimum, and some of those rejected would reach or exceed it. This risk is taken when a decision is made to use a certain score point as the standard, a decision essential to an effective personnel management system. Scientific research on the tests enables the user of the system to estimate with greater precision the probable loss through misclassification and the likely gain through correct classification.

J. E. UHLANER

4. BUSINESS STUDENTS

The various kinds, purposes, and formats of tests that are characteristic of many educational fields are also found in business education. However, there are two especially prominent features of measurement and evaluation in business education that arise from its vocational objectives and from the nature of some of the occupations for which preparation is being made. The first special feature of tests in business education is the evaluation of attitudes, personality, and other personal attributes of students. The second feature is the preponderant use of performance tests (in contrast to essay or short-answer measures) to assess proficiency in typewriting, shorthand, and some aspects of bookkeeping and clerical and distributive occupations.

Evaluation of personal attributes. Reports of employers' dissatisfaction with employees' personal attributes, rather than with their technical job skills, have heightened the sensitivity of business teachers to the development of character and personality and to psychosocial factors. Whether teachers should evaluate the personal traits of their students has been debated. Those who oppose such evaluation by teachers emphasize the weakness of the instruments for personality assessment that are available to the business teacher and the limited extent to which the classroom teacher can make discriminating assessments of as many as 150 or more students each semester or year, especially when general impressions rather than formal measures are used; opponents particularly stress "the failure [of specialists] to find [any] clear-cut relationships between personality . . . and occupational choice or success . . . [so that] our current knowledge of the role of personality . . . in work is impressionistic or, when quantitative, largely superficial" (Super & Crites 1962, pp. 516–517).

Those who favor teachers' evaluations (and who might be unaware of the findings of specialists) hold that, whatever the difficulties with reliable and valid assessment, personal attributes cannot be ignored among students receiving vocational training. However, great care in making such evaluations and a conservative view of their accuracy and validity are required. As Hardaway has observed, when any of these personal trait measures "ask direct questions about a student's attitudes, feelings, preferences, and social adjustments, the results should not be taken too seriously for purposes of evaluation" (1966, p. 44). Enterline is among the many who have cautioned against combining achievement and trait estimates into a single measure, urging that the two be handled separately (Popham 1960).

Performance testing for occupational skills. Measurement in business education can most conveniently be described if the term "skills" is used to designate those tasks prominently involving the chaining, or sequencing, of muscular movements, such as shorthand, typewriting, and the operation of some office machines. The acquisition of mastery of such skills is a relatively long-drawn-out process that cannot be forced. Also, testing and teaching are closely merged; practice activities usually consist of performance by students under essentially testlike conditions. Certain aspects of clerical, secretarial, and distributive education courses also involve frequent use of performance tests because some areas of these courses do not lend themselves very well to paper-and-pencil measures. Although bookkeeping and accounting are sometimes described as having skill components (penmanship, neatness in ruling forms), such features grow less important as machine methods replace manual entries and are, in any event, trivial in relation to the cognitive, or intellectual, factors of the knowledges and principles involved in bookkeeping and accounting.

In performance testing for occupational skills the major problems are those of test administration conditions, control over test difficulty, modes of scoring, reliability, validity, and standards. The developmental and cumulative nature of the process of skill acquisition requires control over several conditions if changes in test scores over time are to be attributed wholly to changes in skill, not confounded by other factors. One requirement is to hold test length constant during nontrivial portions of the training. Another consideration, mildly applicable to typewriting and strongly applicable to shorthand, is control over the difficulty of test materials. One or more of three difficulty indexes are used: stroke intensity (average number of typewriter strokes per dictionary word), syllabic intensity (average number of speech syllables per dictionary word), and percentage of common words (those among the 500, 1,000, or 1,500 most common words in the language). For years, tests have been constructed on the assumption that a stroke intensity of 5.0 and a syllabic intensity of 1.40 are average for the vocabulary of business communication. However, West's reanalysis (1968) of Silverthorn's vocabulary of written business communications (1955) revealed a mean stroke intensity of 6.0 (including spacing and punctuation) and a mean syllabic intensity of 1.54, showing that the conventional figures are serious underestimates of the true values.

Concerning grading practices, some educators advocate marking on the basis of improvement, presumably as a means of motivating the poorer student. Other educators feel that in view of the characteristic slower rate of gains in skill as mastery increases, grading on the basis of improvement rewards the poorer student at the expense of the more able one. It is further argued that vocational objectives require that marketable skill, or employability, be the criterion for assigning grades. However, that basis for grading presupposes the availability of reliable employment standards. Such standards exist for a few, but not for most, of the pertinent occupational skills. In the absence of employment standards that permit absolute grading, relative grading (the so-called marking on the curve) is often employed.

Typewriting.   Some of the knowledges required for typewriting can be tested with paper-and-pencil measures. (An example of a possible test question might be "Pica type provides __ spaces to the horizontal inch.") The first-year typewriting achievement tests developed by one publisher, for example, include a 60-item multiple choice test of basic information, in addition to performance tests in both the first-year and second-year tests. However, the dominant testing in typewriting consists of two types of performance tests: straight copy typing and production work (based on realistic office typing tasks). Straight copy typing is wholly a school training task that has no counterparts outside of the classroom except in many employment tests, including Civil Service tests. Such typing is intended as a measure of stroking skill per se and commonly calls for word-for-word copying of perfectly printed prose; no judgments are required (except, sometimes, for word division), and errors are not corrected. Performances are scored for speed (words per minute) and for the number of errors. The two scores may be recorded separately or combined, as has been traditional, into one or another of various composite scores in which a penalty for errors is deducted from a speed score. However, the uninterpretability of a composite score, which conceals rather than reveals the details of performance, has become increasingly apparent to educators and employers. Separate scoring, giving more weight to speed than to errors, is supported by two findings: (1) the very high reliability of speed scores versus the low reliability of error scores, and (2) the moderate correlations between straight copy speed and speed at realistic typing tasks, as contrasted with the low correlations between straight copy errors and stroking errors on realistic typing tasks (West 1969). Despite these findings, much employment testing, partly because of the cost of scoring production tests, still consists exclusively of straight copy measures, using rather rigorous error standards. In fact, straight copy performance has been the focus of attention for so many years that substantial compilations of data exist as a basis for standards, namely, an average of 28 gross words per minute (wpm) in five-minute timings on copy of 1.50 syllabic intensity (or 5.60 stroke intensity) after one semester of training and an average of 38 wpm after two semesters; the number of errors, however, averages ten in five minutes throughout first-year training (Robinson 1967).

Production work, the second and far more consequential kind of typing performance introduces the component of decision-making about placement, or arrangement, of materials on the page for the typing of letters, tables, reports, and the like. Production testing may or may not include correction of errors and may be carried out either under time-limit conditions (work score) or work-limit conditions (time score). With a fixed work time for all and with more work assigned than can be completed in that time, the speed measure, or work score, is the amount of work done in that time (wpm or number of items per hour). With the amount of work held constant the speed measure is the time taken to complete that work, or the time score. Among teachers, however, scoring production typing for speed is a relatively recent development, employed by few teachers. As yet, the modest compilations of production performance scores among students do not provide an adequate basis for standards. Work-limit and time-limit conditions are exhibited in a number of standardized, published typewriting tests (see Buros 1961; 1965). The various methods used by teachers and test specialists for scoring production typing are discussed by West (1969); some of these methods, unfortunately, parallel the composite scores traditionally used for straight copy testing.

Some teachers evaluate students on the basis of typing techniques during the early weeks of instruction, rather than on the basis of speed and accuracy of performance. However, the practice of rating technique has not been shown to have merit; evaluating at all times on the basis of both speed and accuracy of performance seems preferable.

The near-zero correlations between stroking skill and intelligence support the general thesis that the typewriter is a writing tool for persons at all levels of intelligence, thus making aptitude testing inappropriate. However, if for some reason selection of those of high aptitude is desired, the "Tapping Test" is available (see Buros 1965).

Stenographic and secretarial skills. The notoriously high attrition rates among shorthand students suggest the desirability of careful selection of students. A number of aptitude tests are reviewed in Buros (1965), and general experience suggests that those of less than average intelligence or those who are deficient in the mechanics of English and whose verbal abilities are modest have little chance of success in shorthand. However, intensive remedial work might salvage some students whose initial abilities are not adequate.

There are three criteria of stenographic performance: note-taking (dictation) speed, transcription speed, and quality of the transcript. A number of components presumed to contribute to proficiency in these three areas are sometimes subjected to measurement during training. One component is shorthand oral reading rate (tested from both familiar and unfamiliar perfectly written textbook shorthand, from homework notes, and from familiar and unfamiliar dictated matter). Another component is shorthand vocabulary, as measured by word-list tests for the common words or for knowledge of theory (the ability to apply principles of the shorthand system to the construction of unfamiliar words) or both. On these tests the shorthand is sometimes written from slow dictation (about five to ten seconds per word or phrase), sometimes from a printed list. If written from dictation, the shorthand may or may not be transcribed. Interim measures are also used for the assessment of dictation and transcription skills; among such measures is transcription in longhand from textbook shorthand and from heavily practiced or from new dictated matter, sometimes scored purely for the agreement of the words transcribed with the words dictated, ignoring letter form. Practice and test dictation is commonly at a smooth, measured rate, without interruptions, although some educators have advocated so-called office-style dictation, which includes interruptions and word changes. However, because of the difficulty of standardizing office-style dictation, such dictation is inadvisable as a basis for formal assessment of proficiency, although it might be useful as a training procedure for a common office situation.

Measurement of the outcomes of high school shorthand instruction has tended to focus on transcription quality alone, at a fixed dictation rate of 80 wpm. Among college trainees, terminal writing speeds of 100 wpm and higher are expected. There has been little recognition of the desirability of assessing differences in shorthand writing speed (by dictating at several speeds and grading, in part, on the basis of the highest dictation speed whose notes can be acceptably transcribed on the typewriter). It is similarly unfortunate that little attention has been given to speed of typewritten transcription, estimated to average 14 wpm (timed from completion of dictation to completion of transcript) after two years of high school instruction (Wanous 1940). Accordingly, aside from the number or percentage of high school students who can transcribe, with at least 95 percent accuracy, about five minutes of business-letter material dictated at 80 wpm, no detailed information about the typical levels of transcription speed and transcription quality that accompany various dictation speeds exists as a basis for national standards at terminal stages of shorthand instruction.

As with typewriting, the problems of measuring stenographic proficiency concern scoring and control over the difficulty of test materials. An appropriate weighting of the factors of dictation speed, transcription speed, and quality of the transcript has not yet been made available. On transcription quality, "mailability" is subject to various definitions. Three categories of errors have been advocated by Hardaway (1966) and Balsley (Popham 1960): minor errors (not involving deviations from the dictation and readily correctable by erasure), major errors (acceptable deviations from the dictation or errors readily correctable by erasure), and disqualifying errors (those requiring complete retyping); penalties for each type of error are assessed accordingly. Difficulty factors associated with the vocabulary of the dictation have traditionally been handled by dictating on a "standard word" basis (so many speech syllables, rather than dictionary words, per minute), using a syllabic intensity of 1.40 as representative of a business vocabulary. However, West (1968) has shown 1.54 to be the mean syllabic intensity of a business vocabulary; in addition, Hillestad (1962) and Uthe (1968) have shown syllabic length of words to be an extremely weak predictor of errors in shorthand notes. Percentage of uncommon words (beyond the 1,500 most common words) is the more important factor. Adequate preparation of students for the vocabulary

of stenographic employment requires the use of a syllabic intensity of 1.54 as the basis for the "standard word" and the use of a vocabulary index (the percentage of words in the dictation beyond the 1,000 or 1,500 most common words).

Most of the related knowledges that contribute to stenographic or secretarial proficiency are incorporated into office practice, clerical practice, and secretarial practice courses, which are given after direct instruction in the skills and which integrate the various skills and knowledges involved. Here, the objective, short-answer, paper-and-pencil measures of spelling, grammar, business information and procedures, business arithmetic, filing, employer-employee relations, and so forth are common. The early stages of business English and communications courses also use short-answer measures of fundamentals of grammar and language usage and of knowledge of the principles of letter and report writing. Actual letter writing is, of course, the major focus and is measured by essay tests.

Business machines, and business arithmetic. On the whole, duplicating, calculating, bookkeeping, dictating, and electronic data-processing machines are the major machines included in school training for which performance tests are dominant. In preparing masters for machine duplication, the student is evaluated on the basis of the quality of the copies made and, sometimes, on the time it took to prepare the master. For typewritten transcription from dictation on cylinders, disks, or tape, a terminal training standard per hour of about seven to nine two-paragraph to three-paragraph letters of average length has been recommended by one national association. For calculating and bookkeeping machines, high skill is commonly sought, and measurement of speed of work is the prevailing practice: so many sums (or postings) per hour. Data processing is a relatively new area of business education, and no clear curricular or measurement practices have yet emerged.

Business arithmetic also uses performance tests, sometimes timed (for measures of fundamental operations). Objective tests are also common. (A sample question might be "0.25 as a common fraction equals _____.") In scoring problem tests it has been advocated that one point be allotted to each operation or step required to reach a solution (Hardaway 1966).

For office and clerical occupations, apart from

typewriting and other tasks using machines, most testing is objective, covering business information and office procedures. While some aspects of filing are readily assessed through short-answer measures, performance tests using "practice sets" (collections of miniature letters and business papers) are also employed.

Distributive occupations. Most of the knowledges involved in retail merchandising and selling are measured by various objective tests of the short-answer variety. However, cooperative work-experience programs are common and typically call for observation and rating of the student-employee's work behavior by his supervisor and by the program coordinator, using formal rating sheets. Similarly, ratings of in-school activities by teachers and fellow students (setting up a window display, classifying and making simple weaves of fabrics, wrapping packages, role-playing in a sales situation) are also common. The problems again are ones of reliability and validity of ratings; also, personality characteristics are difficult to assess reliably. For clerical tasks in distributive occupations, performance tests cover the operation of a cash register, using charge tokens, writing sales receipts, and so forth.

Testing in the nonskill areas. The major nonskill areas not discussed earlier—that is, those areas not prominently involving muscular movements—are bookkeeping and accounting and the social business subjects. Business English, although not a skill, was treated earlier because it is an adjunct of secretarial training. Distributive education, also discussed earlier, has some skill components.

Bookkeeping and accounting. Bookkeeping and accounting parallel typewriting and stenographic skills in that the volume of realistic classroom practice done under the teacher's supervision provides many opportunities for the student's work and work habits to be observed. However, formal measures of the knowledges and procedures involved in journalizing, in posting, and in preparing and analyzing financial statements are regularly used. Journalizing and posting processes, as well as vocabulary and aspects of theory, are readily assessed by short-answer objective tests. Performance tests are also needed to measure the achievement of objectives not well covered by short-answer measures or by the tests that accompany textbooks. It is important to design such test items "so that a mistake in arithmetic or

theory in one phase of the problem will not render the whole test worthless" (Hardaway 1966, p. 225); such a requirement leads to many short, independent items rather than one long problem, and the requirement applies, as well, to problem testing in business arithmetic. In scoring bookkeeping problems, "problem-point" scoring has been advocated: one point for each operation and decision involved in completing each test item (Andruss 1943). "Practice sets" often used for daily work in much of the instruction may be accompanied by objective test items, the answers to which are drawn from the practice-set work under open-book conditions. In addition, the practice-set work itself is often scored for correctness of entries and for neatness.

Social business subjects. The unique objectives of the social business or basic business subjects, such as economics, consumer education, introduction to business, and business law, are wholly within the cognitive domain, with no psychomotor, or skill, components. Accordingly, with few if any exceptions, short-answer, objective tests predominate in such courses. These measures "range all the way from the simple knowledge of specifics; through interpretation, application to life problems, and analysis of relationships and principles; to the more complex synthesis of ideas that will enable the student . . . to evaluate many kinds of evidence" (Hardaway 1966, pp. 188–189). In the social business subjects the problems of testing differ sharply from those of the vocational skills. The objectives of social business courses are less easy to specify in operational terms, less stable, and more resistant to quantification than those of vocational skills courses. The issues concern what to teach and, therefore, what to test, rather than the testing process itself.

Published and standardized tests. Buros' *Mental Measurements Yearbook* is the source of evaluative reviews of commercially published tests. These tests are sometimes adequately validated and standardized and sometimes not. *Tests in Print* (Buros 1961) contains 53 listings of business education tests. The leading publishers of instructional materials for business subjects also provide a substantial amount of test materials: in the textbook; separately bound but accompanying and parallel to the textbook, section by section; and in-house organs and other publications of professional associations, usually available without cost to the business teacher. These various tests are probably more carefully constructed than the typical teacher-made test, but they are not in any true sense of the word the outcome of full-scale test development; the tests do not include validation, norms, and the like. Special care must be exercised in judging the adequacy of textbook-related tests for the overall objectives of instruction in a given area. Finally, the "Tests, Measurements, and Research Techniques in Business Education" section in the research listings in spring issues of *National Business Education Quarterly* includes mention of (unpublished) tests developed by researchers in various business education areas.

BIBLIOGRAPHY

ANDRUSS, HARVEY 1943 *Ways to Teach Bookkeeping and Accounting.* Cincinnati, South-Western.

BUROS, OSCAR K. 1961 *Tests in Print.* Highland Park, N.J., Gryphon Press.

BUROS, OSCAR K., ed. 1965 *Sixth Mental Measurements Yearbook.* Highland Park, N.J., Gryphon Press.

HARDAWAY, MATHILDE 1966 *Testing and Evaluation in Business Education.* 3rd ed. Cincinnati, South-Western.

HILLESTAD, MILDRED C. 1962 "Factors That Contribute to the Difficulty of Shorthand Dictation Material." *Delta Pi Epsilon Journal,* 4, no. 4:2–18.

National Business Education Quarterly Published by the National Business Education Association.

POPHAM, ESTELLE L., ed. 1960 *Evaluation of Pupil Progress in Business Education.* Seventeenth American Business Education Yearbook. New York, Eastern Business Teachers Association and National Business Teachers Association.

ROBINSON, JERRY W. 1967 "The Relation of Copy Difficulty to Typewriting Performance." *Delta Pi Epsilon Journal,* 9, no. 2:9–24.

SILVERTHORN, JAMES E. 1955 "The Basic Vocabulary of Written Business Communications." Ed.D. dissertation. Bloomington, Indiana University.

SUPER, DONALD E., AND JOHN O. CRITES 1962 *Appraising Vocational Fitness by Means of Psychological Tests.* Rev. ed. New York, Harper.

UTHE, ELAINE F. 1968 "An Evaluation of the Difficulty Level of Shorthand Dictation Materials." *Delta Pi Epsilon Journal,* 10, no. 4:1–18.

WANOUS, SAMUEL J. 1940 "Transcription Standards in Business Correspondence." Ph.D. dissertation. University of Pittsburgh.

WEST, LEONARD J. 1968 "The Vocabulary of Instructional Materials for Typing and Stenographic Training—Research Findings and Implications." *Delta Pi Epsilon Journal,* 10, no. 3:13–25.

WEST, LEONARD J. 1969 *Acquisition of Typewriting Skills.* New York, Pitman.

LEONARD J. WEST

TESTS, STANDARDIZED

See STANDARDIZED TESTS.

TEXTBOOKS

1. ROLE IN EDUCATION   Lee C. Deighton

2. PRODUCTION   Austin J. McCaffrey

3. SELECTION AND DISTRIBUTION   Peter Smith

1. ROLE IN EDUCATION

The essential and defining characteristic of textbooks is that they are designed for students as written guides to the subject content of a course of study. The physical form of the textbook is not significant. It may be hardback or softback. It may be printed, mimeographed, or photographed. It may be no more than a sheaf of the lecturer's notes as, for example, in some Latin American and African countries. Although textbooks are usually associated with schools and colleges, the formal school is not an essential context for textbooks. They are also used for religious instruction in churches, in correspondence education and home study, in industry training programs, and in television education courses.

Functions. The basic task of a textbook is the presentation of data from the subject field, such as mathematical data, dates, or descriptions of physical characteristics—the basic items agreed upon as facts by the community of scholars and practitioners in a field. The data presented by the textbook may also be of a higher order: concepts, rules, and other generalizations. These are the working materials for students and scholars in any field. They are set forth to the student by a variety of means, and in this essential function the textbook is a presenter. Handbooks—such as those used by engineers—dictionaries, and almanacs are also presenters of information; yet they are not commonly used or regarded as textbooks. They lack certain other essential elements of the textbook, the most important of which is explication.

The textbook explains the relationships among the data it presents. It is sometimes observed that one memorizes data but learns relationships. This is another way of saying that data are usable only as their relevance and significance are perceived. Data may be related as to time or size order, cause and effect, likeness and difference, and so on. The textbook sets forth relationships in the organization of knowledge, as generally accepted by scholars or practitioners in the field, in varying range and depth depending upon the competence and maturity of the student audience. In this role, the textbook is an explicator.

Relationships and functions may be presented graphically in charts, diagrams, photographs, and drawings. Contemporary textbooks make far greater use of graphic devices to organize and dramatize relationships of data than their early prototypes, but it might be observed that even the hornbook of colonial days provided illustrations. Graphics are more useful and necessary in some subject areas than in others; indeed, it may be argued that graphics are wholly unnecessary in a field such as literature. To the degree that a textbook uses graphics, it is an illustrator.

In every school subject, skills of one sort or another are among the objectives or desired outcomes. The skills may be manual, as in typing or in machine maintenance and operation. They may be manipulative, as in mathematics and in foreign language. They may be interpretive, as in history or literature. Whether or not skill development is a considerable part of the school subject, it is generally agreed that the opportunity for application of concepts and other generalizations is required. It is the ability to use what has been learned that indicates whether or not it has been learned.

The textbook, in contrast to all other kinds of books, contains exercises, study questions, and practice materials. Thus, a novel or a biography may be used as a text in literature or social science courses; these books appear on the shelves of trade bookstores and are the normal stock in trade of these stores. But if these books are supplied with study questions and other teaching apparatus, they become textbooks, and the trade bookstores will not stock them. In recent years, trade editions of novels, biographies, and works of other genres have been used, largely in softcover, in college and secondary school courses. They have been used as textbooks; but lacking the characteristic textbook content of study questions, exercises, and practice materials, they are not textbooks.

Range and variety. Textbooks come in a great variety of sizes, shapes, and organization. They may consist entirely of the writing of one author or an author and collaborator, or they may consist of materials from a great number of writers with interstitial comment by the compilers. This is the nature of literary anthologies used in secondary schools and colleges and of many textbooks used in the social and behavioral sciences in colleges.

To an increasing degree, the textbook requirements for school and college courses are no longer met by a single voluminous book. The most obvious example is the instructional material for reading in the primary school. The basic book placed in the young reader's hands consists of brief reading passages and pictures. There are no study questions, there is no presentation of the basic data of the writing code, there is no explication, there are no paradigms presenting solutions of problems. The primary basic reader is by itself an incomplete textbook. It is, in fact, merely an exercise book in which the child applies skills and data learned elsewhere. The full textbook apparatus of beginning reading includes not only the reader but practice books, tests, charts, flash cards, and other materials designed to present, to explicate, and to provide data and skill training.

At the college level and to an increasing degree in secondary schools, there is a tendency to use a variety of textbook materials, each for a specific purpose or element of a course. This practice requires adequate storage and transport facilities and depends upon the availability of textbook materials. This dependence grows less as publishers increase their lists of shorter and ancillary materials.

Among these ancillary materials are the programmed text materials. Beginning in the late 1950's, publishers provided a considerable variety of programmed text materials in a wide array of subject fields. These programs were designed to permit each student to proceed at his own pace, with immediate feedback on the correctness of his response and with an opportunity to master each step in a process before going on to the next. Programs which covered the whole of a course content met with less success in the schools than those which dealt with a single portion of a course. Programmed materials have not been widely adopted in the schools and colleges and have been far more generally used in industry and the military.

Textbooks within systems of materials. Since 1950 it has become increasingly clear that reading is neither the only means of learning nor always the best. The theory and practice of Comenius, Montessori, and others have new meaning for educators today. The invention and development of a host of new media have provided alternatives to the printed page and opportunities for many different learning experiences.

It is quite clear that one cannot learn to speak a foreign language by reading it or learn pitch, rhythm, melody, and harmony from printed music. Recordings, radio and television performances, and direct experience in the presence of performers are more productive. Language laboratories have the additional power of adjusting to individual needs. Except for the very talented, it is probably impossible for the learner to understand a process simply from reading about it. Mitosis, plant growth, or chromatography can best be illustrated by motion pictures rather than by static diagrams. The performance of a drama on film or live television may add dimensions of reality that the printed page cannot present.

Thus, certain instructional tasks can be more successfully performed in one medium than in another. Unfortunately, research has not been directed toward discovering the limitations and strengths of the particular media or toward providing the most effective combination of these media. Yet, in most school classrooms more than one medium of instruction is in use. Even in those classrooms heavily dependent upon printed materials, such materials include not only textbooks but newspapers and magazines.

Any system of operations rests upon an analysis of objectives and leads to considering and trying alternative methods of reaching those objectives. A system of instructional materials would be established in terms of the objectives of instruction and would make use of particular media for tasks to which they are best suited.

In practice, instructional systems in rudimentary form are now supplied by publishers. In addition to the basic textbook, there are achievement tests, practice books, recordings, overhead transparencies, filmstrips, films, books of supplementary readings, special unit studies, and teachers' manuals.

The history of teachers' manuals over the past three decades shows a number of interesting changes. At the outset of this period, they were provided almost exclusively for elementary school teachers. They were comparatively simple and were limited to the task in hand: the orderly presentation and handling of student instructional materials. Manuals for secondary school

and college teachers consisted primarily of keys to exercises and solutions to problems. In the late 1940's two trends emerged simultaneously. First, the elementary teachers' manuals expanded to include general theory of instruction and child growth and development. As a consequence, the elementary teacher was confronted for each elementary school subject with a manual of 300 to 400 pages. Second, a demand arose for larger and more elaborate manuals for secondary school teachers.

A reaction then set in as teachers realized that they were being given more printed assistance than they could use. Innovations, such as teachers' annotated editions of student textbooks, were introduced, and separate manuals were reduced in size.

It seems likely that as instructional objectives in the schools become clarified, teachers' manuals will relate the instructional materials more closely to objectives. Methods and materials for adaptation to individual learning rates will become more specific and more adequate, and the conditions of instruction in the schools will require far more effective teachers' manuals than those now available.

Value of the textbook. Within any system of instruction or within any system of instructional materials, the textbook plays certain unique roles. To view a textbook as a reservoir of information is to view it in its least valuable and least useful light. It is not possible for any written record to be completely current and up-to-date. It is not the function of a textbook to compete with the daily newspaper, but even the newspaper is at a disadvantage in reporting the news in competition with radio and television. To view the textbook as a compendium of current information is to see it as forever out-of-date.

However, the textbook may also be regarded as what it really is—an instructional tool. As such, its function is to provide an orderly introduction to a discipline or subject area. Since it provides an introduction only, it is obliged to report only such data from a field as an introduction requires or only such data as are required to meet the instructional objectives of the course of study.

Orderliness of presentation is an essential goal and a high value for any system of instruction. Jerome Bruner (1960) and Robert Gagné (1965) argued that there is a basic structure in the disciplines and that the goal of instruction is to locate and reproduce this structure by stages. Whether or not there are such disciplinary structures, it is possible to create a learning structure as the means of introduction to a discipline. Conceivably, in a complex and highly interrelated world, several learning structures might be devised for a single discipline.

Whatever the point of entry, the textbook introduction to the discipline proceeds from simple to complex, familiar to unfamiliar, and—insofar as possible—concrete to abstract. New terms are defined and explained when they are first introduced. Concepts are developed and enriched by use in varying contexts. Maps, charts, graphs, and tables are placed close to the portions of the text which explain or make use of them. Assumptions as to previous knowledge are kept to a minimum, and if there is any hazard in making such an assumption, a review of required information can be introduced before new material is begun.

The ultimate objective of the textbook is to permit the student to proceed on his own, by providing the basic facts, concepts, and generalization required for further study. Among these is a description of the methods of inquiry within the discipline, for the historian, for example, asks different questions, seeks different kinds of evidence, and evaluates data differently from the biologist, the physicist, or the literary scholar. Textbooks may be fairly criticized for having paid insufficient attention to methods of inquiry, but it is likely that they mirrored a similar deficiency in curricula.

The second unique role of the textbook is to afford the student a means of reviewing and reorganizing his knowledge. The audiovisual media, by contrast, are transient; they rely upon the student's memory for continuing carry-over. The printed page may be consulted readily through index and table of contents; the book is available to refresh the memory. (It may be noted in passing that one difficulty with programmed textbooks is the lack of an adequate index. The audiovisual media are safest and most effective when they are anchored to and integrated with textbook materials.)

Limitations of textbooks. It was noted previously that certain kinds of learning experiences cannot be presented through the printed page.

This fact alone argues against the sole or heavy dependence upon the textbook. Other limitations also suggest that the textbook should not be used as the only instrument of instruction.

A modern textbook serving as an introduction to a discipline must necessarily be highly selective in its content. A textbook cannot present all that is known about anything. Nor can it be wholly current in the information it provides. Supplementary materials, current journals, magazines, and reports are needed to update textbook content.

The most serious limitation of the textbook lies in the generality of its address. In the main, textbooks are produced for a nationwide market and cannot take into account significant regional variations. Even when textbooks are produced for such a particular market as the urban schools, there is of necessity a generalizing of the urban situation. A second limitation in generality of address arises from the necessity to speak to the entire spectrum of student abilities within a given grade level. While some textbooks are designed for less able students and some for superior students, these attempts fail because the spectrum of abilities within such large groups as the less able and the superior are still too great to be met by a single textbook. The ultimate solution to the problem of providing for individual differences would be an endless array of materials covering the same content at different levels of difficulty. This leads to the difficult question of whether the less able student should be exposed to the same content more simply written or to different content. Is it possible to explain mitosis, or the electoral college, or the second law of thermodynamics simply enough so that all can master it?

The pragmatic answer to the problem is that the average textbook be addressed to the large middle group in ability levels and that teachers not rely on the textbook to do all the work but mediate, as necessary, between textbooks and students.

Like aspirin and atomic energy, textbooks are capable of misuse. In the hands of poorly prepared or poorly motivated teachers, they can be treated as tracts to be memorized or can be made the sole instrument of instruction in the classroom. The instances of misuse do not arise inevitably from the nature of textbooks, however, and may be corrected without totally banning the textbook from school use.

Essentiality of textbooks. There are records of textbooks having been in use in the schools of ancient Greece and Rome. They disappeared with the schools they served in early medieval times and did not reappear until some time after the introduction of the printing press and movable type. It is recorded that university professors protested the appearance of printed books as threatening to their security and to the importance of their lectures.

School books appeared in America in colonial times, the most famous of them written by Noah Webster. Standard works in arithmetic, geography, and history appeared in the early nineteenth century and enjoyed long lives and widespread use. Among the most widely used were McGuffey's readers, which carried little method but much moral instruction. Textbooks have been associated with schools for as long as schools have been known.

There are practical reasons for the present dependency of schools upon textbooks. They serve as a guide to instruction for the teacher and stable orientation for the students. One-third of the teachers in U.S. schools stay for only three years. Their preservice training, in general, does not prepare them for the classroom responsibilities they face. Many very able teachers at all school and college grade levels find it possible to teach brilliantly without textbooks, but even they will place in the hands of their students a syllabus or course outline which serves the basic orienting purpose of the textbook. It is noteworthy that a survey completed by the National Opinion Research Council in 1966 reported that "the textbook is still the dominant teaching tool in the college as it is in the secondary school" (Ennis & Schlipf 1966).

In 1967, Mark Van Doren had this to say about the textbook:

It is hard to imagine this country without school books. Inded it is impossible; for then we should not have this country as it is, nor would it be a country at all as countries go these days, each one of them bent upon carrying its share of civilization's burden. Any people deserving of the name is a thinking, feeling people. All of its members may not think and feel alike, but they do think and feel, and the rest of the world is aware of this. And the habit starts early, in the young.

With us it is an old habit, and school books have everything to do with the way it is kept up. From the first primer to the latest textbook in the rarest science, from the hornbook to the illustrated guide, school books have maintained a central, controlling position in our common life. . . .

Our people came from everywhere. And if they have become one people here, the school book has been the chief instrument through which that miracle was performed. It was a quiet instrument, making no great noise in the marketplace. When traffic stops and children alight from a school bus, the objects they carry are nothing but bundles of words. Nothing but; as if anything could make more difference in their lives, or in the general life of mankind. Those books are the common denominator not merely of the country's educational effort, formally considered, but of its culture: a thing that branches out in countless directions, but here is the base, the root. And the college student in his room, or in some corner of the campus library, still has not departed from that base, though he may think so, and it is proper that he should. He is simply at a later stage of the process by which the country's minds are being liberated and enlarged to do whatever in time they may see fit to do. . . . (Van Doren 1967)

BIBLIOGRAPHY

BRUNER, JEROME S. 1960 *The Process of Education*. Cambridge, Mass., Harvard University Press.

ENNIS, PHILIP, AND FREDERICK A. SCHLIPF 1966 "Copying and Duplicating Practices in American Education: A Report of Surveys Undertaken by the National Opinion Research Council." *An Economic Media Study of Book Publishing*. New York, American Textbook Publishers Institute and the American Book Publishers Council.

GAGNÉ, ROBERT M. 1965 "Learning and the Content of Instruction." *The Conditions of Learning*. New York, Holt. Pages 172–204.

VAN DOREN, MARK 1967 *School Books*. Statement published by the American Educational Publisher's Institute. New York, The Institute.

LEE C. DEIGHTON

2. PRODUCTION

The term "textbooks" as used in this article refers to materials employed by school or college students as standard works on a particular skill or subject. They are designed for classroom use, with appropriate vocabulary, illustrations, student exercises, and teacher aids. They range from the preprimer to the technical, medical, and scientific materials used in graduate education. With few exceptions, the textbooks used in American schools are produced and distributed by commercial publishing companies.

Reliance upon private publishers rather than

government agencies to produce the textbooks used in the nation's schools is the practice in every country in the Western world. Only in countries that do not have private publishing does the state produce textbooks. There are many obvious advantages to private publishing of educational materials. When a number of companies produce textbooks, there is a wide choice available for selection in every subject area. Both the quantity of books and their variety of format and presentation increase as the number of publishing firms grows. Competition among several firms for the same market produces better books, more frequently and more thoroughly revised. Because of the range of materials available to the schools, it is not possible for a single point of view to dominate the schools or a national curriculum to prevail. Private publishing firms, in order to succeed, must be sensitive to educational trends and produce textbooks which are responsive to the needs of society.

Publishing process.   The process of publishing a textbook for elementary or secondary schools differs sharply from the process of publishing any other sort of book. Although a few trade books are commissioned, in general, all elementary school and secondary school textbooks are commissioned; that is, educators are sought out to work on a project. Almost never does a textbook manuscript arrive at a textbook publisher's office unsolicited. A textbook project begins with the determination by the publisher that a new teaching method or subject concept will find acceptance in the school market and that his editorial staff is competent to work in the subject field. The next step is a search for authors. At this stage in the process of trade-book publishing, the publisher seeks a trained, experienced writer who has demonstrated his professional skill. The textbook publisher has no such reservoir of experienced writers to draw upon: he must rely upon scholars and expert teachers, some of whom may never have written for children before. With editorial guidance and trial-and-error experience, the authors often quite literally learn to write instructional materials. In the process of developing these materials the role of the editor is crucial. Experienced writers in any field appreciate the help of an editor who is both a critical reader and a competent rewriter. In creating instructional materials the editor contributes skill in organization, in managing syntax, in determining

that technical terms are carefully defined at their first appearance, and so on.

The textbook manuscript is generally written by scholars and teachers during evenings, weekends, and vacation periods and usually takes from three to five years to complete. At various stages of revision the manuscript is tested in whole or in part in classroom use. This developmental research is in the main relatively casual, because, as the writers of *Research for Tomorrow's School* have noted, "models for product research in education have not been developed, so that no one is sure what such research can and should attempt to do" (Cronbach, Suppes, et al. 1969). These authors note that the development of standardized tests is an exception. Despite the lack of rigorous models and despite the difficulties, publishers of educational materials attempt to discover prior to publication what these materials will do for different kinds of students in different classroom situations.

The editorial role varies with the project and with the quality of the author's manuscript. It may consist only of copy editing and design; it may require reorganization, rewriting, and help to the author in refining his thought. At the maximum, the publisher's editorial role passes beyond intervention to creative contribution in which the editor becomes the author's silent partner. This degree of cooperation may occur at any level, but it is more likely to be found in elementary and secondary school projects than in college publications. Usually, the manuscript for a college textbook requires less editing. It is written according to a preconceived plan agreed on by both author and publisher, often as a commissioned work and normally with an advance payment against royalties.

The editorial establishment of the publisher includes editors who work with the manuscript and designers and artists who plan and create the physical appearance of the finished product and prepare or supervise the preparation of maps, drawings, and other graphic materials. A single high school textbook may require five years from beginning to publication, with at least nine months required for production from the time the manuscript is finished. Editorial work is not limited to working with manuscripts in hand but extends in its research and development stage to study, experiment, and investigation of new methods, new media, and new content. The expenses and salaries required for these efforts are a significant part of the publisher's editorial expenses.

The term "plant costs" refers to expenses in making the printing plates from which the books will be printed. These costs include the expense of composition, or setting type, casting proof, making corrections, and arranging the type in pages. They also include the expense of artists' drawings or photographs and the production of engravings which will become part of the printing plates. The last element of plant expense is the plates themselves.

The term "inventory cost" refers to the expense of printing and binding an edition. The production of books for sale involves costs not found in other industries. The expense of making a printing press or bindery line ready to operate is a substantial part of the total production cost. Printing and binding orders must therefore be as large as prudence permits in order to minimize the cost of each book. The publisher must often order an inventory that will last for two years. In addition, many state agencies which contract with publishers require the publisher to maintain an inventory of adopted books within the state. Experience shows that this required inventory is twice the number of copies sold in a given year. Finally, the states and large cities require publishers with whom they contract to keep available a supply of an adopted book for a period of five years. All of these factors require the publisher to maintain a considerable inactive inventory with capital that is not working or with funds borrowed at increasingly high rates of interest (Deighton 1967).

Editorial costs, plant costs, and inventory costs represent the publisher's investment in research and development and in capital goods. The publisher's printing plates and inventory are among his assets, along with cash and accounts receivable. The investment required in textbook production varies from book to book or from series to series. A series for an elementary school subject, including workbooks, manuals, tests, and other related materials, requires an investment of $1 million to $1.5 million. A single text in history or science for secondary school use may require an investment of $50,000.

A report issued by the National Education Association in 1968 discusses adequate levels for textbook expenditures, citing the high cost of developing textbooks. It notes:

> Most textbooks are developed over a period of many months or even years as educator and scholar, artist and editor contribute their talents to the research, writing, illustrations and validation of teaching methodology that are requisites of good textbooks. The preparation of a textbook or a textbook series frequently requires an investment of a million or more dollars. (American Educational Publishers Institute 1968, p. 19)

Early textbooks. The variety of printed instructional materials available today was completely unknown in colonial times. Very often in colonial schools only the teacher owned a book, or each student brought a book from home. The basis for the establishment of schools in colonial America was the need to teach the young settlers reading skills so that they could read the Bible.

The child's first instructional material was the hornbook, a short wooden paddle on which a piece of paper had been pasted. The paper carried the alphabet, numerals, the Lord's Prayer, and other brief religious sentiments as space permitted. For protection the paper was covered by sheets of transparent horn. After the hornbook the child used a primer, not to be confused with contemporary books of this designation. *The New England Primer*, the most commonly used in early American schools, carried a rhymed alphabet, a brief statement of Puritan theology, John Cotton's "Spiritual Milk for Babes," and the "Shorter Catechism."

In general, the school books used in colonial times and even later were of English origin. As American printing facilities expanded, they were printed on American presses. A spelling book was printed on the first American press at Cambridge, Mass., before 1650. The book is thought to have been Edmund Coote's *English Schoolmaster*. For the teaching of spelling, the spelling book carried an alphabet, exercises, rules, and lists of hard words. But the spelling book was likely also to be used for reading instruction, and for this purpose it contained psalms, prayers, writing models, and a short catechism. When Noah Webster began teaching in 1778, he discovered that all the available textbooks were imported from England. Since they contained sentiments of loyalty to the British Crown, they seemed to him inappropriate for children of an independent America. Within a short period of years, Webster produced a speller, a grammar, and a reader. In his reader and in subsequent textbooks, he introduced American writings, American history, and American geography. He encouraged his friend Jedediah Morse to prepare the first series of American geographies. During Webster's lifetime his readers and grammar were displaced by works of other Americans, but his *American Spelling Book*, known as the "Blue-backed Speller" and originally prepared in 1783, continued in use for a century, with more than 70 million copies sold. So great was its authority and so wide was its use that it was judged largely responsible for the establishment of a common language across the continent.

As schools developed and multiplied in the early national period, more textbooks became available in all of the common school subjects. In general, the content of the books was to be memorized. Exercises were provided only for formal application of rules, with little effort to stimulate student thought or inquiry. It was not until after 1875 that science texts provided for laboratory work, and only in botany were the students directed to practical applications and in this case only to collection and arrangements of specimens.

As the number of schoolchildren increased, competition grew up between rival systems of instruction and between the printers who provided for the expanding market. As a result of competition, printers took thought as to how to make their books more attractive. Better paper and cleaner type were introduced. Maps and pictures were improved, and an effort was made to provide content more interesting to children.

Toward the middle of the nineteenth century graded readers began to appear. The McGuffey readers are doubtless the most famous of these. More than 122 million copies had been sold by 1920. Gradually the concept of graded textbooks in all subjects developed, as the one-room school gave way to buildings in which children were grouped according to age. The early textbook author decided on his subject, wrote his book, and then looked for someone to print it. The printer was the publisher. However, after the Civil War the textbook field became much more complex, and the textbook publisher emerged with the functions of surveying the market, arranging for distribution, and assembling the experts necessary to produce a good text.

In early years the pupil brought to the classroom the books he found at home, so that he and the teacher would have books to use. Each pupil was given an assignment in the book he happened to have, and the teacher heard the recitation. As the result of such changes as the increase in enrollment brought about by the expansion of free public education, the development of common courses of study, the improvement of teaching procedures, and the separation of pupils into rooms and grades, it became necessary to have uniform textbooks in each grade and in all schools under the same jurisdiction. This resulted in more systematic teaching and learning procedures and in more effective teaching plans.

New influences on textbook production. Research studies in child development inaugurated at the beginning of this century have provided new knowledge about how children grow and how they learn. The results of these studies have enabled publishers to produce textbooks designed for students' changing needs.

As book publishing moved into the modern era, the products of the industry were changed markedly by four major influences: (1) child psychology, (2) the improvement of printing and binding, (3) research by authors and publishers, and (4) the development of textbook publication as a specialized industry.

These new influences appeared at a time when the United States was undergoing astounding technological and social changes. The frontiers were being pushed back; the economy was changing from an agricultural to an industrial base; the development of the gas engine and electric current made possible new and speedier modes of transportation and communications; immigrants were entering the country by the millions; child labor legislation was restricting factory employment of young boys and girls; colleges and universities were turning their attention to the art of teaching; and many states were legislating compulsory education for all children.

From the colleges and universities came pronouncements on the need for teachers to know something about child psychology, the methodology of teaching, individual differences, and testing procedures. Emphasis shifted to some degree from subject matter to the teaching process. This was an inevitable development as the pupil population became more diverse and the changing social structure began to require differentiated instruction. Authors and publishers of textbooks became aware that the learning process required increased attention.

At the same time that teacher training was going through a rigorous change, scholars in the universities and textbook publishers initiated research projects to review such factors as appropriateness of content and vocabulary and the sequential placement of material.

Little attention was concentrated on the physical aspects of books during the early decades of American history. Books were published in small quantities without color; illustrations were poorly done; paper was of an inferior quality; size of type was determined without consideration of the age and physical maturity of the reader; covers were dull; binding was weak; and margins and space were usually not considered of any importance. This has all changed. As a result of the joint efforts of teachers, administrators, authors, publishers, manufacturers of books, and specialists in the graphic arts industry, today's textbooks are attractive, appealing, and durable.

The nature of textbooks and textbook publishing has changed radically during the second half of the twentieth century. World War II and the ensuing scientific advances during the cold war in the late 1950's had a dramatic impact on educational publishing. It has become accepted that a single textbook can no longer serve as the sole instructional tool. The textbook of today serves only to introduce the student to a subject area. The expansion of knowledge in every field is so obvious that the old notion of a textbook as "covering the field" has disappeared. Although the textbook remains the most effective way of presenting an organized body of knowledge in sequential order to the student, its traditional format is increasingly subject to modification.

Multilevel texts are being produced to compensate for individual differences. Reading laboratory series are being offered, consisting of boxed sets of multilevel reading materials that allow students of varying abilities in the same classroom to begin reading, each at his own proficiency level, and to progress as fast and as far as his individual capabilities will allow. Books are being published to incorporate the results of curriculum studies; to provide high adult interest motivation at elementary levels of difficulty for adult basic education; and to include increased coverage of minority groups and their contributions to the development and growth of America.

Paperbound books are increasing in importance as supplementary aids and as central instructional tools. One of their important advantages is that they can make current knowledge and art forms available to children and youth without long delay.

Systems of instructional materials are appearing more frequently on publishers' lists. Since supplementary teaching aids are considered today to be a necessary addition to the classroom, publishers have produced a variety of instructional lists. Publishers contract with graphic arts companies to develop films or filmstrips to accompany their textbooks or to produce slides and transparencies. For elementary science, individual equipment is provided for laboratory experience. Books are developed to complement television courses. For foreign-language instruction, publishers provide films, filmstrips, tapes, and records to accompany their textbooks. Workbooks, programmed books, mechanical display and testing devices, planetarium supplies, and standardized tests of aptitude and achievement are part of the publisher's stock in trade.

The events after World War II also had a profound effect on the curriculum of the schools. Wartime testing programs revealed the lack of scientific and mathematical understanding among school graduates. The vision of the scientific era which was beginning impelled educators, parents, and concerned citizens to voice their feelings on the need for curriculum reform. The first round of this reform emphasized scientific and technically related subjects and was directed toward middle-class and upper-class students, primarily college-bound. The study groups eventually turned their attention to modern foreign languages, English, social studies, art, business education, health, home economics, industrial arts, music, physical education, safety education, and vocational education. These curriculum studies had an important influence on textbooks. Some study groups published their own materials in cooperation with a single publisher. Others put the materials in the public domain, to be used by all publishers in creating new courses of study.

More recently curriculum reform has concentrated on the needs of the urban pupil. The demand for materials more relevant to city life and the cultural background of urban students is being met by the publishers. The introduction of preschool programs and compensatory education requires new materials geared to the under-achiever and the less advantaged child. Materials are being developed to give the high school drop-out the skills and training necessary to become a useful and productive citizen.

New instructional methods have also influenced educational publishing. The increased emphasis on individualized instruction inspired such innovations as team teaching, ungraded schools, learning laboratories, programmed instruction, advanced placement courses, and courses for the slow achiever. Technological teaching aids such as computers, television, opaque and overhead projectors, films, and filmstrips require a new type of subject matter presentation in textbooks and other printed materials of instruction. Publishers are involved in experimental projects with microfiche, microfilm, and computer-assisted instruction. It is probable that many new forms of instructional material will emerge in the next decades.

Purchases of textbooks have declined somewhat in recent years as a percentage of total educational expenditures. During the 1960's, in the elementary and secondary schools purchases averaged a little more than 1 percent of school budgets. After a decade of annual increases, the total of textbook sales for elementary and secondary schools leveled off in the late 1960's at close to $400 million, as determined by the annual statistical surveys of the American Educational Publishers Institute. On the other hand, college textbook sales had continued to increase, primarily because of rising enrollments. For 1969, college sales were estimated at $345.85 million. Changes in per pupil expenditure for textbooks are slight from year to year but over the 1960's were steadily upward, reflecting the increase of production costs during the period. In 1968 the average textbook sale per pupil amounted to $7.25 for the elementary grades, $10.92 for high schools, and $44.40 for colleges.

There are some 200 educational publishing firms in the United States, of which 90 are of sufficient size to report earnings in the annual statistical survey of the industry. In the elementary and secondary school field, no single publisher commands more than 15 percent of this market.

In the ten years prior to 1968, 12 publishing houses offered their stock for public sale. Some 40 mergers and acquisitions took place during the period. In some cases, publishing firms combined in order to serve different levels of education or to produce other instructional tools. In other cases, communications and electronics firms sought out publishing houses to produce materials for their new means of communication. Some associations were formed to provide the facilities required to deal with large government contracts, such as those involving military training and Job Corps camps. The rapid growth of education and new trends and developments in instructional materials required a large increase in publishers' capital and considerable diversification of product.

American Educational Publishers Institute. The educational publishing industry has established a professional trade association, the American Educational Publishers Institute. This association consists of over 100 members who produce 95 percent of all the instructional materials used in the schools. Formed in 1942 as the American Textbook Publishers Institute, the AEPI represents producers of textbooks, reference books, maps and globes, and other materials of instruction. The institute operates through a system of committees of member publishers. It presents the industry position to educators, the government, and the public. The institute maintains liaison committees with the Great Cities Research Council, the National Education Association, the Education Media Council, the American Association of Junior Colleges, the American Council on Education, and other public and private groups concerned with education. The institute cooperates with state textbook directors and the Book Manufacturing Institute in maintaining a manual entitled *Official Manufacturing Standards and Specifications for Textbooks.* In addition to its annual survey of industry statistics, the AEPI throughout the year disseminates to members information significant to educational publishers. The institute informs its members of developments within the educational community and brings to their attention the concerns of educators and government officials. The AEPI headquarters is in New York City, with additional offices in Washington and Chicago.

The International Publishers Association. The book industry also participates in the International Publishers Association, which has its headquarters in Geneva. The association first met in

Paris in 1896, and its purpose was to permit publishers to meet and exchange ideas on a worldwide basis. Until recently it was primarily concerned with trade books, but since 1965 there has been an education group within the association, reflecting the increased emphasis on education around the world. The education group meets annually during the Frankfurt Book Fair to discuss such matters as educational research, copyright, the influence of government on the flow of ideas, and ways of promoting the widespread use of books on an international scale.

BIBLIOGRAPHY

AMERICAN ASSOCIATION OF SCHOOL ADMINISTRATORS 1967 *Curriculum Handbook for School Administrators.* Edited by Forrest E. Conner and William J. Ellena. Washington, D.C., The Association.

AMERICAN EDUCATIONAL PUBLISHERS INSTITUTE 1968 *Guidelines for an Adequate Expenditure for Instructional Materials.* Washington, D.C., National Education Association and the American Educational Publishers Institute.

BENNION, GRANT M. 1967 "The Economics of Publishing: The Cost of Books." J. N. Hook, ed., *Publishers and English Teachers: Allies in Education.* Champaign, Ill., National Council of Teachers of English. Pages 15–21.

CARPENTER, CHARLES 1963 *History of American Schoolbooks.* Philadelphia, University of Pennsylvania Press.

CRONBACH, L. J., P. SUPPES, et al. 1969 *Research for Tomorrow's School.* New York, Macmillan.

DEIGHTON, LEE C. 1967 "The Publishing Process." J. N. Hook, ed., *Publishers and English Teachers: Allies in Education.* Champaign, Ill., National Council of Teachers of English. Pages 1–8.

GOODLAD, JOHN I., et al. 1966 *The Changing School Curriculum.* New York, Fund for the Advancement of Education.

LITTLEFIELD, GEORGE EMERY 1904 *Early Schools and School-books of New England.* Boston, Club of Odd Volumes.

NIETZ, JOHN ALFRED 1966 *The Evolution of American Secondary School Textbooks: Rhetoric and Literature, Algebra, Geometry, Natural History (Zoology), Botany, Natural Philosophy (Physics), Chemistry, Latin and Greek, French, German, and World History as Taught in American Latin Grammar Schools, Academies and Early High Schools Before 1900.* Rutland, Vt., Tuttle.

SMITH, DATUS C., JR. 1966 *A Guide to Book Publishing.* New York, Bowker.

The Bowker Annual of Library and Book Trade Information. Sponsored by The Council of National Library Associations. New York, Bowker.

WHIPPLE, MONTROSE, ed. 1931 *The Thirtieth Yearbook of the National Society for the Study of Education.* Part 2: *The Textbook in American Education.* Bloomington, Ill., Public School.

AUSTIN J. MCCAFFREY

3. SELECTION AND DISTRIBUTION

For every field of school study, educational publishers have provided a variety of textbooks and ancillary materials. Although superficially they appear to be much alike, the books differ in several important respects—for example, in style, level of organization, and depth of coverage. These differences are sufficient to require criteria and procedures for selection.

Responsibility for selection. The state, local, or private board of education has legal responsibility for the selection and purchase of textbooks. This is a responsibility which the board must have because it involves the expenditure of funds entrusted by law to the board. (With few exceptions, textbooks are furnished free to elementary and secondary school students in the United States.) As a practical matter, textbook selection and purchasing is delegated by the board of education to professional educators who are in the best position to make recommendations on such matters. In most instances the board is required to approve the textbook selection which is recommended by these professional educators.

School officials attach great importance to the selection of textbooks because the textbook is the core around which subjects are taught. In a very real sense, the textbook is the curriculum. Over the years the term "adoption" has been used to denote the purchase of textbooks. Adoptions take place on a state level, in school districts, or in private school systems.

State versus local adoption. Local school boards, sometimes with the guidance of a multiple listing prepared by the state education agency, select elementary textbooks in 27 states and secondary textbooks in 32 states. A state selection system is practiced by 23 states for elementary textbooks and by 18 states for secondary textbooks. California adopts a single text for its elementary school subjects, with additional texts adopted sometimes for some subjects by local school districts.

Since the early 1940's, no state has changed from school district adoption to state adoption. One state has changed from state adoption to school district adoption, and several states have modified their state adoption systems to increase the number of textbooks available at the local level.

Basic and multiple adoptions. A textbook adoption at the state level may be either a basic or multiple selection. A basic selection involves the choice of one or two texts for each subject area by the state board of education. All the school districts in the state must use the chosen book or books. The advantage of the basic selection is that a pupil transferring from one school district in the state to another will not change textbooks in the process since a more or less standardized curriculum exists for that state. A multiple selection system provides three to six texts for each subject to be adopted and leaves the choice of one of these texts up to the individual school districts. The multiple system provides for a greater freedom of choice on the part of the districts and allows them to account for differences in learning capabilities of their students. A disadvantage of both of these state systems is that the choice must be made by the school districts from only those materials approved for state adoption. The states where the school districts adopt their texts without state approval are known as open territory states, a term which refers to the fact that the districts may purchase whatever materials they feel best meet their own needs.

No rules can be formulated for how all schools should select the materials that will help students learn. Children differ, schools differ, and communities differ. Recognition of such differences has led to state and local autonomy in the selection of teaching and learning materials. This is particularly true in the selection of textbooks.

Many educators believe that the interests of the schools are best served with a maximum of alternatives made available to local school districts. This permits freedom of choice, adaptations to local needs, and direct communication with the producers of materials of instruction. For this reason various proposals advocating a national curriculum involving the selection of text materials at the federal level have not received serious attention.

Adoption periods and cycles. Educational officials have expressed increasing concern over the difficulty of avoiding an accumulation of obsolete instructional materials. There has been an unprecedented overhaul in the elementary and secondary school curriculum resulting from the curriculum study groups. For example, in the field of mathematics there were three major revisions in materials between 1960 and 1970. Biology, physics, and chemistry are quite different subjects than they were a decade ago. The results of continuing research call for new approaches to the teaching of English and social studies. The practical and fine arts have also come under close scrutiny. Adoptions of text materials for periods of

six years or longer limit severely the opportunities to use the newer materials and to provide adequately for individual pupil needs. The survey "Textbook Purchasing," made by *School Management* in March 1966, confirms this point of view. Educators reported that where local school districts had authority to select and purchase textbooks there were more adoptions of newer materials than in state-adoption states. The trend is definitely toward more frequent adoptions; adoptions for four-year and five-year periods have become more common than five-year to six-year adoptions.

Although old texts are not necessarily inadequate, they do have certain intrinsic drawbacks. For example, a book published in 1970 would actually have been written at least two years earlier. It may have been edited and updated to the time of publication, but basically it is a book reflecting the state of knowledge in 1968. Especially in the sciences this is a dangerously long time lag.

The *School Management* survey concluded that state adoption practices severely hamper the efforts of local school districts to provide the most modern texts for their students. The reason is that the districts may purchase only from the state-approved list. Once the approved list is published, it stays in effect for a given number of years; districts wishing to purchase new texts during that period are limited to the list even though new and superior books may appear during the period.

More than 35 percent of the districts in the closed, or state-adoption, states had not purchased new reading texts in the five years preceding the survey, as opposed to 22 percent in the open states. Of the closed group, almost seven out of ten indicated that delay was caused by the state adoption cycle—that is, the time for new reading texts had not yet arrived.

Cycling increases the time between publication and adoption. Most cycles run for five-year periods in major subject areas. Conceivably, a book may not find its way into many classrooms until five years after publication. By most standards that book is already obsolete when it comes into use, but cycling delays its entry into schools which could have used it four or five years earlier.

Selection committees. Whether texts are selected for a whole state, for a school district, or for a private school system, the process is essentially the same. The first step involves the appointment of a selection committee composed of professional educators. Although it is clear that the state, local, and private boards of education have the legal authority for the adoption of textbooks, it should be equally evident that it is in the best interests of education to place the selection of textbooks in the hands of professional personnel.

Choosing personnel for the textbook selection committee is a responsibility of the superintendent of education in the state, the school district, or the private school system. This responsibility is exercised by the superintendent personally or delegated to an administrative staff member. In either case, supervisors and principals in the school system are consulted and invited to recommend competent classroom teachers to work on the committee. The superintendent designates a chairman for the committee or instructs the committee to name a chairman at its first meeting. The chairman is personally responsible for keeping the administrators informed of the committee's work.

The person responsible for the appointment of the selection committee makes sure that all its members fully understand the purposes of the committee. He takes time to see that committee members understand the reasons for the present textbook evaluation, the purposes of the courses for which textbooks are being selected, and the educational philosophy of the school system that will use the texts. The committee members must develop rules or follow established ones for the adoption, to guarantee that all parties concerned are given fair and equitable treatment.

Once the committee is selected, its membership usually becomes public knowledge. Experience indicates that attempts to keep secret the committee's existence or the names of its members are futile and counterproductive. Teachers who will be using the books in the future form the core of the selection committee. However, the committee usually also includes administrative personnel, curriculum specialists, and school librarians, who are sometimes more familiar with the products of publishers than are the teachers.

The selection committees vary in size but are generally large enough to provide for diverse views and judgments, yet not so large that they become unwieldy and inefficient. The size of the committee depends on whether a single textbook, a series of textbooks, or a continuity of textbooks is under consideration. If a textbook for a single grade is to be selected, classroom teachers from the grade above and the grade below the designated level of the textbook are often included. If a series of textbooks for successive grades is to be selected, each grade affected is usually represented. For most purposes a committee of seven to 11 members is ideal. However, smaller committees are effective when they are empowered to utilize the services of consultants or to establish subcommittees for specific purposes.

The committee's function requires that it be given sufficient time to study, to examine, and often to use the materials submitted by the publishers for adoption. One of the first tasks of the committee is to decide on its goal. The committee's next task is to formulate temporary criteria for evaluating the books under consideration.

Frequently, in the state-adoption states, a textbook commission is appointed by either the state board or the state superintendent. Because such a commission is usually called upon to make adoptions in a variety of subject areas, it appoints advisory selection committees composed of professional educators who assist with adoptions in their own subject area specialties.

Bookmen.   The publishers' representatives play an important role in disseminating new educational ideas among school personnel, since they describe the new features in the texts they present for adoption. They also assist the work of selection committees by highlighting the main features of the texts under consideration. They help the committees in building criteria for evaluation of textbooks by presenting the theories upon which their books are based, explaining how subject matter is organized, and demonstrating the use of supplementary aids provided with the texts.

The continuing contact of the professional bookman with educators helps publishers take the pulse of education. The bookmen keep managerial and editorial staffs informed of trends in the field and report to their firms the varied educational needs of school systems throughout the United States. They help bring prospective authors, consultants, and manuscript reviewers to the attention of editors and managers.

The work of the bookman starts when the superintendent notifies him of the impending adoption and the procedures that must be followed. When the bookman learns who the members of the selection committee are, his firm may provide them with sample books and other material. Usually, adoption procedures permit the bookman to call on committee members individually to explain the features and characteristics of his books.

Once the committee members have had an opportunity to study the books, the teachers' guides, and the promotional material, the bookman is invited to meet with the committee at a specified time. The bookman makes a presentation and answers committee members' questions. Sometimes he is accompanied to the meeting by an editorial adviser or an educational consultant made available by his firm. If his company's book is chosen, the bookman serves as the liaison between the school district and the editors on any questions that may arise.

Distribution. Upon completion of the selection process, the school districts place orders with the publishers. The publishers then ship texts either from their warehouses or directly from the binderies.

In 20 states, mostly those having state adoptions, the publishers are required by law or administrative regulation to maintain a supply of books in book depositories. These depositories are run by private companies, with books shipped to the depositories on consignment by the publisher. Usually the state department of education designates a depository as the authorized one for the state. The depository functions by receiving and consolidating textbook orders from the various school districts and either filling these orders with books that are in inventory or forwarding the orders to the publishers. The depositories, which are located in the South and the Far West, developed because school officials in the early 1900's felt their geographical distance from the publishing centers in the Midwest and on the east coast would preclude rapid delivery of books. However, since then publishers have opened centralized and regional warehouses in various parts of the United States, permitting improved distribution to their customers. Improved book distribution is undoubtedly one of the reasons why no new state textbook depositories have been created since the 1930's.

Manufacturing standards. Representatives of the American Educational Publishers Institute and the Book Manufacturers Institute have worked cooperatively with the National Association of Textbook Directors since 1960 to recommend improvements in the quality and durability of the physical components of books. One result of this activity has been the joint adoption by 15 states of standards and specifications for any textbooks marketed in those states. These standards and specifications are viewed as guides in the remaining 35 states. In addition to field testing the books, the group of publishers, manufacturers, and state officials has retained a testing firm to conduct studies in the laboratory. Publishers produce books for a national market on the basis of those state-adopted specifications. If publishers were requested to deviate from this practice to attempt to meet a different set of standards for individual states or school districts, the cost of these books would be increased considerably. The situation would be further complicated by the difficulties in determining in advance the number of copies of a book to be printed. In addition, the problem of inventories, separate accounting, and different deadlines for deliveries would be considerable.

State printing. State printing of elementary textbooks exists only in California, principally because of its large state printing facility and the fact that a single text is used throughout the state for most elementary subjects. Under contract arrangements with the state, publishers lease printing plates to the state printer, who then prints and binds the texts. However, the California educational community has expressed its dissatisfaction with the single-text system at the elementary school level and has prevented its extension to the secondary school level. From time to time other states have explored the possibility of printing texts, but studies have shown that such a system is economically feasible only if single-text adoption is in effect throughout the state.

Contracts. States and school districts have a wide variety of statutes and administrative regulations dealing with the purchase of textbooks. Some have provisions requiring that textbooks be offered for sale on terms equal to those offered at the same time to any other school district in the nation.

The joint committee of the American Educational Publishers Institute and the National Education Association, in *Guidelines for an Adequate Investment in Instructional Materials* (1968b), published recommendations for school textbook expenditures. For elementary school (grades 1–6), $42 should be spent for each new pupil; to replace materials, $14 for every pupil enrolled should be spent annually. For secondary school (grades 7–12), $63 should be spent for each new pupil, and $21 annually per pupil to replace materials.

School officials budgeting for textbook purchases usually need to increase the amount they invest between 6 percent and 10 percent over the previous year, depending upon enrollment trends and the subject matter included in the adoption. Since most textbooks are used from four to six years, usually only one major series must be purchased in any given year. For example, in one year reading texts may be the principal item in the text budget. The next year mathematics might be the main subject, followed in successive years by science and social studies. During the four to six years a text is in use, it is necessary to replace a certain number because of normal wear and loss.

College textbooks. The selection and distribution of textbooks in colleges differs significantly from procedures in elementary and secondary schools. Except in large freshman or sophomore courses, the selection of a college text is left to the individual professor. In courses involving many instructors, the chairman for the course or a committee appointed by him makes the selection. The adoption period is typically, but not always, for a period of two or three years. Since there are no state regulations governing college textbooks, the adoption period is not predetermined, and textbooks may be changed at the end of a single year if the choice has proved unwise or if a superior new book is published. The college professor or course chairman notifies the local college bookstore weeks in advance of the textbook he intends to use the following term. The college bookstore orders from the publisher and sells to the college student.

College department chairmen are called upon by a representative of the college textbook publisher, who is known as a college traveler. His responsibility includes procuring manuscripts for future college textbooks as well as seeking adoption of existing texts.

BIBLIOGRAPHY

AMERICAN EDUCATIONAL PUBLISHERS INSTITUTE 1966 *Publishers and English Teachers: Allies in Education.* Papers presented at the 1966 convention of the National Council of Teachers of English. Edited by J. N. Hook. Washington, D.C., American Textbook Publishers Institute and the National Council of Teachers of English.

AMERICAN EDUCATIONAL PUBLISHERS INSTITUTE 1967 *Guidelines for Textbook Selection*, rev. ed. Washington, D.C., National Education Association and the American Textbook Publishers Institute.

AMERICAN EDUCATIONAL PUBLISHERS INSTITUTE 1968a *Annual Survey of the Textbook Publishing Industry, 1967.* Compiled by Stanley B. Hunt and associates. New York, Statistics and Accounting Committee, American Educational Publishers Institute.

AMERICAN EDUCATIONAL PUBLISHERS INSTITUTE 1968b *Guidelines for an Adequate Investment in Instructional Materials.* Washington, D.C., National Education Association and the American Educational Publishers Institute.

AMERICAN EDUCATIONAL PUBLISHERS INSTITUTE 1968 *State Textbook Selection Practices: A Comprehensive Survey.* New York, American Educational Publishers Institute.

"Textbook Purchasing" 1966 *School Management*, 10, no. 3:4–31.

PETER SMITH

THAILAND

The kingdom of Thailand (formerly Siam) is centrally located in mainland Southeast Asia. Although surrounded by nations recently emerged from colonial rule, Thailand has never been colonized. Its ability to remain independent was due both to the outstanding leadership of the Chakri dynasty (1768 to present) and to the practical need for a buffer state between the British and French colonies in the area. Although Thailand's population is the largest of the mainland Southeast Asian countries and its rate of population increase is among the highest in the world, its currency is fairly stable, and its annual rate of economic growth is among the highest in the world.

Ethnically the Thai constitute the majority of the population. Cambodian, Lao, and Vietnamese minorities, located largely in the northeast region, are quite small. Chinese and Malays are numerically significant; although Chinese nationals are less than 2 percent of the total population, persons of Chinese ancestry make up an estimated 10 percent of the population, and Malays probably are more than 3 percent of the population. Most Malays reside in the southern provinces that were formerly a part of British Malaya. Special educational problems are encountered in these areas largely because of cultural and linguistic conflicts between the home and the school.

Educational development. As in most of Southeast Asia, early education in what is now Thailand was monastic and almost exclusively for males. Among the early Westerners to visit Thailand were some French missionaries who arrived in 1662 and established mission schools. King Narai, suspecting their motives in establishing such schools, maintained tight controls over them.

The present (Chakri) dynasty has promoted educational and cultural development from its beginning in 1768. The first three kings (Rama I, II, and III) were authors in their own right and encouraged great outpourings of literary works. Contact with the West increased during the reign (1809–1824) of Rama II, and more Christian mission schools were established.

It is almost impossible to discuss fundamental reforms that have shaped modern Thailand without mentioning King Mongkut (Rama IV) and his son, King Chulalongkorn (Rama V). Both were tutored in Western ways and in the English language by English governesses. After Chulalongkorn ascended the throne in 1868, he established the Royal Command School, or Palace School, on the palace grounds. The first secular school in Thailand, it is important because its reason for existence became one of the guiding principles of Thai education, namely, that the training of the civil service was a prime purpose of education. As Chulalongkorn modernized and expanded the functions of government, the need arose for a larger civil service, and more schools were established. In addition, some secular public instruction was introduced into the monastic (*wat*) schools. This step made it possible to introduce and expand public instruction with a minimum of capital outlay.

The existence of large numbers of schools created the need for a system of education. The Department of Education was established in 1887; it became a ministry five years later, and in 1898 the National Scheme of Education was introduced. This scheme was revised several times in the following decade. Chulalongkorn University was established in 1917, and the first compulsory education act, passed in 1921, made school compulsory for all children of both sexes between the ages of seven and 14; however, the royal decree handed down at the time required only four years' attendance.

The 1930's brought revolution, a form of constitutional monarchy, and new educational reform. The 1936 amendment to the National Scheme of Education produced the basic organizational scheme used today. The requirement that provinces have at least 50 percent adult literacy in order to be fully represented in Parliament produced a rapid expansion of elementary education.

In Thailand, as in other countries of the area, World War II interrupted educational progress. Although three new institutions of higher education were founded during this period, there was a general decline in academic standards.

Structure. As the result of reforms begun in 1960, the seven years of primary education are divided into four years of lower primary schooling (*pratom* 1–4) and three years of upper primary education (*pratom* 5–7). Two years of kindergarten followed by one year of preprimary education are offered in only 60 out of a total of more than 22,500 government primary schools and are not required steps in the educational ladder.

The five years of secondary education are also divided into two cycles: a three-year lower secondary cycle (*maw saw* 1–3) and a two-year upper cycle (*maw saw* 4–5). A third year of upper secondary education is required in some vocational programs. Higher education programs range in length from two to six years.

A total of 28,235 students were enrolled in Thailand's seven universities in 1966. Thammasat University had the highest enrollment, 12,264, followed by Chulalongkorn, 7,945, Medical Sciences, 2,928, Kasaetsart, 2,739, Chiengmai, 1,522, Silpakorn, 528, and KhonKaen, 309. Of this total, 1,408 students were studying at the master's level and four at the doctoral level. Not included in the totals were 810 students pursuing master's degrees at the National Institute for Development Administration and 110 graduate students enrolled at the SEATO Graduate School of Engineering (in 1967 renamed the Asian Institute of Technology). The College of Education also enrolled 4,353 undergraduate and 88 graduate students.

The establishment of three new universities (Chiengmai in 1964, KhonKaen in 1964–1965, and the University of the South in 1968) marked a divergence from two major trends in Thai higher education: (1) the virtual monopoly of the capital city, Bangkok, over higher educational facilities, and (2) the principal role of the universities as exclusive training schools for the civil service. Before this, each of Thailand's other universities was established and often operated by a government ministry primarily for the purpose of training its own and prospective personnel. For example, Thammasat was founded by the Ministry of Interior (as the University of Moral and Political Sciences), Kasaetsart by the Ministry of Agriculture, and Medical Sciences by the Ministry of Public Health. The College of Education, established in 1954 by the Ministry of Education, is the only higher education institution under the supervision of the Ministry of Education.

Degree programs are offered at one or more Thai universities in the following fields: arts, education, engineering, science, architecture, commerce, accounting, political science, law, economics, social administration, journalism, pharmacy, dentistry, liberal arts, public administration, medicine, agriculture, public health, veterinary medicine, forestry, rural economics, fisheries, irrigation engineering, painting and sculpture, archaeology, and decorative arts.

There are no private universities in Thailand.

Teacher education. There are four basic levels of teacher qualification, although there are specializations within each level. Teacher-training schools offer students who have completed grade 10 a two-year program, and village institutes have a five-year program for those completing grade 7; elementary education certificates are conferred by both types of institutions. Secondary education certificates are awarded by teachers colleges to those who complete a two-year course after grade 12. Bachelor's and master's degrees in education are conferred by the College of Education and the faculty of education of Chulalongkorn University.

Vocational education. The two fundamental guiding principles of Thai education—training personnel for the civil service and promoting national consciousness through universal primary education—began to conflict as early as the 1930's. Because secular education was from its inception oriented toward preparation for the elite government civil service, it was inevitable that conflict would arise as increasingly larger numbers of Thais were exposed to an education designed both to promote national consciousness and to make them eligible for the elitist secondary education. Vocational educational programs thus were established to prevent excessive pressure for government employment from the burgeoning numbers of graduating secondary students.

Vocational education has not been popular in Thailand. Since entry into vocational streams or schools is often associated with failure to meet acceptable standards in the academic schools, few students voluntarily enter. In the mid-1930's, in an effort to accord higher status to vocational education, the Ministry of Education adopted a policy of employing graduates of lower vocational schools as primary school teachers. Along with prestige came new entrants, and lower vocational schools almost immediately were filled to capacity. However, when this policy was abandoned a few years later, enrollment in these schools dropped drastically.

Thailand continues to invest heavily in public technical and vocational education despite the rather unimpressive record of this approach to training skilled manpower.

Curriculum. Thai students follow a prescribed curriculum at every level of schooling. The study of English as a foreign language is compulsory beginning in *pratom* 5. At the secondary level, there are a variety of programs available, ranging from the three streams in the academic schools (science, arts, and general) through a host of vocational programs, but the curriculum for each is strictly defined. Even at the higher education level, elective subjects are very rare, though the College of Education follows a liberal policy in this respect.

There is a heavy reliance upon rote learning, even to the point of utilizing unison chants in the classroom to memorize material. At the higher education level, lectures are delivered at dictation speed and virtually complete recall is demanded at examination time. Classroom environment is very formal by Western standards. To pose a question to a professor (or even an instructor) is to question his competence and threaten his status. Students are neither required nor encouraged to engage in outside reading.

Administration and supervision. The administration of Thai education is highly centralized. Prior to the mid-1960's the Ministry of Education was responsible for administering all Thai education except for the universities. By 1968 the situation had changed substantially: administration of primary education had been transferred to the Ministry of Interior, and the National Education Council had been established with authority to formulate educational policy at all levels of Thai education. The latter organization also provides administrative support to the Thai universities. The Universities Development Commission was established in 1968 to better serve the needs of Thai higher education.

The Ministry of Education continues to administer secondary schools, teacher-training and other vocational schools, and the College of Education. The administrative structure includes 12 regional education officers, 71 provincial (*changwad*) education officers, and a host of district (*tambol*) education officers.

Trends. One problem facing Thailand is that of adequately responding to pressure for increased educational opportunity. In Thailand, as in many other countries at a comparable stage of development, the geographical distribution of educational facilities makes it most difficult to implement policies for the equalization of educational opportunity. The Bangkok-Thonburi metropolitan area has approximately one-third of all the secondary educational facilities in the country, even though its population is less than one-tenth of the total. Prior to 1955 all of the higher educational facilities in Thailand were also located in the metropole. The government has already taken the steps of establishing provincial universities in Chiengmai, KhonKaen, and Songklah and of better distributing secondary schools, but many years will pass before the average Thai village youth can be said to have educational opportunity comparable to that of the metropole resident.

Thailand also struggles with its educational wastage problems. In 1964, for example, more students failed grade 1 than were enrolled in both levels of secondary education in the same year. Almost 90 percent of all Thai students entering grade 1 fail to enter grade 5. Of every 1,000 Thai students entering grade 1, about 105 will enter grade 5; 30 to 40 will enter grade 12; and 6 will enter a university.

Thailand struggles to overcome the linguistic barrier—the need to know English, Russian, German, or French in order to obtain technological information—that impedes its access to technology necessary for development. It cannot rely upon its own educational system to generate new knowledge. In 1968 the Universities Development Commission was founded with the initial task of formulating a strategy for overcoming this handicap. It assigned top priority to Thailand's achiev-

ing a reasonable level of self-sufficiency in the basic sciences and economics and to greatly improving the quality of English language instruction in the nation's schools.

BIBLIOGRAPHY

HARPER, RAY G., AND SOMCHAI WUDHIPREECHA 1968 *Education in Thailand: Educational Planning at the Local Level.* Bangkok, Educational Planning Division, Ministry of Education, and Michigan State University.

KRAFT, RICHARD J. 1968 *Education in Thailand: Student Background and University Admission.* Bangkok, National Education Office and Michigan State University.

SHAW, ARCHIBALD B., AND THAMRONG BUASRI, eds. 1968 *Teachers in Thailand's Universities: An Analysis and Forecast.* Bangkok, National Education Office and Michigan State University.

THAILAND. MINISTRY OF EDUCATION 1958 *Educational Developments in Thailand, 1949–1957.* Bangkok, The Ministry.

WRONSKI, STANLEY P., AND KAW SAWASDI PANICH 1966 *Education in Thailand: Secondary Education, Manpower and Educational Planning in Thailand.* Bangkok, Educational Planning Office, Ministry of Education, and Michigan State University.

KENNETH L. NEFF

THEATER, CHILDREN'S

Only in the last century has the concept of a theater for children been recognized in the Western world and especially in the United States. With growing concern for the intellectual and aesthetic development of the child, it is only natural that live theatrical performance should be used as an additional means of education.

Plays can acquaint children with their literary heritage, history, and mythology, as well as the ways by which other people meet problems. Children can also absorb moral values and attitudes which are inherent in the development of the play. The live quality of the performance carries an emotional charge that makes its content unforgettable.

Types. Children's theater is defined as formal drama for children where the production is of primary importance and where the producers are most concerned with providing a true theatrical experience for the child in the audience. There are three different types of productions for children: those performed by children; those performed by adults; and those performed by a mixed cast of children and adults, with the children playing parts suited to them in age and type. Of the three, the last type tends to provide the best theater for children, assuming that there is a high standard of production.

Creative dramatics, another form of dramatic activity for and by children, is the process of dramatically creating extemporaneous situations and stories under the guidance of a trained leader. It is not audience oriented, and its importance to the child rests in the process rather than the product. Improvisation in current adult theater practice has many similarities to creative drama. Both creative dramatics and children's theater are essential to the aesthetic and emotional development of the child, but they must be regarded as separate activities. Creative drama should never be considered theater.

A children's theater needs to recognize the age level of the audience for which the play will be performed. Some theaters have a separate series of short, simple plays for children under seven. Children's audiences are usually divided into three groups: three to six years, seven to 12 years, and 13 to 16 years.

The plot for a children's play needs a strong story line which can be developed clearly through action rather than long speeches; the play should have characters who are individualized and believable. The message should be inherent in the story. The language should be appropriate to the play but not patronizing to the child. A child deserves an artistic level of production which utilizes imagination and good taste equal to that of adult theater.

American and European patterns. In the United States, children's theater activity varies greatly depending on the producer and the sponsor. There are approximately 1,500 producing units, which include professional companies, college and university theaters, community theaters, high schools, service organizations, recreation programs, museums, and other groups. About 200 organizations act only as sponsors to bring productions into communities. About 10 million children a year see live theater performances.

Most training for careers in children's theater takes place in colleges and universities. More than 350 institutions produce plays for children, and about 250 offer courses in children's theater and creative dramatics.

The major part of children's theater activity has been privately financed or indirectly subsidized on a local basis through such agencies as municipal recreation programs and state universi-

ties. The federal government through the U.S. Department of Health, Education, and Welfare has provided funds to schools for children's theater as a form of educational enrichment.

In Europe the pattern of children's theater activity is quite different. Most producing units are permanent professional companies with complete staffs, a stable repertory of plays, their own theater, and a state subsidy. A typical example is the Theater of Friendship in East Berlin, which in 1966 had an acting company of 40, a technical staff of 55, a play repertory of 15, its own 500-seat theater, and an annual budget of 2.5 million marks. In the Soviet Union there are over 50 such theaters.

Most of the European theaters have strong ties with the public school system; children are brought to specific productions which are subsequently discussed in the classroom. These theaters also employ full-time pedagogues who work directly with the schools to reinforce educational values.

The majority of the important state-subsidized theaters for children are in Eastern Europe, where the governments have a strong belief in the power of the drama as a teaching tool.

History. Although the ancients left no record of theater specially for children, we know that there were children in the audience at the Greek dramatic festivals during the fifth century B.C. Theater was a family as well as a religious and civic affair, and everyone attended, the child drawing what value he could from the performance. The Greek tragedies, based on history and legend, contributed to the child's knowledge of his city and its culture.

From the Orient there are records of shadow plays and puppet and doll theater, which passed on legends, history, and culture.

During the Middle Ages the church used drama —miracle and mystery plays—to teach the Bible to an illiterate society. Children participated in some of these plays, portraying the Christ child and young shepherds in *The York Nativity*, the victims in *The Wakefield Slaughter of the Innocents*, and the boy Jesus in the temple. In some cases older boys played women's roles.

According to Winifred Ward (1958), the first true theater for children was created in 1784 by Stephanie de Genlis, governess to the children of the duke of Chartres. She was a friend of Rousseau and an educational innovator who believed strongly in the rights of the child. She felt that children would learn more easily if they enjoyed what they were doing and tried to make even their amusements instructive. She had a theater constructed for her young charges to perform in and wrote moral plays for them to produce.

The history of children's theater from then until about 1900 was one of isolated professional productions of classics for child and adult audiences. Only in the twentieth century were theaters producing primarily for children established.

During the nineteenth century children in the United States occasionally had an opportunity to see a dramatization of a story considered appropriate for them—for example, *Rip Van Winkle*, *Tom Sawyer*, and *Little Lord Fauntleroy*.

The first consciously educational program in American children's theater was the Children's Educational Theatre established in 1903 by Alice Minnie Herts. Over its six-year life-span the theater produced children's plays on a high artistic level for the Russian-Jewish immigrants on the lower east side of New York. Not only did the theater provide worthwhile entertainment for the children in the poor neighborhood, but it also helped acquaint them and their parents with the culture of their new country. This theater helped social settlements like Hull House in Chicago and groups like the Neighborhood Playhouse in New York create similar programs.

In 1921 the Chicago Junior League produced its first play for children; by 1928, 50 different chapters had children's theater programs. Today, league chapters sponsor or produce plays in more than 100 cities, often performing in public schools without admission charge. The Junior League is now beginning to concentrate on community sponsorship of professional children's theater productions.

In 1925, two children's theaters which were to establish the pattern for most of the educational programs in the United States were started. Winifred Ward of Northwestern University's school of speech founded the Children's Theatre of Evanston, Ill. Two years later the Evanston public schools became cosponsors of the theater, which still produces a full season of children's plays and trains university students for work in children's theater. In 1925 the Goodman Theatre of the Chicago Art Institute also began a program of children's plays. Charlotte B. Chorpenning became director of the children's theater and began

writing plays for children, which became part of the repertory in theaters throughout the country.

In 1922 the Heckscher Foundation in New York City started a children's theater, and Clare Tree Major assumed its management. She left this program to create one of her own and by 1928 had developed a program of touring plays that was active until the 1950's. For many children a production by the Clare Tree Major Company was the only theater they had ever seen.

The depression years fostered a period of consolidation in children's theater activity. In 1933, Dorothy L. McFadden created Junior Programs, Inc., a nonprofit organization which booked professional entertainment for children throughout the United States, encouraged the writing of new plays for children, and promoted active community sponsorship of good children's entertainment.

The Federal Theatre Project of the Work Projects Administration included theater for children as an integral part of the program, thus providing imaginative entertainment while creating jobs for unemployed theater artists. In 1933, Hazel Glaister Robertson established the Palo Alto Community Children's Theatre, which still produces plays for the entire community, using local children. In 1934, Grace Price in Pittsburgh, Pa., developed a company of young professionals who toured schools throughout the region until the 1950's. In the late 1930's, Dina Rees Evans began a summer program for children at Cain Park in Cleveland Heights which continues to provide classes in crafts as well as in theater arts.

By the 1940's there were significant programs in children's theater developing in professional, community, and educational areas. Many colleges and universities not only produced children's plays but also offered courses in this new field. In 1947, Monte Meacham established the Children's World Theatre, which toured professionally until Meacham's death in 1955. Meacham's company performed at the Barbizon Plaza Theatre in New York City prior to each tour; this helped establish the current professional pattern of production.

During the 1950's and 1960's children's theater became an accepted part of theatre programs in educational institutions throughout the country. Many community theaters added a children's series to their regular schedule. In the professional theater, children's companies increased to over 100 in the east coast area alone. The activity and importance of children's theater is still developing. It is yet to be used and supported to its full educational potential.

Organizations. A dedicated group of workers in children's theater met at Northwestern University in 1944 at the invitation of Winifred Ward and formed the Children's Theatre Conference (CTC) to promote work in children's theater and creative dramatics, to raise standards of production and of informal work with children, and to encourage excellence in training in the field. Hazel Glaister Robertson was elected the first chairman.

In the early 1950's the CTC became a division of the American Educational Theatre Association. With a membership of over 1,500, the CTC at its annual meetings draws workers from all types of children's theater and creative dramatics programs. At this time the CTC is the only concerted voice of child drama in the United States.

In 1964 the British Children's Theatre Association invited workers in children's theater throughout the world to attend a festival and to discuss the possibility of organizing an international association. As a result of this meeting the International Association of Theatres for Children and Youth (ASSITEJ) was formed in Paris in 1965 with an executive committee of representatives from 12 nations (Great Britain, the Soviet Union, France, Czechoslovakia, the Netherlands, Belgium, West Germany, Italy, East Germany, Rumania, Canada, and the United States). Gerald Tyler of Great Britain was elected its first president.

The association expects to make available information about world children's theater, to promote high artistic standards, to encourage the establishment of national centers of children's theaters, and to assist with international tours and translations of plays. Approximately 22 nations have national centers which are affiliated with the ASSITEJ. The CTC provides representation for the United States.

BIBLIOGRAPHY

BROCKETT, OSCAR GROSS 1968 *History of the Theatre.* Boston, Allyn & Bacon.

BROCKETT, OSCAR GROSS 1969 *The Theatre: An Introduction.* 2nd ed. New York, Holt.

CHORPENNING, CHARLOTTE BARROWS 1954 *Twenty-one Years With Children's Theatre.* Anchorage, Ky., Children's Theatre Press.

DAVIS, JED HORACE, ed. 1968 *A Directory of Children's Theatres in the United States.* Washington, D.C., American Educational Theatre Association.

DAVIS, JED HORACE, AND MARY JANE WATKINS 1960 *Children's Theatre: Play Production for the Child Audience.* New York, Harper.

EEK, NAT, ed. 1966 *Children's Theatre in the U.S.A.* Norman, Okla., published for the Children's Theatre Conference of the American Educational Theatre Association by Laird Printing.

GOLDBERG, MOSES HAYM 1969 "A Survey and Evaluation of Contemporary Principles and Practices at Selected European Children's Theatres." Doctoral dissertation. Minneapolis, University of Minnesota.

HEWITT, JANICE C. 1969 "The Development of the International Association of Theatre for Children and Young People With Particular Emphasis on the United States' Participation." Master's thesis. Lawrence, University of Kansas.

MAWER, MURIEL, et al. 1951 *Children's Theatre Manual: A Guide for the Operation and Organization of a Non-profit Community Children's Theatre.* Anchorage, Ky., Children's Theatre Press.

NICOLL, ALLARDYCE 1966 *The Development of the Theatre.* 5th ed. London, Harrap.

WARD, WINIFRED 1958 *Theatre for Children.* 3rd ed., rev. Anchorage, Ky., Children's Theatre Press.

NAT EEK

THORNDIKE, EDWARD L.

Edward L. Thorndike was an American psychologist, educator, lexicographer, and pioneer in educational research. The groundwork for research into learning was provided in 1913–1914 by his three-volume *Educational Psychology*, which set forth precepts based on his experimental and statistical investigations. These precepts—which covered such wide-ranging topics as teaching practices and individual differences between students and such administrative concerns as promotion decisions and grouping according to ability—came to dominate professional thinking.

While such men as John Dewey and Robert M. Hutchins influenced the philosophy of education, Thorndike and those whom he inspired wrote reading and arithmetic books for pupils, school dictionaries and spelling lists, tests, and pedagogical guidebooks and teachers' manuals. Because, however, it is far more difficult to assess influence in the operations of many thousands of American classrooms than to analyze ideas in the words of educational theorists, Thorndike's contributions are taken largely for granted.

The man and his career. In its external details, Thorndike's life was uneventful and circumspect; its drama lay in his genius (his IQ was estimated at nearly 200) and in the tumultuous times to which his work bore such marked reference. Born in Williamsburg, Mass., on August 31, 1874, of a family line resident in New England since 1630, Thorndike, like a surprising number of other notables of his day, was reared in a clergyman's household. But in an era when science was challenging religion as a source of truth, when inquiry and universal education threatened dogmatism and sectarian inculcation, and when a career in the church was becoming less attractive than life in the laboratory, Thorndike rejected even his father's liberal brand of Methodism for an agnostic secularism. Yet, in his evangelical regard for science, Thorndike transferred to science a religious-like belief in the possibility of personal and societal salvation. Science was, he said repeatedly, "the only sure foundation for social progress."

Thorndike grew up in a household where excellence was expected, for the children of a minister were to be models for the congregation in all matters. In academic performance the Reverend Thorndike's children complied, all earning excellent grades and winning the scholarships which made college studies possible. In addition, all established academic careers: Ashley as a professor of English, Lynn as a historian, and Mildred as a high school English teacher; eventually all three Thorndike brothers taught at Columbia University. Edward Thorndike's children continued this scholastic brilliance but turned, like their father, from literary to scientific and mathematical careers. All four children earned Ph.D. degrees: Elizabeth Frances in mathematics, Edward Moulton and Alan in physics, and Robert Ladd in psychology. Thus, from his own boyhood, when his parents encouraged early reading and supervised homework, to his own close guidance of his children's schooling, Thorndike brought a high degree of personal involvement to his professional study of education.

Because of the church's requirement that a minister be moved regularly, Thorndike grew up in eight New England towns before 1891, when he left home to enter Wesleyan University in Middletown, Conn. Never feeling at home anywhere in his childhood, when he possessed the power to decide for himself he chose to stay put: he spent 40 years at Teachers College, Columbia University, spurning other positions offered, and built a home at Montrose, N.Y., at age 33. He died there on August 9, 1949, near age 75, leaving his widow, Elizabeth Moulton, whom he married in 1900, and their four grown children.

The early moving about left Thorndike with pronounced shyness and social uneasiness, helping to make the lonely privacy of research a comfortable world. His educational work also displays a certain nonsocial cast. Unlike the psychologies of the progressive educators with whom he shared many beliefs, Thorndike's educational psychology was not a social one. To him learning was an essentially private, organic undertaking, something that happened under one's skin, in the nervous system; the "connections" of interest to the teacher were properly those between stimulus and response—not the interactions between individual students, which concern those who view a class primarily as a social group.

During Thorndike's youth the United States fully entered the age of industrialization and urbanization. The mill towns of New England were part of the industrial revolution that was attracting hundreds of thousands of immigrants a year to manufacturing jobs and making Boston, Pittsburgh, Chicago, and New York great, if trouble-plagued, cities. Coming to New York City in 1897 to complete his doctoral studies at Columbia University, Thorndike was to remain there for the rest of his life, except for a brief tenure from 1898 to 1899 as a teacher of psychology and pedagogy at the College for Women of Western Reserve University in Cleveland, Ohio.

It was understandable that an urban setting would be attractive to the modern academic man, particularly to the man of science; it was in the cities that industrial wealth built museums, libraries, and laboratories, and it was there that philanthropic foundations had their headquarters. Such foundations as the Carnegie Corporation of New York, the General Education Board, and the Commonwealth Fund established the Institute of Educational Research at Teachers College, to which Thorndike devoted his energies almost exclusively from 1921. It was at this time that the wealth and centrality of New York City were helping to make Columbia a great national university and its Teachers College the most important center for the training of the leaders in public education in the United States. By 1900 all leading American universities were, like Columbia, in urban settings. Moreover, the leadership of public education nationally was passing into the hands of the superintendents of big-city school systems and to their counterparts in the state capitals and in the Federal Bureau of Education.

By the turn of the century, elementary education in the United States was virtually universal; thereafter, the task was to extend secondary schooling to the entire nation. The need for teachers was great. Although the normal schools, frequently rural institutions, continued to train many teachers, departments of education became common within universities after 1900. Thorndike first arrived at Teachers College in 1899, when its status was changing from that of a private normal school to the education department of Columbia University. Because universities were preeminently places of research, their departments for training teachers and school administrators partook of the prevailing atmosphere favoring scholarly and scientific inquiry. In leaving Western Reserve for Teachers College, Thorndike abandoned a traditional training school for a place which he quickly helped make a center for the scientific study of education and for the training of educational researchers. As its dean, James Earl Russell, recalled: "In developing the subject of educational psychology . . . for students in all departments, Professor Thorndike has shaped the character of the College in its youth as no one else has done and as no one will ever again have the opportunity of doing" ("Personal Appreciations" 1926, p. 460).

In addition to urban resources and leadership for research and to the prestige accorded science by the universities, there was another incentive for expanding educational research: the widespread desire in educational circles to have teaching recognized as a profession. Schoolmen were aware of the high total of public spending for education and shared the prevailing faith in schools as critical agencies of character training and national development. Even in an occupation marked by low prestige, minimal preparation, a preponderance of women, high turnover, and legal dependence upon boards of laymen, professional status was regarded as an attractive, realizable goal.

One of the characteristics claimed by an occupational group seeking professional status is its possession of a large and growing body of expert knowledge. The function of research was to replace the folklore of the teaching craft with scientifically verifiable assertions. Thorndike acknowledged after 30 years of work that research had yielded only a few answers to the practical questions raised by school operations (1928). He maintained, however, that a true profession awaited those who patiently researched fundamental educational questions. The principal barrier was not, he believed, the limitations of science, but the traditional conservatism and inertia characteristic of institutionalized education.

A psychology for educators.   At Teachers College, Thorndike taught psychology to large numbers of teachers and school administrators. In his early courses and in such books as his *Notes on Child Study* (1901a), *Principles of Teaching, Based on Psychology* (1906), and *Education: A First Book* (1912), he tried to inform educators of what was already known of human nature and human variation, of what had been written about behavior and learning by such creative psychological thinkers as Scotland's Alexander Bain and William James at Harvard, under whom Thorndike had once studied. Increasingly, however, he turned away from concentrating his efforts on converting teachers to a scientific attitude and away from deducing educational precepts from existing psychological thought. Instead, he began to construct a new educational psychology —one more in keeping with the experimental and quantified directions laid out by the "new psychology" being developed in German and American research centers.

The scientific requirement.   As much as he admired the brilliance, humane perceptiveness, and stylistic elegance of William James' *Principles of Psychology*, Thorndike was of that new generation of younger psychologists who, after 1895, sought to sever psychology's ties with "mental philosophy" by rejecting armchair theorizing, avoiding such philosophical concepts as "soul," and opting for the methods, language, and standards of physics and experimental biology. He was deeply impressed by the painstakingly precise observations of animal behavior by Charles Darwin, by the methodological controls in the memory studies of Hermann Ebbinghaus, and by the statistical inventiveness of Sir Francis Galton and Karl Pearson. Discussions in the summer of 1900 with the famed experimentalist Jacques Loeb at the Marine Biology Laboratory at Woods Hole, Mass., finally convinced Thorndike that his real talent lay in "doing science," and that he "ought to be shut up and kept at research work" (Jonçich 1968, p. 265).

Lacking mechanical aptitude, Thorndike never incorporated into his research the elaborate instruments found in Wundt's Leipzig laboratory and among Titchener's students at Cornell, or favored by Charles Judd, another important educational psychologist. Thorndike's approach was basically observational and problematic: place the subject in some problem (test) situation—seeking to escape from a confining place, having to rank his attitudes, choosing the correct response among several alternatives to avoid a mild shock—then observe the behavior aroused and report it in quantitative form. The typical Thorndike experiment was a simple paper-and-pencil investigation, like the first he ever attempted: as a Harvard graduate student he tried to measure children's responsiveness to unconscious cues by giving candy rewards to those correctly guessing the number or object he had in mind.

Lessons from animal studies. Despite his typically simple approach, Thorndike is credited with two research techniques basic to modern psychological studies of animal behavior: the maze and the problem box, both of which were invented for his now-classic study of learning, *Animal Intelligence* (1898). A thoroughgoing Darwinist, Thorndike was convinced that, because of evolutionary continuity, the study of animal behavior is instructive to human psychology. Hence, when he had difficulty in securing human subjects, Thorndike switched easily from children to chickens in his Harvard studies.

A significant portion of *Animal Intelligence* is a critique of the uncontrolled observation and casually acquired anecdotal reportage prevalent in what little comparative psychology existed in the 1890's. The faulty methods, Thorndike declared, contributed spurious data and led to unwarranted interpretations. The most serious error was attributing to animals a higher order of intelligence than would be justified by scientific observations of animal behavior. His own painstaking research with cats and dogs, and later with fish and monkeys, convinced Thorndike that the process of animal learning rested not on some form of reasoning and not even on imitation. Learning depends, instead, upon the presence of some situation or stimulus (S) requiring the animal to make various, more or less random responses (R); as a result of such trial and error, the correct, or most adaptive, response is eventually made (for example, hitting a lever to escape a box or to reach

food). The effect produced by the appropriate response is a sort of reward: it may be escape, food, sex, or a release of tension (in animals and humans) or an experienced feeling of success or other learned rewards (in humans alone). The effect acts physiologically, creating or reinforcing a neural connection between that response and the situation which provoked it; repetition of that or a similar stimulus becomes more readily able to produce the previously successful response, and inappropriate responses are forgone. Learning has taken place.

Reward: the key to learning. The basic principle which Thorndike formulated to account for the S-R connection is the law of effect; in the language of such later psychologists as Clark Hull and B. F. Skinner, this is a reinforcement theory of learning.

If, as Thorndike maintained, human behavior represents primordial attempts to satisfy native and learned wants, then an effective, positive, and humane pedagogy is one which facilitates the making of desired and successful responses, forestalls incorrect responses, and is generous with rewards; a poor teaching method, on the other hand, carelessly permits wrong responses and then must punish them to prevent their becoming established as bad habits. Initially Thorndike assumed that reward and punishment were equal opposites, effects evenly capable of causing learning. Reward is preferable since it is more efficient to forestall inappropriate responses by producing and rewarding desired behavior than by punishing incorrect responses; a positive pedagogy is preferable to a punitive one. As a result of empirical studies undertaken in the late 1920's and 1930's, however, Thorndike concluded that he had been mistaken earlier. Punished responses are not weakened as rewarded connections are strengthened; despite common sense and tradition, punishment may actually enhance the probability that an undesired response will be repeated.

Thorndike was virtually the first educator to give theoretical and empirical attention to effect, although reward and punishment had been given practical attention by generations of schoolmen. Still, the pedagogical emphasis at the turn of the century centered on punitive and repressive measures and on fault-finding. In 1906, Thorndike warned teachers that the most common violation of human nature was the failure to reward desired behavior. In propounding the law of effect, then,

Thorndike gave a psychologist's support to those educational philosophers, like John Dewey, and those founders of progressive schools, like Marietta Johnson, who wished to make schools more humane and to have them better relate educational methods to the nature of childhood. However, because of his articulation of another law of learning—the law of exercise—Thorndike's psychology differed from that progressivist thinking which emphasized spontaneity and favored student selection of activities and freedom from a planned curriculum sequence and from drill. (The law of exercise states that once a given response is made to a particular stimulus, each recurrence of that stimulus tends to recall that response; hence, an S-R bond is being strengthened. The educational implication of the law promotes drill, or practice, of desired responses and careful teacher attention to forming appropriate habits.)

Education as specific habit formation. Accepting William James' views, Thorndike wrote:

Intellect and character are strengthened not by any subtle and easy metamorphosis, but by the establishment of particular ideas and acts under the law of habit. . . . The price of a disciplined intellect and will is eternal vigilance in the formation of habits. . . . Habit rules us but it also never fails us. The mind does not give us something for nothing, but it never cheats. (1906, pp. 247–248)

A radical educational theory stressing freedom, spontaneity, inner direction, and "unfolding," one that "stands out of nature's way," was to Thorndike a "something for nothing" pedagogy. In its place, Thorndike's psychology required the careful ordering of learning tasks, as in the *Thorndike Arithmetics* (1917), which he prepared for school use; practice (exercise, drill) with reward; and measurement of progress through frequent testing, preferably by standardized tests so that more reliable estimates of learning could be had.

Another "something for nothing" educational theory—this one from the conservative, formalistic right wing of educational opinion—was the belief in mental (formal) discipline: that various mental or perceptual faculties are strengthened by being exercised upon some formal, preferably difficult task; that the study of a rigorously logical subject, like geometry, promotes logical behavior; and

that practice in accurate copying transfers to other behavior, making one more accurate generally.

Some skepticism about transfer of training had already developed, on a priori grounds, before Thorndike published the first major empirical challenge to this widely held theory (1901b). The proponents of more modern subjects—vocational courses, the modern languages, physical education, even the sciences—had attacked formal discipline and faculty psychology because the defenders of the classical studies had based classical domination of the curriculum primarily on the grounds that these difficult and abstruse subjects, which were unappreciated by pupils, had tremendous transferability value, just as lifting the heaviest weights develops muscle power better than lighter burdens do. Between 1901 and 1924, Thorndike's research supported those educational reformers who believed that a subject or skill should be included in the curriculum because of its intrinsic value, and not because of unproved assertions about transfer power.

Education as a science. In his *Educational Psychology*, Thorndike wrote: "We conquer the facts of nature when we observe and experiment upon them. When we measure them we have made them our servants" (1903, p. 164). Equally as important as empiricism to Thorndike's psychology was his emphasis on measurement and quantification; poorly prepared by the schools in mathematics and largely self-taught in statistics, Thorndike became the educational world's major exponent of the use of science's universal language of description, numbers. His theme was, all that exists, exists in some amount and can be measured. He introduced the first university course in educational measurement in 1902, and two years later he wrote the first handbook for researchers in the use of social statistics, *An Introduction to the Theory of Mental and Social Measurements*.

Educational and intellectual tests. The movement toward testing was the primary outcome of attempts to translate qualitative statements (Mary seems to be having trouble in reading) into quantitative and comparable terms (In grade 5.6, Mary tests at 4.4 in reading comprehension and 4.7 in vocabulary knowledge). Standardized achievement tests in school subjects were built on centuries of use of teacher-made tests. What the twentieth century added was the standardization necessary for reliability and comparison of results from class to class. Professionally written and administered to thousands of pupils, using norms based on nationwide samples of students, achievement tests were created for every level of schooling, from primary through graduate school, including tests for out-of-school adults at various age levels. In 1921 use of these tests was established when 2 million pupils took standardized tests of academic achievement; thereafter, growth in use and development of tests was virtually taken for granted. Thorndike contributed several works on construction of tests and devised various tests of his own: rating scales for handwriting, drawing, and composition; tests of oral and silent reading skill, geographical knowledge, English usage, spelling, reading and reasoning; and college entrance tests and law-school entrance examinations.

Intelligence and scholastic aptitude tests have a far shorter history but have been even more crucial in shaping school practices (like promotion policies, grouping, and grading) and professional and public thinking. Alfred Binet's point scale, developed in France early in this century, is the landmark contribution. But before such testing could have great educational or social impact, it was necessary to find means of adapting the individually administered, Binet-type artifact tasks to groups using paper and pencil. This did not come about until World War I, when the U.S. Army commissioned psychologists to prepare and administer tests to aid in classifying recruits. Thorndike was a member of the Committee on Classification of Personnel from 1917 to 1919 and supervised work on the Beta form (the form for illiterate recruits); it and the Alpha form (for literates) were administered to 2 million soldiers by 1919, the world's first effort in the mass measurement of intelligence. Within three years, 1 million schoolchildren took similar tests, many of them the National Intelligence Test which a group of former army psychologists, including Thorndike, had developed. He later devised the CAVD (sentence completion, arithmetic, vocabulary, following directions) intelligence examination and a nonlanguage scale (for illiterates).

Aside from the kind of general intelligence measurements which concern educators most, Thorndike was interested in other types of aptitudes, believing that intelligence is not a unitary or general factor but is constituted of millions of discrete stimulus-response bonds; any intelligence test is simply a selective sample-taking of all the possible learned connections that might be present. Thorndike believed that since individuals differ, primarily by heredity, in their relative ability to form connections (that is, to profit from experience, to learn), and since any one individual is unevenly endowed in the ability to form connections of different types, tests of intelligence-in-general may miss certain aptitudes useful for vocational counseling, hiring programs, or selection of employees for special training programs.

In 1914, Thorndike began devising tests for use in locating persons with clerical aptitudes and interests and thereby fathered personnel-selection psychology in business and industry. In 1918 he headed the wartime search for men with aptitude for learning to fly. To try to prophesy flying success was itself a pioneering venture in a day when hardly a flying school existed in the United States and the aircraft industry was yet unborn. Such wartime experience in measuring aptitudes was continued in Thorndike's later research into vocational guidance for schools. He advocated special efforts and new departures in vocational education for those schoolchildren—perhaps as much as a third of the total—who "may learn only discouragement and failure" from much of the existing curriculum (Jonçich 1968, p. 473). The vocational education movement lagged, however, with the decline of public interest in the 1920's and the massive unemployment of the 1930's.

Studying human variation. The new instruments for measuring ability and achievement and especially the widespread use of these instruments inspired new knowledge of and intensified concern with individual differences. "It is useless to recount the traits in which men have been found to differ, for there is no trait in which they do not differ," Thorndike wrote in *Individuality* (1911, p. 6). The new educational psychology, he said, must reject classical psychology's assumption of a typical mind from which pattern there were only rare departures; it must study individual minds, be a differential psychology which describes, explains, and seeks to make predictions about human variation.

Society's commitment to universal schooling must not, Thorndike believed, obscure its responsibility to every individual and its respect of difference. While psychology will, as a science, search for universal laws explaining human behavior, the pedagogical art, Thorndike believed, must recognize that it is individuals who act, who learn or refuse to learn.

> The practical consequence of the fact of individual differences is that every general law of teaching has to be applied with consideration of the particular person . . . [for] the responses of children to any stimulus will not be invariable like the responses of atoms of hydrogen or of filings of iron, but will vary with their individual capacities, interests, and previous experience.   (1906, p. 83)

Of these sources of variation, the most important in Thorndike's view was differing capacities —differences caused primarily by genetic inequalities. To the persisting debate about heredity and environment, Thorndike offered comparative studies of twins, siblings, and unrelated individuals, of family histories, and of school eliminations (what we call dropouts). His findings convinced him that heredity is the primary determinant of intellectual difference and, because such other traits as personal morality, civic responsibility, industriousness, and mental health correlate positively with intelligence, that genetic endowment is the critical variable for welfare and social progress. So, in the interest of improving the human gene pool, he espoused eugenics.

In an age when psychoanalysis introduced arresting concepts of the primitive motivations of mankind, when the arts made a virtue of the "natural," when such educational theorists as G. Stanley Hall espoused a naturalism in education which urged teachers to step aside lest they interfere with nature's way, Thorndike offered dissent. Investigations of original nature and its differing expressions in individuals is not an end in itself, he argued. To find that heredity shapes human potential more than does a favorable environment does not end society's responsibility to improve its institutions, any more than the discovery of gravity was an excuse to cease man's efforts to fly. "The art of human life is to change the world for the better," Thorndike wrote in *Education: A First Book* (1912, p. 1). "Only one thing [in man's nature] is unreservedly good, the power to make it better. This power of learning . . . is the essential principle of reason and right in the world," he wrote in *Educational Psychology* (1913–1914, Vol. 1, pp. 281–282).

It is to institutions called schools and universities that modern societies assign most of the formal stimulation of this power of human learning. For his efforts to improve the abilities of educational institutions to capitalize upon learning potential Thorndike received much recognition during his lifetime: the presidencies of and honorary memberships in numerous American and international scientific and educational associations, honorary degrees from many universities, and election to the National Academy of Sciences. A most appropriate award, the Butler Medal in gold, was bestowed upon Thorndike by Columbia University in 1925 "in recognition of his exceptionally significant contributions to the general problem of the measurement of human faculty and to the applications of such measurements to education" (Jonçich 1968, p. 487).

SELECTED WORKS BY THORNDIKE

1898   "Animal Intelligence." *The Psychological Review, Monograph Supplements*, 2, no. 4:whole No. 8.

1901a   *Notes on Child Study.* New York, Macmillan.

1901b   "The Influence of Improvement in One Mental Function Upon the Efficiency of Other Functions." 3 parts. With Robert S. Woodworth. *Psychological Review*, 8 no. 3:247–261; no. 4:384–395; no. 6:556–564.

1903   *Educational Psychology.* New York, Lemcke and Buechner.

(1904) 1913   *An Introduction to the Theory of Mental and Social Measurements.* 2nd ed., rev. New York, Teachers College Press.

1906   *Principles of Teaching, Based on Psychology.* New York, A. G. Seiler.

1911   *Individuality.* Boston, Houghton Mifflin.

1912   *Education: A First Book.* New York, Macmillan.

1913   *Educational Administration: Quantitative Studies.* New York, Macmillan.

1913–1914   *Educational Psychology.* Vol. 1: *The Original Nature of Man.* Vol. 2: *The Psychology of Learning.* Vol. 3: *Work and Fatigue, Individual Differences and Their Causes.* New York, Teachers College Press.

1917   *Thorndike Arithmetics.* Books 1, 2, and 3. Chicago, Rand McNally.

1923   *Psychology of Algebra.* New York, Macmillan.

1928   "Curriculum Research." *School and Society*, 18:569–576.

1935   *Thorndike-Century Junior Dictionary.* Chicago, Scott Foresman.

1940   *Human Nature and the Social Order.* New York, Macmillan.

1962   *Psychology and the Science of Education: Selected Writings of Edward L. Thorndike.* Edited by Geraldine Jonçich. New York, Teachers College Press.

THORNDIKE, EDWARD L., AND ARTHUR I. GATES 1929 *Elementary Principles of Education.* New York, Macmillan.

THORNDIKE, EDWARD L., et al. 1928 *Adult Learning.* New York, Macmillan.

THORNDIKE BIBLIOGRAPHIES

"Annotated Chronological Bibliography, 1898–1925" 1926 *Teachers College Record*, 27, no. 6:466–515.

"Publications From 1898 to 1940 by E. L. Thorndike" 1940 *Teachers College Record*, 41, no. 8:699–725.

"Thorndike's Publications From 1940 to 1949: A Bibliography" 1949 By Irving Lorge. *Teachers College Record*, 51, no. 1:42–45.

SUPPLEMENTARY BIBLIOGRAPHY

CALLAHAN, RAYMOND 1962 *Education and the Cult of Efficiency.* University of Chicago Press.

CREMIN, LAWRENCE A. 1961 *The Transformation of the School: Progressivism in American Education, 1876–1957.* New York, Knopf.

CURTI, MERLE 1935 *The Social Ideas of American Educators.* New York, Scribner.

JONÇICH, GERALDINE 1968 *The Sane Positivist: A Biography of Edward L. Thorndike.* Middletown, Conn., Wesleyan University Press.

MURCHISON, CARL, ed. 1936 *A History of Psychology in Autobiography.* Vol. 3. Worcester, Mass., Clark University Press.

O'CONNELL, GEOFFREY 1938 *Naturalism in American Education.* New York, Benzinger Brothers.

"Personal Appreciations" 1926 *Teachers College Record*, 27, no. 6:460–465.

GERALDINE JONÇICH CLIFFORD

TORT LIABILITY OF SCHOOL DISTRICTS AND SCHOOL PERSONNEL

A tort is a legal wrong committed against a person or against property; it is a violation of a general standard of conduct, a violation which results in personal injury or property damage. The general standard of conduct is conduct which reasonable people may expect others to observe as they go about their daily lives.

Generally, one cannot claim that the person committing a tort, known as the tort-feasor, violated a written statute. Instead, the accuser's claim is that the tort-feasor acted in such a way as to cause injury to the accuser's person or property. If this act was contrary to what could reasonably be expected of the tort-feasor under the circumstances and if this violation of the standard of conduct is legally recognized as one for which the tort-feasor is required to pay money to the accuser, the tort-feasor is liable for his tort in a civil court proceeding.

The money a tort-feasor must pay to compensate the accuser for the harm he has sustained is called damages. Factors for which money damages are awarded in a tort case include medical expenses, pain and suffering, and lost wages. If the conduct of the tort-feasor is a particularly outrageous or offensive violation of the reasonable standard of conduct expected of him, the civil court will add to its award of regular damages

to the injured person an amount of money known as exemplary, or punitive, damages. These damages constitute a civil, or private, fine against the tort-feasor and are analogous to the fines imposed by a criminal court.

There are two major types of torts—intentional and negligent. Intentional torts, those deliberately committed by a tort-feasor, include assault and battery, defamation, trespass, and false imprisonment. Some intentional torts also can be crimes, and a tort-feasor can be required by a civil court to pay money damages to compensate the injured person and also be required by a criminal court to pay a fine or suffer imprisonment as a criminal. A negligent tort is a tort that, although not intended, was committed in disregard of the rights or reasonable expectations of another person. This is the area of tort law which has given rise to the most litigation, including lawsuits resulting from automobile accidents and injuries incurred on public school and private school land. Some state legislatures have made particularly wanton and irresponsible disregard of others' rights (for example, reckless driving) a crime.

As society becomes more complex, as people live closer and closer together, and as there continues to be a general breakdown of formal lines in society marking the divisions between what is considered "good" or "bad" and "moral" or "immoral," civil courts are calling more types of behavior negligent torts and assessing money damages for them. Legal recognition of the liability of school employees for tortious conduct is one aspect of the expansion of the law of torts.

Torts by school personnel. Laws in some states grant immunity from tort liability to public school employees. The extent of this immunity is usually set by statute, and the statutes vary from state to state, especially in regard to torts resulting from personal dishonesty or the commission of a crime.

In states in which legislation or court decisions do not grant immunity, there are a number of tortious acts for which school personnel may be held liable.

Negligence. Most of the suits brought against school employees allege that an employee has been negligent. The fifth edition of *Black's Law Dictionary* defines "negligence" as "the omission to do something which a reasonable man, guided by those ordinary considerations which ordinarily regulate human affairs, would do, or the doing of something which a reasonable or prudent man would not do."

A person claiming injury because of the negligent tort of a school employee must show that the employee owed him a legal duty; that the employee, by an act or a failure to act, breached that legal duty; and that the breach of duty was the actual and legal cause of the injury. The act or failure to act by a school employee invariably relates to his duty to adequately supervise pupils; that is, the main issue in most negligence suits against school employees is whether the employee provided proper supervision of the pupil at the time the pupil was injured.

To avoid liability, the school employee must provide the kind and quality of supervision of pupils which the so-called reasonable man would provide under the same circumstances. How the reasonable man would or should act is only vaguely defined in common law cases, and the standard of conduct applied by courts may sometimes be unrealistic. In 1937, A. P. Herbert, in *Misleading Cases in the Common Law*, defined the "reasonable man" on the basis of conduct called reasonable in several court decisions:

> He is an ideal, a standard, the embodiment of all those qualities which we demand of the good citizen. . . . He is one who invariably looks where he is going, and is careful to examine the immediate foreground before he executes a leap or a bound; who neither star-gazes nor is lost in meditation when approaching trapdoors or the margin of a dock . . . and will inform himself of the history and habits of a dog before administering a caress; . . . who never drives his ball until those in front of him have definitely vacated the putting green which is his own objective; who never from one year's end to another makes an excessive demand upon his wife, his neighbors [or] his servants . . . who never swears, gambles or loses his temper; who uses nothing except in moderation, and even while he flogs his child is meditating only on the golden mean. . . .

The reasonable man is considered to possess the physical qualities of the tort-feasor, but he does not have the tort-feasor's temperament or set of personal habits; excuses such as "I was excited," "I didn't think," "I was drunk," "I am stupid," or "I was insane" generally do not exempt a person from living up to the reasonable man standard.

Applying the foregoing principles, it may be said that school employees must provide adequate supervision of pupils and a safe place for them at all times when the pupils are under the direct jurisdiction of the school. The duty of proper supervision includes instructing pupils in the possible dangers of certain educational activities. Clearly, therefore, an athletic team coach or a physical education teacher must do more to avoid tort liability than a classroom teacher. In 1958 a California appellate court, considering a case in which an injured pupil was moved after his injury, noted that "the amount of caution involved in the exercise of ordinary care, and hence required by law, increases or decreases as does the danger that reasonably should be apprehended" (*Welch* v. *Dunsmuir Joint Union High School District*, 326 Pac. 2d 633 at 638). In 1970 the California supreme court stated:

> [Supervision of students] is necessary precisely because of the commonly known tendency of students to engage in aggressive and impulsive behavior which exposes them and their peers to the risk of serious physical harm. . . . [A]dolescent high school students are not adults and should not be expected to exhibit that degree of discretion, judgment, and concern for the safety of themselves and others which we associate with full maturity. . . . Recognizing that a principal task of supervisors is to anticipate and curb rash student behavior, our courts have often held that a failure to prevent injuries caused by the intentional or reckless conduct of the victim or a fellow student may constitute negligence. (*Dailey* v. *Los Angeles Unified School District*, 2 Cal. 3d 741 at 748)

This description of a student is in sharp contrast to the high regard in which students are held by the courts when First Amendment "free speech conduct" is at issue. The fact that the supervisory power of school personnel over the free speech activities of students has been lessened considerably by the courts should not be construed to mean that the responsibilities of school employees for the safety, health, and general physical well-being of students on school grounds have in any way been decreased. The standard of ordinary care which would be exercised by a reasonable man under all the circumstances still abides.

However, a school employee has no duty to anticipate or foresee danger to a pupil caused by the sudden willful misconduct of a fellow pupil if there was no reasonable basis for believing that the pupil would misbehave in that way. Even if a teacher is temporarily absent from his class when an injury occurs, tort liability will not ensue if the danger which suddenly developed could not reasonably be said to have resulted from or been caused by the teacher's absence. If a pupil has been injured despite adequate supervision and instruction, the teacher will not be liable if the injured pupil is cared for in a reasonable manner.

The usual legal defenses against negligence are available to a school employee; however, when pupils are involved, these defenses are of little value. The defense that the injured person knowingly assumed a risk and, therefore, is solely or partly responsible for his injury is virtually inapplicable, except perhaps if the pupil is injured while voluntarily attending an extracurricular event. The contributory negligence defense may be invoked if the injured pupil did not fulfill the duty of reasonable care which he owed himself. The degree of care the pupil must exercise, however, is that expected of a reasonable child, considerably less care than that expected of a reasonable man.

In 1970 a school employee could be liable for unintentional injuries to pupils only if the injury resulted from the employee's violating his duty—that is, if the injury was the employee's fault. However, in this era of liability insurance, it is difficult to predict whether courts will continue to look for fault before finding negligence tort liability in school cases, especially when hazardous conditions exist, such as during chemistry experiments or athletic activities. Absolute liability by school employees regardless of fault—strict liability—may become a part of tort law in the future.

Intentional torts. There are several intentional torts—that is, acts committed deliberately which result in injury to another person or to his property—for which school employees may be liable, including assault, battery, false imprisonment, and trespass. Intentionally putting another person in apprehension of immediate harmful or offensive contact constitutes assault; no actual contact is necessary. Battery is intentionally touching in a harmful or offensive manner another person or something closely attached to him. If a school employee intentionally and unreasonably confines a pupil to a fixed area and the pupil is conscious of his confinement, the employee may be liable for false imprisonment. If a school employee intentionally goes without permission onto another person's private land, he may be liable for trespass.

Courts do not permit recovery of damages resulting from these four torts if the act of the school employee either is consented to by the person claiming injury or is privileged. If a school social worker or truant officer is invited into a pupil's home, he is not liable for trespass; however, if he forces himself into a home, he is liable. In schools in which corporal punishment of pupils is permitted either by contract or by state law, a teacher who spanks a child is doing a privileged act and no tort liability accrues; however, if the threat of the spanking and the spanking itself are cruel and vicious in nature, the bounds of privileged conduct are exceeded, and the teacher may be liable for assault and battery. If the privilege extends only to teachers, then other school employees, such as janitors and secretaries, may be liable for assault and battery. In cases involving private schools, provisions in the contract between the school and the parents concerning penalties for misbehavior may apply. Privilege is also relevant in false imprisonment cases. A teacher generally has authority to specify the area in which a pupil must stay during school hours and for a reasonable time thereafter. Accordingly, a teacher may require a pupil to stay after school for a specified period of time in a detention classroom; however, if the pupil is kept for an unreasonably long time or is kept in an inappropriate place (for example, in a dark boiler room), liability for false imprisonment may result because any privilege that did exist was exceeded.

There are other intentional torts for which a school employee may be held liable. For example, he may be liable for the tort of conversion if he takes possession of someone's personal property and exercises the rights of ownership over it.

If a school employee knowingly makes a false statement with the intention of making another person act on the basis of that statement and a student is thereby injured, the employee is liable for deceit. This kind of case arises when a teacher deliberately lies about one of his former students to a college placement officer and, as a result of the lie, the student is denied admission to the college.

A school employee may be liable for defamation if he injures someone's reputation by communicating to others matters which tend to hold the person up to hatred, contempt, or ridicule;

matters which cause others to avoid the person; or matters which cause injury to the person's occupation. Generally, truth is a defense against a charge of defamation. Statements which appear defamatory on their face are privileged if they are not made with malice and are made to protect or advance one's own legitimate interests, are made to protect others, are in the public interest, are fair comment on public matters, or are fair and true reports of official proceedings or public meetings. For example, a school counselor advising a pupil's doctor or prospective employer is privileged. In some states, statutes expressly limit the classes of persons to whom personal information about pupils may be given.

Invasion of privacy involves the infringement of someone's freedom from unreasonable publicity or the commercial use of his likeness or personality. Thus, if a teacher discusses a pupil in a book the teacher has written, he may be liable for the tort of invasion of privacy. Liability does not ensue if the teacher can show that the pupil and his parents consented to the publicity or that the pupil was so well known that the added publicity amounted to fair comment.

If a school employee deliberately inflicts mental distress which is beyond the amount permissible because of his privileged position and which causes physical or mental illness—for example, if a teacher so terrorizes a pupil that the pupil becomes ill—then the employee is liable for a tort.

A school employee who interferes in the domestic relations between a husband and wife when such interference is not essential to performance of his job is also committing a tort.

School and school district liability. An important question for a school or a school district is whether it can be held liable for torts committed by its employees in the performance of their jobs. Any such liability is based on the legal principle *respondeat superior* (literally, let the superior answer).

The principle definitely applies to private schools, so that if a pupil in a private school is injured through the negligence of a teacher, the pupil may sue both the teacher and the school for damages. An injured pupil will want to sue the school as well as the teacher because the school probably has more money with which to pay damages. This is particularly important in cases in which the injury is great and the money damages demanded by the injured pupil are so high that the negligent teacher is unable to pay them.

Whether the doctrine of *respondeat superior* applies to public schools depends on state law. A public school is part of a public school district, which is a government agency. It is a rule at common law—a rule which originated in the 1788 English case *Russell* v. *Men Dwelling in County of Devon* (100 Eng. Rep. 359) and which was first introduced into American law in the 1812 case *Mower* v. *The Inhabitants of Leicester* (9 Mass. 247)—that governments are immune from tort liability. Therefore, a school district is only liable for the torts of its employees if the legislature or courts of the state in which it is located have acted to permit tort suits to be brought against school districts.

In the 1950's and 1960's, decisions in several important cases criticized the tort immunity rule. These cases included *Molitor* v. *Kaneland Community Unit District Number 302* (20 Ill. 2d 555 [1959]), *Muskopf* v. *Corning Hospital District* (55 Cal. 2d 211 [1961]), *Lipman* v. *Brisbane Elementary School District* (55 Cal. 2d 224 [1961]), *Holytz* v. *City of Milwaukee* (115 N.W. 2d 618 [1962]), and *Spanel* v. *Mounds View School District Number 621* (118 N.W. 2d 795 [1962]). These courts viewed the rationale behind the tort immunity rule (originally that "the king can do no wrong") as harsh, unfair, and outmoded. They also considered the argument that the tort immunity rule should be maintained to protect public funds and public property to be untenable when, in the words of the Illinois supreme court in the Moliter case, "public education constitutes one of the biggest businesses in the country."

Even in states which generally adhere to the tort immunity rule, courts have usually acted to permit suits for some torts. For example, some courts have held school districts liable when their employees were responsible for maintaining a nuisance or committed torts while performing a proprietary function. In general, a nuisance results from using one's property in a way which causes damage or injury to one's neighbors. Nuisances for which public agencies have been held liable include operating an open sewer and having an inadequate rainwater drainage system from public property. A proprietary function is any nongovernmental function performed by a government agency. Courts throughout the United States have varying interpretations of the term.

In *Morris* v. *Mount Lebanon Township School District* (393 Pa. 633, 144 Atl. 2d 737 [1958]) a school district's operation of a swimming pool as part of a summer recreation program was deemed a proprietary function, and in *Sawaya* v. *Tucson High School District No. 1* (78 Ariz. 389, 281 Pac. 2d 105 [1955]), use of a grandstand at a school football game was considered proprietary. On the other hand, use of a playground during summer vacation was considered governmental in *Shields* v. *School District of City of Pittsburgh* (408 Pa. 388, 184 Atl. 2d 240 [1962]).

In states which do not follow the tort immunity rule, a school district is liable under the *respondeat superior* doctrine for the torts of its employees which are committed while the employees are performing job responsibilities. In some states, a school district will pay not only those tort damages awarded against it but also those awarded against its employees. However, school districts are generally forbidden by law to pay exemplary, or punitive, damages awarded against one of their employees, because such damages should be paid directly by the person who did the outrageously offensive act.

If a school district is located in a state which does not follow the tort immunity rule, it may also be liable for injuries incurred by children who are trespassers on school property. Liability accrues if the children's trespassing is induced by the existence of an attractive nuisance—that is, an area in which children are likely to play and are also likely to be injured—and if the school district does not take reasonable steps to prevent injury.

Insurance. Many insurance companies issue policies covering virtually every type of tort liability to which a school or a school employee is exposed. Although school districts which are protected by state law need not spend public funds to insure themselves against tort liability, individual school employees, who may not be protected by these laws, may purchase such liability insurance.

BIBLIOGRAPHY

American Law Reports, 57 ALR 419; 120 ALR 1376, with supp. 60 ALR 2d 1198; 75 ALR 1196, with supp. 56 ALR 2d 1415; 161 ALR 367; 140 ALR 1058.
DAVID, LEON T. 1936 *Municipal Liability for Tortious Acts and Omissions*. Los Angeles, Sterling Press.
DAVIS, KENNETH CULP 1958 *Administrative Law Treatise*. St. Paul, Minn., West.
DEBONIS, JOSEPH A. 1967 "Teacher Liability for Pupil Injuries: Duty of Supervision." *Maine Law Review*, 19, no. 1:111–116.
DILLON, JOHN F. 1881 *Commentary on the Law of Municipal Corporations*. 3rd ed., rev. Boston, Little, Brown.
DUGAN, THOMAS A. 1962 "Teachers' Tort Liability." *Cleveland-Marshall Law Review*, 11, no. 3:512–520.
HARPER, FOWLER V., AND FLEMING JAMES, JR. 1956 *The Law of Torts*. Boston, Little, Brown.
HENSON, HAROLD E. 1959 "Schools and Teachers: Tort Liability in Our Changing Society." *Kansas Law Review*, 8, no. 1:124–131.
HERBERT, A. P. 1937 *Misleading Cases in the Common Law*. London, Methuen.
PROEHL, PAUL O. 1959 "Tort Liability of Teachers." *Vanderbilt Law Review*, 12, no. 3:723–754.
PROSSER, WILLIAM L. 1955 *Handbook of the Law of Torts*. 2nd ed. St. Paul, Minn., West.
ROADY, THOMAS GOLMAN, JR., AND WILLIAM R. ANDERSON, eds. 1960 *Professional Negligence*. Nashville, Tenn., Vanderbilt University Press.
VAN ALSTYNE, ARVO 1964 *California Government Tort Liability*. California Continuing Education of the Bar, Practice Book No. 24. Berkeley, University of California Printing Department.

THOMAS A. SHANNON

TOTALITARIANISM AND COMMUNISM, TEACHING ABOUT

Instruction about Communism and totalitarianism has been at least as much a political question to be decided by political leaders as it has been an educational question to be decided by professional educators. During the last three decades, public opinion regarding instruction about Communism has shifted radically. During World War II, educators paid little attention to Communist ideology and the Soviet political system. At that time the primary concern was winning the war, and as the Soviet Union was an ally, little was to be gained by stressing the differences between the Soviet and the American political systems.

Public opinion toward the Soviet Union hardened during the cold war, from the late 1940's to the mid-1950's. During this period, Senator Joseph McCarthy of Wisconsin launched a crusade against what he called internal subversion by Communists in high-ranking governmental positions. Many Americans believed that their society, including its educational system, had been infiltrated by Communists. As a result, schools tended to avoid instruction about Communism and the Soviet Union, and teachers who avoided the topic of Communism were safe from harassment. Some civic organizations even asserted that it was better not to expose students to Communist ideas for fear that students would be deceived and find such ideas attractive.

From 1955 to the mid-1960's, public opinion

changed and citizens increasingly began to demand that schools include units or entire courses on Communism. What caused this shift is not entirely clear, although some attribute it to lessons drawn from the experience of American soldiers who defected during the Korean war. It was widely reported that some Americans held as prisoners by the North Koreans became confused and disoriented by Communist propaganda. Reportedly, these Americans were not so aware as they should have been about the strengths of the American political system and the shortcomings of Communism and so were deluded into believing that Communism was preferable to American-style democracy.

The alleged brainwashing of American prisoners contributed to a demand that the schools teach the advantages of the democratic system and the evils of Communism more effectively than they had in the past. This demand was met in part by the enactment of local and state requirements relating to the study of Communism. No reliable data regarding local requirements exist, but the number of states requiring instruction about Communism grew from one in 1962–1963 to 12 in 1965–1966 (Cox & Evans 1967). The fact that only 12 states had such requirements should not be interpreted as a sign of apathy on the part of the other states, for many of them provided leadership in other ways: by issuing policy statements about instruction in Communism, by publishing syllabi for schools to use, and by encouraging the preparation of courses and units on Communism.

Public pressure to require schools to provide instruction about Communism reached its peak between 1961 and 1965. Although such other topics as sex education and black studies have subsequently attracted more attention, many more schools, particularly secondary schools, now teach about Communism than did in the 1950's.

Three approaches. Most social studies teachers lack sufficient training to teach the concepts of totalitarianism and Communism well. More important, deciding what to teach about Communism and totalitarianism or whether to teach these topics at all may not be up to the teachers. Often those who pressure schools to teach about Communism and totalitarianism are uninterested in having students examine these topics rationally. Rather they wish to use instruction about totalitarianism and Communism to instill in the students a particular set of values and moral principles. Teachers who customarily teach using

the method of scientific inquiry and value clarification are frustrated when told that they must teach topics from certain value positions using carefully selected empirical evidence and making appeals to authority.

The types of teachers who teach about Communism may be grouped as follows: those who consider themselves to be "cold warriors," those who view themselves as "bridge builders," and those who aspire to be "rational inquirers."

The militantly anti-Communist teacher, or the cold warrior, believes that courses on Communism should primarily teach students how to cope with the Communist enemies of the United States. He often uses syllabi that compare the "blessings" of American democracy and the "evils" of Communism and that present an idealized picture of American social, political, and economic life contrasted with the least attractive aspects of life in China or the Soviet Union. Communist theory, expansion, and subversion in the United States are usually treated at length to give students the impression that their nation is besieged by a tireless, clever, united enemy. As a result, the students are told, all Americans must be ever vigilant against such a danger.

The second kind of teacher, the bridge builder, is anxious to further peace and thinks his role is to promote international understanding. Believing that wars begin in the minds of men, he promotes positive, friendly attitudes toward the people of Communist nations. Such a desire affects the topics this teacher selects and the way he teaches them. For example, he may emphasize the history and culture of the Soviets and the Chinese and spend less time on international Communism. When this teacher describes existing Communist systems, he stresses that men have alternative ways to organize political, social, and economic life, and he asserts that each nation has a right to choose the ways that make sense to its own historical and cultural development. In his desire to promote attitudes conducive to world peace, this type of teacher may also distort reality. For example, in confronting students who have strong anti-Communist attitudes learned from parents and friends, the teacher may espouse a more radical view than he believes in, in hopes of making the students take a more moderate position.

Finally, some social studies teachers may try to impart the skills and attitudes of scientific inquiry to their students. These teachers, the rational inquirers, teach about the Soviet Union, China, and other Communist countries because these nations exist and are important for an understanding of world affairs. By requiring students to support claims with facts or evidence, they try to eliminate prejudices.

Those teachers who wish to examine Communism impartially are faced with a number of problems. Having only three or four weeks or, at most, a semester to study about Communism, they must choose which Communist nation and which brand of Communism to concentrate on. They must then decide which aspect of that nation's society they will dwell on—its political system, economic system, foreign policy, attitudes toward minority groups, cultural and intellectual life. Further, they must be aware that such choices, which may be made subjectively, may determine in large part the impression students will derive from their study of Communism. The teacher's task would be much easier if he could rely upon accurate material. Unfortunately, much that has been written is biased and inappropriate. Finally, the teacher who adopts a scholar's position may find himself in serious trouble with citizens who want schools to produce militant anti-Communists.

Totalitarianism. Totalitarianism is a term that has been applied to many different political systems: Nazi, Fascist, and Communist. Few, if any, Communist states fully satisfy the elements required by the definition of totalitarianism.

The term "totalitarianism" has highly emotional origins. It was first used by the mass media as they conjured up the systems of terror used by Fascist Italy, Nazi Germany, and the Soviet Union to control their citizens. Scholars began to use the term in the 1940's and 1950's. Perhaps most influential in formulating the definition of this term were Carl Friedrich and Zbigniew Brzezinski (1956). On the basis of a careful analysis of Nazi Germany, Fascist Italy, and the Soviet Union, they concluded that totalitarian systems had six essential elements: an official ideology, a single party led typically by one man, the systematic use of terror by the secret police for control of the population, a monopolistic control of mass communication, a near-complete monopoly over weapons, and central control of the economy. Other scholars have suggested that other features are central to totalitarian states, including a tendency toward total bureaucratization and a desire to acquire territory.

Some scholars reject the entire concept of totalitarianism as worthless. For example, they object to linking Nazi Germany, Fascist Italy, and the Soviet Union under the same term, claiming that the differences between these nations are blurred when they are treated by the same concept. However, others believe that "totalitarianism" is useful as a relative term rather than an absolute category. For example, regimes may be less totalitarian than they were previously, or one may identify totalitarian trends in a particular society.

Courses on totalitarianism are much less common in the schools than courses on Communism. In general, instruction about totalitarianism is likely to be included in a course on Communism. Teachers have been encouraged to help students recognize the ways in which all regimes having totalitarian tendencies—whatever their professed ideologies—threaten democratic institutions and practices. Teaching about totalitarianism has its difficulties too. It requires more abstraction than teaching about existing Communist states and instructional material about totalitarianism is more scarce than instructional material about Communism. Students who understand the concept of totalitarianism may become aware of a number of political systems that contain totalitarian features and perhaps may even recognize some totalitarian tendencies in their own society.

BIBLIOGRAPHY

Cox, Roy L., and David Evans 1967 "The Study of Communism." *The Clearing House*, 41, no. 6:376–378.
Ebenstein, William 1962 *Totalitarianism: New Perspectives.* New York, Holt.
Friedrich, Carl J. 1968 *"Totalitarianism: Recent Trends." Problems of Communism*, 17, no. 3:32–43.
Friedrich, Carl J., and Zbigniew K. Brzezinski 1956 *Totalitarian Dictatorship and Autocracy.* 2nd ed., rev. Cambridge, Mass., Harvard University Press.
Mehlinger, Howard D., ed. 1965 *The Study of Totalitarianism: An Inductive Approach.* Bulletin No. 37. Washington, D.C., National Council for the Social Studies.
Miller, Richard I. 1966 *Teaching About Communism.* New York, McGraw-Hill.
Wirsig, Marie 1966 "What an American Secondary School Student Should Know About Communism." Ph.D. dissertation. University of Denver.

Howard D. Mehlinger

TRADE AND INDUSTRIAL EDUCATION

Trade and industrial education is a large and significant part of the total area of vocational education. In general, trade and industrial education is concerned with occupations ranging from the highly skilled to those which are less complex and which border upon unskilled occupations. It also includes a variety of service occupations. Initially, the emphasis was on construction, manufacturing, and trade, but finding a precise definition of trade and industrial education has been complicated by the fact that new and emerging occupational education fields which could not be conveniently categorized in other areas have been assigned to this one. In a sense, trade and industrial education has become a catchall for education in a variety of occupations, including machinist, practical nurse, policeman, dental assistant, landscape architect, foreman, and supervisor.

Historical background. Where and when trade and industrial education began is difficult to determine, but one can surmise that some elements of trade and industrial education were present when a father first taught a son to hunt and to help provide for the needs of the family or tribe. Later, as man advanced from savagery to civilization, the need for a variety of skills increased.

Most of what we know about early societies is derived from evidence of man's skill and creativeness. The Hittites, Phrygians, Phoenicians, and Egyptians all left traces of their highly developed skills. The temples of Trajan and Hadrian, the buildings of Pericles in the golden age of Greece, and the roads and bridges of the ancient Roman empire still stand, although eroded by time, as positive evidence that in some way skill in a trade was developed and transmitted from culture to culture.

Craftsmen formed clubs, guilds, or other groups to protect, maintain, and extend their industrial achievements. For the most part a father-son or family relationship existed as a means of transmitting skills, and the ancient system of apprenticeship grew in importance with time. Europe during the Renaissance and Reformation encouraged the guilds and the apprenticeship system, and in some places formal schools were organized strongly related to trade and industrial education. But it was apprenticeship which presented the clear evidence of trade and industrial education.

Colonial America. Colonists brought to America the institutions of their European culture. It is not surprising, therefore, that apprenticeship flourished in the American colonies. Apprenticeship was recognized and regulated by colonial laws and represented one of the fundamental educational institutions of the time. Apprentice-

ship was an acceptable alternative for the boy or girl who could not pay for another type of education.

In colonial times the master provided food, clothing, and shelter for his apprentices. Apprentices were generally taught to read and write, the degree of development depending largely upon the needs of the occupation. Religious training was an important aspect of colonial apprenticeship. Finally, all apprentices were taught the skills of the trade and learned the scientific and mathematical aspects of the occupation.

These elements were under legal jurisdiction, in the form of an indenture of apprenticeship, in which the rights of both the employer and the apprentice were identified. Both boys and girls could become apprentices in recognized occupations. Occupations which did not require skill, such as minding cattle, were not involved in the apprenticeship system.

Trade and industrial education, in the form of apprenticeship, served a direct social function by providing a way for a young person to become a productive member of society; furthermore, apprenticeships prevented orphans from becoming a burden upon colonial society. Both voluntary and involuntary systems of apprenticeship existed, and both types were regulated by law. In their wills, parents frequently directed that their children be apprenticed.

National period to the twentieth century. Apprenticeship suffered a serious setback with the rise of the factory system, but it did not drop out of existence. Concurrently with the rise of educational consciousness in the United States in the 1820's, new forms of trade and industrial education developed. In the beginning the somewhat formalized system of trade education was vested in societies of craftsmen. The most illustrious of these societies was the General Society of Mechanics and Tradesmen, which was founded in 1785 and is still in existence. Most of the societies conducted classes and maintained libraries for the education of their members.

Lyceums, mechanics' institutes, and special schools grew rapidly prior to the Civil War. Evidence seems to suggest that these developments were part of an effort to maintain the fundamental facets of apprenticeship.

After the Civil War the trade-school movement in education produced such schools as the New York Trade School in New York City, the Hampton Institute in Hampton, Va., the Williamson

Free School of Mechanical Trades in Philadelphia, and the California School of Mechanical Arts in San Francisco. Most of these schools were private ventures; although some were entirely free, most required at least a modest tuition. Despite the extensive development of such schools it was not until the twentieth century that the elements of trade and industrial education began to show up in public education. After the Civil War the manual training movement in education did not in theory provide an occupational-type trade and industrial education; it did in practice, however, include many skills for employment. The need for industrial education with a definite occupational purpose was clearly evident.

The vocational movement. In 1906 the National Society for the Promotion of Industrial Education (now called the American Vocational Association) was founded and had as its purpose the development of trade and industrial education throughout the United States, supported in part by financial aid from the federal government. The leaders of the NSPIE were seeking to gain for secondary schools an emphasis similar to that which had developed for those colleges established under the provisions of the Morrill Act of 1862. For 11 years the Congress, the NSPIE, and the public at large discussed the merits of a federal aid bill and the need for trade and industrial education. Finally, the Smith-Hughes Act, signed in 1917, provided in part for cooperative arrangements between the states and the federal government to develop programs of trade and industrial education in the public schools.

Educational principles. During the 11-year period of study of trade and industrial education prior to the passage of the Smith-Hughes Act, the NSPIE, through its publications, national conferences, and study groups, examined thoroughly many directly and indirectly related facets of trade and industrial education, including the size of the program needed and its potential value to society. Federal, state, and local public officials, representatives of chambers of commerce, members of national labor and educational organizations, and many public service groups participated in this study. In the judgment of these groups it became obvious that vocational education could in fact promote the general welfare, and a number of principles for trade and industrial education began to emerge.

There was little doubt in 1906 that the task of trade and industrial education was to promote industrial efficiency and to increase the economic reward of boys and girls who were to enter industrial occupations. It was certain that the proposed field of education under consideration extended beyond manual training but did not include the area of engineering, even though both of these extremes were thought to be a part of the continuum of vocational education. Attention was therefore focused upon that schooling which dealt with training of direct value to the industrial worker. The introduction of industrial education into the public school system required adoption of a broader view of what public education should accomplish. Only in a setting of the best of public education could trade and industrial education prosper.

Thus, it was felt that all trade schools should be open to all: sex, creed, color, or nationality should not bar anyone from an education. All trades should be taught, and the aim of the trade schools should be to give the best preparatory and practical education possible. Therefore, the instructors should have considerable experience and skill in the practical operations of trades. Also, much of the instruction should be individualized. Trade schools, to be successful, must depend upon a system as well organized and as broadly managed as that of the public schools. Furthermore, there should be public control of all trade schools, with representatives of labor on the boards of directors of the schools.

Trade and industrial courses for boys and girls, it was argued, must have a broad scope and must do more than provide for learning of a trade. For example, the outlook of the future worker should be molded. The movement for industrial education should not merely seek to fit into the existing school system most easily and economically; rather, it must demand a radical readjustment of obsolete ideals and methods in public schools. The movement for industrial education should not fix its attention solely or chiefly upon the needs of the children of the poorest families who must begin to earn money at the earliest moment allowed by law. The education of workers in trade or industry is a public necessity; it should not be a private function but a public one, conducted by the public at public expense.

From more than 50 years of experience in vocational education, it would appear that the stated principles of trade and industrial education are sound. However, from time to time the principles must be interpreted in the light of social and economic developments. (It should be noted that the change comes in the interpretation of the principles, not in the principles as such.) The reinterpreted principles must then, of course, be implemented.

There is no evidence to indicate that any new principles of trade and industrial education have emerged since 1906–1917. The foundation principles have been reinterpreted and supported by such legislation as the Smith-Hughes Act (1917), the George-Deen Act (1936), the George-Barden Act (1946), the Vocational Education Act of 1963, and the Vocational Education Amendments of 1968. These acts expanded the range of occupations served by trade and industrial education, in accordance with social and occupational changes and needs. As society and technology continue to change, other interpretations will be necessary.

Enrollment. It took almost 45 years for enrollment in trade and industrial education to reach 1 million persons (in 1960); yet, during the 1960's the enrollment nearly doubled.

Enrollment in trade and industrial education increased approximately 76 percent from fiscal year 1960 through fiscal year 1968. Such an increase was due to a number of factors. New area vocational schools were opened that offered programs predominantly in trade and industrial education. A noticeable increase in public relations activity throughout the United States brought these programs to the attention of a larger number of people. The programs established under the Manpower Development and Training Act of 1962 have encouraged states to organize similar programs on a continuing basis. Increased appropriations resulting from the Vocational Education Act of 1963 have made it possible to finance a number of new programs. Increased demand for goods and services and shortages of skilled craftsmen and other trained industrial workers have encouraged communities and schools to develop programs to meet this increased demand for skilled workers.

A study of the distribution of enrollment in secondary schools, postsecondary schools, and adult programs indicates that well over 50 percent of the total enrollment is composed of adults who are seeking to retrain or upgrade themselves for new employment opportunities.

Expenditures. From 1917 through fiscal year 1964 all appropriations of federal funds to the states were based on occupational categories.

Since fiscal year 1965, however, allocations of federal funds have been made in part upon the basis of the people to be served—primarily secondary school students, postsecondary school students, and adults.

In 1967 total federal, state, and local expenditures for vocational education amounted to more than $1 billion; over 23 percent of this amount was spent for trade and industrial education. For each federal dollar, approximately $2.82 of state and local funds were spent. Nearly 74 percent of the total spent on trade and industrial education came from state and local funds. The federal expenditures more than quintupled in the five-year period between 1962, when $11.4 million was spent, and 1967, when $61.7 million was spent. In 1962 the average federal expenditure per enrollee was $11; in 1967 this amount increased to $41.

Although expenditures per enrollee have increased significantly, the amount allocated is small compared with other federal funding.

Scope of instruction. The greatest diversity of occupations for which training is given falls in the area of trade and industrial education. More than 150 different occupations are included among the enrollments. Those occupations whose enrollment in 1968 was between 100,000 and 150,000 included firemen and auto mechanics. Occupations with a 1968 enrollment of between 50,000 and 100,000 included metals and machine shop, foremanship and supervision, welding, drafting, electrical work, and law enforcement. Those occupations with an enrollment of between 10,000 and 50,000 were carpentry, graphic arts, plumbing and pipe fitting, construction and maintenance, and many others. Other occupations classified as part of trade and industrial education include those of commercial artists, cosmeticians, cooks and chefs, radiographers, industrial atomic energy workers, instrument repair and maintenance men, dressmakers, marine workers, foundry workers, barbers, bakers, meat cutters, waiters and waitresses, and others. The wide scope of the various trade and industrial occupations makes the task of precise identification very difficult. However, in the near future all occupations will have identifying numbers which will make comparisons with occupational need more exact.

Follow-up of graduates. Each October the U.S. Office of Education receives from the states a report of a follow-up study of graduates of trade and industrial education programs. Of the 154,684 students who completed program requirements in 1967 in trade and industrial education programs, nearly 60 percent were available for placement. Most of those students who were not available for placement entered the armed forces or continued school full-time. Of the students available for placement, over 75 percent were placed in a field related to the field for which they were trained; nearly 20 percent were placed in a field unrelated to their training; a small percentage were either placed part-time or unemployed. One of the interesting aspects of the follow-up study is the evidence that through trade and industrial education many students find what they are vocationally suited for and are thus motivated to continue in school full-time.

Teacher recruitment and training. The vast majority of the teachers for trade and industrial education are recruited from industry. In most instances such persons complete teacher-training requirements concurrently with actual teaching. A few preservice programs for trade and industrial teachers, lasting four or five years, are in operation.

Two principles concerned with the selection and training of teachers have been established: (1) The teacher of trade and industrial education must be competent in the subject he teaches, and (2) he must have teacher-education experiences in order to help him transfer his skills and knowledge to his students.

The concept of adequate and successful work experience is valid and deeply rooted. It is through successful work experience that a person learns the skills, technical knowledge, and customs of the occupation he will be teaching. Although work experience provides the basis for instructional content, what is more important is that it gives the teacher insight into the occupational environment for which he is preparing students.

In 1967 a total of 132,581 teachers were involved in the vocational education program in the United States; nearly one-third were trade and industrial teachers. Approximately 41 percent of the trade and industrial teachers were recruited from business and industry as part-time teachers. Nearly 38.5 percent of the teachers were employed full-time in either a secondary or postsecondary school.

An estimated 150 percent increase in the total number of trade and industrial teachers needed during the 1970's requires that the entire area of teacher education be reviewed. Significant change in the practice of selecting trade teachers from industry is not likely to occur. However, a variety of experimental teacher-education programs may be developed which will provide some new sources of teachers. First, in order to facilitate the employment of teachers, state certification requirements will need to be reviewed and adjusted; second, a massive in-service teacher education program is needed in order to upgrade and update the occupational and pedagogical skills of trade and industrial teachers.

Labor market needs. It is anticipated that in the near future labor market supply-and-demand data will be perfected to the extent that statistics related to specific occupations can be properly interpreted. At present there is strong doubt that demand data and supply data are comparable. The problem is not unsolvable; only recently, however, has the necessity to clarify these issues become evident.

An expanding technology and a growing labor market focus attention upon the need to provide additional in-school programs for young persons who are preparing to enter the labor market; the need to provide a greater opportunity, in the public school sector of the educational system, for both employed and unemployed persons to make adjustments in their occupational potential; and the necessity to provide significant attention to the special needs of both youth and adults who have not received adequate training to prepare them for occupations.

The Vocational Education Amendments of 1968 provided a mandate to public education to extend and expand trade and industrial education programs in the secondary and postsecondary schools of the United States. Such expansion should be organized so that no student in school full-time will graduate without a salable skill, no student will drop out of school who cannot be absorbed into the labor market, and no person, employed or unemployed, will be denied the opportunity to have further occupational preparation at public expense.

There is no easy solution to the problem of relating training to market need, but there are a number of strategies by which this goal can be achieved at least partially. The advisory committee system (which was invented by vocational education), if properly used, can help keep the school program reasonably related to actual occupational needs. If there are school employees who are knowledgeable about local, state, and national labor market information, the trade and industrial program has an excellent opportunity to coincide with occupational need. However, a problem far more serious than possible divergence of training and need is that of making trade and industrial education widely available. It is difficult for a student to prepare for an occupation in trade or industry if his school does not offer a suitable program.

BIBLIOGRAPHY

ANDERSON, LEWIS FLINT 1926 *History of Manual and Industrial School Education.* New York, Appleton.

BARLOW, MELVIN L. 1963 *Principles of Trade and Industrial Education.* Austin, University of Texas, Division of Extension.

BARLOW, MELVIN L. 1967 *History of Industrial Education in the United States.* Peoria, Ill., Charles A. Bennett.

BENNETT, CHARLES A. 1926 *History of Manual and Industrial Education Up to 1870.* Peoria, Ill., Manual Arts Press.

BENNETT, CHARLES A. 1937 *History of Manual and Industrial Education, 1870–1917.* Peoria, Ill., Manual Arts Press.

NATIONAL SOCIETY FOR THE STUDY OF EDUCATION 1965 *National Society for the Study of Education. Sixty-fourth Yearbook, Part 1: Vocational Education.* Edited by Melvin L. Barlow. University of Chicago Press.

ROBERTS, ROY W. 1957 *Vocational and Practical Arts Education: History, Development, and Principles.* New York, Harper.

U.S. COMMISSIONER OF LABOR 1893 *Industrial Education, 1892. Eighth Annual Report.* Washington, D.C., Government Printing Office.

U.S. COMMISSIONER OF LABOR 1902 *Trade and Technical Education, 1902. Seventeenth Annual Report.* Washington, D.C., Government Printing Office.

U.S. COMMISSIONER OF LABOR 1911 *Industrial Education, 1910. Twenty-fifth Annual Report.* Washington, D.C., Government Printing Office.

U.S. OFFICE OF EDUCATION 1963 *Education for a Changing World of Work: Report of Panel of Consultants on Vocational Education.* Washington, D.C., Government Printing Office.

U.S. OFFICE OF EDUCATION 1968 *Vocational Education: The Bridge Between Man and His Work.* Washington, D.C., Government Printing Office.

U.S. OFFICE OF EDUCATION 1969 *Vocational Education and Occupations.* Washington, D.C., Government Printing Office.

MELVIN L. BARLOW

TRAINING PROGRAMS, SMALL BUSINESS

1. COMPANY PROGRAMS

Technical and vocational training in the mechanical and industrial arts and crafts gives the trainee skills and knowledge which may be applied widely in problem-solving situations on the job.

The need for vocational training has always existed. Modern programs are an outgrowth of the European guild system; in the United States they date from prerevolutionary times and the first indentured apprentices. However, in the United States the industrial revolution all but destroyed the tradition of the master craftsman passing on his cherished trade secrets to a few select students. As sophisticated machines were developed and mass production became the foremost factor of industrial economics, it became apparent that industry would require a steady and large supply of skilled and semiskilled craftsmen. From this need grew the modern concept of technical and vocational education in industry and the public schools.

Early programs. Early programs dating back to 1937 were utilitarian in the extreme. Often, training was inadequate; students were taught just enough to perform a few rudimentary functions. Too many entrepreneurs failed to equate training with profit. They viewed it as temporary overhead, something they had to put up with in varying degrees. Not until the Manpower Development and Training Act of 1962 did vocational education mature. This act made it possible for businessmen to obtain assistance in the form of cost-sharing from the U.S. Department of Labor and the department's Bureau of Apprenticeship and Training.

Prior to the passage of the Manpower Act, small companies depended almost exclusively on the public school system for their supply of workmen. But little, if any, dialogue existed between the business and the educational communities. Vocational education in the schools, which began in 1917 with the passage of the Smith-Hughes Vocational Education Act, placed primary emphasis on the so-called homemaker arts. The result was that the majority of public schools offered no training for jobs in industry.

Through its cooperative approach, the Manpower Act has drawn industry into closer contact with education. There has been an expansion of training activities within the manufacturing and service industries and a substantial improvement in the quality of training.

Trainees. Until 1969 trainee programs in the vocational and technical fields were limited to persons with a high school or trade school background. Principally, trainees were young men who enjoyed working in the manual and technical areas and who did not intend to go to college. But in a rapidly expanding economy, the demand for these young men has always been greater than the supply.

In 1960, when the economy began to undergo an unprecedented boom, industry as a whole was confronted with a severe shortage of skilled workers. Even the industrial giants—such as IBM, General Motors, and the Pratt and Whitney Aircraft Division (United Aircraft Corporation)—felt the squeeze, but they had sufficient capital to finance advanced in-house training programs. Through the lure of high salaries and generous fringe benefits, which in the vital defense industries included exemption from military service, the big firms captured a large percentage of available trainees. The shortage was therefore felt most acutely by small manufacturing firms.

Although Manpower Act assistance helped the small shop compete in the job market, it did not completely alleviate the shortage of job candidates. One solution to this problem has been to train persons whose academic backgrounds are incomplete or even nonexistent and who have a long history of joblessness—such as school dropouts, the socially and culturally deprived, and the physically handicapped. The training of these so-called hard-core unemployables has required a new educational approach. Small shops have pioneered in the development of programs which train disadvantaged people to successfully hold complex technical jobs.

Perhaps one of the greatest contributions to retraining programs has been made by the contract tool and die industry. As a matter of economic survival, tool and die shops were motivated to train the "untrainable." By 1970, program concepts and techniques which rival, and often surpass, those established by big business had been developed. The fundamental premise has been that anyone who is willing to learn can be taught a valuable skill. The tool and die industry has taken persons whose functional literacy is barely measurable and turned them into machine operators and skilled technicians. Moreover, job placement and job retention figures average above 90 percent.

Teaching techniques. The trend among small shops has been to formalize on-the-job training so that the trainee is taught not only actual production techniques but also new technological advances. Therefore, "classrooms" are often found at or near the job site itself.

Functional approach. Before a trainee even enters the shop he is given intensive instruction. For those whose functional literacy is low, instruction includes learning the fundamentals of English and mathematics. Often, the functional approach —teaching only the skills that directly relate to job functions and job problems—is used in training programs. For instance, the student first brushes up on basic mathematics and fills in the gaps in his background; he then moves on to more advanced mathematics—such as trigonometry and algebra—but he is not asked to concern himself with theory. Instead, his instruction relates directly to specific problems he will encounter on the job. He is taught how to use mathematical tables and learns the shortcuts of algebra. The functional approach makes it possible for a trainee in the tool and die industry to learn enough algebra in a few hours to handle almost anything that may occur in a tool-making situation.

Programmed instruction. Programmed instruction can be used by both literate and low-literacy trainees. In 1970, 69 percent of all programmed learning was job oriented (American Society of Manufacturing Engineers 1969).

Programmed instruction is not a new concept but dates back to the experiments of Sydney L. Pressy of Ohio State University in 1928. There are several kinds of programmed instruction, but the most common one in use today is the linear approach, developed in the 1950's by B. F. Skinner of Harvard. Skinner's theory is that if material is correctly programmed, or sequenced in "chapters," every student can master the chapters, provided he is allowed to progress at his own pace (Lumsdaine & Glaser 1960).

An outstanding example of programmed instruction has been in use at the Arrow Tool Company in Wethersfield, Conn. At Arrow, numerical-control machine tools have been used as teaching machines. The operations of these machine tools are controlled by a tape which has been created by a computer. The student works with the machine by using what is known as a manuscript, a documented step-by-step analysis of the creation of a part. As the machine cuts the part, the trainee follows the manuscript through each sequence; at the same time, he performs simple functions and keeps a check on the progress of the cutting.

It has been possible to gear the production process to the trainee's ability to ingest information. At first the trainee makes simple parts which require little in the way of skills; later he produces parts which are more complex. Each part produced in this way becomes a separate learning experience. Within four weeks the student has learned to read a manuscript and to follow its instructions, to know what to expect from various cutting tools, and to operate the machine. These are, of course, very specific lessons, but enough general information is in them to allow for an understanding of the capabilities of various other machine tools.

Making the student responsible for operation and inspection of the machine tool prevents him from stumbling through the learning process without having to pay attention, as he could do in a classroom lecture. Like any effective teaching device, the numerical-control machine tool presents information, requires responses by the trainee, and gives immediate feedback to let the trainee know whether his response is correct or not. To build confidence, the machine tool allows the trainee to work on his own and to control his own rate of progress.

Instructor-coach method.   The instructor-coach method, which allows a trained person to help learners, has met with great success in training programs in small shops. In this method a skilled workman is taken into a company classroom where he is given special teacher training and sensitivity training which provide him with a better understanding of the trainees with whom he will be working. The workman is then put in charge of a group of trainees. His function is that of both foreman and teacher. As larger numbers of workmen are promoted to instructor-coach status, more people are able to enter the company at the bottom.

Teaching aids.   A variety of teaching aids are in wide use, particularly in the apprentice and preapprentice training areas. Most of them have been used effectively in small-shop programs.

Special books.   The National Tool, Die and Precision Machining Association, with an industry endowment, has developed an assortment of teaching materials and aids.

The association has developed a series of special textbooks designed for low achievers and for those whose emotional makeup has caused them some difficulty in the past. These texts are structured so that the confusion often caused by the presentation of single concepts surrounded by a circle of multidimensional ideas is eliminated. It is left to the student to relate one concept to another. If this proves too difficult, he is given personal attention by an instructor. In this way he is not in strict competition with his classmates, and his ego remains intact.

Vocational coloring books, also developed by the association, are used in training culturally deprived persons. Like a child's coloring book, pictures of machines with the components marked are presented. For example, a picture might be labeled: "This is a spindle; the piece is mounted on the spindle; color it blue." Sounds simple but it works.

Electronic devices.   The rear-screen projector, a television-like apparatus which presents pictures (often with sound tracks) on a screen, is a widely used device in vocational training. The student can control the film so that he can absorb its message at his own pace; the projector is lightweight and portable, and the trainee can carry it home with him; the range of instructional materials that can be shown on the projector is unlimited; and its cost is low.

Among the other electronic and semielectronic devices in use in the small shop are tape recorders, slide and motion picture projectors, the Didak Programmer, which presents questions on a paper reel, and the Videosonic viewer, which shows slides and presents tape-recorded commentaries.

Setting up a training program.   A well-planned training program requires money and the cooperation of top management. Getting this cooperation might mean that one or two people must be convinced of the need for training, or it might mean that a company's policy must be revamped. A major policy change might involve drawing up a brief for management on the results—such as lowered costs or improvements in workmanship—obtained by other companies in the field.

Basically, there are three types of job training. First, there are highly organized programs in technical-vocational or trade schools and in special training shops as well as apprenticeships; all of these are administered by special instructors or training specialists to produce top-notch craftsmen. Second, there is that job training which is handled by the line supervisor in a department, with outside facilities and organizations playing only an incidental role. Third, there is job rotation on a planned or unplanned basis to provide incidental job experience. These forms of job training take place in apprenticeship, on-the-job, and near-the-job programs.

Apprenticeship programs. Apprenticeship programs are established to train persons in the crafts or trades that require a wide range of skills and knowledge and mature, independent judgment. The untrained worker is given comprehensive training in all the practical and theoretical aspects of his trade or craft. It has been found that properly supervised apprentices do not constitute a financial loss; as the apprentice masters new skills he applies them to productive work.

Small companies have found that properly supervised apprentice programs have increased productivity, bolstered worker security, improved product quality, reduced the need for supervision of graduates of apprentice schools, increased the versatility of the company, and opened up a source of future supervisors, technicians, and instructors.

The trend in apprentice training is to give as much on-the-job experience as possible by eliminating from the program those things which are nonessential and emphasizing what must be known in order to practice a trade. Presently, the United States has a shortage of apprentices. To improve this situation, apprentice training programs can be shortened from the usual four years for most crafts and trades and can be made less expensive and more effective. However, to achieve these ends new programs must be carefully planned and administered.

On-the-job training. A common mistake is to assume that near-the-job training is the same as on-the-job training. On-the-job training takes place only when a worker is learning on his production assignment.

The most common and efficient method of on-the-job training for most companies, and the one with which people are most familiar, is four-step job instruction training (JIT), adopted by industry during World War II. The first step in the JIT program is the preparation of the trainee by putting him at ease, explaining what the job is, and explaining its importance. The second is a step-by-step presentation of the job. The instructor explains and demonstrates the various aspects of the job. As reinforcement, the trainee then repeats the explanation and tries each step himself. The third step is a performance tryout; the trainee does his assigned job under supervision. The last step is the follow-up; the trainee works on his own, but his work is inspected regularly. Because the JIT method is quite flexible, many variations of it have come into popular use. In one of the more successful of these, the student and teacher change roles. This points up any mistakes the pupil might make.

JIT is used primarily to teach manipulative skills; when applied to more complex tasks, it often produces disappointing results. Inadequate supervision is another pitfall; although the method is flexible, it requires uniform application throughout the plant, and experienced instructors should direct and assist new ones. Also, many foremen who have used JIT in the past may need a refresher course in the method.

Near-the-job training. Instruction both in the classroom and on the line for specific assignments is more common than strictly on-the-job training. An example of this type of program is one at Hughes Aircraft in Fullerton, Calif. Hughes, engaged in supplying electronics parts and systems to defense agencies, must meet exacting standards. Thus, the assembly worker who does the vital wrapping, harnessing, and soldering of parts must be exceptionally reliable. This demand is met by establishing high, uniform standards in all areas of classification and by administering lengthy written and practical tests to make sure workers are well qualified to meet the standards. New workers are carefully selected and trained; older workers are given refresher training. These tests and refresher courses cost Hughes only the time the worker is off the floor, about $10 worth of equipment for each person, and the bonus pay for about six instructors. In return, the company gains a flexible work force with a professional attitude, uniform assembly, improved reliability, and reduced inspection costs.

Future challenge. The challenge facing both large and small industries is to somehow meet the continuing shortage of skilled workers. Although there were more training programs in 1970 than ever before, there were still not enough to keep pace with technological advances and a growing economy. Because the nation's rate of growth has shown no signs of a permanent slowdown, even greater numbers of skilled workmen will be needed in the future. As a matter of necessity small shops must start new training programs and upgrade those already in progress.

BIBLIOGRAPHY

AMERICAN SOCIETY OF MANUFACTURING ENGINEERS 1969 *Creative Manufacturing Seminars.* Technical Paper MS69–607. Dearborn, Mich., The Society.

HARDMAN, WILLIAM E. 1963 *In-plant Training.* Waterford, Conn., National Foremen's Institute, Bureau of Business Practice, National Sales Development Institute.

HARDMAN, WILLIAM E. 1965 "Training From Scratch." *American Machinist*, 109, no. 13:98–99.

HYMAN, I. HARRY 1960 "The Craftsman—Today's Vanishing American." *American Machinist*, 104, no. 7:121–124.

HYMAN, I. HARRY, AND WILLIAM E. HARDMAN 1962 "Training the 'Green' Worker." *American Machinist*, 106, no. 6:113–115.

LUMSDAINE, ARTHUR A., AND ROBERT GLASER, eds. 1960 *Teaching Machines and Programmed Learning: A Source Book.* Washington, D.C., National Education Association.

STATON, THOMAS F. 1960 *How to Instruct Successfully: Modern Teaching Methods in Adult Education.* New York, McGraw-Hill.

"The Training Explosion" 1966 *American Machinist*, 110, no. 12:entire issue.

WILLIAM E. HARDMAN

2. FEDERAL PROGRAMS

More than 95 percent of the U.S. business population is engaged in small business enterprises. Nearly 40 percent of U.S. business activity is conducted by these enterprises, which provide employment for approximately 34 million people. The economic health of the American people depends substantially upon the health of small business firms.

The number of small business enterprises started each year is greater than is generally realized. In the late 1960's new incorporations alone averaged 200,000 per year. When the number of new sole proprietorships and partnerships is added, the total must be much higher. Unfortunately, the number of failures is also very high. According to Harold Clark, the two prime reasons for these failures are inadequate capitalization and insufficient management knowledge and skill.

In 1953, Congress enacted a law setting up the Small Business Administration as an independent agency, on a year-to-year basis, to help small businesses overcome these two serious inadequacies and to meet other persistent problems. In 1958, Congress made the SBA a permanent agency. The SBA in 1969 employed approximately 4,000 persons at its Washington, D.C., headquarters and in 73 field offices.

The definition of the term "small business," which is fairly flexible, includes sole proprietorships, partnerships, and corporations. For the purpose of making loans, the SBA generally defines a small business as a wholesale concern with annual sales not exceeding $5 million, a retail or service business with sales or receipts not exceeding $1 million, or a manufacturing concern with not more than 250 employees. Higher limits apply in certain cases, depending upon the industry. Other standards also apply in government contract assistance and in the small business investment company program.

The SBA engages in a variety of loan programs to assist in the establishment, maintenance, and development of small business. These loan programs, designed to assist firms which cannot secure commercial bank loans, are a principal concern. In addition, the SBA provides assistance in securing government contracts or subcontracts and in exploring foreign trade possibilities. As of 1970 the SBA provided the only significant assistance program available to small business in the United States.

Training services. To improve the management of small business concerns, the SBA provides a diversified program of services. One aspect of the program provides services prior to the establishment of a business and in particular for the assistance of disadvantaged persons. Another aspect assists owner-managers who are struggling to put a new business on its feet. A third aspect assists those who have management problems associated with growth, rapid technological change, competition, and foreign trade.

Business enabling services. Business enabling services of the SBA are classified under the following headings: management training (courses and teaching materials), management counseling, foreign trade assistance, technology utilization, and management publications.

Management training. Training for those already engaged in business and for those planning to embark on business ventures is provided in formal courses of instruction, conferences, problem clinics, and workshops. In fiscal 1968 there were 2,558 instances of these programs, involving 84,326 enrollees. Cumulatively, from the start of the assistance programs through fiscal 1968, there had been 11,218 instances involving a total of 453,203 enrollees.

Management courses involve the largest number of enrollees among actual and prospective small business personnel. The courses typically cover from six to eight subject areas, with one meeting devoted to each subject. Follow-up courses are provided to deal with single management functions, such as personnel management, marketing, accounting, communications, and community relations.

Sponsorship of the courses is arranged jointly by the SBA and universities, colleges, distributive education units, trade and professional associations, and local business and civic organizations. The training sessions are organized and planned by SBA specialists, who provide administrative advice and guidance and furnish the instructional materials. For the actual teaching of the courses, experienced educators, successful businessmen, management consultants, accountants, lawyers, small business managers, and university professors are employed. In some communities, management courses are offered over local educational and commercial television stations.

Specialized courses are offered to meet the needs and interests of local communities. Among these are courses in federal contract administration, which cover bid preparation and submission, patents, contract requirements, negotiations, and disputes and appeals. Other special courses are provided in export trade. These courses include such topics as selling in foreign markets, correspondence, contracts, shipping, documentation, and credit and financing.

Management conferences are the second most popular of the formal training procedures. These conferences are cosponsored by local banks, chambers of commerce, educational institutions, trade associations, and civic groups. Typically, these are one-day conferences which include speakers, panel discussions, work sessions, and question and answer periods. The conferences are usually devoted to a single area, such as exporting, taxes, or crime prevention. The tax conferences, under the leadership of qualified tax experts, cover the

impact of taxation on business management decisions. The crime prevention conferences cover such problems as shoplifting, employee pilfering, burglary, forgery, and bad checks.

Problem clinics are small group meetings (5–15 persons) of manager-owners who are brought together by the SBA and cosponsoring organizations. Under the guidance of a leader supplied by the SBA, the participants learn from each other by sharing experiences.

Workshops for prospective small business owners are conducted by SBA specialists and cosponsoring groups for the purpose of reducing the high proportion of failures among new businesses. These workshops are significant because so many failures are due to inadequate preparation and analysis prior to the opening of a business.

The SBA workshops usually last one day. They emphasize the need for technical and managerial experience and for understanding what knowledge is required in the fields of financing, law, and management. Information is provided on sources of assistance. During the workshops the following subjects are discussed: initial capital requirements and sources of financing; locating a business; buying a going concern; types of business organization; business regulations, taxes, and insurance; and management needs of a small business.

Conduct of the management training programs is not left to chance. The SBA publishes a coordinator's kit for use by leaders and instructors in formal courses, workshops, problem clinics, and management conferences. The kit contains a basic guidebook for planning and conducting the programs, together with loose-leaf items issued from time to time. These items include case studies, lectures, outlines, methods for starting courses, and suggestions for speakers.

A series of booklets containing management subject presentations is available for instructors. These booklets are part of a package to aid the instructor in preparing sessions on a particular topic. The package contains a teaching outline, a lecture, visual aids, handouts for class members, case materials, suggested homework assignments, and a bibliography. Special instructive materials are available for the workshops for prospective small business owners, including directions for planning and conducting sessions, work sheets, handout materials, and visual aids.

The SBA has prepared a wide variety of visual

aids for use in training sessions. A set of 12 to 15 overhead transparencies has been prepared for each management subject presentation. Another set, coordinated with the lecture script, is available for the prospective-owner workshops. The SBA also makes 16-mm. movies and television tapes for use in training programs. These are available to all educational institutions and other organizations which cosponsor small business training programs with the SBA. Films and tapes are available not only on basic management subjects but also for training programs in foreign trade and crime prevention.

Management counseling. The function of SBA management counseling is to provide individual assistance to small business owners or to prospective owners. Information and advice are related to all phases of successful management of a going business, a business to be established, or a business about to be liquidated.

SBA management counseling is available under two programs: Counseling at the Local Level (CALL) and Service Corps of Retired Executives (SCORE).

Under the CALL program, SBA specialists in the 73 field offices provide individual counseling and information services to small businesses wherever they operate. These services cover marketing, accounting, product analysis, production methods, research and development, selling to the government, and foreign trade. Counseling is also available on specific types of business enterprises.

CALL specialists operate at field offices, at key business cities away from SBA offices, and even in remote places previously outside the usual operation area of an SBA field office. They take SBA services to locations where the public ordinarily has no easy access to a field office. The SBA's resources and services are thus made available to the distant, to the disadvantaged, and to those who have difficulty in getting to a regional office.

In April 1964 the SBA announced its intention to create a service corps of retired executives (SCORE) to advise small businessmen. In July 1964 the first pilot program was started in Washington, D.C. In October of the same year SCORE became a national program with 1,000 volunteers available for service. By 1969 there were 3,200 volunteers, and nearly 51,000 small businessmen had been assisted through the program.

In the SCORE program emphasis is given to the very small retail and service business unit unable to pay for expert services. Some small firms call for a SCORE review simply to get a fresh slant on operations and to make a going business more profitable. SCORE services are also available to assist an ailing business or to advise those who contemplate entering a business.

The collective experience of SCORE volunteers spans the full range of American enterprise. Volunteers include retailers, production analysts, office managers, lawyers, engineers, accountants, economists, bankers, advertising and public relations men, sales managers, wholesalers, controllers, plant managers, procurement specialists, management consultants, scientists, foreign trade specialists, product designers, and applied research experts. Their services are free except for actual expenses.

Foreign trade assistance. To increase small business participation in export trade, the SBA provides a program of counseling and training to give small businesses assistance and information on export opportunities.

SBA specialists work closely with the Department of Commerce in cosponsoring conferences and seminars in which trade experts from both government and private industry share their knowledge with businessmen and help them explore and assess foreign trade prospects. Small businessmen have an opportunity to hear and meet with experts in such allied fields as manufacturing, packaging, shipping, and distribution.

Technology utilization. The rapid expansion of technological growth presents a serious challenge to the entire industrial community. The SBA's Technology Utilization Program is designed to keep the small manufacturer informed about technological advances and to motivate him to apply relevant innovations and new processes, techniques, and materials.

Through conferences, seminars, workshops, individual counseling, and publications on new products, new processes, and new methods, the SBA's Technology Utilization Program attempts to interest small firms in acquiring the latest information and brings small manufacturers into contact with the wealth of scientific and engineering information generated by government-sponsored research and development.

Major contributors to this ever-growing accumulation are such agencies as the Department of Defense, the National Aeronautics and Space Administration (NASA), the Atomic Energy Commission (AEC), the Department of Agriculture, the Department of Labor, the Department of the Interior, and the Department of Health, Education, and Welfare.

The SBA selects and publishes technological innovations resulting from the research and development programs of NASA, the AEC, and other federal agencies. These unique collections of technical advances are directed to small manufacturers to encourage the application of new technology for their potential commercial benefit. Included in these publications is information about selected government-owned patents. A variety of new or improved products, processes, and materials which are available for private exploitation on a nonexclusive, royalty-free basis is described.

Management publications. Management assistance publications are designed to help small business owner-managers exercise efficient management of their companies. These publications discuss problems of practical interest to large cross sections of management as well as present facts and figures in brief, readable, nontechnical form.

The material in these publications is original. It is written by independent experts in many fields to fit the needs of small business. Most authors contribute their work as a public service. Nine different classes of management assistance publications are available for use by individual owner-managers and as support for SBA's various management assistance services. Five of these series, which are leaflet-type publications, are distributed free through SBA offices. Mailing lists are maintained for three of these series.

The series Management Aids for Small Manufacturers deals with functional problems in small plants and concentrates on subjects of interest to administrative executives. The series Small Marketers Aids is designed for retail, wholesale, and service firms on subjects of interest to administrative executives. The series Technical Aids for Small Manufacturers is intended for the top technical men in small concerns. In many firms the administrative and technical officials are one and the same; in others there may be technical specialists to supervise certain parts of a company's operations.

To clarify the differences in content and approach of the three aids series, here are a few typical titles: Management Aids—*Using Census Data in Small Plant Marketing, Checklist for De-*

veloping a Training Program; Small Marketers Aids—*Pointers on Display Lighting, Accounting Services for Small Service Firms;* Technical Aids—*Value Analysis for Small Business, Judging Your Electric Power Needs.*

The series Small Business Bibliographies is devoted to individual types of businesses or functions of management. Bibliographies were developed in response to needs revealed in SBA's counseling work, and their most direct application is in counseling.

Management Research Summaries is a series of leaflets which summarize the findings of reports published under the SBA grant research program. They cover a wide variety of subjects in the broad area of managing, financing, and operating small business enterprises.

Four series of booklets are for sale at nominal prices from the Superintendent of Documents, U.S. Government Printing Office, Washington, D.C. 20402. These include *Aids Annual,* a compilation of individual issues from the three aids series. *Management Aids for Small Manufacturers Annual, Small Marketers Aids Annual,* and *Technical Aids for Small Manufacturers Annual* contain publications from their respective series. Annuals furnish small business owner-managers with permanent reference sources for the material originally published in the three aids series.

The Small Business Management Series is devoted to more comprehensive discussions of special management problems in small concerns. Thirty-four such volumes have already been published. Typical titles include *A Handbook of Small Business Finance, Ratio Analysis for Small Business, Profitable Small Plant Layout,* and *Small Store Planning for Growth.*

The Starting and Managing Series describes the problems of starting and operating specific types of small enterprises. The single exception is the first volume in the series—*Starting and Managing a Small Business of Your Own*—which does not deal with a specific type of business. Representative titles include *Starting and Managing a Service Station* as well as *Starting and Managing a Small Dry Cleaning Business.*

The volumes of the Small Business Research Series contain the results of academic or other professional research projects in small business management. The primary audience is the individual serving small business rather than the owner-manager. Typical titles include *The First*

Two Years, Problems of Small Firm Growth and Survival and *Interbusiness Financing—Economic Implications for Small Business.*

*James S. Reed

TRANSFER OF TRAINING

The influence an existing habit exerts on the learning, retention, or performance of another habit is referred to as transfer of training. If the influence of the first habit improves performance on the second habit, positive transfer of training has occurred. In other cases the influence of the first habit may interfere with or inhibit the learning of the second habit; in such cases negative transfer of training has taken place.

To determine transfer of training experimentally, the scientists can have an experimental group learn Task A and then learn Task B. At the same time, a control group can learn Task B without having learned Task A. The amount and sign (positive or negative) of transfer are determined by comparing performances in Task B. If the experimental group surpasses the control group in the performance of Task B, positive transfer has occurred. However, if the control group performs better than the experimental group, negative transfer has taken place. The amount of transfer is indicated by the extent of the difference between the performances of the experimental group and the control group on Task B. No completely satisfactory measure of amount of transfer of training has been devised. However, the amount (percentage) of transfer can be measured by subtracting the control group's score from the experimental group's score in Task B, dividing the remainder by the control group's score, and multiplying the result by 100.

Significance of transfer. When transfer is defined in this rather simple and precise way, its significance in education may be overlooked. However, transfer is central to the entire learning process. This is because transfer does not merely occur from one relatively discrete task to another but is also involved in the cumulative trial-to-trial increments that are depicted by learning curves. Also, in a real sense, a failure in remembering may be thought of as the failure of transfer of training to occur between the learning situation and the circumstance under which remembering is to take place. Furthermore, in very many complex tasks the different parts of the same task interact with each other during the processes of learning and remembering according to general principles of transfer.

Even within the limited context of transfer from one learning situation to another, however, it should be apparent that the problem of transfer lies at the heart of the problem of education. Education takes place in school settings and academic environments, but it is hoped that the results of the educative process will be manifested in situations outside of school that may or may not bear a close resemblance to classroom situations. To the extent that transfer between the classroom and the outside world does not occur, educational effort has been wasted.

It is widely held that a most important goal of education has to do with teaching students how to learn rather than with imparting particular skills. In a rapidly changing world in which many skills swiftly become obsolete, it is obvious that the student who learns how to learn will have an advantage over the student who merely learns a set of specific habits and skills. Learning how to learn is an important facet of transfer.

Stimulus generalization. It should be carefully noted that transfer always involves two habits or aspects of habits, one of which exerts an influence on the other. In the preceding paragraphs, these habits have been labeled Task A and Task B. Each task or habit, moreover, can be analyzed into situational or stimulus (S) components on the one hand and response (R) components on the other. Thus, we could speak of Task A as being composed of S_1-R_1 and Task B as consisting of S_2-R_2.

One of the least complicated examples of transfer of training is the phenomenon of stimulus generalization. For example, in a simple learning situation a child might be trained to approach and open a particular small white box that contained, on each training trial, a piece of candy. If the child is now tested with another, similar box, he will probably approach and open this new box even though it has never been presented to him before. The greater the similarity between the box used in the test and the box that had been used in the original training, the greater the likelihood that the child will generalize his habit to the new situation.

The practical consequence of this state of affairs is that in simple training situations, such as teaching a child to obey a verbal command, it is not necessary to teach the child to make the proper response under every conceivable set of environmental circumstances, tones of voice, or sources of command. What is learned in one situation is very likely to be transferred to other similar situations without further training.

When stimulus generalization effects occur, they are always examples of positive transfer of training. This is because the same response is produced in both Task A and Task B (R_1 and R_2 are the same). Negative transfer effects can be produced by requiring the learner to alter his responses to familiar signals. If similar rather than identical stimuli are used in Task B, smaller amounts of negative transfer will be produced. Doubtless a great deal of confusion and a good many traffic accidents would be caused if the traffic regulations were suddenly changed to require drivers to stop at green lights and to proceed at red lights. Such a change would produce large amounts of negative transfer because the stimuli in Task A and Task B are the same, but the responses have been reversed.

General principles of transfer. Two general principles regarding transfer of training emerge. First, the amount of transfer of training, without regard to whether the transfer is positive or negative, will depend on the similarity of the stimuli eliciting the responses in Task A and Task B— that is, on the similarity between S_1 and S_2. Second, the sign of the transfer (positive or negative) will depend on whether the response learned in Task A is appropriate to Task B. If R_1 (in Task A) is appropriate in Task B, transfer will be positive. If R_1 is inappropriate in Task B, transfer will be either nonexistent or negative. Maximum negative transfer should occur when the stimuli eliciting the responses in Task A and Task B are identical and when the response learned in Task A is actually opposed to the response required in Task B (such as stopping instead of starting at the green light).

Effects between trials. Transfer also occurs between successive trials of practice or periods of training on the same task. In order for improvement to occur over a block of trials or practice periods, what is learned on Trial 1 must be remembered until Trial 2, and the circumstances of Trial 2 must be sufficiently similar to those of Trial 1 to allow transfer of training to occur. Trial-to-trial training within a single task is usually conducted under circumstances that are relatively ideal for the production of positive transfer. However, it is worth noting that the fastest improvement will occur under circumstances that maintain the constancy of training conditions from trial to trial as much as possible.

Effects within a task. In many practical training situations it is not possible, or even desirable, to maintain absolute constancy of the circumstances under which training occurs over several successive practice periods. Not only is a considerable amount of gratuitous environmental variation likely to take place, but the nature of the task itself is likely to change under the conditions of practice. The apprentice, the journeyman, and the expert are not doing exactly the same things with only different degrees of proficiency. What the concert pianist does differs in kind as well as in degree from what the beginning piano student does. In part, this qualitative difference develops during the career of each person as he acquires skill; thus, it can be inferred that the kind of practice that is appropriate for the novice is not necessarily the kind of practice that will be beneficial to the expert.

Part of the qualitative difference in performance associated with different levels of proficiency stems from the fact that complex skills tend to be made up of a number of component skills, and these components probably combine in different ways in the performances of the novice and the expert. A simple example of what is meant is involved in what is called response learning. Training involves the linking of responses to stimuli; however, in many cases, the response itself must be learned before such linkage can take place. Response learning or familiarization is a component part of most kinds of learning, verbal and motor, although response learning is perhaps easier to demonstrate in motor skills situations. For example, a novice baseball pitcher cannot learn to respond effectively to his catcher's hand signal to throw a curve ball until he has learned how to throw a curve.

Whole versus part problem. The problem of the composition of complex skills goes beyond the simple matter of stimulus familiarization and response learning. Another aspect of the problem of composition is involved in the question concerning the kind and amount of transfer that can be expected from practice on the parts of a task to performance on the whole task. A general answer cannot be given to this question because not all learning situations can be analyzed in terms that permit making appropriate measurements, but from the cases that can be analyzed some useful hints may emerge. In some skills the combination of the subskills into the whole performance can be stated rather simply. For example, many skills involve simultaneous performance with the right and left hands, and the whole performance will not be adequate unless both hands are performing properly at the same time. The pianist must play correctly with both hands simultaneously if the music is to be properly played. Under such circumstances it is frequently observed that if the right hand is performing correctly for a certain proportion of the time and the left hand is performing properly for another specifiable proportion of the time, the proportion of time that the whole performance will be correct can be predicted by multiplying the two proportions. Thus, in a two-handed tracking task if the right hand is "on target" .25 of the time and the left hand is on target .30 of the time, the subject is apt to be on target with both hands about .075 of the time. A piano student who can play correctly with his right hand .70 of the time and with his left hand only .20 of the time will have both hands performing properly at the same time about .14 of the time. Under these conditions, it is obvious that much greater improvement of the whole performance will result from improvement of the weaker component than from equal improvement of the stronger component. If the piano student improves with the left hand (only) so that he is correct with this hand .40 of the time, his total correct performance will approximately double by jumping from .14 to .28. However, if he improves his stronger hand performance (only) to an equal degree (from .70 to .90), his total performance will only increase from .14 to .18. Clearly, then, the most dramatic improvement will occur under conditions where the student is able to improve the worse rather than the better aspects of his performance. As a rule, most practice time should be devoted to attempting to overcome faults rather than to trying to improve further the areas of strength.

Remembering and forgetting. If transfer of training plays a dominant role in the acquisition of habits, it plays a no less important part in the subsequent performance and retention of the habits. The circumstances of remembering are frequently somewhat different from the circumstances of acquisition, especially in practical educational situations as opposed to laboratory situations for the study of remembering and forgetting. Thus, remembering will occur only to the extent that the stimulus components of the memory situation are adequate to elicit the proper responses to be remembered. Looked at in this way, the concept of memory is forced into the conceptual framework of studies on stimulus generalization and transfer of training.

From an educational point of view, one of the most serious deficiencies in the application of transfer theory to educational practice involves the lack of similarity between the situations under which skills are learned in school and the situations under which these skills must be applied later on. Frequently, school subjects are taught in abstract or artificial contexts that bear little apparent relation to the world outside the academy. It is not surprising to find, therefore, that people sometimes do not make the best use of the education they have received. For example, one of the faults of the "old" mathematics was that it was often taught in such a way that the student did not perceive the relationship between the kind of mathematical training he had received and the real-life problems that could be solved mathematically. It is not necessary that all educational effort serve some immediate end to which the training can be applied or that all learning be carried on under circumstances as close to real life as possible. However, skills should be learned under a wide enough variety of circumstances so that when an opportunity to apply a skill arises, the student is able to perceive that the skill is applicable in the situation.

Transfer of training plays an additional role in determining the amount of remembering. In some instances it can be shown that forgetting occurs because of active interference occasioned by negative transfer of training. When this transfer occurs as a result of the learning of material that is interpolated between the time of original learning and the later measurement of retention, psychologists speak of retroactive inhibition. Thus, in the experimental design shown in Table 1, if the experimental group is inferior to the control

Table 1

GROUP	ORIGINAL LEARNING	INTERPOLATED LEARNING	RECALL AND RELEARNING
Experimental	Task B	Task A	Task B
Control	Task B	———	Task B

Table 2

GROUP	FIRST LEARNING	SECOND LEARNING	TEST OF RETENTION
Experimental	Learn Task A	Learn Task B	Task B
Control	————	Learn Task B	Task B

group in the recall and relearning of Task B, retroactive inhibition has taken place.

If the interference is between a preexisting habit and the retention of a more recently learned habit, it is proper to speak of proactive inhibition. In the diagram of an experimental design for the study of proactive inhibition shown in Table 2, if the experimental group is inferior to the control group in the recall and relearning of Task B, then proactive inhibition has occurred.

Taken together, failure of stimulus generalization and negative transfer of training in the forms of retroactive and proactive inhibition are responsible for a great deal of the everyday forgetting of habits acquired both in and out of school.

Formal discipline and insightful learning. Early views of transfer of training were oriented toward the doctrine of formal discipline, which held that the proper business of education was to train the powers of the mind; the doctrine presupposed a type of transfer that was at once too great in amount and too general in character. The doctrine of formal discipline with its almost unbreakable ties to a faculty psychology did not last long into the twentieth century. However, the educational objectives implicit in the doctrine are still very much alive. We continue to hope that students will acquire in school habits that will generalize very widely and be applied to the solution of novel problems and to new learning situations. This kind of objective is implied when people state that education should teach people how to think or that the goal of education should be to teach the student how to learn for himself. One cannot dispute the desirability of these goals; it is necessary, however, to inquire into the best means for attaining them.

A closely related issue in the psychology of learning has been raised by the gestalt school, whose members have held that productive, creative, and permanent learning is achieved by insight rather than by blind rote acquisition. Much of the gestalt emphasis in education has been on the problem of arranging learning situations in such a way that the student can understand, see through, or have insight into the problem he is trying to solve. In the gestalt conception of learning, practice serves not so much to "stamp in" correct habits and "stamp out" incorrect ones (to use Thorndike's phrase) as it does to present the problem to the learner in such a way that there is an opportunity for insight to occur. The practice that takes place before the attainment of insight is generally held to be ineffective and irrelevant. Insight may be recognized by the fact that the resulting improvement occurs suddenly, tends to be permanent, and transfers readily to other similar situations. Of course, these views are in considerable opposition to more traditional and mechanistic views of learning such as those embodied in Thorndike's law of exercise and the general belief that practice makes perfect.

Almost from the first demonstration of insightful behavior in human learners, it has been possible to interpret such insights as examples of transfer of training. For human beings insight seems to occur most readily under circumstances where the learner can bring previously established habits and skills to bear upon the solution of a new problem. In this context, the utility of practice as a vehicle for carrying the conditions for insight can be reinterpreted; practice can instead be seen as a vehicle for aligning the conditions of stimulus generalization and positive transfer of training.

Insight, learning sets, and learning to learn. Harlow's work on learning sets (1949) provided the basis for an interpretation of insightful learning. In essence, Harlow caused monkeys to learn to solve many different visual discrimination problems, one after another. The early problems in the series tended to be solved by blind, rote, mechanical means. Progress tended to be uncertain and slow. However, monkeys that had previously solved a large number of discrimination problems were able to solve a new problem of the same general class rapidly and easily. Their performances on these later problems bore two of the hallmarks of insightful solution: suddenness and permanence of learning. These experiments on learning sets reemphasized the general importance of learning to learn as a factor in education.

The general implication of the work on learning sets is that the ability to solve a particular problem easily and efficiently (to solve it with insight) is greatly dependent upon having solved a considerable number of similar problems in the past. It may be suggested that the learning of rudimentary habits and the solving of simple problems by trial-and-error methods involve more than the simple learning of those habits and the solving of those problems; concomitantly, a more general expertise concerning the whole class of problems is being established that eventually will allow the student to exercise expert critical judgment and to solve specific individual problems with great facility. However, two limitations should be noted. First, although it may be expected that the cumulative transfer effects that are signalized in the formation of learning sets may not be confined to the exact class of problems under consideration, it would be imprudent to assume that there will be much generalization between widely different classes of problems. For example, it is probably not true that the attainment of great sophistication in the field of dramatic criticism will have a large positive transfer effect for the solving of mathematical problems. The second limitation is that although the work on learning to learn may establish an attractive objective for education, it must be remembered that the formation of learning sets rests upon the acquisition of many particular habits and rudimentary skills, the learning of which may be slow, tedious, and laborious, particularly in the beginning stages. In short, the findings on learning sets do not offer an easy solution to all of the problems of education.

Historical and bibliographical notes. The pioneer studies of transfer were those of Thorndike and Woodworth (1901a; 1901b). From the results of his investigations, Thorndike was able to advance his well-known theory of "identical elements," which held that one habit will be helpful in acquiring a second habit to the extent that the two tasks have elements in common. Problems of measurement and experimental design have been discussed by Gagné, Foster, and Crowley (1948) and by Murdock (1957). Similarity-of-task relationships in transfer of training have been studied very intensively. The early work of Robinson (1927) and Bruce (1933) as well as Osgood's theoretical summary of some of the similarity relationships (1949) deserve to be mentioned. Osgood's analysis has been extended and made more specific by Martin (1965). A summary of the findings on stimulus generalization can be found in Hilgard and Marquis (1961), and the role of inter-

ference in remembering and forgetting is discussed by Underwood (1957) and by Underwood and Postman (1960). The classical gestalt work on insightful learning is by Köhler (1925), and Katona (1940) has extended some of the findings to the human learning situation. Harlow's paper on learning sets (1949) is the classical study in this area. Postman and his colleagues (Postman 1964; Postman & Schwartz 1964; Keppel & Postman 1966; Postman & Stark 1967; and Schwenn & Postman 1967) have published a series of experiments on learning to learn. General summaries of the work on transfer of training and a discussion of some of the problems associated with work in this area can be found in Battig (1966), Deese and Hulse (1967), Ellis (1965), Hall (1966), McGeoch (1952), Osgood (1953), and Underwood (1966).

BIBLIOGRAPHY

BATTIG, WILLIAM F. 1966 "Facilitation and Interference." Edward Alfred Bilodeau, ed., *Acquisition of Skill.* New York, Academic Press. Pages 215–244.

BRUCE, ROBERT WALLACE 1933 "Conditions of Transfer of Training." *Journal of Experimental Psychology,* 16, no. 3:343–361.

DEESE, JAMES EARLE, AND STEWART H. HULSE 1967 *The Psychology of Learning.* 3rd ed. New York, McGraw-Hill.

ELLIS, HENRY CARLTON 1965 *The Transfer of Learning.* The Critical Issues in Psychology Series. New York, Macmillan.

GAGNÉ, ROBERT M., HARRIET FOSTER, AND MIRIAM E. CROWLEY 1948 "The Measurement of Transfer of Training." *Psychological Bulletin,* 45, no. 2:97–130.

HALL, JOHN FRY 1966 *The Psychology of Learning.* Philadelphia, Lippincott.

HARLOW, HARRY F. 1949 "The Formation of Learning Sets." *Psychological Review,* 56, no. 1:51–65.

HILGARD, ERNEST ROPIEQUET, AND D. G. MARQUIS 1961 *Conditioning and Learning.* 2nd ed. Revised by Gregory Adams Kimble. New York, Appleton.

KATONA, GEORGE 1940 *Organizing and Memorizing: Studies in the Psychology of Learning and Teaching.* New York, Columbia University Press. A reprint was published in 1967 by Hafner.

KEPPEL, GEOFFREY, AND LEO POSTMAN 1966 "Studies of Learning to Learn: III. Conditions of Improvement in Successive Transfer Tasks." *Journal of Verbal Learning and Verbal Behavior,* 5, no. 3:260–267.

KÖHLER, WOLFGANG 1925 *The Mentality of Apes.* Translated from 2nd rev. ed. by Ella Winter. New York, Harcourt.

MARTIN, EDWIN 1965 "Transfer of Verbal Paired Associates." *Psychological Review,* 72, no. 5:327–343.

McGEOCH, JOHN ALEXANDER 1952 *The Psychology of Human Learning.* 2nd ed. Revised by Arthur L. Irion. New York, Longmans.

MURDOCK, BENNET B., JR. 1957 "Transfer Designs and Formulas." *Psychological Bulletin,* 54, no. 4:313–326.

OSGOOD, CHARLES E. 1949 "The Similarity Paradox in Human Learning: A Resolution." *Psychological Review,* 56, no. 3:132–143.

OSGOOD, CHARLES E. 1953 *Method and Theory in Experimental Psychology*. New York, Oxford University Press.

POSTMAN, LEO 1964 "Studies of Learning to Learn: II. Changes in Transfer as a Function of Practice." *Journal of Verbal Learning and Verbal Behavior*, 3, no. 5:437–447.

POSTMAN, LEO, AND MARIAN SCHWARTZ 1964 "Studies of Learning to Learn: I. Transfer as a Function of Method of Practice and Class of Verbal Materials." *Journal of Verbal Learning and Verbal Behavior*, 3, no. 1:37–49.

POSTMAN, LEO, AND KAREN STARK 1967 "Studies of Learning to Learn: IV. Transfer From Serial to Paired-Associate Learning." *Journal of Verbal Learning and Verbal Behavior*, 6, no. 3:339–353.

ROBINSON, EDWARD S. 1927 "The 'Similarity' Factor in Retroaction." *American Journal of Psychology*, 39, nos. 1–4:297–312.

SCHWENN, ELIZABETH, AND LEO POSTMAN 1967 "Studies of Learning to Learn: V. Gains in Performance as a Function of Warm-Up and Associative Practice." *Journal of Verbal Learning and Verbal Behavior*, 6, no. 4:565–573.

THORNDIKE, EDWARD L., AND R. S. WOODWORTH 1901*a* "The Influence of Improvement in One Mental Function Upon the Efficiency of Other Functions. II. The Estimation of Magnitudes." *Psychological Review*, 8, no. 4:384–395.

THORNDIKE, EDWARD L., AND R. S. WOODWORTH 1901*b* "The Influence of Improvement in One Mental Function Upon the Efficiency of Other Functions. III. Functions Involving Attention, Observation and Discrimination. *Psychological Review*, 8, no. 6:553–564.

UNDERWOOD, BENTON J. 1957 "Interference and Forgetting." *Psychological Review*, 64, no. 1:49–60.

UNDERWOOD, BENTON J. 1966 *Experimental Psychology*. 2nd ed. New York, Appleton.

UNDERWOOD, BENTON J., AND LEO POSTMAN 1960 "Extra-experimental Sources of Interference in Forgetting." *Psychological Review*, 67, no. 2:73–95.

ARTHUR L. IRION

TRANSFORMATIONAL GRAMMAR

The term "transformational grammar" refers to any of several closely related views of the nature and study of language and of linguistic description. It is also used to refer to any particular linguistic description which conforms to these views. Finally, it may refer to a grammar (of any language) which contains at least one so-called transformational rule or its equivalent.

The notion of transformational rule arose in the early 1950's when Noam Chomsky, then a junior fellow at Harvard University, attempted to formulate the grammar of a natural language as a so-called formal system of rules and found a number of inadequacies in the prevailing view that the syntactic structure of a sentence is just its constituent structure—that is, a labeled bracketing of the sentence's word or morpheme components into hierarchically arranged, nonoverlapping phrases.

The motivations for and efficacy of these notions can, of course, be appreciated only within the context of the transformational grammarian's conception of the goals of linguistic research. He assumes that the main desideratum is to construct a theory of linguistic intuitions—that is, first, an account of what an ideal, expert user of a language must know in order to interpret utterances correctly or to create arbitrary utterances in his language and, second, an account of how that knowledge is acquired by infants. In such a psycholinguistic approach, one must distinguish clearly between the formal knowledge a person must have, his so-called linguistic competence, and the behavior he may exhibit in which some of this knowledge is put to use, his so-called linguistic performance. Thus, to speak correctly, a person must be able to distinguish between well-formed utterances of his language and those of other languages (or of no language), between the sounds of his language and other sounds, and between the way meanings are expressed in his language and other possible ways. However, his actual speech is determined only in part by this linguistic knowledge, since characteristically a person's performance is subject to many other factors, such as memory span, motor skill, attentiveness, state of health, familiarity with the topic, emotional stress, fatigue, and ambient noise conditions, none of which can be viewed as features of one's language per se.

Moreover, no two speakers of a language have exactly the same conception of what belongs to that language, and accordingly we must suppose that an exact description of one speaker's competence will differ, albeit only slightly, from that of another's.

The transformational grammarian favors a well-known strategy of research—namely, that of model-building and constant search for corroboration of models by measuring their predictions against observations. The grammar of a language is viewed as a predictive theory of sentencehood in that language. Since there is no "longest" sentence in a natural language, there are an infinite number of sentences to be described. The grammar assigns at least one description to each sentence, but the grammar must itself be finite in length if it is to represent a portion of a person's knowledge. It follows that the grammar must contain productive rules which construct a large, indefinite number of different descriptions from a finite number of different elements. This feature of productive rules accounts, then, for a speaker's ability to understand or use an indefinite number of novel utterances of his language. Such a view leaves unanswered such questions as how a person manages to understand utterances which are grammatically incorrect and badly pronounced, fragmentary, or even nonsensical when taken literally, but it does provide a basis upon which these important problems might someday be approached.

An enormous body of evidence has been assembled, from English principally but also from a variety of other languages, to support the claims of transformational grammarians. Although few details of their formulations remained unchallenged and unaltered during the ten years of feverish activity in this field of research from 1960 to 1970, no serious objection succeeded in altering the basic notions.

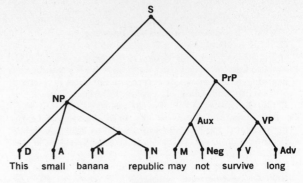

Figure 1

ABBREVIATIONS

A	adjective	NP	noun phrase
Adv	adverb	P	preposition
AdvP	adverb phrase	Pass	passive agent
AP	adjective phrase	Pfct	perfective aspect
Aux	auxiliary phrase		phrase (HAVE +
BE	copula verb		PPl)
Cmp	complementizer	PP	prepositional
	of embedded S		phrase
Comp	comparativizer	PPl	past participle
	in AP	PrP	predicate phrase
D	determiner	Prt	particle
Deg	degree modifier	PS	passive auxiliary
	of A		phrase
Gen	genitive suffix for	Q	question marker
	nouns	S	sentence
Gnd	gerund suffix	Tns	tense suffix
HAVE	perfective verb	V	verb
M	modal	VP	verb phrase
N	noun	∅	null symbol
Neg	negative particle		

Immediate-constituent analysis. Traditionally, the syntactic structure of a sentence has been conceived of as a hierarchy of nonoverlapping (immediate) constituents, representable in the form of a labeled bracketing or branching diagram. This claim—namely, that the phrase structure of a sentence is just its constituent hierarchy—succeeds in accounting for a small number of linguistic intuitions. For example, for a large family of cases the constituents are just the most easily substitutable and paraphrasable parts of the sentence, in terms of which, presumably, we

understand the meaning of the whole. Thus, in the sentence *This small banana republic may not survive long*, we can easily replace or paraphrase such parts as *this small banana republic* (the tiny peasant country), *banana republic* (Latin nation), *may not survive long* (probably won't last), or *survive long* (endure); but other sequences of words from the sentence are not thus paraphrasable, such as *small banana* or *republic may*. Such facts are nicely represented by the branching diagram shown in Figure 1, since the easily extracted functional parts are each dominated by one of the labeled nodes in the tree. But in other cases (for example, the sentence *Hasn't this theory been rejected?*), a bracketing unfortunately adds little or no insight, since few elements can be grouped with a neighbor into a functional unit.

Another virtue of the conception of syntactic structure as representable by a single labeled bracketing is that certain cases of grammatical ambiguity and convergence in form can be thus explained. For example, in the utterance *They could have been returning veterans*, a speaker of English recognizes two different sentences, paraphrased differently as either *They could have been some returning veterans* or *They could have been returning some veterans*. This fact is exactly captured by the plausibility of the claim that an English grammar would automatically assign two different constituent-trees to such an utterance (Figures 2a and 2b).

But again there are a great many other sentences which do not seem to be elucidated by representation as a labeled bracketing of constituents. For example, there is no justification for assigning two different trees to the sentence *Bill likes Jill more than Will*, since whatever argues for a particular immediate-constitutent diagram

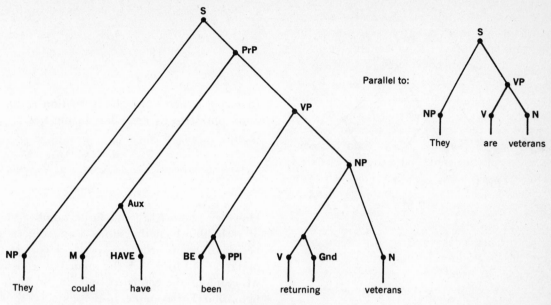

Parallel to:

Figure 2a

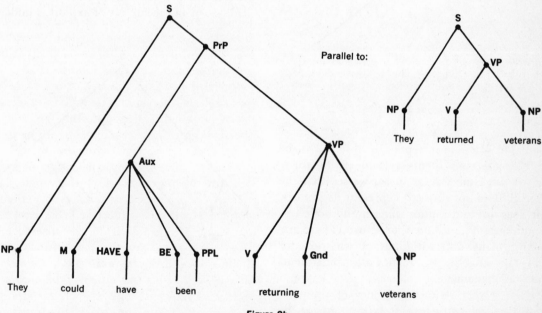

Parallel to:

Figure 2b

in the interpretation *Bill prefers Jill to Will* will also argue for it in the alternative interpretation *Bill prefers Jill, but Will prefers her less so*.

Similarly, the branching diagrams of the sentences *Mongolia is anxious to cooperate* and *Mongolia is awesome to contemplate* are identical, and the great difference in the way they are interpreted cannot plausibly be attributed to the meanings of *anxious, cooperate, awesome,* or *contemplate,* for many other words can replace

these, but there is always this same kind of difference in the interpretation which is given to the two utterances.

Another reason to suspect that this mode of grammatical description is inadequate is the ubiquity of sentences containing functional phrases which are *not* immediate constituents. Compare the two synonymous sentences shown in Figures 3a and 3b. Since we interpret 3a in part in terms of the meaning of a node V_1, namely,

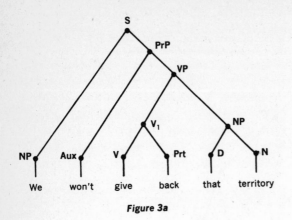

Figure 3a

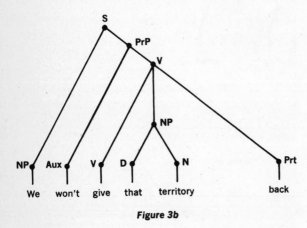

Figure 3b

return, and since we interpret 3b in terms of the same ultimate constituents, related among themselves in the same way as in 3a, we see that the tree of 3b does not correctly represent its phrases, for it does not and cannot contain any node corresponding to V₁, *give back*, or return. There are, in short, many different kinds of sentences for which the analysis by immediate constituents would be inadequate.

Finally, a very serious deficiency of the view that the syntactic structure of expressions can be captured by an analysis into immediate constituents is the impossibility of characterizing certain indispensable grammatical functions or relations. For example, there is no doubt that we interpret sentences in part in terms of the subject and object relations which are inherent in certain pairs of noun phrase and verb. But nothing in the immediate-constituent structure of sentences marks those relations except for the simplest declaratives of the form noun phrase plus verb plus noun phrase, in which we might construe the subject relation to be the relation which exists between

a noun phrase and its neighbors in the tree

In such a sentence the object relation is that of a noun phrase to its neighbors in the tree

However, there is an indefinite number of cases of verbs in which the subjects and objects must be identified in order to specify a correct interpretation but for which the immediate-constituent structure of the sentence contains no such configuration. For example, in the sentences shown in Figures 4a and 4b the configurations of immediate constituents and their syntactic types are identical, yet in 4a the subject of *exploit* is understood

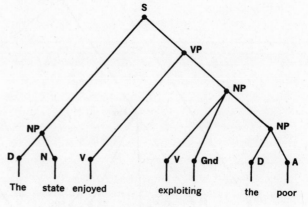

Figure 4a

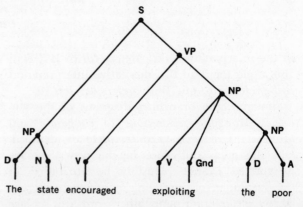

Figure 4b

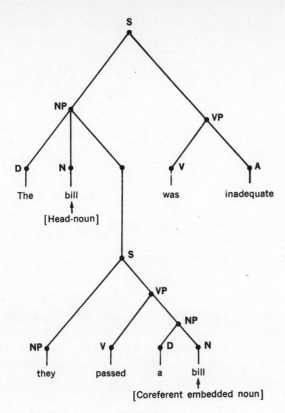

Figure 5

Briefly, the use of a transformational rule presupposes the existence of an underlying abstract representation of each sentence to the derivation of which the rule is applied. This representation reveals the constituent structure of the sentence in a branching diagram of labeled nodes. Sequential diagrams serve to specify less abstract representations of that sentence by rearranging, altering, or deleting certain branches of its diagram. For example, we may interpret a relative-clause modifier of a noun to be a subordinated sentence inside the (dominating) noun phrase. Then, the sentence *The bill they passed was inadequate* may be construed to contain an embedded sentence *They passed a bill.* A more abstract representation of the original sentence, its so-called deep structure, might be sketched as in Figure 5.

Thus, the general transformational rule which connects this underlying representation to the more concrete version would specify that whenever a noun phrase in the embedded sentence is coreferent to the head-noun of the noun phrase, it is shifted to the front of its sentence and converted to the corresponding WH-word, in this

to be the noun phrase *the state,* while in 4b the subject of *exploit* is not *the state* but *someone* (else).

Transformational analysis. For these and other reasons, Chomsky proposed that the syntactic form of a natural-language sentence can be represented only by means of a more abstract device than an immediate-constituent tree, though the virtues of such an analysis cannot easily be given up. In particular, he would first assign to a sentence a more abstract tree, representing much more directly its meaning; then he would formulate in the associated grammar of the language the transformational rules which connect these two trees. Thus, the grammar of a natural language is no longer a set of complex node-expanding rules alone but rather a set of much simplified node-expanding rules of formation (to generate the deep-structure trees) and a set of tree-deforming rules of transformation (to map deep-structure trees onto surface structures). Correspondingly, the syntactic structure of a sentence generated by such a grammar would no longer be only a single hierarchy of its constituents but rather a set of such trees at various levels of abstraction.

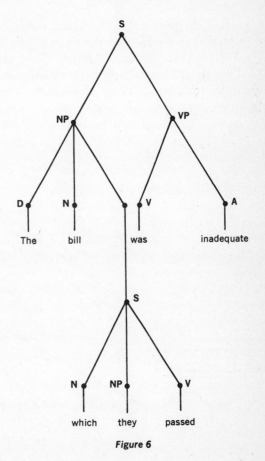

Figure 6

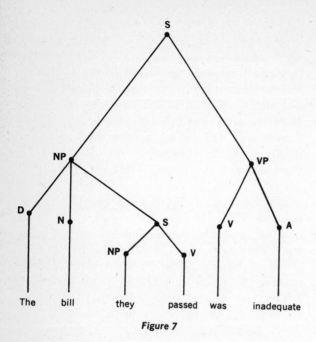

Figure 7

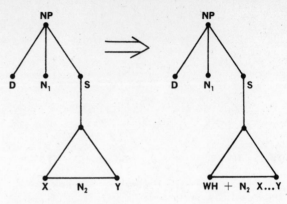

N_1 is coreferent to N_2
X,Y are variables
WH + N_2 represents the WH-word *which*

Figure 8

case *which*, yielding the structure depicted in Figure 6.

A subsequent rule would permit the deletion of this WH-word under certain conditions, in this case yielding the pronounceable surface structure of the sentence in question, as shown in Figure 7.

The rule of WH-shift then captures the grammatical derivations generalized by the illustrations in Figure 8, from which many details have been omitted.

As evidence in favor of this new view, we might reformulate several of the difficulties encountered in immediate-constituent analysis to see how a transformational analysis might illuminate them. The phrase structure of the utterance *Hasn't this theory been rejected?* is revealed by assuming that it has an underlying deep structure of the form depicted in Figure 9.

Four main transformational rules apply to this utterance: passive, agent ellipsis, question, and affix, yielding the successively less abstract representations depicted in Figures 10a, b, c, d. The only phrase of the sentence which has remained

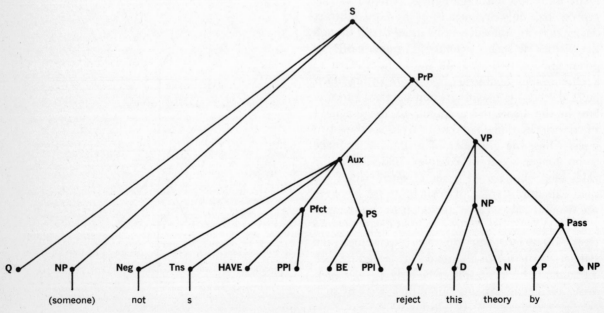

Figure 9

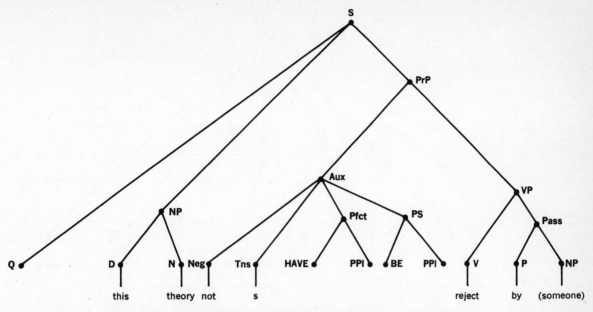

Figure 10a. *By passive rule, interchanging subject-NP and object-NP*

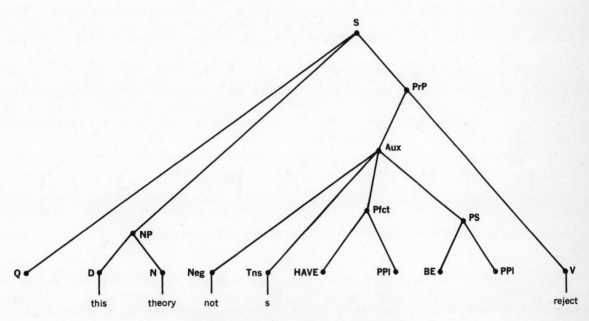

Figure 10b. *By optional deletion of agent phrase*

unaltered during the derivation is, then, the patient–noun phrase *this theory* (that is, the so-called logical object of the verb, the receiver of the action), which ends up as the subject of an interrogative passive. The semantically significant phrase structure is given by 9, but the pronounceable sentence is given by 10d. Such a derivation and its underlying deep structure and associated transformational rules are justified just in case each of these elements of the analysis is separately and independently supported by insightful applicability to a large number of other cases—that is, just in case each element permits the formulation of some more or less deep generalization.

The case of *Bill likes Jill more than Will* is quite transparent to any traditional grammarian, and the relevant rules of ellipsis are not difficult

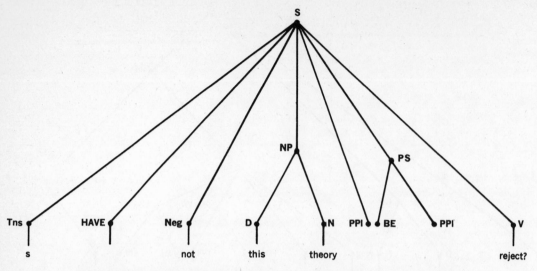

Figure 10c. By question rule, interchanging subject-NP and first elements of auxiliary

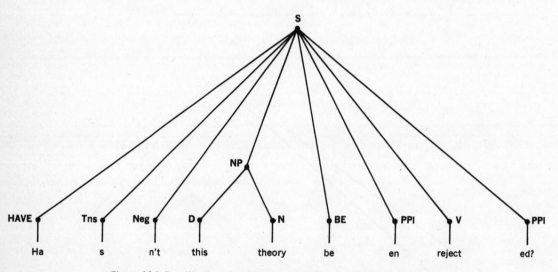

Figure 10d. By affixation of endings on immediately following verb bases

to justify, though there is still some question as to the underlying structure. One reasonable, though perhaps insufficiently abstract, view would be that underlying this utterance are two different complex structures, as shown in Figures 11a and 11b. Each contains an adverb of degree which includes a comparative modifier, itself containing an embedded sentence, which would be different in the two cases.

The transformational rules involved would be (principally) comparative—ellipsis and affix—yielding the stages of derivation shown in Figures 12a, b, c, d. Thus, we can say that a person can interpret this utterance in two ways, because he may associate to it two different organizations of

phrases, namely 11a or 11b, which happen to be mapped by otherwise motivated rules of ellipsis for repeated elements into the same pronounced utterance.

Leaving aside the cumbersome details, we may interpret the difference between *Mongolia is anxious to cooperate* and *Mongolia is awesome to contemplate* to devolve upon the contrast in deep structure and derivation between the trees shown in Figures 13a and 13b. At the same time, we see how it happens that in 13a *Mongolia* is understood as the agent of *cooperate*, while in 13b it is construed as the patient of *contemplate*. It is also now easy to formulate well-supported rules and constraints to permit the derivation of *It is*

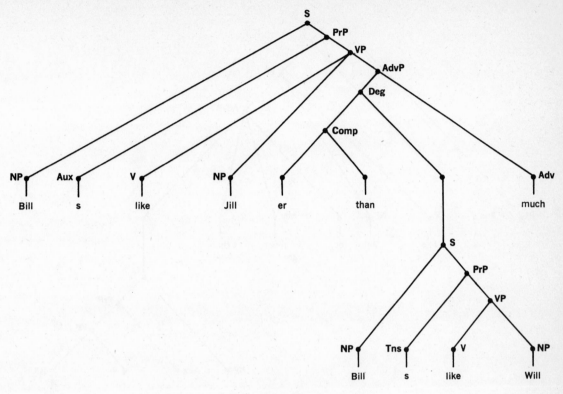

Figure 11a

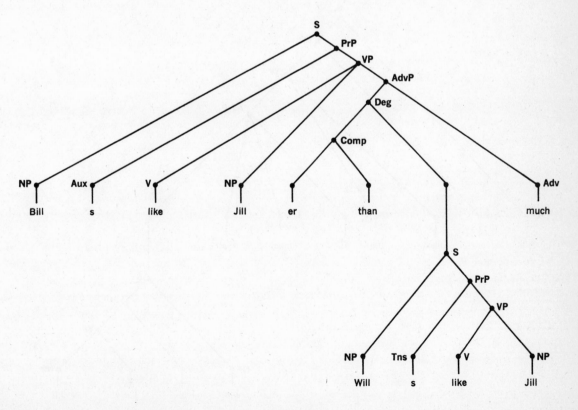

Figure 11b

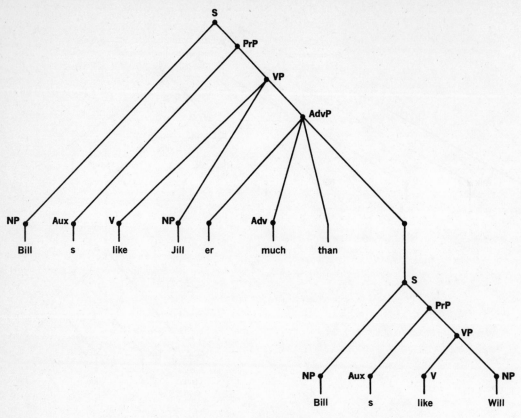

Figure 12a. *From 11a by comparative shift of than + s to end of sentence*

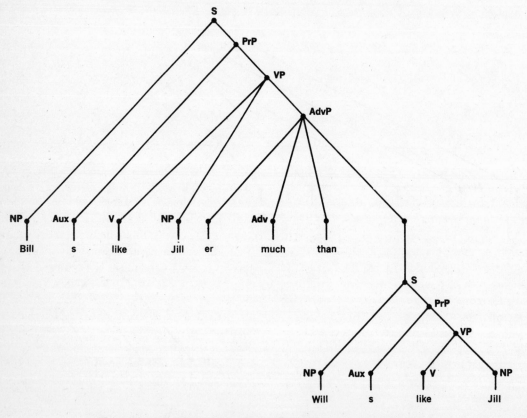

Figure 12b. *From 11b by comparative shift of than + s to end of sentence*

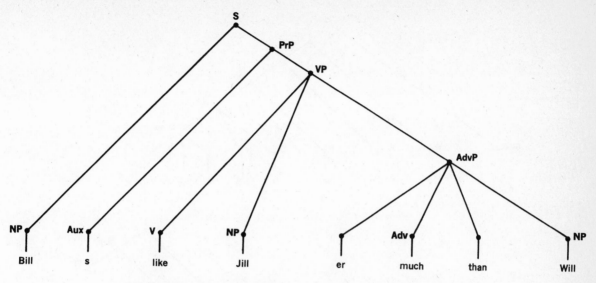

Figure 12c. *From 12a or 12b by ellipses of coreferent NP's and identical verbs*

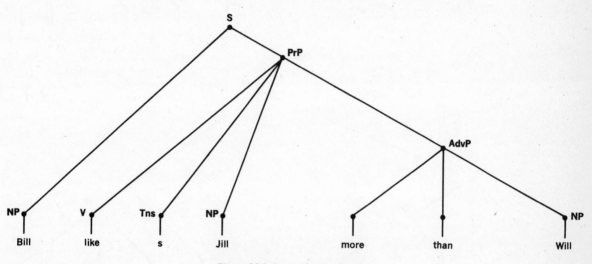

Figure 12d. *From 12c by affixation*

awesome (for someone) to contemplate Mongolia but not for **It is anxious for Mongolia to cooperate (with someone)* or for **It is anxious (for someone) to cooperate with Mongolia.*

Continuing, we will now be able to represent the fact that 3a and 3b are interpreted identically by formulating independently justified rules to derive them from the same underlying structure, as shown in Figure 14; the relevant rule shifts the second member of a complex verb like *give back* out beyond the nominal object.

Finally, the difference between 4a and 4b is elucidated by a justified derivational contrast beginning with the deep structure shown in Figures 15a and 15b.

In such transformational analyses the applica-

bility of a rule may in general be subject to certain conditions. These conditions include the presence of a certain category type in the tree—as in 15a and 15b where V_x is distinguished from V_y or in 13a and 13b where A_x is distinguished from A_y—or the requirement that a certain category must be coreferent with another—say, for ellipsis, as in 12a or 12b to 12c. As analyses are made more and more subtle to account for more sophisticated distinctions, it appears that in the deepest trees distinctions must be represented which are closer and closer to what we would ordinarily and intuitively interpret as semantic properties of words and expressions. We must employ such notions as stative-dynamic, *verbum dicendi*, adjective of feeling, verb of motion,

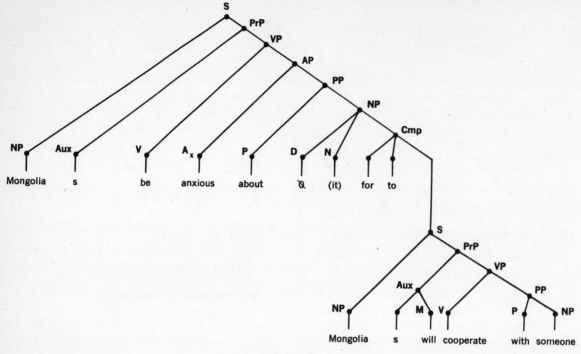

Figure 13a

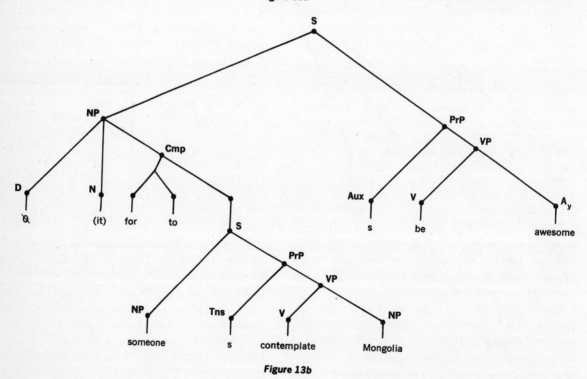

Figure 13b

locative, and human-nonhuman. Thus, the deeper the syntactic representation provided, the more it comes to resemble a picture of the meaning of a sentence.

Another point of importance in understanding the so-called transformational approach concerns the significance of linguistic universals. Since the interpretation of an observation depends critically upon the theoretical framework within which it is supposed to play a role (just as the evaluation

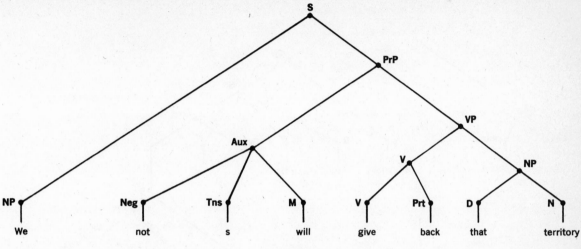

Figure 14

of a theory depends critically upon what observations it is intended to account for), it follows that at every turn the linguist must not only seek to formulate rules to describe observed linguistic phenomena but must simultaneously attempt to justify his overall conception of linguistic description. That is, his interpretation of given observations will depend essentially upon his basic, and sometimes not yet clearly stated, assumptions about the form of all natural languages, his view of what is to be taken as universally true of all languages.

For example, we note that there are no reflexive passives in English—that is, an English speaker will not generally accept as grammatically well formed such utterances as (a) *Himself was shaved by John* or even (b) *John was shaved by himself.*

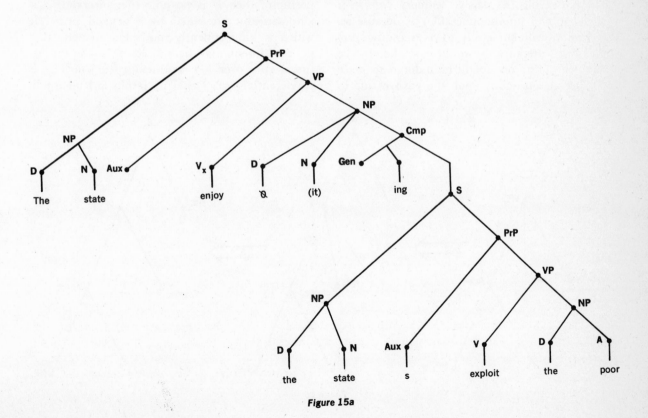

Figure 15a

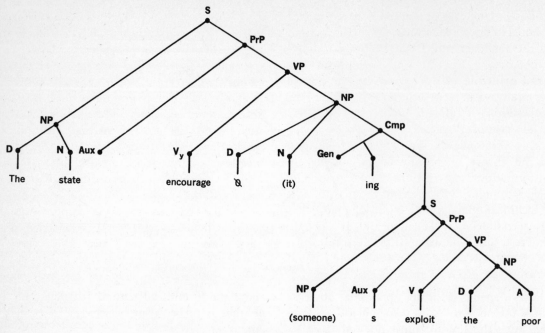

Figure 15b

Utterance *a* may be eliminated from the output of a grammar of English, say, by ordering the reflexive rule after the rule which assembles passives, when it will no longer apply, either because the subject-form *he* will not undergo the reflexivization (leaving the passive sentence *John was shaved by John* unpronounceable) or because reflexivization will not apply to a preceding pronoun. But utterance *b* would not thereby be eliminated. Thus, one might be induced to place some special constraints upon the passive rule to prevent utterance *b*. However, if the rule has roughly the form depicted in Figure 16 (in which the first operation shifts the subject NP_1 into an agent phrase [Agent] with preposition *by*, and the second shifts the object NP_2 to the vacated subject position), then it is possible that utterance *b* is automatically prevented by a general principle which is independently motivated—namely, that no constituent may be shifted by a transformational rule over a constituent with which it is coreferential (see Postal in Jacobs & Rosenblum

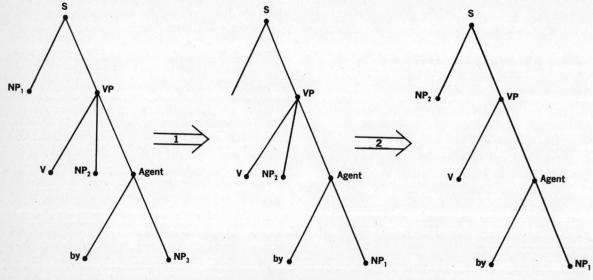

Figure 16

1968). But for the case of utterance *b*, the underlying subject and object *are* coreferential, for that is just the condition which determines the choice of *self*. Thus, a linguist who believes in this universal principle will not constrain the passive rule specially to prevent utterance *b*; rather, the first operation is already prohibited by this universal "crossover" principle.

In this brief sketch nothing has been said about the theory of pronunciation adopted in a transformational description of a language, the so-called phonology. Phonological description is more technical than syntactic and therefore less readily accessible to the layman and of less general interest. Suffice it to say that the transformational phonologist has shown how a more general account can be given of pronunciation and pronounceability by adopting a more abstract view of how underlying forms and the application of ordered and, in part, transformational rules determine pronunciation (see Chomsky & Halle 1968).

Unsolved problems. Supporters of any worthwhile view are apt to give the impression that they believe themselves to have solved all relevant problems. But the hallmark of any substantial field of knowledge is that it ultimately generates more and harder problems than it solves. The questions now raised by transformational grammarians are baffling and sophisticated. Some of the basic notions underlying this field of research have been entertained and accepted for many centuries. For example, the idea that the internal organization of concepts in a sentence is not revealed directly by the sequence of words itself goes back at least as far as the period of Cartesian logic and grammar and probably to the sixteenth-century scholastics.

Many difficult and baffling problems remain unsolved: the relation between logic and sentences; the correct representation of derivational morphology in word formation; and the analysis of conjunctive expressions, of illocutionary or performative expressions, or of nominal compounds. At the end of the 1960's there was a serious conflict between two schools of thought: proponents of a transformationist view, with a generative semantics and elaborate use of much ramified and very abstract deep embedding of simple trees, and proponents of a lexicalist view, with an interpretive semantics and less abstract tree structure but greater elaboration of the lexicon and greater use of lexical features.

A most important result of the transformational grammatical studies since 1960 has been the opening up of new areas of research. As we deepen our analyses of natural-language sentences and formulate deeper and wider generalizations about language, we can hypothesize more and more specifically about man's inherent linguistic capacities, about the presuppositions concerning linguistic form which every baby must bring to his language-learning tasks, and, finally, about the a priori conceptions in terms of which men view their world.

Perhaps specific practical applications may someday be discovered for this knowledge, though at present no one can realistically claim that grammatical analysis, transformational or otherwise, is directly useful for any practical purpose. (Thus, there is no reliable evidence known to support the frequent claim that foreign languages may be taught better, more effectively, or faster on the basis of one view of grammatical structure than of another.)

On the other hand, those insights which are to be gained from a knowledge of linguistics may be of inestimable value to a language teacher or an information-retrieval engineer in covert and unspecifiable ways. Finally, it seems reasonable for high school students to be told as much about the results of contemporary linguistic research as they would normally learn of modern physics or economics, for language is man's most intrinsic and characteristic trait.

BIBLIOGRAPHY

BACH, EMMON 1964 *An Introduction to Transformational Grammars.* New York, Holt.

BACH, EMMON, AND R. HARMS 1968 *Universals in Linguistic Theory.* New York, Holt.

CHOMSKY, NOAM A. 1957 *Syntactic Structures.* The Hague, Mouton.

CHOMSKY, NOAM 1965 *Aspects of the Theory of Syntax.* Massachusetts Institute of Technology, Research Laboratory of Electronics, Special Technology Report No. 11. Cambridge, Mass., MIT Press.

CHOMSKY, NOAM A. 1966 *Cartesian Linguistics: A Chapter in the History of Rationalist Thought.* New York, Harper.

CHOMSKY, NOAM A. 1966 *Current Issues in Linguistic Theory.* New York, Humanities Press.

CHOMSKY, NOAM A. 1966 "Topics in the Theory of Generative Grammar." T. A. Sebeok, ed., *Current Trends in Linguistics.* Vol. 3: *Theoretical Foundations.* The Hague, Mouton. Pages 1–60.

CHOMSKY, NOAM A. 1968 *Language and Mind.* New York, Harcourt.

CHOMSKY, NOAM A., AND MORRIS HALLE 1968 *The Sound Pattern of English.* New York, Harper.

FODOR, JERRY A., AND JERROLD J. KATZ 1964 *The Structure of Language: Readings in the Philosophy of Language.* Englewood Cliffs, N.J., Prentice-Hall.

JACOBS, RODERICK A., AND P. S. ROSENBLUM 1968 *English Transformational Grammar.* With an epilogue by Paul Postal. Waltham, Mass., Blaisdell.

LANGACKER, RONALD W. 1968 *Language and Its Structures: Some Fundamental Linguistic Concepts.* New York, Harcourt.

LANGENDOEN, D. TERENCE 1969 *The Study of Syntax.* New York, Holt.

LEES, ROBERT B. 1960 *Grammar of English Nominalizations.* Publication No. 12. Bloomington, Indiana University Research Center in Anthropology, Folklore, and Linguistics. Reprinted by Mouton in 1964 and 1966.

LENNEBERG, ERIC H. 1967 *Biological Foundations of Language.* With appendices by Noam Chomsky and Otto Marx. New York, Wiley.

REIBEL, D. A., AND S. A. SCHANE 1969 *Modern Studies in English: Readings in Transformational Grammar.* Englewood Cliffs, N.J., Prentice-Hall.

ROBERT B. LEES

TRANSPORTATION AND SCHOOL BUSING

School buses are operated by most school systems in the United States. These vehicles have played a significant role in the development of American education, and they are indispensable to the modern system of school operation. They have brought educational opportunities to rural children, aided in the tremendous suburban development since 1945, and are now contributing to remaking inner-city districts by transporting pupils for interchange between schools.

History. Pupil transportation developed from the cooperative efforts of individual families to provide horsedrawn transportation for their children to schools beyond walking distance from their homes. In 1838, Horace Mann enunciated the necessity of pupil transportation by pointing out that it was impossible to have a schoolhouse located near the homes of all pupils. By 1869, Massachusetts had authorized taxation to raise transportation funds. All states had publicly supported school transportation services by the early 1920's.

The first vehicles used for pupil transportation were privately owned wagons or carriages. They were supplied by designated individuals through cooperative agreement among interested families and became a part of the public school system. Farm wagons were often converted for pupil transportation by adding full-length seats and protective canvas covers. Such vehicles were used by enterprising individuals who contracted to transport children of the community to a neighboring school for a negotiated fee. In the early 1900's special school wagons offering such luxuries as upholstered seats, glass windows, and coal-fired heaters for use on winter days were commercially manufactured.

By the second decade of the twentieth century motor vehicles were being used, such as private automobiles and trucks with special bodies for seating purposes. Automobiles were sometimes used to tow trailers which had been built for transporting children.

Shortly after World War I truck-manufacturing plants in the United States began to make truck chassis which were convertible to pupil transportation use. Such chassis, outfitted with bodies built by local blacksmith shops or by enterprising school bus operators, became a common sight on the nation's developing system of roads and highways.

During the period of rapid expansion in the use of motor vehicles, made possible largely through the use of truck chassis, body construction developed through the use of a variety of designs. Many units were constructed by owner-drivers and consisted of little more than wooden frames covered with canvas for protection against the weather. Some were built by master craftsmen who designed body structures strong enough to support an overturned vehicle without collapsing. Manufacturing plants began to specialize in truck bodies to be used for pupil transportation. This led to a wide range of vehicles in terms of suitability, safety, and comfort for children. School boards began to specify construction standards as a safety measure. Consequently, hundreds of variations in specifications for buses developed, and assembly-line production was thereby made practically impossible. For example, buses to be used in different states, even in different districts within a state, had to be hand produced because of required differences in door dimensions, the number and kind of windows permitted, seat height and construction, and a great number of other variants. Because of these conditions, it appeared that modern technology could not be used to mass-produce acceptable buses.

In 1939 representatives of state education agencies were invited to attend a national conference with representatives of chassis and body manufacturers for the purpose of establishing bus construction standards which would be acceptable throughout the United States (Featherston & Culp 1965). At the conference, representatives of state education agencies agreed on basic construction standards for school buses. The agreement, which was quickly adopted by most states, enabled manufacturing concerns to build uniform specialized vehicles for pupil transportation. (National school bus chrome, a distinctive color used only for painting school buses, is an example of one of the standards recognized in most areas of the country.) This cooperative effort has continued. National conferences are held periodically to enable state representatives to update technological standards for school buses.

Organization of transportation services. The boards of education responsible for school systems containing a number of individual schools with transported pupils should authorize a special staff for managing, operating, and supervising the transportation program. Such staff would include superintendents or directors of transportation and the associates needed to handle the responsibilities of buying, operating, and maintaining school buses; designating routes to be used and pupils eligible to ride the buses; developing safety procedures; training and supervising drivers; and managing a complex system which must have daily consideration.

While organization patterns for transportation services may vary considerably from one school system to another, two essential elements of such organization are quite basic: (1) there must be specific designation of the officials responsible for transportation affairs and (2) the officials must be competent to deal with the many highly specialized problems in the transportation service. Individuals responsible for transportation services must have a broad knowledge of educational policies and procedures and possess the highly specialized background essential in managing a transportation fleet, operating adequate safety programs, and providing the overall management which is essential to an acceptable system of busing. Unfortunately, provisions for the adequate education of transportation officials are entirely too limited.

In small school districts and in private schools buses are generally managed and supervised by administrative officers, such as the principal of the school or a designated associate. Transportation services must receive the administrative and managerial attention demanded by such a large operation costing tremendous sums of money and involving the safety and welfare of large numbers of children. The principal reason for the lack of appropriate attention springs from the fact that the bus service began primarily from the efforts of parents to get their children to schools, while other aspects of the educational program were developed through the efforts of professional teachers and administrators. Modern developments have tended to overcome this, but transportation is still generally considered an auxiliary part of the school program.

The most important aspect of pupil transportation is that it has extended educational opportunity to rural children. Distance is no longer a factor in the availability of education. It is not unusual for children to bus 30 miles to a consolidated school. In sparsely settled areas of the country children ride buses more than 100 miles a day to attend modern consolidated schools where a wide variety of educational services are available. The result of this development has been to provide comprehensive educational programs for rural children which differ little from those provided by urban and suburban schools.

But transportation is not limited to rural areas. Since 1948 the greatest growth in pupil transportation has been recorded in urban and suburban areas. In such places traffic congestion makes it virtually impossible for children to walk to school, and public demand has developed for increased services by government agencies, including school systems. Moreover, school integration or efforts to secure cultural-social-ethnic balances in school systems have created a large demand for transportation or school busing in city and suburban districts. Under such conditions school buses often serve a dual purpose; they transport children from their homes to school centers and then transport pupils from one school campus to another to satisfy enrollment policies adopted by boards of education and their supporting communities.

In addition to transporting children to and from school, buses transport pupils to athletic contests and musical performances, to sites of historical interest, and on field trips of every description.

Busing for racial balance. Since 1965 considerable attention has been given to providing racial balance in schools, particularly in areas where de facto segregation prevails. (De facto segregation is caused by geography or similar conditions as contrasted with de jure segregation— that caused by definite plans or actions by controlling boards of education or other governmental units.) Busing students for neighborhood exchange has been inaugurated in a number of school systems, particularly in large metropolitan areas, but there is still considerable controversy about the legality of such bus services. The courts have not laid down clear definitions of what boards of education may do or must do in cases where de facto segregation occurs. The weight of available evidence, however, indicates that school authorities must assume the burden of initiating plans and procedures for desegregation in the public schools and that the role of the courts is to determine whether such actions and procedures comply in good faith with constitutional requirements. In the absence of court decisions which would halt or prohibit bus services between schools for the purpose of establishing racial mixture or balance, it appears that the service is likely to expand in the years ahead.

Service for parochial school students. Tax-supported transportation services were initially provided only for students attending public schools. This practice was based on the traditional separation of church and state and with only scattered or sporadic challenges continued to be almost universally accepted until the close of World War II. Gradually, more and more interest was expressed in the concept that transportation represented a service to pupils and not to schools, the so-called child benefit theory, which derived from a U.S. Supreme Court decision in 1930 permitting public funds to be used to purchase textbooks for parochial school pupils (*Cochran* v. *Louisiana State Board of Education*, 281 U.S. 370). This concept and the fact that pupil transportation was frequently a voluntary service offered by boards of education gave support to the view that boards of education were, therefore, free to provide services for parochial school students. On the basis that transportation is a service to children, local boards of education began to provide bus services for parochial school students, in some instances specifying that the service would be provided only when circumstances would not require additional operating expenses. Such busing on a permissive basis gradually spread, and efforts to invalidate the practice largely failed.

In 1947 a New Jersey law permitting the expenditure of public funds for transportation of parochial school pupils was challenged, and the U.S. Supreme Court ruled in *Everson* v. *Board of Education of Ewing Township, N.J.* (330 U.S. 1) that the statute did not violate the First and Fourteenth Amendments to the Constitution. Subsequently, state courts found that state constitutions did not permit the use of state tax funds for transporting private or parochial school pupils, and states began to amend constitutions and pass laws specifically authorizing bus services for nonpublic school attendance. This proved to be a popular movement, and in 1967, Wisconsin became the 22nd state to provide publicly supported transportation for children attending parochial schools.

Many states still deny tax-supported transportation services to children who attend parochial schools, but the extent of the practice of authorizing such services in the United States indicates that there will be changes in this area.

Instructional use of buses. The school bus has proven itself not only as a means for making educational opportunity available to students but also as an instructional tool of high potential. As noted above, buses transport thousands of pupils to athletic contests and musical performances, to sites of historical interest, and on field trips. It is not unusual to see a school bus hundreds of miles from its home town district as it transports pupils to destinations chosen by those who plan educational experiences for children. In addition to serving as a means of transportation, the bus-riding experience itself offers many educational opportunities to learn traffic safety and individual responsibility for one's conduct and behavior.

Trends. School bus design, manufacture, maintenance, operation, and supervision are steadily becoming more highly specialized and professional. Manufacturers are spending large sums of money in developing better equipment which will provide greater comfort and safety for student passengers. School boards are providing professionals to direct and manage transportation systems. Drivers are being trained for the highly skilled job of safe and effective driving of buses. Specialists are being employed to make purchases, provide adequate records and accounting, and administer all other aspects of a transportation program which is steadily growing in magnitude.

Bus services have been extended to atypical children and those who have educational needs which can be met only by limited, special schools. Those involved in adult education programs and compensatory education programs, as well as service groups closely allied to education, such as scouting organizations, are being increasingly served by the use of buses owned and operated by public school systems.

BIBLIOGRAPHY

FEATHERSTON, E. GLENN, AND DELOS P. CULP 1965 *Pupil Transportation.* New York, Harper.

DELOS P. CULP

TRUSTEES

See GOVERNANCE IN HIGHER EDUCATION.

TUNISIA

Education in Tunisia is organized in accordance with the Education Reform Law of November 4, 1958, which stipulates that education is to be provided for all Tunisians regardless of race, sex, creed, or social status. The law also stipulates that education is compulsory for all children between the ages of six and 12 and that it is free at all stages.

The Secretariat of State for Education is generally responsible for everything concerning education and has full authority over all educational institutions. However, other ministries supervise some institutions. Among these ministries are the Secretariat of State for Public Works and Housing and the Secretariat of State for Public Health.

Tunisian education is centrally financed. The education budget has risen considerably since the late 1950's, and in the mid-1960's it accounted for approximately 25 percent of the national budget.

Structure. Although the state has not assumed the responsibility of providing public schools for the preprimary stage, there are independent bodies which establish, supervise, and finance such schools.

Children enroll in the six-year primary school when they are six years old. At the end of the sixth grade they take an examination for the primary education certificate. In 1959 the state instituted a ten-year plan designed to increase enrollment in primary education.

Postprimary education is of two types: terminal intermediate education and secondary education. To enter either type of postprimary schooling a student must take an entrance examination. The aim of terminal intermediate education is to provide students with further general education and to prepare them for vocational activities in a three-year program in the general section, commercial section, or industrial section. Some of the intermediate schools give a fourth year of practical training or greater specialization. Education at the intermediate stage ends with the intermediate education certificate.

Secondary education aims at developing the mental and practical abilities of youth and preparing them either to work in specialized activities needed by the country or to pursue higher education. The secondary stage is divided into two stages, each of which lasts three years.

The course in the first year of the first stage is of a general nature. At the beginning of the second year, the student enters one of three sections: the general section, the economic section, or the industrial section.

A student in the second stage of secondary education may choose from a variety of sections. The student who chose the general section at the first stage now selects the modern literary, classics, science, mathematics, or primary teacher-training section. Study in most of these sections ends in the baccalaureate certificate (secondary education certificate). However, study in the primary teacher-training section ends in the diploma of completion of pedagogical studies.

A student who chose the economic section at the first stage must select either the economic section or the commercial section in the second stage. Study in both of these sections ends in the economic baccalaureate certificate.

A student who chose the industrial section at the first stage enrolls in the mathematics techniques section or the industrial techniques section. Study ends in the diploma in industrial education at the end of the fifth year and the technician's diploma at the end of the sixth year.

Students who leave the secondary education program after completing only the first stage obtain a secondary school diploma.

Before Tunisia obtained its independence in 1955, higher education had been available only in such educational institutions as El Zeitouna University, the Higher Studies Institute, and the Tunisian School of Administration. In 1961 the

State Secretariat of Education founded the University of Tunis, which now has faculties of arts and humanities, mathematics, physics and natural sciences, law, economics and political science, medicine and pharmacy, and Islamic law and jurisprudence. Study in these faculties (with the exception of the faculty of medicine and pharmacy) lasts four years and ends in the bachelor's degree.

Among the many institutes and specialized higher schools now affiliated with the University of Tunis are the Dramatic Arts School, the Higher School of Commercial Studies, the Bourguiba Institute of Living Languages, the Audiovisual Aids Center, the Atomic Physics Center, the Social Studies Research Center, and the Economic and Social Research Center. Among the institutes not affiliated with the University of Tunis are the Higher School of Law, the Higher School of Agriculture, the National School of Administration, and the Tunisian School of Fine Arts.

Teacher education. Primary school teachers are prepared in the primary teacher-training section of the secondary stage of education. However, teachers at the intermediate and secondary stages are prepared in the École Normale Supérieure, the École Normale de Professeurs Adjoints, and the Centre National d'Étude et de Formation Pédagogique. These three institutes are affiliated with the University of Tunis.

The program of study in the École Normale Supérieure lasts three years and prepares future secondary school teachers. Students are selected from the holders of the baccalaureate by means of a competitive examination. This school grants the B.A. degree in arts, education, and science and education. The École Normale de Professeurs Adjoints gives a two-year course for future teachers of the intermediate schools and the first stage of the secondary school. Students are selected from the holders of the baccalaureate or any secondary school diploma. Study leads to the certificat d'aptitude de professeur adjoints.

The Centre National d'Étude et de Formation Pédagogique, which is affiliated with the École Normale Supérieure, gives a one-year course which leads to a certificate in higher studies in pedagogy.

Adult education and literacy. After independence, Tunisia started to utilize popular enthusiasm to combat illiteracy. Teachers were called on to volunteer to teach the illiterate. However, this attempt was not very successful. In 1958 the state launched the first organized literacy campaign. Yet by the early 1970's, illiteracy among Tunisians over the age of ten amounted to nearly 69 percent.

Methods and materials of instruction. The primary school curriculum includes Arabic, French, arithmetic, practical skills, applied works, photography, songs, physical training, environmental studies, and moral and social education.

The curriculum of the terminal intermediate school for the general section includes Arabic, French, English, history and geography, religion and civic education, mathematics, science, drawing, laboratory work, physical training, and an optional subject.

The curriculum of the industrial section for boys is the same as that of the general section; however, the hours of study devoted to laboratory work and technical drawing are increased.

The curricula of the scientific and mathematical general sections of the secondary school include a second foreign language, history, geography, mathematics, sciences (including practical work), physical education, and philosophy.

Trends. Since its reform in 1958, Tunisian education has stressed the ancient and modern linguistic and cultural heritage of Tunisia and has paid attention to the history and geography of the Islamic world in general and the Arab Maghreb in particular. Further, it has kept pace with the needs of the country and the developments of the modern world. Finally, both primary and postprimary education have been made more widely available to compensate for past insufficiencies.

WAHIB I. SAMAAN

TURKEY

Formal education in Turkey consists of primary school (*ilkokul*) for five years; intermediate school (*ortaokul*) for three years; upper-secondary school (*lisé* or trade school) for three years; and higher or professional training, which ranges from two years of training for teachers of intermediate schools to six years for those aspiring to become physicians.

Beyond the primary school, which is by law free and compulsory for all children between the ages of seven and 12, there are two systems of secondary education. The general educational system includes the intermediate schools, the *lisés*, and the universities; the vocational-technical system encompasses trade schools, vocational institutes, and higher technical and professional schools and technical universities. The primary goal of the first system is to provide general education in a formal academic setting. The main goal of the second system is to train technicians, secretaries, and others who aspire to enter trade and technical occupations. The first type of education is intended to be theoretical, the second practical or applied. There is much overlapping between these two systems, and students may transfer from one system to the other.

The great majority of students attend public schools. However, there are private schools, which at the secondary level are divided into three types: private Turkish schools, minority schools (for example, Greek, Armenian, and Jewish), and foreign-operated schools. With the exception of the minority schools, these private schools are attended by Turks wishing to enter a prestigious university either in Turkey or abroad. Although the sources of income of these schools are private or foreign, the Ministry of Education closely supervises their curricula, examinations, and other important administrative and organizational matters; the ministry also gives or withholds permission to open and operate new schools.

Since 1923, when the Turkish republic was proclaimed, there has been phenomenal growth in education as measured by attendance and general literacy rates. During the 1927–1928 academic year there were only 497,300 full-time students attending schools at all levels. By the 1960–1961 school year the total school enrollment had increased to nearly 3.4 million. In 1927–1928 only 3.7 percent of the population was in school; by 1960–1961 the figure had risen to 12.2 percent. The most marked increase in attendance has been in primary schools, where enrollments jumped from 27.6 percent of the six-to-11 age group in 1935 to an estimated 81 percent in 1964. Some of the results of this increase in schooling have also been impressive. For example, in 1927–1928 only 10.6 percent of the total population was literate; by 1960–1961, 39.6 percent of the population was literate (Kazamias 1966; Kazamias & Massialas 1965).

Organization and administration. The Ministry of Education supervises and controls all public education in the republic of Turkey. The minister of education has almost absolute power over decisions affecting the administration of all schools. In discharging this power the minister is assisted by two permanent undersecretaries and several directors who are in charge of primary, secondary, higher, vocational, technical, private, physical, and teacher education. The directors are also in charge of the nation's fine arts activities, antiquities, museums, and libraries. The directors of primary and secondary education are very important because they control either directly or indirectly the administrative organization and curriculum of the schools; in addition, they make all personnel decisions for these schools. The director of secondary education deals directly with each secondary school, whereas the director of primary education exercises control through the provincial inspectors.

Primary-school inspectors, who are connected with the Ministry of Education through the governor of each of the 67 provinces, perform a variety of services which include inspection, research, instruction, and guidance. Overall, the complicated network of inspection and control includes ministerial inspectors-general, directors of education (with authority in a specified department or region), primary-school inspectors, deputy inspectors, and education officers (operating at the subprovincial levels, known as *kazas*). The local school director or principal (*müdür*) is the ministry's lowest supervisory agent. His responsibilities include inspecting the daily classroom work of the teachers and making sure that course outlines are both available and carefully followed. In addition, the principal meets regularly with the teachers to ensure that educational policy is followed; at the end of each school year he evaluates the performance of each teacher for promotion or transfer purposes.

In the formation of policy the minister of education is assisted by the Supreme Council of Education, which consists of high-ranking officials in various ministries, rectors of the universities, deans of faculties, inspectors, school principals, and teachers. Meeting at least once every three years, the council concerns itself mostly with educational policies dealing with curriculum matters and school regulations. The Board of Education and Training functions as a permanent advisory committee whose responsibilities include the examination of textbooks, the preparation of courses of study, and the critical review of proposed educational legislation.

With the exception of private schools, which generate their own revenue, the primary financial responsibility for all schools rests with the central government. Although provincial and village governments contribute toward public-school expenses (for example, paying the salaries of the nonteaching school personnel), such matters as teachers' and administrators' salaries, travel costs, and medical expenses are borne by the state. Expenses of building and maintaining public primary schools are borne by the province or local community, although the central government often assists in the building of rural schools. Since 1936 there has been a movement toward a centralized system of financing public education. In 1935 only 47 percent of the total school expenditure was underwritten by the central government; by 1948 this figure had risen to 88 percent. There has also been a movement to allocate a higher percentage of the national budget to education. Between 1932 and 1963 the percent of the national budget given to education rose from 9.3 to 16.3.

Curricula and methods of instruction. Under the Ottomans, Turkish education was the domain of the Islamic religious doctors known as *ulemas*. The primary school (*mekteb*) historically was closely supervised by the local imam (the parish priest) and the *muhtar* (village headman), and was expected to emphasize Islamic instruction and the Ottoman language and literature. The *medrese*, the prevalent religious higher school, provided an Islamic education, was free, and prepared students for the priesthood. Both the *mekteb* and the *medrese* reflected the outlook and the goals of the Ottoman society and symbolized "reaction, conservatism, and a static state of affairs" (Kazamias 1966, p. 92).

An effort to centralize the schools and to provide a European education was begun in the early part of the nineteenth century. In the mid-1850's two important schools were created which pushed forward the movement toward Westernization— the Mülkiye and the Imperial Lisé of Galatasaray, in Istanbul. Both institutions functioned as training schools for government officials and were open to all ethnic groups in the empire. The *lisé*

was patterned after the French *lycée* which traditionally stressed an academic curriculum. This *lisé* became the model for all subsequent Turkish *lisés*. The French influence on Turkish education was introduced primarily through this institution, although in the 1960's the American concept of the comprehensive school began to gain support, particularly among American-trained Turkish educators.

Primary schools. The five-year primary schools in Turkey emphasize the emotional, social, and intellectual development of the child. According to the directorate of primary education, the objectives of primary education include learning hygienic ways of living, utilizing the senses more efficiently, developing the ability to make sound judgments, learning scientific methods of thinking, grasping the principles of a good family life, and developing patriotic and democratic feelings. Furthermore, the school is expected to instill in the young Turkish child pride for being the son of a great nation with an honorable history. The Turkish educational system makes an attempt to meet these ambitious objectives through a program of studies including study of environment (for only the first three years of primary school), Turkish, history, geography, civics, natural sciences, domestic science (offered only during the fourth and fifth years), mathematics, drawing, manual work, writing, and music. Special instruction in agriculture is offered to children in rural primary schools, and physical education is offered to those attending urban schools. The primary school pupil has, on the average, 26 hours of formal instruction a week. Much of this time is given to Turkish-language instruction (about one-third of the total time); agriculture occupies one-fourth of the time in the rural schools, and mathematics takes about one-fourth of the time in both rural and urban schools.

Pupils are promoted from one grade level to the next on the basis of marks received during the year. At the end of the fifth year all children are required to take school-leaving examinations; if they pass them, they receive the primary-school leaving certificate (*ilkokul diplomasi*), which automatically admits them to the intermediate school. The examinations stress ability in the Turkish language (the only subject where both oral and written tests are required), but all other subjects are included.

With the exception of the differences between

rural and urban schools, there are virtually no variations in the course of study in primary schools throughout the country. The weekly timetables which are based on the 1948 curriculum are uniformly applied to schools in all the provinces; no deviation is allowed. Teachers are issued detailed instructions concerning examinations, daily lessons, holidays, and other matters relating to curriculum and instruction. A teacher's guide lists the objectives of education and elaborates the pedagogical, social, and psychological principles upon which these objectives are based.

Secondary schools. Secondary education is divided into intermediate schools and upper-secondary schools. The objectives and curricula of the three-year intermediate schools (*ortaokuls*) include developing national consciousness and feelings of patriotism; protecting the values of Turkish culture and history; respecting the constitution and the laws of the Turkish republic; improving the ability to read, write, and speak correctly; choosing a suitable job; and developing moral character.

The instructional program to be followed in all intermediate schools is based on a 32-hour weekly schedule which provides for instruction in Turkish, history, geography, civics, mathematics, physics (offered only during the last two years), chemistry (only in the last two years), natural sciences, elements of commercial practice, agricultural work, gardening, handwork (for boys) or domestic work (for girls), a foreign language (French, English, or German), physical education, drawing, music, and free work (team work conducted in the library, classroom, laboratory, garden, or workshop). Humanistic subjects consume by far the largest portion of the instructional program (about 35 percent). The second largest allotment of time is that given to science and mathematics (21 percent). Offerings in commerce and in agriculture consume 6 percent of the time. The emphasis on Turkish language and culture is not unrealistic, especially since the reforms of the Kemalist revolution sought to "Turkicize" the people by providing a new set of Turkish ideals (not Ottoman), by eliminating religion from state-related activity, and by introducing a new Turkish Latin alphabet to replace the Arabic script. The curriculum of the schools as a whole sought to implement the principles of the revolution by making Turks more conscious than they

were under the Ottomans of their unique cultural heritage and pre-Islamic past.

The *ortaokul* comes under the authority of the director of secondary education, who controls this type of school through the appointment of principals, lesser administrators, and teachers. In all cases the provincial governor or provincial director of education acts as the representative of the central government. If the *ortaokul* is part of a secondary school which includes the upper levels, it is run by the principal of the upper school. Most intermediate schools are coeducational, except in large cities where relatively large enrollments permit separation.

To be promoted from one grade to the next, a student must maintain passing marks in each class. If the student fails two or three of the approximately 14 courses he takes, he has to repeat the entire year of studies. At the end of the three-year intermediate school the students take an examination on all of the subjects. Success on this examination enables them to obtain the intermediate-school leaving certificate, which is necessary in order to continue in an upper-secondary school, a three-year teacher-training school, or a technical or commercial school.

The *lisé*, which is the nation's predominant and most-sought-after upper-secondary school, has its roots in the Ottoman past. A school originally known as *sultani* (patterned after the French *lycée*, the English grammar school, and the German *gymnasium*) was designed to provide a general, humanistic education for a small group of elite youth who aspired to enter the universities or to be recruited into the imperial bureaucracy. Mektebi Sultani, the first *lisé* in Turkey, was established in 1868. Later, this institution came to be known as the Imperial Lisé of Galatasaray; it has continued to enjoy great prestige and certain privileges (for example, both Turkish and French are used as languages of instruction).

During the first year of the three-year course of studies at the *lisé*, all courses apply uniformly to all students; during the second and third years, *lisé* classes are divided into science and arts sections. Turkish language and literature is offered all three years and, as in the primary and intermediate schools, consumes a disproportionate amount of the weekly instructional time. The following courses are also offered at all levels and in all sections of the *lisé*: history, geography, mathematics, natural sciences, physics, chemistry, foreign languages, physical education, and military training. Psychology is offered during the second year, and philosophy, logic, and sociology are offered the third. Students must continue taking the foreign language they elected in the intermediate school. Students may also choose to study a second foreign language, drawing and handwork, or music.

In addition to the *lisé*, which still maintains elitist characteristics because it generally recruits pupils from the middle or upper socioeconomic strata, there are vocational, technical, and commercial schools. These schools offer programs at the intermediate and upper-secondary levels. The technical institutes for girls provide a five-year postprimary course. The curriculum of these schools is the same as that of the *ortaokuls* except that more courses for the girls' roles as housewives are offered (for example, dressmaking, the domestic arts, and child care). The technical institutes for boys admit primary school graduates and are divided into two cycles. In the three-year cycle—or intermediate technical school—more than half of the instructional time is devoted to such general subjects as Turkish, history, and geography; the remainder of the time is given to practical and professional subjects. The second cycle, which lasts two years, offers some courses in general education but emphasizes training in the different branches of industry. Forging, laminating, and joinery (woodworking and metalworking) are compulsory subjects for all boys. Students are expected to spend at least 75 percent of the time in vocational subjects and practical courses. The subjects and the nature of the work vary according to the section in which students are enrolled—metallurgy, mines, electricity, or textiles. Upon completion of the two-year course, students may enter an industry as specialized workmen or foremen, or they may enter a *lisé*, their work in the institute being considered the equivalent of that in an intermediate school.

In addition, there are schools for imams, commercial schools, and normal schools for teachers. The normal schools offer the equivalent of a secondary school education (both middle and upper) and prepare primary school teachers. Secondary school teachers are graduates of a university or a teacher-training college.

Although the government has tried to expand and upgrade vocational and technical education, this type of schooling continues to attract students from lower classes who are intellectually less competent than those attracted by the academic schools. Unless society begins to place a higher premium on this type of education, the government will not be able to change the image of these schools.

Higher education. Most matters concerning university education come under the directorate of higher education. Higher technical or specialized schools are under other appropriate directorates of the Ministry of Education, except for such schools as the School for Nurses and the School of Navigation, which come under the ministries of public health and communication, respectively.

Higher education is offered in four universities, two teacher-training colleges, seven pedagogical institutes, one commercial teacher-training college, one technical teacher-training college for women, two technical teacher-training colleges for men, four colleges of commerce and economics, seven secretarial schools, 26 technician schools, the School for Applied Fine Arts, the Academy of Fine Arts, and the Higher Islamic Institute. Robert College of Istanbul, founded by Protestant missionaries in 1863, follows the American pattern and issues bachelor's and master's degrees in liberal arts, commerce, and engineering.

The institutions which enjoy university status and special legal privileges are the four general universities—the University of Ankara, Ataturk University, the University of the Aegean, and the University of Istanbul—and the three technical universities—the Technical University of Istanbul, the Technical University of the Black Sea, and the Middle East Technical University. The most prestigious institution of all is the University of Istanbul, which was established after the fall of Constantinople in 1453. This university has faculties of medicine, law, letters, science, economics, and forestry; schools of dentistry, pharmacy, and foreign languages; and institutes of journalism and economic development.

In order to be admitted to a university a student must hold a secondary-school leaving certificate (*olgunluk*), granted upon successful completion of the course of study and passage of an examination. University entrance examinations are also required of all secondary school graduates. The competition for admission into a university is very strong because there are very few places for students in higher education. It has been estimated that less than 2 percent of the school-going population is enrolled in higher educational institutions (Kazamias & Massialas 1965).

Trends. There has been a concerted effort on the part of all Turkish governments to democratize education—to make education available to more and more Turkish citizens and to provide practical or vocational education for those who are interested.

Despite these efforts, however, there are still some social and educational conditions which make the quest for democratization extremely difficult. For example, there are great inequalities in educational opportunities between urban and rural populations. In ten nonurban provinces less than 5 percent of the total population attends primary school as compared to the national average of 10 percent. In these regions less than 30 percent of the school-age population attends school. It has been estimated that in the early 1960's one-third of all Turkish villages had no schools (Eastmond 1964). Overall, it has been estimated that only 65 to 75 percent of the appropriate age-group is enrolled in primary school (*ibid.*).

The dropout rate is also serious. For example, only 50 percent of the children enrolled in the first grade of primary school in 1956–1957 reached the fifth grade. Similar attrition rates exist in secondary schools. The ones most affected by this are girls and students who live in rural communities. Little progress has been made in increasing the school enrollments of girls. The enrollment in Turkish schools as a whole is 36 percent female and 64 percent male. The boy-girl enrollment disparities are more striking in the postprimary schools, where only about 23 percent of those attending are girls.

The elitist character of the *lisé* has been mentioned above. A study conducted in 1962–1963 reinforced the notion that the *lisé* was designed for affluent youth who aspire to white-collar positions (Kazamias 1966). For example, of the sampled students who were enrolled in the *lisés*, 44 percent had parents with white-collar occupations as opposed to 17.5 percent whose parents were skilled or unskilled workers. Likewise, a low proportion of students in comparison to the distribution of the total population came from agricultural backgrounds. Seventy-seven percent of the students in the sample aspired to a white-collar job, but only 57 percent expected to be able to find placement in such a job.

Another major problem facing Turkish education today is connected with the type of curriculum offered in schools. At all levels of education there is an overemphasis on the Turkish language and literature and related subjects. Although scientific subjects are included, they are not emphasized. Further, facilities and laboratory experiences are lacking, and the expository style of instruction which is prevalent in the schools prevents students from receiving an adequate introduction to scientific concepts and modes of thinking. The social sciences are also inadequately stressed. In addition, the ordinary *ortaokul* or *lisé* provides instruction in few commercial or professional subjects. In order to acquire secretarial or mechanical skills, a student must attend a separate trade school, and many youngsters do not take this avenue since these schools are not socially prestigious. Because of the value attached to an academic education, students prefer to attend a *lisé* rather than a commercial or trade school, although they know that with a commercial or trade diploma they have more chances for gainful employment upon graduation.

BIBLIOGRAPHY

EASTMOND, JEFFERSON N. 1964 *Availability and Efficiency of Schools in Turkey.* Ankara, Research and Measurement Bureau.

KAZAMIAS, ANDREAS M. 1966 *Education and the Quest for Modernity in Turkey.* University of Chicago Press.

KAZAMIAS, ANDREAS M., AND BYRON G. MASSIALAS 1965 *Tradition and Change in Education: A Comparative Study.* Englewood Cliffs, N.J., Prentice-Hall.

BYRON G. MASSIALAS

TYPEWRITING, TEACHING OF

Courses in typewriting are conducted at every level from the intermediate grades of the elementary school through the college and university. Persons who learn typewriting usually expect to type their own correspondence, school reports, compositions, and the like (personal use), or they expect to type someone else's correspondence, reports, forms, tabular data, and so on, in exchange for payment (vocational use).

Goals. The goals of typewriting courses are speed and accuracy in operating the typewriter, efficiency in using the machine for the production of typewritten material, mastery of a mass of related technical information, and improvement of the learner's language skills. These four goals are not necessarily of equal importance; the purpose of a particular school's course may call for stressing some goals above others.

Skill goals. Typing skill is expressed in words a minute and errors a minute, as measured by a test consisting of the copying of paragraph material for an assigned number of minutes. To balance long and short words, typists and their teachers consider every combination of five consecutive strokes, characters, and spaces as a word. Thus, 30 words a minute is 150 strokes a minute, or 2½ strokes a second. An error is a word or a number with one or more misstrokes in it or in the space (and punctuation mark, if there is one) following. A failure in spacing, centering, underscoring, or carrying out other directions is also considered an error. The lowest echelon of civil service typing jobs has as the minimum skill qualification the ability to type 35 five-stroke words a minute with not more than one error a minute, for five minutes of paragraph copying. Some civil service tests count actual words, and when such tests include an abnormal number of long words, applicants' scores drop sharply even though their performance is normal.

The skill attainable by a given student depends on his innate learning ability, motor coordination, aggressiveness, and many other personal characteristics. His achievement is influenced, too, by his equipment (new typewriter better than old, electric better than manual, etc.), his teacher's performance, and the instructional materials used. Of all the factors involved, however, the most important is time. The length of a course largely determines the average skill outcome; conversely, a skill commitment will determine the length of the course that must be provided to fulfill the commitment.

Given 45-minute class periods, a manual typewriter in good condition, and a competent teacher, the average high school teen-ager with no pronounced learning disability will perform on five-minute paragraph-copying tests, within one error a minute, as follows: 30 words a minute after 75 periods, 40 words a minute after 150 periods, 47 words a minute after 225 periods, 51 words a minute after 300 periods. Older learners, because of their motivation and stronger background, acquire typing skill in less time. Junior college and business school students, for example, usually achieve 50 words a minute in about 200 periods and 60 words a minute in approximate-

ly 300 periods. The reputed high skills of older learners are often a reflection of some previous training received in high school and post-high school classrooms (Rowe et al. 1967, vol. 2, p. 18T).

If a curriculum planner is committed to a goal of, say, 50 words a minute for vocational office trainees and if he must achieve this goal within the framework of the economy-class program that is offered in most high schools (manuals, single basal textbook, 30 to 45 students in a class), he must provide the equivalent of 300 periods of 45 minutes each—a two-year, once-a-day program (with allowances for absences, test days, and other lost instructional periods).

If the planner must accomplish that goal in less time, if he aspires to a higher skill goal, or if he designs a program for children of lower learning acquisitiveness, he must explore innovations that—despite their higher cost—offer some hope of improving achievement: longer periods, better equipment, overhead projectors, multichannel recorded instruction, supplementary books, closed-circuit television, pacesetter instruments, individual instruction, and so on.

Production goals. The number and kinds of production experiences in the classroom vary with the length and purpose of the course. In the first semester of a typical two-year course, two-thirds of the time is devoted to building skill and one-third to applying it, so the list of applications is brief. The ratio of skill time to application time steadily alters, however, so that by the fourth semester one-third of the time is for skill and two-thirds for application, and the list of applications is endless. The average alumnus of a 300-period course should be able to type correctly anything that has vocabulary and purpose he understands.

An expression of production goals includes not only an enumeration of different kinds of applications but also a specification concerning the student's rate or speed of production at each stage of the course. Wanous (1949) suggests the following as reasonable rates of production in terms of paragraph-copying speed: letters, 75 percent; tabulations, 40 percent; rough drafts, 50 to 60 percent; manuscripts and statistical copy, 75 percent.

In another approach to stating production goals as rates (Rowe et al. 1967), the number of strokes the average typist would have tapped if he were striking keys instead of taking time for other machine manipulations, such as indenting, skipping from column to column, centering, backspacing, and so on, is computed. With appropriate stroking allowances included in the word count of a task, production material is equated with ordinary paragraphs, so that production goals can be defined in terms of specific words a minute instead of percentages. In this system scores should be within one word a minute, plus or minus, of the student's paragraph-copying speed, and the school's regular words-a-minute speed expectation can be applied to production tasks.

Production goals, therefore, involve two expressions: first, a citation of applications to be experienced; and second, a statement of the rate expectation at a particular point in the course, which may be expressed by a percentage formula or by a speed figure based on the production counting system.

Technical goals. The typist is responsible for the arrangement and correctness of what he types. To implement this responsibility, he must also receive systematic instruction in computing and setting margins; centering; numbering pages; addressing; inserting expressions of courtesy in correspondence; paragraph spacing; spacing after punctuation marks; sequencing punctuation marks at the end of quotations; displaying headings, subheadings, and lists; selecting and using proper business forms; and a myriad of other technical details. The typist must also learn to use carbon paper, make corrections, prepare duplicating stencils and masters, respond to revision marks, compose footnote references, and so on. Most technicalities are painlessly learned by the trainee as by-products of his production practice and require little discussion per se.

Language arts goals. Every typewriting course involves a great deal of practice in the language arts. Trends are in the direction of increasing emphasis on this aspect of typing.

The typist must learn many sets of language arts rules—the rules for dividing words, for example, and for expressing figures. The typist gets much spelling practice, too, for the 75,000 words that the average student pumps through his fingers each semester involve innumerable repetitions of the 5,000 or 6,000 words of a basic business vocabulary, and serve to develop automatic reflexes in the fingers, to teach the fingers to spell, as it were. He also develops many editorial skills, because of his need to proofread his typing. He gets composing practice from creating routine letters of acknowledgment, inquiry, reservation, and the like, and his copying of business letters and reports leaves a residual sensitivity to commercial phrasing and expression.

So valuable are the correlative language arts skills that many schools are modifying their typewriting program in order to emphasize them. Typewriting is widely taught in elementary school, not primarily because typing skill per se is desirable, but because typing practice reinforces children's acquisition of language skills.

Special books for persons who can already type consist wholly of language arts drills, which are made more appetizing and functional because they are designed for quick execution on the typewriter. There is also a programmed instruction series so arranged that the typewriter is used as a teaching machine (Brendel & Near 1964).

Goal combinations. Any formal expression of typewriting course goals will include all four goal areas. One course differs from another primarily in the relative weighting given each area and the length of time allotted to it. An elementary school program of 60 to 70 periods may accent skill and language arts, with only token attention to technicalities and production. A junior high school program may be similar, but being longer, can include more focus on production and some attention to the technicalities. A college-preparatory personal-use course will concentrate on skill and the technicalities of typing college term papers, with less attention to language arts and to other production tasks. The full vocational program will place great emphasis on skill and production, much stress on the technicalities, and moderate accent on language arts.

Content and method. The content of a typing program should, of course, depend on the selected course goals. Typewriting courses in public educational institutions commonly set general objectives for each semester or other course segment in these seven areas: speed and accuracy, correspondence, tabular data, printed forms, documents and reports, related technical information, and creative and language experiences. Under the general objectives are subsumed the fine points to be included. When given in detail, these can make a long list; one state guide uses ten pages for a complete outline of content (Liles & Liles 1968).

The plan of content organization will depend on the teaching method used in the institution.

Millions of people have learned typewriting in classes where all the students do the same thing at the same time, under a teacher's immediate direction. This group-cadence pattern is standard in most public schools and colleges. Because the teacher must strive mightily to adjust the program to match the different abilities of the individuals in the class, he needs maximum textbook help. His text, therefore, will be one that is organized into daily lessons, with groupings that parallel the school's report card schedule. This is the design of today's most widely used typewriting textbooks, which are distinguished as much by their helpfulness to the teacher as by their ability to make learning easier for the student.

An equal number of people have mastered typewriting through individual-advancement plans, in classes where each student forges ahead as rapidly as his energy and abilities permit, regardless of what classmates do. This method is standard in small business schools and in a number of adult and evening classes. Interest in the individual-advancement approach, which lost ground to the group approach, is resurging because of the impact of programmed instruction and because of the wider range of ability among typewriting students. Programmed instruction accommodates greater latitude in learning acquisitiveness and opens vocational doors to those who were formerly screened out. The main new thrust in training materials is toward more and better programmed instruction for persons who previously had been unable to learn typewriting at a functional level because they could not maintain a group-cadence pace.

Whether it is programmed or not, a book designed for independent progress must be organized in tiny, sequential steps, with directions and instructions expressed very clearly and at a reading level within the grasp of all learners. Whichever method of instruction is used, the teacher manuals and teacher editions of typewriting textbooks provide enough material, and in sufficient variety, to implement successful, systematic programs for steady growth in basic typing skill.

Similarity to other studies. In typewriting instruction the universal teaching activities are more or less the same as in other studies. The standard class-management factors—comfort, interest, discipline, and so on—are the same, too.

In principles of learning, typewriting is also like other disciplines. Even the fact that raw typewriting is a motor skill does not materially affect the psychological principles involved; the motor skill quickly becomes an intellectual one the moment it is applied to any useful purpose, since understanding and thought are immediately required (Russon & Wanous 1960). The familiar teaching precepts, such as "Repetition is valueless unless it is made purposeful and meaningful," are as pertinent to typing instruction as to other studies.

In a few respects, however, the teacher's tasks differ slightly from those in other disciplines. Lesson preparation, for example, is likely to be easier because of the extraordinarily detailed lesson structuring—minute by minute, exercise by exercise—in most of the typing texts. Grading is also less of a problem, because of the concreteness of the typed papers and the words-a-minute criterion and because day-by-day grading is meaningless. It doesn't matter how good a typist was, only how good he becomes; so past skill performances are never averaged with present ones. Paper handling, on the other hand, is a greater problem, because typewriters generate avalanches of paper.

There are two aspects of instruction in typewriting that are unique and merit a close view: the building of skill (speed and accuracy) and the application of that skill.

Skill building. Any unbridled drive for speed will result in so many errors that accuracy is jeopardized. Any unbridled drive for accuracy will result in so grave a slowdown that speed is jeopardized. The problem of the teacher, therefore, is to build both accuracy and speed without letting one jeopardize the other.

The following are some of the ways in which the teacher can help a student build speed and accuracy simultaneously:

(1) Insist on proper operating posture at all times—body erect, eyes on the copy, feet squarely on the floor, body a handspan from the machine and centered opposite the J key. Deviation from correct position induces muscular strain, which invites errors and leads to slowdowns.

(2) Build skill with short drills (three minutes or less), in which a student can truly maintain full effort, instead of long, fatiguing ones. For testing, three- and five-minute periods are best.

(3) Use material that is easy to type (short words, common words, high-frequency words, correct-motion words) and easy to understand, with a theme that is interesting, not admonitory.

(4) Conduct a typing "preview" before timed writings that are intended to build skill rather than merely to test the student's present achievement. A typing preview is preliminary selection and practice of words that are likely to be speed or accuracy pitfalls. When students have previewed a passage, they are able to type it more fluently and, therefore, more profitably for habit formation.

(5) Insist on the student's citing a specific speed goal and accuracy goal for each skill drive. No one ever typed well without intending to.

(6) Watch scores to note repetition saturation. Trainees do better and better as they repeat material, but only up to a point; any practice selection has a value limit.

(7) Have each student keep a daily record of his timed-writing achievement. Knowing what he has done is his best motivation for doing better next time. Knowing the average of his class and the school norm, if any, is also a help.

(8) When a student does self-supervised practice, such as remedial drill, be sure he uses the correct procedure: for speed gains, repeat single lines; for accuracy gains, repeat blocks of lines in paragraph form.

(9) Provide frequent rests. A tired learner types neither accurately nor rapidly.

Any speed campaign that completely ignores or disregards accuracy is to be avoided, as is any accuracy campaign that completely ignores or disregards speed. Students should never be asked for speed scores without being asked for accuracy scores, and vice versa. Production work should never be so hard that it forces learners to slow down or make errors. Production material should be as thoroughly copy controlled as skill-building material.

Application. The purpose of developing typing skill is to apply it. A course in typewriting, therefore, involves not only training in the skillful operation of the typewriter but also training in the proper arrangement of typed material, the steps in its production, and the building of a good production rate.

Typing is in such general use that standard conventions (spacing and placement of material, for example) have become established in the various areas of application—letters, tables, forms, manuscripts, etc. These conventions are discussed and illustrated in all basal textbooks, most of which outline a three-step sequence for the student

to follow in building his understanding: (1) study a facsimile model; (2) copy the model; (3) use the model as a guide to solve problems involving similar material presented in unarranged form.

The number, kind, and difficulty of the problems in a particular text are keyed to the ability of the students to whom the book is addressed. A vocational course for slower learners would include more experiences in filling in simple forms than would a secretarial training course, for example.

Because the correct array of typed material is standardized, the steps for producing each kind of material efficiently are also standardized. The student is therefore trained by the inductive method; he is shown what steps to take for each different task and drilled in taking those steps. One of the important contributions of textbooks is their itemization of steps in production, presented in words and illustrations, so that the sequences will be very, very clear.

If students are given many production jobs to do and there is no pressure on them to get the jobs done quickly, the students are likely to do their production work slowly. If the jobs are hard, in terms of either arrangement or content, the student is likely to work at a careful pace, far below his paragraph-copying speed. Extended intervals of production practice represent a potential hazard: if students do all their production jobs slowly, they will not be able to build their speed to higher levels.

Production routines, therefore, must include frequent timed exercises—production timed writings, they are called—in which learners are impelled to use their full power, instead of a fraction of it, in producing typed material. The frequency, duration, and content of production timed writings vary with the level of the course and with the degree of emphasis that a particular textbook places on this aspect of training. The general pattern is for the teacher and class together to analyze particular tasks or groups of tasks, discuss them so that there is no doubt as to the procedure, and then see how much of the work can be done in an assigned number of minutes and deduce a score (production words a minute) that can be recorded for comparison with past and future scores. There is evidence that building production power with the frequent use of production timed writings is an excellent procedure for building basic skill itself—even that it is preferable to build skill by production timed writings rather than by paragraph copying (Crawford 1960).

Background. The history of instruction in typewriting is the story of a seesaw battle to reconcile three factors that keep getting in each other's way: speed, accuracy, and production. Teachers are likely to mirror the stage that was in ascendance when they themselves or their teachers were in training.

Before 1900 most arguments concerned the shape of the keyboard and plans for fingering the keys. It was assumed that anyone who knew what fingers to use would automatically be expert. By 1900 there was agreement that the modern keyboard arrangement is the best one; that all eight fingers should be used; that control should be by touch; and that the diagonal-zone fingering system should be adopted. It was also beginning to be realized that there is more to typewriting than knowing which finger to move.

The early 1900's saw dozens of approaches for developing touch control of the keys. Emphasis was put on filling in blank keyboard charts. Some schools required students to recite the keyboard before touching a machine. Psychologists cautioned against tolerating any errors, and teachers developed an obsessive horror of mistakes, requiring students to repeat an exercise until it was done perfectly. They reasoned that speed would come as a by-product of the repetitions necessary to get perfect copies. Teachers also felt a dread of keyboard peeking and invented all manner of devices to prevent it, ranging from blanking the keys to shielding the keyboard from sight by an apron.

By 1920, however, the pendulum had reversed. It was conceded that accuracy did not result from demanding perfect copies; that speed did not come as a by-product of working for accuracy; that blanking or shielding the keys had no effect on eye control; and that the jump from keyboard drills to production work was staggering. Students were urged to press for speed, on the basis that anyone who could type rapidly could also type accurately by the simple expedient of slowing down a bit and that if errors recurred it would be possible to analyze them and prescribe drills to remedy the inaccuracies. It was also argued that production should be postponed, because it would make students slow down if introduced too soon.

But there were skeptics, and when World War II came along, with its urgent need for office production, they had their field day. Study after study showed that operators made so many errors because of the speed philosophy with which they had been trained that they had no production power at all.

Dissatisfaction was common all through World War II and into the 1950's. Caution crept into the classroom. Less emphasis was put on all-out speed and more on error control. The phrase "with not more than one-half an error a minute" reappeared in teaching guides. Attention began to settle on correct operating procedure—technique. Production problems, which had been relegated to the back of the textbook, were introduced, in simplified form, in the early lessons. Teachers sought ways to build a more useful, more productive skill. The deadly ten-minute timed writing began to lose out to the livelier, more valuable five- and three-minute writings. Some pioneers ventured to time students' production exercises. The typing preview made its appearance.

The late 1950's and the 1960's brought a marked simmering down of extremes in the speed-versus-accuracy conflict. The search for a safe middle ground led to universal stress on correct posture and good operating technique. The search also led to two new approaches to the development of skill.

One of these is pacing: Set a safe pace, nudge it upward bit by bit until accuracy shows strain, then slack off slightly to a better-than-before safe pace. The pacing can be accomplished by the teacher's signals, by sound cues, or by a pace-setting instrument.

The other is copy control—practice on material so easy (or made so easy by preview or repetition) that the student can type it faster than he can other material and with no or few errors. Having established a new rate on the very easy material, the student transfers the new rate to copy of intermediate difficulty and then to copy of greater difficulty. A study by Weaver (1966) has reinforced and extended the copy-control concept. Using a computer and thousands of student papers, Weaver was able to ascertain which motions of keyboard control helped and which hindered speed, as well as which helped and which hindered accuracy at five different speed ranges, and he did this separately for manual and for electric machine operators. It is possible, thanks to Weaver, to prescribe skill-development drills as readily as remedial drills.

The search for a way to build speed and

accuracy was paralleled by a search for a way to assure a high production rate. The result is an emphasis on frequent production-timed writings, which provide pressure for better production rates and develop production power while building skill, rather than after building it. The ultimate test of success in the typing course is the learner's demonstration of his ability to use the typewriter correctly in the rapid production of properly arrayed typewritten materials.

BIBLIOGRAPHY

BRENDEL, LeROY A., AND DORIS NEAR 1964 *Spelling Drills and Exercise: Programmed for the Typewriter.* New York, McGraw-Hill.

COOK, FRED S., et al. 1965 *Gregg Junior High Typing.* 2nd ed. New York, McGraw-Hill.

CRAWFORD, THOMAS JAMES 1960 *The Effect of Emphasizing Production Typewriting Contrasted With Speed Typewriting in Developing Production Typewriting Ability: An Abstract.* Monograph 97. Cincinnati, Ohio, South-Western Publishing.

LILES, PARKER, AND ZENOBIA T. LILES 1968 *A Guide for the Improvement of Typewriting Instruction.* 2nd ed. Atlanta, Ga., State Department of Education.

LLOYD, ALAN C. 1968 "Typewriting Futures." *Business Education World*, 48, no. 8:17–18.

ROWE, JOHN L., ALAN C. LLOYD, AND FRED E. WINGER 1967 *Gregg Typing, 191 Series.* 2nd ed., 2 vols. New York, McGraw-Hill.

RUSSON, ALLIEN R., AND S. J. WANOUS 1960 *Philosophy and Psychology of Teaching Typewriting.* Cincinnati, Ohio, South-Western Publishing.

WANOUS, S. J. 1949 "How to Get Better Results in Production Typewriting." *UBEA Forum*, 4, no. 2:13–15.

WEAVER, DAVID H. 1966 "An Experimental Study of the Relative Impact of Controllable Factors of Difficulty in Typewriting Practice Material." Ph.D. thesis. Syracuse, N.Y., Syracuse University.

ALAN C. LLOYD

U

UNGRADED SCHOOLS

See Nongraded elementary schools; Nongraded high schools.

UNION OF SOVIET SOCIALIST REPUBLICS

The Union of Soviet Socialist Republics is a multinational federation of 15 union republics. After China and India, the Soviet Union has the world's third largest population, composed of 26 major nationalities and some 140 minor national groups. The Soviet Union is ruled by a single-party national government which constitutionally legitimizes its legislative, judicial, and executive power in the name of the dictatorship of the proletariat—a union of workers and peasants under the leadership of the Communist Party.

It is a nation where all land, all means of production, all private (and most personal) property, and all social services, including education, have been nationalized and are controlled by the state. Despite regional and linguistic diversity, the Soviet Union boasts the world's largest unified and uniform educational system.

Education in the Soviet Union has become its largest industry. In 1968, for example, about 77 million persons, almost one-third of the total population, were enrolled either in formal educational institutions (60 million) or in diverse types of on-the-job manpower training/retraining programs and short-term courses (17 million). The 230,000 formal educational establishments of different types and levels were manned by 3.1 million teachers and instructors of various ranks. Total employment in Soviet education was 7.2 million, about 9 percent of the entire employed labor force of the Soviet Union. Soviet expenditures on education were approximately 4.2 percent of the gross national product.

Development. During the more than five decades of Communist rule the different sectors of the educational system have expanded at different rates, reflecting the relative priorities assigned by the state. Because it inherited a relatively extensive system of primary and secondary education from Imperial Russia, the Soviet Union's drive toward universal primary and secondary schooling has produced only about a $4\frac{1}{2}$-fold expansion in enrollment since the Revolution of 1917. Having inherited a small and highly selective system of specialized, higher, and university education, the Soviet regime made the utmost effort to expand and diversify this type of training. As a result, enrollments increased almost 47-fold between 1914 and 1968, to approximately 8.5 million. In Imperial Russia, adult education and part-time higher and specialized education were virtually nonexistent; they were established after 1917 and were expanded particularly during the post–World War II period. Enrollments in the formal vocational and skilled-manpower–training programs increased about 20-fold between 1914 and 1968. On-the-job training and apprenticeship and occupational retraining programs multiplied about 25 times in the same period.

These long-term trends reflect the adjustment of the Soviet school system to an unprecedented expansion and diversification of demand for education. Further, it was recognized by the nation's leaders that universal literacy and thus compulsory primary education were necessary for political integration and social transformation, and that diversified professional and manpower training was needed for the speedy development of industry and for the transformation to collectivized agriculture.

Prerevolutionary period. In the prerevolutionary period there was a wide diversity of secondary schools; for each type of school, however, there were uniform curricula, syllabi, and textbooks. These practices resulted in furcation—that is, the division of schooling into several different programs; although each student had to take a standard program of a specific type, he was free to choose between different schools and different tracks.

Period of experimentation (1917–1931). Just as the Revolution of 1917 destroyed the old social order, so it destroyed the old multitrack schools. In October 1918 the establishment of the new nine-year unified labor school was decreed. The instructional programs in these schools were to be based on the principle of transferability—that is, the pupils in all schools throughout the country were to follow identical instruction programs so that grade-syllabi sequences would interlock. In 1920, three recommendations were made in regard to the curricula: education was to be secularized completely, and all religious teaching was to be abolished; labor activity was to be introduced and used as an instructional method; and delineations between subjects of instruction were to be abolished so that subjects in the same topical area would be blended. (For example, the physical universe area would include mathematics, physics, chemistry, and biology.) This curricular method came to be known as the complex method of the labor schools. The complex method dominated the Soviet instructional process in the 1920's; labor activity was the moving spirit of the new education and the "withering away of the school" was proclaimed as the ultimate goal.

This experimental period was unique in other respects as well. The educational system was highly permissive and innovative and was marked by courageous and brilliant experimentation with the ideas of such liberal Western educators as Dewey, Kerschensteiner, Decroly, Parkhurst, and Montessori. Some radicals advocated that formal schooling be replaced completely by labor practice and the mere observation of life and environment. "Learning through doing" led to the notion of the group or brigade method of instruction, which called for dividing the task of learning the multiplication tables among various members of the brigade, for composing of collective poems and developing literary appreciation while building roads, and for scrubbing floors as a means of teaching the laws of physics.

Collectivism was practiced to such an extreme that individual learning was replaced by group practice and individual grading by criteria of group performance. Social and political participation overshadowed all other learning pursuits. The teacher's authority was nonexistent, all textbook learning was rejected, parental authority was castigated as a survival of capitalism, and the family was sentenced to wither away along with the school and the state.

The traditional school restored (1931–1958). The academic chaos of the experimental period, which was subsequently condemned as a period of impotence, came to an end in 1931. In response to the pressure of industrialization and the growing demand for high-level technical and scientific manpower, the Central Committee of the Communist Party, along with the Soviet government, proposed a different approach to education. The task was set as that of preparing fully literate persons for *technicums* and higher-education establishments—persons who had acquired the fundamentals of knowledge (physics, chemistry, mathematics, languages, geography, and so forth). Although the schools were still operating under the Marxist-Leninist slogan "unity of theory and practice," this slogan was now interpreted to mean that classroom instruction in the fundamentals of sciences came first and that practical application of science in the formation of work habits followed. Soviet education thus returned to the time-tested, traditional methods of instruction.

In accordance with new pedagogical principles expounded by Anton S. Makarenko, a gifted Soviet educator, emphasis was placed anew upon discipline and obedience. The essence of Makarenko's educational ideas was that the demands by the group (collective) or by society should take priority over individual wishes. Individual fulfillment would be realized by the renunciation of self-interest in favor of group interest; the collective, through sanctions or rewards, would foster the ideal of working with conscious discipline for the benefit of society. The aims of education were therefore to bring an individual to the point where all his views, beliefs, and acts were in harmony with those of a wider group. Although paying great tribute to these ideals, Soviet pedagogy began to emphasize individual performance and achievement as a measure of contribution to society: individual learning and grading as measures of basic academic knowledge were restored in the schools, social and political participation were pushed into the realm of extracurricular activity, and student interference with teaching was curtailed and the authority of the teacher and the parent was restored.

In the early 1930's the ten-year school was established with a standard curriculum and a uniform syllabus for each subject, and rigorous promotion examinations were introduced. The establishment of this pattern marked the beginning of a 25-year period of relative stability in which polytechnical instruction and labor activity in the schools ceased to be actively discussed. The majority of the "experimental" educators of the 1920's were purged or silenced after the "pedology" purge of 1936.

Recent adjustments. In the mid-1950's new problems emerged. With the expansion of secondary school enrollments, the secondary school was called upon to prepare not merely candidates for entry into higher education but also persons capable of entering practical work activity. This led to the 1958 Khrushchev reform, which attempted to supplement with mandatory labor activity the theory taught in regular classes by traditional and conservative methods. The reform (which lasted only until 1964) promised to reshape radically the instruction programs in the direction of greater production specialization by giving students vocational education and by requiring them to work in industrial enterprises up to 20 hours a week.

The Soviet educational structure also underwent changes. Until the mid-1930's the primary-intermediate-secondary school had a 4–3–2 grade structure. In the 1930's, 1940's, and 1950's the structure was 4–3–3. In 1958 the Khrushchev school reform created a 4–4–3 structure, with the extra year being devoted almost entirely to labor-polytechnical education in the general-education school. In early 1964 the Soviet government abruptly decreed the elimination of the major features of Khrushchev's educational program, and in August of that year the Central Committee of the Communist Party and the U.S.S.R Council of Ministers decreed a cutback from a program length of 11 years to the prereform length of ten years.

There were four major reasons for these structural changes. First, the Stalinist educational system was designed to develop a learned, technocratic elite; trained primarily in the single-track academic stream of the secondary schools, this elite subsequently gained entry into higher education. Second, in the late 1940's and early 1950's, secondary schooling expanded more rapidly than any other component of the educational system and the output of secondary school graduates substantially exceeded available places for higher education. Third, the need emerged to adjust the strictly academic secondary curriculum to the requirements for diversified and vocationally oriented training. And fourth, the reforms ran into trouble when the quality of secondary schooling began to deteriorate and when it was discovered that prolongation of the secondary schooling by a year devoted largely to production training did not justify itself in most cases: students neither learned the laboring skill nor were better prepared for life.

The 1964 change transformed schools to a 4–4–2 grade structure and eliminated vocational training and part-time production employment in the upper grades of secondary schools. The schools went back to the prereform instructional methods and curricula with one major modification—Western techniques in teaching various courses (particularly in the sciences) with the aid of programmed texts were introduced.

Administration. Since 1917 the Soviet educational system has undergone a number of structural changes in response to policy shifts. Each of these Soviet school reforms has been an attempt to revamp the school structure and to modify the contents of instruction through the edicts of the Soviet government and the Communist Party.

Legislation and administrative regulations pertaining to structure and operation of schools, contents of instruction, teacher-employment practices, use of textbooks, and so forth—in short, all major aspects of educational policy and practice—originate with the national government. An individual educational institution follows the existing laws and regulations issued by the ministry in charge of one sector of the educational system. The existence of several ministerial jurisdictions over Soviet education is a reflection of the Soviet conception of the functions of education.

In addition to the general-education schools, which are administered by the 15 republic ministries of education and by a central coordinating body (the U.S.S.R. Ministry of Public Education), there are subsystems of specialized schools designed to provide functional education and occupational training. Hence, secondary-level vocational education is coordinated by a set of ministries and committees for vocational-technical education; professional higher and paraprofessional specialized secondary education is administered by a group of secondary specialized and higher-education ministries, which also oversee advanced-degree training and research. On-the-job training, apprenticeship, occupational upgrading, and retraining programs are supervised by a score of industrial ministries as well as by the ministries of agriculture, health, and education. The ultimate coordination of these diverse ministerial administrations in such matters as enrollment quotas, school facilities, and funds rests with the U.S.S.R. State Planning Commission, which is directly responsible to the U.S.S.R. Council of Ministers.

The heads of individual educational institutions are primarily concerned with the day-to-day implementation of the state-set syllabi. They also oversee the disbursement of funds allocated annually from the national budget for the operation of each school and educational institution. Thus, the decision-making role of the individual educational administrator in the Soviet Union is circumscribed by the regulations and requirements which originate outside the particular school or educational institution.

Soviet aims. Soviet leaders view eduation as an effective means of achieving social change and economic development. In the Soviet Union there is an inseparable relationship between the system of education and the society it is designed to serve. The basic aim of Soviet education, therefore, is to prepare an individual for service in a collectivist society which is said to be presently in a transition from socialism to communism.

By identifying themselves with the common good of this collectivist society, the Soviet state and its single, ruling Communist Party subordinate the physical and mental training of individuals to serve their needs. The individual is provided with the opportunity to develop his personal abilities only within the confines of choice determined by the state on the basis of the broad social, political, and economic objectives postulated in the national development plans and policy guidelines, which are promulgated jointly by the top administrative organs of the government and the Central Committee of the Communist Party.

Education and ideology. The fundamental distinguishing characteristic of Soviet educational policy and practice is the replacement of the concept of individual or private benefit with the concept of service to society. In line with this, Soviet education sets itself a much broader task than mere transmission and development of knowledge: it aims at providing the nation's youth with the functional skills that will be most useful to the nation's development. It also seeks to remold the character of the individual by inculcating a uniform pattern of prescribed beliefs, social attitudes, normative sentiments, and behavioral values consonant with Communist ideology. As a result, all educational institutions in the Soviet Union are required to propagate Communist ideology through their curricular programs and organized extracurricular activities. In primary and secondary education all courses in the humanities and social sciences expound the Communist outlook. All higher-education students must take indoctrination courses which promote Communist values. The ultimate aim of all these practices is to create the new Soviet man.

According to the Marxist precepts of education, this new Soviet man will attain complete unity of mental and physical labor for service to society in the Communist millennium, where unity of theory and practice are fully achieved and all differences between mental and manual labor are finally eliminated as a source of exploitation and social distinction.

In accordance with these ideals, the Soviet school is called upon to prepare well-rounded individuals who have mastered the foundations of academic knowledge and who are at the same time capable of productive physical labor. Also called upon to instill in the young the desire to be useful to society, the school is intended to create patriotic and loyal citizens who take an active part in producing the material wealth and the social values needed by Soviet society.

Education in the national plan. There is, however, a conflict between these ideals and the conditions prevailing in the Soviet Union. With the advance of technology and the increasing complexity of industrial organization, Soviet education must necessarily provide more functional and more specialized training—which furthers rather than eliminates the division of labor and thus ultimately negates the Marxist ideal of a well-rounded education. To cope with this problem, national educational planning is superimposed by the state upon all types and levels of schools. Soviet educational planning sets up a scale of requirements for various types of specialized labor training to ensure that the proper number of qualified students are channeled into each type and level of training. But as a result, Soviet students find that their program of education does not necessarily coincide either with their preferences or with the aspirations of their parents.

The three major pillars of the Soviet system of centralized national planning are called national balances—balances of materials, finances, and labor. The labor balance consists of a checkerboard method of estimating and projecting labor figures for each occupation and each industrial sector. The personnel who set the labor balance specify the types of education, training, and experience needed for occupations. In this way, the nation's demand for educated personnel is derived. The source of supply in the labor balance involves detailed tabulations by occupation, education, and place of future employment of the new additions to the labor force. The majority of these new labor-force entrants are youths between the ages of 15 and 20. Their assimilation into the labor force simply means the termination of their formal education upon obtaining some level of occupational preparation. This, in turn, means that all Soviet educational institutions on the secondary-school level and beyond are given annual admission quotas. Each educational establishment decides how it will fill its quota. Each Soviet educational institution selects its students on the basis of merit (both academic and political) and in accordance with a national, uniform set of rules and requirements. Each institution trains its students in accordance with nationally prescribed curricula and syllabi.

Once the training chore is completed, each institution receives its placement schedule for that year's graduating class. In this way the targets for education beyond intermediate school (that is, beyond grade 8) are derived on the basis of the national manpower plan. The various specialized networks of the educational system are thus integrated into national planning through admission quotas for each specific type of training and through a national placement system. The obvious

complexity of this process calls for a great diversity of educational institutions grouped into networks to fulfill specific functional needs. Diversity in Soviet education is the result of the need for occupational specialization; unity is achieved through national planning for each specific functional network of education.

Preschool education. The consolidated, two-stage preschool facilities (day nurseries and nursery schools) provide child care for infants (aged six months to three years) and young children (aged three to seven). Preschool institutions range from boarding (six-day week), to full-day (12 hours), to part-day (four to six hours) schools. Some schools operate on a year-round basis; others, particularly in rural areas, are seasonal in operation. Preschool facilities are financed in large measure by local economic enterprises, by trade unions, and by fees from parents; their availability therefore varies greatly from locality to locality. The child care services are supervised by the republics' ministries of health (which also certify the employment of doctors and nurses); instructional content is determined by the ministries of public education (which also certify the appointment of preschool teachers). Nursery schools offer extensive instruction in reading, writing, and arithmetic for children between the ages of five and seven in addition to organized games and a program in health, music, and art. Apart from the convenience it provides to working parents, the preschool offers educators a unique opportunity to influence children's early development.

The Soviet government has placed great emphasis upon the expansion of preschool education, especially since 1950. Between 1950 and 1968, enrollments multiplied almost ten times, and in 1968 some 9 million children (about 36 percent of the age group) were accommodated in more than 75,000 day nurseries and nursery schools.

Primary and secondary education. The only Soviet educational institutions which do not aim at specialization are the general-education primary and secondary schools.

General-education schools. General-education schools consist of the four-year primary school and the four-year junior secondary school, with both components constituting the eight-year or incomplete secondary school. The four-year junior secondary school is then followed by the two-year senior secondary school. All three schools constitute the ten-year or complete secondary school. The school-entry age is seven; the normal age at completion of the ten-year school is 17. In the late 1960's the Soviet Union had more than 85,000 primary schools, more than 55,000 eight-year schools, and 40,000 ten-year schools.

School attendance is determined by school district boundaries, which encompass several schools with different levels of grades. Upon completion of the lower grade level, pupils are transferred to schools which have the complement of higher grades. This accounts for the great variation in the size of schools, with many (particularly rural) four-year primary schools being small, and large (particularly urban) ten-year schools having enrollments of several thousand students. About 90 percent of all eight-year and ten-year schools operate on two shifts. Because of insufficient school transportation and the failure of many consolidation drives, the Soviet Union still has many one-room, one-teacher schools in rural areas. The major reorganizational drive in the early 1970's aims at nationwide transfer of the fourth grade from the four-year school to the eight-year school. This shift is to be accompanied by a conversion of instruction in the fourth grade from general teaching (one teacher for all subjects) to subject teaching (separate teachers for each subject). This step is viewed as transitional to the ultimate closing of the small four-year primary schools.

The major variant in the Soviet general-education school is the language of instruction. About 60 percent of all schools use the Russian language in instruction. In all schools which use the local language in instruction, Russian is a compulsory subject. The Russian-language schools operating in a particular republic or national district where the local language is other than Russian offer the local language and its literature as optional subjects. Until 1958 a two-language formula, with Russian and local languages as compulsory subjects, was adhered to throughout the Soviet Union.

Uniform curricula and prescribed syllabi prevail throughout the Soviet Union. About 37 percent of the instruction in the ten-year school is devoted to mathematics, nature studies, biology, physics, chemistry, and astronomy; about 40 percent is devoted to Russian language and literature, local language and literature, art, music, history, social studies, geography, and at least one foreign language; and about 23 percent of the time is given to physical education and applied vocational subjects (workshops, polytechnical education, and technical drawing). In grades 1 through 4, instruction is carried out by one teacher for all subjects; beginning with grade 5 each subject is taught by a teacher who is a specialist in the specific field.

Until the mid-1950's, promotion from one grade to another (starting with grade 4) was based on annual examinations covering each subject of instruction. With a few minor exceptions, where aptitude and ability testing was occasionally given to ascertain occupational proficiency, most Soviet examinations and tests measured achievement. Promotions are now based on cumulative grading, with the exception of grades 8 and 10, in which nationally prepared achievement examinations are given; these examinations are based on each subject's contents for the respective school level (that is, an eight-year or ten-year school). The national tests are given not merely to rank pupil performance but also as a means of ensuring schools' adherence to national syllabi.

Annual enrollment in grades 1 through 4 in the late 1960's was about 115 percent of the respective age group (seven- to ten-year-olds) because of the presence of repeaters and overaged pupils. In the intermediate grades (5 through 8), about 90 percent of the age group (11 through 14) was in school. In the senior grades (9 and 10), only about 37 percent of the age group (15 to 16) was attending school. These data indicate that the senior secondary school still remains highly selective, with entrance requirements in grade 9 set in such a way that only about half of those completing grade 8 continue on to grade 9. Among those who do not enter the ninth grade of the general-education secondary school, more than half attend either the vocational-technical schools —which prepare youth for various skilled and semiskilled occupations—or enter specialized secondary semiprofessional schools (*technicums*). Thus, only a very small fraction of students completing the eighth grade do not continue their education.

General secondary education in the Soviet Union culminates at the end of grade 10 with a national oral and written examination for the certificate of secondary education. These examinations are conducted by individual schools, which each May receive from the ministries of education the questions for the examinations. The examinations are designed to cover the contents of a given subject in accordance with the national syllabus. Such major subjects as language, mathematics, and the sciences may have both written and oral parts; others (history, geography, and so forth) are conducted orally only. The results are entered, along with the student's cumulative grade record, on the certificate of secondary school completion (which is required for entry into higher education). Secondary school marks are weighted heavily in the consideration for admission to higher education.

Special primary and secondary schools. The Soviet Union operates a number of special schools for mentally retarded or physically handicapped children. These schools follow the programs of the general education schools but make adjustments to suit the special needs of their pupils; these adjustments include provision of more individualized instruction, use of special teaching aids, teaching of special-skill trades, and so forth. Since the 1920's the enrollments in these schools have remained relatively stable and small.

There also are a small number of schools (with limited enrollments) which in the 1960's developed experimental programs—such as using a foreign language as the language of instruction in all subjects beginning with grade 5, or giving more intensive and advanced teaching in mathematics and sciences. Most of these schools are affiliated with universities, pedagogical institutions, or foreign language institutes, and serve as laboratory schools. In the same category, but dating back to the prerevolutionary period, are the schools for artistically gifted children; most of these schools are directly attached to the conservatories or to the ballet or performing-art establishments.

The general-education schools have still another variation, the boarding and the extended-day schools established in the late 1950's. Despite the great publicity given to boarding schools, the high cost (covered only in small part by boarding fees) of operating these facilities has stifled their development. In the late 1960's, for example, boarding schools accommodated about 1 million pupils (about the same number in the late 1950's); about 3.3 million students were enrolled in extended-day schools. Far from being schools for the elite, boarding schools accommodate primarily orphans, children of widows or unmarried mothers, and other types of deprived or problem children. The curriculum does not differ significantly from that in the regular day schools; however, vocational and occupational subjects usually are taught more extensively. The extended-day schools are designed mostly for the children of working parents. The program consists of supervised study and recreational activities on the premises of the regular school in addition to regularly scheduled classroom instruction identical to that in the regular general-education school.

Schools for working and rural individuals. Soviet schools for working and rural youth and adults, part-time in nature, parallel general-education primary and secondary schools and are administered by the same organs. These schools provide the equivalent of general education for working youth and adults who have not completed regular day schools. Most of them operate in the evening; some provide education on an alternating-shift basis. Of the 20,000 schools in this category, about 12,000 are separate units (mostly on the premises of industrial plants); the remainder use regular school facilities for evening instruction.

Vocational-technical schools. A separate network of vocational-technical schools is operated on the senior secondary level by the U.S.S.R. Ministry of Vocational-Technical Education and its counterpart ministries in the republics. The approximately 1,300 vocational-technical schools accept eighth-grade graduates and prepare semi-skilled and skilled workers in programs which last from six to 18 months. Although some general-education subjects are taught, most programs concentrate on specific vocational or occupational topics. They emphasize workshop or apprenticeship skills and are designed to be terminal without being equivalent to upper secondary education. To qualify for certificates of completed secondary education, persons finishing vocational schools must obtain further secondary education by enrolling in part-time schools for adults.

On-the-job occupational training programs. Programs for on-the-job, individual, or group-apprenticeship training are given on a variety of levels by industrial, agricultural, and other business enterprises. On-the-job training and apprenticeship programs accept working youths, adults, and current dropouts. Unlike vocational schools, which usually require the completion of an eight-year education, there are no minimal educational entrance requirements. Training is handled by individual enterprises but is coordinated by the U.S.S.R. Ministry of Vocational-Technical Education in cooperation with other ministries controlling specific functions. About one-third of persons undertaking this training are being retrained or are taking job-upgrading courses. Access to further formal education is available only through supplementary schooling for adults.

Technicums. The separate network of specialized secondary schools (*technicums*) has two levels: the four-year *technicums* for graduates of the eighth grade of the intermediate school, and the two-year advanced *technicums* for graduates of the ten-year school. About one-third of all *technicums* have advanced programs only; the remainder have both advanced and intermediate programs. *Technicum* instruction is offered in about 380 different occupational specialties covering such fields as industry, transportation, construction, agriculture, commerce, paramedical studies, pedagogy, library science, and the fine arts. The curriculum of a four-year *technicum* devotes approximately half of its time to general academic and general technical subjects; the rest of the time is taken by specialized and applied training. In addition to providing training leading to certificates of subprofessional qualification, *technicums* are considered equivalent to the upper secondary school; *technicum* graduates are eligible for admission to higher educational institutions on an equal basis with graduates of the general-education schools.

Depending upon the field of training they provide, *technicums* are operated by the different functional ministries. For example, industrial ministries are in charge of various *technicums* for technicians, ministries of public health are in charge of paramedical *technicums,* and ministries of education are in charge of preschool and elementary school teacher-training *technicums.* The overall planning of facilities and enrollments for each specialty field is coordinated by a division for semiprofessional education of the U.S.S.R. Ministry of Higher and Secondary Specialized Education. Admission to *technicums* is based on entrance examinations for a specific course of study. There are three types of programs for each specialty—day, evening, and extension correspondence. In the late 1960's more than 4.1 million students were enrolled annually in *technicums.* About half of each year's graduates enter industrial and transport fields, and about one-eighth are paramedical personnel; the remainder are teachers or specialists in agriculture and business. *Technicum* graduates who receive a diploma are usually assigned to jobs which they must keep for three years; however, those in the top 5 percent of their class are permitted to apply for higher education immediately upon graduation.

Higher education. Of all the Soviet advances in the development of education since the October Revolution, few have received as much notice as higher education. Today there are more than 40 universities and more than 740 institutes of higher learning (*VUZ*). Universities provide faculties for study and research in a variety of fields in the sciences and humanities. Some *VUZ* establishments are large, multifaculty engineering schools (polytechnical institutes) and others are highly specialized engineering schools for mining, civil engineering, metallurgy, transportation, and so on. Also included in the *VUZ* category are agricultural, medical, economics, law, arts, and pedagogical institutes. Soviet institutions of higher learning offer training in more than 345 different specialties in more than 20 branches of knowledge. The training lasts from four to six years, depending upon the field of specialized study. Medical education lasts six years; most university and engineering programs last from five to 5½ years. Pedagogical and agricultural training lasts four years. About one-third of the instructional time is devoted to general sciences; the remainder is used for professional specialization. Within the latter, narrow specialization takes up some 20 percent and on-the-job practical experience some 15 percent of the student's time. Competition for entry is rather keen, with only 20 percent of the age group and less than half of the ten-year–school graduates entering higher studies. All applicants must have completed their secondary education in a ten-year school or *technicum.*

Total employment in higher education has surpassed 1 million. The entire network of higher education is administered by the Soviet Union's Ministry of Higher and Secondary Specialized Education.

Higher-education institutions have three types of programs: full-time day, part-time evening, and extension-correspondence divisions. More than 4.3 million students are participating in these programs; most are enrolled in day or extension-correspondence programs. No degrees are granted for completion of studies; instead, graduates receive a diploma which bestows upon them a professional title. Graduates are assigned to jobs for a period of three years. About 40 percent graduate as engineers, some 8 percent as agricultural field specialists, more than 7 percent as physicians, more than 35 percent as teachers for secondary schools and universities, and the remainder as professionals in the fields of business, commerce, arts, and culture. The 40-year trend in the production of professional graduates from Soviet higher education reveals preference for specialists in engineering and applied sciences: about 65 percent were trained in these fields. About 25 percent of all graduates were trained as teachers.

Special-purpose higher education. In addition to the regular higher-education institutions, the Soviet Union operates several networks of closed-access higher education—higher military schools and academies (U.S.S.R. Ministry of Defense), higher schools of the Communist Party of the Soviet Union, and higher managerial-training academies. Admission is through competitive examinations and "appointment" by the respective service. Exact enrollments are unknown, but are likely to be several hundred thousand.

Advanced training, research, and degrees. About half of the higher-education establishments and about 400 research institutions (which do not offer regular higher education) conduct advanced "aspirantura" training (lasting three years) and award, upon the successful defense of a dissertation, the degree of candidate. (Aspirantura programs enroll individuals who aspire to academic or research careers.) Entrants must have the higher-education diploma. Annual aspirantura enrollment in the late 1960's was less than 100,000; approximately 22,000 candidate degrees were awarded. The second advanced degree is the doctorate and is awarded exclusively on the basis of research and publications. Some 1,700 doctorates were awarded annually in the late 1960's. All advanced-degree training programs are supervised by a national agency, the Supreme Attestation Commission. This agency also certifies academic appointments in institutions of higher learning and research appointments in research institutions.

Trends. In the 1970's further expansion of enrollments on the upper-secondary and postsecondary levels is to be expected, with the number of graduates from the tenth grade, *technicums,* and higher education probably increasing by 50 percent by 1980. In regard to this expansion, however, a major problem remains in the rural areas. Although there is nationwide eight-year education, and 60 to 70 percent of the age group attends upper-secondary grades (9 and 10) in urban areas, a high dropout rate is common in rural areas. Despite uniform curricula, the actual standards of instruction continue to vary, largely because of the rural-urban differences in the quality of facilities and teachers.

It is unlikely that the Soviet Union will ever adopt an unrestricted choice of courses; the need for multiple streaming and differentiation of school programs (but each program with a fixed subject track) has been acknowledged, but the Soviet government is reluctant to adopt this reform.

The government's attitude is to preserve the general-education ten-year schools, which are to be primarily concerned with the preparation of students for further education in *technicums* and institutes of higher education. The government also wishes to keep the separate networks of schools specifically aimed at training skilled and semiprofessional workers on the secondary level and specialized professional personnel in institutions of higher learning. It is unlikely that the philosophy and practice of maintaining these separate subsystems of general and specialized education will change in the foreseeable future so that the concept of the comprehensive school may be embraced; because Soviet educational philosophy is firmly rooted in the conviction that man is destined to perform a specific working task, it is unlikely that the concept of functional education will be altered.

In the summer of 1964 the U.S.S.R. Ministry of Public Education was set up to supervise all aspects of curricular development. Its research arm, the Academy of Pedagogical Sciences, is in charge of educational research in the Soviet Union. In March 1969 the Central Committee of the Communist Party outlined for the Academy of Pedagogical Sciences the major research tasks essential for transition to universal ten-year secondary education. Not only did the Central Committee decree the qualitative improvement of both the contents and methods of instruction in each subject, but it also made mandatory further research in educational and social psychology. For several decades both have been in official disrepute: they have been noted as areas not merely of neglect, but of official taboo for more than 40 years. Studies in personality, ability, psychometry, sociometry, attitudes, and learning and thought processes as well as age-ranked psychological and physiological measures of aptitude are all areas where pedagogical research in the Soviet Union was viewed as off-limits because of preconceptions about personality development and learning processes.

The school reforms and especially the departure into the realm of studies of human behavior reflect the Soviet Union's determination to improve upon the present educational product—a man who, although reasonably well educated and technically competent, is often socially irresponsive, apathetic, and, at times, irresponsible. They reflect a determination to bridge the gap between the present Soviet reality and the ideal upbringing of the new Soviet man.

BIBLIOGRAPHY

ALT, HERSCHEL, AND EDITH ALT 1959 *Russia's Children: A First Report on Child Welfare in the Soviet Union.* New York, Bookman.

BEREDAY, GEORGE Z. F., WILLIAM W. BRICKMAN, AND GERALD H. READ, eds. 1960 *The Changing Soviet School.* Boston, Houghton Mifflin.

BEREDAY, GEORGE Z. F., AND JAAN PENNAR, eds. 1960 *The Politics of Soviet Education.* New York, Praeger.

BOWEN, JAMES 1962 *Soviet Education: Anton Makarenko and the Years of Experiment.* Madison, University of Wisconsin Press.

COUNTS, GEORGE S. 1957 *The Challenge of Soviet Education.* New York, McGraw-Hill.

DEWITT, NICHOLAS 1961 *Education and Professional Employment in the USSR.* Washington, D.C., National Science Foundation.

DEWITT, NICHOLAS 1967 "Educational and Manpower Planning in the Soviet Union." George Z. F. Bereday and Joseph A. Lauwerys, eds., *The World Year Book of Education 1967.* New York, Harcourt. Pages 219–239.

GRANT, NIGEL 1964 *Soviet Education.* Baltimore, Penguin.

HANS, NICHOLAS A. 1963 *The Russian Tradition in Education.* London, Routledge.

HECHINGER, FRED M. 1959 *The Big Red Schoolhouse.* New York, Doubleday.

KING, EDMUND J., ed. 1963 *Communist Education.* New York. Ryerson.

KOROL, ALEXANDER G. 1957 *Soviet Education for Science and Technology.* Cambridge, Mass., MIT Press.

ROSEN, SEYMOUR M. 1963 *Higher Education in the USSR: Curriculums, Schools and Statistics.* U.S. Office of Education Bulletin 1963, No. 16. Washington, D.C., The Office.

SHORE, MAURICE J. 1947 *Soviet Education: Its Psychology and Philosophy.* New York, Philosophical Library.

SIMON, BRIAN, AND JOAN SIMON, eds. 1963 *Educational Psychology in the USSR.* Stanford, Calif., Stanford University Press.

NICHOLAS DEWITT

UNITED ARAB REPUBLIC

Education in the United Arab Republic is a constitutional right guaranteed to all citizens by the state. It is free in all state schools and compulsory in the primary stage.

Administration. The Ministry of Education is responsible for all education below the higher education stage, which is supervised by the Ministry of Higher Education. The Ministry of Culture, the Ministry of Social Affairs, the Ministry of Health, and the Ministry of the Treasury also supervise some educational institutions.

Since 1939, some of the authority and responsibility of the Ministry of Education have been vested in the local educational directorates (now numbering 28).

To further local initiative, a local administration law (No. 124 of 1960) divided the republic into administrative units; these units include governorates, towns, villages, and groups of villages. The units are represented by councils which share responsibility for education with the educational directorates. Governorate councils are in charge of academic and technical secondary schools and teacher-training institutes: town councils are responsible for primary and preparatory schools; and village councils are entrusted with primary schools.

The state provides the financing for all public educational institutions and offers grants to some private schools. The rate of expenditure on education has constantly increased. For example, in the 1953–1954 school year the education budget represented 3.8 percent of the general national revenue; by the 1964–1965 school year it had risen to 5.7 percent of the gross national product.

Structure. Children between the ages of three and six attend nursery school. Education in these schools is neither compulsory nor free. Children enroll in the compulsory six-grade primary school when they are six years old. This stage is followed by a three-grade preparatory stage and a three-grade secondary stage. The secondary certificate, obtained at the end of the secondary stage, allows students to attend the nation's higher institutes and universities.

Primary education. Many primary schools follow a two-shift system (one in the morning and the other in the afternoon). This system has been adopted as a remedy for the shortage of school buildings and as a means of making the best possible use of existing facilities. About 38 percent of the primary schools followed this system in the early 1970's.

Preparatory education. The preparatory stage is considered an intermediate stage of education. It provides education for those students between the ages of 12 and 15 who have completed their primary studies and who have passed a preparatory school entrance examination (held at the end of the sixth grade).

Although the ministry is expanding compulsory education, it intends to restrict preparatory education. Hence, not more than 20 percent of those who have completed their primary education enter the preparatory stage. About 75 percent of these students go to the government schools, and 25 percent attend the private schools.

Preparatory education aims at discovering the abilities and aptitudes of the students, at developing these bents, and at guiding students into a suitable program of secondary education. This stage ends with a nationwide exam; successful students receive the preparatory certificate.

Secondary education. Secondary education comprises general secondary education and technical secondary education. The preparatory school graduates whose grades allow them to enter secondary education (about 40 percent of the students who pass the preparatory certificate examination) are distributed as follows: 40 to 45 percent enter secondary school; 30 percent enroll in technical secondary school; 11 percent attend teacher-training institutes, which prepare teachers for primary schools; and the remainder join the work force.

General secondary education is designed to enrich the physical, mental, and moral life of young people. It also aims to prepare those who do not intend to continue beyond this stage to earn their living and provides suitable education for those who want to attend higher educational institutions. General secondary education ends in a nationwide exam, and those students who pass receive the general secondary certificate.

Technical secondary education is divided into industrial, agricultural, and commercial forms; it aims at supplying the country with technicians who are able to supervise projects in business and government enterprises and who can guide the production processes in the right direction. Students who pass an examination at the end of this program receive the technical secondary certificate of education.

Higher education is provided by universities, by institutions supervised by the Ministry of Higher Education, and by unaffiliated institutions of higher education.

Each of the United Arab Republic's five universities (Cairo, Alexandria, Ain-Shams, Asyût, and al-Azhar) has a number of faculties which provide undergraduate as well as postgraduate studies. Institutes for higher specialization are affiliated with most of these faculties. Each university controls its own affairs to a great extent, and the teaching staff is free to set the curricula and courses of study.

Holders of the general secondary certificate join the faculties according to the sum total of their marks. Holders of the technical secondary certificate who have obtained a total of more than 70 percent may join the faculties of commerce, agriculture, and engineering. The required number of years of study is not the same in all faculties. However, students in the science faculty can get a bachelor's degree in arts or social science after four years of study; study in the faculties of engineering and of dentistry lasts for five years. Study in the faculty of medicine requires seven years, which includes one year of practical training.

Most of the higher institutes not affiliated with the universities but supervised by the Ministry of Higher Education were established recently to prepare skilled technicians. These institutes include technological institutes for the study of the scientific and applied bases of industry, agriculture, and commerce; such vocational institutes as the School of Languages, the Higher Institute of Social Services, and the Institute of Home Economics; and the institutes and colleges of arts.

To attend these institutes, students must have either the general or the technical secondary certificate. Study lasts four years and ends in the bachelor's degree.

The Ministry of Higher Education also runs a number of industrial, agricultural, and commercial training centers in which the length of study ranges between 12 and 18 months. Only holders of the general or the technical secondary certificate may enroll.

Institutes which offer higher studies but are affiliated with neither the universities nor the Ministry of Higher Education are either private institutions or institutions run by international organizations in cooperation with the U.A.R. government. These institutes offer training programs and supervise study and research leading to degrees. Among these institutes are the National Institute for Planning, the Institute of Public Administration, the Higher Institute for Arab Studies, and the Higher Institute for Coptic Studies.

Teacher training. Teachers are prepared in several kinds of institutes and colleges. The teacher-training institutes prepare primary school teachers. Holders of the preparatory certificate attend these schools for five years. The teachers colleges affiliated with the universities also prepare teachers. Holders of the general secondary certificate attend these colleges for four years. The faculty of education affiliated with Ain-Shams University enrolls graduates of the faculties of arts, sciences, and agriculture for one year. Graduates can continue their higher studies in this faculty to obtain the M.A. or the Ph.D. in education. Colleges which offer technical education in agriculture, industry, and commerce prepare some of their students for teaching. They accept holders of the general or the technical secondary certificate. The program of study lasts four years.

Literacy. The work to combat illiteracy on a national basis started about 1922. However, these early efforts dwindled in the 1930's; in 1944 the responsibility for this campaign was transferred to the state. In 1945 the Ministry of Education established a special literacy department to carry out the campaign, and the new department soon opened literacy classes. However, it was discovered in 1952 that the efforts spent in this field were not very fruitful. To remedy this situation, the literacy campaign was redirected into a program of expanding primary education. This program lasted from 1952 to 1959. In 1959 a stage of evaluation and planning was begun. A comprehensive plan for the future was made in 1962 and 1963.

According to the 1960 U.A.R. census, 70 percent of the population over ten years old was illiterate.

Methods and materials of instruction. The primary-stage curriculum includes religion, Arabic, songs, arithmetic, geometry, history, geography, civics, general science, physical training, handicrafts, and art. Suitable audiovisual aids are widely used.

The preparatory-stage curriculum includes religion, Arabic, one foreign language, civics, history, geography, mathematics, general science, art, and practical studies.

The curriculum in the first year of the secondary general stage includes religion, Arabic, two foreign languages, mathematics, biology, physics, chemistry history, geography, Arab society, physical training, military training, drawing and history of art, and practical studies. In the second and third years, the literary section offers additional courses in sociology and philosophy; the scientific section stresses mathematics and science.

Trends and problems. There is great interest in scientific educational planning at all stages. This is evident in the drawing up of educational plans and in the formation of planning committees to coordinate national policies of education, to make suitable programs for the implementation of these policies, and to expand education into the countryside while taking into full consideration the country's economic and social needs. There is also considerable expansion of education, especially at the primary stage.

Colleges and higher institutes have also been established. Among these are the Institute of Mining and Oil at Suez, the Higher Industrial Institute at Port Said, the Institute of Electronics at Menouf, and the Institute of Chemical Industries at Aswan. Cairo University has also opened a branch in Beirut.

However, the great expansion in U.A.R. education has led to such problems as inadequate school buildings, overcrowded classrooms, insufficient teachers, and declining academic standards. And despite the growing trend toward local administration and decentralization in education, the people show little interest in educational affairs.

WAHIB I. SAMAAN

UNITED BUSINESS SCHOOLS ASSOCIATION

The United Business Schools Association is an association of independent colleges and schools offering resident programs predominantly in the field of business career preparation. It is a national association to which institutions, not individuals, belong. Many of its member schools have been in operation for over 100 years. The UBSA is an affiliate of the American Council on Education.

Program. Throughout the years since its establishment, the UBSA has supported legislation to aid students who desire to include in their education an occupational skill rather than just an academic or liberal arts program. Such legislation includes the 1966 G.I. Bill (Public Law 89–358), which extends educational benefits to armed forces veterans who plan to continue their education. Similar assistance is available to war orphans and war widows. Business and commercial schools are specifically defined in the law as an approvable type of educational institution which the veterans, war widows, or orphans may attend.

The Federally Insured Student Loan Program of the Higher Education Act of 1965 enables students in business and commercial schools to receive low-interest loans of up to $1,500 a year, guaranteed by the federal government. Other programs for which proprietary business schools and colleges are eligible include the College Work-Study Program and the National Defense Student Loan Program.

Business schools are involved under contract in a number of training programs sponsored by the federal government. Under these programs the government pays the tuition of the student under an individual referral, or a number of students under a group referral, for a course which will give the student a marketable skill and enable him to compete in a job market for which he would otherwise not qualify. One of the best-known programs is the Manpower Development and Training Program, established under the Manpower Development and Training Act of 1962 (P.L. 87–415). Vocational rehabilitation and Indian adult education are among the many programs in which business school facilities are extensively used.

In 1967 the UBSA began a series of pilot projects under the MDTA to equip individuals with new or upgraded employable skills. The series is administered by the UBSA for the U.S. Office of Education (USOE) and is carried out in conjunction with local state employment services and the U.S. Department of Labor. Under contract, state governments similarly administer programs of an ongoing rather than demonstration type with individual schools.

For over 50 years business schools have been noted as pioneers in the training of the handicapped. Specially designed typewriters, adding machines, and calculators are often provided to help handicapped students acquire skills which might otherwise be impossible for them. This is another example of under-contract training through the Vocational Rehabilitation Act of June 2, 1920, as amended.

The UBSA publishes *The Compass,* a monthly journal, for its members and for others interested in postsecondary business education. *The Compass* includes articles on current legislation, member schools' activities, government programs (many prepared by federal and state officials), and other areas of interest to business school administrators. It has a circulation of 4,500 copies.

The UBSA guidance department publishes a number of brochures of interest to students planning to attend business schools and to guidance counselors who seek information about business education. These publications include *Your Career as a Secretary, Accounting for Your Future,* and *Don't Overlook the Business College.* The guidance department also issues reprints of articles from magazines and newspapers which are of use to guidance counselors and students.

The *Directory of Accredited Institutions* is published each year by the Accrediting Commission. It lists all the member institutions by state and includes their addresses and the names of the principal administrators. The ethics and standards of practice are published separately in the criteria. All publications are available free upon request to educators, parents, and students.

UBSA members receive the *Bulletin,* a newsletter issued at irregular intervals which contains the most recent information on accreditation and association programs and elections. The *Bulletin* serves as the internal publication for members of the association.

At an annual convention in the autumn, new officers are presented, panel discussions and general meetings are held, and well-known government and industrial figures speak to the members. Discussions include current topics of interest to business schools such as legislation, public relations, and new educational innovations. The convention banquet is highlighted by the presentation of awards and a speech by an outstanding American educator, legislator, or industrial leader.

Organizational structure. UBSA officers include a president, president-elect, past president, secretary, and treasurer elected for one-year terms of office. In addition, the United States is divided into six regions and 12 districts, with a director elected from each to serve for three years on the UBSA board of directors. Standing committees include committees on educational standards; business ethics; regional and state associations; membership; allied members liaison; finance, budget, and audit; awards and recognition; legislative; ballot counting; and public relations. Additional committees are formed when necessary.

The Accrediting Commission for Business Schools (ACBS) is a professionally independent arm of UBSA. It was established by the UBSA to accredit schools as one-year or two-year business schools, junior colleges of business, or senior colleges of business. In 1956 the USOE, pursuant to P.L. 82–550 and subsequent legislation, designated the ACBS as a nationally recognized accrediting agency for the accreditation of business schools. Although the ACBS accredits schools, the UBSA is the membership organization of which some 450 schools are now accredited. To become a UBSA member, a school must be accredited.

Membership. Membership in UBSA includes over 550 schools in the United States, Canada, and Latin America which seek higher standards of education in independent, postsecondary business schools. These schools, including nearly 50 junior colleges of business and seven senior colleges of business, educate accountants, data processors, secretaries, court reporters, typists, and other skilled employees employed in the nation's white-collar work force.

There are state and regional associations of business schools throughout the United States. Most of the schools belonging to state and regional associations are UBSA members. Their goals are similar to those of the UBSA but are regional in scope so as to encompass state and local differences in training and employment requirements.

All member schools must maintain placement services for their own graduates as well as graduates of other UBSA member schools. This free lifetime placement is one of the services which makes attendance at a UBSA school attractive to a number of students. Employers also look to UBSA schools for skilled employees.

History and development. On December 12, 1912, the first organized group of business school administrators met to create definite guidelines delineating the purposes and practices of private business schools. This was the beginning of what

was 50 years later to become the United Business Schools Association. Two groups—the National Association and Council of Business Schools and the American Association of Business Schools—unified in 1962 to become the present UBSA. Thus, the history of the UBSA dates back over nearly 60 years of service and dedication to the ideals of business education.

Over the years the UBSA has grown both in membership and in recognition by others as a responsible organization with a clear purpose, that of upgrading the standards in business schools to give a quality education to America's business-oriented students. The UBSA has increased its activities to include testimony upon invitation before congressional committees, statements to various national advisory councils, liaison with other educational organizations, encouragement of new developments in accreditation standards, and promotion of an overall recognition of the business school graduate as an important asset to the American business community and the nation.

The offices of the UBSA and its Accrediting Commission are located at 1730 M Street NW, Washington, D.C. 20036.

RICHARD A. FULTON

UNITED KINGDOM

Four administrative systems regulate education in the United Kingdom. Since three-quarters of the United Kingdom's total population of 55 million live in England, the English system is the most important. It is directed by the Department of Education and Science, located in London. In Scotland, education is the responsibility of the secretary of state for Scotland, who is located in Edinburgh; in Wales it is administered by the secretary of state for Wales (except for higher education, which is regulated from London); and in Northern Ireland it is directed by the Northern Ireland government, which in internal matters is independent of the British Parliament.

The legal basis for education in England is the 1944 Education Act, which created for the first time a central ministry, established secondary education for all children, and continued the practice of giving financial support to denominational schools. The law was an all-party measure inspired by a wartime idealism aimed at achieving "equality of opportunity." It implied a modification of hitherto accepted elitist concepts, took a more instrumental view of the function of education, and increased intervention by the central government. At the same time, education became a controversial political issue. The dissensions about English education may be seen as one facet of the balance, always disputable in a democracy, that must be struck between the occasionally conflicting principles of liberty and equality.

The English approach to education has differed radically from that of the Continent. It may be viewed as largely empirical and pragmatic; moreover, intellectualism has been less esteemed. Instead, character-formation, based on moral and often religious values, has been especially emphasized. The fostering of group loyalties, which act as a cohesive political and social force, has often been preferred to the encouragement of individualism. Historically, the purpose has been to educate the gentleman rather than to train the professional. Such an approach has its demerits, however, and there is evidence that it is being increasingly questioned.

Administration. The central government, acting in partnership with local government, is responsible for developing and administering educational policy. The Department of Education and Science is headed by a secretary of state who holds cabinet rank and is assisted by three ministers of state. All four officers are political appointees. The top civil servant of the department is the permanent undersecretary. The department has general branches for schools, further education, universities, teachers, and science, as well as a number of specialized sections for health, buildings, planning and statistics, law, and information. The secretary of state directs and controls education: he establishes minimum standards for the provision of education; sanctions building programs; regulates teacher training, supply, and certification; acts as the arbiter between the central government and local authorities, particularly in the financing of education; supports directly by grants a few special educational institutions; and promotes educational research. His actions may be considered as more oblique than direct; in smaller matters he acts not only by mandatory regulations, orders, and circulars but also by making suggestions through handbooks and pamphlets. He exercises no direct responsibility for the running of schools, is not the employer of teachers (who are servants of the local education author-

ities), and has no power to prescribe programs and textbooks.

The Department of Education and Science is assisted in its tasks by a number of other organizations. Nominally reporting directly to the secretary of state are her majesty's inspectors, who act as the secretary's eyes and ears in the schools. Central advisory councils draw up reports on matters remitted to them; the Schools Council for the Curriculum and Examinations, representing many educational interests, also tenders advice. Financial recommendations in university matters are made by the University Grants Committee (central government grants to the universities, which cover most of their expenditure, are made every five years).

At the local level, 163 local education authorities (LEA's) are responsible for all schools and institutions of further education, as well as for most teacher-training colleges. The LEA's are established by the elected councils of counties and county boroughs. Each council sets up an education committee, consisting of councilmen and coopted members, to act as the LEA for the area. Each LEA has as its top permanent official a chief education officer. All educational staff are LEA employees.

The LEA may not prescribe curricula or textbooks; this is the prerogative of the head teacher in a school. The head teacher is nominally responsible to a board of governors or managers, who represent many local interests but in practice wield little power. The freedom of the school—and even of the individual teacher—to regulate matters regarded as primarily pedagogical is highly prized. Although parent-teacher associations exist, their influence is very limited.

This network of educational administration has been described as one of checks and balances, the mainspring of which is held to be the "partnership" between the Department of Education and Science and the LEA. In recent years it has shown signs of stress: the politicization of education has caused conflicts when the elected central and local governments have been of differing political views. Moreover, the expansion of education has entailed the central government's bearing a larger financial burden; it has, therefore, tended to intervene more at the local level, although discreetly and with some reluctance.

Historical development. This reluctance on the part of the central government to intervene in educational matters has deep historical roots, entwined around the nineteenth-century tradition of laissez-faire. Not until 1833 did Parliament first vote money for education, and not until as late as 1902 was there an educational system as such. By 1840 a government committee on education had been established to inspect elementary schools, then mainly in the hands of the Anglican church, for grant purposes. A system of payment by results was later introduced. Thus, the state supplemented money raised by charity.

In secondary education the so-called public independent schools such as Eton, Winchester, and Rugby began to prosper, providing an education not only for the aristocracy but also for the newly rich upper-middle class produced by the Industrial Revolution. Particularly in these institutions, religious values, gentlemanly conduct, and patriotic fervor—rather than scholastic prowess—were inculcated. At the same time, measures were proposed to reform the old local grammar schools.

Further state intervention could not, in fact, be long deferred. The increasing urban population had gained the franchise in 1867. The demand soon arose for nondenominational, compulsory, free, and universal education. The 1879 Education Act instituted local school boards to provide compulsory education for children between the ages of five and 13, either by building schools themselves or by supporting existing denominational schools. The boards were to administer central government grants and to use local taxes (rates) to pay for education. The new board schools were permitted to provide nondenominational religious instruction; the denominational schools continued to teach religion as before. Thus, a dual system of state and "voluntary" schools was created.

Some schools under this system developed beyond the elementary stage and became known as higher grade schools. Some even launched into the teaching of technical and commercial subjects. The 1895 Bryce Commission recommended that they should be considered secondary schools.

Embodying other recommendations of this commission, the 1899 Board of Education Act instituted a central authority for the first time to "advise and supervise" on educational matters. This new board, under a president (a politician usually without cabinet rank), survived until 1944.

External industrial and commercial pressures and the need for a more highly literate labor force finally impelled the government to establish a more elaborate educational framework. The 1902 Education Act replaced the school boards with LEA's but continued the dual system of state and voluntary schools. Free places were offered in the reorganized secondary grammar schools, thereby creating an educational ladder by which the poor could attain higher education. In 1918 the leaving age was raised to 14. Despite political prejudice and economic crises, a new view of secondary education as a right for all children gained ground, particularly after the Hadow Report of 1926. This report recommended a break in schooling at 11, when children, unless selected for grammar schools, should proceed to senior schools.

The 1944 Education Act again reorganized and extended the system. A central ministry supplanted the Board of Education, but the powers of the LEA's were not diminished. Denominational schools qualified for capital grants and were aided, in certain circumstances, with grants for current expenditure. (Since 1966 these schools —mainly Anglican and Catholic—have received grants of up to 80 percent of capital and maintenance costs.) The leaving age was set at 15, although this provision was not implemented until 1947. Secondary education was provided free for all children from the age of 11 in grammar, technical, and modern schools—in effect, a tripartite system. But the grammar school, entry to which was determined by a competitive examination, continued to carry the most esteem because it led to higher education.

Since 1944 no major legislation has been passed, but a number of administrative measures and reports have affected considerably the workings of the system. In many areas the tripartite system has been replaced by one of comprehensive secondary schools. The leaving age is to be raised to 16 by 1972. Reforms in secondary curricula and examinations are in progress or under debate. The Crowther Report of 1959, dealing with the education of adolescents, recommended a massive extension of schooling and the establishment of part-time education for all children up to the age of 17. The 1963 Newsom Report, which studied the needs of the average and below-average secondary pupil, established priorities in the field and recommended vast changes in curricula and methods. The Robbins Report of 1963 reviewed the future pattern of higher education. The Plowden Report of 1967 reviewed primary education and the transition to secondary education. The 1968 Report of the Public Schools Commission proposed measures for integrating these independent schools into the state system. All these developments, although not yet resulting in any comprehensive new legislation, have nevertheless promoted reforms.

Finances. The financing of education is shared roughly equally by the central government and the LEA's. Expenditure almost trebled during the 1960's. In the late 1960's an average of more than $500 was spent on each of the nation's 9.5 million students. This money included also such related items as school meals, milk, maintenance grants, the youth service and physical training, transportation, and residence costs for teacher trainees. The total expenditure also amounted to approximately 6 percent of the gross national product (if "related items" are omitted, the balance represents 5 percent of the GNP).

Some three-fourths of all local taxes are spent on education; the heaviest charge on the LEA is that of teachers' salaries, which account for about half of local expenditure. Of the remainder, 22 percent is spent on capital costs and 17 percent on running costs.

Public school system. In the late 1960's there were more than 8.3 million children enrolled annually in primary and secondary schools. Just under 50 percent stayed on beyond the statutory leaving age, and at age 17 or over, 18 percent of the age group were still in school. The trend to later leaving has recently become very marked. In 1970 the overall teacher-pupil ratio was 1 to 23. There were 250,000 immigrant children in schools, of whom 44,000 required special tuition in English (the official policy is to assimilate immigrants as quickly as possible into normal classes).

Preprimary and primary education. The demand for places in kindergartens and play groups for the 3–5 age group far exceeds the supply; this shortage was highlighted in the 1967 Plowden Report. To the 500 official nursery schools must be added more than 200 independent, locally organized play groups recognized by the education department. The official policy is to double the present provision, so that 15 percent of the children will be enrolled annually in full-time nursery education.

Of the 23,000 state primary schools, which edu-

cate 4.5 million children annually, 9,000 are denominational schools. Primary schools educate pupils for six years (ages five to 11). They are coeducational and are divided into infant and junior departments. The infant school receives children at the age of five, the compulsory age for beginning school. Catering exclusively to children between the ages of five and seven, it is a distinctively English institution. It is often characterized by vertical or "family" grouping, in which each class contains pupils from the whole age range. The purpose is for the younger children to be inducted into school life by the older children. Teaching takes place within the framework of the integrated day, in which children work individually at will on set tasks according to their interests. This is one of the most successful areas of English education.

Junior schools enroll children from the age of seven to the age of 11. The 1967 Plowden Report found that on criteria relating to standards of work, discipline and personal relationships, the balance of the curriculum, and teachers' competence, 33 percent of children were being educated in "good" and 5 percent in "poor" primary schools. But teachers still work under difficulty: the average class size in 1970 was 32, and 6.7 percent of the classes contained more than 40 pupils; moreover, 15 percent of the pupils were being educated in buildings constructed before 1903. It is reckoned that by the time they are seven or eight years old, children will have learned to read and can move on to a fuller curriculum which includes not only communication but also environmental studies, the arts, physical education, a foreign language, mathematics, and science. The junior school provides this wider curriculum.

Secondary education. After secondary education was extended in 1944 to all children from age 11 to school leaving and beyond, a tripartite system evolved in which the academically gifted (or those identified as such) went on to grammar schools, the less gifted went to technical schools, and the bulk attended modern schools. In fact, the technical school, which never took more than 5 percent of the children, failed to survive, leaving a bipartite system in which some 20 percent (depending on local school provision) of the primary school graduates were educated in grammar schools and the rest in modern schools. Selection for the grammar school was based on the competitive 11+ examination, which included intelligence tests and papers in arithmetic and English. Although later efforts were made to attenuate selection procedures for the grammar school, the system was considered unsatisfactory by many LEA's. The "parity of esteem" between secondary schools allegedly established by the 1944 act did not correspond to reality.

Since 1947, comprehensive secondary schools have sprung up in some areas to supplant the former segregation of able students from less able students by separate schools. Within these comprehensive schools, however, there is no uniform means of distinguishing between students of unequal caliber: some schools group children by ability or by key subjects, and others keep heterogeneous grouping within the age range, with progressive differentiation. Of the 5,700 secondary schools (1,000 of which are considered denominational), there are about 1,000 comprehensive schools. In 1965, comprehensive schooling became official policy and LEA's were required to draw up plans for secondary reorganization. The officially favored structure was for an all-through comprehensive school for the 11–18 age range. Another, more revolutionary scheme allowed for a new division of compulsory education, with a first school for pupils between the ages of five and nine, a new type of middle school for students aged nine to 13, and a senior school for students 13 years old and up. In 1970 the obligation to plan for comprehensive schooling was withdrawn; the grammar school, offering an eight-year course leading to a full graduation qualification, was reprieved. Thus, today, many structural forms of secondary education exist, and the ultimate pattern of English secondary education is likely to remain unclear until the end of the century.

Further and higher education. Postsecondary education is given in colleges of further education, evening institutes, technical and commercial colleges, colleges of art, colleges of agriculture, colleges of education, polytechnics, technological universities, and universities. Many of these institutions have both full-time and part-time programs, evening classes, day-release programs, and "sandwich" programs (in which the student alternates between long spells of employment and study).

Those institutions not belonging to the higher education sector accept for vocational, industrial, or commercial training or for further general education those students who may have no more than the statutory minimum of education. In late 1968, there were more than 3.1 million full-time or part-time students. At present such institutions are having to face a massive increase in the numbers in sandwich programs and a steady growth in the number of full-time students. Moreover, of the total insured work force under 18 in the late 1960's, nearly 24 percent were receiving some form of part-time, day-release education. Many programs are available, the most well-known being those that prepare students for the qualifications of the City and Guilds Institute and for the national certificates and diplomas, which may be obtained in many vocational and professional specializations.

In addition to the institutions mentioned above, adult education is carried out through extramural work, through the Workers' Educational Association, and by many voluntary and local organizations.

The polytechnics, the universities, and the colleges of education constitute the field of higher education. The nation's 30 polytechnics, relatively recent creations, have been set up side by side with the traditional universities in what has become known as the binary system; as yet, they lack the prestige attached to the traditional universities. Although they concentrate on providing applied science, engineering and technology, and business and management programs, many polytechnics offer social science and humanities programs as well. A recent creation has been the Open University, for study by means of television and correspondence. Although some polytechnics still offer lower-level programs, most students take the degree examinations of the Council for National Academic Awards (an autonomous body granted a royal charter in 1964 to award degrees to those successfully completing approved programs other than in universities).

The 35 full universities range from modern technological universities such as Loughborough to more traditional universities such as London or the medieval foundations of Oxford and Cambridge. These are more selective institutions, and entry to some is highly competitive. In 1968–1969, there were more than 177,000 university students studying for a bachelor's degree each year; 26 percent were studying science, 22 percent arts subjects, 21 percent social sciences, 16 percent engineering and technology, 11 percent medical subjects, and 4 percent other subjects. The phenomenon of recent years has been the rise in the numbers studying the social sciences. There were also more than 38,000 postgraduate students, of whom 23,000 were engaged in research degrees and 4,800 in one-year teacher-training courses. One in four postgraduates was a foreigner.

In the 160 colleges of education the more than 125,000 students preparing for teaching were mainly enrolled in three-year courses not leading to a bachelor's degree.

The Robbins Report of 1963 had predicted that by 1981–1982 the total numbers in higher education would rise to 510,000, but a more recent forecast by the education department now estimates the figure for that year as 727,000, or some 25 percent of the age group. All forecast figures up to the present have proved to be underestimates.

The problems facing further and higher education concern the optimum size of the student body, student financing, staff-student ratios, type and organization of programs, and type of student residences. The overall problem is one of cost: its solution depends upon the degree of priority given to further and higher education over other sectors of education or over other areas of national welfare. In addition, there is also a general problem of definition of higher education: it now seems as though the North American type of higher education, with a great gradation and variety of institutions, rather than the traditional European concept of the university, will prevail.

Education of exceptional children. Although gifted children (insofar as they can be identified) are still largely placed in grammar schools, the official policy is to integrate as far as possible the mentally or physically handicapped into a normal school. There are, however, special schools for the extremely physically handicapped and for children whose IQ ranges from 55 to 75.

Private sector of education. The private sector of education comprises some 3,600 nonstate, fee-paying schools in which are educated 450,000 pupils—some 6 percent of the school population. The denominational schools mentioned previously and the direct-grant grammar schools are not included in these figures because they receive funds from the central government. All other private schools must be formally registered and may seek recognition from the Department of Education and Science as being "efficient." Only one-third of private school pupils are boarders.

The most well-known schools in the private sector are the 200 independent institutions known as public schools. These schools educate only 2 percent of pupils aged 13–18, but their alumni occupy 20 percent of university places. A few schools are of medieval origin, such as Winchester College (founded by William of Wykeham), but the majority date from the Victorian period. Sporadic attempts have been made to widen their social recruitment. Some idea of their former influence may be gleaned from the fact that between 1918 and 1955, Eton and Harrow, two of the more famous schools, provided 36 percent of all Conservative members of Parliament and 45 percent of all cabinet ministers. This leadership role of the public schools is steadily declining as access to higher education becomes more easy, but critics claim that the existence of such schools still allows the wealthy to buy privilege and influence for their children.

Curricula and methods. The latitude of the school principal in regard to curricula and methods has already been mentioned. In fact, the only curriculum subject that must legally be offered is nondenominational religious instruction, although the parent has the right to withdraw his child from such classes if he so desires. (The law also prescribes that each school day must begin with an act of worship, but again stipulates the right of withdrawal.)

In primary education the aim is to teach the basic skills and to orient the child to further knowledge. In secondary education the bright child is subjected to a rigorous academic curriculum, the basic components of which are English, a foreign language, mathematics, and science; however, this curriculum may include the study of as many as ten subjects for five years. Prescribed syllabi for examinations administered by eight examining boards (all save one of which are attached to universities) tend to limit the curriculum content. In the last two or three years of secondary schooling (grades 12 and 13) as few as two subjects may be taken as examinable subjects, although optional subjects may also be studied. This limitation of subjects is termed specialization or study in depth and would seem to be a peculiarly English phenomenon at this top academic secondary level. For the average student in the less prestigious secondary modern school or not in the top streams of a comprehensive school, the curriculum is more flexible, although there is at present much experimentation as to the form it should take. In general, many North American curriculum projects and ideas in the teaching of science, mathematics, and modern languages have been taken up and adapted. In this respect the language laboratories to teaching machines, is on the increase.

The typical teaching method may be described as that of the Socratic dialogue rather than the magisterial exposition. For the younger children and the less gifted there is much use of the project method. In science great stress is laid upon experimental work performed by the pupils themselves; in languages the audiovisual methods are well developed. The use of educational technology, from language laboratories to teaching machines, is on the increase.

Examinations. The main school examinations are run by the eight examining boards already mentioned. After five years of secondary education the more academic pupils may take the general certificate of education (ordinary level) examination. This, despite its name, is a subject and not a certificate examination. In the late 1960's more than 625,000 candidates took this examination each year, with over 2 million subject entries. The success rate was 59 percent, and the most popular subjects were English language and literature, mathematics, geography, French, history, and biology. After a further two or three years, at about the age of 18, the brightest pupils will take the general certificate of education (advanced level) examination, but this time usually in only two or three subjects. At present, success in these examinations admits a student to many postsecondary programs and also exempts him from certain professional and vocational entrance requirements. The general certificate of education, with a combination of passes at ordinary and advanced levels in English, mathematics, a foreign language, one science, and another subject, is the usual minimum necessary (but not sufficient) qualification for entry to higher education.

For students of lesser ability there is a certificate of secondary education examination, which is taken at about age 16 and is also a subject examination. In the late 1960's some 207,000 candidates took this examination each year; the most

popular subjects were English, mathematics, geography, history, and technical drawing.

Examinations are mainly of the conventional essay type, although objective testing is increasingly being tried out. Assessment is external to the school, but experiments in internal assessment and in continuous assessment are being carried out. A further experiment is the development of a scholastic aptitude test for those seeking university entrance.

Teacher education and teachers. In colleges of education, which are run by the LEA's and in some cases by religious denominations, academic and professional training is concurrent. The three-year course culminates in the award of a teacher's certificate. A few students may stay on for a fourth year to take a B.Ed. degree. Graduate teacher trainees are educated separately in university departments, where they follow a one-year professional program. In both types of training the actual teaching practice lasts about three months. About 123,000 students enroll annually in training, and numbers are continuing to increase.

Responsible for teacher training are the 20 area training organizations, all but one of which are attached to universities. Their duties include recommending the certification of new teachers to the Department of Education and Science and the promotion of in-service training and educational research.

In 1970 there were 322,000 full-time teachers in schools. Shortages of infant-school teachers and of mathematics and science teachers continue, and there is much wastage in the profession because of poor salary and promotion prospects.

Scotland, Wales, and Northern Ireland. The educational systems of Scotland, Wales, and Northern Ireland differ in several ways from the education system in England. In Scotland the legal basis is the 1946 Education Act, which largely duplicates the 1944 act for England, although the Scottish central authority exercises greater power than does the English education department. Primary education is for children between the ages of five and 12. Students are then admitted to a three-year course in a junior secondary school or to a five-year course in a senior secondary school. Some 35 percent of the students, as compared with 20 percent in England, follow the five-year academic course. In any case, distinctions are not so rigid, and "comprehensivization" has not encountered so much opposition as in England. There are no denominational schools, and religious instruction is not obligatory.

Since 1970, primary and secondary education in Wales has been a purely Welsh responsibility. In Welsh-speaking areas, which comprise 25 percent of the population, the language of instruction is Welsh. Welsh is also taught in practically all primary schools.

Although educational organization in Northern Ireland is broadly similar to that in England, many grammar schools are run by religious denominations, as in the Irish Republic.

Trends. In the years to come, the United Kingdom may see an improvement in the provision of preschool and primary education, particularly in new buildings, and further controversy regarding the secondary education system. The choice of whether to introduce comprehensive schooling or to retain a bipartite structure may eventually be made by local authorities. There may be a vast expansion in the numbers staying on at school beyond the statutory leaving age, even after it is raised to 16; this will mean a rethinking of curriculum for what is already termed the new sixth form.

In the general field of curriculum and methods, a growth of interdisciplinary and prevocational programs, accompanied by a greater use of educational technology, may occur. Some modification of the rigid examination system, which in the past tended to determine curricula, may be made. Finally, there will probably be an expansion in postsecondary education. The greatest area of growth here will probably be in the polytechnics. The colleges of education may also cease to be monotechnic, becoming either liberal arts colleges with an education component or preparing also for other professions and paraprofessions related to teaching.

The central problem in British education will, however, remain that of preserving the best in an old and proven tradition while educating the individual for the new technological society.

BIBLIOGRAPHY

BARON, GEORGE 1965 *A Bibliographical Guide to the English Educational System.* London, Athlone.
BARON, GEORGE 1966 *Society, Schools, and Progress in England.* Oxford, Pergamon Press.
HUNTER, S. LESLIE 1968 *The Scottish Educational System.* New York and London, Oxford University Press.
MONKS, T. G. 1968 *Comprehensive Education in England and Wales.* Slough, England, National Foundation for Educational Research.
OSBORNE, GERALD STANLEY 1966 *Scottish and English Schools: A Comparative Survey of the Past Fifty Years.* London, Longmans. Published in 1967 by the University of Pittsburgh Press.
SMITH, W. O. LESTER 1967 *Education in Great Britain.* 5th ed. New York and London, Oxford University Press.

W. D. HALLS

UNITED NATIONS EDUCATIONAL, SCIENTIFIC AND CULTURAL ORGANIZATION

The United Nations Educational, Scientific and Cultural Organization (UNESCO) is a specialized agency with the distinctive role of contributing to peace and security "by promoting collaboration among the nations through education, science and culture" (UNESCO 1945, Article I). But it also represents the latest internationally organized effort of men and governments to promote, as an end in itself, the achievement of a stronger world intellectual community.

The pursuit of these two essential objectives—contributing to peace and strengthening the world intellectual community—has required a great amount of experimentation and innovation and has been conducted under UNESCO's leadership, through collaboration among governments as well as among individuals and nongovernmental organizations. The diversity among national cultures has required much compromise in the process of program formulation. The complexity of its work, combined with the depth of conviction that its role is an important one, has sustained UNESCO's determined efforts since its inception to establish policies and programs in a format acceptable to all its members.

UNESCO has grown from the 28 member nations attending the first General Conference in 1946 to 125 eligible members at the 1968 session; its annual budget has grown from approximately $7 million in 1947 to $38 million in 1968, not including about $30 million of United Nations Development Program projects which UNESCO administers. In addition, UNESCO is being called upon to play a central professional role in programs separately funded by UNICEF, the International Bank for Reconstruction and Development, and some other international organizations.

Fundamentally, all of UNESCO's activities have been educational in the sense in which the preamble to its constitution called for the construction of "the defenses of peace" in the minds of men. The division of its program tasks into education, science, culture, and mass communications must be seen as a convenient operational means of furthering this basic objective of the attainment of peace and the advancement of the common welfare. The achievement of an acceptable program strategy was difficult because of the different emphases and priorities member states saw as desirable.

Origins and structure. The more obvious roots of UNESCO were in the efforts made at the end of World War II to fashion a world system of organizations to guide nations in avoiding war and advancing human welfare. In this sense, UNESCO was to be an integral part of the intergovernmental political framework for the promotion of peace. Its creation was based upon the belief that in the attainment of peace and human welfare a substantial amount of constructive effort is required through positive cooperation in education, science, and culture as well as in such fields as trade, finance, health, nutrition, and disarmament and in the adjustment of political disputes.

But UNESCO also had roots in the historic efforts of men to build an intellectual community; this had led in the days of the League of Nations to the calling of a committee on intellectual cooperation. This committee focused upon such matters as the conditions of intellectual life, including the need for assistance to individual nations; intellectual property rights; university cooperation; and the international coordination of bibliographical research (McMurry & Lee 1947). The committee also concerned itself with the achievement of international understanding through education. In 1924 the Institute for Intellectual Cooperation was established by the Assembly of the League of Nations. Somewhat later the league formed the International Organization for Intellectual Cooperation, thereby giving a new focus and a somewhat stronger base to initiative in international intellectual cooperation. These very modest and tentative efforts served primarily to stimulate some awareness of the need for concern with transnational intellectual interests. They served, moreover, as precedents in the planning of UNESCO.

In UNESCO's constitution the objectives of peace and intellectual cooperation were both incorporated in the language of Article I, Paragraph 1:

> The purpose of the Organization is to contribute to peace and security by promoting collaboration among the nations through education, science and culture in order to further universal respect for justice, for the rule of law and for the human rights and fundamental freedoms which are affirmed for the peoples of the world, without distinction of race, sex, language or religion, by the Charter of the United Nations.

But the constitution went further, reflecting especially the proceedings of the Council of Allied Ministers of Education in London during World War II, and attempted to define how UNESCO would make this contribution (Article I, Paragraph 2). The organization would collaborate in the efforts to advance mutual knowledge and understanding of peoples by various means of mass communication and would recommend those international agreements seen as necessary to promote the free flow of ideas. UNESCO would promote popular education and the spread of culture by suggesting desirable educational methods and by aiding members to develop their educational activities and to advance the ideal of equality of educational opportunity without prejudicial distinctions. UNESCO would maintain, increase, and diffuse knowledge; conserve and protect the world's heritage of books, works of art, and monuments of history and science and recommend the necessary international conventions to the nations concerned; encourage international cooperation in all intellectual activities, including cultural exchanges of experts and materials; and initiate methods of international cooperation to give peoples of all countries access to published materials produced by any of them.

The intention to make UNESCO an essential part of the United Nations system, as decided at the San Francisco United Nations Conference on International Organization, was fulfilled by making it an intergovernmental organization, controlled and financed by the same governments which, in the main, would also control the rest of the UN system. Provision was made for a formal agreement between UNESCO and the UN under the coordinating leadership of the Economic and Social Council.

The intellectual origin of UNESCO was also clear. It was reflected principally in constitutional provisions for an executive board to be composed of outstanding intellectual leaders, who, with the director-general, would guide the execution of UNESCO's program. The constitution also provided for the establishment by each member state of national commissions or cooperating bodies which were to "function as agencies of liaison in all matters of interest to" UNESCO (Article VII). These national commissions or cooperating bodies, to be made up of representatives of interested educational, scientific, and cultural bodies, were to be advisory to the General Conference and to their own governments. Finally, the constitution emphasized the use of nongovernmental organizations in the fields of education, science, culture, and mass communications by giving UNESCO the authority to make "suitable arrangements for consultation and cooperation" with such organizations "and to invite them to undertake specific tasks, including 'appropriate participation by representatives of such organizations on advisory committees set up by the General Conference'" (Article XI).

This much background concerning UNESCO's origin and nature is essential to understanding the slow rate of progress in achieving a consensus among member states as to just how the new organization was to be utilized in its dual and broadly educational mission. In virtually every session of the General Conference and of the executive board there have been suggestions and pressures for program additions, amendments, or deletions which stem from varied, sometimes divergent, interpretations of UNESCO's purpose or from differing judgments as to the way in which UNESCO can best contribute to peace, to strengthening intellectual cooperation, or to serving the special interests of individual nations. As both the educational agency of the United Nations and an organization for promoting worldwide intellectual communication, UNESCO has been offered a myriad of program suggestions individually interesting and frequently appealing but often beyond the organization's capacity for performance or beyond the financial resources provided by governments. But, perhaps most important, a balance had to be achieved between the influences brought to bear by governments and those stemming more directly from nongovernmental interests.

International influences. A number of major international factors influenced the early development of UNESCO. One was the fact that the U.S.S.R. did not join UNESCO until 1954 and, therefore, did not participate in the early fashioning of UNESCO's basic program.

A second factor was the Chinese civil war, which prevented the millions of mainland Chinese from participating in UNESCO activities.

A third consideration was the burgeoning number of newly independent states which joined UNESCO as well as the United Nations in the 1950's and 1960's, long after UNESCO's constitution had gone into effect and a program pattern had been established. This resulted in extraordinary new pressures upon UNESCO to provide a vast range and quantity of developmental assistance in education, science, and culture.

Closely related was a fourth international development, the determination of the UN family to accept major responsibilities in promoting economic and social development in the underdeveloped nations. UNESCO undertook to implement this international effort in addition to meeting the new responsibilities it found in adjusting its own normal program to meet the demand of the enlarged membership.

Finally, there was the marked decline in the post–San Francisco mood of euphoria concerning the prospects for an increasingly rational approach in building a peaceful world community. Critical tensions developed, affecting the relationships among all nations and influencing UNESCO's policy-making and program-making process. The revival of nationalism—an obstacle to international cooperation—became evident throughout the world. While it made more obvious the need for contributions by UNESCO which were envisaged in its constitution, it undermined the prospects for UNESCO to make such contributions on a substantial scale.

The concepts and substance of education, science, and culture have been undergoing extraordinary changes as the result of research, discoveries, and applied technology. Hence, there has also been a need for fundamental changes in the focus and methods of UNESCO's efforts.

Scope of activities. The scope of UNESCO's work has been determined by the interplay of many factors. It is vast in range by almost any standards unless compared with the magnitude of the world's needs. These needs far outweigh what UNESCO is authorized to do as well as what it is capable of doing. One way of understanding the scope and hence the complexity of the tasks of the organization and its member states is to examine the official biennial program and budget adopted at the General Conference in 1968. But that document cannot provide a full sense of what has been going on over the years, of the experiences gained, and of the cumulative impact UNESCO has had since 1946 in almost every one of its member states. For this, one would need to visit individual member states and consult with government and professional people in the intellectual and cultural community.

Such a study would reveal that UNESCO has three main approaches to its work: (1) strengthening international intellectual cooperation, (2) providing aid and assistance in the context of the development process facing a large proportion of its member states, and (3) promoting agreed-upon universal norms and standards believed to be essential and fundamental to the attainment of greater understanding and peace.

Strengthening intellectual cooperation. It was clear in the earliest discussions about the establishment of UNESCO that its primary concern would be with facilitating communication within the worldwide intellectual community. Although at the preparatory meetings in San Francisco and in London there was considerable debate over whether a single international organization should be established covering education, science, and culture or whether there should be a separate organization in each field, there was never much doubt that the basic need for international organization in these fields arose from the lack of communication within the world's intellectual community. It was the same need that had been recognized during the interwar years by the League of Nations. Therefore, as soon as UNESCO was established, it embarked on intensive efforts toward developing new channels for transnational and international intellectual cooperation.

Scholars in the natural sciences most quickly articulated the kind of help they wanted from UNESCO. They had had experience in the organized promotion of communication—indeed the world's natural scientists were probably better organized than any other part of the intellectual community. Scientists were aware of what was needed and had a strong sense of community;

this was particularly evident in the work of the International Council of Scientific Unions (ICSU). This nongovernmental body had for several decades served as the coordinating organization for physicists, mathematicians, biologists, astronomers, botanists, and many other specialists in the natural sciences. The ICSU played a leading role in helping UNESCO develop the means for stimulating communication not only in the natural sciences but also in all other intellectual areas within its concern and jurisdiction.

The pattern of UNESCO's efforts toward strengthening the means for intellectual cooperation is varied. Assistance has been provided in the development or strengthening of international professional nongovernmental organizations. The ICSU was strengthened; new groups were created, such as the International Council of Philosophy and Humanistic Studies, the International Political Science Association, the International Sociological Association, the International Economic Organization, the International Social Science Council, the International Council of the Arts, the International Council of Museums, the International Music Council, and the International Association of Universities. Financial assistance has been given to establish or strengthen central secretariats to carry on the work of these professional bodies and to conduct international seminars, meetings, and conferences; in many instances, UNESCO has utilized these organizations in the execution of its own programs, thereby widening its own impact and strengthening the role of the organizations in relation to professional centers and individuals on a worldwide basis. This has been especially true when cooperation with UNESCO involved organizing international meetings or publishing and distributing reports, scientific studies, and other materials.

UNESCO has also contributed to increasing communication among intellectuals internationally by organizing conferences on such subjects as data and information processing (1959), adult education (1960), oceanographic records (1960), hydrological research (1964), problems of youth (1964), illiteracy problems (1965), and the biosphere (1968). Such conferences, worldwide or regional, have brought together scholars, publicists, and governmental personnel and have usually led to the publication of materials for the intellectual community as a whole.

A third kind of effort to strengthen the intellectual community is found in the establishment of advisory committees, which bring into UNESCO's program-making process individual scientists, educators, and cultural leaders who serve to stimulate the exchange of ideas and the development of communication facilities throughout the world. Such advisory committees have been created for a large variety of subjects, including school curriculum development, science education, adult education and literacy, seismology, and standardization of scientific documentation. Over a period of several years the intellectual community was mobilized through advisory committees to help in the preparation of a cultural and scientific history of mankind and in the so-called East-West Mutual Appreciation Project (formally, the Mutual Appreciation of Eastern and Western Cultural Values Project).

A fourth kind of need in strengthening intellectual cooperation has been in the field of documentation, that is, in developing means by which research findings from throughout the world may be made available in systematic fashion to individual scholars. UNESCO estimates that in the natural sciences alone more than 2.5 million articles are published annually in 50,000 to 60,000 journals in addition to the publication of vast numbers of books and pamphlets. Comparable figures probably exist for educational and cultural publications. UNESCO has sought to improve the situation by publishing bibliographies, by encouraging the standardization and dissemination of specialized documentation, and by applying electronic methods to the cataloging and retrieval of information.

UNESCO has also been concerned with the development of international and regional research facilities—such as the European Nuclear Research Organization, the International Institute for Educational Planning, the International Brain Research Organization, and the International Cell Research Organization—and with focusing attention upon neglected areas of research. It has prompted surveys of trends in research in the natural and social sciences.

Finally, UNESCO's publications are an integral part of its contribution to strengthening intellectual cooperation; they derive from research, conferences, expert groups, sponsored research, and similar efforts. UNESCO itself reports that during its first 20 years more than 4,000 titles were published (including multi-

language editions). They have been principally of two kinds: documentary—for example, UNESCO's *Statistical Yearbook, Index Translationum, International Yearbook of Education,* and *Study Abroad*—and statistical or analytical, referring to such subjects as television, technical education, arid zone problems, and effective urbanization. Some publications are more philosophical and are "aimed at stirring thought on certain problems"; these include the journal *Impact of Science on Society* and publications on urbanization, race, international conflicts, and other topics. Most of UNESCO's publications cannot be categorized—they include such journals as the *Copyright Bulletin, Museum, International Social Science Journal,* and the *UNESCO Courier.* UNESCO adds about 50 titles a year to its list of publications.

Thus, by a wide variety of means, UNESCO has strengthened the network of international intellectual communications. This was UNESCO's primary concern in the early years and was based on the nature of previous transnational and international collaboration. It was a concern that reflected the immediate and often articulated interests of specialists and of governments in the relatively highly developed countries which constituted the hard core of UNESCO's membership in the early years. Newly developing countries, as they became members of UNESCO, also became interested in establishing international cultural communications, although they lacked much of the intellectual infrastructure that is essential for effective cooperation with the more advanced countries.

This preoccupation with intellectual cooperation, according to UNESCO's constitution, was expected to contribute to peace and security. At any rate, it was assumed that this would be an effect of UNESCO's focus upon intellectual cooperation and that it was not necessary to give such program efforts a particular emphasis or slant to ensure a maximum contribution to peace. That the intellectual community of all nations was being drawn into closer cooperation was believed to be a contribution in itself. Some of the special program activities, such as studies of race, tensions, international conflicts, and human rights, were considered to have a bearing upon reducing tensions among member states.

Providing development assistance. In expressing its concern with strengthening the international intellectual community, UNESCO, at least by implication, also indicated its concern with strengthening the intellectual resources within individual nations. It did not initially become directly involved in the development of these resources—for example, universities, school systems, libraries, or museums—except as part of a passing postwar responsibility for reconstruction needs growing out of wartime damages. As more nations with weak intellectual infrastructures joined UNESCO and as UN members accepted greater responsibility for providing technical assistance to the large number of nations classified as newly developing, UNESCO was required to devote major attention to the creation and development of institutional and other resources in the areas of education, science, and culture. To a degree the efforts toward strengthening international intellectual cooperation provided a framework, and preparation for their participation in the intellectual cooperative process became an articulated objective of developing nations. What they needed first and foremost, however, were those educational, scientific, and cultural institutional infrastructures that were basic to their development. It was inevitable and imperative that UNESCO, as the world's principal international organization in education, science, and culture, should aid these nations.

The basic task of UNESCO in this endeavor has been to provide assistance in educational development at all levels. Assistance has been offered through conferences, seminars, advisory groups, fellowships, technical assistance experts, and other means. The extent of the assistance has been substantial, however one measures it, and aid has been directed toward solving some of the most critical problems facing developing countries. UNESCO has collaborated in major educational conferences in Africa, Asia, and Latin America to assist the countries of each region to discuss and identify their common needs and to develop specific goals. They have focused upon means for attaining goals in primary and secondary teacher education and in university education. It has been UNESCO's objective to assist nations in setting practical targets and in planning realistic policies. Difficult questions are discussed in terms of the priorities to be given to different levels of educational development, taking into consideration the availability of national resources.

Assistance efforts have also involved perplexing professional problems with curriculum content and teaching methods. The question of what the place of science teaching, technological education, and social studies should be has assumed major importance in deliberations about and assistance for educational development. Probably the most dynamic program of UNESCO has been that focused on educational planning: (1) promoting understanding of the concept of planning in education, (2) training for educational planning, (3) promoting research, and (4) promoting the establishment of institutions for training for educational planning in individual countries and regions and linking these through fellowships and publications with the UNESCO International Institute for Educational Planning at Paris. School construction has also been a field for major assistance efforts.

Through UNESCO it has been possible to launch a campaign for stimulating worldwide concern with the problem of illiteracy. In a number of countries, including Algeria, Ecuador, Guinea, Iran, Mali, and Tanzania, pilot projects have been established to test methods and evaluate the results of massive literacy programs. An increasing effort is being made by UNESCO to promote the development of the social sciences as disciplines at appropriate levels in the educational programs of newly developing countries; centers for social science research focused especially upon development problems have been established in Vienna, Rio de Janeiro, and New Delhi.

To help strengthen the development of the intellectual infrastructures of developing nations, UNESCO has emphasized library development and the development of publishing facilities for educational material, including textbooks and dictionaries. At the same time UNESCO has actively promoted dissemination of knowledge about the resources and techniques of mass media which relate to informal public education and which can be used more systematically in formal education. Special attention has been given to the potential of stationary satellites as a means of supplementing school education, especially in large countries such as India. Here again, UNESCO has promoted important research and training projects as in Strasbourg, Quito, Manila, and Dakar.

The amount of assistance given by UNESCO using funds from outside its own budget—that is, as executive agency for the United Nations Development Program—has exceeded very considerably that available under UNESCO's regular budget. UNESCO is deeply involved in education, the most fundamental aspect of the development process in most of the developing countries.

Promoting universal norms. UNESCO is concerned not merely with providing technical services toward strengthening worldwide intellectual cooperation and the educational resources of newly developing countries; it also has an essentially normative function which constitutes the third aspect of its work. Its value commitments, stated clearly in the constitution in terms of human rights, are made apparent in the execution of its program activities. These rights are also the subjects of special efforts to secure their implementation.

The basic norms are the human rights referred to in UNESCO's constitution and the United Nations Charter and further explicated in the Universal Declaration of Human Rights and in several covenants adopted by the General Assembly of the United Nations. In its various program efforts UNESCO always emphasizes the need to avoid discrimination on the basis of race, sex, or color as essential to the attainment of its goals. This principle appears not only in resolutions of the General Conference authorizing specific programs but also pervades the speeches and papers of the director-general in his discussions of UNESCO's missions or the scope of particular programs. The *UNESCO Courier*, a unique publication for an international organization, has an obvious editorial commitment to these same values and to the belief that it is urgently necessary for mankind to work incessantly toward their attainment as part of the search for peace.

In addition to the promotion of human rights as an integral aspect of its program services, UNESCO undertakes direct promotion of such values in separate program activities—for example, in their promotion through conferences and publications on education about human rights. Similarly, UNESCO has developed cooperative projects among schools in different countries which emphasize teaching about the UN and the achievement of international understanding. Cooperation among youth organizations has been fostered for the same purposes.

UNESCO fashioned and adopted a special international recommendation and convention in 1960 condemning in education all those distinctions which are founded on race, color, sex, language, religion, political or other opinions,

national or social origins, and economic conditions or birth (UNESCO 1966). One of the most interesting efforts in this direction was UNESCO's sponsorship of a project which focused on compiling scientific evidence related to race and racial distinctions and the factors which contribute to racial prejudice. UNESCO also instituted a special program to further mutual understanding in an attempt to guide relations between Asia and the West; the project lasted about a decade and sought to influence the educational systems of all nations. Finally, reference should be made to UNESCO's sponsorship of several international conventions now in effect and intended to guide the conduct of ratifying states: the Universal Copyright Convention (1952); the International Convention for the Protection of Cultural Property in the Event of Armed Conflict (1954); and the so-called Florence Convention, or more formally the Convention on the Importation of Educational, Scientific, and Cultural Materials (1950).

Progress. Both the very extraordinary range and variety of UNESCO's efforts—which member states authorized—and the essential nature of UNESCO as a facilitating agency help to explain why it has been difficult and why it has taken so long for UNESCO to achieve an agreed focus and program strategy. It explains, also, why UNESCO has come to mean so many different things to different people. It explains perhaps most of all why the impact of UNESCO is not easily seen.

Some aspects of UNESCO's evolution deserve special emphasis. First of all, it is clear that since its establishment UNESCO has become firmly rooted as an essential institution in the world community. It is today the principal world center through which member states seek by multilateral means to promote international action for the advancement of education, science, and culture. It is equally recognized as a major instrument for coalescing the interests of the world's nongovernmental intellectual community. It is thus both an agent of member states and a stimulant in its own right for governmental as well as nongovernmental policy and activity in the broad spectrum of education, science, and culture.

Second, the member states have found ways of achieving balance and strategy in UNESCO's program-making process. The early conflict over whether all UNESCO's activities must make a demonstrable contribution to peace has been largely forgotten, not only because such a relationship is difficult to establish or predict but also because of the uncertainty of governments concerning the kind of peace they really want. There has developed within UNESCO a kind of faith that any cooperation in education, science, and culture will eventually contribute in some manner to the prospects for peace. Member states have clearly not wanted vigorous and effective international efforts in education and the mass media which might influence the attitudes and opinions of their people on international topics. Both prevailing nationalistic emotions and the tensions in contemporary international politics have favored avoiding debate on whether UNESCO's program should always seek to contribute directly and immediately to the prospects for world peace.

Third, the critically underdeveloped character of the educational, scientific, and cultural resources of the great majority of UNESCO's member states continues to pose both organizational and program problems. Because of the insistent needs of these nations for technical assistance, the organization's attention has tended to shift toward these needs to an extent that has led some of the more developed nations to feel that UNESCO faces a crisis of identity. It is believed by some that UNESCO is in danger of becoming primarily an operational agency for dispensing assistance and that it may thereby lose its status as an institution for high-level educational, scientific, and cultural advancement and cooperation. This issue will be especially important in the future because of the voting strength of the less developed countries, which is generally in inverse proportion to their capacity to pay and their state of development in education, science, and culture.

Fourth, like all United Nations agencies concerned with assisting the less developed countries, UNESCO faces serious financial restrictions. This is likely to be the case for some years to come. UNESCO's budget has increased considerably since 1947, especially in respect to its development assistance component, but the increase hardly reflects the magnitude of the problems in education, science, and cultural development facing the world community today. In large measure the financial problem is a result of the policy (thus far) of most of the principal member states to channel their assistance funds through bilateral rather than multilateral agencies and to focus upon bilateral or regional means for cooperation in education, science, and culture. These approaches are controlled by prevailing nationalistic sentiment in the context of very tense international politics. To a small extent it may also be due to the member states' evaluation of UNESCO's administrative capabilities and its ability to marshal technical expertise on a worldwide basis.

Fifth, it may be noted that UNESCO's program areas have developed at different rates. Greatest progress was made initially in the field of the natural sciences. Not only was the transnational community of natural scientists ready for more systematic international cooperation, but also the prevailing concern of most member states after World War II was to quickly develop their scientific resources to stimulate technological and industrial development. This desire was echoed by most of the newly developing countries as they became members of UNESCO. As the development efforts of the United Nations got underway in the 1950's and early 1960's, it became increasingly clear that for many countries an equally great or perhaps even greater need lay in the development of educational systems, curricula, and the teaching profession. A shift of emphasis occurred therefore in the educational component of UNESCO's program and budget. The social sciences, which had long been neglected, were given somewhat more emphasis. Neglect was a reflection, in part, of the status of the social sciences as disciplines. It was also a reflection of the uneven development of the social sciences in otherwise highly developed countries and, therefore, uneven support from these governments. Perhaps most important, the neglect of the social sciences reflected a suspicion, especially in less modernized countries (but not unknown in the more developed ones), of the potential effect that rational study of social relationships might have upon the authority structure of traditional societies. However, the imperative importance of the social sciences in national development planning and in coping with some of the social consequences of industrialization and of modernization in agriculture now impels UNESCO member states to place more emphasis upon this component of the organization's program. To fulfill the needs of less developed countries, mass communications programs have been strengthened. The development of mass media as a means of promoting international understanding tends to be avoided, however, because of the nationalistic sentiments which underlie contemporary international tensions.

In comparison with its programs in education, science, and mass communications, UNESCO's cultural programs are less easily defined and have tended to be of less intensity. Unless one defines "culture" in terms of the responsibilities which have bureaucratically been grouped in a section of the UNESCO secretariat, it is clear that the term "cultural activities" must overlap with education, science, and mass communications. UNESCO's cultural activities have included saving the historic treasures threatened by floods caused by the Aswan Dam, helping to restore the art treasures of Florence after the flood of 1966, and making an appeal to the world to help save historic treasures in Venice.

Reviewing UNESCO's formative years and its present promise, one can see why it is an intriguing enterprise and why it continues to have a high emotional, intellectual, and political appeal. The reasons lie in its organizational nature and in its program focus; in both respects there has been a high degree of innovation. As an international organization focused upon education, science, and culture, UNESCO is unique in modern times. It is completely international, its policies and programs formulated by international agreement among member states and administered under the direction of international civil servants. It is intergovernmental, but it has extensive direct contacts with nongovernmental institutions and persons concerned with the advancement of the educational, scientific, and cultural interests of mankind. It collaborates with other UN organizations concerned with the promotion of peace. Its mission is the distinct one of helping to build the world's intellectual community and of responding to the special educational, scientific, and cultural needs of underdeveloped countries. It mobilizes financial resources on the basis of capacity to pay and dispenses them for activities identified as international needs.

UNESCO's varied program activities have been on a larger scale and have covered a wider range of problems than have those of any previous international organization in this area. UNESCO developed new ways of collaboration which have served to make it a center for intergovernmental collaboration and have enabled it to reach directly the people who can benefit from the advancement of education, science, and culture.

BIBLIOGRAPHY

DUNN, FREDERICK S. 1950 *War and the Minds of Men.* New York, published for the Council on Foreign Relations, by Harper.

LAVES, WALTER H. C., AND CHARLES A. THOMSON 1957 *UNESCO: Purpose, Progress, Prospects.* Bloomington, Indiana University Press.

MCMURRY, RUTH EMILY, AND MUNA LEE 1947 *The Cultural Approach: Another Way in International Relations.* Chapel Hill, University of North Carolina Press.

SATHYAMURTHY, T. V. 1964 *The Politics of International Cooperation: Contrasting Conceptions of UNESCO.* Geneva, Droz.

SATHYAMURTHY, T. V. 1967 "Functional International Cooperation: UNESCO." *International Studies,* 8, no. 4:361–385.

SHUSTER, GEORGE N. 1963 *UNESCO: Assessment and Promise.* New York, published for the Council on Foreign Relations, by Harper.

THOMAS, JEAN 1962 *U.N.E.S.C.O.* Paris, Gallimard.

UNESCO 1945 *Constitution of the United Nations.* Publication No. 367. Paris, The Organization.

UNESCO 1966 *What Is UNESCO?* 5th ed. Paris, The Organization.

UNESCO 1969 *Approved Programme and Budget for 1969–1970.* Paris, The Organization.

U.S. NATIONAL COMMISSION FOR UNESCO 1963 *Basic Documents* (United Nations Educational, Scientific and Cultural Organization). Washington, D.C., U.S. Department of State.

WALTER H. C. LAVES

UNITED STATES ARMED FORCES INSTITUTE

The United States Armed Forces Institute is an agency of the Department of Defense which provides supplementary educational opportunities for men and women on active duty in the armed forces. The institute makes available an enormously wide variety of academic and technical courses at the elementary, secondary, and college levels. Since it began operations early in World War II, well over 6 million course enrollments have been processed through USAFI. Courses are offered for personal enrichment, as preparation for a career or further academic work in civilian life, or as a supplement to military training. The institute's central headquarters in located in Madison, Wis. (USAFI, Madison).

Administration. USAFI's operations are directed and supervised by the Directorate for Education Programs and Management Training, Office of the Deputy Assistant Secretary of Defense for Education. In order to provide direct and expeditious service to military personnel stationed throughout the world, three overseas USAFI's are presently in operation: USAFI, Alaska, operated by the Department of the Air Force; USAFI, Caribbean, operated by the Department of the Army; and USAFI, Hawaii, operated by the Department of the Navy.

The overseas USAFI's perform most of the same functions as USAFI, Madison, with a number of exceptions. Thus, all work on the development of USAFI courses and tests is done at USAFI, Madison, and all educational materials are centrally procured from there. USAFI, Madison, is also the permanent repository for records of enrollees' educational achievement and is the only USAFI authorized to report this achievement to educational institutions and other interested agencies.

Military personnel may enroll in USAFI courses by mailing an application form directly to the nearest USAFI. They may also enroll at registration sections, located at military installations, where USAFI course materials are stocked and issued. There are close to 200 such registration sections in operation at installations in the United States and overseas. The serviceman-student pays only a small, nominal fee for enrollment in his first course. Provided that his progress is satisfactory, he is then eligible for any other USAFI courses and services without additional cost. No classes are conducted at Madison; all enrollees study at their respective posts or installations, by means of either group study classes, correspondence, or self-teaching.

A computer complex is operated at USAFI, Madison, in order to expedite service to students in the field, to reduce record storage space, to maintain greater accuracy in student records, and, in general, to make student services at USAFI more responsive to needs in the field.

Ties with civilian education. From USAFI's beginnings in World War II, policy direction of the institute has been strongly influenced by the civilian educational community. Prominent educators were directly involved in the development and administration of the USAFI program during the war years, and this relationship has continued through the close association of the professional staff at USAFI with their civilian counterparts at the university-college, technical school, high school, and pre-high-school levels.

A formal relationship has been established with the Commission on Accreditation of Service Experiences (CASE) of the American Council on Education. CASE maintains liaison with the Office of the Deputy Assistant Secretary of Defense for Education and with secondary schools, colleges and universities, regional accrediting associations, and other organizations interested in accreditation. The commission is composed of 12 civilian members appointed by the president of the American Council on Education, who is an ex officio member.

All USAFI courses at the high school and college levels and in technical subjects have been evaluated by CASE for conformance with accepted educational practice. CASE issues recommendations as to how much credit should be granted for given USAFI courses, and these recommendations are published by the American Council on Education for the information of civilian educational institutions. USAFI does not itself grant academic credit for courses—only civilian institutions and agencies may do this or may issue diplomas and equivalency certificates. Upon a student's request, USAFI, Madison, will report results on high school and college level tests to the educational institutions of his choice. The actual granting of credit or equivalency certification is then a matter to be decided by the institution or state department of education concerned.

Selection of course materials. The textbooks used in most USAFI courses are the same as those frequently used in civilian classrooms. USAFI textbooks are selected through the cooperative efforts of publishers, national professional associations, educational specialists employed at USAFI, and nationally recognized authorities.

USAFI obtains information on the textbooks most frequently used in various subject areas in representative junior colleges, colleges, and universities and selected elementary and high schools. An initial review and selection of texts is made by analysts at USAFI, and three to five appropriate texts are submitted to a panel of subject matter specialists who evaluate the texts and make recommendations. Final selections are viewed by the Directorate for Education Programs and Management Training in Washington. When suitable standard editions of textbooks cannot be found, USAFI arranges to have the materials developed by educational specialists. Study guides, instructors' manuals, and tests are also specially developed for most USAFI courses.

Education programs.   For servicemen who have not finished elementary or high school, USAFI has courses and tests leading to high school equivalency. For persons who have graduated from high school and are thinking of college, USAFI offers courses at the college freshman and sophomore levels. For those thinking of a job instead of college after they leave the service, the institute has courses in many different vocational and technical areas.

USAFI offers two distinct education programs: (1) the range of courses developed by the institute itself at Madison, Wis., which includes elementary and high school programs and technical courses; and (2) the participating college and university program, in which some 6,000 courses are offered through 50-odd colleges and universities. The latter program is based on individual contracts with the institutions concerned, under which the institution develops and provides the requisite educational materials and guides the student through the course. The serviceman pays for the course materials, and USAFI pays for the instructional services.

Methods of instruction.   Originally, correspondence was the only method of instruction in USAFI courses. However, two additional approaches have since come to be employed: self-teaching and group study classes. In correspondence courses, students receive systematically prepared lesson materials which take them step by step through the work of the course. At each step they submit written lessons for grading and evaluation, and the lessons are usually returned with helpful comments and suggestions to aid them in their work. In self-teaching courses, the students do not submit lessons but proceed on their own.

Group study is conducted in the same manner as formal school courses, with experienced instructors and regularly scheduled classes. These classes are organized and conducted by the separate military services, and the textbooks and course materials are provided by USAFI. Many basic and intermediate courses (see below) are taught this way, but this approach is also widely used for college-level courses. Whenever a sufficient number of persons at an army camp, an air force base, or a naval station are interested in taking a particular course, a class may be established for them.

Basic and intermediate courses.   For servicemen who have not finished elementary school, USAFI offers courses at the basic and intermediate levels, grades 1 through 8. Courses in the first six grades (the basic level) are conducted primarily in group classes, under the direction of qualified instructors. Major subjects include reading, arithmetic, science, geography, and history.

High school courses.   At the secondary school level, USAFI offers all the courses given by the average civilian high school. The subjects in greatest demand include algebra, American history, English composition and literature, and bookkeeping and accounting. High school courses are conducted through both the correspondence and the self-teaching method of study. Correspondence students within the continental United States send their written lessons to USAFI, Madison; those stationed elsewhere, to their respective overseas USAFI's. Lessons sent to USAFI, Madison, are graded and evaluated by instructors at the extension division of the University of Wisconsin. A high school course is completed when the student makes a satisfactory score on the USAFI end-of-course test in that subject.

College study.   Through the 50-odd colleges and universities participating in its programs, USAFI offers a wide range of courses in the humanities, the social sciences, the natural sciences, and the field of business. Among the more prominent courses and subject areas are mathematics, English composition and literature, history, psychology, modern foreign languages, business administration, biology, and physics. Work in a given course is satisfactorily completed when the student achieves a passing score in a standardized USAFI test in that subject.

Technical and language courses.   USAFI's many technical and trade courses give servicemen an opportunity to supplement their military training by learning principles and developing skills that may be applied in their military occupations. These courses may also help prepare servicemen for vocations in civilian life. Many of those technical subjects having the highest levels of participation are directly related to military assignments: auto mechanics, television, radio for beginners, elementary electricity, and elementary photography. Other subjects offered include farming, forestry, aeronautics, and carpentry.

USAFI works closely with another Defense Department agency, the Defense Language Institute, in the development of spoken-language courses. Tests are used to validate achievement in spoken languages both for military purposes and for recognition by civilian institutions in terms of granting credit for speech proficiency.

General Educational Development. To help the services meet the challenge of steadily increasing demands upon their educational facilities, USAFI has evolved an integrated program called General Educational Development extending in range from basic literacy through high school equivalency. This program, designated the USAFI Core GED Program, has been primarily designed with an eye to increasing the efficiency of the individual in his military assignments.

The Core GED Program is meant for the man who does not care to follow civilian education course by course for specific credit, but who is seeking rather to make up his individual deficiencies so as to attain either eighth grade or high school equivalency as rapidly as is consistent with solid accomplishment.

Constructed largely from existing course materials which have been adapted and augmented with special instructions to meet immediate needs, the Core GED Program is an ever-evolving, ever-developing curriculum, designed to keep abreast of the needs of the services. It is under constant revision as improved methods are developed and newer materials become available.

Courses within the Core GED Program have been grouped at three general levels: beginning, pre-high-school, and high school. The basic objective is to advance each man as far as possible in the time available—beginning students to the stage of functional literacy, pre-high-school students to eighth grade equivalency, and high school students to high school equivalency.

Although the above represents the core program, General Educational Development may also take in more advanced levels. Thus, there are available USAFI tests geared to validate an individual's level of educational achievement in various areas, which take into account both his formal studies, in USAFI and elsewhere, and the knowledge and experience he has gained informally. Such tests may provide the basis for recognition of his advanced standing by colleges and universities, regardless of the level of study he has formally completed.

Testing and reporting services. Testing has always been an important part of the USAFI education program. Four types of tests are available from USAFI: end-of-course tests, designed to test mastery of specific USAFI courses; General Educational Development tests (high school and college), standardized to measure the extent to which all the educational experiences of a serviceman, including his informal or self-educational experiences, have contributed to his ability to carry on a program of general education; subject examination—standardized to measure achievement in various high school and college subject areas, regardless of the source from which the knowledge was obtained; and basic and intermediate achievement tests—designed to measure general educational achievement at grade levels 1 through 9 (these tests are used for military purposes only; results are not available to civilian educational institutions).

There is no charge to the serviceman for USAFI testing services, and prior enrollment in a USAFI program or course is not necessary. Upon the serviceman's application, testing materials are forwarded by USAFI to the test control officer who signed his application form. The tests are administered under rigidly prescribed testing procedures.

The original versions of these tests were developed during World War II and were based upon the thesis that an adult learns a great deal informally, that the knowledge thus acquired can be measured, and that the individual may thereby be placed at an educational level higher than that indicated by his formal education. Servicemen have availed themselves widely of these tests and their subsequent revisions. It is estimated that some 2 million military personnel have attained high school equivalency by successfully passing the battery of high school GED tests. These results have been widely accepted both by colleges and universities and by industry in lieu of formal high school graduation. Additionally, advanced college standing has been granted to numerous military personnel as a result of passing college-level GED tests.

On July 1, 1965, the general examinations of the College-Level Examination Program, sponsored by the College Entrance Examination Board, replaced the college-level GED tests, which had been in existence since 1943. The general examinations consist of a battery of five tests in

English composition, history and other social sciences, the natural sciences, the humanities, and mathematics.

To facilitate testing, many military installations have set up testing sections, where USAFI tests are stocked and administered. Close to 300 military installations in the United States and overseas provide in this way immediate access to testing services. Strict accounting controls are in effect at USAFI, Madison, for safeguarding the security of USAFI tests.

Certificates of completion and official USAFI reports are issued by USAFI to servicemen and servicewomen who successfully complete USAFI courses and tests. Permanent records of such educational achievement are kept in each student's personnel file. For many hundreds of thousands of service personnel, educational requirements for admission to service schools and for military promotions have been fulfilled through USAFI. Also, as previously indicated, USAFI reports work completed to given civilian institutions at the student's request.

Historical review. On December 24, 1941, the War Department authorized the establishment of a correspondence school to be known as the Army Institute. Its mission was to provide educational opportunities for enlisted personnel of the army.

Actual operations of the institute began at Madison, Wis., on April 1, 1942, in a building donated by the University of Wisconsin. The institute's initial program consisted of 64 courses in technical education and a few academic subjects at the secondary and junior-college levels. In addition, several hundred university and high school courses were made available through the institute by the extension divisions of participating colleges and universities under contract with the federal government.

In September 1942 the institute's offerings were made available to the personnel of the navy, marine corps, and coast guard. The agency's name was changed to the United States Armed Forces Institute in February 1943, and it has been known popularly as USAFI ever since. In July of that year, commissioned personnel were made eligible to participate in USAFI's programs. In 1946, Secretary of War Robert P. Patterson established the institute as a peacetime educational activity.

In 1949, USAFI was placed under the Armed Forces Information and Education Division of the Office of the Secretary of Defense. Shortly thereafter, however, in January 1950, administration of the institute was vested in a civilian director in order to assure the stability and continuity of its operations. Since that date USAFI has been administered as a field agency of the Office of the Deputy Assistant Secretary of Defense for Education, Washington, D.C.

Ben M. Zeff

UNITED STATES COAST GUARD AUXILIARY

The U.S. Coast Guard Auxiliary is a civilian, nonmilitary, voluntary organization of owners of boats, airplanes, and radio stations. The organization, which was originally authorized by an act of Congress in 1939, is administered by the U.S. Coast Guard.

The functions of the auxiliary as stated explicitly in the congressional act are to promote safety and effect rescues on and over the high seas and in the navigable waters; to promote efficiency in the operation of motorboats and yachts; to foster a wider knowledge of and better compliance with the laws, rules, and regulations governing the operation of motorboats and yachts; and to facilitate the other operations of the coast guard. To perform these functions, the auxiliary relies upon two educational programs—one for its members and one for the public. The educational programs are usually conducted by the basic, local unit of the auxiliary, the flotilla, or the next higher level, the division. The flotilla consists of ten or more vessels; the division consists of five or more flotillas in the same geographic area.

Public education program. The public education program of the auxiliary is its largest and most important service. This program consists of four different courses offered annually through the 17 district offices of the auxiliary. The activities of the coast guard and of the auxiliary are not limited to coastal waters but extend to navigable waters in the interior. The four courses for the public are designed to meet the varying needs of the U.S. boating population.

The outboard motorboat handling course is designed for the novice operator of outboard motorboats. It consists of a single lesson lasting from two to three hours. The purpose of the course is to provide the basic knowledge required for safe outboard motorboat operation. The course covers boat construction and terminology, lifesaving devices, overloading, state and national legal requirements, seamanship, rules of the road, fueling, aids to navigation, recommended equipment, and boat handling.

The safe boating course is designed for vacationers at beach and summer resort areas, where boats are operated for a relatively short period of time. The course consists of three lessons one day a week over a three-week period. The subject matter is more involved than that given for novices in the outboard motorboat handling course.

The hunter-fisherman course, also a one-lesson course, is designed for the sportsman-boater.

The basic seamanship course is the most important of the courses offered by the auxiliary to the public. It consists of eight lessons together with homework and practice extending over an eight-week period. The course covers boat construction, maneuvering, charts and compasses, marlin-spike seamanship, aids to navigation, rules of the road, legal responsibilities, and safe operation of craft.

All of the public education courses are taught by qualified coast guard auxiliary instructors. These instructors are qualified by years of experience on the water, by study of their subjects, and by special courses in practice teaching and teacher training. In the late 1960's more than 180,000 persons a year enrolled in the public education courses.

Public education in boating is also carried on though a major program in the courtesy examination of motorboats. Courtesy examinations are undertaken by qualified members of the auxiliary only upon specific request of the owners. The examinations are free, and boatmen who pass the the courtesy motorboat examination are given a decal, the Seal of Safety, to display on their boats. The regular coast guard and most state enforcement officials will not board a boat displaying this emblem unless there is an apparent violation of regulations in operation or equipment.

The CME is conducted only by auxiliary members who have received special training and have qualified as examiners. Part of this training is a thorough study of state and federal laws pertaining to recreational boats. The CME covers equipment and other essentials of safe boating. It therefore amounts to a private course of instruction. The CME program has been welcomed by the boating public, with examinations rising in number to over 180,000 a year in the late 1960's. The seriousness of the program is indicated by the fact that only slightly more than half of the boats inspected pass the examination.

Internal auxiliary training. Membership in the auxiliary is open to all U.S. citizens and nationals over 17 years of age who own at least 25 percent interest in a boat. The ownership qualification is waived in certain cases, and in 1944 membership was extended to owners of radio stations and aircraft.

There are auxiliary membership training programs at three levels. The first program is designed to assist the basic qualification status; the second is designed to prepare basically qualified members to become instructors or courtesy examiners; and the third consists of courses in the seven operational specialties. A member who completes all seven specialty courses automatically qualifies for operational membership. Courses at all three levels are directed by members who have qualified as instructors by expertness in subject matter and by passing the instructor course. The courses are usually offered and conducted by the flotillas.

There are 17 criteria for basic qualification. These range from knowledge of the history and organization of the coast guard through flag etiquette and official orders to communications, seamanship, piloting, and principles of marine power plants. Upon joining the auxiliary, the individual becomes a conditional member and is given a year to complete basic qualification. He is accorded this status after passing a written examination and a practical examination.

The coast guard provides instructional materials which are published as auxiliary manuals. The U.S. Coast Guard Institute offers correspondence courses in mathematics for navigators, piloting, celestial navigation, and meteorology. The flotillas and divisions conduct regular courses to assist conditional members in achieving basic qualification.

Training for the roles of courtesy examiner and instructor is conducted at the flotilla and division levels. Instructional materials and course outlines for this training are also prepared by the coast guard. Annual refresher courses and seminars for examiners and instructors are strongly recommended but are not required. The course for instructors is central to the entire auxiliary operation, since only those members who pass this course are qualified to instruct in public education or internal membership training programs.

Courses covering operational specialties are presented by qualified members of the auxiliary at flotilla and divisional locations. Preparation for these specialties, however, also involves independent study. The coast guard has developed a training text for each specialty and makes course outlines and reading lists available for each subject. The operational specialties are seamanship, navigation, communications, search and rescue, patrol procedures, weather, and auxiliary administration as well.

Development. Since the late 1930's small boat ownership in the United States has increased at an extraordinary rate. In 1939 there were 300,000 registered motorboats and 4,000 auxiliary yachts; by 1969 there were over 7.8 million motorboats and 576,000 yachts. In 1939 the coast guard received 14,000 calls for assistance and effected 8,600 "in peril" rescues of vacationing boatmen. It was discovered that most of the calls for assistance arose either from ignorance of basic seamanship or of the law. The need for an associated civilian group to carry on a massive educational program and to assist in coast guard operations became clear. At the recommendation of the coast guard, Congress in 1939 created the coast guard reserve, a nonmilitary organization with a three-year membership.

As World War II drew closer, it became evident that the coast guard, a uniformed military service, required a full military reserve force. Therefore, in February 1941, Congress passed an act creating such a reserve and renaming the original reserve the coast guard auxiliary. During the war the auxiliary performed a wide range of essential services, and its original functions were necessarily put aside. By 1947 the auxiliary had returned to its former purpose: to promote safety and efficiency in the operation of motorboats and yachts primarily through courtesy examinations and classroom instruction.

The growth of the auxiliary's programs has continued at an accelerated rate. In 1957 there were some 40,000 courtesy motorboat examinations; in 1968 there were 180,172. In late 1960 there were 92,411 men and women enrolled in the public education courses; by the end of the decade the number had grown to over 180,000.

Membership in the auxiliary had reached 25,000 by 1967. It was expected that the number might be quadrupled in the succeeding decade.

This description of the coast guard auxiliary has dealt primarily with its education programs. Qualified auxilary members engage in many other operations associated with the coast guard functions of maintaining pleasure craft safety standards. Its work in search and rescue operations and in patrol of regattas and races is substantial. In 1968, for example, the record showed 158 lives saved, 4,563 regatta patrols, and 8,938 boats assisted.

Since 1955 the auxiliary has annually sponsored a four-day visit to the U.S. Coast Guard Academy for a limited number of high school students who have the potential of qualifying as cadets. The purpose of the visit is to acquaint students with the academy and with career opportunities in the coast guard. The auxiliary units pay travel expenses.

*Edward James Ard

UNITED STATES INFORMATION AGENCY PROGRAMS

The United States Information Service (USIS), overseas operational arm of the United States Information Agency (USIA), is usually described as the government's foreign propaganda mechanism. Its activities normally include such traditional propaganda devices as television programs, press releases, and radio programs with messages designed to further short-range national policies. However, the USIS does much more than distribute conventional propaganda; it also has long-range objectives, and its activities embrace many measures necessary to produce total support of national policies. These long-range programs, which often are described as cultural exchange, place heavy emphasis on educational activities.

USIS offices are staffed ordinarily by a country public affairs officer and his two principal assistants, an information officer and a cultural affairs officer, and by a varying number of supporting officers concerned with mass media, libraries, and cultural exchange. Local foreign service employees, whose positions are relatively permanent, outnumber Americans about five to one at an average post and are the backbone of all USIS installations. The American staff acts primarily in a planning and supervisory capacity and serves for limited periods of time, usually two to four years.

Before the USIA became an independent agency under an executive order by President Dwight D. Eisenhower in 1953, the USIS had been administered by the Department of State as authorized by the Smith-Mundt Act of 1948. It has since been guided by both statutory and executive direction as to its mission and functions. President John F. Kennedy made a formal statement of mission on January 25, 1963, in a memorandum to the director of the USIA. The president said:

The mission of the U.S. Information Agency is to help achieve U.S. foreign policy objectives by (*a*) influencing public attitudes in other nations and (*b*) advising the President, his representatives abroad, and the various Departments and Agencies on the implications of foreign opinion for present and contemplated U.S. policies, programs and official statements.

The advisory function is to be carried out at various levels in Washington, and within the Country Team at U.S. diplomatic missions abroad. While the Director of the U.S. Information Agency shall take the initiative in offering counsel where he deems it advisable, the various departments and agencies should seek such counsel when considering policies and programs which may substantially affect or be affected by foreign opinion. Consultation with the U.S. Information Agency is essential when programs affecting communication media in other countries are contemplated.

U.S. Information Agency staffs abroad, acting under the supervision of the chiefs of mission, are responsible for the conduct of overt public information, public relations and cultural activities —i.e., those activities intended to inform or influence foreign public opinion—for agencies of the U.S. government except for Commands of the Department of Defense.

The influencing of attitudes is to be carried out by the overt use of the various techniques of communication—personal contact, radio broadcasting, libraries, book publication and distribution, press, motion pictures, television, exhibits, English-language instruction, and others. (Memorandum . . . 1963, p. 9)

According to President Kennedy's statement, the agency should fulfill its goals by following two general principles. First, individual country programs should promote the country and regional objectives expressed by the president in official policy pronouncements. Second, agency activities should promote public support abroad for a peaceful world community of independent and free states, free to choose their own future and their own system so long as it does not threaten others' freedom. Activities should stress the strength and dynamism of the United States and its qualifications to lead efforts toward world peace. Attempts to distort or frustrate policies and the objectives of the United States must be uncovered and resisted. These activities should emphasize the harmony between American policies and other peoples and governments by stressing those aspects of American life which will encourage understanding of American policies. This statement of mission, establishing both short-range and long-range goals not originally defined, gave the information agency considerably more latitude than did President Eisenhower's executive order and the Smith-Mundt Act.

Binational cultural centers. Long-range operations are sometimes carried on by the USIS through direct means—for example, by supporting such cultural and educational programs as binational cultural centers and English-teaching institutes. In the case of educational exchange programs, the USIS acts as the overseas agent for the Department of State, which has statutory responsibility for the activity. USIS support of binational cultural centers usually consists of teachers' salaries, textbooks, and teaching equipment. In most cases, policy is left to a binational board of directors which derives its authority from international agreements. Whether or not there is a binational center in a given country usually depends primarily on the political climate and the need. Most Communist and many neutral countries do not welcome such a working relationship with the United States. In 1970 there were 127 such centers. Where they exist, programs usually include English teaching, seminars and forums on a wide range of subjects not necessarily in support of U.S. objectives, concerts, lectures, and other cultural activities.

If there is no binational center in a country, direct activities of the USIS are larger and more varied. When the USIS carries on cultural and educational programs directly, they are normally developed around the nucleus of a library.

Libraries. American overseas libraries are a major operational unit of the USIS and the principal showcase of the United States government's information and cultural exchange program abroad. With minor exceptions all government libraries abroad are operated by the USIS. The exceptions include certain technical libraries maintained by the Agency for International Development, commercial libraries maintained by embassies and consulates abroad, and armed forces libraries, which serve primarily members of the forces and their dependents. According to USIS officials, there were 159 USIS libraries and 62 reading rooms in 84 countries as of 1968. In addition, the USIS assisted 130 binational centers (113 of them in Latin America) which maintained small libraries, averaging about 4,000 volumes each.

Functions. USIS libraries support not only overall informational and cultural objectives but clearly defined national political and economic goals as well. Since each library operates according to a plan developed by individual United States missions abroad and approved in Washington, D.C., operations in no two countries are identical.

Because the library service was originally staffed by American professionals who had a tradition of objectivity, administrators of the program sought to follow the same principles in further planning the functions of overseas libraries. Believing that libraries should be objective, even on such issues as democracy and Communism, the administrators tried to keep library operations free from all political influence. Members of Congress who appropriate the money to finance the program have consistently contended, however, that the libraries should be used to achieve policy objectives.

During the hearings conducted in the early 1950's by the late Senator Joseph McCarthy of Wisconsin, the search for Communist subversion of the federal government led to severe restrictions on the use of books written by Communists or their sympathizers and on books about Communism. A few books were burned and others withdrawn from the overseas library shelves. These restrictions were later modified to permit use of such books when they could be shown to make a positive contribution to the objectives of the information program—such as exposure of Communist aims and tactics.

Currently country public affairs officers are instructed that the American library is a special-purpose library designed to reach specific audiences and groups. The overseas posts are called

upon, however, to achieve a balance between the special purpose of the library and its function as a community center. It is the American idea of the library as a community center that the USIS seeks to portray as one of the strong institutions of a modern democracy. Like the domestic American library, the overseas library cooperates with schools, civic groups, business and professional organizations, research institutes, and local officials in every way possible. The overseas libraries are much like their counterparts in America in physical appearance. Whenever possible they are centrally located at street level so that they are easily accessible to the public. They are equipped with standard American library equipment and furnishings. On the average they are open to the public about 48 hours a week, the majority operating in the evenings and on Saturdays, with some open also for a brief period on Sundays.

Most USIS posts also conduct a book-translation program under which American books are translated into other languages and published at moderate prices. The program is closely identified with the library's needs and operations. In addition, there usually is a book-presentation program which presents key individuals with single volumes of American works or institutions with collections of varying size. Most libraries also maintain a stock of musical scores and recordings to attract music lovers. In many countries bookmobiles carry books, films, and records to areas that are not easily accessible, and rotating collections are loaned to public or institutional libraries.

In many parts of the world where by long tradition books are regarded as so valuable that they must be kept under lock and key, the USIS provides the only circulating library available to the public. Another objective of the libraries is to provide a practical demonstration of American library methods as an aid in preparing local libraries to meet the rising demands of rapidly increasing literacy in newly developing countries. The open shelf policy—the freedom to browse among collections—is a special characteristic of the American library not found in most other countries.

USIS libraries encourage local librarians who are interested in improving their own library services to make use of study and reference materials on library science and American library practice and to observe and discuss such matters of interest as cataloging, reader advisory service, reference works, and book selection with the USIS library staff. The USIS sponsors workshops and seminars on library practices and invites librarians from local schools, universities, and other institutions to take part. The United States government also has helped many foreign librarians to come to the United States for advanced library training.

Among substantial changes in the library program during the 1960's have been a sharp decline in children's library activities, a reduction in the number of American librarians overseas from 113 to 28 (these have been replaced by locally employed librarians), an increase in the number of USIS libraries in Africa from 12 to 52, and a reduction in Europe from 69 USIS libraries in 1955 to 26 in 1967.

Book selection. Selection of new books for the library shelves is the responsibility of the country public affairs officer (CPAO) at each post. Each book collection is expected to contain a balanced representation of points of view on such controversial topics as politics, labor, and religion. He may choose from a weekly list of recommended books made up by an internal USIA committee, or he may order books not so listed. Recommended books make up the great majority of selections, however. The USIA also sends out packets of books which the agency believes are particularly useful in promoting program objectives. The CPAO is also at liberty to remove books from the library shelves when, in his opinion, changing program requirements make it advisable. Each CPAO manages the libraries under his jurisdiction autonomously, although he must follow certain general policy guidelines in book selection.

Some books are selected because of their utility in counteracting hostile propaganda; others are chosen because they explain the interest of the United States in other nations, because they display the American intellectual, artistic, and spiritual heritage, or because they provide useful information about the United States, its people, culture, institutions, policies, problems, and achievements. Books by American authors on other subjects may also be used. Despite the many differences to be found in individual libraries, all make use of certain basic Americana and reference books, as well as many volumes on science and technology, medicine, agriculture, engineer-

ing, the social sciences, education, economics, and political science.

In those countries where library facilities are otherwise limited, USIS collections may also include selected world classics, such as works by Shakespeare or Plato, which have had an important influence on American life and education. Light reading is minimized, although some fiction is included because it attracts patrons to the libraries and also because some American fiction contains intrinsic program values. Support for American studies courses given in foreign schools is an increasingly important library function, and some books are selected for this purpose. Emphasis is on an effective reference service in each library to ensure that accurate information about the United States is readily available to local government officials, news media, educators, and others seeking such information.

Newspapers and periodicals are an important part of the services offered by all USIS libraries. Some newspapers and periodicals are delivered by air mail so that foreign audiences are able to keep abreast of developments in the United States. Overseas libraries are supplied with a list of 500 American periodicals from which they may order subscriptions. About half the periodicals in USIS libraries are selected from this list; the remainder are chosen from other sources. A total of about 1,000 different magazines is in use.

USIS libraries vary widely in size, content, facilities, resources, and programs. The collections abroad total more than 2 million volumes, of which about 24 percent are in local languages. The percentage is somewhat higher in such areas as Africa, where there are fewer people who read English, and the general policy is to increase the percentage of volumes written in local languages. Collections at individual posts range in size from about 1,500 volumes to nearly 40,000 in the largest library, which is located in Buenos Aires. Binational center libraries aided by the USIS had 588,879 volumes on their shelves in 1967, a circulation of 757,050 for that year, and visitors or readers numbering 2,228,049.

The USIA has been expending about $6 million a year in operational costs for the library program. However, the amount available for book and magazine purchases has been declining as the purchase costs have steadily continued to increase. In fiscal year 1967, for example, the agency received about $710,000 from Congress for purchase of books, with which nearly 153,000 volumes were procured, according to USIS officials. This compares with an appropriation of about $800,000 in 1963, when approximately 201,000 books were purchased. In short, the number of books and magazines purchased each year has been declining even more rapidly than the amount of money appropriated.

Popularity. In some cases, notably in Germany and Japan, American libraries have become so much a part of the life of a foreign community that when budgetary considerations have required the USIS to discontinue its operations the local citizens have taken over and continued the operation at their own expense, with the USIS donating its book collection. The USIS libraries, which are patronized most heavily by students and youth, are usually the best-known symbol of American "presence" in foreign countries. Attesting to this is the fact that USIS libraries are most often singled out for attack during anti-American riots or demonstrations, which have come into increasing vogue in recent years as a means of applying political pressure. The youthful patrons of the libraries are often participants in the demonstrations. Physical attacks on USIS libraries, ranging from broken windows to complete sacking and demolition, totaled an estimated 130 by December 1967. Nevertheless, the underlying popularity of the libraries is clearly shown by attendance and book circulation. In the 1966–1967 fiscal year, total attendance at information centers and libraries was 19,601,409, and book circulation was 4,812,677. Although libraries in some countries have been forced to close during periods of political tension, sometimes—for example, in Indonesia—they have also been urgently invited to reopen when conditions changed.

Cultural and information centers. The USIS cultural or information center ordinarily includes, in addition to the library, an auditorium in which daily programs of films, recorded music, English lessons, lectures, and concerts are typical activities. Often art and other traveling exhibits are displayed in the center. Through activities such as seminars, cultural programs, and English teaching, the centers attempt to promote understanding between the people of the particular country and the United States. Forum lecturers—sometimes specialists in American life and culture—are often drawn from the academic or business community of the host country. Like the forums,

seminars cover a wide range of topics, such as world issues and the teaching of English as a second language; they are usually devoted to subject matter concerning the United States but may be devoted to matters of primary interest in the host country.

Foundations. In some countries the USIS may assist in the administration of an American educational foundation or an English-teaching institute. As in the case of the binational centers, the foundations are governed by a binational board of directors and rest on bilateral international agreements. The foundations were authorized by the Fulbright Act of 1946 to administer the use of surplus foreign currencies for both the travel expenses of foreign university students, teachers, research scholars, and lecturers to the United States and the travel and living expenses abroad of Americans in similar professions. The American ambassador invariably is honorary chairman of the board of directors, and all American members of the board are appointed by him. Usually the active chairman is an American, sometimes the country public affairs officer; usually the cultural affairs officer is a member.

Informational activities. Although to a great extent the information officer acts as an agent of the USIA "fast" media—the press, radio, motion pictures, and television—his responsibilities are often much broader, encompassing locally generated activity.

The fact that communication patterns vary from country to country accounts for most of the differences in media emphasis between the various information officers' programs. Where literacy levels are low, the press rudimentary, and radio receivers scarce, the information officer will carry the USIS message through mobile units touring the country with films, simply illustrated pamphlets, and cartoon books. In other countries where radio listening may be widespread, the information officer may operate a USIS radio station equipped to prepare local programs, which may include sound tapes of Voice of America short-wave broadcasts as well as tapes made by local announcers, commentators, and artists. In relatively sophisticated countries, low-priced books may be one of the most effective means of reaching a target audience.

In almost every country, the film library is one of the most popular USIS facilities. Individuals or organizations are able to borrow any of hundreds of films from these libraries for private or public showing. Projectors may also be borrowed, and if there is to be a large enough audience the USIS may also furnish a projectionist and a portable generator. The repertoire includes many how-to-do-it educational films and documentaries which support long-range objectives. The Motion Picture Service and Television Service of USIA have the capacity to record films in 50 languages. In addition, many dialects are recorded by local posts. The USIA estimates that hundreds of millions of people annually view USIS films.

With the development of the communications satellites and the growing number of television sets, the use of television as an outlet for USIS films has added an ever-increasing prime audience. Television's impact on the formation of attitudes in many countries influenced the 1970 USIA budget, which included a substantial increase in the television allocation and a decrease in the funds marked for motion pictures.

Exhibits are an important segment of the work of all USIS posts. The nature of the exhibits, whether cultural or informational, varies widely. In some countries, emphasis may be on art, literature, or science, whereas in others, simple portrayals of American life are planned for less sophisticated viewers. Many of the exhibits are prepared in Washington, D.C., but others are arranged at the posts. These local exhibits often are designed to publicize economic-assistance projects in the host country.

The Voice of America. The Voice of America (VOA), the official radio broadcasting service of the U.S. government, is located in the United States but is the one medium which can and does enter the homes of those living abroad without any public commitment on the part of the listener. To hear the Voice of America, it is not necessary to attend a film showing, to visit a library, to talk to an American, or to attend an exhibit. It is the only element of the U.S. government that communicates directly with people across geographical lines and the only agency that can reach populations of most Communist countries. It is at the same time a propaganda and educational effort.

Although many of the VOA's programs are devoted to political analyses, U.S. opinion roundups, and news reviews, time also is earmarked for educational and cultural programs featuring forum lectures, seminars, and book reviews. Music is regarded not only as entertainment but also as a means to portray American life, and the programs cut across historical, educational, cultural, and religious lines. Some are used to show the interest and talent of American youth in cultural areas, another series is programmed around music in industry to give evidence of the cultural interests of American laborers. Another program, "Musical Folkways," is designed to portray the historical development of the United States. Many VOA programs are prepared in the country in which they are to be broadcast. They are sent by telephone or mail to Washington, D.C., and are then transmitted back over the air.

Historical background. The progenitor of the USIA was the Committee on Public Information, created by President Woodrow Wilson in 1917. Wilson appointed George Creel, editor of the *Rocky Mountain News*, to the chairmanship of what was to be the U.S. government's first systematic and well-financed excursion into international propaganda. The Committee on Public Information controlled both the government's domestic and overseas propaganda activities and administered the voluntary censorship program for the duration of World War I. The original purpose of the committee was to coordinate and facilitate distribution of government news, but Creel, youthful and imaginative, soon built a huge organization designed to stimulate domestic and overseas interest in support of the war. He established American reading rooms abroad and brought foreign newsmen to the United States. The Creel committee was under constant criticism from the press, which resented Creel's "voluntary" censorship, and from Congress, which was wary of the committee's increasing involvement in propaganda activities. Congress abolished the Committee on Public Information in 1919.

Although the period between the two world wars saw the development of the propaganda battle via shortwave radio, with the Soviet Union, Germany, Japan, and Britain as the principal participants, the United States sought to ignore the growing barrage of propaganda from both Fascist and Communist sources and tried to keep channels of communication open. It was not until 1938 that the U.S. government made its first tentative move toward engagement in psychological warfare with the establishment of the Interdepartmental Committee on Cooperation with American Republics. The committee was created through executive action of President Franklin D. Roosevelt in order to promote solidarity in the western hemisphere against the substantial propaganda efforts of the Nazis. By 1940 it was evident that a larger effort was needed, and in August the Office of Coordinator of Commercial and Cultural Relations Between the American Republics was established with Nelson Rockefeller as its head. The committee's activities, one of which was dissemination of information, were carried on in a number of fields. The organization was renamed the Office of Coordinator of Inter-American Affairs in 1941 and, in 1945, the Office of Inter-American Affairs.

In July 1941, with war imminent, President Roosevelt established the Coordinator of Information by executive order and named the then Colonel William J. Donovan as chief. Although the organization was conceived primarily as an intelligence-gathering effort, Donovan, with the tacit approval of the president, soon set up the Foreign Information Service with Robert Sherwood in charge. On February 24, 1942, Sherwood's group began broadcasting as the Voice of America.

The Office of War Information was created early in the war by executive order. The office consisted of two branches: the Foreign Information Service under Sherwood, and the other agencies—with the exception of the Coordinator of Inter-American Affairs under Nelson Rockefeller—combined under a domestic branch. The remaining duties of Donovan's Coordinator of Information office were transferred into the Office of Strategic Services—a forerunner of the Central Intelligence Agency.

Preparing for a peacetime information operation, the Department of State in December 1944 established the position of assistant secretary of state in charge of public and cultural affairs. When President Harry S. Truman abolished the Office of War Information in August 1945, the State Department took over its operations as well as those of the Office of Inter-American Affairs and placed them under the assistant secretary. Later they were given separate status within the department.

Initial statutory authority for a peacetime program was provided by the Smith-Mundt Act of 1948. This continues to be the basic legislation under which the USIA operates, although it has been materially expanded under the Reorganization Plan No. 8 of 1953 and the Fulbright-Hays Act of 1961.

A wartime assignment. A unique role was assumed by the USIA in 1965, when the agency was assigned the responsibility for all psychological warfare in Vietnam. At that time USIS operations in Vietnam ceased to exist as a separate entity, and the Joint U.S. Public Affairs Office, headed by the USIS country public affairs officer, was established. In earlier wars, civil and military propaganda efforts had been largely compartmented. As the United States began to assist the Vietnamese government in its pacification efforts, the range of psychological operations proliferated and came to include activities by the military forces in combat and activities among civilians in the war areas. In addition, the Agency for International Development (AID) and the USIS conducted economic-assistance programs for the entire civilian population of Vietnam. The USIS had the basic equipment, organization, and personnel to fill the urgent need for improved coordination of the psychological efforts, and the agency drew the assignment from President Lyndon B. Johnson on the advice of the National Security Council. In addition to providing policy guidance to the many organizational divisions created by the inclusion of personnel from the Military Assistance Command Vietnam and the AID mission under the Joint U.S. Public Affairs Office, the USIS also engaged in the usual information and cultural operations throughout Vietnam.

BIBLIOGRAPHY

ALLEN, GEORGE V. 1961 "Books and the American Image." *Atlantic Monthly*, 207, no. 5:77–80.

BARRETT, EDWARD W. 1953 *Truth Is Our Weapon.* New York, Funk and Wagnalls.

CREEL, GEORGE 1920 *How We Advertised America.* New York, Harper.

DIZARD, WILSON J. 1961 *The Strategy of Truth: The Story of the U.S. Information Service.* Washington, D.C., Public Affairs Press.

ELDER, ROBERT E. 1968 *The Information Machine: The U.S. Information Agency and American Foreign Policy.* Syracuse, N.Y., Syracuse University Press.

"Evaluating the Overseas Library Program" 1953 Statement by Robert L. Johnson, administrator, International Information Administration. *The Department of State Bulletin*, 29, no. 734:77–82.

HENDERSON, JOHN W. 1969 *The United States Information Agency.* New York, Praeger.

Memorandum from President John F. Kennedy to Edward R. Murrow, Director of USIA 1963 Department of State, *Newsletter*, no. 30, October 1963, p. 9.

SORENSON, THOMAS C. 1968 *The Word War: The Story of American Propaganda.* New York, Harper.

STEPHENS, OREN 1955 *Facts to a Candid World: America's Overseas Information Program.* Palo Alto, Calif., Stanford University Press.

THOMSON, CHARLES A. H. 1948 *Overseas Information Service of the United States Government.* Washington, D.C., The Brookings Institution.

THOMSON, CHARLES A. H., AND WALTER H. C. LAVES 1963 *Cultural Relations and U.S. Foreign Policy.* Bloomington, Indiana University Press.

U.S. DEPARTMENT OF STATE 1953 "Policy on Selection of Books in IIA Libraries." *The Department of State Bulletin,* 29, no. 733:58–59.

JOHN W. HENDERSON

UNITED STATES MERCHANT MARINE ACADEMY

The United States Merchant Marine Academy is one of five federal service academies and is operated by the Maritime Administration, an agency of the U.S. Department of Commerce. It is located at Kings Point, N.Y., on the north shore of Long Island, and is commonly referred to as Kings Point. It offers a four-year program leading to the degree of bachelor of science and is accredited by the Middle States Association of Colleges and Secondary Schools. Each graduate is awarded a license as a third mate or third assistant engineer and the commission of ensign in the U.S. Naval Reserve. The student body numbers about 1,000, with over 700 in residence at Kings Point and the rest in training aboard ships at sea. The academy was established to prepare young American men for careers as deck or engineering officers aboard ships of the U.S. Merchant Marine. One of the conditions for admission is the signing of an agreement to serve as a licensed officer in the U.S. Merchant Marine for at least five consecutive years after graduation.

The U.S. Merchant Marine consists of all commercial U.S. flag vessels and crews engaged in the foreign and domestic transport of cargo and passengers. Although the ships are owned and operated by private shipping companies, they provide logistic support to the military services in times of emergency; the U.S. Merchant Marine is often called the "fourth arm of national defense."

The Kings Point graduate joins his ship as a fully qualified junior officer and immediately takes charge of a watch on the bridge or in the engine room. Deck officers are responsible for navigation, cargo handling, vessel maintenance, and shipboard safety. Engineering officers are responsible for maintaining and operating all the ship's machinery—including propulsion, auxiliary, refrigeration, and deck equipment.

Curriculum. The educational program of the U.S. Merchant Marine Academy consists of three years ashore at Kings Point; one year is spent at sea aboard merchant ships. Each resident academic year is 11 months in duration, with a rigorous program of study in order that professional and degree requirements may be met within the three-year period.

Kings Pointers select either the nautical science curriculum leading to service as deck officers or the marine engineering curriculum for preparation as engineering officers. One section of entering midshipmen, selected from the top 10 percent of the class, voluntarily embarks upon a dual license curriculum and receives both deck and engineering training. This experimental program, pioneered by the academy in 1965, anticipates technological changes in the industry which may call for highly trained officers possessing both deck and engineering proficiency.

In addition to the attainment of professional excellence, midshipmen are provided with mathematical and scientific knowledge, a basic general education, and a familiarity with the problems of maritime operations to prepare them for executive positions when they move ashore after careers at sea.

The nautical science curriculum includes such professional subjects as seamanship, communications, navigation, naval architecture, meteorology, safety of life at sea, cargo handling, gyrocompass principles, electronics, international law of the sea, and marine transportation. The marine engineering program includes such technical subjects as machine shop, engineering graphics, marine machinery repair, statics, dynamics, thermodynamics, strength of materials, hydraulics, internal combustion engines, marine refrigeration and air conditioning, electrical engineering, and marine engineering. Each curriculum also includes a certain number of hours in mathematics, physics, chemistry, English, history, foreign language or comparative culture, business and maritime law, economics, labor relations, marine insurance, ship's medicine, physical education, and naval science. Each curriculum is composed primarily of required courses; however, a midshipman with the necessary academic standing may add one elective course each quarter. One set of electives deals with various aspects of work aboard nuclear-powered vessels. In addition to midshipmen, several groups of trainees for the nuclear-powered ship *Savannah* have been trained at the academy's Nuclear Study Center and other facilities.

Transfer credit may be awarded for any course completed at another college which is equivalent to a course offered at the academy. Validation credit may also be awarded in certain subjects upon passing an examination administered at the academy. A student may then substitute courses from the list of electives to complete his academic program.

Because the merchant marine operates with the navy in time of war, an understanding of naval procedures by its officers is essential to successful cooperation. Candidates for admission to the Merchant Marine Academy must meet the qualifications for naval reserve midshipmen. All midshipmen take a prescribed program of naval science courses, taught by naval officers, which leads to a commission, upon graduation, as an ensign in the U.S. Naval Reserve. The graduate is then under obligation to remain in the naval reserve for six years and to maintain his status by completing correspondence courses and undergoing training duty.

Sea year. After one year at the academy, during which the midshipman takes introductory courses in all areas of study, he is assigned to several different types of merchant ships for a year. This is a unique work-study situation in which the ship serves as a laboratory. The midshipman is introduced to life at sea, and he becomes familiar with the work done aboard ocean vessels. In addition, he is issued a sea project manual containing assignments which he completes and forwards to the academy for grading. The midshipman also receives voluntary instruction from ships' officers while observing and performing some of the duties of a junior officer. Academy training representatives in New York, New Orleans, and San Francisco assign midshipmen to the ships and oversee their progress.

Regimental life. The academy is military in character; midshipmen are organized into a regiment. The regimental program provides an opportunity to practice leadership as midshipmen officers, a system of strict discipline in which infractions of regulations incur demerits and punishment, and the standing of watches. Regimental life is considered essential to the development of leadership ability, self-discipline, a sense of responsibility, and the ability to adapt to the rigorous life at sea.

In addition to his participation in the military routine of the regiment, the Kings Pointer may take part in student government and such extracurricular activities as publications, musical groups, special interest and hobby clubs, debates, and social affairs. An arts and world affairs series brings a program of cultural activities to the campus throughout the year. Participation in religious activities and attendance at services in the Merchant Marine Memorial Chapel are voluntary. In addition, there are an intramural athletic program and scheduled intercollegiate competition. Liberty is granted as a matter of privilege.

Admission. Appointment to the academy begins with an application to the appropriate nominating authority, usually a member of Congress, requesting that the applicant's name be submitted in nomination to become a candidate for admission. A candidate must meet general and scholastic requirements, including high school graduation or its equivalent and qualifying scores in certain College Entrance Examination Board tests. Candidates are ranked in order of merit by an objective evaluation of all credentials. Then they are selected competitively to fill academy vacancies through a quota system based on each state's representation in Congress. The candidate must then pass a physical examination conducted by the U.S. Navy for appointment as a midshipman, U.S. Naval Reserve, and must meet security requirements.

The US. government bears the major portion of academy costs, including tuition, quarters and subsistence, and medical and dental care. While at the academy, each midshipman receives a yearly allowance for required uniforms and textbooks. During the sea year a monthly salary is paid by the shipping companies.

History. The U.S. Merchant Marine Academy was developed from a program of merchant marine officer training which began in 1891, when the federal government authorized the assignment of cadets aboard ships receiving mail subsidies. In 1938, when the handling of training by shipping companies proved unsatisfactory, the federal government took over the program. The training program was conducted solely aboard ship at first, but temporary shore facilities were later established. The permanent academy was begun in January 1942 at the Walter P. Chrysler estate, whose 13 acres formed the nucleus of the present 68-acre campus. A building program was started in May 1942, and the academy was dedicated on September 30, 1943. In his dedicatory message, President Franklin D. Roosevelt summed up the purpose of the academy: "This academy serves the Merchant Marine as West Point serves the Army and Annapolis the Navy."

During World War II the academy berthed at one time as many as 2,700 cadets taking a short course which included training aboard ships in combat zones. The academy graduated 6,634 officers during the war. The four-year course was instituted with the class entering in September 1945, and authorization to grant a degree, accreditation, and permanency legislation followed. Over 4,000 midshipmen have graduated from the academy's four-year program, and there have been over 13,000 graduates since the founding of the academy.

BIBLIOGRAPHY

CARSE, ROBERT 1964 *Your Place in the Merchant Marine.* New York, Macmillan.

CRUMP, IRVING 1958 *Our Merchant Marine Academy, Kings Point.* New York, Dodd, Mead.

KENNEY, NATHANIEL T. 1955 "Kings Point: Maker of Mariners." *National Geographic,* 108, no. 5:692–706.

McLINTOCK, GORDON 1968 *Your Future in the Merchant Marine.* New York, Rosen.

EVERETT H. NORTHROP

UNITED STATES OFFICE OF EDUCATION

The United States Office of Education, a unit in the Department of Health, Education, and Welfare (HEW), is the federal agency to which Congress has assigned primary responsibility for education. Its legislative mandate is to collect statistics and facts which show the condition and progress of education, to diffuse information which will help to establish and maintain efficient school systems, and to otherwise promote the cause of education. The office does not, however, have authority to operate or oversee a national educational system—states are responsible for their own educational systems. Nor does the office control or coordinate the 40 or so federal agencies connected with educational programs.

As Congress enacts new educational legislation, the number and type of programs administered by the Office of Education increase. In 1970 there were over 70 programs designed, for example, to provide scholarships, fellowships, and loans to undergraduate and graduate students, to help build libraries and laboratories, to finance the purchase of textbooks and laboratory equipment, and to support research programs involving educational policy and practice. Through its many and varied programs, the office serves several major functions in addition to collecting and disseminating educational statistics and information and providing a mandatory annual report on education to Congress.

The office administers grants for educational purposes to states or other educational constituencies and monitors the use of the funds by its guidelines and regulations. The grants are usually for specified purposes, and usually there is a formula determined by Congress for computing who gets how much for what purpose. The office also awards contracts or grants to colleges, universities, states, and industrial groups for research and related activities, ranging from individual projects to major laboratory programs. It provides consultative services for state departments of education, colleges and universities, school systems, groups of educators, governmental agencies, and international organizations and helps agencies with their educational programs as well. For example, it works with the Department of State in selecting educational attachés for embassies overseas and in finding teachers for programs to aid developing nations.

Established in 1867, the office grew very gradually until the National Defense Education Act of 1958 increased its staff and budget. Its staff grew from 250 employees in 1950 to 2,113 in 1965 and to 2,642 in 1970. Its budget showed a similar rate of growth—for example, the total agency budget increased from $602 million in fiscal 1962 to $4 billion in 1967. The 1970 budget, most of which was for disbursement to other educational agencies, totaled $3.8 billion, compared to a total federal expenditure for education of more than $12 billion. State, local, and private agencies spent well over $40 billion.

The office is headed by the commissioner of education, who is appointed for an indefinite term by the president and confirmed by the Senate. The commissioner, who is responsible to the secretary of health, education, and welfare, has primary responsibility for carrying out the assignments given directly to the office by Congress, by the president, or by the secretary of health, education, and welfare. As chief administrative officer, the commissioner maintains liaison with the executive, legislative, and judicial branches of government.

The office is organized into bureaus, some of which carry out programs for specific kinds of learners (for example, the Bureau of Education for the Handicapped conducts programs for the handicapped). Other bureaus perform specific functions for all learners (for example, the Bureau of Library and Educational Technology). Bureaus are composed of divisions, which operate specific programs. Situated in Washington, D.C., the office has nine regional offices throughout the United States.

Role of Congress. Throughout its history the Office of Education has had numerous problems related to federal-state interactions and internal operations. These problems arose out of the issue of federal control of education and out of the apparent contradiction of having a federal office of education in a system which prides itself on the sanctity of local control. With neither a congressional mandate nor a constitutional imperative, the office has not had authority or precedent for any direct involvement in the affairs of schools. Largely because it fears critics' charges of federal control, the office has always waited for congressional directive and avoided an active role in establishing a national educational policy or exerting direct pressures for educational reform. Consequently, its internal structure has developed in response to congressional programs rather than to the needs of an integrated organization with clear lines of authority for control of operations.

A variety of almost successful attempts at educational change have invariably fallen short of their goals because of compromise necessitated by fear of federal control. The very promising "curriculum revolution" of the 1950's and 1960's is an example of the office's inability to see innovative theory put into practice. Based on the idea that the school curriculum should reflect new learnings, the curriculum reform movement brought scientists and scholars concerned with educational reform into direct contact with the office (and with the National Science Foundation as well). To some extent the "revolution" was hindered by its own insistence that curriculum improvement could single-handedly bring about major changes in the schools. However, the office was unable to see the new curricula put into enough

schools so that their effectiveness (or lack of effectiveness) could be demonstrated.

In contrast, the National Science Foundation, which is chartered by Congress and began development of new curricula and instructional materials in 1957, was not inhibited either by congressional scrutiny or by the fear of being charged with federal control. It supported development of new curricula and instructional materials for every grade level in science and mathematics, and it financed in-service programs to train teachers to use them.

Until the mid-1950's, the office preferred to supply information through publications and to provide advice only in those limited areas of specialization where advice was sought. As greater sums of money were allocated and more legislation for new programs was enacted, the office took a more positive role in educational leadership, mostly by controlling funds voted by Congress for rather specific purposes.

Internal organization. Because it awaited congressional direction, the office evolved an organizational structure designed to accommodate the housing of new programs as they were mandated by legislation. The management and staffing of these units were controlled by specialists who were concerned with their own discipline rather than with the office as an institution. The commissioner of education as an appointed official usually had only three years in office. As soon as he arrived, he set about restructuring the organization, either because of congressional or White House pressure or because of the natural tendency of an incoming administrator to seek to redefine the role of the office. Because of the turnover of top management, there evolved a cadre of technicians and professionals who saw commissioners come and go. These more permanent members developed procedures which became self-perpetuating and "traditional." Tension arose between the professionals who had authority because of their competence and the managerial technicians who had authority because of their long tenure and civil service rank.

This tradition-based organization, in which the real power was vested in autonomous units, characterized the office until the late 1950's, when the outpouring of new legislation and moneys made this atomistic structure unworkable. However, to the staff and to that portion of the educational public they served, this system seemed to work—despite the fact that there was no overall consistency in how specialists operated in the various office divisions and virtually no concept of financial or management systems development. Nevertheless, new programs designed to meet the challenge of space exploration and combat racial discrimination in education could not be adapted to the existing structure. The essential task was to develop a system for coordinating activities which had been divided among subunits of employees. The result was, of course, a bureaucracy, a system in which general rules circumscribe all action.

In this institutional transformation, the specialist was replaced by the generalist who could manage programs, and power was shifted from the operating units to the office of the commissioner, which grew drastically from 1950 to 1970.

Finally, the transformation meant that many of the old liaisons, external and internal, were obsolete, and new ones had to be formed. In keeping with the character of the new institution, these were required to be impersonal—from institution to institution rather than from individual to individual. The office has not been able to make this transformation with ease, and there are still vestigial remains of the old order.

The early years. When President Andrew Johnson appointed Henry Barnard the first commissioner of education in March 1867, it was in response to decades of prodding, much of it by Barnard himself. Although Barnard, like his successors, had a vision of how he could transform American education, he soon learned that transforming that vision into reality was an impossible task. With his three clerks, he planned a series of compelling reports on the state of American education and how it might achieve reform. But this did not seem to be what Congress wanted. With a contrariness that was to become characteristic, Congress, chiding Barnard for not setting up a new educational system for the freed slaves, regarded any departure from mere statistics collection as meddling in federal control. Barnard remained in office only three years, during which he saw his appropriations reduced annually and the department relegated to the status of a bureau in the Department of the Interior in 1869.

John Eaton, who succeeded Barnard, was instrumental in setting up a program for the annual collection of educational data. Nathaniel H. R. Dawson followed Eaton, continuing his efforts

and establishing a division of statistics in the bureau. Collecting statistics and disseminating information were to dominate the bureau until the mid-1950's.

Paradoxically, during this same postwar Reconstruction period, Congress proposed some drastic changes in education. The Hoar Bill, drawn up in 1870, proposed general aid to the common schools and sought to establish a common system of education throughout the country as a means of developing an educational system for the South. Although this bill never came to a vote in Congress, it established federal concern with the common school and marked the first of a series of attempts to use federal aid for educational improvement. The Perce Bill, two years later, proposed a national educational fund, to be financed from the sale of public land. The money was to be allocated to local school districts on the basis of population. This bill, the Burnside Bill of 1879, and the Blair Bill (which passed the Senate in 1884, 1886, and 1888 but never cleared the House) represented an attempt to establish direct federal aid to education. They were defeated because of fear of federal control.

For the next three decades Congress was unwilling to grant the office any new functions despite the efforts of some strong commissioners who sought to broaden its role. New legislation did, however, broaden the work of the office by adding money and authority to make grants.

In 1862, five years before establishing a department of education, Congress created the Department of Agriculture with the mandate to acquire and diffuse useful information on subjects connected with agriculture. In the same year Congress passed the first Morrill Act, providing for grants of land or land scrip to the states for support of colleges of agriculture and mechanics. A succession of acts through 1917 reaffirmed the importance attached by Congress to agricultural education. All of these acts providing federal funds required that participating states contribute matching funds, a principle later embodied in general education legislation. In 1887 the Hatch Act provided for cooperative state-federal support of agricultural experiment stations to be operated as part of the land-grant colleges.

In 1890 the second Morrill Act put the office (still only a bureau) in the grant business. This second land-grant law was designed to make permanent annual grants available to certain qualified institutions of higher education (that is, mechanical and agricultural schools) with the requirement that the institution must report on the disbursement of the funds. Although the office had little opportunity to exercise discretion —the grants were categorical and based upon a formula—disbursing money gave it more status and power than dispensing statistics.

In 1914 the Smith-Lever Act established a co-operative state-federal extension service, also lodged in the land-grant colleges, primarily for education of adults at work on farms. All of these programs provided support for colleges; all of them bypassed the department of education except to note that, in accordance with its establishing law, the office was to report to Congress on the operation of the land-grant program. The cooperative programs, although providing federal funds, have been completely free of charges of federal control, a circumstance seldom noted in debate over general federal aid to education.

In 1917, Congress passed the Smith-Hughes Act, which provided aid for the first time to schools below the college level. The act provided funds to states on a matching basis for preparing teachers, supervisors, and directors of agricultural subjects and teachers of trade, industrial, and home economics subjects. The act created as an independent agency a federal board of vocational education and required each participating state to establish a state board. The commissioner of education was a member of the first federal board, but its chairman was the secretary of agriculture. In 1933 the federal board was transferred by executive order to the Department of the Interior, the board became merely advisory, and administration of the federal vocational education programs was finally the responsibility of the Office of Education, then in the Department of the Interior. The Smith-Hughes Act added nothing to the status or funds of the federal education agency, but it did set a pattern of channeling federal funds for schools through the states.

World War I through the New Deal. Despite new money and authority, the history of the office from World War I through the New Deal era was, for the most part, one of hostility or apathy on the part of Congress and of less than enthusiastic support from the educational community. Education was not the national priority

issue, even to those progressives who saw it as the vehicle for achieving new social goals.

Proposals to give the bureau the status of a cabinet department, such as that contained in the Smith-Towner Act of 1919, were never approved. Nor did the office get an increased budget. In 1900 the budget of the office was about $1.3 million, by 1920 it had reached $32.4 million, and by 1930 it had fallen back to $12.6 million. The bulk of the funds were to be disbursed, but the funds to hire a staff to do the disbursing were meager: large administrative staffs were suggestive of federal control.

Although the commissioners during this period did initiate change, it was always through the permissive clause "to promote the cause of education" rather than through any direct attempt to legislate new mandates.

The depression of the 1930's and the subsequent attempts of the New Deal at social as well as economic engineering demanded federal action to stabilize the economy and repair the social fabric. Although there were no separate bills enacted for education as such, much of the legislation from 1930 to 1940 provided funds for educational purposes. The Public Works Administration, the Emergency Relief Administration, and a myriad of other agencies supplied money for construction of public works, including public schools and universities. There are some estimates that as much as $1 billion went directly or indirectly into school building programs. The Civilian Conservation Corps established a financial resource for vocational training programs, which were carried out under the jurisdiction of the office; the Works Progress Administration created employment, some of which was in educational projects; and the National Youth Administration, created by executive order in 1935, provided both relief and employment for youths 16–25 years old. A new liaison was established between the educators and the social planners, with education viewed as an important means of social transformation.

World War II to the present. World War II and subsequent military actions once again provided legislative mandate for new roles for the office. The office played a significant role in administering moneys disbursed under the Lanham Act of 1941, which provided funds for school construction, maintenance, and equipment and for child care facilities to ease the financial pressures on communities close to military bases and defense plants. Federal programs in vocational training for war production workers, for food production training, and for engineering, science, and management war training were administered by the office. It also carried out programs providing visual aids service and student loans.

The renewal of military activity during the Korean war necessitated funds for schools in communities surrounded by nontaxable military property, and Public Laws 815 and 874 were passed in 1950 to provide financial compensation to the schools. The government spent an increasing amount of money in the 1960's on the implementation of these laws, commonly known as the impact laws. P.L. 874 marked the first granting of federal funds to school districts for general operating costs; there was no earmarking of funds, which the districts could then use at their discretion. The lesson of this act was not lost on the office: if aid must be categorized, find a broad, popular category, and then allow schools relative freedom in how to use the money. This lesson was very useful in 1965, when the designation "poverty" helped get general aid funds to urban school systems.

The National Defense Education Act of 1958, the Civil Rights Act of 1964, and the Elementary and Secondary Education Act of 1965 made education a public issue and led to a major reorientation in American education and in the office as well. Changes had already begun to appear as the result of the Cooperative Research Act of 1954 (P.L. 531), which gave the office, for the first time, discretionary power to do something other than follow an imposed pattern of granting money. P.L. 531 specifically empowered the commissioner of education to "enter into contracts or jointly financed cooperative arrangements with universities and colleges and state educational agencies for the conduct of research, surveys, and demonstrations in the field of education." This very broad mandate carried with it a modest block of money, since it was not earmarked. The Cooperative Research Program also had important implications for staffing. Until the post–World War II period, a good proportion of office staff had come from school systems and state departments of education, since the functions of the office were related to operational programs in

schools. Moreover, the office's self-image as a group of "resource people" who gave advice to the profession had led to the development of corps of specialists. The specialist, usually a former schoolman or former professor at a school of education, saw his function as maintaining liaison with the professional education group in his area of specialization through providing consultation in the office or in the field, attending professional society meetings, or preparing printed materials. In some cases, specialists held offices in professional societies; a prevalent view was that in these relationships the office was the captive of the National Education Association. The staff for the Cooperative Research Program also came from schools of education, but these staff members were affiliated with the research-oriented university community rather than with specialists. This different affiliation, combined with the fact that the new group had some freedom in how they awarded their funds, led to some competition between the researchers and the specialists. It also foreshadowed some problems of the late 1950's.

The Soviet launching of Sputnik 1 in 1957 intensified both popular and professional doubt concerning the quality of American education. We had obviously fallen behind in the science curriculum. Where else were we inferior? Education suddenly took on international overtones, and, because of the climate of opinion, it was suddenly possible to enact, in the National Defense Education Act of 1958 (NDEA), all the ideas which had been brewing for almost a century. This act contains ten titles which provide for such aid as loans to students in institutions of higher education; financial assistance and fellowships for strengthening science, mathematics, and modern language instruction; identification and encouragement of able students; counseling and guidance training; centers for research and development in foreign languages; research in more effective educational use of media; area vocational education programs; and improvement of statistical services of state educational agencies.

The NDEA established a policy for federal aid to education which transformed the Office of Education. First, university scientists and mathematicians and, later, artists and social scientists responded to the demands for new curricular materials by designing the new mathematics and new science courses. This new reference group, however, was not exclusive to the office, because Congress, still suspicious of the office and still not certain that it could handle this new charge, installed some of the curriculum programs in the National Science Foundation. Thus, Congress managed once again to set up an alternative to increased responsibility for the office in planning educational reform. In addition, more of the new personnel who came to manage these new programs were from liberal arts colleges and graduate faculties than from schools of education; these generalists had a broader range of interests and managerial skills than the specialists did. It was in this period that the office began its transition from a fairly homogeneous institution to a bureaucracy.

The Civil Rights Act of 1964 led to a demand for equality and directed the attention of the office to a different aspect of American schools. The office was put in a new role of policing compliance with the desegregation statutes, although the Department of Health, Education, and Welfare, into which the office had been incorporated, and the Department of Justice made the major decisions. This again signaled, to some at least, no confidence that the office could handle the new task. The Office of Economic Opportunity also assumed major responsibilities in both early childhood and community education. Nevertheless, the civil rights movement and the attack on poverty probably more than any other forces led to the development and passage of the Elementary and Secondary Education Act of 1965 (ESEA), the most powerful impetus to change of status and organization in the history of the office.

This act was remarkably comprehensive. Under its five titles there were vast sums available for aid to schools in poverty areas and funds for textbooks. Other titles authorized new supplementary education centers and a national network of educational laboratories. Money was also made available to state education agencies for the purpose of self-improvement.

The ESEA provided the financial assistance necessary to reform education, but it also called into question the ability of the office—at least as it was then constituted—to carry out the task. With the passage of the ESEA, the office's budget had suddenly soared to billions of dollars—the Office of Education had the third largest budget of any government agency. The need for a drastic reorganization was almost as widely accepted

within the office as it was outside. The office and a series of commissioners were brought into contact with new groups which reinforced the movement toward fundamental change.

In 1965 the administration of President Lyndon B. Johnson appointed a special task force composed of administrative experts from high-level government posts outside the office to overhaul it completely. The change was accomplished in less than one year, and a completely new organization emerged, with leaders who had broad interests replacing specialists at every level. More than just signaling the changing of the guard in the office, the ESEA marked the arrival of the office as a new power with great potential in American education. Not only did it have the power of vast sums of money, it also added a network of federally related educational research laboratories and supplementary education centers throughout the country. The office had almost overnight become a major financial partner with every school district in the United States.

The reorganization of the office after the passage of the ESEA considerably strengthened the office of the commissioner and enabled him to control and coordinate the activities of four newly created bureaus. Later, other bureaus were added, again as new legislation was enacted. A by-product of the 1966 reorganization was the creation of the new post of assistant secretary for education in the Department of Health, Education, and Welfare. This official was to coordinate, at the secretary's level, education and education-related activities.

Rapid and enormous growth continue to present the same problems which confront other popular sectors of governmental administration. New legislation continues to develop, and the office finds new roles; from 1963 to 1970 more educational legislation was passed than in the entire history of the office prior to that time.

Suggestions for reforming the organizational structure of the office of education are still abundant in Washington. Some think the agency ought to be autonomous, with a cabinet representative for education. As educational activity increases, it will be instructive to watch the office adapt to new roles. Unfortunately, in recent years we have witnessed the legislative process and the practical demands of implementation weaken programs noble in intent. The Office of Education is unquestionably a permanent and significant factor in determining the course of American schools. Whether or not a centralized, bureaucratic organization can successfully administer future educational policies remains to be seen.

FRANCIS A. J. IANNI

UNIVERSITIES IN THE UNITED STATES, HISTORY OF

The modern American university came into being in the three or four decades after the Civil War. The ferment of reform in higher learning that marked those years took many forms and resulted in a variety of institutional arrangements. Because of this variety and because in the United States there is no formal definition of what is and what is not a university, it is difficult to date precisely the beginnings of the university movement or, indeed, all the roots and sources of that movement. Most generally, the rise of the university marks the institutionalization of new definitions of knowledge and learning: knowledge was always expanding and always changing; it was not given but must be sought for; learning was not familiarity with the known but knowing how to find out something new. This new attitude toward knowledge changed the place and purpose of higher education in American society. Higher education was called upon to foster the search for new knowledge necessary to meet the ever-changing needs of modern society, to train intelligence and direct it to the service of society and mankind, and to prepare students for many different, complex leadership roles in a complex society. These expectations form the essence of what may be called the university ideal.

The formal, institutional manifestation of this ideal and of the rise of the modern university in America was the establishment of graduate schools (professional and academic) devoted to research and to preparing students for specific careers. The university mode of organizing higher education can be said to have become predominant when these commitments to research, specialization, and professionalism effectively penetrated the undergraduate college—the traditional home of general, or liberal, education. The two phases overlap, of course; research and professional instruction penetrated the undergraduate curricula of some institutions before other institutions had even begun adopting the research mode at the graduate level.

But the rise of the university can be roughly divided into these two phases, dating the first from 1870 to 1920 and the second from 1890 to 1945. By the end of World War II, the university mode of organizing instruction was generalized to all institutions of higher education except those few quite self-consciously general education institutions which maintained a common curriculum of "great books" or of introductions to selected disciplines for all undergraduates.

The roots of university reform. In the late nineteenth century, several significant challenges to older American conceptions of knowledge and its usefulness in a democratic polity caused the dominant conception of the role of higher education institutions to change from that of transmitting a given body of knowledge to that of seeking and disseminating new knowledge. Chief among these challenges was the ever-widening scope and increased power of scientific thought. Biblical criticism, physiological psychology, and Darwin's theory of evolution all demonstrated that science was extending its demand for empirical verification over matters of man and his spirit, which until that time were thought to be firmly and safely in the realm of philosophy and religion. Science, especially Darwin's epoch-making hypothesis, forced a reconsideration of the finality of revealed religious knowledge, in particular the biblical account of man. And if biblical knowledge and explanations were unsure, was any body of nonscientific, nonempirical knowledge acceptable?

University reform sprang from the negative answer so many American academics gave to that question. Science's demonstrated success in providing new explanations for observable natural phenomena forced many leading educators and thinkers, who had themselves once believed in a fixed body of knowledge, to question the wisdom of basing higher education on the foundation of revelation. The most fundamental facts and explanations concerning man's social and physical environment and his own humanity needed explication and empirical, or what they called scientific, testing. Such needs suggested a higher learning far different from that embodied in the sectarian antebellum college.

The very growth of the United States challenged its people and its leaders. The immense economic, social, and political problems connected with the Civil War and Reconstruction revealed how complex an increasingly industrialized and urbanized society had become. The failure of Reconstruction policy and the widespread selfishness and corruption of the period from 1865 to 1890—the Gilded Age—led many educated Americans to feel that there was a leadership gap in America. They rejected both the extreme democratic doctrine that any man was fit to hold any government office and the aristocratic doctrine that any cultivated gentleman, solely by reason of his culture and breeding, was a natural leader. Instead they believed that the proper leaders in a democracy were men with special training that enabled them to understand and manage the great complexities of a modern society. The United States needed lawyers, doctors, engineers, geologists, and economists to help shape and control the physical and social environment. American society gradually turned to institutions of higher learning to train them.

In order to meet the demand for trained leaders, these institutions replaced the ideal of transmitting a fundamentally fixed curriculum with the university ideal of seeking and transmitting new knowledge. A complex society constantly presented new problems to its leaders; only an institution committed to the discovery and transmission of new knowledge was equipped to train future leaders to meet these new problems successfully. At the same time, society's demands that institutions of higher education and their staffs supply knowledge and expertise directly applicable to current problems reinforced the pressures on colleges to direct their energies to the search for new knowledge. These demands and the responses to them made higher education increasingly important to the whole society.

The Gilded Age's immersion in material values and official corruption and American society's concomitant failure to deal with pressing social problems repelled a growing body of Americans. For them, the university and the search for new knowledge it embodied became both a refuge from the Gilded Age and a place from which they could gain the power and the skills that would enable them to serve and to change their society.

The example of the German university significantly shaped their vision. Much credit for university reform must go to the efforts of students and young faculty members, especially those who, in ever-increasing numbers (perhaps 10,000 in the nineteenth century), pursued postbaccalaureate studies in German universities. In 1895–1896 (the peak year), 517 Americans were matriculated at German institutions (Vesey 1965); almost all of them and their predecessors compared the American college unfavorably with the German university. What most impressed Americans about the German universities in the second half of the nineteenth century was their salutary effect on German industrialization and national unification. Germany sustained a tremendous economic growth not unlike that of the United States but without—the American students felt—succumbing to the materialism, corruption, and social callousness they saw at home. These students credited the German university with creating this more desirable society, attributing the university's effectiveness to its power to bar the unqualified from civil service or leadership positions, to its dedication to research and the application of new knowledge to the problems of an industrializing society, and to its success in conferring social prestige on trained intelligence. When American students and young faculty members considered changing the society they found distasteful, they took heart from the example of the German university and sought to transfer what they considered its strengths to the United States.

Graduate and professional schools. The American university differed from the American college most obviously in its commitment to high-quality professional training programs. Scores of independent professional schools in medicine, law, engineering, and theology sprang up in the United States late in the eighteenth century and early in the nineteenth. A movement got under way after 1820 to affiliate many of these independent schools with already existing colleges and to endow new professional schools to be built alongside existing colleges. Despite these nominal connections, however, before the Civil War these professional schools remained extraordinarily independent of the colleges with which they were affiliated. In most cases, this independence meant low standards of admission (virtually anyone with the equivalent of a secondary education who could pay the fee qualified) and poor pedagogy limited either to rote recitation or to the apprenticeship model. Few, if any, of these schools sought to teach the general principles upon which practice rested. The university revolution transformed the professional schools: the central institutions exerted stricter control;

standards for admission and graduation rose; professional school faculties began to seek new knowledge and to train students not merely to imitate their teachers but to understand general principles of practice so that they could improve upon the methods of their predecessors. In many cases this transformation entailed the professional school's becoming a graduate school itself, requiring the B.A. or its equivalent for entrance.

Harvard was the first institution in the United States to reform its professional schools to conform to the university ideal. Prior to reform, the medical school, for instance, had operated essentially as a proprietary institution, in which a small body of Boston doctors offered a one-year course of lectures. Student fees for the lectures and for the degree constituted the lecturers' only remuneration. Since the student was required to attend two years of lectures in order to earn the degree, he repeated in his second year what he had done in his first and paid the fee again. Little provision was made for practical training; students were expected to gain actual experience with patients by assisting practicing physicians during the summer months or on the job after graduation. The absence of practical training meant that the capacity of the teaching hospital did not limit class size. The lecture method made large classes feasible; the fee system made them attractive. Harvard's medical school—which was better than most—and most other professional schools run on this model strove, therefore, to increase the student body, paying little attention to the quality or prior training of the students.

Charles W. Eliot, Harvard's reform-minded president from 1869 to 1909, believed that fulfilling the university ideal's commitment to training leaders required professional schools with high academic standards. Under Eliot, Harvard established or significantly upgraded professional schools of medicine, dentistry, veterinary medicine, divinity, law, engineering, and agriculture and established programs leading to graduate degrees in mining and petrography, forestry, and (in the early twentieth century) business administration and education. Although these programs were not equally successful, each developed a rigorous curriculum and contributed significantly to the advancement of knowledge in its field. The price of such rigor, however, was high, as Eliot's reforms at the medical school indicate. Raising admissions standards and lengthening the medical training course to three years reduced the number of fee-paying students; committing the school to research required expensive laboratories; encouraging practical training in the school rather than on the job required hospital facilities. And all these changes required a larger faculty working longer hours.

Few schools in the nineteenth century possessed Harvard's financial resources, and consequently, few could afford more than a gradual upgrading of their professional divisions. It might be noted that perhaps the best professional school in the nineteenth century, the Johns Hopkins School of Medicine, founded in 1873 but not opened until 1893, had, with its companion teaching hospital, an endowment of more than $3.5 million, considerably more than the total endowment of most universities at that time.

The most important professional school that the evolving universities established, however, was the graduate school of arts and sciences—dedicated to the professional training of scholars, most of whom became university teachers themselves. Founding a graduate school of arts and sciences was considerably cheaper than founding other professional schools, for the undergraduate college shared much of the capitalization and salary costs. But the graduate school of arts and sciences became so significant in university reform because it embodied better than any other professional school the ideal of seeking knowledge to advance the general welfare. Here the university ideal of disinterested research could flourish.

Johns Hopkins University opened in 1876 with a generous endowment for its time and a strong commitment to advancing knowledge by encouraging original research and training original researchers. This university created the first ongoing, self-perpetuating, fully staffed and fully committed graduate doctoral program in the United States. The Hopkins program differed significantly from earlier, less formal doctoral programs at Yale, Harvard, and Columbia. The latter programs offered little systematic training, the students taking undergraduate courses and doing independent reading. Hopkins designed special courses and laboratory exercises for the graduate students. Harvard, prodded by the success of the Hopkins experiment, quickly emulated that system, as did Columbia a bit later and Yale considerably later.

Thus, what had been experimental in the late

1870's and 1880's became general in the 1890's. In 1900, 14 universities, responsible for awarding 90 percent of the legitimate doctorates that year, organized the Association of American Universities (AAU). They joined together in an effort to bring some order to the field of graduate education by defining standards, requirements, and purposes of advanced study. That these 14 universities included representatives of the three major kinds of institutions of higher learning that existed in the late nineteenth century indicates how comprehensively professional training in scholarship had spread in a quarter of a century. Five of these schools—Columbia, Harvard, Pennsylvania, Princeton, and Yale—erected their graduate programs upon old, originally religious, if not sectarian, collegiate foundations; five others—Catholic University of America, Chicago, Clark, Johns Hopkins, and Stanford—were new, private universities, established with a strong commitment to professional education; the remaining four—California, Cornell, Michigan, and Wisconsin—were rising land-grant universities, committed to adding the highest quality of tertiary education to the public education systems in their states.

The doctoral degree. Educational reformers considered the certification of professionals for leadership roles as the university's most important function. The awarding of earned, advanced degrees was for them crucially symbolic of the salutary impact the university would have on society. The most important degree was the doctorate, awarded for study and research beyond the undergraduate level. (This generalization excludes the M.D., which had long been awarded to graduates of medical schools whatever their prior education and the nature of their work in medical school.) Some reformers spoke of making the master's degree a significant measure of postgraduate competence and expertise (or at least teaching proficiency) in a profession or a discipline, but efforts in that direction generally failed. Until the 1870's the M.A. in the United States, as in England, was strictly an honorary degree, usually awarded automatically to any bachelor of arts of three years' standing who was able to show evidence of good character and willing to pay a small fee. Harvard abolished the automatic master's degree in 1872 in order to use that degree to certify advanced study. Even though some schools followed suit, many others did not, and

the degree remained somewhat of a debased currency.

The doctorate rather than the master's became the symbol of advanced achievement. In the nineteenth century, doctoral students sought the Ph.D. primarily, although some earned doctor of science degrees, and a few, the doctor of jurisprudence. Graduate schools of arts and sciences awarded almost all of these doctorates. After 1920 the graduate professional schools began to award doctoral degrees—sometimes the Ph.D., sometimes the professional doctorate, such as the Ed.D., D.Eng., and D.B.A.—to signify that the recipient had done research that extended the boundaries of knowledge in that particular profession or in the basic fields of knowledge which underlay that profession. Yale awarded the first Ph.D. degree in 1861; Harvard followed in 1873, Columbia in 1875, and Johns Hopkins in 1878. In 1900 approximately 250 students earned legitimate doctorates (another 130 received honorary doctorates or doctoral degrees from institutions which offered no graduate-level instruction [Berelson 1960]).

Although the AAU could not agree upon a definition of the standards and purposes of graduate instruction, the broad outline of the successful program was clear. The doctoral degree distinguished the university-trained scholar from others on the basis of his demonstrated capacity to make an original contribution to knowledge—to fulfill, in other words, the university ideal. The student's capacity for advancing knowledge was judged on the basis of the work he did in the laboratory or seminar in preparing his doctoral dissertation, the final embodiment of the student's contribution. The laboratory in the natural sciences and the seminar in the social sciences and the humanities were the most characteristic devices for graduate training. Modeled on those in the German universities, they were designed so that a professor (himself an experienced scholar) and a few students could examine data—biological slides or historical documents, for example—and jointly discover new interpretations or explanations of the data. The professor was not simply to use laboratory apparatus to demonstrate to a class how certain conclusions were reached—the usual procedure for many years in American colleges— but genuinely to involve his students in a search for new knowledge.

Laurence Vesey (1965) identified the essence of the seminar method as the personal relation it fostered between teacher and students. Thus, the method's success depended, perhaps too much, on the leader's personal magnetism and inspirational quality. In theory the experienced scholar was to work in seminar or laboratory with the students as equals, inspiring them to search for truth and encouraging their independence; as often as not, however, strong-minded, inspiring scholars used the seminar or laboratory to mold disciples. But despite these very real problems, the seminar or laboratory method remains central to advanced training, for it embodies most clearly the commitment to discovering new knowledge which is vital to the university ideal.

When a student had completed his explorations in the seminar or laboratory and, presumably, discovered new data or a new interpretation of older data, he presented his results in a dissertation which he defended as his original contribution to knowledge. From the very beginning, the doctoral dissertation promised more than it delivered. Relatively few dissertations fulfilled the university ideal of significantly advancing knowledge. Nevertheless, the Ph.D. has steadily grown in prestige. Earning this degree became nearly synonymous with making an original contribution to knowledge and came to differentiate, unfairly and inaccurately, at least in the early years, scholars contributing to knowledge from other educated people. The implication that those without doctoral training would not and could not advance knowledge was manifestly untrue in the late nineteenth century, when very few Americans had received doctoral training—including many of those directing doctoral seminars in leading universities—and when men who had at most a college education were responsible for many of the period's great intellectual advances.

University reformers did their best to ensure that earning the doctorate and contributing to knowledge did become synonymous, first by vastly increasing doctoral enrollment and, second, by restricting, wherever possible, college teaching positions to holders of advanced degrees. Before 1890, American universities had awarded fewer than 1,200 doctorates of all kinds; by 1900 about 250 doctorates were awarded each year; by 1925 more than 1,200 were awarded each year; and 25 years later 6,633 doctorates were awarded. The popularity of the doctoral degree increased more than that of any other degree. Part of this popularity stems from the simple intellectual attrac-

tion that advanced studies hold for increasing numbers of students. It also reflects the fact that the doctorate became a requirement for those desiring to teach in any American university and in most American colleges, and as the twentieth century advanced, for those wishing to do research in industry or government. As access to university and research positions was restricted to those holding the doctorate, there soon developed a very high correlation between doctoral training and contributing to knowledge.

Just as important as the actual discovery of new knowledge was the scholar's duty to communicate that knowledge. The establishment of a vast number of scholarly journals and monograph series in which doctoral students and scholars could publish their discoveries encouraged such communication. At the same time, these specialized publications expanded the separation between the university-trained scholars and other educated men, because the former wrote now for the specialized audience of the scholarly journal rather than for the nonacademic audience of, for instance, the *Atlantic Monthly*. Individual universities published the earliest of the scholarly serials, largely as outlets for the work of their own faculty and students. Johns Hopkins was the pioneer in this field, publishing the first numbers of six major serials between 1878 and 1886. Other universities quickly, if not so prolifically, followed suit. In the 1890's such newly founded national scholarly organizations as the American Economic Association and the American Historical Association attempted to replace the serial publications based in individual universities with national journals published by each association. This attempt generally succeeded only in adding national journals to the list of those already being published at individual universities.

In the nineteenth century many universities, including Johns Hopkins, Harvard, and Columbia, started printing and publishing offices of their own, which gradually grew into today's prestigious university presses. Established originally to supervise the printing of serials catalogs, presidents' reports, syllabi, and so on, the printing offices soon began to offer book-publishing services to faculty and students unable to find commercial houses willing to publish specialized work unsuited to the popular market. How important university encouragement of scholarly communication had become is indicated by the fact that the University of Chicago, upon opening in 1892, immediately established a publishing office (which later became the university press) that in its first decade published 200 separate titles, including 11 scholarly journals.

Thus, university reformers came to define the most sought-after product of the university ideal as the scholar, and they established Ph.D. programs and scholarly publishing facilities to realize their goals. Because these definitions of scholarly merit were easily standardized from discipline to discipline and much more easily judged than contributions to social reform or the general welfare, which the university ideal also sought to stimulate, the essence of the American university as it moved into the twentieth century came to be identified with advanced degrees and with scholarly publication.

Finances. Implementation of the university ideal was enormously expensive. The student-teacher ratio declined dramatically; faculty demanded time and money to pursue new knowledge and prepare work for publication; the commitment to research and professionalization demanded better laboratory equipment, more extensive libraries, and vast facilities for clinical training. The university ideal could not have been effected without new sources of funding. The $50,000 that Abbott Lawrence gave Harvard to found the Lawrence Scientific School in 1847 was reportedly the largest single gift to an institution of higher education before the Civil War. Antebellum colleges normally relied on student fees, subventions from interested religious denominations, and gifts from local citizens conscious of benefits stemming from the college's presence. These sources nearly always proved inadequate even to the restricted purposes of the antebellum college.

Support for the implementation of the university ideal came from three sources: large gifts from businessmen and philanthropists, the most important source in the late nineteenth century; grants from private foundations established by businessmen/philanthropists like Andrew Carnegie, John D. Rockefeller, and Russell and Margaret Olivia Sage, which were especially crucial in the early part of the twentieth century; and a steadily increasing contribution from municipal, state, and federal governments, a source of support that has become the most important since World War II. These gifts include

Johns Hopkins' 1873 gift of $7 million to establish a university and hospital in Baltimore, John D. Rockefeller's $35 million given between 1890 and 1920 to found and support the University of Chicago, the General Education Board's gifts totaling $60 million to several universities to fuel the great endowment drive of 1902–1924, and Congress' appropriation of almost $200 million in the first year of the Higher Education Act of 1965 (U.S. Office of Education . . . 1968). There have been spectacular donations from a few individuals, but it should be noted that giving to higher education has been very widespread in the United States. Annual alumni drives, for example, have become increasingly important.

It is not easy to account for this generosity on the part of reputedly anti-intellectual businessmen and on the part of governments democratically chosen by a supposedly anti-intellectual, pragmatic people. The support of universities by these individuals and groups was prompted by several factors, among them the university ideal's commitment to the training of professionals to manage society more efficiently and more soundly. University research was funded because new knowledge was of immense importance to industry, to defense, and to social welfare. The wealthy businessmen who gave to universities directly, or indirectly through foundations, were performing the role of the "steward of wealth"—the most wealthy (and therefore, according to social Darwinism, the most fit) believed themselves responsible for aiding the whole society by investing some of their earnings in institutions like schools, libraries, and churches that furthered the general welfare. By means of large grants, wealthy individuals probably also expected to purchase for themselves a certain amount of respectability in a society still suspicious of new wealth. The university ideal of research benefited financially from being associated with the undergraduate college, of which alumni held fond memories and on which an increasing number of Americans placed their hopes for the social mobility of their children. Moreover, the competition between public and private universities for prestige stimulated a rivalry between supporters of public and of private education that swelled contributions on both sides. Generally, the financial support for higher education came from men and institutions devoted to the success of the democratic experiment and to the American dream of equality of opportunity. The democratic experiment required the educated leadership that the university was expected to train; equality of opportunity required the open access to leadership positions on the basis of ability and merit that the university was thought to provide. The American people's huge and diffuse investment in universities was a popular vote of confidence in an institution devoted to serving a democratic society.

Nationalization of research. In the twentieth century the impetus behind the search for new knowledge and its application has slowly shifted from the universities to national scholarly and research organizations and to the governments and private foundations which finance research. Of course, most scholars still carry on much of their research in university buildings as part of being professors, but their financial support, their inspiration, and their sense of direction and purpose now come from extrauniversity sources. In the nineteenth century the president of an academic institution guided academic reform intellectually as well as administratively and provided much of the impetus and the direction for original research. He controlled his professors' access to research time and money, their promotions, and their access to public recognition—in short, he distributed academic rewards almost exclusively. The typical professor thus felt his primary affiliation and responsibility to the president and to his university rather than to the standards and purposes of his discipline as defined by the nation's leading scholars in that field.

The first challenge to this conception of university reform came between 1880 and 1905, when leading scholars organized 15 national disciplinary associations: the American Chemical Society (1876), the Modern Language Association of America (1883), the American Historical Association (1884), the American Economic Association (1885), the Geological Society of America and the American Mathematical Society (1888), the American Academy of Political and Social Science (1889), the American Society of Zoologists (1890), the American Psychological Association (1892), the American Astronomical Society and the American Physical Society (1899), the American Philosophical Association (1900), the American Anthropological Association (1902), the American Political Science Association (1903), and the American Sociological Association (1905).

By sponsoring annual meetings at which re-

search papers were read and scholarly journals in which they were printed, these disciplinary associations facilitated communication among scholars, directed their attention away from their universities toward the standards and goals of research defined by the national community of scholars in that discipline, and provided an alternative, suprauniversity structure in which academics could strive for recognition. This alternative system served to inspire scholarship among the professoriat in a way that supplemented the efforts of the university president. As Barry Karl, upon whose insights much of this section rests, put it: "The development of national associations in various academic fields served not only to facilitate intellectual communication in the disciplines, but also to provide resources for publication and to move individuals into national professional prominence, visible above the spires and turrets of their particular institutions" (1968, 1006–1007).

Between 1910 and 1930 further redistributions of academic power and initiative took place which finally supplanted the university and its president as the leading loci of the university ideal. After 1890 the university's claim to be certifying experts coincided nicely with a growing public demand for increased rationality, honesty, and impartiality in public affairs. Academic participation in decision-making on questions as diverse as conservation, taxation, and public health characterized political reform in the Progressive Era. The economic, military, and diplomatic mobilization of World War I only increased the demand for academic expertise. With the government demands for expert opinion supported by objective, scientific research came business demands for research in management techniques and product development. Capitalizing on this situation, individual professors and groups of professors during and after the war developed national research organizations which were, in effect, greatly expanded versions of the national disciplinary organizations created in the previous era. The National Research Council (1916), the American Council of Learned Societies (1919), and the Social Science Research Council (1923) were designed to assemble research money from private foundations, from industry, and from local, state, and federal governments and to distribute that research money among the scholars the councils judged most competent. This mode of organization represented a commitment by the academics—as scholars rather than members of a university—to a national research effort and to the creation of direct relations between the academics and the segments of society demanding their research. It is not entirely clear why the university system as organized before 1910 was inadequate to handle the accumulation and distribution of these moneys. Barry Karl (1968) suggests that universities and their leaders were too conservative to recognize these new sources of income and to involve the universities in political action and reform. It might be further suggested that the system of separate and rather isolated universities offered no means of ranking scholars nationally within a discipline. Research consumers, seeking the best men for their purposes, turned not to the universities but to the national scholarly organizations and councils whose leaders could identify top men in various subspecialties throughout the country.

Through their control of the distribution of funds, leaders of these, in Karl's phrase, research "trusts," joined in later years by leaders of the large foundations and of government research organizations like the National Science Foundation and the Defense Department, initiated and molded the directions and purposes of academic research in the United States. Universities continued as the locus of most research and as the beneficiaries of much of the research money, but they became increasingly passive in this process, acting as homes for scholars whose money and goals came from outside the universities. This shift has been gradual, affecting some disciplines, especially the natural and the policy-oriented social sciences, more rapidly than others. But massive governmental and foundation involvement in financing research—sometimes contributing well over half of a university's budget—has made it very nearly complete. The university, which initiated the movement to discover and apply new knowledge for the improvement of man and his society, has now become, in effect, a dependent unit in an overall national research effort.

The university and the college. By the middle of the twentieth century, the university mode of approaching higher education had come to dominate all phases of higher education, including the liberal arts college, the traditional home of general, nonprofessional education. Universities awarded more than twice as many bachelor's de-grees as liberal arts colleges (that is, colleges without graduate programs), and virtually all faculty members teaching undergraduates had been trained in the university graduate school.

The university ideal clearly committed the universities to instruction beyond that of the traditional college curriculum, and almost all university reformers strove to build universities by adding graduate and professional programs to the existing college rather than by building new foundations. This agreement left the relationship between the emerging university and the traditional college quite fluid. University reformers had to decide how the seminar method, the search for and transmission of new knowledge, the commitment to service and leadership training, and the advanced and professional degree programs were to affect the undergraduate college's traditional concern with liberal and general education.

No European nation faced this problem. In England the three chartered universities served as umbrella institutions for collections of separately endowed and largely self-governing colleges, which carried on instruction chiefly in the liberal arts. Although the universities undertook some professional education in law, medicine, and theology, they did not become generally committed to the university ideal of research and service as American reformers understood this ideal until the twentieth century. Research and most advanced instruction in arts and science in England centered in research institutes and academies, which were quite separate from the university structure. Where England had colleges but no university in the American sense, Germany and France had great universities but no colleges in the English or American sense. The Continental universities which served the Americans as models relied on secondary schools, the *gymnasium* and the *lycée,* to provide general education. Graduates of these schools came directly to the universities to begin specialized work leading to positions in the learned professions, the civil service, or the military. The European student attended the *gymnasium* or the *lycée* at the same age that his American counterpart attended the last two years of high school and the first two years of college; he began his professional training while the American was still pursuing general education. American reformers, impressed with the German example and concerned with bringing university education to as many as possible, struggled with the issue of when to introduce specialized, professional education to young people. Each reformer and institution answered this complicated question somewhat differently. The responses of three different university presidents—Daniel Coit Gilman at Johns Hopkins, Charles William Eliot at Harvard, and Charles Richard Van Hise at the University of Wisconsin—represent the most important models of university-college relations and, in their sequence, demonstrate the university ideal's steady encroachment on the undergraduate college.

Daniel Coit Gilman and the graduate school. Daniel Coit Gilman (1831–1908) was president of Johns Hopkins University from its opening in 1876 until 1901. An 1852 graduate of Yale and librarian, professor of geography, and secretary of the school of science there from 1855 to 1872, Gilman grew deeply discouraged with Yale's conservative definition of higher learning, which relegated scientific study to an inferior position in the university. In 1872, Gilman left New Haven and possible advancement at America's third oldest college to become president of California's new land-grant college at Berkeley. There he set out to establish the foundations of a college offering both liberal arts and scientific courses and to develop an agricultural training program in accordance with the terms of the Morrill Act. The college had neither the money, the students, nor the public support to pursue the university ideal; Gilman's major reform battle at Berkeley involved bitter controversies with various farm groups that complained of the irrelevance of college training to actual agricultural problems.

In 1873, Johns Hopkins, a wealthy Quaker merchant, willed $7 million for the creation of a university, medical school, and hospital in Baltimore. In 1874 the trustees chosen in Hopkins' will, advised by presidents Eliot of Harvard, Andrew D. White of Cornell, and James B. Angell of the University of Michigan, chose Gilman to execute Johns Hopkins' desires. Gilman now had the facilities with which to engage in an enterprise different from college-building. He had money; he felt that Baltimore, unlike California, had enough colleges nearby to make building another large undergraduate institution unnecessary. The new institution had no traditions or prior commitments to prevent him from implementing his conception of the university ideal. For Gilman

the questions of how to define the university ideal institutionally and how to relate it to traditional college instruction were easily settled. In his inaugural address in 1876 he stated that the college "implies, as a general rule, restriction rather than freedom; tutorial rather than professorial guidance; residence within appointed bounds; the chapel, the dining-hall, and the daily inspection. The College theoretically stands *in loco parentis*; it does not afford a very wide scope; it gives a liberal and substantial foundation on which the university instruction may be wisely built" (Gilman 1898, p. 14). On the other hand, the university was to offer the student personal and intellectual freedom, professorial guidance, and a "wide scope." But Gilman wanted to maintain a separation between the institutions. He expected the college to change little; rather, university instruction was to be built on top of the four-year college curriculum. Johns Hopkins University, therefore, opened in 1876 with a small traditional college and a separate graduate school offering advanced work in most of the liberal arts and sciences. Within two years Gilman and his faculty defined a program leading to the Ph.D. that required each student to participate in a departmental seminar and to publish an original contribution to knowledge. Gilman also established scholarly journals at Hopkins for the work of staff and students. One of his most far-reaching innovations was the provision of large fellowships, which allowed graduate students to finance their work beyond the bachelor's degree. Gilman was concerned both with attracting able men to a new and unproved kind of training program and with increasing the rewards that society offered the man of trained intelligence. Of the university reformers of his era, he was the most assiduous in urging higher faculty salaries and higher material rewards for research.

In developing Johns Hopkins University, Gilman gave first priority to encouraging scholarly research and contributions to knowledge. He had no doubt, and indeed tirelessly stressed, that the scholarly pursuit of knowledge would produce results ultimately useful for society. In his inaugural speech he defined the university movement in the United States as "a reaching out for a better state of society than now exists; it is a dim but an indelible impression of the value of knowledge; it is a craving for intellectual and moral growth; it is a longing to interpret the laws of creation; it means a wish for less misery among the poor, less ignorance in schools, less bigotry in religion, less suffering in the hospital, less fraud in business, less folly in politics; it means more study of nature, more love of art, more lessons from history, more security in property, more health in cities, more virtue in the country, more wisdom in legislation; it implies more intelligence, more happiness, more religion" (*ibid.*, pp. 12–13). But Gilman left the relation between scholarship and society somewhat vague. He stressed the university ideal's search for new knowledge and new explanations for observed phenomena but neglected somewhat that ideal's concern with effecting social reform and providing trained leadership. Because Hopkins focused on training scholars who would continue the research tradition rather than on training social and political leaders, Gilman was less inclined than most reformers to intrude university methods into the traditional college. Most reformers reversed the priorities, which led them to reason that university methods must be extended into the college if they were to affect enough students to make a significant impact on the larger society. Isolating university methods in the separate graduate school with its small number of students, as Gilman advocated, blunted the university movement's capacities for improving American society.

Charles William Eliot and the elective system. Charles William Eliot (1834–1926), the president of Harvard University for 40 years (1869–1909), offers a striking contrast to Gilman on these issues. When Eliot assumed the reins of the oldest and richest university in the United States, its students, its alumni, and its rather elitist, old-stock, Brahmin supporters were deploring the college's limited influence in preventing or tempering the political and social immorality of the Gilded Age. Eliot, a Brahmin himself, shared this discontent and lamented Harvard's failure to produce the leaders it once had produced. In pressing for university reform, Eliot sought primarily not to increase knowledge but to train leaders more effectively. Despite his Brahmin background, he repudiated the aristocracy of birth and supported the Jeffersonian idea of an aristocracy of the intellectually talented. Higher education, he believed, could best serve and most effectively reform its society by identifying and training that intellectual aristocracy.

Eliot and his supporters blamed Harvard's shortcomings on its rigid adherence to a curriculum and a pedagogy no longer relevant to the complexities of an urban, industrial civilization. In many ways Eliot's ideas were traditional: colleges could best train leaders by disciplining and exercising their minds; proper mental discipline came from pursuing a subject in depth. Eliot criticized the antebellum college because its insistence, in an era of rapidly expanding knowledge, on a curriculum common to all students served to keep all instruction elementary and superficial. Because each undergraduate had to study every subject taught at the college, adding a new subject to the curriculum required a corresponding reduction of time spent on other subjects. The trivium and quadrivium of the colonial college had become by 1860 a plethora of short and superficial introductions to a great many subjects.

Eliot's reforms rested on his contention that the antebellum curriculum was too superficial and too easy to winnow effectively the intellectually gifted from the mass of students. He raised admission standards at the college, appointed more rigorous faculty members, and demanded (rather unsuccessfully) harder work from the undergraduates. In advocating the earned M.A., he suggested that a truly educated leader needed five years of liberal education rather than four. He restricted admission to Harvard's professional and vocational schools to holders of the bachelor's degree; he lengthened the law and medical school programs to three years.

Eliot was not traditional in defining the contents of a properly rigorous curriculum. A chemist, Eliot shared Gilman's faith in scientific advance, and he welcomed the expansion of knowledge and urged the immediate insertion of new subjects in the curriculum. Eliot resolved the conflict between his desire for depth and his desire for an inclusive curriculum by repudiating the concept that all educated men must study the same subjects in the same way. Instead, he established the elective system (he did not invent it), which, fundamentally, allowed undergraduates to choose freely the courses and subjects that appealed most to them from among the many the college offered. The elective principle allowed Harvard to offer more subjects and courses than an individual could take in four years and to add new subjects and courses without reducing the number of faculty or courses in other fields. Eliot also expected the system to encourage students—at least the best ones, with whom he was most concerned—to explore certain subjects in great depth. Thus, the elective principle enabled Eliot to modernize the curriculum and at the same time to increase its capacity for disciplining the mind and identifying the intellectually talented.

Full implementation of the elective system at Harvard took almost 20 years, as Eliot fought to overcome the objections of the traditionalists among faculty, alumni, and trustees. Between 1890 and 1910, Harvard students enjoyed absolutely free election of courses; thereafter, concentration, distribution, and general education requirements tempered the elective principle at Harvard. The elective principle spread to many colleges in the late nineteenth century and to almost all colleges in the twentieth century, although never in its pure form. The elective principle was nearly always accompanied by requirements that each student concentrate his electives so as to major, or specialize, in a single field and that he take some work outside his field of specialization.

But in whatever form the system spread, it profoundly altered the American college by introducing the ideal of pursuing new knowledge. Instituted to affect undergraduates, the elective system was most profoundly and immediately effective in changing the functions and the character of the college faculty. An elective curriculum included general introductory courses and various levels of advanced specialized courses, thereby providing both the depth of treatment that Eliot desired and opportunities for undergraduate professors to search for and contribute to knowledge. Where all courses in the common curriculum had to be general enough to appeal to all students, faculty members under the elective system could design specialized courses around their own research interests. While the commitment to a common curriculum restricted faculty size because it limited the number of courses taught, the elective principle had no such limit and encouraged an enlargement of the faculty far out of proportion to the increase in the student body. As the faculty grew in size, each member had more time to spend on his own specialized subject. Typically, a professor taught one general course and two or three advanced courses on topics on which he was doing research.

The effect the elective system had on the college was not a part of Eliot's original purpose. He was interested primarily in selecting and training leaders and gave the discovery of new knowledge and the training of research scholars a relatively low priority. Only when his own faculty, more impressed with Gilman's implementation of the university ideal than with Eliot's, threatened to move to better research facilities at competing universities like Johns Hopkins did Eliot grant faculty members individual research time, construct research laboratories and libraries, and adequately fund facilities for training the advanced research scholar. At Hopkins a fully articulated training program for the research scholar had existed from the very beginning and set the tone for the whole university; at Harvard such training grew slowly and hesitantly out of the undergraduate program and for many years remained subordinate to the purposes of that program. In 1872, Harvard outlined residence and dissertation requirements for the M.A. and Ph.D. but made no provision for graduate course work—graduate students were expected to supplement undergraduate courses with independent study supervised by college faculty members. Three years later a few faculty members voluntarily offered courses of directed reading especially for graduate students, but these courses attracted more undergraduates than graduates. This experience helped Eliot and his faculty redefine research instruction and college instruction simply as different levels in a single progression from elementary to more specialized courses within each field. The advanced courses simply capped that progression. Undergraduates and graduates were expected to progress from the elementary to the highly advanced levels, well-prepared graduate students perhaps dispensing with the elementary level and undergraduates perhaps forgoing the highly advanced level.

But Eliot envisioned no separation between the college and the graduate school, and he urged students to move back and forth as occasion, ability, and desire indicated. He saw Harvard's graduate courses as opportunities for the intellectually talented undergraduate to explore subjects in greater depth. The success of Johns Hopkins forced Eliot and Harvard to recognize the graduate department's duty to train professional scholars as well as leaders, but Eliot never acceded to the demand of some of his more professionalized faculty that the graduate school become a separate institution, with standards and purposes different from those of the college. When, in 1890, the college and the graduate school were separated for administrative purposes, Harvard placed the instructional responsibility for both schools in a single faculty of arts and and sciences, which was charged with the responsibility of offering a common course of study for undergraduates and graduate students. In Eliot's day that faculty focused primarily on the problems and concerns of undergraduate instruction and on the goal of producing well-informed and well-disciplined leaders. But as the twentieth century and academic professionalization proceeded, faculty attention at Harvard (and at other universities organized on its model) shifted more and more to the problems and concerns of graduate instruction and to the encouragement of original research and scholarly publication, with a consequent neglect of the special problems of general undergraduate education.

Charles Van Hise and the "Wisconsin idea." Charles Richard Van Hise (1857–1918), who served as president of the University of Wisconsin from 1903 to 1918, greatly expanded the university's functions in society. Gilman and, to a greater extent, Eliot implied that the university's ultimate justification lay in its long-run contribution to society; Van Hise declared that the highest aim of the university, especially the state university, was to serve its society directly. Van Hise, a prominent geologist and conservationist, received his bachelor of metallurgical engineering degree from Wisconsin in 1879, joined its instructional staff in geology in 1882, and received the first earned Ph.D. given by the university in 1892. As president he inherited the state university's traditional creed that public service was the university's highest duty, and he dramatized and publicized that creed into the nationally known "Wisconsin idea." In his inaugural address of 1904 he outlined the land-grant institution's three tasks: to prepare the student for his lifework and for effective citizenship; to advance knowledge; and to facilitate the application of knowledge to the economic, social, and political problems of the people.

Van Hise was not responsible for any particular improvements in preparing students for their lifework and for effective citizenship. What is significant is how little attention his administration gave to general, unspecialized education at any level. Wisconsin's colleges of Letters and Science,

of Agriculture, and of Engineering each offered both undergraduate and graduate degrees. Even the undergraduate division of the College of Letters and Science, the university's largest division, focused on vocational education. Before 1903 this college included separate schools which granted vocational bachelor's degrees in education, music skills, commerce, library training, journalism, physical education, social service, and manual arts. Van Hise combined these schools into a single college program granting a single degree, and he allowed undergraduates to elect individual courses. But he expected most students to major in some vocational field; by 1910 over three-quarters of the undergraduate body did so. The university ideal of professionalism and specialization had clearly triumphed over the old-time college.

But the main thrust of Van Hise's administration was not undergraduate vocational training. Nor did it concentrate on training research scholars (as at Hopkins) or training leaders (as at Harvard). Rather, Van Hise stressed the connection between advancing knowledge and applying those advances to bettering the life of the people of the state. This connection underlay the Wisconsin idea. Van Hise, more than any of his predecessors, encouraged research and scholarship at Wisconsin. Indeed, research pervaded all parts of the university, both graduate and undergraduate; in the 1890's the College of Letters and Science began to require a dissertation on the graduate school model from all undergraduates. But Van Hise supported research that promised a fairly immediate application, believing "that every fundamental discovery yet made by the delving student has been of service to man before a decade has passed" (Curti & Carstensen 1949, p. 88).

Van Hise emphasized two ways of relating research to the service of mankind. First, he encouraged, indeed expected, faculty members to serve the state government as experts and advise on issues ranging from improving agricultural methods to equalizing tax burdens. By 1908, at the height of Wisconsin's progressive movement, 41 faculty members were sitting on one or more state commissions, chiefly regulatory ones. Although university scholars had previously served business and government as experts, Van Hise was the first university reformer to make that relation explicit, to publicize it aggressively, to assert the primacy of such activity, and to direct it toward the public rather than the private interest.

One example of expert involvement in politics was Charles McCarthy's famous Legislative Reference Library. McCarthy, a part-time professor at the univerity (which was located only a few blocks from the state capitol), offered a bill-drafting service for legislators. McCarthy took a general outline of a lawmaker's legislative goals and, after consulting his extensive record of legislation from other states and talking with experts from the university faculty, wrote a bill that carried out the legislator's intent—whether McCarthy agreed with it or not. McCarthy's service and other expert involvement in politics assumed that the scholar's search for truth made him an ideal, impartial adviser to government administrators. The disinterested scholar-expert could, the theory went, execute the political and social wishes of others without imposing his own—often unconscious—biases, and he was obliged to do so whatever his personal beliefs. This concept of the academic expert, whatever its limitations, enjoyed enormous popularity in the early twentieth century, and much of this naïve faith in the capacity of the expert continues to this day.

Second, Van Hise sought to relate research and application in improving the lives of the people of the state through the university's extension movement, which would, he hoped, "carry light and opportunity" to every citizen (*ibid.*, p. 563). "I shall never be content," he wrote, "until the beneficent influence of the University reaches every family in the state" (*ibid.*, p. 88). Such was his ideal of a state university. To fulfill this ideal, he created the extension division in 1908 as a separate unit of the university. This division was designed to supplement the agricultural extension work that had been so prominent in the 1890's and to ensure that the fruits of knowledge accumulated at Madison would reach all citizens of the state. This dissemination process would occur, not only indirectly through improved leadership, improved legislation, and improved administration, but directly through short two-week courses for farmers, mechanics, and housewives; through correspondence courses; through debate materials sent to every Wisconsin high school; and through the classes that university professors held in communities throughout the state.

With Van Hise the university revolution was complete; the Wisconsin idea clearly foreshadowed the multiversity. Wisconsin combined research, professional and specialized training, and the academic expert's involvement with social improvement more successfully than Hopkins or Harvard had done in the nineteenth century. Yet the Wisconsin formulation had serious weaknesses. Van Hise's emphasis on immediate service directed the university ideal's concern with improving society toward short-term rather than long-term goals and sometimes involved universities too closely in society and government that they might best have served by taking a more critical stance. Van Hise, like so many university administrators, discovered no formula for allocating university support satisfactorily between pure and applied research. But the most serious deficiency of the Wisconsin formulation of the university ideal was that it allowed research, specialized training, and public service to take precedence over liberal education and critical inquiry into human values and social purposes.

BIBLIOGRAPHY

BARZUN, JACQUES 1968 *The American University: How It Runs, Where It Is Going.* New York, Harper.

BELL, DANIEL 1966 *The Reforming of General Education: The Columbia College Experience in Its National Setting.* New York, Columbia University Press.

BEN-DAVID, JOSEPH, AND RANDALL COLLINS 1966 "A Comparative Study of Academic Freedom and Student Politics." *Comparative Education Review,* 10:220–249.

BEN-DAVID, JOSEPH, AND AWRAHAM ZLOCZOWER 1962 "Universities and Academic Systems in Modern Societies." *Archives Européennes de Sociologie,* 3, no. 1:45–84.

BERELSON, BERNARD 1960 *Graduate Education in the United States.* New York, McGraw-Hill.

CHURCH, ROBERT L., et al. 1965 *Social Sciences at Harvard, 1860–1920.* Edited by Paul Buck. Cambridge, Mass., Harvard University Press.

CORDASCO, FRANCESCO 1960 *Daniel Coit Gilman and the Protean Ph.D.: Shaping of American Graduate Education.* Leiden, The Netherlands, E. J. Brill.

CURTI, MERLE, AND VERNON CARSTENSEN 1949 *The University of Wisconsin: A History, 1848–1925.* 2 vols. Madison, University of Wisconsin Press.

CURTI, MERLE, AND RODERICK NASH 1965 *Philanthropy in the Shaping of American Higher Education.* New Brunswick, N.J., Rutgers University Press.

EDDY, EDWARD DANFORTH, JR. 1957 *Colleges for Our Land and Time: The Land-Grant Idea in American Education.* New York, Harper.

ELIOT, CHARLES W. 1898 *Educational Reform: Essays and Addresses.* New York, Century.

FARMER, PAUL 1950 "Nineteenth-century Ideas of the University: Continental Europe." Margaret Clapp, ed., *The Modern University.* Ithaca, N.Y., Cornell University Press. Pages 3–24.

FLEMING, DONALD H. 1954 *William H. Welch and the Rise of Modern Medicine.* Boston, Little, Brown.

GILLISPIE, CHARLES C. 1950 "English Ideas of the University in the Nineteenth Century." Margaret Clapp, ed., *The Modern University*. Ithaca, N.Y., Cornell University Press. Pages 27–55.

GILMAN, DANIEL COIT 1898 *University Problems in the United States*. New York, Century.

HALSEY, A. H. 1962 "British Universities." *Archives Européennes de Sociologie*, 3, no. 1:85–101.

HAWKINS, HUGH 1960 *Pioneer: A History of the Johns Hopkins University, 1874–1889*. Ithaca, N.Y., Cornell University Press.

HERBST, JURGEN 1965 *The German Historical School in American Scholarship: A Study in the Transfer of Culture*. Ithaca, N.Y., Cornell University Press.

HOFSTADTER, RICHARD, AND WALTER P. METZGER 1955 *The Development of Academic Freedom in the United States*. New York, Columbia University Press.

HOFSTADTER, RICHARD, AND WILSON SMITH, eds. 1961 *American Higher Education: A Documentary History*. Vol. 2. University of Chicago Press.

JAMES, HENRY 1930 *Charles W. Eliot: President of Harvard University, 1869–1909*. Boston, Houghton Mifflin.

JENCKS, CHRISTOPHER, AND DAVID RIESMAN 1968 *The Academic Revolution*. Garden City, N.Y., Doubleday.

KARL, BARRY D. 1968 "The Power of Intellect and the Politics of Ideas." *Daedalus*, 97, no. 3:1002–1035.

KERR, CLARK 1963 *The Uses of the University*. Cambridge, Mass., Harvard University Press.

LEDUC, THOMAS 1946 *Piety and Intellect at Amherst College, 1865–1912*. New York, Columbia University Press.

LUBOVE, ROY 1965 *The Professional Altruist: The Emergence of Social Work as a Career, 1880–1930*. Cambridge, Mass., Harvard University Press.

MACHLUP, FRITZ 1962 *The Production and Distribution of Knowledge in the United States*. Princeton, N.J., Princeton University Press.

McCARTHY, CHARLES 1912 *The Wisconsin Idea*. New York, Macmillan.

MILLETT, JOHN D. 1952 *Financing Higher Education in the United States*. New York, Columbia University Press.

MORISON, SAMUEL ELIOT, ed. 1930 *The Development of Harvard University Since the Inauguration of President Eliot, 1869–1929*. Cambridge, Mass., Harvard University Press.

NEVINS, ALLAN 1962 *The State Universities and Democracy*. Urbana, University of Illinois Press.

PAULSEN, FRIEDRICH 1906 *The German Universities and University Study*. New York, Scribner.

PETERSON, GEORGE E. 1964 *The New England College in the Age of the University*. Amherst, Mass., Amherst College Press.

ROSS, EARLE D. 1942 *Democracy's College: The Land-Grant Movement in the Formative Stage*. Ames, Iowa State College Press.

RUDOLPH, FREDERICK 1962 *The American College and University: A History*. New York, Knopf.

RYAN, W. CARSON 1939 *Studies in Early Graduate Education: The Johns Hopkins, Clark University, the University of Chicago*. New York, Carnegie Foundation for the Advancement of Teaching.

SOLBERG, WINTON U. 1968 *The University of Illinois, 1867–1894: An Intellectual and Cultural History*. Urbana, University of Illinois Press.

STORR, RICHARD J. 1953 *The Beginnings of Graduate Education in America*. University of Chicago Press.

SUTHERLAND, ARTHUR E. 1967 *The Law at Harvard: A History of Ideas and Men, 1817–1967*. Cambridge, Mass., Harvard University Press.

U.S. OFFICE OF EDUCATION. OFFICE OF ADMINISTRATION MANAGEMENT. EVALUATION DIVISION 1968 *Fact Book: Office of Education Programs, June 1968*. Washington, D.C., Government Printing Office.

VANCE, MAURICE M. 1960 *Charles Richard Van Hise: Scientist Progressive*. Madison, The State Historical Society of Wisconsin.

VESEY, LAURENCE R. 1965 *The Emergence of the American University*. University of Chicago Press.

ROBERT L. CHURCH

UNIVERSITIES, INTELLECTUAL ROLE OF

Any effort to define the intellectual role of the American university leads to an awareness of the number of other roles it has undertaken, particularly during the twentieth century. The majority of parents and students are convinced that the university's major role is vocational, making possible entry into the professions and business. In the minds of others, social status is the predominant reason for attendance and academic motivations are secondary. When the Morrill Act of 1865 created the land-grant colleges, another very practical role was assumed by the university, that of preparing students for agriculture and engineering. Since the late 1930's industry and government have asked the university to take on the role of adviser and researcher in matters relating to everything from defense to food and drugs. Still another role has emerged, stimulated by external pressures and by the university's own humanitarian and democratic concerns. This is the function of ameliorating undesirable social or political conditions in the university neighborhood or region by participating in social planning and action.

As all these developments continue, the basic purpose of the university remains unclear to the lay observer. He becomes disturbed when he hears the university called a supermarket where everyone may shop for what he chooses and is sure to find something he can use. And the university itself is sometimes equally disturbed and often moves confusedly in the midst of demands that it take on the adaptability of a chameleon.

Yet when it takes the time to examine itself, the university invariably arrives at the conclusion that its paramount reason for being is its intellectual role. And it defines this role as two-pronged: the pursuit of truth for its own sake and the development of wisdom. Both parts of the definition presuppose objectivity and academic freedom, and both carry with them the desirability of, if not the necessity for, the kind of meditative atmosphere which only a separation from society can bring about.

The pursuit of truth and the development of wisdom are sometimes suspect, especially when they represent a withdrawal from society and, almost paradoxically, an evaluation of its affairs. In the intellectual role of critic, a university is bound to create animosities and antagonisms, and it sometimes is constrained to appraise negatively the very agencies or individuals upon whose goodwill its future existence depends. Thus, the university is *within* the world even though it purports not to be *of* it. And if it is to fulfill this intellectual role honestly, it must accept and wrestle with the dilemmas that are inherent in such a role.

Problems of role definition. There is an anomaly of sorts in the fact that the intellectual role of the university in our society should need definition or explanation. One would suppose the university to have established such a role over the centuries in ways that precluded even the semblance of a challenge. One would expect its place in the affairs of men to be firm and sure. Indeed, this is partially true, for it does have a place. The recurring question, however, is the nature of that place. Endless controversy arises in regard to the real or alleged purposes of the university; pressures representing disparate points of view are exerted as society changes its character or its motives or its criteria of achievement and success; bitter words are exchanged between members of the academic community and those who surround it. And even within the university's own confines, battles rage unceasingly and sometimes threaten to leave it drained and powerless.

The reasons for this anomaly are both historical and current. There has never been agreement as to whether the university should be for the few or the many; whether it should strive to create men of wisdom or skilled practitioners; whether its relation to society should be active or passive, one of leadership or comment and criticism; whether it should affirm that certain values are immutable or stand ready to cast any value aside; whether it should react and adjust to the external changes and influences surrounding it or stand aloof. From the university's beginnings in medieval times, some or all of these questions have been debated, and they are debated no less today.

Under such circumstances the basic intellectual function of the university has always been in a precarious state, and in modern times the precariousness is even more pronounced. In academic circles the life of the mind has become one of many lives; the world of thought has become one of many worlds. The modern university is more inclusive than ever before, more diverse, more complex, and thus more difficult to comprehend as a universally accepted institution with clearly agreed-upon motivations. And there is no likelihood that any consensus is in the offing. The opposite is more apt to be true, and the battle lines will continue to be drawn. In the United States the struggle is more acute and less likely to be settled because the needs of the society are contrary to what the traditionalists in the university would like to make its major concern.

Pressures on the university. To speak of the intellectual role, therefore, is to speak of an aspect of the university that is forced to resist or adapt to pressures from many quarters if it is to retain its preeminence in academic life. These are pressures which frighten or exhilarate, depending upon one's point of view.

Mass education. There is, for example, the pressure of mass education. An aristocracy of learning can now exist only as part of a much larger and more comprehensive objective. As a democratic nation, the United States may often fumble and stumble. It has its high and low points in reputation and achievement. This is understandable, for to a very great extent it treads on previously unexplored ground. If it truly practices what it professes, then this country dedicates itself to abolishing ignorance among all its people. No other nation has so thoroughly embraced this concept or made such strong efforts to have it permeate the consciousness and the conscience of its citizenry. Whoever believes in the United States believes all its people must be educated. Otherwise, the first precept under which the republic was founded, equality of opportunity, is made meaningless.

Mass education, therefore, is the United States' insurance that democracy may thrive, for without it the decision-making power of the people is weakened and even manipulated, their ability to change their status is lessened, and their expectations are placed within arbitrary limits not of their own choosing. The nation's failure to achieve this is evidenced in urban and rural blight, in extremism and violence. Mass education means lifting every individual to the level where his potential has a fair chance of being realized. This goal is necessarily the preoccupation of all levels of the academic system.

Thus, the university's dilemma engendered by the pressure of mass education is self-evident. It is constantly fearful that its responsiveness to mass educational needs will dilute the quality of its intellectual achievements, cause it to compromise its standards, or take attention and support away from the academic elite for whom it is also responsible. The university is equally fearful that it will be too far removed from the realities of modern society to be an effective contributor to the solution of current problems. Whichever direction the university follows will make it the target of criticism; if it provides for both mass and elite education, major changes in philosophy, techniques, and even structure will be necessary.

Science and technology. Another pressure affecting the university's intellectual role is brought about by the enormous strides of science and technology. For a long time now there has been clear recognition by the academic world that this pressure has caused an imbalance in intellectual preoccupations. The rapidity with which new scientific concepts have emerged, giving birth to a succession of new pragmatic possibilities, has captured the public imagination. Technological achievement, surrounding the society with an aura of materialism, brings comfort to the body but does little for the soul. The so-called liberal studies in the university have grown steadily weaker as they have found it more and more difficult to establish their relevance in a society oriented to the technological specialist. This is the age of the doer rather than the thinker, the manager rather than the meditator. Its accent is on immediacy; its approach to problems is too often facile and expedient.

The tragedy of this decline in the influence of liberal studies in the university is all the more poignant because it is unnecessary. The implications of scientific discovery for the philosopher, the artist, or the writer are so profound that they open great new opportunities which could be a strengthening influence upon liberal studies. The emphasis on science and specialization raises philosophical, historical, ethical, and social questions which could well be part of the core of the curricula in their related disciplines. The study of such questions belongs in the background of every truly educated person, regardless of the ultimate direction of his career.

The liberal studies are no more immutable than any other academic disciplines; yet too little has been done to transform the natural reluctance of their proponents into a desire for change. More than ever before, science and technology require a foundation of philosophical and cultural understanding; this foundation can deepen rather than threaten the intellectual role of the university.

A sidelight on the pressure of science and technology has been the revulsion against it by a minority of youth. They are troubled by their experience with a society where ideas are largely rated by their salability, where convictions too often seem secondary to compromise, and where democratic ideals lag behind pragmatic realities. In an inchoate way some of these young people appear to be trying to pull the society back to a more contemplative life deeply rooted in basic values. Others are simply lashing out, either because of their own confusion or as the result of being manipulated. For both groups, the extremism they sometimes espouse to call attention to their cause becomes self-defeating. What it accomplishes all too often is a further hardening of conservatism among adults and an alarming increase in general suspicion of all intellectual matters and activities.

There is little question, however, that the university does react to this academic revolt. It reexamines its present forms and attitudes, its policies and techniques, and frequently finds itself guilty as charged. It even changes as a result of the examination. Yet, it does all this out of fear and guilt rather than out of positive conviction. And its uneasiness probably stems from the fact that its intellectual role is weakened still more instead of being made stronger by this new pressure upon it and upon society as a whole.

Political activism. The university faces still another kind of student and faculty activism, which is politically rather than intellectually motivated and which has little or nothing to do with curricular matters. It is a revolution against the structure of the institution and the mores of society, against any sort of unilateral authority on or off the campus. Like most revolutions it stimulates extremist actions and breeds abuses. But like most revolutions it comes about because there is a core of justification at its center.

It may be that an intellectual eagerness lies behind this attitude of revolt, but the outward manifestations tend steadily toward the acquisition of political power on campuses. And this power, once acquired, is likely to be wielded more to change the nonintellectual aspects of student and faculty life than to make curricula more relevant. Students, and some faculty also, are engrossed in the social, economic, and political problems of the country as never before, engrossed not only in examining them critically but more and more in active efforts to change them in ways that run counter to previously accepted American traditions and values. The intellectual part of such examination is more and more a side issue; the real attraction lies in the sense of movement, the identification of an enemy, the call to the barricades, the planning of strategy, the mounting of a campaign, and the excitement of a confrontation, with its possible victories and dangers.

The American university is traditionally ill-equipped to cope with such activism. It has always believed itself to be an evolutionary rather than a revolutionary instrument of change. It has never been a political arena like its Latin American counterpart, for example. Even during periods of national stress, particularly war periods, it has adapted to demands upon it without sensing any major shift in its essential role. But these other stresses and pressures, whether national or related to the campus itself, are not so easily turned aside. And in dealing with such pressures the university may find itself often putting intellectual considerations aside while it struggles for its own survival. It may find itself yielding to the demands for relevance to such an extent that the more timeless, more reflective, more philosophical preoccupations of man will be relegated to quite different sorts of institutions of the "think-tank" variety, purposely uninhabited by faculty and students.

External pressures.   One other type of pressure affecting the university's intellectual role is the pressure of external influences of many sorts which combine to limit and constrain the institution.

The first of these influences is reflected in the research activities of the university. In academic life, research by faculty and students is a precious component of institutional strength and guarantees the expansion of knowledge. When pursued in its broadest and most basic forms, research becomes the lifeblood of the intellectual body, whether it is the individual or the institution as a whole. However, there is a disinclination to support broad and basic research unless evidence can clearly be given that it will contribute in very practical ways to the needs of society. Such practicalities relate to business and industrial needs, to technological development, and often to matters of military necessity. Under these circumstances the humanistic studies are slighted, and one major part of the intellectual spectrum remains unsupported. State and federal legislatures or large industrial complexes are rarely moved to invest their resources in pure research that is an intellectual exercise without immediate practical ends. And since these external agencies provide by far the major share of research opportunity, the university is faced with the dilemma of starving itself or eating too much of the wrong food.

Another external influence is the control of the public university by those who hold the purse strings. Simple accountability for expenditures can become a detailed examination of every academic program, existing or contemplated, and educational decisions may come to be made from outside the university. When this continues unchecked, the nature of the institution must change to suit the predilections of whatever political force is in control. Obviously, if the university is to be proscribed in its general activities and planning by outside agencies, the effect upon its freedom of movement and intellectual breadth can only be negative. It is only a short step from this stage to being told directly and completely what may and may not be taught or explored.

There are significant reasons for the existence and growth of these and other external influences. Not the least of them is the reaction of legislators and the general public to student and faculty activism. The university, always under a certain amount of suspicion because it deals with ideas, frequently unpopular ideas, has its future threatened by those who blame it for the behavior of the younger generation. Since the adult population is largely conservative, it tends to reject bitterly any far-ranging freedom of thought for the university. The university faces more clearly than ever the centuries-old problem of justifying its existence as a completely free institution.

The increase of public higher education makes the problem even more acute, since dependence upon public funds always carries with it the potentiality, if not the reality, of public censure and control. The atmosphere surrounding the university and public officialdom is too often one of tension. Such an atmosphere is hardly conducive to the encouragement of innovation or the easy adjustment to necessary change. Instead of being bold in its adaptations to the new conditions of society, conditions calling for sweeping revisions not only of curricula and techniques but even of educational concepts, the university is constrained to be overly cautious. It has always been deliberate in movement; but its deliberateness may become even more marked, since it moves with a constant threat of reprisal when any innovative effort backfires. It can thus become a supremely conservative institution incapable of meeting the needs of a democracy that intends to practice what its ideology reflects.

Trends in the university. The many pressures that converge upon the American university, particularly the public university, combine either to sap the institution's intellectual life or to create distractions and diversions which complicate its efforts to keep major emphasis upon the world of the mind. The university cannot stand aside from the major issues facing society, not only because all these issues have intellectual roots which need to be uncovered for all to recognize but also because it has within it much to offer for the pragmatic resolutions of such issues. The new university is at the center of man's concerns, not on the periphery. Thus, its responsibility is augmented by an urgent necessity to *do* as well as to think about what must be done. And whenever this is the case, there is danger that the intellectual life will suffer.

It is possible, however, that out of this new realignment of purposes and the energies they engender, a new concept of the intellectual role can emerge. Such an intellectual role, linked to the personal development of individuals as sharing equally in the benefits of a democratic society, can enhance the development of character as well as intellect. It can couple the power of intellectual inquiry with the university's direct efforts to work for a more just society and thus create individuals with moral courage, with dedication to worthy goals, with strong beliefs in human progress. It can take the new leisure created by technology and transform it from a source of potential boredom to one of cultural awareness. The man of the future will have much of his life available for ends nobler than those of economic survival. The university in its intellectual role can nourish his awareness of opportunities for self-development and his involvement with the social action of the time.

The major tasks of the university remain what they have always been: the development of the individual's intellect and character and the attainment of wisdom by the advancement and extension of knowledge. Knowledge without wisdom breeds arrogance; intellect without character breeds danger. There is little to be gained if there is no connection between brilliance of mind and sense of responsibility. And there also is little to be gained in the destruction of values if there are no new ones, valid in a democratic society, to substitute for the old.

When the university performs its task properly and effectively, a person emerges who can find for himself a stable economic life technically or professionally; who can weave richer and deeper patterns of living through his cultural awareness and appreciation; who can assume a position of activity and even leadership in the expansion of knowledge and the pursuit of truth; who is constantly aware of the swiftness of change in modern civilization and is receptive to such change; who can be moved to understand and desire world peace; who understands the responsibilities of freedom together with its rights and insists upon these responsibilities and rights for others as well as for himself; and who is motivated to help solve the major social problems of his age. In its intellectual role, the university couples intellect with character, it joins thinking with doing, and it places the educated man squarely in the center of his society and keeps him there.

Samuel B. Gould

UNIVERSITY COUNCIL FOR EDUCATIONAL ADMINISTRATION

The University Council for Educational Administration is an organization of 59 major universities which offer doctoral programs in educational administration. The goals of the UCEA are to conceptualize the essential elements in quality programs of preparation; to achieve innovations in existing preparatory programs and assess these innovations; to increase the supply of superior candidates for leadership preparation; to create and test new instructional materials and methodologies; to provide professors of educational administration opportunities to evaluate the relevance and utility of important research findings, new instructional materials and methodologies, emerging theories, and other developments pertinent to improvement; to establish a firmer knowledge base in educational administration and to devise better ways to disseminate new knowledge; and to interpret the role of educational leadership in society, the need to improve leadership, and the ways leadership might be improved.

Program. The UCEA sponsors and conducts activities designed to improve school administration through interuniversity cooperation. Research in educational administration is fostered through national and regional seminars and task force activities on subjects which have potential for study. Large-scale patterns for research involving a number of member institutions are created. Consultant help is provided to personnel in member universities who are initiating proposals for research projects. Information about foundations, government offices, and other funding agencies is made available to member universities. Dissemination of research findings and knowledge about program development is accomplished through workshops, seminars, publications, and tape-recorded descriptions of innovations which are in preparation.

Career development seminars, planned and produced by the UCEA, are hosted and financed by volunteer member institutions. These seminars are designed to provide in-service learning experiences for professors of educational administration. There have been programs on such subjects as theory in administration; new perspectives in the training of educational administrators; the case method of teaching; community analysis and administrative decision-making; changing perspectives in education; computer concepts and educational administration; the community college in a changing world; collective negotiations and educational administration; educational administration from an international perspective; public policy in relation to urban education and the

American Negro; and knowledge production and utilization in educational administration.

Task forces provide opportunities for professors interested in particular subjects to explore, develop, organize, and plan cooperatively for the dissemination of concepts pertinent to these subjects. Such subjects have included recruitment and selection of candidates for preparatory programs, internships in educational administration, common and specialized learnings for various administrative personnel, social sciences and the preparation of educational administrators, professorship in educational administration, institutional roles for the continuing education of school administrators, programs of specialized preparation for school personnel administration, emerging roles of state departments of education, and preparation of educational leaders for large urban school systems.

New instructional materials developed by individual professors, teams of professors, and staffs are disseminated by the UCEA to both member and nonmember universities. The most elaborate of these materials involve simulation of several administrative roles within an existing but anonymous school district. Available simulation materials include general background filmstrips and tape recordings on the community and school system as well as materials specifically pertinent to the roles of superintendent, assistant superintendent for instructional services, assistant superintendent for business management, secondary school principal, and elementary school principal. Other instructional materials available through the UCEA include written and tape-recorded case studies, films, programmed texts, and recorded lectures by eminent professors. Materials under development involve the use of computer-assisted instructional exercises and gamed simulations. Use of innovative instructional materials and methodology is encouraged through descriptive publications, institutes in which new methods and materials for preparing administrators are demonstrated, and tape-recorded presentations by professors illustrating effective methodologies.

Advanced graduate students of educational administration in member universities are served by the UCEA through a program which includes distribution of listings of publications, preparation of informative literature about the UCEA activities, promotion of graduate student attendance at career development seminars and other meetings, dissemination to member universities of personal data about graduate students who desire to be considered for faculty appointments as professors of educational administration, and regional seminars designed especially for graduate students.

Three periodicals are sponsored by the UCEA. The UCEA *Newsletter*, printed five times each year, contains news about current or projected UCEA programs and activities. Although the major emphasis is placed upon news stories, special sections are devoted to descriptions of new instructional materials and prints and reprints. The latter consists of synopses of unpublished essays, occasional papers, reports of university institutional research, and other documents which are made available to the UCEA for distribution without cost.

The *Educational Administration Quarterly*, a professional journal, provides a forum for dialogue among professors, graduate students, research-oriented practitioners, and social scientists. Editorial policy for the journal is formulated by an eight-man editorial board. The editor is a professor in a UCEA member university who has been granted free time by his university to perform his editorial duties. The editor of the quarterly serves in the position for three years.

The third periodical sponsored by the UCEA is *Educational Administration Abstracts*. Approximately 100 journals are reviewed for each issue in an effort to select articles relevant to educational administration. Nine section editors review periodicals and assign pertinent articles to approximately 60 abstractors, who prepare indicative abstracts for dissemination. Overall direction of the operation is handled by a general editor, who is in charge of the content of the publication, and a managing editor, who is responsible for technical aspects of printing and preparing the abstracts for distribution. An editorial commission meets annually to discuss policy and procedural matters related to the publication.

Organizational structure. UCEA policies are formulated by a nine-member board of trustees, which meets three times each year. Three members of the board are elected annually for three-year terms by representatives to the UCEA plenary session, which is composed of one representative from each of the member institutions. Convened twice a year, the plenary session examines the financial statements of the organization, receives an audit of the council's assets and liabilities,

makes decisions relative to the annual budget, nominates candidates for election to the board, and elects board members. Representatives to the plenary session serve as official liaison among the universities, the board, and the UCEA central staff. The central staff, composed of an executive director, a deputy executive director, and two associate directors, implements the policies of the board of trustees, develops ideas and programs to achieve the goals of the organization, coordinates activities, and disseminates information resulting from research and development projects.

Membership and financial support. Membership in the UCEA is on an institutional basis. All professors associated with the program for preparing educational leaders in a university which qualifies for membership are automatically eligible to participate in and contribute to the activities of the organization. Approximately 1,000 professors in 59 universities are involved in various aspects of the UCEA program. An institution applying for membership must meet the following criteria: it must have awarded doctoral degrees in educational administration; it must be willing and able to engage in research and development activities within a framework of interuniversity cooperation and communication; it must be part of a well-established college or university and have available special strengths in disciplines other than those in schools of education; it must have enough specialists in educational administration and in other areas of professional education to ensure an adequate and well-balanced preparatory program; it must have identifiable ways of contributing to the improvement of educational administration at the local, state, national, and international levels; it must have personnel with the capacity and the motivation to help solve some of the professional problems which stand in the way of the advancement of educational administration; and it must have a planned program to advance the profession of educational administration over a five-year period.

Financial support for the UCEA comes from annual fees paid by member universities and from contributions by individual universities, foundations, and governmental agencies for special programs and projects.

History and development. Proposed originally in 1954 by members of the Cooperative Program in Educational Administration (Middle Atlantic Region), the establishment of the UCEA was facilitated in 1955, when the W. K. Kellogg Foundation made a grant to Teachers College, Columbia University, to support planning. At an open meeting of representatives from major universities in February 1956 a recommendation was made to proceed with plans for organizing the UCEA.

From 1956 until 1959 the central office for the organization was located at Teachers College, with faculty members devoting part of their time to directing the development of the council. During this period the constitution and bylaws were written, and the purposes of the organization were defined. Thirty-four universities became charter members of the organization. In 1959 the UCEA central office was moved to its present location on the campus of Ohio State University, and a small full-time professional staff was assembled.

UCEA headquarters are located at 29 West Woodruff Avenue, Columbus, Ohio 43210.

BRYCE M. FOGARTY

UNIVERSITY PARTICIPATION IN PUBLIC AFFAIRS

The university has been catapulted to great prominence and prestige as a consequence of the continually growing and strategic role of knowledge in a developing industrial and urban society; society's dependence upon tradition in decision-making has given way increasingly to the systematic application of knowledge in the solution of problems. The continuing evolution of society stimulates even greater demands for information and knowledge. The university is a primary source of knowledge in this increasingly knowledge-centered society. Thus, the changing nature and needs of society have inevitably drawn the university into a major and visible role in many of society's affairs.

The modern demands on the university sometimes lead people to view the university as simply a producer of useful knowledge. Seen thus, the university becomes little more than an economic unit in society, with no more claim for uniqueness than any other economic unit. But no university worthy of the name is merely a factory for producing and packaging utilitarian knowledge; it is far more. Its most uniquely creative—and fragile —function is that of social critic. Successful execution of this role requires the university to main-

tain both its independence in society and the integrity of its commitment to objectivity. Indeed, institutional and individual independence and commitment to objectivity are essential to the university in all its roles—as teacher of knowledge and values, as creator of knowledge for its own sake as well as for outside use, as a catalytic agent in the problem-solving activities of society, and as a critic in society.

From the time the Western university developed out of the medieval cathedral school, it has had as some of its roles the scholarly quest for knowledge, the provision of a liberal education, and the provision of specific vocational and professional training. These roles have long coexisted in some tension. For example, while scholarly research and teaching complement and reinforce each other, they compete for the use of time and resources; further, exclusive devotion of academics to one could destroy the other. This is true of the relationship between all of the university's roles. Neither academics nor society may safely treat the university as if it were a single-purpose institution. The university is governed best when the complementary potential of its various roles is carefully fostered and the potentially competitive and inconsistent relationships are avoided or carefully managed.

The university's growing role in public affairs results in a great diversity of activities. These commitments can perhaps be described most simply as the involvement of the university in solving social problems. As with the university's other roles, participation in public affairs offers a challenging potential as well as danger.

The knowledge-centered society. In the early stages of industrialization, society's capital was embodied primarily in machines, but this has changed as the industrialization process has matured. Increasingly, the largest and most strategic investment has been made in the human resources and efforts which have been devoted to problem-solving and innovation in the production process (Boulding 1953). "Today, the economically significant industrial property is not the machine, but the design, and not so much the design as the capacity to innovate design in process and product. This is scarcely (physical) property at all, but is rather a capacity inhering in an organization" (Piel 1961, pp. 274–275). It is, in other words, the organization of human knowledge and the human capacity to create new knowledge.

Knowledge has become a highly valued input in the production processes of society as a consequence of the application of science to the activities of man. This change has given rise to research and development activities in universities and in industry, activities which have been collectively termed the knowledge industry (Machlup 1962; Slichter 1958). The systematic application of science leads to an increase in the rate at which knowledge accumulates and thus also in the rate at which the existing stock of earlier knowledge becomes obsolete. As science causes the economy to become more dependent upon knowledge for its continued growth and vitality, the organization of knowledge shifts in emphasis from the conservation, retrieval, and communication of knowledge to the creation of knowledge.

One of the most characteristic features of industrialization and technological change is an intense specialization in organization, function, and decision-making. At the same time, the process of specialization creates a far more intense interdependence among society's social, economic, and political components. Communities in modern society are faced by increasingly complex problem-solving which requires an ever-widening span of knowledge for choice among an ever-increasing number of alternatives. Increasing specialization and complexity put a progressively greater premium on coordination and planning in the application of knowledge. Although the university, as other large-scale organizations, has some difficulty in coordinating its own activities, its capacity for objectivity and the wide range of knowledge at its command have an obvious relevance to society's problem-solving. In a society increasingly dependent on new knowledge for continued growth, the capacity for creating knowledge has made the university a strategic institution.

Pathologies of the knowledge-centered society. Over the years, the United States has transformed itself from a traditional society of many small localized decision systems, organizations, and communities that were viable and reasonably self-sufficient into an industrial society of functionally specialized large-scale organizations frequently managed from a regional or national decision-making level. The United States now has specialized, large, national decision systems concerned with, for example, housing, highways, welfare, education, and public health. These specialized decision systems frequently transcend the scale of even the largest city. Since such decision systems are usually focused around a single specialized function, they are vertical organizations in nature and do not relate well across society; they do not respond easily either to broad, complex social problems or to more general needs or goals. The restructuring of public and private decision systems into large-scale, highly specialized independent organizations works reasonably well for specialized problem-solving, but it is disastrous for the integrated decision-making upon which depend the viability and development of the human community.

The problem is illustrated by the processes involved in creating more effective highway systems. The specialized national and state highway organizations generally give little or no consideration to the possibility that in some cases mass transit or other forms of transportation might be a more desirable alternative; neither do they often consider the external effects of their decisions: the destruction without replacement of low-income housing, the massive congestion of some local areas, and the depopulation or isolation of others. These external effects of highway decisions are generally treated by professional highway engineers as someone else's—that is, the community's —problems. Few of the large, specialized, national decision-making systems, public or private, are capable of integrating their various functions at the community level.

Under the impact of the changing scale and intense specialization of organization and decision-making, there has been a breakdown in effective community, both local and national. In fact, the concepts of national sovereignty and community self-sufficiency are probably obsolescent ideas at this point. In any case, there has been a massive increase in the minimum size of the effective community, whether one is dealing in terms of decision-making at community, state, or national levels. It is clear that under present institutional arrangements many of the strategic elements of decision-making have passed beyond the immediate control of specific local, state, or national governments to higher social aggregates.

As a consequence of the breakdown in its capacity for community problem-solving, society faces a rising incidence of severe social pathologies, particularly in urban life. The Kerner Report (*Report of the National Advisory Commis-*

sion . . . 1968) and the urgent writings of social analysts such as Brown (1965), Clark (1965), Abrams (1964), Mumford (1967), Harrington (1963), Galbraith (1958), and Sanford (1967) provide recent and vivid testimony. These pathologies generate problems related to jobs, education, housing, transportation, medical services and health, inadequate income, pollution, civil order, and justice; they all greatly pressure the university to become involved in solving such problems.

This breakdown in the ability to master community problem-solving or decision-making is testimony to the fact that the capacity to create technical change has outrun social invention to manage that change. Consequently, we are today destroying man, his natural environment, and even his society. The potential for redressing this imbalance between our knowledge of science and technology and our knowledge of man and his social systems is to a great extent found in the university.

Public affairs as a university role. The American university has long had major involvement in public affairs. What is new today is the overwhelming pressure (arising from modern society's need for broad access to knowledge for problem-solving purposes) for a university-wide commitment. This pressure is now felt in private as well as public institutions, in small community colleges as well as large universities, and in the arts-and-science college of a university as well as in its professional schools. No major part of any institution is exempt. Higher education is now creating a public-affairs mission equaling its social commitment to teaching and research.

University public affairs today involves such a wide range of activities that it is difficult to define the term "public affairs" precisely. It includes teaching and research as well as service activities in urban planning, organization, and administration, in community, regional, and national economic development, in medicine and health, in resource conservation, and in science and technology. It also includes training Peace Corps volunteers and performing research on aerospace systems.

Some think of public affairs as simply the service part of the classical trinity of university functions—teaching, research, and service. This is not an adequate notion, for many public affairs activities involve not just service but teaching and research as well. The teaching of urban planners and sanitary engineers, for example, can be regarded as both teaching and a public service. University research to find a means of ridding mankind of cancer or controlling environmental pollution is both research and a public service. Such applied problem-solving has also led to contributions to basic scientific knowledge. University public-affairs commitments thus usually involve some mixture of teaching, research, and service functions.

University public affairs includes those activities in which the university or one of its members has conscious commitments to a role in the problem-solving efforts of society. It involves the outreach of the university to society, the extension of the university's special competence and resources to organizations and to individuals outside the university (Carnegie Foundation . . . 1967). It is the response of the university to what it perceives to be primary local, state, regional, or national community needs. Thus, it is problem-solving–oriented university teaching, service, or research in which there is a major public interest and which is structured on the basis of the university's understanding of the priorities of social need and the constraints of the university's special competencies, resources, and societal environment.

From their founding, many public universities have been committed in part to public service and to training the new professionals of a rising industrial society. The Morrill Act of 1862 founded the land-grant colleges around an explicit commitment to education and to public service. This commitment was made concrete primarily in the application of science to the improvement of the productivity, material well-being, and social status of the two largest components of the laboring classes of the nineteenth century, farmers and industrial laborers. The land-grant college and the associated institutions that it helped to build in rural areas have transformed the productivity, welfare, and social class of the now successful commercial farmer to an extent that would astonish its founders. In terms of deliberate national commitment, the land-grant college is certainly the beginning of higher education's mission in U.S. public affairs (Eddy 1957).

The land-grant tradition generated a set of university institutional arrangements that constitute one major historical model of university public affairs. The basic-research and applied-research activities in agriculture developed around the problem-solving focus of an agricultural experiment station. In the effort to move knowledge effectively from the university campus to the farm and rural user, the Cooperative Extension Service was created in 1914. This organization provides for a university field staff in local communities and attempts to relate the campus to the community, thus providing a means for facilitating community-problem identification and the direction of university knowledge toward the problems selected for university action. Since 1960 the focus of the informal educational activities of the Cooperative Extension Service has broadened in many states from agricultural and rural community concerns to include many urban community activities.

Many public and private universities have also created general extension programs for continuing adult education, usually as formal educational programs provided in the evening hours and frequently in locations removed from the university campus. The extension programs have provided specific vocational training, continuing education for various professions, and general cultural enrichment (Ziegler 1964).

In recent years, both general education and cooperative extension programs have been pulled into the service of urban community development. On about half of the land-grant university campuses the various extension organizations have been combined in a coordinated, university-wide public affairs outreach system reporting to the president of the university rather than to one or several deans.

However, many university public affairs activities take place outside the context of the university's extension framework. This is because some public affairs activities are carried on without the development of formal university programs or because the program of activity develops as a logical part of the regular teaching or research of the university. Thus, many of the professional schools independently carry on quite varied public affairs activities for the continuing education of their own professional groups. Some on-campus teaching programs attempt to expose students to learning situations outside the university classroom by putting them into public-service or social-action situations. In other cases, graduate research programs use outside organizations as a type of laboratory by supplying problem-solving research and education for these organizations.

In a few states, unique relationships were forged between the university and state government, creating a partnership which saw the university serving a critical role in training future state government personnel, in planning and leading state economic development, and in analyzing state problems. On occasion, the university has been deeply involved in the design of legislation in a broad range of areas. One of the products of university-government collaboration is the university institute of government or of government research. In an often closely interrelated process, public administration developed both as an academic field and as a profession. This development occurred early in private as well as public universities; some of the most distinguished U.S. schools of public administration are in such private institutions as Syracuse University, Harvard University, and Princeton University.

Individual universities have often developed unique relationships with specific industries where such industries have constituted a major and strategic element in the well-being of the region or state. For example, the University of Minnesota has long committed resources to research on the technology of mining and, since World War II, has increased its research on the utilization of low-grade iron ore in an attempt to offset the decline in economic activity and employment that occurred in the northern part of Minnesota as the ores from the high-grade Mesabi range were depleted. There is, in fact, a general national pattern of specialized public affairs commitments arising from geographic location and from the nature of the resource base of the area served by a given institution.

During World War II a unique relationship developed between the university science community and the federal government; they combined resources to produce an atomic bomb earlier than the German government. Ever since, university scientists in the United States have worked on a wide range of weaponry and national defense problems. Funding supplied by the Department of Defense, the National Aeronautics and Space Administration, and the Atomic Energy Commission has made major demands upon the university but has also built much of the current U.S. university capacity for physical science research. The creation of the National Science Foundation to sustain pure science after the war was a final element in the attempt to institutionalize university physical science in the service of national interest.

One of the most distinctive public affairs missions developed by U.S. universities since World War II has been in international programs. Both public and private higher education in the United States have become increasingly involved in a wide range of activities, extending from helping to build various institutions abroad, particularly educational institutions, to becoming involved in various types of foreign economic development and development-planning activities.

Other national public affairs commitments have developed in recent years. For decades this society has been investing major resources in medical research; the result has been the production of much new medical knowledge. However, there exists a great and growing gap between the type of care available in a limited number of high-quality centers of medicine and the level of medical care available to most Americans. The Heart Disease, Cancer, and Stroke Act of 1964, as amended, attempts to close that gap by developing a new set of regional institutions for the delivery of medical care and knowledge. University medical schools have generally become the contractors or members of the contracting consortia in the development of the regional medical programs authorized under the act. Additional legislation expanding mental-health care and the training of health professionals also calls upon university resources in a major way.

The experience in medicine is eloquent testimony to the fact that investment in research alone rarely ensures that the knowledge thus created will be utilized by society. If new knowledge is to have social value, it must be used. This normally requires the creation of some institutional arrangement that connects the university with society. Some of these institutional arrangements are operated by the university, some by commercial users of knowledge, and some by agencies of the state.

Increasingly since World War II, legislation has been enacted which directly or indirectly calls upon the university to provide its expertise and resources in the solution of urgent societal problems. Practically all of the national efforts to improve the rate of development of lagging or depressed economic areas and industries in the United States have involved the universities directly. This is the case in Appalachia and in such other regional development areas as the Ozarks and the northern lake states.

Paramount in recent years have been the pressures that have mounted as a result of the crisis of the city, which is facing pathologies that seem to threaten its very existence. Congressional legislation related to manpower development and training, the Job Corps, poverty, urban housing, and urban redevelopment calls upon university competence. Urban research centers and programs are proliferating. The demands on the university range all the way from requests for applied research on specific problems to insistence that the university take action itself to help solve the problems of urban ghettos. Indeed, a characteristic of the urban crisis is the pressure for direct university involvement in the political conflicts and day-to-day action of the social institutions lying at the center of the problem.

Issues and problems. The public affairs role of the university arises as society is confronted by problems about which the university is the most capable and relevant source of knowledge. If the university has the knowledge and expertise that society needs, the university must have a very good reason to refuse to respond to the most urgent of society's needs, particularly when there is no good alternative source of this knowledge. Refusal without adequate reason will lead to a general withdrawal of societal support for the university. Since public funding constitutes the major source of university financing for all public and an increasing number of major private universities, the university may be in jeopardy if it does not respond thoughtfully to society's needs.

The university's social responsibility is to give society what it needs, however, not what it wants. There is often a difference. Thus, the university's responsibility as a social critic is most serious. Society, through its public and private organizations, often asks of the university things that would serve society only poorly or not at all. Similarly, many real social needs tend to go long unrecognized. The university's responsibility in public affairs is to exercise its role of social critic —to identify genuine social needs, to establish priorities as best it can, and to respond whether it has been asked to do so or not.

The university is also often asked to involve itself in commitments in which it has no legitimate role. Consulting firms and other private and public organizations are often better equipped to handle these needs. Other requests would make the university an agent of partisan interests; such activities are inconsistent with the true nature and limits of a university. The university must be careful to commit its limited resources to public affairs activities that are legitimate for a university and are of major social significance.

University public affairs involves the university in the application of its critical capacities in the most fundamentally creative and sensitive social processes. This is clearly a role fraught with danger. There are dangers to the university whether it accepts or rejects a general commitment to public affairs (Ward 1966). If the university rejects this role or fails to perform it adequately, society has little choice but to put its problem-solving, applied-research, and educational resources into some other institutional arrangement, such as public and private research institutes, private firms providing educational services, and the action agencies of government. This is now occurring to some extent. If such were to become the general institutional pattern for societal problem-solving, it would probably not be long before most of society's investment in research—applied as well as basic—would be channeled through these other institutions. This creates the possibility that these institutions could become the intellectual cutting edge in a number of academic areas. If this were to occur, the university would become a weak competitor for research scholars and might even be stripped of its role as society's primary knowledge center in these academic fields.

General acceptance by the university of a broad commitment to public affairs also seriously endangers the university as an institution. The broader the commitment to public affairs and the greater the involvement in society, the greater the danger to the integrity of the university. This is true in several senses. Public affairs missions are generally complex and expensive. The typical U.S. university is presently engaged in an extensive range of activities, and its resource base is often seriously strained. To take on additional responsibilities without adequate financial support could endanger the entire university structure. The university is not a surrogate for society, and it may not safely allow such an expectation to persist. There is a limit to its capacity, resources, and resilience.

The integrity of the university also lies in its freedom to pursue and communicate knowledge and its freedom to choose its missions and the means of implementing such missions. However, any society imposes restraints on individual and institutional social choice. Deep involvement with society always carries with it the implicit danger of loss of many of the university's freedoms to make choices as well as of erosion of the university's basic objectivity. Without objectivity and the freedom to make choices, the university has lost its primary reason for being.

On the other hand, there are implicit in a general public affairs mission many new opportunities for the university to add to its capacity in its older roles and to open new channels for further development as society's primary knowledge-creating center.

The whole of the university has never fully appreciated the creative potential that derives from the combination of action with thought. The capacity for undisturbed reflective thought is essential to the nature of a university, but thought in continuing isolation leads to intellectual sterility. The World War II experience in large-scale, mission-oriented research demonstrated the acceleration in creativity possible in an environment which combines pure and applied scientists, theorists, mathematicians, and engineers in a continuing dialogue. The idea that science contributes to technology in a one-way fashion is a simple notion of a complex process and does not stand inspection (Kranzberg 1967; 1968). If the university maintains a thoughtful role in public affairs, it has a far larger potential for creativity and knowledge.

This is not a new notion. In 1936, Alfred North Whitehead wrote (on the occasion of Harvard's tercentennial):

> In the process of learning there should be present, in some sense or other, a subordinate activity of application. In fact, the applications are part of the knowledge. For the very meaning of the things known is wrapped up in their relationships beyond themselves. Thus unapplied knowledge is knowledge shorn of its meaning.
>
> The careful shielding of a university from the activities of the world around is the best way to chill interest and to defeat progress. Celibacy does not suit a university. It must mate with action. (p. 267)

This call to action is not an invitation to replace the public and private agencies of action in society with the university. The university's institutional role in action is still one of education rather than direct decision-making. The university involved in public affairs may properly provide intellectual input, information, problem identification, analysis of alternatives for decision, and the education of decision-makers. It may also organize to bring itself closer to decision-processes for the effective extension of this knowledge. In short, the university may participate directly in the action process only when it is using the action environment as a laboratory for experimental research or as a demonstration model for social innovation; the role of the university in public problem-solving is essentially that of a catalytic and cooperative agent.

Individual faculty and students are not so constrained as the university. The participation by individual academics—while on leave or otherwise outside their formal university obligations—as decision-makers in those action processes they believe important enriches the university. Indeed, academic freedom ensures the right of academics to participate as individuals in anything they choose. However, academic freedom does not exempt anyone from the laws of society or from the normal university criteria for the academic performance of students and faculty.

Certainly, each university need not be equally and deeply involved; nor must it be committed to the same set of public affairs activities. Universities are not equally committed to certain of the older roles that characterize higher education. However, the realistic options for higher education as a system involve commitment to public affairs activity. It is necessary, however, to project a philosophy of public affairs appropriate to a particular university's special competence, resources, and environment. The university must stake out clearly the primary areas in which it is prepared to act in public affairs. The university must aggressively maintain and exercise the positive power of choice through avoidance of unrealistic expectations about its roles. There are many mythologies and unrealistic expectations held both within and without the university; these must be dealt with if a genuinely successful public affairs mission is to be mounted.

The university must accept the task of fashioning some coherent role in public affairs. In doing so it faces a great challenge, for there are many dangers as well as opportunities in expanding the capacity and the social meaning of the university.

However well developed in some parts of the university, the public affairs role remains inchoate as a university-wide commitment. At the heart of the problem lies the need in each institution to develop an integrating philosophy of public affairs adapted to the capacities and environment of the institution. In developing its role in public affairs the university must sustain a high level of consciousness in its decision-making. Its task is one of continued judicious choice in matching its highly specialized and limited resources to a set of societal demands that range from the relevant and urgent to the nonsensical and from the dangerous and controversial to the generally agreed upon. Despite the discomfort of many and the resistance of some, we are well down the path toward a university-wide role in public affairs.

BIBLIOGRAPHY

ABRAMS, CHARLES 1964 *Man's Struggle for Shelter in an Urbanizing World.* Cambridge, Mass., MIT Press.

ASHBY, ERIC 1958 *Technology and the Academics: An Essay on Universities and the Scientific Revolution.* London, Macmillan.

BOULDING, KENNETH E. 1953 *The Organizational Revolution: A Study in the Ethics of Economic Organization.* New York, Harper.

BROWN, CLAUDE 1965 *Manchild in the Promised Land.* New York, Macmillan.

BUSH, DOUGLAS 1964 "The Humanities." *Daedalus*, fall: 1219–1237.

CARNEGIE FOUNDATION FOR THE ADVANCEMENT OF TEACHING 1967 *The University at the Service of Society.* Sixty-second annual report for the year ending June 30, 1967. New York, The Foundation.

CLARK, KENNETH 1965 *Dark Ghetto: Dilemmas of Social Power.* New York, Harper.

COLEMAN, JAMES S. 1967 "Toward Open Schools." *The Public Interest*, no. 9:20–27.

COLEMAN, JAMES S., et al. 1966 *Equality of Educational Opportunity.* Washington, D.C., U.S. Office of Education.

CONOT, ROBERT 1967 *Rivers of Blood, Years of Darkness.* New York, Bantam.

EDDY, EDWARD D., JR. 1957 *Colleges for Our Land and Time: The Land-Grant Idea in American Education.* New York, Harper.

GALBRAITH, JOHN KENNETH 1958 *The Affluent Society.* Boston, Houghton Mifflin.

GALBRAITH, JOHN KENNETH 1967 *The New Industrial State.* Boston, Houghton Mifflin.

GLAZER, NATHAN 1967 "Housing Problems and Housing Policies." *The Public Interest*, no. 7:21–51.

HARRINGTON, MICHAEL 1963 *The Other America: Poverty in the United States.* Baltimore, Penguin.

JACOBS, JANE 1961 *The Death and Life of Great American Cities.* New York, Random House.

KERR, CLARK 1963 *The Uses of the University.* Cambridge, Mass., Harvard University Press.

KRANZBERG, MELVIN 1967 "The Unity of Science-Technology." *American Scientist*, 55, no. 1:48–66.

KRANZBERG, MELVIN 1968 "The Disunity of Science-Technology." *American Scientist*, 56, no. 1:21–34.

MACHLUP, FRITZ 1962 *The Production and Distribution of Knowledge in the United States.* Princeton, N.J., Princeton University Press.

MORRISON, ROBERT S. 1962 "The University and Technical Assistance." *Daedalus*, spring:319–340.

MUMFORD, LEWIS 1967 *The Urban Prospect*. New York, Harcourt.

NEVINS, ALLAN 1962 *The State Universities and Democracy*. Urbana, University of Illinois Press.

PERKINS, JAMES A. 1966 *The University in Transition*. Princeton, N.J., Princeton University Press.

PIEL, GERARD 1961 *Science in the Cause of Man*. New York, Knopf.

PRICE, DON K. 1965 *The Scientific Estate*. Cambridge, Mass., Harvard University Press.

Report of the National Advisory Commission on Civil Disorders 1968 New York, Bantam.

ROSSI, PETER H. 1964 "Researchers, Scholars and Policy Makers: The Politics of Large-scale Research." *Daedalus*, fall:1142–1161.

SANFORD, TERRY 1967 *Storm Over the States*. New York, McGraw-Hill.

SLICHTER, SUMNER H. 1958 "The Industry of Discovery." *Science*, 128, no. 3339:1610–1613.

U.S. PRESIDENT'S NATIONAL ADVISORY COMMISSION ON RURAL POVERTY 1967 *The People Left Behind*. A report. Washington, D.C., Government Printing Office.

WARD, JOHN WILLIAM 1966 "The Trouble With Higher Education." *The Public Interest*, no. 4:76–88.

WEISS, PAUL 1964 "Science in the University." *Daedalus*, fall:1184–1218.

WHITEHEAD, ALFRED NORTH 1936 "Harvard: The Future." *Atlantic Monthly*, 158, no. 3:260–270.

ZIEGLER, JEROME M. 1964 "Continuing Education in the University." *Daedalus*, fall:1162–1183.

JAMES T. BONNEN

UPWARD BOUND

In 1965 the Office of Economic Opportunity (OEO) funded 17 pilot projects with the aim of designing a program to help prepare high school students from low-income homes for a college education. These projects—known as Upward Bound—were patterned after the special educational programs which had been set up in 1964 by several colleges and universities for the same purpose. Aided by foundation grants, these special programs had concentrated on improving the basic skills needed for a college education, especially those used in reading and mathematics.

No doubt influenced by the public support for the Head Start program, the OEO sought to identify the new Upward Bound program as a Head Start for teenagers. Upward Bound received statutory recognition when it was incorporated into the 1967 amendments (section 222 of Title II) of the Economic Opportunity Act of 1964. According to the legislation, the goal of Upward Bound is to motivate inadequately prepared high school students from low-income homes and tutor them in the skills requisite for success in college.

Administration and finance. As with practically all antipoverty programs, Upward Bound's resources fell far short of need. According to the OEO, funds for fiscal 1965 totaled only $2.5 million. Remedial education is expensive—the annual cost of maintaining a student in Upward Bound is about twice the average public high school expenditure per student. At the level of funding during fiscal 1970, with $28.3 million available, Upward Bound was able to enroll only about 24,000 students, or about 4 percent of those who could have benefited from the program. These figures showed little change from fiscal 1967, when 249 projects, supported by $28.1 million, enrolled 23,000 students.

The OEO established a unique administrative arrangement for Upward Bound by violating its own cardinal maxim that, wherever feasible, funds made available to the office should be channeled through Community Action Agencies. For all practical purposes, the OEO, in October 1965, turned over administration of Upward Bound to Educational Associates, Inc., a private nonprofit organization, awarding it a contract to operate the program on the basis of costs plus fixed fees.

Spokesmen for Upward Bound stated that the separation of the project from the Community Action Program was necessary to sell the program to colleges and universities. Of 294 projects operating in fiscal 1970, none was funded through a Community Action Agency.

Upward Bound was transferred to the Office of Education effective July 1969.

Curriculum. The Upward Bound program usually consists of a six-week to eight-week summer session in residence on a college campus. There is at least one follow-up program during the academic year which provides academic support and motivates students to pursue higher education. Most of the students enter the program after the 10th or 11th grade. They thus have the opportunity to attend two summer sessions. Each sponsoring institution designs the summer course of study and a program of extracurricular activities. Frequently, classes consist of small discussion groups. Although allowing wide variation among projects, the OEO guidelines established a general pattern. In addition to the academic curriculum, programs provide athletics, social recreation, and exposure to a variety of culturally enriching activities, including visits to theaters, exhibits, and museums.

Teaching staff. The teaching staff is composed of college and high school teachers in addition to art, speech, and other specialists as deemed fit. Ideally, instructors and other staff members are selected by the project director for their interest in students from poor homes and their ability to relate to them in and out of the classroom. Many of the colleges have at least one teacher who spends part of his time during the year with students when they visit the campus. In many urban areas the students travel to the college at least once a week for tutoring sessions. This arrangement is more difficult to accomplish in rural areas, where students find it expensive or difficult to visit the campus. To alleviate the problem, tutor-counselors have been sent to rural areas, and local teachers have also helped.

Results. In view of Upward Bound's goal—to prepare enrollees to gain admission to college and remain there until graduation—it seems that the program has been remarkably successful. Some 70 percent of all Upward Bound graduates during the program's first five years entered college; two of every three who entered college in 1967 were still enrolled by spring of their sophomore year. The college academic record of former Upward Bound enrollees was about the same as that of other students who entered college in 1966.

Follow-up data on Upward Bound enrollees who dropped out of the program and the information available concerning students admitted into the program are largely inadequate. A sample survey conducted for Upward Bound in 1968 showed that the grades of enrollees conformed closely to the grades of other students in their high schools. However, since most Upward Bound students were from poor and nonwhite homes, it was likely that they attended poorer high schools and had below average achievement scores (as measured by American College Testing Service).

Many colleges operating Upward Bound programs pledged to accept a certain number of students, provided they satisfactorily completed the summer program. Although the Ivy League colleges did accept graduates of the Upward Bound program, it was mainly a token gesture of admitting one or two. Thus, many students enrolled in community or junior colleges, teachers colleges, or similar institutions with relatively low admission requirements and not excessively rigorous standards. About 80 percent of the black Upward Bound students enrolled in Negro colleges. The high college admission and survival rate of Upward Bound students was evidently due in part to careful screening by the colleges, which lessened the risk of accepting poorly motivated or underachieving students. In addition, some col-

leges lowered their admission standards to accept Upward Bound students. However, based on the available fragmentary data, it appears that Upward Bound did improve the participants' chances of entering college.

The need of Upward Bound graduates for financial help presented an obstacle to college attendance. The Office of Education has estimated the average yearly financial need of an Upward Bound student to be $2,065. Of the nearly 5,000 Upward Bound students who entered college in the fall of 1967, 75 percent received financial assistance to complete the year of schooling.

The Office of Education, on the basis of its fiscal 1971 level of operations, estimated that approximately 6,000 Upward Bound students would enter colleges during the year. Aside from numerous private and state scholarships available to poor students, the federal government helps college students in four major ways: college work-study payments, educational opportunity grants; National Defense Education Act loans, and federal loan guarantees.

Conclusion. Given the fragmentary data available on the operations of Upward Bound, only a tentative judgment can be made about the program. The future impact of Upward Bound on students and higher education is as yet unknown; however, the program has brought to the surface the need for providing a remedial program for students who possess intellectual capacity but who nevertheless have failed in school. This type of effort is far more expensive than providing the right kind of education within the school system in the first instance. As much as any other antipoverty program, Upward Bound reflects a change in societal attitudes toward offering youths a second chance to acquire a college education.

SAR A. LEVITAN

URBAN EDUCATION

1. SCHOOL SEGREGATION, DESEGREGATION, AND INTEGRATION   Irwin Katz

2. HIGHER EDUCATION   Julian H. Levi

1. SCHOOL SEGREGATION, DESEGREGATION, AND INTEGRATION

Although openly avowed policies of racial segregation are rapidly disappearing from the educational scene in the United States, de facto separation of white and nonwhite pupils continues to prevail in all regions. According to a report of the U.S. Commission on Civil Rights, "Racial isolation in the schools . . . is intense whether the cities are large or small, whether the proportion of Negro enrollment is large or small, whether they are located North or South" (1967, p. 7). In this article the focus will be on racial imbalance involving Negroes, since they are the largest and most isolated nonwhite minority group in big city schools.

Dentler and Elsbery point out that in the 20 largest central cities in the nation, "the evidence suggests that 70 percent of all Negro pupils attend schools that are composed of 90 to 100 percent Negro pupils" (1967, p. 307). Dentler and Elsbery estimate that by 1975, unless new policies are instituted, 80 percent of all Negro pupils in these cities will be attending 90 to 100 percent Negro schools.

In some small cities and rural areas the outlook for full desegregation is more promising. A survey of eight small cities in the North and South, conducted in October 1970 by the New York *Times*, indicated that these communities were able to achieve racially balanced school enrollments without reducing educational standards (Rosenthal 1970).

The move toward complete elimination of de jure segregation in the South was spurred by the U.S. Supreme Court decision of October 1969 ordering an immediate end to all dual systems. However, de facto segregation patterns still prevail in most areas of the South, particularly the urban areas. In September 1970, James T. Wooten, a correspondent for the New York *Times*, estimated that two-thirds of the 3.1 million Negro pupils in the 11 southern states were still attending schools with all-black or predominantly black enrollments (Wooten 1970).

The major cause of racial isolation in urban public schools appears to be residential segregation. Pettigrew (1969) notes that over 80 percent of all Negro Americans who live in metropolitan areas reside in central cities, whereas over half of all white Americans who live in metropolitan areas reside in suburbs. But even a gradual movement of Negro families into the suburbs will probably not in itself reduce racial separation, since present trends indicate they will be forced into new ghettos.

Another factor contributing to de facto school segregation is what Pettigrew (1969) refers to as "the anti-metropolitan nature of school district organization." He notes that the major urban areas of the nation are divided into large numbers of independent school districts (as many as 75 in the Boston metropolitan area and 96 in the Detroit metropolitan area). This type of school district organization tends to effectively preclude any intermixing of central city and suburban school populations.

A third factor is the growing preference of white parents for private schools. In the 20 largest cities, according to Dentler and Elsbery (1967), approximately four out of ten white pupils are enrolled in private schools. On the other hand, only one out of every ten Negro students attends a private school.

Racial composition of enrollments. The effect of racial composition of school and class enrollments on the intellectual, behavioral, and emotional development of students is a topic that has been debated in the United States ever since the 1954 U.S. Supreme Court decision outlawing segregation in the public schools. Beyond dispute is the fact that academic performances of Negro youths are on the whole lower than those of whites. This was documented by a nationwide survey of 645,000 pupils in over 4,000 public elementary and secondary schools that was conducted by Coleman and others (1966) for the U.S. Office of Education.

Coleman and his associates found that on objective tests of scholastic achievement and ability the average scores of Negroes at every grade level studied were about one standard deviation below white norms. That is, about 85 percent of the Negro school population tested below white averages for their grade levels. The racial gap in achievement, when expressed in terms of Negro and white score distributions, remains fairly constant in the North throughout the school years, whereas in the South it grows progressively larger from grade 1 to grade 12. These findings are generally consistent with the results of previous, more limited surveys of Negro and white scholastic achievement and with the day-to-day observations of teachers and school administrators in racially integrated schools.

What relationship exists between the racial composition of student bodies and the racial gap in academic achievement? The information most relevant to the question comes from comparative studies of pupils in segregated and desegregated situations, a type of research that is beset by many special difficulties. Pettigrew (1969) observes that the investigator in this realm is by definition a disturber of the equilibrium of educational and political establishments and, therefore, can expect to encounter frequent refusals of cooperation from school systems, hidden biases in officially released data, and constraints against pursuing certain lines of inquiry. Apparently, the most common political barrier to research is refusal to cooperate. Although the Coleman survey had been specifically ordered by the U.S. Congress, about 30 percent of the school systems selected for the survey did not participate. The nonparticipation rate was almost as high in the North and West (28 percent) as in the South and Southwest (35 percent).

There are also special technical difficulties associated with desegregation research. In the ideal investigation one would compare the academic progress of students with similar family background and initial ability who had been randomly assigned to learning environments that were identical in all respects except the one critical factor of racial composition. But actual field conditions rarely permit a fully satisfactory research design. Pettigrew (1969) mentions a number of commonly encountered technical difficulties: the nonrandom assignment of students to various types of schools (for example, middle-class Negroes are more likely to be represented in desegregated schools and neighborhoods than are lower-class Negroes), the nonrandom treatment of students within schools (for example, ability grouping), the high attrition in Negro samples owing to the subject's dropping out of school and their residential mobility, the noncomparability of social-class categories across racial lines, and artifactual effects in evaluation studies associated with temporary spurts of motivation and other biasing phenomena (for example, the Hawthorne effect).

With so many problems associated with research on desegregation, it is not surprising that until the early 1960's little research of any consequence had been done. Commenting on the dearth of unequivocal information about Negro performance in desegregated schools, Katz wrote: "Reports on the academic progress of Negro children in desegregated schools are on the whole inadequate for drawing any conclusions about the

effects of biracial environments upon Negro performance" (1964, p. 396). Most of the evidence that could be found at that time presented a favorable picture of Negro students' academic adjustment in racially mixed settings.

Stallings (1959), for example, reported on the results of achievement testing in the Louisville, Ky., school system in 1955–1956, the year prior to total elimination of legal segregation, and again two years later. Gains were found in the median scores of all pupils for the grades tested, with Negroes showing greater improvement than whites. However, the report gave no indication whether the gains for Negroes were related to increased interracial contacts. Indeed, a closer examination of the Louisville situation (Katz 1964) indicated that the best Negro gains were actually made by children who remained in segregated classrooms and could only be attributed to factors other than desegregation, such as a general improvement in educational standards.

As another example of the equivocal nature of early evidence on effects of desegregation, Hansen (1960) reported data for the District of Columbia public schools, which were supposed to show year-to-year gains in student progress following systemwide desegregation in 1954. But the data were not broken down by race. Given the existence of a rigid system of ability grouping, as well as a steadily increasing predominance of Negro students in the Washington schools, it seems reasonable to attribute the academic gains to an ambitious program of educational improvement rather than to racial mixing.

Early research on Negroes in racially mixed settings was also carried out in a study of Negro graduates of segregated southern high schools who attended integrated colleges, situated mostly in the North. The academic progress of over 9,000 Negro students who had been helped to enroll in interracial colleges during a 15-year period was reviewed by the National Scholarship Service and Fund for Negro Students (1963). The NSSFNS report stated that 55.9 percent of the students had grade point averages of B− or better, 32.4 percent were in the C+ to C− range, and only 0.7 percent had averages below C−. No grades were listed for 11 percent. Fewer than 5 percent withdrew from college for any reason, as compared with a 40 percent dropout rate for all students in the nation. It should be noted that these Negro students were carefully selected for their academic qualifications. Nonetheless, the NSSFNS experience demonstrates that qualified southern Negro youth can function effectively in predominantly white colleges of good quality.

Coleman Report. The Coleman Report, *Equality of Educational Opportunity*, released in 1966, indicated that the most important in-school correlate of individual achievement for both Negroes and whites was the peer environment— that is, the characteristics of the student body as a whole. Thus, the academic attainment of both Negro and white pupils, when their family background characteristics were equated, was more closely related to the educational proficiency of their classmates than to all objective school characteristics together (such as curriculum, expenditure per pupil, physical facilities, and size of class) or to all teacher characteristics together (such as type of education, experience, verbal ability, and attitude). In the upper grades the apparent influence of the quality of the student body on individual achievement was two to three times greater for Negro pupils than for white pupils.

Another student body characteristic related to the minority pupil's performance was the racial composition in the school. The higher the proportion of whites in a school, the higher the level of Negro achievement; and the apparent effect was cumulative through time. The seeming impact of desegregation can be illustrated by comparing test scores in reading comprehension for Negro high school students in the metropolitan North who never had a white classmate with scores of metropolitan northern Negroes with similar family backgrounds who attended racially mixed schools from the early grades. Figures from the Coleman Report, when consolidated, show that Negro ninth graders in predominantly white classes whose first interracial experience occurred in the primary grades had an average score of 48.2. This was about five points below the white norm for the same region but less than two points below the national norm of 50.0. In contrast, Negro ninth graders who had never had white classmates averaged 43.8—almost ten points below the white regional norm. Thus, it seems as though desegregation reduced the racial achievement gap by almost half. (The results based on Negro 12th graders are similar, but perhaps less convincing because of a possibly high rate of Negro dropouts after the ninth grade.)

Additionally, the test scores of Negroes in majority white classrooms showed much more variability than did those of whites.

When the influence of the student body's educational background and aspirations was controlled, the relationship between racial composition of schools and Negro test scores appeared to be sharply reduced. Hence, Coleman and his associates concluded that the apparently beneficial effect of having a high proportion of white classmates did not come from racial composition per se but from the higher educational background and aspirations that they found, on the average, among white students.

Also associated with the amount of interracial contact were the scholastic attitudes of Negroes. The higher the proportion of whites in the school, the more likely were Negro children to feel that success and failure depended upon what they themselves were able to accomplish rather than upon circumstances beyond their control. This perception of personal efficacy was strongly related to Negro achievement. With or without family background characteristics equated and discounted, this perception accounted for about three times as much variance in the test scores of Negroes as of whites at the higher grade levels, in both the North and South. However, on another attitude that was less closely related to Negro test performance, desegregation seemed to have an adverse effect: Negro children in racially mixed classrooms tended to rate themselves lower in intellectual ability than did Negroes who were racially isolated. Apparently, the positive effect on Negro performance of an enhanced sense of personal efficacy outweighed the detrimental effect of lowered self-esteem, since the actual achievement of desegregated Negro children was relatively high.

Finally, the Coleman Report presented data on the percentages of white students whose questionnaire responses indicated a preference for all-white "close friends" and all-white classrooms. Quite consistently, the effect of desegregation on white attitudes appeared to be favorable. White children who began their interracial school experiences in the first three grades tended to have less preference for all-white friends and classes than did other white students.

Analyses of the Coleman Report. Because of the time pressures under which it was prepared, the Coleman Report devoted relatively little attention to the effects of desegregation. The U.S. Commission on Civil Rights (1967), therefore, undertook to analyze more thoroughly certain portions of the Coleman data and to carry out new investigations on the problem of desegregation. The commission's report is largely concerned with the question of what the relationship is between racial composition of school enrollments and Negro performance. To answer the question the following differences between racially mixed and racially isolated classrooms were controlled by means of cross-tabulations: (1) quality of educational services available, (2) academic ability and social class background of classmates, and (3) academic ability and home background of the Negro students.

Controlling for these three sets of factors, the commission found a consistent relationship between racial composition of the classroom and Negro verbal achievement. Negroes in predominantly white classes tested higher than those in classes with no white students or only a minority of whites. In the metropolitan Northeast the average differences in favor of Negro students attending majority-white classes were substantial, averaging about one year of academic growth for ninth grade Negro pupils. However, average test scores of Negro pupils never reached the level of white scores. Consistent with the findings of the Coleman Report, the benefits of desegregation appeared to be greatest for those Negro children whose biracial contacts began in the early grades.

With regard to the achievement of white children, the commission found that their test scores were not adversely affected by the presence of Negro classmates, provided the latter were not in the majority.

In another reanalysis of the Coleman data, McPartland (1969) compared the relative influence of classroom and school desegregation on the achievement test scores of over 5,000 Negro ninth graders in the Northeast, controlling for students' social-class background. He found that the only Negro students who appeared to derive benefit from attendance at predominantly white schools were those in majority-white classes within the school. He concluded: "As far as differences in their achievement are concerned, the students in segregated classes may as well be in segregated schools as desegregated ones" (p. 97). Even Negro

students in predominantly Negro schools seemed to benefit from being in a class composed mainly of whites. Partitioning students by program of study or by ability track did not greatly reduce the apparent effect of classroom composition, except for one group—those in the lowest of three ability tracks.

Despite the thoroughness of the additional analyses of the Coleman data that were done by the U.S. Commission on Civil Rights and by McPartland, they could not transcend the basic limitations of those data. The Coleman survey tested children at a single point in time and hence could not provide definitive answers to questions of causality; moreover, it used a sample from which several major cities were excluded. Also, the nonresponse rate on important questionnaire items was high enough to allow the possibility of serious factual distortions. For example, a large proportion of children did not know the educational levels of their parents, a key variable. These and other limitations of the Coleman data have been discussed by Dyer (1968), Weinberg (1968), Pettigrew (1969), Gordon (1967), Dentler (1966), and others.

Additional studies on integration.   Even with its limitations the Coleman survey stands as the landmark investigation of the correlates of school racial composition. But it points up the need for longitudinal studies. An investigation of this type was conducted in Richmond, Calif., by Wilson (reported by U.S. Commission on Civil Rights 1967), who used both longitudinal data and students' initial mental ability scores upon entering school. Even when differences among individual students in social-class background and initial mental maturity were taken into account, the social-class composition of the student body as a whole had a strong effect upon academic growth. The effect was stronger on Negroes than on whites. The influence of school racial composition was substantially less than that of social-class composition. However, the number of Negroes in predominantly white schools was really too small to permit an adequate evaluation of the effect of racial environment independent of the social-class effect.

In evaluations of school busing programs, although the results of various studies (reviewed by Weinberg 1968) are not entirely consistent, the general trend of findings suggests favorable academic outcomes for Negro children who are bused to predominantly white schools, with white children who have Negroes bused to their schools suffering no measurable decrements in their development.

Compensatory education in Negro schools. No general discussion of the complex relationship between racial balance and academic achievement would be complete without evaluating the effectiveness of compensatory programs in ghetto schools. Pettigrew (1969) makes the point that since the initiation in 1959 of the widely publicized Higher Horizons project in New York City, and similar early childhood programs elsewhere, pedagogical efforts directed at improving the academic performance of lower-class children have been put forward as an alternative to racially integrated education. He sees this alternative as both financially attractive (backed as it is by federal funds, under Title I of the Elementary and Secondary Education Act of 1965) and politically expedient, since it tends to reduce pressure from integrationist elements in the community.

Since compensatory efforts are seen by many school and government officials as an alternative to desegregation, the U.S. Commission on Civil Rights (1967) examined the effectiveness of such programs in St. Louis, New York City, Syracuse, Philadelphia, Berkeley, and Seattle. It found them to be generally ineffective. Similarly, Gordon and Wilkerson (1966) concluded from their own nationwide survey of compensatory programs that where evaluative studies had been conducted, the reports typically showed ambiguous outcomes.

Of course, the general failure of ghetto compensatory programs in the past does not necessarily mean failure of future and radically different programs. Furthermore, to limit the alternatives to either integration or compensatory programs may be an error. An optimal educational strategy would seem to entail combining the two measures as needed.

Mediators of desegregation effects. The reports of the U.S. Commission on Civil Rights (1967) stressed the distinction between a merely desegregated school and an integrated one. The term "desegregation" refers only to the racial composition of student enrollments, while "integration" involves the sociopsychological quality of the interracial contact. Calling attention to the Coleman survey's finding of greater variability of Negro test performance in biracial classrooms,

Pettigrew (1969) observes that merely desegregated schools can be either effective or ineffective, can boast genuine interracial acceptance or intense interracial hostility. In short, a desegregated school is not necessarily a good school. The commission's analysis indicates that in desegregated schools where most teachers reported no racial tension, Negro students scored higher on verbal achievement tests, had more definite plans for attending college, and had friendlier attitudes toward whites than did Negroes in schools with high tension levels.

Four-factor model. In a series of experiments set up with students, Katz (1964) and his associates sought to clarify the factors that determine whether biracial contact will have beneficial or detrimental effects upon the intellectual performance of Negroes. Although most of the studies were of college students, there is reason to believe that the results are also applicable to elementary and secondary school pupils. All of the findings are consistent with a four-factor model of Negro achievement in biracial settings, which can be summarized as follows:

(1) *Low probability of success.* Where there is marked descrepancy in the educational standards of Negro and white schools or where strong feelings of inferiority are acquired by Negro children outside the school, minority-group newcomers in integrated classrooms are likely to have a low expectancy of academic success; consequently, their achievement motivation should be low.

(2) *Social threat.* Given the prestige and power of the white majority group, rejection of Negro students by white classmates or teachers should tend to elicit emotional responses—fear, anger, and humiliation—that are detrimental to intellectual functioning.

(3) *Failure threat.* When academic failure entails disapproval by significant others—parents, teachers, and perhaps also classmates—low expectancy of success should elicit emotional responses that are detrimental to performance.

(4) *Social facilitation effect.* On the other hand, acceptance of Negroes by white peers and adults should have a social facilitation effect upon their ability to learn by motivating them to adhere to white standards of academic performance; anticipation that high performance will win white approval should endow scholastic success with high-incentive value.

Cross-racial comparisons. In a provocative article, Pettigrew (1967) shows how the social comparison concepts of experimental social psychology and sociology can be applied to the dynamics of the biracial classroom. He proposes a broad hypothesis which is consistent with the empirical findings and interpretations of Katz (1964), as well as with data from field studies of desegregation. Pettigrew suggests that "many of the consequences of interracial classrooms for both Negro and white children are a direct function of the opportunities such classrooms provide for cross-racial self-evaluation" (1967, p. 287). It follows from such a hypothesis, he continues, "that the more opportunities for cross-racial self-evaluation a school provides, the greater the consequences. And it also follows that those children for whom peers of the other race become referent should evince the largest changes" (*ibid.*). In fact, the U.S. Commission on Civil Rights found that in predominantly white classrooms Negro children with close white friends showed both higher achievement and higher education aspirations than Negroes having no close white friends.

Pettigrew's hypothesis specifies consequences of desegregation and not simply benefits. He discusses the conditions under which cross-racial comparison would arouse anxious expectations of failure in Negro students. But he concludes that on balance the consequences of such comparison appear to be beneficial. The two federal studies did in fact reveal higher performance levels among Negro children in predominantly white classrooms.

Trends. In an authoritative[1] overview of trends and methods in urban desegregation, Dentler and Elsbery (1967) point out that in the 20 largest cities in the United States segregation continues its annual increase and is nowhere being reduced or prevented. Each of these cities has planned or has in operation a small number of limited remedies—free choice enrollment, grade structure revision, school pairing, busing, and the like—but only a few cities have potentially comprehensive programs of desegregation in operation. As examples of comprehensive programs, Dentler and Elbery mention Cleveland's "supplementary center," where pupils are brought together for part of the day for enriched and remedial instruction; a school-clustering effort in Baltimore; and in Boston, the privately financed and operated Metropolitan Council for Occupa-

tional and Educational Opportunities program, under which a few hundred Negro children are being bused from the city into the schools of six cooperating suburban school districts. Dentler and Elsbery believe that although the Boston program is very small, it represents the most significant mechanism operating in the largest cities, because it involves urban-suburban cooperation.

According to these experts on urban desegregation, none of the limited techniques, alone or in combination, can prevent segregated education in the largest central cities. Nonetheless, the programs should be continued and extended, because they stimulate progressively greater commitment to comprehensive programs. Dentler and Elsbery state:

> It is unlikely that federal, state, or local agencies will take giant steps to remedy a problem unless there has been experience in the small interim steps. Limited programs . . . also serve to thaw an otherwise frozen complex of local school customs and mores. . . . Well planned, well implemented, yet limited desegregation schemes should be encouraged. Hasty mechanical experiments should be avoided; they harm some students, and they *depress* confidence in the desirability of comprehensive school integration. (1967, p. 310)

A comprehensive plan which Dentler and Elsbery find promising is the educational complex, "an administratively and geographically bounded network of public schools whose chief officer has the authority and the means to increase integration among staff and students in the member schools, and to make the best local adaptation of schools to student needs and to the reduction of ethnic isolation" (1967, p. 311). The schools in a complex would be proximate enough that students could be quickly bused from one to another for maximum utilization of special services and facilities. Perhaps the most important strength of the educational complex idea is that it offers a concrete way of moving from neighborhood-based school systems to larger districts and paves the way for educational parks. Its main weaknesses are that it requires substantial administrative and staff reorganization and, unless combined with other techniques, may provide only limited desegregation in many central cities.

Another promising desegregation concept mentioned by Dentler and Elsbery is the educational park, "a very large consolidated unified school plant, built in a campus-like arrangement and zoned to serve many surrounding neighborhoods, subcommunities, or combinations of communities" (1967, p. 313). In the 20 largest cities, educational parks have been proposed and to some extent planned in New York, Chicago, Philadelphia, and Detroit.

Educational parks would be too expensive for cities to build unless they received substantial federal aid. Further, the desegregation potential of big city parks would necessarily be limited unless they involved consolidation of mainly white suburban school districts with increasingly Negro inner-city districts.

An essential element in the strategy recommended by Dentler and Elsbery for implementing urban-suburban park programs, in addition to obtaining federal and state participation, is the consistent emphasis at the local level upon the ways in which these innovations will provide improved educational services, not only for minority groups but also for all citizens and their children.

BIBLIOGRAPHY

COLEMAN, JAMES S., et al. 1966 *Equality of Educational Opportunity*. Washington, D.C., Government Printing Office.

DENTLER, ROBERT A. 1966 "Equality of Educational Opportunity: A Special Review." *Urban Review*, 1, no. 5:27–29.

DENTLER, ROBERT A., AND J. ELSBERY 1967 "Big City School Desegregation: Trends and Methods." *Papers Prepared for National Conference on Equal Educational Opportunity in America's Cities*. Washington, D.C., Government Printing Office. Pages 305–324.

DYER, HENRY S. 1968 "School Factors." *Harvard Educational Review*, 38, no. 1:38–56.

GORDON, EDMUND W. 1967 "Equalizing Educational Opportunity in the Public School." *IRCD Bulletin*, 3, no. 5:1–3.

GORDON, EDMUND W., AND DOXEY A. WILKERSON 1966 *Compensatory Education for the Disadvantaged: Programs and Practices, Preschool Through College*. New York, College Entrance Examination Board.

HANSEN, CARL F. 1960 "The Scholastic Performances of Negro and White Pupils in the Integrated Public Schools of the District of Columbia." *Harvard Educational Review*, 30, no. 3:216–236.

KATZ, IRWIN 1964 "Review of Evidence Relating to Effects of Desegregation on the Intellectual Performance of Negroes." *American Psychologist*, 19, no. 6:381–399.

MCPARTLAND, JAMES 1969 "The Relative Influence of School and of Classroom Desegregation on the Academic Achievement of Ninth Grade Negro Students." *Journal of Social Issues*, 25, no. 3:93–102.

NATIONAL SCHOLARSHIP SERVICE AND FUND FOR NEGRO STUDENTS 1963 *Annual Report 1962–1963*. New York, The Service and Fund.

PETTIGREW, THOMAS F. 1967 "Social Evaluation Theory: Convergences and Applications." David Levine, ed., *Nebraska Symposium on Motivation*. Vol. 15. Lincoln, University of Nebraska Press. Pages 241–311.

PETTIGREW, THOMAS F. 1969 "The Negro and Education: Problems and Proposals." Irwin Katz and Patricia Gurin, eds., *Race and the Social Sciences*. New York, Basic Books.

ROSENTHAL, JACK 1970 "Small Cities Hail Full Integration." New York *Times*, October 18, 1970, part 1, p. 1.

STALLINGS, FRANK H. 1959 "A Study of the Immediate Effects of Integration on Scholastic Achievement in the Louisville Public Schools." *Journal of Negro Education*, 28, no. 4:439–444.

U.S. COMMISSION ON CIVIL RIGHTS 1967 *Racial Isolation in the Public Schools*. Vol. 1. Washington, D.C., Government Printing Office.

WEINBERG, MEYER 1968 *Desegregation Research: An Appraisal*. Chicago, Integrated Education Associates.

WOOTEN, JAMES T. 1970 "Schools 1: Still a Long Way to Go in South." New York *Times*, September 6, 1970, part 4, p. 4.

IRWIN KATZ

2. HIGHER EDUCATION

Since 1950 universities and colleges in the United States have been increasingly affected by urban growth and change. By 1970 the national population had grown to more than 200 million and the rate of increased centralization had accelerated. By that time more than 70 percent of the national population was located in the 200-odd standard metropolitan areas of the United States, and most American institutions, including colleges and universities, were within urban settings.

Moreover, profound population shifts and changes occurred within metropolitan districts themselves. The *Report of the National Advisory Commission on Civil Disorders* (1968), known as the Kerner Report, stated that there was "accelerating segregation of low-income, disadvantaged Negroes within the ghettos of the largest American cities. . . . From 1960 to 1966, the Negro population of all central cities rose 2.4 million, 88.9 percent of total national Negro population growth" (pp. 389, 390). The same report concluded that the United States was rapidly separating into two increasingly distinct societies and that by the late 1980's this split could be so deep that unity would be almost impossible. By that time, whites, settled in the suburbs, the smaller central cities, and on the edges of large central cities, would be totally cut off from blacks, who would be heavily concentrated in the large central cities.

Enrollment growth. Enrollment in American colleges and universities experienced more than a fourfold increase from 1940 to 1968. This increase—from 1.7 million to 6.9 million—resulted not only from an increase in population but also from an increase in the percentage of young people attending college (U.S. Bureau of the Census 1970).

As a result of urban growth and change, the city college or university has been particularly affected by increased enrollments. The Association of Urban Universities estimated that, as of 1968, city institutions claimed 17.7 percent of the full-time student enrollment in the United States, 31.1 percent of the part-time enrollment, and 20.8 percent of all students. Because of the demands of increased enrollment, new institutions had to be created—such as the University of Illinois' campus at Chicago Circle and Cleveland State University (founded in 1923). Older institutions, such as Wayne State University, founded in 1868 in Detroit, were incorporated into the state public system. Others, such as the University of Pittsburgh, developed special affiliation arrangements with the state public system.

The growth in student enrollment has been a particular response to societal pressures. For example, the new technology sends the part-time student back to school for further training. Northeastern University in Boston, Wayne State University in Detroit, and Temple University in Philadelphia are typical of places where in-service training programs have been developed at the request of private or public employers.

Furthermore, the national policy toward education as expressed in the Upward Bound and Talent Search programs, which were directed at providing college opportunities for young black men and women, is of particular significance to nonresidential institutions in central city locations, where the costs of education are lessened by the absence of residence requirements. The result is that the student mix in the city institution is indeed diverse. The pressures from a changing student body—that is, new kinds of students with less favored backgrounds, often poorer preparation, and more diverse ethnic and national origins—combined with a greatly increased enrollment, pose a particularly difficult challenge to the urban institution. Moreover, sheer growth in institutional size in response to enrollment pressures has produced urbanism around the campus.

Expansion of facilities. Colleges and universities tend to remain on their original sites because of the prohibitive capital costs of abandoning existing plants and facilities. Uncontrolled city growth and change occur about them; thus, these institutions are increasingly confronted with central city problems. The need for institutional expansion, generated by increased enrollment and research and training activities, often exacerbates relationships between the institution and the surrounding communities.

Demand for new facilities for higher education has been estimated by the U.S. Office of Education to require an expenditure of more than $2.1 billion per year until 1975 for construction. Logan Wilson of the American Council on Education forecasts that by 1980 it will be necessary to double the size of every existing American institution of higher education and, in addition, to create 1,000 new institutions with an enrollment of 2,500 each.

These demands can be met only through acquisition of land area, usually a specific site adjacent to existing campus. Wide separation of academic facilities—of laboratories and libraries—leads to inefficiency or unwarranted duplications. In cases of medical school and related hospital expansion, patient care requires immediate proximity.

Moreover, these problems tend to be most acute in the cases of long-established universities and colleges. Their sites, determined long ago, have been subjected to the full cycles of city growth, change, and deterioration. As institutions with long histories of effective research and training, colleges and universities have taken on the major responsibilities of furthering the new technology. Unstable and sometimes chaotic social conditions in the surrounding communities hamper the ability of colleges and universities to discharge their academic responsibilities.

Federal support. Recognizing that colleges and universities needed both expansion area secured through urban renewal and a compatible adjoining community, section 112 of the Housing Act of 1959 authorized federal assistance to those urban renewal projects which involve colleges and universities without regard to zoning requirements that redevelopment be primarily residential. Further, it provided that, under certain circumstances and upon execution of a certificate of expenditure by the college or university, institutional expenditures made for acquisition of land, demolition of buildings, and relocation services could be treated as local noncash grants-in-aid. Thus, a municipality in collaboration with an institution of higher education could obtain, through federal recognition of institutional expenditures, matching federal urban-renewal assistance; the institutional expenditure, upon certification, provided the required local contribution.

In 1961 the legislation was enlarged to include hospitals as eligible institutions. Thus, as of 1970, approximately 200 universities, colleges, and hospitals were being assisted through this legislation. In the case of the University of Chicago eligible, noncash, local, grant-in-aid expenditures exceeded $14 million; this enabled the city of Chicago, in collaboration with the university, to obtain $42 million in federal urban-renewal assistance.

Research. There has also been a marked increase in research activities in colleges and universities with the rise in student enrollment. According to reports from colleges and universities and federal agencies, about $613 million was spent for basic research on college campuses in fiscal year 1962 (U.S. Congress . . . 1963). Enterprises of this magnitude and complexity generate demands for space, facilities, and employment.

Almost half of the $613 million appropriated for basic research on college and university campuses went to the National Institutes of Health, the U.S. Office of Education, the Office of Vocational Rehabilitation, the Public Health Service, and the National Science Foundation. Significant portions of this amount supported work and research in urban-related problems. Since 1962 the level of support has materially increased. It is also significant that 90 percent of total federal research funds in that year were distributed to 100 educational institutions within the United States, more than 70 of which were located in major urban centers (*ibid.*).

The university and the community. In the early 1950's a number of universities—particularly Columbia University, the University of Pennsylvania, and the University of Chicago—undertook community stabilization and improvement programs in conjunction with community organization affiliates.

For example, the West Philadelphia Corporation, under the aegis of the University of Pennsylvania, has provided a variety of planning, development, and educational services to the west Philadelphia community, including the development in collaboration with the Board of Education of Philadelphia of a new model high school in the area.

The University of Chicago, through the departments of psychiatry and pediatrics, respectively, of the Pritzker Medical School, operates a mental health project and a child care center in the Woodlawn community. The university's Graduate School of Education, in collaboration with the Woodlawn Organization and the Chicago Board of Education, operates an experimental school district directed at improving educational opportunities, research, and training for 4,000 children in public schools in Woodlawn.

The Children's Bureau of the Department of Health, Education, and Welfare administers a program of grants to institutions of higher education for training professional personnel in the field of child welfare; funds for traineeship grants and short-term training activities are also available. In 1965 an amendment to the Social Security Act of 1935 awarded special-project grants to schools of medicine and dentistry and to teaching hospitals affiliated with schools of medicine. These grants provided comprehensive health care for school and preschool children of low-income families. Accordingly, a number of university-affiliated medical schools and hospitals have undertaken the operation of outpatient clinics and medical centers for such purposes.

Title I of the Higher Education Act of 1965 authorized the commissioner of education to make grants to strengthen community-service programs of colleges and universities. Funds available under this title are distributed according to a state-approved plan, which requires that local academic resources be focused upon problems viewed as crucial by state public authorities. The 1968 amendments to the Higher Education Act authorized continued funding of the community-services program in the amount of $10 million for 1969, $50 million for 1970, and $60 million for 1971 (*College and University Reporter*, vol. 2, par. 14214).

Section 703 of the Housing and Urban Development Act of 1965 authorized the secretary of housing and urban development to make grants to any local public body or agency to assist in financing specific projects for neighborhood facilities and provided specifically that any such project may be undertaken by such a body or agency either directly or through an approved nonprofit organization. Under this provision a social services center is being erected on the campus of the University of Chicago to serve the adjoining Woodlawn community.

Educational planning. Since capital funds available to municipalities prior to the 1930's were limited to public works, such as roads, parks, and playgrounds, educational planning in the American university was primarily directed to physical planning and centered in schools of architecture and design. Inauguration of public housing, slum clearance, renewal, and neighborhood conservation programs after 1930 generated interest in the social aspects of city planning. As of 1968, 73 universities, including six Canadian institutions, offered higher degrees in various planning fields, such as city planning and architecture and design.

Moreover, as the urban crisis deepened, special interests developed among existing university disciplines, departments, and schools, often in multidisciplinary lines. For example, the Columbia University School of Law and the Arthur Garfield Hays Civil Liberties Program of the New York University School of Law have undertaken studies and education in social welfare law. Schools of education, such as Teachers College in New York City and the Graduate School of Education of the University of Chicago, have undertaken research and training in problems of urban education. Textbooks and other teaching materials thought more appropriate for urban students have been produced, and teachers, paraprofessionals, and cadres of other specialists have been trained specifically to deal with the problems of urban education.

The Elementary and Secondary Education Act of 1965—particularly Title III, which provided for supplementary educational centers and services, and Title IV, which provided for regional facilities to conduct research in improving elementary and secondary education—has led to broad university participation in educational planning. The U.S. Office of Education has founded regional laboratories under Title IV all over the country. These laboratories involve consortia of institutions, so that each regional laboratory usually includes representatives from at least ten universities. Although the work that has been done by these laboratories varies widely, there has been a tendency to concentrate on the preparation of teaching materials.

Student scholarship and fellowship funds are provided under a variety of federal programs. In fiscal 1968, Congress appropriated $500,000 for fellowships in city planning and urban studies and $11 million for research and studies relating to housing and urban problems. Both programs are administered by the Department of Housing and Urban Development (*College and University*

Reporter, vol. 2, par. 14723). The National Science Foundation provides grants to doctoral candidates in the social sciences, and the surgeon general provides support for public health service fellowships and traineeships as well as support for research fellowships in community health services.

BIBLIOGRAPHY

College and University Reporter. Published semimonthly by Commerce Clearing House.
LEVI, JULIAN H. 1964 *Municipal and Institutional Relations Within Boston: The Benefits of Section 112 of the Federal Housing Act of 1961*. University of Chicago Press.
Report of the National Advisory Commission on Civil Disorders 1968 New York, Bantam.
Urban Affairs Reporter. Published semimonthly by Commerce Clearing House.
U.S. BUREAU OF THE CENSUS 1970 *Statistical Abstract of the United States: 1970*. 91st ed. Washington, D.C., Government Printing Office.
U.S. CONGRESS. HOUSE. COMMITTEE ON EDUCATION AND LABOR 1963 *The Federal Government and Education*. Report presented by Mrs. Green of Oregon, chairman of the special subcommittee on education. 88th Cong., 1st sess. House document No. 159. Washington, D.C., Government Printing Office.

JULIAN H. LEVI

URBAN INTERN PROGRAM, NATIONAL

The Urban Intern Program of the Department of Housing and Urban Development (HUD) meets the department's needs for a regular input of especially competent recent college graduates. The program is designed to give these young people a firm understanding of the urban development processes and the purposes for which HUD has been established.

An understanding of the relationships between the various activities, programs, and objectives of the department is essential for all HUD professional, technical, and managerial employees who will eventually play a key role in program administration. It is, therefore, necessary for the department to provide the training which will ensure such understanding, regardless of the initial job assignment of the individual, his career goals, or the educational preparation he has had for his initial assignment.

Purposes and implications. The Urban Intern Program is concerned primarily with orienting young men and women to major federal urban development programs and program interrelationships both within HUD and with other, related federal programs. The program also serves to integrate the intern quickly into the regular work force. The one-to-one relationship between the urban intern and his supervisor-sponsor and carefully chosen initial assignments also provide for accelerated professional development for those interns having a field of occupational specialization. The combination of these elements makes it possible for the intern to make significant contributions to the department much sooner than otherwise would be expected. In defining the purposes of the urban intern program, it is essential to recognize that the program is a key element in HUD's recruitment programs and manpower-planning programs.

These programs are based on the recruitment of 20 percent to 30 percent of HUD's annual professional turnover through the intern program. The annual input and sound development of superior talented young people affect other portions of the department's regular manpower development program. There is, for instance, a career educational program designed to give qualified HUD employees an opportunity to compete for one year of full-time graduate level education at the department's expense. Employees who came to HUD through the intern program make up over 80 percent of those selected for this advanced training opportunity.

Administration. The HUD Urban Intern Program is the responsibility of management in every organizational component of the department in Washington, D.C., and in each regional office. The basic responsibility for administration of the program rests with HUD's director of personnel, with the assistance of an urban intern coordinator, who concentrates on the recruitment, assignment, and training aspects of the intern program. There is an intern training committee in each geographical area having an intern program. These committees evaluate the individual intern training plans, the intern training, progress, the effectiveness of sponsors, and the effectiveness of the total program in each area. The Employee Development and Training Division of the Office of Personnel in Washington provides technical supervision of intern training.

Selection. HUD seeks out students with better than average academic records and with histories of campus leadership and extracurricular participation, especially in student electoral politics, at both the graduate and undergraduate levels. The program is open to all candidates of high caliber in the major technical and professional fields within the department. Although many interns have had special urban development courses, these courses have not been a requirement for those individuals who are otherwise educationally qualified.

Every effort is made to recruit an intern group which is broadly representative in terms of geographic location, racial groupings, and sex. Although urban intern candidates who are attorneys must meet department standards and other occupational specialists must meet the Civil Service Commission's occupational examination requirements, most urban interns are selected after they have qualified in the Federal Service Entrance Examination. Some interns are also selected by means of the Management Intern Examination. HUD employees who meet the qualification standards may also be appointed to the program.

Elements. On-the-job training and sponsorship constitute the major aspect of the urban intern training plan, supplemented by seminars, conferences, assigned readings, and rotational work assignments within HUD, in local and state government agencies, in neighborhood organizations, and in federal agencies. In some cases, after-hour academic study is also part of the intern's training. Normally, each intern is assigned to a specific position for which his education, interests, and experience have qualified him. He begins his internship in this position by performing a regular but challenging job to the extent permitted by his experience. His supervisor-sponsor directs his work from the beginning, so that when the time comes to design an individual training plan for the intern, the sponsor will know the intern's capacities and interests.

There is one basic department-wide urban intern program. Regional offices have the authority to add additional optional program elements to the general basic program.

There are three major elements in the basic Urban Intern Training Program. These basic elements are orientation, initial productive assignments, and rotation assignments.

The initial orientation consists of an explanation of HUD programs, functions, and organization, together with a detailed explanation of the urban intern program itself. There are some lectures, but there is an increasing use of case studies, problem-solving, work groups, and field trips.

The initial productive assignments consist of three months of meaningful work assignments in the intern's designated organization. The purpose is to introduce him to some of the more challenging work of the organization and to serve as a transition from academic life to the more production-centered work of HUD.

Each urban intern in the basic program must have rotational assignments in all major HUD program areas. There is a minimum of 12 weeks required rotation outside of his own major organization, with two assignments of no less than four weeks each. A longer period of rotation is required of urbanist interns.

The following six additional program elements are also required as part of the basic program: sponsorship, readings, reports, evaluations, one-year training program, and on-the-job training.

A sponsor is a senior staff member who, for the intern training period at least, is in direct supervisory line with the intern and is generally in the same occupational or professional field as the intern. The sponsor is expected to work out the initial assignments for the intern and later, with the help of the intern, to plan a series of rotational experiences and other training for him. The sponsor reviews the required written reports and makes additional training assignments to the intern throughout the entire training period.

All urban interns are required to have at least one major reading assignment in each of the following subject areas: the general problems and processes of urban development, the economic aspects of housing and urban development, and the human and social problems in urban development. Sponsors may assign additional reading in the professional or technical area of interest and may also give interns special assignments in the housing and urban development fields. The HUD library publishes a bibliography particularly pertinent for urban interns, and most interns have reading assignments in the professional architectural and housing journals.

Written reports on all phases of the program, including the rotation assignments, readings, conferences, and field trips, are required of all interns. The program itself requires the reports on at least a quarterly basis, and the sponsor may require additional regular reports or special reports at any time he thinks appropriate. These reports keep the sponsor advised of the intern's progress and give the sponsor a measure of the intern's ability to express himself and an opportunity to assist the intern in learning to write reports. All reports are forwarded to the intern training committee at the evaluation times.

In addition to regular face-to-face evaluations and discussions, the sponsor is required to prepare two written evaluations of the intern's progress and effectiveness. These written evaluations, the intern's reports, and his rotational assignment schedule are reviewed by the local intern training committee prior to an evaluation interview. The interview usually includes both a discussion regarding the value of specific training assignments and also questions to test the intern's knowledge and understanding of HUD programs. The committee meets to evaluate the individual intern's program at the end of the fifth month and again at the end of the tenth month of internship and recommends appropriate action at each time.

The intern who satisfactorily completes a one-year internship is promoted to the next major salary level on such satisfactory completion. Unsatisfactory performance results in separation from the department or reassignment to a less demanding job some time before the end of the training period.

Since on-the-job training is the key element in the internship program, the majority of an intern's time is spent in actual work situations. The requirement that sponsors have an initial work assignment plan is designed to encourage the planning of challenging, meaningful assignments.

Optional features. HUD organizations participating in the urban intern program are permitted to add the following program elements.

Intern seminars meet periodically to discuss major HUD program and urban development problems. The seminars may consist of discussions of papers prepared by interns or of lectures and discussions by HUD staff members or by outside urban development experts. Customarily, the later phases of the intern seminar program are controlled by the interns themselves, with each intern required to serve as coordinator and chairman for at least one of the seminars. This optional feature is almost always part of the program.

The federal requirement for one year of continuous experience before an employee is permitted to participate in paid training programs outside the government is waived in the case of urban interns. Intern sponsors may assign interns to special training sessions and outside, after-hours academic training, with the approval of the training committee. HUD pays all of the training costs for programs which are directly job-related and three-fourths of the cost of after-hours courses which are related to the broad purposes of the department.

HUD program managers develop special technical and professional training sessions for interns to supplement the regular intern training. Supplemental training is not usually permitted during the first three months of internship and is most logically included sometime during the last six months of the training period. This supplemental technical and professional training usually consists of formal classroom or seminar training supplemented by a plan which sequences the work assignments to enhance technical and professional development. Occupational programs for auditors, appraisers, and market analysts are typical and include considerable structured, classroom-type training along with specially designed practical work experience.

History.   The Urban Intern Program had its genesis in the worldwide urban crisis and the corresponding urban development manpower shortages which have been developing since World War II. Ever since the early 1950's, there has been a growing need for skilled technicians and managers in urban development on all levels of government. The Urban Intern Program, which began as the Housing Intern Program in 1956, was developed in response to these needs. In its initial developmental stages, the program was to be an occupational training program tied to a positive recruitment program focusing on recent college graduates. Because of the personal interest of Housing and Home Finance Agency (HHFA) administrator Albert M. Cole, the training portions of the intern program were reworked to give participants a general understanding of urban development and an in-depth understanding of the existing programs then under the jurisdiction of the HHFA.

It was decided that the internship concept appeared to be the most likely to meet the broad training objectives established. This concept, modeled after the approach used by the medical profession, focused on initial identification of participants with occupational categories and even specific jobs. An intern's initial assignments within the agency serve as a background for his subsequent understanding of other HUD program areas.

The program has maintained a one-to-one relationship between the intern and his professionally skilled sponsor-supervisor, but the specific training techniques and the subject matter of the training have been under constant evaluation and change. Initially, most of the seminars and conferences which the interns attended were staffed by experienced housing and urban development professionals in the federal service. By the second year of the program's history this fixation on internal problems and programs began to change, so that now, with the exception of a two-week orientation program, almost all of the conferences and seminars focus on broad urban development problems, and most utilize resource people from outside the department. The most recent changes in the program are those which are intended to give the intern some intense experiences at the neighborhood or local government level. These experiences provide a better understanding of the practical program administration policies involved in administering and managing programs with broad objectives which must also accommodate the many local issues and problems affecting decision-making at every level.

Since the intern program is an adult-learning situation, there is necessarily a considerable amount of direct intern participation in the design of his training program and in the design of group activities. This participation has increased significantly since the program's inception, with the most drastic increases in the late 1960's.

Evaluation of techniques and approaches goes on almost continually, and there is always an evaluation by participants at the end of the year. Evaluations to see if the program is meeting the basic manpower-planning objectives for which it was founded have been less frequent; the HUD management staff, has, nevertheless, expressed confidence that the program is successful.

The program initially had 36 participants; during the late 1950's and early 1960's the number doubled and reached as high as 300 by the late 1960's. The retention rate for interns has maintained a fairly constant level: Periodic checks on turnover indicate that interns have a lower turnover rate than other professional employees within HUD, and, when compared to other training programs in the federal government and in private corporations, the urban intern turnover rate has run slightly below that of most other programs. The retention rates of organizations in HUD are very often related to the advancement profiles of the interns in that organization. Although logic would imply that those organizations with the lowest average age would be the most difficult for an intern to find advancement in, this has not proved to be the case. As a matter of fact,

HUD management has found that those organizations with the highest average age of the professional employees—those which need the intern program the most—have special problems in making the program work. So far, the most successful approaches to solving these special organizational problems have involved rather intensive educational efforts among the older staff and a more careful selection and sponsorship of the interns in these organizations.

On the whole, then, the Urban Intern Program is considered a successful, worthwhile venture for the department itself. In addition, HUD officials have felt from the beginning that an intern who leaves to go to a local government job carrying out the programs that HUD administers at the national level cannot be considered a loss to the program. The most recent survey made of the occupational fields in which former interns are now engaged and the retention rate within the department indicate that of all the interns employed since 1956, about 75 percent are now engaged in urban development at some level of government or in a private organization serving local, state, or federal urban development program areas.

FREDERICK H. AREND

URBAN MINORITIES

---

1. SCHOOL ACHIEVEMENT   David J. Fox and
                                             Valerie Barnes

2. EDUCATION OF IMMIGRANTS   Joe L. Rempson

---

1. SCHOOL ACHIEVEMENT

There are few more disturbing sets of educational data than the data on the educational achievement of minority group children in urban schools. For any of the minority groups of current concern and for all formal aspects of educational achievement, the data present a picture of consistent and serious retardation behind the normative data for the particular measure or behind comparable data available on the same measure from majority group children.

For the purposes of this article more than 200 studies were reviewed, and the data from 43 representative studies were summarized. Nearly all studies reported retardation, and thus the substance of the data analyses presented is simply a consideration of the extent of retardation for the different minority groups which the studies identify and of the sensitivity to change of retardation as reflected in the reports of school programs principally financed under Title I of the 1965 Elementary and Secondary Education Act.

Each study included in this article met five criteria:

(1) It reported data specifically for children in one or more of the ethnic minority groups of concern or for children who were defined as disadvantaged.
(2) It based the appraisal of achievement on a standardized test.
(3) It reported the data in grade equivalents.
(4) It provided some basis for determining that an urban community was involved.
(5) It reported the number of cases as well as the grades in which testing was done. (This criterion may seem superfluous or naïve, but several studies were eliminated because they never mentioned either sample size or grade of testing.)

Groups included. Although any group which consists of less than 50 percent of the population of an urban area can be considered a minority group, only those studies concerned with the minority groups which were of greatest educational concern in the late 1960's were selected for review. This rationale turns attention to three groups of children—black, Puerto Rican, and those defined as disadvantaged in reports of school programs financed under Title I of the Elementary and Secondary Education Act. (It should be noted that the majority of the data on Puerto Ricans was obtained from the study made by Goodman and his associates [1956]. By 1970 no other achievement data specifically on this minority group had been reported.) Although ethnic breakdowns of the disadvantaged group, when available, indicated that black and Puerto Rican children predominated, in some urban areas significant proportions of white children were included as well, since they met the income, residential area, or father's occupation criterion used in the particular study to define a disadvantaged child. For comparison purposes, data available for two other groups of children—Spanish American (most often children of Mexican parents) and American Indian—were also included. This last group, the least urban of the five groups for whom data are reviewed, is included for two reasons. First, American Indians are slowly beginning to receive more attention in educational circles. Second, the data from the Indian children who typically have lived in the same area for their entire lives provide a useful contrast to other minority groups among whom there are mobile segments. No applicable data which met the criteria mentioned could be obtained for schoolchildren of Oriental American descent.

Procedure. In those studies where achievement scores were reported for more than one grade, the two grades were singled out at which achievement was the highest and lowest, or in which the retardation was the least and the greatest. In those instances where only one grade was reported, the one grade was considered as the highest in achievement for that study. These scores were then compared both to the expected norms for that grade and to a non-minority group of children, usually white, when such comparative data were included in the original study.

To estimate the extent of retardation from the norm in those studies which did not report the month of the school year during which the tests were administered, one convention had to be arbitrarily applied. In these instances, time of testing was consistently set at midyear—that is, the fifth month of the year. Furthermore, if both pretest and posttest data were mentioned in the study, only the pretest data were selected for inclusion in this article.

Results. For black children an overall median of 1.09 years' reading retardation in relation to the norm was found among the best scores, and a median of 1.91 years of retardation was observed among the worst results. When the reading achievement scores of black and white children were compared with these same studies, the difference between the groups ranged from 2.2 years in the best scores to 2.8 years in the worst scores. In other words, the white children were typically performing above grade level, and so the black children were further behind the white children than behind the norms. Analysis of the grades during which the best and worst scores occur both in comparison to the norms and to the white children indicates that (as would be expected) the lower the grade, the less the retardation; or, as the grade level increases, so does the extent of the

reading deficiency. Thus, although the median retardation in relation to the norm is two years, in the tenth and 12th grades the gross retardation is practically twice that in most instances. Finally, although a majority of these studies represent either normative samples of achievement or the effects of segregation or of integration on performance, the few which do report compensatory programs (A. Harris et al. 1968; Jonsson 1966; U.S. Commission . . . 1967*b*) appear to suggest slightly lower retardation than those which did not provide such programs.

Arithmetic achievement of black children indicates 1.8 years of retardation when the best scores are compared to the norms and more than twice this amount (4.1 years) in the worst scores. From the available comparisons with white children, the pattern of retardation is similar to that with the norms.

The reading and arithmetic achievement scores of other separately identifiable minority groups are also below the norms. Among the best scores for Puerto Rican children, reading retardation is 2.3 years, and it is 3.43 years in the worst group of scores (Coleman et al. 1966; Goldberg 1967; Goodman et al. 1956). The Puerto Rican children did better in arithmetic than in reading; the highest and lowest scores were 1.6 years and 2.1 years below the norm, respectively. For the remaining minority groups, Spanish American and Indian children, the meager evidence available indicates that at best both these groups are approximately 1.5 years below the norms (Charles 1964; Coleman et al. 1966; Zintz 1963).

Most reading and arithmetic achievement data for disadvantaged populations were obtained from evaluations of compensatory educational programs supported under Title I of the Elementary and Secondary Education Act which were in effect during the school year 1966–1967. Bearing in mind the varied ethnic composition of this group, it is interesting to observe a median retardation of 0.91 year in the best scores in reading and 1.8 years in the worst scores. The fact that both of these scores are almost one-half year less than the retardation levels observed with black, Puerto Rican, Spanish American, and Indian children raises speculation as to whether the choice of sites for compensatory education programs might have been sufficiently selective to produce the comparatively lower reading deficiencies. Arithmetic achievement among disadvantaged children ranged from approximately one-half year to three years below the norm level.

Retardation in an academic area, as expressed in grade equivalents, is a complex phenomenon to consider, since it belongs to that family of measures such as height and weight in which the overall range expands as the child grows. Thus, being ten pounds underweight has different meaning for a five-year-old, who is expected to weigh about 41 pounds, than it does for a ten-year-old, who is expected to weigh about 70 pounds. But in the same sense one could argue that reading six months below the level expected at the end of the second grade has different meaning from reading six months below the level expected at the end of the sixth grade. Because of this constantly expanding range in the level of reading expected as a child progresses through the grades, children may look to be falling further and further behind although an examination of their learning rates would reveal steady and consistent progress for them. Figures 1 and 2 illustrate this construct.

Figure 1 presents the achievement of child A who is at normal levels of achievement when first tested at the end of the first grade and who proceeds through school at a normal rate of learning so that at the end of each school year he tests at the norm. Children B and C also test at normal levels initially but thereafter exhibit different

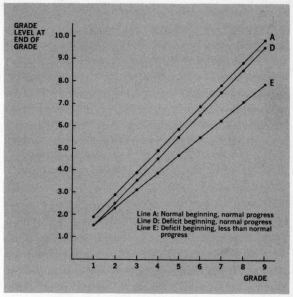

Figure 2. *Progress of three children at different rates from different starting points*

patterns of less than normal progress. Child B progresses at 80 percent of the normally expected rate and therefore gains 0.8 year each grade rather than the expected 1.0 year but maintains his pace year after year. Child C too begins at normal levels and initially progresses 0.8 year but then truly does begin to fall further and further behind, progressing only at 70 percent of normal in grades 3 and 4, at 60 percent in grades 5 and 6, at 50 percent in grades 7 and 8, and at 40 percent in grade 9. Child B, progressing at a steady 80 percent, is only 0.2 year behind at grade 2 but 1.6 years behind by grade 9. Child C also is only 0.2 year behind at grade 2 but is 3.2 years behind by grade 9. Clearly these are children who pose entirely different problems in the learning and teaching situation. Yet both are generally described as being subject to increasing retardation as they progress through the grades.

Figure 2 repeats the graph for child A, who began and progressed normally. It presents the profile of achievement for child D, who when first tested shows an achievement level below normal but who thereafter progresses at normal rates. However, whenever tested he shows the same amount of retardation as he had when first tested. Child E on the other hand combines both kinds of retardation: he begins with an initial deficit and progresses at slower than normal rates so that he falls further and further behind not only the

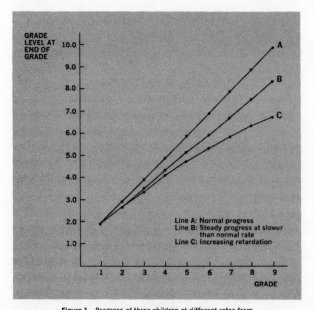

Figure 1. *Progress of three children at different rates from the same starting point*

Table 1. Percent of norm achieved by black children in reading

STUDY	GRADE								TYPE OF CHANGE
	1	2	3	4	5	6	7	8	
Anderson 1956						58			
Brazziel & Gordon 1963							73		
Cooper 1964				73	67	65	77	71	no change
Dressler 1967*		82	82						
Dressler 1967†		77	70						
Goldberg 1967			86			77			
Hansen 1960						78			
A. Harris 1968	83	82	89						better
HARYOU 1964			71			63		71	no change
Henton & Johnson 1964				67		72			
Jonsson 1966*		77	94			86			better
Jonsson 1966†		73	66			65			no change
Kaplan 1962			89			94			
Kennedy et al. 1963		76	77	64	78	75			no change
Osborne 1960						71		68	
Stallings 1959						77		77	
U.S. Commission . . . 1967a			91			75			
U.S. Commission . . . 1967b‡	95	90	69						worse
U.S. Commission . . . 1967b**	106	99	76						worse
U.S. Commission . . . 1967b††			69	73	65				no change
U.S. Commission . . . 1967b**			71	78	69				no change
Mean proportion of achievement	94.7	82.0	78.6	71.0	69.8	73.5		71.8	

* Children bused to nonsegregated schools   † Children not bused   ‡ Educational Improvement Program children
** No compensatory program   †† Madison Area compensatory program

norm but the amount of his initial retardation as well.

To provide some insight into which of these models best fit the data reported in various studies on retardation, the reading data of the studies reviewed in this article were reanalyzed to identify what proportion of normal expectancy the children studied had achieved in each of the grades for which separate data were reported. The data derived from this analysis are presented in Table 1 for black children and Table 2 for disadvantaged children.

A consideration of Table 1 reveals two basic findings: one is apparent from scanning the bottom row and the second from scanning the right-hand column of the table. The bottom row presents the mean percent of normal expectation actually achieved, and beginning in grade 2 it remains relatively steady in the range of 70 to 80

percent. The right-hand column indicates for the separate studies whether or not there was any change in the proportion of normal level achieved. The reanalysis was completed for every study for which data were reported separately for at least three different grade levels. For six of the ten studies for which this analysis was possible, there was no statistically significant drop in the proportion of grade level achieved. (The test of significant differences between percents used for this analysis is sensitive to the observed difference, the number of cases, and the point in the continuum of percents where the differences have occurred. Thus, the same observed difference may be significant in one study and not in another.)

Looking at the data this way one can also pinpoint when in the educational sequence the worsening occurs. Consider the bottom row, which presents, for each grade in which there are at least

Table 2. Percent of norm achieved by disadvantaged children in reading

STUDY	1	2	3	4	5	6	7	8	TYPE OF CHANGE
Badal 1968								73	
Birmingham . . . 1967			64	60	70	71	70	69	no change
Boston . . . 1967		92	84	71	69	71			worse
Boyles et al. 1967							58		
Chattanooga . . . 1967				64		58	71		better
Delaven & England 1966				93	87	82			worse
Florida . . . 1967							60		
Fox 1967					82	90			
Fox et al. 1968*		93	84	83	81	81			worse
Fox et al. 1968†		79	76	75	76	81			no change
Fox et al. 1968‡		75	79	81	79	76			no change
J. Harris 1967		91	84	76	79	77	72	72	worse
Indiana . . . 1967		77	72	59	73	71	72		no change
Levine 1966							72		
Long Beach . . . 1966	67	67	77	56	55	49	56	59	worse
Michigan . . . 1967		73	66	64	62	68			no change
Sacramento . . . 1967		80	73	88	92	87			better
St. Louis 1967					82	83	83		no change
Steinhoff 1967		74		72	77				no change
Wrightstone 1960								67	
Mean proportion of achievement		80.1	75.9	72.5	76.0	74.6	68.2	68.0	

* More Effective Schools sample † Control schools sample ‡ Special Service schools sample

three items, the mean proportion of normal expectation achieved. The one serious drop occurs between grades 3 and 4—a drop from 78.6 percent to 71.0 percent. After grade 4 the data remain relatively stable, with the observed (but not statistically significant) drops between grades 4 and 5 and 6 and 8 more than balanced by the improvement from grade 5 to grade 6, so that children studied in grade 8 were still achieving 71.8 percent.

The data in Table 2 for the heterogeneous grouping of disadvantaged children present the same picture of predominantly no change in status (for seven of the 14 studies analyzed for direction of change) but do not pinpoint grade 4 as a trouble spot in the same way. Instead, major drops occur from grade 2 to grade 3, grade 3 to grade 4, and grade 6 to grade 7.

When the proportions of grade achievements from Tables 1 and 2 are graphed, Figure 3 results. Here the same line works as a line of best fit for both black and disadvantaged children. The line suggests that they are slightly behind when first tested in either grade 1 or grade 2 and that thereafter their rates of progress are slower than normal—that is, they behave like child E in Figure 2.

This suggests that efforts concentrating on the early childhood years may be successful in eliminating the initial deficit but will not have any long-range effect in eliminating retardation among minority group children unless the problem of less than normal rate of progress through the later school years is also solved.

Explanations. Various explanations of slow development of minority children have been offered. These explanations can be grouped into four categories—social-environmental, school situational, physiological, or genetic-racial. The social-environmental group, typified by Deutsch (1960), Hunt (1961), Coles (1967), and Bernstein (1961), argues that there are sufficient inhibiting

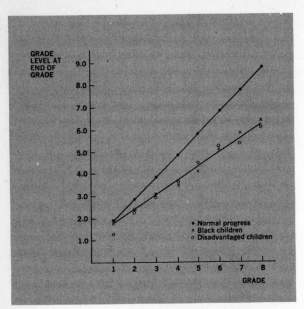

Figure 3. *Normal progress and line of best fit for black and disadvantaged children in reading*

and depressing environmental factors in the life space of black and disadvantaged children to diminish their motivation in school (and particularly in testing situations) and to distract them from their functioning in school so that only a fraction of their normal potential is ever at the service of their cognitive demands. One could subdivide this group further. One subgroup consists of social scientists such as Coles who have considered these social forces so serious and so inhibiting as to be pathological and thus not easily susceptible to manipulation except through deep social change. The second subgroup consists of social scientists such as Deutsch, Hunt, and Bernstein who have treated the social difficulties involved as less pathological and therefore easier to remedy.

A different dimension of the environment argument is the view that it is not the home or cultural environment which is defeating the child but the situation he faces in the urban ghetto school. This view ranges from discreet critics of curriculum and methodology like Clark (1965) and Passow (1963) to the blunter critics of method, organization, and curriculum like Kozol (1967), Holt (1964), and Kohl (1967) and the critics of the school and teachers' motivation like Hatchett (1967) and Herman Ferguson (Bigart 1968), who refer to the educational genocide which a school system oriented toward the white middle class perpetrates on black and other poor

children. In this view the progress noted in the studies reviewed here represents what the children have achieved despite the irrelevance of much of what they study, their inability to identify with the content of the texts, the inappropriateness of method, and the hostility and low expectations of teachers.

The discrepancy between these different views as to which aspects of the environment are at the root of the disadvantaged child's slower progress culminated in the late 1960's in the clear separation of those who felt school integration was the basic goal toward which the urban schools should strive from those who argued for local control and the creation of black schools for black children. Those who saw the basic lack by minority children as social and cognitive experiences and interactions felt that schooling was the logical means to provide children with a socially and an ethnically integrated daily experience which would be more varied than that provided in a school attended only by minority children. Those who saw the problem as one of the inadequacy of the components of the school argued that segregation per se was not the key evil but that a total reorganization of the educational power structure was needed to place the power in the hands of those who would use it for the benefit of the minority children.

An alternative source of explanation lies not in the environmental but in the physiological domain. The general lack of interest in physiological explanations of social behavior which characterized the social disciplines throughout the 1940's and 1950's continued until the mid-1960's. Then, primarily because of concern with underdeveloped countries, studies and papers began to appear noting that malnutrition, ill health, and drug addiction during pregnancy as well as nutritional deficiencies in early childhood had direct effects on the cognitive development of children. Given the higher incidence of these prenatal and postnatal conditions among the poor of all ethnic groups, this argument would explain lower rates of progress as attributable to this physiological crippling of the learning potential of many poor children, while maintaining that their genetic potential was not different from that of the socially favored class.

At the end of the 1960's the oldest argument of all to explain differential functioning was renewed—the argument based on genetic differences in capacity for complex cognitive processes among different ethnic groups.

This view in a sense dismisses all of the arguments above as efforts to explain away the data and as symptomatic of a refusal to deal with the simplest explanation for these data: that some social or ethnic groups of children within the society are indeed less able to function in the current school situation. Ultimately, those who hold this view come to the conclusion that differences in intellectual capacity or academic potential are based on race. This view, long argued by Garrett (1960) and some educators and politicians in the southern United States, was advanced anew as the 1960's closed by Jensen (1969) and Shockley (1965).

Obviously, because the data reviewed in this article come from surveys and are primarily descriptive rather than experimental in nature, they cannot be used to test the validity of any of the explanations. All these data support each theoretical position since the data do provide a need for a theory explaining retardation. Jensen, however, argues that in addition to explaining retardation, any theory must also satisfactorily explain what he refers to as the failure of compensatory programs whether at the early childhood level or later in the school sequence. He argues that programs such as Head Start or the variety of school programs funded under Title I of the Elementary and Secondary Education Act essentially sought to implement the social-environmental or school situational arguments and by "failing" have in essence provided evidence of the lack of validity of these arguments.

Of course, even if Jensen's argument is true it would not dismiss the alternative physiological argument based not on genetic differences but on those factors in the life space of the pregnant woman who is poor which directly affect her child from the moment he is conceived and after he is born. Nor would it dismiss the argument of the serious critics of the schools who claim that Title I and Title III programs have not involved any change in the power structure of the urban school but simply have meant giving the same people who have not educated the children of the poor during the regular school day and year additional funds so they can fail for longer days and during the summer as well.

Critical to recognize, however, are two false assumptions of those who have dismissed compensatory education as a failure. The first assumption is that the programs have existed long enough for change to take place. The second and more serious assumption is that these have been "programs" in any true educational sense and so represent a valid test of the possible impact of truly remedial and compensatory education. Report after report which cites data indicating no effect also cites the lack of time for program planning, the lack of time or effort to train or retrain teachers, the lack of materials and curricula developed for the "new" programs, and the delayed start of programs owing to procrastination in funding.

The school achievement of the urban child of black, Puerto Rican, Mexican, or disadvantaged background is the focus of a growing debate. The danger is that the introduction of the genetic argument will make the 1970's a decade of ever-hardening positions and of studies and efforts to prove or disprove the obvious rather than a decade of serious inquiry into the explanations and the development of successful remedies.

BIBLIOGRAPHY

ANDERSON, WILLIAM F., JR. 1956 "Instructional Problems of Integration." *Phi Delta Kappan*, 37, no. 8:353–359.

BADAL, ALDEN W. 1968 *Evaluation Report: ESEA Program of Compensatory Education.* Oakland, Calif., Research Department, Oakland Public Schools.

BERNSTEIN, BASIL 1961 "Social Structure, Language and Learning." *Educational Research*, 3:163–176.

BIGART, HOMER 1968 "Ferguson Gives Plan for Schools." New York *Times*, March 14, 1968, p. 36.

BIRMINGHAM PUBLIC SCHOOLS 1967 *Evaluation Title I Program, 1966–67 School Year.* Birmingham, Ala., Board of Education.

BOSTON PUBLIC SCHOOLS 1967 *Annual Title I Report: P.L. 89–10.* Boston, Board of Education.

BOYLES, MARION, JESS ELLIOTT, AND VERA TRELAND 1967 *1966–67 Evaluation Report.* Atlanta Public Schools.

BRAZZIEL, WILLIAM F., AND MARGARET GORDON 1963 "Replications of Some Aspects of the Higher Horizons Program in a Southern Junior High School." *Journal of Negro Education*, 32, no. 2:107–113.

CHARLES, C. M. 1964 "Bicultural Children and Science Achievement." *Science Education*, 48, no. 2:93–96.

CHATTANOOGA PUBLIC SCHOOLS 1967 *Evaluation Report, Title I 1966–67: Strengthening Basic Communication and Mathematics Skills.* Chattanooga, Tenn., The Public Schools.

CLARK, KENNETH 1965 *Dark Ghetto: Dilemma of Social Power.* New York, Harper.

COLEMAN, JAMES, et al. 1966 *Equality of Educational Opportunity.* Washington, D.C., Government Printing Office.

COLES, ROBERT 1967 *Children of Crisis: A Study of Courage and Fear.* Boston, Atlantic–Little, Brown.

COOPER, BERNICE 1964 "An Analysis of the Reading Achievement of White and Negro Pupils in Certain Public Schools of Georgia." *School Review*, 72, no. 4:462–471.

DELAVAN, FRANK, AND MORRISON C. ENGLAND 1966 *Evaluation of ESEA Programs and Services for the Educationally Disadvantaged*. ED 013 128. Sacramento, Calif., Sacramento City Unified School District.

DEUTSCH, MARTIN 1960 *Minority Group and Class Status as Related to Social and Personality Factors in Scholastic Achievement*. Monograph No. 2. New York, Society for Applied Anthropology.

DOWNING, GERTRUDE L., et al. 1965 *The Preparation of Teachers for Schools in Culturally Deprived Neighborhoods*. (The Bridge Project.) New York, Queens College, City University of New York.

DRESSLER, FRANK J. 1967 *Study of Achievement in Reading of Pupils Transferred From Schools 15 and 37 to Peripheral Schools to Eliminate Overcrowding, to Abandon an Obsolete School and to Achieve a More Desirable Racial Balance in City Schools*. Buffalo, Division of Curriculum Evaluation and Development, Buffalo Public Schools.

DUVALL COUNTY PUBLIC SCHOOLS 1967 *Evaluation Title I Program, 1966–67*. Jacksonville, Fla., Duvall County Board of Public Instruction.

FLORIDA STATE DEPARTMENT OF EDUCATION 1967 *Title I Evaluation Forms, 1966–67*. Tallahassee, Fla., The Department.

FOX, DAVID J. 1967 *Expansion of the Free Choice Open Enrollment Program*. New York, Center for Urban Education.

FOX, DAVID J., et al. 1968 *More Effective Schools Program*. New York, Center for Urban Education.

FRANKEL, EDWARD 1967 *Grade Reorganization Preparatory to the Establishment of the Four Year Comprehensive High School*. New York, Center for Urban Education.

GARRETT, HENRY E. 1960 "Klineberg's Chapter on Race and Psychology." *Mankind Quarterly*, 1:15–22.

GOLDBERG, MIRIAM 1967 "Factors Affecting Educational Attainment in Depressed Urban Areas." A. Harry Passow, Miriam Goldberg, and Abraham J. Tannenbaum, eds., *Education of the Disadvantaged*. New York, Holt. Pages 31–61.

GOODMAN, SAMUEL M., LORRAINE K. DIAMOND, AND DAVID J. FOX 1956 *Who Are the Puerto Rican Pupils in the New York City Public Schools?* Puerto Rican Study Research Report. New York City, Board of Education.

HANSEN, CARL F. 1960 "The Scholastic Performances of Negro and White Pupils in the Integrated Public Schools of the District of Columbia." *Harvard Educational Review*, 30, no. 3:216–236.

HARRIS, ALBERT J., et al. 1968 *Continuation of the CRAFT Project: Comparing Reading Approaches With Disadvantaged Urban Negro Children in Primary Grades*. ED 020 297, BR–5–0570. New York, Division of Teacher Education, City University of New York.

HARRIS, JOHN H. 1967 *A Program of Compensatory Efforts for the Educationally and Culturally Deprived of Metropolitan Nashville–Davidson County*. Nashville, Metropolitan Schools.

HARYOU (HARLEM YOUTH OPPORTUNITIES UNLIMITED) 1964 *Youth in the Ghetto: A Study of the Consequences of Powerlessness and a Blueprint for Change*. New York, HARYOU.

HATCHETT, JOHN F. 1967 "A Study in Educational Perfidy." *Afro-American Teachers Forum*, November-December 1967.

HENTON, COMRADGE L., AND EDWARD E. JOHNSON 1964 *The Relationship Between Self-concepts of Negro Elementary-school Children and Their Academic Achievement, Intelligence, Interests and Manifest Anxiety*. Cooperative Research Project No. 1592, ED 00 32 88. Washington, D.C., U.S. Office of Education.

HOLT, JOHN 1964 *How Children Fail*. New York, Pitman.

HUNT, J. McV. 1961 *Intelligence and Experience*. New York, Ronald Press.

INDIANA STATE DEPARTMENT OF PUBLIC INSTRUCTION 1967 *1966–67 Title I Annual Report*. Part A. Indianapolis, The Department.

JENSEN, ARTHUR 1969 "How Much Can We Boost I.Q. and Scholastic Achievement?" *Harvard Educational Review*, 39:1–123.

JONSSON, HAROLD A. 1966 *ESEA Title I Project in the Berkeley Unified School District: A Short Summary of Activities and Evaluation for the Spring Semester 1966*. Berkeley, Calif., Berkeley Unified School District.

JUSTMAN, JOSEPH 1965 *Stability of Academic Aptitude and Reading Test Scores of Mobile and Non-mobile Disadvantaged Children*. New York, Bureau of Education, Programs, Research, and Statistics, Board of Education.

KAPLAN, JOHN 1962 "New Rochelle." U.S. Commission on Civil Rights, *Civil Rights U.S.A.: Public Schools, Cities in the North and West*. Washington, D.C., The Commission. Pages 33–103.

KENNEDY, WALLACE A., VERNON VAN DE RIET, AND JAMES C. WHITE, JR. 1963 "A Normative Sample of Intelligence and Achievement of Negro Elementary School Children in the Southeastern U.S." *Monographs of the Society for Research in Child Development*, 28, no. 6, Serial No. 90.

KOHL, HERBERT 1967 *36 Children*. New York, New American Library.

KOZOL, JONATHAN 1967 *Death at an Early Age: The Destruction of the Hearts and Minds of Negro Children in the Boston Public Schools*. Boston, Houghton Mifflin.

LEVINE, DANIEL 1966 *Raising Standards in the Inner-city Schools*. Washington, D.C., Council for Basic Education.

LONG BEACH UNIFIED SCHOOL DISTRICT 1966 *Evaluation of the Compensatory Education Program, ESEA Title I*. Long Beach, Calif., The District.

MICHIGAN DEPARTMENT OF EDUCATION 1967 *Annual Data Summary and Evaluation Report, 1967*. East Lansing, Mich., Evaluation and Research Section, Bureau of Educational Services.

OSBORNE, R. T. 1960 "Racial Differences in Mental Growth and School Achievement: A Longitudinal Study." *Psychological Reports*, 7, no. 2:233–239.

PASSOW, A. HARRY 1963 "Education in Depressed Areas." A. Harry Passow, ed., *Education in Depressed Areas*. New York, Teachers College Press. Pages 332–351.

SACRAMENTO CITY UNIFIED SCHOOL DISTRICT 1967 *Evaluation of ESEA Program and Services for the Educationally Disadvantaged, 1966–67*. Sacramento, Calif., Board of Education.

ST. LOUIS 1967 *1966–67 Title I Evaluation*. St. Louis, State of Missouri.

SHOCKLEY, WILLIAM 1965 "Is the Quality of the United States Population Declining?" *U.S. News and World Report*, November 22, 1965, pp. 68–71.

STALLINGS, FRANK H. 1959 "A Study of the Immediate Effects of Integration on Scholastic Achievement in the Louisville Public Schools." *Journal of Negro Education*, 28, no. 4:439–444.

SEINHOFF, CARL R. 1967 *Improved Educational Services in Selected Special Service Elementary and Junior High Schools*. New York, Center for Urban Education.

U.S. COMMISSION ON CIVIL RIGHTS 1967a "Educational Consequences of Segregation in a California Community." *Racial Isolation in the Public Schools*. Vol. 2 of the report of the U.S. Commission on Civil Rights. Washington, D.C., The Commission. Pages 165–206.

U.S. COMMISSION ON CIVIL RIGHTS 1967b "Evaluation of Education Improvement Program, Philadelphia, Pa., and Madison Area Project, Syracuse, N.Y." *Racial Isolation in the Public Schools.* Vol. 2 of the report of the U.S. Commission on Civil. Rights. Washington, D.C., The Commission. Pages 243–252.

WRIGHTSTONE, J. WAYNE 1960 "Demonstration Guidance Project in New York City." *Harvard Educational Review*, 30, no. 3:237–251.

ZINTZ, M. 1963 *Education Across Cultures.* Dubuque, Iowa, W. C. Brown.

DAVID J. FOX and VALERIE BARNES

2. EDUCATION OF IMMIGRANTS

During the years from 1890 through 1924 the problem of assimilating the members of minority groups into cities became prominent. The groups in question were immigrants. Between 1890 and 1914, 15 million immigrants came to the United States. World War I interrupted this wave, and the immigration quotas of 1921 and 1924 brought it to a virtual halt. There had been two previous immigrant waves. The first, between 1815 and 1860, had brought 5 million immigrants, and the second, between 1860 and 1890, had brought 10 million.

The new immigrants, as those in the second group were called, came mainly from southern and eastern Europe; the first immigrants had come chiefly from northern and western Europe. The second group were the least educated, the least skilled, and the least advanced of the immigrants. Although the frontier closed in 1890, the very year that the wave got under way, conditions were ripe for this new group. Markets and resources opened up by imperialism and new and expanding industries occasioned by the revolutions in agriculture, industry, and business all combined to accelerate vastly the need for cheap labor.

The new immigrants were also the first to settle principally in the cities; with the exception of the Irish, the older immigrants tended to locate primarily inland. This fact created the necessity of accommodating in the city a large, unskilled, and poorly paid labor force. The suffering and hardship that this situation caused made for slum conditions of an unprecedented magnitude.

Americanization. "Americanization" represented the response of the nation to this problem. Conceived at first as teaching the new immigrants English and citizenship, later (particularly after World War I) it came to mean much more—the reconstruction of their social life and the improvement of their neighborhood life (Berger 1956; Cremin 1961).

The role played by the school in this Americanization effort—which is to say the relationship between the school and the new immigrants—is a largely ignored chapter in the history of school-parent relations and, more broadly, in the explication of the role of the school in American society.

An attempt to sketch that role meets with difficulty. The information upon which to draw is too often incomplete and imprecise. For example, little is known about the role of the school in the conduct of factory classes and labor union classes or about the work of home teachers. The annual reports of superintendents and school boards—practically the only primary source data on the subject—often give, for example, attendance and not enrollment figures or enrollment and not attendance figures; in some cases, they list mothers' classes separately and in other instances include them with day classes. Such barriers notwithstanding, the general outlines of school-parent relations during the period under study can be authentically sketched.

The problem of assimilating the new immigrants and the part played by the school in this process did not, of course, end in 1924; it continued, although on a diminished basis, for roughly 20 more years. It was not until after 1940 that the United States Bureau of the Census ceased to give attention to immigrant groups, thereby signaling that the process was no longer an important element in American life. Nothing happened subsequently that basically altered the outlines of that period, which includes the years during which the Americanization movement was at its zenith, 1916–1919.

Approaches. The school sought to reach the new immigrants through night or evening schools, day schools, home teachers, and the school center movement. The school also helped to conduct some fatory classes and labor union classes.

Night schools. The most important approach was the night schools. Here, typically for two hours a night for two or three days a week, the new immigrants were taught English and citizenship. The night schools were slow in getting started, however, and many cities never established any (Berger 1956; Thompson 1920). In 1914–1915, 25 years after the influx of new immigrants began, 62 percent of the cities with a foreign-born population of over 1,000 reported having no public school programs for the education of this population. Four years later, when the Americanization movement was tapering off, this situation was hardly better: 53 percent reported having no such provisions (Thompson 1920). Often, classes were conducted in places outside the school—for example, in neighborhood houses, churches, and libraries. In 1923–1924, New York City, for example, held twice as many classes in neighborhood houses as in schools, and during the same year the Massachusetts department of education reported that 968 classes were held in the school and 493 were held outside the school (New York City . . . 1914–1925; Massachusetts . . . 1926).

Day schools.   In comparison to night schools, there were few day schools. Most of these schools were set up for the convenience of the immigrant mothers who attended them; others were set up to provide schooling for working immigrants who could not attend night school.

Home teachers.   The use of home teachers never became a widespread practice. New York City, for example, although in the forefront in providing for the new immigrants and although subjected to pressure by settlement houses and the Public Education Association, never adopted the practice (Berger 1956). Practical difficulties were deterring factors—for example, the amount of time involved, unfavorable home conditions, and the immigrants' lack of receptiveness to the idea.

California pioneered in the use of home teachers with the Home-Teacher Bill of 1915, which permitted local school boards to employ one home teacher for every 500 pupils in attendance. Boards of education in all the large cities of the state took advantage of this permissive legislation. Behind it lay a motive that extended beyond Americanization—to prevent family disorganization by bridging the gap that often occurred between children and older family members as a result of the children's American education.

The nature of the attack on the problem of family disorganization and the broader meaning that Americanization came to have are captured in the following descripton of a mothers' class activity:

Visits were made by groups [of foreign-born mothers] to the Field Museum, where the films "The Chronicles of America" were shown, followed by a visit to a section of the Museum, with com-

petent guides to explain the exhibits. The Chicago Art Institute, on three separate occasions, opened Fullerton Hall for lectures by Mr. Dudley Craft Watson. The course of lectures was called "How to Know the Art Institute." On each occasion, Mr. Watson gave a stereopticon lecture to the members of our Mothers' Classes on the treasures of the Art Institute. And in each instance the lecture was followed by a visit to the galleries to find the work of art of which Mr. Watson had spoken. (Chicago . . . 1926, p. 128)

The home teachers usually held two classes a week, lasting two hours each session. The meeting place was a mother's home, a neighborhood location, or the school. Contacts were usually made through the child, the focus being on non-English-speaking mothers. The goal was to persuade the mother to attend a mothers' class.

School center movement.   The most ambitious attempt at Americanization was the school center movement (also referred to as the community center movement or the community school movement), which spanned the years between 1900 and 1924. The school became the center of neighborhood life. In these schools, a "nation-wide program for the purposeful organization of neighborhood life" was to be conducted (Glueck 1927b, p. xi). The centers, it was thought, would serve to make the new immigrants a genuine part of American life and to halt the disintegrating influences resulting from modern industrialism. The centers were also to serve as a democratizing force, not merely by bringing all groups together in cooperative living and working but also by permitting them to run the centers themselves. Self-government and self-direction were to be two of their hallmarks. Toward these ends, the school was to be the meeting place, the polling place, the employment center, the branch library, the health center, the music center, the art gallery, the gymnasium, the concert center, and the home of all formal and informal education (Berger 1956; Cremin 1961; Glueck 1927b; Ward 1915).

Although prior to 1900 many states enacted laws that permitted extended use of the school for such functions as those mentioned (the first state was Indiana, in 1859), a conscious attempt to make the school a center of community life did not occur until around 1900 (Berger 1956; Glueck 1927b). Edward J. Ward took the first step by establishing school centers in Rochester, N.Y., during the years 1907–1909. With this accomplishment, the school center movement gained momentum and peaked in 1924, by which time 32 states and the District of Columbia had enacted legislation providing for extended use of the public schools. Excluding night school, only 5 percent of the schools in Glueck's national survey (1927a) used the school as often as once a week for two types of activities or twice a week for one type of activity. Most frequently, these schools were located in rural areas. In all areas, recreation was the chief reason for their use, and only rarely were they used for some of the functions envisioned for them by those who most strongly advocated the establishment of school centers.

Factory classes. Not until the drive to improve immigrant education began in 1919 did the school come to play a significant role in the conduct of factory classes. Until that time, these classes were operated chiefly by the factories themselves, with the teaching being done for the most part by anyone declaring himself capable of the job (Leiserson 1924). After 1919 the most common arrangement was for the school to supply teachers and materials. It had been only three years earlier, when the presence of a large number of non-English-speaking workers came to be considered a danger to industry and the community, that most large industries had established factory classes in some form.

The annual reports of some school systems—for example, Cincinnati, Milwaukee, and Pittsburgh—make no mention of factory classes, however. For the 1925–1926 school year the New York City superintendent of schools reported having as few as six of these classes, while during this same year the Chicago superintendent indicated having 49 of these classes. Although figures for Boston could not be obtained for this year, the state of Massachusetts, which alone among the states financed 50 percent of the cost to the school board of factory classes, had 199 of these classes. This figure is in comparison with 866 evening schools and 523 neighborhood classes in Massachusetts. Typically, the factory classes were held before and after work, with the employer paying the worker for one-half of the time spent in class.

Labor union classes. Almost no information is available about the role of the school in the conduct of labor union classes. Annual school reports do not even mention this activity. Thompson (1920) reports that the practice did exist, indicating that the labor unions supplied the pupils and the school provided the teacher and the building. As the most successful example of this arrangement, he cites the International Ladies Garment Workers' Union in New York City, which in 1919 supplied attendance for 19 evening classes. Leiserson (1924) mentions these classes, too, but does not say anything about the role of the school in their operation.

Except for graduation exercises and, after 1920, open house night in many schools, these classes were practically the only scheduled contacts the school had with the new immigrants (Matthews 1966; Olsen 1954). The Parent-Teacher Association, which might have been expected to provide a vehicle for contact, had just been founded in 1897. In 1920 it had fewer than 200,000 members in 38 states, and although by 1926 it had over a million members in 47 states, few of these members were new immigrants. Thus, around this time, the association adopted a two-year recruitment program to attract immigrants (Hedger 1924; Reeve & Lombard 1927). There is no indication that it was successful, however.

Recruitment. Recruitment for school programs was one of the methods whereby the school sought to help assimilate the new immigrants, and it posed some important problems. In general, the new immigrants did not, on their own initiative, make contacts of any kind with the school. For example, Leonard Covello, the prominent New York City educator born of immigrant parents, confides: "In all of her years in America, my mother never saw the inside of a school. My father went only once . . ," (1958, p. 22). Speaking generally, Matthews observes that "parents learned about America from their children but their contacts with the school were almost none. . . . They paid a visit to the school only if sent for and this would ordinarily be a summons because of misconduct on the part of the child. Proximity to the school buildings made no difference" (1966, p. 312).

Devices. A wide variety of devices were employed to cope with the immigrants' lack of contact with the school, including press notices in the various tongues, notices posted in public places (printed in the various tongues), handbills, letters, notices taken home by children, notices put in payrolls, help of immigrant pastors, use of indigenous leaders, house-to-house canvassing, paid recruiters, baby-sitting services for immigrant mothers, slides in movie theaters, and word of mouth (U.S. Department of Labor . . . 1917; 1918; 1921; 1923; Farrington 1916; Hedger 1924).

City-wide recruitment campaigns were also conducted in some areas—for example, Detroit, Mich., Ansonia, Conn., Minneapolis, Minn., Johnstown, N.Y., and Wilmington, Del.—under the auspices of a variety of social, civic, and economic groups; mass meetings of interested groups (immigrant and other) were sometimes held to generate ideas and action; and, as already mentioned, some businesses set aside specific hours on certain days when the new immigrants might attend classes, sometimes paying these immigrants for the time they spent in class (Fernandez 1920; National Americanization Committee . . . 1915; Thompson 1920; U.S. Department of Labor . . . 1918; Woodward 1920).

In 1923 the Bureau of Naturalization even came out with a list of suggestions as to how to hold the interest of the new immigrants. Included among these suggestions were some that had been tried—for example, prizes for papers and debates on Americanization and public recognition of citizenship by presentation of graduation and naturalization certificates and prizes (U.S. Department of Labor . . . 1917). At least two cities, New York and Pittsburgh, socialized their evening schools, combining or alternating instruction with recreation (Thompson 1920).

Degree of success. In general, these recruitment devices were not successful. A New York City superintendent of schools, for example, confessed that the social gatherings for the new immigrants in that school system made no difference in attendance at school-sponsored programs. Even in those instances where some of these devices were comparatively successful—for example, some of the mass meetings and some of the city-wide campaigns—attendance dropped "as rapidly as it rose, with few students remaining in the school except those who came for a definitely felt need which the school was so fortunate as to discover and satisfy" (California . . . 1922a, p. 7).

The figures support this description. On the basis of his study Thompson (1920) estimates that, in the first place, with a reasonable amount of publicity, the night schools attracted only 5 to 10 percent of the non-English-speaking population (even the intensive city-wide recruitment campaign in Detroit attracted only about 5 percent of this population); and that, in the second place, once attracted, only 33 to 50 percent remained, schools in Boston, Chicago, Cleveland, Detroit,

and New York City being cases in point. Thompson's study also revealed that for every five cities that started schooling for the new immigrants, three dropped it, and for every ten classes that were started, nine were dropped—and this situation prevailed with respect to communities of all types.

A later report from Massachusetts, one of the most progressive states in its Americanization efforts, supports Thompson's account (Massachusetts . . . 1926). It stated that fewer than 3,000 of the 146,000 illiterate immigrants (those who were unable to read or write any English) were enrolled in Americanization classes and that of a total of 442,000 adult immigrants in the state, a maximum of 7 percent were registered in these classes.

The studies and reports of others (Abbott 1917; Berger 1956; Fernandez 1920; Miller 1916; U.S. Department of Labor . . . 1917) also support Thompson's findings. According to the Bureau of Naturalization (U.S. Department of Labor . . . 1917), the greatest success at Americanization occurred in places with a small foreign-born community where a "sense of personal guardianship" prevailed. Of course, the attempt to reach the Jewish immigrants was singularly successful, but this success can be attributed more to the efforts of the Jews than those of the school (National Council . . . 1921–1930; Matthews 1966).

The school centers fared no better than the night schools in reaching the new immigrants, and like the night schools and classes, these centers came and went. Although there was citizen participation in the operation of some of these centers, participation being one of the principles on which the centers were founded, that participation was not widespread and apparently did not include the new immigrants to any significant extent (Glueck 1927b). Rather than serving to bring people together, many of the centers in time came instead to be used by private groups for their own purposes (Berger 1956).

As for the use of home teachers, the practice never gained much of a foothold outside California. The reports of the California department of education (1922a; 1926) imply that in California it met with no more success as regards attendance than the day and night schools.

Enrollment and attendance. The data on enrollment and attendance at factory classes and labor union classes are no more informative. Before the school got involved in 1919, the factory classes, with their totally untrained teachers, were generally a disaster. Although the cooperation of the school made a difference, the extent to which it improved the programs is not reported in any of the available literature. Whether, at the same time, the statement of a leader of a national labor union with 175,000 members is a clue to the success of labor union classes can only be surmised. He is quoted as saying, "We are not getting all the people, but we get enough to run the classes. . . " (Leiserson 1924, p. 22). Unfortunately, the lack of data makes impossible a comparison regarding enrollment and attendance among the various Americanization activities.

Failure to reach immigrants. The explanation for the failure of the school to reach the new immigrants lies in factors related to the school and to the new immigrants.

School-related factors. On the part of the school, at least five factors were involved. First, all recruitment efforts tended to be on a hit-or-miss basis, and in many instances recruitment was not even attempted (Farrington 1916; Matthews 1966). For example, press notices were commonly printed in English, posters were infrequently used, and few cities used cooperating committees of foreigners.

Second, the new immigrants were not involved in the planning or operation of the programs. Plans were made for them, not with them (Fernandez 1920).

Third, the schools for the new immigrants were poorly organized and administered (Covello 1958; Miller 1916; Thompson 1920). Invariably, no one person was assigned this task, and therefore there existed no overall central direction.

Fourth, the instruction in the schools was poor. For years the teaching was done by nonprofessionals; gradually, day-school teachers replaced them, but the performance level of these teachers, who had been working all day, was low. To get a competent core of these teachers in the first place was difficult because of the short school terms and the limited number of evenings. Thus, the provision for instructors (as well as principals) was makeshift. The prevailing idea was that "any individual who possessed a fair knowledge of English and the vernacular of the students could successfully teach adult immigrant classes" (Sharlip & Owens, 1925, p. v.). The instructors, therefore, were generally "left to their own devices, with

the injunction to teach English and maintain classes of a satisfactory size" (Thompson 1920, p. 164).

There was no pedagogic theory as to teaching the new immigrants, and no attempt was made to individualize instruction. The same approach was used with them as with children. For example, Abbott reports that in one of the steel mills in Cleveland men were found copying "I am a yellow bird. I can sing. I can fly. I can sing to you"; in another mill they were found reading "Little drops of water, little grains of sand" (Abbott 1917, p. 242). The adult content was hardly more inspiring, as demonstrated by the tone of one of the textbooks: "In this book we shall study the organization of our government, and the work which it performs. We shall see that it is a representative government, that its welfare depends upon the interest which the citizens take in it. Do you think, then, that every new American should be familiar with the history of our country, which abounds in glorious deeds and great achievements?" (Webster 1919, p. 5).

An investigation by the Federal Bureau of Education (now the U.S. Office of Education) in 1914 revealed that a state of "chaos existed in this important phase of education" as "few established and well-approved standards existed, and practically all methods were in the experimental stage" (Wheaton 1916, p. 339). Not until 1919 was the first real drive made to rectify this situation (Thompson 1920).

Finally, the school centers were victims of one of one of the forces that had been a factor in their creation: modern industrialism. Increasing urbanization brought about increasing opportunities for new forms of leisure-time activities with which the school was not able to compete, such as the movie theater and the dance hall. Moreover, it was often difficult to recruit volunteers for the centers, and in some cases, dissension among local committees that ran the centers had a destructive influence.

External factors. Beneath these five school-related factors that help to explain the failure of the school to reach the new immigrants lay other contributing forces. One was the lack of financial support for school programs. In 1920 evening school appropriations did not exceed 1 percent of the total appropriations for all school purposes, and six years later the situation was about the same (Glueck 1927a; Thompson 1920).

Another and more inclusive force involved a mixture of philosophy and social policy. Abbott points out that "the general American attitude has in the past been that the immigrant is only a one-generation difficulty and that all we had to do was to see that the children got a good American education and then we need have no anxiety about the future of the country" (1917, p. 234). This attitude was part of an overall viewpoint about school-community relations. Although there was a time in the early history of the public school when there was a close relationship between school and neighborhood, that time passed as the state assumed increasing control over education and as the United States became increasingly industrialized. Therefore, in 1897, Alice McLellan Birney thought it necessary to start what became the National Congress of Parents and Teachers to revitalize that once close relationship (Anderson & Gores 1948; Bittner & Lombard 1923; Olsen 1954; Pierce 1950). Not until after World War I did the school itself begin to make some noticeable effort to reach the parents. The new immigrants, therefore, rather than being the beneficiaries of a community-oriented school policy, were instead a factor in its revitalization, receiving such belated proceeds as those described above.

It took outside forces, particularly federal intervention, to help extend that policy. Acting under congressional statute, in 1915 the Bureau of Naturalization began a cooperative effort with the public schools to give the Americanization attempts of these schools some organized direction based on sound pedagogic practices (U.S. Department of Labor . . . 1917). In January of the next year, under the auspices of the Federal Bureau of Education, the National Conference on Immigration and Americanization held in Philadelphia gave impetus to a change in the concept of Americanization. This change involved shifting the emphasis from mastery of English and teaching of citizenship to comprehensive training in the American way of life, a change that had been signaled three years earlier at a conference sponsored by the North American Civic League for Immigrants (Berger 1956; Cremin 1961). Through such practices as adult education and community-center programs and the efforts of such persons as Jane Addams and Lillian D. Wald, the settlement movement, which began about the same time that the new immigrant wave got under way, also greatly influenced the community policy of the school (this, incidentally, being its underlying motive).

Otherwise, the school was not standing still. Forces for change were operative from within in the form of progressive education, and the school system in general was being modified during this period. There was a rapid growth in the number of high schools; compulsory attendance and child-labor laws were enacted; enlightened provisions were made for the instruction of the handicapped; library services were extended; and the professional teacher emerged. But the school's attempt to reach the new immigrants and the nature of that attempt were less a result of the school's volition than a response to pressures and incentives from the outside (Berger 1956; Cremin 1961). It should indeed be observed that, except for the "steamer" classes, in which immigrant children were supposed to learn English rapidly, the school did little to adapt to the children's needs (Abbott 1917; Covello 1958; Matthews 1966). Hardly more could be expected of the school for the parents of these children.

Immigrant-related factors. In relation to the new immigrants themselves, there were seven factors that help to explain the failure of the schools to secure immigrants' participation in activities sponsored for them.

First, reasons of personal inconvenience kept many away—for example, overtime work, night work, illness, fatigue, change of jobs, deprivation of social life, and distance from school (Abbott 1917; Sharlip & Owens 1925; Thompson 1920). Although there were complaints about the poor instruction, less than 15 percent of the new immigrants themselves reported leaving for this reason. One survey (Abbott 1917) revealed that the reason most frequently mentioned by the immigrants for nonattendance was that the teacher did not speak their language. Although the immigrants felt that if one of their own were teaching, attendance would increase, there is nothing to indicate that this would in fact have been the case.

Second, the new immigrants were self-reliant. Through their mutual aid societies, most of them attended to their own economic and social needs (Handlin 1951; Jones 1960). A survey in Cleveland, for example, showed that the Slovenians had 72 mutual aid societies, the Bohemians 68, and the

Jews over 150 (Miller 1916). This situation minimized the need of the new immigrants to reach back to the school. Many new immigrant groups even established their own schools, although not with much success.

Third, the new immigrants lived a compartmentalized life. Each group lived in a defined section of the city. This factor, combined with their self-reliance, helped to insulate them from the world outside.

Fourth, the new immigrants were not participators. Aside from their religious life and their membership in the mutual aid societies, their participation in organized life was limited mainly to informal activities. The more organized the mutual aid societies became, the less the new immigrants participated in them (Handlin 1951).

Fifth, the new immigrants lacked a tradition of familiarity with a school system, as the school systems in their countries existed primarily to serve the upper classes (Covello 1967; Handlin 1951). Hence, they tended to look upon the school as an instrument of authority, as part of the government, which, in their minds, was "an evil to be kept at arm's length, rather than . . . an instrument lying conveniently at hand " (Jones 1960, p. 231).

Sixth, the new immigrants were not driven by utopian visions, or, for that matter, even by the anticipation of a better order. Rather, they were "pessimistic, resigned, unhopeful of changing the existing order of things" (*ibid.*). Conservatism was their sociopolitical style.

Last, there existed no school crisis or basic school problem that served to focus attention on the school and therefore on school-related concerns. Most of the immigrant children adjusted to the school, and although other school issues might have been raised to the crisis point, none was.

The school clearly was not prepared to reach out to the new immigrants, and the new immigrants were not ready to respond to the school, much less reach out to it. Nevertheless, some of the new immigrants were reached. Thompson (1920) suggests that they tended to be the very able or the very poor. In a more recent study, Matthews (1966) indicates that they were those in the upper socioeconomic strata. Greer's study (1969) of immigrants and Negroes in the public schools of New York City and Berger's study (1956) point to the same conclusion. That the

school did not, in any case, play a significant role in the assimilation of the new immigrants is the consensus of the authors of these more recent studies; the economy is given credit for being the primary impetus to assimilation. On the basis of data on 542 pupils in Boston and 478 pupils in New York City—all in English classes for immigrants—Thompson went so far as to conclude that "very few individuals get any adequate return for their time and effort, while many are actually worse off than when they began" (1920, p. 231).

Implications. Five important lessons emerge from the history of urban minority school-parent relations from 1890 to 1924. The first is one of conception. The term "school-parent relations" is commonly used to refer to the working relationship that exists between parents and school. To be sure, urban minority school-parent relations include this element, but more basic is the effort of the school to help assimilate, or Americanize, a minority group. To speak of urban minority school-parent relations, therefore, is to speak of the school as an instrument of assimilation or, more broadly, as an agent of social change. It is fundamentally this sobering conception that must guide the actions of the school in urban minority school-parent relations if these relations are to have significant consequences.

The second lesson is that, on its own initiative, the school is unlikely to be an agent of change in relation to urban minority groups. For this to occur on any noticeable scale requires pressure and incentive from the outside.

The third lesson is that, however ideally suited the school may be as an agent of change by virtue of its relationship to parents (and other citizens), it is set up not to change parents but to educate their children. To have any chance of making significant headway in reaching parents and in changing them, it must set up a separate structure for this purpose. This effort includes bringing into concert the organization, personnel, and knowledge to do the job. The task can hardly be successfully imposed upon the traditional school structure.

The fourth lesson is that a school-parent relations program aimed at low-income minority groups faces certain structural barriers created by cultural patterns and by social class and class-related attributes. Indeed, one of the most striking facts is that the reasons given for the failure of the new immigrants to respond to school initiatives are the same in most instances as the reasons which are advanced today for the failure of low-income minority groups to respond to similar school initiatives (Rempson 1967; 1969).

The period under study clearly suggests that impersonal methods of recruitment do not work. Given the shortcomings of the efforts of the school, however, it leaves unresolved the questions of whether more personal methods will be more successful and whether providing these groups educational experiences will, in itself, make much of a difference. However, to the extent that this period provides a guide, it shows that the school, given its traditional structure and resources, is not likely to crack the structural barriers that stand between it and low-income minority groups.

From this conclusion, the fifth and final lesson follows: given the resources of the schools and the limits imposed upon them by public expectations and support, to ask the school to play a dominant role in the assimilation of a low-income minority group population is asking it to do more than can realistically be expected. The answer to just what role the school can reasonably be expected to play in this process must be sought as much in the experiences of the present as in those of the past.

BIBLIOGRAPHY

ABBOTT, GRACE 1917 *The Immigrant and the Community.* New York, Century.

ANDERSON, HOMER V., AND HAROLD B. GORES 1948 "The School as a Recreative Center." *School Executive*, 67, no. 10:45–56.

BERGER, MORRIS I. 1956 "The Settlement, the Immigrant and the Public School: A Study of the Influence of the Settlement Movement and the New Migration Upon Public Education, 1890–1924." Ph.D. dissertation. New York, Teachers College.

BITTNER, WALTON S., AND ELLEN C. LOMBARD 1923 *Parent-Teacher Associations.* U.S. Department of the Interior, Bureau of Education, Home Education Circular No. 3. Washington, D.C., Government Printing Office.

CALIFORNIA. DEPARTMENT OF EDUCATION 1922a *Immigrant Education Manual.* Bulletin No. 5A. Sacramento, The Department.

CALIFORNIA. DEPARTMENT OF EDUCATION 1922b *Thirtieth Biennial Report of the Superintendent of Public Instruction for the School Years Ending June 30, 1921, and June 30, 1922.* Sacramento, The Department.

CALIFORNIA. DEPARTMENT OF EDUCATION 1926 *Thirty-second Biennial Report of the Superintendent of Public Instruction for the School Years Ending June 30, 1925, and June 30, 1926.* Sacramento, The Department.

CALIFORNIA. DEPARTMENT OF EDUCATION 1932 *Handbook for Home Teachers.* Bulletin No. 20. Sacramento, The Department.

CASTLE, A. W. 1939 *Home Classes for Foreign-born Mothers.* Bulletin 295. Harrisburg, Pa., Department of Public Instruction.

CHICAGO. SUPERINTENDENT OF SCHOOLS 1926 *Annual Report of the Superintendent of Schools.* Chicago, Board of Education.

COVELLO, LEONARD 1958 *The Heart Is the Teacher.* New York, McGraw-Hill.

COVELLO, LEONARD 1967 *The Social Background of the Italo-American School Child.* Leiden, Netherlands, E. J. Brill.

CREMIN, LAWRENCE A. 1961 *The Transformation of the School: Progressivism in American Education, 1876–1957.* New York, Knopf.

DEWEY, JOHN 1902 "The School as a Social Center." *Elementary School Teacher*, 3, no. 2:79.

DEWEY, JOHN 1962 "The School as a Social Settlement." John Dewey and Evelyn Dewey, *Schools of Tomorrow.* New York, Dutton. Pages 205–228.

EPSTEIN, MAX 1930 "A Comparative Study of the Intelligence of Children of Foreign Parentage." M.A. thesis. New York, Teachers College.

FARRINGTON, FREDERIC E. 1916 *Public Facilities for Educating the Alien.* U.S. Department of the Interior, Bureau of Education, Bulletin 1916, No. 18. Washington, D.C., Government Printing Office.

FERNANDEZ, ALICE B. 1920 *The Problem of Adult Education in Passaic, New Jersey.* U.S. Department of the Interior, Bureau of Education, Bulletin 1920, No. 4. Washington, D.C., Government Printing Office.

GLUECK, ELEANOR T. 1927a *Extended Use of School Buildings.* U.S. Department of the Interior, Bureau of Education, Bulletin 1927, No. 5. Washington, D.C., Government Printing Office.

GLUECK, ELEANOR T. 1927b *The Community Use of Schools.* Baltimore, Williams & Wilkins.

GREER, COLIN 1969 "Immigrants, Negroes and the Public Schools." *Urban Review*, 3, no. 3:9–12.

HANDLIN, OSCAR 1951 *The Uprooted.* New York, Grosset & Dunlap.

HANDLIN, OSCAR 1962 *The Newcomers.* Garden City, N.Y., Doubleday.

HEDGER, CAROLINE 1924 *Parent-Teacher Associations and Foreign-born Women.* U.S. Department of the Interior, Bureau of Education, Home Education Circular No. 5. Washington, D.C., Government Printing Office.

"Interview With Leonard Covello" 1969 *Urban Review*, 3, no. 3:13–19.

JONES, MALDWYN A. 1960 *American Immigration.* University of Chicago Press.

LAWS, GERTRUDE 1935 *Public Schools and Parent Education.* California, Department of Education, Bulletin No. 22. Sacramento, The Department.

LEISERSON, WILLIAM M. 1924 *Adjusting Immigrant and Industry.* New York, Harper.

MASSACHUSETTS. DEPARTMENT OF EDUCATION 1926 *Annual Report for the Year Ending November 30, 1926.* Parts 1 & 2, Document No. 2. Boston, The Department.

MATTHEWS, SISTER MARY F. 1966 "The Role of the Public School in the Assimilation of the Italian Immigrant Child in New York City, 1900–1914." Ph.D. dissertation. New York, Fordham University.

McCARTHY, JESSIE H. 1917 *Where Garments and Americans Are Made: Story of Sicher System of Factory Education for Americanization of Foreigners.* New York, Writers Publishing.

MILLER, HERBERT A. 1916 *The School and the Immigrant.* Cleveland Foundation Survey Committee.

NATIONAL AMERICANIZATION COMMITTEE AND THE COMMITTEE FOR IMMIGRANTS IN AMERICA 1915 *Americanizing a City: The Campaign for the Detroit Night Schools.* Conducted by the Detroit Board of Education. New York, The Committees.

NATIONAL COUNCIL OF JEWISH WOMEN 1921–1930 *The Immigrant,* vols. 1–10.

NEW YORK CITY. BOARD OF EDUCATION 1914–1925 Annual Reports of the Superintendent of Schools. New York, The Board.

NEW YORK CITY. BOARD OF EDUCATION 1948 *The First Fifty Years: A Brief Review of Progress, 1898–1948.* Fiftieth annual report of the superintendent of schools. New York, The Board.

OLSEN, EDWARD G., ed. 1954 *School and Community.* 2nd ed. Englewood Cliffs, N.J., Prentice-Hall.

PIERCE, TRUMAN M. 1950 "The Growing Trend Toward Lay Participation in Education." *Peabody Journal of Education,* 28, no. 3:161–166.

REEVE, MARGARETTA W., AND ELLEN C. LOMBARD 1927 *The Parent-Teacher Associations, 1924–1926.* U.S. Department of the Interior, Bureau of Education, Bulletin 1927, No. 11. Washington, D.C., Government Printing Office.

REMPSON, JOE L. 1967 "School-Parent Programs in Depressed Urban Neighborhoods." Robert A. Dentler, Bernard Mackler, and Mary E. Warshauer, eds., *The Urban R's: Race Relations as the Problem in Urban Education.* New York, published for the Center for Urban Education by Praeger. Pages 130–157.

REMPSON, JOE L. 1969 "An Exploratory Study to Help Increase the Number of Parents Who Make In-school Contacts in Low-income Urban Area Public Elementary Schools." Ed.D. dissertation. New York, Teachers College.

SHARLIP, WILLIAM, AND ALBERT A. OWENS 1925 *Adult Immigration Education.* New York, Macmillan.

THOMPSON, FRANK V. 1920 *Schooling of the Immigrant.* New York, Harper.

U.S. DEPARTMENT OF LABOR. BUREAU OF NATURALIZATION 1917 *The Work of the Public Schools With the Bureau of Naturalization.* Washington, D.C., Government Printing Office.

U.S. DEPARTMENT OF LABOR. BUREAU OF NATURALIZATION 1918 *Second Year of the Work of the Public Schools With the Bureau of Naturalization.* By Raymond F. Crist. Washington, D.C., Government Printing Office.

U.S. DEPARTMENT OF LABOR. BUREAU OF NATURALIZATION 1921 *Suggestions for Americanization Work Among Foreign-born Women.* Washington, D.C., Government Printing Office.

U.S. DEPARTMENT OF LABOR. BUREAU OF NATURALIZATION 1923 *Suggestions for Securing and Holding Attendance of Foreign-born Adults Upon Public School English and Citizenship Classes.* Washington, D. C., Government Printing Office.

U.S. IMMIGRATION COMMISSION 1911 *Abstract of the Report on the Children of Immigrants in Schools.* Washington, D.C., Government Printing Office.

WARD, EDWARD J. 1915 *The Social Center.* New York, Appleton.

WEBSTER, HANSON H. 1919 *Americanization and Citizenship.* Boston, Houghton Mifflin.

WETMORE, FRANCES K. 1920 "Industrial Classes." *Training Teachers for Americanization.* By John J. Mahoney. U.S. Department of the Interior, Bureau of Education, Bulletin 1920, No. 12. Washington, D.C., Government Printing Office. Pages 43–48.

WHEATON, H. H. 1916 *Establishing Fundamental Standards in the Education of Immigrants.* U.S. Department of the Interior, Bureau of Education. Washington, D.C., Government Printing Office.

WINKLER, HELEN, AND ELSA ALSBERG 1920 "Home and Neighborhood Classes." *Training Teachers for Americanization.* By John J. Mahoney. U.S Department of the Interior, Bureau of Education, Bulletin 1920, No. 12. Washington, D.C., Government Printing Office. Pages 49–58.

WOODWARD, ELIZABETH A. 1920 *Report on Elementary Education of Non-English-speaking Adults: Survey and Tendencies of Work, 1919–1921.* Washington, D.C., National Education Association, Commission on Revision of Elementary Education.

JOE L. REMPSON

URBAN SCHOOLS

1. ORGANIZATION

The organization of urban schools in the United States is largely an institutional response to the particular needs of a large, diversified population. The school structure is fundamentally a product of American political institutions and ideology. Traditionally, education has been viewed as a state and local function. Although schools operate within the context of a local governmental structure, the independence of school administration is a strong tradition in the United States.

City school systems may have the special legal status of completely independent government organizations or, in some instances, may be semiautonomous administrative structures under their state governments. Every city school system is administratively independent of the city governmental structure and operates under a board of education which is usually elected but sometimes appointed to office. Those city systems which have complete independence are often referred to as fiscally independent districts. The power to collect taxes and spend its own funds distinguishes the fiscally independent district from the dependent one. In the less common dependent district, city and state funds are allocated to meet costs. Appropriations by the city may be made in a lump sum, as in New York City, or on the basis of predetermined costs, as in Philadelphia. Under the latter procedure, controls exercised by the city government over the schools can be much greater.

Most observers have generally assumed that fiscal independence gives the school system a greater degree of autonomy and lessens its dependence on the city government. Some studies indicate, however, that fiscal independence does not necessarily result in separation from the politics of the city (James et al. 1966; Gittell & Hollander 1968). The pressure for increased financial support and the constant need for voter approval of tax increases often require school district leaders to work directly with city officials. The financial independence supposed to result from organizational independence is also questionable, since independent districts generally suffer a loss of state aid (Gittell & Hollander 1968). Nevertheless, the great majority of cities whose school populations are greater than 100,000 have independent school districts.

The state and the city. Although the extent of direct state involvement in the affairs of city school districts varies from state to state, state education departments are generally concerned with setting broad educational and teaching standards. They are also very much involved in the distribution of state aid for educational purposes. Almost all states, particularly those with large urban populations, increased their allocation of funds to local school districts during the 1950's and 1960's, and state aid has become an increasingly important source of support for city school districts. However, special state concern with the problems of urban education only began to emerge in the late 1960's. As of 1970 most state education departments did not yet have divisions for urban education. Legislative antagonism and insensitivity toward city needs have contributed considerably to creating a reserved attitude in state departments of education toward the special circumstances of city school districts.

The informal contact between professional educators employed by the state and the city is an important source of assistance to both. Through their cooperative efforts state policy has been influenced by and sensitized to urban needs in several states. For the most part, however, large cities exercise a very limited role in the development of state educational policy (Masters et al. 1964; Usdan 1963). State aid formulas often reflect this lack of urban influence in the disproportionately low distribution of state funds for education to large city school systems.

The mayor. Regardless of whether or not a district is fiscally independent of the city government, certain relationships between cities and school districts continue to be relevant to the urban school structure. Mayors, for example, as the chief elected city executives, are often held responsible for school policy, even though they may have only limited authority over it. In dependent districts the mayor's role is more direct than in independent ones, because he determines to a considerable extent the share of city revenue to be allocated for educational purposes. The mayor is greatly influenced in his evaluation of educational needs by the professional educators and the school board; he must, however, set priorities in consideration of total city needs. Educational expenditures constitute the largest share of city budgets.

Negotiations on teachers' salaries in several both fiscally independent and dependent cities have directly involved their mayors, particularly in the final stages of settlement. Otherwise, most mayors have been careful to remove themselves as much as possible from educational matters. The tradition of school independence is rather carefully observed for fear of political reprisals by the voters and accusations of interference from the professionals. On school integration issues civic groups in several cities have attempted to involve their mayors in school integration issues, most often, however, without success (Gittell & Hollander 1968). Generally the mayors suggest that such matters must be determined by professional educators or school officers.

The boards of education. The board of education is the policy-making body for every urban school district. The method of selecting the school board is directly related to its status. Almost all fiscally independent districts elect school board members, generally in off-year, nonpartisan elections, and members are most often elected at large rather than by wards. A number of dependent school districts, particularly in the larger cities, have appointed school boards. In such cities the mayor usually appoints members of the board for a term overlapping his own. In the 1960's the appointment procedure in three large cities (New York City, Chicago, and Philadelphia) was modified by the provision for a selection panel to recommend to the mayor possible candidates for membership on the school board. This procedure was intended to reduce political influence.

The board of education's independence of the

city government is in keeping with the strong tradition of separating education from all other city functions and of keeping it apolitical. Periodically, recommendations emerge, particularly from academic sources (Henry & Kerwin 1938; Eliot 1960), to abolish the boards and establish education as a division or department of city government under the mayor. These suggestions have always been short-lived, however, because of strong opposition from several areas, especially from the professional educators in the system.

In the United States the board of education usually has from six to 15 members. For the most part, the members of the board of education are recruited from the middle and upper classes and are recognized community leaders who have established some prior role in educational circles. According to a study by the U.S. Office of Education, boards of education largely include professionals (such as doctors and lawyers) and business-management people (White 1962). Seldom are board members blue-collar workers, teachers, small businessmen, or lower-management people. Most boards include some minority group representation, and the average age of members is generally over 50. Board members are unsalaried and assume their positions as a civic responsibility. However, in some instances board membership can be a stepping-stone to other political offices.

As the chief policy-making organ of the school system, the school board must meet regularly to determine guidelines for the administrative staff. Because it seldom has a large staff directly and wholly responsible to it, the board must rely on the superintendent and other school professionals for most of its information and recommendations. Any weakness or ineffectuality of the board of education is often attributed to this lack of staff and to the limited time board members can devote to school affairs because of their part-time, unsalaried status. The strength of school boards varies from city to city and may be related directly to the character of leadership on the board itself. One author, himself a board member, noted the frustrations school board members experience in the face of overwhelming problems and a lack of time and resources (Pois 1964). Often, the school board will be sensitive to and caught up in day-to-day administrative problems and eschew long-range policy issues.

The great dependence of boards of education on the superintendent of schools makes his appointment one of their key functions. Their other major concerns are budgetary and financial policies, especially in the fiscally independent districts. Personnel matters are yet another aspect of school decision-making on which boards must focus considerable attention.

Superintendent and administrative structure. The increased size evident in large-city school systems and the growing specialization of labor within them have steadily complicated the role of the chief school administrative officer, generally referred to as the superintendent of schools. Until the beginning of the twentieth century, the office of superintendent in many cities was shared by two officials appointed separately by the board of education—a business manager, who usually had the upper hand, and a school administrator. Their tasks were divided according to their titles, and the distinction in their roles was the source of divided authority and conflict (Cronin 1965). Administrative reorganization in most cities has since revised that structure, establishing a single chief administrator to whom all staff members are responsible.

The superintendent generally has advanced academic credentials in education and considerable training and experience in school administration. In the urban school structure increasing staff size, professionalism, and centralization have resulted in a sizable headquarters staff operating under the superintendent. The superintendent is hired by the board of education under a contract, generally for a four-year to six-year period. In many of the larger cities the superintendent has risen within that city's school system. In the 1960's there was some tendency to go outside the local system to fill the superintendent's office, but there remains strong, internal pressure to appoint a superintendent familiar with the local structure.

Some authors have noted the precariousness of the superintendent's job in large cities and have suggested that his average length of tenure is diminishing (Talbott 1966). The rather sensitive issues which have developed as a result of the vast changes in city population and of the pressing educational needs in urban areas are part of the mounting pressure on the superintendent. Educational failures are often attributed to him, a fact which probably explains his shorter term in office.

The administrative structure of the urban school system has increased in size and complexity over the years, thus greatly enlarging the scope of the superintendent's responsibilities. The student population, however, has not expanded in proportion to the significant increase in all types of specialized personnel (Gittell & Hollander 1968).

The establishment of rather strict merit and seniority systems has restricted the administrative discretion of the superintendent. Often he cannot choose his own administrative assistants and personal staff and must reply on people who have risen within the system. In most urban school districts the administrative hierarchy comes from the teaching ranks. Principals and assistant principals, who are the administrators of individual schools, must be experienced teachers and are promoted by examination. Oral and written examinations are often required by school regulations. Movement beyond the school to district headquarters is based either on a further required examination or on experience as a school administrator. This procedure closes off the system to outsiders and administrators of noneducational institutions. Headquarters staff members are generally experienced field personnel who have been promoted into their positions. Even in the more specialized areas—such as budgeting, public relations, and personnel—staff members must rise through the teaching and administrative ranks. This procedure generally excludes people from other school systems from these jobs and binds the superintendent to an in-house staff.

The larger the school system, the more likely it is to have a complex headquarters structure. Generally, there are certain key divisions in the central staff: secondary and elementary school needs are usually handled separately, and the central organization also contains special education, budgeting, planning, and major curriculum subdivisions. Programs for audiovisual aids and school guidance are found in almost every school headquarters operation. Since increasing federal aid has been given for special programs, project directors and staffs have been established at central offices to coordinate them.

A city school system may have from three to 60 assistant superintendents in charge of its major divisions, which vary according to the size of the city and the extent of its bureaucracy. Most urban school systems have become highly professionally oriented; specialists in many areas of education serve as directors or supervisors of headquarters staff in their particular areas. These specialists form policy for the system as a whole, and their policy decisions are implemented through headquarters directives to school principals and regional staff. In some cities curriculum coordinators serve as two-way liaisons between the central headquarters and the schools. All central headquarters operations are administratively under the superintendent, who is responsible for the performance of the entire administrative staff and of each school in his district.

In some of the larger cities, only a few or as many as 30 regional districts may exist; to avoid overcentralization, district or field superintendents are appointed to supervise these regions. In some cities, field administrators operate from headquarters; in others, local field offices and staffs have been set up. Mounting concern with the alleged unresponsiveness of headquarters staff in many cities has resulted in the delegation of increased discretion in decision-making to regional field administrators. Generally, however, headquarters personnel retain strong controls over citywide policy, and limited policy-making power is delegated to local field administrators.

The superintendent is responsible for implementing all school policy for the school district (National Education Association . . . 1965). With the help of his headquarters and field staffs he must develop priorities, recommend broad policies to the board of education, and make short-range decisions regarding curriculum standards, pupil policy, and personnel policy. Superintendents are increasingly required to play a strong public relations role. Many superintendents in large cities appear regularly on television and radio and are subject to the public's and teachers' protests and demonstrations on major issues. Another part of the superintendent's job is the effective management of a large amount of public funds, since school costs are the largest single item of local expenditure in every city.

The principal. The administration of the individual school is the responsibility of the principal and his assistants. Although the principal's discretion may be circumscribed by a centrally prepared curriculum plan or by preestablished budget and personnel procedures, he is immediately responsible for the operation of his school and the actual educational process. He is also the immediate liaison with the school's constituency—parents, children, and teachers. Principals in an average city elementary school are responsible for about 300 to 500 students, 15 to 30 teachers, and additional special personnel. Secondary schools may be double or triple in size. Assigned by headquarters to a particular school, principals in most cities do not have legal tenure; however, they rarely are removed from their job or rank. In cities whose principals do have tenure, they are protected by the usual provisions of tenure law which limit dismissal to proven misconduct in office.

The principal is viewed by many as a key figure in school administration because he can set the tone and general character of the school. Moreover, even within the limits of central controls, individual principals may be more or less innovative in their attempts to strengthen the educational experience. Too often, however, promotion to higher administrative rank may depend upon running a tight ship and making as little trouble for the headquarters staff as possible.

Supervisory staffs in several cities are organized into professional associations, often by school level and rank. Their primary interest is to protect their members' status and salaries, but their concern with maintaining sound educational standards is growing. These associations are participants in policy-making through their public statements and the pressure they put directly on the board of education and on city and state officials.

Teachers. Teachers constitute the largest body of school personnel in any urban school structure. Requirements for teaching certification vary in different cities from an examination to an approved college program in education. State requirements are often used, and most systems require practice teaching and a college degree for a regular teaching license. Because of the shortage of teachers in some areas, however, these requirements are sometimes reduced for substitute or temporary teaching status. In some urban areas, teachers with temporary licenses constitute a majority or close to a majority of the staff. Civil service laws in most states and cities establish minimum hiring standards and protection against unfair firing practices.

Teacher organizations and unions proliferated during the 1960's and have now emerged as a significant influence in school affairs. Union leaders are important participants in school policy-making, and the union contract is one of the more important documents of school policy, particularly in the areas of working conditions,

salaries, and fringe benefits. Priorities for the allocation of school funds are greatly influenced by the settlement of salary levels made with the teachers. In several of the larger cities, unions and other teacher organizations have been directly involved in other areas of school policy, often with the result that provisions concerning educational practices become an integral part of the contract arrangement. Such matters as team teaching, class size, and compensatory educational programs have become issues for negotiations. The American Federation of Teachers, for example, adopted a national policy favoring the More Effective Schools program (a compensatory education program initiated by the United Federation of Teachers in New York City) and has sought its adoption in several cities. Teacher organizations and unions have worked with school administrators on problems of recruitment and training as well. In some cities the union has shared directly in the campaign for teacher recruitment.

Educational interest groups. In addition to the formal school organization in urban communities, some informal participants are important in school policy-making. Specialized educational interest groups function in every urban area and may have small professional staffs to carry on a large part of their role. They usually consist of reform-oriented citizens who watch over the school system on a citywide basis. Often these groups are supportive of the system and serve to help in securing more funds for school purposes. They are seldom critical of the total system but may attack a particular program or encourage adoption of a new approach or project. Boards of education, superintendents, and school administrators are usually in close contact with these groups.

The parent associations in each school are an important part of the individual school program. Their power as reported by most research is quite limited (Campbell et al. 1965), but they do reinforce the system and its efforts. Their interest in the local school and its structure and their particular concerns with their own children's educational needs determine to a large extent the focus of their energies.

The decision of the Supreme Court in 1954 on *Brown* v. *Board of Education of Topeka*, which called for school desegregation, stimulated civil rights and local ad hoc groups in urban areas to become increasingly involved in educational issues. In fact, many school systems have established human relations divisions to cope with increasing pressures in this area. Civil rights groups have largely concerned themselves with the integration issue, but they are also directly involved in matters related to minority groups and compensatory educational needs. Prior to the 1954 Supreme Court decision, school decision-making power was rather closely held by the professionals, particularly those at district headquarters. Currently, there is greater responsiveness to pressures for opening channels of communication to community groups, and several school systems have encouraged the creation of citizen committees and community participation in certain aspects of decision-making.

Trends. The most significant trend in urban school reorganization, particularly in the larger cities, is the movement toward greater decentralization and increased community participation. This movement was an outgrowth of the 1954 Supreme Court decision (*Brown* v. *Topeka*). Civil rights groups took up the challenge of integration and exposed the great inequities in city schools, focusing on the lack of adequate programs and facilities in the ghetto communities. The general failure of subsequent integration efforts as well as of compensatory educational programs indicated the inadequacy of the urban school structure and its insulation from community interests and demands. Several studies of urban school systems identified obsolete procedures, poor recruitment methods, and overcentralization as causes of educational failure (Gittell & Hollander 1968; Havighurst 1964).

In the 1960's many educators thought little could be accomplished with special programs without revision of the total school structure. Consequently, reformers and, particularly, ghetto groups began pressing for school reorganization in several large cities. The pressure is now toward a more equitable balancing of community and professional roles. Most reform plans call for an increased role for the local community through the election of local school boards and the delegation of personnel, budget, and curriculum powers to these boards. In several states legislation has been introduced to provide for city action on school problems; in other states more specific legislation calling for restructuring of city school systems has been recommended. These efforts are likely to be expanded in coming years, and the largest city school districts will probably become more decentralized. The extent of community control granted to local boards may vary, but they certainly will be given an increasingly direct role in educational policy-making.

Many educators believe that conflicts between professional teachers and urban residents will decrease as urban school systems become decentralized. Reformers hope that once urban parents can formally express their interest in the schools through elected boards with some measure of power, urban public school systems will be revitalized. Moreover, the educator, who now often sees himself as the public's adversary, may enhance his professionalism when he is more accountable to the public he serves. The overall impact of decentralization and community control, therefore, is expected to be the formation of a greater number of reform-minded public school policies.

BIBLIOGRAPHY

BERUBE, MAURICE R., AND MARILYN GITTELL, eds. 1969 *Confrontation at Ocean Hill–Brownsville.* New York, Praeger.

CAMPBELL, ROALD F. 1966 "Is the School Superintendent Obsolete?" *Phi Delta Kappan,* 48, no. 2:50–58.

CAMPBELL, ROALD F., LAVERN L. CUNNINGHAM, AND RODERICK F. McPHEE 1965 *The Organization and Control of American Schools.* Columbus, Ohio, Merrill.

CHANDLER, BOBBY JOE, LINDLEY J. STILES, AND JOHN I. KITSUSE 1962 *Education in Urban Society.* New York, Dodd, Mead.

CRAIN, ROBERT L. 1968 *The Politics of School Desegregation: Comparative Case Studies of Community Structure and Policy-making.* Chicago, Aldine.

CRONIN, JOSEPH M. 1965 "The Board of Education in the 'Great Cities,' 1890–1964." Ed.D. dissertation. Palo Alto, Calif., Stanford University.

ELIOT, THOMAS H. 1960 "Towards an Understanding of Public School Politics." *Teachers College Record,* 62, no. 2:118–132.

FANTINI, MARIO D. 1968 In "Implementing Equal Educational Opportunity." *Harvard Educational Review,* 38, no. 1:160–175.

FANTINI, MARIO D., MARILYN GITTELL, AND RICHARD MAGAT 1970 *Community Control and the Urban School.* New York, Praeger.

GITTELL, MARILYN 1967 *Participants and Participation: A Study of School Policy in New York City.* New York, Praeger.

GITTELL, MARILYN, AND ALAN HEVESI, eds. 1969 *The Politics of Urban Education.* New York, Praeger.

GITTELL, MARILYN, AND T. EDWARD HOLLANDER 1968 *Six Urban School Districts: A Comparative Study of Institutional Response.* Praeger Special Study Series. New York, Praeger.

HAVIGHURST, ROBERT J. 1964 *The Public Schools of Chicago: A Survey.* Board of Education of the City of Chicago.

HENRY, NELSON B., AND JEROME G. KERWIN 1938 *Schools*

and City Government: A Study of School and Municipal Relationships in Cities of 50,000 or More Population. University of Chicago Press.

JAMES, HENRY THOMAS, JAMES A. KELLY, AND WALTER I. GARMS 1966 *Determinants of Educational Expenditures in Large Cities of the United States.* Stanford, Calif., Stanford University, School of Education.

LEVIN, HENRY M., ed. 1970 *Community Control of Schools.* Washington, D.C., Brookings Institution.

MASTERS, NICHOLAS A., ROBERT H. SALISBURY, AND THOMAS H. ELIOT 1964 *State Politics and the Public Schools: An Exploratory Analysis.* New York, Knopf.

MAYOR'S ADVISORY PANEL ON DECENTRALIZATION OF THE NEW YORK CITY SCHOOLS 1967 *Reconnection for Learning: A Community School System for New York City.* A report. New York, The Panel.

NATIONAL EDUCATION ASSOCIATION. EDUCATIONAL POLICIES COMMISSION 1965 *The Unique Role of the Superintendent of Schools.* Washington, D.C., The Commission.

NATIONAL EDUCATION ASSOCIATION. RESEARCH DIVISION 1961 *Administrative Practices in Urban School Districts, 1958–59.* Washington, D.C., The Association.

NATIONAL EDUCATION ASSOCIATION. RESEARCH DIVISION 1966 *Fiscal Dependence and Independence of Local School Systems.* Washington, D.C., The Association.

POIS, JOSEPH 1964 *The School Board Crisis: A Chicago Case Study.* Chicago, Educational Methods.

RUBINSTEIN, ANNETTE, ed. 1970 *Schools Against Children: The Case for Community Control.* New York, Monthly Review Press.

SMOLEY, EUGENE R. 1965 *Community Participation in Urban School Government.* Cooperative Research Project, No. S-029. Baltimore, Johns Hopkins University.

TALBOTT, ALLAN R. 1966 "Needed: A New Breed of School Superintendent." *Harper's,* 232, no. 1389:81–87.

USDAN, MICHAEL D. 1963 *The Political Power of Education in New York State.* New York, Teachers College.

WHITE, ALPHEUS L. 1959 *Characteristics of Local Board Policy Manuals.* Washington, D.C., U.S. Office of Education.

WHITE, ALPHEUS L. 1962 *Local School Boards: Organization and Practices.* Washington, D.C., U.S. Office of Education.

WHITE, ALPHEUS L. 1963 "An Analysis of School Board Organization." *American School Board Journal,* 146, no. 4:7–8.

MARILYN GITTELL

2. STAFF DEVELOPMENT

Recruitment and retention of certified personnel have almost always been problems in American educational systems. Throughout most of U.S. history, great cities and agricultural regions have suffered alike from a shortage of qualified teachers. During the nineteenth century and the early part of the twentieth, as the industrial revolution and the successive waves of European immigrants transformed a nation of farmers, villagers, and plantation employees into a predominantly urban civilization, the difficulties of staff development in city schools were severe. This situation existed until the depression began in 1929.

Teacher supply and demand. On the surface the situation that existed in the early years of the depression would seem to be an exception to the general statement that the supply of teachers has never been equal to the demand. At that time approximately 200,000 potential teachers living in metropolitan areas could not obtain positions.

However, what appeared to be a surplus of staff was in large part the result of increased class size and a reduced curriculum. Although English teachers sometimes taught classes of 50 students, instructors in art, Latin, and other so-called fringe areas were no longer recruited. In many towns and cities, supervisors returned to the classrooms. Also, many thousands of men who had lost jobs in industry and commerce turned toward teaching.

This apparent reserve of teachers hardly prepared school officials for the sudden drought that lay just ahead. There is evidence that, when personnel appeared to be so readily available, administrators of metropolitan schools became more selective. Although this factor served to raise professional standards, it also caused picayune criteria to be used for certification. Esoteric and often useless courses were required of undergraduates at teacher-training institutions. In addition, some states like New Jersey stopped the expansion of teachers colleges; instead, entrance requirements for students were made so high that few applicants were admitted.

The contrast between urban and agricultural regions during the depression is interesting to note. Montana tried to swell the number of new enrollees at the State Normal College by offering to pay their railroad fares from distant points. This offer indicates the scarcity of teachers in western states, with their widely scattered rural schools, in a period when the great cities were enjoying a temporary respite from the teacher shortage.

The diminution of available teaching positions during the depression aggravated the difficulties confronting urban schools when World War II caused a severe manpower shortage. What had been a seller's market became the reverse after 1941.

Teacher shortages. The greatest problem in urban education since the early 1940's has been the paucity of new personnel. During World War II, American public schools employed 125,000 teachers on emergency or substandard licenses because certified teachers were unavailable. At that time, 14 percent of the classroom teachers could not meet the minimum requirements, which ranged from a high school diploma to a master's degree. Suburbs were least affected by the shortage, and rural areas suffered as usual, but the problem became increasingly worse in the big cities in the postwar period. To illustrate, in September 1958, New York City had approximately 500 unfilled positions when it opened its classrooms.

In the case of New York, about 80 percent of the vacancies were in the junior high schools— a typical situation in city school systems throughout the United States. Of the many reasons advanced for recruitment difficulties in the junior high schools, only a few can be cited here. Recognized authorities, such as Gesell, have described preadolescent children as volatile, emotional, and hard to handle (Gesell et al. 1956). In addition, a large number of recalcitrant youths must remain in junior high school because of compulsory-age laws. These same youngsters drop out shortly after they enter senior high school or just before. Thus, hoping to have fewer discipline problems, many junior high school teachers move on to grades 10 through 12.

Another reason for the upward migration of junior high school teachers is the intellectual challenge of advanced subject matter. A mathematics teacher who must cover simple arithmetical computations with his seventh grade class may seek an opportunity to teach solid geometry or calculus to bright 17-year-olds. On the other hand, the stimulus of the curriculum itself is of relatively little importance at the elementary school level, and teachers who choose to teach at that level usually do so chiefly because they like younger children. Therefore, the junior high schools constantly lose teachers to the high schools and gain very few from the elementary schools.

Subject-area shortages. The incidence of teacher shortages in large school systems is related to subject areas as well as to grade levels. In some areas there is an abundance of teachers; in other areas there is a severe shortage. For example, potential teachers of social studies are relatively numerous, and very often college students who have majored in that field are unable to obtain positions unless they agree to give instruction in other areas. Many accept assignments in elementary schools, where they take the places of thousands of teachers on maternity leaves.

On the other hand, a 1968 survey made by the National Education Association, Research Division (1969) shows that in several subject fields the problem of filling positions has remained rather constant in large cities throughout the 1960's. In decreasing order the areas of shortage are industrial arts, special education, mathematics, trade subjects, girls' physical education, remedial reading, speech, and science. School psychologists and librarians are also badly needed in most urban school systems.

Educators' difficulties. At every level and in every subject area the two great barriers to effective recruitment of teachers in large cities are salaries and working conditions. In the period from 1920 to 1940, city schools had the highest salary schedules in the country, but by the 1950's the salaries of urban school teachers had consistently fallen below those of their suburban colleagues. There were various causes for this decline. The transfer of some industries from the cities to the surrounding suburbs and the exodus of a large part of the middle class reduced the tax base of the municipalities. In several states the political structure prevented the cities from getting back more than a small share of tax funds they contributed to the state treasury. Mayors and councilmen, in reaction to inflation and dwindling resources, often made drastic cuts in the budgets submitted by city boards of education.

The cities thus could no longer point proudly to high salaries as an attraction for new teachers. At the same time, working conditions deteriorated seriously. Plans for the construction of new buildings and the repair or modernization of old ones lagged far behind needs. As a result, teachers and students were often housed in obsolete structures, some of which were firetraps. Faced with more pupils than the schools could hold, thousands of principals resorted to administrative devices such as double sessions, split shifts, and overlapping programs. Some pupils arrived at school as early as 7 A.M. and left after lunch; others came as late as noon and left at 5 P.M. In addition, many schools adopted short-time schedules, which generally shorten the day by one hour and thus deprive students of up to 200 hours of instruction each year.

Simultaneously, the character of the pupil population changed. Those middle class families that did not flee to the suburbs often sent their children to private or parochial schools. Thus, a large part of the student population in public schools consisted of indigent Afro-American children whose parents had come from the South and, in some cities, of children from Puerto Rico and other Latin American countries. For example, early in the 1960's more than half the enrollment of the New York City public elementary schools consisted of Afro-American and Puerto Rican pupils. The school population in Washington, D.C., is 90 percent black, with widely divergent dialectical differences. Los Angeles not only has a growing black population but also has a large number of Mexicans, American Indians, and Orientals.

In the 1950's and even into the 1960's, only a relatively small number of teacher-training institutions made any change in curriculum or personnel to meet the new and demanding challenges of the changing pupil population. For example, until the late 1960's teacher-training institutions had few courses dealing with Afro-American culture or the special problems of children learning English as a second language. Consequently, new teachers were ill-prepared to enter classrooms in the ghetto schools. Many teachers foundered and resigned in anger and disgust; others simply refused appointments to ghetto schools, thus leaving numerous vacancies to be filled by long-term substitutes who were even less equipped and less qualified to handle the task. Many classes consisted of reluctant and retarded learners: some became dropouts or "pushouts" (those students aged 16 or over who are generally truants or very disruptive in the classroom and are consequently strongly urged to get their working papers rather than to graduate); other students gave vent to their frustrations through antisocial behavior. Most supervisors, burdened by administrative and disciplinary matters, found little time to help and support the new teachers on their staffs. The teaching-learning process grew less and less efficient year after year.

In all the great cities a dilemma arose regarding the assignment of new teachers. The residential sections attracted more than enough personnel to staff their schools, but the reverse was true in the slums and business districts. Therefore, great numbers of novices were assigned to schools far from their homes, sometimes in neighborhoods which they feared.

Pupil-teacher ratios. The pupil-teacher ratio in most large school systems climbed considerably during the period after World War II. A 1968 survey revealed that eight cities under study (Baltimore, Chicago, Cleveland, Houston, Los Angeles, Milwaukee, Philadelphia, and St. Louis) exceeded the national average pupil-teacher ratio of 23:1, in one instance (St. Louis) by as much as 5.1 pupils per teacher (National Education Association . . . 1969).

Another index of the viability of a school system is the number of professionals that it employs for every thousand children that it enrolls. Here again, the suburbs have an advantage over the large cities. Various surveys conducted during the 1960's showed that urban schools have as few as 50 professionals per thousand children, whereas richer towns in the outlying areas employ as many as 75 professionals for the same number of pupils. Striking differences favoring the suburbs are evidenced regarding the supply of school nurses, school librarians, and school psychologists. For example, according to National Education Association, Research Division data (1967), Washington, D.C., had a ratio of 1,377 pupils per school librarian, in sharp contrast to neighboring Arlington County, Va., which had a ratio of only 459 pupils per librarian. Similar contrasts were found in comparisons between Baltimore and Baltimore County (2,317:1 and 787:1, respectively); Milwaukee and Racine (10,508:1 and 1,432:1, respectively); San Francisco and Berkeley (1,958:1 and 750:1, respectively); and Los Angeles and Long Beach (26,354:1 and 1,138:1, respectively).

Recruitment and licensing practices. By 1960 most large cities had taken definite steps to relieve personnel shortages. Los Angeles sent a team of recruiters as far as the eastern seaboard to publicize the benefits of teaching in a balmy climate and to interview applicants, some of whom were experienced teachers in other large cities. (This form of pirating, while frowned upon by many educators, became a rather common practice.) Detroit and Chicago, among many other cities, set up systems for combing the United States. As the black population increased in urban schools, recruitment expeditions to Afro-American colleges in the South became more numerous each year.

The situation can be summarized as follows:

This competition for the services of qualified teachers has caused a remarkable rise in recruitment activities. Many school systems now prepare attractive brochures and send them to teacher-training institutions. A number of cities and states have set up recruitment offices. These officials send out literature, give talks at colleges and attend teachers' conventions in the hope of persuading likely young men and women to accept positions. (Atkinson & Maleska 1965, p. 386)

Cities vary in their approaches to licensing. In Boston and Philadelphia, state certification and a brief interview are required. In Chicago and other cities, candidates must pass a national teachers' examination. In New York City, the board of examiners, which was established by state law in 1912, acts almost autonomously and screens all applicants for every school license up to and including the position of high school principal. Even in the 1950's, when shortages were so extreme, the board of examiners continued to give a battery of written and oral tests to each applicant for a regular teacher's license. Several times during the 1950's and 1960's, the abolishment of the board of examiners or a reduction of its powers was strongly recommended by outside agencies. Black militants and civil rights leaders, noting the paucity of Afro-Americans, especially in the supervisory ranks, accused the examiners of perpetrating racial injustice and joined in the demand for their removal. On the other hand, organizations such as the United Federation of Teachers have cautioned against the scrapping of a merit system that helps to prevent such evils as patronage and nepotism.

It should be pointed out that New York has been considered the city where the least amount of political chicanery or personal favoritism in the selection of teachers and principals takes place. Whether this virtue outweighs the faults of inflexibility is a controversial issue open to debate.

Assignment of new teachers. Once an applicant has succeeded in obtaining a teaching license, a decision must be reached as to the school at which he will teach and the specific position that he will occupy. Here the procedure in a large city differs greatly from the practice in a small town. In small towns, usually the superintendent or the principal will find and hire a person who seems especially fitted for the job in question. But in most urban school systems, sheer numbers hinder such refinements.

Whatever their size, all large urban school systems give some measure of authority to personnel officers at headquarters. These officials often assign new teachers and take into account wherever possible such factors as the number of vacancies in the individual schools and the distance of the school from the licensee's home.

Efforts have been made to humanize and decentralize what has often become an assembly-line process. The principle of mutual consent is often followed, especially in those cases where appointees have recently served as substitute or student teachers in ghetto schools. A brief letter from the teacher and a supporting statement from the supervisor are usually sufficient to effect the assignment.

Los Angeles is one of the cities that has sought to match the new teacher with the position most suited to his talents and interests. There the personnel officer sends the appointees to area superintendents, who try to determine in informal interviews the schools that best fit the personalities and backgrounds of the newcomers. New York City, in its decentralization program, has adopted a similar plan: new teachers are interviewed and assigned by each of 30 field superintendents, sometimes in the presence of the local school board.

Most urban school systems urge their principals to recruit teachers, and some even give them permission to hire qualified people on the spot. This practice, although commendable for its flexibility and encouragement of initiative, has dangerous aspects. Sometimes the principal in an economically favored district is able to take the most highly qualified applicants while his colleagues in the inner-city schools have a limited choice or can find no one to fill urgent vacancies. Therefore, most personnel officers at headquarters try to effect a compromise between rigid central control and complete local autonomy in hiring teachers.

The staffing problem. Regardless of the placement methods used, one problem that has plagued all urban school officials is the staffing of inner-city classrooms. In addition to the factors mentioned previously, it is well known that many teachers who have served in such classrooms exercise their right to transfer after a certain number of years (three years in New York and five years in Chicago, for example). This right to transfer creates a spiral of inequities. Legions of experienced teachers are instructing children who already have many advantages from their home environments. In the meantime, inexperienced teachers fill the gaps in the slums each year. Thus, the children who need help most are instructed by novices who, in effect, learn their trade at the expense of the pupils. (It should be stated that suburban administrators are usually pleased to get veterans from the urban schools, especially those who have taught in the slums. Apparently daily experiences in difficult areas serve to keep many teachers from falling into a rut.)

Quota systems and other administrative inventions have made only a small dent in this self-perpetuating structure. (The quota system is a device whereby an "index" of the percentage of regular appointees—as opposed to substitutes—is established, and schools having more than the quota of regular teachers will not receive any new regular appointments.) Some observers have recommended forced rotation of teachers as a solution. But others point out that such a step would cause more problems than it would solve. Teachers' organizations have gone on record as opposing rotation, and even if the idea were put into effect it might cause a great number of early retirements. More important, it would bring to the ghetto disgruntled (and sometimes biased) teachers, many of whom would complain that they had already "served time" in good faith while waiting for the day to be transferred to residential areas.

Early in the 1960's, New York City tried to remedy this situation by suggesting that inner-city teachers who take special courses and fulfill other criteria receive a yearly bonus of $1,000. Charles Cogen, then president of the United Federation of Teachers, labeled the bonus as combat pay, and black leaders regarded it as an insult.

Whether experienced or inexperienced, most teachers in the ghetto have not been effective. As is widely known, scores of ghetto students on achievement tests attest to that fact. The causes are almost as numerous as the teachers, and the listing of the causes in order of importance depends upon the standpoint of whoever presumes to judge. Some of the reasons, it is safe to say, have not yet been discovered.

Many urban administrators sincerely declare that even the most zealous black teachers and white teachers who are relatively free from prejudice seldom succeed in bringing their classes in ghetto schools up to national norms on standardized tests. Staff members usually cite home environments and the tremendous mobility of the families as the chief causes. But some communities, searching for other answers, claim that the entire school setting, ranging from selection of

supervisors to components of the curriculum, needs to be reconstructed.

Amidon and Flanders (1963), Ryan (1960), and others have conducted studies of successful teaching practices, but there is obviously a great need for research centering specifically on the effective teacher in the black ghetto. In view of the numerous failures, the success of such organizations as the national Teacher Corps and VISTA deserves attention and investigation.

Preservice and in-service training. A large number of young urban teachers give up in despair each year. Among the chief causes of their failure are irrelevant and theoretical courses at college and a lack of sustained and helpful guidance from principals and other supervisors.

In recent years officials on the campuses and in the urban schools have taken positive steps to remedy defects on both fronts. Teacher-training institutions have started to introduce black studies and courses in Puerto Rican culture. Among the most promising new practices is the gradual induction of college students into teaching through a system that involves frequent observations in classrooms during the sophomore year of college, participation once or twice a week in classroom activities during the junior year, and assignment to a ghetto school as a student teacher during the senior year. Future teachers are given practical courses that stress field work with the community, especially in urban slum areas. There is an increasing use of experienced teachers and administrators from the public schools as instructors in methods courses. Greater emphasis is placed on proper handling of discipline, daily routines, and classroom management. Courses in human relations and sensitivity training are given, and members of minority groups are involved in teacher-training programs.

In the schools themselves, some of the most helpful practices that have spread from city to city during the 1960's are the assignment of a master teacher as an on-the-job "teacher trainer" for a small group of neophytes and the creative use of television, films, and other media. When a team-teaching approach is adopted, new teachers receive support and stimulation from daily collaboration with experienced colleagues. Another helpful practice is the cooperation of school systems with colleges and universities in a fifth-year, or intern, program that bridges the gap between preservice and in-service education. In preparing future teachers, there should also be greater emphasis on demonstration lessons.

New approaches. In recent years both federal and state authorities have focused their attention on the enormous problems that face teachers and supervisors in large urban schools. As a result, an increased amount of funds has been allocated to the cities. Innovative and constructive practices in curriculum, instruction, and staff training have encouraged through the use of money provided for by the 1965 Elementary and Secondary Education Act (especially under Title I and Title III). These funds are obtained either directly from the federal government or indirectly through the state department of education.

In 1966, acting under the provisions of Title IV, the U.S. Office of Education organized 20 regional laboratories to improve schools, especially those in urban areas. As of 1970, 15 of these laboratories still existed and were beginning to make progress in the development of meaningful programs and materials. For example, the Center for Urban Education in New York City has produced Instructional Profiles, a series of cards to help newly appointed schoolteachers in grades 3 and 4 in the preparation of lessons for every subject area. This laboratory also has created a new curriculum for social studies, relevant to the urban child's needs and designed to promote the active involvement of the teacher and the class in the life of the community.

Another promising trend in urban schools is the use of paraprofessionals. The first major effort to reduce the alarming number of clerical chores handled daily by teachers was made in Bay City, Mich., in 1953 under a grant from the Ford Foundation's Fund for the Advancement of Education. Since then the movement has gained tremendous impetus, and the scope of the tasks handled by teacher aides has increased. In 1970, in the New York City schools alone, there were approximately 30,000 school aides and paraprofessionals, whose range of activities extends from patrolling the lunchroom and running a mimeograph machine to tutoring small groups of children selected by the teachers for special help. In many large cities a promotional ladder is being developed for this relatively new corps of workers from the indigenous population.

Probably the most important feature of the growth of the paraprofessional movement is its relation to the concept of decentralization that has swept through urban communities. In city after city, parents and local spokesmen have demanded the right to participate in, and even control, the decisions that affect the destinies of children. At first, school officials offered some resistance to the tide of discontent, but most administrators have begun to seek constructive ways to effect a true partnership with the community. Obviously, the road to be traveled together is fraught with pitfalls for both groups, but in the end it may lead to the discovery of educational solutions that have remained hidden for centuries. One thing is certain: in the era ahead, urban staff development will no longer be the province of only the professionals.

BIBLIOGRAPHY

AMIDON, EDMUND J., AND NED A. FLANDERS 1963 *The Role of the Teacher in the Classroom: A Manual for Understanding and Improving Teachers' Classroom Behavior.* Minneapolis, Paul S. Amidon and Associates.

ATKINSON, CARROL, AND EUGENE T. MALESKA 1965 *The Story of Education.* 2nd ed. Philadelphia, Chilton.

GESELL, ARNOLD, et al. 1956 *Youth: The Years From Ten to Sixteen.* New York, Harper.

NATIONAL EDUCATION ASSOCIATION. RESEARCH DIVISION 1967 *23rd Biennial Salary Survey of Public School Professional Personnel, 1966–67: Data for Systems With Enrollments of 12,000 or More.* Research Report 1967–R12. Washington, D.C., The Association.

NATIONAL EDUCATION ASSOCIATION. RESEARCH DIVISION 1969 *Teacher Supply and Demand in Public Schools, 1968.* Research Report, 1969–R4. Washington, D.C., The Association.

RYAN, DAVID G. 1960 *Characteristics of Teachers: Their Description, Comparison, and Appraisal.* Washington, D.C., American Council on Education.

U.S. OFFICE OF EDUCATION 1969 *Fall 1968 Statistics of Public Elementary and Secondary Day Schools: Pupils, Teachers, Instruction Rooms, and Expenditures.* By Robert H. Bass and Betty J. Foster. Washington, D.C., Government Printing Office.

EUGENE T. MALESKA

3. SLUM SCHOOLS

A slum may be defined as an overcrowded, rundown, poverty-stricken residential area which is usually found within a city. The presence of schools in such areas is not a recent phenomenon in the United States, since slums developed in many large cities during the massive immigration of the late nineteenth and early twentieth centuries. Then as now, administrators in urban slum schools were confronted with problems of overcrowded classes, special pupil needs, teacher shortages, and inadequate funds. The current urban scene, however, differs in several respects, and these differences have further complicated the operation of such schools. Four present-day developments are local pressure for decentralization and community involvement, legal requirements for racial desegregation, collective bargaining by teacher organizations, and the growth of federal aid to education. Each of these trends has implications for the urban slum school. However, the major influence, which is basic to many other present-day developments, is the changing urban population.

Urban population. The population of metropolitan areas in the United States has grown continuously since the founding of the country. In 1790 the first United States census showed two dozen communities with more than 2,500 inhabitants, but only 5 percent of the population resided in such centers. By 1920, 50 percent of the population was living in urban districts. In 1960, 61.3 percent of the population lived in 189 standard metropolitan areas identified by the U.S. Bureau of the Census. It has been predicted that by 1980 over 90 percent of the American people will be living in urban areas (Gordon 1963). Although the process of urbanization has continued at a rapid pace, the suburbs in these areas have recently experienced greater growth than the cities. In the 1960's the population of several large cities in the East and Midwest declined, as did their school enrollments; however, slums and slum schools are still of great concern because as the cities shrink, the relative size of the slum population increases.

The continued existence of slum schools is partly due to pupil population increases within attendance zones, but it is more significantly due to the array of social and economic conditions arising from the changing urban population.

Foreign immigration. American slums were first inhabited by immigrants from overseas who began to arrive in great numbers at the end of the nineteenth century. The new arrivals tended to settle first in the older and less desirable areas of the city. Members of each immigrant group formed their own neighborhood, as they found security in solidarity. After a time, each group moved outward from the inner city and became less segregated. Economically, the newcomers usually began on the lower rungs of the employment ladder, and they were also confronted by social prejudice and hostility. Later, the makeup of the inner city changed as the children of immigrants

grew up and left home, their parents died, and immigration was cut in the early 1920's by federal legislation. Today, only the bare outlines of many former ethnic neighborhoods remain. Many children of immigrants such as Italians, Jews, and Hungarians have created more affluent neighborhoods. The newer groupings are based more on economic status than on religious and ethnic origins, but the connotations of ethnic labels have yet to be erased (Glazer & Moynihan 1963).

Racial minorities. Much of the present-day urban slum population is black. The proportion of Negroes to total population during the early days of the United States was higher than it is now. From 1790 to 1830, 20 percent of Americans were Negro. With the abolition of slave traffic and massive European immigration, the proportion declined to little more than 10 percent and has remained fairly stable.

Although there were increasing black populations in Philadelphia and Chicago after 1880 and almost 100,000 Negroes in New York City in 1910, it was during World War I, when industrial activity was calling for increased manpower, that the surge northward to the cities began. When the usual cheap labor supply from European immigration was cut off, employers turned to the Negroes. The South was becoming industrialized, easing the need for unskilled rural labor, and many Negroes moved to northern cities looking for work. Even though the flow decreased somewhat during the depression, it swelled again when mobilization for World War II began. At the same time that the Negro population was arriving in the inner city, the more prosperous whites were moving to the suburbs. Between 1950 and 1960 the 12 largest U.S. cities lost over 2 million white residents and gained nearly 2 million Negro residents.

Another relative newcomer to the urban scene, also an American, is the Puerto Rican. The 1960 census indicated that 900,000 residents of the continental United States were of Puerto Rican birth. Although New York City is the home of almost three-quarters of the Puerto Ricans in the continental United States, a dispersion to other areas has begun, and since 1957 only 60 percent of the net migration has been to New York City (Goldberg 1968). Even though the number of new arrivals has fallen off and will probably remain low, the present high birthrate in this group indicates that Puerto Ricans will constitute an increasing proportion of New York City's population (Glazer 1963).

Increasing nonwhite enrollments in slum schools also include Mexican-Americans, in the southwestern states, as well as Orientals. The white enrollment includes the descendants of immigrants who have not managed to escape poverty. Seeking employment, the Anglo-Saxon indigents of Appalachia have migrated to cities in the Great Lakes area, particularly.

In terms of preponderant numbers, however, the population change in urban slum areas has been from white to nonwhite. One reason for this change has been that those moving away from the slums have been predominantly white. Other reasons are that there is a higher birthrate among nonwhites than among whites and that relatively fewer nonwhite children attend parochial or private schools. If present trends continue, white pupils could be in the minority in the schools of most large northern cities by 1980 (Glatt 1965). The administration of the slum school requires an awareness of the implications of this population change in racial as well as cultural terms.

Children and parents. The children of the slum school show high rates of social maladjustment, behavorial disturbance, and academic retardation. Most slum children are socially disadvantaged; that is, they come from populations which have in common such characteristics as low economic and social status, low educational achievement, marginal employment, minimal civic participation, and limited preparation for upward mobility. These people are handicapped not only by depressed social and economic conditions but also, in many instances, by ethnic and cultural class status (Rudman & Featherstone 1968).

Granting the existence of exceptions, an understanding of slum school pupils and their functioning in school often depends on an awareness of cultural differences, child-rearing practices, sex-related personality differences, the development of verbal ability, and the nature of low academic motivation found in the slums.

Cultural differences. The residents of urban slums possess cultural attitudes which often differ from those dominant in the broader society. As a result, their children come to school handicapped because they have been denied many social experiences other children have had. The total environment, including such influences as the home, the street, social and political agencies, and the

mass media, constitutes the "hidden" curriculum, which affects the child's reactions to the formal school curriculum (Fantini & Weinstein 1968). One example of a deleterious cultural effect is the high dropout rate among Negroes. Among the reasons for this are greater family reliance on income from children, the inflexibility of slum schools, and the low self-image of slum children.

Child-rearing practices. Child-rearing practices in slums differ from those common in non-slum areas. Some lower-class parents exercise control over their children by harsh corporal punishment, which the children often expect as their proper due. But the role of each parent in child rearing varies with the racial or ethnic group and has correspondingly different effects. For example, the absence of a strong father figure in many lower-class Negro homes has a deleterious effect on the educational aspirations of boys in particular. Greater employment discrimination against black men than against black women has lowered male prestige and encouraged the development of a matriarchal society in the Negro slums (Pettigrew 1964). Compounding the problem is the fact that a high proportion of Negro mothers work and therefore have relatively little time for participation in school matters.

In contrast, the patriarchal family style is found among Puerto Rican, Mexican-Americans, and Appalachian whites. Here the father is usually present, and stern paternal control of the entire family typically prevails.

Sex-related personality differences. Sex-related personality differences also vary between different racial and ethnic groups. In the lower-class Negro family, girls are favored more than boys, and in their mothers they have models, which the boys lack. Negro females as a group stay in school longer, do better academically, and achieve more after leaving school than do Negro males. Among Puerto Ricans, Mexican-Americans, and Appalachian whites, parents either favor boys over girls or display no preference (Moynihan 1965).

Verbal ability. The child of the disadvantaged home is often severely handicapped in attaining verbal ability, a skill of key importance to good performance in school and also on tests of intelligence. An enriched environment provides models and experience with patterns of standard English, while a deprived one fails to offer the kinds of experiences that facilitate the development of verbal ability (Bloom 1964). In the slum home the scarcity of objects of all kinds, the frequent lack of parental attention, the lack of travel experiences, and the presence of malnutrition and physical neglect all tend to create a restrictive environment whose effects may be irreversible.

Low motivation. The prevalence of pupils with low academic motivation is a marked feature of the slum school. The characteristics of such children vary; however, the following are frequently noted. The poorly motivated pupil has little interest in delayed rewards. He is more peer conscious than he is teacher conscious. Academic achievements that would make him noticeable among his peers are often avoided. He judges academic standards on the basis of getting by. He feels little need to complete tasks. Escape through daydreaming is common. Especially among boys there is hostility toward school authorities (Farquhar 1968). The high incidence of such characteristics in many urban slum classrooms suggests the difficulty of the task confronting the administrators and teachers.

Teachers. Research knowledge concerning desirable teacher behavior is still limited. Teaching skills can vary greatly and still be effective. There is some experimental evidence that a significant relationship exists between desirable outcomes and the tendency of the teacher to be approving, to provide emotional support, and to accept the feelings of pupils (Gage 1966). Other findings suggest that the successful teacher understands and interprets to the class the reasons behind the facts which he teaches. Encouragement of student participation—giving pupils opportunities to engage in discussions and problem-solving rather than having them listen exclusively to lectures by the instructor—is also desirable. The expectations the teacher has for the slum school child are important; if the teacher anticipates low achievement, then little achievement results, and a self-fulfilling prophecy is established.

Effective school staffing is a challenge even in the affluent suburbs. In the slums, teacher recruitment and assignment are complicated by a variety of factors (Levenson 1968). The poor image of the city, drab and often hazardous surroundings, large classes, the continued use in some cities of examinations and eligibility lists, uncertainty about interracial relationships, and the prevalence of retardation and discipline problems, even if less than feared, are deterrents to recruitment. An assignment to the slum school is often a

temporary one except for the highly committed teacher. With the extension of collective bargaining, seniority has assumed increasing importance among the considerations in granting assignment options. Thus, in many large cities the slum school is staffed to a large extent by relatively inexperienced teachers, most of whom are white. Those who stay do so because they receive satisfaction from the response of their pupils (Wayson 1966).

Curriculum. The aim of the curriculum for the disadvantaged child, like the aim of curriculum generally, is maximum improvement of the learner's abilities. These abilities may be due in greater or lesser proportion to nature or nurture, a controversy which has been revived recently (Jensen 1969), but the curriculum is essentially concerned with the child as he is rather than with the disputed causes for his being so (Bloom 1964; Hunt 1969).

The traditional curriculum, rigidly scheduled and uniform throughout the system, is particularly inadequate for the child raised in a slum environment. Adaptations are essential to make the curriculum more relevant to the background and the daily experiences of the pupil (Loretan & Umans 1966).

A variety of proposals for adaptations have been made. One plan regarding procedures for course selection would permit each slum school to make its own curriculum decisions within the broad limits set by the central board of education; planning time would be provided to teachers involved in curriculum revision. In regard to course content, curriculum guides for slum schools have been developed which emphasize the use of listening and reading materials employing familiar neighborhood experiences rather than abstractions alien to the slum child. Another reform, attempted with seeming success, involves the use of individual programmed units in an ungraded setting so that the child can proceed according to ability. In still another plan, social-action projects have been used as the focus for learning. Whatever the approach, the aim has been to make the curriculum more effective through increased relevance to the child's experience and through concern with the emotional as well as the intellectual needs of the disadvantaged learner (Taba & Elkins 1966).

Compensatory education. The major thrust of reforms in curriculum planning for the culturally disadvantaged has been toward compensatory education. Compensatory education has been defined as "programs, practices, techniques and projects designed to overcome the deficiencies of children from culturally disadvantaged homes to enable them to fulfill the fundamental purposes of education" (Chicago. Public Schools 1964).

This concept is not new. For many years most school systems have offered the disadvantaged pupil additional attention, special assignments, tutoring, and a number of other aids. In most states special services for handicapped pupils are provided by increased financial assistance: class size is kept small, special equipment is used, and paraprofessionals are employed. More recent is the recognition that handicaps are due not only to physical, mental, and emotional factors but also to environmental deprivation and that society has a stake in alleviating these handicaps.

Interest in additional experimentation with compensatory programs was stimulated in large northern cities by the Ford Foundation's Gray Area Project in the early 1960's. The major impetus came in 1965, when federal funds became available through Title I of the Elementary and Secondary Education Act. In 1968, 9 million American children had some contact with Title I programs (U.S. National Advisory Council . . . 1969).

A wide variety of compensatory programs have been undertaken. Many are locally funded. Among the features frequently included are remedial work in communication skills, field trips, expanded music and art programs, extended guidance services, special library activities, and medical, dental, and psychological care.

Additional supportive personnel, such as social workers, enrichment teachers, team-teaching leaders, counselors, and paraprofessionals, have been utilized. Most of the programs have been conducted during school hours, although many types have been held on Saturdays, after school hours, and during summer vacations. The term "compensatory education programs" has been dropped in most large school systems because the compensatory components are interlocked with the regular school programs, making the components difficult to identify clearly and evaluate properly.

Preschool programs such as Head Start are compensatory in purpose although originally ad-

ministered under the Office of Economic Opportunity. The goal of preschool programs is to marshal those resources which can benefit the child's total development: health care, nutrition planning, and social services, as well as academic education. A significant innovation was the direct involvement of slum parents. Improved child health and more community interest in child care have been observed, but there has been little evidence that preschool programs have lasting effects upon mental growth and development (Elkind 1969).

Conclusive evidence as to the effectiveness of compensatory education programs in general is also lacking. Although the wide variation in content and quality has prevented any statistical evaluation on a nationwide scale, there are programs in several school systems which have been judged effective in terms of positive, identifiable changes such as improvement in reading scores (U.S. National Advisory Council . . . 1969).

The progressive administrator of the slum school recognizes that curriculum effectiveness—that is, the successful intervention between the child and the environment—requires a strategy for blending available resources and procedures into an integrated program. These resources and procedures include teacher selection and in-service training programs, teacher attitudes and skills, administrative insight, discipline, regulations, textbooks and other equipment, special services, and involvement with the neighborhood—in fact, the entire spectrum of school life. Even if innovative, a new curriculum in a traditional middle-class setting has little value for slum children. The impact of the curriculum upon the slum child is thus dependent upon the prevalence of a dynamic philosophy in which unorthodox flexibility is welcome, not suspect.

Administration. The slum environment exacerbates administrative difficulties in a number of ways. Two areas in which these difficulties may be illustrated are school-community relationships and the provision of physical facilities.

School-community relationships. In 1966 in New York City there was an eruption of community pressures for direct involvement in the formulation and execution of local school policy. These pressures are not characteristic of slum districts in all metropolitan areas. In many American slums, although the latent forces are there and parental interest in better education for children is widespread, the lines of communication between school and home are tenuous and a coalescence of leadership is not yet evident. The reasons for this are manifold. Pupil mobility is great and therefore class attendance is often not continuous. There is considerable reluctance to visit schools because some parents are embarrassed by their own limited education and many are concerned about appearing in an alien setting. Poor adult reading ability often minimizes the effects of written materials.

Although the reverberations of the New York City confrontation have led to a concentrated effort in most big cities to improve school-community understanding, the gap remains a sizable one. One common approach has been to increase the number of minority-group members in administrative posts, particularly in human relations bureaus. Based to some extent upon the experience with Head Start, a policy in some systems has been to employ as teacher aides people who actually live in the slums and who, it is hoped, will help to interpret school programs to the neighborhood.

Decentralization plans have been widely studied, and in the largest cities such reorganizations are increasingly common. There are conflicts, for on one hand there is pressure from groups who fear that creating local districts may tend to freeze slum boundaries, while on the other hand there is pressure from groups calling for community control. In the middle of such struggles is the school principal, who also faces conflicts between collective bargaining agreements made with teachers on a city-wide basis and the adaptations demanded by the local district (Cronin & Crocker 1969).

Looming in the background of such turmoil is the federal government's interest in the implementation of local plans to reduce, if not eliminate, de facto segregation. As whites continue to leave the cities and as slums spread and become increasingly populated by blacks and other minority groups, the achievement of racial integration in the schools becomes extremely difficult. Attempts at involving the largely white suburbs in metropolitan integration plans have thus far produced negligible results. Hartford, Conn., and Rochester, N.Y., have undertaken exchanges with neighboring school systems, but even there only a small percentage of slum school children have participated.

Physical facilities. The provision of adequate school facilities is also affected by demographic factors. The prediction of school construction needs, for example, depends upon an accurate estimate of probable attendance. In slum districts this is complicated, since there are numerous shifts in population, as well as migration in and out. In some slum schools the annual number of student transfers equals or exceeds the total enrollment of the school. In addition, in the slum, where zoning is often weak and enforcement lax, the deleterious effects of overcrowding on the schools are magnified, because slum children have already been subjected to the psychological onslaughts of overcrowding in their home environments. A stable, less pressurized school setting could contribute to some release and a semblance of serenity, if only for five hours a day.

Urban renewal and expressway construction, common occurrences in the slums, have special impact on the schools. Population shifts caused by widespread demolition create imbalances in nearby schools; some are underenrolled and others overcrowded. Sudden, widespread family moves play havoc with long-range school building programs, which are often plagued by long delays. Although there may be later benefits from new housing projects and highways, the slum child's continuity of attendance, already highly irregular, becomes worse.

Rapid overcrowding in certain districts and delays in new building construction have led to a variety of emergency measures. These are particularly evident in slum schools, where time-buying palliatives create other difficulties.

A common device is to use all available space in the building for classrooms. This in turn can mean the loss of special-activity facilities such as libraries and guidance rooms. Another procedure is to increase class size. Usually, the classes are already too big. In some cities secondary schools have longer days to facilitate half-day sessions or overlapping sessions. Thus, pupils in early or late classes may have to travel in darkness during the winter season, with attendant hazards. The boundaries of school districts are occasionally changed to reduce the imbalance of attendance among different schools. When this is done, travel distances may become noticeably unequal for different children, they may be exposed to traffic hazards, and neighborhood loyalties may be undermined.

Mobile or prefabricated structures are sometimes employed. Although these have improved in quality, they may arouse community resentment because the quarters are often regarded, perhaps unjustifiably, as substandard and as a symbol of discrimination. The rental of nearby facilities such as churches, libraries, and social agencies is frequently undertaken. Some parents dislike such steps because use of these buildings separates some children from the rest of the student body, travel problems may develop, and special school activities are sometimes missed. Occasionally, parents object to the use of church facilities, expressing concern that their children may be influenced by alien religious propaganda; more common is the view that the principle of separation of church and state is endangered by such arrangements.

A more controversial measure is to divide the school day into half-day sessions, which still exist in several large cities, especially in slum districts. Community opposition to such procedures is evident even though the school administration may try to compensate by adding staff and supplies.

The most drastic step to overcome building shortages is to transport pupils to schools where there is available room. Frequently, the nearest school is one some white pupils have left to attend a neighborhood parochial school, and the sending school is often one in a Negro section. When the transportation plan means a change in the racial balance, a tense situation is likely to develop.

Such procedures to overcome building shortages are not unique to the slums. Nevertheless, in most cities the use of stopgap measures is greater in the slums than elsewhere.

Although the school housing situation in many American slums remains bleak, there have been signs of improvement, and there are some slum areas which now contain outstanding examples of modern school architecture—Franklin Delano Roosevelt High School in New York City and Giddings Elementary School in Cleveland, Ohio, are two good examples.

Need has stimulated innovation. Expensive site and construction costs have led to joint apartment-school projects, prefabricated mini-schools,

and the use of air rights over freeways and railways. The trend toward extended summer activities has led to increased installation of air-conditioning. The interest in parent education has generated new concepts in community school planning.

In addition, federal legislation to provide funds for certain types of school construction may prove to be an important source of aid. After several false starts, coordination of planning between school, municipal, state, and federal officials has improved and holds great promise for the future.

BIBLIOGRAPHY

BLOOM, BENJAMIN S. 1964 *Stability and Change in Human Characteristics.* New York, Wiley.

CHICAGO. PUBLIC SCHOOLS 1964 *Compensatory Education in the Chicago Public Schools.* Study Report No. 4. Chicago, The Public Schools.

CRONIN, JOSEPH M., AND JULIAN D. CROCKER, JR. 1969 "Principals Under Pressure." *The Urban Review,* 3, no. 25:34–37.

ELKIND, DAVID 1969 "Conceptions of Intelligence." *Harvard Educational Review,* 39, no. 2:319–337.

FANTINI, MARIO D., AND GERALD WEINSTEIN 1968 *The Disadvantaged: Challenge to Education.* New York, Harper.

FARQUHAR, WILLIAM W. 1968 "Academic Motivation and Inner City Schools." Herbert C. Rudman and Richard L. Featherstone, eds., *Urban Schooling.* New York, Harcourt. Pages 197–213.

GAGE, NATHANIEL L. 1966 "Desirable Behaviors of Teachers." Michael Usdan and Frederick Bertolaet, eds., *Teachers for the Disadvantaged.* Chicago, Follett. Pages 4–12.

GLATT, CHARLES A. 1965 "Selected Demographic Factors That Affect School Planning: A Look at Four Northern Cities." *Urban Education,* 2, no. 1:35–49.

GLAZER, NATHAN 1963 "The Puerto Ricans." *Commentary,* 36, no. 1:1–9.

GLAZER, NATHAN, AND DANIEL PATRICK MOYNIHAN 1963 *Beyond the Melting Pot.* Cambridge, Mass., MIT Press.

GOLDBERG, GERTRUDE 1968 "Puerto Rican Migrants on the Mainland of the United States." *IRCD Bulletin,* 4, no. 1:1–8.

GORDON, MITCHELL 1963 *Sick Cities.* New York, Macmillan.

HUNT, JOSEPH McV. 1969 "Has Compensatory Education Failed? Has It Been Attempted?" *Harvard Educational Review,* 39, no. 2:278–300.

JENSEN, ARTHUR R. 1969 "How Much Can We Boost IQ and Scholastic Achievement?" *Harvard Educational Review,* 39, no. 1:entire issue.

KRISTOL, IRVING 1967 "Common Sense About the 'Urban Crisis.'" *Fortune,* 76, no. 5:233–234.

LEVENSON, WILLIAM B. 1968 *The Spiral Pendulum: The Urban School in Transition.* Chicago, Rand McNally.

LORETAN, JOSEPH O., AND SHELLEY UMANS 1966 *Teaching the Disadvantaged.* New York, Teachers College Press.

MOYNIHAN, DANIEL PATRICK 1965 "Employment, Income and the Negro Family." *Daedalus,* 94, no. 4:745–769.

PETTIGREW, THOMAS F. 1964 *A Profile of the Negro American.* Princeton, N.J., Van Nostrand.

RUDMAN, HERBERT C., AND RICHARD L. FEATHERSTONE, eds. 1968 *Urban Schooling.* New York, Harcourt.

TABA, HILDA, AND DEBORAH ELKINS 1966 *Teaching Strategies for the Culturally Disadvantaged.* Chicago, Rand McNally.

U.S. NATIONAL ADVISORY COUNCIL ON THE EDUCATION OF DISADVANTAGED CHILDREN 1969 *Fourth Annual Report.* Washington, D.C., Government Printing Office.

WAYSON, WILLIAM W. 1966 "Source of Teacher Satisfaction in Slum Schools." *Administrator's Notebook,* 14, no. 9:1–4.

WILLIAM B. LEVENSON

4. DYNAMICS OF SLUM SCHOOLS

The urban slum school in many industrialized Western societies is one variation on the theme of the standard public school. Therefore, certain features of the standard school must be described before the characteristics of the slum school can be examined. The references cited have been limited to the United States, but similar conditions exist elsewhere in the world.

Standard school model. The standard school consists of a building designed like a small factory and located in and serving the children of a residential neighborhood of ½ to 1 square mile, depending on the population density. The school population includes students, who attend in accordance with compulsory attendance laws, and a paid staff. Parental participation in school matters is part-time and indirect.

The functions performed in the standard school proliferate each decade, as what is expected of education expands beyond the historic functions of inducing literacy and computational skills and transmitting the cultural heritage. Among other functions expected of the schools in the 1970's are custodial care and management of children, the fostering of emotional and social growth, the remediation of diagnosed learning disabilities, and the evaluative sorting of students in anticipation of future schooling. Teachers in standard schools, under conditions stimulated by professionalization and unionization, function not only as parent surrogates but also as a group of commuting, tenured, upwardly mobile functionaries of the state. Changes in the role of the teacher have been so marked that schools must now be characterized as organized work stations in a fluid labor market.

Activities. Standard schools have become increasingly uniform to the point where curricular and operating differences between school districts and even geographical regions are negligible (Coleman et al. 1966), yet the cited functions are so complex as to be mutually contradictory. Moreover, under conditions of rapid social change, the activities undertaken within schools are often only weakly associated with fulfillment of the functions.

The activity consuming the most time is the practice of social control through rituals of deference, courtesy, and docility training (Henry 1963). Instruction through the use of workbooks, basal texts, group lectures, audiovisual demonstrations, and student group projects is the second most time-consuming activity. Other activities include physical exercise, occasional exposure to arts and crafts, and leadership training through a variety of student-government affairs. All activities are profoundly standardized, although staff members have some freedom to diversify routines and to introduce special projects. The success of the standardized activities, which are supposed to fulfill the school functions, is measured in two ways: Students take tests, most of them standardized, which enable the staff either to register success in fostering cognitive growth or to prescribe remedies where failure is noted; and the staff members rate the students' social conduct. On the basis of the two sets of records, students are judged as more or less competent in achievement and social conformity.

Status structures. The staff status structure and the pupil sociometric structure reflect the social norms which are pivotal to the standard school (Gronlund 1959). The staff members, with state sanction, place the greatest prestige and authority in the hands of the principal and the vice-principal. Tenured teachers with the most experience in the management of the custody and sorting of students are given next highest status. Teachers generally regulate the organizational routines and, as disciplinarians, maintain social control over the students. Among the students, prestige is accorded to peers in terms of manifest achievement on tests and compliance with the rituals of deference and impulse control.

Social contract. There are variations along all of these dimensions within standard schools. Yet, a cultural model emerges in which the manifold functions of the school converge in the concept of a social contract: In return for a negotiated wage and job security, the school staff members agree to oversee the day-to-day cognitive, social, and emotional development of the neighborhood's children along lines that are generally believed by adults to be desirable. As party to the contract, the child is rewarded by being sorted favorably if he understands that his presence is obligatory under the law and if he complies with the social norms—that is, to sit still, be quiet and well-mannered, exhibit deference to elders, and perform at a rate prescribed by the teacher. The child who cannot internalize these norms during the years from kindergarten through second grade is defined as a problem child and may be remanded to a different setting for special treatment. Under standard operating conditions, about one in every ten children qualifies as a problem child (Dentler et al. 1967).

The social contract depends upon community legitimation of the terms (Altshuler 1970). Both parents and taxpayers must believe that the direction and content of the socialization the staff members oversee is socially desirable. Teachers must believe that their pay, job security, and community approval are roughly commensurate with their ability to deliver the type and quality of custodial and academic supervision the community desires. Above all, each student must be prepared by parents and peers to play his part under the contract. This preparation antecedes enrollment; it is grounded in a convergence between family, peer group, and school norms and is established during the preschool years.

Slum schools. The standard school is able to operate because both the community and the school staff share certain values. However, in the slum schools there are no such shared values; the environment and the culture of the urban slum neighborhood undermine the contractual foundation upon which the standard school rests. Every service institution, even one with less complex functions and more adaptable norms than the public school, relies for its viability upon a matrix of supportive relations with other institutions. When the matrix is broken, the institution may persist under the impress of law or custom, but its services will warp under the strain. The warping of the school depends for its completeness upon the warping of a host of related institutions.

Slum environment and culture. A slum is not necessarily the most socially disorganized, most highly congested residential area in a city. The wealthiest residential district of a city may be more densely populated, more congested by traffic, and less communal than a slum neighborhood. Nor is a slum a racial ghetto; in fact, a slum may

include diverse income groups and facilities (Dentler 1968).

Environmentally, an urban slum is a substandard location exhibiting an extremely suboptimal utilization of land. The buildings are often deteriorated and unsanitary. Municipal services—such as garbage collection, traffic control, fire and police protection, health care, and recreation programming—are generally very low in quality of delivery and frequency of coverage compared to other areas in the same city. In turn, an urban slum reflects extremely high levels of morbidity, criminal victimization, and exploitation in the commercial sphere.

Culturally, urban slums vary greatly (Dentler 1968). Some serve as residential neighborhoods of last resort; some offer temporary haven during a process of upward mobility or assimilation; and some are ideal as places of opportunity, offering insulation from kin, protection against easy detection by agents of the law, or chances to experiment with deviant life-styles and occupations. Social scientists have repeatedly cautioned against any assumptions about the cultural organization of slum neighborhoods, for some are highly organized and profoundly communal, whereas others are pathologically disorganized and fragmented by subcultural differences and intergroup tensions (Valentine 1968; Fuchs 1966).

No generalizations are completely valid, but many urban slums do exhibit cultural patterns which are worth noting. High unemployment, underemployment, severe and extensive welfare dependency, and high residential mobility from tenement to tenement often nurture a slum subculture organized around these motifs: (1) cultural isolation fostered by fear of the community beyond the slum and by the erection of territorial boundaries around ethnic groups; (2) heavy reliance upon kin for mutual economic aid and protection against outside threats—including intrusions of agents of the state; and (3) a protective, dependency-oriented, sometimes rigid rearing of children from birth through age seven or eight, followed thereafter by strong emphasis upon autonomy.

School buildings. The slum school is located within a suboptimal environment. It is most often sited amid abandoned tenements, burnt-out retail stores, vacant warehouses, and shutdown factories. If the school building is old, it may be rat- and vermin-infested and on the verge of condemnation. Even if it has been recently built, expensively designed, and handsomely appointed, it strikes the local eye as anomalous, alien, and deserving of suspicion. In either case, it may be locally defined as the target of vandalism. (Parents and local adult residents seldom, if ever, participated in the planning of schools built before the 1960's. Indeed, this kind of citizen participation is still extraordinarily rare.) Finally, old or new, the urban slum school is usually overcrowded with students, understaffed, and poorly or inappropriately equipped (Miller & Woock 1970).

Staff, student, and parent interaction. The triangle of interaction between school staff, children, and parents so basic to the standard public school is broken in the urban slum school. The staff is not recruited from the school neighborhood or from neighborhoods with comparable social-class, ethnic, and life-style characteristics. Composed of college graduates licensed to teach, as it must be under state law, the staff is economically and culturally alien to the slum neighborhood. The lack of congruence goes far beyond race and social class to encompass belief systems and views of self and others (Herriott & St. John 1966).

Parental avoidance of the schools often prevents the development of meaningful relationships between staff and parents. Thirty years of educational research on parent-school relations within low-income urban neighborhoods verifies the fact that parents are generally not involved in school affairs (Dentler et al. 1967). It must be understood, however, that parents suffering from insecurity, welfare dependency, illness, and victimization cannot be expected to participate actively in the affairs of a manifestly alien institution except under carefully designed community relations programs. Few, if any, agents of the school are able, let alone disposed, to build such programs.

The career paths of public school teachers further undermine staff-parent relationships. In city systems, newly licensed teachers tend to be assigned initially to slum schools. The staff turnover rate is often the highest in the city, and the rate of demand for assignment by veteran teachers the lowest. Upward mobility in the teaching field means reassignment to a school outside the slums and ultimately to a school in the suburban, affluent fringe of the city (Boykin 1964). Efforts to change this career path by offering compensatory pay to teachers in slum schools or by changing

assignment policies have been resisted by teachers' unions and organizations. Yet, not all teachers follow this path. For teachers with strong moral and social ideals, assignment to a slum school is desirable. Some other teachers who are assigned to slum schools make an effective personal adjustment. However, the adjusted veteran teacher is sometimes defined, either locally or by teachers at large, as too inept to improve his position, and his adjustment becomes a stigma.

As a result, the rapport between parents and staff is very tenuous, and internal staff stability is hard to maintain. The staff is most likely to consist of young recruits experiencing "culture shock" and uncertain about their ability to carry on, together with veteran teachers stigmatized for their long identification with a slum school. A vigorous and inventive principal can improve these conditions, but the same career conditions also move administrators away from slum schools. Moreover, the principal of a slum school who does not follow the standard school model may risk censure from peers and superiors who count on him to maintain that standard (Hentoff 1966), even though he may succeed locally.

Slum children. Although urban slum children want to go to school and aspire to and are capable of school success in the same way as most nonslum children, they do not arrive in first grade prepared in advance by parents and peers to accept the social contract. The terms of the contract described earlier are disturbingly novel; the rituals of deference and waiting one's turn and the procedural routines so vital to the standard school are strange. To conform effectively, the child must know something in advance about why the conformity is expected (however mythical the rationale may be) and how to achieve it for himself. Given time, the slum student is socialized to the academic rituals as readily as any other student. However, by fourth grade, when the school social pattern has become clear to every slum child, the difference between what is expected in school and what is expected within the peer culture of the streets has reached a stage of unbearable conflict. To conform to one is to become alienated from the other (Passow 1970).

In the standard public school a close watch is maintained, even in the early grades, to diagnose children as retarded, disturbed, maladjusted, physically handicapped, or intellectually gifted. In the more affluent community there is ample time for reconsideration by school staff and parents. In the slum school, however, the entire evaluating and sorting process gets truncated. It matters little whether ability grouping and tracking are practiced or avoided. It is difficult, because of scarce resources and ineffective diagnostic techniques, to accurately identify the children who are gifted or who need remedial help. In addition, diagnostic sorting is usually completed long before the child is socialized to the novel demands of the school, and second chances are rare.

School failure. All these factors contribute to what may be called school failure—that is, the diffuse effects of functional dislocation. The activities programmed by the staff cannot be accomplished; the skill-building exercises go untried; procedural routines are disrupted daily by grave emergencies of illness, accidents, and panic; the concerns of home and neighborhood life—many of them incomprehensible to the staff or objectionable when manifested inside schools—penetrate the confines of hallway and classroom. The staff concludes that school routines cannot be played out, at least by conventional rules. Yet, these routines are the only ones the staff are trained and paid to provide. New teachers often search for modifications in the routines, but the administration, the veteran staff, and the older children are often in agreement about what one beginning teacher identified, quoting students, as "the way it spozed to be" (Herndon 1965).

In the substandard, slum school the delicate balance of staff status structures with student sociometric structures breaks down from one or another sector of the network each day. It breaks down severely enough to make the repairs that suffice in the standard school insufficient. Innovative modifications in the rules of the game fail, since other parties—including parents and children—view them as threats to the balancing effort. The alternative to modification becomes an almost grotesque insistence upon adherence to convention.

At the extreme, the grotesque result evolves in this fashion: Administrators behave as if the school were functioning well. At the same time, they overreward and publicize student conformity and school achievement. The teaching staff takes pride in playing out its part "in spite of" all obstacles. Special recognition is given to veteran teachers who preserve firm adherence to social controls (euphemistically termed classroom management) and who strictly observe the rituals of drill and recitation.

For their part, the slum schoolchildren behave as if they accepted the social controls and as if they were learning to read, write, and multiply. In exchange for public compliance, they are promoted rather than suspended, expelled, or remanded to another institution. A child's illiteracy and his inability to survive high school often come, therefore, as a stunning surprise to his parents.

Impact on the slum community. Slum school failure and the "as if" behavior it spawns have had a vital impact on the slum community. At first, the uneasy legitimacy of the institution was strengthened. The school seemed to some parents to be what it always was. It never worked well, but it was viewed as the warmest, quietest, and safest place for children to be housed during the day. It might have been an alien institution built by unknown officials of the city and staffed by adults from other places and ways of life, but what went on within its walls offered no new source of anxiety. The actual, individual, developmental damage did not materialize till later, when it was pointless to place blame (Miller & Woock 1970). The norms and the routines of the school seemed to be indelibly internalized.

The few children who found their way swiftly and accurately to conventional academic success were rewarded. Some slum schoolchildren, the chosen few, went to academic high schools and even to colleges and professional schools. The rate of success, slightly above zero as it was, was enough to reinforce the success theme of American culture. The few who made it out of the slums confirmed the belief in the adequacy of the standard educational system of the dominant culture. Although slum dwellers may have suspected those who intruded upon their territory, the belief of many of the slum dwellers in the educational values of the dominant culture was profound (Altshuler 1970).

Slum school failure forced the school staff into projections of idealism: One "does one's best—and more." This projection, while not commonplace, enabled teachers to respect themselves and selected peers in terms of the oldest standards in the profession: dedication, self-sacrifice, and service to the poor.

The standard school values were thus distorted within the slum. The "as if" behavior and the celebration of staff and occasional student success —such masking devices basic to the substandard, slum school in the United States since at least 1900—attempted to hide the actual high rate of failure (Janowitz 1969). Popular conceptions aside, the children of Irish and European immigrants entering city slum schools in the early twentieth century were no better educated than today's *chicanos*, Puerto Ricans, and Negroes. Moreover, Negro children in these schools were as badly served by the public school system in 1900 as they are today (Greer 1969).

Social and economic changes are causing the public to lose faith in the legitimacy of the standard school. Today, parents demand more from the schools than a safe haven, employers demand more than a supply of cheap and abundant manual laborers, and teachers want to live something other than the dedicated life. As parents protest, the school's authority structure deteriorates, causing the social controls within the school to deteriorate accordingly. What is more, anger builds when the slum dwellers realize that the outcomes of the historic arrangement are almost irreversible and that the illiterate, under-socialized slum school student seems destined for a lifetime of income insecurity.

Effect on the standard model. The standard school itself has come under critical reconsideration by parents, educators, and social scientists. It appears that the standard model cannot be used as a guide for upgrading substandard, slum schools. The Coleman Report strongly implied that the standard school has been able to operate mainly by relying upon family and social class support (Coleman et al. 1966). The standard school has weathered attack because, although it may fall far short of the educational ideal, it has seemed, under economically and culturally secure conditions, to do no harm. The standard model has now collapsed in urban slum areas because it has ceased to have family or social class support. Even economic equalization of pupil expenditure and capital budgets from district to district will have negligible results (Fox 1967) if the values inherent in the standard school are not changed.

Since 1965, the civil rights movement in the cities has generated a widening disenchantment with the quest for equal educational opportunity through racial and economic desegregation of the schools. The concentration on upgrading segregated slum schools that took place from 1965 to 1968 also proved a source of disenchantment, as the futility of importing the standard school model into the city slum schools via extra movies and remedial programs became clear.

Remedies. When remedies are explored, scale presents the greatest challenge. In 1969 the U.S. Office of Education estimated that 9 million public school students came from households with average incomes of $4,000 or less. About 80 percent of these children attended schools within central cities or in adjacent industrial suburbs. Industrial relocation, suburbanization of the middle-income and upper-income groups, and rising isolation of the urban poor are at the core of the problem. An urban education task force report to the secretary of health, education, and welfare in 1970 estimated that the federal government would have to invest between $7 billion and $14 billion in large-city school systems in the 1970's if the resource imbalance between these systems and those in the affluent suburbs were to begin to be redressed.

A valuable conceptual scheme for a school system that might prove viable within the substandard urban setting has been devised by Janowitz (1969). He called for holistic reordering of the cultural premises and organizational conditions under which teachers and pupils interact. He pointed to urgently needed modifications in districting, grade structures, internal divisions of labor, authority structures, community relations, teaching roles, classroom management, and teacher education. His formulation is emphasized because it systemically identifies the many changes that would have to be introduced (many of them simultaneously) if the substandard school is to meet the needs of the society it serves. One can differ with the Janowitz model without disagreeing that comprehensive change is necessary to reduce the rate of student failure.

Attempts to replace the standard school model are being made in hundreds of urban communities. In some places, educational parks, or facility megastructures which seek to pool plant, staff, and services in a way that greatly enlarges the framework of the neighborhood and the purview of the school as a vast campus (Wolff 1970), are being built. In other districts, community control and the hiring of local residents as semiprofessionals and paraprofessionals in the school may bring parents and staff closer together. Elsewhere, "nonschool schools," which establish programs within work settings, museums, stores, parks, and neighborhood streets, attempt to make a school's curriculum relevant to the students. Finally, performance contracting, computers, and audiovisual aids are being used to try to improve slum schools.

The trend toward greater community control of schools has been directly countered by the unionization of teachers and school administrators. Militant teacher unionism has often presupposed continuation of the standard school, albeit with improvements in the quality of the model—such as reduced class size and lighter teaching loads. Nevertheless, because citizen participation and teacher unionism involve reallocations of resources and authority, they may themselves produce rapid changes in the design of the standard school.

BIBLIOGRAPHY

ALTSHULER, ALAN A. 1970 *Community Control: The Black Demand for Participation in Large American Cities.* New York, Pegasus.

BOYKIN, ARSENE O. 1964 "Demographic Factors Associated With Intra-system Teacher Mobility in an Urban School System." Ph.D. dissertation. Urbana, University of Illinois.

COLEMAN, JAMES S., et al. 1966 *Equality of Educational Opportunity.* Washington, D.C., Government Printing Office.

DENTLER, ROBERT A. 1968 *American Community Problems.* New York, McGraw-Hill.

DENTLER, ROBERT A., BERNARD MACKLER, AND MARY ELLEN WARSHAUER, eds. 1967 *The Urban R's: Race Relations as the Problem in Urban Education.* New York, published for the Center for Urban Education by Praeger.

FOX, DAVID J. 1967 "Issues in Evaluating Programs for Disadvantaged Children." *Urban Review,* 2, no. 3:5, 7, 9.

FUCHS, ESTELLE 1966 *Pickets at the Gates.* New York, Free Press.

GREER, COLIN 1969 "Immigrants, Negroes, and the Public Schools." *Urban Review,* 3, no. 3:9–12.

GRONLUND, NORMAN E. 1959 *Sociometry in the Classroom.* New York, Harper.

HENRY, JULES 1963 *Culture Against Man.* New York, Random House.

HENTOFF, NAT 1966 *Our Children Are Dying.* New York, Viking.

HERNDON, JAMES 1965 *The Way It Spozed to Be.* New York, Simon and Schuster.

HERRIOTT, ROBERT E., AND NANCY H. ST. JOHN 1966 *Social Class and the Urban School.* New York, Wiley.

JANOWITZ, MORRIS 1969 *Institution Building in Urban Education.* New York, Russell Sage Foundation.

MILLER, HARRY L., AND ROGER R. WOOCK 1970 *Social Foundations of Urban Education.* Hinsdale, Ill., Dryden.

PASSOW, A. HARRY, ed. 1970 *Reaching the Disadvantaged Learner.* New York, Teachers College Press.

VALENTINE, CHARLES A. 1968 *Culture and Poverty: Critique and Counter-proposals.* University of Chicago Press.

WOLFF, MAX 1970 *The Educational Park: A Guide to Its Implementation.* With Alan Rinzler, ed. New York, Center for Urban Education.

ROBERT A. DENTLER

5. DIVERSITY IN URBAN SCHOOLS

Diversity among people who associate together can be functional or dysfunctional. The urban public school is both strengthened and weakened by great diversity among students and between students and staff. The important differences to be dealt with in this article are not those resulting from individual personality or from the fact that parents, pupils, and administrators, by virtue of their various positions, have different parts to play. These roles are complementary, and, to the extent that all participants agree on the rules of the school game, the rights of the clients are the obligations of the professionals and vice versa. However, performance of roles is governed not only by common expectations for oneself and for others but also by diverse expectations resulting from diverse social backgrounds. It is the gap between the social worlds of different groups of students and between those of some students and their teachers which create problems for the urban public school.

Any society is characterized by its own way of life, by its own set of beliefs and values, in short, by its own culture. But a modern industrial society is not homogeneous. It encompasses many regional, ethnic, and socioeconomic groups, which share elements of the national culture but have distinguishable subcultures of their own. Some aspects of culture are more relevant to an educational system than others. The all-important cultural differences for schools are differences in commitment to and preparation for academic achievement and differences in beliefs about appropriate teacher and pupil behavior. In these respects children from various subcultures arrive in school very differently equipped.

Some statistics will indicate the extent of background differences between groups of public school pupils. Rose and Rose (1965) attempted to determine the number of groups that face discrimination in the United States and the size of each group. They concluded that almost one-fifth of all Americans, not counting Catholics, are minorities in the sense of being targets of discrimination, including Negroes (10.5 percent of the total population), Jews (3 percent), Spanish-Americans and Mexican-Americans (2.9 percent), Orientals (0.5 percent), Puerto Ricans (0.5 percent), and American Indians (0.3 percent). In addition, large numbers of Americans in other ethnic groups are foreign-born or the children of foreign-born parents. Thus, Glazer and Moynihan (1963) estimated that, in 1960, 19 percent of New York City's population were foreign-born and 28 percent were the children of foreign-born Americans. As for income, in 1962, 28 percent of the households in the United States had annual incomes of less than $3,000; 28 percent had incomes between $3,000 and $6,000; 28 percent, between $6,000 and $10,000; and 15 percent, over $10,000 (Lasswell 1965). These income and ethnic group statistics are national. Among public school pupils in large cities the percentage of low-income families is lower and the percentage of nonwhite families is higher.

Heterogeneity in pupil background, however, is not found within most urban classrooms. It is ironic that belief in the value of heterogeneity has grown simultaneously with decreases in actual social mixing. Of necessity, the rural one-room school mixed ages, sexes, abilities, and social backgrounds. As communities grew, educators chose to sort children into age grades, ability groups, boys' schools and girls' schools, trade schools and grammar schools, and schools for whites and schools for Negroes or Indians. As a result of shifts in educational philosophy, one form of segregation after another has been challenged. However, suburbanization and the growth of the nonwhite population in center cities, patterns of urban renewal and housing development, and decisions on highway construction have intensified the economic and racial divisions between metropolitan neighborhoods and therefore between their schools.

According to Havighurst (1963), the larger the city, the smaller its percentage of mixed-class schools and the larger its percentage of homogeneous middle-class or lower-class schools. Thus, in Detroit 16 percent of the elementary school pupils attend middle-class schools, 52 percent attend mixed-class schools, and 32 percent attend lower-class schools; however, in Chicago the figures are 19 percent, 35 percent, and 46 percent, respectively. Herriott and St. John (1966) divided the

National Principalship Study sample of elementary schools in 41 cities into quartiles according to the background of parents. Over one-half of the parents of students in schools in the top quarter were college-educated professional or business people with annual incomes of over $10,000, and about 90 percent of the parents of students in schools in the bottom quarter were unskilled or semiskilled workers with high school educations or less and family incomes of under $5,000.

In the first grade, 97 percent of white children in the United States, 97 percent of Negro children in southern cities, and 72 percent of Negro children in northern cities are in schools in which they are in the majority. Other minority group children are not usually in schools in which their own group predominates but are often in schools with Negroes (Coleman et al. 1966). The U.S. Commission on Civil Rights (1967) found that among school-age Negro children in Chicago and Philadelphia 89 percent and 72 percent, respectively, were in schools whose student bodies were 90 to 100 percent Negro. In New York City, 56 percent of all Negro and Puerto Rican children were in schools whose student bodies were 90 to 100 percent Negro and Puerto Rican.

The plight of poor and minority group pupils isolated in schools with others of similar backgrounds can be measured either in terms of dissatisfaction and turnover of teachers or in terms of alienation and underachievement of pupils. The Coleman (Coleman et al. 1966) and U.S. Commission on Civil Rights (1967) reports relate these effects to economic or ethnic segregation. Some black power spokesmen and other observers maintain that the responsibility for pupil failure rests with the schools, because deprived pupils do not have teachers who understand them, believe in them, and know how to teach them. Several writers have seen teacher-pupil cultural or racial differences as dysfunctional (Clark 1965; Carmichael & Hamilton 1967).

The idea of a dysfunctional culture gap between teachers and pupils is not new. In the 1940's the proposition was advanced that teachers, being middle class, hold middle-class values which cause them to reject and discriminate against lower-class pupils (Warner et al. 1944). Charters (1963) summarized the pre-1960 evidence on the social origins and values of teachers and the influence of these values on classroom behavior, and he concluded that Warner's proposition remained an unproved hypothesis. However, today it is the ethnic or racial gap between teachers and pupils rather than the economic gap that concerns many observers. Moreover, new evidence as to cognitive and motivational differences between people of diverse backgrounds suggests that one reason why 20 years of research into the teacher-pupil gap proved sterile was the excessive concern of researchers with values. Values may be society-wide and part of the culture that all share. Subcultural differences which are crucial for the schools may be of a different type.

Teacher-student background differences. Teachers are undoubtedly members of the middle class. Whether the index used is educational level, current income, or occupational status, teachers rank above the average American. Thus, 95 percent of teachers in the United States but only 9.8 percent of other persons over 25 hold at least a bachelor's degree (U.S. Department . . . 1967). All teachers, but only 12.8 percent of American wage earners, are professionals. Mason (1961) found that over one-half of the employed spouses of beginning teachers were teachers or other professionals. Although the average salary of teachers is lower than that of most other professionals, it is 10 percent above the mean salary of all employed workers (National Education Association 1960). In 1966 a national sample considered teaching the 29th most prestigious of 90 occupations listed (Cohen 1967). There is no question but that teachers' status as a group is somewhat above the average for all occupations.

It is, however, the social-class origin of teachers rather than their present status which has been considered the key to their cultural values and norms. Does the typical teacher grow up in a middle-class or a working-class home? The question is usually answered in terms of the occupational and educational level of his parents. The fathers of teachers come from all occupational levels, and over one-half are either blue-collar workers, farmers, or low-status white-collar workers. Therefore, a larger percentage of teachers are upward mobile than is the case in other professions (Mason 1961; Davis 1965). However, in comparison with all Americans of their own or their pupils' generation, a larger percentage of teachers are the children of professionals, business managers, and farmers and a smaller percentage are the children of blue-collar workers and low-status white-collar workers.

Teachers' parents generally have more education than do the parents of teachers' contemporaries or their pupils. Data on income levels in the homes in which teachers grow up are scarce, but roughly 11 percent of the elementary school teachers surveyed in the National Principalship Study reported that their families' incomes had been in the top quarter in their community, 33 percent in the second quarter, 45 percent in the third quarter, and 11 percent in the bottom quarter (Herriott & St. John 1966). In short, most teachers grow up in homes of moderate income.

In general, therefore, in comparison with public school pupils, a smaller percentage of teachers are from lower-class homes and a larger percentage are from upper-class homes. Moreover, the large family size and small private school attendance among pupils from the lowest strata must be taken into account. Therefore, if both teachers and pupils were distributed among classrooms across the United States completely at random, in any one year perhaps more than one-third of all pupils would have teachers from higher social class backgrounds than their own, and in the course of 12 years pupils would probably be exposed to teachers from all backgrounds.

Socioeconomic match by classroom. Since distribution is not random, knowledge of the overall socioeconomic match tells one little about the classroom match of pupils and teachers, and this match by classroom has not been the subject of systematic research. There is some evidence of a correlation between the social background of teachers and the social background of their pupils. For instance, among elementary school teachers sampled for the National Principalship Study, 64 percent of the teachers in schools whose pupils had the highest socioeconomic status had white-collar fathers. However, only 43 percent of the teachers in schools for lower-class pupils had blue-collar fathers (Herriott & St. John 1966). The greatest teacher-student social gap thus occurs in schools for the lower classes. Even if all teachers from working-class backgrounds were concentrated in these schools (and they obviously are not), they would be too few to fill all the teaching posts. Moreover, it is likely that most teachers who are working-class in origin would not have been as deprived in their youth as the pupils they would teach.

Ethnic and community matching. Overall, the number of minority group members being trained as teachers is too small to allow ethnic matching in the classroom, even if such matching were public policy. A National Education Association analysis of 1960 census data showed that about 9 percent of all teachers in the United States are nonwhite (Cohen 1967), but 17 percent of American pupils are nonwhite (U.S. Department . . . 1967). In one national sample of beginning teachers, only 5 percent were Negroes and 1 percent were other nonwhites. The nonwhites were concentrated in the Southeast, so that the proportion in the North and in the West was under 3 percent (Mason 1961).

The Coleman and U.S. Commission on Civil Rights reports have made available data on teacher-pupil congruency by race and ethnic group. White children throughout the United States are usually taught by white teachers. Negro children have Negro teachers if they live in the South but have more white than Negro teachers if they live in other regions. Oriental children in secondary schools sometimes have Oriental teachers. Other minority group children—Mexican-Americans, Puerto Ricans, American Indians— in spite of their language handicap, rarely have a teacher with their own linguistic background (Coleman et al. 1966). In Philadelphia, for example, in 1961, 37 percent of the teachers and 53 percent of the pupils were Negro (U.S. Commission . . . 1962). The black teachers were distributed so that there were roughly one-third fewer black teachers than black pupils in all districts.

The religious background of teachers and their pupils has been little studied, but National Principalship Study data on elementary schools in 41 cities may be representative of the situation in large cities across the United States. Congruency is greatest in schools whose students are lower middle class. In upper-class schools a larger percentage of pupils than teachers are Jewish; in lower-class schools a larger percentage of teachers than pupils are either Jewish or Catholic (Herriott & St. John 1966).

Teachers and their pupils can also be matched (or mismatched) with respect to the type of community in which they grew up. Of the elementary school teachers in cities with populations of 50,000 or more sampled in the National Principalship Study, 16 percent came from rural areas, 37 percent came from villages or small cities, and only 46 percent came, as did their pupils, from large cities (*ibid.*). Of the 67,000 teachers

sampled in the Coleman study, about 40 percent had spent most of their lives in the localities in which they were teaching, and this percentage was higher for the teachers of Negroes and Puerto Ricans (especially in metropolitan areas) than for the teachers of other minority groups or whites (Coleman et al. 1966).

Charters concludes a discussion of the social origins of teachers with this modal description: "American teachers may be characterized as predominantly college-educated, native-born, Protestant, white, middle-aged, married females of middle class and possibly rural or small town origins" (1963, p. 721). He warns, however, that such a description does not take into account variations from the norm or the systematic nature of such variations. It must also be added that the description does not take account of the selective influence of the characteristics of pupils on the characteristics of teachers in individual schools.

Subcultural differences among pupils. The school-related attitudes and behaviors of pupils in slum schools become clearer if compared with those of children in middle-class schools. Two cautions are necessary if the importance of the comparison is to be properly understood. First, all pupils in slum schools do not come from poor, uneducated, or unstable families; nor do all pupils in middle-class schools come from middle-income, well-educated, and stable families. Second, parents and children, whether they are poor or affluent and whether they are members of a minority group or the majority group, do not all exhibit the modal characteristics associated with their social backgrounds. Remembering these reservations, one can profitably consider the influence of social class and ethnic group membership on pupils' commitment to and preparation for school achievement. An excellent reference source on this subject is Joan Roberts' *School Children in the Urban Slum* (1967).

Values and attitudes. Oscar Lewis (1966) has stated that in the culture of poverty, people are aware of middle-class values and may even claim some of them as their own, but they do not live by them. According to Kluckhohn and Lockwood (1953), the dominant American values, those of the middle-class majority group, are activistic, individualistic, and future oriented, but variant class and ethnic subcultures are passivistic, collectivistic, and present oriented. Rosen (1959) tested that hypothesis on a sample of mothers of diverse social and ethnic backgrounds. There was much overlap, but lower-class mothers were less apt than were middle-class mothers to indicate activistic, individualistic, and future-oriented (that is, achievement) values.

A cross-cultural study of the qualities which blue-collar and white-collar parents in Italy and the United States hope for in their children found that essentially the same class differences existed in both countries, the middle-class parents stressing self-control and working-class parents emphasizing obedience. This difference was seen as the result of universal occupational differences between white-collar and blue-collar workers as to closeness of supervision, degree of self-reliance, and amount of work with things, people, or ideas. Blue-collar parents, whose own work is with things and is closely supervised, will see the importance of obedience but will not strive to develop in their children self-reliance or interest in people and ideas (Pearlin & Kohn 1966).

Another study found support for the theory that the values given highest priority by people are those which are seen as both important and uncertain of attainment—internalized standards of conduct among middle-class parents and respectability among working-class parents (Kohn 1959). Respectability is of more concern to parents than to children, of more concern to the upper working class than to the lower working class, and of more concern to those Gans (1962) called "routine-seekers" than to "action-seekers." Walter B. Miller (1958) was referring to action-seeking lower-class youths when he identified six "focal concerns" of those in lower-class culture: avoiding trouble with officials, being tough, being smart (in the sense of having the ability to outwit and not be "taken in"), having exciting experiences, having autonomy (although lower-class youths may have a need for the external controls they resent), and believing in fate. The child who comes to school with such focal concerns will obviously be a challenge to his teacher.

A belief in fate or luck rather than in the efficacy of one's own efforts is generally characteristic of people who cannot realistically hope to succeed without outside intervention (Rotter 1960; O. Lewis 1966). The Coleman Report gives the percentages of 12th-grade pupils surveyed who disagreed with the statement that good luck is more important for success than is hard work: 89 per-

cent of whites, 70 percent of Negroes in the metropolitan Northeast, 57 percent of Negroes in the nonmetropolitan South, and 53 percent of Puerto Ricans (Coleman et al. 1966).

Many studies have found differences between social classes in the levels of aspiration expressed by parents for their children and by adolescents for themselves. In view of the difficulties that stand in the path of lower-class or minority-group youths, the puzzle is not why there are differences in the mean levels of aspiration but why the differences are so small. For example, the Coleman Report found that an especially high level of motivation was reported by Negro students (Coleman et al. 1966). According to Lott and Lott (1963), Negro and white high school seniors in Kentucky have many values and aspirations in common; however, although the Negroes verbalize their belief in education, they do not pursue this objective as strongly as do white students. A projective test indicated the Negroes' lower need for achievement (designated "N–ach"). Similarly, the Negro mothers in Rosen's sample wanted much education for their sons, but the boys themselves had lower N–ach scores than did the boys of any other ethnic group (Rosen 1959).

One study of attitudes toward public schools found lower-class parents less negative than middle-class parents, more likely to mention teachers when evaluating the job schools are doing, and more likely to feel schools do not pay attention to children from poor families (Cloward & Jones 1963). Lower-class parents generally feel more cut off from their children's schools than do middle-class parents and are more hesitant to initiate contact with school authorities (Eddy 1967).

The studies reviewed here have focused on mean differences, but they have all reported much divergence from the mean. In fact, across subcultures, values are more alike than they are different. Variations occur less in respect to values than in respect to focal concerns, less in respect to goals than in respect to the belief that goals can be realized or the willingness to struggle to achieve them.

Child rearing and personality. In the culture of poverty the family does not cherish childhood (O. Lewis 1966). Working-class homes are "adult-centered," and middle-class homes are "child-centered" (Gans 1962). The instability and pressures of life among lower-class people and the facts that families are often larger, fathers often absent, and mothers often at work mean that children get less attention (Langner & Michael 1963; Liebow 1967). Some researchers have noted a lack of interest among the lower class in personality characteristics which differentiate one individual from another and which contribute to the development of a sense of self-identification (Wortis et al. 1963). Young children are not pushed to learn self-control or skills. They are criticized less but also praised less than are middle-class children. Less emphasis is placed on postponing satisfaction or on planning for the future.

Among the lower class, parent surrogates—older siblings, grandmothers, foster parents—often share in the care of the young child and may confuse him because they hold different standards of acceptable behavior. Discipline is apt to be authoritarian rather than democratic, physical rather than verbal. Social control is achieved by shame and threats of punishment, not by reasoning and encouragement of the development of internal controls (Bronfenbrenner 1958). Lower-class children achieve independence from adult authority at an earlier age than do middle-class children; the peer group thus assumes a more important role as socializing agent (Ausubel & Ausubel 1963).

The personality difficulties common among lower-class or minority-group children (Dreger & Miller 1960) may be caused, at least partially, by their having been "undersocialized—resulting in an acting out of problems which we label character disorders" (Langner & Michael 1963, p. 442). The personality problems of some lower-class children may also be a result of the stresses and strains in their own lives and in those of their parents. Albert Cohen and Harold Hodges, Jr., (1963) describe the life situation of lower-class workers on the San Francisco peninsula as being characterized by constricted experience, powerlessness, deprivation, and insecurity. The lower-class person's adaptation to this situation includes intolerance, suspicion of the unfamiliar and of the motives of others, extrapunitiveness, pessimism, fatalism, and alienation.

The matriarchal family organization, so common among lower-class Negroes and assumed to be so destructive to the development of ego strength in boys (Rainwater 1966; H. Lewis 1967) is not characteristic of the Puerto Rican or Mexican-American subcultures (Heller 1966). But even though he may be present and dominant, the lower-class father typically does not provide his son with the role model of a happy, successful man; the father's low status is a source of shame to himself and his family (Liebow 1967). The self-concept of the nonwhite child is further depressed through internalization of color prejudice (Pettigrew 1964).

In short, lower-class children are raised in homes in which the standards and methods of discipline are generally unlike those in the school, in which adults relinquish to the peer group much of their socializing role, and in which ambivalence toward authority, aggressiveness, fatalism, apathy, and a negative self-concept may be learned from the culture if not acquired as a result of the frustrations of life.

Cognitive development. It is well established that performance on tests of mental ability and achievement is related both to socioeconomic status and to racial background. Although the overlap is always great, the mean scores of lower-class whites or Negroes are below those of middle-class or upper-class whites or Negroes, and at each status level the mean score of Negroes is below that of whites (Dreger & Miller 1960).

Both environmental and testing factors combine to produce such differences. Birth defects and nutritional deficiencies, common among the poor, can affect intellectual functioning (Pettigrew 1964). Being born into a large family or a fatherless home is also detrimental, probably because the child receives minimal attention (Deutsch & Brown 1964). The lower-class child lacks the constant coaching of adults and the stimulation of a home rich in material objects. The cumulative nature of environmental deprivation is indicated by the increasing test score differences between classes or racial groups as the children grow older (Coleman et al. 1966).

Achievement and ability tests are not in any sense culturally unbiased; in fact, these tests are designed to determine the degree to which a child has assimilated a culture appropriate to modern life in America—that is, a middle-class culture (Coleman et al. 1966). The importance of early training in the home to the development of language fluency and the ability to use language for other learning is well recognized and the subject of much research. Bernstein (1961) analyzed the speech styles of working-class and middle-class people: the former style is "restricted" in meanings and syntax, and the latter is "elaborated," allowing much more scope in communication. Olim, Hess, and Shipman (1967) found a significant relation between social class and the type of language and control mothers used to instruct their children, on the one hand, and those children's cognitive performance, on the other. Working-class children tend to have a "motoric" orientation; middle-class children tend to have a "conceptual" orientation (D. Miller & Swanson 1960). These orientations are related to the type of discipline and rewards used by mothers (*ibid.*). Riessman (1962) contrasts the patient, persevering, "slow gifted" lower-class child to the quick, facile, flexible middle-class child.

In summary, therefore, many of the lower-class children entering slum schools are already handicapped in the race for advantaged roles in society. Their subcultures have not provided them with interests, motives, skills, or attitudes toward themselves or toward those in authority that are as functional for school learning as those normally acquired by middle-class children. It would seem that the handicap could be overcome only with the help of teachers who understand its nature and have confidence in their pupils and in their own professional competence to meet the pupils' needs.

Teachers' attitudes and expectations. Teaching attracts and retains people who have certain attributes. One attribute is being female; more than two-thirds of all public school teachers and three-quarters of elementary school teachers are women (National Education Association 1962). In addition, future teachers usually achieve lower intelligence test scores or grade-point averages than do other college students (Davis 1965). Among one group of undergraduates studied, wanting to work with people and not especially wanting to make a lot of money correlated strongly with choosing a career in education (*ibid.*). Similarly, when Mason (1961) compared the occupational values of beginning teachers with those of a sample of students in all fields, he found that the teachers' interest in being helpful and in working with people was much higher than that of the comparison group and their interest in making money was much lower.

Socialization. Socialization into professional roles takes place in training institutions and on the job. Through formal instruction and through informal association with faculty members, fellow students, and veteran professionals, prospec-

tive and beginning teachers gradually learn professional values and attitudes as well as teaching skills and knowledge (Charters 1963; Corwin 1965). Experience in the classroom during either student teaching or a first job is especially likely to produce changes in attitudes. For example, scores on the Minnesota Teacher Attitude Inventory (MTAI), which rise during the college years, drop following practice teaching, indicating that attitudes toward children have become less permissive and warm (Rabinowitz & Rosenbaum 1960). Those who continue to teach a second year have more favorable attitudes toward schools and pupils than those who do not, but they stress the need for professionalism in teaching and tight classroom discipline (Sorenson et al. 1966). Walberg (1968) found that students rate themselves less favorably following practice teaching. He attributed the decline in self-concept to a conflict between the teachers' personality need to establish rapport with children and the role demands of teaching. Rabinowitz and Rosenbaum described the changes in teachers' attitudes during the first years on the job as follows: "Teachers became less concerned with pupil freedom and more concerned with establishing a stable, orderly classroom in which academic standards receive prominent position" (1960, p. 317).

Teaching situations. Some "reality shock" and attitude changes follow teaching experience in any setting. However, the specific teaching situation also influences new teachers. A comparison of student teachers who volunteer for and those who are assigned to New York City public schools for disadvantaged pupils indicated that the volunteers were less rigid, authoritarian, or negative in their perceptions of these schools and more self-confident and interested in humanitarian service (Langberg & Freedman 1965). The supervisors of beginning teachers in systems with predominantly working-class pupils tend to stress discipline, organization, and task performance; in middle-class schools teachers are evaluated more on social skills (Turner 1965).

In large cities, beginning teachers are especially likely to be assigned to slum schools. They are typically given no special training to develop the competencies necessary to deal with the cognitive and motivational style of their pupils. On-the-job supervision, where available, tends to stress meeting the needs of the organization rather than the needs of pupils (Corwin 1965, chap. 1; E.

Fuchs 1967). From experienced teachers the novice usually learns to blame the pupils or the administration for his difficulties rather than himself. Groff (1963) reported on the dissatisfaction of teachers in schools serving Negro or Mexican-American ghettos in a large city. The most common reason for teachers' leaving ghetto schools was characteristics of their pupils, a reason mentioned by 42 percent of the teachers studied. Deficiencies in the administration and organization of the school came next, mentioned by 38 percent of the teachers. Shortcomings of the teachers themselves was third, mentioned by 22 percent. Becker (1952) was the first to identify horizontal mobility—away from slum schools where careers often began, through a series of transfers, to schools whose clients were more acceptable to the teacher—as the typical career pattern of teachers in large cities. Difficulty in producing changes in students' skill and knowledge levels, difficulty in disciplining students, and the unacceptability of students' morals were cited by teachers as reasons for leaving ghetto schools. A minority stayed, revised their expectations, and learned new teaching and disciplinary techniques. A number of subsequent studies with larger samples have confirmed Becker's findings as to both the prevalence of the desire to transfer away from slum schools and the reasons for that desire (Havighurst 1964, chap. 16; Herriott & St. John 1966).

Wayson (1966) interviewed 42 teachers who had been in slum schools for more than five years and 20 teachers who had left or were planning to do so. The "stayers" were motivated to remain in ghetto schools by their freedom from community pressures and extra classroom obligations and by the characteristics of slum children that they perceived as complementary to their own personality needs. The "leavers" were motivated by frustration over the low academic achievement of disadvantaged pupils and by a desire for recognition from professional superiors. Neither social-class origin nor race distinguished the two groups. Both stayers and leavers had lower-middle-class backgrounds: Negro stayers were like white stayers; Negro leavers were like white leavers.

The stayers and leavers described by Becker and by Wayson defined the role of teacher differently. One of the problems faced by those being socialized into any occupational role is lack of consensus as to role expectations; teaching is no exception (Getzels & Guba 1955; Gross et al.

1958). Record (1964) described convincingly (although without offering empirical evidence) six types of teachers often found on the faculties of schools for the disadvantaged: the indifferent, the frightened, the status-striver, the custodian, the secular missionary, and the teacher's teacher (who is professionally interested in subject matter and students and in bringing the two together). The new teacher must choose between such role models and also reconcile their conflicting definitions with those of the principal, the parents, and the pupils. Failure to resolve the divergent expectations of significant others and to find a role which satisfies personality needs as well is probably an important cause of dissatisfaction among teachers in slum schools.

Influence of teacher's background. What part does the social-class and ethnic background of teachers play in their attitudes and role performance? Charters (1963) found little empirical evidence showing that teachers hold attitudes typical of their backgrounds or guide their classroom teaching accordingly. Differential allocation of rewards and punishments to middle-class and lower-class children, which obviously occurs (Davidson & Lang 1960), can be explained as a function of the students' preparation for academic competition rather than as a function of the middle-class orientation of teachers.

There is some evidence that ethnic difference may be more of a barrier between teacher and pupil than is social-class difference. Teachers have been found to be very unaware of the social backgrounds of pupils from ethnic cultures different from their own (Ulibarri 1960). Expectations for minority-group pupils on the part of majority-group teachers are often very low (Clark 1965; Anderson & Safar 1967). Children perceive very well their teachers' feelings toward them, and achievement tends to adjust to teacher expectations (Davidson & Lang 1960; Rosenthal 1966). Moreover, black students have been found to underestimate the favorable attitudes of white teachers toward them (Amos 1952).

Gottlieb (1964) demonstrated that white and black teachers' perceptions of the same pupils can be quite different. Children who seemed happy, cooperative, energetic, and ambitious to black teachers seemed talkative, lazy, high-strung, and rebellious to white teachers. Gottlieb's sample of 39 black teachers and 57 white teachers was drawn from six inner-city schools in a medium-sized midwestern city. Among both racial groups, dissatisfaction increased with years of teaching experience, but white teachers criticized the shortcomings of students and felt that training programs should be more realistic, whereas black teachers criticized the physical setting of the school and felt that teachers should be more carefully selected and more thoroughly trained in how to teach skills. Since the black teachers were younger than the white teachers and more apt to come from backgrounds similar to those of their pupils, it is difficult to determine whether their greater personal identification with the pupils was the result of greater ethnic, economic, or generational congruity. Gottlieb's findings are intriguing and suggest the importance of further studies, under controlled conditions, of the effect of racially matching teachers and pupils.

Incongruence in urban schools. Lawrence Fuchs contrasted the achievement orientation of Peace Corps volunteers in the Philippines with the native attitude of "bahala-na":

> More than anything else, volunteers wanted to succeed in doing something significant. . . . Imbued with the ideals of their own culture, the volunteers came to a land that had for more than 50 years given verbal endorsement to those very same ideals, while retaining a way of life at variance with them. . . . The deepest meaning of "bahala-na" (It doesn't matter, never mind) is that conditions of life are unchanging and unchangeable. To American volunteers restlessly anxious to improve the world almost everything mattered desperately, at least at first. (L. Fuchs 1967, pp. 66, 108)

Young teachers, like Peace Corps volunteers, want to succeed at doing something significant. They want to help children acquire skills and knowledge. Assignment to a low-income neighborhood means for many teachers entering a cultural world very different from the one in which they grew up and went to college. People in both cultures hold many of the same values but differ radically in their focal concerns, their outlooks on life, and the degree to which they encourage self-confidence, self-discipline, and readiness for learning in their children.

Unfortunately, teachers of low-income children ordinarily do not completely bridge the cultural gap between their world and that of their pupils. Their only contacts with lower-class life occur in the school, and from this perspective their view of the community is inexact and stereotyped. Having had different childhoods, they do not really understand or identify with their pupils (Eddy 1967). However, the incongruence in the situation is not necessarily the result of the background gap between teachers and pupils but of barriers that keep them apart and the fact that teachers have few supervisors who help them understand subcultural differences and the commonalities beneath these differences.

A second type of incongruence in the urban school is the considerable gap between the academic needs of lower-class pupils and the ability of most teachers to meet those needs. The preschool socialization of competence is as incomplete for the teachers as it is for the pupils. Knowledge of how children learn or of how to teach those who do not teach themselves is still very incomplete. Stodolsky and Lesser (1967) urged, as a step toward meeting the educational needs of the disadvantaged, the assessment of each child's pattern of mental abilities and the matching of instructional strategy to the child's particular strengths and weaknesses. Ausubel (1963) suggested a threefold teaching strategy for slum children. First, initial learning material should be geared to the learner's state of readiness. Second, each learning task should be mastered and integrated with previous learning before new tasks are introduced. Third, learning materials optimally organized to facilitate efficient sequential learning should be used.

The attitudes and role expectations of teachers, although somewhat influenced by their own social origins, are more significantly influenced by the needs, traditions, norms, goals, and assumptions of their profession, their school system, and their school. The urban school is distant from its lower-class community not primarily because its personnel are middle-class but because its task definition is too narrow, its curriculum is too inappropriate, its professional leadership is too inadequate, and its criteria of success are too traditional to ensure the rewards of achievement for either pupils or teachers. The urban school "culture" is as foreign to most beginning teachers as it is to lower-class pupils.

A third type of incongruence, then, is that between the personality needs of teachers and the opportunities for satisfying those needs in urban schools. Beginning teachers are eager to use their abilities to help people. To varying degrees, depending on individual personality structure, they also need success, status, recognition, and self-actualization. The slum school rarely affords many of these satisfactions. Teachers who leave slum schools are frustrated by the low academic achievement of their pupils and by the lack of recognition from professional superiors (Wayson 1966). The teacher in the slum school must somehow develop the competence to help children to achieve, and he must receive the recognition such accomplishment deserves.

Teachers who remain in slum schools are apparently motivated by characteristics of slum children they perceive as complementary to their own personality needs. This finding is important. A recognized principle in the sociology of the family is that successful marriage can be built on complementary as well as similar personality needs, interests, or values. Analogously, diversity of cultural background may not stand in the way of the successful interaction of teacher and pupil in the urban school if cultural understanding matches eagerness to help and if professional training is geared to the learning needs of the pupil.

BIBLIOGRAPHY

AMOS, ROBERT T. 1952 "The Accuracy of Negro and White Children's Predictions of Teachers' Attitudes Toward Negro Students." *Journal of Negro Education*, 21, no. 2:125–135.

ANDERSON, JAMES G., AND DWIGHT SAFAR 1967 "The Influence of Differential Community Perceptions on the Provision of Equal Educational Opportunity." *Sociology of Education*, 40, no. 3:219–230.

AUSUBEL, DAVID P. 1963 "A Teaching Strategy for Culturally Deprived Pupils: Cognitive and Motivational Considerations." *School Review*, 71, no. 4:454–463.

AUSUBEL, DAVID P., AND PEARL AUSUBEL 1963 "Ego Development Among Segregated Negro Children." A. Harry Passow, ed., *Education in Depressed Areas*. New York, Teachers College Press. Pages 109–141.

BECKER, HOWARD S. 1952 "The Career of the Chicago Public School Teacher." *American Journal of Sociology*, 57, no. 5:470–477.

BERNSTEIN, BASIL 1961 "Social Structure, Language and Learning." *Educational Research*, 3, no. 3:1–15.

BRONFENBRENNER, URIE 1958 "Socialization and Social Class Through Time and Space." Eleanor E. Maccoby, Theodore M. Newcomb, and Eugene L. Hartley, eds., *Readings in Social Psychology*. 3rd ed. New York, Holt. Pages 400–425.

CARMICHAEL, STOKELY, AND CHARLES V. HAMILTON 1967 *Black Power: The Politics of Liberation in America*. New York, Vintage.

CHARTERS, W. W., JR. 1963 "The Social Background of Teaching." Nathaniel L. Gage, ed., *Handbook of Research on Teaching*. Chicago, Rand McNally. Pages 715–813.

CLARK, KENNETH B. 1965 *Dark Ghetto: Dilemmas of Social Power*. New York, Harper.

CLOWARD, RICHARD A., AND JAMES A. JONES 1963 "Social Class: Educational Attitudes and Participation." A. Harry Passow, ed., *Education in Depressed Areas*. New York, Teachers College Press. Pages 190–216.

COHEN, ALBERT K., AND HAROLD M. HODGES, JR. 1963 "Characteristics of the Lower Blue-collar Class." *Social Problems*, 10, no. 4:303–334.

COHEN, ELIZABETH G. 1967 "Status of Teachers." *Review of Educational Research*, 37, no. 3:280–295.

COLEMAN, JAMES S., et al. 1966 *Equality of Educational Opportunity*. Washington, D.C., Government Printing Office.

CORWIN, RONALD G. 1965 *A Sociology of Education*. New York, Appleton. See especially Chapter 1, "Schools in Process."

DAVIDSON, HELEN H., AND GERHARD LANG 1960 "Children's Perceptions of Their Teacher's Feelings Toward Them Related to Self-perception, School Achievement and Behavior." *Journal of Educational Psychology*, 29, no. 2:107–118.

DAVIS, JAMES A. 1965 *Undergraduate Career Decisions: Correlates of Occupational Choice*. Chicago, Aldine.

DEUTSCH, M., AND B. BROWN 1964 "Social Influences in Negro-White Intelligence Differences." *Journal of Social Issues*, 20:24–35.

DREGER, RALPH M., AND KENT S. MILLER 1960 "Comparative Psychological Studies of Negroes and Whites in the United States." *Psychological Bulletin*, 57, no. 5:361–402.

EDDY, ELIZABETH M. 1967 *Walk the White Line: A Profile of Urban Education*. Garden City, N.Y., Doubleday.

FUCHS, ESTELLE 1967 *Teachers Talk: A View From Within Inner City Schools*. New York, Project True, Hunter College.

FUCHS, LAWRENCE H. 1967 *Those Peculiar Americans: The Peace Corps and American National Character*. New York, Meredith.

GANS, HERBERT J. 1962 *The Urban Villagers*. New York, Free Press.

GETZELS, JACOB W., AND EGON G. GUBA 1955 "The Structure of Roles and Role Conflict in the Teaching Situation." *Journal of Educational Sociology*, 29:30–40.

GLAZER, NATHAN, AND DANIEL PATRICK MOYNIHAN 1963 *Beyond the Melting Pot*. Cambridge, Mass., MIT Press.

GOTTLIEB, DAVID 1964 "Teaching and Students: The Views of Negro and White Teachers." *Sociology of Education*, 37, no. 4:345–353.

GROFF, PATRICK J. 1963 "Dissatisfactions in Teaching the Culturally Deprived Child." *Phi Delta Kappan*, 45, no. 2:76.

GROSS, NEAL C., WARD S. MASON, AND ALEXANDER W. McEACHERN 1958 *Explorations in Role Analysis: Studies of the School Superintendency Role*. New York, Wiley.

HAVIGHURST, ROBERT J. 1963 "Urban Development and the Educational System." A. Harry Passow, ed., *Education in Depressed Areas*. New York, Teachers College Press. Pages 24–45.

HAVIGHURST, ROBERT J. 1964 *The Public Schools of Chicago*. Chicago Board of Education.

HELLER, CELIA 1966 *Mexican-American Youth: Forgotten Youth at the Crossroads*. New York, Random House.

HERRIOTT, ROBERT, AND NANCY H. ST. JOHN 1966 *Social Class and the Urban School*. New York, Wiley.

KATZ, IRWIN 1964 "Review of Evidence Relating to Effects of Desegregation on the Intellectual Performance of Negroes." *American Psychologist*, 19, no. 6:381–399.

KLUCKHOHN, CLYDE, AND FLORENCE LOCKWOOD 1953 "Dominant and Variant Value Orientations." Clyde Kluckhohn, Henry A. Murray, and David N. Schneider, eds.,

Personality in Nature, Society and Culture. New York, Knopf. Pages 342–357.

KOHN, MELVIN L. 1959 "Social Class and Parental Values." *American Journal of Sociology,* 64, no. 4:337–351.

LANGBERG, GEORGE, AND PHILIP I. FREEDMAN 1965 "Self Selection of Student Teachers." *Integrated Education,* 3, nos. 4 and 5:34–40.

LANGNER, THOMAS S., AND STANLEY T. MICHAEL 1963 *Life Stress and Mental Health.* New York, Free Press.

LASSWELL, THOMAS E. 1965 *Class and Stratum: An Introduction to Concepts and Research.* Boston, Houghton Mifflin.

LEWIS, HYLAN 1967 "The Family: Resources for Change." Lee Rainwater and W. Yancey, eds., *The Moynihan Report and the Politics of Controversy.* Cambridge, Mass., MIT Press.

LEWIS, OSCAR 1966 "The Culture of Poverty." *Scientific American,* 215, no. 4:19–25.

LIEBOW, ELLIOT 1967 *Tally's Corner: A Study of Negro Street Corner Men.* Boston, Little, Brown.

LOTT, ALBERT J., AND BERNICE E. LOTT 1963 *Negro and White Youth: A Psychological Study in a Border State Community.* New York, Holt.

MASON, WARD S. 1961 *The Beginning Teacher: Status and Career Orientations.* Final report on the survey of new teachers in the public schools, 1956–1957. Washington, D.C., U.S. Department of Health, Education, and Welfare.

MILLER, DANIEL R., AND GUY E. SWANSON 1960 *Inner Conflict and Defense.* New York, Holt.

MILLER, WALTER B. 1958 "Lower Class Culture as a Generating Milieu of Gang Delinquency." *Journal of Social Issues,* 14, no. 3:5–19.

NATIONAL EDUCATION ASSOCIATION 1960 "The Financial Rewards of Teaching." *NEA Research Bulletin,* 38, no. 2:49–55.

NATIONAL EDUCATION ASSOCIATION 1962 "Profile of the Metropolitan Teacher." *NEA Research Bulletin,* 40, no. 3:67–74.

NATIONAL EDUCATION ASSOCIATION. RESEARCH DIVISION 1965 *What Teachers Think: A Summary of Teacher Opinion Poll Findings, 1960–1965.* Washington, D.C., The Association.

OLIM, ELLIS G., ROBERT D. HESS, AND VIRGINIA C. SHIPMAN 1967 "Role of Mothers' Language Styles in Mediating Their Pre-School Children's Cognitive Development." *School Review,* 75, no. 4:414–424.

PEARLIN, LEONARD I., AND MELVIN L. KOHN 1966 "Social Class, Occupation, and Parental Values: A Cross National Study." *American Sociological Review,* 31, no. 4:466–479.

PETTIGREW, THOMAS F. 1964 *A Profile of the Negro American.* Princeton, N.J., Van Nostrand.

RABINOWITZ, WILLIAM, AND IRA ROSENBAUM 1960 "Teaching Experience and Teaching Attitudes." *Elementary School Journal,* 60, no. 6:313–319.

RAINWATER, LEE 1966 "Crucible of Identity: The Negro Lower Class Family." Talcott Parsons and Kenneth B. Clark, eds., *The Negro American.* New York, Houghton Mifflin. Pages 160–204.

RECORD, WILSON 1964 "Changing Attitudes of School Personnel." *Integrated Education,* 2, no. 5:26–43.

RIESSMAN, FRANK 1962 *The Culturally Deprived Child.* New York, Harper.

ROBERTS, JOAN I., ed. 1967 *School Children in the Urban Slum.* New York, Free Press.

ROSE, ARNOLD M., AND CAROLINE B. ROSE, eds. 1965 *Minority Problems: A Textbook of Readings in Intergroup Relations.* New York, Harper.

ROSEN, BERNARD 1959 "Race, Ethnicity and the Achievement Syndrome." *American Sociological Review,* 24, no. 1:47–60.

ROSENTHAL, ROBERT 1966 *Experimenter Effects in Behavioral Research.* New York, Appleton.

ROTTER, JULIAN B. 1960 "Generalized Expectancies for Internal Versus External Control of Reinforcement." *Psychological Monographs,* 609.

SORENSON, GARTH, SHIRLEY SCHAEFER, AND ERNEST HYMAN 1966 "A Teacher Drop-out for MTAI?" *California Journal of Educational Research,* 17, no. 2:91–95.

STODOLSKY, SUSAN, AND GERALD LESSER 1967 "Learning Patterns in the Disadvantaged." *Harvard Educational Review,* 37, no. 4:546–593.

TURNER, RICHARD L. 1965 "Characteristics of Beginning Teachers: Their Differential Linkage With School System Types." *School Review,* 73, no. 1:48–58.

ULIBARRI, HORACIO 1960 "Teacher Awareness of Sociocultural Differences in Multicultural Classrooms." *Journal of Applied Sociology,* 45, no. 1:49–55.

U.S. COMMISSION ON CIVIL RIGHTS 1962 *Civil Rights U.S.A.: Public Schools, Cities in the North and West.* Washington, D.C., Government Printing Office.

U.S. COMMISSION ON CIVIL RIGHTS 1967 *Racial Isolation in the Public Schools.* Washington, D.C., Government Printing Office.

U.S. DEPARTMENT OF COMMERCE. BUREAU OF THE CENSUS 1967 *The American Almanac: The U.S. Book of Facts, Statistics, and Information.* 88th ed. New York, Grosset & Dunlap.

WALBERG, HERBERT J. 1968 "Personality-Role Conflict and Self-Conception in Urban Practice Teachers." *School Review,* 76, no. 1:41–49.

WARNER, WILLIAM LLOYD, ROBERT J. HAVIGHURST, AND M. B. LOEB 1944 *Who Shall Be Educated: The Challenge of Unequal Opportunities.* New York, Harper.

WAYSON, WILLIAM W. 1966 "Securing Teachers for Slum Schools." *Integrated Education,* 4, no. 1:31–38.

WORTIS, H., et al. 1963 "Child-rearing Practices in a Low Socioeconomic Group." *Pediatrics,* 32, no. 2:298–307.

NANCY H. ST. JOHN

URUGUAY

Education in Uruguay is best characterized as a federally controlled, equalitarian, tuition-free, coeducational, and single-track system of public schools. Schools are available to citizens and foreigners alike without regard to race, sex, or social class. Although this tradition began with the Public Education Law of 1826, the Law of Common Education of 1877 established the pattern and spirit of Uruguayan education. This law is commonly known as the Vareliana reform because José Pedro Varela was able to fashion the Uruguayan system of education in just one decade of his short life. Varela formed his educational philosophy in association with two well-known friends, Domingo F. Sarmiento, of Argentina, and Horace Mann, of the United States.

An elementary education is obtained by most

school-age children in the country, and Uruguay has a literacy rate in excess of 90 percent. The majority of illiterates are found among the elderly people who have remained unschooled.

Uruguay spends about 3 percent of its total national income for education each year; this represents from 20 to 23 percent of the annual federal budget. Education consistently receives the largest single appropriation in the Uruguayan budget. The national legislature directly appropriates funds from general revenues of the treasury to finance education. Although educational institutions may accept gifts and donations from private sources, they receive no revenues from tuition because schools are tuition-free.

Organization and administration. The federal constitution of 1951 established the present guidelines for education in Uruguay. Article 68 guarantees freedom of education and permits parents to choose teachers and schools for their children. Privately operated educational institutions providing free education for a given number of students may be exempt from payment of national and municipal taxes in accordance with Article 69. The constitution affirms the compulsory nature of primary education and provides that higher, secondary, primary, teacher-training, vocational, technical, and artistic education in public institutions shall be governed by one or more autonomous councils. Other state educational services are administered by autonomous councils when determined by the legislature. These autonomous councils operate under the auspices of the Ministry of Public Instruction and Social Welfare.

Education is the function of the central government. The Ministry of Public Instruction and Social Welfare is a combined organization with responsibilities for education, culture, and welfare. The minister is a member of the president's cabinet. He is directly assisted by an undersecretary, by a director-general, and by section directors.

Three autonomous councils make policy and give direction to elementary and secondary education: the National Council for Primary and Teacher Education, the National Council for Secondary and Preparatory Education, and the National Council for Vocational and Technical Education. Higher educational administration is the responsibility of the Central University Council, another autonomous group. The authority of the ministry is mainly political; therefore, most technical matters are handled by the autonomous councils, which operate independently but in cooperation with each other. Each council is responsible for educational functions and problems within its own sphere of operation.

Private schools are supervised by the ministry and are given accreditation upon approval. Students who graduate from accredited schools are entitled to the same academic recognition and opportunities as those who have graduated from official schools.

Elementary education. Preschool establishments are known as kindergartens or kindergarten classes. Kindergartens are located primarily in Montevideo and are intended for children between the ages of three and six. Kindergarten classes are held around the country for five-year-olds. Children of working mothers may be enrolled in kindergartens operated by a social welfare institution known as the Children's Council.

Although the curriculum varies in accordance with the type of kindergarten, the emphasis is generally on character training and psychological and physiological development. Play activities are alternated with music, poetry, drawing, story telling, and rhythmic exercises in day care and boarding kindergartens.

Teachers for preschools are prepared in programs and courses sponsored by the ministry. Handbooks and curriculum guides are given to teachers for resource and reference purposes.

The general aim of public elementary education is "the full development of the child's personality, particular attention being given to any special gifts discernible at an early age." Education is compulsory for children between the ages of six and 14, or for six grades. More than 90 percent of the Uruguayan children in this age bracket attend school. Enforcement of the compulsory education law, however, becomes difficult in sparsely settled areas. Attendance policies are defined in the Children's Code, which was written by the Children's Council (formed in 1933 for the express purpose of protecting the welfare of children "from gestation to majority"). Article 83 of the code states that parents or guardians may be fined if their child misses more than three days of schooling a month without legitimate reasons. Article 79 lists the legitimate reasons for nonattendance: the child has completed primary school before the age of 14, he lives more than

2½ miles from school without available public transportation, he is not a permanent resident of Uruguay, or he has a physical or mental handicap.

Elementary schools fall into rural and urban categories. Schools in these categories are classified as four-year incomplete (or first-grade) or six-year complete (or second-grade) schools; there are a few third-grade schools which offer an additional year of instruction for children who do not plan to attend secondary school. The classification of schools into grades is not synonymous with classification of children into grades. Most four-year elementary schools are located outside populated centers. Six-year schools are located primarily in Montevideo.

The government provides other types of schools which serve children who are unable to participate in the regular public schools. Establishments for the mentally and physically handicapped are known as open-air, seaside, riverside, mountainside, or preventive schools. Farm schools give training in agriculture, and mobile schools move from place to place in order to provide specialized training for rural children and adults in vocational and technical topics.

The primary school curriculum includes arithmetic, Spanish, drawing, writing, handicrafts, and singing during the first two years. Civics, moral instruction, geography, physics, chemistry, and biology are introduced in the third year of study. Attention is given to the study of man, nature, and society. Religious instruction is not given in public schools.

Secondary education. The purposes of secondary education are generally defined in terms of the preparation of students for life in the home, nation, and world; for advanced studies; for vocational and professional competence; for leisure activities; and for cultural development. These objectives apply to all secondary education, whether academic, vocational, technical, or pedagogical in nature.

General academic education. The lyceum has traditionally been the academic secondary school. It began in 1830, the date of the first constitution, as a school for upper-class children. The school remained selective in nature until 1935, when an organic law made secondary education an integral part of the public school system. The lyceum no longer serves an exclusively elite function because it is tuition-free and open to those who qualify academically. The bachelor's certificate, which allows the successful candidate to enter university programs, is granted by the lyceum.

In 1963 the New Plan of Secondary Education established basic and advanced cycles of three years' duration each. The advanced cycle is further divided into a two-year phase which emphasizes academic exploration and cultural development, and a one-year preprofessional course. The preprofessional year is a differentiated program (in terms of courses and activities) for students who plan university careers and is designed to prepare them for admission to a professional program at the university.

The curriculum in the general academic secondary school includes Spanish, English, French, literature, mathematics, natural sciences or biology, physics, chemistry, natural history, cosmography, philosophy, economics, sociology, music, art, physical education, and manual arts. The student spends 36 hours a week in the classroom.

Vocational and technical education. The vocational and technical branch of secondary education began in 1879 with the enactment of a law which provided for training in crafts. A higher industrial council was formed in 1915, and in 1934 a directorate for industrial education was begun. The National Council for Industrial Education was created in 1942 and made autonomous in 1943. Industrial and technical schools are collectively known as the University of Labor.

Vocational schools are dedicated to the improvement of worker effectiveness through training in applied arts, schooling in intellectual and technical subjects, continuing education, and instruction in a full spectrum of vocational courses. Vocational and technical education is offered in several types of schools. Specific programs are available in mechanics, electronics, construction, home economics for girls, graphic arts, naval industries, commerce, industrial education for teachers, forestry, dairy farming, agriculture, and so forth. Private industries and religious groups maintain schools and are allowed to confer their own diplomas.

Vocational and technical schools accept students who have completed primary schools or who are at least 12 years old. Most programs last two years. All students are required to take mathematics, drawing, hygiene, Spanish, geography, and moral and civic education in addition to their vocational training.

Teacher education. The normal institutes

have traditionally been the schools which have prepared elementary school teachers. These institutions generally accept students who have successfully completed at least three years of secondary school, who are under 30, and who can meet established mental and physical standards. The four-year curriculum provides a balance between subject-matter and professional courses. The first years of the program include courses in psychology, logic, philosophy, Spanish, French or English, mathematics, natural sciences, music, and some professional subjects. The final year concentrates on practice teaching, teaching methods, philosophy of education, music education, sociology, and law. The title of teacher is conferred upon the graduate.

Further specialization in science or music, in special education, in kindergarten education, and in supervision, as well as training for those who would become teacher-directors or inspectors, may be obtained in the Magisterial Institute of Superior Studies.

Teachers for secondary schools are trained in the Artigas Teachers' Institute, founded in 1949. As a general rule, the school accepts students who are at least 18 years old and who have obtained the bachelor's certificate (or who have a valid teacher's certificate from a normal school). Students major in a subject-matter area such as philosophy, history, geography, literature, Spanish, English, biology, chemistry, or music. Each area of specialization has its own curriculum. Courses in education are required in each of the majors. Upon successful completion the candidates receive the title of professor and are qualified for employment in secondary schools without competitive examinations.

The Institute for Higher Education was founded in 1929 as a three-year institution for the preparation of teachers of Spanish language and literature.

The Uruguayan Federation of Teachers is the official organization for teachers. This body is concerned with the general welfare of teachers and represents them in such matters as professional negotiations, improvement of the profession, working conditions, tenure, retirement, and grievances. The Statute of Teaching Personnel defines the regulations, limitations, benefits, and employment practices applicable to teachers. Salary schedules are fixed by the legislature and are based on length of service, level of teaching, and subject matter taught. Some subject-matter specializations are rewarded more than others. Even though salaries of teachers are not considered to be large, regular increments, tenure, and financial stability do attract people to the profession.

Higher education. The University of the Republic of Uruguay is the nation's only university. At the time the university was officially inaugurated, in 1849, it controlled primary and secondary education. The university is autonomous and is located in Montevideo. Each faculty operates as a separate unit under a dean. There is no central campus; rather, each faculty has its own facilities in Montevideo. The university does have some branches for agricultural studies in Paysandu, Salta, and Cerro Largo.

Even though each faculty operates independently, governing bodies coordinate activities of the total university. The Organic Law of 1958 specifies current organization and guidelines for the university. The law provides for four governing bodies. The Central University Council is charged with administration, supervision, discipline, budgeting, and policy formation for the university. The rector of the university presides over the body, which is made up of one representative from each faculty and nine representatives from the General Faculty Assembly.

Faculty councils have direct administrative responsibilities for their respective faculties. The dean is each council's presiding member and is assisted by five elected professors, three alumni members, and three students. Faculty councils perform essentially the same functions for the college as the central council performs for the university.

The General Faculty Assembly (three professors, two graduates, and two students from each of the ten faculties) and the Faculty Assembly (15 elected faculty members, ten graduates, and ten students) are consulting bodies. The assemblies represent their faculties in matters relating to curricula, and they elect the rector of the university and the faculty deans.

Staff. Faculty members become civil servants when selected and appointed by their faculties. They do not have tenure as do other government civil servants. Most professors are hired on a part-time basis, and only approximately 7 percent of the total staff is considered full-time. Teaching and research are performed by directors of institutes, chiefs of departments, chaired professors, directors of schools, and by contract, adjunct, and assistant professors. A professor may accept a "total dedication" project contract if he renounces all official and private activities which are unrelated to the contract. He will receive extra compensation beyond his salary if he agrees to work at least 44 hours a week.

Students. Students admitted to the university must pay only for books and supplies. Needy students may qualify for financial aid in the form of interest-free loans. A welfare organization known as the Department of Student Welfare supervises social, economic, health, counseling, food, housing, physical education, and cultural services for students.

The official student organization is the Uruguayan Federation of University Students. Students have representation on all councils and faculty assemblies in accordance with the 1958 law. Student representation has been traditional in Uruguay since 1908.

Almost half of the students enrolled in the university follow careers in law and medicine (27 and 20 percent, respectively). Economics attracts about 11 percent of the students, and architecture is next with 8 percent. All other faculties and schools vie for the remaining third of the students. About 60 percent of the students are men.

Degrees. Most professional programs require five years of study. Law, medicine, and engineering have six-year programs. Each faculty has two-year, three-year, and four-year semiprofessional programs as well as its programs for professional degrees. Students who do not have the bachelor's certificate—but who have taken vocational courses in the University of Labor—may pursue studies which lead to diplomas in public administration, nursing, midwifery, dental technology, physiotherapy, and laboratory technology.

Trends. In the years to come, preprimary education will be extended to reach more children between the ages of four and six. The length and quality of schooling for children in rural areas will increase. Secondary education will soon become compulsory through grades 7, 8, and 9. This will change enrollment patterns dramatically. The University of Labor will continue its rapid enrollment increases because the government wants more terminal programs for youth. The government also recognizes that manpower needs for business and industry demand the education of greater numbers of skilled workers. Uruguayan needs are being accentuated in scientific, business, and educational fields. Law and medicine will still be popular among students because of traditional prestige, but the proportion of students attending these colleges will decline. Considerable support is present for the establishment of a faculty of education at the university.

AUGUSTUS F. FAUST

V

VENEZUELA

Education in Venezuela is compulsory and free for children between the ages of seven and 13; the right to education has been a constitutional guarantee since the national educational system began in 1864. Venezuela's present educational system is defined in the Organic Law of Education of 1961, which established both the general objectives and the specific organization and administration of education at all levels. Although changes in organization may be made by presidential decree or ministerial resolution, most changes follow the spirit of the 1961 law.

Legal provisions for education, however, can be misleading; although such provisions may describe the ideal, they seldom correspond to actual conditions. Thus, despite legal requirements, education languished during the 1952–1958 dictatorship of Marcos Pérez Jiménez (Sánchez 1963). After the fall of Pérez Jiménez in 1958, the country was faced with a tremendous backlog of demands for education. The present legal bases for national education, established by the Democratic Action Party, are an attempt to eliminate these quantitative gaps by implementing an educational philosophy first enunciated by the party's erstwhile educational spokesman, Luis Prieto Figueroa, in 1941. The major premise of this philosophy is that education is the means by which the masses of the country may be incorporated into the democratic processes (Martz 1966). The primary educational goals, according to party precepts, were immediately to expand education at all levels and to stress the expansion of secondary vocational programs, teacher training, and adult education (Alexander 1964).

Venezuela's success in achieving these goals is shown by dramatic increases in enrollments of stu-

dents. Between 1958 and 1967, primary enrollments rose 75 percent; secondary academic, 227 percent; secondary vocational, 379 percent; university, 265 percent; and higher normal, 315 percent. On the other hand, enrollments in secondary normal schools decreased nearly 22 percent.

Administration and organization. The tremendous expansion of education since 1958 has required substantial increases in expenditures. The national educational budget represents about 18 percent of total government expenditures. Educational finances are raised on federal, state, and local levels, and all three levels operate schools. Increasingly, however, national schools and financing predominate. At the federal level the Ministry of Education provides most funds for education. Other ministries also contribute through the operation of specialized schools for agriculture, social work, aviation, and military training.

At the primary and secondary levels of education, the overriding principle of organization is centralization. Although state, local, and private-school authorities have some power to make decisions, most decision-making power resides in the Ministry of Education.

For every educational activity there is a ministry department, division, or section which determines or, in the case of universities, recommends policy. Other ministry bodies are responsible for implementing these decisions.

The ministry includes directorates for primary and normal education (including adult education), secondary and higher education, and vocational secondary education. Each directorate supervises the schools under its control, develops and promulgates curricula, and is the final arbiter of degrees granted.

The administration of public primary and secondary schools is carried out through the adoption of standard operating procedures. These procedures include nationwide salary scales for teachers, standardized programs of study, national supervision of programs, and standardized teacher-training programs. The teachers of any one grade level in any one type of school are expected to follow faithfully the sequence of learning experiences, the textbooks, and the practical exercises determined by ministerial committees and outlined in ministerial guides. The ministry does not exercise such direct control over private primary and secondary schools. It does, however, exercise indirect control, for ministerial decisions determine whether these schools and their degrees will be recognized. Although the freedom of private education is constitutionally guaranteed, there is continuing conflict between the proponents of public and of private education. Since the late 1960's heated debate has been waged over the power of the ministry to establish standard textbooks for all Venezuelan schools.

Further centralization of schools is effected through the ministry's supervision of educational planning, audiovisual materials development, guidance, and scholarship programs.

The organization and administration of higher education are marked by several contradictory patterns. The public universities and the higher normal schools are under the control of the ministry and are governed in much the same way as are public primary and secondary schools. Private universities, on the other hand, while empowered to establish their own programs, are indirectly controlled because their degrees are recognized only at the pleasure of the government.

The administration of the national universities is complex. Each relatively autonomous faculty and school maintains its own governing body which decides on curricula, expenditures, admissions, and degrees. Administration and control are further complicated by student and alumni representation on all university governing bodies; this long-defended principle of "co-government" serves to create additional confusion in the administrative procedures followed by the national universities.

Coordination among universities remains a problem. Neither legal grounds nor historical precedent encourage coordination, and each university jealously guards its independence. The National University Council has been established to assist in coordination but, as an ex officio body, has been relatively ineffectual.

Primary education. Primary education in Venezuela includes both preprimary education, which is neither obligatory nor available everywhere, and primary education, which lasts six years. Pupils normally enroll in primary school at the age of seven. Primary school teachers are usually trained in secondary normal schools.

While the growth of primary education since 1958 has been remarkable, primary schools still do not enroll all Venezuelan children between the ages of seven and 13; about 26 percent of this age group remains outside the school system.

In rural areas, particularly in the remote Andean and Amazon regions, both registration and attendance are well below the national average. This situation results from three factors. First, the population within these regions is scattered, making location of schools problematic and travel to and from school difficult. Second, rural economic conditions place heavy financial burdens on parents, who can afford neither the direct cost of clothing and transportation for their children nor the indirect cost of not having children to assist in working. Third, rural schools are frequently one-room schools which offer instruction through only the third or fourth year of primary school.

Despite the fact that there have been improvements in these remote rural areas, more than one-half of the rural schools remain one-room buildings relatively untouched by the educational revolution sweeping the more urban and geographically more accessible areas of the country.

Secondary education. Venezuelan secondary education includes both academic and vocational programs. The academic secondary schools (the public *liceos* and the private *colegios*) are generically referred to as secondary education. While nonacademic secondary education has grown substantially in the recent past, academic secondary schools continue to enroll more than 60 percent of the total secondary student body. It remains the desirable form of schooling, both for the prestige it confers on its students and for its almost-certain guarantee of university admission to graduates.

Academic education. Secondary academic education consists of five years of study, divided into two cycles. The first cycle, three years in duration, is general in nature; the second cycle requires students to specialize in either humanities or sciences. Either form of specialization leads to the *bachillerato* (secondary academic certificate) and to university admission. Examinations for the *bachillerato* are rigid. In 1966, for example, the pass rate was only 68.4 percent in humanities and 52.7 percent in sciences.

Teachers in the academic secondary schools are usually graduates of higher normal schools or universities. There are, however, many teachers who have received only secondary normal training (16 percent) or secondary academic training (14.6 percent).

Vocational education. Vocational secondary education consists of nine different programs of study offered in separate schools; the programs vary as to length, degrees conferred, and provision of future educational opportunities.

The largest vocational secondary program is that which prepares teachers for the primary schools. This program has been particularly emphasized by the government since 1958. Enrollments in the normal schools have followed closely the expansion of the primary school system. Normal-school training programs last five years and lead to the degree of *normalista*. A teacher with this degree is officially qualified to teach at the primary level. The degree also entitles the student to apply for admission to a higher normal school or, in rare instances, to a university. Untrained teachers and teachers requiring special training in new subject matter may receive in-service education in the Professional Improvement Institute.

Other vocational secondary programs have received increased attention since 1960, expanding nearly fivefold in the number of students enrolled. Students in the industrial program study three years for the title of operator, four years for the title of expert, and six years for the title of technician. Commercial-program students obtain the title of office assistant after two years of training, secretary after three years, commercial expert after four years, and commercial technician after five years. Students in agriculture are called agricultural experts after three years and agricultural mechanics after four. Study in the arts program lasts from two to four years. Other students enroll in the three-year mechanics program, four-year nursing program, four-year social-work program, or ten-year music program.

Higher education. Higher education in Venezuela is provided by universities, higher teacher-training institutes, the National Polytechnic Institute, and military schools.

Universities are national, public, or private. The four national universities are publicly funded. For a long time these institutions were autonomous, but in September 1970 a university reform law was passed, ending the virtual autonomy of the universities in Venezuela. The law authorizes the government to replace the autonomous university councils with government-appointed councils, which control the activities and direction of the universities. National universities are open to all Venezuelan students who have received the *bachillerato* or, in some cases, degrees from other secondary and higher institutions. There is no tuition, nor are there entrance examinations. The two private universities are similar in structure to the national universities. The public universities are under direct supervision of the Ministry of Education and therefore do not have autonomy.

All three types of universities are composed of separate faculties and schools which offer a variety of professional training programs, usually lasting five years. The traditionally preferred programs of law, medicine, and civil engineering continue to dominate enrollments.

There are two higher teacher-training institutions, in Caracas and in Barquisimeto. Each is a four-year institution which prepares teachers for secondary schools, although a few graduates go on to study at the university.

The National Polytechnic Institute, founded in 1962, offers technical training at the higher-education level to graduates of secondary industrial schools who have had at least two years of work experience. Other secondary graduates may, on occasion, also gain admission.

Informal education. There are numerous informal educational programs which range from intensive adult-education programs sponsored by the Ministry of Education to on-the-job programs sponsored by private industry. Perhaps the most influential of these informal programs is that of the National Institute for Educational Training (INCE), a semiautonomous institution begun in 1960. INCE offers training programs in industrial and commercial fields, in literacy, and in agricultural topics. INCE is a response to the need for immediate training of middle-level technicians. By law, any enterprise which has ten employees or more must have at least 5 percent of these employees in apprenticeship positions which pay the employee for time spent in INCE training.

Another semiautonomous institution, the Venezuelan Institute for Community Action, provides training programs for rural community leaders and assists in the organization of rural development programs. Through the Venezuelan Institute for Scientific Research, special training of scientists is undertaken.

Methods and materials of instruction. Both content and methodology of instruction in primary and secondary education are standardized. Methods and materials are prescribed by the Ministry of Education in course outlines which include not only the specific topics to be covered but also the sequence of these topics, the practical exercises, and the examinations.

Curricula are intended to be comprehensive. For example, in the second year of academic secondary education, students receive 34 hours of instruction a week in Spanish, mathematics, geography, history, biology, English, art, manual training, civics, and physical education. In the third year, manual training and art are eliminated, but chemistry and physics are added and the total weekly instruction rises to 40 hours. Extensive course offerings are particularly characteristic of the secondary academic schools, which are expected to provide total general education to students prior to university admission.

Centralized decisions on curricula and methods do not always prove effective. One study showed that despite centralization, schools, especially those in remote areas, often do not follow the standardized programs (Acosta Saignes 1965).

At the university level, programs are established by individual faculties and schools. Attempts have been made since the late 1950's to standardize curricula, employ full-time professors, and improve teaching methods by stressing the use of textbooks and library materials rather than the copying and memorization of lecture notes. These efforts proceed slowly, however.

Trends and problems. Since 1958 the major goal of Venezuelan education has been to get children into the schools. The success of this effort has been remarkable, particularly in light of the backlog of educational needs, the high birthrate, the great number of children of school age, and the country's geographical problems. However, the quantitative expansion of education has made more glaring the qualitative defects. Getting more children into school has not eliminated or even substantially reduced the high dropout rate at all levels of education, enrolling more students in secondary and higher-level vocational programs has not alleviated the nation's need for qualified manpower at both intermediate

and advanced levels; and increasing rural enrollments has neither made rural life more attractive and productive nor facilitated the adjustment of rural migrants to urban life.

The attrition rates of primary and secondary education are very high. Calculations made in the late 1960's indicate that only one pupil in four completes the sixth year of primary school. At the secondary academic level, only one student in three completes the fifth year. Attrition rates are similarly high in other secondary and higher education programs (Instituto para el Desarrollo Económico y Social 1968).

High attrition rates cause several problems. The production of graduates at each level of education is costly because much of each year's expenditure is devoted to students who then drop out; in addition, the employment prospects of students who do not graduate are poor because much more stress is given to degrees obtained than to number of years of education completed. These problems are especially prevalent in rural areas, where retention rates are considerably below national averages.

Why attrition rates are high is a question still open to debate. Frequently cited reasons are the economic strains put on families in keeping their children in school; the system of yearly examinations, which prevents promotion from grade to grade; and the irrelevance of school curricula, particularly for students from rural areas and from urban low-income areas.

School feeding programs, scholarships, free textbooks and classroom materials, guidance programs, in-service teacher-training programs, and intensified supervision have been introduced to improve the schools' retention power. These are only partial solutions, however. The government has begun what may prove a more direct solution: the reorganization of the primary and secondary school system. When completed, the reform will provide for eight years of general education for all students. This would be followed by three years of specialized education in either university preparatory or vocational programs. The proposed reform will reduce the emphasis now given to secondary academic education and will postpone selection of students for different programs until they have had greater experience with general secondary education.

Although university enrollments have expanded, universities still do not provide graduates in sufficient quantities to meet national manpower needs. Most students continue to enroll in medicine, law, and civil engineering programs, and secondary academic students continue to aspire to university admission in these fields (Ruscoe 1968). Further, the scientific and technical manpower needed for the country's petroleum, petrochemical, and steel industries remains in short supply (Roche 1967).

The universities' failure to meet national needs was exacerbated by their sometimes overzealous defense of autonomy. It is true that autonomy on occasion was reprehensibly violated by the government, but autonomy also allowed the universities to ignore pressing national issues. Universities have been the political training grounds for many of the nation's political leaders (Friedmann 1965), and university students have played a positive central role in the nation's politics (Alexander 1964); however, university students have also disrupted university and national life.

It was to counter undue university autonomy that the Venezuelan government enacted its university reform law of 1970, ending the autonomy of the universities. Two quite different routes have also been followed by the government in its attempt to reform higher education. First, the government has created new types of institutions which bypass the national university system. For example, Oriente University was established in 1961 directly under the supervision of the Ministry of Education. Because Oriente does not have autonomy, the government has been able to introduce such notable reforms as the prohibition of student political activity within the university, the introduction of preprofessional general education, and the provision of scientific and technical teaching and research by full-time professors for full-time students. In 1967 the ministry was empowered to establish other higher education institutions outside the national university system. These institutions are to be experimental universities, university colleges, and institutes of research and technology.

Second, the Law of the Universities was revised through executive decree in 1967, thus bringing the government into direct confrontation with the national universities. National universities are now forbidden to engage in political propaganda and partisan politics contrary to national interest or disruptive of education. Students are now permitted to repeat a year of studies only twice and must pay US$25.00 for each course repeated.

Only regular students may now be elected to university governing bodies; and repeaters, part-time students, and students who have completed course work but not taken their degrees are not considered regular students. This should, it is hoped, encourage students to graduate at a normal rate and discourage the professional student–politician.

Unfortunately, the reforms of primary, secondary, and higher education have not attacked directly another problem which confronts Venezuelan education: the marginal communities. These communities, which do not participate fully in national life and institutions, are to be found both in rural areas and in the cities. In the rural areas many communities of peasants and Indians survive only haphazardly and are largely untouched by national economic, political, and educational activities (Layrisse & Wilbert 1966). Efforts have been made since 1958 to improve and expand rural education, to develop rural leadership, and to provide adult education. Nonetheless, much of rural Venezuela remains peripheral to national development.

The situation is similar in the rapidly growing urban areas, where urban slums sprawl into the surrounding countryside. It has been estimated that one-fourth of the residents of Caracas are slum dwellers (Hall 1966). The number of slum-dwellers expands annually, as migration from the rural areas continues unabated even though urban living conditions are poor, job opportunities are limited, and city services are overtaxed. Efforts have been made to provide these urban marginal communities with entry points into the national system. Catholic priests, women's groups, foundations, and private business have attempted to enlist community support within the slums to finance and supervise schools. However, these efforts are at best designed only to meet immediate needs with whatever funds and labor are available. National educational policy has yet to follow the lead set by private efforts, and there are no government educational programs specifically designed for the slums. To the observer these urban marginal settlements remain the most pressing challenge to the educational revolution now taking place in Venezuela.

BIBLIOGRAPHY

ACOSTA SAIGNES, GLADYS DE 1965 *Investigación sobre materiales de la escuela Venezolana.* Caracas, Universidad Central de Venezuela.

ALEXANDER, ROBERT JACKSON 1964 *The Venezuelan Demo-*

cratic Revolution: A Profile of the Regime of Rómulo Betancourt. New Brunswick, N.J., Rutgers University Press.

FRIEDMANN, JOHN 1965 *Venezuela: From Doctrine to Dialogue.* Syracuse, N.Y., Syracuse University Press.

HALL, GEORGE 1966 "Fundación Creole: The First Decade." Fundación Creole report. Mimeographed. Caracas.

INSTITUTO PARA EL DESARROLLO ECONÓMICO Y SOCIAL 1968 *Educación: La Gran Urgencia.* Caracas, The Institute.

LAYRISSE, MIGUEL, AND JOHANNES WILBERT 1966 *Indian Societies of Venezuela: Their Blood Group Types.* Monograph Series No. 13. Caracas, Editorial Sucre.

MARTZ, JOHN D. 1966 *Acción Democrática: Evolution of a Modern Political Party in Venezuela.* Princeton, N.J., Princeton University Press.

ROCHE, MARCEL 1967 "Social Aspects of Science in a Developing Country." *Science Teacher,* 34, no. 1:25.

RUSCOE, GORDON C. 1968 "Individual Decisions and Educational Planning: Occupational Choices of Venezuelan Secondary Students." *International Development Review,* 10, no. 2:20–25.

SÁNCHEZ, GEORGE I. 1963 *The Development of Education in Venezuela.* Bulletin 1963, No. 7. Washington, D.C., U.S. Office of Education.

GORDON C. RUSCOE

VETERANS EDUCATION

See FEDERAL EDUCATIONAL ACTIVITIES: OVERVIEW. G.I. BILL OF RIGHTS.

VETERINARY MEDICINE, EDUCATION FOR

The objective of veterinary medical education is to prepare people, through classroom instruction and research, to perform the following roles: preventing, curing, or alleviating disease and injury in animals; preventing or controlling the transmission of disease from animals to man; and contributing to knowledge in all branches of medical science.

Formal education in veterinary medicine was provided as early as 1740, when a privately owned riding academy in Lyon, France, included "instruction on equine medicine" in its curriculum. The first English college of veterinary medicine was established in London in 1791; the first successful veterinary medical school in the United States, the Boston Veterinary Institute, was organized in 1854. All of the small private veterinary colleges in North America have now been replaced by colleges which are integral parts of well-recognized, publicly supported universities. Of the existing veterinary schools in the United States, the oldest is that of Iowa State University of Science and Technology, organized in 1879 (Hay 1964).

In 1970 there were 18 colleges of veterinary medicine in the United States and three in Canada. They had a total enrollment of almost 5,500 students, including 490 women, and about 1,850 faculty members (American Veterinary Medical Association 1970). Of the faculty members in schools of veterinary medicine in 1968, 57 percent belonged to basic science departments, 42 percent were in clinical departments, and 1 percent were in public health departments. Twenty-seven percent of the faculty members held both a D.V.M. (doctor of veterinary medicine) and a Ph.D. degree, 19 percent held a Ph.D. only, 50 percent held a D.V.M. only, and 4 percent held other degrees (Gay 1968).

Educational programs. All veterinary medical colleges in the United States require applicants for admission to have completed a minimum of two years of preprofessional course work at an accredited university; however, most successful applicants have from three to four years of such training. For example, in one first-year class at Auburn University, the average amount of preprofessional work completed by students was 3.65 years; 28 percent of the students had B.S. degrees, and 3 percent had M.S. degrees. Veterinary medical schools suggest that applicants have a firm academic foundation in English, chemistry, mathematics, and biology. Traditional requirements of background in specific animal sciences are generally being diminished. In some instances, it is possible for a highly qualified applicant to be admitted even if he has no agricultural course credits or practical experience with livestock. Most schools are encouraging applicants to take a number of electives in the humanities as well as the traditional science courses (such as physics, genetics, inorganic and organic chemistry, and zoology).

Curriculum. Students at veterinary colleges devote some 5,000 classroom hours over a period of four years to traditional courses dealing with bacteriology, immunology, histology, biochemistry, physiology, pharmacology, genetics, radiobiology and roentgenology, pathology, parasitology, public health, preventive medicine, surgery, obstetrics, toxicology, nutrition, laboratory animal medicine, and medical jurisprudence and ethics.

Currently, the majority of veterinary colleges are actively studying and revising their curricula in order to better equip their graduates to meet both the challenges of changing trends in agricultural methods and the growing demand for veterinary scientists to participate in meeting general medical and public health needs. This demand stems from the fact that veterinary medical education, although generally similar to other medical education, includes study of comparative medicine (Gay 1968). It is this broad study of many species—including man—that enables the veterinarian to make important contributions to medical knowledge.

The curriculum changes taking place involve rearrangement of the sequence of courses, reallotment of time, and introduction of new course material. Since scientific knowledge is expanding at an almost inconceivably rapid rate and since it does not seem wise to extend the time required to train veterinarians, course content is being modified to emphasize basic principles or concepts rather than facts; specialized instruction is generally being reserved for postgraduate, internship, or residency training. In addition, many schools are attempting to integrate instruction in basic and applied science.

The conventional curriculum traditionally provided for basic science courses in the first two years of veterinary medical school and applied or clinical courses in the last two years, the course work in pathology being considered the link between the two areas of study. However, both medical schools and veterinary colleges are increasingly crossing departmental and disciplinary lines to present a type of integrated, correlated, or cooperative teaching effort. For example, at the medical school of Case Western Reserve University, both clinical and basic subjects are taught in about equal quantities each year by interdisciplinary committees. However, this type of plan requires much cooperation in organization and presentation, and difficulties arise when personnel changes occur. Veterinary colleges are striving more toward a so-called diagonal type of integration, in which both basic and clinical material is taught in all four years, the percentage of clinical material increasing each year and the percentage of basic material decreasing.

Some educators feel that, on campuses having both medical and veterinary colleges, instruction in many basic subjects can be given to medical and veterinary students in common courses. Such courses are being offered at four universities in the United States and are being planned at others.

Teaching methods. The standard method of instruction at colleges of veterinary medicine is the lecture method. This method is being modified at most schools to include more demonstrations and more student participation. The increasing availability of excellent textbooks allows instructors to assign reading material on basic subjects rather than lecturing about them, freeing class time for discussion. In addition, visual aids—slides, overhead projection, movies, and closed-circuit television—are increasingly being employed. The use of television facilitates the demonstration of techniques, and television can be employed in lectures, laboratory classes, seminars, and small-group conferences. Videotapes of course work provide a permanent record for future use.

Most colleges are investigating the effectiveness of using autotutorial devices to supplement or partially replace conventional lectures. Booths or carrels which are equipped with single-concept film loops and projectors, slide sets, tape recordings, and pertinent written notes or guides can be employed. Those colleges planning new facilities are frequently providing for permanently assigned individual study areas for students, located in a room in which a variety of laboratory facilities is available. Limited laboratory study can be performed in conjunction with the autotutorial materials. Eventually, computerized and other types of programmed instruction will probably also be used. These autotutorial devices will not replace the teacher but merely divert some of his efforts to developing and maintaining teaching aids to supplement his usual classroom and laboratory instruction.

Postdoctoral education. Since the responsibilities of veterinarians are becoming more diversified, requiring a broader range of scientific knowledge, it is generally felt among teachers of veterinary medicine that the D.V.M. degree should represent completion of a program of study oriented toward basic science and that concentrated learning in a certain specialized discipline should occur in postdoctoral training. Such training is available in M.S. and Ph.D. programs, in internships or specialty residencies, and in practically oriented continuing education courses.

Holding a graduate research degree, such as an M.S. or a Ph.D., is considered necessary for teaching and research in veterinary medicine. Degree candidates obtain advanced training in one aspect of veterinary medicine and are required to complete an original research project, which forms the basis for a thesis.

For clinicians, participation in an internship and residency program (in lieu of M.S. or Ph.D. training) is becoming an increasingly important source of training in specialty areas (for example, toxicology or neurosurgery). In residency programs an intensive research project leading to a thesis or dissertation is not required. However, in order to become certified, the specialist not only must complete his training and experience but also must pass a comprehensive examination administered by the appropriate specialty board. This certification assures the public that the specialist has advanced training and experience which qualify him to perform his specialty.

Continuing education has become a necessity in all fields of medicine because scientific knowledge is constantly changing at a rapid pace. Veterinary colleges have instituted and are expanding continuing education programs, which include intensive short courses offered both on and off campus, programmed-instruction courses, audiotapes, phonograph records, and even statewide closed-circuit television programs.

Students' expenses. The direct cost to the student of veterinary education varies considerably with the college one attends, the campus and geographical area in which it is situated, and the books and equipment one is required to purchase. Since medical books, microscopes, instruments, and related equipment are expensive, veterinary education tends to be much more costly than liberal arts education.

Licensing. In order for a veterinarian to practice in the United States, he must be a graduate of an accredited school of veterinary medicine and pass the comprehensive examination prescribed in the "practice act" of his state. The board of veterinary examiners of the state administers the examination, which may have written, practical, and oral sections. Many states use the written examination compiled and administered by the National Board of Veterinary Examiners. Some of the states using this examination will not require a veterinarian who has moved to the state shortly after initial examination to repeat this part of their licensing requirements.

Career opportunities. In 1970 there were approximately 30,000 veterinarians in the United States and Canada, and an estimated 1,150 new graduates join the profession each year (American Veterinary Medical Association 1970). The demand for veterinarians greatly exceeds the supply, and, based on the current rate at which new doctors are being graduated, it has been projected that there will be a shortage of over 12,000 veterinarians in the United States by 1975 and a shortage of over 20,000 by 1985 (Joint Committee . . . 1965). However, as a result of the Health Manpower Act of 1968, increased federal aid is being given to veterinary educational facilities to help eliminate the disparity between demand and supply.

Private practice. Over two-thirds of all veterinarians in the United States are engaged in private clinical practice—that is, in diagnosing and treating animal diseases, in preventing the spread of these diseases to man, and in ensuring the provision of a wholesome food supply. The veterinarian's practice may be primarily farm animals, pet and recreational animals, zoo animals, or even laboratory animals (American Veterinary Medical Association 1966; Joint Committee . . . 1965).

Over 8,500 veterinarians care for farm or food animals, which are so vital to human health and welfare. The practitioners also cooperate with veterinarians employed by the federal government or by state governments in the eradication or control of major livestock diseases, such as tuberculosis or brucellosis, both of which are communicable to man (American Veterinary Medical Association 1966; Joint Committee . . . 1965).

About 55 percent of the families in the United States have a pet of some kind, and approximately 5,000 veterinarians concern themselves with the treatment of these pets. Veterinarians in this type of practice protect people against diseases which can be transmitted to man from pets, such as rabies, leptospirosis (rat fever), ringworm, bacterial infections, and psittacosis. About 3,000 hospitals in the United States specialize in the treatment of pet animals (American Veterinary Medical Association 1966; Joint Committee . . . 1965).

Most veterinary practitioners have occasion to serve a client with an exotic pet, such as a skunk, a squirrel, a snake, or a monkey. There is a growing demand for specialists in the treatment of zoo animals and exotic pets, which require different care than do conventional pet or farm animals. One can imagine the differences in medicinal dosages or surgical techniques required to care for a one-pound Chihuahua dog, a two-ounce parakeet, or a 10,000-pound elephant. Many veterinary practitioners are also needed to care for laboratory animals used in research.

Government service. Veterinarians have been engaged in the eradication of livestock diseases, including those communicable to man, since 1884, when the Bureau of Animal Industry became a part of the U.S. Department of Agriculture (USDA). Veterinarians working as members of state government or federal government agencies or as private practitioners have been responsible for decreasing the incidence of cattle tuberculosis from 5 percent in 1917 to 0.1 percent in 1965. The incidence of brucellosis in cattle and swine has decreased from 16 percent in 1937 to less than 1 percent in 1965, and its incidence in man has dropped from 6,000 cases in 1947 to approximately 400 cases in 1965.

Veterinarians direct meat and poultry inspection programs for the federal government and for state and local governments. In addition, veterinarians employed by the Agricultural Research Service of the USDA are responsible for broad research programs designed to develop a clearer understanding of the basic mechanisms of disease (Joint Committee . . . 1965).

Since 1943 veterinarians have been employed by the U.S. Public Health Service. Over 100 veterinarians occupy key positions in a variety of programs in sanitation, laboratory animal medicine, comparative pathology and physiology, industrial health, epidemiology, infectious diseases, air pollution, and radiological health, as well as cancer, cardiovascular, and kidney disease research. The importance of the veterinarians' work is indicated by the fact that there are 138 diseases shared by man and other vertebrates. The need for veterinarians to participate in public health programs is increasing tremendously.

Veterinarians are also involved in the work of the Food and Drug Administration. The establishment in the mid-1960's of the Bureau of Veterinary Medicine within the administration reflects the importance of their activity. A number of antibiotics, hormones, patent drugs, and other chemicals are added to animal feeds, and it is the responsibility of the veterinarian to determine whether humans consuming meat and other products from animals given such feeds will be adversely affected by the use of the chemicals (*ibid.*).

Veterinary officers in the armed services work closely with physicians and other health personnel to prevent disease and promote the health of military personnel. Veterinarians are also involved in the space research programs using experimental animals. Some 60 air force veterinarians are members of the biomedical teams for such programs (*ibid.*).

The federal government and various veterinary colleges assign veterinarians to serve in the veterinary medical aid programs of the United Nations' Food and Agriculture Organization (FAO) and World Health Organization (WHO).

The services of veterinarians are also utilized by state, county, and city health and agricultural departments. Part of the task of these departments is to cooperate with federal services in eradicating or controlling the diseases common to man and animals. Veterinarians employed by local governments may also supervise local processing of food derived from animals (*ibid.*).

Institutional work. The 18 veterinary colleges in the United States employ well over 1,000 veterinarians to serve in teaching, research, and extension or continuing education programs. The research and extension activities of veterinary medical schools are expanding rapidly. Veterinarians are also employed by other educational institutions offering courses in animal science, agriculture, biology, or medicine. Medical schools are employing an increasing number of veterinarians to teach comparative medicine. Animal models are being used to study human illnesses, such as arthritis and diseases of the respiratory and nervous systems, and to study immunology. As these research efforts continue, veterinarians will be needed to assume important and expanded roles in comparative medicine and laboratory animal medicine.

Other opportunities. Private industry's need for veterinary scientists is increasing rapidly. In the food processing, animal feed, and drug industries, veterinarians, because of their broad basic training, play valuable roles in research and development and in promotion of new products. Veterinarians employed by private pharmaceutical firms supervise development, production, and testing of approximately $150 million worth of drugs and biological products (that is, serums, vaccines, and other medicinal preparations made from living organisms and their products).

Environmental pollution and its effects on the health of human and animal populations are major concerns of society. Since air, water, and food contamination which adversely affects animals can also affect the people who depend on those animals as a source of food, the importance of veterinarians in the ecology movement is obvious.

Professional organizations. The American Veterinary Medical Association (AVMA) is a voluntary professional organization for veterinarians in the United States. The association was founded in 1863 as the United States Veterinary Medical Association and had an initial membership of about 40. In 1970 its membership exceeded 20,000.

The association is composed of 54 constituent associations, representing veterinarians in each of the 50 states, in U.S. territories and possessions, and in the federal government and the armed forces. The association publishes two journals—the *Journal of the American Veterinary Medical Association* (semimonthly) and the *American Journal of Veterinary Research* (monthly).

Associated with the AVMA are 51 other organizations representing various interest or occupational areas in veterinary medicine—for example, the American Animal Hospital Association, the American Academy of Veterinary Cardiology, and the American Association of Equine Practitioners. In addition to these 51 organizations, there are seven specialty boards concerned with special individual competence in certain disciplines. These organizations, recognized by the AVMA, are the American Board of Veterinary Public Health, the American Board of Veterinary Radiology, the American Board of Veterinary Toxicology, the American College of Laboratory Animal Medicine, the American College of Veterinary Microbiologists, the American College of Veterinary Pathologists, and the American College of Veterinary Surgeons. Each specialty group sets its own training and experience standards and gives comprehensive examinations to determine whether individuals should be certified as specialists.

The AVMA is the accrediting agency for all United States and Canadian veterinary medical schools. Accreditation is determined by the association's Council on Education, organized in 1936. The council, a member of the National Commission on Accrediting, attempts to promote active progress in the educational programs of veterinary colleges, with full accreditation of each college as the ultimate goal. (All 18 veterinary colleges in the United States have some level of AVMA

accreditation.) The council encourages schools to meet its requirements and assists them in doing so. Upon request, the council works with newly organized schools or colleges, so that eligibility for accreditation may be established by the time the first class is graduated. The council studies teaching and research methods with the objective of progressively improving the quality of veterinary medical education. It also constantly studies the need to establish new courses to enable veterinarians to meet changing societal demands.

BIBLIOGRAPHY

AMERICAN VETERINARY MEDICAL ASSOCIATION 1966 *Dimensions of Veterinary Medicine.* Chicago, The Association.
AMERICAN VETERINARY MEDICAL ASSOCIATION 1970 *Today's Veterinarian.* Chicago, The Association.
CHRISTENSEN, G. C. 1963 "Veterinary Medical Education: A Rapid Revolution." J. F. Smithcors, ed., *The American Veterinary Medical Profession: Its Background and Development.* Ames, Iowa State University Press. Pages 641–665.
GAY, WILLIAM I. 1968 "Opportunities for the Veterinary Scientists in Medical Research." *Journal of the American Veterinary Medical Association*, 153, no. 8:1033–1039.
HAY, JAMES P. 1964 "Veterinary Medicine." Allan Murray Cartter, ed., *American Universities and Colleges.* 9th ed. Washington, D.C., American Council on Education. Pages 144–147.
JOINT COMMITTEE ON VETERINARY EDUCATION SPECIAL TASK FORCE 1965 *Veterinary Medicine.* A project of the American Veterinary Medical Association and the American Association of Veterinary Medical Colleges. Chicago, American Veterinary Medical Association.

B. F. HOERLEIN

VIETNAM

| 1. NORTH VIETNAM | Vu Tam Ich |
| 2. SOUTH VIETNAM | Glenn C. Atkyns |

1. NORTH VIETNAM

The 1946 constitution of the Democratic Republic of Vietnam (North Vietnam) provided for equal cultural rights to all citizens regardless of race and sex; for free and compulsory education for all pupils; and for state responsibility for ensuring the implementation of these principles. The principle of free education was reaffirmed in the 1960 constitution, which replaced the 1946 document.

Controlled by the government and by the Workers' Party of Vietnam, usually known as the Lao Dong Party, the educational system of North Vietnam is administered by the Ministry of Education, which is in turn directed by the Council of Ministers. The council has direct jurisdiction over all ministries and full authority to annul or revise the decisions, regulations, and instructions issued by any lower body.

In accordance with the principle "combination of state forces and people's forces," expenditures for education are shared by the state and the people, who make so-called voluntary contributions to pay for school buildings.

Structure and organization. On September 2, 1945, the Democratic Republic of Vietnam was proclaimed and a provisional government set up. One week later, President Ho Chi Minh signed a decree forming an official anti-illiteracy department to help improve the cultural level of workers, peasants, and the urban poor—the vast majority of whom did not know how to read or write. At first, the village was the basic unit for the fight against illiteracy; the village was later replaced by the district and the province. In the early 1960's the Ministry of Education claimed that illiteracy had been eradicated in the delta and middle regions of North Vietnam.

Complementary education. A program of complementary studies in Vietnamese, mathematics, and basic science has been created for those who know how to read and write. Complementary education has been carried out in regular schools for party cadres and for peasants and workers, in spare-time courses, in evening courses, in short-term courses, and in correspondence courses. For more advanced students there are programs on the secondary-school level. Each province has its secondary school for adults. Secondary schools for workers and peasants have been opened in Hanoi and in various provinces. In the early 1960's more than 1.2 million persons annually finished public complementary courses. In addition, military services and the units of the North Vietnamese People's Army have their own complementary courses.

Primary-secondary education. An educational reform carried out in 1950–1951 created a nine-year unitary school divided into three levels: a four-year primary level, a three-year elementary level, and a two-year secondary level. Half of each day was expected to be devoted to study; the other half was to be spent in production and defense work. In 1956 the whole system was recast and the general-education course was extended to ten years, as recommended by the General Education Congress. Now there are four-year first-

degree schools, three-year second-degree schools, and three-year third-degree schools. In 1957 new regulations for the ten-year general-education course were adopted. The reform was aimed not only at improving the quality of education but also at promoting the wide diffusion of public education.

Each village in North Vietnam now has a first-degree school. There is a second-degree school for every two villages, on the average. Certain districts in very populous provinces such as Thanh Hoa and Nghe An have two or three third-degree schools. In Hanoi and its suburbs, there are more than 15 third-degree schools.

In addition, new types of primary-secondary schools have been set up in North Vietnam. There are special schools where pupils are offered courses in general education and are guided toward either an agricultural or an industrial specialization. These schools are not considered professional or technical institutions. Another new type of school is found in the mountain regions, where children of ethnic minorities receive a complete general education in their own language and a technical education aimed at meeting the agricultural or industrial needs of their province.

Higher education. Higher education has apparently expanded steadily since 1956, especially with the refoundation of the University of Hanoi, which has faculties of mathematics and physics, chemistry, biology, and social science. This university is a state institution financed from public funds. It is headed by a rector and three prorectors. Each faculty is administered by a dean with the help of university and faculty councils.

Between 1956 and 1960 eight institutions of higher learning were created. These include the Polytechnical Institute of Hanoi, which offers diploma courses in mechanical engineering, electrical and radio engineering, metallurgy, mining, geology, building engineering, and industrial food chemistry; the Institute of Education of Hanoi, which has faculties of letters, history, geography, foreign languages, mathematics, physics, chemistry, and biology; the Institute of Education of Vinh, which has a faculty of letters and a faculty of mathematics; the Institute of Medicine and Pharmacy, which has faculties of medicine and pharmacy; the Institute of Economics and Finance, which offers courses in industrial economics, commerce, agriculture, transportation, foreign relations, statistics, planning, and finance; the Institute of Agriculture and Forestry, which offers courses in agriculture, forestry, fishery, veterinary medicine, and agricultural engineering; the Institute of Hydraulics and Electrical Engineering; and the Institute of Telecommunications. With the exception of the Institute of Education of Vinh, all the institutes were founded in Hanoi.

The annual student enrollment in higher education in the mid-1960's is said to have been 26,300. In addition, hundreds of students have been sent every year to study in the Soviet Union, Mainland China, Poland, East Germany, and other Socialist countries.

Technical and vocational education. Special attention has been paid to technical and vocational education because of the urgent need for skilled industrial workers, technicians, engineers, statisticians, teachers, professors, doctors, and so forth. The Ministry of Specialized Secondary and Higher Education administers specialized training in such fields as agriculture, communications, public health, fine arts, music, and finance. Secondary technical or vocational schools are open to persons who have completed seven years of general education; these schools offer a three-year course as well as evening and correspondence classes for working people. Upon completion of the three-year course, students may be admitted to higher technical schools. In the mid-1960's about 100,000 students were enrolled annually in secondary technical education.

In addition, on-the-job training is offered to qualified workers, to party personnel, and to members of mass organizations. State farms, businesses, factories, governmental agencies, and units of the North Vietnamese People's Army have their own technical and vocational programs and schools. For instance, the School for Training Information Officers and the Institute for Training Medical Officers are operated and administered by military personnel.

Since 1957, scientific and cultural cooperation between North Vietnam and the countries of the Socialist camp have enabled thousands of Vietnamese students and workers to go to the Soviet Union and Mainland China to receive training in factories, technical schools, and universities. In addition, foreign experts have been invited to come to North Vietnam to direct the training of professional personnel.

Curricula and textbooks. Since August 1945, Vietnamese has reportedly been used as the language of instruction at all levels. The Ministry of Education has stated that only by teaching in the mother tongue and upholding its position in schools can the young generations be made to foster the national language and to be patriotic. The government feels that only in this way can it build a genuinely national democratic education, make such education popular among the people, and create conditions for the mass of the people to be receptive to technology.

An important development in the early 1960's was the simplification and betterment of the scripts of several *montagnard* languages, so that they could be used to fight illiteracy among the ethnic minorities. The Thai, Meo, and Tay-Nung groups now have their own scripts.

Civics is given special attention in the general-education curriculum. Political indoctrination, in the form of a systematic Marxist-Leninist ideological education, is stressed at all levels, since the aim of schooling is not only to provide pupils with scientific and practical knowledge but also to prepare them for the building of socialism.

The program of instruction in the first four years of general education includes Vietnamese, arithmetic, history, geography, health education, gardening, agriculture, and political discussion of current events (from the third grade on). From grades 5 through 10, students are given instruction in national literature, mathematics, history, geography, political studies and current affairs, biology, physics, chemistry, foreign languages, technical drawing, hygiene, music, philosophy, economics and agriculture, physical education, moral education, and (for girls) home economics.

The government and the Workers' Party make full use of the school system to instill loyalty to the regime. To this end, the preparation of curricula and textbooks is tightly controlled by the government. Students at all levels are exposed to Marxist-Leninist ideology along with the regular academic subjects. Textbooks reflect the importance given to national salvation, Socialism, hatred for American imperialism, and national reunification. These topics are contained even in books dealing with hygiene. Reading selections include many stories and anecdotes about the heroism of North Vietnamese soldiers and of members of the National Front for the Liberation of South Vietnam.

Teachers and teacher training. Because of the rapid expansion of education and school enrollment, there has been an increasing demand for teachers at all levels. In 1965 the teaching strength in general-education schools of all levels was said to be 79,000, as compared with 35,000 in 1960.

A number of French-trained teachers continued to be employed during the late 1950's, but they were "readjusted" to the needs of the new educational system through courses and conferences organized by the Ministry of Education. Importance was given to the training of a new generation of teachers from among the youth who had grown up in the Indochina war (1946–1954) usually known as the resistance war.

Complementary-education courses and schools require thousands of teachers having at least the qualifications of a graduate of a second-degree school (grades 5–7). To meet this great demand, general-education teachers, college students, upperclass students in complementary education schools, and even a number of cadres in state offices are used.

The Hanoi Institute of Education and the Vinh Institute of Education admit secondary school graduates and offer a curriculum of three to four years' duration. They produce fully qualified secondary school instructors. Teachers of lower grades in general-education schools are trained in various normal schools. One type of normal school admits pupils who have completed the fourth grade and offers a three-year course. Another accepts those who have finished the seventh grade for a one-year course. There are also normal schools for training teachers for ethnic minorities.

In technical and higher education, the shortage of qualified teachers has been a big problem. A number of secondary school teachers having extensive knowledge and professional experience have been promoted to the rank of university assistants. The best college graduates have been selected to be university trainees under the guidance of professors or foreign experts. A number of students who have completed their studies in the Soviet Union or other Socialist countries have been appointed as technical or higher education instructors.

Trends. Education in North Vietnam has undergone rapid expansion, especially since 1954. The government claims that 95 percent of the people are literate. The masses of workers and peasants—and their children—are given access to all degrees of schooling. Importance is placed on the education of women and ethnic minorities. Although figures supplied by the government cannot be verified and are probably overstated, present educational endeavors are far more intensive and widespread than those under French rule.

The active participation of the people in building and equipping schools and in fostering teachers has significantly contributed to the development of education. This support appears to be the result of well-organized indoctrination efforts and of the close relationship between the schools and the needs of the people.

However, the rapid expansion of education also has its drawbacks. Teaching standards have inevitably been lowered because of the shortage of such teaching aids as maps and laboratories. The supply of qualified teachers and researchers has not been able to meet the needs of an ever-increasing school enrollment. Despite effective popular support, North Vietnam is still short of school buildings; consequently, teaching is impaired by the size of classes, which sometimes have as many as 70 or 80 pupils.

BIBLIOGRAPHY

BUTTINGER, JOSEPH 1967 *Vietnam: A Dragon Embattled.* 2 vols. London, Pall Mall Press.
FALL, BERNARD B. 1960 "North Viet-Nam's Constitution and Government." *Pacific Affairs*, 33, no. 3:282–290.
SACKS, I. MILTON 1959 "Marxism in Vietnam." Frank N. Trager, ed., *Marxism in Southeast Asia*. Stanford, Calif., Stanford University Press. Pages 102–170.
VU TAM ICH 1959 "A Historical Survey of Educational Developments in Vietnam." *Bulletin of the Bureau of School Service*, 32, no. 2:1–135.

VU TAM ICH

2. SOUTH VIETNAM

The constitution of the Republic of Vietnam, promulgated April 1, 1967, has education specifically and firmly implanted within it. Article 10 states:

(1) The State recognizes freedom of education. (2) Basic education is compulsory and free of charge. (3) University education is autonomous. (4) Talented persons who do not have the means will be given aid and support to continue their studies. (5) The State encourages and supports research and creative work by citizens in the fields of science, letters and the arts.

However, the constitution must be interpreted in terms of Vietnamese concepts. By "freedom of education" the Vietnamese mean equality of opportunity to engage in academic competition for the limited number of student openings in a particular school at a particular level; this is not to be confused with the American concept of providing a school opening for every student who wishes to attend school through at least the secondary level and frequently through the community college level. In this regard the Vietnamese are more like the French, from whom their educational structure is derived in part. By "basic education" the Vietnamese mean the first five years of school. In practice, basic education is not available to every child; however, the government clearly intends to provide compulsory and free basic education and has made considerable strides in pursuit of this goal. The provision that the university is autonomous is also subject to interpretation; Article 58 provides that the president of the republic shall appoint the rector of the university, an action performed by the faculty in many European universities. Nevertheless, the university has greater autonomy than the secondary or elementary schools. The constitution, without mentioning education specifically, ensures equal opportunity through provisions which prohibit discrimination because of sex or religion; it also states that "minority compatriots will receive special support so that they can achieve the same rate of progress as the population as a whole."

The Republic of Vietnam's constitution provides educational direction through Article 92, which states that "Culture and Education must be part of National policy based on people, science, and human nature," and through Article 93, which establishes the Culture and Education Council to advise the government in preparing and carrying out educational policy. (A similar council existed prior to the 1967 constitution.) The council has the power to select representatives to report on matters of concern to the National Assembly, and the constitution states that the council may give opinions on bills in its area of competence before they are debated by the National Assembly. The council's opinions carry weight in the deliberations of the legislature. Officials who administer the schools frequently refer to council statements as the basis for policies. The president of the republic appoints one-third of the members of the council, and two-thirds are elected by public and private cultural and educational organizations and by parents' and teachers' associations. The term of service is four years. The vice-president of the republic is chairman of the Culture and Education Council.

Administration. The government carries out educational policy through the Ministry of Education, which is divided into departments of higher education and research; secondary, elementary, and mass education; technical and vocational education; and youth.

The Ministry of Education controls curricula, pupil selection, teacher education, teacher assignments to schools or geographical areas, school finance (including teachers' and administrators' salaries), and school construction (except for the hamlet schools, which are built by the Ministry of Rural Development) for all public institutions of learning from the elementary level through the university level. The ministry also controls the curricula of the private secondary and elementary schools. A system of school inspectors is employed by the ministry to maintain control over the curriculum and to maintain liaison between the field and the central offices in Saigon.

The Ministry of Rural Development and the military services also have responsibilities for education. The Ministry of Rural Development builds the hamlet (elementary) school in a hamlet or village that has recently been recovered from the Vietcong (Communist insurgents) and staffs it for two years. After two years the school and the teacher come under the direction and finances of the Ministry of Education (the assumption being that the area is now militarily secure). The military services make a major contribution by training soldiers as mechanics, pilots, and construction workers and in a myriad of other fields that have application to the civilian economy when the soldiers are released. Not to be underestimated is the training given in problem analysis and decision-making to Vietnamese officers attending such military institutions in the United States as the U.S. Army Command and General Staff College.

Coordination of educational activities takes place at the ministry level between the different agencies of government. The educational system is supported by the central government from the general treasury rather than from specified tax revenues. Only approximately 2 percent of the gross national product is spent on education.

The highly centralized government administration is a heritage from both the Chinese and the

French. It is also a practical necessity until more South Vietnamese leaders of high caliber and flexibility can be developed. The classical examination system was employed by the Chinese for selecting members of the fixed administrative hierarchy. In 1075, after obtaining independence, the Vietnamese adopted the Chinese system of compulsory examinations for public office; they introduced literary competitions to determine the grade of an official soon after. With conquest by the French came the French-imposed school system. It had the series of examinations characteristic of French education and was employed to help select the small number of administrators whom the French chose from the indigenous population (literacy actually declined under French domination). It was with this administrative and educational background that an again-independent Vietnam came into being in 1954.

The present civil service system reflects this adherence to educational qualifications. At the same time the educational system tends to be, as under the French, classically oriented, with a heavy emphasis on memorization rather than on the solving of practical problems. The combination of a limited number of persons with secondary or higher education and the type of education provided in Vietnamese schools accounts in part for the need of a centralized government to make maximum use of the trained manpower.

The limited number of highly educated older persons, the larger number of young graduates, the special training afforded to the military officers, and the demand for flexible leadership as the Republic of Vietnam enters the industrial age help explain why there are so many relatively young government and business leaders in a country that venerates the aged as having wisdom.

To the extent that there is decentralization in the educational system, it is at the elementary level. Elementary schools are administered by geographical regions or districts. The provincial education official is appointed by the Ministry of Education. However, he also answers to and usually obtains his funds for the schools, including salaries for teachers in many cases, from the province chief—the military governor of the province, who controls most military and civil matters in the area. After 1971 the province chief was to be an elected official.

Structure, Although basic education is free, it is not compulsory in practice because the government has not furnished enough classrooms and teachers for all who wish to attend. As a result, many parents pay to send their children to private school for at least a couple of years. Approximately 75 percent of the age group go to elementary school; about 66 percent of these attend public schools. By law, instruction in the elementary and secondary schools must be conducted in Vietnamese.

Elementary   education. Elementary school teachers complete the 11th grade and take a two-year normal-school program. Because of a teacher shortage, many elementary teachers have only an emergency preparation, which means that they have completed the 11th or 12th grade and a three-month course in pedagogy. Some hamlet school teachers have even less preparation. The normal-school graduate is paid twice as much as the emergency teacher.

The expansion of elementary education has been phenomenal, reflecting the thirst for education on the part of the people and the determination of the government to provide it. In 1954, when the Vietnamese achieved independence, there were 441,000 grade school pupils; by 1968, enrollments surpassed 2 million. It was estimated that in the early 1970's, 85 percent of the children in this age group would be in school, a point beyond which some experts believe a developing country usually cannot be expected to go.

Many public schools have two sessions. Classes are large; public school classes have more than 60 students in some instances. Some 63 percent of the population is literate (by UNESCO standards, able to read and write something), a third more than under the French.

Secondary education. Secondary schools, vocational-technical schools, and agricultural schools are centrally controlled. Teachers and administrators are hired, assigned, and supervised by the Ministry of Education in Saigon. Secondary school teachers are university graduates, usually from the faculty of pedagogy. Those who teach vocational-technical subjects are expected to be graduates of the Phu Tho Technical Institute, but the school graduates too few teachers to meet the demand. Some teacher trainees take jobs in industry.

Approximately two-thirds of the secondary students are in private schools. Contrary to situations in some other countries, the public secondary school is the prestige school in the Republic of Vietnam. Class size in the public secondary school does not exceed 60; by contrast, private schools frequently have up to 120 in a class. It is the normal practice, in the larger cities, for the public school teacher to teach in a private school as well. If his teaching reputation is excellent, he may receive a very high salary from the private school. Since the secondary teacher has only a 16-hour to 18-hour load and need not be available except for his classes, holding two positions is quite feasible.

Public education is characterized by a rigorous examination system. For example, in 1967 only about 60 percent of those taking the examination to enter the sixth grade (secondary school) passed. Many students who passed did not attempt to continue their studies. The result is that only 25 percent of primary school graduates enter secondary school. At the end of the 11th grade the first part of the baccalaureate examination is taken, and approximately 40 percent pass. At the end of the 12th grade the second part of the baccalaureate examination is taken, and again about 40 percent pass. Some students leave school for economic or other reasons. Only about 19 percent of those between the ages of 12 and 17 are in school. In Saigon, which contains a considerable refugee population, the figure is only 10.5 percent.

Higher education. Higher education is provided by three public universities, two private universities, one technical institute, one agricultural college, and five normal schools. The University of Saigon, founded in 1955, is centrally located in the capital city. The University of Hué, opened in 1957, is in the historic capital in the north; the University of Can Tho, established in 1966, is in the Mekong Delta. The private University of Dalat, founded in 1957, is the only university in the highlands. The private University of Van Hanh, opened in 1964, is located in Saigon. The normal schools are distributed around the country.

The University of Saigon was created after Vietnam had been divided into two countries. It had its nucleus in a large number of faculty and students from the University of Hanoi who fled south. Prior to the establishment of the University of Saigon, there were in Saigon a medical center and a faculty of law affiliated with the University of Hanoi.

The University of Dalat is a privately managed property of the Roman Catholic bishops of Vietnam. It was established, in the words of its first chancellor, the Archbishop Ngo Dinh Thuc, brother of the late president Diem, "to contribute its share to the important assignment of forming an elite for the nation." Van Hanh University, a private Buddhist institution, is a project of the Vien Hoa Dao (the organization for executing the dharma). Both the University of Dalat and Van Hanh University have received government financial support.

Although the Ministry of Education has a department of higher education and research, the universities enjoy a special position and respond only to the minister of education, from whom they must obtain funds. Since the beginning of higher education in 1955 there has been a major increase in enrollment, but expansion in enrollment has not been accompanied by a corresponding increase in facilities and teaching staff. Professors commute from Saigon to the University of Dalat or to the University of Can Tho to teach.

Students who pass the second part of the baccalaureate examination may register for a university course and obtain printed copies of the lectures. Only in the faculties of medicine and pedagogy, where government scholarships are provided and the student must pass an entrance examination, is attendance at lectures mandatory. Students graduate by passing annual examinations, but only a small percentage of those enrolled in faculties other than medicine and pedagogy take the examination. A recently passed mobilization law removes any student from draft exemption unless he takes the examinations and does well on them; presumably this will result in more students taking the examination and fewer registering at the university who do not have serious academic intent.

Methods and materials of instruction. Education in the Republic of Vietnam is designed to be "humanistic, nationalistic, and scientific." This tripartite goal has been expressed by both the National Council and the 1964 National Conference on Education. The curricula to implement these goals are centrally controlled.

Elementary education. Major advances have been made in elementary education and literacy. Credit in part is due to the Vietnamese language and its written development. The efforts of a French missionary, Alexander of Rhodes, culminated in 1649 in a catechism employing a Romanized script for the Vietnamese language and a Vietnamese-Latin-Portuguese dictionary. This written language, Quoc Ngu, replaced the Chinese characters and was taught to schoolchildren beginning around 1915. After World War I a group of young men, the Tu Luc Van Doan (or Self-reliance Literary Club), took up the task of purifying the language. Their writings are studied today as examples of simplicity of style and clarity of exposition. These efforts laid the foundations for the present written language. The Latin script, six tone signs, and three vowel signs provide for a phonetic written language of great facility: children learn to read in three to four months.

The goals of mass education in Vietnam appear to be the development of literacy and health and the inculcation of moral, scientific, economic, national, international, and community and home values. In each of the first five years of school there is instruction in civics, arithmetic, handicrafts, health, reading, and science. In the second year, history and geography are added. In the last two years, child care information is provided to the female pupils. Free textbooks are provided for each of the subjects.

Elementary schools are gradually being converted to community schools and are adding such new subjects as agriculture and animal husbandry. The 1964 National Education Conference proposed a change from the single elementary curriculum to four curricula—delta, highlands, coastal regions, and city—which recognized economic and other differences.

Historically, rote teaching has been used almost exclusively at the elementary levels in Vietnam. Thus, South Vietnamese teachers have required an extensive program of in-service training in the use of newly available elementary textbooks. A center for instructional materials, under the Ministry of Education, furnishes books, develops other educational materials for elementary schools, and provides educational radio broadcasts.

Secondary education. The secondary school has two cycles. The first cycle (grades 6 through 9) offers Vietnamese, history-geography, civics, a modern foreign language, natural science, physics-chemistry, and mathematics. The amount of time devoted to subjects other than Vietnamese and a modern language is limited. An hour of instruction each week is supposed to be given in drawing, music, physical education, handicrafts (for boys), and home economics (child care for girls); however, these courses are not always available. In the cities there are frequently no facilities for physical education.

The second cycle (grades 10 through 12) has four tracks: modern literature, classical literature, mathematical sciences, and experimental sciences. Vietnamese, history-geography, civics, philosophy, a modern language, physics-chemistry, mathematics, natural science, physical education, and home economics (child care for girls) are present in all four tracks. The time allotted to each subject varies by track, except for the subjects of history-geography and civics. In addition, the modern literature, mathematical sciences, and experimental sciences tracks require a second modern language. A classical language replaces the second modern language in the classical literature track. About 70 percent of the students take English as the first foreign language. French is the next most popular.

The secondary school relies almost exclusively on the lecture method. Although partially occasioned by the large class size, it also reflects traditional practice. The students take and memorize copious notes. In science areas there are some practical demonstrations. However, only a few secondary schools have the facilities for student experiments.

The Ministry of Education, through laboratory schools attached to the pedagogical faculty at the University of Saigon and 11 selected pilot schools, is experimenting with a comprehensive high school curriculum which includes industrial arts, home economics, and business education. The new curricula seek to emphasize problem-solving. Textbooks for the secondary schools are being written by Vietnamese scholars and printed under Ministry of Education auspices.

The demonstration high schools at the faculties of pedagogy at the universities of Saigon and Hué are also used to exhibit more diversified teaching methods. Along with this teacher-training development there is an effort—in science education, in particular—to improve instructional methods in the rural areas through local workshops which concentrate on the use of locally available and inexpensive materials for demonstrations and experiments.

Vocational education is conducted in four coeducational secondary-level polytechnic schools, five all-male technical schools, and 12 of 18 planned junior technical schools. Students spend half of their time in shop training and half in related classroom activities. Programs vary from school to school but generally include forging and welding, machine-shop work, sheet metalworking, automotive and diesel mechanics, electricity, and woodworking. The coeducational schools include business administration and home economics. The Phu Tho Polytechnic Institute is the only higher education institution of a technical nature.

Agricultural high schools at Bao-Loc in the central highlands, at Hué on the north coastal area, and at Can Tho in the Mekong Delta provide a limited program of study in agriculture.

Higher education.   The universities of Saigon, Hué, Can Tho, and Dalat are organized on the European pattern, with separate faculties for each area of study. These faculties include letters, science, pedagogy, law, medicine, dentistry, pharmacy, architecture, and business administration. Van Hanh University is organized differently. It provides instruction in letters, social work, and Buddhist studies; it also has a language center. Instruction is ordinarily by lecture. However, many enrolled students do not attend the lectures. Library facilities are still exceedingly limited.

Trends and problems.   There are three major problems in South Vietnamese education: minority education, the relevancy of the curriculum, and the effects of the war.

The South Vietnamese desire to assimilate their minorities into the dominant culture. The Chinese, the largest foreign minority, number more than 1 million and constitute between 6 and 7 percent of the population. Under the French, the Chinese in Vietnam were allowed to retain their Chinese citizenship and to appeal to China for protection of their special rights. As many as 400,000 Chinese came to Vietnam after the invasion of China by Japan in 1937, and most settled in the cities of South Vietnam. In 1956, South Vietnam granted Vietnamese nationality to all Chinese born in the country and forbade any

foreigner to engage in certain professions and industrial, commercial, and agricultural enterprises. Some Chinese left the country; some, married to Vietnamese women, carried on their business in the wife's name. The regional administrative associations, by which the Chinese had enjoyed considerable powers of self-government, were abolished in 1960. Until recently the private Chinese schools relied on educational authorities in Taiwan to validate their efforts and grant the graduation certificate; these practices are now forbidden. Almost all Chinese have now adopted Vietnamese citizenship, but the old ties continue. Most Chinese children attend private Chinese schools. Inspectors insist that instruction be given in Vietnamese, but once the inspectors leave, instruction frequently reverts to Chinese. Chinese resistance to assimilation offends nationalist feeling and precludes the serious offering of Chinese as a first foreign language in the secondary schools.

The highland minorities are native to the area but are of a different racial stock and language. The highland child is allowed an additional year to complete the elementary grades because of the language difference. Slow progress toward assimilation of this minority group is being made.

The Republic of Vietnam's changing economy demands a larger number of citizens with a secondary education that includes useful economic skills. Unfortunately, Vietnam's historic ideal of the educated man is that of a "cultured" person who tells others what to do and who does not perform work which will get his hands dirty. Secondary education is seen as a means of reaching higher education and as a cultural acquisition rather than as a means of enhancing productivity. Because of this outlook, the vocational courses are given only in addition to the standard curriculum; the agriculture student thus has more than 40 hours of weekly class, as opposed to 26 hours for the student in a traditional school.

War is the most serious impediment to educational development. It absorbs money and manpower, including male teachers. It also presents the problem of the absorption of ex-soldiers into the economic and social life of the nation, a problem that the limited school system is unprepared to solve.

There is, however, a thirst for education by the people and a commitment by government officials to increase the opportunities. In 1939, under

French rule, there were approximately 5,000 secondary students in North and South Vietnam; in contrast, as of 1971 there were over 470,000 in South Vietnam alone. Educational progress is being made despite the war. With peace the educational prospects would be bright indeed.

BIBLIOGRAPHY

BUTTINGER, JOSEPH 1962 *The Smaller Dragon.* New York, Praeger.

BUTTINGER, JOSEPH 1967 *Vietnam: A Dragon Embattled.* 2 vols. New York, Praeger.

FALL, BERNARD B. 1963 *The Two Vietnams: A Political and Military Analysis.* New York, Praeger.

GLENN C. ATKYNS

VISTA

See WORK AND TRAINING PROGRAMS, FEDERAL: VISTA.

VISUAL PERCEPTION AND PERCEPTUAL LEARNING

Definitions of the term "perception" may be assigned to two categories: those which emphasize perception as product or achievement and those which emphasize perception as process (Hochberg 1956; Garner et al. 1956; Natsoulas 1967). These emphases are combined in the following statement: Perception consists of the internal processes that operate on the physical energies impinging on the receptors, resulting in the attainment of information about the environment. A number of aspects of this statement should be noted: (1) The term "perception" is limited to sensory experiences which are initiated by physical energies that originate in the external environment and impinge on the sensory receptors. (2) The term "perception" is reserved for experiences which are referred to the external environment. "Seeing stars" after a blow on the the head is not an example of perception, nor is a hallucination or an eidetic image. (3) Visual perception is initiated by optical (retinal) stimulation, but it is not determined exclusively by optical stimulation. Other variables contribute to the determination of perception.

The similarities between the human eye and the camera have been frequently noted (Wald 1950). Such comparisons are somewhat instructive, but it is probably the differences between the ocular system and the camera that account for the great utility of the human eye as a system for extracting information. First, the human ocular system is a coordinated binocular system. Second, the ocular system has moving components and is part of a larger system—the body, which is also typically in motion. Most important, the ocular system is one component in a larger perceptual system, which is distinguished by selector and comparator mechanisms at various levels. These mechanisms act to select certain aspects of the incoming stimulation by blocking or neglecting other aspects. They also compare contemporary inputs with memories or traces of previous inputs. When we add to these three considerations the recognition that the perceptual system is in the service of an organism whose behavior is planful, the limitations of the comparisons between the camera and the ocular system become apparent.

Ontogeny of perception. At the beginning of life there is "blooming buzzing confusion." This was William James' description of the newborn infant's visual world. For many years this speculation was accepted as fact. The newborn child's visual world was considered to be an undifferentiated, continuously changing aggregate of light points. Gradually, by trial and error and adventitious reinforcement, order and stability emerged. The chief justification for this description of the infant's perceptual world was that it conformed to the empiricism that generally prevailed in psychology during its early development. However, new experimental investigations have produced data which have upset the traditional view. The data strongly imply that the newborn human infant possesses a significant repertoire of perceptual capabilities.

Experimental objectives. The experimental investigations have been initiated only recently; therefore, it would be premature to list the capabilities exhibited by the newborn. Instead, we will briefly discuss the experimental procedures that have been used to study the question. The principal methodological objectives of a study of infant perception are (1) to secure a stable behavioral response that will reflect perceptual discrimination reliably and (2) to identify the variables of the optic array that control the discrimination. Both of these requirements apply as well to studies of adult perception. However, the impossibility of verbal communication and the presence of greater behavioral lability create special difficulties when infants are studied.

The stimulus preference method. The problem of knowing what the preverbal infant sees—the response problem—can be solved by recognizing that any measurable overt response can be used as a perceptual indicator as long as it is stable and is, or can be made to be, contingent on visual stimuli. The direction of gaze is an example of a naturally occurring response to visual stimuli. Head turning is not spontaneously contingent on visual stimuli, but the desired contingency can be established by training procedures. Once a response has been selected, the experimenter can make it serve to indicate what the infant sees by noting whether the response occurs differentially when several distinct stimuli are exhibited simultaneously. If the response is differential, the stimuli have been discriminated. Consider the case of a hollow hemisphere and a flat frontal-plane projection of the sphere presented for simultaneous viewing to a supine infant. At programmed intervals an automatic camera photographs the corneal reflections on the infant's eyes. The photographs are examined to determine the location of the imaged object relative to the pupil, and in this way the direction of gaze is determined. If the infant has looked significantly more often at either of the two stimuli, then the investigator concludes that the infant can discriminate between them. This testing procedure is called the stimulus preference method. The premise is that no preference can be exhibited without prior discrimination. Instructive studies with the stimulus preference method have been reported by Fantz (1965), Salapatek and Kessen (1966), and Hershenson (1967) in studies of form perception and by Walk and Gibson (1961) in studies of depth perception.

Operant conditioning. Operant conditioning procedures provide the opportunity for establishing stimulus-response contingencies by training. The following is an illustration. In the presence of a frontal parallel circle, a head movement to the right activates a switch which brings into view a favorite toy. The same head movement, in the presence of a frontal parallel elliptical shape, does not lead to the reinforcing event (toy). Eventually the infant will turn his head consistently when the circle is present and only rarely when the ellipse is present. Next, the infant is shown a circle rotated in space so that its projective (retinal) shape is equivalent to that of the frontal parallel ellipse. If the conditioned head turning occurs, then we may infer that shape constancy prevails. If head turning does not occur, suggesting that the slanted circle is not discriminated from the projectively equivalent ellipse, then shape constancy is absent. Experiments following this format have been reported by Bower (1966; 1967).

Ordered responses. These procedures can establish the existence of perceptual capabilities, but we also need to identify more precisely the stimulus variables that control the discriminatory response. If an infant distributes his gaze unevenly between a triangle and a circle, is he discriminating form in the gestalt sense or only angularity compared to curvature? To answer this question, the test stimuli must be chosen to represent specifiable variations along a single stimulus dimension—for example, angularity. Then the stimuli are tested in pairs to determine if an ordered set of responses is obtained that is coordinate with the variations along the stimulus dimension. When an ordered set of responses is observed, we may conclude that an effective stimulus has been isolated. A discussion of this procedure can be found in Hershenson (1967).

Selective principles. What determines the perceptual world of the infant? It seems mandatory to grant that the infant's perceptions are governed by variables of optical stimulation. The visual world of the infant is a function of optical stimulation (J. Gibson 1950; 1966; Epstein & Park 1964). But it also seems necessary to recognize that an account entirely in terms of optical stimulation will not suffice. For a variety of reasons, but chiefly because of a fundamental equivocality in the relationship between optical stimulation and the environment, some additional principles must be at work to determine the perceptual world (Ittelson 1960). The nature of these principles can only be guessed. One such principle may be a preference for minimal change, or for that change which can be specified by the least amount of information (Hochberg 1957; Johansson 1964; Wallach 1959). For example, investigations have revealed a preference for attributing motion to a surrounded object and not the surrounding and a preference for seeing a rigid turning tridimensional object instead of a continuously deforming planar object. These preferences, or selective principles, provide a primitive but essential way of resolving the ambiguity of the relationship between optical stimulation and the environment, and they are prerequisite to the effectiveness of optical stimulation. Admittedly, this formulation lacks precision. Some more exact statement or new alternative will be needed to complete the explanation of what determines the infant's perceptual world.

Perceptual processing. What part does optical stimulation play in determining the perceptual world of the more mature perceiver? The answer is that optical stimulation continues as an important determinant, but that very often it is processed stimulation. The link between stimulation and perception is mediated by intervening processes. Therefore, to understand perception we need to understand the processes that operate on the incoming stimulation. The four forms of processes are (1) selection and differentiation, (2) comparison with memory, (3) assessment in the assumptive context, and (4) linguistic processing.

Selection and differentiation. The first level of processing is selection and filtering (Egeth 1967; Haber 1966; Steinfeld 1967; Broadbent 1958). The perceptual system is usually tuned to respond selectively to a fraction of the total contemporary stimulation and to filter out the balance. This selectivity is manifested in greater clarity and promptness of the response to the variable to which the observer is attuned. At the same time, the observer may reject the stimulation for which he is not set, or he may provide an attenuated response. These tuning and filtering mechanisms have effects similar to the mechanisms that operate in man-made receiver systems such as radio receivers. But the nature of the mechanisms in the perceptual system is more complex than a radio receiver, since the perceptual tuning and filter systems are not preset and fixed but are highly flexible.

Differentiation is a special case of selection (Gibson & Gibson 1955; Tighe & Tighe 1966). Differentiation is an instance of selection which consists of learning to respond to variables of stimulation that have been previously neglected. The most important use of this type of selection is differentiation of higher-order variables which have previously been disregarded in favor of lower-order variables. Examples of higher-order variables are ratios and gradients of stimulation, such as intensity ratios and gradients of optical texture. Although these variables may be present as potential stimuli, they may not be effective initially. Subsequent differentiation of these variables

puts perception under the control of variables that are more likely to lead to stable, veridical perception than are the locally specified stimulus correlates—for example, the retinal image corresponding to an object.

Comparison with memory. Stimulation leaves traces of its occurrence which persist after the source of stimulation is removed. These traces may be impermanent, fading rapidly with elapsed time, or they may be more lasting. Both types of traces are involved in perception, but we will confine ourselves to the more permanent memory traces (Wallach 1949; Hochberg 1968). The simplest case is the trace that is correlated with a specific target. Thus, exposure to a given word will deposit a trace whose strength will increase with frequency of exposure. The influence of these traces can be noted in the fact that the recognition threshold for words is inversely related to frequency of prior exposure (Broadbent 1967).

A somewhat more complicated case is the trace of the perceptual experience associated with a stimulus input. For example, frequent input of perspective transformations associated with perceived extension in depth serves to establish a trace complex made up of representations of perspective such as converging lines and perceived extensity. Later, when a fractional perspective cue is presented, the associated depth perception is elicited (Gregory 1963).

Compound memory traces of correlated visual and nonvisual stimulation may be formed. Recurrent association of auditory and visual stimulation may deposit a compound trace. These compound traces may account for the influence of concurrent auditory stimulation on the response to visual stimulation. A word may be seen more clearly if it is read aloud to the observer during exposure (Smith 1967). Another example is the correlation of body movement and visual stimulation (von Holst 1954). As an object is approached head-on, the retinal image undergoes symmetrical expansion. As a result, when such approaching movement is executed, the memory trace of symmetrical expansion is aroused. If the trace is matched by actual symmetrical expansion of the image, a stable, stationary environment is perceived. If the transformation of the image does not match the trace, some change of the position of the object is perceived.

The assumptive context. The typical history of perceptual experience contains numerous recurrent regularities in the relationships involving optical stimulation (Kilpatrick 1961; Epstein 1967). Objects located at varying distances tend on the average to subtend visual angles that are inversely proportional to their distance. Objects that rotate or swing like a hinged door exhibit lawful transformations of projective shape. The foregoing are examples of regularities involving the relationship between the environment and optical stimulation. In addition, we become aware of environmental regularities. The size of most objects is not variable, although some exceptions are recognized—for example, the size of a balloon. The contours of objects are usually continuous and unbroken. The textures of man-made surfaces tend to be composed of uniform elements. These regularities and many more like them, some in exaggerated and others in attenuated form, lead to the development of an assumptive context for the evaluation of retinal stimulation. The generalized assumptions contribute to veridical perception, but their role in perception has usually been illustrated in demonstrations of illusory perception. The normal rectangular appearance of the "distorted room" is a familiar example (Ittelson & Kilpatrick 1961).

Linguistic processing. Language and perception are related on several levels. The structure and corpus of the language condition our conceptualizations of the structure of the environment, and these conceptualizations condition our readiness to make particular discriminations (Brown & Lenneberg 1954; Whorf 1950). These effects may facilitate or inhibit perception. Many instances of cross-cultural differences—for example, anthropological reports of differences in ability to discriminate color—may reflect differences in the resources of the native languages of various cultures. Although such effects of language are important in determining behavior, many psychologists doubt that perceptual sensitivity is materially affected in the manner implied by the anthropological evidence.

Nevertheless, there are a number of ways in which language could affect perception. Two of these possibilities have been investigated experimentally. (1) Verbal processing of the stimulus may determine the memory trace of the event and in this way affect perception on a subsequent occasion of the stimulus (Herman et al. 1957). (2) Verbal processing may affect the discriminability of stimuli by creating a compound stimulus that consists of a visual stimulus and the verbal responses that have been associated with the stimulus. If the verbal responses are distinctive, the result will be enhanced distinctiveness. For example, learning the names of the letters *b* and *d* may enhance their discriminability. On the other hand, if the verbal response is associated with more than one stimulus, these stimuli may be harder to discriminate (Epstein 1967).

Modification of perception. It is clear from the preceding section that perception is modifiable. Most occasions of perceptual learning can be classified into two categories: (1) learning to respond to new stimuli and (2) learning new responses to old stimuli. In the first case, learning consists of responding to aspects of stimulation that previously had been neglected. In the second case, learning is a matter of reevaluating stimuli and learning to respond to these stimuli in different ways.

New stimuli. The enrichment studies are good examples of learning to respond to new stimuli (Tighe & Tighe 1966; Epstein 1967). Animals— for example, rats—are reared from birth in different visual environments. In the enriched environment a number of visual forms are continuously exposed. In the comparison environment a matched littermate is reared without any forms in view. At a preselected age the animals are subjected to a form-discrimination test. The typical result is that the animal reared in the enriched environment exhibits superior form discrimination. Exposure to visual forms provides an opportunity for differentiation of the stimulus variables that distinguish the forms. Although it is possible that these results are peculiar to hooded and albino rats, it does not strain credibility to propose that enriched visual environments will have salutary effects on human infants.

The effects of training on perceptual discrimination represent another example of the learned modification of perception (Gibson 1953). In some experimental demonstrations of training effects it is difficult to classify the underlying change. Some effects are simply instances of associative learning with no accompanying enhancement of sensitivity. This is probably the case for the claims that color-blind observers can be trained to discriminate hue. Improved performance probably rests on learning to associate color names with brightness differences. In the main, however, where training does affect perceptual sensitivity, the result may be attributed chiefly to differentiation—that is, learning to respond to new stimuli.

The training procedure usually takes the form of controlled practice in judging the same or similar test stimuli. The factors that can regulate the magnitude of the practice effect are the amount of practice, reinforcement or correction, and the sequence of judgments. The following generalizations about these factors are permissible: (1) The amount of improvement resulting from practice is a negatively accelerated function of the amount of practice. The greatest improvements occur early in practice. (2) The effects of practice are increased if each judgment is followed by appropriate reinforcement or correction. But improvement may occur in the absence of controlled reinforcement. (3) Practice will be more effective if a sequence of tests can be provided which begin with simple discriminations and increase the difficulty of discrimination progressively.

New responses. The second type of perceptual learning is a reevaluation of stimulation—learning new responses to old stimuli. This type of reevaluation has been observed in a variety of studies of perceptual discrepancy or conflict. The most prominent examples are the investigations of adaptation to optically induced transformations of stimulation (Rock 1966; Epstein 1967). These transformations are brought about by interposing a special medium—for example, a prism—between the eye and the environment. A right-angle prism properly oriented and worn in eyeglass frames will produce a known amount of tilt in the visual scene. The presence of optical tilt leads to a condition of conflict or discrepancy: (1) Objects which have a familiar orientation appear in an anomalous orientation; for example, a bookcase may seem tilted 30 degrees to the left. (2) The perceived orientation of objects and the consequences of behaviors guided by the perceived orientation are discordant. (3) When the observer engages in normal movement—for example, walking down a corridor—parts of the visual scene appear to move in and out of view in an unaccustomed manner.

The right-angle prism is only one of several optical devices that have been used, and the precise nature of the discrepancy will vary with the character of the medium—for example, sideways displacement and minification. The central finding in these studies is that adaptation occurs.

With continued exposure to the optical transformation, the world begins to resume its pre-experimental appearance. Only a few investigators have reported complete adaptation, but the typical finding of partial adaptation may be due to practical limitations on the length of the exposure period.

Adaptation is a striking example of perceptual plasticity. There is still considerable disagreement about the precise nature of the underlying modification. Nevertheless, the variety of accounts that have been proposed all fit the general formulation that the stimulation has been reevaluated.

Perception and education. There has been considerable progress in working out the details of particular types of perceptual learning phenomena. However, very little work has been done to help locate perceptual learning in the more general context of learning phenomena. In advance of this synthesis the student of the educational process will have to be cautious in applying the facts and hypotheses of perceptual learning to the questions in his field.

BIBLIOGRAPHY

BOWER, T. G. R. 1966 "Slant Perception and Shape Constancy in Infants." *Science*, 151, no. 3712:832–834.

BOWER, T. G. R. 1967 "Phenomenal Identity and Form Perception in an Infant." *Perception and Psychophysics*, 2, no. 2:74–76.

BROADBENT, DONALD E. 1958 *Perception and Communication*. New York, Pergamon Press.

BROADBENT, DONALD E. 1967 "Word Frequency Effect and Response Bias." *Psychological Review*, 74, no. 1:1–15.

BROWN, ROGER W., AND E. H. LENNEBERG 1954 "A Study in Language and Cognition." *Journal of Abnormal Social Psychology*, 49, no. 3:454–462.

EGETH, HOWARD 1967 "Selective Attention." *Psychological Bulletin*, 67, no. 1:41–57.

EPSTEIN, WILLIAM 1967 *Varieties of Perceptual Learning*. New York, McGraw-Hill. See Chapters 2–4, 5 (especially pages 107–116), 7, and 9.

EPSTEIN, WILLIAM, AND JOHN PARK 1964 "Examination of Gibson's Psychophysical Hypothesis." *Psychological Bulletin*, 62, no. 3:180–196.

FANTZ, R. L. 1965 "Ontogeny of Perception." Allan M. Schrier, Harry F. Harlow, and Fred Stollintz, eds., *Behavior of Nonhuman Primates*. Vol. 2. New York, Academic Press. Pages 365–402.

GARNER, W. R., H. W. HAKE, AND C. W. ERIKSON 1956 "Operationism and the Concept of Perception." *Psychological Review*, 63, no. 3:149–159.

GIBSON, ELEANOR J. 1953 "Improvements in Perceptual Judgments as a Function of Controlled Practice or Training." *Psychological Bulletin*, 50, no. 6:401–431.

GIBSON, JAMES J. 1950 *The Perception of the Visual World*. Edited by Leonard Carmichael. Boston, Houghton Mifflin.

GIBSON, JAMES J. 1966 *The Senses Considered as Perceptual Systems*. Edited by Leonard Carmichael. Boston, Houghton Mifflin.

GIBSON, JAMES J., AND ELEANOR J. GIBSON 1955 "Perceptual Learning: Differentiation or Enrichment?" *Psychological Review*, 62, no. 1:32–41.

GREGORY, RICHARD L. 1963 "Distortion of Visual Space as Inappropriate Constancy Scaling." *Nature*, 199:678–680.

HABER, RALPH N. 1966 "Nature of the Effect of Set on Perception." *Psychological Review*, 73, no. 4:335–351.

HERMAN, DAVID T., RICHARD H. LAWLESS, AND RICHARD W. MARSHALL 1957 "Variables in the Effect of Language on the Reproduction of Visually Perceived Form." *Perception and Motor Skills*, 7, no. 2:171–186.

HERSHENSON, MAURICE 1967 "Development in the Perception of Form." *Psychological Bulletin*, 67, no. 5:326–336.

HOCHBERG, JULIAN E. 1956 "Perception: Toward the Recovery of a Definition." *Psychological Review*, 63, no. 6:400–405.

HOCHBERG, JULIAN E. 1957 "Effects of the Gestalt Revolution: The Cornell Symposium on Perception." *Psychological Review*, 64, no. 2:73–84.

HOCHBERG, JULIAN E. 1968 "In the Mind's Eye." Ralph N. Haber, ed., *Contemporary Theory and Research in Visual Perception*. New York, Holt. Pages 309–331.

ITTELSON, WILLIAM H. 1960 *Visual Space Perception*. New York, Springer.

ITTELSON, WILLIAM H., AND FRANKLIN P. KILPATRICK, eds. 1961 "The Monocular and Binocular Distorted Rooms." Franklin P. Kilpatrick, ed., *Explorations in Transitional Psychology*. New York University Press. Pages 154–173.

JOHANSSON, GUNNAR 1964 "Perception of Motion and Changing Form." *Scandinavian Journal of Psychology*, 5, no. 3:181–208.

KILPATRICK, FRANKLIN P., ed. 1961 *Explorations in Transactional Psychology*. New York University Press.

NATSOULAS, THOMAS 1967 "What Are Perceptual Reports About?" *Psychological Bulletin*, 67, no. 4:249–272.

ROCK, IRVIN 1966 *The Nature of Perceptual Adaptation*. New York, Basic Books.

SALAPATEK, PHILIP, AND WILLIAM KESSEN 1966 "Visual Scanning of Triangle by the Human Newborn." *Journal of Experimental Child Psychology*, 3:155–167.

SMITH, WILLIAM M. 1967 "Visual Recognition: Facilitating of Seeing by Saying." *Perception and Psychophysics*, 2, no. 2:57–58.

STEINFELD, GEORGE 1967 "Concepts of Set and Availability and Their Relation to the Reorganization of Ambiguous Pictorial Stimuli." *Psychological Review*, 74, no. 6:505–522.

TIGHE, LOUISE S., AND THOMAS J. TIGHE 1966 "Discrimination Learning: Two Views in Historical Perspective." *Psychological Bulletin*, 66, no. 5:353–370.

VON HOLST, E. 1954 "Relations Between the Central Nervous System and the Peripheral Organs." *British Journal of Animal Behavior*, 2, no. 3:89–94.

WALD, GEORGE 1950 "Eye and Camera." *Scientific American*, 183, no. 2:32–41.

WALK, RICHARD D., AND ELEANOR J. GIBSON 1961 "A Comparative and Analytical Study of Visual Depth Perception." *Psychological Monographs*, 75, no. 15:whole No. 519.

WALLACH, HANS 1949 "Some Considerations Concerning the Relation Between Perception and Cognition." *Journal of Personality*, 18, no. 1:6–13.

WALLACH, HANS 1959 "The Perception of Motion." *Scientific American*, 201, no. 1:56–59.

WHORF, BENJAMIN LEE 1950 *Four Articles on Metalinguistics*. Washington, D.C., Foreign Services Institute.

WILLIAM EPSTEIN

VOCABULARY DEVELOPMENT

Vocabulary development is usually thought of as the process of increasing one's store of words and meanings. The point of view in this article is that vocabulary development consists of a great deal more and must include word power, which is the power to deal effectively with new words and with new meanings for old words when they are encountered. Vocabulary development therefore consists of both knowledge and skills.

Word knowledge includes a knowledge of specific words and specific meanings, but more fundamentally, it includes a knowledge of how words acquire meanings and of how they convey meanings. The skills of vocabulary development are the skills required to work out a meaning for a word through use of context clues and clues provided by word parts.

The status of vocabulary. The common view is that the size of a person's vocabulary is directly associated with the level of his intelligence. There is some justification for this common view but no justification whatever for the view that one can increase his intelligence by increasing his vocabulary. However, vocabulary items still have a dominant place in verbal intelligence tests and in tests used for placement in schools, industry, and the military.

There are two reasonable justifications for the use of vocabulary items in such tests. First, words are symbols that the individual uses for coping with his environment. The more words he commands, the more discriminations he can make and use effectively. Cross-cultural studies have indicated that some societies do not have words or concepts found in the Western world and that the language available determines the adaptation of a society to its environment. What is true for a society is held to be true for individuals.

The second justification for reliance upon vocabulary items in testing is that they measure the individual's ability to acquire and utilize significant items from his environment. Whether or not this ability is associated with intelligence or is intelligence, the concept embraces a significant principle in vocabulary development: Word meaning does come from experience.

The emphasis upon the size and range of vocabulary measured by tests carries two unfortunate implications. The first is that mere size of vocabulary is its most significant aspect. The second is that vocabulary is the most important element of language power in general. This notion obscures the importance of the structures of a language. English structures themselves carry meaning. Basil Bernstein (1958) reports that studies of language deprivation in England show a deficit in the knowledge and use of structures, which results in poverty of expression. In short, size of vocabulary is by no means the only determinant of language facility.

The system of basic English derived by C. K. Ogden is built upon a list of only 850 words. It was designed for use in international communication on the assumption that any English passage —except for one with specifically technical and scientific terms—could be translated into these 850 words. The force and effectiveness of this list gained from two peculiarities which give English its extraordinary flexibility. First, by the addition of adverbs to common verbs, the so-called two-word verbs are created with a great range of meanings. Thus, *turn in* can stand for *retire*, as well as *hand over* or *betray*; *get ahead* can stand for *prosper*, as well as *advance*, and so forth. Second, in English nouns modify nouns to a degree not found in other Western languages. Thus, we can say *brook trout* and avoid the necessity of creating a new term.

The great flexibility of English structure makes it unnecessary to reach very far into the stock of more than 600,000 words in the language. Mere size of vocabulary is thus not likely to be the most significant aspect of vocabulary for the individual. One has only to recall Winston Churchill's reliance upon common words to realize what can be done with them: ". . . we shall fight on the beaches, we shall fight on the landing-grounds, we shall fight in the fields and in the streets, we shall fight in the hills; we shall never surrender. . . ."

Whether or not vocabulary is a measure of intelligence, it is almost certainly a measure of achievement. Vocabulary is a means through which intelligence operates. If for no other reason, vocabulary development merits the status it now has in our society.

Kinds of vocabulary. In common usage a person's vocabulary is considered to be the range of words he uses in ordinary speech or writing. It is more accurate to note that there are at least four kinds of vocabulary—oral, writing, listening, and reading—each with its own range and uses.

Oral vocabulary consists of words actively used in speech. Words slip in and out of this stock. Nonce words, created for a particular moment or occasion, are picked up and dropped. Changes in circumstances and in age produce changes in the words that a person uses actively in speaking. The total range of these words includes those used in business, trade, or profession and those used socially, whether in the context of a locker room or of a formal dinner. The significant character of oral vocabulary is that it is actively used by the speaker in unrehearsed situations.

Unrehearsed speech is usually under the constraints of time and the attention of listeners. The speaker, even in dialogue with one other person, is required to act quickly in order to avert interruption or the wandering of the listener's attention. This time constraint limits the opportunity for searching out the exact word. It is understandable, therefore, that the language of ordinary speech is relatively limited in range and that the person who is quick and ready in locating the words he wants is marked as having a large vocabulary.

Writing vocabulary varies considerably from oral vocabulary. When writing is entirely colloquial, however, and merely substitutes for face-to-face speech, it may vary little. In more formal writing the occasion, the subject matter, and the audience may require words seldom encountered in ordinary speech.

For many, the act of writing is uncomfortable and even abnormal, and it produces a freezing self-consciousness which calls forth words seldom heard in the writer's speech. By contrast, there are the professionals for whom writing provides the leisure to search out words to carry precisely the determined meanings.

Writing vocabulary, like oral vocabulary, consists of words actively used. Since it is not under constraint of time, it may have substantially wider range than the vocabulary of unrehearsed speech.

Listening vocabulary is the stock of words to which one responds with meaning and understanding in the speech of others. This speech may or may not be unrehearsed. In public addresses and in most radio and television statements, the speaker's words have been written out. Words in a listener's vocabulary are not necessarily those which he projects in his own active use. They may have a minimum of meaning for him. The range of listening vocabulary is wider than that of oral or writing vocabulary, since it includes words which the listener has not mastered sufficiently to use in his own speech and writing. The apt example of such a listener is the child who can respond with understanding to words he cannot himself formulate.

Reading vocabulary is the stock of words to which one responds with meaning and understanding in the writing of others. Here, there is no constraint of time whatever. Context provides clues to meaning just as with the listening vocabulary, but the context is recorded and may be studied, whereas the context in listening is fleeting and can be brought back only with difficulty and seldom with certainty. In addition, formal signals and word affixes are open to inspection in reading, whereas they may be missed in listening.

It seems probable that reading vocabulary is more extensive than listening vocabulary and that the two do not coincide. A reader can deal with a word that he cannot pronounce, but he may therefore fail to recognize it when it is spoken. It is a safe estimate that reading vocabulary is the most extensive of the four kinds of vocabulary: speaking, writing, listening, and reading.

Measurement of vocabulary. The measurement of vocabulary has proceeded in two directions. The first pertains to words themselves: their frequency of use and their difficulty. The second pertains to the extent of an individual's reading vocabulary. These measures involve serious sampling problems, which have not been wholly resolved.

The validity of a word frequency count depends upon the currency of the source materials. If the study is designed to measure the use of words over several centuries, the problem of selecting source materials is virtually insoluble. If the study is designed to measure the frequency with which words appear in the writings of a particular contemporary moment, factors of change in reading consumption must be taken into account. Thorndike and Lorge (1944) included in their frequency count some 3,000 pages of Gibbon's *The Decline and Fall of the Roman Empire.* The appropriateness of this sample is questionable, since few have ever read the work in its entirety, and few read any portion of it today. If the frequency of word use is important, computer analysis may now be applied on a grand scale to overcome problems of sampling, but the value of frequency counts is questionable for educational purposes.

The measure of word difficulty assumes that words have characteristics of length, shape, abstractness, and so forth which make them innately easy or difficult to recognize and use. Unquestionably, certain words are more difficult to pronounce than others. Some words are persistently difficult to spell for all ages of man. In the beginning levels of reading instruction, the word *the* is rated as a "hard" word, because the initial phoneme is difficult to pronounce. The basis of such judgments is common experience. A word may be difficult for a particular person or even for a particular age group to spell or pronounce, but it does not seem permissible to apply a generalizing label of "hard" or "easy" to any word. The analysis of word difficulty finds its chief use in elementary school courses. Since the difficulty of a word may be overcome by instruction, it would seem that usefulness might be a better criterion for introducing a word than difficulty.

The second kind of vocabulary measurement is the estimation of an individual's vocabulary. Here the problem of sampling is very great, since the validity of a sample depends upon full knowledge of the universe it is intended to represent, and the extent of an individual's reading or listening vocabulary is unknown and is not open to inspection. Response to a particular group of words tells nothing about potential response to any other group. It seems unlikely that any device can measure the whole range of a person's reading or listening vocabulary. The means employed to measure a child's preschool listening vocabulary, for example, rely upon reports from the child himself and employ such devices as turning through the pages of a dictionary at random. Methods of this sort do not usually produce verifiable results.

Word power. The use of vocabulary items in tests and the measurement of vocabulary, word difficulty, and the like represent a static view of language. Usually, the tests assume a single fixed meaning for a word and assume that a student "knows" a word if he can respond to one of its meanings. In the Introduction to *The Teacher's Word Book of 30,000 Words* (Thorndike & Lorge 1944), this sentence appears:

A teacher should decide concerning many words which occur in books or articles to be read by the class, whether to have the class learn the word well enough so that the ability to know the sound and the important meaning or meanings of the word where they see it will be a permanent part of their stock of word knowledge, or merely inform them of its meaning temporarily so that they can understand and enjoy the reading matter in which it occurs. (p. 252)

There is some question as to whether anyone can learn a word so that it becomes a permanent part of his word stock by being informed of the word's meaning temporarily, as stated in the passage above. More important, there is another possibility (not considered by Thorndike and Lorge) for teachers. This is the teaching of word power, the power to deal with a new word or a new meaning independently when it is first encountered. Vocabulary grows when a person learns new meanings for familiar words as well as when he acquires wholly new words. Acquiring meanings is a lifelong process, but there are specific strategies and information that can make the effort rewarding at any stage.

The cognitive goals in building word power are straightforward: (1) the ability to estimate and validate meanings, (2) the ability to recognize when new meanings occur, and (3) the ability to recognize figurative language. The parallel affective goals are development of an interest in words and willingness to spend time and effort in acquiring and using word meanings and in using them precisely.

The linguistic base. The development of word power has both a linguistic base and a semantic base. In part, the linguistic base involves an understanding of the meanings in a sentence carried by sentence structures. But more specifically to vocabulary development, the linguistic base involves word signals and affixes.

The word signals that carry meaning include *-s, -es, -ed, -en, en-, 's,* and *'d.* The *-ed* ending attached to a verb signals past time, and it is a relatively reliable signal. The forms *-s* and *-es* added to nouns signal the plural. However, *-s* may also indicate present time and singular number when it is added to the base form of a verb.

The *'s* carries three different meanings depending upon the situation. When it is added to a Class 1 word (noun), the genitive form is created and establishes the meaning of possession, belonging, or direct association with respect to the following noun. When *'s* is added to a noun or pronoun followed by a participle, however, it may be a contraction of either *is* or *has.*

Similarly, the *'d,* if affixed to a noun or pronoun, may signal either *had* or *would.* The *-en* form has great versatility since it may be a signal of the past participle, as in *written* and *bitten,* or of the plural, as in *children.* It may also appear as a prefix, as in *enrich,* or as a suffix, as in *wooden* or *frighten.*

The affixes which contribute meaning are of three sorts: prefixes, suffixes, and combining forms. The most prominent of the combining forms derive from Latin and Greek and are the forms of words used in those languages to combine with other words or word parts in the formation of new words. Several combining forms may appear at the beginning or end of English words —for example, tele*phone,* *phono*graph, and *graph*ology.

In a living language, word composition is an ongoing process. It proceeds by joining an element to an established base. This base may be a free form, which appears independently, or a bound form, such as *vis* or *clud,* which has no independent existence as a word. American English is distinguished by the flexibility with which word composition occurs. We may join two or more Class 1 words (nouns) and produce *airline, airway,* and *airport.* We may join Class 2 words (verbs) with complements and modifiers and produce *readout, printout, input, output, dogooder, pacesetter,* and *feedback.*

It should be noted that the consistency with which word formation occurs in speech does not appear in the written language. Thus, *drugstore* appears as one word and *grocery store* as two; there is also the case of *hairpin, hair net,* and *hair-trigger.* There appear to be no rules or set procedures followed by printers and editors to represent what in speech is a single compounded word.

Apart from the base words (free forms) and the roots (bound forms), the most important and useful word parts for vocabulary development are the suffixes. E. L. Thorndike, who undertook a study of English suffixes, observed: "Correct responses to suffixes is not a luxury in the comprehension and use of English, but a necessity" (1941, p. 64). The usefulness of suffixes derives from two functions they perform: signifying specific meaning and indicating word class or part of speech.

The suffix meaning may be quite specific, as with *-ee, -cide, -ist, -able (-ible, -ble), -ful,* and *-less.*

For other suffixes the meaning may be generalized to such translations as "pertaining to" (*-acious, -ative, -ish*) and "state, condition, or being of" (*-ment, -ness, -ion*).

Equally important is the use of suffixes in English to indicate word class, or part of speech. It should be noted that English speakers transfer a word from one class to another by use of suffixes. Thus, the noun *man* becomes the adjective *manly* by addition of *-ly*. The verb *use* becomes an adjective by the addition of *-able*. This use of suffixes enormously expands the resources of the language without the necessity of creating specific, discrete, unrelated words for each new meaning situation. Moreover, an understanding of the process permits the learner to acquire whole clusters or families of words with central meanings deriving from the base word.

The suffixes which regularly identify a word as Class 1 (nouns) are *-ment, -ness, -ion (-tion), -ence (-ance), -ity, -ure, -ism, -ist, -th,* and *-age.* Two suffixes identify Class 2 words (verbs): *-ify* and *-ize.* The suffixes which identify Class 3 words (adjectives) are *-ish, -y, -ous, -ful, -less, -like, -ive, -most, -able (-ible),* and *-ant.* There are no suffixes which appear only in Class 4 words (adverbs).

Prefixes are neither as numerous nor as productive of meaning as suffixes. There are perhaps no more than ten common prefixes, such as *mal-, mis-,* and *non-,* that have a single invariant meaning. Two of the most common prefixes, *in-* and *un-,* have several meanings. As a consequence, when the learner comes upon a new word containing these prefixes, he cannot depend upon them as a source of meaning in the word.

In sum, the linguistic basis for the development of word power lies in formal word elements, such as inflectional signals (*-d, -ed, -s,* and so forth), and in roots, base words, and affixes.

The semantic base. A number of semantic principles are basic for an effective vocabulary program. Among the important ones are these:

(1) Most words in common use have more than one meaning. The more familiar the word, the more meanings it has: the word *run* has about 90 meanings, for example. Some words have meanings that are directly opposite. The word *with,* for example, means both "in opposition to" and "as an associate of."

(2) The meaning of a word which applies in a particular situation is determined by the context of other words with which it is used. Context always determines meaning. Context sometimes illuminates the meaning of a word by a variety of clues, which will be discussed later.

(3) Meaning comes from experience. A person may have experience with a word in the presence of what it refers to or in the presence of other words.

(4) A single encounter with a word cannot reveal all of its meanings.

(5) Since meaning comes from experience, and one person's experience differs from that of his fellows, communication occurs only when there is an overlap of common, shared experience. A complete communication of meaning is usually impossible.

These five semantic principles are critical in vocabulary development. They inform and enlighten vocabulary study, but more important, they limit vocabulary instruction. When they are transgressed or forgotten, misinformation and misunderstanding result.

A semantic problem arises when words do not carry their regular lexical meanings. The tendency of the unsophisticated reader is to take words always at their face value, to read literally when literal meaning is not intended.

In the figurative use of words, meanings are deliberately stretched for emphasis or color. The pages of the daily newspaper are filled with examples, notably in the headlines. The following were culled from one issue of the New York *Times*: President Urged to *Spur* Campaign on Rural Poverty; Reminders of War *Touch* Ceremony in East Room; Vietcong *Pin Down* Government Battalion; U.S. *Presses* Europe for Gold Support; Professors *Spur* Ferment in Madrid; Construction Program Changing *Face* of South Vietnam; G.O.P. Governors *Map Platform.*

While metaphor in newspaper headlines derives from the constraints of available space, in other writing its purpose is to heighten meaning. This it does by exaggeration and by the juxtaposition of words and concepts not normally used together. In most instances the common meanings of the words do not fit. An examination of metaphor is therefore quite properly a part of the development of word power, the power to deal with new words and new meanings.

Idiom is another instance of words not having their accustomed meanings. (The word *idiom* as used here refers to a phrase whose meaning differs from the sum of meanings of the words composing it.) Consider the idiom *look in*, for example. The ordinary meaning, with the words having their common significance, appears in the following:

Did you look in the closet for your gloves?

Two quite different meanings are to be found in the two following statements:

Jack didn't have a *look in* for the presidency.
We will *look in* on the Johnsons this evening.

In the latter two sentences, the meaning of *look in* cannot be derived from the lexical meanings of *look* and *in*. The words constitute an idiom with meanings of its own.

Changes in meaning. The processes by which words lose and acquire meanings may be observed in the pages of any dictionary which provides etymologies, or the processes may be studied under the guidance of linguists in such books as *Words and Their Ways in English Speech* (Greenough & Kittredge 1961).

An understanding of the processes by which words lose old meanings and acquire new meanings is essential in development of word power. The first goal of instruction is to make the learner aware that change occurs, not just over historical periods but frequently in short spans within a lifetime. Greenough and Kittredge give the following example of meaning change:

The Latin *persona* means properly "a mask" such as the ancient actors wore. (*Per-*, "through" and *sonare* "to sound," since [an] actor "talked through" the large mouth of his mask.) This meaning we may call *A*. Such masks were typical of various parts or *roles*, and thus arises *A + B*, "a dramatic character as indicated by the appropriate mask." Then *A* disappears and *B* remains, so that *persona* means "a character or *role* in a play." To *B* is then added a further modifier (*C*), "one who represents," and we have *B + C*, "one who represents a dramatic character," "one who takes a *role*." Next *B* disappears, so that *persona* means merely "a representative." *C* is then modified by the addition of "the church" (*D*), and we get *C + D*,

"the representative of the church (persona ecclesiae) in a parish." Finally the main idea of *C* ("representative") disappears, and *parson* in the sense of "parish priest" results. (1961, p. 268)

Change in meaning occurs by a generalizing process of degeneration and by a particularizing process in which meaning is sharply narrowed. In both processes, old meanings tend to drop away. In current English, *thing*, *way*, and *place* are examples of generalized words of such vagueness as to be useful when precision of meaning is not wanted. A special case of degeneration is the social language formula such as *How do you do*. Other examples are the space-holders *well*, *you see*, *you know*, or *I mean*. Another example of degeneration occurs with words used to express generalized favor or disfavor such as *great* and *terrible* and, recently, *bomb* and *cool*.

The process of particularizing meaning is illustrated by the example of *liquor*, which once referred to any matter in a liquid state, to the liquid portion of any secretion, to the product of a chemical process, or to a solution used in an industrial process. Now almost universally, it is used to refer only to a drink manufactured by distillation.

The particularizing process does not always result in the fading of old meanings. When information scientists seized the term *bit* to describe a unit in communication, its specialized meaning was confined to their science.

Many words have affective values in addition to their use as labels. These values stem from the culture and are learned by the young through admonition, praise, punishment, and reward. Words are thus said to connote more than they specify. Psychologists have established that some words produce anxiety responses. The degree to which any word produces anxiety or another emotion in an individual depends, however, upon his experience with the word and his experience in the real world of things, people, and events.

Changes in the meanings of words are interesting historically and interesting in themselves. They are useful elements in the development of word power because they reinforce the principle that words are not counters. They are not like numbers or scientific formulas which have fixed, single, and invariant meanings.

This variable nature of word meanings produces problems in communication. What a word means to any person is the result of his experience with it, and the experience of one person differs from that of another. Communication is possible only because of the overlap of common experience. In a particular situation, a particular person may succeed in giving his audience a shade of meaning that is peculiar to his own experience. This "meaning" may not be found recorded in even the largest dictionaries. Dictionaries record only generalized experiences with words and cannot possibly take into account the countless private happenings in which the circumstances contribute to meaning.

In general, the individual acquires meanings by attentive experience with a word in varying contexts. This is as true of common words as it is of specialized technical terms. Since most words in common use have a variety of meanings, it follows that the full range of meanings in a word can never be acquired in a single encounter. It also follows that the learner should be encouraged to become aware of shifts in the meaning of common words as he meets them.

Developing word power. When the reader encounters a new word or an old word used in an unfamiliar context, he may ignore it, consult a dictionary, conclude that the writer made a mistake, or work out the meaning from clues provided. It is essential in developing word power to establish a bias in favor of the writer, an assumption that he knows what he is saying.

Since a dictionary may not always be at hand, it is useful to know something about clues to word meaning. Clues derive from context and from word parts. Use of these clues may seldom provide full and certain knowledge, but the clues can provide enough knowledge to permit the reader to proceed with understanding.

Word-part clues. A great many English words have been derived directly from Latin or indirectly from Latin by way of other languages. A common feature of these Latin derivatives is the root, or stem, used in Latin for word-formation. Among these are *ject, clude, fect, fer, struct,* and the like. There are significant difficulties in the use of these roots in deriving meanings of English words. Many Latin stems have more than one meaning, and there is no a priori way of knowing which meaning is present. In many English words the base meanings have proceeded far from the Latin meanings: for example, it is of little value to the learner of English to know that *perceive,*

receive, and *deceive* are all derived from the Latin *capere.* Also, the spelling of the Latin root is often quite different from the spelling of the English word derived from it.

The use of word parts to work out a meaning for an unfamiliar word is limited by the specific information these parts provide. The most helpful are those that have a single invariant meaning. Combining forms such as *lith, phone,* and *photo* are the most reliable. Perhaps a dozen may profitably be called to the learner's attention.

Prefixes present several problems. As previously noted, there are no more than ten common prefixes having a single invariant meaning, although there are many more or less commonly used prefixes of value, particularly those deriving from technical and scientific fields.

In a great many words absorbed from Latin and French, the force of the prefix is no longer felt in English, because it may have been lost in Roman times, when new words were created for purposes of emphasis or style by the addition of a prefix which did not alter the meaning at all. In some instances, the prefix lost significance after the word came into English. Nonetheless, a knowledge of prefix meanings and of the forms of prefixes is useful in getting at word meanings. It is helpful to know, for example, that *in-* becomes *ir-* before *r, il-* before *l,* and *im-* before *p* and *b.* The prefix *com-* becomes *cor-, col-, co-,* or *con-,* depending upon the following letter. The prefix *ad-* makes eight different accommodations of this sort.

Prefixes with several meanings, such as *in-, de-, dis-, un-,* and *trans-,* need not be avoided. Their successful use requires careful study, but this study can be rewarding even if no other result follows than understanding that *trans-* does not always signify "across," *un-* does not always mean "not," and *de-* does not always mean "down." Thus, in *transalpine,* the prefix means "beyond." In *untie,* the prefix means "reversal of." In *defunct,* the prefix means "totally."

Suffixes provide a substantial amount of information. There are a half-dozen which signify agency, "one who" or "a thing that": *-ist, -ier, -ler, -ster, -ess,* and *-grapher.* Several are regularly used as diminutives: *-ock, -ule, -cle, -kin,* and *-let.* It is important to note that the letters forming these suffixes may not in fact be suffixes at all but a part of the base word itself. In general, the suffixes used for word-class transfer or word-class identification contribute no meaning to the word in which they appear: *-y*, *-ize*, *-ment*, and so forth.

There is one hazard to be avoided at all costs in the use of word parts: the practice of adding prefix, root, and suffix to produce a "literal meaning." The sum of the parts is substantially less than the whole of an English word. The literal meaning is often wholly unrelated to current English meaning. But more important, the additive process leads to a single meaning. Nothing could be more obstructive to vocabulary development than the idea that a word has only one meaning.

English base words. A great many English words have been composed or compounded from shorter English words. Thus, the words *act*, *form*, and *press* lead to a great store of formatives. Recognition of these base words within longer words will provide clues to meaning. The use of base words in vocabulary study is not to be confused with the now-discredited practice in elementary reading instruction of "finding the little word in the big word," which led to finding *eat* in *beat*.

English base words are properly used only as they combine with other free forms or with recognizable affixes. A word such as *depend* may be treated as a base word leading to *independent*, *dependencies*, *dependable*, and other words. It is useful to call attention to changes in spelling when base words combine with suffixes. In some instances, vowels are dropped: *reveal* becomes *relevant*, and *appear* becomes *apparent*. In other instances, vowels are changed: *defy* becomes *defiant*. In some words, a letter is added: *arbor* becomes *arboreal*, and *obey* becomes *obedient*. In some words, the final consonant is changed or dropped: *number* becomes *numerical*, *attend* becomes *attention*, and *offend* becomes *offensive*.

There is one limiting factor in the use of base words: the existence of multiple meanings. One meaning of a base may carry over into one group of formatives, while a second meaning carries over into another group of formatives. More often the formatives may carry either meaning. Thus *move*, meaning "to arouse sympathies," and *move*, meaning "to change position," both lead to *mover* (as in "movers and shakers" or "movers of furniture"), to *unmoved* (as in "sympathies not aroused" or "unchanged in position"), and to *moving* (as in "a moving appeal" or "a moving van").

Context clues. It would be extremely difficult to design an experiment to prove or disprove the hypothesis that we get most of our understanding of words through observation of context. Yet this seems likely to be the case. We do not get meanings from a dictionary, since a dictionary is only a record of common significations taken from contexts. Some meanings are acquired through seeing or hearing a word used in the presence of the thing or event it names, as with labels and signs. No significant study of the effects of television upon acquisition of words and meanings has appeared, but it seems likely that the instructive effect of this medium is very strong.

Context always determines which of a word's many meanings is intended—that is, context always determines meaning. Occasionally, context illuminates meaning by the use of deliberately contrived clues. When context operates in this way, it reveals only one meaning of a word, and it seldom clarifies the whole range of this meaning. The acquisition of meanings through the use of context is therefore gradual and accumulative. There are other limiting conditions: the success of context clarification depends upon the previous experience of the reader (the clues provided may have no meaning for him); for most readers the enlightening context must be close enough to the target word so that the relationship is obvious; the substantive connection of context and target word must be clear (Deighton 1959).

The following clues are consciously planted by writers in order to assist readers in determining meaning:

(1) Definition. Outright definition is signaled by expressions such as *By this we mean . . .* and *We use this term to signify. . . .* The usual pattern is to equate the unfamiliar terms with the known or familiar by some form of the verb *be*.

(2) Example. Signal words usually precede the clarifying example: *such as, such, like, especially, for example, other, this* or *these, in the way that*. Many of these signal words also operate structurally as sequence signals relating an utterance to one that has preceded.

(3) Modifiers. The meaning intended for a word can be identified by phrase or clause modifiers. In examples (a) and (b) below, the modifier attaches to the word being illuminated. In examples (c) and (d), the modifier attaches to another word.

(a) There are several ways of determining *validity*, which is a measure of whether a test covers the ground it is supposed to cover.

(b) There is increasing use in education of *systems analysis*—identifying goals, determining alternative means of reaching them, and evaluating the means chosen.

(c) You have a situation of *cognitive dissonance* when a person holding one belief is faced with a contrary belief or set of facts.

(d) A person is *field-dependent* or *independent* according to whether he depends on others or himself for his goals and sense of direction.

(4) Restatement. The writer may give a term the meaning he intends by use of synonyms or other words which restate the term in question. One clear and frequent method of restatement is the use of an appositive which follows the word to be illuminated and is usually separated from it by a comma. For example:

(a) One test in wide use is the *"in-basket,"* a collection of memoranda, letters, and other papers requiring action, such as might reach an executive's desk in a day.

(b) Establishing the *criterion* of a test, the qualities it is to measure, is the first step.

Restatements are conscious efforts by the writer to make his meaning clear. As with the method of examples, there are signal words and mechanical devices which indicate that an elaboration or restatement is to follow. Parentheses and dashes are among these devices. Among the signal words are *in other words, that is* or *i.e., to put it another way, what this means,* and *which is to say that.* The simplest and perhaps most frequently used signal word is *or.* It appears with a synonym and is usually signaled as a restatement by being enclosed in commas.

The word to be illuminated may itself be set off by devices or signal words, as in the examples below.

(1) Recently it has been suggested that people differ according to whether they minimize small differences (level) or accentuate small differences (sharpen) when judging.

(2) Learning to read in one's native language is learning to shift, to *transfer,* from auditory signs for the language signals to visual or graphic signs for the same signals.

(3) In the early grammars, the first large division of the book was usually devoted to *orthography*—the letters of the alphabet, their kinds and uses, the formation of syllables, and the spelling of words.

Inference. The writer who consciously undertakes to illuminate the meanings he is applying to words will use definition, example, modifiers, and restatement. Textbook writing and other careful exposition provide many clues to meaning. Most writing is not of this kind, however, and as a result, context clues are not frequently found. Nonetheless, it seems likely that we do acquire most of our word meanings from context. How does this happen in the absence of outright clues?

From internal evidence in a passage, it is possible for the reader to infer meaning for an unfamiliar word. As the word appears in new and shifting contexts within the same article or book or in other materials, the reader can test his inferred meaning. It is by this process that one discovers new meanings for familiar words: *field* means one thing in agriculture, quite another in surgery, and still another in physics. This process of gathering details, making connections, reading back and forth across a passage, and locating relationships requires attentive and persistent effort. The process is difficult to learn and difficult to teach since it requires a rigorous analysis of the text.

Occasionally the process of inferring meaning is assisted by structural connections in the text. Awareness of how these connections operate is perhaps just as important as awareness of signal words and other outright clues planted by the author. Structural connections are employed by a writer as a matter of style or of rhetoric, but they are nonetheless useful in illuminating the meaning of unfamiliar words. There are three general kinds of structural connections.

In the first type of connection, parallel sentence structure, an unfamiliar word or meaning may appear in parallel position with a familiar word, and the reader may properly infer a meaning relationship. An example is "Dialogue gives sparkle and life, but it can easily be overdone. Do not employ it for *trivialities;* do not let it become mere patter."

The second type of structural connection, repetition of key words, establishes the necessary connection between the unfamiliar word and the explanatory context. An example of repetition is the following: "Because of the time-consuming character of the procedures, wars might readily be finished before *retaliatory economic measures* could be put into effect. . . . Even the war between Italy and Abyssinia was far advanced before it was decided to apply economic sanctions."

Connecting words are the third type of structural connection. To establish connections between sentences in a discourse, writers of English use an abundance of sequence signals. These differ in function from the signal words used to identify examples and restatements. Note the several connecting words, indicated in bold-face type, in the following passage. (The italics appear in the original text to emphasize the difference between phonics and phonemics.)

. . . modern English spelling is not hopelessly chaotic. Most of **that** spelling is patterned. **It** is basically phonemic in its representation with *patterns of letters* rather than *single letters* as the *functioning units* of the representation. It is **this** fact that makes the *phonics* approach to reading and to spelling less than satisfactory. (Fries 1963, p. 169)

Summary. The proper goal of instruction in vocabulary development is word power, the power to deal with unfamiliar words and unfamiliar meanings of familiar words when they are encountered. Two major resources are available for this instruction: a study of context operation and a knowledge of word parts and word-formation. Since it appears likely that we acquire most of our words and meanings from context, the study of how context operates is the single most productive method of instruction. The contribution of word parts is specific and substantial, but there are serious limitations in their use.

Vocabulary development, to be effective, must be securely grounded on semantic principles. Perhaps the most important of these are that most words in common use have several meanings and that word meaning comes from experience.

Development of word power has affective goals as well as cognitive goals, and the most important affective goal is a growing interest in words. Without this interest, vocabulary development is slow and uncertain. With this interest, the learner moves on his own with high motivation.

BIBLIOGRAPHY

BERNSTEIN, BASIL 1958 "Some Sociological Determinants of Perception." *British Journal of Sociology*, 9:158–174.
DEIGHTON, LEE C. 1959 *Vocabulary Development in the Classroom.* New York, Teachers College, Bureau of Publications.
FRIES, CHARLES C. 1963 *Linguistics and Reading.* New York, Holt.
GREENOUGH, JAMES, AND GEORGE LYMAN KITTREDGE 1961 *Words and Their Ways in English Speech.* New York, Macmillan.
THORNDIKE, EDWARD L. 1941 *The Teaching of English Suffixes.* New York, Teachers College, Bureau of Publications.
THORNDIKE, EDWARD L., AND IRVING LORGE 1944 *The Teacher's Word Book of 30,000 Words.* New York, Teachers College, Bureau of Publications.

LEE C. DEIGHTON

VOCATIONAL CHOICE, BACKGROUND FACTORS

Choosing a vocation is a modern concept. Two hundred years ago social class and tradition were dominant factors in determining one's occupation. A young man did not choose an occupation—he was expected to enter either his father's occupation or one of his father's choosing. The nonconformist escaped to make his own way as a soldier of fortune, a sailor, or an emigrant to a new world.

Occupations, careers, and vocations. Vocational choice involves choice of occupation and of career. An occupation is a collection of tasks performed for pay in some organized way because others need to have them done. A career is the sequence of occupations engaged in by an individual during his lifetime, including positions held early and late in one's life, such as the unpaid working position of student and the nonworking paid position of pensioner.

The concepts of occupation and career are often confused, even in professional and scientific writing, because many middle-class persons have only one occupation throughout their working lives. The occupation thus becomes the individual's career. The term "vocation" might best be reserved for the occupation chosen and engaged in for a substantial period of time because it is appropriate to the individual's abilities, interests, values, and desires. The term "occupation" is then reserved for a set of tasks engaged in for pay, and the term "career" denotes a lifetime sequence of positions and occupations.

The occupational structure. Depending on the definitions used, there are some 30,000 occupations in the United States, each having hundreds or thousands of positions (that is, specific posts at which one does a given type of work). Even when positions are grouped as occupations in which essentially similar sets of tasks are performed, their numbers are too great for easy use in vocational guidance, vocational education, and even personnel selection. Occupational analysis and classification have therefore become well-developed specialties.

The basic terms used in occupational classification are "field" and "level." Fields are areas of work determined by the nature of the activity engaged in, by the content of the work, by the type of function performed, or by the interests and values which are expressed and satisfied in doing the work. Fields of work are, for example, social service (teaching, social work), business contact (sales), business administration and control (including accounting), technology, science, culture, and arts and entertainment. In contrast, levels are distinguished not by the activity or content but by the amount of intellectual ability and education required, by the degree of responsibility, and by the prestige and income associated with the work. Commonly used levels are the professional and managerial, semiprofessional and low-level managerial (including sales), skilled (both blue collar and white collar), semiskilled, and unskilled. Levels identified by the amount of education required are, for example, university, specialty training (postsecondary school but not four-year college), and extensive or short-term on-the-job training. The classification developed by Anne Roe in 1956 is that most frequently used by counselors today; that devised by the U.S. Department of Labor in 1965 is most widely used in employment work.

According to the Roe classification, there are levels within levels—for example, certified public accountants rank higher than accountants, and within each specialty there are junior, senior, and other grades. Thus, we have the concept of occupational or career ladders, normal pathways of advancement from one level to another.

Stages of a career. It is natural to analyze careers, which can be life histories, in terms of stages of life, such as childhood, adolescence, adulthood, and old age. During childhood vocational development consists largely of trying out various self-concepts in fantasy—for example, playing teacher, fireman, or engineer. Adolescence has been found to be an exploratory stage when school subjects are tried out and majors are chosen, when clubs and part-time jobs provide opportunities to use different kinds of skills, and when various social and occupationally related roles can be tried. During early adulthood the individual begins to establish himself in a chosen occupation. In middle adulthood he tends to keep on doing the kind of work he has previously done with success. Only exceptional men and those who have been uprooted by events break new ground and establish themselves in a new field at this point in their careers. Finally, aging brings a slowing down of the pace of work and eventually retirement.

Educators have been particularly concerned about the exploratory stage of careers but much less aware of needs at other stages. However, as technological change and population trends make society increasingly aware of the vocational education needs of adults, more attention is being paid to continuing education and retirement recreation. Also, the discovery of the importance of the early formative years of growth and of the role which self-concepts play in vocational development has brought recognition that vocational guidance, not for choice but for development, is very relevant during childhood. Fantasy is not useless; it is functional.

The awareness of the exploratory nature of the adolescent years has not, however, resulted in the development of effective programs of vocational exploration. The junior high school, which developed as a means of helping youths explore a variety of offerings before having to choose one course of study in high school, has now been recognized as a failure in this respect. Teachers of skills and of knowledge still find it difficult to plan courses which permit exploration instead of requiring mastery. Just as senior high schools became preparatory for college, business, and skilled trades, junior high schools became preparatory for high school.

But preparation is meaningless if some appropriate goal has not been decided upon. Exploration is therefore in order. Psychologists, counselors, curriculum specialists, teachers, and personnel specialists need to work together to devise effective methods of vocational exploration and self-exploration, so that schools may provide direction and motivation in preparatory education. Sound vocational goals are not identified early—they emerge late. Vocational guidance in the secondary school should not be guidance in the choice of an occupation or of a career; rather, it should be guidance in the development of potential vocational aptitudes, interests, and goals (Super & Overstreet 1960).

Career patterns. Four major types of career patterns have been found in men, according to sociologists: stable, conventional, multiple-trial, and unstable. These same patterns, with some variation and two additional patterns—doubletrack and interrupted—have been found in women.

Stable career patterns are those in which one prepares for a field of work, enters it, and remains in it for the bulk of his career. High-level occupations, such as engineering, medicine, and skilled trades entered from apprenticeships, lend themselves to this characteristically middle-class pattern. Another career sequence, the conventional pattern, involves one or more changes of occupation before stabilizing in one occupation and remaining in it for the rest of the working career. Many executives and some skilled occupational persons who have worked their way up the job ladder adhere to this mobile, middle-class pattern. Multiple-trial careers are characterized by fairly frequent changes from one occupation to another, without remaining long enough in any one of them to become stabilized. Unstable career patterns resemble these but have some periods of stability which are interrupted for either personal (psychological or familial) or social (economic or political) reasons. Although these two patterns occur at all socioeconomic levels, they are most common at the lower levels.

For women stable and conventional career patterns may involve only employment, only homemaking (stable), or both employment and homemaking (conventional). Multiple-trial and unstable career patterns are found among women, but women may also pursue double-track (homemaking and employment simultaneously) or interrupted (employment-homemaking-employment) career patterns.

Cultural anthropologists have examined careers from a somewhat different perspective and have categorized them as either responsive or expressive. Responsive careers are characterized by the pursuit of occupations which are approved by and typical of the individual's family or socioeconomic group. This type of career is found most often among members of the immobile upper and lower classes. In contrast, expressive careers are those in which individuals respond to internal, not external, pressures—they seek to be fulfilled, to express their interests, and to use their abilities in their occupations. These careers are found primarily among members of the mobile middle class, who are free to do what seems best for them.

Because educators have tended to assume that everyone follows a stable career pattern, they have generally failed to recognize that career patterns have important implications for education. Few educators have asked what the nature of guidance and education should be for unstable, multiple-trial, and interrupted careers (Super 1957).

Determinants of choice and success. There have been many studies of the determinants of occupational choice, success, and satisfaction, far fewer investigations of the determinants of career patterns, and still fewer long-term studies of careers. This situation came about partly because early formulations saw the problem of choosing an occupation in simplistic terms: it was only a matter of fitting a square peg into a square slot. Also, researchers and their sponsors were reluctant to begin long-term studies—long-term financing has generally been viewed as having a deleterious effect on productivity, and researchers desire projects that bring immediate recognition. As a result, cross-sectional or short-term studies were undertaken which focused on choice of occupation and performance in a particular job rather than on career development and adaptation in moving from one position to the next.

Education is one of the principal determinants of occupational and career choice and success. Those who have more education qualify for higher levels of occupational employment, and those who do best in the preparatory activities of school and college are most highly recommended for later employment. If the education has been at all relevant, they are also the best prepared to do the work for which they are employed.

Socioeconomic status is another factor in occupational and career choice and success. It determines the opportunity one has to learn about, try out, and develop skill and interest in various activities, and it gives one the opportunity to choose from a variety of educational and occupational alternatives. When asked what he would like his children to do as adults, the typical semiskilled factory worker in North America says "something better than what I do"; when asked what that might be, he does not know. When asked the same questions, a typical middle-class worker says that it is up to the child to decide, but he can name a number of differing and interesting possibilities. The middle-class child grows up knowing about some of these possibilities—he sees a number of adults who model various roles, and he knows he can choose between these roles. However, the lower-class child sees only the model of the semi-skilled parent and his similarly employed neighbors. Higher level occupations and the education needed to enter them are not real to him.

Intelligence, as measured by verbal or quantitative reasoning tests, is closely related to socioeconomic status and to education. High status generally means exposure to many intellectual stimuli and to educational experiences. In some cases, superior intelligence may lead to substantial educational achievement and thus to higher socioeconomic status. With or without education, intellectually endowed persons tend to advance more rapidly in employment, to be more successful in demanding occupations, and to have more stable and satisfying careers.

Intelligence consists of the related but semi-independent abilities to reason with verbal, numerical, and spatial symbols. Reasoning is a basic aptitude which manifests itself somewhat differently depending upon the situation. Most learning is verbal—even when the subject is numerical.

Special aptitudes which are relatively independent of reasoning ability have also been found to play a part in occupational choice, success, and career development. Spatial visualization, the ability to judge shapes and sizes, plays an important role in scientific and technical work as well as in certain semiskilled occupations. Perceptual speed and accuracy in identifying and differentiating letters and numbers are important in the keeping and use of records. Various combinations of basic aptitudes produce functional aptitudes, such as mechanical, artistic, and musical aptitudes. Manual dexterities play a part in determining the choice of and initial adaptation to such semiskilled jobs as that of assembly worker.

Interests have been defined as tendencies to like, to seek, and to engage in certain kinds of activities. They may be assessed by a simple question concerning preferences, by a series of questions constituting an inventory and scored in complex ways, or by information or attention tests. Most of what we know about the development and predictive validity of interests has been determined from studies of inventories. Inventoried interests have been shown to be better predictors of occupational choice and stability than mere expressions of preferences in middle-class (expressive career) boys and young men. But professed interest is at least as good a predictor in boys and young men who, coming from responsive environments, know what they are expected to do, say they will do it, and do it regardless of their underlying interests. Interests, unlike aptitude and training, are rarely related to degree of success—they tell something of what a person will choose to do but little of how well he will do it.

Values are somewhat more fundamental than interests, for they indicate what a person seeks in an activity. For instance, people who like to understand why and how things work (intellectual or theoretical values) tend to be interested in social work or education. Some values, such as an appreciation of positive change, the support of human relationships obtained from associates, and independence from supervision, do not have clear occupational outlets. These extrinsic, or context, values tend to be more important in semiskilled occupations, which are easily entered and left, whereas intrinsic, or content, values (such as intellectual stimulation, creativity, and altruism) tend to be stronger in higher level occupations, which require more of a commitment from the worker.

Even more fundamental than values and interests are needs, drives resulting from the lack of something essential. The basic needs, often called survival needs, are physiological. Higher level needs have more opportunity to manifest themselves—for instance, in choice of occupation—when basic needs have been at least partially met: it is easier to be concerned about beautiful surroundings when one has enough to eat. The higher level needs propel men in different directions according to their capacities, interests, and experiences. However, since most needs can be met in a variety of ways, needs are less clearly related to occupational choice and careers than are aptitudes and interests.

The tendency to act in a given way in a given situation is known as a personality trait. Traits also have little bearing on occupational choice and success—they are more indicative of style and manner in playing a role than they are of the role that will be chosen. Teachers, for example, have different personalities. Some are friendly, and others are cool and detached; some are more interested in people, and some are more interested in their subject matter. However, they may all be equally successful in organizing and presenting their subjects.

Implications for education. Education is the key to occupational choice and success and to career development. For society to be democratic and for people to have the opportunity to move to appropriate occupations, educational opportunity must be genuine. Educational institutions, aided by guidance and counseling services, must do what they can to make up for the socioeconomic deficiencies of homes which do not expose children to varied, appropriate role models.

Individual differences in abilities, interests, and personality require corresponding variety in curricula, methods, and materials. One function of educational and vocational guidance has been to take these differences into account in educational planning and instruction. We know what to do and how to do it. What is still needed is a sufficient number of trained personnel with time to use their knowledge and skill for these purposes in schools which have curricula and facilities flexible enough to make possible the recognition of individual differences.

Individualized education seems an elusive goal, but an educational system which recognizes the realities of the occupational structure, of life stages, and of career patterns must work toward this end if it is to help people develop their potential.

BIBLIOGRAPHY

BOROW, HENRY, ed. 1964 *Man in a World at Work*. Boston, Houghton Mifflin.

OSIPOW, SAMUEL HERMAN 1968 *Theories of Career Development*. New York, Appleton.

ROE, ANNE 1956 *The Psychology of Occupations*. New York, Wiley.

SUPER, DONALD E. 1957 *Psychology of Careers: An Introduction to Vocational Development*. New York, Harper.

SUPER, DONALD E., AND M. J. BOHN, JR. 1970 *Occupational Psychology*. Belmont, Calif., Wadsworth.

SUPER, DONALD E., AND PHOEBE L. OVERSTREET 1960 *Vocational Maturity of Ninth Grade Boys*. In collaboration with Charles N. Morris et al. Horace Mann-Lincoln Institute of School Experimentation, Career Pattern Study, Monograph 2. New York, Teachers College Press.

SUPER, DONALD E., et al. 1957 *Vocational Development: A Framework for Research*. New York, Teachers College Press.

U.S. DEPARTMENT OF LABOR 1965 *The Dictionary of Occupational Titles*. 3rd ed. Washington, D.C., Government Printing Office.

ZYTOWSKI, DONALD G., ed. 1968 *Vocational Behavior: Readings in Theory and Research*. New York, Holt.

DONALD E. SUPER

VOCATIONAL EDUCATION

1. HISTORY

Americans have always respected the efficacy of physical labor. Having confronted and conquered nature in order to build the country, they consider the ability to deal with the natural environment a part of their national character. This commitment to physical struggle and the manipulation of nature has figured prominently in debates on American education. From the beginning, Americans have tried to combine the physical and intellectual in learning. Manual labor, it has been argued, enhances man's ability to think, stimulating his mind by invigorating his body. Moreover, in the early days of the United States work with one's hands broke down traditional social class distinctions; in a society where all labored to survive, work was a moral and economic necessity, giving the rich and the poor a common bond.

Pre-Civil War antecedents. Before the Civil War, attempts to integrate manual and intellectual activities in education took a variety of forms. Future ministers, fearful that their theological studies would alienate them from the daily experiences of those they ministered to, engaged in manual labor as part of their seminary training. Artisans and mechanics, already committed to working with their hands, organized workingmen's institutes designed to advance their scientific and literary knowledge in a congenial social setting. The model factory towns of Lowell and Lawrence, Mass., tried to broaden the educational experiences of their laborers during the 1820's and 1830's by establishing literary and cultural clubs.

Manual work in itself was considered a beneficial educational experience. In the growing cities of antebellum America, philanthropists sought to modify the damaging effects of social change—the loss of social control and the increase in poverty and delinquency—by teaching children how to labor. Finding city children, especially among the poor and the immigrant populations, inadequately prepared for jobs in modern society, philanthropic and religious societies founded classes for the teaching of manual skills. Reform industrial schools were also established to prevent vagrant children from entering into lives of crime. These schools combined the lessons of the common school with a healthy dose of manual labor. Rarely, however, did the philanthropic or reform schools reach more than a very small proportion of city youth.

These varied activities attested to concern in the pre-Civil War period that both physical and mental training should be part of the education of Americans. But it is important to note that in a society still in the process of formalizing its educational institutions, in which only a minority of children attended school, these activities did not center in the common school. Manual work and learning, antebellum Americans believed, occurred in a variety of situations outside the classroom. Not until the late nineteenth century did manual education become a part of public education.

The late nineteenth century. In 1878, John D. Runkle, president of the Massachusetts Institute of Technology, helped usher in a new era of American education with these words: "There is a growing feeling that our public education should touch practical life in a larger number of points; that it should better fit all for that sphere in life in which they are destined to find their highest happiness and well-being" (Bennett 1937, p. 341). Runkle called for the introduction of the "manual element" into the schools, asking that the traditional responsibilities of public education be significantly enlarged.

Runkle was not alone in his plea. Calvin M. Woodward, professor of mathematics and applied mechanics at Washington University in St. Louis, was also actively seeking to bring manual instruction into the public school classroom. As dean of the university's polytechnical institute in the 1870's, Woodward organized workshop classes to give his students a knowledge of tools and their uses. Convinced of the necessity for even more formal and extensive shop instruction, he sought and received support for the opening in 1880 of the Manual Training School, to provide preliminary training for those who wished to enter the polytechnical institute. Woodward quickly became the leading manual training advocate in the United States. He enlarged his conception of manual education, arguing that it was essential to relevant schooling for all pupils, regardless of their career goals.

Both Woodward and Runkle considered that formal instruction in classroom shops provided a basis for the understanding of complex industrial processes. Both men proposed workshops patterned after those used at the Imperial Technical School of Moscow under the directorship of Victor Della Vos. These workshops separated instruction from actual production and made the former rather than the latter the goal of training. By learning how to use hand tools through a series of systematic and formal exercises of increasing complexity, students gained respect for labor and learned the values of precision, diligence, and logic—in short, the training necessary for success in a modern industrial society. Woodward and Runkle held that individuals lacking these characteristics could not have personal success and could not contribute effectively to the nation's industrial progress. Therefore, manual education was deemed necessary for all children, whether their future lay in manual production or not.

Woodward and Runkle helped crystallize support for classroom manual instruction. Alternatives to their Russian workshop system were offered, some of which called for more emphasis on training for a trade, others of which identified everything from kindergarten clay-modeling and paper-cutting activities to adult mechanical-drawing classes as manual education. In time, large numbers of American laymen and educators came to believe that manual instruction should be given in the public schools and that the principles of effective labor were best learned in the classroom. To a great extent, these attitudes reflected the emergence of a set of common assumptions about an idyllic antebellum United States and also showed the effects of industrial change appearing in the decades after the Civil War.

Idealization of antebellum America. After the Civil War, many Americans came to assume that the United States had once been a homogeneous rural society in which institutions such as the home, shop, school, and church functioned harmoniously. Each institution met its obligations and, as important, aided other institutions in meeting theirs. They shared in the education of all children. In the home, the child learned morality and simple literary skills. In the shop, he learned his future vocation, with the home serving this purpose for girls. At school, he learned to communicate and to engage in abstract thinking, in addition to undergoing further inculcation in moral and social values. The model form of vocational education at this time was the apprenticeship system, in which the artisan taught the young person the skills of a trade. Ideally, apprenticeship served as an extension of the home and the shop, integrating the two into a setting for specialized vocational training.

To Americans of the late nineteenth century these pre-Civil War institutions seemed to demonstrate an example of ideal social harmony. As one writer on education summarized this attitude, "The little red school house did its work well, because the cottage home, the little white church, the little shop and the town meeting were neighbors co-operating in the training of youth for the duties of life" (Massachusetts Board of Education 1893, p. 79).

American educators did not realize that these assumptions were only partially valid. In a society with open land and a shortage of labor, the apprenticeship system had never been as stable as the educators of the late nineteenth century believed. Nor had American society ever been as homogeneous and unified as the rhetoric professed. But the belief in an idyllic, harmonious, preindustrial past persisted, growing more prominent as industrialization and urbanization created more disharmony and fragmentation in society.

Effects of social change. In the decades after the Civil War, America underwent a major transformation. Heterogeneity took the place of homogeneity. Rural youths moved increasingly to the city, where they mingled with immigrants and alien ways of life. Children growing up in the cramped quarters of the city could not test their physical prowess in meadows or woods but instead ran free in the streets. No longer did society look to the artisan for its products; now the factory dominated industrial life. Those who worked in the urban industrial environment lost the sense of achievement which comes from individual completion of a product and lost any conception of themselves as producers. Also, rapid industrial change made it difficult to transmit skills from one generation to another, and the traditional method of learning a vocation—the apprenticeship system—was rendered impotent. Young people therefore lacked a systematic means of preparing for a vocation and confronted their economic future untrained and exposed to the insecurities of a seemingly anarchic environment. All these developments, American educators of this period argued, had led to a denigration of manual labor itself. As apprenticeship disappeared and youths were unable to identify with the craftsman or artisan, they rejected manual labor as inferior. The sense that the United States was losing its commitment to manual labor and the fact that the country lacked sufficient skilled workmen for the industrial economy were underlying reasons for the concern with manual training.

Although belief in the existence and methods of the harmonious, preindustrial past was not new in the late nineteenth century, having appeared before the Civil War, this belief now became a national article of faith and had momentous consequences for American schools. In spite of the fact that educators believed in the institutions of the idealized past, they realized that these institutions were no longer effective and, therefore, called upon the school to act as a surrogate for the home, the shop, and in many cases the church. In many urban areas at the turn of the century, girls were introduced to sewing and cooking in an effort to preserve homemaking skills. Boys received woodworking instruction so that they could become acquainted with physical labor. By 1920, most school systems in the country offered some manual education at every grade level.

Perhaps the most striking example of the social uses of manual education was its application to the emancipated slaves of the South. National interest in manual training for Negroes developed largely through the efforts of General Samuel Chapman Armstrong (founder of Hampton Institute in Virginia), Booker T. Washington (founder of Tuskegee Institute in Alabama), and northern philanthropists. For Washington, industrial education was only tangentially related to specific trades and skills. Most of what was taught at Hampton and Tuskegee had little to do with either modern industry or agriculture, for the black man, Washington argued, had to be provided with an education which would inculcate the principles of productive labor and fundamental moral values. Such knowledge would help the newly emancipated Negro to make a place for himself in society. Therefore, Washington urged manual training as the central educational experience for the black man in the period just after the Civil War.

The emergence of public support. The manual training movement laid the groundwork for a system of vocational schooling. The spokesmen of this movement helped pressure the public school to train individuals for the industrial economy, asserting that industrialization had destroyed the apprenticeship system and no other traditional institution stood ready to provide vocational instruction. After 1900 these pressures were further intensified by published studies which showed that, despite growing attendance figures, children were continuing to drop out of school at high rates and that school dropouts appeared to suffer in the job market. Simultaneously, Germany was emerging as an industrial power with an elaborate system of industrial and technical education, demonstrating the possibilities of using vocational training to aid national economic progress.

In 1906 the Massachusetts Commission on Industrial and Technical Education, known as the Douglas Commission after the governor who appointed its members, gave these themes formal and noteworthy support in a report which was to be a watershed in the history of vocational education. The report offered new evidence that the school prepared youth inadequately for the industrial economy. One of its major findings was that in Massachusetts alone 25,000 children between the ages of 14 and 16 were out of school and that most had left not out of economic necessity but because school seemed irrelevant to their vocational needs. Working now at unskilled, dead-end jobs in industry and with little hope for advancement or for the possibility of training, these young people were wasting some of their most valuable years, a waste neither they nor society could afford. The commission suggested that manual training, where rationalized as training for the industrial job market, was nothing more than a cruel hoax. It had become "a cultural subject mainly useful as a stimulus to other forms of intellectual effort—a sort of mustard relish, an appetizer—to be conducted without reference to any industrial end. It has been severed from real life as completely as have the other school activities" (Massachusetts Commission . . . 1906, p. 14). The philosophy of manual training which called for instruction in the underlying principles of work was inadequate; individuals needed not principles but specific skills for specific jobs. Moreover, the commission declared, public school educators should not have control of vocational schooling. Rather, trade schools should be established under independent auspices, allowing the schools to accommodate their programs more directly to local industrial needs.

Considered by some to be the Magna Carta of vocational education, the Douglas Commission's report achieved instantaneous success as its findings on Massachusetts were quickly generalized to apply to the country at large. Although not the first statement in support of practical vocational training—commercial courses had been organized for more than a decade and a limited

number of trade schools had been established before 1905—it provided a focus and rationale for this type of training.

The National Society for the Promotion of Industrial Education shaped this rationale into a political organization. Two New York City educators, Charles R. Richards and James P. Haney, founded the society in 1906, almost simultaneously with the appearance of the Douglas Commission's report (Cremin 1961; Krug 1964). The society devoted itself to propagandizing for vocational training and to uniting varied groups with an interest in this field. The society also brought together nationally prominent businessmen, labor leaders, social workers, politicians, and educators and soon went beyond the initial proposals of the Douglas Commission to support multiple forms of vocational education.

The society's main concern was less with how and what trades were taught than with the acceptance of vocational training as the responsibility of public education. This nonspecific approach to the support of vocational training was undoubtedly necessary, for the society contained some groups fiercely at odds with one another. This opposition was strongest between the National Association of Manufacturers and the American Federation of Labor. The business community had early expressed its approval of vocational schooling as a means of increasing industrial efficiency through the creation of a ready supply of skilled labor. Indeed, a few large corporations—American Telephone and Telegraph and Carnegie Steel were two prominent examples —had actually established corporation schools at the turn of the century to assure themselves of trained workers. In most cases, however, corporations and smaller businesses pressured the public schools to undertake basic vocational training.

Another reason why businessmen, particularly those associated with the National Association of Manufacturers, advocated trade schooling was that they saw it as a means of preventing union control over job entry. This attitude in turn helped shape the early thinking of union officials toward trade schooling. "The trade schools thus far in existence," wrote one union leader in 1886, "have been nothing more nor less than the breeding schools for scabs or rats . . ." (Cremin 1961, p. 36). Although a few unions instituted some trade programs to help their members adjust to technological innovations, most clung to the idea of job security and higher wages as the best kind of economic protection.

In the years between the Douglas Commission's report and World War I, the hostility between management and labor over the purposes of vocational education lessened. Union officials recognized the widespread public support for the teaching of trades and realized that extensive vocational schooling was a probability whether the unions participated or not. In a major statement in 1910, a committee of the American Federation of Labor condemned schools established by management and opted for broadly based public trade schools which combined shop and general instruction, classes for workers already on the job, and union-sponsored programs. That same year, the National Education Association's Committee on the Place of Industries in Public Education submitted an extensive report (National Education Association 1910) in support of vocational training as a fundamental aspect of education at all levels. By the 1920's, then, labor leaders and educators had joined management in the movement for vocational education.

The movement was significantly strengthened by the inclusion of groups agitating for agricultural education. Pointing to the early passage of the Morrill Act (1862), which established land-grant colleges, farm lobbyists pushed for governmental action to bring technical education to agriculture. In 1887 the farm lobbyists helped secure the Hatch Act, establishing federally assisted agricultural stations. In 1890 the "Second Morrill Act" provided still further federal funds to land-grant colleges offering instruction in the "industries of life." Throughout the farm belt in the 1890's and first decades of the twentieth century, men like Henry Wallace and William Dempster Hoard worked tirelessly to convince farmers and educators that agricultural instruction belonged in the schools at all levels if this type of instruction and schools in general were to prosper in rural areas. These men stressed the possibilities of agricultural efficiency through science, which would make the farm more attractive than the city, and they sought to make the schools more relevant institutions. Indeed, even the Douglas Commission in urban-industrial Massachusetts had made vocational instruction in agriculture part of its recommendations.

Federal assistance. Between 1906 and 1917 governmental support for vocational schooling significantly expanded. By 1910, 29 states had passed legislation in support of some form of practical education. Yet, state-by-state activity was time-consuming, inefficient, and insufficiently standardized to be satisfactory. Under the auspices of the National Society for the Promotion of Industrial Education, the advocates of vocational schooling turned to the federal government in a massive and coordinated effort to secure legislation for trade training. Drawing upon an already established tradition of federal financing for agricultural education, which was intensified by a series of legislative proposals between 1907 and 1914 to expand aid for rural vocational schooling, the society combined nationwide propagandizing with lobbying in Washington to gain congressional backing. With Charles A. Prosser, the society's newly appointed secretary, playing an important role in achieving compromise agreements, Congress passed the Smith-Lever Act in 1914, again in support of federally assisted agricultural extension programs. Congress also created the nine-member Commission on National Aid to Vocational Education, which was to present legislative recommendations for improving vocational training.

The recommendations of the Commission on National Aid to Vocational Education (U.S. Congress . . . 1914) were foregone conclusions. The four congressional members had previously spoken in favor of federal aid to vocational education; the remaining five appointees all belonged to the National Society for the Promotion of Industrial Education. Compiling the readily available material, much of it supplied by the society, the commission reported that the "development of vocational education at the present time is a matter of urgent concern to the nation" (Hawkins et al. 1951, p. 550) and strongly urged federal financing. The commission called for appropriations to pay for the training and salaries of teachers and supervisors of agricultural and industrial subjects. It also defined broad categories of vocational education and specifically recommended that all funds be directed to three kinds of public vocational programs—full-time trade schools, part-time classes, and evening instruction designed for individuals already on the job—all of which had to be given in "schools or classes supported and controlled by the public" (U.S. Congress . . . 1914, vol. 1, p. 73). In a major innovative move the commission also proposed the establishment of the Federal Board for Vocational Education, with supervisory and administrative powers. President Woodrow Wilson urged support of the commission's recommendations, for with the advent of World War I skilled workers were necessary for national preparedness. Thus, legislation introduced by Representative Dudley M. Hughes and Senator Hoke Smith, both of Georgia, received Congressional approval in February 1917 as the Smith-Hughes Act.

The Smith-Hughes Act brought to fruition the efforts of more than a decade to improve vocational schooling. Adopting the recommendations of the Commission on National Aid to Vocational Education with only slight modifications, Congress made governmental support of vocational education a national commitment. The Smith-Hughes Act was directed at institutions of lower than college level and was designed to help young persons over 14 years of age receive training for useful technical employment. Although the states retained the initiative in shaping their vocational programs, the Federal Board of Vocational Education received supervisory authority (Blauch 1933).

Although the Smith-Hughes Act was not the first legislation to provide federal assistance to schooling, this act significantly enlarged the government's responsibility for educational change. Simultaneously, however, by sharply distinguishing vocational from general education, the act aggravated an already-existing conflict between these two educational groups. Vocational educators now jealously guarded their activities from the encroachments of traditional and "cultural" educators, while the latter frequently found themselves at odds with the purposes and methods of vocational schooling. The conflict became a dominant theme in American education after the Smith-Hughes Act.

Vocational guidance. The emergence of vocational education as a major function of public schooling revived some fundamental questions about how educators were to know which courses best prepared students for the job market and how each student was to decide which vocation he was most suited for. The explicit commitment to vocational schools and the multiplication of vocational course offerings in high schools and the newly established junior high schools caused these questions to be raised more insistently than ever before. Vocational guidance seemed to offer

some answers, although such counseling would ultimately become more concerned with plant efficiency and the categorization of students than with the coordination of individual pupil interests and industrial needs.

No institution played a more influential role in initially publicizing the possibilities of vocational guidance than the Boston Vocation Bureau, which was founded in 1908 as a philanthropic endeavor to be managed in close alliance with the public schools. Under Frank Parsons, a prominent Boston reformer, the bureau promised to bring science to career selection by introducing an elaborate system for measuring and comparing jobs and individuals, conditions in the job market, possible earnings in particular vocations, and the individual's chances for success. Parsons hoped that choosing a vocation would thus be done "in a careful scientific way, with due regard to . . . aptitudes, abilities, ambitions, resources, and limitations, and the relations of these elements to the conditions of success in different industries" (Parsons 1909, pp. 3–4). Under Parsons' successors, especially Meyer Bloomfield, who became director in 1909, the bureau quickly became a major influence in the Boston schools. It sponsored special classes to train school counselors, published pamphlets on local industries, and advised the school system on efficient methods of guidance. Through its work in Boston, the bureau achieved prominence throughout the United States as other cities moved to establish systems for counseling their students.

Although the Boston Vocation Bureau's conception of vocational guidance depended in theory upon a close understanding of the relationship between schooling and industry and the needs of an industrial society, vocational guidance in practice became concerned with channeling the student efficiently through school. By the mid-1920's, as the number of courses expanded and pupils were required to make ever-increasing choices as to what they should study, vocational guidance became a means of categorization. With the growing use of educational testing, which was stimulated by the use of IQ tests during World War I, counselors spent most of their time placing students in programs appropriate to their aptitudes and intellectual capabilities. Criticism of this emphasis appeared frequently after 1920, especially from those who wanted the school to take a more active role in job placement and from those who wanted guidance counselors to receive broader psychological training which would enable them to provide therapeutic counseling as well as course-scheduling information. Despite this criticism, vocational guidance has continued as primarily a means for the placing of students in different courses.

Between the world wars. The Smith-Hughes Act established vocational schooling as a national commitment and proved very important during and after World War I. Training for jobs during the war became a national priority, and vocational education achieved a prominence few would have predicted. Federal support for vocational training rose from $1.5 million in 1918 to $7 million in 1927, while enrollment in industrial, agricultural, home economics, and commercial programs financed by federal, state, and local governments went from an insignificant figure to more than 900,000 in the same period.

The 1930's brought further commitment but little organization. While public school officials were forced to cut back funds for their educational programs, the Civilian Conservation Corps included vocational training and vocational guidance among its activities, seeing itself as a bridge between school and job. The National Youth Administration, established in 1935, functioned as an early work-study program by taking youth off the streets and off the unemployment rolls. For the next eight years, thousands received part-time employment and schooling which included guidance counseling, placement service, job training, and recreation activities. By 1939 more than 2 million individuals were taking vocational education courses. Within and outside of school systems, vocational training had become a dominant theme of American education.

Yet, vocational education never achieved universal support. The distinction drawn by the Smith-Hughes Act between traditional and vocational educators developed into open hostility as each group condemned the other for corrupting the goals of American education. Vocational schools were accused of providing second-class education and serving as dumping grounds for those unable to succeed in an academic environment. Vocational educators retorted that equality of educational opportunity demanded varied school programs to fit the needs of a variety of students. School systems, hard-pressed financially, frequently failed to provide adequate funding for the relatively expensive vocational program, forcing outworn machinery and outdated instruction upon the students. Often, vocational educators themselves had little knowledge or understanding of the modern industrial economy for which they were supposedly trying to prepare their students. And, finally, the distinction between vocational education as a means of teaching social values and strengthening character through work and vocational education as a means of training for a specific job in the economy, a distinction drawn at the turn of the century, was never fully clarified. Many—educators and laymen alike—never understood what the shops in elementary and secondary schools were for. As the United States stood on the eve of World War II, vocational education had become an established feature of the educational system, but it remained a subject of controversy and confusion.

After World War II. During the years after World War II, greater recognition than ever before was given to the roles of industry, the armed services, and community and junior colleges in vocational training, and the federal government increased its funding. The contemporary controversies in American education as a whole have been reflected in the problems of vocational education in the postwar period. During the 1950's and especially after the 1957 launching of Sputnik 1, the schools were increasingly criticized for failing to provide high-quality academic programs. Vocational education was attacked for being insufficiently academic and for teaching skills no longer demanded by the economy. In 1956 the number of white-collar workers—professional, managerial, clerical, and sales—exceeded blue-collar workers for the first time. When combined with the acceleration of automation, this development made the traditional stress on manual occupations seem particularly outmoded. Pressure developed to emphasize basic principles fundamental to many vocations and to introduce new occupational categories, such as health services and technical training, into vocational schooling. The largest area of growth was the technical programs, which increased from less than 100 in 1950 to around 600 by the early 1960's. This growth was hastened by the National Defense Education Act of 1958, which provided funds for technical training. In 1962, Congress passed the Manpower Development and Training Act to upgrade the nation's work force. The following year, the Vocational Education Act provided for new programs, buildings, and teacher training.

Vocational education became a focus for social reformers in the early 1960's. Job training was seen as one means of increasing the social mobility of the poor and of defusing the social "dynamite" in the cities. Programs for school dropouts and for the growing number of "unemployables" emphasized work skills. Learning-and-work programs such as the Job Corps and the Neighborhood Youth Corps became important features of the War on Poverty in the mid-1960's. Minority groups increasingly demanded that more relevant and marketable skills be taught in the schools.

Contemporary controversies in vocational education may seem unique, because automated society poses questions rarely asked before. Yet, a great deal of continuity with the past does exist. The struggle between general educators and vocationalists for control of vocational programs remains unresolved, as does the question of whether such programs should be given in separate schools or in comprehensive high schools. Despite increased federal expenditures, vocational schooling is still often stigmatized as second-class education. As the 1970's began, it was clear that vocational education had not yet moved significantly beyond the formulations, practices, and assumptions of the Smith-Hughes era and that a dramatic rethinking was necessary.

BIBLIOGRAPHY

BENNETT, CHARLES A. 1926 *History of Manual and Industrial Education Up to 1870*. Peoria, Ill., Manual Arts Press.

BENNETT, CHARLES A. 1937 *History of Manual and Industrial Education, 1870 to 1917*. Peoria, Ill., Manual Arts Press.

BLAUCH, LLOYD E. 1933 *Federal Cooperation in Agricultural Extension Work, Vocational Education, and Vocational Rehabilitation*. U.S. Office of Education. Bulletin No. 15. Washington, D.C., The Office.

BREWER, JOHN M. 1942 *History of Vocational Guidance: Origins and Early Development*. New York, Harper.

COHEN, SOL 1968 "The Industrial Education Movement, 1906–17." *American Quarterly*, 20, no. 1:95–110.

CREMIN, LAWRENCE A. 1961 *The Transformation of the School: Progressivism in American Education, 1876–1957*. New York, Knopf.

DOUGLAS, PAUL H. 1921 "American Apprenticeship and Industrial Education." Ph.D. thesis. New York, Columbia University.

FISHER, BERENICE M. 1967 *Industrial Education: American Ideals and Institutions*. Madison, University of Wisconsin Press.

HAWKINS, LAYTON S., CHARLES A. PROSSER, AND JOHN C. WRIGHT 1951 *Development of Vocational Education*. Chicago, American Technical Society.

KRUG, EDWARD A. 1964 *The Shaping of the American High School*. New York, Harper.

LAZERSON, MARVIN 1971 *Origins of the Urban School: Public Education in Massachusetts, 1870–1915*. Cambridge, Mass., Harvard University Press.

MASSACHUSETTS BOARD OF EDUCATION 1893 *Report of the Committee Appointed to Investigate the Existing Systems of Manual Training and Industrial Education*. Boston, The Board.

MASSACHUSETTS COMMISSION ON INDUSTRIAL AND TECHNICAL EDUCATION 1906 *Report*. Boston, The Commission.

MEIER, AUGUST, AND MILTON MELTZER 1966 *Negro Thought in America 1880–1915: Racial Ideologies in the Age of Booker T. Washington*. Ann Arbor, University of Michigan Press.

NATIONAL EDUCATION ASSOCIATION 1910 "Report of the Committee on the Place of Industries in Public Education." *Journal of Proceedings and Addresses*. Pages 652–773.

PARSONS, FRANK 1909 *Choosing a Vocation*. Boston, Houghton Mifflin.

PROSSER, CHARLES A., AND CHARLES R. ALLEN 1925 *Vocational Education in a Democracy*. New York, Century.

U.S. CONGRESS. HOUSE. COMMISSION ON NATIONAL AID TO VOCATIONAL EDUCATION 1914 *Report*. 63rd Cong., 2nd sess., H.D. 1004. 2 vols. Washington, D.C., Government Printing Office.

WELTER, RUSH 1962 *Popular Education and Democratic Thought in America*. New York, Columbia University Press.

MARVIN LAZERSON

2. TRAINING OF TEACHERS

The adequate training of teachers for vocational education was seen as imperative to the success of vocational education programs by early leaders in the field. Although many accomplishments can be identified in contemporary vocational education programs, the problem of providing adequately trained teachers and other professional personnel remains among the most critical areas of consideration in the expansion of vocational and technical programs.

The problem has become more complex as the role of vocational education has been expanded. Early programs of vocational education, encouraged by the Smith-Hughes Act of 1917, were related to agriculture, home economics, and trade and industrial occupations. The role of vocational education was gradually expanded by succeeding federal legislation until the Vocational Education Act of 1963, which provided that training be made available for all occupations not requiring a baccalaureate degree and emphasized serving the occupational educational needs of all individuals.

This emphasis implies the provision of a broader range of programs in terms of occupations and in terms of levels of instruction in order to accommodate the broad range of abilities and interests of youth and adults.

The Vocational Education Amendments of 1968 provided resources for a great expansion in vocational and technical programs and earmarked funds for the expansion of programs for particular groups such as the disadvantaged and the handicapped (until recently these groups were not considered a responsibility of vocational education). Legislation has also placed emphasis on several other program dimensions, including the occupational aspects of guidance and counseling, orientation to the world of work, occupation exploration, cooperative education, work-study programs, job placement, and follow-up.

In response to the need for a more sophisticated labor force owing to expanding technology, the growth of vocational and technical programs at the post-high-school level, particularly in junior and community colleges, has been phenomenal. This growth will continue as the job market continues to require increasing numbers of the labor force to have training at this higher level. Vocational programs have also continued to serve large numbers of adults in need of retraining. This need has been magnified by the introduction of new materials, methods, and equipment into the job market.

The challenge of providing adequately trained teachers for vocational and technical education courses is very great because of the variety of occupations, levels, and types of institutions in which programs are offered and because of the range of abilities and ages of individuals to be served. The problem is compounded by the fact that teacher education programs of the traditional type have not always been appropriate for the kinds of teachers needed in vocational education.

History. The literature on the beginnings of vocational education points to the persistent need for well-qualified teachers. Reports of the National Society for the Promotion of Industrial Education, formed in 1906 (now the American Vocational Association), and the Commission on National Aid to Vocational Education, created by Congress in 1914, make clear that it was no accident that teacher training was given significant attention in the Smith-Hughes Act.

The Smith-Hughes Act. The Smith-Hughes Act, passed in 1917, provided that $3 million be allocated to agriculture; $3 million to trade and industrial and home economics education (not more than 20 percent of which could be used for home economics); $1 million for teacher training (not less than 20 percent or more than 60 percent of which could be used for the training of teachers in agriculture, trade and industry, or home economics); and $200,000 for the establishment of the Federal Board for Vocational Education.

As a condition for eligibility, each state was required to create a state board for vocational education, responsible for developing and administering its vocational education program. Although the Federal Board for Vocational Education is no longer in existence, the state boards have continued to be the structures to which funds flow from the federal government and through which programs are developed and administered in the states.

Many individuals and groups who were instrumental in the development and passage of the Smith-Hughes Act expressed concern for providing adequately trained teachers for the new programs. They were convinced that there was neither an appropriate pattern nor programs of teacher education in existence which would meet the need. Therefore, the responsibility for providing properly trained personnel was clearly identified and placed with the state boards. The Smith-Hughes Act states that in order to secure appropriations each state board must prepare plans outlining all aspects of the program of vocational education for which the appropriations are to be used.

Responsibility of state boards. The provisions of the Smith-Hughes Act are important not only as historical background but also because the act established a philosophy and a pattern of operation in vocational education and vocational teacher education which has persisted through the years. Each succeeding vocational education act up to and including the Vocational Education Amendments of 1968 reflected three basic principles that first appeared in the Smith-Hughes Act: first, that the state board must develop a plan to be approved at the federal level, a plan indicating the state's scheme for providing vocational education and including information on instructional personnel; second, that responsibility for the preparation of teachers and other vocational education personnel and the establishment of minimum qualifications are responsibilities of the state board; and third, that federal funds under each of the acts can be spent for teacher-training purposes.

Thus, final responsibility for teacher education programs rests with the state boards for vocational education. The patterns whereby states meet this responsibility vary from state to state. During the school year of 1960–1961, for example, 40 percent of the states met their responsibility for teacher education through existing teacher education institutions; 38 percent of the states met the responsibility through joint programs conducted by the state boards for vocational education and by one or more teacher education institutions; 19 percent followed a system which involved the state board for vocational education, a teacher-training institution, and local boards of education; and the remaining 3 percent followed combinations of these plans (U.S. Panel of Consultants . . . 1963).

Nature of training. One of the strengths of vocational education has been its ability to keep open numerous sources of teachers. Full-time teachers of agriculture, home economics, and office occupations (business education) are prepared through baccalaureate programs. Full-time teachers in trade and industrial education, in contrast, are often recruited from the occupation for which training is to be given. The selection criteria for these teachers emphasize competence and success in the occupation rather than the completion of a degree. Teachers for health occupations usually are recruited from the occupations, in which case they have met the degree or other training requirements of the occupations and hold licenses if such are required. In the case of teachers for highly technical occupations, emphasis is again placed on their success in the occupation. Typically, those recruited have had formal training appropriate for success in their field. This training might include a degree in engineering or an associate degree in a technical field. Often, however, these teachers have not had any courses related to learning theory or teaching methodology.

The challenge of teacher training is magnified by the large number of part-time teachers required, particularly in adult programs, which comprise as much as 50 percent of the vocational education enrollment. In addition, it has been the practice to staff adult programs with specialists recruited from business, industry, agriculture, health, and other related fields. Except for those who enter teaching with a degree in education, the initial thrust of teacher training in vocational education is to provide teaching and other educational skills necessary to meet certification requirements and improve teaching efficiency.

In addition to recruiting teachers from many sources, a second important dimension of vocational teacher education is the upgrading of teachers in terms of the content and skills related to the particular occupations they are teaching. This dimension has become increasingly important as the rate of change in occupations reflects the accelerated rate of technological change.

The general education needs of regular teachers are also important for vocational teachers. Although many vocational teachers who are recruited lack baccalaureate or higher degrees, they are encouraged to complete degrees. As a result, the number of degrees held by vocational teachers who have been in the field a number of years compares favorably with those of teachers in other fields.

Institutions and enrollments. A wide range of institutions are now involved in preparing teachers and other professional personnel for vocational and technical education. Early efforts were concentrated to a great extent in the land-grant institutions. Although the land-grant institutions are still important in this special area, programs have been greatly expanded so that the majority of state universities involved in other teacher education programs contribute to the training of vocational and technical education teachers.

The increasing concern across the United States to provide all individuals with occupational competencies which will make them employable and the sizable increase in federal funds to stimulate new programs mean that the need for teachers for vocational and technical education programs will continue to increase. Using past data on teacher enrollments in training programs and teachers employed, the Division of Vocational and Technical Education (U.S. Department . . . 1968a) has predicted for 1975 teacher education enrollments of 121,000 in preservice education programs and 124,000 in in-service education programs.

The term "teacher education" is sometimes used generically to include support and administrative personnel in vocational and technical education. However, the task of providing training in a broad range of competencies for this large group poses many additional challenges. As programs expand in terms of types of occupations, types and levels of instruction, kinds of institutions, and types of support services, new kinds of specialists will be needed in increasing numbers. The Division of Vocational and Technical Education (U.S. Department . . . 1969) has also predicted that by 1975 the number of administrative and ancillary personnel will have risen to 13,540 at state and local levels, compared to about 7,150 in 1965.

Vocational categories. Teachers of vocational education are usually identified by the service area of their competency—for example, agriculture, distributive occupations, or health occupations. In the writing and implementation of the Smith-Hughes Act of 1917, the early leaders in vocational education sensed an inadequacy in the structure and methods of the training programs of that day and emphasized several categories of vocational teachers, while the states developed certification requirements by service area. Although modifications have been made, certification requirements and teacher education programs are for the most part identified according to a service category.

Agricultural occupations. Traditionally, all teachers in agriculture have come through the teacher education programs provided in the land-grant colleges. These programs are located within colleges or departments of agriculture and have strong ties to colleges or departments of education. Prior to the Vocational Education Act of 1963 instruction in agriculture was directed toward preparing youth and adults for production agriculture or toward upgrading their skills in this area. Typically, farm boys who had taken agriculture programs in high school were recruited for these programs.

The Vocational Education Act of 1963 brought new challenges to traditional programs. The task of preparing instructional personnel became more complicated than under previous legislation because the act broadened the responsibility to provide training to all persons, including the disadvantaged and handicapped, and for all occu-

pations not considered to be professional. In addition to curriculum changes in college programs, opportunities are now being provided for cooperative experiences in business and industry.

Business and office occupations. Programs in the area of business and office occupations became eligible for federal support under the Vocational Education Act of 1963. The system of teacher education in business education at this time was similar to that in general education. Although at present these teachers continue to teach courses that enable youth to become employable, teacher education programs need to expand in order to provide instruction in a broader range of office occupations, including those related to data processing. Several states, in addition to making significant curriculum changes in teacher education programs, have made provisions for recruiting teachers from the business world, particularly for such programs as data processing in postsecondary institutions. Significant efforts have also been made in providing in-service activities for business-education teachers to upgrade their office-related skills.

Distributive occupations. The Vocational Education Act of 1963 broadened the states' authority to provide preparatory programs in distributive education in addition to the cooperative programs between the schools and distributive businesses (both wholesale and retail) which had been provided previously. This act has made possible and encouraged an expansion in the size and number of distributive teacher education programs. In general, however, these programs appear to be understaffed and underdeveloped to meet the need for teachers in a field with a rapidly expanding labor force. Full-time teachers usually have been provided through baccalaureate programs, many of which are closely allied to departments of commerce in colleges. Part-time teachers have often been recruited from the business world.

Home economics occupations. The home economics teacher is prepared through the baccalaureate route. Prior to the Vocational Education Act of 1963, home economics programs were directed at developing students' abilities and understanding in the area of home and family life and at helping them to live as informed citizens. The 1963 act provided that new funds could be used only for employment training in occupations requiring knowledge and skills related to home economics (such jobs as waitress, homemaker aide, child-care aide, and hotel and motel keeper). It was the intent that these programs be added to rather than replace the traditional home economics program. The development of new programs has undoubtedly been hampered by the lack of teachers with appropriate experience and training to develop and teach courses in occupations related to home economics.

Health occupations. Teacher education for the health occupations was provided in the past primarily as a part of trade and industrial teacher education. Potential teachers were recruited from the various health occupations—for example, registered nurses for practical nurse training programs and dental hygienists and dental assistants for dental assistance programs. The Health Amendments Act of 1956 provided for expanded training in health occupations. These amendments were administered as Title III of the George-Barden Act of 1946, and succeeding vocational education acts have given rise to additional program expansions. Several states are developing teacher education programs specifically geared to the needs of the health occupation teacher.

Technical occupations. Technical education programs are provided mainly at the post-high-school level in junior and community colleges, technical institutes, and other postsecondary institutions. In order to staff these programs, it has been necessary to compete directly with business and industry. Nearly all technical areas of occupational preparation are becoming more specialized, with workers in business and industry requiring training in depth. The challenge to educators is to recruit and retain teachers with depth, breadth, and currency of experience in the technology to be taught as well as with teaching skills. Such a challenge dictates close cooperation with business and industry.

The practice has been to recruit persons from business and industry who have demonstrated competence in the technology and to provide them with the teaching skills through in-service programs. However, this practice does not solve the problem of keeping these teachers current with the technology in their fields. Successful solutions to this problem have included short-term workshops and institutes, often in cooperation with an industry, trade, or professional association or supplier; university courses related to the technology;

and return to business and industry for additional experience.

Trade and industrial occupations. The traditional approach to securing teachers in trade and industrial occupations has been to recruit skilled craftsmen and then to provide them with general education teaching skills on an in-service basis. One limitation of this method has been that teachers' salaries have not been competitive (particularly at the secondary school level) with the earnings of well-qualified craftsmen. In addition, there has been increased concern on the part of many school administrators that a degree should be at least one of the qualifications for teaching. A number of approaches have been developed which attempt to recruit persons who have already developed some occupational competence into baccalaureate programs. The problem remains that if a person is well qualified in an occupational area, the school must still be competitive with industry to retain his services.

Implications of the 1968 amendments. The Vocational Education Amendments of 1968 have been funded and have substantially increased support for vocational and technical education. The need to extend vocational and technical education opportunities exists in every state. It does not, therefore, seem unreasonable to expect that state and local resources will be made available far in excess of funds needed to meet the matching requirements of the Vocational Education Amendments of 1968. The Division of Vocational and Technical Education (U.S. Department . . . 1969) has predicted an enrollment of 14 million in vocational education programs by 1975, which is almost double the 1968 enrollment. This increase will require nearly a doubling of the number of professional personnel.

The task of preparing instructional personnel will be complicated by some of the new categories of personnel and programs identified in the act and by several other factors which will affect all areas of education. First among these other factors is education technology, which is developing at a rapid rate. Sophisticated equipment is already available that greatly increases learning efficiency. The real challenge to education is to identify and develop educational content appropriate to the many occupational areas and to program that content for use with appropriate instructional media. Included in the newer media and methods is the expanded use of programmed material on an individual basis, which involves not only wider use of programmed texts but also the combination of these texts with other media, such as audiotapes, slides, and filmstrips. Electronic student-response systems will become more widely used, as will closed-circuit television. The computer has already been proved to be an appropriate tool for teaching and learning, and its extensive use should prove financially feasible by the end of the 1980's, if not sooner. The greatest potential limitation to its effective use may be the lack of capability to properly organize and adapt the content for use with this new media.

New staffing and scheduling arrangements will also affect the requirements for the training of educational personnel. The concept that all teaching personnel should be equally competent and the resulting practice of assigning classes of approximately equal size to each teacher is giving way to a differentiated staffing pattern, with teaching teams that include paraprofessionals. Students are being taught in groups of varying size, depending upon the content and media used.

Perhaps the greatest challenge to educators, particularly vocational educators, is keeping teachers abreast of the rapid changes in technology in their fields. New products, materials, equipment, and methods can make occupational skills partially obsolete unless ways are found to update experience.

The Vocational Education Amendments of 1968 identified several aspects either new to vocational and technical education or requiring expansion that will involve new dimensions in teacher preparation. Among these aspects is the provision of occupational guidance, orientation to the world of work, and exploratory occupational experiences at the elementary, middle school, junior high, and high school levels.

Another area of challenge for vocational teacher education is the preparation of teachers for students with special needs. Among such students are those with academic, socioeconomic, and physical handicaps. The serving of these students, until recently, was not necessarily considered as a part of the role of vocational education. The Vocational Education Amendments of 1968 allocated significant amounts of money for programs to serve these groups. It has been projected that by 1975 more than 4,000 teachers will be needed (in addition to those already teaching) with the necessary vocational competence and special training to work successfully with handicapped students (U.S. Department . . . 1969).

The act also emphasized the need to expand cooperative and work-study programs. This expansion will create the need for staffs with the knowledge and skills to coordinate programs with business and industry. The expansion of the school into the community to a greater degree than at present will certainly require new talents and working relationships.

Other aspects of the program envisioned by the Vocational Education Amendments of 1968 include expansion of programs in occupations related to home economics and consumer education. The amendments encouraged home economics educators to give greater consideration to social and cultural conditions and needs, especially in economically depressed areas. This direction will require new emphasis in teacher education programs in homemaking.

The 1968 amendments also stressed the need to serve youth in urban areas and made provision for residential demonstration schools. These residential schools are to be designed for those young people from central city areas and rural poverty areas who can best be served by being removed from their environment. The schools envisage a full range of health, guidance, and counseling services in addition to providing occupational skills. Staffs for such schools need to have new and different talents than those required of the more traditional staffs.

Trends. Vocational teacher education programs must expand if needs are to be met. This expansion will require organization of the programs' resources. Although there has been a trend toward the development of vocational teacher education departments, far too many colleges and universities serve only one or a limited number of the service areas or locate their programs and resources in a number of different schools, departments, or colleges. The result is that there is too little cooperation among the services. If all needs are to be met, the trend of bringing the expertise of the various service areas together should be encouraged. Although there are unique differences in teacher education needs among the services, there are many common elements.

A more rigorous recruiting program for teachers must be developed. In addition to recruiting high school graduates and former vocational students into preservice training programs, maximum effort should be made to recruit prospective teachers from business, industry, and the military. Differentiated staffing will make possible the use of a broader range of personnel.

The effectiveness and efficiency of vocational and technical education programs will depend on their leadership as much as on their teachers. The more than 4,000 projected leadership positions additional to those already in existence that must be filled by 1975 (*ibid.*) will be at both state and local levels and will include directors, deans, supervisors, teacher trainers, researchers, and curriculum specialists. In addition to training these leaders, all administrators of both secondary and postsecondary institutions must be provided with greater knowledge of the requirements and operational patterns of vocational and technical education programs. They will thereby be better equipped to make decisions affecting vocational and technical education and, ultimately, all education.

BIBLIOGRAPHY

BARLOW, MELVIN L. 1967 *History of Industrial Education in the United States.* Peoria, Ill., Charles A. Bennett.

BARLOW, MELVIN L., AND BRUCE REINHART 1968 *Profiles of Trade and Technical Teachers: Comprehensive Report 1968.* Los Angeles, Division of Vocational Education, University of California.

COON, BEULAH I. 1965 *Home Economics Instruction in the Secondary Schools.* Washington, D.C., Center for Applied Research in Education.

HAWKINS, LAYTON S. 1962 *Development of Federal Legislation for Vocational Education.* Chicago, American Technical Society.

LEE, EDWIN A. 1938 *Objectives and Problems of Vocational Education.* 2nd ed. New York, McGraw-Hill.

MAY, ARTHUR B. 1930 *An Introduction to Vocational Education.* New York, Appleton.

NATIONAL SOCIETY FOR THE STUDY OF EDUCATION. COMMITTEE ON VOCATIONAL EDUCATION 1968 *Vocational Education.* Edited by Melvin L. Barlow. University of Chicago Press.

U.S. DEPARTMENT OF HEALTH, EDUCATION, AND WELFARE 1967 *Administration of Vocational Education: Rules and Regulations for Administration of Vocational Education Programs Under Provisions of Federal Vocational Education Acts.* Vocational Education Bulletin No. 1. Washington, D.C., Government Printing Office.

U.S. DEPARTMENT OF HEALTH, EDUCATION, AND WELFARE 1968a *Vocational Education: The Bridge Between Man and His Work.* Prepared by the Advisory Council on Vocational Education. Washington, D.C., Government Printing Office.

U.S. DEPARTMENT OF HEALTH, EDUCATION, AND WELFARE 1968b *Vocational and Technical Education, Annual Report, Fiscal Year 1966.* Washington, D.C., Government Printing Office.

U.S. DEPARTMENT OF HEALTH, EDUCATION, AND WELFARE 1969 *Vocational and Technical Education, Annual Report, Fiscal Year 1967.* Washington, D.C., Government Printing Office.

U.S. PANEL OF CONSULTANTS ON VOCATIONAL EDUCATION 1963 *Education for a Changing World of Work: Report Prepared at the Request of the President of the United States.* Washington, D.C., Government Printing Office.

VENN, GRANT 1964 *Man, Education, and Work: Post-secondary Vocational and Technical Education.* Assisted by Theodore J. Marchese, Jr. Washington, D.C., American Council on Education.

WRIGHT, J. C., AND CHARLES R. ALLEN 1929 *Efficiency in Vocational Education.* New York, Wiley.

MERLE E. STRONG

3. ADULT PROGRAMS

Vocational education faces the challenge of ensuring that people are equipped with marketable skills in a changing world of work. The very existence of vocational-technical education depends upon its ability to provide meaningful instruction that meets the needs of business and industry and its ability to minister to the needs of the individual at whatever level he may be in the educational, social, or economic structure. Programs operated under the Vocational Education Amendments of 1968 represent the largest organized effort to stabilize unemployment at the lowest possible level and to reduce or eliminate occupational shortages.

The jointly financed local-state-federal programs of vocational-technical education had their inception with the Smith-Hughes Act of 1917.

History. When Congress passed the 1968 Vocational Education Amendments, it repealed all previous vocational education measures except the Smith-Hughes Act of 1917.

Early legislation. In one respect the 1917 act is unique—the funds were not authorized for it; they were directly appropriated. It is congressional practice now to authorize funds, which means that in each session Congress can decide how much of the authorized funding it will actually appropriate for each program; the authorization only establishes a ceiling.

The funds appropriated for the 1917 act were to continue "annually thereafter" or at least until repeal of the act. The Smith-Hughes Act provided for the salaries and training of "teachers, supervisors, and directors of agricultural subjects and teachers of trade, home economics and industrial subjects" on the traditional dollar-for-dollar matching basis. (One dollar of federal funds may be used to match one dollar of state or local funds.) Also, funds could be spent for studies and reports to aid vocational education.

While the Department of Health, Education, and Welfare still receives about $7.2 million under the Smith-Hughes Act, it spends the money on programs stimulated by the 1968 amendments, including adult education.

The 1917 act created the Federal Board for Vocational Education (no longer in existence), a powerful body that reported directly to Congress. It had three citizen members, representing commercial, agricultural, and labor interests. As time and conditions changed, legislation was altered to meet changing needs. The George-Deen Act of 1936 provided funding on a matching basis for distributive education. The programs authorized by this act emphasized the updating and upgrading of adult workers already employed in the distribution and marketing fields. Preparatory programs were limited to cooperative training, wherein skill development was provided on the job by an employer and related instruction took place in school as a part of a regular high school program. In addition, a teacher-coordinator worked with each trainee and with each employer. This arrangement tended to link the school and the employing establishment closely together, thereby making the school a meaningful adjunct of the business community. The coordinator in his business contacts was in a position to promote adult vocational education programs with establishments both within and beyond the cooperative education structure.

1940's and 1950's. In 1946 the George-Barden Act expanded vocational education materially. This act was amended in 1956 to include practical nurse education and training in the health occupations. Enrollments in the health fields have been largely at the adult level. Practical nurse training has attracted a preponderance of women, 55 percent of whom are 20 years of age or older (Tate & Knopf 1968).

Training for the fisheries industry was added about the time the health occupations program came into being. Although enrollments have never been high in this area, the major thrust has been training adults rather than preparing youth for jobs in commercial fishing. There has been, however, revived interest on the part of some governmental agencies in providing federally based training programs for the fishing indus-

try. Interest in oceanography on the part of technical educators may stimulate some states to provide adult programs that meet the manpower demands of the fishing industry.

The advent of the Soviet satellite Sputnik 1 in 1957 stimulated the passage of the National Defense Education Act of 1958. This legislation authorized the training of technicians in occupations important to the national defense.

1960's and 1970's. The Vocational Education Act of 1963 increased badly needed funding to update programs in the areas of distribution and marketing, home economics, agriculture, health occupations, trade, and technical and industrial education, and it added training in office education. The act made funds available for training such groups as high school youth, postsecondary school youth, adults enrolled in school full time or part time, and all persons with special needs.

The Vocational Education Amendments of 1968 have been characterized as a charter for important changes in emphasis for American education. The 1968 act is designed to assist the educational community in breaking down the barriers between the academic, general, and vocational curricula so that no person will be denied an opportunity to prepare for work that suits him.

The amendments substantially increased the level of federal appropriations for vocational education from $260 million for 1968 to $542.1 million for 1969, to $857.65 million for 1971, and to $910.15 million for 1972.

The most important element of the legislation, however, is that it opens up opportunities for vocational administrators throughout the United States to tailor programs to the needs of individuals. The new legislation is specifically oriented toward those people needing training, especially urban ghetto residents and similarly disadvantaged persons.

The Smith-Hughes Act of 1917 and the George-Barden Act of 1946 set forth legislative determinations that training be directed toward supplying trained manpower for certain areas of the economy. In the dynamic economy of the 1960's, the Vocational Education Act of 1963 gave the vocational education community greater flexibility, requiring that training be focused primarily upon gainful employment. The newer legislation consolidates the Smith-Hughes and George-Barden acts into the amended basic framework of the 1963 act. Federal vocational education funds are now authorized for a wide range of training focused on individual and community needs.

Purposes. The primary purpose of vocational-technical education is to make training programs and services readily accessible to prepare individuals for employment. The programs are designed for people in high school and postsecondary school and for those who have completed or discontinued their formal education, those already in the labor market, and those with special handicaps.

The vocational or technical training and re-training is given in schools or classes and includes fieldwork, laboratory work, and remedial or related academic and technical instruction. Such training may be provided under contractual agreement with a state board of vocational education or a local school. The purpose and design of the training program must be to prepare individuals for gainful employment as semiskilled or skilled workers, technicians or subprofessionals, in recognized occupations or in new and emerging occupations. Opportunities also prevail to prepare individuals for enrollment in advanced technical education programs not relating to the professional sphere or requiring a baccalaureate or higher degree.

Occupational choices in vocational and technical fields may be facilitated through vocational guidance and counseling, either individually or in groups. Job placement, follow-up, and other auxiliary services related to occupational choice, training, and success on the job may also be supported by government funds.

Federal impetus to adult education. Federal funds are made available to state boards of vocational education through a letter-of-credit arrangement with the U.S. Office of Education. Such funding is used principally for salaries of vocational teachers, teacher educators, coordinators, supervisors, and directors. Salaries of the supporting ancillary service workers are also reimbursable under the provisions of the Vocational Education Amendments of 1968. Grants to the states may be used in accordance with approved state plan provisions.

As of the early 1960's, of the more than 26 million employed skilled workers, close to 853,000 were enrolled in vocational trade and industrial courses supplemental to their daily employment. However, this figure represents only 3.2 percent of the total skilled workers in the labor force and is only about 20 percent as great as the potential

demonstrated by the state of Washington, where in that same period 14.1 percent of the skilled workers were enrolled in vocational courses.

In the 1950's the number of craftsmen increased 11.5 percent, while enrollments in vocational trade courses increased 15.1 percent. Thus, adult enrollments increased almost 4 percent above the number of persons coming into the skilled craftsman category. Enrollments increased 28 percent from 1960 to 1967 (Bowler 1968).

A preliminary report prepared by the U.S. Office of Education for 1969 indicates an increase of 2.1 percent in adult enrollments. Although this total growth figure may seem low, it is made up of state enrollments that fluctuate greatly. For example, New Jersey adult vocational enrollments increased 157 percent, while Massachusetts showed a decline of 44.6 percent, matching that of Utah. Total enrollments in vocational education programs in 1969 were more than 7.98 million. Of this total, 38.2 percent were adults. Secondary school enrollments accounted for more than 51 percent.

Teachers. Adult vocational education programs serve those who have already entered upon an occupational pursuit and those preparing to enter an occupation. Therefore, teachers must be expert in an occupational field, skilled in dealing with persons preparing to enter an occupation, and qualified to work with persons already employed in an occupation. Special preparation in teaching adults is also needed.

Teachers of supplementary courses frequently are recruited from the ranks of day school staffs. Others may be workers employed in plants, businesses, and governmental agencies. Of the seven vocational-technical education fields, only in trades and industries are teachers without degree qualifications likely to be found. While many trade teachers do hold baccalaureate degrees, qualification as a successful tradesman may take precedence over the degree. Hence, the graduate of a two-year community college with the prescribed state plan occupational qualifications may be found teaching shop work. Such a person, when adequately prepared in teaching methodology, is usually a successful adult education teacher because he knows the problems of his students.

Preparation. Effective programs in adult education can be maintained only if a continuous supply of highly qualified instructional personnel is available. Traditionally, home economics and agriculture have developed their teachers through the degree programs of the four-year institutions. With a new emphasis on gainful employment in home economics (that is, employment in a wage-earning occupation, such as working as a waitress, as a dietician aide, or as a child-care aide), teachers should come into programs from business and industry as well as from four-year colleges. Examples of the areas from which teachers might be recruited include the food or hospitality industry, the needle trades, and the field of institutional management.

Agriculture-related occupations are receiving increased emphasis in some two-year institutions. Teachers with successful employment records might be found and employed directly from establishments dealing in seed, feed, and grain, from food-processing plants, and from agencies employing grounds keepers and horticulturists. Certainly, in areas where knowledge of conditions in business or industry is important to success on the job, persons with occupational experience should be employed as teachers.

The popularity of the two-year community college has increased the demand for well-qualified and experienced teachers. Many presently employed workers with two years of college could be recruited and encouraged to complete one or more degree requirements while teaching adults.

Recruitment techniques. Advertising has been used with satisfactory results to locate specialists in certain occupational fields. For example, capable "automotive engine tune-up and automotive front-end alignment specialists" have been recruited for teaching through blind ads in a metropolitan daily newspaper. Success tends to increase where the recruiting school system has a good image.

Individuals helpful in locating teachers of adults are school administrators, who may be encouraged to seek the assistance of advisory committee members in recruiting capable teachers; supervisors, teachers, and school board members, who might be urged to identify likely teaching prospects from among friends, associates, and acquaintances; supervisors and administrators, who may invite teachers in related fields to qualify for teaching in vocational education; and administrators, who may contact military personnel in their search for qualified shop and laboratory teachers. Informal brainstorming on the part of supervisors, teachers, and administrators at state and local meetings is helpful in identifying other worthwhile recruitment techniques. Teaching candidates recruited directly from business and industry should have available to them teacher-training courses that are up-to-date and dynamic.

Promoting adult classes. Since World War II, manpower shortages have been prevalent in most areas of the economy. At times the shortages have been limited to certain specialized fields, but they have persisted. There has also been an imbalance between supply and demand in the labor market. These conditions indicate the need for expanded adult education programs.

Adult vocational-technical programs—even when they are of excellent quality—will not grow of their own accord. They must be publicized. The story of successful programs must be retold often and through a variety of media to promote healthy program expansion.

The authors of the Smith-Hughes Act of 1917 foresaw the need to publicize training opportunities. The preamble to the legislation states that it is "an act to provide for the promotion of vocational education; to provide for cooperation with the States in the promotion of such education. . . ." Regardless of whether adult programs are reimbursed under any one of several federal acts, the need for publicizing training opportunities is still a vital element in program growth and development.

Advisory committees are important adjuncts to successful adult vocational-technical education. These groups can assist in promotional work of the school. In addition, they can be an important source of information for the planning of new courses and units.

Business and industry can be brought into the promotional and developmental activities of a school through serving as program cosponsors. Local chambers of commerce have been acting in this capacity for many years. Enlightened management in many organizations now recognizes that vocational courses do not cost—they pay.

Planning and organizing. An adult education program must be carefully planned and organized. Planning should include such things as developing performance objectives, determining program scope, establishing staff size and qualifications, budgeting, securing funds, and specifying course content. It must take into account such factors as equipment, materials, supplies, travel, and salaries. Programs should be based upon the needs of individuals and the manpower requirements of business and industry.

Financing patterns tend to vary widely among states. Programs under public supervision and control should be developed in cooperation with the state board for vocational education. Usually, local, state, and federal funding are obtainable. Where the use of federal funds for vocational adult activity seems desirable, contact with the state director of vocational education should be made while the program is in the exploratory stage. The state director, in his decisions relative to the use of federal funds, is governed by the federal acts, pertinent rules and regulations, and the state plan for vocational education. Where programs qualify for federal funding, at least dollar-for-dollar matching is a possibility.

Impact on the work force. Vocational-technical education programs for adults have developed and expanded rapidly to meet a wide range of diverse needs. The increasing cooperation between business, industry, and the schools has resulted in greater satisfaction on the part of the business sector with the schools' training efforts. The need still remains, however, for greater sensitivity on the part of educators to the supply-and-demand factors in the labor market.

The general report of the Advisory Council on Vocational Education (U.S. Department of Health . . . 1968*b*) indicates how vocational adult programs are affecting the development of the nation's manpower. According to the report, although in the future more people will spend more time continuing their education to meet specific job requirements, the program of continuing education is neither sufficiently broad nor sufficiently extensive to meet present needs. In nearly every occupational field, the report continues, employment opportunities exceed the availability of postsecondary preemployment instruction, and instructional needs for trained manpower exceed the total capacity of the present public school program to provide for these manpower needs. Moreover, many workers who desire occupational training have not been able to obtain it because appropriate programs were not accessible to them.

The report also points out that many educators in leadership positions have failed to recognize the importance of vocational education for employed persons and have not promoted its development. Lack of initiative and imagination in exploring new occupational fields have had the effect of restricting program offerings to those that had been commonly provided in the past. In addition, related training for apprentices at school has had severe limitations. Among these were the lack of adequate classroom space and appropriate instructional equipment and materials for many types of courses, which caused some programs to be removed from the public schools; and the fact that craftsmen used as teachers for related training and skill training of apprentices and journeymen were not given adequate opportunities to learn modern instructional methods.

Expenditures. Adult vocational programs are generally short-term programs in a given occupation and are attended on a part-time basis. While there have been several states and many communities which have long offered excellent programs in adult education, in general, adult education has been slow to develop in most parts of the United States. Many communities have been reluctant to assume the added financial burden in view of the difficulty of providing adequate budgets for the already existing public education. Therefore, adult education in most states and communities has, until recently, been totally or nearly self-supporting through student fees.

The Vocational Education Act of 1963 provided additional funding and an emphasis on meeting the needs of individuals. It is interesting to see how the states have applied efforts in meeting the problems of workers and how expanded programs have had an impact on the work force. The information below was taken from annual state reports covering the period since funding under the 1963 act became available.

Supplementary programs for employed adults showed great gains in many states in the number of programs operated, the diversity of course offerings, and the employment areas served. Demand for supplementary training also increased.

State and local staffs organized and conducted programs to prepare middle managers and supervisors to meet the manpower needs of their areas. Courses offered by one eastern state totaled 15 and included techniques of supervision, waste reduction, and job economics and fundamentals of management. Another state offered 56 programs for 70 different industrial organizations. Community colleges have been among the institutions providing adult supervisory training.

Vocational education health programs offered training in an increased number of occupations to persons ranging in age from 16 to 60. Included were both short-term and long-term assistants (workers at a skill level approaching that of an aide) and the two-year associate degree program for registered nurses. The adult programs offered supplementary training to persons who were already employed but who needed to update their skills.

A 6.4 percent increase in adult vocational education enrollments was recorded during 1966 for the United States as a whole. Meanwhile, adult enrollments rose 15 percent in Minnesota, and South Carolina marked an increase of nearly 12 percent. Mississippi opened 83 new adult classes in office education alone. Georgia at the same time provided adult training in all 21 of its area schools.

Alabama upgraded employees in office, sales, construction, metal-working, and service occupations for which employers had reported shortages. New curricula offerings for adults in food services, building trades, transportation, traffic management, law enforcement, banking, real estate, and small business management were opened in other states.

Progress was made in several states in providing opportunities in the field of health occupations for persons with prison records and for disadvantaged persons from low-income families. Criteria were adopted that permit the admission of selected former inmates who otherwise meet all requirements for trainees as established by the schools.

More than 400,000 farmers and farm workers attended agricultural courses, predominantly in agricultural mechanics and farm management, in 1967. Television programs in farm management for young and adult farmers were instituted by the Minnesota state government.

In the distributive education field, tourist promotion and development and merchandise control were areas where short-term classes were made available on a much larger scale than formerly. Six states that previously had not reported any adult enrollments provided training during the 1967 school year.

The demand for improved services in nursing homes and extended care facilities stimulated cooperation among many health agencies and vocational educators in developing plans for up-grading staffs and for preparing qualified workers for these institutions. To serve nursing homes better, the states trained service aides, nursing assistants, and physical and occupational therapy aides.

Greater emphasis has been placed on consumer education in adult home economics programs. Preparatory and supplementary training for service occupations were provided for adults in every state. These adult programs served widely different needs, including those of persons receiving public assistance and of migrant and other low-income groups. To alleviate shortages of hospital food-service workers, courses were opened for adults in several institutions. In Tennessee, for example, adults were trained as aides for Head Start programs, while in Colorado, 18 centers conducted programs to help adults deal more effectively with the dual role of homemaking and outside employment.

In the field of office occupations, California developed a program aimed at adults from culturally deprived and low-income groups wishing immediate employment as stenographers and clerk-typists. Adult education enrollments in technical education programs gained more than 12 percent in 1966. Adult programs enrolled many more students than secondary and postsecondary programs. Enrollments in adult trade and industrial education increased 20.2 percent above the 1966 level. This figure means that 162,000 more persons were in training in 1967 than in 1966.

Manpower programs. In 1968, Secretary of Labor W. Willard Wirtz indicated that programs were achieving success in the area of manpower development but that certain goals had yet to be achieved. He identified the remaining segments of unemployment as the hard-core unemployed, who need skill training, literacy training, and successful work experience to develop new motivation and become stable, productive workers; the seasonably unemployed, who are fully prepared to work all year and yet constitute one-fifth of the unemployed force; the unemployed young people struggling to bridge the gap between school and work; the unemployed and inactive older workers, whose energies and talents are wasted because of inadequate opportunities, outmoded traditions, and discrimination; the unemployed and underemployed members of minority groups—Negroes, Puerto Ricans, American Indians, Mexican-Americans, and others—who need special help to catch up with the majority; and the jobless handicapped, many of whom could become employable if given rehabilitation and other services.

The impact of existing programs may be ascertained through a review of enrollments and completions in institutional and on-the-job manpower training programs. The *Manpower Report of the President* (U.S. Department of Labor 1968) credits the manpower development program for accomplishing substantial reductions in the length of individual unemployment.

A pattern of both progress and retrogression emerges relating to the impact of training and education on nonwhites. The growing number of Negro families with moderate incomes or better, the increase in the number of Negro males graduating from college, and the growth in representation of Negroes in professional, technical, and other white-collar occupations augur well for this group that has been able to take advantage of available opportunities. At the other end of the scale, however, are the Negro rural poor and slum dwellers. Although advances have been made, as evidenced by the reduction in the proportion of families with incomes of less than $3,000, many slum residents appear to be in a deteriorating economic position.

In an effort to reach the hard-core unemployed among the American Indians, the Bureau of Indian Affairs established several residential employment-training centers. Programs initiated under the Economic Opportunity Act of 1964 are expanding educational, training, and work-training opportunities for Indians. Programs under the Manpower Development and Training Act of 1962 also have had an impact on training reservation Indians, for whom a number of specific projects have been designed. The federal and state employment service systems are also strengthening their services to Indians.

The Vocational Education Amendments of 1968 focused on a serious problem confronting the disadvantaged. U.S. President Lyndon Baines Johnson at that time described the obstacles confronting disadvantaged groups in the labor market as remediable through vocational-technical adult education programs. He said that enrollments in institutional programs, both in the regular program and in the manpower program, grow with available resources provided schools undertake the task of rehabilitating persons and

preparing them for employment. Many ancillary services are needed, said Johnson, and while they are expensive, they return a high yield to the taxpayer. Therefore, he concluded, as the services expand, the unemployment rate may be expected to decline.

Cooperative efforts. At the local and state levels, vocational administrators are likely to be involved with the coordination and operation of programs funded from a wide range of sources. This situation means they may be directly concerned with the quality of the program and the level of funding.

Staffing at the state level in vocational-technical education, to ensure sufficient numbers of people for participation in the multitude of planning, organizational, and developmental meetings, presents a difficult budgetary problem. To make the most effective use of scarce resources and to avoid duplication and confusion, coordinated plans must be developed.

Coordinated planning. Coordinated planning was begun in April 1966 with the establishment of the Federal-State Manpower Development Planning System (now the Office of Manpower Development), launched with the cooperation of the Manpower Administration, the U.S. Office of Education, and the Community Action Programs of the Office of Economic Opportunity. The Welfare Administration, the Vocational Rehabilitation Administration, the Economic Development Administration, and the Department of Housing and Urban Development later became participants. Each of these agencies instructed its national and regional staffs to assist in the development of state and local plans.

In March 1967, this form of interagency cooperation was restructured as the Cooperative Area Manpower Planning System (CAMPS) under the coordination of the Department of Labor. In its first year of work CAMPS involved the federal administrators of major manpower programs in joint program planning for 1968 and subsequent years. This joint planning focused on local areas, where coordinating committees were important to the systematic exchange of information about resources and the adjustment of responsibility for providing services. These local committees were composed of representatives from each participating federal agency and public and private local and community agencies. Local plans were submitted to the state coordinating committees, which combined them within a single document. The state plan also included plans for the areas not covered by local committees, particularly where significant program resources are available from one or more participating agencies.

Regional coordinating committees were established in each of the 11 regions of the Bureau of Employment Security. Each participating federal agency designated an appropriate regional representative to serve on the committee to review and approve state plans, provide technical assistance to the state committees, and review results periodically in light of state and national goals. As of 1968, there were seven regional committees, conforming to the regional geographic areas for manpower administration. Statewide coordinating committees operate in each of the states and in the District of Columbia, Puerto Rico, and the Virgin Islands.

President Johnson proposed that CAMPS, started in 1967, be established on a long-term basis. This system links federal, state, and local resources in a coordinated effort to reduce unemployment and underemployment. The program called for by the president—Job Opportunities in the Business Sector (JOBS)—is aimed at a partnership between government and industry to train and hire the hard-core unemployed. Essentially, the partnership involves the government's locating and identifying the unemployed and the company's training them and offering them jobs. The company bears the normal cost of training, as it would for any of its new employees. But with the hard-core unemployed there are extra costs, and these are paid by the government.

Manpower forces against poverty were scheduled to expand through the Concentrated Employment Program (CEP) as well as through CAMPS. The Model Cities Program, with its strong emphasis on manpower development, is another manpower force against poverty; on a smaller scale, the one-stop neighborhood service centers represent still another. In addition, the Special Impact program makes possible an intensive attack on unemployment and poverty in particular slum areas through business and community development.

Contributing to these efforts are the Human Resources programs of the federal and state employment service systems. These programs represent a marshaling and reorientation of facilities and services, with the goal of helping the disadvantaged qualify for and obtain meaningful jobs.

Several major projects initiated by private industry have furnished valuable experience also. In Detroit, for example, the New Detroit Committee, established in 1967 with representation from most of the city's larger businesses, carried out some very successful projects for recruiting and training the disadvantaged, primarily among Negroes. The New York Urban Coalition, also organized in 1967, differs from the Detroit project in that it includes labor and civic as well as business leaders, but its purpose is much the same. Also in 1967 the steel industry and the steelworkers' union secured federal help in upgrading steelworkers and training unemployed workers to take the place of those who were promoted to better jobs.

Manpower training. The 1966 *Manpower Report of the President* called for special emphasis on serving those who are severely handicapped socially and educationally. The secretary of labor, in consultation with the secretary of health, education, and welfare, accordingly directed that 40 percent of the training effort henceforth be aimed at severely disadvantaged unemployed adults, 25 percent at disadvantaged youth, and 35 percent at lessening skill shortages in the occupations for which manpower training is appropriate. These relative priorities were unchanged as of the early 1970's.

The numerical goal of manpower training for 1967 was a total of 250,000 trainees. Of these, half were to be provided with institutional training—that is, with occupational preparation in classrooms and other educational facilities—and half were to be trained on the job. The institutional training program was thus expected to fund projects authorizing training for 125,000 trainees during 1967 and the on-the-job training program (OJT) 125,000 trainees. Of the 125,000 OJT openings, 72,500 were to be in coupled programs combining training at the job site with some classroom instruction. At least 15,000 manpower trainees were to be residents of communities officially designated as redevelopment areas.

The manpower training program in 1967 substantially surpassed its goal. Institutional programs provided for 132,300 trainees, including those from redevelopment areas (the most severely depressed communities in economic terms). The number of OJT training openings exceeded the

OJT planning quota, reaching a total of 152,700 by the end of the year, of whom 54,600 were to be in coupled projects of job training.

Indications are that industry will become more involved as a partner in the training of manpower. The Concentrated Employment Program is expected to have its greatest impact in reducing unemployment in city ghettos and depressed rural areas. The Human Resources Development Program is expected to remain the main force of employment services programs.

Critical and systematic evaluation should be implemented if unworkable and uneconomic efforts are not to waste federal monies and community staff resources. Local school administrators and state vocational-technical supervisory personnel should explore ways to participate actively in this evaluation effort and to assume a role of responsibility in the generation, cooperation, and coordination of the many programs that affect the adult vocational-technical education structure.

Problems and trends. Adult education in the 1970's has a great opportunity for service. While skill development is important to the individual and to business and industry, the higher the employment rate, the greater becomes the need for auxiliary services. For example, there is a growing need for schools to establish guidance centers for adults. Vocational guidance should be the foundation of such an effort, but counsel and expert advice should be available to adults on a variety of subjects. Counseling in such areas as consumer education, personal grooming, debt management, ability to get along with others, and job placement should be open to adults seeking to make a better adjustment to life.

Some adult programs tend to suffer from the same problem that affects secondary schools. They tend to involve too much mass production activity, with too little attention to the needs of the individual. The quality control effort on the part of the institutions often is nonexistent. Adult education has a unique opportunity to provide missing auxiliary services to its clientele. It is to be hoped that the Vocational Education Amendments of 1968 will make possible many personal services for those enrolled in programs for adults, the disadvantaged, and the handicapped. Adequate funding for matching purposes is the key to providing these services.

BIBLIOGRAPHY

BOWLER, EARL M. 1968 *Enrollments in Adult Trade and Industrial Education.* Washington, D.C., Division of Vocational and Technical Education, U.S. Office of Education.

TATE, BARBARA L., AND LUCILLE KNOPF 1968 *Nurse Career-Pattern Study.* New York, National League for Nursing, Research and Development.

U.S. DEPARTMENT OF HEALTH, EDUCATION, AND WELFARE 1968a *Education and Training: Learning for Jobs.* Sixth Annual Report of Department of Health, Education, and Welfare to Congress. Washington, D.C., Government Printing Office.

U.S. DEPARTMENT OF HEALTH, EDUCATION, AND WELFARE 1968b *Vocational Education: The Bridge Between Man and His Work.* Prepared by the Advisory Council on Vocational Education. Washington, D.C., Government Printing Office.

U.S. DEPARTMENT OF LABOR 1968 *Manpower Report of the President.* Washington, D.C., Government Printing Office.

EARL M. BOWLER

4. ADVISORY COMMITTEES

Belief in the ability of citizens' advisory committees to help develop sound educational policies and programs has long permeated the field of public education in the United States. Citizens' committees have been involved in formulating practically every aspect of school policy, objectives, programs, and operations. In the area of vocational and technical education, administrators and teachers involved with the preparation of youth and adults for careers in various sectors of the economy have called upon representatives from industry, trade, business, agriculture, the professions, and organized labor (all of whom will here be referred to as representatives from industry) for cooperation and guidance in organizing, conducting, and evaluating school programs. It is estimated that over 100,000 private citizens are serving voluntarily as members of advisory committees organized by local schools and school systems, public and private vocational and technical schools, community colleges, rehabilitation institutions, and various antipoverty programs.

Services provided by advisory committees. In spite of their designation as advisory committees, which is meant to preclude involvement in school and educational administrative matters, citizens' committees perform many services which may be considered operational or cooperative. For example, committees established by vocational and technical schools for specific occupational programs have been found to engage in more than 30 specific cooperative activities related to various aspects and stages of the education process. A brief examination of the services rendered by these occupational committees will serve to give an idea of the broad range of operations with which advisory committees are concerned.

Recruiting, selecting, and placing students. Industry representatives on various occupational committees assist the schools in their recruitment endeavors by visiting feeder schools, civic clubs, and meetings of other appropriate groups in order to encourage young people and their parents to consider the benefits of vocational and technical education. Committee members often aid in the selection process by assisting in the development of aptitude tests and in the screening of applicants for admission. They also provide the schools with information concerning the aptitude and the educational and experiential background necessary for obtaining entry-level jobs in specific areas of their sectors of the economy.

At the other end of the educational process, the committee members help to place students in appropriate jobs. Not only do they place and hire graduates for full-time jobs, but they often provide summer or part-time work for students as part of cooperative programs with the schools. The industry representatives also arrange field trips to plants and businesses for students and counselors, provide the schools with free guidance literature concerning various industries, businesses, and professions, and assist in the development of aptitude, achievement, certification, and licensing examinations related to the initial employment of graduates in various fields of work.

Assistance with the educational program. Citizens serving on occupational advisory committees render many services related to the actual program of instruction in the vocational and technical schools. They help to (1) develop and review course content to ensure that it meets the current needs and demands of industry; (2) evaluate the adequacy of laboratories, shops, and equipment; (3) prepare and review budget requests for needed equipment and supplies; (4) obtain equipment and supplies on loan, as gifts, or at special prices; (5) establish and maintain libraries of reading materials and visual aids concerning the various opportunities in industry and other fields; (6) establish standards of proficiency to be met by the students; (7) develop school policy regarding the kinds and volume of production work

required of students so that this work will be of instructional value in the educational program; (8) develop special programs called for by federal and state legislation; (9) develop evening-school courses for employees; and (10) arrange for school courses related to apprenticeship or on-the-job training.

Assistance to teachers. Many occupational advisory committees perform certain services which are of direct help to technical and vocational education teachers. They often conduct in-service training programs and arrange for instructors from industry to assist the regular teachers in the classroom. In the area of financial assistance, the committees often find summer employment for teachers and in unusual circumstances subsidize salaries in order to help the schools obtain qualified instructors. Funds are often provided by the advisory committees to enable teachers to attend regional and national meetings of industry and teacher organizations. At times the committees arrange special meetings of teachers to establish cooperative relationships between the schools and industry. Finally, to serve the interests of the schools, students, and teachers, the committees often aid in the establishment of teacher qualification requirements.

Student recognition. Aware of the need to recognize and reward exceptional performance in vocational and technical schools, many citizens' committees give prizes to students and scholarships and other types of assistance to outstanding graduates who wish to continue their education in technical institutes, teacher-training institutions, or other institutions of higher education.

Public relations. Since good public relations is important to the fulfillment of the goals of vocational and technical education, many committees do their best to assist the schools in this area. Committee members often attend meetings in support of vocational and technical education which are called by local and state school officials or by legislative groups. The committees also provide speakers to address trade and civic groups on the subject of relevant training programs in the schools. Further, to bring the activities of the schools to the attention of the public, the committees often provide news stories about the various school programs to the local news media and to magazines published for specific industry, trade, business, or professional groups.

Benefits of service on advisory committees. There are several factors which motivate employers and their representatives to serve on advisory committees. Employers are always in need of well-trained personnel to fill jobs in their offices and plants; they also want to keep to a minimum the cost of recruitment and training of new employees. It is thus to the employers' benefit to see that school programs in vocational and technical education are well planned and well executed. It is also to their advantage to support manpower development and other antipoverty programs which attempt to compensate for the inadequacies of many schools and school systems. The high cost of these remedial programs has further convinced industry representatives of the need to help schools improve their vocational education courses and to assist educators in motivating young people to better prepare themselves for the world of work.

Although the need for a continuing supply of educated and trained employees provides the most significant motivation for service on advisory committees, participation in school programs also provides a certain personal satisfaction for public-spirited employers and their staffs. Membership in the committees affords these citizens the opportunity to engage in an educational activity that gives them prestige in their communities. By providing awards and financial aid to individual students, many industry representatives satisfy a desire to feel and be considered altruistic and philanthropic. By helping schools, committee members fulfill what they feel to be their civic and community responsibilities and discharge personally felt moral and social obligations to help young people prepare themselves to become productive citizens. Finally, employers and their representatives find that participation in school and educational affairs allows them to capitalize on the public- and customer-relations benefits which come from such activity.

Sophisticated vocational and technical education administrators, in seeking industry representatives to serve on their advisory committees, try to appeal to as many of these motivating factors as possible. Further, they arrange for a variety of activities during each school year which will express their appreciation to those who do serve on the committees. School publications, such as course catalogs and annual reports, list the names

and company affiliations of all committee members. Bulletin boards are often covered with pictures of the committee. School administrators also frequently award certificates of appreciation at dinners honoring the citizens' groups.

Types of advisory committees. There are five general types of advisory committees: occupational advisory committees, which we have been discussing above; general advisory committees for an entire school or local school system; joint apprenticeship committees; state advisory committees on vocational education; and the National Advisory Council on Vocational Education.

Occupational advisory committees. The great majority of industry-education advisory committees are of the occupational variety. Almost all vocational and technical education programs offered in publicly supported institutions have established some form of committee to serve in an advisory capacity to instructors for a specific occupational program or to department heads for a group of related occupational education and training programs. For example, if a school is offering several courses in the construction trades, there may be an advisory committee for the construction trades department and subcommittees for individual courses such as bricklaying, carpentry, and electricity. There may, on the other hand, simply be advisory committees for each individual trade but no general committee for the entire department. In the large vocational and technical schools there may be anywhere from 25 to 75 or more such committees, depending upon the number of programs and courses offered.

Membership in occupational committees is usually drawn by the school officials from frontline supervisory and middle-management staff in companies employing large numbers of people skilled in a particular trade, occupation, or profession. Owners of small companies may also serve on such committees. If the occupational education program is preparing students for jobs and careers in a unionized trade or industry or for some paraprofessional field such as practical nursing, representatives from the union and trade or professional associations will ordinarily be appointed to the advisory committee. Members are usually those individuals in a company or organization who are directly responsible for hiring and training new employees. The number of members on a committee, including school staff, may be as small as five or as large as 15. The size depends on such factors as the number and scale of companies in the community employing people engaged in the occupation for which the school is training its students and the number of unions and trade associations concerned.

The frequency with which occupational committees meet varies from once a year to once a month or more, depending on the variety of activities in which a committee is engaged. For example, if a committee or subcommittee is drawing up a new course of study, it may meet several times a month for three or four months. If a committee is asked to do little or nothing during the school year, one *pro forma* meeting a year would be considered sufficient. Obviously, any school administrator who calls his committees together for only one meeting a year is not utilizing the advisers very effectively. However, it should be noted that while a committee may meet infrequently, its members and other industry people are often called upon by instructors and department heads for on-the-spot advice, information, and assistance.

Prior to 1963 many state departments of education had issued regulations, either to implement specific state laws or as a result of administrative decision, which required vocational and technical education programs to utilize occupational advisory committees. The Vocational Education Act of 1963, with its implementing rules and regulations issued by the U.S. Office of Education, requires local school administrators to consult with employers and other individuals who have skills in and substantive knowledge of the occupational field for which the school system is offering a program. Thus, all state departments of education now insist on the formation of occupational advisory committees for every specialized course of instruction offered by local schools and school systems.

General advisory committees. Unlike occupational committees, general advisory committees are purely advisory in nature. They are established for the purpose of assisting school officials in the development of the broad range of vocational and technical education courses offered in schools, school districts, community colleges, or area vocational schools. This type of committee helps both in the planning of objectives and policy in view of local needs for vocational and technical education

and in the determination of the relative emphasis and priority that should be given to the various elements of the program. Once policy and priorities have been agreed upon, the members of the committee usually engage in activities to obtain public support, any needed legislation, and funds.

Membership in general advisory committees is usually drawn from the ranks of top-level management—that is, from among directors of personnel, plant superintendents, vice-presidents of large companies, and presidents and owners of small organizations. Also serving on such committees are high-level representatives of various local and state agencies, economic development groups, and trade, professional, and labor organizations. Every effort is made to include representatives from the major public and private sectors of the economy in the community or regional area. The number of members on the committee may be as small as 15 or as large as 30, depending on the level of industrial development of the community served by the school. The committees usually meet from two to six times a year, the frequency being determined by the extent to which the head of the school or school system desires to benefit from committee services.

While the establishment of general advisory committees is recommended by a number of state departments of education, it is required by only a few states under certain specified conditions. The number of general advisory committees in existence is not large, but it is expected that as vocational and technical education administrators become more and more involved in developing long-range plans for their programs, this type of committee will receive greater acceptance and become more widely utilized.

Joint apprenticeship committees. Local joint apprenticeship committees exist for many skilled crafts in a number of cities. Membership usually consists of six people—three from labor and three from management—involved in the craft or trade which the committee is serving. While the primary responsibilities of the committees involve selection, training, education, and placement of apprentices, many educators turn to the local JAC for advice concerning the development, execution, and evaluation of their occupational education programs. The committees also work with school officials on related educational programs for on-the-job apprentices. Apprenticeship committees usually meet once a month to conduct their business; those that are also serving as advisory committees convene again in that capacity.

The JAC concept is promoted by the Bureau of Apprenticeship and Training of the U.S. Department of Labor and by state apprenticeship agencies, not by educators. For this reason, and because the committees are basically concerned with apprenticeships rather than with school programs, most vocational and technical education administrators are opposed to utilizing a JAC as a school advisory committee. They much prefer to establish a school occupational advisory committee which will cooperate with the JAC but remain separate from it.

State advisory councils. The 1968 amendments to the Vocational Education Act of 1963 contain a section which is unique in the history of U.S. federal legislation on vocational education. This section makes federal aid to a state under Title I of the act contingent upon the establishment of a state advisory council and specifies the areas of interest and expertise which must be represented on the council. For example, the members must include a person or persons familiar with the vocational needs and problems of labor and management of the state, representing schools and colleges with vocational education programs, representing manpower and vocational education agencies in the state, and knowledgeable about the educational needs of the handicapped and of the poor and disadvantaged. The law also describes the functions and responsibilities of the state councils and requires that they report their evaluations and recommendations to a national council established by the law. The amendments thus went far beyond the original 1963 act, which required the establishment of a state advisory council only if the state board for vocational education did not include representatives from certain segments of the economy and which contained no statement of function or requirements for staffing of the councils.

The 1968 amendments had a great effect on vocational education at the national, state, and local levels. The establishment of state councils strengthened the concept and influence of local advisory committees and served to provide a link between local groups and the national council.

The National Advisory Council on Vocational Education. The 1963 Vocational Education Act established an advisory committee to provide the U.S. commissioner of education with advice on the national administration of the act and an advisory council to the secretary of the Department of Health, Education, and Welfare to study vocational and technical education programs and to recommend needed improvements. These two groups were replaced in 1968 by the National Advisory Council on Vocational Education, whose 21 members are appointed by the president of the United States.

The amendment which established the national council specifies that it shall advise the commissioner on vocational education programs supported by aid under Title I of the act, review the administration, operation, and effectiveness of programs under the title and make annual reports of its findings and recommendations to the secretary of HEW, and conduct independent evaluations of these programs and publish and distribute the results of its studies.

Impact of state and federal legislation. The enactment of the 1968 amendments to the Vocational Education Act, along with legislation existing in many states, makes it almost mandatory for technical and vocational education administrators to establish and utilize advisory committees at the local, state, and federal levels. The field of vocational and technical education has become unique in the extent to which it involves leadership from the private sector of the nation. During the more than 50 years that vocational education has received major assistance from the federal government, the services of citizens' advisory councils have been both eagerly sought and readily available.

BIBLIOGRAPHY

AMERICAN ASSOCIATION OF SCHOOL ADMINISTRATORS. EDUCATIONAL RESEARCH SERVICE 1968 *Citizens Advisory Committees.* ERS Circular No. 3. Washington, D.C., The Association.

AMERICAN VOCATIONAL ASSOCIATION 1957 *Vocational Advisory Committees.* Washington, D.C., The Association.

BURT, SAMUEL M. 1967 *Industry and Vocational-Technical Education: A Study of Industry Education Advisory Committees.* New York, McGraw-Hill.

BURT, SAMUEL M. 1968 "Three-year Program Plan for Your Advisory Committee." *American Vocational Association Journal,* September:13–14.

RIENDEAU, ALBERT J. 1967 *The Role of the Advisory Committee in Occupational Education in the Junior College.* Washington, D.C., American Association of Junior Colleges.

U.S. DEPARTMENT OF HEALTH, EDUCATION, AND WELFARE 1960 *Organization and Effective Use of Advisory Committees.* By Sam Wilson King. Washington, D.C., Government Printing Office.

SAMUEL M. BURT

VOCATIONAL EDUCATION IN THE SCHOOLS

1. SECONDARY SCHOOLS   Edwin L. Rumpf

2. POSTSECONDARY TECHNICAL
   TRAINING   Joseph T. Nerden

3. CURRICULUM TRENDS   Lane C. Ash

1. SECONDARY SCHOOLS

Secondary school vocational education is that organized program of studies at the high school level which has as its objective the development of salable occupational skills in an individual to prepare him for employment and for assuming a place in society. Upon completion of this program of studies, the individual is usually granted a high school diploma.

Despite the vast educational opportunities available to people in the United States, only recently has any great concern been expressed regarding the kind of education that is made available. In 1945, C. A. Prosser defined the issues involved in vocational education in the statement now referred to as the Prosser resolution. Prosser stated that although 20 percent of the youth of secondary school age were being prepared for college and another 20 percent were being prepared vocationally to enter an occupation, he did not believe "that the remaining 60 percent of our youth of secondary school age will receive the life adjustment training they need and to which they are entitled as American citizens—unless and until the administrators of public education with the assistance of the vocational education leaders formulate a comparable program for this group" (Keller 1955, p. 84).

The ensuing years brought much discussion and many conferences on life adjustment education, but vocational education never received the emphasis that Prosser had envisioned. Education in the secondary school was largely directed toward preparing students for college entrance rather than preparing students who would become employed immediately upon leaving school for jobs. The proper balance between educational preparation in the secondary school and preparation for the future needs of those being educated has still to be achieved.

Background. The need for vocational education at the college and university level was recognized well before any state or federal legislation provided support for secondary school vocational education. During the period of colonial development, institutions of higher education were established in response to the need to prepare individuals for the ministry and for certain other professions. However, persons prepared for medicine and law by serving a form of apprenticeship before institutions of higher education offered formal preparation for these professions. Private institutions provided these educational opportunities before they became available in the public colleges. Mays (1948) suggested that development of secondary school vocational education followed the same steps from some form of apprenticeship to the gradual establishment of a few private training schools to the institution of public training schools or classes. Roberts (1957) also supported the idea that private and philanthropic schools were the forerunners of schools of public trade, which came into prominence in the early 1900's.

Vocational education at the secondary school level received tremendous impetus in 1917 with the passage of the Smith-Hughes Act. This legislation provided federal funds that could be matched with state or local funds to support vocational education programs below the college level in the fields of agriculture, trades, homemaking, and industry as well as teacher-training programs in these fields.

Between 1917 and 1946 other vocational education laws were passed which were terminal in nature. The Vocational Education Act of 1946, commonly known as the George-Barden Act, provided for a permanent authorization of funds, extended the provisions of the Smith-Hughes Act, and included support for vocational education in distribution and marketing, the latter having first been federally supported ten years earlier. Fisheries occupations were also included, and later legislation included health occupations and area vocational education programs.

The Vocational Education Act of 1963 was a compromise between the old and the new. The Smith-Hughes and George-Barden acts were continued, but their provisions were liberalized. The traditional occupational categories included under these acts—agriculture, distribution and marketing, home economics, and trades and industry—were greatly broadened. Training in agriculture was extended to include those jobs which were related to agriculture. Support could now be given to training for gainful employment related to home economics. Training in distribution and marketing was no longer restricted to persons who were employed but could include in-school preparatory programs.

The new emphasis under the 1963 act was evidenced by vocational education programs directed toward the people to be served. These included persons in high school, those who had completed or left high school, employed persons who needed training or retraining, and persons who had special needs which could not be met in the regular vocational education program. For the first time federal vocational education funds could be used to construct area vocational education schools.

The Vocational Education Amendments of 1968 made a complete break with the past. The George-Barden Act was repealed, and only the funds authorized by the Smith-Hughes Act were retained, with the stipulation that expenditures must be in accordance with the new law. Completely gone were the traditional occupational categories. A permanent authorization was provided for the basic grant programs in the states; these were, in the main, like those first supported under the Vocational Education Act of 1963, which permitted support of training for any occupation not generally considered to be professional or requiring a baccalaureate or higher degree. Great emphasis was placed upon programs for the disadvantaged, including the handicapped, with special funds set aside for these categories and for postsecondary education programs. Other parts of the law provided the authorization of funds for exemplary programs, consumer and homemaker education, cooperative vocational education, work-study, demonstration residential schools, curriculum development, and preservice and in-service development of professionals.

Research activities were to be shared between federal and state agencies. Other provisions in the law required that there be more comprehensive planning with greater involvement of state and local personnel.

Nature of programs.   Vocational education in the secondary schools of the United States varies from little or nothing to quite sophisticated and comprehensive programs. The absence or inadequacy of programs is due to a variety of reasons, ranging from the community's indifference to the needs of its students to the belief that some other form of education is best suited to the needs of students at this stage in their development. In some cases, especially in the rural areas where the number of students is small, the financial investment required and the practical inability to establish a comprehensive program militate against the establishment of an adequate program. On a national basis, the variety of educational opportunities is significant. The problem is to provide the student with the right kind of vocational education opportunity at the right time and place.

Philosophy.   Opportunities in secondary school vocational education are provided for the same reason that vocational education was created—to meet a social need for an educated labor force. Hence, as a function and responsibility of public education, secondary school vocational education must be responsive to the changes and needs of contemporary society. The orientation must be, as the Advisory Council on Vocational Education reported in 1968, toward social, educational, and manpower considerations.

A number of forces have shaped secondary school vocational education. Some people believe that students at this level are too young to warrant the expenditure needed to develop salable skills. Others contend that time taken for vocational education could better be expended in improving the general education skills of the individual. Some believe that all occupational skill development should be postponed until later in life and that only general and cultural educational experiences should be included in the high school program. Some members of the labor force look upon vocational education efforts as a threat to their security and as a means of providing cheap labor which would be in direct competition with them. Some view vocational education as an instrument which would create a working-class society and which would forever block its participants from any further educational progress. Others view expenditures for vocational education as a direct subsidy to prospective employers and suggest that the schools should not try to perform a function that is the responsibility of the employer.

On the other side of the question, many believe that the high school student who will not enter a program of higher education but who expects to enter the labor market upon leaving school should have the right to be more adequately prepared to play his role, whatever it might be (Venn 1964). Many high school students have performed most capably on the job when engaged in a cooperative vocational education program. It is unrealistic to assume that all students should pursue a college preparatory program when only about 20 percent of all high school graduates finish college. The high school vocational student still has the opportunity for further education, as he must meet the same state requirements for high school graduation as any other student. As much consideration and concern should be given to the student who will enter the labor market immediately as has traditionally been given to the college preparatory student.

Purposes. Until the passage of the Vocational Education Act of 1963, the stipulated purpose of federally supported vocational education programs in the public schools was to train individuals for useful employment. Although the term "useful employment" was generally interpreted to mean gainful employment, it was broad enough to permit support of programs in home economics, which prepared persons for work as homemakers. Since the homemaker or wife was not usually paid a formal wage, this was considered useful rather than gainful employment.

By 1963 the close correlation between the individual's educational achievement and his future economic level was recognized. Simultaneously, vocational education was being looked upon as an instrument of social and economic accomplishment which must demonstrate the benefits derived from it in order to merit any public financial support. Therefore, it was mandated that any vocational education program supported under the 1963 act had to be designed to lead to gainful employment. All of the traditional occupational categories—agriculture, distribution and marketing, health, home economics, trades and industry, and technology—were so recognized, except the home economics programs which prepared persons as homemakers. Business and office occupations, referred to specifically in the law, were also classified as being eligible for support. Under the 1963 act, vocational education was rather broadly defined and included support for any program which would prepare the individual for gainful employment in any occupation not generally considered to be professional and not requiring the baccalaureate or higher degree.

The word "purpose" has been used in a special way in the vocational education acts to refer to the uses for which federal funds may be expended. The 1963 act specified six purposes: (1) vocational education for persons in high school; (2) vocational education for persons who had completed or left high school; (3) vocational education for persons who needed training or retraining; (4) vocational education for persons who had academic, socioeconomic, or other handicaps which prevented them from succeeding in the regular vocational program; (5) construction of area vocational education school facilities; and (6) ancillary services intended to improve the quality of the program. Of these six purposes, only the second and third would not normally be included in or directly related to secondary school vocational education.

When the purposes of the earlier vocational education laws are compared with those of more recent laws, it is apparent that the purposes have become much broader in their intent and application.

Growth. Although reporting requirements relating to federally supported programs have varied, making it difficult to compare data on secondary school vocational education on a long-term basis, some general trends are apparent.

Venn (1964) reported a 50 percent increase in secondary school attendance from 1950 to 1960, while during this same period enrollment in federally supported vocational education classes showed less than an 8 percent increase. He estimated that no more than 4 or 5 percent of the high school graduates in any year completed a full-time preemployment curriculum which received federal financial aid.

Draper (1967) felt that the number of persons pursuing vocational education programs at the high school level should be greatly increased. He determined that before 1963 only about 15 percent of secondary school students were involved in specifically vocational programs; a more appropriate group should include 40 to 50 percent of the student population, in Draper's opinion.

Extent. The extent of secondary school vocational education may be viewed in a number of different ways. One can look at the absolute number of students involved; the percentage of enrollment that this group represents of the total enrollment in vocational education at all levels—primary, secondary, and postsecondary; the percentage of enrollment that this group represents of the total secondary school enrollment; and other similar measures. Each gives some indication of the educational opportunity that is available to students in high school today and provides a rough measure of the progress that still must be made.

In 1962 the Panel of Consultants on Vocational Education, studying the nationwide program of vocational education, reached these conclusions:

> Wide variations exist among the States, and among the schools in the States, in the vocational curriculums offered for high school students. The scope of the typical high school program is narrow in relation to needs of the present day. . . . Many young people in high school need special occupational instruction if they have not been able to adjust to the regular school program and lack interest and motivation. (U.S. Office of Education 1963, p. 157)

The panel's study also reported that for the school year 1960–1961 there were slightly more than 1.7 million in-school youth enrolled in vocational education. This number represented approximately 13 percent of the slightly more than 13 million youth in the total population who were 15 to 19 years old.

In 1967 the Advisory Council on Vocational Education reported that secondary school enrollments in vocational education had increased by more than 43 percent in 1966 over the 1964 fiscal year and constituted 50 percent of the total enrollment in vocational education (U.S. Congress . . . 1968). The advisory council also noted that by 1966 the national average of secondary school students (grades 9–12) enrolled in vocational education had risen to 25.4 percent; enrollments among states varied, however, from 10.5 to 50.6 percent. Slightly more than 3 million of the almost 12 million students enrolled in grades 9 to 12 in secondary schools in the United States were in vocational education programs. From 1966 to 1967 vocational enrollments increased by almost 0.5 million to 3.53 million in the secondary schools.

Despite this seemingly broad opportunity for vocational education in the secondary schools, the report stated that the growth in enrollment was still inadequate to fulfill the needs of the young people who should benefit from vocational education.

Integration of curricula. At the beginning of the twentieth century secondary education had as its major goal the preparation of students for college. Most individuals who did not aspire to attend college or who could not afford to do so started their working life with the barest minimum of a so-called general education. The many employment opportunities available to the high school graduate did not require that the individual have any occupational skills before taking a job.

The decrease in the number of European immigrants who had salable occupational skills, the inefficiency of employing unskilled workers, the increase in technology, the greater percentage of students remaining in high school, and an expanding economy were the factors which combined to promote popular support for federal legislation for vocational education. Leaders in the field of vocational education, however, had little faith that general school administrators would provide the necessary leaderhip to ensure the success of bona fide vocational education programs within the existing educational structure. Consequently, the resultant legislation and administrative procedures had the effect of establishing requirements which were so different from those for general education that vocational education was interpreted to be separate from the educational program then in existence.

As the number of students graduating from high school increased, the percentage of students going to college decreased. Gradually, there developed a general awareness that high school students needed a differentiated preparation based on their expected postgraduate plans. Leading educators recognized the need for change and gave voice to their beliefs in a variety of ways. Some, as Edmonson and his associates reported, stated:

> Secondary education should not be limited to general education; it should include also a dynamic program of vocational education. Vocational education includes all activities directed by the school for the specific purpose of preparing individuals for successful participation in different fields of service. General education refers to all other activities directed by the school, namely, those having no reference to the particular fields of service in which individuals hope to engage. (1948, pp. 376–377)

This statement clearly conveys the thought that together vocational and general education should constitute the secondary education experience of every individual.

Conant (1959) stated that the three main objectives of a comprehensive high school were to provide a general education for all students, to provide good elective programs for those who wished to use their skills immediately after graduation, and to provide satisfactory programs for those whose vocations would depend on their subsequent education in a college or university. Conant further suggested that students should not be classified according to clearly defined and labeled programs or tracks, such as college preparatory, vocational, or commercial. Instead, he believed that the school should attempt to provide an individualized program for every student.

The vocational education program does not take the place of general academic education but rather supplements and enhances it for students who want to be trained for a particular occupation. It provides part of a well-rounded program of studies which attempts to develop competent workers and citizens. In an effort to integrate the various educational elements in a comprehensive program, the U.S. Office of Education has begun developing a system of education known as the Educational System for the 70's.

Issues and problems.   Since the Soviet Union's launching of Sputnik 1 in 1957, there has been an increasing emphasis upon improving the degree of educational achievement of students at all levels. Courses in mathematics and science that previously had been offered only in the colleges and universities have been added at the secondary school level. Persons who previously had questioned the inclusion of vocational education offerings in the high school curriculum gained further support for their views because of the increased emphasis on academic subjects. For many, the issue of general education versus vocational education at the high school level was no issue at all. The rigors of the times, they contended, required that all persons should be given as much general education as possible during their high school experience. Specialization, as it related to vocational education, should be postponed until the postsecondary school period.

Opponents of this point of view believed that a general education experience was not suited to the vast majority of students who would not be going to college. The number of dropouts, estimated to total 1.7 million from 1960 to 1970,

and the educational problems of large-city ghetto residents further attested to the need to reexamine the educational program at the high school level. It was seen that what was needed was an educational program that would provide each individual with the opportunity to develop both general and vocational competencies.

An attempt was made to respond to the criticism that the offerings were too narrow and not relevant. Regulations for the Vocational Education Act of 1963 were written to permit support of clusters of closely related occupations as well as of specifically recognized occupations (U.S. Office of Education 1966). Advisory committees were used to ensure that vocational education would be geared to the needs of the individual and to the job that he would be required to perform.

A number of problems had to be solved before vocational programs could be expanded. Among the major problems were the lack of sufficient funds for construction and program operation, the lack of qualified personnel, the lack of meaningful communication with the general public, an unsympathetic attitude on the part of administrators and teachers, the requirement for local matching funds, and the emphasis on college and academic preparation.

The Advisory Council on Vocational Education noted in its 1968 report that programs for high school youth were limited in scope and availability. Other matters that required improvement, according to this report, were long-term planning at all levels and preparedness to meet changing or emergency conditions; in addition, vocational education should be made more generally available and greater financial support should be provided for vocational education (U.S. Congress . . . 1968).

Types of schools.   Federal agencies responsible for vocational education have emphasized the importance of the quality of the educational program rather than concentrating on the kind of facility or organizational structure to offer the program. Accordingly, the states have offered vocational education programs in a variety of facilities and institutions. Experience has shown that very successful secondary vocational education programs can be provided in various settings.

Generally, vocational education programs are offered under the auspices of the local education agency in such schools as the comprehensive high school, the vocational-technical high school, and the area vocational-technical school. The student may be enrolled in a school in which the program is totally self-contained—that is, where all aspects of the educational program are given within the same facility—or in one in which the program involves shared-time—that is, where the student attends one school for the vocational portion of his educational experience and receives the remainder of his educational experience in a "home" high school.

Comprehensive high school. The term "comprehensive high school" refers to a school at the secondary school level which provides curricular offerings sufficiently broad to meet the educational needs of a majority of its students. Educational experiences are provided for those who plan to go on to college and for those who plan to enter directly into some form of employment. A student enrollment of 1,500 or more in the comprehensive high school would increase the possibility of accomplishing this objective. The many small high schools in the United States find it difficult to be truly comprehensive. Some professional educators reject the idea that a satisfactory vocational education program can be provided in a small, so-called comprehensive high school. As the number of students enrolled in high schools varies, the comprehensiveness of the program in meeting the educational needs of the entire student body also varies.

In fiscal 1966, 17,066 schools offered vocational education. Of this number, 15,592, or approximately 91 percent, were regular or comprehensive secondary schools (U.S. Congress . . . 1968).

Vocational-technical high school. The vocational-technical high school is a school at the secondary school level which offers only vocational-technical education programs. The educational program is usually self-contained, offering all subjects necessary to enable students to qualify for high school graduation in addition to the specialized vocational-technical subjects.

Of the 17,066 schools offering vocational education in fiscal 1966, only 431, or about 2.5 percent, were listed as vocational-technical secondary schools (U.S. Congress . . . 1968).

Area vocational education school. There are four different types of area vocational education schools: specialized high schools, comprehensive high schools with vocational education departments, technical or vocational schools offering

postsecondary programs, and junior and community colleges or institutions of higher education with departments or divisions of vocational education. The state or local educational agency is required to provide such schools to qualify for federal vocational education funds for construction purposes under the 1963 act. In addition, the institution so established has to be available to all residents of the state or of an area designated by the state board for vocational education.

In order to satisfy the need for additional vocational education facilities, construction was begun on 443 state projects during the 1965 and 1966 fiscal years, with an expected total expenditure of more than $271 million, of which almost $104 million was to come from federal funds.

Of the 443 construction projects, 72 were specialized high schools, and 181 were departments of high schools. Thus, 253, or 57 percent, of these 443 vocational education facilities would ultimately offer more opportunity to high school students.

Impact of 1963 act. The Vocational Education Act of 1963 had an impact on every facet of the vocational education program in the United States and its possessions. The intent of the act was to provide services to people without regard to predetermined occupational groupings, whereas previous acts had supported training for persons in specific occupational categories.

Increased appropriations under the 1963 act enabled the states and school districts to develop new programs so as to meet increased demands for service, skilled, and other industrial workers. Total enrollment in vocational education programs increased substantially; the average annual increase was 14 percent during the three years after the act was passed, compared with an average annual increase of approximately 4 percent for the three years before.

Federal financial support for vocational education under the 1963 act stimulated greater state and local expenditures for the program. Federal support increased as follows: 1964, $55 million; 1965, $157 million; and 1966, $234 million. State and local expenditures during these years were as follows: 1964, $278 million; 1965, $448 million; and 1966, $566 million.

The 1963 act required that no less than 3 percent of the state's allotment be expended for ancillary services to improve the quality of vocational education in the state. The states reported almost 5 percent expended for ancillary services in 1965; in 1966 the expenditure for this purpose exceeded 10 percent.

The 1963 act, in addition to providing for the individual's needs, also focused the requirements of the national economy. To further ensure that vocational education programs would be related to the demands of the economy, the law provided that cooperative relationships should be established between the system of public employment offices in the state and the vocational education agencies. Formal agreements describing these arrangements at the state level were required by federal regulations, and a copy of the agreement was made a part of each state plan of vocational education.

Another provision in the law required that the state board have certain representation; in the words of the act, members of this group would include "persons familiar with the vocational education needs of management and labor in the State, and a person or persons representative of junior colleges, technical institutes, or other institutions of higher education which provide programs of technical or vocational training meeting the definition of vocational education." If the state board did not have such representation, it had to establish an advisory council which would consult with the state board in administering the state plan. By 1968, 49 advisory councils had been established in states and territories in which the state boards lacked the required representation. The experience with these advisory councils indicated that they functioned with varying degrees of success, some having little or no effect on the vocational education programs in their states. This poor record of performance was probably instrumental in causing new provisions for state advisory councils to be included in the Vocational Education Amendments of 1968.

Although the lack of adequate staff at the federal level militated against a comprehensive federal staff reorganization, state and local agencies, after the 1963 act, were able to increase administrative staffs and reorganize them so that they were directed toward a functional approach in administration.

Research was greatly strengthened by the act's provision which required that 10 percent of the funds appropriated be retained by the commissioner to pay part of the cost of research and training programs and of experimental, development-

mental, and pilot programs. At the federal level a division of research was established. By 1965, 44 states had established research coordinating units; at about the same time, two national vocational education research centers were established —one at Ohio State University and the other at North Carolina State University at Raleigh.

The 1963 act broadened the scope of curriculum activities to include office occupations, programs related to agriculture and home economics, and training of persons having academic, socioeconomic, and other handicaps. Expanded efforts in these and other areas of vocational education were noted at local, state, and federal levels.

In attempting to make vocational education programs more relevant to modern needs, many state and local education agencies used 1963 act funds to make studies and surveys to develop and improve vocational education programs. These efforts also tended to involve other community agencies interested in vocational education.

The Vocational Education Act of 1963 permitted greater program flexibility, made possible new areas of service, and greatly increased the financial support to the states. The provision for construction of area vocational education school facilities, the emphasis on research and experimentation, and the recognition that vocational education was an important instrument in solving the nation's manpower problems were direct beneficial results of this legislation.

Influence of the 1968 amendments. The Vocational Education Amendments of 1968 are expected to determine certain trends and directions in educational philosophy and practices. Elaborating on the provisions of the 1963 act, the 1968 amendments emphasized the fact that vocational education programs rather than vocational courses should be developed which would be responsive to both the needs of people and the economic needs of the nation. There seemed to be a movement away from basing program development on the traditional occupational categories and toward a much broader approach.

It is believed that vocational education programs and philosophy will have a strong influence on academic and general education programs. Some educators, who believe that vocational education has developed separate and apart from the established system, propose that vocational education be made an integral part of all education. Amalgamation is now proceeding much more slowly than the best interests of all parties concerned warrant.

Since the law stipulates that 10 percent of the federal funds must be expended for the education of the handicapped and 15 percent for the disadvantaged, these groups are expected to receive more vocational education services. Perhaps as important as meeting the vocational education needs of these groups is encouraging cooperation among persons with special knowledge of and responsibility for related services in special education, vocational rehabilitation, and vocational education. By using a team approach, professional persons representing various disciplines can contribute their special skills to meeting the needs of the individual. A variety of vocational and related needs can be recognized and dealt with through this joint effort.

Closely related to the provision of services for the disadvantaged and the handicapped and equally significant for the educational needs of all persons is the concept of the "zero" reject. This implies that no one coming to the educational system for service should fail. No longer should the individual need to adjust to the system. On the contrary, the system should adjust to the needs of the individual, whatever they may be, so that he may achieve success in terms of his interests and capabilities. To accomplish this goal the individual and the professional personnel working with him must recognize what the obstacles are and then make sound plans to overcome them. Since the solutions to many of these problems may lie outside the province of educational experts, a team approach has been suggested; this would combine the skills of the educator with those of people in other disciplines related to the particular needs of each individual.

As the zero-reject concept is more widely accepted, education for employment will become broader and will include basic education whenever this is essential for the individual to perform successfully. There will be closer articulation between vocational education and all other areas of education. A person in the educational system moving toward the objective of occupational competency will be afforded experiences at the elementary school level which will prepare him for occupational education experiences later in his career. Similar articulation will smooth the way for further education or work after high school.

The 1968 law could well be the instrument which will galvanize the general public into action to ensure that a balanced program of education is provided which is geared to the individual's interests, needs, and abilities; to ensure that the high school student will not need to fail first before he is given an opportunity to study vocational subjects; and to ensure that the student who is not planning to attend college will receive as much consideration as has been accorded traditionally to the student who is preparing to enter college.

BIBLIOGRAPHY

AMERICAN ASSOCIATION OF SCHOOL ADMINISTRATORS. COMMISSION ON IMPERATIVES IN EDUCATION 1966 *Imperatives in Education*. Washington, D.C., The Association.

CONANT, JAMES B. 1959 *The American High School Today: A First Report to Interested Citizens*. Carnegie Series in American Education. New York, McGraw-Hill.

DRAPER, DALE CARLTON 1967 *Educating for Work*. Washington, D.C., Department of Secondary-School Principals, National Education Association.

EDMONSON, JAMES BARTLETT, JOSEPH ROEMER, AND FRANCIS BACON 1948 *The Administration of the Modern Secondary School*. New York, Macmillan.

"Education and Automation: The Coming World of Work and Leisure" 1964 National Association of Secondary-School Principals, *Bulletin*, 48, no. 295:entire issue.

KELLER, FRANKLIN J. 1955 *The Comprehensive High School*. New York, Harper.

MAYS, ARTHUR B. 1948 *Principles and Practices of Vocational Education*. New York, McGraw-Hill.

NATIONAL SOCIETY FOR THE STUDY OF EDUCATION. COMMITTEE ON THE CHANGING AMERICAN SCHOOL 1966 *The Changing American School*. Sixty-fifth Yearbook, Part 2. Edited by John I. Goodlad et al. University of Chicago Press.

NATIONAL SOCIETY FOR THE STUDY OF EDUCATION. COMMITTEE ON VOCATIONAL EDUCATION 1965 *Vocational Education*. Sixty-fourth Yearbook, Part 1. Edited by Melvin L. Barlow et al. University of Chicago Press.

ROBERTS, ROY W. 1957 *Vocational and Practical Arts Education*. Exploration Series in Education. New York, Harper.

The Transition From School to Work 1968 A report based on the Princeton Manpower Symposium, May 9-10, 1968, organized by the U.S. Department of Labor, U.S. Department of Health, Education, and Welfare, National Manpower Policy Task Force, and The Woodrow Wilson School and the Industrial Relations Section. Princeton, N.J., Princeton University.

U.S. CONGRESS. SENATE. COMMITTEE ON LABOR AND PUBLIC WELFARE 1968 *Notes and Working Papers Concerning Administration of Programs Authorized Under Vocational Education Act of 1963, Public Law 88–210, as Amended*. Prepared for the Subcommittee on Education, March 1968. 90th Cong., 2nd sess. Washington, D.C., Government Printing Office.

U.S. OFFICE OF EDUCATION 1963 *Education for a Changing World of Work: Report of the Panel of Consultants on Vocational Education*. OE–80021. Washington, D.C., Government Printing Office.

U.S. OFFICE OF EDUCATION 1966 *Administration of Vocational Education*. Vocational Education Bulletin No. 1. Washington, D.C., Government Printing Office.

VENN, GRANT 1964 *Man, Education, and Work: Postsec-ondary, Vocational and Technical Education.* Washington, D.C., American Council on Education.

"Vocational Education: Time for Decision" 1965 National Association of Secondary-School Principals, *Bulletin,* 49, no. 301:entire issue.

EDWIN L. RUMPF

2. POSTSECONDARY TECHNICAL TRAINING

Technical education programs have an occupational orientation and are intended to augment the manipulative skills of an individual planning to enter the world of work. Technical education is training for those occupations which are oriented toward engineering, manufacturing, and industry. With the emergence of a broader definition of technical education supported by federal legislation and with the new urgency in many fields to adapt business procedures along technological lines, technical education has broadened its scope to include not only the fields of engineering, manufacturing, science, and research but also business, the health industry, agriculture, and the distributive occupations. Many new kinds of occupations have appeared which involve few, if any, manipulative skills but which require high levels of specialized technical knowledge. Combinations of two broad fields—for example, agriculture and distribution—result in technical types of occupations which relate to both fields, such as agribusiness technician jobs. Other combinations, such as business and industry, industry and the health fields, and distribution and metallurgy, are revealing new types of technical education needs which, in turn, lead to new classifications of technical occupations.

History. Technical education in the United States began in the early 1800's, when several large cities and some universities provided specialized educational opportunities to enable young men to prepare for the mechanical arts. With the passage of the Morrill Act in 1862, land-grant colleges were established, and public attention was directed toward the need to prepare individuals for responsibilities in the rapidly growing industrial society.

The Morrill Act did much to make the country aware of the need for individuals capable of assuming the responsibilities of designing, building, and staffing for the emerging industrial nation. Most of the institutions of higher education that received encouragement at the time and which engaged in education for the agricultural

and mechanical arts were two-year postsecondary schools. These schools served a rather small enrollment compared to the traditional four-year institutions. Growth of technical education programs was slow, largely because the status and respectability of technical education was slow in developing. The dominant role of the liberal arts curricula relegated technical education to a secondary position in the public consideration, and to a considerable degree this situation has persisted up to the present day.

Post-World War I. Technical education also received considerable stimulus from the Smith-Hughes Act of 1917. With the rapid growth of industry in the country during World War I and with the increasing need for skilled personnel, some of the secondary schools that received federal reimbursement funds under the Smith-Hughes Act used these funds to develop technical occupational training for high school youth. Technical high schools sprang up in many of the large cities.

The Soviet launching of Sputnik 1 in 1957 forcefully directed the attention of the United States to the urgent need for more technically trained personnel. The U.S. Office of Education (USOE), through its Trade and Industrial Education branch of the Vocational Education Division, called a national conference in 1957 to plan for and organize technical education opportunities in the schools. Vocational education personnel from each of the states were invited to participate and to assist in the development of a philosophy of technical education for the future. The conference stimulated extensive action on the part of the states directed toward developing technical education at the secondary and postsecondary levels. Even as late as 1957, technical education still had reference largely to the fields of research, science, manufacturing, and industry, and little attention had been given to the other fields of business, health, agriculture, and distribution.

National Defense Education Act. The urgent need for technically trained personnel received the attention of Congress in 1958 with the passage of the National Defense Education Act (NDEA). This act emphasized the need for public awareness of and action on those phases of education which concerned the sciences and the technical elements of education. As a result of the efforts of the American Vocational Association, the USOE, and the American Technical Education Association, the 1958 act provided funds for stimulating technical education on both the secondary and postsecondary levels and fostered a national awareness of the possibilities of area vocational programs and area vocational institutions.

The act specified that the instruction offered must be of a technical nature and in the interest of the national defense. The technician-training phases of the NDEA had an immediate impact upon public school education. Postsecondary technical education, which had long been struggling for recognition, became energized. Programs of instruction were expanded, and enrollments grew rapidly. In the secondary education programs emphasis was again placed upon technician training for occupations of a technical nature, and rapid growth occurred in programs for such areas as mechanical drafting, architectural drafting, industrial electricity, and industrial chemistry. Area vocational schools on the pattern established by several highly industrial northeastern states were analyzed, and the pattern was adapted to the needs of other localities. The passage of the NDEA was thus the turning point in the public and governmental philosophical and financial support for technical education.

Program growth.   As of 1968, technician education programs in secondary schools had enrollments of 36,286 in full-time day school programs and 104,746 in postsecondary programs. The number of technical education schools had increased from 405 in 1963 to 1,697 in 1968, and it was estimated that 1975 enrollments would triple the 1968 levels and require approximately 1,900 new vocational-technical school (U.S. Department of Health . . . 1970).

The growth in need for technically trained personnel has been apparent since the 1920's. However, during the 1960's, increasing industrialization, the introduction of many more labor-saving devices, and the appearance of new products and new processes as a result of advances in electronics, pneumatics, and hydraulics resulted in pyramiding requirements for technically trained personnel. The age of automation and of tape-controlled and computer-controlled living will unquestionably require greater numbers of technicians in the future.

All of these factors have produced a decline in the number of jobs requiring manipulative skills. Many of these hand skills can be more rapidly,

accurately, and economically performed by automated equipment. Manpower is thereby released for training in other technical areas. For example, a need exists for engineering support personnel and support technicians for research and development. In the rapidly expanding health field many different kinds of technicians are needed for work in hospital laboratories, operating rooms, and medical and dental complexes. Business, with its rapidly expanding adaptation of the computer to problems of inventory, sales, and distribution, also requires greater numbers of technically trained people. Efforts are being made by technical education facilities, both public and private, to accommodate these growing needs.

Areas served.   Technical education serves many levels of employment and many kinds of individuals. Young men and women in secondary and postsecondary schools prepare for technical occupations on a variety of levels; employed persons who require updating and upgrading of their occupational skills attend institutions which provide technical instruction.

For many years industrial apprentices had received their technical instruction in secondary-level institutions largely because they entered employment prior to graduation from a high school program. Now, with many industries requiring apprentices to have a high school diploma, the need exists for a higher level of technical instruction. Thus, many apprentices complete their technical instruction in postsecondary institutions and move toward an associate degree. Extensive adult education programs for the updating and upgrading of technical skills are offered in the area vocational-technical programs, technical institutes, and community and junior colleges. In an effort to serve these employed adults, single courses, series of courses, and entire programs of technical education are offered at the convenience of the enrollees. Programs are conducted in the late afternoons and evenings, and often the adults in these programs outnumber the full-time day school enrollees.

Program duration and structure.   Because the meaning of technical education has expanded so considerably since the early 1960's, technical instruction must be offered on many different levels to meet many different needs. For example, some technicians employed in laboratories have relatively simple routine tasks to perform, yet they are called technicians. The preparatory technical education for individuals who fill these kinds of low-level technical occupations is one of short duration. Indeed, technical programs for certain types of laboratory activities may be as short as six months. Other kinds of technical occupations require extended periods of training, and in the secondary schools this period may be as much as four years. Thus, in several of the technical high schools in large cities, programs which prepare mechanical draftsmen, industrial electronics technicians, and similarly skilled personnel start in grade 9 and often continue through the 13th year.

In postsecondary technical education, efforts are made to keep instruction to the two-year time limit of a junior college, a community college, or a technical institute. Graduates from such two-year programs generally earn an associate degree, and about 25 percent of those completing such programs go on to four-year institutions and complete work for a baccalaureate degree. Under funds provided by the federal government through its several vocational acts, technical programs are conducted on the secondary level in comprehensive high schools, in area vocational schools or service centers, and in vocational high schools.

Technical education has grown rapidly on the secondary level. Area vocational programs or service centers provide both vocational and technical occupational training for a region, and enrollees, who attend on a half-day basis, are students from cooperating high schools, counties, or school districts. The initial costs of construction and the recurring costs of instruction are shared by the cooperating school districts. The regionalization of the technical education offerings makes possible a wider selection of technical occupations to students.

The same regionalization principle has been carried over into the postsecondary field, and many postsecondary area technical education centers and area vocational-technical centers have been established. Postsecondary technician training is often provided within the operational structures of junior and community colleges. These institutions used to restrict their instruction to the academic or college transfer program. With the growing need for technically trained personnel, however, and with the need for technically prepared people to staff posts in the other business, agriculture, and health segments of the economy, such institutions have begun to broaden their programs to include occupational training as one of their most important branches of instruction.

Efforts have been made to allot all technical education to the postsecondary level, but much doubt exists that individual needs or the manpower needs for technically trained personnel can be successfully met by this effort alone. Since the greater proportion of enrollees in vocational-technical programs are drawn from the lowest socioeconomic strata of society, the delay in offering technical education until the postsecondary years would tend to lose qualified young people, particularly at a time when their motivations are highest and the needs of the economy are greatest. Hence, it appears that in the foreseeable future technical education will continue to be offered on both secondary and postsecondary levels.

The USOE reports that in 1966 only 7.2 percent of all of those individuals served by any kind of occupational training were accommodated by postsecondary institutions and that by 1975 the projected percentage would be only 8.7 percent (U.S. Department of Health . . . 1968). On the other hand, it was also reported that the secondary institutions providing both vocational and technical education served 50 percent of all those needing occupational training (*ibid.*), and this percentage is expected to be maintained through 1975.

Specialized programs. One of the areas that has received concentrated attention from a variety of professional groups is the engineering-oriented technician-training programs. These programs provide the support personnel for engineers, research personnel, and scientists. The program of instruction for these individuals consists primarily of applied mathematics and science. Graduates of such programs are called engineering aides, technicians, or engineering technicians. Their responsibilities largely involve acting as a liaison between the engineers and craftsmen or between research personnel in an industry and the production and manufacturing personnel. The postsecondary institutions that provide this kind of instruction tend to recruit engineers as teachers and to relate the programs of instruction closely to the engineering profession. The Engineers Council for Professional Development takes an unusual interest in the development of the engineering-technician programs and functions as an accrediting agency.

Since private technical institutes and institutes of mechanical technology and mechanic arts were in existence for many years prior to public school involvement in technical education, these private schools and a few universities have taken a proprietary interest in technical education. Believing that the preparation of the engineering technician is largely one which should be reserved to specialized institutions, representatives of the private schools and universities made strong representations before Congress when the 1963 Vocational Education Act was being discussed in congressional committees. The opposition by these private-interest groups was shortsighted, however, since the need for technically trained personnel has continued to grow steadily, and there is little likelihood that even with the prospect of new institutions and new programs of technical education the manpower needs for technicians will be met.

Issues and problems. The issues and problems which face technical education today are much like those which have been associated with it from its inception.

Status. The primary problem is that the vocational-technical education curricula traditionally have been regarded as secondary in importance to the academic curricula. Efforts are being made to establish their equality with other forms of education. Part of this striving for status and recognition may be noted in the efforts of many postsecondary institutions to be included within such accreditation procedures as are generally accorded the regular academic institutions. The American Vocational Association, coordinating its accreditation activities with those of the National Commission on Accrediting and its affiliated regional accrediting associations, has done much to promote acceptance of the concept that vocational education, as a fundamental segment of all education, must be accorded the same treatment in the matter of accreditation as that enjoyed by other academic institutions. The American Vocational Association sees the acquisition of accreditation by vocational-technical schools as one of its major thrusts in the 1970's. Status, recognition, and the possibility of accreditation have caused many of the high school-level technical programs to evolve into postsecondary education, and by the same token some two-year technical education

programs have been tending toward four-year college programs. Future efforts will be made to stabilize the drive toward recognition and accreditation in the hope that the movement will not by its own momentum project institutions into the four-year category.

Enrollees. With the acceptance of technical education as a valid form of education and as an area whose status is equal to that of academic education will come a change in the number and quality of enrollees. The bulk of the students in vocational and technical education have been drawn from the lowest socioeconomic strata of society. They have generally been the children of workers rather than of professional men. With adequate recognition for technical education, this situation could change and with it could come a tremendous growth in enrollments. Also, broadening the concept of technical education to include the preparation of highly skilled personnel for fields other than industry, manufacturing, science, and research creates the likelihood that children from middle-class and upper-class families may in time enroll in the technician education programs offered in the fields of business, agriculture, distribution, health, and others.

Funding. With the passage of the Vocational Education Act of 1963, federal funds to build and house the educational programs required for technical education were available for the first time. Area schools committed to vocational and technical education were constructed. With the passage of the 1968 Vocational Education Amendments, further expansion was encouraged and greater appropriations were authorized to provide for the operation of buildings and programs.

Also included in the 1968 amendments were provisions for the preparation of teachers, supervisors, and administrators. Staffing such programs has presented perplexing problems, and with the rapid growth of institutions of technical education in the future, the staffing problem will become even more significant.

The 1968 amendments provide many opportunities for creative thinking and innovations that should bring greater assurances of success to the technical education movement. The possibility that secondary-level technical education may be used as preparation for postsecondary technical education was written into the new amendments. In the past secondary-level technical education had to provide a terminal job for each enrollee, although the instruction might at times have been such that the graduate could have gone on to an institution of higher learning. The 1968 amendments make it possible for a day-school student to enroll in a secondary school program, knowing in advance that upon graduation he would go on to postsecondary technical education in a technical institute, community college, or area vocational-technical school. The results of such a procedure may mean that many more enrollees will be motivated to seek postsecondary technical education.

Cooperative programs. Several other issues and problems challenge the growth of technical education. The costs of equipping a program of technical education in a technical institute, a community college, a technical education center, or a technical service center are high. Maintaining the currency of equipment is also expensive. The total costs involved represent more of an expense for the public institutions than the tax base can usually withstand. Hence, more attention must be given to the establishment of cooperative technical education. Students might thereby receive much of their laboratory experience on a part-time basis during employment in the field, while reserving the classroom and technical education aspects of their programs to the home institution. This structure would eliminate the need for elaborately equipped laboratories in such areas as metal work, electronics, and chemical unit operations. The skills and knowledge generally acquired in expensively equipped laboratories would be provided and underwritten by the industries in the vicinity of the technical center, with the result that many more programs might be started.

Cooperative education has long been a successful form of vocational and technical education, and joining the professional and the private sectors of the economy into a single cooperative effort may provide the solution to meeting the costs of technical preparation. To stimulate and encourage cooperative enterprises, the 1968 amendments make it possible for cooperating employers to be reimbursed by the government for their training costs.

Gaps. Another problem facing technical education is the serious gaps in the structure of technical education. The present high school programs emphasize preparation for the college-bound student, and to some extent this situation is replicated in the postsecondary junior and community colleges. Technical education offerings oriented toward the world of work are not always available for many of the young people who wish this kind of instruction. Unless steps are taken in many of the comprehensive institutions, both secondary and postsecondary, many people will not receive the type and quality of technical education they desire. The problem involves the entire educational establishment, and certain philosophic modifications must occur before equal emphasis is placed upon preparation for work and preparation for higher education.

Organizational patterns. There are many school districts which cannot alone support adequate programs of technical education on the secondary or postsecondary levels. Because of the rather rigid organizational patterns under which school districts operate, the likelihood of adjacent or contiguous school districts coordinating their educational needs and efforts to promote a common institution is remote. The organizational patterns of the school systems in many instances are the crux of the problem, and until steps are taken to eliminate some of the antiquated operational patterns, the preparation of technicians on a national scope will be retarded. These steps would require changes in the school district regulations to permit consolidation or regionalization and would necessitate a commitment on the part of school administrators and school boards to organize their schools for better service to the enrollees.

Curriculum patterns. In the past curriculum patterns for technical education were geared largely to individual occupations or to clusters of occupations. The continuation of this procedure will present certain difficulties, since the instructional areas included in mechanical, electrical, construction, electronic, civil, and nuclear engineering technologies have many elements in common. Although the needs of the several professions are different, the technical subject matter is similar enough to warrant a core approach. Further broadening of the technologies into clusters and the adjustment of the curricula to accommodate the cluster trend would further implement the development of technical education. The core approach would be especially effective in less populated areas, where adequate enrollments for several different technical areas of instruction are difficult to assemble on a continuing basis.

BIBLIOGRAPHY

U.S. DEPARTMENT OF HEALTH, EDUCATION, AND WELFARE
1968 *Vocational and Technical Education, Annual Report, Fiscal Year 1966.* Washington, D.C., Government Printing Office.

U.S. DEPARTMENT OF HEALTH, EDUCATION, AND WELFARE
1970 *Vocational and Technical Education, Annual Report, Fiscal Year 1968.* Washington, D. C., Government Printing Office.

JOSEPH T. NERDEN

3. CURRICULUM TRENDS

Vocational curricula derive from the needs of the times. They are organized to provide learning experiences for those who would prepare themselves for employment in a particular field of endeavor. In the development of curricula it is necessary to consider social and technological change and the effects these have upon occupations and preparation for entry to them. For the purposes of this article, the term "curriculum" will include curriculum materials—described in the Vocational Education Amendments of 1968 as "materials consisting of a series of courses to cover instruction in any occupational field in vocational education which are designed to prepare persons for employment at the entry level or to upgrade occupational competencies of those previously or presently employed in any occupational field" (P. L. 90–576).

Developments before World War II. Organized curriculum development at public expense started with the effort of the Federal Board for Vocational Education to develop instructional materials immediately after the passage of the Smith-Hughes Act in 1917. Curricula for vocational education did not exist prior to that time. They had to be created. Whereas the first of these were responsive to the training needs of World War I, the content of later instructional materials reflected the requirements of the schools as the federal board saw them at the time.

The Smith-Hughes Act provided authority for the federal government to assist the states in the promotion of vocational education and in the training of teachers in agricultural, trade, industrial, and home economics subjects. Under the provisions of the act vocational education was to be an integral part of the public school system in the United States. It was to be part of a well-rounded program of studies aimed at developing competent workers and citizens. Programs were to be administered by state boards for vocational education.

The 1917 act placed on the Federal Board for Vocational Education the duty of making studies, investigations, and reports which could be used to aid the states in the establishment of vocational schools and classes, thus ensuring curricula that were realistic at that time. One purpose in granting federal aid for vocational education was to secure the establishment of practical standards of vocational education and to stimulate the states to accept these standards.

Therefore, it is not surprising that in a statement of its policies in 1917, the Federal Board for Vocational Education emphasized the fact that vocational schools and classes were not fostered under the Smith-Hughes Act for the purpose of giving instruction to retarded, incorrigible, or otherwise subnormal individuals; instead, such schools and classes were to be established and maintained for the explicit purpose of giving thorough vocational instruction to healthy, normal individuals so that they might be prepared for profitable and efficient employment. The federal board aided the states in establishing vocational education and in giving instruction in vocational subjects by issuing bulletins, circulars, and announcements dealing with the various phases of studies carried on in its research department. These efforts are still continued to some extent. The more recent publications have been curriculum guides useful at all levels.

For many years vocational courses were organized to give dominance to one subject or group of experiences—such as shop experiences, drawing, science, or mathematics. The experiences, items of information, or topics in the predominant subject were arranged in some effective order of progression. It was believed that subject matter should be arranged to give, at the time each job was taught, the drawing, the sciences, and the mathematics required for the successful performance of the job.

For many years curricula published by the federal board and later by the U.S. Office of Education (USOE), with which it was merged in 1933, outlined the manipulative and technical instructional material which the student, apprentice, or journeyman worker should master for his trade. No attempt was made to detail the various job procedures, but for each job outlined, operational and technical information was presented. The publications were not intended to be used for self-instruction by students but were to be used by competent vocational instructors as manuals to assist them in better organizing their methods of instruction. This method of organizing instructional material in vocational education is still used in the suggested curriculum guides published by the Division of Vocational and Technical Education of the USOE.

Fundamental to developing courses of study in vocational education was the job analysis. As a preliminary step in outlining suggested courses of instruction in a trade, an analysis was made to classify similar jobs in the occupation. This analysis was not in any sense a course of study or plan of instruction; it was merely an inventory of many of the jobs in the trade and included the technical information that was necessary for each job. The technical information and manipulative skills listed in the analysis were to be acquired by the student during his learning period. When the jobs listed in the inventory were properly grouped and outlined, the classification that resulted could be used as the basis for courses of instruction to meet special training conditions for almost any training situation or trainee.

In 1935 the Division of Vocational and Technical Education of the USOE undertook the preparation of outlines of instruction, covering a selected number of occupations and subjects, for use by the educational advisers and instructors in Civilian Conservation Corps camps. For this purpose a small committee was formed consisting of persons experienced in analyzing occupations for teaching content and in planning lessons in vocational subjects. This was the typical way of preparing curriculum materials in vocational education. The committee made a study of the specific requirements of a number of Civilian Conservation Corps camps in order to determine the kind of material most needed. Numerous trips were made to the camps and advice was sought from individuals actively engaged in different phases of the conservation work-program. Two types of instructional material were selected to meet this need: a manual for instructors and outlines of instruction in 15 occupations and subjects (Civilian Conservation Corps 1935).

In the preparation of the outlines no attempt was made to provide informational subject matter. It was assumed that the instructor would be an experienced workman who already knew his trade and only needed assistance in organizing the subject matter and suggestions as to methods of teaching. The outlines provided typical lesson analyses useful to the instructors as guides for

teaching or as guides for the preparation of instructional outlines covering occupations not included in the series prepared by the committee.

War efforts. From 1940 to 1945 the public vocational schools conducted short, single-skill training programs for many thousands of industrial workers. Because the war required the emergency training of nearly 7½ million persons who would go directly into production, it was necessary for vocational schools to revise their instructional practices and also to develop suitable instructional materials. A practical approach influenced the development of both instructional practices and materials. Units of instruction were planned to include processes and information required in the actual industrial job, while instructional methods were adapted to the particular production procedure in the industry for which the workers were being trained.

The U.S. Office of Education set up the Instructional Materials Section to aid the states in the development, coordination, and distribution of instructional materials. The states, too, cooperated with each other in the development and dissemination of instructional materials. When two or more states had a mutual need for certain types of instructional material, they pooled their efforts in conducting such projects. Curriculum laboratories were established where necessary in both state and local programs; some of these are still in operation.

The preparation of instructional materials in curriculum laboratories was an outstanding development of the program known as Vocational Training for War Production Workers. Each state had the opportunity to secure promptly the most up-to-date material developed anywhere in the program. Moreover, the material was specifically for war training purposes under specially selected conditions. The states helped one another and benefited greatly from the materials developed in these curriculum laboratories. A pattern for planning and cooperation had been established.

Panel of consultants. In 1961, President John F. Kennedy requested the appointment of an advisory body to be charged with the responsibility of reviewing and evaluating the current vocational education acts and making recommendations for improving and redirecting the program. This advisory body, which came to be known as the Panel of Consultants on Vocational Education, made its report late in 1962.

In reporting on their inquiry into curriculum

and instructional materials, the panel members noted the complicated system which exists in vocational education because of the wide range of occupational fields in the total program.

The panel found that various responsibilities for curriculum development existed at federal, state, and local levels. The federal government had responsibility for gathering and disseminating information concerning curriculum materials contemplated or under way. It also had the responsibility for coordinating projects in this field which were subsidized by federal funds so that unnecessary duplication of effort could be avoided and new fields might be developed. Its primary function was coordination of effort.

The state education agency, the panel reported, had the responsibility of coordinating work in curriculum development within the state. It could also undertake the task of specific curriculum development where special needs were present.

The panel found several agencies and organizations active in curriculum development. The armed forces developed instructional material for their own use in training military and civilian personnel; some of the material had direct application for use in vocational schools. Manufacturers of tools, machines, and technical equipment had done much. Education agencies contributed a great variety of materials ranging from simple materials prepared by course instructors and duplicated within the school to comprehensive manuals published in quantity and made available to institutions throughout the United States. Much of the locally prepared material was prepared to meet local needs, and frequently the quality of its content and reproduction process was poor.

Further, the panel stated that a considerable number of commercial publishers gave attention to the needs of vocational and technical education. Some of them produced materials as part of a larger publishing program; others confined their efforts to vocational and technical education.

The panel's analysis revealed that in many states materials were developed for trade and industrial programs, mainly in instructional materials laboratories. Some made their products available to other states, while others limited the distribution of materials to schools within the state. The panel discovered a heavy concentration of effort in a relatively small number of fields; for most, commercial publications were readily available. Much duplication of material was found; this duplication indicated the need for coordination of effort on the national level. The states, however, helped to meet the need for instructional materials in programs too small to interest the commercial publishers. There was not adequate dissemination of information about the available materials at the local level; too often the instructor who might have used the materials did not know they existed. Pride of local authorship and unwillingness to use materials developed by others handicapped the distribution and use of some locally developed curriculum materials. Some of the state-produced materials used poorly planned formats, lacked sufficient illustrations, and were printed in unattractive form. The panel concluded that perhaps some of these difficulties might have been lessened if the task had been concentrated in fewer, better-equipped, and more adequately staffed laboratories.

Recommendations. The panel recommended that the production of instructional materials for vocational courses be recognized as vital to an effective national program and that

(1) One or more instructional material laboratories be established to produce and distribute vocational instructional materials; (2) It be a responsibility of the Office of Education to (a) Establish and administer instructional materials laboratories through contractual arrangements with a State department of education, a college, a university, or a large school district; (b) Develop policies for the operation, coordination between centers, production of the materials, and distribution of materials produced in these centers; (c) Finance the operation of these centers; (3) An adequate quantity and an appropriate quality of instructional supplies, tools, instruments, and equipment be recognized as essential to good instruction. (U.S. Office of Education 1963, pp. 240–241)

The Vocational Education Act of 1963 contains many provisions which were, in fact, recommendations from the report of the panel of consultants. However, although the act authorized funds to be expended for the acquisition, maintenance, and repair of instructional supplies, teaching aids, and equipment, no specific amounts were stipulated by the statute. Largely because of this, little progress was observed in implementing the recommendations of the panel concerning curriculum materials in vocational education.

However, the emphasis in vocational education

was changed from occupational training as such to training and retraining in any occupation which would serve the needs of the people.

Curriculum guides. From 1963 to 1969 the Curriculum–Instructional Materials Section of the Division of Vocational and Technical Education of the USOE developed a number of suggested curriculum guides designed to meet the needs of schools which were to conduct programs in new and relatively less attended courses. Subject matter was selected on the basis of national need as perceived by the program specialists employed in the vocational division, and guides were developed for such topics as grain, feed, seed, and farm supplies technology; planning and organizing an export trade education program; organizing a dental assistant training program; hotel and motel housekeeping; instrumentation and automatic control; vending machine repairs; and water and waste-water technology.

Typically, these curriculum guides were jointly developed by a large number of specialists in vocational education. The need for a particular curriculum was agreed upon only after a canvass of state requirements by staff experts. For example, to publish a postsecondary curriculum guide in a particular technology would require the advice and counsel of a specialist in technical education, a specialist in the administration of post-secondary programs, a curriculum specialist, an education editor, a contract officer, and the chief of the organizational unit responsible for curriculum development in the vocational division. A decision would be reached as to which qualified institution or author was to prepare the manuscript. Contractual arrangements would be made, and ultimately a manuscript would be received by the USOE. The manuscript would then be edited for conformity with the government style manual and other vocational education publications, corrections would be made, and a committee of experts would review it for suitability, level of difficulty, and probable acceptance by instructors in the field. The ensuing publication would be distributed in limited quantities to the states for such utilization as vocational education authorities saw fit.

National curriculum clinic. In 1967 vocational education specialists concerned with curriculum development met in Kansas City, Mo., at the National Curriculum Materials Clinic sponsored by the USOE. A number of recommendations were made for curriculum development programs which would meet the needs of the 1970's. It was suggested that the USOE develop broad guidelines for state curriculum development activities, for which materials would be produced by the coordinated efforts of educators and representatives of the private sector; that each of the states designate a person with responsibility for liaison with other states and the USOE; that regional clinics be held so that teacher educators and local and state personnel could participate in the preparation of instructional materials; that instructors be aided in obtaining greater insight into the teaching-learning process and the function of instructional materials; and that curriculum guides be accompanied by materials which would aid teachers of special groups, such as older workers and the disadvantaged, to accommodate to the needs of these students (U.S. Office of Education. Bureau of Adult, Vocational, and Library Programs 1967).

Advisory council. The Vocational Education Act of 1963 provided for the appointment of the Advisory Council on Vocational Education to review the administration of programs conducted under the vocational education acts and to make recommendations for improvements. The council's report contains numerous references to curriculum as well as recommendations for improvements (U.S. Office of Education. Advisory Council on Vocational Education 1968).

The council noted that only a few of the many suggested curriculum guides had been printed. Curtailment of the funds authorized by the 1963 act limited the ability of the USOE to develop new curricula for use by the states. The council found that there was an increase in the number of curriculum specialists employed at the state level; however, in spite of the encouragement provided by Congress, many states had done little or nothing in this area on an organized basis. Many local school districts reported the development of new courses; for the most part these were based on the traditional occupational categories. While it was clear that some progress had been made in curriculum development since 1963, it fell far short of meeting the nation's needs. Noting the paucity of curriculum development efforts, the council stated, "Probably 10 times as much money has been spent on curriculum materials for physics (taken by 5 percent of the high school students) as has been spent on the 100 or more occupations commonly taught in vocational education" (U.S. Office of Education. Advisory Council on Vocational Education 1968, pp. 389–390).

The advisory council observed that there was a trend toward greater individualization of instruction and that programs which separated vocational and general education detracted from both; when they were brought together they served to improve and enhance each other. The council noted significant objectives and assumptions in vocational education: that in planning, the fact must be accepted that not all students learn in the same way, nor will they learn the same things under the same circumstances; that program planning must be done on the assumption that "schools fail students" rather than that "students fail school"; that programs should place greater responsibility upon the student for his own education and for making decisions; that more comprehensive programs are needed to accommodate a greater variety of individual needs and differences; that teachers are becoming managers of the learning environment rather than purveyors of information; that, as education, like society, becomes more complex, the team strategy for planning becomes essential; and that it must be recognized that education can no longer be planned within the confines of the school but must be coordinated with community resources and agencies.

The council made an administrative recommendation to the commissioner of education that two to four centers for curriculum development in vocational education be established. No action was taken on this recommendation.

Federal legislation. As with earlier legislation which grew out of the recommendations of advisory bodies, the Vocational Education Amendments of 1968 contained many provisions that were directly related to the recommendations of the advisory council. Congress, in the section of the law on curriculum development in vocational and technical education, provided for appropriate assistance to be given to state and local educational agencies to develop curricula for new and changing occupations and for coordinating improvements in, and dissemination of, existing curriculum materials; and it authorized generous appropriations for this purpose.

It is significant that in spite of numerous studies by government commissions and a national conference, so little has been done. These bodies have recognized the fundamental fact that cur-

riculum is basic to the teaching and learning processes in vocational education and that its importance merits national leadership.

The Vocational Education Act of 1963 provided authority for the appropriation of funds for research and certain training programs. Projects funded by the act included studies apparently directly related to present and future needs in such areas as electromechanical technology, the cluster concept in trade and industrial education, biomedical equipment technology, occupational instruction for school-alienated youth, technical training for industrial radiographers, specialized programs for poor learners for use in noneducational settings, training of personnel in health services, and the training of law enforcement officers.

A long-range project was designed in the belief by some that too many schools are unrewarding to their students, who are alienated by a series of failure experiences. Students tend to believe the learning environment is hostile and custodial rather than that it can be involving and challenging. Many teachers fail to appreciate the individual differences in students. There has been a lack of well-defined objectives, and measuring procedures are inadequate to determine whether the student has achieved those objectives which are set for him.

Federal projects. In recognition of the failure of the educational system to provide meaningful experiences for the whole student population, the U.S. Office of Education promoted the innovative Education System for the 70's, known popularly as the Organic Curriculum, where there would be no discrete demarcation between academic and skill training (Bushnell 1967). This educational design for the high school level would provide comprehensive education for all students. The graduates of the comprehensive secondary school would be as well trained vocationally and academically as those completing specialized vocational or college preparatory programs. This is a program in which all students would succeed —the curriculum would be interesting and challenging and would be built upon student motivations. The learner would start at his own level when he enters the system—computerized programming would aid in determining his level and would prescribe the educational experience to be offered next. Program objectives would be behavioral and would be stated specifically and in measurable terms. The ingredients of such a high school program would be designed so as to ensure the attainment of these objectives.

More than 16 local school districts in 13 states are experimenting with this new program. Federal support for the program was withdrawn in June 1970; the program continues under the encouragement of a nonprofit corporate identity.

Industrial programs. One of the most recent developments in occupational preparation is the expanding effort of private industry to discover procedures and techniques which are effective in helping the hard-core unemployed become self-sufficient and productive workers. While much of this kind of vocational preparation is still at the experimental level, some notable successes have been achieved by several companies. From these achievements have come some guidelines and cautions regarding training that have implications for curriculum and its use in a new instructor-student setting and relationship. It is now suggested that the scene of the learning experience be nonschool oriented; that, as with good vocational education practice, learning experiences be absolutely job related; that instruction be geared to the lowest levels of understanding among students; that modular media be utilized, with each succeeding unit reinforcing the preceding one; that all training have a discernible purpose which is related to the trainee's job; and that gradually the trainee be brought to the point where he can begin to direct his own performance in training and on the job.

One large corporation reported success in selecting, training, and holding workers formerly considered unemployable by revising a long-standing apprenticeship program in such a way that hiring standards were lowered; youth were hired on the basis of what they could do and not screened out for what they had not done in school. This more flexible employment practice required a preapprentice training program. Undereducated youth were hired who ordinarily would not have qualified. They were paid while they learned what they needed to know to bring them up to the level where they would be able to enter the skilled trades apprentice training program. The company did not lower the standards of the apprenticeship program; it opened up a new route to get into it.

This and other experiences in training the so-called unemployables caused the company to change its ideas about what constituted training.

At first the best craftsmen were assigned as instructors on the theory that the men who knew the job best could teach it best. It was discovered that the instructors were not teaching tools and tolerances. They were teaching reading, writing, and arithmetic. They had correctly sensed what was needed, but this kind of training was not their specialty. Instead, fundamental education specialists were called in to conduct two programs: the first, to raise the students' educational level to the equivalent of the fourth grade; and the second, to take them from the fifth grade through the eighth. Students attended class two hours a day for ten to 12 weeks as a part of their paid working schedule. From the day a man was hired he was working on projects that had a real purpose—not make-work projects. These helped to give him a true sense of accomplishment, and they also made it clear that the company was not patronizing him.

Programs and materials. In 1969 the vocational division of the USOE published a report of a nationwide survey of the curriculum materials available in the states which cooperated in the study. Over 800 specific curriculum titles were included with instructions for obtaining them.

At the National Conference on Curriculum Development in Vocational and Technical Education in 1969 the conferees concluded that the single most important factor which determines what will be taught is the curriculum and the materials that accompany it; that results will vary according to the teacher's ability to use the materials effectively; and that the need for rapid expansion of vocational education programs cannot be met until an adequate program of curriculum development is in continuous operation. The educators recommended that a nationwide plan for training curriculum specialists be established; that all vocational-technical curriculum materials be cataloged; that materials be made uniform in format; that information on available curricula be disseminated to all teachers; that regional and state curriculum centers which meet standards for ensuring efficiency, effectiveness, and quality of work be established and operated; that in-service training programs be developed which can be used by the states to prepare vocational-technical teachers in the better use of curriculum materials; and that plans be implemented for the coordination of all curriculum activities (Barlow et al. 1969).

Prospects. Existing curricula in vocational-technical education are inadequate to prepare workers for present and future needs. The rapid change in technology, the wider range in educational background of persons who must be trained to become employable and to progress in their occupations, and the anticipation of labor shortages as production needs and the call for services increase demand training and retraining of a different kind than had been offered previously. This cannot be accomplished without the development of new and appropriate types of curricula to serve the many varied needs of workers and employers.

In the immediate future there will be new and intensive efforts at curriculum development to serve the needs of those who have been left behind in the schools: the educationally disadvantaged, the economically disadvantaged, and the socially disadvantaged. New training schemes will be devised for older workers; for persons with physical, mental, or emotional handicaps; for school dropouts and for high school graduates who have apparently completed their formal education but have no skills to make them employable; and for persons of high intellectual capacity who are able to prepare for highly skilled technical occupations.

Attention will be given to flexible scheduling in secondary schools. This will be computer-generated: different structures may be requested for courses in each program—for example, large group lectures, shop or laboratory periods of varying lengths, small group discussions, and independent work in resource centers. These would be scheduled in modules for varying numbers of students and varying amounts of time. Flexible scheduling would thus considerably modify the sterile, restrictive, manual scheduling so prevalent in the secondary school at the present time and would open the way to student activities which previously could not be included in the school because they could not be scheduled.

Curriculum planning is now trying to fulfill such recently recognized needs as basic education which is occupationally oriented, stimulating, and of interest to those who must make decisions about their future vocational education; preoccupational curricula which would help elementary and junior high school pupils discover facts about the world of work and thus be able to make more informed educational and occupational choices; curricula which would meet the single-purpose job needs of various persons; curricula which would upgrade persons employed in lower-level entry positions, thus opening up job opportunities for those who are unemployed, underemployed, or relatively unskilled; remedial vocational education curricula which would rehabilitate dropouts, inmates of correctional institutions, and able but unmotivated persons; pretechnical curricula which would prepare those who lack some academic requirements to enter postsecondary programs; and many more high-level technical curricula which would prepare the vast number of personnel needed in present and future technical occupations.

The trend is toward more cooperative, part-time work experience programs in which full-time students at both secondary and postsecondary levels are employed part of the time in supervised work which is directly related to the in-school program of studies; the need for curricula in this work-learning situation is unlimited.

The trend is toward greater involvement of all interested parties in the development of vocational curricula—for example, the armed forces, private industry, organized labor, public and private training institutions, and scholars representing other disciplines. Public education authorities will coordinate the efforts of various agencies, arranging programs rather than merely directing vocational education.

The trend is toward increased federal-state cooperation in curriculum development and teacher utilization. Arrangements will be made for increasing federal leadership and coordination of state laboratory activities; this will promote wider use of the materials which will be produced for a greater range of areas of instruction. There will be continual in-service training of teachers in creative instructor-trainee relationships which utilize new methods and materials for improved occupational preparation.

BIBLIOGRAPHY

BARLOW, MELVIN L., DAVID ALLEN, AND JAMES R. D. EDDY 1969 *A Guide for the Development of Curriculum in Vocational and Technical Education.* A report of the National Conference on Curriculum Development in Vocational and Technical Education, Dallas, Texas, March 5–7, 1969. Los Angeles, Division of Vocational Education, University of California.

BLAUCH, LLOYD E. 1935 *Federal Cooperation in Agricultural Extension Work, Vocational Education and Rehabilitation.* U.S. Office of Education Bulletin 1933, No. 15. Washington, D.C., Government Printing Office.

BUSHNELL, DAVID S. 1967 *An Education System for the 70's.* Washington, D.C., Aerospace Education Foundation Conference.

CIVILIAN CONSERVATION CORPS 1935 *Instructor's Manual and Outlines of Instruction.* Vocational Series Manual and Outlines Nos. 1–15. Washington, D.C., Government Printing Office.

COMMISSION ON NATIONAL AID TO VOCATIONAL EDUCATION 1914 *Report.* Vol. 1. Washington, D.C., Government Printing Office.

FEDERAL BOARD FOR VOCATIONAL EDUCATION 1917 *Statement of Policies.* Bulletin No. 1. Washington, D.C., Government Printing Office.

MALLORY, BERENICE 1964 "Curriculum Developments." National Association of Secondary-School Principals, *Bulletin*, 48, no. 296:51–65.

McGARVEY, GEORGE A. 1940 *Bricklaying, an Analysis of the Trade.* U.S. Office of Education Vocational Division Bulletin No. 208, Trade and Industrial Series No. 60. Washington, D.C., Government Printing Office.

MUSSER, W. DANIEL 1946 *Vocational Training for War Production Workers.* U.S. Office of Education Bulletin 1946, No. 10. Washington, D.C., Government Printing Office.

U.S. OFFICE OF EDUCATION 1963 *Education for a Changing World of Work: Report of the Panel of Consultants on Vocational Education.* OE–80021. Washington, D.C., Government Printing Office.

U.S. OFFICE OF EDUCATION. ADVISORY COUNCIL ON VOCATIONAL EDUCATION 1968 *Vocational Education: The Bridge Between Man and His Work.* Washington, D.C., Government Printing Office.

U.S. OFFICE OF EDUCATION. BUREAU OF ADULT, VOCATIONAL, AND LIBRARY PROGRAMS 1967 *National Curriculum Materials Clinic: Vocational and Technical Education, Manpower Development and Training Education.* Kansas City, Mo., January 17–19, 1967. Washington, D.C., Government Printing Office.

WRIGHT, J. C. 1926 *The Supervision of Vocational Education.* New York, Wiley.

LANE C. ASH

VOCATIONAL EDUCATION RESEARCH

The role of research and development in vocational and technical education has been paradoxical. Probably more than any other type of education, vocational education must have the systematic capacity for changing its structure, content, and procedures to accommodate changing occupational and societal requirements. Traditionally, however, the field has been characterized by its emphasis on practice and experience. There has been neither a scientific tradition nor a system for planned change.

Background. The Smith-Hughes Act of 1917 and the George-Barden Act of 1946 provided the means for developing a research and development system for vocational education on a scale equal to the agricultural, medical, and other research traditions. Unfortunately, adequate investments in vocational education were not made. What modest funds were allocated were focused primarily on operations research designed to answer social bookkeeping questions rather than to resolve fundamental problems and enhance the knowledge base.

For most of the duration of reimbursed vocational education, the government, particularly the U.S. Office of Education (USOE), has not been especially active in the areas of research activity, employing research personnel, disseminating research results, and encouraging and coordinating research in the states. This passive attitude was expressive of limited faith in the utility of research for vocational education; thus, there was inadequate commitment to invest the funds needed for the development of a more viable and pervasive research and development capability.

Regrettably, there still exists a widespread misunderstanding of research and development—its capacity and its limitations. The beliefs remain that research can produce instant answers, that researchers work in isolation from real world problems, and that there is inadequate interaction between research producers and consumers. This state of affairs, however, is not unique to vocational and technical education.

Research in vocational and technical education is characterized by problems and constraints similar to those of research in the field of general education. While promising advances have been made in recent years, elements of research and development activities are still characterized by insular, sporadic, and fragmented efforts devoid of a theoretical base or a conceptual framework. The research team and interservice and interdisciplinary research are more the exceptions than the rule. Effective experimentation and pilot programs are often lacking. Demonstrations and other dissemination techniques are not adequately provided or articulated. Sustained programmatic efforts are limited. The long-range planning, systematic coordination, and effective communication needed to secure an additive effect through research and development efforts are too often absent.

Until the provision of research and development funds under the Vocational Education Act of 1963, a majority of the research was conducted by graduate students who, at best, were interns and not qualified researchers. Too often their studies were descriptive and superficial. Perhaps even more important were the limitations of problem selection. In too many instances, problems selected were isolated or localized and concentrated on the past rather than the future; they were, therefore, insignificant in terms of their implications for improving programs or contributing to a knowledge base.

Federal intervention. Because earlier vocational education legislation permitted only limited investments in research and development, little was accomplished in relation to the gross needs of an increasingly complex and interrelated economy and society. Recognizing these historical deficiencies, Congress included in the Vocational Education Act of 1963 provisions for developing a sustained research and development thrust in vocational education. Specifically, the act authorized 10 percent of the new funds for use by the U.S. commissioner of education to make grants for research and experimental, developmental, pilot, and training programs.

The allotment to the states permitted funds to be used for ancillary services and activities to ensure quality in vocational education programs (including experimental programs), development of instructional materials, and periodic evaluations. Unfortunately, limited investments were made and few programs were initiated. The 1968 Vocational Education Amendments provided for a 10 percent authorization of research and development moneys. These funds were divided, half going to the commissioner and half to the states for research and development activities. This authorization, if adequately funded, should permit continued emphasis on projects and programs of national significance at the same time that it will facilitate the growth of research and development at the state level.

Despite erratic appropriations by Congress for the research and development portion of the act, some progress has been made in developing research, development, dissemination, and training capacities in vocational education at the state and national levels.

Research and development centers. There was widespread support for the establishment of national research and development centers. The U.S. President's Panel of Consultants on Vocational Education recommended the establishment of centers, and the American Vocational Association in 1963 passed a resolution calling for the establishment of a national center. With the active support of the assistant commissioner for vocational education, a national center for research and leadership development in vocational and technical education was established at Ohio State University in 1965. A second center, the Center for Occupational Education at North Carolina State University at Raleigh, was established in the same year.

The Center for Vocational and Technical Education at Ohio State University is engaged in six major areas: state leadership in vocational-technical education, curriculum development in vocational-technical education, vocational-technical teacher education, vocational-technical education for the occupationally disadvantaged, vocational development and adjustment, and the change process in vocational and technical education.

The program of the Center for Occupational Education at North Carolina State University at Raleigh focuses on the following areas: occupational adjustment in the South, shaping flexible vocational behavior of youth, policies and policymaking for occupational education, development of professional personnel, evaluation of occupational education, and occupational education for areas in economic transition.

State research coordinating units. For states to meet the challenge of providing adequate vocational programs, the need existed for systematic coordination and exploitation of each state's research and development capacities. Accordingly, in 1965 the commissioner of education sent a memorandum to state departments of education and universities asking them to submit proposals for establishing state research coordinating units.

The call for the establishment of research coordinating units for vocational education in the states represented an attempt to meet congressional criticisms, one of which was that research in vocational education was sporadic, uncoordinated, and directed chiefly toward program operation (Goldhammer et al. 1969). The invitation to submit proposals was accepted by 25 states and prompted 22 additional states to establish research coordinating units.

A 1965 statement of the role of the research coordinating units identified the following broad objectives:

(1) To build an atmosphere within a state that is receptive to research—especially

among state staff, school leaders, and government legislators;

(2) To stimulate projects, ideas, and understanding of research;

(3) To provide leadership in research-related activities, such as seminars and special conferences;

(4) To coordinate state education research efforts in the state agency and with other state government and professional agencies and professions;

(5) To serve as consultants on research ideas and projects that forward vocational education;

(6) To disseminate information that enables others to utilize recent research findings;

(7) To identify research training needs and personnel;

(8) To work toward the identification of basic issues and problems needing research;

(9) To develop long-range plans for research;

(10) To gather or assist in gathering needed data for a potentially computer-based system of educational information; and

(11) To work closely with research and development centers and with U.S. Office of Education (USOE) personnel in coordinating the total research effort (U.S. Office of Education. Advisory Council on Vocational Education 1968).

These state research coordinating units were institutionalized by Congress in the 1968 amendments, which provided for their support.

Educational Resources Information Center. Over $64 million was appropriated for research, development, and training in vocational and technical education from 1965 through 1969. This investment of unprecedented magnitude generated large numbers of research reports, curriculum materials, and related publications which, to be effective, had to reach the hands of users. The Educational Resources Information Center (ERIC) in the USOE is the national information, retrieval, and dissemination system for American education as well as a decentralized system of 19 clearinghouses, each focusing on a different substantive area of education.

The ERIC Clearinghouse on Vocational and Technical Education is affiliated with the center at Ohio State University. In addition to acquiring, indexing, and abstracting research,

instructional materials, and related reports, the clearinghouse is responsible for information-analysis activities. The clearinghouse makes monthly contributions to *Research in Education, Current Index to Journals in Education,* and the publications of central ERIC, which cover the entire educational field. In addition, it publishes *Abstracts of Research and Related Materials in Vocational and Technical Education* and *Abstracts of Instructional Materials in Vocational and Technical Education* quarterly and provides an annual cumulative index. Material for the annual *Manpower Research Inventory,* prepared under the auspices of the Federal Interagency Committee on Manpower Research, is indexed and abstracted by the Vocational-Technical Clearinghouse and published by the Department of Health, Education, and Welfare. All of these information tools provide researchers and practitioners access to the significant literature of the field.

Full text of the documents in the system are available either on microfiche or facsimile copy from the ERIC Document Reproduction Service. For the first time in history, fugitive materials are available to the field. In addition to providing fundamental information tools, the Vocational-Technical Clearinghouse has commissioned a number of review and synthesis papers on the service fields of vocational education and on problem-centered topics. These review and synthesis papers provide a means of coordinating and integrating a wide range of related reports around certain focal areas and establish a bench mark for researchers and practitioners.

The clearinghouse and the center have worked closely with state research coordinating units to develop state information systems for vocational and technical education which utilize the entire ERIC system. The further development of this integral subsystem will contribute to more rapid utilization of research and related products by a wide range of user groups, thereby decreasing the gap between knowledge and practice.

Priorities. After the passage of the Vocational Education Act of 1963, vocational education research activities sponsored by the USOE centered on providing several kinds of supporting services to the new vocational education research community. These services include the sponsorship of programs to stimulate and implement new research; to provide assistance to those preparing proposals for research grants; to develop new research talent through workshops, seminars, and institutes; to expand and strengthen state research capabilities; and to disseminate meaningful research results (Bushnell 1969).

In 1965 the Bureau of Research, in cooperation with other bureaus in the USOE, established several specific priorities. These priorities focused upon problem areas in vocational education, with recognition given to existing major social or cultural facets of each area.

The first priority research area was program evaluation, whereby appropriate procedures were examined for adapting job projection and survey information to the planning requirements of local schools.

The second area was vocational education resource development. Studies in this area focused upon the need for identifying the numbers, qualifications, and forces of staff personnel to fill the projected needs of the expanding vocational program.

Vocational guidance and career choice process was the third priority area, in which attention was addressed to the problem of assisting both vocational guidance counselors and individual counselees. Research was directed toward answering questions concerning how concepts of work are formed, how individuals become motivated to pursue a given career, and what satisfactions are derived as a person moves through his working career.

The fourth area was organization and administration, where work was directed toward the improvement of existing organizational structures for vocational education at state and local levels.

New careers, the fifth priority area, supported research designed to establish innovative vocational-technical education programs for new careers in the personal services.

From 1965 through 1969 research funds available under the Vocational Education Act of 1963 were approximately $65 million. Approximately 65 percent of these funds supported demonstration and pilot efforts and research projects. Approximately 25 percent supported the work of the two national research centers and the state research coordinating units, and 10 percent was spent on training (U.S. Department . . . 1970).

In viewing these overall research priorities and the total amount of $64 million expended between 1965 and 1969, it is significant to note that 80 percent of that money was invested in individual research and development projects (Bushnell 1969). Priorities established by the USOE are subject to modification and redirection periodically, based on research and development outcomes, local needs, and the changing sociopolitical context.

Major developments. Research in vocational education must provide the capacity for self-renewal. Without this capacity, a systematic program of education for occupational competence and career development soon becomes stagnant and obsolete. With the growing research, development, and training efforts in vocational and technical education, there have been a number of significant and promising developments characterized by their interservice and interdisciplinary emphases.

Economics. Since 1968 there have been growing limitations on the amount of public funds for the support of education as a result of increased competition for the dollars that are available. With limited funds, public policymakers must make allocation decisions for supporting programs with the greatest economic yield and social benefits. Research on the economics of vocational and technical education is essential for making informed decisions concerning the allocation and effective utilization of educational resources. Valid economic models and data must be available to support these decisions. An increased amount of research on the economics of education has been undertaken as a basis for future policy decisions.

Research in the area of the economics of vocational and technical education has centered on the benefits of occupational training versus the cost of this training. Problems inherent in this general research thrust include determining alternative social costs when education and training are not available as well as determining intrinsic social benefits from vocational education.

Studies in the area of the economics of vocational and technical education indicate that this type of education is a sound investment for society when compared to general education or college preparatory programs for students who do not go to college (Warmbrod 1968).

Organization and administration. Research in the organization and administration of vocational and technical education has been extremely diverse, with the majority of the studies focusing upon a specific state or local problem. Comprehensive surveys have been made in at least 30 states for the purpose of adjusting state legislation or policy relating to the organization and administration of vocational education. These studies have generally related to the organization of vocational education administrative units within area schools, junior colleges, or university branches.

Although research relating to policy and planning at the national level has provided few definitive answers to pervasive organizational problems, the body of research has made seven specific recommendations (Lee et al. 1968; Levitan 1963; Venn 1964).

First, occupational education should become an integral part of the total education system and a responsibility of every segment of the system. Second, continuing occupational education should be provided for everyone. Third, occupational guidance and counseling should be improved, and placement and guidance should be provided for dropouts. Fourth, on leaving school all high school youth should be equipped with marketable occupational skills or with preparation for further education. Fifth, initial placement services should be the responsibility of the school. Sixth, there should be a closer relationship between occupational demands and occupational education curricula. Seventh, there needs to be a partnership between the vocational education establishment and private business and industry.

Curriculum development. A majority of earlier efforts in vocational education curriculum development were directed toward determining the specific skills required for a job or occupation through job or task analysis. In this kind of analysis, certain manipulative skills were identified and then used as the basis for curriculum development. However, because of the increase in occupations which require a high degree of knowledge and a low degree of manipulative skill, new forms of occupational analysis have been developed which are based on cognitive skills and factors rather than on manipulative tasks (Evans & Brandon 1965). Furthermore, a recent development has been the emphasis on meeting the physical and social needs of learners while they are acquiring specific knowledge and skills.

A major research thrust in curriculum development has been the job-cluster approach. This methodology identifies a core of knowledge and skills common to several jobs. A person prepared in such a training program would thus be able to obtain entry-level employment for jobs within a large family of occupations. He should also be better prepared to adjust to job demands which change with new technological developments.

Another area of emphasis in vocational education curriculum research has been the development and utilization of specific performance objectives, along with appropriate criterion measures for their use in curriculum design. Besides making possible more realistic training sequences, this methodology can provide for more tangible methods of curriculum evaluation. It can also provide a rational basis for curriculum modules that may be used in the development and utilization of small, specific training units.

In spite of the impressive value of performance objectives in education, demonstrated primarily in military and industrial training programs, these objectives are not yet widely used in public vocational education. Some people find it difficult to think of objectives in terms of student performance. Others are afraid that such objectives will not include intangibles, thought to be of major importance. Some expect performance objectives to reduce the teacher's influence.

But all of these reasons for avoiding performance objectives are based on misunderstandings. The major persistent difficulty delaying the widespread emergence of courses based on performance objectives is that of providing the necessary development time and talent. Preparation of a set of sequenced course objectives clearly defining what the successful student will be able to do, the conditions under which he is expected to perform, and the criteria by which his success will be judged is a demanding and difficult task. Nevertheless, the benefits are apparent, the techniques and methods are available, and it seems likely that vocational and technical education courses will be based increasingly on performance objectives.

Perhaps the most significant curriculum development activity of the 1970's has been the Education System for the 70's project (ES'70). This massive project, sponsored by the USOE and 19 school systems across the United States, brings together and utilizes both the principles of the behavioral-objective approach to curriculum development and the job-cluster approach to occupational skill development (Popham 1969). In this project the traditional disciplines of mathematics, science, English, and social studies along with the area of vocational education have been rigorously analyzed in an effort to identify behavioral objectives that relate to the development of desired academic skills. These performance objectives are then combined to form a flexible curriculum which attempts to minimize academic overlap and to make each learning objective an integral part of a larger organic whole.

Program evaluation.   In recent years the evaluation of vocational education programs has been given a high priority in research funding (U.S. Office of Education. Division of Adult and Vocational Research 1966). This priority status has stimulated important new developments in several areas of program evaluation.

One major area of investment has been in evaluation systems—that is, evaluation models that encompass a total administrative agency to provide credible information for educational decisions. A common point of departure within these models has been an emphasis on the development and verification of appropriate goals and objectives for individual training programs or for entire systems or agencies. From these stated program goals, self-evaluation criteria are determined that will indicate when these goals have been met. Data and data sources are then identified that will provide appropriate criterion measures, and administrative feedback channels are identified to provide inputs to decision processes that will redirect program activities to meet originally stated program goals (Starr 1967).

Another area of emphasis has been the utilization of planning, programming, and budgeting systems (PPBS). Specially directed efforts to familiarize vocational education administrators and program planners with the advantages, requirements, and limitations of PPBS have been made in the form of in-service training-materials development and PPBS training seminars, clinics, and institutes (McGivney & Nelson 1969).

In the past student follow-up studies have constituted a major segment of program evaluation studies. These studies have certain common deficiencies. They fail to report on persons when occupational skills and resulting employment come about through nonschool activities, they infer unwarranted causal relationships, and they are weak in methodological design (Little 1969). However, a significant positive development in these kinds of studies has been the comparison of vocational trainees with nontrainees. In these studies such variables as employment security, initial earnings, and long-range earnings have been examined among high school graduates. It has been found that graduates with vocational education are generally in a more favorable economic position than their nonvocationally trained counterparts (Warmbrod 1968).

With the continuing high priority on research directed toward the evaluation of vocational education, it appears that future areas of emphasis and investment will be in the evaluation of total vocational education structures and in areas directed toward the accreditation of vocational and technical education offerings.

Guidance and career development.   The process of selecting and adjusting successfully to a career is a complex problem that is not well understood or effectively handled by many persons —especially young people. Providing the opportunity to acquire employable skills is not sufficient preparation for the world of work. Past research indicates that the majority of youngsters of junior high school age are not aware of occupational alternatives that may be available to them at a later date (Campbell 1968). Moreover, too many students in both junior and senior high schools see a college education as the only educational objective when other objectives may be more appropriate for their individual requirements (*ibid.*).

One of the major developments in the area of guidance and career development has been the emphasis on developing programs of career guidance which begin in the elementary school and extend through the secondary school. Such programs serve to extend the youngster's occupational horizons and provide a realistic core of occupational understanding, as a result of which the more traditional course work takes on new meaning. They also expose the youngster to career options and help him to develop a better knowledge of himself.

Campbell's research (*ibid.*) indicates that vocational guidance and counseling should be available throughout the total school experience to point the student toward a realistic occupational choice. If made early, this choice is helpful in generating greater motivation toward education in general. The fact that the student may change his mind several times prior to making a final vocational choice is of little importance (Evans, Mangum, & Pragan 1969).

Impact. The classical view of research is that its purpose is the generation of knowledge for knowledge's sake; a more pragmatic viewpoint pervades vocational and technical education. There is a concern that investments in research and development substantially contribute to qualitative programmatic changes. In such areas as agriculture, medicine, and the physical sciences, the impact of research is primarily attributable to sustained programmatic support. This support has given rise to a network of special agencies created to stimulate, conduct, and coordinate research, development, and diffusion activities. These systems have established and maintained essential structures and linkages that allow operational problems to generate research activities that move across the continuum of fundamental research, development, and testing to the utilization of research results in operation settings. If a comparable impact is to be secured from research and development efforts in vocational education, the message is obvious: Sustained programmatic support is essential.

Recognizing multiple causation and the complex milieu within which educational programs function, it is difficult to assess the precise impact of educational research. In any event, a certain minimum amount of time is necessary to identify problems, conduct the needed research, report the findings, implement new programs, and determine the consequences of these programs. Since 1965 represents the first year in which funds of any appreciable amount were available for vocational education research, it is too early to try to assess the long-term impact of investments since then.

It is apparent, however, that research and development have had a substantial impact on programs of vocational and technical education. New curricula have been developed and installed, new procedures for leadership development have been instituted, more sophisticated management procedures prevail, systematic evaluation is being conducted, and a wide range of techniques and modes of instruction have been adopted. Most important, there is a new appreciation for the role of research and development as a means of planning, developing, and improving programs.

Although it is too early to establish a clear cause-and-effect relationship between research expenditures and general impact, one significant accomplishment is clear: recognition of the need for research, the need for preparing capable re-search personnel, and the need for organizations and administrative mechanisms and procedures capable of achieving the most economical benefits from these research expenditures (Evans, Mangum, & Pragan 1969).

BIBLIOGRAPHY

ASHMUN, RICHARD D., AND ROGER A. LARSON 1970 *Review and Synthesis of Research on Distributive Education.* 2nd ed. Columbus, Center for Vocational and Technical Education, Ohio State University.

BUSHNELL, DAVID S. 1967 *An Education System for the 70's.* Washington, D.C., Aerospace Education Foundation Conference.

BUSHNELL, DAVID S. 1969 *Past, Present, and Future Priorities for Vocational Education Research.* Proceedings of the National Conference on Research. Stillwater, Oklahoma Research Coordinating Unit, Oklahoma State University.

CAMPBELL, R. E. 1968 *Vocational Guidance in Secondary Education: Results of a National Survey.* Columbus, Center for Vocational and Technical Education, Ohio State University.

CHADDERDON, HESTER, AND ALYCE M. FANSLOW 1966 *Review and Synthesis of Research in Home Economics Education.* Columbus, Center for Vocational Technical Education, Ohio State University.

EVANS, RUPERT N., AND GEORGE L. BRANDON 1965 "Research in Vocational Education." *Vocational Education.* Sixty-fourth Yearbook of the National Society for the Study of Education, Part 1. University of Chicago Press. Pages 264–279.

EVANS, RUPERT N., GARTH L. MANGUM, AND OTTO PRAGAN 1969 *Education for Employment: The Background and Potential of the 1968 Vocational Education Amendments.* Ann Arbor, Institute of Labor and Industrial Relations, University of Michigan.

GOLDHAMMER, KEITH, et al. 1969 *Research Coordinating Unit Program Evaluation.* Corvallis, Center for Educational Research and Service, Oregon State University.

GREISSMAN, EUGENE B., AND KENNETH G. DENSLEY 1969 *Review and Synthesis of Research on Vocational Education in Rural Areas.* Columbus, Center for Vocational and Technical Education, Ohio State University.

HOLLOWAY, LEWIS D., AND ELIZABETH E. KERR 1969 *Review and Synthesis of Research in Health Occupations Education.* Columbus, Center for Vocational and Technical Education, Ohio State University.

HOUSEHOLDER, DANIEL L., AND ALAN R. SUESS 1969 *Review and Synthesis of Research in Industrial Arts Education.* 2nd ed. Columbus, Center for Vocational and Technical Education, Ohio State University.

LANHAM, FRANK W., AND J. M. TRYTTEN 1966 *Review and Synthesis of Research in Business and Office Occupations Education.* Columbus, Center for Vocational and Technical Education, Ohio State University.

LARSON, MILTON E. 1966 *Review and Synthesis of Research in Technical Education.* Columbus, Center for Vocational and Technical Education, Ohio State University.

LARSON, MILTON E. 1969 *Review and Synthesis of Research: Analysis for Curriculum Development.* Columbus, Center for Vocational and Technical Education, Ohio State University.

LEE, ALLEN, et al. 1968 *Vocational Education: General Education Situation Study.* Monmouth, Teaching Research Division, Oregon State System of Higher Education.

LEVITAN, SAR A. 1963 *Vocational Education and Federal Policy*. Kalamazoo, Mich., Upjohn Institute for Employment Research.

LITTLE, KENNETH J. 1969 *Review and Synthesis of Research on the Placement and Follow-up of Vocational Education Students*. Columbus, Center for Vocational and Technical Education, Ohio State University.

McGIVNEY, JOSEPH H., AND WILLIAM C. NELSON 1969 *Program, Planning, Budgeting Systems for Educators*. Vols. 1–3. A final report, Leadership Series 18 and 19, Bibliography Series 3. Columbus, Center for Vocational and Technical Education, Ohio State University.

MEYER, WARREN G., AND WILLIAM B. LOGAN 1966 *Review and Synthesis of Research in Distributive Education*. Columbus, Center for Vocational and Technical Education, Ohio State University.

MOSS, JEROME 1968 "The Past Is Prologue." *Review of Educational Research*, 38, no. 4:434–440.

PAUTLER, ALBERT J., AND CARL J. SCHAEFER 1970 *Review and Synthesis of Research on Trade and Technical Education*. 2nd ed. Columbus, Center for Vocational and Technical Education, Ohio State University.

PHILLIPS, DONALD S., AND LLOYD D. BRIGGS 1970 *Review and Synthesis of Research on Technical Education*. 2nd ed. Columbus, Center for Vocational and Technical Education, Ohio State University.

POPHAM, JAMES W. 1969 "Focus on Outcomes: A Guiding Theme of ES'70." *Phi Delta Kappan*, 51, no. 4:208–210.

STARR, HAROLD 1967 "A Model for Evaluating State Programs." *American Vocational Journal*, 42, no. 9:13–14.

STREICHLER, JERRY 1966 *Review and Synthesis of Research in Industrial Arts Education*. Columbus, Center for Vocational and Technical Education, Ohio State University.

TUCKMAN, BRUCE W., AND CARL J. SCHAEFER 1966 *Review and Synthesis of Research in Trade and Industrial Education*. Columbus, Center for Vocational and Technical Education, Ohio State University.

U.S. CONGRESS 1968 *Notes and Working Papers Concerning the Administration of Programs Authorized Under Vocational Education Act of 1963, Public Law 88–210, as Amended*. Washington, D.C., Government Printing Office.

U.S. DEPARTMENT OF HEALTH, EDUCATION, AND WELFARE 1970 *Educational Research and Development in the United States*. Washington, D.C., Government Printing Office.

U.S. OFFICE OF EDUCATION 1963 *Education for a Changing World of Work: Report of the Panel of Consultants on Vocational Education*. OE–80021. Washington, D.C., Government Printing Office.

U.S. OFFICE OF EDUCATION. ADVISORY COUNCIL ON VOCATIONAL EDUCATION 1968 *Vocational Education: The Bridge Between Man and His Work*. Washington, D.C., Government Printing Office.

U.S. OFFICE OF EDUCATION. DIVISION OF ADULT AND VOCATIONAL RESEARCH 1966 "Guidelines for Adult and Vocational Research." *Journal of Human Resources*, 1, no. 1:78–83.

VENN, GRANT 1964 *Man, Education, and Work: Postsecondary, Vocational and Technical Education*. Washington, D.C., American Council on Education.

WARMBROD, J. ROBERT 1968 *Review and Synthesis of Research on the Economics of Vocational-Technical Education*. Columbus, Center for Vocational and Technical Education, Ohio State University.

WARMBROD, J. ROBERT, AND LLOYD J. PHIPPS 1966 *Review and Synthesis of Research in Agricultural Education*. Columbus, Center for Vocational and Technical Education, Ohio State University.

WENRICH, RALPH C. 1970 *Review and Synthesis of Research on the Administration of Vocational and Technical Education*. Columbus, Center for Vocational and Technical Education, Ohio State University.

ROBERT E. TAYLOR and AARON J. MILLER

VOCATIONAL SCHOOLS, PRIVATE

Private vocational schools are concerned with training for explicitly stated occupational objectives rather than for academic degrees, as are most colleges. The flexible operations and diverse training programs provided by private vocational schools are the direct outcome of their private ownership and, in the case of most schools, of a quest for profits. The profitability of private vocational schools, like that of all business enterprises, is directly related to their capabilities for satisfying consumer demands. Since services at the schools are utilized directly and principally by students, the training courses and even their scheduling reflect students' specialized occupational interests and time preferences. Government agencies, contracting with the schools primarily for services to disabled and disadvantaged persons, also exert some impact upon the schools' operations. Private business firms are the major source of employment for the schools' graduates and therefore have important influences upon the training content of most occupational courses.

Historical development. Private vocational schools, also known as specialty schools, have had a long economic development in the United States. Predominantly proprietary rather than nonprofit, these schools have evolved structurally and functionally in response both to changing training requirements in occupations and to the development of new jobs. Many of the innovations in courses, teaching materials, and methods first introduced by private vocational schools were later adopted by other institutions. In addition to adapting their training programs to the economy's technological complexity and multiplicity of services, these schools have demonstrated that institutional instruction can be provided more efficiently than on-the-job training for numerous occupations.

Under the apprenticeship system, proprietary masters provided practical education in the United States throughout the eighteenth century; they preceded the first trade schools, also privately operated, which arose at least as early as the first quarter of the nineteenth century. By the middle of the nineteenth century many business schools, once again private and proprietary, had been founded in response to the needs of expanding national and international commerce.

Marked technological innovation and material growth after the Civil War provided a stimulus to the private schools and also demonstrated the schools' capacity for adapting to rapidly changing business and industrial needs. By 1925 greatly curtailed immigration had the economic effect of foreclosing a major source of skilled workers, and this naturally meant that more of the available labor force had to be trained by such resources as the specialty schools. The passage in 1917 of the Smith-Hughes Vocational Education Act provided important encouragement to the practical instruction offered in public secondary schools, while also reflecting the great need for expansion of all training facilities.

Probably the major period of proprietary school growth occurred after World War II, in response to the training requirements of war veterans and their opportunity to pursue such training under the liberal benefits of the G.I. Bill. At the same time, growth and sophistication in numerous fields—including engineering, electronics, and medicine—created many quasi-professional openings for technicians. The technician ranked below the professional in qualifications and responsibilities, but his position was higher than that of the craftsman or skilled worker.

Apprenticeships and on-the-job training were inadequate means of preparing persons for many of these new occupations, and either most public high schools and the growing number of community colleges failed to serve the total number of persons seeking instruction or else the nature and length of the curriculum were considered unsatisfactory by many prospective students.

Neglect of vocational education. Despite the prominence of vocational schools as a training resource for well over 100 years, a comprehensive census of the private vocational schools has not been made. Even less is known about the number and diversity of courses offered by the schools.

Such neglect exists despite the fact that most young Americans do not graduate from four-year colleges or universities and hundreds of thousands of them do enroll in the specialty schools each year.

The minor regard for the operations of private schools bears some similarity to the relative inattention given, until recently, to vocational education in the public schools. The Vocational Education Act of 1963 and amendments to the act in 1968 aimed to strengthen various aspects of the programs found in public schools throughout the United States. However, even a marked expansion in, for example, the number of school counselors with adequate knowledge of the labor market and of training opportunities will not immediately counter the often unrealistic views held by many parents and their children on the necessity of getting a college degree. The consistent and effective public demand for raising the number and percentage of college graduates in the adult population has been further stimulated by the goal of equalizing educational opportunity. This goal has been widely acknowledged as a laudable one for a democratic nation in which many talented youngsters from low-income families still lack the financial resources to attend college. At the same time, inadequate concern has been shown for acquainting parents and their children with the numerous positions available to students who, although lacking aptitude for or interest in a college education, are able to complete a vocational education course.

Schools, students, and programs. The first serious attempt to estimate the number of specialty schools and to consider their various programs was made in 1964. Clark and Sloan (1966) estimated there were more than 35,000 of these schools, with an enrollment exceeding 5 million. Their calculations for all specialty schools yielded a figure greater than the total number of public and private secondary schools and institutions of higher learning. However, these figures included schools offering both vocational and leisure-time training programs.

A study by Belitsky (1969) disclosed a total of 7,000 private schools limited to vocational education and serving approximately 1.5 million students during the 1966–1967 school year. The schools were divided into four broad occupational categories: trade and technical (3,000 schools with 835,710 students), business (1,300 schools with

439,500 students), cosmetology (2,477 schools with 272,470 students), and barber (294 schools with 15,876 students). These conservative estimates were based upon sample returns from 1,200 schools to a questionnaire and on supplemental information provided by associations representing the four types of schools. The numbers of cosmetology and barber schools were precise because their respective associations conduct an annual census. The United Business Schools Association had a memberhip of 500 schools and maintained a record of 800 other business schools. Although the National Association of Trade and Technical Schools, established in 1965, had only 200 member schools, it had a mailing list of nearly 2,400 schools.

As these data show, the majority of students attended trade and technical schools. The combined enrollments in this category and in the business schools accounted for 80 percent of all students. However, the impact of the cosmetology and barber schools is also considerable, because they train most of the persons entering such occupations.

The data also revealed that the average annual enrollment at all types of occupational training schools was quite small—less than 5 percent enrolled more than 2,000 students annually. The average business school enrolled less than 350 students annually; this figure exceeded the average enrollment in the trade and technical schools by 20 percent and was much greater than the typical enrollments in the cosmetology and barber schools.

One explanation for the small size of most vocational schools is that the practical and problem-solving aspects of the courses are of primary importance. Since only short periods of time can be spent in large classrooms, the costs of machinery and adequate space for special programs necessarily limit the size of a school building and its staff. Second, the schools are widely distributed geographically—often in cities of less than 100,000 persons as well as in several sections of heavily populated metropolitan areas. (For example, two-year community colleges are often found in several sections of a state, and their enrollment is therefore typically smaller than the enrollments of the one or two public universities in the state.) A third reason for the small size is related principally to the trade and technical schools, which collectively offer the greatest diversity of courses;

individually, however, these schools tend to train for single or related occupations, which accounts for the great number of highly specialized schools.

The specialized nature of courses and the primary objective of preparing students for employment prompts most schools to maintain close but informal contacts with employers. Course content is readily modified as a result of frequent exchanges of information. Changes in course emphasis naturally reflect innovations made in the employers' plants, offices, and laboratories. The contacts also create mutual trust and give the schools a significant source for their important service of placing graduates in jobs; often employers will send their representatives to the schools to recruit students who are nearing graduation.

The various courses provided by the private trade and technical schools train persons for employment in every major industry. More than 200 different occupational courses were recorded in a survey of about 550 vocational schools (Belitsky 1969). Some of these courses—such as auctioneering, automobile damage appraisal, bartending, baseball umpiring, farriery, fire and explosion investigation, neon glass blowing, Swedish massage, time study engineering, and watchmaking—are offered in few, if any, other types of institutions.

According to this survey the six major training categories (based on the number of courses in each category) were, in descending order, data processing, electronics, medical services, drafting, automobile maintenance and related services, and radio-television. Although most manpower projections consider the three largest areas of training (data processing, electronics, and medical services) to be growing very rapidly in terms of employment opportunities, the other three categories also offer numerous job openings. Drafting may be allied with the electronics industry and the still-important construction industry, and a radio-television course may include training in the repair of color television sets. Automobile repair also provides many job openings for competent workmen.

Less than 60 percent of all courses were included in the above six categories. Other important categories in which courses were offered included commercial arts; construction; fashion design; needle trades; shoemaking; food preparation, processing, merchandising, and service; interior design and related services; major and minor appliance repair and servicing; machine shop;

photography; printing; promotions, sales, and related services; tool and die design; various forms of transportation and traffic management; and welding. In addition, courses in aerospace engineering technology, waste and water reconversion, gardening, hotel-motel management and related services, and many others, although listed only by a few schools, are also among the areas of growing job opportunities.

Aspects of instruction. Examining the form and means by which a productive service is provided is the best way of gaining an appreciation and understanding of the productive agent—in this case, the private vocational school. The service is, of course, instruction or training, which has the objective of preparing students for direct employment.

The instruction at vocational schools is offered under practical conditions. Indeed, ultimate job sites are often simulated, and students spend a major share of each day in a shop or laboratory setting where visual aids and operative equipment are the common components of training. Only a small amount of home study is required for many of the courses, because only those theoretical or academic concepts which are relevant to the performance of a job are dealt with. Moreover, the concepts are carefully and immediately integrated with the practical phases of instruction. For example, a course in auto mechanics includes only the physics of combustion and of electrical hydraulics that pertains to automobiles.

A related aspect of instruction is the presentation and testing of course material in short sequential units in order to reinforce previously learned material. This practice also gives the student a sense of achievement because he is informed of his progress continually rather than only at the conclusion of a term or semester.

Another significant feature of the instruction at many private vocational schools is the training offered at various levels of accomplishment within a group of related occupations. For instance, in one school students may shift their concentration from a radio-television repair course to a more sophisticated course in electronics technology, or vice versa, depending on their demonstrated aptitudes and interests. Some schools offer courses in different occupational fields and allow students to alter their specialty course. These options are naturally advantageous to students who would otherwise fail their courses or be compelled to accept the dissatisfactions of employment in an occupation that is not their foremost preference.

A final aspect of the instruction is directly the result of course selectivity. Since the students select occupational courses which they prefer, they are much more likely to be motivated than they would be in the absence of such free choice. Several previously mentioned components of the instruction, such as the various levels of training and small classes, have such a strong appeal for the students that they contribute to rather high student motivation. Thus, the instruction is especially attractive and useful to students who want short, intensive courses containing only a minimum of the academic content which had posed a threat to many of them when they were enrolled in the public schools.

Students' backgrounds and needs. The occupational courses in private vocational schools are necessarily a function of the educational levels, ages, and employment experiences of the students. Although typical students, according to one study (Belitsky 1969), are recent high school graduates, many of them have considerably less education, and others have even attended college. In all likelihood, the students' average level of formal education has risen more rapidly than the average educational requirement for admission to private vocational schools. More than 40 percent of the trade and technical schools surveyed still had at least one course requiring less than a high school education for admission, and 10 percent of the schools had a course requiring a maximum of only six years of schooling.

Along with the discrepancies between admission standards and most students' actual attainments, there is a discrepancy between the number of students enrolled and the number of students that can be accommodated. A majority of vocational schools have the capacity to expand their enrollments, particularly during afternoons and evenings; therefore, a sizable number of persons who are considered educationally disadvantaged could be enrolled.

The diversity of formal education among students is indicative of the schools' flexibility in accommodating students of different backgrounds and needs. Student bodies include high school dropouts with no occupational training; high school graduates of general education programs that lacked any specific preparation for work; high school graduates who did not pass the private vocational schools' aptitude tests in algebra or even arithmetic; persons preparing for licensable occupations; college dropouts, college students, and college graduates desiring an otherwise unavailable course, such as computer programming; and persons for whom the formal education requirements are relaxed because they have several years of employment experience and are currently unemployed or finding it difficult, as a result of physical disabilities, to remain in their present occupations.

In addition to taking their students' educational preparation into account, school owners and administrators adjust the scheduling of courses to the requirements of students, who are in fact considered clients. For some courses, new students are enrolled as often as once a week in courses that have already begun, although new students are usually accepted every two months. Students can also attend either day or evening sessions, and they can choose to attend on a full-time or part-time basis. Courses given by members of the National Association of Trade and Technical Schools ranged in length from half a week to 130 weeks—the median was 40 weeks (*National Association of Trade* . . . 1968). Most of these courses require twice the time when taken on a part-time basis. The option of enrolling in a course either full-time or part-time and the great variations in course length give the students considerable flexibility in scheduling. Finally, the schools usually operate throughout the year, permitting the ambitious student to complete an already compact course most expeditiously.

Once he is enrolled in a private vocational school, the typical student's major challenge is having adequate funds to finance the period of his education. Only a small minority of students attending trade and technical schools can rely upon parents or personal savings to pay for all their schooling—more than 60 percent are compelled to work part-time. The school owners' practice of accepting deferred payments is a useful, although limited, form of financial assistance available in most schools. Under this practice, students may elect to pay tuition in installments throughout the year rather than in one or two lump sums.

Despite financial pressures, the student dropout rate in private vocational schools is lower than the dropout rates for either high school or college students, partly because of the self-selection of

courses (Belitsky 1969). Nevertheless, financial problems are still the major reason why students in the proprietary schools fail to complete their courses, and the next most important reasons cited—family problems and securing a full-time job—also suggest the presence of financial difficulties. School owners report that only about 15 percent of the students dropping out fail to complete their courses because of lack of ability (*ibid.*).

Accreditation. Like other educational institutions, private vocational schools usually apply for accreditation on a voluntary basis. Hygienic rules are established by the states for the barber and cosmetology schools; state and federal laws influence the scope of training for a limited number of technical occupations, including commercial pilot, ship radio officer, and tractor-trailer driver. In general, however, business, trade, and technical schools are evaluated by private accrediting groups.

Accrediting teams evaluate a school on the basis of its success in meeting its self-stated objective. About 500 of an estimated 1,300 business schools are members of the United Business Schools Association, a recognized accrediting body. In contrast, only about 10 percent of all trade and technical schools are members of the National Association of Trade and Technical Schools (NATTS), which received its accrediting designation from the U.S. commissioner of education in 1967, approximately two years after the association's establishment.

Less than half of all states license and regulate private vocational schools, and comparatively few of these states carefully supervise the instructional programs offered by the schools. Therefore, a visiting team from an association like NATTS is the principal means of accrediting trade and technical schools. The NATTS team consists of industry experts who examine the course content and instruction in their relevant fields. A member of the NATTS accrediting commission checks the school's business practices, including job placement records and student recruitment procedures, especially when a school's representatives are paid on a commission basis. Impressions of students are garnered through several random interviews.

Specialty schools may also be evaluated when they are in competition with other private schools or public schools for government-financed training. Hence, under the Manpower Development and Training Act the private schools must be used when their training is equivalent to that provided by public schools or agencies and can also be provided at a lower cost. The 1968 amendments to the Vocational Education Act of 1963 enabled the public secondary schools to utilize the facilities of the proprietary schools for training which they cannot offer. Presumably, a public school would show some concern over the quality of instruction its students received in the proprietary schools, and this could lead to at least an informal type of evaluation.

Outlook. Private vocational schools will probably gain wider recognition in the 1970's from various sources, including the public schools and private business organizations, and will probably act more often in concert with the public vocational schools, which will ensure continued growth in student enrollments.

The private vocational schools are likely to remain more experimental than public schools in initiating new courses (such as computer programming) and revising old courses. Risk-taking (including the possibility of failure) seems to be more acceptable to and even expected of proprietary schools, and, of course, many useful innovations can result only from what are initially considered daring attempts.

The organization of the proprietary schools enables them to operate with a flexibility that is absent from most public vocational schools. If funds are available, a private school may expand or revise its services in direct response to student needs or to the advice of its instructors. In contrast, the typical public school desiring new equipment or teaching aids needs the approval of one or even several departments of a local government; in addition, a new course in a public school must usually receive approval of the school board, which does not meet regularly and usually cannot revise its allocation of funds during a fiscal year.

Each course in a proprietary school has a precise employment objective, whereas the programs in a public school usually attempt to fulfill a broader purpose. The variety of courses available in the specialty schools is, therefore, not likely to be found even in the several high schools of a metropolitan area. It would be virtually impossible for the public schools to incorporate the numerous short-term courses offered by private schools into their training programs; the attempt could, in

any case, be economically wasteful, because some training resources might then remain unused. In addition, unlike many of the community colleges that have been concerned with student transferability to four-year colleges, most private vocational schools have been content to remain non-degree-granting (or terminal) institutions.

For these reasons, it may not be feasible for public vocational schools to compete with proprietary schools. Instead, cooperative ventures between the two types of schools, as recommended in the 1968 amendments to the Vocational Education Act, could be mutually advantageous. Such joint ventures would increase the motivation and educational alternatives of many high school students. An additional effect could be the lowering of the dropout rate in high schools as students are enabled to enroll part-time in vocational courses unavailable in the public schools.

Those who have completed their formal education will probably have the opportunity to attend proprietary vocational schools under several government-supported programs. Major programs, in addition to those serving war veterans and physically and emotionally handicapped persons, will include those provided by the Manpower Development and Training Act and the Guaranteed Loan Program; under the latter, the government guarantees loans and pays part of the interest costs. Moreover, Congress may raise the maximum amount of loans and pay part of the principal on the loans—some Congressmen have even suggested that the federal government should issue up to 100,000 grants annually to disadvantaged persons desiring to attend proprietary schools.

Most jobless persons with employment experience who enroll in specialty schools are referred to the schools on an individual basis for retraining under the Manpower Development and Training Act. Although this has been a useful way of accommodating individual needs, it is likely that groups of persons will also be sent to the schools under the act.

The growing relationship between the private occupational school and business firms will be demonstrated in two major ways. First, more private firms will subcontract with the specialty schools to meet their training needs. Second, the acquiring of specialty schools by numerous corporate enterprises will result in greater consolidation of ownership, in increased franchising of schools, and, ultimately, in an even closer approximation of the schools' training courses to specific industry requirements.

BIBLIOGRAPHY

American Trade Schools Directory. Queens Village, N.Y., Croner Publications. Published annually.

Barber Schools, Barber Students & Barber Statistics. Columbus, Ohio, National Association of Barber Schools, Inc. Revised annually.

BARLOW, MELVIN L. 1967 *History of Industrial Education in the United States.* Peoria, Ill., C. A. Bennett.

BELITSKY, A. HARVEY 1969 *Private Vocational Schools and Their Students: Limited Objectives, Unlimited Opportunities.* Cambridge, Mass., Schenkman.

CLARK, HAROLD F., AND HAROLD S. SLOAN 1966 *Classrooms on Main Street: An Account of Specialty Schools in the United States That Train for Work and Leisure.* New York, Teachers College Press.

Directory of Accredited Institutions and Operating Criteria. Published annually by the Accrediting Commission for Business Schools.

HOYT, KENNETH B. 1962 *An Introduction to the Specialty Oriented Student Research Program at the State University of Iowa.* Iowa City, State University of Iowa.

JOHNSON, ELOISE LETSON 1967 "A Descriptive Survey of Teachers of Private Trade and Technical Schools Associated With the National Association of Trade and Technical Schools." Ed.D. dissertation. Washington, D.C., George Washington University.

LOVEJOY, CLARENCE E. 1967 *Lovejoy's Career and Vocational School Guide.* New York, Simon and Schuster.

Milady State Board Cosmetology Guide. 17th ed. 1971. Bronx, N.Y., Milady.

National Association of Trade and Technical Schools Directory 1968 Washington, D.C., The Association.

State Barber Laws. Columbus, Ohio, National Association of Barber Schools, Inc. Revised annually.

A. HARVEY BELITSKY

VOLUNTARY SUPPORT OF HIGHER EDUCATION

Voluntary support of higher education consists of funds provided by individuals, foundations, businesses, and government. Such support is necessary because the rapid growth of higher education has brought economic strain and financial worries. Each year there has been a dollar gap between what students pay for their education and what it costs the colleges to educate them. Consequently, the colleges have dipped into capital (endowment) and pleaded for generous help from alumni, friends, corporations, and the federal government as well.

Private colleges, for example, which depend almost entirely on tuition and fees, endowment income, and gifts, are having a particularly difficult time. *Fortune* magazine, in studying the plight of private institutions, gave its report this headline: "Private Colleges: A Question of Survival" (Norton-Taylor 1967). For its survey *Fortune* selected 20 private institutions which were among the wealthiest in the United States. The magazine pointed out that if these colleges raised tuition charges to meet projected deficits ranging from $45 million to $110 million a year in the 1970's, they would either "price themselves out of the market or, at best, become exclusive academies for the wealthy elite" (p. 153).

Early philanthropy. It is generally thought that American philanthropy—like American higher education—began with what is now Harvard University. John Harvard bequeathed half of his estate to found the college in 1636. In 1641 three men, friends of the new college, were sent to England to seek additional support for that colonial institution.

The first alumni fund was established at Yale in 1890, but it was not until after 1930 that most colleges and universities organized to obtain unrestricted funds from their alumni on an annual basis.

John D. Rockefeller's first gift to the University of Chicago was $600,000 in 1890, and his last gift to that institution, $10 million in 1910, brought his total contributions to the university to nearly $35 million. Between 1885 and 1893, Senator and Mrs. Leland Stanford provided more than $20 million for the original endowment of Stanford University. There were other substantial gifts to private universities in the early years of the twentieth century, notably those of George Eastman to the University of Rochester and those of Edward S. Harkness to both Harvard and Yale universities.

Fund-raising campaigns. Although multimillion dollar gifts continue to be made by single donors and large bequests to educational institutions may be even more numerous today, the intensive capital campaigns since the late 1940's have operated from a much broader base. For example, a campaign for $25 million conducted by the Massachusetts Institute of Technology between January 1948 and June 1951 went $700,000 over the goal, with 10,632 individuals contributing. These individual gifts were mostly from alumni, and they amounted to 24 percent of the total. Business and industrial firms provided 26 percent of the total, and the other 50 percent came primarily from foundations and from a few other sources.

The goal of the MIT campaign was modest when compared with some which followed almost immediately. A figure of $82.5 million shook the educational fund-raising firmament when it was announced as the goal of "The Program for Harvard College." In quick succession there followed the announcement of campaigns of $53 million for Yale, $60 for Princeton, $98 million for MIT, and $100 million for Stanford.

Interestingly enough, all of these campaigns reached their goals. Most of them were included in a special study of capital campaigns completed between 1959 and 1963 which was produced in December 1964 by the Council for Financial Aid to Education. In that survey 265 institutions raised $812,603,000 against a total goal of $774,954,000.

Much of this lifting of fund-raising sights was stimulated by the Ford Foundation, which in 1960 began its special program in education. This program was designed to help private colleges and universities raise themselves to regional or national centers of excellence. The foundation offered challenge grants, which in most cases had to be matched by the institution on a two-for-one or three-for-one basis.

Not all of the large capital campaigns have had a Ford Challenge Grant built into them, nor have they all been carried out by private institutions. The statewide system of the University of California raised over $24 million for each of the years between 1964 and 1967. At the beginning of 1965 the University of Michigan announced a capital campaign for $55 million, and when it was concluded within three years the university had raised $72.8 million.

A survey of educational fund raising published by the John Price Jones Company annually reports gifts and bequests to a selected list of 50 colleges and universities. In the decade from 1920 to 1930 the 50 institutions in the survey reported gifts and bequests totaling $556 million. Now these same institutions raise more money in two years than they formerly did in ten. In the five years from to 1963 to 1968 the same 50 institutions raised from $373 million in the poorest year to $504 million in the best year (*American Philanthropy in Higher Education* 1969).

The interest of foundations in education is borne out by the studies of voluntary support of education which have been made since 1954 by the Council for Financial Aid to Education. General welfare foundations have provided 25 percent of the grant total of all the surveys made by the council between 1954 and 1968. They are the second largest source of funds for colleges and universities and may be considered the largest single source if individuals are divided into two categories—alumni and nonalumni individuals.

Corporate aid. The newest source of voluntary financial aid to higher education in the United States is the business corporation. Since 1954, business has provided a little better than 15 percent of the total support contributed to colleges and universities. In addition, the corporation has become an important source of funds—in the form of scholarships and fellowships—for the ever-increasing number of high school graduates who want to go on to college.

The advent of business upon the educational fund raising scene as a substantial source of financial support for higher education was not simply a matter of fortuitous coincidence. There were certain factors which made the corporation a logical prospect for important assistance. However, it is doubtful that business would have moved so swiftly to support institutions of higher education had there not been corporate leaders who stepped forward to articulate the situation and to establish a guide to corporate donation policy.

History. Corporate giving originated with the campaigns and national war chests instituted during World War I by the American National Red Cross and other organizations which undertook fund-raising drives systematically directed at attracting philanthropic support. The war chests were followed by community chests, but even so corporate giving dropped off after World War I, even during the prosperous years before the crash of 1929.

Tax exemptions on charitable gifts had been granted to individuals as early as 1917 to promote contributions for war campaigns. In the early 1930's, as the federal government initiated emergency relief operations on a large scale to combat the effects of the depression, it became apparent that private health and welfare agencies were needed more than ever before and that something had to be done if these agencies were to obtain any corporate support.

The Federal Revenue Act of 1935 ushered in a new era in corporate giving when it permitted business firms to take deductions of up to 5 percent of pretax net income for contributions to charitable and educational organizations. However, not much happened immediately, and, according to U.S. Treasury statistics of income, only $30 million was contributed by business in 1936. This amounted to 0.39 percent of corporate net profits that year.

Although no great share of corporate giving was to go to education until the 1950's, a sharp increase in total corporate giving began in 1942, and by 1945 the figure had reached $266 million, which represented 1.24 percent of corporate net income. Until 1948 no attempt was made to ascertain education's share of total contributions made by corporations. The National Industrial Conference Board estimated that in that year education received $24 million from companies, or about 10 percent of their total gifts.

By 1950 colleges and universities had had a number of years of experience with the crowded conditions of the postwar era, when large numbers of World War II veterans went to college with the help of the G.I. Bill. Taking a look at the population statistics and at the trend of the growing percentage of high school graduates seeking admission to college (about 50 percent in the late 1960's as compared with 16 percent in 1940), the institutions, and particularly the private ones, looked ahead with considerable foreboding to the tidal wave of students headed their way.

Council for Financial Aid to Education. At about this same time, a handful of top business executives—first individually and later collectively —also took a hard look at what was happening to the colleges and at the importance of the future strength of higher education to the growth and prosperity of business. These five businessmen, each of whom was identified with a top executive position in a major corporation, were Frank W. Abrams, Standard Oil Company of New Jersey; Irving S. Olds, United States Steel Corporation; Walter P. Paepke, Container Corporation of America; Henning W. Prentis, Jr., Armstrong Cork Company; and Alfred P. Sloan, Jr., General Motors Corporation. To these names should be added the name of Dr. Frank H. Sparks, who served as the catalyst in bringing these five high-powered individuals together.

These men were the incorporators in 1952 of the Council for Financial Aid to Education. The council, which began operation in 1953, was to function as a fact-gathering and an information-disseminating agency. It sought to measure the

financial needs of institutions of higher learning, as projected by them for a decade and also to determine the flow of gift money from various sources of support. At about the same time the CFAE began the first of a series of continuing biennial studies of corporate support of higher education in which the major companies reported both the dollars they were contributing and the areas of education to which these funds were going.

The business community, assured of reliable data on the financial needs of colleges, next sought guidance on how to construct effective programs of support. On this problem the CFAE was able to bring to bear the thinking and experience of a number of large corporations which had pioneered aid-to-education programs. The council began to develop a broad collection of case histories and to evolve a rationale of corporate support which helped companies to think through the important first steps in establishing programs of assistance. Over the years the council's consultation service has been expanded to provide additional data and guidance to corporations wishing to establish, evaluate, and expand their aid-to-education programs.

At the time that the CFAE was established, there was considerable doubt about the legality of unrestricted corporate gifts to colleges and universities. This doubt was put to rest in 1953, when two of the council's founders, Frank W. Abrams and Irving S. Olds, successfully helped to shepherd the case of the *A. P. Smith Manufacturing Company* v. *Barlow et al.* (26 N.J. Super., 106) through the Supreme Court of New Jersey. This case was followed in almost all other states by the enactment of permissive legislation for corporations to make certain kinds of gifts to nonprofit organizations.

In 1953, when the CFAE began operation, total corporate support for education was estimated at about $80 million. Corporate support has grown continuously, and as programs increased the companies became more sophisticated in their approaches and in their programs, which were well thought out and geared to long-range corporate goals.

As part of its effort to raise the level of support for higher education, the CFAE carried on a continuing program of information. This program has included the writing and distribution of special pamphlets and statistical studies for both business firms and colleges. In the early days the council prepared and distributed a series of special pamphlets on the major financial needs of the various types of educational institutions. One critical need which the CFAE, along with many others, helped to document and publicize was that of faculty salary improvement. In 1956 and 1957 the Ford Foundation made grants for this purpose to every private, accredited four-year college and university. This extraordinary philanthropy provided nearly $260 million and started a dramatic rise in faculty salaries.

In seeking ways to inform the general public about the importance of higher education and the reasons for supporting it, the CFAE was fortunate to win the cooperation of the Advertising Council, which agreed to include a nationwide campaign for higher education among the public service campaigns for which it obtained media acceptance. Beginning in 1956, this campaign has annually helped generate a favorable climate of opinion in which colleges can more effectively seek financial support, and the themes of the campaign, "Give to the College of Your Choice" and "College Is America's Best Friend," have become well known.

In 1958 the CFAE, which by this time had become well known to college administrators for its studies of educational philanthropy and also for its work in persuading more corporations to support higher education, started the first of 25 presidents' seminars, in which more than 1,000 college and university administrators met for two and a half days to be counseled by experienced consultants and to discuss staffing and operational procedures for effective college development.

The financing for these seminars came from four major foundations—the same four which had been supporting the work of the CFAE since it began operation. These were the Carnegie Corporation, the Ford Foundation, the Rockefeller Foundation, and the Alfred P. Sloan Foundation. These foundations supported the council for the first ten years of its activities. Since 1963 the program of the CFAE has been supported by many of the country's leading business firms.

Other agencies. Although playing a unique role in encouraging greater voluntary support of higher education, particularly from corporations, the CFAE was not the only agency whose influence was felt by both corporations and colleges in raising the level of business support of education. The Na-

tional Industrial Conference Board has been prominent among business organizations which have sought to study the implications of corporate giving and to report on managerial policies as they were evolved. The Council of Executives on Company Contributions, made up of the contributions officers of approximately 70 large national corporations, was established by the NICB. This group usually meets twice a year to discuss common problems of corporate philanthropy. Once a year a seminar is held at which contributions officers outside the membership can meet to study and discuss new developments in company giving policies.

Educational organizations. A number of educational organizations have greatly helped colleges and universities to organize for fund raising on a continuing basis and to call on business and industrial firms for financial assistance. In 1948, Dr. Frank H. Sparks, president of Wabash College, and Dr. Thomas E. Jones, president of Earlham College, called upon Indiana industrialists to seek financial support for their two institutions. They later persuaded presidents of 13 other private liberal arts colleges in the state to join them. The Associated Colleges of Indiana became the first of 39 state and regional associations representing more than 500 privately supported colleges and universities which present a unified approach to business and industry for financial support. In 1958 it was voted to set up a national office to serve as a coordinating center and clearinghouse to be known as the Independent College Funds of America. Most of the member colleges and universities are four-year, degree-granting institutions which are accredited.

A number of other private colleges also have incorporated for joint fund raising among business and industrial firms. Notable among these is the Council for the Advancement of Small Colleges, which has assisted a number of small private colleges to obtain accreditation and to strengthen their academic programs and educational services in other ways. There also are several associations of private junior colleges. The private two-year institutions, with few exceptions, have not organized as effectively as many of the four-year institutions to aggressively seek voluntary support.

The American Alumni Council also has been instrumental in serving educational fund raisers, including those persons on the staffs of colleges and universities who are concerned with annual alumni funds.

Development officer. By 1950 there had appeared on the educational fund raising scene a new member of the college administrative team known as the development officer. The development officers settled on the American College Public Relations Association as the organization which could help them organize and provide expanding opportunities for professional advancement. There is no doubt that college fund raising has produced a number of development officers who are professional both in their methods and in their results.

Federal aid. Individually, and collectively through their various education associations, college and university presidents have let it be known that they are looking to the federal government for a good deal more money in the future than has come their way in the past. A commission financed by the Carnegie Corporation to study the future of higher education and headed by Dr. Clark Kerr recommended in 1968 that if the United States was to get the "quality and equality" from higher education which it needs, then increased federal aid was essential. It was recommended, for example, that federal aid should increase to $13 billion a year by 1976.

At this point, it would seem logical to ask whether the institutions are asking for so much from the federal government because they expect so little from the private sector. Perhaps it was the predictions of growth which caused the institutions of higher education to look to the federal government for such large amounts in addition to private support.

Future needs. The projections of future growth in enrollments and needed expenditures suggest that voluntary support of higher education also needs to reach a figure by 1975 that would be about double the 1965 total. On the basis of its studies, the CFAE believes that this would mean a figure close to $3 billion that would be needed by 1975 for the support of higher education. If corporations and business firms were to continue to produce approximately 15 percent of

total voluntary support, this would mean that by 1975 business giving to higher education should reach at least $450 million.

The goals of voluntary support for higher education would seem neither unrealistic nor unattainable—although to reach them certainly will take some doing. Contributions from some large foundations may have topped out so far as higher education is concerned. However, the prospects are bright for greatly increased contributions from individuals, both those who are alumni of the colleges and those who are friends of the institutions, and from business corporations. Despite the steady increase in voluntary support by individuals and by business firms to all causes, it should be noted that the average American still gives less than 4 percent of his taxable income (as against the 30 percent permissible by federal law) and that the corporation is currently contributing at a level of only about 1 percent of pretax net income where the federal tax law permits 5 percent.

Government participation has rarely eliminated the need for philanthropy. On the contrary, it has often spurred philanthropy to greater effort. This is particularly evident in education and health programs, where government grants requiring matching funds have created the need for increased philanthropic participation.

Each college and university will have to build a strong case for itself, articulate it well, and aggressively present the story to all who might be expected to care what happens to the institution. As someone has said, "You never know how far you can reach 'til you stretch."

BIBLIOGRAPHY

American Philanthropy in Higher Education 1969 New York, John Price Jones.
COUNCIL FOR FINANCIAL AID TO EDUCATION 1964 *College Capital Campaigns*. New York, The Council.
Foundation News. New York, Foundation Library Center. Published bimonthly.
Giving USA. Published annually by the American Association of Fund-Raising Counsel.
NORTON-TAYLOR, DUNCAN 1967 "Private Colleges: A Question of Survival." *Fortune*, 76, no. 5:153–154+.

HOLGAR J. JOHNSON

WAR COLLEGES

The war colleges, which are also called the senior service schools, stand at the summit of the pyramidal structure that makes up military education. In the three major services this level is represented by the army, navy, and air war colleges; in the military establishment as a whole, this level is represented by the National War College and the Industrial College of the Armed Forces.

The commanding position of the war colleges within military education is reflected in their criteria for selecting the officers who attend them, in their stated purposes, and in their educational philosophies. Prerequisites for selection by one of the colleges are attainment of the rank of lieutenant colonel or its equivalent, active military service of 15 to 20 years, and, frequently, attendance at lower or intermediate level professional schools.

All of the war colleges prepare students for high-level military command, staff, and policy-making positions. Although the service colleges place greater emphasis on strategic concepts more directly related to the parent service, the National War College emphasizes military policy and operations at the level of the National Security Council.

The war colleges impart broad knowledge and esoterica rather than the basic information and technical know-how which characterize military education at lower levels. The general orientation of the curricula reflects the educational philosophies of the schools, in which the model of the civilian professional school plays a prominent role. There is a characteristic emphasis on providing the students with the intellectual tools for future professional work—for example, through research and writing. Academic freedom and conflicting viewpoints are stressed. At the same time, however, the locus of the colleges within the military authority structure forces important compromises when it comes to translating the academic model into practice.

Origins and evolution. The immediate rationale for the establishment of the first war colleges at the end of the nineteenth century was to give senior officers a theoretical background for their duties and a broader perspective on warfare and military strategy. In this respect the movement on the part of a few officers calling for an expansion of officer education amounted to an increased concern for the requirements of a professionalized corps of officers and to something of an intellectual awakening.

Until that time, officer education had been limited to attendance at the Military Academy at West Point and the Naval Academy at Annapolis, founded in 1802 and 1845 respectively. These institutions were primarily concerned with preparing students for early career assignments through the teaching of basic military skills. From about the end of the Civil War, the training given at these academies was supplemented by training at specialized schools. Among the first of these was the School for the Application of Cavalry and Infantry, which opened at Fort Leavenworth, Kan., in 1881.

Although the army was the first to prepare the ground for a war college by dispatching one of its officers abroad to study existing institutions, it was the navy that actually first established such a college, in 1884. The Naval War College, as it became known, led a precarious existence during its first 25 years, and it was not until 1911 that the notion of higher education for officers had gained sufficient support to permit the launching of an annual course rather than the six-week summer program that had been its principal offering until then.

Meanwhile, the Army War College had been established in 1901 as part of a sweeping reform of the service carried out by Secretary of War Elihu Root. The primary innovation instituted by Root was the creation of the general staff. By gearing education at the Army War College to the preparation of officers for positions with the staff and by assigning planning tasks to its personnel, the founders of the Army War College gave it more explicit missions than the Naval War College during its initial period of functioning. Hence, it quickly became an integrated part of the service.

During both world wars, military education such as was provided by the war colleges was among the few military activities to be curtailed or actually suspended. When the schools were reopened after World War I, the changes that were made presaged some of the revamping and restructuring of the colleges that took place as a result of World War II.

An early sign of recognition that modern warfare required knowledge of extramilitary matters was the establishment of the Army Industrial College in 1924. Drawing heavily on World War I experiences in economic mobilization, the curriculum of the college included instruction in such subjects as the procurement of matériel to meet military needs and the organization required for wartime mobilization of private industry. Originally limited to army officers, by 1930 the college had taken on the character of a joint military school, with an enrollment representing both army and navy officers.

A similar broadening of senior military education took place within the structure of the Army War College late in the interwar years. The students were encouraged to think in terms of national policy rather than of the individual services. In their committee work they tackled such topics as the institutional structures required for the planning and execution of national security policy, the coordination of military and civilian policies in foreign affairs, and economic warfare.

The experiences of the military in World War II set in motion many of the changes instituted in the military educational system after the war. The simultaneous consideration of economic, social, scientific, political, and purely military matters in the policies and actions of the war highlighted the importance of providing officers preparing for high-level command and staff positions with a broad professional perspective. The extensive use of joint service planning and operations during the war continued after the war—for example, in the plans for extending joint military education. In the emphasis on providing instruction in politico-military matters as well as on joint education and training, postwar developments were to intensify trends established during the war.

The need for an institution which would prepare officers for positions in national security agencies was recognized and acted on even before many of these agencies were established by the National Security Act of 1947. In early 1946 the National War College was established in Washington, D.C., as an institution to which all the military services could send students. At about the same time, the Army Industrial College was reconstituted as a joint service school. Both the Industrial College of the Armed Forces, as it was renamed, and the National War College were placed under the supervision of the joint chiefs of staff.

The National War College rapidly became the principal military institution for the study of national security. Although the service colleges initially deferred to the National War College, they soon broadened their own scope of study of national security to include the consideration of political, economic, and social conditions affecting the use of force. This was done in recognition of the limited number of officers from each service that would be selected to attend the National War College and of the need for knowledge among the general corps of high-ranking officers of the factors determining national security policies.

This broadening of scope was first manifested at the Air War College (established in 1947), which, as an institution serving a newly established service, was less encumbered by traditions and past experiences. When reestablished in 1949, the Army War College too gave greater emphasis to areas of study covered by the National War College. At the Naval War College such a broadening of the curriculum had to await the introduction of a second-year course in 1955. The latter dealt largely with joint level operations and was intended for officers likely to be selected for high rank. The lectures delivered at the Air War College in 1964–1965 indicate how strong the emphasis on nonmilitary matters had grown by that time. During this particular term, close to half of the lectures dealt with other than strictly military matters, notably international politics and politico-economic aspects of foreign areas.

This broadening of the curricula moved the war colleges closer to the model of the university professional school, which, as described by Barber (1963), had "as one of its basic functions the transmission to its students of the generalized and systematic knowledge that is the basis of professional performance" (p. 20). At the same time, however, there were factors counteracting the trend toward making the colleges conform to the model of academic professional schools. Foremost among these were instructional methods at the colleges, particularly the system of having the faculty perform advisory and administrative rather than teaching or research tasks, the extensive use of formal lectures by invited speakers, and, with some exceptions, the absence of an elective study program. The colleges remained largely unchanged with respect to these features until the mid-1960's, when two review panels simultaneously proposed important modifications in the curricula and methods of instruction.

Administration. The differences between the war colleges and civilian professional schools are highlighted by the arrangements for administration and supervision of the colleges. Whereas the university-affiliated professional school maintains a considerable degree of financial and intellectual independence toward its parent institution and toward the profession whose future members it trains, the war colleges are enmeshed in military structures, particularly those having functions related to education and training.

At the war colleges overall controlling authority and administrative responsibility generally rest with the commandant. He is usually a distinguished military man who occupies this position for a period of three years. Although decisions regarding curriculum, course materials, and instructional methods are generally made by the colleges, they follow the guidelines laid down by the numerous agencies which supervise military education. General responsibility in this area lies with the assistant secretary of defense for manpower and the secretaries of the respective services. Policy decisions that affect the colleges

directly are made by the joint chiefs of staff for the joint institutions and by the services for the senior service colleges.

There are considerable differences in the systems used for supervising officer education. In the army and the navy, supervisory responsibility for the schools is scattered among a variety of agencies. Many of these—for instance, the agencies within the general staff which supervise the Army War College—are responsible for education as well as the more practically oriented training activities carried out at specialized schools.

By contrast, the air force used the opportunity to design new structures at the time of its establishment as a separate service. It gathered all its educational facilities under one roof and made them, along with their administrative structures, a major air force command—the Air University.

Although financial dependence has placed the war colleges in a less autonomous position with respect to their parent institutions than civilian professional schools, the war colleges are also more responsive to the requests and suggestions made by members of the military profession. Close contact and cooperation with the various services or with joint military agencies is ensured, among other things, through the frequent rotation of the military members of the faculties. The students who come fresh from the field to spend one year at the colleges also ensure that the schools will remain in tune with latest operational experience.

However, mechanisms also exist to counteract the restrictions on the independence of the colleges that may result from the supervisory and monitoring system. The diffusion of responsibility among several agencies concerned with military education has given the army and navy war colleges, in particular, considerable autonomy and freedom of action. Several of the colleges have boards of visitors, which include civilian educators as well as military men. The boards have not infrequently represented the interests of the colleges before high-echelon civilian and military agencies. Finally, the prestige of the colleges within the military establishment also guarantees that they will retain as much of an independent position as is feasible, given their locus within military authority structures.

Students, faculty, and curricula. The five war colleges annually enroll some 940 officers. The Army War College has the largest number (224 in

1970), followed by the Air War College (215), the Industrial College of the Armed Forces (180), and the Naval War College (180). The National War College had 140 students in 1970. From 65 percent to 85 percent—the lower figure pertains to the Naval War College, the higher to the Army War College and the Air War College—of the students at the service colleges come from the parent service of that college, with the remainder coming from other services and a sprinkling from civilian agencies. At the National War College and the Industrial College space is evenly apportioned among personnel from each of the three main services and civilian agencies. In addition, there is some representation of the marine corps and the coast guard. At the National War College the civilian contingent consists primarily of foreign service officers; the Industrial College enrolls personnel from a large number of government agencies with functions related to economic mobilization.

All of the colleges have resident faculties composed mostly of officers. These officers generally have the rank of colonel or its equivalent. There is rapid turnover, with the average tour of duty somewhere between two and four years.

Compared to the faculty of civilian professional schools, the war college faculty does relatively little teaching of courses or lecturing. It serves primarily in a planning and supervisory capacity; among other things, members of the faculty prepare course materials and syllabi, lead discussion groups and elective seminars, and advise the students concerning their individual research projects. In the 1960's, however, attempts were made to strengthen the role of the faculty by providing, for example, more opportunities for teaching.

All of the colleges have ten-month terms. With the exception of the joint service schools, they use a standard curriculum and provide the same courses of instruction for all students attending a particular college. At the National War College, for instance, the curriculum is divided into 11 parts, each taking from two to four weeks. After an introductory survey of the world situation, subsequent courses deal with elements of national power, the formulation of national security policy, the implementation of national security policy in strategic areas, defense management, and the problems and prospects of major geographic regions. The curriculum emphasizes contemporary affairs. In the syllabi which describe the course of study, the topics are formulated as problems in strategic planning or foreign affairs, and the students are expected to contribute to their solution.

Although the lecture plays a much less prominent role than previously, it still appears to be the most important method of instruction at the colleges. A lecture is given almost every day throughout the ten months. It is most frequently delivered by an outside speaker. Increasingly, however, lectures by individual speakers are being replaced by panel discussions with several experts as participants. The lectures or panel discussions are followed by question periods, and generally the speakers remain for informal conferences with smaller numbers of students.

The large majority of lecturers are drawn from the military, the civilian government, and the university world, approximately one-third from each sphere for all the colleges combined. Individual variations among the colleges include a much smaller proportion of military men lecturing at the Industrial College and the National War College.

To provide for active involvement of the students, the colleges employ such devices as discussion groups, seminars, and committee work. The last is used to give practical training in solving problems of policy or operations. The class is divided into committees, each of which is assigned a problem for which it prepares a written solution. The solutions are then chosen for formal presentation and critique before other small groups or the entire college. The students' research and communication skills are promoted through the requirement at all the colleges of a thesis. Broadly representative of the areas covered in the courses, the topics of the theses generally reflect the students' past experience or training. In addition to developing writing ability, the thesis work emphasizes library research and skill in oral presentation. In the absence of examinations, written work, and in particular the thesis, is important to the evaluations of the students made by the faculty and submitted to the parent service.

Research. The research efforts of the war colleges have been sporadic and less successful. Research or advanced study groups, composed mainly of faculty but with some student participation, have existed at each of the colleges at one time or another; however, they have not been able to engage in sustained research in national security. Among the reasons given for the past failures of the colleges in this respect are inadequacy of personnel and other resources, the rapid rotation of the faculty, and the difficulty of avoiding research activities simply directed at producing staff studies for operational agencies.

Critique and reform. The war colleges have not attracted a great deal of interest among civilian scholars of education or among those studying the military profession. Academicians studying the war colleges have most frequently been motivated by a strong personal interest in these institutions. Two works, in particular, are exceptions in that their authors have attempted a systematic treatment of senior military education. The most exhaustive description and evaluation of the colleges available to the public is contained in *Soldiers and Scholars*, written by John W. Masland and Laurence I. Radway (1957). In *The Professional Soldier*, by Morris Janowitz (1960), education at the senior colleges is examined, with particular reference to professional formation.

With civilian educational researchers showing scant interest in the war colleges, the continuing reappraisal of the colleges that is necessary to keep them responsive to changing needs has been left largely to the institutions themselves and to military educational specialists. The faculties and the boards of visitors have been important sources of suggestions for reform. The opinions of the students have also been elicited in several surveys of war college graduates. These surveys have given special emphasis to the graduates' opinions of the utility of war college education in their subsequent assignments.

However, suggestions for more thoroughgoing reforms have generally originated in specially convened boards charged with the review and study of officer education in an individual service or in the military as a whole. Thus, the revamping of the war college system after World War II was the work of several review boards functioning simultaneously. In the mid-1960's officer education was under consideration both by an army board to review army officer schools (the Haines Board) and by a group convened by the assistant secretary of defense for manpower (the Morris Board). Both groups submitted their reports in 1966

(*Report of the Department* . . . 1966; *Officer Education* . . . 1966).

The recommendations of the boards with respect to war college education demonstrated an ambition to make the schools conform more closely to the ideals of the professional school and the institution of higher learning. Both boards favored the introduction of more true electives into the military professional school system. The Morris Board recommended that measures be taken which would ensure that the qualifications of the faculty were made consistent with the purposes and objectives of the schools. Up to that time, assignments of faculty to the colleges had frequently been made by persons with limited capacity to evaluate the qualifications of an officer for this particular task. The board also found that several of the colleges lacked civilian educational advisers. It recommended that such positions be created where they did not exist and that measures be taken which would increase the attractiveness of such positions where they did exist. In the late 1960's most of these recommendations were being implemented at the colleges.

BIBLIOGRAPHY

BARBER, BERNARD 1963 "Some Problems in the Sociology of the Professions." Kenneth S. Lynn et al., eds., *The Professions in America*. Boston, Beacon. Pages 15–34.
CRAWFORD, ELISABETH T. 1967 "Education for Policy Roles: An Analysis of Lecturers and Reading Materials at Selected War Colleges." Paper presented at the 62nd annual meeting of the American Sociological Association, San Francisco, Calif., August 28–31, 1967.
JANOWITZ, MORRIS 1960 *The Professional Soldier*. New York, Free Press.
LYNN, KENNETH S., ed., AND EDITORS OF DAEDALUS 1965 *The Professions in America*. Boston, Beacon.
MASLAND, JOHN W., AND LAURENCE I. RADWAY 1957 *Soldiers and Scholars: Military Education and National Policy*. Princeton, N.J., Princeton University Press.
Officer Education Study, Vols. 1–3 1966 Washington, D.C., Office of the Assistant Secretary of Defense, Manpower.
Report of the Department of the Army Board to Review Army Officer Schools, Vols. 1–4 1966 Washington, D.C., Department of the Army.

ELISABETH T. CRAWFORD

WASHINGTON INTERNATIONAL CENTER

The Washington International Center is a project operated by the Meridian House Foundation, a nonprofit educational organization. The center provides an introduction to the United States for government-sponsored visitors from abroad who are involved in training, education, or observation programs. Established in 1950, the center now has served nearly 90,000 visitors (87,598 as of December 31, 1970, from 151 countries and territories, at the rate of about 5,000 a year).

The center is financed by a contract, largely funded by the Agency for International Development and to a lesser extent by the Bureau of Educational and Cultural Affairs in the Department of State and the Department of the Army. A few participants are on fellowships from the United Nations, the Asia Foundation, the Ford Foundation, the National Science Foundation, and so on. Some special programs are funded by grants or private contributions, including those conducted under an agreement with the Japanese Productivity Center.

Programs. The center's regular week-long orientation program begins every Monday morning with an introductory session and initial briefing on Washington, D.C., continues through Friday afternoon with a series of seminars and tours, and concludes with an optional trip to Mount Vernon and other places of historic interest Saturday morning. The overall theme of the program is an explanation of the current values of American society; its purpose is to enhance the visitor's adjustment and accommodation to living in the United States during his stay.

The principal topics covered in the orientation are: characteristics of the American people, major facets of a society in transition, the American educational system, the economy, the political process, and race relations. A seminar format is followed, emphasizing group participation. Speakers are authorities in their respective fields and are drawn largely from the six universities in the area. Supplementing these seminars are a tour of Capitol Hill, a morning spent visiting a public high school, and, on the first day, a trip to a shopping center for firsthand observation of typical facilities for daily life.

Special Programs. Special programs are tailored to the needs of particular visitors such as high government officials, business and labor leaders, journalists, educators, and students and may run from one to five days. Programs can be provided in whole or in part in Spanish, Portuguese, or French. The center also has translating equipment for use by interpreters.

Other special programs routinely conducted are a seminar on American life for large groups of foreign military officers eight to ten times a year and annual conferences for senior Fulbright-Hays scholars from abroad and young business interns sponsored by the Association Internationale des Étudiants en Sciences Économiques et Commerciales (International Association of Students in Economics and Commerce) who come to the United States on summer exchange training programs.

Volunteers. An integral part of the center's orientation program is offering opportunities for visitors to meet Americans informally and to experience varied facets of American life. Both are provided through the volunteer organization associated with the center, which includes 200 working volunteers, who serve regularly in specific assignments, and some 500 host families as of January 1971.

A paid staff member works with each of the seven volunteer service committees: Airport Reception, Capitol Hill Tour, Escort, Functional Living, Home Hospitality, Hospitality, and Reception and Information. Through their organized activities, visitors meet Americans informally all through the week. Volunteers welcome incoming visitors at the airports, receive them at the center, act as hostesses at the Monday morning and Friday afternoon coffee hours, arrange invitations for hospitality in area homes, and serve as tour guides and escorts to a wide variety of events in the Washington community. Involved in nearly every aspect of the center's work, the volunteers play an essential role in helping foreign visitors adjust to U.S. life.

Services. About three-fourths of the participants in center programs have just arrived in the United States. Center staff members and volunteers make hotel reservations for them and meet them at airports and terminals. Housing advice and assistance are provided also for those remaining in the city for extended study or training periods. Most participants proceed from their orientation program to enter American universities or to embark on training programs or observation tours.

Two booklets prepared by the center for program participants are *Overseas Visitors in Washington*, a compendium of practical information for newcomers, and *Washington, Where to Go, What to See*, an area guidebook including suggested walking tours. The Meridian House Foundation publishes more generalized information in its *Handbook for Travels to the U.S.A.*, which government sponsors distribute overseas. This is issued also in Spanish and Portuguese. The foundation compiles *A Directory of Religious Services in Foreign Languages in the Washington Area* as a public service.

The center maintains contact with its former participants through a free quarterly newsletter, the *International Exchange News*, sent to them after they return home as well as by personal replies to their letters. Edited as an alumni newsletter, the *News* features reports and items sent in by readers. (In 1970 the circulation was 56,000 in 151 countries and territories.)

History. The Washington International Center was opened in March 1950 as part of the postwar reconstruction effort. It was administered by the American Council on Education (ACE) at the request of the U.S. government. The center's scope later expanded to include government-sponsored visitors on the educational exchange and technical cooperation programs as they evolved after implementation of the Marshall Plan.

In 1959, Meridian House was purchased with a grant to ACE from the Ford Foundation. The following year, the Meridian House Foundation was created to assume ownership of Meridian House and operation of the center. Since December 1960, the center has conducted its programs in the house, formerly a private mansion which has been called the finest example of French residential architecture of the Louis XVI period in the United States. It was designed by John Russell Pope, architect of Washington's National Gallery of Art and the Jefferson Memorial.

As a nonprofit cultural and educational organization, the Meridian House Foundation's purpose is to help develop and coordinate citizens' efforts to serve international visitors. Although its resources are limited, the foundation helps to finance several of the nongovernment-sponsored programs conducted by the center. The foundation also assists financially and administers the Hospitality and Information Service for Diplomatic Residents and Families in Washington and the International Visitors Service Council of Greater Washington Organizations. The foundation also provides administrative support for the National Council for Community Services to In-

ternational Visitors, composed of more than 80 community service organizations and about 30 private national programming agencies throughout the United States.

ARTHUR L. RICHARDS

WEBSTER, NOAH

Noah Webster (1758–1843) was born in West Hartford, Conn. After a period of tutoring by his local pastor, Webster entered Yale at the age of 16, graduating four years later. There was no further formal education for the man who was to become America's greatest lexicographer.

In January 1798, Noah Webster directed a letter "To the Governors, Instructors, And Trustees of the Universities And Other Seminaries of Learning in the United States." In this letter he stated some principles which guided not only the production of his own dictionaries but also the production of other later dictionaries and indeed the development of linguistics into our own time. He wrote:

> The truth is, a language is not only formed but must arrive to a tolerable state of perfection before a grammar of that language can be constructed. Languages are not formed by philosophers but by ignorant barbarians; and as nations advance in knowledge, new words and new combinations of words are added to their language to express the new ideas which they may acquire. Men speak before they write, and usually hundreds of years have elapsed from the foundation of a nation or state before the people have had any written language. . . . Thus in every instance *grammar is built solely* on the *structure of language.* . . . Grammars are made to show the student what a language *is*, not how it ought to be. . . . (Webster 1953, pp. 174–175)

Behind this extraordinary address to the academic community lay 20 years of thought and study. From his early experience in teaching, Webster perceived the need for American school textbooks based upon the American language and the American experience to replace British books widely in use. He wrote the three-part *A Grammatical Institute of the English Language*, of which the first part was the famed *American Spelling Book* (known as the "Blue-backed Speller"), the second a grammar, and the third a reader. Leaving the field of teaching, he prepared five lectures on the English language, which he delivered to audiences from Charleston to Boston.

Webster was concerned with establishing regularity and simplicity in spelling; for a time he proposed with Benjamin Franklin a radical simplification of spelling. In the end he surrendered to the overwhelming opposition of public opinion, contenting himself with dropping the *u* in words such as *colour* and *honour* and with dropping the *k* in words such as *publick*.

In pronunciation Webster sought a norm of simple diacritical marking which represented his native New England speech but which could be accommodated to regional American variations. For both spelling and pronunciation he introduced new syllable divisions, dividing between two consonants, as in *adven'ture*, in contrast to usage in textbooks imported from England. He ridiculed the affectations of his leading British competitor, Thomas Dilworth, who split such words as *brave* and *save* into two syllables.

In grammar Webster fought an enduring battle against the prescriptions laid down by Bishop Robert Lowth in England and found comfort in the insights of the British critic John Horne Tooke, who castigated not only Lowth but Dr. Samuel Johnson. Webster was dissatisfied with his own published grammar and acknowledged that it had been overshadowed by the work of an American competitor, Lindley Murray. His own efforts were to seek a grammar in the usage of good writers rather than in the authority of those British grammarians who had erected a grammatical structure based upon analogy with Latin. Webster observed several times that no adequate grammar of English had been composed.

In June 1800, Webster had inserted in the newspapers of New Haven, Conn., the following announcement:

> Mr. Webster of this city, we understand, is engaged in completing the system for the instruction of youth, which he began in the year 1783. He has in hand a Dictionary of the American Language, a work long since projected, but which other occupations have delayed till this time. The plan contemplated extends to a small Dictionary for schools, one for the counting-house, and a large one for men of science. The first is nearly ready for the press—the second and third will require the labor of some years.
>
> It is found that a work of this kind is absolutely necessary, on account of considerable differences between the American and English language. . . . Some new words are introduced and many more new significations are annexed to words, which it is necessary to explain. . . .   (Warfel 1936, p. 289)

The announcement was greeted with derision, in part because it was considered presumptuous of an American to attempt what the famed Dr. Johnson had done so well. However, the attack was also a response from political adversaries whom Webster had offended while editor of a succession of Federalist newspapers. He observed in a letter to Jedediah Morse on July 30, 1806: "The question at issue is whether an *American citizen shall be permitted to correct and improve English books* or whether we are bound down to receive whatever the English give us" (Webster 1953, p. 269). On another occasion he wrote: "It is impossible to improve in knowledge while we take it for granted that the books we have cannot be improved" (*ibid.*, p. 291).

The Compendious Dictionary was published in 1806. The dictionary for schools, containing about 30,000 word entries, was published the following year. Both were based upon John Entick's *Spelling Dictionary*, produced in England. Webster added 6,000 words to Entick's word list for the *Compendious Dictionary*.

Work had started on the complete dictionary, and early in 1807 Webster announced his design in a letter to "Friends of Literature in the U.S." He explained that existing dictionaries had not properly taken into account the origin and history of English and had produced unsatisfactory definitions through faulty research: "In our own language the primitive senses of words are in some cases totally lost or greatly obscured, which renders the definitions imperfect; and some of its idioms are scarcely explicable without resorting to the original ideas of the words. . . . I propose to compile a complete Dictionary of the English Language, inviting to my assistance the instructors of the principal seminaries of learning with whom I can most conveniently correspond" (*ibid.*, pp. 272–273). The letter concluded with an appeal for funds to carry forward the project.

Webster was well aware that in justifying the production of a new dictionary it was necessary to attack the well-established dictionary of Dr. Johnson, a formidable undertaking. He did this with the best grace possible, always taking care to compliment Johnson's powers. His criticism was nonetheless direct and forthright. "In the history of the English language," he wrote in October 1807, "the author has proved himself very imperfectly acquainted with the subject. . . . This part of Johnson's work, as well as his Grammar which is extracted from Wallis' Grammar, if they are not 'contemptible performances,' to use [Horne] Tooke's language, are wretchedly imperfect" (*ibid.*, pp. 284–285).

Webster enumerated the following defects in Johnson's work:

(1) The insertion of a multitude of words that do not belong to the language, words such as *adversable, advesperate, adjugate, abstrude, injudicable, spicosity,* and *balbucinate;*

(2) An injudicious selection of authorities, among whom "Sir Thomas Browne seems to have been a favorite. . . . The affectation of Latinity was indeed a common vice of authors from the revival of letters to the age of Queen Anne; but Browne, in attempting to write Latin-English, exceeded all his contemporaries, and actually rendered himself unintelligible" (*ibid.*, p. 286). On another occasion Webster wrote: "It was most injudicious in Johnson to select Shakespeare as one of his principal authorities" (*ibid.*, p. 330).

(3) The inclusion of vulgar and cant words, many of them found in Shakespeare;

(4) A lack of accurate discrimination among the different senses of words;

(5) A lack of care "in defining words nearly synonymous, or rather words which bear some portion of a common signification" (*ibid.*, p. 287).

(6) The use of quotations that throw no light on the definitions;

(7) The inaccuracy of the etymologies. "Let me only add what I am prepared by a minute examination of this subject to affirm, that not a single page of Johnson's Dictionary is correct: every page requires amendment or admits of material improvement" (*ibid.*, p. 291).

In a letter of November 12, 1807, to Joel Barlow, Webster stated his objectives: "My improvement will consist in *adding* all the legitimate words which are now used and which are not in English dictionaries; second, in rendering the definitions far more precise, and in exhibiting what may be called the *specific* differences of signification . . . ; third, in developing the origin and history of numerous *families* of words . . . ; fourth, to settle the orthography of words . . . ." (*ibid.*, p. 298).

In late 1807, Webster believed that he could complete the dictionary within five years, but at some time in that year he faced two realities: supporting funds would not be provided in any substantial sum, and he would have to halt his progress for a period in order to study languages. He had finished entries for two letters when the need for this study became clear to him. During the next ten years he mastered 20 languages, including Chaldean, Syriac, Hebrew, Arabic, Ethiopic, and Persian. His studies were summarized in a "Synopsis," which he intended to publish as a reference appendix to the dictionary. The "Synopsis" and the study of languages were completed in 1817, but the "Synopsis" was never published, and the manuscript rests in the rare manuscript room of the New York Public Library.

The purpose of the language studies was to seek out the historic origins of English words and to locate their roots, or radicals, as Webster termed them. He believed, on the basis of his studies, that "the families of man" originated in Central Asia and that their progress could be traced by their languages. He believed that many European languages retained primitive words and that these origins were obscured in Greek and Latin. He traced many English words to the early inhabitants of Great Britain before the invasions of Germanic and Scandinavian groups. He was aware of Sanskrit but did not have access at the time of compilation to the substantial German studies of the language which appeared in the 1830's and 1840's.

Webster's income derived chiefly from royalties on his books and from proceeds of various newspaper enterprises. The newspapers disappeared one by one, and the royalties were minimal. He moved from Hartford to Amherst, Mass., where he could live at less expense. Here he helped found both Amherst Academy and Amherst College and entered into state politics. From time to time small sums arrived from benefactors, notably John Jay.

Amherst in the 1820's was not the most likely

place for a lexicographer to advance his work, and it is a matter of wonder that Webster was able to acquire here the books he needed. He brought to his work a knowledge of law, for he had become an attorney in Hartford. He was acquainted with medicine as a result of a year of study in epidemiology. He kept abreast of the sciences, and he was for many years active in politics. This breadth of direct experience, as well as his wide reading, accounts for the range of his vocabularies.

The hostility which greeted the 1800 announcement of his dictionary plans continued for many years. The spelling books and the *Compendious Dictionary* were targets of criticism that Webster felt compelled to answer, sometimes caustically. One of his critics, John Pickering, published a volume entitled *Vocabulary, or Collection of Words and Phrases (Which Have Been) Supposed To Be Peculiar to the United States.* This work contained a direct attack upon Webster for alleged errors and for the introduction of Americanisms into his dictionaries. Webster replied in a 64-page letter, printed as a pamphlet. This letter to John Pickering of December 1816 was not only a reply but a statement of Webster's position on language and lexicography. It is strikingly contemporary in tone. Webster observed, for example, that "the terms used by the common people of a country are as genuine and legitimate as those used by a poet or historian and as necessary, nay, more necessary. . . . The business of a lexicographer is to collect, arrange, and define, as far as possible, *all* the words that belong to a language. . . . On professional topics, the arts, sciences, and in local description, the use of technical and local words is not only justifiable but necessary" (*ibid.*, pp. 349–350). He also observed: ". . . a living language must keep pace with improvements in knowledge and with the multiplication of ideas" (*ibid.*, p. 368). "In this country new objects, new ideas, and new associations of ideas compel us either to invent new terms or to use English words in a new sense" (*ibid.*, p. 346). It is difficult now to realize how radically these views differed from the authoritarian traditions of Webster's times.

By 1824, Webster had proceeded through the letter *R*. In the summer of that year, with a loan of $1,000 from one of his married daughters, he went with his son to France. Here he investigated new scientific terms. From Paris he went on to Cambridge, England, where the university libraries were put at his disposal. Here in 1825 he wrote his last dictionary entry. He had originally planned to have the dictionary published in England, and on his behalf Senator Daniel Webster had prevailed upon Congress to pass a law exempting the importation of his books from the tariff. But English printers were otherwise occupied, and Webster returned home. *An American Dictionary of the English Language* was published in New Haven in two volumes in 1828.

The work contained some 70,000 entries and a Preface, which once again set forth Webster's views on the nature and history of language in general and of English grammar in particular. The etymologies were far more extensive and useful than any previously provided. The definitions were remarkable for succinctness and discrimination. In sum, *An American Dictionary* was a scholarly work of the highest distinction, the first produced in America and the last for many years. In England the dictionary was immediately acclaimed; in the United States the old animosities were set aside in a mixture of astonishment and jubilation over a genuinely American achievement. During the winter of 1830–1831 Webster, then 73 years old, spent two months lobbying for passage of an improved copyright bill. During those months Congress adopted his *American Dictionary* as its standard, and more than 100 congressmen signed an endorsement of Webster's textbooks and dictionaries.

The first American edition of 2,500 sets was soon exhausted, but Webster could find no printer to undertake another. He was compelled to mortgage his Amherst home in 1840 for funds to underwrite the second printing. After Webster's death the dictionary was taken over by the G. & C. Merriam Company, which guided the work through a succession of revisions and editions of varying scope.

The second edition of 1840 is known as the revised edition. In 1847 the rights and stock had passed to the G. & C. Merriam Company, of Springfield, Mass. This company engaged a Webster son-in-law, Professor Chauncey A. Goodrich of Yale, to edit a new and revised edition in 1859. In 1864 a new edition was published, with three times the number of entries in the 1828 original. This edition was popularly known as the unabridged edition. In 1890 the international edition appeared, and in 1909 the new international edition was published with over 400,000 entries. In 1934 the international was revised again and was published as *Webster's New International Dictionary, Second Edition. Webster's Third New International Dictionary of the English Language, Unabridged* appeared in 1961 and at once aroused serious adverse criticism; the second edition continued in high favor and active use, although within a decade it could be obtained only at a substantial premium.

There have been only three other American dictionaries comparable in scale to the unabridged Webster's edition: *The Century Dictionary* (1889–1891), Funk and Wagnalls' *New Standard Dictionary* (1893), and the so-called Webster's *Imperial Dictionary of the English Language* (1904). The last of these was prepared by a Chicago publisher and was not in the direct line of descent from Noah Webster.

There have been a number of shorter works, such as *The American College Dictionary*, published by Random House; *Webster's New Collegiate Dictionary*, published by G. & C. Merriam Company; *Webster's New World Dictionary*, published by World Publishing Company; *The Random House Dictionary of the English Language*, published by Random House; and *The American Heritage Dictionary of the English Language*, published by the American Heritage Publishing Company and Houghton Mifflin.

BIBLIOGRAPHY

SCUDDER, HORACE E. 1881 *Life of Noah Webster*. Boston, Houghton Mifflin.
SHOEMAKER, ERWIN C. 1936 *Noah Webster, Pioneer of Learning*. New York, Columbia University Press.
WARFEL, HARRY R. 1936 *Noah Webster, Schoolmaster to America*. New York, Macmillan.
WEBSTER, NOAH 1953 *Letters*. Edited, with an introduction by Harry R. Warfel. New York, Library Publications.

LEE C. DEIGHTON

WHITE HOUSE FELLOWS

The White House Fellows program was established in October 1964 by executive order for the purpose of enabling the U.S. government to benefit from the services of large numbers of bright, able, and talented citizens not ordinarily seeking careers in government. The program was a result of the concern expressed by John W. Gardner, then president of the Carnegie Corporation, and shared by President Lyndon B. Johnson that the contributions of such citizens were not directly benefiting the government and the nation except in times of national crisis, such as during a war.

The President's Commission on White House Fellows was appointed to select young leaders from a wide variety of backgrounds, interests, and professional pursuits—who had not as a rule received their academic or professional training in the field of government—to serve for a year as special assistants to the president's staff, cabinet members, and other top decision-makers. White House Fellows were to be given an opportunity for participation, not just observation.

Selection process. Any citizen of the United States between the ages of 23 and 35 who believes that he has "marked leadership qualities and unusual promise of future development," as well as an ability to function effectively at the highest levels of the executive branch, may apply for the White House Fellows program. The competition is extraordinarily keen: in the first six years of the program, only 103 White House Fellows (between 15 and 20 each year) were chosen from over 8,000 applicants. Applications are usually submitted between October 1 and January 1 for the White House Fellows year beginning in September. Candidates may be nominated by universities, colleges, professional associations, or other groups, but the majority of candidates apply on their own initiative. A screening committee of the president's commission reads and rates the applications, referring the most impressive ones to panels in 11 regions (coinciding with the Civil Service regions) for further screening. The regional panels designate a number of regional finalists, interview them, and recommend national finalists to the commission. After extensive interviews over a period of several days, the commission makes its choices known to the president, who then appoints the White House Fellows.

Although leadership can be a difficult quality to define, it is felt that mature leaders are capable of recognizing leadership; hence, the commission's selection process for White House Fellows involves the judgment of established leaders across the United States.

At the national level, the first chairman of the commission was David Rockefeller; C. Douglas Dillon was the second, Judge William H. Hastie the third, and Arthur Flemming, appointed by President Richard M. Nixon in April 1969, was the fourth chairman. Other members of the commission have included corporate executives, members of the president's cabinet and the federal judiciary, bankers, lawyers, and distinguished men and women from other professions. The regional panels have been composed of similarly prominent local and regional leaders. In all, some 180 persons participated in the five selection cycles from 1965 through 1970.

Job assignments. As special assistants, White House Fellows have performed various functions for their respective principals. A few Fellows become top staff assistants to cabinet secretaries and agency heads; others are assigned developmental and coordinating responsibilities in particular substantive areas. Often, Fellows serve as troubleshooters, working on whatever problem requires immediate attention in the highest ranks of their agencies and departments.

In carrying out such responsibilities, Fellows have sometimes been able to make contributions to government policies or programs. For example, a report by a White House Fellow formed the basis for important changes in the government's migrant labor program; one Fellow's survey of natural resources in an American island territory led to the development of a master plan to protect the territory's resources; another Fellow formulated a new and successful program for involving ghetto youngsters in cooperative profit-making enterprises.

The 1968–1969 group of White House Fellows was the first to serve under two administrations, and some Fellows played significant roles in the transition between the Johnson and Nixon presidencies. A number of the Fellows were given the responsibility of coordinating and transmitting their departments' "transition papers"—that is, the analyses of programs and problems prepared by outgoing officials for their successors. Early in the Nixon administration, the postmaster general and the director of the Office of Management and Budget designated the White House Fellows assigned to their departments as their top staff assistants. Another Fellow became an assistant armed forces aide to President Nixon.

The contributions of White House Fellows in the early years of the program prompted President Johnson (as quoted in White House Fellows program brochures) to observe in 1967: "Two years ago when we established the White House Fellows program, we thought that its main benefits would be educational, serving chiefly the Fellows themselves. Today we are not so sure who gains the most, the Fellows or the government they serve."

Education program. Despite their services to the government, White House Fellows would argue that the immediate benefits of the program flow mainly in their direction. First of all, their job experience gives them a unique opportunity for understanding the operations of one government department or agency, including the style and methods of top decision-makers, as well as an opportunity for service. In addition, the president's commission operates an education program which provides Fellows with an understanding of areas of government outside of those to which they have been assigned as well as a knowledge of the major issues and problems with which the government must cope. In this way, the education program supplements job experience.

In a typical year's education series, White House Fellows meet with all cabinet members, with other important officials in the executive branch, and with leading figures in the legislative and judicial branches of government. In exploring substantive areas over which the government has some jurisdiction and exploring the government's problems, Fellows may also meet with governors, mayors, sociologists, urban planners, representatives of interest groups, international economists, several levels of foreign service officers, foreign policy-makers, fiscal experts, businessmen, labor leaders, and commentators from the press and academic circles.

Since the program's inception, White House Fellows have studied urban problems in Chicago, New York, Atlanta, San Francisco, and other cities. The 1969–1970 Fellows traveled to Europe and the Middle East, and the 1970–1971 Fellows visited Latin America, seeing firsthand the problems other nations face and gaining new perspectives on the United States' role in world affairs. Fellows have spoken with the scientists who have made possible the nation's accomplishments in space. They have witnessed U.S. Marine training exercises and boarded ships and submarines. They have talked to politicians and government officials of both parties and at every level. These activities and conversations have helped Fellows develop an increased understanding of the nature of the challenges and opportunities facing American society today and a greater sensitivity to the role of federal government.

Financing the program. During its first years, the White House Fellows program was supported entirely by private grant funds. Major support was provided by the Carnegie Corporation and the Ford Foundation, and David Rockefeller made a sizable personal donation to the commission. Gradually, however, the costs of the program have been shifted to the federal government. At first, each White House Fellow received a stipend paid from private grant funds; now Fellows are paid salaries by their respective departments and agencies. At present, the private grant funds, handled for the commission by the Smithsonian Institution, bear the cost of the education program and a portion of the cost of the selection process. Grants to the president's commission for the support of the White House Fellows have also been made by the Richardson Foundation, Inc., of North Carolina and the United States Steel Foundation.

Evaluation. Has the White House Fellows program, exciting as a concept, proved to be valid and successful? It is still too early to make a final judgment as to the program's ultimate success, since the program has been in operation less than a decade. However, the idea of allowing novices and outsiders to participate in the governmental process at the highest levels has proved workable. The program has shown that the sources of leadership in the United States are of endless variety and that any of these sources can provide persons and ideas capable of meeting society's and government's needs. The 103 young Americans chosen as White House Fellows by 1970 have come from such professions as medicine, architecture, journalism, social work, teaching, and corporate business; they represent most of the 50 states and hold degrees from 53 colleges and universities across the United States; they have been men and women, black and white, and of various religious beliefs and political persuasions. In spite of diverse backgrounds and the fact that few White House Fellows have been trained in government, the common denominator among the Fellows has been successful performance on the job.

There is, in addition, a common phenomenon that occurs with White House Fellows, one which seems to indicate that the program is achieving desirable goals. After serving in Washington for a year and returning to their own communities and earlier pursuits, most White House Fellows have felt compelled to continue their efforts to promote the common good. Since leaving Washington one former Fellow has accepted the challenge of directing the public works activities of one of the largest cities on the east coast; another is currently serving as executive secretary to the mayor of a major west coast city. One former Fellow, in addition to resuming his academic duties at an urban university, is designing a revised plan for his city that will coordinate educational and health services in one of its most disadvantaged neighborhoods.

Obviously, White House Fellows are already regarded as a cadre of willing and experienced citizens who can be tapped for further public service. Several former Fellows have been named to top jobs in state government, including that of state finance director. At the national level, some Fellows who served during the first two years of the program have been called back into service; former Fellows were appointed as an assistant postmaster general and a deputy undersecretary of the Department of Health, Education, and Welfare by the Nixon administration.

As the White House Fellows program proceeds, the increasing number of Fellows will be able, by sharing their experiences and by serving interchangeably at the local, state, and national levels, to help build a renewed feeling of closeness between the various levels of government and also between government and the people. Meanwhile, this much is already clear: the United States still produces leaders capable of fulfilling government's and society's needs. All that is required is that the talent be recognized.

Emphatically not a recruiting program, the White House Fellows program has served, nonetheless, to emphasize the need and the opportunity that exist for young citizens in government participation and has shown the benefits that can result from such participation.

STEPHEN P. STRICKLAND

WHITEHEAD, ALFRED NORTH

Alfred North Whitehead (1861–1947), the English mathematician and philosopher, became well known as an educationist after he delivered his brilliant address, "The Aims of Education: A Plea for Reform," in January 1916. This address is the most famous of his 16 essays on education—all written between 1911 and 1936. Whitehead's influence on education springs also, and almost as much, from some of the books in which he set forth his world-view after he migrated to the United States in 1924.

Background and career.   Whitehead's teaching career consisted of 39 years in mathematics (26 at Trinity College, Cambridge, and 13 at the University of London) and 13 years in philosophy at Harvard. He was, however, concerned with education at all levels, and he served on governing committees of many different types of schools.

He was born on February 15, 1861, at Ramsgate in East Kent, the son of a successful schoolmaster and grandson of another. As he was considered a frail boy, he was privately educated by his father until he was 14, when he was sent to Sherborne, then one of the best although not one of the most prestigious of England's public schools. There he received the usual predominantly classical education but was excused from some of the Latin to devote more time, under a first-rate master, to mathematics. A good football player, he became both captain of the games and head of the school (that is, the chief of the prefects, boys who had complete charge of discipline outside the classroom). In dedication to duty and in the exercise of authority by persuasion Whitehead early became an example of the public school Englishman at his best.

Whitehead's formal instruction as a student at Trinity College, Cambridge, was entirely in mathematics for honors. His advanced education in the humanities came from his own reading and from a sort of daily Platonic dialogue (as he called it) with friends, both as a Fellow of Trinity College and in the society of students known as the Apostles.

The fellowship and appointment to the staff followed soon after he got his degree. Most of his research at Cambridge dealt with the foundations of mathematics; this culminated in *Principia Mathematica* (1910–1913), written with his former pupil Bertrand Russell. After moving to London in 1910 he wrote the superb, popular *An Introduction to Mathematics* (1911). He then resumed the teaching of applied mathematics, of which he became professor in the Imperial College of Science and Technology. Challenged by the problems of educating the masses, he took on a good deal of administrative work at the University of London as well as in various other educational institutions. At the same time he wrote three highly technical but also philosophical books on the foundations of physical science. His pre-

eminence as a philosopher of science led to an invitation to join the Harvard faculty when he was 63. There his interest turned quickly from the philosophy of science to the philosophy of civilization and metaphysics.

Bertrand Russell remembered that "Whitehead was extraordinarily perfect as a teacher [of mathematics]. . . . He would elicit from a pupil the best of which a pupil was capable" (1956, p. 97). Many former Harvard and Radcliffe students remember his lectures—loosely organized philosophic talks—as the best part of their college experience.

"The Aims of Education."   In the Preface to his *The Aims of Education and Other Essays*, Whitehead wrote that "the whole book is a protest against dead knowledge, that is to say, against inert ideas" (*The Aims of Education and Other Essays* 1959, p. v, hereafter cited as *Aims*). In the title essay he explained that by inert ideas he meant "ideas that are merely received into the mind without being utilised, or tested, or thrown into fresh combinations" (*Aims*, p. 1). Whitehead first became concerned about the teaching of mathematics in the secondary schools of England, but he extended his attack and his own philosophy of education to the teaching of all subjects to pupils of all ages, and his message was meant to be pertinent in all countries. Although almost every reformer has fought the mere learning of algebraic rules and formulas, dates, and other information, Whitehead's attack has become classic in its unequaled clarity and vigor, the positive insights that accompanied it, and its hard-headed realism. He also had a genius for epigrammatic utterance: sentences like "you may not divide the seamless coat of learning" (*Aims*, p. 18) have had an enduring influence upon teachers who know little of his general position.

There is a good deal of anger in Whitehead's attack on dead knowledge. He thought such pseudoteaching not just useless but also wicked: "It must never be forgotten that education is not a process of packing articles in a trunk. Such a simile is entirely inapplicable. It is, of course, a process completely of its own peculiar genus. Its nearest analogue is the assimilation of food by a living organism" (*Aims*, p. 51).

The statement of purpose—"the students are alive, and the purpose of education is to stimulate and guide their self-development" (*Aims*, p. v)—was not meant to rule out other purposes, such as the transmission of the most valuable achievements of a culture to the next generation or the production of individuals whose trained intelligence will serve their country well. Whitehead valued these aims, but he insisted that it is only by the well-guided self-development of children that schools can effectively realize any worthy aim.

All historians of education are aware of earlier advocates of self-development as a basis for education. Henry W. Holmes (Schilpp 1951), writing about Whitehead's view, mentioned similar ideas held by John Dewey, Friedrich Froebel, and Froebel's predecessors, but concluded that this idea is deepest of all and has most sweep in Whitehead.

There is no formal definition of the educative process in Whitehead's writings. The statement closest to a definition is "education is the acquisition of the art of the utilization of knowledge" (*Aims*, p. 3). Whitehead did not value knowledge for its own sake:

> Pedants sneer at an education which is useful. But if education is not useful, what is it? Is it a talent, to be hidden away in a napkin? Of course, education should be useful, whatever your aim in life. It was useful to Saint Augustine, and it was useful to Napoleon. It is useful, because understanding is useful. (*Aims*, p. 3)

"Understanding" does not here refer to the intellectual grasp of ideas. It refers rather to the comprehension of life by means of ideas in a sense which includes more than logical analysis. Whitehead conceived this kind of understanding as the final desideratum of education on its intellectual side.

Curriculum. The disconnection of subjects in teaching was a constant horror to Whitehead. In 1916 he was urging teachers to develop in their pupils a sense of the wide power of ideas by using the concepts of the variable, of functions, and of rates of change to exhibit in graphs "the quantitative flux of the forces of modern society. . . . The curves of history are more vivid and more informative than the dry catalogues of names and dates. . . ." (*Aims*, p. 13).

Whitehead presented the need for curricular unity in these words:

> There is only one subject-matter for education, and that is Life in all its manifestations. Instead of this single unity, we offer children—Algebra, from which nothing follows; History, from which nothing follows; a Couple of Languages, never

mastered; and lastly, most dreary of all, Literature, represented by plays of Shakespeare, with philological notes and short analyses of plot and character to be in substance committed to memory. Can such a list be said to represent Life, as it is known in the midst of the living of it? The best that can be said of it is, that it is a rapid table of contents which a deity might run over in his mind while he was thinking of creating a world, and had not yet determined how to put it together. (*Aims*, pp. 10–11)

Unfortunately, the English system of uniform examinations of school pupils, set by outside examiners, was an obstacle to Whitehead's approach. The essays he wrote in England are all peppered with denunciations of the examination system. He thought that better curricula and better teaching are possible only if teachers are free to attempt them. Since the school is "the true educational unit," outside authorities should examine the schools rather than the individual scholars.

In his attack on another established practice, Whitehead had powerful allies, especially in the United States. The following passage shows his version of a view he shared with John Dewey:

> . . . what is the point of teaching a child to solve a quadratic equation? There is a traditional answer to this question. It runs thus: The mind is an instrument, you first sharpen it, and then use it; . . . Now there is just enough truth in this answer to have made it live through the ages. But for all its half-truth, it embodies a radical error which bids fair to stifle the genius of the modern world. . . . The mind is never passive; it is a perpetual activity, delicate, receptive, responsive to stimulus. You cannot postpone its life until you have sharpened it. Whatever interest attaches to your subject-matter must be evoked here and now; whatever powers you are strengthening in the pupil, must be exercised here and now; whatever possibilities of mental life your teaching should impart, must be exhibited here and now. That is the golden rule of education, and a very difficult rule to follow. (*Aims*, pp. 8–9)

(However, Whitehead thought that there is good reason to teach the solution of quadratic equations to at least some pupils—if quadratic equations are part of a connected curriculum.)

Freedom and discipline. The doctrine of the rhythmic claims of freedom and discipline advanced by Whitehead is based on his view that mental growth is essentially cyclical. The cycle begins with free exploration marked by wonder, "the stage of romance"; proceeds to the acquirement of technique and detailed knowledge, "the stage of precision"; and reaches fruition in a final stage of romance, marked by the free application of what has been learned, "the stage of generalisation." Whitehead suggested that if the schoolroom teaching of a subject is to be as successful as the process of learning one's native language, for example, it should begin with free exploration, with guidance and discipline provided but not systematized or allowed to become dominant; it should proceed to the disciplined mastery of a body of precise, detailed knowledge that has been carefully limited to essentials; and it should conclude with enjoyment of the power of knowledge in use.

In recommending that the order of learning tasks be guided in this way, Whitehead rejected as based on a false psychology the assumption that the pupil's progress should be uniformly steady. He also rejected the assumption that the easier subjects should be studied before the harder ones. "On the contrary, some of the hardest must come first because nature so dictates, and because they are essential to life" (*Aims*, p. 25). For example, the infant's first intellectual task is to attach meanings to sounds; the child's is to correlate sounds with shapes; both are tasks of appalling difficulty. When he comes to study mathematics, the elements of algebra may be harder to grasp than more advanced material.

By using the word "rhythm" Whitehead meant to emphasize the plurality of learning cycles—cycles big and little, early and late, in phase and out of phase with each other. (The stage of precision in language studies may occur while the study of science is still in the first, romantic, stage, for example.) Romance must be present in every stage, or interest dies. Whitehead attributed the success of the Montessori system to its recognition of the dominance of romance in early childhood; but no one could be more insistent than Whitehead on the need for disciplined learning later on. Indeed, in Whitehead's view, all three stages—romance, precision, and generalization—should be present at all times; the cycles represent alternations in their dominance. Traditional teaching recognized only the stage of precision.

Whitehead warned against supposing that he was advancing a method that could be learned

and then applied on schedule by any teacher to any group of children. The individual teacher of a subject must have an intimate awareness of the progress of the pupils and must judge what next in the way of freedom and discipline their self-development calls for. A teacher who cannot elicit enthusiasm for the essential ideas and techniques of the subject and who does not make the class glad that he is there is not worth his salt. But Whitehead was not so foolish as to assume that the good teacher must have genius.

Whitehead's conception of the rhythm of education shows some similarity to the one which T. Percy Nunn, of the University of London, expounded originally in 1905. Nunn (1920) said that Whitehead's conception was independent of his own. Whitehead himself never discussed the writings of other philosophers of education; probably he did not study them much.

General and special education. Whitehead warned against viewing general and special education as antithetical. Although general purposes naturally have priority over special ones until the child reaches the age of about 16, general education itself requires attention to special focuses since only in this manner can the pupil learn to "see the wood by means of the trees" (*Aims*, p. 10).

Throughout general education the business of studying a subject, Whitehead held, is not so much to produce knowledge as to form habits. Thus, the study of natural science should enforce a union of thought and firsthand observation, whereby observation becomes exact, and imagination is strengthened.

Whitehead seldom speaks of general knowledge; he refers instead to culture:

> Culture is activity of thought, and receptiveness to beauty and humane feeling. Scraps of information have nothing to do with it. A merely well-informed man is the most useless bore on God's earth. What we should aim at producing is men who possess both culture and expert knowledge in some special direction. (*Aims*, p. 1)

Whitehead rests his case for special studies not only on the fact that expert knowledge is indispensable in the modern world but also on the idea that the vitality of education requires them since pupils' interests are naturally specialized. Furthermore, he pointed out, "nothing but a special study can give any appreciation for the exact formulation of general ideas, for their relations when formulated, for their service in the comprehension of life" (*Aims*, pp. 18–19). The final gift of special studies is the sense for what Whitehead called "the ultimate morality of mind"—style:

> It is an aesthetic sense, based on admiration for the direct attainment of a foreseen end, simply and without waste. . . . The love of a subject in itself and for itself, where it is not the sleepy pleasure of pacing a mental quarter-deck, is the love of style as manifested in that study.
>
> Here we are brought back to the position from which we started, the utility of education. Style, in its finest sense, is the last acquirement of the educated mind; it is also the most useful.
>
> . . . Now style is the exclusive privilege of the expert. (*Aims*, pp. 19–20)

Mathematics and technical education. The contribution of mathematics—the science in which Whitehead was expert—to a liberal education was the subject of his first published address on education, "The Place of Mathematics in a Liberal Education," given in 1911 (*Essays in Science and Philosophy* 1947). He argued that mathematics, properly taught, develops three closely related abilities: (1) the power of clearly grasping abstract ideas, a power which can be gained only by choosing a group of abstract ideas which are important, clear, and definite, and by learning to analyze and generalize them, (2) the habit of thinking logically, including the ability to recognize imprecise ideas, to be aware of one's assumptions, and to reason well, and (3) the capacity to apply abstract ideas to the concrete universe, including both nature and society. In discussing the first ability, Whitehead called it a positive error to begin with mathematical ideas in their clear, refined forms and to try to impart these; rather, the start must be made with the ideas as they actually exist in the child's mind, and the child must be shown how to civilize them. In discussing the second ability, he called for rigor and for brevity in the material used. What gets in the way of the third ability, he said, is the time consumed on silly examples and in learning algebraic manipulations which lead nowhere; he called for "one hour of the Caliph Omar, to burn up and utterly destroy all the silly mathematical problems which cumber our text-books" (*Essays in Science and Philosophy* 1947, p. 181).

In 1917, Whitehead delivered an address, "Technical Education and Its Relation to Science and Literature" (*Aims*). Some of the things he considered are now outdated, but most of the ideas are of permanent value. For example, he pointed out that the importance of scientific knowledge cannot be realized apart from technical applications and that technical education is needed for the proper development of all human beings. Whitehead also held that the antithesis between technical and liberal education is fallacious. He urged the inclusion of literary study in the technical curriculum, and he recommended that the curriculum concentrate on getting the pupils to enjoy literature. "It does not matter what they know, but the enjoyment is vital" (*Aims*, p. 89).

The classics. In 1919, Prime Minister David Lloyd George appointed a committee to inquire into the position of classics in Britain's educational system; it reported after two years of hearings. Although Whitehead was the only Fellow of the Royal Society among the 19 distinguished members of the committee, he did not often take stands against the majority. His subsequent essay, "The Place of Classics in Education" (*Aims*), was not a minority report. Its defense of the classics, however, is rather different from the committee's in that Whitehead does not place the value of Latin and Greek for most students in the learning of the languages, which are seldom remembered, nor in the grammatical training, but rather in being instrumental to a firsthand appreciation of the unity of civilization and to an enrichment of the students' intellectual character. It is here that Whitehead made his oft-quoted assertion, "moral education is impossible apart from the habitual vision of greatness" (*Aims*, p. 106).

University education. In describing the rhythm of education, Whitehead considered the whole period of mental growth from infancy to manhood as one grand cycle, in which the years spent at a college or university should be dominated by the spirit of generalization. He did not say much else about university studies while he was in England, where the reform of schoolteaching was his chief concern. Universities are, however, the topic of the five pieces on education which he wrote in the United States. The first, "Universities and Their Function" (*Aims*), makes the point that is most central: Since books are cheap and research can be done in institutes, a university is justified only if it unites the young and the old in the imaginative consideration of learning.

He believed that the young are naturally imaginative, and he assumed that they are in college because they want to be there. He placed a high value on personal contacts between professors and students, but he assumed that regular lectures are basic. Whitehead's message concerns what is said in lectures: "For successful education there must always be a certain freshness in the knowledge dealt with. It must either be new in itself or it must be invested with some novelty of applications to the new world of new times. Knowledge does not keep any better than fish" (*Aims*, p. 147).

As we might expect, Whitehead recommended the closest possible contact of theoretical studies with vocational practices in the professional schools of universities.

The philosophy of organism. The philosophy of organism is Whitehead's name for the well-articulated metaphysical system which he developed between 1924 and 1928 after he came to Harvard as professor of philosophy.

The philosophy of organism grew from several sources; the central one was the collapse of the Newtonian physics in which Whitehead himself was educated. His own work on the foundations of mathematics and physics was another source, and his habitual ways of understanding history and literature constituted a third. It would be incredible if his long experience as an educator and his reflections on education were not at work as a fourth source of his world view. The reader of his metaphysics is struck by its harmony with Whitehead's views on education. (Since he had already published his main ideas about education, it would be an anachronism to suppose that the philosophy of organism was their basis. His views on education represent convictions that were aroused by his varied experiences with educational practice in England and can stand on their own feet. In his metaphysical books there are a few brief discussions of education but no references to his educational essays; nor did reprintings of the essays lead him to insert references to his metaphysics.)

Whitehead did change his mind about God, probably gradually, between 1915 and 1924. He had been an agnostic for many years, but in *Science and the Modern World* (1925) he argued that a coherent world view requires a conception of God, and in *Religion in the Making* (1926) he set forth his conception of religion. Whitehead's metaphysics culminated in a new philosophical theology, which has been its most influential element. (None of Whitehead's essays on education show their author's position with regard to theism.)

Whitehead was convinced that certain features of human experience—notably becoming and perishing, individuality and interdependence, intrinsic value and external utility, derivation from the past and deviation from its course, compulsion, self-determination, and purpose—are rooted, and in some definite way related to each other, in the very nature of things. He was equally convinced that we can never do more than approximate a coherent, universally applicable conceptualization of reality. He offered his system of speculative philosophy, set forth in *Process and Reality* (1929), as an interwoven set of suggestions. So far as Whitehead was successful, he noted and overcame every major dualism of European philosophy. His is a philosophy of process, although it does not contend that only process is real. It cannot without fatal distortion be classified as a form of any familiar "-ism," and it is too original to be called eclectic.

The philosophy of organism was devised as an alternative to scientific materialism—the view that nature basically consists of matter or purely physical energy which simply moves from place to place and that values arise only in minds. Whitehead, refusing to accept "substance" as a fundamental concept, analyzed the world process into becomings, or atoms of process. (A substantial thing consists of associated chains of becomings.) The underlying energy of process, always passing on to new incarnations, he called creativity. It is a firm principle of Whitehead's that, although past becomings are fixed and cannot be shaken off in a present becoming, their influences do not completely determine how they will be synthesized in the present; therein lies the freedom of the present becoming, its measure of self-determination. Whitehead's choice of the name "philosophy of organism" reflects the fact that an organism determines the integration of its own parts. In human experience, one's personal past, the external environment, and the bodily processes by which the environment enters into the experience are all emotionally charged factors in the person-now. It is the person-now that turns them into a privately enjoyed unity of feelings that is rather like what William James called a pulse or drop of experience, although it is not necessarily conscious. The basic factors in an occasion of experience are not clear and distinct perceptions; Whitehead was as critical of the Humian tradition as of the Newtonian.

In Whitehead's system change is always interpreted as becoming-and-perishing. He works on the principle that becoming is intelligible only as actualization of potentialities. The Platonic strain in his metaphysics comes out most strongly in his doctrine that a novel synthesis must be able to draw into itself qualities, patterns, and ideal aims which have not been realized in the environment from which it grows. It is one function of God, in Whitehead's system, to provide these possibilities; indeed, God is the eternal reservoir of all "forms of definiteness," these being in themselves timeless, pure potentials. (This complex conception of Whitehead's is something like the simple one that Platonic Ideas have their being in God's mind.) In addition to being the original source of novelty and forms of order, God, as Whitehead conceived Him, is the everlasting conserver of what is achieved in and by the temporal world; thus, He "grows" as the sum of finite becomings increases. He is not omnipotent, nor is He the only real being. He is both immanent in the world and transcendent, and every finite becoming both transcends Him and becomes immanent in Him.

In Whitehead's theory of the generic constitution of individual becomings, the roles of causation and of individual purpose are nicely interlocked. Life is the characteristic of those organizations of becomings which show a marked degree of initiative in their reactions to the causal pressures of their environments; our human reason is our discipline of spontaneous initiatives. The concept of adventure—so important, as "romance," in Whitehead's philosophy of education —is central to his theory of life and to his concept of civilization. A traditional way of being alive, or a tradition in art, provides a basis which permits variations, up to a point; when they are exhausted, decay follows—unless there is adventure guided by discipline.

Whitehead's conception of order is based on the idea that an environment is ordered in proportion as it favors the attainment of complex ends. There are many types of order and disorder and many species of importance, or value; but, since Whitehead always thought of things as composite, aesthetic value easily became central in his view. Those organizations of process which must reject the novelty that arises in their environment rank lower than those which can appropriate it in aesthetic contrast with the old so that a new and more complex harmony can be experienced. Moral goodness and truth are servants of harmony; the essence of evil is mutual destruction.

In the final chapter of *Science and the Modern World* (1925), "Requisites for Social Progress," Whitehead urged that aesthetic values be emphasized in education: the habit of active interest in the variety of individual values which emerge in nature and in art and other human enterprises will give depth and breadth to minds whose intellectual training is necessarily specialized.

Adventures of Ideas (1933) is, after *Science and the Modern World*, the most widely read of Whitehead's metaphysical books. In Part 4 he applied his metaphysical principles to elucidate the nature of beauty, truth, art, adventure, and peace. He defined a civilized society as one which exhibits these five qualities. By peace he meant a religious attitude which is "primarily a trust in the efficacy of beauty" (*Adventures of Ideas*, p. 367). (Whitehead, always realistic, held that religion can be very bad, and that it sometimes has been.) This fourth part of the book and the historical chapters (in which progress is practically identified with the gradual displacement of force by persuasion) have been irreplaceable sources of wisdom to many people concerned with education for civilization. Chapter 3 of Whitehead's short earlier book, *Symbolism: Its Meaning and Effect* (1927) offered sociological insights which have tempered the positions of both reformers and conservatives.

Whitehead is sometimes erroneously called an anti-intellectual philosopher. He had faith that nothing is intrinsically closed to theoretical understanding. An epistemological realist, he held that our knowledge is of things, not of ideas; but things are infinitely complex, and the disclosure is never complete. He said again and again that our finite thought can proceed only by making judicious abstractions; but he called "dogmatic" all thinkers who, after fastening on some important feature of what exists and developing a precise theory of that feature by a method appropriate to it, claim that they have omitted nothing that could be significant. When he criticized scientific materialism he said that its adherents committed what he called the fallacy of misplaced concreteness by mistaking an abstract system of material particles for the concrete reality of nature. He was likewise sharply critical of several views which became prevalent in his later years: mechanistic theories of life, behaviorism, the assumption that linguistic phrases adequately express ideas, and the view that our mathematical truths are only tautologies (he believed that they concern forms of process).

The targets of Whitehead's philosophical criticism have an obvious kinship with that preoccupation with formularized settled knowledge against which he protested in his essays on education. As he then placed his hope on the pupil's joyful discovery of the power of ideas to illuminate experience, so Whitehead as a philosopher sought the widest possible understanding. The question he wanted men to ask of every new idea was not simply "true or false?" nor only "does it solve the present problem?" but "how far can it take us?"

Influence on education. No study seems to have been made of Whitehead's effect on British or American teaching; perhaps no reliable detailed analysis of it can be made. Something, however, can be said now about its extent and character.

Whitehead did not discuss the school as an instrument for bringing about a more democratic society; so far as educators concentrated on that issue, he did not influence them. Since he never wrote a book-length elaboration of his convictions about education into a systematic theory, it is not surprising that while some American philosophers took up his ideas, no influential teachers' college became predominantly Whiteheadian. Nevertheless, he was and is read by countless students of education. His work has become classic: chapters on Whitehead were added to the 1968 edition of Robert Ulich's *History of Educational Thought* and the 1970 edition of Robert R. Rusk's *Doctrines of the Great Educators.*

The main effect of Whitehead's educational essays has been to warn and to inspire. They have done this for a great many teachers, even outside the English-speaking world. Substantial specific influence in England has mainly depended on an occasional headmaster's being so impressed that he could bring about some realization of Whitehead's ideals even in the face of the examination system. In the same individual but influential manner, some directors of American private schools have responded—Katherine Taylor and her successors at the Shady Hill School in Cambridge,

Mass., are good examples. Programmed instruction and the movement toward programmed schools militate against Whitehead's influence. Earlier, the advocacy of core curricula benefited from it.

On the whole, Whitehead's reflections on civilization have meant more to educators than his metaphysics has. The influence of the latter has been indirect and fairly nebulous; for every reader who achieved a clear understanding of the philosophy of organism, hundreds settled for vague impressions. Some of these hundreds are nonetheless its enthusiasts; more have dismissed it as impossibly obscure (especially in England) or as soft because of its idealistic and theistic elements. Among sympathizers with philosophies of process, the majority consider John Dewey's less ambitious one—a theory of the ongoing experience-continuum, not of all existence—a sufficient basis for educational thought. Yet in view of widespread lack of interest in metaphysical systems, the influence of Whitehead's is unusually vital. (Dewey's response was a mixture of admiring agreement and puzzled disagreement.) Harold Dunkel (1965) and Frank C. Wegener (1957) have written books which endeavor to apply the philosophy of organism to education.

SELECTED WORKS BY
ALFRED NORTH WHITEHEAD

1910–1913 *Principia Mathematica.* 3 vols. With Bertrand Russell. Cambridge University Press.

1911 *An Introduction to Mathematics.* London, Williams & Northgate; New York, Holt.

1917 *The Organization of Thought, Educational and Scientific.* London, Williams & Northgate. Includes five essays on education, two of which are not republished elsewhere: "The Principles of Mathematics in Relation to Elementary Teaching" (1912) and "A Polytechnic in War-Time" (1917).

1919 *An Enquiry Concerning the Principles of Natural Knowledge.* Cambridge University Press.

1925 *Science and the Modern World.* New York, Macmillan.

1926 *Religion in the Making.* New York, Macmillan.

1927 *Symbolism: Its Meaning and Effect.* New York, Macmillan.

1929 *Process and Reality: An Essay in Cosmology.* New York, Macmillan.

1929 *The Function of Reason.* Princeton, N.J., Princeton University Press.

1933 *Adventures of Ideas.* New York, Macmillan.

1938 *Modes of Thought.* New York, Macmillan.

1947 *Essays in Science and Philosophy.* New York, Philosophical Library. Includes "The Place of Mathematics in a Liberal Education" (1911), "Education and Self-Education" (1919), "Science in General Education" (1921), "Historical Changes" (1930), "The Study of the Past—

Its Uses and Its Dangers" (1933), and "Harvard: The Future" (1936).

1953 *Alfred North Whitehead: An Anthology.* Selected by F. S. C. Northrup and Mason W. Gross. New York, Macmillan.

1959 *The Aims of Education and Other Essays.* New York, Macmillan. Includes "The Mathematical Curriculum" (1913), "The Aims of Education" (1916), "Technical Education and Its Relation to Science and Literature" (1917), "The Rhythm of Education" (1922), "The Rhythmic Claims of Freedom and Discipline" (1923), "The Place of Classics in Education" (1923), and "Universities and Their Function" (1928).

SUPPLEMENTARY BIBLIOGRAPHY

"Centennial Issue: Alfred North Whitehead, 1861–1947." 1961 *Educational Theory,* 11, no. 4:entire issue.

DEWEY, JOHN 1937 "Whitehead's Philosophy." *The Philosophical Review,* 46, no. 2:170–177.

DUNKEL, HAROLD B. 1965 *Whitehead on Education.* Columbus, Ohio State University Press.

EMMET, DOROTHY M. 1967 "Whitehead, Alfred North." Paul Edwards, ed., *The Encyclopedia of Philosophy.* New York, Macmillan and Free Press. Volume 8, pages 290–296.

FRANKENA, WILLIAM K., ed. 1965 *Philosophy of Education.* New York, Macmillan.

NUNN, T. PERCY (1920) 1945 *Education: Its Data and First Principles.* 3rd ed., rev. London, E. Arnold.

RUSK, ROBERT R. 1970 *Doctrines of the Great Educators.* 4th ed. New York, St. Martin's.

RUSSELL, BERTRAND 1956 *Portraits From Memory and Other Essays.* London, Allen and Unwin.

SCHILPP, PAUL A., ed. 1951 *The Philosophy of Alfred North Whitehead.* 2nd ed. New York, Tudor. Contains a "Bibliography of the Writings of Alfred North Whitehead, Published Through January 3, 1951," compiled by Victor Lowe and R. C. Baldwin.

ULICH, ROBERT 1968 *History of Educational Thought.* 2nd ed. New York, Van Nostrand.

WEGENER, FRANK C. 1957 *The Organic Philosophy of Education.* Dubuque, Iowa, W. C. Brown.

VICTOR LOWE

WOMEN, EDUCATION OF

1. HISTORY   Kathryn Kish Sklar

2. CONTINUING EDUCATION   Vera M. Schletzer

3. JOB REENTRY TRAINING   Prudence B. Randall

1. HISTORY

Although the same historical forces have shaped both the course of American education and the development of women's education, they have often influenced the education of men and women in different ways. Thus, in the seventeenth century, when college education was primarily professional education and the major professions were closed to women, women were not included in the small and privileged number who attended college. The education of women was not neglected but was rather in keeping with the general utilitarian aim of educating young people with a view toward their future social role. The family, the apprentice system, and the church were for the vast majority of early colonists the most influential agencies of education. And although the broad aim of education, grooming for future social roles, was the same for men and women, the results were different—women were prepared for a domestic role and men were not. The dramatic transformation of women's education that occurred in the nineteenth century was a response to the development of teaching as a profession. For the first time a profession was open to women, and the formal schooling of girls therefore became desirable. As other professions opened to women in the late nineteenth and early twentieth centuries, the education of women became a major theme in American education.

Yet, the scope of women's education has been influenced not only by the overall growth of education but also by the changing roles that women have assumed in American society. Thus, in the twentieth century as well as the seventeenth, women's education has been determined by the roles society provides for women.

Although educational opportunities have steadily expanded for women since colonial days, there have been some unexpected reverses. For example, proportionately to the population, more women earned advanced degrees in 1930 than in 1950. Only in the 1960's, when new cultural trends affecting women's social roles had supplanted those of the 1950's, did women begin to equal the educational achievements of the 1920's. Educational opportunity alone has not, therefore, determined the level of women's education.

Seventeenth and eighteenth centuries. Like most cultural forms in the American colonies, the education of women in the seventeenth century was patterned after the English example—that is, young women were prepared primarily for their future roles as wives and mothers, and their education was limited to what their homes or the master to whom they were apprenticed could provide. Throughout most of the colonial period, the main agency of education was the home, which consisted not only of the nuclear family but also of apprentices of both sexes and a variety of relatives. According to the English tradition the master of this extended family was responsible for the education of all the young people in his charge. In both Massachusetts and Virginia, laws passed in 1642 made this traditional requirement a legal one. Indeed, a Virginia law of 1672 gave the county courts the power to place all children whose parents were not able to bring them up as apprentices to tradesmen and families, who were then responsible for educating the males until they were 21 years old and the females until they were 18 years old (Woody 1966). Education consisted mainly of learning a trade, but rudimentary reading ability was also expected. In Massachusetts all heads of families were required to teach their charges to read and understand both the major laws of the colony and the tenets of the Puritan faith.

This early emphasis upon the home or family as the major agency of education set the stage for the future development of women's education. However, according to Bernard Bailyn (1960), the master of the American family could not exert the same authority traditionally enjoyed by the English family head because in the new world "the entire apparatus of authority had been weakened" as a result of "disruption and transplantation in alien soil." Thus, Bailyn says, alternative educational forms began to evolve, and during the eighteenth century town schools and evening schools for apprentices became widespread. Yet, the most important development for women was not the growth of these institutions, from which they were still largely excluded until the end of the eighteenth century, but the development of a different attitude toward education. Education came to be regarded not as an automatic transmission of a traditional culture, but, in Bailyn's words, as "deliberate, self-conscious, and explicit." This change in attitude expanded the role of the mother—she was not only to nurture but also to educate her children. Although much research remains to be done on the changing nature of the colonial family, it is clear that by the end of this period the mother had begun to replace the male family head as the person most responsible for educating their sons and daughters.

Benjamin Rush's *Thoughts Upon Female Education*, an address delivered in 1787, marks an important turning point in women's education. Rush makes explicit the changes that have gradually transformed American attitudes toward the education of women, emphasizing the role of women in the education of children and pointing out the inadequacy of contemporary female schooling to provide women with the kind of education that will be necessary for them if they are to assume this larger social and cultural burden. Reviewing the tendency of Americans to adopt British customs in educating women, Rush called for a specific form of female education that would be accommodated to American society. Since the male heads of families were too occupied with their life outside the home, he said, "a principal share of the instruction of children naturally devolves upon the women. It becomes us therefore to prepare them by a suitable education, for the discharge of this most important duty of mothers" (Rush 1798, p. 76).

During the eighteenth century a provincial culture had developed in the colonies, and in the numerous schools for young women that had been established girls were taught cultural accomplishments that were more appropriate to English than to American society. After a year or two in a "dame school"—an institution on the British model that resembled a kindergarten where rudimentary reading was taught in the home of a local woman—the secondary education of girls consisted primarily of writing, composition, painting, drawing, French, dancing, and sewing. American girls were being educated for a domestic life, but one that mirrored the ornaments of English society rather than one that enabled them to educate their own sons and daughters. Rush set the tone for the next century in the education of women when he declared that "it is incumbent upon us to make ornamental accomplishments yield to principles and knowledge in the education of our women" (*ibid.*, p. 87).

Nineteenth century. Many advances made in women's education in the early decades of the nineteenth century arose from women's newly explicit but long-practiced role as educators of the young. Although Thomas Jefferson's celebrated plan for education in Virginia did not include girls, he gave his own daughters a solid education "to enable them when mothers, to educate their own daughters and even to direct the course for their sons" (Woody 1966, vol. 1, p. 275). At this time, when the new nation was striving to prove its worth, the sentiment most widely expressed with regard to female education was that which appeared in an early issue of the first journal devoted to education, the *Ameri-*

can *Annals of Education.* "Science," Catharine Beecher declared, "would never reach its acme, while the influential half of our race, to whom the training of the rising generation is committed, were left in ignorance of it" (1827, p. 222).

Many academies and seminaries were established in the early 1800's to provide women with a secondary education equal to that of men. Emma Willard's school for girls at Troy, N.Y. (founded in 1821), Catharine Beecher's at Hartford, Conn. (1824), Zilpah Grant's at Ipswich, Mass. (1828), Mary Lyon's at South Hadley, Mass. (1837), and George B. Emerson's academy at Boston, Mass. (1823), were only a few of several institutions founded exclusively for women. This group of New Englanders knew one another well, and their pioneer efforts were enhanced by the knowledge that they were part of a widespread movement. Therefore, they enjoyed a sense of common purpose that was lacking in earlier academies, such as John Poor's at Philadelphia (chartered in 1792), Sally Pierce's at Litchfield, Conn. (1792), and Timothy Dwight's at Greenfield Hill, Conn. (1785). Although these eighteenth-century academies had offered a course of study equal to the best in contemporary secondary education, they had failed to capture the public imagination and had remained economically marginal institutions (without endowment). With the exception of Poor's academy, they had no legal basis, such as a charter of incorporation or a board of trustees. In contrast, the seminary movement of the early nineteenth century, under the leadership of Emma Willard and Catharine Beecher, sought to establish institutions for women on a permanent basis—with endowments, a charter, and a board of trustees. These later academies were therefore able to solicit funds in addition to the tuition paid by students, to construct buildings, and to provide financial security for seminary teachers. To a large extent the leaders of this seminary movement met with a responsive public which financed buildings and purchased school equipment, even if it did not always go so far as to endow the academies. This movement was also enhanced by the spirit of expansion and optimism that characterized the first decades of the nineteenth century—numerous academies and seminaries were founded at a rapid rate in the North, South, and West.

The experience of one prominent member of the seminary movement, Catharine Beecher, reveals the nature and the national dimensions of this movement that so significantly altered the character of women's education in the United States. In its broad outlines, Catharine Beecher's career is typical of those of her dedicated contemporaries who recast women's education. Taught at home in a school run by her mother until she was ten years old, Miss Beecher did not receive a systematic or thorough education. She subsequently attended Miss Pierce's Academy at Litchfield for six years, but in her *Educational Reminiscences and Suggestions* (1874) she stated that she did not take full advantage of the intellectual side of the academy and devoted these years primarily to developing social graces and preparing for marriage. Only when her own marriage plans were terminated by the death of her fiancé in 1823 did she turn to teaching as a means of livelihood. For a few years in Hartford she conducted a one-room secondary school for girls that differed little from the one she attended in Litchfield. In 1827, however, she established her school on a seminary pattern, received a charter, and chose a board of trustees who aided her fund-raising efforts.

Equipped with a staff of six teachers, the Hartford Female Seminary divided its pupils into classes according to age and ability and occupied its own ample building with several recitation rooms, a large study hall, and a library. All these were innovations in the education of women. Catharine Beecher struggled to reform the contemporary practice whereby a girl's family sent her not to one institution for several terms but to several institutions for one term in the belief that she could thereby profit from the virtues that each school offered. To correct this haphazard enrollment policy, Catharine Beecher refused to admit girls for less than a full course of study (usually lasting two terms), and she devised a more sequential curriculum designed to foster real rather than superficial knowledge in her students. In keeping with the contemporary mood of expansion, Catharine Beecher left her flourishing Hartford academy in 1832 and went to Cincinnati to establish another seminary, which was successful because she attracted a staff of teachers and enjoyed local patronage. The extent of the growth of seminaries during this period is shown by the fact that numerous opportunities for secondary female education existed in Cincinnati; in addition to Catharine Beecher's Western Female Institute, there were nine other female academies listed in the *City Directory* by 1836, several of which were of as high quality as Catharine Beecher's. Natural science, moral philosophy, history, mathematics, and literature were taught along with the subjects traditionally taught to women, such as music and drawing.

The greatest impetus to the growth of women's education was the parallel growth of common schools. Since seminaries were primarily training grounds for the teachers who were so urgently needed to staff the enormously increasing numbers of small primary schools, men like Horace Mann, Thomas Gallaudet, Thomas Burrowes, and Calvin Stowe who led the common school movement also actively supported the female academy movement. The cause of women's education therefore became inextricably combined with the cause of popular education. Catharine Beecher left her Cincinnati academy in 1837 to become a publicist—as did many of her contemporary educators—for the combined causes of popular education and the creation of normal schools for women.

With the aid of male educators like Horace Mann, Catharine Beecher campaigned to establish teaching as a woman's profession. At female seminaries throughout the nation many young women, like Lucy Larcom, were channeled into teaching careers. As she described in her autobiographical *A New England Girlhood*, the young Miss Larcom left New England for Godfrey, Ill., where she enrolled in Monticello Seminary (founded in 1838) and began a career as a teacher with the encouragement of the principal of the seminary. The National Board of Popular Education, an organization founded by Catharine Beecher, placed more than 400 women from the East in teaching positions in the West. By the 1850's higher education for women had become nearly synonymous with normal schools. Although most women who profited from the expansion of women's education did not become teachers, the development of teaching as a career for women provided a rationale for women's education and vastly increased their educational opportunities.

In 1839 the first state normal school was established at Lexington, Mass., and it was exclusively for women. Statistics from Philadelphia show to what extent the work of the elementary schools had come into the hands of women (Woody 1966): in 1842 there were 82 male and 699 female teachers. By 1872 there were 101 normal schools in the United States—48 aided by states, 44 affiliated with other institutions, and nine self-supporting. By 1875 the affiliated institutions were more frequently colleges or universities than female seminaries, as earlier.

Women teachers were desirable because they were willing to work for less money than men. For instance, in the 1840's in Maine men received an average monthly salary of $15, whereas women received less than $5; and in Vermont, Connecticut, New York, Indiana, and Michigan male teachers' salaries were more than double the women's salaries. In the first decades of the nineteenth century, women were considered competent to teach in summer school but not in the winter session when the older boys attended. By the 1850's, however, women teachers outnumbered men by more than two to one, and by 1890 two-thirds of American teachers were women (in urban areas more than 90 percent were women).

The growth of normal schools and the teacher-training role of seminaries also greatly influenced public secondary education for women, because the example set by the female students in such academies was frequently responsible for opening the doors of local high schools to women, as had been the case in George Emerson's Boston academy for young women. The first public high school for girls was opened in Worcester, Mass., in 1824, and within two years others were established in New York City and Boston. Separate high schools for girls were economically wasteful, however, and as the number of public high schools increased, girls were generally also admitted and given the same course of study as boys. Coeducational high schools were established at Bridgewater, Conn., in 1826, at Providence, R.I., in 1838, and at Hartford, Conn., in 1847. Although the growth of high schools was slow before the Civil War, from 1865 to 1890 their number increased enormously; by 1890 twice as many girls as boys graduated from high schools.

The trend toward widespread secondary education of girls was firmly established in 1850. However, college education for women remained a rarity—only a handful of experimental colleges received women. Oberlin began the movement toward coeducation in 1837, and Antioch followed shortly thereafter. But later, after the Civil War, coeducation was not confined to newer, radical institutions; it was adopted by such older, conservative universities as Boston University in 1869 and the University of Pennsylvania in 1877. In 1870 one-third of American colleges were co-educational (excluding technical schools and the colleges established expressly for women), and by 1880 the proportion of coeducational institutions had risen to 50 percent (Woody 1966). Coeducation had become the norm in American higher education, both public and private, by the turn of the century, and it was this dominant sentiment that was responsible for the coeducational basis upon which such great private institutions as Stanford University and the University of Chicago were founded.

The arguments in favor of coeducation were that separate education was economically wasteful; that women, as the equals and not the inferiors of men, deserved an education equal to that provided for men; that any institutional separation of the sexes was "unnatural" and artificial; and that coeducation could exert a "refining" influence upon young men. With the exception of the economic factor, all these advantages were viewed as disadvantages by those who opposed coeducation. Opponents argued that coeducation threw over the traditional and "natural" relationship between men and women and that college women would become coarse and college men effeminate. Most important was the argument that women were intellectually unable to do college work and that any attempt on their part to do so would injure their minds and weaken their bodies. Edward H. Clarke, at one time a professor at Harvard, denounced coeducation in a widely read book entitled *Sex in Education* (1873), wherein he argued that by straining their intellects beyond their capabilities women would suffer physiological disabilities which would render them unfit for their more essential roles as wives and mothers. The continued health and scholarly success of women in coeducational institutions was proof against Clarke's arguments. (From 1870 to 1900 the number of women in coeducational schools increased sixfold, while the number of men increased only threefold.)

Equally important was the example of scholarship set by the female students enrolled in women's colleges. It was from 1870 to 1900, when the debate over the scholarly ability of women was at its height, that most women's colleges were founded. Although these colleges were varied both in character and in educational goals, they were united in an effort to demonstrate the capabilities of women for serious academic study. By 1868 there were only four women's colleges authorized to grant the B.A. degree—Elmira and Vassar colleges, Ingham University, and Rutgers Female College. Although some of these colleges initially introduced courses in household economy, none of them offered such courses by 1868. Rather, they and such subsequent women's colleges as Smith, Wellesley, Bryn Mawr, Barnard, and Radcliffe (then called the Society for the Collegiate Instruction of Women) deliberately shaped their admissions policy and their course offerings to conform to the highest academic standards.

1900 to 1970. Harvard faculty who taught at Radcliffe and Columbia professors who taught at Barnard confirmed beyond any doubt that their women students were academically equal if not superior to their students in the coordinate male college. The high academic standards set by these early women's colleges settled the argument in favor of higher education for women, and from 1900 to 1930 the enthusiastic response of women to their new opportunities in higher education matched the enormously expanded academic field that was now open to them. In fact, the proportion of women among total college students increased from 21 percent in 1870 to 47 percent in 1920 (Newcomer 1959).

The 1920's was a high point in women's education—there were three girls graduating from high school for every two boys—and it seemed as though higher education would become as much a matter of course for women as for men. However, despite opportunities, the proportion of women in college from the 1920's to the 1960's declined, and not until the 1960's was the record of the 1920's matched.

By the 1950's it was clear that women's education is powerfully shaped by changing attitudes toward women's role in society and that women respond more strongly to these attitudes than they do to the availability of educational opportunities. In the 1920's the attitude toward women was enormously liberal; however, in the 1930's, 1940's, and 1950's this attitude was replaced by one which emphasized the traditional roles of women in their homes and families. By 1950 the percentage of women among total college students had dropped from the 1920's high of 47 percent to a low of 30 percent; and whereas at the end of the 1920's, 40 percent of the master's degrees and 15 percent of the doctorates were earned by women, these figures had dropped by 1950 to 25 percent and 9 percent, respectively. Statistics gathered by the Women's Bureau of the U.S. Department of Labor during the 1960's indicate, however, that the percentage of women earning bachelor and graduate degrees is slowly but surely rising to match the level reached in the 1920's.

Outlook. Two trends seem to indicate that the course of women's education in the 1970's will be one of further advances rather than a cycle of regression such as that which followed the 1920's. These trends are the overwhelming sentiment in favor of coeducation within institutions heretofore given to separate education and the increasing tendency to redefine work in terms of its usefulness to the individual as well as its usefulness to society. The decisions of Radcliffe to merge completely with Harvard and of Princeton, Yale, and Vassar to become coeducational indicate that the current trend is to think of higher education more in terms of the individual student than in terms of sexual differences. Since this trend is supported by social attitudes, it should lead to a new era of educational and professional advances for women.

New attitudes toward work and gainful employ- may also favorably affect the future development of women's education. As economic prosperity and new patterns of leisure point to a future in which individuals will work because they want to and not because they have to, women will no longer have to justify their educational or professional preparation in economic terms. Economic justifications for the higher education of women have operated as much against the cause of women's education as for it. Traditionally, an economic rationale has led a family to educate its sons first and its daughters last; but as individuals are educated more and more to develop their potential as human beings rather than to provide them with economic security, women should no longer have to justify their educations or their careers in economic terms. Although the history of the education of women in the United States has been shaped by the opportunities opened to women to serve others—whether as in the eighteenth century to serve the family or as in the nineteenth century to serve the common schools—the current trend seems to break with this history and define women's education in terms of what

it can do to develop the potential of the individual, apart from social or economic service.

BIBLIOGRAPHY

BAILYN, BERNARD 1960 *Education in the Forming of American Society: Needs and Opportunities for Study.* Chapel Hill, University of North Carolina Press.

BEECHER, CATHERINE 1827 "Female Education." *American Annals of Education,* 2, no. 5:222.

BEECHER, CATHARINE 1874 *Educational Reminiscences and Suggestions.* New York, J. B. Ford.

CLARKE, EDWARD H. 1873 *Sex in Education, or A Fair Chance for the Girls.* Boston, J. R. Osgood.

LARCOM, LUCY 1961 *A New England Girlhood.* With an introduction by Charles T. Davis. New York, Corinth Books.

NEWCOMER, MABEL 1959 *A Century of Higher Education for American Women.* New York, Harper.

RUSH, BENJAMIN 1798 "Thoughts Upon Female Education, Accommodated to the Present State of Society, Manners and Government, in the United States of America." *Essays, Literary, Moral and Philosophical.* Philadelphia, Thomas F. Bradford, Printer. Pages 75–92.

WOODY, THOMAS 1966 *A History of Women's Education in the United States.* 2 vols. New York, Octagon Books.

KATHRYN KISH SKLAR

2. CONTINUING EDUCATION

The year 1960 marked the beginning of a rapid proliferation of continuing education programs for women at many colleges and universities in the United States. These programs were aimed at mature women who had finished their formal education at some earlier period. The term "continuing education" thus designates a group of programs offered by colleges and universities to provide formal learning opportunities for women who wish to continue their education after an interval usually devoted to pursuits related to marriage and raising children.

Background. In the United States the educational careers of boys and girls between the ages of five and 17 are very similar. Beyond the age of 17, however, wide discrepancies appear. In 1966, for example, only 38 percent of girls aged 18 and 19 were in school, compared to 58 percent of the boys in that same age group. For older persons the differences were even more startling. Among those 20 and 21 years old, 21 percent of the women and 41 percent of the men were attending school. Among those 22 to 24 years old, only 7 percent of the women but 21 percent of the men were attending school. Girls have consistently outnumbered boys among high school graduates, but a much smaller proportion—53 percent of the female high school graduates as opposed to 70 percent of the male graduates—were enrolled in college in 1967 (U.S. Department of Labor . . . 1969).

Since the greatest differences in educational attainment between boys and girls come after the age of compulsory school attendance, it is important to understand the motivation for higher education. Douvan and Kaye (1962) found that in adolescence "boys are actively planning and testing for future work identities, apparently sifting alternatives in an effort to find the role that will fit most comfortably their particular skills and interests, temperamental characteristics and needs. Girls, in contrast, are absorbed much more in phantasy, particularly phantasy about boys and popularity, marriage, and love" (p. 202). Surveys show that the main reason for a girl's dropping out of either high school or college is marriage or pregnancy. In the United States, 50 percent of the women are married by age 20.5 (U.S. Department of Labor . . . 1969).

This absorbing interest in marriage and a family distracts young women from planning for the other realities of their lives. Although nine out of ten women in the United States marry, nine out of ten also work outside the home at some time in their lives (U.S. Department of Labor . . . 1969). Currently, it is estimated that a woman will spend 25 years in paid employment, and the more education she has, the more likely she is to continue working after marriage. More than six out of ten college-educated women in the 45-to-54-year age group and 86 percent of those with five or more years of college were employed in 1968, and long-term trends indicate an even higher proportion by 1980 (*ibid.*).

The fact that a smaller proportion of married women aged 25 to 34, usually with small children, work outside the home points to the emergence of a pattern of work for women: employment immediately after school or college, retirement from the labor force after marriage and the birth of children, and return to paid employment when the children are in school or able to get along without close supervision by the mother.

This second career for women is the primary factor behind continuing education programs. Other pressures are also present, however. Many intelligent women simply want the intellectual stimulation and growth that comes with additional education. Many women who do not work, especially those who had attended college earlier,

want additional education in order to become better wives, mothers, and citizens. The mature woman's educational and vocational plans are greatly influenced by her status as a wife and mother, and many women are interested in preparing for jobs so that they can provide additional financial support for their families.

Program objectives. Most of the continuing education programs for women have two objectives—serving the needs of the labor force and serving the needs of the individual women. The 1960's was a time of high employment in the United States. Professional, technical, and clerical occupations were undergoing rapid expansion, with resultant shortages of trained personnel in many areas. The fact that the population had increasingly higher percentages of nonproductive persons—young people in school for longer periods of time and more retired persons—put an increased burden on people between the ages of 25 and 60 to do the productive work of the society.

These general trends created the conditions that not only opened jobs to women but made women the most readily available resource to meet the needs of the labor force. Hence, there were compelling reasons for making education and training resources more available to them. The country's need for community volunteer workers as well as for intelligent, informed citizens was also cited as a reason for the establishment of special programs for women.

The needs of the women themselves were also to be considered. The period of time women devote to family concerns usually causes some depreciation of knowledge and skills, and at the same time most professions are changing rapidly. The problem for women of entering or reentering the labor force means either undertaking another period of education or training or going into less demanding jobs which do not properly utilize their talents. The desire for additional college education on the part of women who wish to embark upon interesting careers is the major factor behind the continuing education programs for women. In addition to vocational motivations, however, women may have the equally important desires to find new interests, new goals, and a new feeling of importance after their children no longer need their total attention.

Pioneer programs. The early programs in continuing education for women were so diverse in their forms and objectives that they served as prototypes for the more than 200 programs which followed (U.S. Department of Labor . . . 1968). Although some programs aimed at providing specific curricular offerings and others aimed at providing specific services for the mature woman student, most schools found these needs to be interrelated and broadened the scope of the programs over the years to include both.

University of Minnesota. One of the earliest experimental programs and one which provided the widest variety of services was the Women's Continuing Education Program at the University of Minnesota. This program, started in June 1960 under a grant from the Carnegie Corporation of New York, reflected the egalitarian philosophy of this land-grant institution. The objective of the Minnesota Plan, as it was called, was to help each woman reach her individual goal—whether this goal was preparation for a career, more meaningful community participation, or self-enrichment—through utilization of the resources of the university. Many of the opportunities not present in other institutions—for instance, part-time graduate work or transfer of up to three years of accumulated credits—were already acceptable practices at Minnesota.

Although the University of Minnesota already offered hundreds of courses through day school, evening classes, and correspondence, it was still found necessary to augment the curricular offerings for the new continuing education program. Several year-long, interdisciplinary seminars were offered for mature women on a schedule that required them to come to campus only one morning on alternate weeks for a three-hour session. Most of these experimental seminars were accredited at the upper-division level and were taught by senior graduate school faculty. In addition to these seminars, shorter noncredit series in such areas as astronomy, mathematics, and art history were offered both on and off the campus. Many seminars were held in students' homes. Concentrated reading and study-skills workshops and guidance seminars were also offered and proved to be very popular.

In addition to special curricular offerings, the Minnesota Plan, during the first several years of its operation, offered such service as individual vocational, educational, and personal counseling. Counseling, aimed at guiding women in the utilization of the resources available to them, was considered to be the cornerstone of the program and the feature most likely to be adopted by other schools. In addition to counseling, the service aspect of the program included job placement, a small scholarship program, a baby-sitting service, and a newsletter which helped maintain individual interest and motivation.

Radcliffe College. The Radcliffe Institute for Independent Study was founded in 1960 and began operating in September 1961. The original focus of the institute was on women with doctorates or the equivalent in achievement and status whose careers had been interrupted by marriage or some other circumstance. These "associate scholars" were given an annual stipend of $3,000 for part-time appointments along with whatever facilities were needed for serious work. Additional research funds were available for special equipment or materials needed for their work. Provisions were made for associate scholars with degrees in medicine or dentistry to do course work or clinical work in order to qualify again for active practice. The women were not permitted to work toward degrees. The objective was to give the scholars one to two years to work on independent research or a creative project.

From the start the Radcliffe program provided service to a wide group of women, through its career guidance program, which utilized both workshops and individual counseling sessions. Research was also considered an integral part of the project, and a wide variety of studies, ranging from determinations of manpower requirements to individual case histories of talented women, have been carried out.

The scope of the institute has widened since its establishment. In 1963 the Radcliffe seminars, which had been offered since 1950, became the responsibility of the institute. These seminars, originally a series of liberal arts courses, were expanded to include a landscape design program as well as seminars on community problems. Daytime classes in such subjects as literature, history, religion, art, and philosophy are taught on a level appropriate for the college graduate. The classes generally meet for two hours or longer, one day a week, for one or more semesters. The fellowship program was extended to include a few grants for full-time study as well as scholarships for part-time course work and graduate study. The importance of the Radcliffe institute was underscored by its being housed in permanent quarters in 1967.

Rutgers University. Probably the most specific of the early programs of continuing education for women was the Ford Foundation program at Rutgers University for retraining women college graduates in mathematics. This program was started in 1961 because of the shortage of mathematically trained personnel and because the group of nonworking, mature women who had graduated from college was looked upon as a possible resource in helping to meet this shortage. The program is vocationally oriented. Five courses are offered: a review of college mathematics, teaching mathematics, computer programming, calculus, and introductory statistics. In addition to the courses, guidance, tuition, and a placement service are also provided.

Since mathematics has never been a popular subject for women (only 3.1 percent of the bachelor's degrees awarded to women in the United States in 1966–1967 were in the area of mathematical subjects [U.S. Department of Labor . . . 1969]), the main problem of the Rutgers experiment in the beginning years was the small number of interested and qualified students. However, the program was continued and was later expanded to include science courses. First-term enrollments grew from 54 students a year in 1961 to 140 in 1967, and it was estimated that in 1968 more than half of the 600 women who had participated in the program were either working (mostly as teachers) or continuing their education further. Since 1965 the program has been funded in part by a grant from the National Science Foundation. The Rutgers program demonstrates how concrete needs can be met with specific and appropriate action.

University of Missouri. Another early project in continuing education for women was started at the University of Kansas City, now the University of Missouri at Kansas City, in the fall of 1961. This center offers noncredit seminars in various liberal arts subjects as well as seminars devoted to a study of the lives of women. The program also provides day-long forums on women's education which bring together community women to consider problems related to continuing their educations. The group also started a training program to help women become research assistants.

Sarah Lawrence College. The Center for Continuing Education at Sarah Lawrence College, another of the early programs, was established in 1962 under a grant from the Carnegie Corporation. This program is directed toward women who had interrupted their undergraduate college education and to women with baccalaureate degrees who wish to do graduate study. Special counseling is offered to each applicant to aid her in formulating plans, and many women are referred to other institutions within the New York metropolitan area.

Undergraduate students for whom study at Sarah Lawrence seems appropriate are offered special continuing education courses. These are five-point credit courses and parallel courses offered in the regular undergraduate program. After one semester in such a course the student may apply for degree candidacy. If she is accepted, she then takes the courses in the regular curriculum which are appropriate for her. The continuing education courses are designed to help both the student and the college evaluate abilities and motivation.

The pattern of referrals to other institutions by the Sarah Lawrence program led to a unique development—institutional cooperation in granting professional graduate degrees. Shortages in many of the helping professions, such as teaching, social work, school guidance, library science, and remedial reading, have been partially alleviated by joint programs with New York University, the Pratt Institute, and the City University of New York. In most cases, the cooperating institution sets the requirements and fees, provides the faculty, and grants the degree. Sarah Lawrnce provides the physical facilities for giving the courses on a part-time basis and recruits and counsels the students. It also acts as a catalyst in starting the new programs and as the administrative agency in obtaining financial assistance.

Fellowships. These five pioneer programs, then, were the first of the women's continuing education programs. The experiments have grown and prospered. Concurrent with their development, fellowship programs, such as the College Faculty Program of the American Association of University Women Educational Foundation, the E. B. Fred Fellowships at the University of Wisconsin, and the Danforth Foundation Graduate Fellowships for Women, provided additional incentive and financial assistance to mature women for return to graduate school.

Evaluation. Each continuing education program reflects the resources and philosophy of its parent institution. The Minnesota philosophy is to assign and assimilate each function or service of the program into the appropriate university department so that it will become a continuing part of the ongoing university. Thus, the Minnesota Plan involves a group of personnel with a common goal rather than a separate, autonomous department. In view of the more viable growth of the Radcliffe and Sarah Lawrence programs, both of which have a physical and organizational location on campus, it would seem that the Minnesota strategy has certain disadvantages. However, the intangible benefits of assimilating mature women into the campus proper are somewhat compensatory. The physical presence of mature women in classes serves to remind many young women of the necessity for long-range planning in their lives.

Characteristics of returning students. Adults who seek additional education are a self-selected lot. This distinction is particularly true for women, who have fewer extrinsic pressures to continue their education than do men. However, mature women, whose job skills are rusty after years in the home, are likely to feel that education is a necessary prerequisite to successful re-entry into the labor force.

It is obvious that the characteristics of the specific program do much to determine who is attracted to it. The Rutgers program, limited to college graduates with mathematics majors, can appeal to a relatively small student population. A program offering only noncredit courses in liberal arts subjects generally appeals to women whose primary goal is self-enrichment and who have no need to prepare for a job.

Beyond these rather obvious limitations, however, the physical location of the institution itself is important in determining who returns to school. The adult usually must attend a school within commuting distance of home, and home for most women is determined by the husband's job. Finding the right program in the right location is often a matter of chance. Whether a particular school is appropriate for a particular student depends upon the school's resources and how they are deployed, its costs, its curricula, its scheduling of classes, its attitude toward

exceptions to the rules, and its general philosophy of education. A large university located in a metropolitan center can offer more opportunities than a small liberal arts college located in a small town; and what is offered has a great deal of influence in determining who returns to school.

But in spite of the differences in the programs and their sponsoring institutions, the women participating in them have many characteristics in common. The great majority of these women are married, generally to professional men or business executives. They usually have several children and have histories of active volunteer work in their communities. Most of them have been to college, although this is not necessarily a prerequisite for program attendance in some schools. These women are intelligent, interested in culturally and socially significant activities, realistic about their plans and problems, and academically motivated. They are interested in both self-enrichment and in preparing for a career. Some form of teaching is the most frequently chosen vocation, and social science occupations are next in popularity.

Educators have found that the women returning to school are not neurotic, frustrated women seeking to escape from the so-called drudgery of household responsibilities. Most of them enjoy their homes and families and lead active lives. However, since most of them are intelligent and energetic, they are attracted to the rewards and satisfactions of the academic world and the world of work.

In spite of their usually successful academic backgrounds, stable family relationships, and rewarding community activities, these women have one common characteristic that makes the first step back to campus life a frightening one—anxiety or insecurity about their capabilities. This lack of self-confidence was even noticed in the Ph.D.'s returning to Radcliffe. Because of this lack of assurance, their first reception on campus is very important. Once this initial hurdle is cleared, the intellectual satisfactions and normal academic rewards usually provide all the motivation that is needed for a successful educational experience.

Problems of returning students. The lack of self-confidence that mature women often feel in contemplating a return to school results from both real and perceived problems. Since most women returning to school have family responsibilities, they are concerned with effects on relationships within the family. Real problems they face relate to shortage of time, child-care arrangements, housekeeping chores, and financial arrangements. These problems can usually be solved by family cooperation and common sense. The general sócial climate, however, is often such that women are made to feel that anything personally satisfying to themselves is automatically harmful to the family. Much of the individual and group counseling deals with these problems. In general, once the step back to school is taken, most family members seem to benefit from the new interests of the mother by developing new interests of their own, new responsibilities, and new independence.

The problem most frequently mentioned by returning women students is concern about their ability to study and to keep up with new and supposedly higher standards of scholarship. Women also worry about their acceptance by teachers and younger students. Besides these general problems, mature students face the same problems as younger students: course choice, scheduling difficulties, grades, tests, term papers, academic red tape, transportation and parking problems, and so on. Because the mature students more often are transferring from one curriculum to another or from one college to another, the problems of credit transfers and differing prerequisites often exacerbate the other problems. A seemingly small requirement, such as one more course in mathematics or a langauge, might necessitate a year or two of review courses. And, naturally, a required course in physical education has much different meaning for a 45-year-old woman than for an 18-year-old girl.

Since the goal of many students is to enter employment, questions concerning occupational requirements are of prime importance. The problem of finding the job that fits into a certain framework of interests, capabilities, and life-style is complicated by worry over age restrictions, employer resistance, local opportunities, and family responsibilities. Although information about occupational requirements necessarily sets limits on opportunity and achievement, most women still find a satisfactory variety of choices open to them. Shortages existed in many professional fields in the 1960's, and persons who became qualified through education were rarely turned away from employment.

Adjustments. Although most educators talk sincerely of education as a lifelong process, the fact remains that the task of educating increasing numbers of young people puts tremendous pressures on the resources available to most institutions. Moreover, by the end of the 1960's institutions of higher éducation were being challenged on many fronts, particularly as to the relevance of their curricula and teaching methods to minority and disadvantaged groups.

The problems of educating women are not those of curricula and methods so much as they are problems of timing. For the majority of women, the traditional years of college or professional education precede a period of homemaking rather than a period of working. Many women, therefore, need higher education (directed toward either a degree program or refresher courses) at a later time in their lives. The special programs for women try to provide higher education at a time and in such a way that it is appropriate to meet these special conditions.

The matter of bringing about changes in the traditional timing of a college education, however, raises questions about the validity and relevance of many rules and regulations. Many sacrosanct requirements, such as course load, distribution requirements, and prerequisites, were dictated for the sake of convenience or by the supposed requirements of 18-year-olds, not necessarily by any sound educational policy.

However, once the educational lockstep is broken by changing the "when" of a college education, other problems immediately arise. Transfer of credits from one accredited institution to another usually results in loss of credits and in the addition of new sets of requirements. Knowledge gained at nonaccredited institutions or by self-study is often difficult or impossible to validate for credit through proficiency and equivalency examinations. Out-of-state tuition for nonresident students can be a financial burden. New teaching methods, such as programmed learning and televised lectures, are not always utilized in the right way. (Some educators feel that ten-year-olds are mature enough to learn from television while graduate students are not.) Degree requirements, both for individual courses and for broader area distributions, or majors, need to be reviewed more often to determine their current relevance, especially for adults.

Since many women want advanced degrees, the

rules and regulations of some graduate schools prove particularly irksome. Many of these schools insist on full-time study when slower progress is in no way inconsistent with proper educational goals. Many refuse to allow credits to be earned in evening classes, by correspondence, or through independent study, since these methods cannot be as closely supervised. Although the stated goal of most graduate schools is to turn out independent scholars, this goal loses much in its translation into specific requirements which tend to stifle independent scholarship rather than to nourish it.

The problem of timing has some aspects, however, that require new resources rather than rule changes. Most mature women prefer to attend classes during the daytime hours, when their husbands are at work and their children are in school. Block scheduling—that is, a long class session on a once-a-week basis—is an especially convenient way to offer courses but requires faculty time and classroom space that are not always available. Child-care facilities are needed by many young mothers. Some schools provide or help organize this service, but many do not. Laboratory or practicum facilities are often so scarce that they have to be limited to full-time students.

The one service that is most needed by women returning to school is counseling. In general, the students are unfamiliar with the requirements, the resources, and the rewards they can expect. They need especially sensitive and knowledgeable counselors. However, schools which put a low priority on counseling for their typical undergraduate population are not likely to provide counseling for atypical students.

Significance. The programs of continuing education for women are attempts to influence the American system of higher education to adapt itself to the distinctive educational needs of women. The educational opportunities presented are instrumental in returning thousands of women to productive lives, especially in service-oriented positions. In general, these women carry their concern for people from within the home to the community outside the home.

Beyond their aid to the individual woman, the programs are centers of concern for the status of women generally, and their presence on campus has heightened awareness of the potentialities of women and has significantly altered attitudes in the academic world as well in the wider community. If the goal of these programs—making higher education relevant to the needs of women—can ever be truly accomplished, then continuing education for women will rank equally in significance with the establishment of women's colleges and women's obtaining the right to vote.

BIBLIOGRAPHY

DAVID, OPAL D., ed. 1958 *The Education of Women: Signs for the Future.* Washington, D.C., American Council on Education.

DOUVAN, ELIZABETH, AND CAROL KAYE 1962 "Motivational Factors in College Entrance." Nevitt Sanford, ed., *The American College.* New York, Wiley. Pages 199–224.

FRIEDAN, BETTY 1963 *The Feminine Mystique.* New York, Norton.

ITASCA CONFERENCE ON THE CONTINUING EDUCATION OF WOMEN 1963 *Education and a Woman's Life: Proceedings.* Edited by Lawrence Edward Dennis. Washington, D.C., American Council on Education.

NEWCOMER, MABEL 1959 *A Century of Higher Education for American Women.* New York, Harper.

NYE, FRANCES IVAN, AND LOIS N. W. HOFFMAN 1963 *The Employed Mother in America.* Chicago, Rand McNally.

O'NEILL, BARBARA POWELL 1965 *Careers for Women After Marriage and Children.* New York, Macmillan.

SCHLETZER, VERA M., et al. 1967 *A Five-year Report: 1960–1965 of the Minnesota Plan.* Minneapolis, University of Minnesota.

"The Woman in America" 1964 *Daedalus,* 93, no. 2:entire issue.

U.S. DEPARTMENT OF LABOR. WOMEN'S BUREAU 1968 *Continuing Education Programs and Services for Women.* Washington, D.C., Government Printing Office.

U.S. DEPARTMENT OF LABOR. WOMEN'S BUREAU 1969 *1969 Handbook on Women Workers.* Washington, D.C., Government Printing Office.

U.S. PRESIDENT'S COMMISSION ON THE STATUS OF WOMEN 1965 *American Women.* New York, Scribner.

ZAPOLEON, MARGUERITE (WYKOFF) 1961 *Occupational Planning for Women.* New York, Harper.

VERA M. SCHLETZER

3. JOB REENTRY TRAINING

The preparation for a return to a career after the period during which a woman has spent most of her time caring for her home and family is commonly called job reentry training. There are three different times when women most frequently undertake such preparation: when their children enter school, when their children are considered mature enough to be left alone, or when divorce or a husband's death or illness requires a woman to resume her career.

A woman may play several roles in sequential stages of her life: career girl, young wife, mother of preschool children, mother of school-age children, mother whose children have left home, and widow. Job reentry training may be initiated upon an abrupt decision at any stage or may be built into the life and planning of the young career girl, young wife, and young mother.

As home responsibilities lessen and women are freed from household chores, many seek, often unconsciously, to expand domestic work in order to provide evidence that they are fully occupied and indispensable. Domestic work can be expanded to an almost unlimited degree; bored and restless women begin to doubt their purposefulness. A woman's decision to embark upon a program of vocational preparation frequently follows her examination of the opportunities available to her outside the home. Changing social customs have encouraged greater acceptance of the role of the working wife than formerly. A reduction in the size of families, a longer life span, and a shortened workweek make gainful employment and homemaking a feasible combination. Smaller families started at an early age can result in a woman bearing her last child by the age of 30. The heaviest responsibilities related to motherhood may be completed by the age of 45, when the mother still has considerable vitality resulting from present high standards of nutrition and health care.

Formal job reentry training may serve a variety of needs, depending upon women's goals and the point in their lives when they begin the training. The woman who has psychological and social barriers to transcend before actually undertaking further education or applying for a job seeks the type of job reentry training that will provide for discussion of the advantages and disadvantages of the working wife and mother. A woman must evaluate her interests and talents before deciding whether to seek a salaried position or volunteer work. The number of hours a day or week she can afford to spend away from home must be determined, and a plan for managing both home and professional life must be worked out.

Women who have made the decision to resume a career outside the home often undertake training to bring them up-to-date with current developments in their former fields; they may work toward renewing a teacher's certificate or nurse's license, for example, or they may initiate studies in a new area.

Sources of training. The sources of job reentry training are varied. Adult education classes provided by public school systems and institutions of higher education offer courses ranging from tailoring to foreign languages and philosophy. Special

interest groups are frequently formed when enough members of a community demonstrate interest. Correspondence courses and television courses can prove to be stimulating and allow a woman to continue her education in her own home. Specialized schools, such as beauty schools, can offer short-term courses for the returning career woman. State employment agencies and libraries may also offer courses.

Many high schools, junior colleges, liberal arts colleges, and universities make provisions for women returning to school to take limited course loads in degree or nondegree programs. In some instances, institutions drop requirements for a high school diploma or admission examinations and admit nonprofessional trainees (mainly mature women) as special students. Special students can become regular students after they demonstrate that they can successfully undertake college-level work. Flexible scheduling of classes at hours convenient for housewives is intentionally provided. Policies related to accepting transfer credits are often liberal, and educational and employment counseling for the adult woman has been formally instituted. Financial assistance for part-time study is awarded, and nursery services have appeared in order to help the young mother assume academic responsibilities. Job placement and referral services are organized with the specific objective of placing women who are reentering careers.

Countless colleges and universities throughout the United States have independently organized offices of continuing education for women or, with the cooperation of an organization such as a local branch of the American Association of University Women, offer academic, vocational, placement, and counseling services.

Several institutions direct their programs toward a specific field of study. For example, Rutgers, the State University of New Jersey, offers a retraining program in mathematics and science, and Wellesley College in Massachusetts sponsors an institute in chemistry that leads to a master's degree. Refresher courses in nursing, teaching, home economics, and business skills are also popular at many institutions.

Other programs are designed to prepare women to reenter employment as assistants or aides in semiskilled occupations. Courses exist for "gericare" aides, teacher aides, library aides, mental health assistants, nursery school assistants, research assistants, school library aides, and social work aides. Most of these programs are offered by colleges and universities.

Groups sponsoring job reentry training under the auspices of community colleges, adult education divisions of public school systems, or community social service agencies often arrange group tours of local facilities offering employment opportunities for adult women and on-the-job training. A group visit to a department store can help the prospective employee become aware of a variety of positions: clerical, data-processing, merchandising, supervisory, advertising, and retailing. A visit to a hospital may stimulate interest in careers in such areas as admissions, social services, bookkeeping, housekeeping, medical records, and food service supervision. A visit to a bank can expose women to jobs requiring "figure aptitude" such as teller, clerical, data-processing, and supervisory positions.

Types of programs. Programs offered to women considering returning to work are aimed at satisfying a wide range of needs. Orientation workshops discuss employment opportunities and the workings of the business world. Programs of an academic or skills-oriented nature help women to prepare for specific professions. Some workshops offer group counseling to help individual women decide on the course they should pursue in finding jobs that will meet their needs.

Orientation workshops attempt to emphasize the diversity of opportunities available to women seeking employment. Career possibilities suggested by such workshops may include employment by the government, private business, and the civil service; health, education, and library careers; hotel and restaurant management; and market research, public relations, and work in the communications media.

An example of an extensive program is that formally organized by the University of Minnesota to make the university a more efficient and effective resource for adult women. Known as the Minnesota Planning and Counseling Center for Women, it provides counseling and information services for women at all educational levels. It maintains contact with the local metropolitan area in order to refer women to both educational and employment opportunities. Scholarship aid, nursery facilities, and job placement services are provided. In 1966 this center expanded its services by developing a program called Operation: Second Chance. This comprehensive service, offered through more than 60 post-high-school educational institutions, provides advice and counseling to adult women throughout the state.

Another program, the Radcliffe Institute of Radcliffe College, Cambridge, Mass., provides fellowships to enable qualified women to engage in part-time or, occasionally, full-time research or creative work while they still have family commitments. The institute administers a special fellowship program for women physicians engaged in graduate and professional medical training in the Boston area. It also provides fellowships to women for part-time graduate study in colleges and universities in Connecticut, Massachusetts, or Rhode Island. The Radcliffe Seminars sponsored by the institute offer weekly courses to adult women on a credit and noncredit basis. In addition, the institute maintains a guidance laboratory and a research program.

Southern Methodist University in Dallas, Texas, conducts an annual management seminar for women executives that emphasizes the woman's point of view in human relations and work management, as well as management philosophy and techniques. It offers university lectures for women during morning hours and short-term courses and conferences on special subjects, such as the husbandless home.

Some workshops emphasize preemployment testing by offering a one-day or half-day session to assist women in understanding the basic types of questions included in such testing. The session can provide a chance to sample different kinds of tests and to gain experience in a timed group-testing situation, as well as an opportunity to get insight into the purposes of testing. A program of this nature must be conducted by qualified professional psychological services; information about such a program can be obtained most readily from a college or university.

Model workshops. Orientation workshops and short-term courses may be planned by a government or community agency, such as a public library or community center, as well as by a college or university. Although the time available in a short-term course is limited, much can be accomplished. Two models of workshops will be presented here: one of an expository nature and the other of a counseling nature.

Career information workshop. In the fall of 1969 a typical five-session career information series was sponsored jointly by the Cleveland

Public Library and Project EVE, a vocational-educational counseling and information service for adult women under the auspices of Cuyahoga Community College in Cleveland, Ohio. Five two-hour sessions were held in the auditorium of the public library and were designed for the adult woman who wanted to know how to plan for a career and to be better informed about careers before making a decision concerning her education, testing of vocational interests, or returning to work. The first session, "Making Career Decisions," reviewed the labor market and the financial aspects of work. The second session, "Government Employment and Private Business," presented current trends and opportunities in banking and data processing, in clerical and secretarial fields, and in civil service at federal, state, and local levels. Information regarding the use of governmental and private employment agencies was presented. The third session, "Health Careers," reviewed paraprofessional careers in medical records, mental health, physical therapy, and occupational therapy. A fourth session dealt with libraries and education. Current developments in education-related careers—ranging from day care centers, nursery schools, and kindergartens through colleges—were discussed. The speakers in the fifth session provided material related to careers in hotel and restaurant management and in food production and food service. Opportunities in such fields as market research, interviewing, advertising, and public relations were reviewed, and the possibilities of gaining employment in television, radio, and other communications media were discussed.

Each of the sessions was structured as a panel discussion with community representatives presenting information. Among those participating were the director of the Manpower Planning and Development Commission of the Cleveland Welfare Federation, a budget consultant from one of the banks, the director of Cleveland's central volunteer bureau, the employment superintendent of the U.S. Navy Finance Center, the director of education of the Greater Cleveland Hospital Association, the director of personnel from one of the suburban public school systems, the general manager of a local radio station, and a representative of the research and development department of a food corporation.

Psychologically oriented workshop. In contrast to the expository type of workshop, the group counseling workshop has been concerned solely with helping the individual review her personal situation in a small group of women with similar interests. Problems in planning the return to the labor market or education are considered. These sessions are of value to the woman with family responsibilities who is using free time, while her children are growing, in order to prepare for the future. Widows and divorced women have found the sessions helpful in adjusting to new life patterns. As with the expository type of workshops, each session of the short-term course typically deals with a specific question or theme.

The following model for a six-session program has proved to be popular. The first session deals with a review of the ways in which the lives of American women have changed in recent years, and participants are asked to reflect upon how these changes influence their ideas, attitudes, and plans. Each member of the group evaluates her personal situation, considering the needs and attitudes of her husband, children, and herself, as well as the requirements of home management. She evaluates whether reordering the pattern of family life would be worthwhile. The reordering may involve such practical aspects of homemaking as the rescheduling of household chores and perhaps the hiring of household help, the purchase of additional household equipment, the use of frozen and prepared foods, and a general modification and simplification of domestic activity. A husband's attitude needs to be considered, since his adjustment to his wife's new role and to the reordering of a household schedule will affect his approval or disapproval of his wife's reentry into a vocation outside the home. Other members of the family will need to learn new ways of interacting with one another, since increased independence and reliance upon each other may be necessary during those times when the mother is absent from the home. The added cost of returning to work is discussed in terms of such expenses as lunches, transportation, taxes, and clothing.

In the second session each group member analyzes her motivations, past experiences, educational background, skills, personality, and goals. A woman who for a number of years has regularly placed the welfare, security, and growth of other family members ahead of her own may experience guilt in abandoning some of her previous activities. Feelings and expressions of resentment and stress caused by the new role of the wife and mother need to be worked out.

Before selecting the career they wish to pursue, women must determine the extent to which they wish to control or direct other people and be noticed by them on their job, the importance of the job's financial rewards, whether they prefer working independently or under another's direction, what is necessary for a sense of accomplishment and satisfaction, to what extent they desire achieving mastery of a situation, what types of experiences would constitute interesting work activities, and whether they wish to be of service to others and establish interpersonal relationships or select a type of work where altruism and contact with other people are not important factors.

Vocational experimentation, which may have occurred during a woman's years at home as she imagined engaging in a particular career, is also examined during the second session. Through volunteer work and club activities a woman may have held positions of responsibility that she may choose to explore further. The hospital volunteer may have been stimulated to learn more about a career in practical nursing, physical therapy, occupational therapy, recreational therapy, medical social work, medical librarianship, or medical technology. The young woman who volunteered to help in a cooperative nursery may have developed a desire to become a nursery school teacher. The woman whose leisure time activity during her childbearing and family-nurturing years centered on politics and community causes may choose to investigate opportunities for women in the fields of law, politics, or economics. Women are free to enter such fields as securities analysis, computer programming, systems engineering, and real estate. Some religious denominations are accepting women as members of the clergy and church governing assemblies.

The third session of this type of job reentry training series provides for an examination of a woman's present aptitudes and interests and seeks to relate them to specific kinds of work. A variety of questionnaires and experimental materials may be used if psychological guidance in administering and interpreting them is available. An effort is made to assist the mature woman in recognizing her strengths and weaknesses as they apply to potential employment.

A woman may choose to depart from the actual experiences she has had and explore a new field. If the direction she has chosen requires further academic study, she might consider experimenting in order to become accustomed to the student role. For many women, reentry into a formal academic setting is a threatening experience. Periods of concentrated study are tedious and may require a new kind of discipline. Competing with younger students and submitting to measures of evaluation may be accompanied by timidity and hesitation. In order to prepare for such formal situations, a woman might try following a television course. Her patterns of study and tolerance for intellectual discipline need to be tested and exercised. Auditing a course in a nearby community college might serve as a refresher course in both content and method. The woman who had not previously thought of herself as a scholar may discover that with added maturity and the experience of her years at home she can more easily become enthusiastic about studying. Her purposes, commitment, and willpower will probably be stronger than they were during earlier school experiences, which may have served as the setting for social activity as much as for intellectual and vocational preparation. Redefining in a new context her skills learned from homemaking and parenthood can produce a healthy attitude as a woman realizes that she is needed anew.

During the fourth session there is an attempt to learn about current requirements for entering the working world. Women discuss newly developing fields, the kinds of work that mature women can most successfully handle, problems that may occur, the effect of the factor of age, and the merits of full-time, part-time, and temporary jobs. Temporary employment as a means of brushing up on old skills and determining what new ones a woman might wish to acquire is suggested. During the sessions, women consider whether they should automatically reenter their previous fields and occupations by discussing what originally influenced them and whether those interests are still applicable. The women discuss the necessity of gaining new knowledge in order to be of value in certain fields. Of great concern, for example, is the position shorthand and bookkeeping skills hold in this age of dictating equipment, computers, and mechanized office operations. Fact-finding to prepare for the new venture does not always require the help of a formal educational institution. Women considering opening a small business, for example, would need to contact a Small Business Administration office of the United States government. Women interested in entering the real estate field would need to contact a state real estate board. The facts regarding taking civil service tests and renewing old civil service ratings should be investigated through the appropriate government agency.

Finding where appropriate training or education is available for various types of work is the concern of the fifth session. The level of a woman's job reentry training depends upon her previous experience: completion of high school, community college, graduate school, or specialized professional training. Local and state sources of continuing education, as well as the counseling, job placement, and referral services generally available at local or state employment agencies and at schools women have previously attended, are usually satisfactory.

The sixth and final session deals with methods of actually finding a job. Discussions reveal resources for locating job opportunities and review practical job-finding techniques such as résumés, application forms, letters of application, and preparation for job interviews.

Federally assisted programs. Institutions of higher education may qualify for federal assistance under the Community Service and Continuing Education Programs authorized under Title I of the Higher Education Act of 1965. Approved programs have provided counseling, training, or academic instruction specifically for women and have met the objectives of Title I programs as stated: "to apply the resources of institutions of higher education, both public and private, to the solution of community problems by enlarging and extending university extension and continuing education programs" (U.S. Department of Labor . . . 1968, p. 89). Major emphasis is on such community problems as housing, poverty, government, recreation, employment, youth opportunities, transportation, health, and land use.

Financial assistance additional to that provided by federal sources can be obtained through state agencies that have been designated or created by the governor of each state and approved by the U.S. Office of Education.

Special programs in job reentry training have been developed for women with poverty-level incomes and limited education. In 1964 the Women's Talent Corps Institute, funded by the federal government, was organized in New York City. Its formal task was defined as the development of an action-centered approach to the training of women from ghetto neighborhoods for careers in community service. Approximately half of the participants accepted were high school dropouts. The only requirement was the ability to read and write. Ages ranged from 21 to the late 50's; participants were predominantly Negro, Asian, American Indian, and Puerto Rican (9 percent of the group was white). All participants met the U.S. Department of Labor criterion for poverty at the time: an annual income of $3,200 or less.

From the Women's Talent Corps Institute a two-year college program evolved in New York City. Called the College for Human Services, it offers an opportunity to enter careers in physical or mental health fields, legal services, and various social and welfare services. In addition to offering training for semiprofessional positions in a variety of fields, the college assumes responsibility for opening these positions by negotiating for jobs with unions, administrators, and the civil service and has pressed to formulate job descriptions and improve career lines.

A 30-week work-study program designed to open new career opportunities in human services was developed with the cooperation of the U.S. Office of Economic Opportunity and Project Head Start in June 1967. The program provided full-year Head Start staff members with an opportunity to work toward two-year and four-year degrees in early childhood education and related areas. The College for Human Services no longer sponsors the Head Start work-study program but offers similar 36-week work-study programs leading to a two-year associate of arts degree.

A project designed to retrain mature women for clerical employment by updating their skills and rebuilding their self-confidence was initiated at Middlesex County College in Edison, N.J., in 1968. Designated Job Horizons for Women, it was financed by the New Jersey state department of education under Title I of the Higher Education Act of 1965 in response to the demand for clerical personnel in central New Jersey. The one-year certificate program provided training and instruction at the college level for certain skills which enable participants to enter the labor market. Specific attempts were made to develop participants' confidence by helping them understand the adjustment which might be necessary when they assume a new role in society. Students spent 11 to 12 hours a week in study. Counseling was stressed throughout the program, from admission to placement: individual admission counseling was required to help clarify the applicants' objectives and assist them in determining their academic potential, for example.

Conclusion. There is little doubt that a revolution in family patterns has been occurring in the United States in the second half of the twentieth century. According to the U.S. Census Bureau the number of employed women rose from 17.3 million in 1950 to 27.8 million in 1968 —an increase of about 60 percent. During that period the number of men holding jobs rose 16 percent—from 41.6 million to 48.1 million. The removal of external restrictions on women's freedom of choice of careers through mechanization, legislation, and the increased social acceptance of working mothers, along with the establishment of day care centers, has shifted much of the responsibility to women themselves. Thus, a major goal of education for women is the discovery of those skills and abilities which can be employed to make the different stages of their lives most meaningful. Job reentry training emphasizes the role of woman's place as man's intellectual and economic partner, not only as the keeper of his home and mother of his children. Such training is designed to provide information which will enable women to gain optimal fulfillment from active participation in social, political, artistic, or economic career roles outside the home.

BIBLIOGRAPHY

AMERICAN ASSOCIATION OF UNIVERSITY WOMEN EDUCATIONAL FOUNDATION 1966 *New Careers for Women, 1970–80.* Washington, D.C., The Association.

ERIKSON, ERIK 1959 *Identity and the Life Cycle.* New York, International University Press.

SINCLAIR, ANDREW 1965 *The Emancipation of the American Woman.* New York, Harper.

U.S. DEPARTMENT OF LABOR. WAGE AND LABOR STANDARDS ADMINISTRATION. WOMEN'S BUREAU 1968 *Continuing Education Programs and Services for Women.* Washington, D.C., Government Printing Office.

WOLFE, H. B. 1969 "Analysis of the Work Values of Women: Implications for Counseling." *National Association of Women Deans and Counselors Journal,* 33, no. 1:13–18.

PRUDENCE B. RANDALL

WORK AND TRAINING PROGRAMS, FEDERAL

---

1. OVERVIEW	Sar A. Levitan and Garth L. Mangum
2. WORK EXPERIENCE AND TRAINING FOR RELIEF RECIPIENTS	Sar A. Levitan
3. JOB CORPS	Sar A. Levitan
4. VISTA	Sar A. Levitan

---

1. OVERVIEW

According to U.S. government statistics, federally supported manpower programs, devoted mostly to aiding the unemployed and the inadequately educated, carried a price tag of over $2.9 billion in 1970—more than a tenfold increase since 1961. Two major developments combined to generate federal support for training and rehabilitating the unemployed and disadvantaged. The first was the sustained high level of unemployment that began during the latter part of the 1950's and persisted into the mid-1960's. The second, and perhaps the more significant in the long run, was the civil rights movement.

Unemployment was attacked by stimulating the total demand for goods and services, with a consequent increase in employment levels, and by lowering geographical, age, skill, and racial barriers, which prevented many individuals from competing effectively for existing jobs.

The civil rights movement initially focused upon Negro civil and political rights—particularly in the areas of school integration, voting rights, and equal access to public facilities. It soon became clear, however, that Negroes and other deprived minorities could not compete on an equal footing with the rest of the nation without special economic assistance. The solutions appeared to be the same as for general unemployment—more jobs and more training—but there was an essential difference. Without the civil rights movement and the attention it focused upon poverty, reduction of unemployment could have dissolved effective support for continuing public manpower efforts. However, riots in the nation's urban slums, stemming from the unrest among minorities, antagonized and frightened many voters. And tight labor markets after 1965 brought the problem of competitive disadvantage in the job market into sharper relief.

History. Although the federal government was no novice in affecting manpower utilization, the emphasis of its policy has changed radically over the years.

Traditionally, the concern of federal manpower policies has been the supply of labor, both skilled and unskilled. Early examples were the Morrill Act, which established the land-grant college system in 1862 during the period of agricultural expansion and early industrialization, and the Smith-Hughes Act of 1917, which awarded matching grants for vocational education as industrialization entered a more sophisticated stage. Even the federally financed state employment services have been primarily concerned with filling job orders. Only during the depression of the 1930's did manpower policy efforts shift to the demand side in financing public works and work-relief jobs.

During World War II the federal impact upon manpower was pervasive. Not only were millions of persons drafted into the armed forces, but vast numbers were trained and retrained for war production. In addition, wage policies were utilized to channel labor into defense industries. The first G.I. Bill of Rights, enacted in 1944, had a significant impact upon manpower development by assisting 7.8 million veterans in obtaining education and training.

During the 1950's federal manpower policies focused upon expanding the supply of highly skilled and professional labor. The establishment of the National Science Foundation in 1950 and the passage of the National Defense Education Act in 1958 were illustrative of the government's new focus.

Federal manpower efforts continued during the 1960's, but a new dimension was added. No longer was the emphasis on matching the best man with an existing job; instead, providing a suitable job for each man or equipping the man to fill a suitable job took priority.

Serving the undereducated, the undermotivated, and the victims of discrimination demanded not only reorientation of the existing values of manpower agencies but also a whole new set of closely interwoven functions. The agencies neither generated nor sought this reorientation—the new functions were thrust upon them by changing public attitudes and new government commitments. These functions included reaching out to find the discouraged and undermotivated and encouraging them to partake of available services, providing adult basic education and training for entry-level skills to remedy the absence or obsolescence of early schooling, and offering prevocational orientation to expose those of limited experience to alternative occupational choices. To support these educational efforts, the agencies offered training allowances as incentives for those undergoing training, residential facilities for those living in sparsely populated areas or having home environments that preclude successful rehabilitation, and work experience for those unaccustomed to the discipline of work.

Once the disadvantaged completed their training, the agencies strove on their behalf to solicit suitable job opportunities, to subsidize private employment, to create public-service jobs tailored to the needs of those job seekers not absorbed in the competitive market, and to provide relocation allowances for residents of labor-surplus areas in conjunction with special inducements to employers to bring jobs to those stranded in depressed areas. After jobs were found, the agencies provided job coaching to work out supervisor-worker relationships and supportive services—such as medical aid and day care centers—for those needing corrective measures to enter or resume work positions.

Manpower efforts, 1961–1965. Government commitment to help the undereducated, the undermotivated, and the victims of discrimination was realized in the various federal laws enacted and the programs undertaken in the early 1960's.

Area Redevelopment Act of 1961. The first of the new programs aimed at reducing the competitive disadvantage of individuals and groups was the Area Redevelopment Act of 1961 (ARA). Its target was the unemployment concentrated in depressed areas, and its intent was to attract industry and jobs to those areas. The program foundered because the ARA's resources were inadequate to overcome its obstacles—the intransigent forces which restrained the long-term growth of depressed areas and the general slack in the total economy. Moreover, the ARA's resources were frittered away attempting to do too much in too many places.

Manpower Development and Training Act of 1962. The next effort after the Area Redevelopment Act was to expand the training program for the unemployed which had been a minuscule component of ARA. The Manpower Development and Training Act of 1962 concentrated at first on the needs of unemployed family heads who had been members of the labor force for three years or more. Emphasis was placed upon institutional training. Allowances, linked to the average levels of unemployment compensation in the state, were paid through the network of local employment offices. Also, an experimental effort —the Community Work and Training Program— started by the Welfare Administration, was designed so that relief recipients could develop work habits and "work off" the aid received.

In 1963 the emphasis shifted to youth. Unemployment of male adult family heads had dropped sharply, but the level of youth unemployment continued to rise despite overall economic expansion. The original legislation limited expenditures on youths to no more than 5 percent of total training allowances; the 1963 amendments expanded the youth portion of the program to a maximum of 25 percent of the trainees receiving allowances.

Vocational Education Act of 1963. The Vocational Education Act of 1963, and later the 1968 act, enlarged the scope of vocational education to include office and technical occupations and to draw greater attention to those with educational handicaps. Department of Health, Education, and Welfare data show that allocations for vocational education grew from $57 million to $371 million between 1963 and 1970.

Economic Opportunity Act of 1964. In 1964, President Lyndon B. Johnson declared "total war on poverty," but the beginnings of this war were modest. In line with traditional American values, the goal of the war on poverty was not to lift the needy out of poverty but to open the paths of opportunity and self-help to them. The Economic Opportunity Act of 1964, which created the Office of Economic Opportunity, included a series of work-training programs, some conventional and some new but all directed toward employment as the preferred source of income. After federal agencies gained experience in administering these new programs, the antipoverty budget was expected to increase to a level commensurate with the task at hand; but the needed funding never came.

Included in the act were the Neighborhood Youth Corps, set up to provide work experience and income to unemployed youth both in and out of school, and the Job Corps, designed for those youth whose home environment was the major obstacle to successful education, training, and employment. Also included in the antipoverty package were funds for adult basic education, a work-experience program which enlarged the earlier Community Work and Training Program, provisions for limited loans for the self-employed, and the Community Action Program.

The Community Action Program, based on concepts developed by the Ford Foundation's community development (or "gray areas") program and the Juvenile Delinquency and Youth Offense Control Act of 1961, was the heart of the antipoverty act. Practically any project aimed at reducing poverty in a community could be funded by the Community Action Program, provided only that the poor or their spokesmen participated in the planning and execution of the project and that racial discrimination was barred. Although employment and training efforts were offered through the Community Action Program, they accounted for only about 6 percent of the total federal funds expended between 1965 and 1969. Related approvable projects included remedial and preschool education, health services, birth control clinics, housing and home management, consumer education, legal aid, social services, and neighborhood centers.

Old programs expanded. In addition to the new programs that were introduced in the early 1960's, old ones were expanded. New legislation in 1965 authorized the tripling of federal support for the Vocational Rehabilitation Administration, which had been established in 1920 to qualify the physically and mentally handicapped for productive employment; the definition of handicapped was broadened to include impairment due to vocational, educational, cultural, social, environmental, or other factors. The programs of the Vocational Rehabilitation Administration were further expanded three years later.

The budget of the United States Employment Service was also expanded, although perhaps not commensurately with the added work load imposed by the new manpower programs. Department of Labor statistics show that the budget in 1965 was $182 million—more than 50 percent larger than the 1961 budget of $112 million. As a result of the broadened responsibilities and competition from community action agencies and others, the public employment services became concerned with outreach, training, job development, and supportive services.

Elementary and Secondary Education Act of 1965. The emphasis of federal support in 1965 was on education. Far more important than the increase in federal support for higher education was the Elementary and Secondary Education Act of 1965—the largest single commitment of federal aid to education since the G.I. Bill of Rights of 1944 and the first general federal support to the public schools. The act stressed the needs of those school districts with concentrations of poor and educationally disadvantaged children. This was also the year of the Economic Development Act and the Appalachian Regional Development Act, both of which attempted to apply lessons from the experience of the Area Redevelopment Act to generate employment in depressed areas.

Manpower efforts in the late 1960's. The momentum built up by the federal programs initiated between 1961 and 1965 and expanded during the mid-1960's carried through to the late 1960's and early 1970's. A major emphasis after 1965 was placed on improving the administration of the programs and developing viable techniques to reach and train the disadvantaged. To these ends, the private sector was involved increasingly after 1966.

Support and opposition. The 1966 amendments to the Economic Opportunity Act of 1964 added three employment programs (funded at a total of $70 million in 1969). These were Operation Mainstream, which provided jobs on behalf of rural conservation and beautification efforts; the New Careers Program, which provided for the creation of subprofessional jobs; and the Special Impact Program, which emphasized job creation in urban areas with concentrations of poverty. In addition, many formerly poor persons obtained direct employment in community-action neighborhood centers.

The antipoverty program appeared to be in serious trouble in 1967. The Job Corps residential training program had been very expensive. More importantly, in many cities the community action agencies had proved to be a focal point for organized opposition to the local political establishment. Yet, the fact that the Economic Opportunity Act was renewed and funded at $789 million in 1967

—$62 million more than in the previous year—was evidence that its programs were creating their own vested interests and were likely to endure.

Countervailing forces were also apparent in the support for and opposition to a multibillion-dollar proposal to guarantee employment opportunities for all. As an immediate aftermath of serious riots in Newark, N.J., and Detroit in 1967, Congressman James G. O'Hara of Michigan, along with 76 cosigners, introduced a $4 billion bill for emergency public service employment, and Senator Joseph S. Clark of Pennsylvania introduced an emergency employment amendment to the Economic Opportunity Act calling for a $3 billion expenditure over two years. The O'Hara bill never came to a vote. The administration, opposing any budget increase, helped defeat the Clark proposal and also a less costly substitute by Senator Winston L. Prouty of Vermont.

Amendments to the Social Security Act of 1935. The 1967 amendments to the Social Security Act of 1935 demonstrated another area of concern about employment problems. In response to rising welfare costs and widespread allegations that many welfare recipients could and should be earning their own way, Congress attempted to arrest the trend of expanding welfare rolls not only by unsuccessfully attempting to impose limitations on the federal contribution to aid families with dependent children but also by providing incentives for relief recipients to accept employment and by making provisions to improve their employability. This last measure, an expansion of the Work Experience and Training Program initiated under the Economic Opportunity Act, was the Work Incentive Program (WIN). The 1967 amendments called for continuing expansion of funds for training, education, day care, and other supportive services. WIN got off to a slow start in 1968 and 1969 but during 1970 reached an enrollment of 100,000 and outlays of $75 million.

Role of the private employer. Since 1966 a major thrust of the federally supported manpower programs has been to involve private employers in training and employing the disadvantaged. The Manpower Development and Training Act was the first to be affected. Early in 1966 the Department of Labor made plans to allocate two-thirds of the MDTA budget for training and employing the disadvantaged. At the same time the quota for on-the-job training was raised, not only to accommodate more trainees under the limited budget (on-the-job training is cheaper for the government than institutional training because income support is not required) but also to make a direct connection between training and jobs with private employers. It was anticipated that employers reimbursed for the cost of on-the-job training would be encouraged to hire disadvantaged workers they might otherwise avoid.

It was soon realized that the limited subsidies paid to private employers under the MDTA were an inadequate inducement to hire, train, and retain disadvantaged employees. Consequently, in 1967 the administration embarked upon a series of experimental programs to induce employers to hire poorly educated and unskilled workers, especially Negroes, from slum areas. The Concentrated Employment Program was one major effort having this goal. Selectees from the target areas were to be given a two-week orientation course and then placed in jobs or in training programs. However, the goal of placing half of the trainees with private employers did not materialize.

In addition to the Concentrated Employment Program, the Special Impact Program was initiated in 1967 to encourage employers to bring jobs to the slums. The funds allocated to the program were to be used to reimburse employers for the extra cost of hiring disadvantaged workers. In reality, the funds were subsidies to get business firms to locate their industrial plants in or near the slums in five cities selected for the program.

A third experiment, Job Opportunities in the Business Sector (JOBS), was based on the recognition that the government would have to bear the training costs as well as the other costs associated with hiring high-risk workers if such workers were to be trained and employed. In December 1967, the Labor Department announced that it was ready to pay an average annual subsidy of $3,500 to employers who would hire disadvantaged workers selected by public employment offices. The goal was to provide jobs in private industry for 500,000 hard-core unemployed during the succeeding three years, but part of the subsidies to private industry were provided by cutting back on training and work-experience programs.

The National Alliance of Businessmen was organized to coordinate the private sector's involvement in JOBS. Businessmen pledged to hire the disadvantaged unemployed and provide not only jobs and training but also a full range of supportive services needed to encourage the new employees to retain their jobs. The federal government agreed to bear the cost of extra expenses associated with these services.

Directions for the 1970's. The advent of a new administration in 1969 brought few drastic changes in the scope and tenor of federal manpower efforts. The Nixon administration did, however, overhaul selected individual programs. Nearly half of the Job Corps centers were closed and administration of the program was shifted from the Office of Economic Opportunity to the Department of Labor. In addition, the Neighborhood Youth Corps was cut back, restricted to 16-year-olds and 17-year-olds, and refocused from work experience to training.

Efforts to expand substantially the involvement of the private sector, especially through the JOBS program, foundered as the economy experienced a recession. Unemployment rose during all of 1970, and businessmen who were laying off experienced workers could not hire the hard-core unemployed.

The slack economy also dampened the prospects for other groups. With the curtailment of military efforts in Southeast Asia and of overall troop strength, many veterans returned to the civilian labor force only to find jobs scarce, with unemployment soaring from 3.5 percent in December 1969 to 6.2 percent a year later. To assist servicemen prior to discharge, the Department of Defense provided counseling, testing, limited skill training, and job placement through Project Transition. On-the-job training and vocational rehabilitation for veterans were administered by the Veterans Administration.

Another significant development in 1970 was the increased reliance upon the federal-state employment service and the expansion of its duties. To fulfill its traditional role of assisting employers to fill existing vacancies, the employment service used job banks and computerized job matching systems. Moreover, the employment service became involved in seeking out the disadvantaged and attempting to increase their employability or to provide jobs.

Child care became an increasingly important job support activity as the labor force participation of wives and mothers reached unprecedented proportions and efforts to assist adults on welfare (primarily mothers) to secure employment were emphasized.

The major new thrust of the Nixon administration was the decentralization of federal manpower efforts by expanding the role of state and local governments. However, attempts to overhaul the manpower programs of the federal government were frustrated when President Nixon vetoed the Employment and Manpower Act of 1970.

Because the curtailment and consolidation of some of the programs inherited from the 1960's were outweighed by increases in other existing programs and funding of new efforts, manpower expenditures continued to climb in the early 1970's, totaling over $3 billion in fiscal 1971.

BIBLIOGRAPHY

LEVITAN, SAR A., AND GARTH L. MANGUM 1969 *Federal Training and Work Programs in the Sixties.* Ann Arbor, Mich., Institute of Labor and Industrial Relations.

MANGUM, GARTH L. 1969 *The Emergence of Manpower Policy.* New York, Holt.

Manpower Report of the President 1970 Washington, D.C., Government Printing Office.

Special Analyses, Budget of the United States, Fiscal Year 1972 1971 Washington, D.C., Government Printing Office.

SAR A. LEVITAN and GARTH L. MANGUM

2. WORK EXPERIENCE AND TRAINING FOR RELIEF RECIPIENTS

Federal efforts to help welfare recipients enhance their employability and seek jobs were begun and greatly expanded during the 1960's. Originally, Aid to Families with Dependent Children (AFDC), established by the Social Security Act of 1935, was available only when a parent was dead, disabled, or absent. Mothers who were household heads were considered indispensable in the home and therefore unemployable. In 1961, however, an Unemployed Parent (UP) provision was added to AFDC for children who were poor because a parent was unemployed.

The Community Work and Training Program. The presence for the first time of unemployed but employable parents on the AFDC rolls led to the creation in 1962 of the Community Work and Training Program (CWT), administered by the Welfare Administration of the Department of Health, Education, and Welfare. Work projects were established to rehabilitate the unemployed parents and to allow them to work off their relief payments. Adoption of these programs was left to the states. By 1964 only 18 states had established AFDC-UP and only ten had implemented CWT programs. The lack of response was due in part to limitations on the use of federal funds and to a lack of state matching funds. Because federal funds could be used to cover only half of the administrative costs of CWT projects but

up to three-fourths of the costs of social services, states expanded the latter instead of establishing the former.

The Work Experience and Training Program. The primary focus of CWT was retained but its scope substantially enlarged by the Economic Opportunity Act of 1964. Title V established the Work Experience and Training Program (WET) to help welfare recipients and other needy adults "to secure and retain employment [and the] . . . capability for self-support or personal independence." It was hoped that the work experience and training gained on projects, usually in public institutions, combined with vocational training, remedial education, and other supportive services, would help the participants find work and enable them to get off welfare rolls.

The hopes advanced for the program appeared to vary with the social philosophies of its proponents. Some people hoped that malingerers on public assistance, when faced with the choice of receiving relief and having to work for a living, would leave the relief rolls and get jobs. Others expected that participants would develop the "work habit" and that this, in combination with training and other services, would help them secure jobs in the open market. There were also those who viewed Title V as a means of expanding incomes for poor people who could not qualify under the stringent public-assistance eligibility rules, since unemployed parents in a majority of states were ineligible to receive public assistance. Title V would, it was reasoned, circumvent some of the inadequacies of the federal-state public assistance programs by providing to poor families income support that was 100 percent federally funded. About 30 percent of Title V participants were not recipients of AFDC.

Department of Health, Education, and Welfare data indicate that between 1965 and 1969 the federal government spent a total of approximately $370 million on WET projects. Some 228,000 persons were enrolled for an average period of seven months. A total of 344 WET projects were established in every state (except Alabama), the District of Columbia, Puerto Rico, and the Virgin Islands. The content and scope of individual projects varied widely, depending upon the imagination and resourcefulness of project administrators and prevailing economic conditions in the different areas.

Results. Available statistics, although limited, raised questions as to whether the goal of self-support was achieved through the WET program. Although about two-fifths of the enrollees found jobs or entered advanced vocational training, the extent to which participation in the program had significantly contributed to their advancement was uncertain. Furthermore, since employable recipients of public assistance remained on relief rolls for an average of less than nine months, it was not unexpected that many participants in the Title V program, who averaged seven months on a project, secured employment during or after their course of training and work experience. For three-fifths of the enrollees—including those who completed the program and dropouts—no benefits were evident after termination.

Failures. Several built-in obstacles in the public-assistance system militated against the success of the WET program. In most states, all earnings of relief recipients were deducted from the assistance they received. Since the jobs open to recipients frequently paid little more than the basic needs provided by public assistance, there was slight incentive to accept a job. The incentive was further reduced by the difficulty which a recipient had in returning to the welfare rolls upon losing a job. In order to motivate welfare recipients to achieve economic independence, there was a need to provide incentives not available under then-existing legislation.

Although the enrollees' work assignments featured a certain amount of informal vocational instruction, the bulk of these assignments was limited to low-paying, unskilled occupations, understandably because of the trainees' limited skills and educational attainments. In addition, data prepared by the Welfare Administration of the Department of Health, Education, and Welfare show that the proportion of funds going to training and instruction was limited, although it increased from 2 percent in 1966 to 14 percent in 1968. WET-project administrators, however, advanced little evidence that occupational training led to the upgrading of trainees from their former occupational levels. Only 5 percent of the terminees went on to advanced vocational training.

Success. Although Title V left much to be desired as far as achieving its statutory goal was concerned, in a number of areas Title V projects became the employer of last resort; in this respect, projects saved thousands of families from dire want and deprivation. For several years Title V funds supported some 6,000 families in depressed eastern Kentucky, where no alternative employment opportunities were available, and the state made no provision to support employable adults. The eastern Kentucky experience was duplicated on a smaller scale in other areas. Given the legislative mandate, however, the reluctance of administrators to claim credit for these programs was understandable.

Work Incentive Program. In 1967, Congress approved amendments to the Social Security Act of 1935 expanding work experience and training opportunities for relief recipients through the Work Incentive Program (WIN), which replaced both the CWT and the Title V programs.

WIN aimed at a broader variety of work-training situations than either CWT or Title V. It was hoped, among other things, that this plan would reduce relief rolls by requiring "employables" to work. Although WIN funds were largely limited to use by public and nonprofit agencies, relief recipients were provided some incentives to secure economic independence. The 1967 amendments permitted exemption of the first $30 of monthly earnings and work expenses and one-third of the balance before any reductions in public-assistance payments could be made. Also, persons in training programs got up to $30 a month more than their public-assistance allotment. WIN also provided for the creation of public jobs, adopting in principle the concept that government should be the employer of last resort. However, less than 2 percent of the enrollees participated in such projects in 1969 and 1970.

Despite the fears expressed during congressional debates about the harshness of the program, especially the "forcing" of mothers of young children to work, it appeared from the early administrative regulations that such coercion was not likely to occur. A significant portion of the early trainees were simply to be transfers from Title V or CWT projects. The next priority groups were AFDC-UP fathers and youths from AFDC families who were over 16 and neither working nor in school. Mothers with preschool children who did not volunteer for WIN were last on the priority of referral. This fact, in addition to the requirement for adequate day care facilities—facilities which were virtually nonexistent in many places—indicated that mothers were not "forced" into WIN participation.

WIN was administered by the Labor Department in cooperation with the Department of Health, Education, and Welfare and their respective state and local units. In fiscal 1969 and 1970, $102 million was spent on WIN.

Although administration officials had hoped to enroll 150,000 people by the end of fiscal 1970, at the end of September 1970 enrollment was only 103,000. Of a total of 155,000 persons enrolled by mid-1970, some 71,000 were still in training, 25,000 were at work under various arrangements, and over 53,000—more than one-third of all enrollees—had left the program prior to completing their employability plan.

Department of Labor data on 4,800 WIN graduates employed as of February 1970 indicated that the average hourly wage was $2.29 and that graduates were working about 40 hours weekly. The most common occupational categories were clerical and sales and service, each with about one-fifth of the graduates. Another study, of 5,300 graduates in six states at the end of 1969, showed substantial disparities in earnings between men and women: median hourly earnings for men were almost $2.50 but only about $2.00 for women. Thus, even after training and employment, many welfare mothers, especially those with several children, did not earn enough to bring their families out of poverty. Data on approximately 15,600 persons who had terminated through March 1970 showed that only 20 percent (24 percent of males and 17 percent of females) were placed in employment.

These early findings suggested limitations of the WIN program. The earliest terminees were likely to be the most successful because many were transfers from WET projects, many were men, and the labor market in 1969 was tight. But as women, who generally experience less success in the labor market, constituted an increasing proportion of enrollees and as business conditions softened, the success of WIN declined. The inability of WIN to provide adequate child-care services also jeopardized the employability of many mothers of small children.

The proposed Family Assistance Program. In August 1969, President Nixon proposed to substitute for the existing AFDC and WIN programs a Family Assistance Program (FAP). Under this welfare proposal, assistance payments could be made to all low-income families with children, including families with a male head who is employed but earning an inadequate income. A floor would be placed under the wide range of state benefit levels so that a family of four with no other income would receive at least a basic annual payment of $1,600—that is, $500 for each of the first two family members and $300 for each additional member.

The manpower aspects of the family assistance proposal focused upon creating work incentives and helping relief recipients to find employment. Under this plan, the first $60 of a family's monthly income would be disregarded, and benefits would be reduced 50 cents on the dollar for earnings beyond this point. (WIN permits the AFDC mother—most AFDC families are headed by a female—to retain the first $30 of her monthly earnings plus work expenses and one-third of each additional dollar.) In addition, FAP would include a requirement that at least one employable person in each family be employed or in training.

The manpower components of the family assistance proposal were built on the experience of WIN. FAP would provide expanded assistance for day care centers, enabling adults in recipient families to work, and would provide for remedial training and job placement.

The importance of the Family Assistance Program is not only that it would liberalize and extend the work incentives of WIN, an obviously needed improvement, but also that it would guarantee an income to families with an employed head. It was estimated that the families of 1.8 million full-time working poor would be covered by FAP.

The Family Assistance Program recognizes the needs of the many who are employed full time but who work for such meager wages that they continue to live in poverty. And, it reflects the national ideology and presidential preference for "work-fare" over welfare.

BIBLIOGRAPHY

AUERBACH CORPORATION 1970 *An Appraisal of the Work Incentive Program.* U.S. Congress, Senate Committee on Finance, *Reports on the Work Incentive Program,* 91st Cong., 2nd sess. Washington, D.C., Government Printing Office.

LEVITAN, SAR A., AND GARTH L. MANGUM 1969 *Federal Training and Work Programs in the Sixties.* Ann Arbor, Mich., Institute of Labor and Industrial Relations. Part 6.

STATS, JEANETTE 1970 *Door to Opportunity: Title V, Economic Opportunity Act.* Social and Rehabilitation Service, Department of Health, Education, and Welfare. Washington, D.C., Government Printing Office.

SAR A. LEVITAN

3. JOB CORPS

The Job Corps was established in Section 101 of the Economic Opportunity Act of 1964 to prepare youths aged 16 through 21 "for the responsibility of citizenship and to increase their employability . . . by providing them in rural and urban residential centers with education, vocational education, useful work directed toward conservation of natural resources, and other appropriate activities." The assumption underlying this mission was that many youths from impoverished homes had to be removed from their home environments before they could be rehabilitated through training and education. This type of program was believed to be needed because, beginning in the early 1960's, youth unemployment was three times the national average; the number of out-of-school unmarried youths from poor families, most of whom were eligible to enroll in the Job Corps, was about 1 million in 1967.

Administration. The administration of the various Job Corps programs was assigned to the Office of Economic Opportunity (OEO). It established three types of residential centers: men's urban, men's conservation, and women's urban. Enrollees at urban centers received educational and intensive skill training. Persons with more severe educational deficiencies than urban-center enrollees were assigned to conservation centers where basic education and work experience, mostly in conservation, were emphasized. Teachers in all centers were required to be regularly accredited. Counseling and job placement services were to be provided, but actual availability varied widely from place to place.

In early 1971, after six years of operation, the Job Corps had served over 300,000 persons. In mid-1967 the Job Corps reached its peak, operating 123 residential centers with a total enrollment of 42,000.

To operate the urban centers, which, in 1968, contained 60 percent of the Job Corps' population (about equally divided between men and women), OEO turned to private contractors, including such corporate giants as General Electric, IBM, Litton Industries, RCA, and Westinghouse. The contractors were responsible for hiring the faculty. Men's urban centers were operated for the most part on abandoned military installations. These centers ranged in population from 600 to 3,000, averaging around 2,000. Women's centers ranged in population from 300 to 1,100, averaging only 500 enrollees in fiscal 1968.

Forty percent of the Job Corps population was located in conservation centers ranging in population from 100 to 250, with an average of 160 in fiscal 1968. The responsibility for the operation of most conservation centers was delegated to the Departments of Agriculture and Interior. The Economic Opportunity Act authorized contracts with states, but only seven of the 82 conservation centers in 1968 were operated by state agencies. The Departments of Agriculture and Interior or the state sponsor hired the faculty.

The cost of the Job Corps was substantial. During its first six years of operation, more than $1.3 billion was allocated, as follows: in 1965, $183 million; in 1966, $310 million; in 1967, $211 million; in 1968, $285 million; in 1969, $236 million; and in 1970, $144 million. Congress imposed a ceiling of $7,500 per enrollee for fiscal 1967 and $6,900 per enrollee for fiscal 1968. Included in this amount was money for pay and allowances, travel, clothing subsistence, medical and dental care, educational and vocational supplies, and recreation. The actual allotment was higher because, among other things, statutory costs did not include overhead and amortization expenses.

A cut in the 1968 budget forced OEO to close 16 centers, dropping total enrollment from 41,000 to about 33,000. Even more substantial changes were made in 1969. The budget was slashed by nearly $100 million, and 50 centers were closed. With 16,500 enrollees forced out of the program, total enrollment dropped to about 18,000. Persistent criticism that the program was too costly was corroborated by a report of the General Accounting Office. In line with the reshaping of the program, authority for the remaining centers was transferred from OEO to the Department of Labor. In addition, 30 residential manpower centers (so-called mini-centers) were announced as replacements for the closed facilities. By the end of 1970, nine of the new centers had been opened, and sites had been selected and contractors identified for 13 more.

Of the 20,100 enrollees at the end of 1970, 37 percent were at the four men's urban centers; 25 percent at the 12 women's urban centers; 27 percent at the 32 conservation centers; and 10 percent at the nine new residential manpower centers.

By closing some of the more costly (but not necessarily less effective) centers and operating near full capacity, the Job Corps was able to cut training costs per man-year to about $6,270.

Enrollee characteristics.   Since its founding, the Job Corps has tried to attract the most disadvantaged youths; only those youths whose needs could not be met by a less costly alternative were to be enrolled. In 1968, for example, two of every five enrollees had completed eight years of education or less. Their actual achievement levels were even lower: reading and arithmetic comprehension for half of the enrollees was at about the fifth-grade level. Three of every five came from broken homes, and two of every five were from families on relief. Except for a decrease in the proportion from welfare families, these characteristics were little changed through 1970.

Most of the screening of enrollees was delegated to the United States Employment Service and its affiliated state agencies. In addition, Community Action Agencies assisted in their communities. Other groups, including the volunteer Women in Community Service and the Urban League, also contributed.

There has been a high proportion of nonwhite and 16-year-old and 17-year-old enrollees, over 66 percent of the total enrollment and almost 60 percent of the total, respectively, in July 1967. In 1970, 66 percent of the enrollees were 17 and under, and the proportion of nonwhites had increased to nearly 75 percent (61 percent Negro and 13 percent other, primarily Spanish-American).

Racial conflict plagued the Job Corps during its first two years, but thereafter staff members learned how to handle such problems, and few incidents have been recorded since then. The very low retention rate of the youngest enrollees led to teaching difficulties.

Achievements.   The success of the Job Corps in providing basic education has been measured by the improvement of enrollee performance on periodic achievement tests. Analysis of past tests showed that the average rate of learning was probably lower than the public school norm but substantially higher than the corpsman's previous learning rate. Men in urban centers made the greatest progress, followed by those in conservation centers. Women showed the least achievement. There was also a wide variation in achievement rates among centers (U.S. Office of Economic Opportunity . . . 1967).

The quality of vocational education in the Job Corps is more difficult to assess, but the benefits of vocational and basic education seem to be directly related to the duration of training. Of those who stayed longer than six months, 42 per-

cent used their Job Corps skill training compared with only 5 percent of those who stayed less than three months (Louis Harris . . . 1967a).

Although the law authorized a two-year enrollment with possible extensions, the Job Corps had difficulty retaining enrollees. Only one in nine enrollees remained in the corps as long as a year. The average length of stay for terminees in late 1967 was 5.6 months, but 22 percent left the Job Corps within the first month and 43 percent within the first three months. Over the first four years the average stay was only 5.3 months. A particular retention problem was found among younger corpsmen. For 16-year-old and 17-year-old terminees in 1967, the average stay was only 4.2 months (Louis Harris . . . 1967b).

The most significant measure of the performance of the Job Corps in educating and training disadvantaged youths was the improvement in the employment status of former corpsmen. Two conclusions can be drawn from employment rates: first, there is a positive and significant correlation between employment rates and duration of stay; and second, 18-year-olds and 19-year-olds benefited most from the Job Corps experience. The same conclusions can be drawn from wage rates. Those who stayed longer than six months in centers not only had higher wage levels but also made much greater gains over pre-enrollment earnings than those remaining less than six months.

Data on 1967 terminees showed that the percent unemployed dropped and starting hourly wages rose steadily with age (from 16 to 22) at termination, from 60 percent to 42 percent and from $1.41 to $1.82, respectively (Louis Harris . . . 1967a).

Eighteen months after termination, the average hourly wage of August 1966 terminees was $1.90 for men and $1.67 for women, showing gains of approximately 50 percent in each case (Louis Harris . . . 1968).

BIBLIOGRAPHY

LEVITAN, SAR A. 1969 *The Great Society's Poor Law.* Baltimore, Johns Hopkins Press.

LOUIS HARRIS AND ASSOCIATES 1967a *A Study of August 1966 Terminations From the Job Corps.* New York, Louis Harris and Associates. Also found in U.S. Congress, House, Committee on Education and Labor, *Hearings on Economic Opportunity Amendments of 1967.* 90th Cong., 1st sess., Part 1. Washington, D.C., Government Printing Office.

LOUIS HARRIS AND ASSOCIATES 1967b *A Study of Job Corps Non-graduate Terminations.* New York, Louis Harris and Associates. Also found in U.S. Congress, House, *Hearings on Economic Opportunity Amendments of 1967.* 90th Cong., 1st sess., Part 1. Washington, D.C., Government Printing Office.

LOUIS HARRIS AND ASSOCIATES 1968 *A Study of the Status of August 1966 Job Corps Terminees 18 Months After Termination.* New York, Louis Harris and Associates.

U.S. CONGRESS. HOUSE. COMMITTEE ON APPROPRIATIONS 1968 *Hearings on the Departments of Labor, and Health, Education, and Welfare Appropriations for 1969.* 90th Cong., 2nd sess. Washington, D.C., Government Printing Office. Part 6, pages 74–206.

U.S. OFFICE OF ECONOMIC OPPORTUNITY. JOB CORPS 1967 "Educational Gains." Assessment and Research Reports, No. 5. Washington, D.C., Government Printing Office.

SAR A. LEVITAN

4. VISTA

A result of the Economic Opportunity Act of 1964 was the development of a volunteer corps intended to become the channel for the participation of individual citizens in the national effort to combat poverty in the United States and to serve as a national clearinghouse for volunteers, which would supply full-time skilled manpower where shortages were most acute. In addition, it was hoped that the stimulation of volunteer activities would encourage volunteers to enter careers in service to the needy at the end of their "tour of duty" in an organized program. To allay persisting congressional doubts about the necessity of a volunteer corps, it was decided that volunteers would be sent only at the request of a state or local agency or nonprofit organization and would work under the direction of the sponsoring organization. In addition, each state's governor would be given veto power over the use of volunteers in his state. Volunteers in Service to America (VISTA), the domestic equivalent of the Peace Corps, was incorporated into Title VI of the Economic Opportunity Act of 1964.

Since VISTA, at least during the period immediately following the passage of the act, lacked the attractive image and appeal of the Peace Corps, it was initially unable to arouse the desire of young college graduates to work for the alleviation of poverty in their own country. Thus, during its first three years VISTA experienced difficulties in attracting personnel. With intensified civil strife and greater emphasis on domestic poverty, however, interest in VISTA eventually increased.

Volunteers. Following the example of the Peace Corps, VISTA directed its efforts primarily toward attracting college students as volunteers. However, VISTA sought to diversify recruitment to a broader cross-section of the general population. Thus, recruitment was carried on at four levels: at colleges, in competition with the Peace Corps; in communities, often in tandem with college drives; among specific groups, such as retired teachers and senior citizens, who were reached by direct mailings and appeals at organization meetings; and within poverty communities.

After being selected, the volunteer entered a six-week training program, spending the first two weeks in orientation and the next four weeks in on-the-job training in the areas in which he would work. This system—permitting a flow of information on expectations, job performance, and support between the trainee, the sponsor, and the VISTA training center—was intended to make training directly relevant to problems of the volunteer in the field.

In summer 1966, VISTA initiated a program called VISTA Associates to utilize the services of college students full-time during their summer vacations; about 1,600 students served as associates in the summer of 1968. VISTA covered about three-quarters of the cost of this project, and sponsoring agencies covered the remainder. The Citizens Volunteer Corps, utilizing the services of private citizens who donated time to help implement VISTA activities in their own communities, was initiated in 1967. By the end of that fiscal year VISTA stated that 40,000 citizen corpsmen were working with regular volunteers.

As compared to the 1,500 volunteers in 1965, there were some 4,800 full-time volunteers in September 1970 on 428 projects located in every state but Delaware and Mississippi; 4,100 of these volunteers were assigned to projects, and the rest were in training. Requests for an additional 23,000 volunteers, coming from nearly 2,000 private groups and agencies, had been logged in the Washington office. Since the demand for volunteers outweighed the supply, certain criteria were established to determine the selection of projects: (1) the activities had to appear likely to produce improvements in the lives of the poor; (2) the volunteers had to be in direct contact with the poor; (3) the sponsoring organization had to be able to provide supervision; (4) the project had to be located in areas of greatest need according to the indexes of poverty; (5) volunteers had to be invited to serve in the area; and (6) the project had to be approved by the governor.

Activities and accomplishments. VISTA assigned about 85 percent of its volunteers to work with community-action agencies or projects funded by the Office of Economic Opportunity's Community Action Program and the remainder to work with the mentally ill or retarded, the

Job Corps, or other programs under the Economic Opportunity Act of 1964. The volunteers were about equally divided between urban community-action agencies, including delegate organizations (operating CAP projects), and rural projects, including Indian reservations and migrant areas.

Most VISTA volunteers had no special skills or preparation for their assignments. The volunteers were equally divided by sex, were between the ages of 20 and 24, and had some college training. Although no records were kept of the race or previous income of the volunteers, VISTA officials estimated that perhaps 10 percent of them came from the ranks of the poor.

In most cases, the effectiveness of the volunteer hinged not so much on the merits of the project as on the rapport he could establish with the community. VISTA volunteers not only worked with the poor; they lived among them. A common problem of the volunteers was overidentification with their clientele, causing the volunteers to become overcommitted "advocates of the alienated" and, thus, suspect to the rest of the community. Possibly, the skill most needed by VISTA volunteers to function effectively was the ability to empathize with their neighbors' problems but not alienate other community groups.

On Indian reservations and in the hollows of Appalachia, VISTA volunteers launched literacy programs, started libraries and recreational programs for youth, began preschool programs, and organized self-help housing projects. In Eskimo villages reached only by bush plane, volunteers brought the only technical skills or contact with the outside world many of these Americans have ever known. Volunteers brought refrigeration to Eskimo fishermen, helping them to keep their catch fresh until it could be flown to market.

In the cities volunteers developed youth outreach and recreation programs, narcotics addiction control programs, and bail bond projects. In Job Corps centers volunteers counseled Job Corps participants, worked on remedial programs, and organized recreation activities. In mental hospitals VISTA volunteers set up classes and activities to help prepare patients for the world outside. VISTA volunteers supplemented regular staff in schools and workshops for the mentally retarded and developed recreational and tutorial programs.

Volunteers also engaged in somewhat more controversial activities, such as the formation of tenant unions, cooperative buying programs, and welfare rights committees. In the Kentucky mountains volunteers were credited (and blamed) for encouraging local support for campaigns to stop strip-mining and to place privately owned coal reserves under local public ownership. Several volunteers in Newark, N.J., assigned by their sponsor, the mayor's office, to routine jobs as aides and general helpers in county hospitals, released a report on poor treatment and adverse conditions encountered by charity patients. Other volunteers in Newark were dismissed from VISTA after refusing transfer which came as a result of organizing slum tenants to press city hall for improvement in inspection and prosecution of housing code violations.

The Office of Economic Opportunity feared the consequences of spelling out criteria designating "proper" behavior for VISTA volunteers—that is, behavior that would not antagonize the community. Stringent rules would have discouraged many potential dedicated applicants, whom VISTA needed. Thus, a decision to be flexible and to approve applications on a project-by-project basis was reached, with the hope of reducing or scattering the attacks on the program.

VISTA's expenditures during the first six years totaled over $140 million, rising from $3 million in fiscal 1965 to over $35 million in fiscal 1970.

The average annual cost per volunteer was more than $7,000, almost one-quarter allocated for administration. The direct cost of supporting a volunteer, amounting to $3,300 in 1968, was modest by any standard. The volunteer received an annual stipend of $600 and an additional $2,428 for food, lodging, and other living expenses. The balance of the direct expenditures covered transportation, medical care, and social security taxes. The major indirect costs included training, program administration, and recruitment.

SAR A. LEVITAN

WORK-STUDY PROGRAMS, COLLEGE

See COOPERATIVE EDUCATION.

WORK-STUDY PROGRAMS, HIGH SCHOOL

High school work-study programs, also referred to as cooperative education programs or cooperative vocational education programs, can be defined as those programs in which students spend one-half of their time taking courses in high school and one-half of their time working. The curriculum of the work-study student is totally integrated: his courses in high school relate directly to his experiences on the job.

There are many kinds of high school work-study programs. Some programs are specifically designed to serve young people who are alienated and have difficulty in perceiving the value of education as a preparation for life. Other programs are designed to develop a student's skill and ability by placing him in a specific skilled or managerial job and relating his school instruction to the skills he learns on the job. Still other programs do not emphasize specific skills but help students to gain acceptable work habits and attitudes and an understanding of the work world. All high school work-study programs provide for payment of the students by the employer. Payment is considered a valuable characteristic of the program, causing students to relate education to life more effectively.

Organization.   Most high school work-study programs are offered to seniors because the students are then old enough for placement in a wide variety of jobs. For instance, programs that offer training in the merchandising, retail, and wholesale trade areas provide placement in sales and marketing jobs in the senior year. Other programs may offer job experience in the latter part of the junior year. Most programs designed to train students for managerial or highly skilled positions offer job placement at both the junior and senior levels in high school. Those vocational work-study programs designed for alienated youth or students who have difficulty with the usual academic type of education are on a nongraded basis and are available to 16-year-olds.

Work-study programs involving jobs in the private sector are not usually offered to students younger than 16. There are few jobs in business and industry open to students 14 and 15 years old, and child labor regulations hinder the placement of students this young. There are, however, programs that place students in school jobs in, for example, school cafeterias and storage areas; these programs are open to students under 16.

In work-study programs students generally spend half their time on the job and half their time in school. Often they spend the afternoon on the job and the forenoon in school. The school courses are the usual required academic courses coupled with job-adjustment and work-orientation courses which relate directly to the student's job.

Some work-study programs alternate work and school at longer intervals, such as two weeks, six weeks, or one semester, but the half-day alternation is by far the most common in high schools. The longer alternations are usually found in collegiate work-study programs.

Some work-study programs employ a two-platoon system to keep job stations filled all day, with one group of students working in the morning and studying in the afternoon and the other group going to school in the morning and working in the afternoon. This procedure permits a single job station to serve two different students and helps employers in working with the program.

In an effective work-study program the teacher, usually called a teacher-coordinator, makes sure that work and school form an integrated educational experience in which academic subjects as well as the job become meaningful for the student. In the school, the teacher-coordinator helps his students with job adjustment and the development of good work habits, shows them how to apply for a job and get along with fellow workers, and does some skill instruction. He also supervises, instructs, and counsels students while they are on the job, and he consults with employers concerning the progress and problems of individual students. The availability of the teacher-coordinator to the student on the job is generally considered one of the most important aspects of a successful work-study program. A teacher-coordinator typically works with 25 students.

An effective work-study program usually makes use of a consulting or advisory committee to bring joint thought and planning to bear on school, employment, and community problems. The advisory committee normally consists of employer representatives, who give advice on the educational program, find positions for students in the program, and identify common problems encountered by students on the job. The advisory committee also serves as a public relations agent for the program and the school, and it helps to relate the world of work to the educational program.

The essential elements of a successful work-study program are the selection of students, their placement in jobs, their adjustment to a work environment and counseling to that end, and full-time placement upon graduation in jobs for which the students have been trained.

At the start of the selection process the teacher-coordinator administers to his students a battery of tests designed to identify their strengths and weaknesses. He helps his students learn how to conduct themselves in interviews with prospective employers and then arranges job interviews with several different employers.

After the student has been interviewed, one of the cooperating employers selects him as a work-study employee. The teacher-coordinator assists the employer and the student in drawing up agreements which describe the conditions of employment. He also helps secure the necessary work permits and helps the employer gain a better understanding of his role in the on-the-job facet of the work-study program. The necessary forms concerning such labor regulations as those governing working conditions and wage and hour requirements are also completed at the placement stage.

The teacher-coordinator uses counseling to help the student adjust to his job, often employing the team approach. The team consists of the employer, the employee, and the coordinator, and it discusses the student's performance on the job, his strengths and weaknesses, and ways in which he can improve his performance.

Finally, the work-study student graduates from high school and is placed on a job full-time as a result of his training program. The teacher-coordinator assumes an important role in this task. He utilizes all of the resources of the school counseling and guidance services and the state and federal employment services.

Kinds of programs. The many different kinds of work-study programs are usually called vocational cooperative programs, vocational work-study programs, or special purpose work-study programs. Presently there are seven types of vocational cooperative or work-study programs in operation in high schools.

Cooperative work-study programs in office and business education provide classroom instruction and on-the-job training to prepare students for employment and advancement in business and office jobs. Prior to placement on the job, classroom instruction includes such courses as typing, shorthand, transcription, bookkeeping, and business machine operation.

Cooperative programs in distributive education are designed to prepare students for employment in the various areas of marketing, including wholesaling and retailing.

Cooperative programs in home economics are designed to prepare students through in-school instruction and work experience for jobs requiring technical skills in home economics. Such jobs include food service assistant, child care aide, home health aide, and day care center assistant.

Cooperative programs in trade and industrial education are designed to prepare students to enter jobs in the skilled trades or in industry. The in-school phase emphasizes both general employment and specific jobs, and the academic instruction is coupled with specific skill training. On the job the student receives training in several different skills.

Cooperative off-farm agriculture programs have been developed to train young people for the many off-farm agricultural jobs which have emerged in recent years in such areas as grain elevator operations, farm equipment sales, feed and fertilizer sales, farm produce marketing, livestock brokerage, and horticulture.

Combination or interrelated vocational work-study cooperative programs are in operation in many communities, with students being employed in several different vocational fields including office, distributive, trade and industrial, off-farm agricultural, and home-economics-oriented occupations. In some states, these programs are called diversified cooperative programs. Programs of this type are best suited to small high schools where there are neither enough students nor enough training stations to justify a separate work-study program in each occupational area.

Another type of work-study program has been implemented in high schools as a result of the passage of the Vocational Education Act of 1963. The Vocational Education Work-Study Program, described in Section 13 of the act, provides needy students an opportunity to go to school full-time and work part-time in a public agency or institution. The act states that the program shall provide employment only to young people who (1) have been accepted for enrollment as full-time students in a vocational program which meets the standards prescribed by state boards of education and local education agencies, (2) are in need of earnings from such employment to commence or continue their vocational education program, and (3) are at least 15 years of age and less than 21 at the commencement of employment. In this type of work-study program no student is employed for more than 15 hours in any week during which his classes are in session.

In this program, as in all work-study programs, the student's job is related to his in-school instruction and vocational program. In the Vocational Education Work-Study Program, the student is an employee of his school. He is placed for work either in the school or in another public agency, such as courts, hospitals, mental institutions, and departments of public housing, public works, public health, public welfare, fire, and police. Part of the wages paid the student by the public school are reimbursed by the federal government under the provisions of the Vocational Education Act of 1963.

Special purpose work-study programs include those designed specifically for the physically handicapped, the educable mentally retarded, and alienated or disadvantaged youth. Job placement, usually in the private sector, is an integral part of the total program. Student wages are paid by the private employer.

Common elements.   All high school work-study programs share several common elements. They include (1) Paid employment which enables the student-employee to gain the experiences of a full-fledged employee rather than those superficial experiences gained as an observer. (2) The employment of a teacher-coordinator with special training in coordination techniques and with experience in the working world which enables him to instruct, guide, and counsel the student trainee. (3) The use of consulting or advisory committees to bring joint thought and planning to bear on the program.

The work-study curriculum.   The work-study curriculum consists of two main parts, namely in-school and on-the-job instruction.

The purpose of in-school instruction is to make the on-the-job placement experience educationally valuable to the student. The in-school facet of instruction consists of two areas. The first area includes units in general and academic areas that relate to all types of employment and contain information and technical knowledge needed for the development of the student's vocational confidence. The second area consists of units relating directly to the student's job. These units are usually studied by the student on an individual or a small group basis. The student is also enrolled in the academic subjects necessary for graduation.

In-school job-related instruction may include such units as how to apply for a job, employee responsibilities, good work habits, the importance of proper grooming, and laws and regulations affecting workers, including social security and income tax laws. The student is also instructed in the elements of good communication with fellow workers and customers. Particular attention is paid to the relation between the work-study program and the student's work life after graduation from school.

A training plan for each student is prepared by the teacher-coordinator and the student's on-the-job supervisor. It describes the student's activities on the job and aids the teacher-coordinator in coordinating classroom instruction with on-the-job training.

The on-the-job part of the work-study curriculum contributes directly to the student's development of occupational competence. During this part of the curriculum the teacher-coordinator and the on-the-job supervisor join in assisting the student to learn his job.

The on-the-job supervisor is a person designated by the employer who is responsible for orienting the student to his training station. This person also helps the teacher-coordinator determine what skills the student should possess before he is placed on the job. An important responsibility of the on-the-job supervisor is to teach safety practices along with the specific skills involved in the job. He also prepares a periodic evaluation of the trainee's progress and cooperates with the teacher-coordinator in evaluating student performance.

The on-the-job part of the program carries specific responsibilities for the teacher-coordinator. He helps the employer understand the purpose and method of the work-study program. His periodic visits with the on-the-job supervisor help in developing a sound practical program for the student to follow. Quite often problems arise on the job which require the combined efforts of the teacher-coordinator and the on-the-job supervisor to solve. It is usually customary for the teacher-coordinator to keep the employer and the on-the-job supervisor informed of the trainee's progress in school.

Several administrative forms are used in work-study programs. These forms include the student agreement, the cooperative training agreement, and the employer's evaluation form. The student training agreement sets forth some of the conditions of the work situation and describes the duties and responsibilities of the student-employee. It also specifies the number of credits to be given for the on-the-job part of the program and describes other aspects of the program. When signed by the student and the parent, the student training agreement assures their understanding of the student's responsibilities.

The cooperative training agreement describes the student's work activities, his in-school program, and his responsibilities in the overall program. It is approved and signed by the trainee, employer, teacher-coordinator, and parent or guardian. This instrument helps all parties to understand their responsibilities in the work-study program.

The employer's evaluation sheet contains a listing of student performance characteristics, such as attitude, interest, adaptability, ability to learn, quality of work, attendance, punctuality, quantity of work, dependability, initiative, and judgment. The teacher-coordinator consults the employer's evaluation sheet when he thinks it necessary to adjust the program to improve the student's performance on the job.

Advantages. The work-study program has advantages for the student, the school, the employer, and the community.

The high school work-study program allows the student to learn an occupation under actual working conditions and provides him the opportunity to gain technical and related information that is relevant in terms of his job or career goal. Actual working conditions also allow the student to adjust to adult responsibilities in work, relations with other workers, and supervision on the job. The student has an opportunity to gain a better relationship to his peers and to the community. He has an opportunity to be self-supporting and to feel genuine pride and satisfaction in his work and his wages. As a result of the work-study program students often see education as relevant for the first time. In many cases the program brings education back into the real world of work and helps it take on a meaning and significance that otherwise is difficult to attain.

As far as the school is concerned there are numerous advantages to be derived from the program. It enables the school to enlarge its learning facilities since use is made of surrounding businesses and industries as laboratories for learning and earning. A valuable program can be offered without great expenditures for facilities and equipment. The program also helps to tie the school, the community, and business and industry closer together because they all share in the job of preparing well-educated, economically self-sufficient citizens. Another advantage of the work-study program to the school is that it provides an opportunity for the school to evaluate its instructional program in terms of the real world of work.

Some of the advantages shared by employers relate directly to the opportunity to secure competent, well-trained employees. The program also assists employers by providing them with well-selected, motivated workers who have chosen a career in keeping with their interests and aptitudes. In addition, a considerable amount of the burden of employee training is shouldered by the school through the work-study program. Employers also have an opportunity to play a role in helping to keep educational programs consistent with current technological practices in business, industry, and agriculture.

There are many advantages to the work-study program that relate to the community. The program is very effective in helping to develop good citizenship skills. These skills are developed within the framework of the real situation in the community, rather than in the rather abstract framework of an in-school setting. The community also has an opportunity to retain skilled workers because high school students, through the work-study program experience, tend to become employed and continue their employment with community firms.

A study conducted in Michigan (Michigan State Board of Education 1967) of 5,420 people one year after their graduation from high school work-study programs indicated that less than 1 percent were unemployed. More than 60 percent had obtained their current full-time employment within one month of graduation from high school. The study also indicated that the work-study program helped students to go on to further education. For example, 40 percent were enrolled in college or other education beyond high school one year after graduation.

Problems. The availability of good work stations in business and industry is the very essence of an effective high school work-study program. Work stations are usually readily available in high-population areas where there are large numbers of firms. In more sparsely settled areas, however, location of an adequate number of work stations is sometimes difficult. During periods when the labor market is tight and there tends to be a shortage of workers, it is quite easy to find suitable training stations for work-study students. However, as labor demands change and there is a surplus of labor, locating suitable stations becomes more difficult.

Employers are generally anxious to participate in a work-study program because placement of students in their firms tends to provide them with an opportunity to secure better trained personnel. As their contribution to the program, employers are willing to pay work-study students the minimum wage for the position in which they are working and also provide them with on-the-job training. But the training they provide is a cost of production that is not necessarily offset by increased productivity of the worker until much later. This situation, coupled with the competition for jobs during periods of labor surplus, may make it difficult to find a sufficient number of work stations.

Another problem area of the high school work-study program concerns the welfare of the student worker while on the job. It is the responsibility of the school and the teacher-coordinator to make sure that work-study students are not exploited by their employers. An effective work-study program should not serve as a source of cheap labor for business and industry. The effectiveness of federal and state labor regulations, coupled with the guidance of the teacher-coordinator and the cooperation of employers, usually prevents exploitation from becoming a serious problem.

Students in a work-study program usually provide their own transportation to their place of employment. Students unable to provide their own transportation often are unable to enroll in the program. Transportation is more likely to be a problem in suburban and rural areas than it is in highly populated metropolitan areas with easily available mass transportation.

The program also tends to suffer from a problem underlying all other areas of public education, namely, difficulty in securing competent and well-qualified teachers. The requirements for teacher-coordinators in work-study programs are unique. In addition to the necessary background of academic education and teacher preparation,

these persons need experience in business and industry. A teacher-coordinator's effectiveness in helping students face situations on the job depends to a large measure on the experience he has had as an employee in the private sector. A considerable degree of maturity and human understanding is required of effective teacher-coordinators. Therefore, these people are usually those who have had some background of successful teaching experience in schools coupled with at least two years of work outside public education. As a means of providing a more adequate supply of teacher-coordinators, institutions of higher education engaged in teacher preparation are giving more attention to offering preservice and inservice education programs designed to prepare work-study teachers. The job of providing good teacher-coordinators is challenging because they must possess not only the standard professional background but also the ability to work with many other school, community, and governmental agencies.

History. The concept of cooperative work-study education began in 1906 with the inauguration of a program at the University of Cincinnati. This program was on the collegiate level and was a combination of work and study as an integral part of the engineering program. The first high school work-study program started in 1909. It was established, in cooperation with the General Electric Company, at Fitchburg, Mass. In 1910 high school cooperative work-study courses were established in the Cincinnati, Ohio, public schools. In 1911, York, Pa., established an experimental high school work-study program. The first retail cooperative training program, which is a type of high school work-study program, was established in Boston, Mass., and incorporated in the high schools there in 1912. The public school system in Dayton, Ohio, established a cooperative high school in 1914 that was devoted entirely to work-study programs. In 1915 work-study high school programs were established in ten New York City high schools.

In 1917 the Smith-Hughes Act, establishing vocational education as a federally supported high school program, was passed. This legislation encouraged the continued development of vocational cooperative work-study programs in the high schools of the United States. The Vocational Education Act of 1963 gave further assistance to the development of this type of high school program.

BIBLIOGRAPHY

BURCHILL, GEORGE W. 1962 *Work-Study Programs for Alienated Youth.* Chicago, Science Research Associates.

DILLON, HAROLD J. 1946 *Work Experience in Secondary Education: A Study of Part-time School and Work Programs.* Publication No. 394. New York, National Child Labor Committee.

GOLD, MILTON J. 1951 *Working to Learn: General Education Through Occupational Experiences.* New York, Teachers College, Bureau of Publications.

FLORIDA STATE DEPARTMENT OF EDUCATION. DIVISION OF VOCATIONAL, TECHNICAL AND ADULT EDUCATION 1963 *Handbook for Diversified Cooperative Training.* Tallahassee, The Department.

HERMAN, MELVIN, AND STANLEY SADOFSKY 1966 *Youth-Work-Programs: Problems of Planning and Operation.* New York University, Graduate School of Social Work, Center for the Study of Unemployed Youth.

MARTIN, MARIE Y. 1954 "An Evaluation of the Work Experience Program in the Los Angeles City Public High Schools." Ed.D. dissertation. Los Angeles, University of Southern California.

MASON, RALPH E., AND PETER G. HAINES 1965 *Cooperative Occupational Education and Work Experience in the Curriculum.* Danville, Ill., Interstate.

MCINTOSH, MARGERY PHIDELIA 1949 "The Work Experience Program in San Francisco High Schools." Ed.D. dissertation. Stanford, Calif., Stanford University.

MICHIGAN STATE BOARD OF EDUCATION 1967 *Cooperative Occupational Training for Michigan Public Schools.* Lansing, The Board.

OHIO STATE BOARD OF EDUCATION. DIVISION OF SCHOOL FINANCE 1967 *The Ohio Law for State Support of Public Schools.* Columbus, Ohio, The Board.

OHIO STATE UNIVERSITY. THE CENTER FOR VOCATIONAL AND TECHNICAL EDUCATION 1967 *Guidelines in Cooperative Education.* Columbus, The University.

SCOGGINS, WILL 1966 *Labor in Learning: Public School Treatment of the World of Work.* Los Angeles, University of California, Institute of Industrial Relations for Center for Labor Research and Education.

SMITH, HAROLD T. 1963 *Education and Training for the World of Work.* Kalamazoo, Mich., Upjohn Institute for Employment Research.

PRESIDENT'S COMMISSION ON LAW ENFORCEMENT AND ADMINISTRATION OF JUSTICE. Task Force on Juvenile Delinquency 1967 *Task Force Report: Juvenile Delinquency and Youth Crime.* Report on juvenile justice and consultants' papers, with bibliographies. Washington, D.C., Government Printing Office.

TYLER, HENRY T. 1956 *Report of the Study of Work Experience Programs in California High Schools and Junior Colleges.* Bulletin of State Department of Education, Vol. 25, No. 3. Sacramento, Calif., State Department of Education.

UNIVERSITY OF THE STATE OF NEW YORK. THE STATE EDUCATION DEPARTMENT. DIVISION OF INDUSTRIAL EDUCATION, BUREAU OF TRADE AND TECHNICAL EDUCATION 1960 *Vocational Industrial Cooperative Programs.* Albany, N.Y., The University.

THE UNIVERSITY OF THE STATE OF NEW YORK. THE STATE EDUCATION DEPARTMENT. BUREAU OF BUSINESS AND DISTRIBUTIVE EDUCATION 1965 *Cooperative Work Experience Manual for Business and Distributive Education.* Albany, The University.

U.S. OFFICE OF EDUCATION. 1954 *Cooperative Education in the United States.* By Henry H. Armsby. Bulletin No. 11. Washington, D.C., The Office.

VENN, GRANT, AND THEODORE J. MARCHESE, JR. 1964 *Man, Education, and Work.* Washington, D.C., American Council on Education.

WILSON, JAMES W., AND EDWARD H. LYONS 1961 *Work-Study College Programs: Appraisal and Report of the Study of Cooperative Education.* New York, Harper.

HERBERT D. BRUM

WORK SUPERVISOR AS INSTRUCTOR

Nothing in business and industry is more clearly defined than the supervisor's responsibility for production, discipline, and the recruitment of employees. His career may often hinge on his ability to be successful in these efforts. If he is able to meet production schedules, keep his employees in line, and meet his hiring quotas, his chances for recognition and advancement are generally very good. Often the degree to which he is better at this than other supervisors is the degree to which he receives recognition.

Paradoxically, however, he is rarely held accountable for the development of the employees under his supervision. Although better trained employees are usually capable of doing better work than those with less training, the direct relationship of training and production is often overlooked even by the supervisor. The more progressive segments of the business community now recognize the importance of developing people and realize that one of the best ways of accomplishing this task is by holding the supervisor directly responsible for the training that they receive. Quality checks, performance evaluation, and other methods are used to assess employee competence, and the failure of employees to meet proper standards is considered a reflection upon the supervisor's training ability.

Many enlightened industries now recognize that the best supervisors are the ones who work themselves out of a job by allowing their subordinates to increase their own skills through the training process.

Although it is the direct responsibility of the supervisor to see that his employees are properly instructed on all facets of their job, the supervisor himself must not necessarily do all of the training. Training may be done in a centralized school, by a work leader, or in small study groups, but the supervisor must see that the employees are made available for the training and that the training is made available to the employees. He is responsible for the scheduling, work-load rearrangement, and career planning of the individuals under his supervision. This situation holds true whether or not there is a formal plan within the particular business firm and whether or not the supervisor submits a formal progress report.

Training employees. Although the supervisor is responsible for employee training, he is not always an expert instructor. But when no one else can do the training, either because of the nature of the job or the lack of competent instructors, the supervisor is the natural one to take charge.

In large assembly-line operations a supervisor or foreman is generally responsible for the training, but he has available to him—either in his group or assigned in the plant—an officially designated instructor. Often the foreman can request this instructor at any time he sees a need. In other situations the foreman is expected to train the employees himself, usually using accepted on-the-job training methods.

In most jobs employees actually receive very little formal training in relation to the total amount of job responsibility they have. The vast majority of employees learn their work on the job by trial and error, by asking questions, by watching other workers, or by verbal instruction from the supervisor. Although this method is time-consuming and even costly to the business, it is generally the way things are run. Many businesses and industries, therefore, emphasize teaching supervisors the rudiments of on-the-job training. In many instances this training is given to subordinate employees, who in turn train the new employees.

There are some jobs that are best learned in group situations, with follow-up training done on the job. Sales training, for instance, is usually done first in a formal classroom situation, sometimes involving the use of closed-circuit television, whereby the instructor and the other students can evaluate the student's approach. There follows a probationary period when the employee is watched closely by the supervisor as he goes through sales efforts with actual customers.

Sometimes training in the use of new techniques must be done on a group basis either by a traveling instructor or with the students being brought to a central location. The value of group training is twofold. First, large numbers of people can be trained in a relatively small amount of time; second, all of the people learn the new technique the same way at the same time.

When this type of training is left up to the individual supervisors, there is often a lack of commitment and perhaps even a lack of understanding of the new policy or technique on their parts. The supervisors may vary in their teaching abilities so that not all of the employees learn the same amount. Some of the supervisors may delay instruction, with the result that the new practice or policy cannot be instituted at the same time in all parts of the business. In the case of technical innovations, the additional problem may exist that the supervisor himself does not understand the new procedures or technology. In such a situation he must get the information from manuals or specifications.

Company. The size of a company significantly affects the training situation. In smaller companies there is less apt to be a competent training staff. Money and facilities may not be available to develop a centralized training program. What formal training is required may well be accomplished by renting a conference room and bringing the employees in on a one-time basis for a specific training effort, after which the instructors go back to their regular jobs and the training program is disbanded.

Some smaller companies have a full-time training officer who keeps up with changes in the field and is himself a competent instructor. He may conduct the training on a centralized basis by having a few of the employees in at a time; or he may do the training before or after working hours; or he may even go to the job site and train the people individually. There are both advantages and disadvantages to this approach, and its successful application depends a great deal on the capabilities of the particular training officer.

Other small companies have been successful in having the supervisors do all of the training on the job. New concepts are discussed and the training approach is decided upon at frequent supervisory meetings. Supervisors then conduct whatever on-the-job training is required. They may report at their next meeting how successful the training has been and how the new procedure is working.

In larger companies centralized training is available, much of which can be highly specialized because adequate facilities, sufficient budget, and competent instructors can be provided. A training staff can be secured on a permanent or temporary basis, and the training program can be worked out with proper leader's guides, visual aids, handouts, and so forth. Employees can be scheduled for training well in advance and the training given as the work load demands and permits.

But again, in neither the small company nor the large company is the supervisor relieved of his responsibility for training. In smaller companies, even where there is a full-time instructor, the supervisor still must do a large amount of the training on his own because the full-time man can give to each employee only a small amount of time. The supervisor's responsibility for training is total where there is no full-time instructor. In larger companies where there are formal centralized training programs, the supervisor must still fill in the gaps. Although the number of man-hours of training reported each year is high, they account for only about 2 to 3 percent of the total number of man-hours. Moreover, the instructors in these schools may be line supervisors who are borrowed because of their technical competence in certain subjects.

Qualifications. Most instructors in business-industry situations are chosen more for their technical competence than for their teaching ability. Whether the training is to be done on the job by the supervisor or whether the supervisor is borrowed to instruct in the classroom, there are certain skills essential in producing the correct behavior in the trainee. Several methods have been used over the years to train instructors, with varying degrees of success.

The 1960's was a period of important changes in industrial training because greater emphasis came to be placed on learning than on teaching. Supervisors being trained to teach found themselves having to deal with such questions as what the student would be able to do when the training was over rather than the traditional question of what he was going to teach the student. This change in emphasis caused instructor training to take quite a different turn in more progressive organizations.

In the past most instructor training consisted of teaching the supervisors how to prepare lesson plans and giving them instruction and practice in public speaking. They were sometimes given additional training on how to prepare and use visual aids.

During the 1960's instructor training began to put less emphasis on public speaking and more emphasis on student involvement and measuring the results of training. The role of the supervisor as an instructor therefore became one of producing behavioral change, and his success as an instructor was measured in those terms. No longer was it satisfactory to say in a profit-oriented business that the instructor's job was simply to put out the information and the students' responsibility was to get it. Executives had become disenchanted with this approach because they saw no reason to supply large sums of money when the only hope they had of producing more capable workers lay in the degree to which the students were self-motivated. They preferred a system that put pressure on the instructor to find techniques that would force the students to become involved and to demonstrate in the classroom that they were actually able to perform the various tasks. This system would also take advantage of the fact that learning itself is a good motivator.

The effective instructor-training programs are those that allow the supervisors to practice their teaching in a realistic environment and then measure the results of that teaching. Evaluations of teaching focus on the reasons for not producing learning and examine the techniques used to teach certain types of information. For example, instead of suggesting that the supervisor did not use an appropriate gesture or that he leaned on the rostrum too long, the evaluational comments might suggest that a prepared chart on an easel would have been more effective than information written on the blackboard. Once the would-be instructor becomes concerned over the amount of learning that takes place during his teaching, he will be better able to accept training on how to use such devices as visual aids. He then will have a commitment to use these devices because he will have seen their beneficial effects in his own teaching efforts.

Instructional techniques. The supervisor who is a contents specialist must develop his capability as an instructor as well. First, he must learn that teaching is a skill and therefore can be learned. Primary requirements for teaching include both the ability to produce lasting learning in an efficient manner and the ability to get the students involved by using participation techniques and by stimulating their thinking through such means as challenges, controversy, and competition. In this context one of the least effective forms of instruction is the traditional lecture, in which students have nothing more than a passive role. By contrast, students' ability to remember and use information in the acquisition of which they have participated is very high. Students appear to remember a large amount of what they say and do themselves in an instructional setting as opposed to what they hear and see someone else say and do.

There are a number of simple but effective methods for producing greater student involvement. One of the easiest is to have the students respond to a question or a directive in writing. For example, they might be asked the following: "Make a list of the three most important ideas we just discussed"; or "What is the biggest single problem you see facing you in your job?" After a few minutes the instructor can record the information on the blackboard and begin a discussion. Since all of the ideas under discussion will have come from the students, they will be more involved and committed to the subject than if the instructor had made up the list himself.

An expansion of this idea is asking the students to work in small groups of three or four people and to come up with a common list or a single item for that small group. When notations are made on the blackboard or easel, the element of competition, which arises between the groups, tends to increase student interest and involvement.

A third approach is for the instructor to supply the list of items and then have the small groups select certain items according to such categories as the most important or the best or the worst. Thus, a degree of controversy enters the teaching-learning activity in addition to participation and competition, since the groups will probably vary in their opinions.

Communication barriers. There are several built-in stumbling blocks to the instructional process that the supervisor must overcome. First, the fact that he is the supervisor may cause some superior-subordinate conflicts, especially if he insists on forcing this relationship. If, however, the students are able to discern that his interest lies in their learning rather than their recognizing him as the boss, they will more quickly overcome their fears.

Second, a supervisor who is inexperienced as an instructor may use words, codes, abbreviations, or expressions that are familiar to him but unfamiliar to the learner. He may not realize that there are employees who do not know all of the technical names and integral parts of equipment and procedures. Some instructors think the students will not respect them unless they use technical terms and mysterious references. The more enlightened supervisors have learned, however, that they are more respected and more effective when they put the information on the student's level rather than trying to force the student to guess at what certain terms and phrases mean. Many businesses and industries have therefore found it advantageous to begin training programs with a glossary of terms and definitions.

Another way to overcome communication barriers is to use the involvement techniques mentioned above, which enable the teacher to get feedback from the students and thus correct any misconceptions.

Ingredients of successful instruction. Ingredients of successful learning include behavioral objectives, a plan of instruction, use of teaching skills, feedback, and follow-up.

Behavioral objectives. Perhaps the most important single ingredient for producing successful learning is a good set of behavioral objectives. These objectives should specify exactly what students should be able to do at the end of the instruction period and also should list the conditions and restrictions under which this performance is to take place. Such an objective might be worded as follows: "Given the proper forms and reference material, the clerk will be able to enter the information in the correct rows and columns and perform the necessary calculations to arrive at a bottom line total with 100 percent accuracy. This task should be performed in a maximum of 20 minutes." By thus stating the objectives, the supervisor not only will be aware of his goals but also will have an excellent chance to see whether he has been successful in his instruction. An additional benefit is that the student will also recognize his success or failure because the objectives have been clearly stated in behavioral form.

Plan of instruction. The next necessary ingredient for successful instruction is an appropriate plan of instruction which takes into consideration not only the objectives but also the means and methods to be used in achieving them. The lesson plan should include references to the techniques for encouraging student involvement, the visual aids to be used, and an approximate time schedule. A good lesson plan specifies what both the instructor and the students will be doing as the class period progresses. One of the possible dangers of a lesson plan is that the inexperienced instructor may find himself too closely wedded to it and will not have the flexibility that he should have in conducting a successful teaching effort.

Most experienced instructors find that the lesson plan or the leader's guide should be just that—a plan or a guide. They set it to one side for reference, preferring to communicate directly with the students. They circulate up and down the aisles, stand in the back of the room, and move across the floor. They are not inhibited by having to constantly lean over a large book or extensive outline. They may on occasion stop and look at their notes to be sure nothing is overlooked and that there is enough time to complete the lesson, but they do not let such minimal checking handicap their relations with the class.

Use of teaching skills.   The next ingredient for successful instruction is one that has already been discussed—the use of successful teaching skills. These skills may involve the utilization of class participation, individual exercises, case studies, tests, class discussion, and visual aids. But whatever the techniques, they will have been chosen as the most effective means of producing a particular change in behavior in a given group of students on a specific subject at a particular time.

Feedback.   Another requisite for successful instruction, which is also a means of measuring success, is feedback. The involvement techniques already discussed are designed to produce a large amount of feedback. The successful instructor will not wait until the teaching session is over to get his feedback in the form of a final exam. Rather, he will seek as much feedback, at frequent intervals, as he can. He is thereby able to make adjustments as required and continually determine his progress in meeting the stated objectives. The instructor must, however, be flexible enough to adapt his presentation to what he learns from the feedback. In any kind of system there can be no adequate control unless there is adequate feedback.

Follow-up.   The final essential ingredient of successful instruction—follow-up—is one that is the direct responsibility of the supervisor, perhaps more so than any of the other elements. Regardless of what the students are able to do in the classroom or demonstrate for the supervisor in an on-the-job session, the training is not successful unless the employees can perform on the job under normal conditions. It is essential that the supervisor make a diligent effort to check on each employee following any training activity.

Follow-up serves several purposes. First, it allows the supervisor to measure the effectiveness of the training, and it provides some measure of the student's ability to learn. In addition, it allows for modification of the training program if the proper results are not being obtained. Finally, it gives the supervisor a chance to make small corrections without sending the student back to class and without the student's going through another formal training session. Most businesses and industries consider that the effectiveness of training can be significantly increased by the supervisor's making a determined effort to follow-up at least one time on each employee. The time spent usually produces large dividends.

BIBLIOGRAPHY

BROADWELL, MARTIN M. 1969 *The Supervisor and On-the-Job Training.* Reading, Mass., Addison-Wesley.

BROADWELL, MARTIN M. 1970 *The Supervisor as an Instructor.* 2nd ed. Reading, Mass., Addison-Wesley.

MARTIN M. BROADWELL

Y

YEAR-ROUND SCHOOL PROGRAMS

There is no logical reason for closing schools in July and August. The long school vacation during the summer months originated at a time when the economy and culture of the United States were agrarian. Children were needed on the farm and around the home during the planting, growing, and harvesting seasons; organized educational experiences were less important as job qualifications; young people had more opportunities to learn about work, develop vocational skills and competencies, and develop a genuine understanding of community life through actual work experiences. In the 1970's the old school calendar is still kept even though the United States is confronted with a serious shortage of teaching personnel and school facilities and even though there are insistent pressures on young people who will enter the labor market to learn more in school and to learn it better.

The almost universal practice of leaving school plants and teaching personnel idle for two months every year should be carefully reexamined in the light of present circumstances and needs. Various alternatives have been and are being proposed and, to some extent, implemented. A four-quarter, staggered-vacation plan was in use in Bluffton, Ind., as early as 1904. In many communities some year-round school programs are well established, such as vocationally oriented courses in agriculture, home economics, and distributive education. Remedial programs, music programs, arts and crafts programs, and recreational programs also have been operated during the summer months in many school districts. In California children may enroll in awareness-sensitivity groups for the summer or may study marine biology, civil rights, or computer technology. In Washington students

may take a summer course in sailing that meets regularly at a yacht basin. In Illinois children have an opportunity to study the stock market. Whether they attend out of boredom and a desire to escape the confines of the inner city or because they want to widen their learning experience, more and more children are attracted to an increasing number of summer classes.

Some school districts have adopted a variation of year-round schooling in which the students attend school for the usual 36 or 40 weeks but the teachers work an additional ten to 12 weeks attempting to improve the educational program to be offered during the next school year.

Meeting the needs of an ever increasing number of young people and improving the quality of educational programs will, in most communities, require more personnel, more and better facilities, and more money. However, achieving better utilization of existing facilities and personnel by developing a year-round educational program can also help meet these needs.

Year-round schooling has several positive features, both fiscal and educational:

(1) The school plant to be used already exists, fully equipped and ready for use.
(2) Overhead costs for administration and fixed charges, such as insurance and interest, frequently remain fairly constant whether the schools are open or closed during the summer.
(3) Teachers (especially male teachers), if offered full-time employment and, consequently, better annual salaries, will not be forced to leave teaching for other occupations offering greater remuneration.
(4) Since many children, especially those living in towns and cities, have few other con-

structive things to do during the summer months, attending school may be the most useful activity available to them.

(5) Teachers have an opportunity to become better acquainted with students and parents.

(6) The professional growth of teachers is accelerated.

(7) Opportunities are available for improving educational programs and for giving adequate orientation to new teachers.

Although the concept of year-round schooling has been discussed and debated intensely in recent years, most of the discussion has been based upon judgments held by interested parties rather than upon information drawn from carefully designed research. Therefore, increased controversy rather than common agreement on principles and approaches has been the result. The practicality of some of the proposals has seldom been tested other than by trial and error. These proposals have taken different forms and have been advanced for a variety of reasons. In general, however, there are only a few basic plans.

Four-quarter, staggered-vacation plan. A four-quarter, staggered-vacation plan utilizes a 48-week school year divided into 12-week quarters. The student body is divided into four groups, and each group attends school for three quarters, or the usual nine months. However, the vacation period is staggered, so that a different group of students is on vacation each quarter. Teachers may follow the same vacation plan as the group of students they teach or may elect to work all 48 weeks.

Several advantages are claimed for this plan. Theoretically, each child is guaranteed as much instruction time as is normally provided under conventional scheduling, but 25 percent more pupils are taught by approximately the same size staff, using the same number of classrooms, laboratories, libraries, and playgrounds. Pupils graduate on schedule, and double shifts, which shorten each student's school day, are unnecessary. In addition, the need for new buildings and equipment is drastically reduced, thereby alleviating the urgent need of many school districts for more funds.

There are also several problems inherent in a staggered-vacation plan. The first stems from the fact that, if a school is to operate efficiently under the plan, its total enrollment must be divided into four equal groups, and in addition, enrollment in each grade in an elementary school and in each subject in a high school must be approximately the same during each quarter. According to the American Association of School Administrators:

> Optimal conditions must prevail for the theoretical economy to become fully operative, and optimal conditions are not often present. If a school is overcrowded, the all-year plan can help to ease the load: But the full savings can be obtained only if the number of pupils can be divided exactly by four so that a capacity load will be in attendance every quarter. The loads must be exactly divisible by three so that each quarter the pupils in attendance use every room to capacity. Unused classrooms or teachers with substandard loads reduce the theoretical economy. (1960, p. 8)

Thus, it might be argued that unless a school's enrollment is large and unless the number of students in attendance each quarter is about the same, inefficiency rather than efficiency prevails under a staggered-quarter plan.

School systems having relatively small enrollments may find it difficult to register equal numbers in each quarter at the most efficient pupil-teacher ratios. In addition, prevailing family and community living and working habits may make it difficult for any school system to maintain a constant enrollment level throughout the year. Clearly, if parents who have two or more children in school are given an opportunity to choose the quarters their children attend, they will generally want them all to be in school during the same quarters. Furthermore, parents will want vacation schedules for all members of the family to coincide. It is almost certain that relatively few families will urge their children to be out of school in the winter months or in school during June, July, and August. Thus, it seems very probable that a family-elective system will result in a very uneven distribution of pupils over the four quarters. Of course, the school board and the school administrator conceivably could arbitrarily assign pupils so as to equalize enrollment in each quarter. However, anyone familiar with the problems of administering American schools and also with the independence of American citizens would hesitate long before urging such a policy. Getting community acceptance of the dozens of family inconveniences and hardships which the staggered-vacation plan involves is an almost insurmountable obstacle to the plan's efficient operation.

In any case, the economies resulting from the plan may not be as great as some advocates have claimed. In many sections of the country, air conditioning will have to be installed in school buildings before they can be used year-round. Installation and operating costs, especially in old buildings, would be considerable. Teachers' salaries, too, must be adjusted upward for those on full-year teaching assignments, and part-time teachers are likely to be needed throughout the year. Furthermore, a four-quarter schedule will probably result in less efficient bus loads, more months of employment for transportation personnel, and thus greater salary expenditure.

It is also possible that, under a four-quarter plan, juvenile delinquency will increase unless families and community organizations quickly expend time and money to establish community services and facilities for the school-age children out of school in the fall, winter, or spring quarters. (In the summer quarter, traditional work opportunities, camps, and family vacations provide out-of-school students with ways to use their time.) No community should give one-quarter of its schoolchildren 12 weeks of free time without providing supervision or planned programs. If such supervision and programs are provided throughout the year, many of the economies claimed for the four-quarter plan will vanish. Possibly communities exist in which, because of home schedules, community facilities and services, and mild weather, out-of-school children may be kept occupied during all months of the year. However, such communities are rare.

It is also difficult to provide and administer many kinds of extracurricular and scholastic activities under a staggered-vacation plan. For example, the coaches will want all football players to be enrolled in the fall term, all basketball players enrolled in the winter and spring, all track and tennis players enrolled in the spring and fall, and all swimming team members enrolled throughout the year. In addition, the bandmaster, the dramatic coach, the orchestra leader, the debate coach, and the academic teachers interested in certain scholastic events and scholarship examinations will insist on the attendance of certain students during certain quarters.

Forty-eight–week school year. A second plan involves having regular school in session for 48 weeks. There may be a one-month summer vacation, or the four weeks of vacation may be distributed throughout the year (for example, around Christmas and Easter). Advocates of this plan claim that, if it is used, above-average children can easily complete what is now 12 years of schooling in nine years, and children who fail grades can nevertheless complete elementary school and secondary school in the present normal period of 12 years. The longer school year may be voluntary—those who wish to attend for 48 weeks may do so, and those who strongly object to being in school throughout the year may attend only for the present term of about nine months. Alternatively, the plan may be made compulsory by legislation requiring children to be in school all year. In either case, school facilities are used year-round.

Voluntary year-round schooling programs were in operation in Newark, N.J., from 1912 to 1931 and in Nashville, Tenn., from 1924 to 1932. Pupils in these school systems were able to obtain schooling continuously if they so chose, and teachers could teach throughout the year, receiving a commensurate salary increase for their additional work. Both cities discontinued the program, however, primarily because it proved to be too expensive and because serious complaints were voiced that those high school students graduating early were too young for regular employment and too young to succeed in college. It was also claimed that the early graduates were not as well prepared for work or college as high school graduates in other school systems.

In 1955 the Citizens' School Study Council of Fairfield, Conn., studied a year-round–schooling plan under which children would be required to attend classes for at least 11 months every year. It was hoped that, by fully utilizing existing school facilities, expenditures for construction of additional buildings could be reduced. After considerable study, however, it was decided that the social and administrative disadvantages of this plan far outweighed the economic advantages, and the plan was rejected.

Multiple-trails plan. The multiple-trails plan is a proposal for reorganization of the secondary school and is directed toward both educational and economic objectives. Designers of the plan report that it can provide an immediate release of about 25 percent of available classroom space.

Under the multiple-trails plan, the school year

is 11 months long, containing 210 school days. (There is a July or August vacation, and there are the traditional winter and spring vacations.) The length of the school day remains the same, but the day is rescheduled into time modules which vary in length from 15 minutes to 30 minutes, depending on the individual school's decision. Classes are scheduled in terms of time modules, which replace the conventional, longer class periods. (Each class session may be one or more time modules long.) This rescheduling reduces instructional time per week in each subject, but because the school year is longer, the total annual instructional time in each subject remains the same.

Therefore, using a lengthened school year and multiple time modules releases some pupil time, instruction time, and classroom space each school day without sacrificing the school's educational program and makes possible several alternatives. The classroom space released may be used to relieve overcrowding or to accommodate students the school previously could not handle. Teachers may spend their additional free time on such projects as curriculum revision. The additional instructional time and classroom space may be used to provide an accelerated high school program or to meet the needs of individual students through the use of remedial, corrective, and enrichment programs.

An extended school year and modular scheduling can also be used with a program of continuous progress, in which grade levels become insignificant and students proceed through the study of subject areas at their own rates.

Voluntary summer programs. An increasing number of school systems are offering a regular 36-week or 40-week program supplemented by a voluntary summer program varying in length from four weeks to 12 weeks. These summer programs provide for remedial and accelerated work. However, the major emphasis is usually placed on enrichment—that is, on providing educational experiences above and beyond those offered during the regular term. For example, some children may take advanced courses in chemistry, physics, mathematics, creative writing, or painting; some may attend great books seminars, thereby becoming acquainted with some of the great writers and philosophers; some may study foreign languages; and some may take courses which do not fit into their regular school programs, such as

typing (for personal use), nature study, woodworking, music, crafts, or stenography. The experience of communities offering such summer programs indicates that about one-third of the student population attends them.

In such communities, teachers may be hired for a regular nine-month term and given a choice as to teaching summer school. Alternatively, they may be hired on a 12-month basis and given a variety of summer assignments: teaching summer school, preparing curriculum materials, traveling, or attending summer school.

In the summer program, many of the traditional regulations that tend to restrict the pupils' work during the regular school term are removed. For example, some enrichment activities may be offered without credit; thus, the class does not have to meet a minimum amount of time in a given week. The summer program is an opportunity for exploration, experimentation, and enrichment.

The program answers a great many of the needs of communities and school systems. It lends itself to maximum flexibility and adaptation to local needs and to the provision of many activities which cannot reasonably be included in the regular school session. It also provides an opportunity for community participation in planning the schools' activities and for adult education. The additional cost involved is the primary drawback of the summer program.

Summer programs for professional personnel. Keeping the instructional program up-to-date and improving it year after year is both a purpose and a problem of school administration. This problem becomes more urgent and more challenging as the tempo of cultural change accelerates. The consequences of retaining outmoded curricula and instructional methods are serious, far-reaching, and possibly disastrous.

The instructional program cannot be kept relevant by merely adding courses, increasing the number of units required for graduation, or assigning more homework. One of the most fruitful ways to add quality to the school program is to provide for the professional growth of instructional staff members. This growth takes place as staff members study and improve teaching methods, reorganize and revise curriculum content, and gain new insights into how children learn.

Where can time be found to give such serious attention to improving the instructional program?

During the regular school day, teachers are devoting almost all of their time and energies to working directly with pupils. In the hours immediately after school, teachers are too tired to be very imaginative and creative. In the evening they have to do such work as correcting papers and preparing for the next day's class or classes. On weekends teachers must have some relaxation and respite from their work if they are to retain the freshness and vitality so essential to effective teaching. Consequently, in order to ensure the quality and relevancy of their instructional programs, several school districts have in recent years adopted a variation of year-round schooling in which the teachers (employed on a 12-month basis) work 48 weeks and have four weeks of vacation and the pupils attend school for the traditional 36 to 40 weeks.

During the summer weeks when pupils are not in school, teachers, together with administrators and district supervisors, engage in instructional and curriculum planning. They review developments in instructional fields and revise curriculum content accordingly; they carefully think through instructional methods in light of the latest educational research findings; they survey the different instructional materials and equipment that are continually coming onto the market; and they review evaluative procedures and promotion policies.

School board members, supervisors, principals, teachers, and leaders of various community organizations join with the superintendent of schools in deciding what needs to be done and how it should be done. The work done is widely publicized in the community, so that residents will understand the purposes and nature of this part of the total school program.

The summer program may vary considerably from year to year, and even in a single summer different teachers may engage in different activities. Some may take advanced courses at a college or university; some may attend a workshop in the local school district, actually preparing materials to be used during the next school year; some may spend the summer in a professional organization, in a business establishment, in the research laboratory of an industrial plant, on a nature-study expedition, or in foreign countries (for the purpose of getting firsthand knowledge of cultural developments). The program is flexible enough

to make use of numerous kinds of experiences and resources, but through careful planning, all efforts are directed to the common purpose of bringing life and vitality into the instructional program.

There is no rigid requirement that every teacher participate in the summer program. Exceptions are made when participation would impose hardships or extreme difficulties on individual teachers. Maintaining the physical and emotional well-being of every member of the teaching staff is a prime function of this summer program. Therefore, the program should not become entrapped in a rigid pattern that defeats its very purpose.

School systems that develop and operate summer programs for their professional personnel will be confronted with several problems. One is that such a program costs money. It may necessitate an increase in the system's expense budget of 10 to 20 percent. The expenditure of school funds for the professional improvement of individual teachers is a considerable departure from general practice. Unless people in the community understand the purposes of such an expenditure and see that it constitutes a sensible use of school funds, they will not support the program enthusiastically. A further result of the program is that the leadership responsibilities of the administrative and supervisory staff increase tremendously.

The problems are not insurmountable, however, and teachers and administrators who have participated in summer programs for faculty members have identified several positive features of such programs:

(1) Teaching becomes a full-time profession.
(2) Teachers begin the regular school year with a greater sense of security.
(3) Curriculum revision takes place in a relaxed atmosphere.
(4) Greater time can be devoted to the selection of textbooks and other teaching materials.
(5) System-wide workshops and committees give teachers an opportunity to understand other teachers' problems.
(6) As teachers participate in workshops, orientation programs, examinations and discussions of students' records, and the many other activities of the summer school pro-

gram, they become better able to guide and direct students during the regular school year.

(7) There is an opportunity for system-wide, vertical curriculum meetings which contribute to teachers' understanding of the total curriculum.

College-level summer programs. Although the nature of the program varies with the institution, almost all major colleges and universities make effective use of plant facilities and personnel during the summer. The programs, four weeks to 12 weeks in length, include hundreds of courses in numerous fields.

The summer school programs of the smaller teachers colleges have given thousands of teachers, supervisors, administrators, and other school personnel an opportunity to continue their professional preparation without resigning from their positions. The progress that has been made in upgrading certification standards since World War II would hardly have been possible without such opportunities for summer school work. In addition, the insights professional educators have gained from studying child growth and development, educational philosophy, research dealing with actual teaching and learning, and the subject matter they are to teach have affected in a striking way the character and quality of education in school districts throughout the United States.

Two aspects of college and university summer programs are of particular interest to the local school system that is considering the adoption of an extended-school-year program. First, some college administrators have concluded that buildings and equipment and highly skilled faculties are too valuable to be left idle for a quarter of the year. They have realized that the need for educational services does not stop automatically with commencement and begin again with the opening of the fall semester. Second, the nature, scope, and purposes of the summer programs are broadly conceived; a concept of service to the people of the state or region in which the university is located is clearly in evidence. The summer activities constitute part of a continuing educational program that reaches many people and comes to grips with numerous current problems.

Institutions of higher learning which have let their laboratories and classrooms be closed, have let their equipment and facilities remain idle, and have disbanded their instructional staffs and sent them on long vacations during the summer months have missed great opportunities to make an important contribution to the cultural life in the areas they serve.

The nature and purpose of a public school system are very different from those of a major college or university. However, the concepts of flexible organization, a broad educational program, and a wide range of instructional services for members of the community might well be given serious consideration at all levels.

Decision-making on school-year length. If the leadership of a community decides to reappraise the adequacy of the length of the school year, a number of issues should be considered. It must be determined who should be involved in the decision-making process and when they should be involved. Clearly, the superintendent of schools, principals, representative teachers, school board members, and the heads of civic, labor, and business groups should all participate in study and discussion. They need not all work simultaneously, however. Probably the schools' professional staff, with the guidance of the superintendent, should be first to examine such questions as: Is there a need for change in the length of the school year to make the schools more efficient, to economize, or to extend pupil services to improve the quality of education? Have the demands for formal education so increased and the curriculum so expanded that pupils must have more time in school to meet requirements? Does the long period of preparation required of those who assume complex occupational roles suggest the need for acceleration? Any such examination will probably involve serious study of contemporary social, economic, political, and cultural developments, both national and international, and their implications for education. If this study indicates the need for a longer school year, attention should next center on the various year-round–schooling plans which might be adopted. Faculty meetings devoted to discussion of these plans should be held. The discussion should later be broadened to include members of parent-teacher organizations and civic and business groups.

After a consensus has been reached as to what should be done, the proposed program should be widely publicized to gain community acceptance of both the program and a plan for securing any additional revenues needed.

BIBLIOGRAPHY

AMERICAN ASSOCIATION OF SCHOOL ADMINISTRATORS 1960 *Year-round School*. Washington, D.C., The Association.

BULLOCK, ROBERT P. 1962 "Some Cultural Implications of Year-round Schools." *Theory Into Practice*, 1, no. 3:154–161.

CALIFORNIA ELEMENTARY SCHOOL ADMINISTRATORS ASSOCIATION 1960 *Emerging Summer School Practices in the Elementary Schools of California*. Monograph No. 12. Burlingame, Calif., The Association.

CAMMAROTA, CANDIDA GLORIA, JOHN A. STOOPS, AND FRANK R. JOHNSON 1961 *Extending the School Year*. Washington, D.C., Association for Supervision and Curriculum Development, National Education Association.

CHILDRESS, JACK R., AND HARLAN A. PHILIPPI 1964 "Administrative Problems Related to the 11- or 12-month School Year." *High School Journal*, 47, no. 1:230–237.

CINCINNATI BOARD OF EDUCATION. DEPARTMENT OF RESEARCH, STATISTICS, AND INFORMATION 1958 *The Four-quarter School Year: A Status Report With Pertinent Applications to Cincinnati*. Cincinnati, Ohio, The Board.

CITIZENS' COMMITTEE OF THE SEQUOIA UNION HIGH SCHOOL DISTRICT 1960 *The Four-quarter Plan and Other Methods of High School Plant Utilization*. Redwood City, Calif., The District.

EAVES, ROBERT W., MARY F. HAZELL, AND DOROTHY NEUBAUER, eds. 1952 "The Extended School Program." *National Elementary Principal*, 31, no. 5:entire issue.

FLORIDA EDUCATIONAL RESEARCH AND DEVELOPMENT COUNCIL 1966 *Year-round Schools for Polk County, Florida: A Feasibility Study*. Gainesville, University of Florida.

FLORIDA STATE DEPARTMENT OF EDUCATION 1957 *The All-year School*. Tallahassee, The Department.

GEORGE PEABODY COLLEGE FOR TEACHERS. DIVISION OF SURVEYS AND FIELD STUDIES 1931 *The All-year School of Nashville, Tennessee*. Field Studies No. 3. Nashville, The College.

GILCHRIST, ROBERT S., AND EDWIN R. EDMUNDS 1962 "The Value of an Independent Summer Program." *Theory Into Practice*, 1, no. 3:162ff.

GUBA, EGON G., ed. 1962 "The Year-round School." *Theory Into Practice*, 1, no. 3:121ff.

HARTSELL, HORACE C. 1953 "The Twelve-month School." National Association of Secondary-School Principals, *Bulletin*, 37, no. 198:18–33.

IOWA STATE DEPARTMENT OF PUBLIC INSTRUCTION 1962 *Summer School*. Des Moines, The Department.

LEWIS, RUSSEL L. 1950 "The Organization and Administration of Summer Public School Educational and Recreational Programs in Districts Within Metropolitan Areas of the United States." Doctoral thesis. Los Angeles, University of Southern California.

LOS ANGELES CITY SCHOOL DISTRICTS. COMMITTEE TO STUDY THE ALL-YEAR SCHOOL 1954 *The All-year School*. Los Angeles City School Districts.

MCCARTY, DONALD J. 1958 "Is the All-year School the Answer?" *Administrator's Notebook*, 6, no. 6:1–4.

NATIONAL EDUCATION ASSOCIATION. RESEARCH DIVISION 1960 *Extended Work Year for Teachers*. Research Memo No. 1960–45. Washington, D.C., The Association.

NATIONAL EDUCATION ASSOCIATION. RESEARCH DIVISION 1967 "Summer School: Programs for Students, Employment for Teachers." *NEA Research Bulletin*, 45, no. 1:20–24.

NATIONAL EDUCATION ASSOCIATION. RESEARCH DIVISION 1968 *The Rescheduled School Year*. Research Summary 1968–S2. Washington, D.C., The Association.

NATIONAL EDUCATION ASSOCIATION (RESEARCH DIVISION) AND AMERICAN ASSOCIATION OF SCHOOL ADMINISTRATORS 1968 *Summer Enrichment Programs*. Educational Research Service Circular No. 2. Washington, D.C., Educational Research Service.

NEW YORK STATE EDUCATION DEPARTMENT 1967 *Administrative Handbook on Summer Secondary Schools*. Albany, N.Y., The Department.

REMMLEIN, MADALINE KINTER 1964 *Legal Provisions for Summer Schools*. Washington, D.C., Committee on Educational Finance, National Education Association.

Report of the Commission for the Study of a Twelve Months' Use of Public School Buildings and Facilities for Public School Purposes 1960 Raleigh, North Carolina State Department of Public Instruction.

RICH, K. W. 1956 "Present Status of the All-year Secondary School." *California Journal of Secondary Education*, 31:18–24.

THOMAS, GEORGE I. 1965 *Economy and Increased Educational Opportunity Through Extended School-year Programs*. Albany, Office of Research and Evaluation, University of the State of New York.

THOMAS, GEORGE I. 1966 *Extended School-year Designs*. Albany, University of the State of New York.

THOMAS, GEORGE I. 1968 *An Introduction to the Multiple Trails Extended School-year Plan*. Albany, University of the State of New York.

THOMAS, GEORGE I. 1968 *Setting the Stage for Lengthened School-year Programs*. Albany, University of the State of New York.

TRUMP, J. LLOYD 1959 *Images of the Future: A New Approach to the Secondary School*. Urbana, Ill., Commission on the Experimental Study of the Utilization of the Staff in the Secondary School.

TURBEVILLE, GUS 1964 "A Sociologist Looks at the Twelve-month School Year." *Peabody Journal of Education*, 42, no. 3:182–186.

WILLIAM J. ELLENA

YOUTH ORGANIZATIONS

Various types of organizations offer programs for young people. Some of these programs, sponsored by departments of the National Education Association or the U.S. Office of Education, are organized within schools to supplement and enrich a specific area of study; other programs form school chapters or operate within schools with the permission of the local school administration. Some national organizations offer leisure-time programs not only for school-age youngsters but also for people of all ages. The groups described here are representative of all types of organizations providing services for young people.

AMERICAN FIELD SERVICE

The American Field Service is an nonprofit organization concerned with promoting understanding among people throughout the world. Its purposes are to involve high school students in the family, community, and school life of other nations.

Program. The AFS conducts two types of international scholarship programs for high school juniors and seniors. The first program annually brings approximately 2,800 students from 63 countries to the United States to live for one year with an American family and attend the senior year of the local secondary school. The second program is the Americans Abroad Program, which annually provides opportunities for over 1,500 American high school juniors and seniors to live and study in 51 countries. AFS programs are administered in cooperation with volunteer organizations throughout the world and with the help of local volunteer chapters in the U.S. communities where students are placed.

Organization. The AFS is controlled by 50 international trustee members, who meet annually to review policies, guide the development of programs, and elect a 21-member board of directors, which conducts the organization's business throughout the year. In 38 of the 63 overseas countries participating in AFS programs, a small paid staff coordinates the work of volunteers and serves as liaison with international headquarters. In the other 25 countries a private citizen, a binational center director, or a cultural assistant on the U.S. embassy staff handles the representation procedures.

Membership. In the United States there are 2,800 chapters which represent the AFS program in every high school in which an overseas student is placed. These schools are eligible to nominate candidates for the AFS Americans Abroad Program. Each chapter assumes financial responsibility for an overseas student; many chapters also raise funds to assist needy Americans Abroad students.

History. In 1914, Americans residing in Paris organized the AFS as a volunteer ambulance service to assist French hospitals in the evacuation of the wounded from the French war front. Additional volunteers formed both ambulance and trucking units under the command of the French armies. After World War I the remaining funds were used to operate a postgraduate scholarship program for the exchange of American and French students. During World War II the AFS provided ambulance drivers for the French forces and later for the British forces in the Middle

East. Units also served in Italy, France, Germany, and on the India-Burma front. The present international scholarship program, which began in 1947 with 52 students, has sponsored approximately 37,000 overseas students and 19,000 American students.

The AFS has its headquarters at 313 East 43rd Street, New York, N.Y. 10017.

ARTHUR HOWE, JR.

AMERICAN YOUTH HOSTELS

American Youth Hostels, Inc., is a nonprofit association which emphasizes the values of simple and inexpensive travel and offers reasonable overnight accommodations in hostels in the United States. The major educational aims of AYH are to help people of all ages gain greater understanding of the world and other people through its program of outdoor activity and educational and recreational travel and to develop fit, self-reliant, and well-informed citizens.

Program. Each summer AYH plans and sponsors an average of 50 hosteling trips through the United States, Canada, Mexico, Europe, Israel, Turkey, Japan, the Caribbean, and Yugoslavia. The trips, which are priced low enough to offer planned travel to people with limited financial means who have the desire to travel and meet people, range from one week to eight weeks. Each AYH trip is led by a trained leader, and groups never exceed more than ten in number.

AYH issues the *Annual Hostel Guide and Handbook*, newsletters, and bulletins. It offers services to other youth and community organizations such as the scouts, Y's, community centers, and school and church groups. It is cooperating with foundations, businesses, and industries to stimulate travel from abroad to the United States and is trying to establish a chain of hostels throughout the United States to provide inexpensive hostel accommodations at intervals of about 300 miles.

Organization. AYH has a national board of 33 directors, who are prominent citizens and educators. Twenty-five regional councils throughout the United States sponsor year-round activities and projects through more than 90 hostels. AYH is affiliated with the International Youth Hostel Federation, whose membership includes organizations in 47 countries and over 4,250 youth hostels.

Membership. Membership in AYH, which now numbers over 52,000, is open to people of all ages. A member must purchase a hostel pass which is valid for use in all hostels throughout the world. Passes range in price according to age, from $5 to $10 for individuals. The major source of income is from program fees; about 20 percent comes from contributions.

History. The youth hostel idea was first conceived in 1909 in Germany by an elementary school teacher, Richard Schirrmann. Eleven national associations were represented at the first International Youth Hostel Conference, which was held in Amsterdam in 1932. In 1969, of the more than 4,100 youth hostels associated with the International Youth Hostel Federation, there were 752 in Poland, 644 in Germany, 567 in Japan, 265 in England, 206 in France, and 93 in the United States.

In the United States, AYH was founded in 1934 by two schoolteachers, Monroe and Isabel Smith, who started the first American hostel in Northfield, Mass. From its beginning, AYH has been a completely integrated movement. Hostels have been established on farms and in schools, camps, lodges, student houses, and community centers. The first city hostel was opened in May 1965 in Philadelphia in Fairmount Park, when the city turned over the famous colonial Chamounix mansion to a local group for use as a metropolitan youth hostel.

The national office of American Youth Hostels, Inc., is at 20 West 17th Street, New York, N.Y. 10011.

SAM SHAYON

BIG BROTHERS OF AMERICA

Big Brothers of America is a social service organization providing a youth guidance program for boys who do not have normal father relationships. Big Brothers is committed to the principle that every boy needs adult male companionship, and it encourages mature, responsible men to offer friendship and counsel to boys who have been separated from their fathers.

Program. Big Brothers of America serves member agencies in the United States and Canada. It enlists dedicated men from all walks of life and from all ethnic, racial, and national backgrounds to help guide, instruct, and influence young fatherless boys. Volunteers have dedicated themselves to developing positive social and educational attitudes in young boys. As a result of their assignments to Big Brothers, boys have shown

marked improvement in schoolwork and appreciable decrease in juvenile behavioral problems.

Although there is no structured educational program, all men who volunteer as Big Brothers are concerned with helping boys learn the best ways of relating to society. In many instances, referrals to Big Brother agencies come from local schools. In Florida and Michigan several school systems employ regular Big Brother counselors to work with boys from fatherless homes.

The work of Big Brothers is carried out at the local agency level, where volunteers are interviewed and screened prior to being accepted as Big Brothers. Boys are also introduced to the program at the local agency level, where a man and a boy are assigned as a team. No dues or fees are charged either the men or boys, and each man is free to spend as much money as he wishes with the boy.

Organization. In some large metropolitan centers there are three separate Big Brother agencies. In other cities there are two separate agencies, but in most smaller communities there is only one such agency. A large national board determines program policies and standards for all Big Brother agencies. A small paid staff at the national headquarters organizes regional professional staff conferences, regional laymen's council meetings, and an annual meeting at which all agencies are represented. Each local agency has its own board of directors.

Membership. By 1970 there were 192 member agencies in the United States and Canada, with 175 other communities in the process of organizing agencies. Although more than two-thirds of the local agencies receive a portion of their support from local United Fund appeals, much of the work is financed by private contributions from foundations and individuals.

History. The Big Brother concept of one man working with one boy began in 1904 in New York City as a result of a clerk's interest in children's court. The clerk, who was concerned with the increasing rate of juvenile crime, spoke to a church men's club about the problem. As a result, each man in the club agreed to befriend a boy who had experienced behavioral problems. Although other similarly motivated groups joined the movement, Big Brothers of America was not officially organized until after World War II. The BBA undertook a growth and development program which encouraged communities to form agencies.

It sought highly skilled social workers to staff local agencies; launched a public information program; and initiated a research program to determine need, effectiveness, and value for the national organization and its local affiliates.

The national headquarters of the Big Brothers of America is located at Suburban Station Building, Philadelphia, Pa. 19103.

RAYMOND J. HOFFMAN

B'NAI B'RITH YOUTH ORGANIZATION

B'nai B'rith Youth Organization is a youth organization whose purpose is to help young Jewish people achieve personal growth so that they may lead satisfying and socially useful lives in the Jewish community and in the larger community in which they live. The BBYO encourages its groups to participate in a broad program of cultural, religious, community service, human relations, sports, and social activities.

Program. All BBYO activities are designed as learning experiences. The community service program combines fund raising and personal service. Each local chapter is expected to contribute to the International Service Fund. The money is used for leadership training activities within the BBYO and for such other philanthropic organizations as the Leo N. Levi Arthritic Memorial Hospital in Hot Springs, Ark.; the B'nai B'rith Women's Children's Home in Israel; two agricultural settlements in Israel; Camp B'nai B'rith in Starlight, Pa.; UNESCO; CARE; the Kennedy Center for the Performing Arts; and the National College Fund and Service for Negro Students. BBYO groups participate in local Jewish Welfare Fund campaigns, local health drives, and other local institutions. The program also includes tutoring underachievers, taking disadvantaged youngsters to museums and recreational events, collecting books for use in economically deprived areas, and holding discussions with black youths to achieve better race relations.

In the area of personal service, the BBYO sponsors the Adopt-a-Grandparent Program, in which youngsters provide companionship to the aged in or out of institutions. BBYO groups entertain and help children in hospitals, homes, and other institutions. They read to the blind and help the physically and mentally handicapped.

The BBYO has published a series of 13 Judaism pamphlets for use by teen-agers. Titles include *Judaism and Ethics, The Jewish Concept of Man, Judaism and Christianity*, and *A Jewish View of Love and Marriage*. It has also published a series of program guides for its chapters.

Contests in oratory, storytelling, creative writing, sermon writing, and creative arts are held at the chapter level. Local winners proceed through regional and district levels to the international finals at Camp B'nai B'rith.

Organization. The BBYO is a federation of three youth organizations: the Aleph Zadik Aleph, for high school boys; the B'nai B'rith Girls, for high school girls; and the B'nai B'rith Young Adults, for young men and women. Each local chapter has an unpaid volunteer adviser who is supervised by the professional staff of social group workers. Chapters are united into regions, each of which has a youth structure, an adult policy-making structure, and a professional staff structure. Several regions constitute a district, of which there are eight in North America and others in other countries of the free world. The three international organizations have conventions and make legislative recommendations which are reviewed by the international B'nai B'rith Youth Commission, which is the highest governing body. The international director and his staff enforce the policies of the commission and provide the top professional leadership for the organization.

Membership. Because Jewish aspirations are emphasized, membership is open only to Jewish youths. The BBYO has more than 41,000 members in 1,557 groups in communities in the United States and Canada. Approximately 8,000 members are affiliated with groups in other countries. About two-thirds of the organization's support is derived from the parent organization and one-third from membership dues and fees.

History. The B'nai B'rith youth movement originated in 1924 in Omaha, Neb., with a single chapter of 16 boys who opposed the exclusive high school and college social fraternity system. Three other chapters were formed during the same year, and the four groups held their first convention in July 1924. In 1925 the youth organization received official sponsorship by the B'nai B'rith. The first chapter of B'nai B'rith Girls was founded in 1927 in San Francisco. In 1944 the two organizations merged and became the BBYO. After the formation of the B'nai B'rith Young Adults, the three groups became a federation. Since 1950, BBYO membership has doubled.

The B'nai B'rith Youth Organization has its headquarters at 1640 Rhode Island Avenue NW, Washington, D.C. 20036.

MAX F. BAER

BOY SCOUTS OF AMERICA

Boy Scouts of America is a scouting organization committed to character development, citizenship training, and mental and physical fitness. The organization seeks to accomplish its goals through its educational program and the oaths, promises, and codes of the scout program.

Program. Boys eight to 18 participate in the Cub Scouts, Boy Scouts, and Explorers. Cub scouting provides the home-centered, parent-oriented experience; boy scouting provides man-led, outdoor activities; and exploring provides experience in group choice and self-operation. The achievement and advancement system permits a Scout to progress at his own speed. The standards are quite specific in terms of knowledge, skills, and attitudes.

Self-realization, the goal of the advancement process, finds expression in three broad areas: first, the Scout learns clearly identifiable and progressively challenging scoutcraft skills; second, the Scout learns the leadership skills which require demonstrable growth; and, third, under the supervision of skilled counselors, the Scout personally investigates self-chosen fields of vocational or avocational opportunities designed to broaden his horizons.

In the first area, the Scout learns skills that make him more self-reliant while living in the out-of-doors and functioning as a key member of his patrol. He learns that performing his assigned tasks helps his patrol to function skillfully and harmoniously. The Boy Scouts of America operates permanent and primitive camps and provides other camping experiences so that the lessons learned result in group comfort, safety, and harmony for all participants.

The second area of the advancement process gives the boy an opportunity to observe and practice the techniques of leadership. He learns that true leadership is based on each person's ability to share in group action, to understand situations, and to accomplish necessary tasks.

The third area provides the Scout with the opportunity for mature experience. He selects his area of interest and pursues it through his own initiative. The interest areas, known as merit badge subjects, are varied and comprehensive. The Boy Scouts of America offers over 100 merit badge subjects, ranging from such required topics as lifesaving, swimming, first aid, citizenship, and conservation to such elective topics as oceanography, space exploration, surveying, photography, and art. The numbers of required and elective merit badges are so balanced that a Scout develops personal skills and moral values to serve himself and others and still has the opportunity to investigate subjects that may lead to a choice of educational pursuit or a lifetime hobby.

High school boys may join an Explorer post, in which the young man may be involved not only in activities chosen by members of the group but also in the merit badge program leading to the rank of Eagle. The group may select such special career interests as law enforcement, engineering, medicine, graphic arts, airlines management, photography, and sports. Leaders in business, industry, and the professions have cooperated with the Boy Scouts of America in this program. In recent years, girls have joined in Explorer post activities.

Organization. A church, synagogue, school, industry, service club, veterans' organization, or group of citizens may be granted a sponsorship charter to operate a pack, troop, or post program. There are 97,000 such chartered institutions, which provide the volunteer leaders and places for the groups to meet. They also appoint volunteers to coordinate the work of the units with the district committee and the local council. The local council is an administrative geographical division with an elected board of volunteers. The 496 local councils receive direct assistance from 12 regional offices. The National Council is the official body of the Boy Scouts of America. It consists principally of local council representatives. It is represented between annual meetings by an elected executive board empowered to transact all business related to the Boy Scouts of America.

Membership. Boys of all religious faiths, ethnic and racial backgrounds, and socioeconomic levels may join the Boy Scouts. Boys of eight, nine, and ten years of age may join a Cub Scout den or pack; boys of 11 through 17 may join a Scout patrol and troop or an Explorer post at the time they enter high school.

Financing of the program of the Boy Scouts of

America is on three levels. The national office operates on income from its sale of official uniforms and equipment, revenue from advertising in its two national magazines, bequests, and charter fees paid by local councils. Local councils are financed largely through community contributions through the United Fund and from friends of scouting. The individual Cub pack, Scout troop, and Explorer post meets its expenses through weekly dues and money-earning projects.

History. The Boy Scouts of America was founded in 1910 in Washington, D.C. In its first year the combined boy and adult membership was 61,495. By 1930, when the Cub Scout program was officially adopted, the membership had grown to nearly 850,000. By 1969 scouting had served over 45 million members.

The Boy Scouts of America has its national headquarters at New Brunswick, N.J. 08903.

RAYMOND K. NEAL

BOYS AND GIRLS NATIONS

Boys and Girls Nations are summer programs for boys and girls sponsored by the American Legion and the American Legion Auxiliary. The objective of these programs is to provide training for youth in citizenship.

Program. Each summer 100 boys representing 49 states and the District of Columbia and 102 girls representing 49 states, the District of Columbia, and the Panama Canal Zone undergo a week of intensive practical study of the operation of the federal government. The boys and girls are high school juniors chosen from those with the best records of achievement in their respective Boys State and Girls State programs.

Every aspect of the American national government and political party system which can be emulated is employed in the program under the direction of trained volunteer American Legion and auxiliary members. Boys and Girls Nations stress actual participation in the organization and development of political parties. Each delegate is assigned to a mock political party and is encouraged to participate fully in the organization of his party, starting with the organizing caucus, continuing with the formation of committees, and concluding with a mock senate session—complete with the introduction and passage of resolutions and bills.

Delegates are briefed by members of the president's cabinet on current problems confronting the national government. They visit federal departments and institutions, shrines, and historical sites in and around the capital. They tour the Capitol, hear high-ranking congressmen explain House procedure, visit the Federal Bureau of Investigation, meet high-ranking military officers and Civil Service Commission members, see the Supreme Court chamber, and perhaps even have an impromptu visit at the White House with the president.

Organization. The Boys Nation program is administered by the legion's National Americanism Division; Girls Nation is administered by the national auxiliary.

Counselors at Boys Nation are attorneys, schoolteachers, and professional youth counselors; Girls Nation staff are members of the auxiliary's National Girls State Committee, and each has served as president of one of the auxiliary's 52 Girls State programs. The annual programs are arranged by the National Public Relations Division and the executive director of the Washington office.

Membership. Each of the delegates to Boys and Girls Nations, who is designated a senator, has just completed from six to 14 days of study of local, county, and state government structures and administration in Boys and Girls State programs. These programs are financed by the national organization budgets of the legion and the auxiliary.

The American Legion has its headquarters at 700 N. Pennsylvania Street, Indianapolis, Ind. 46204; the auxiliary has its headquarters at 777 N. Meridian Street, Indianapolis, Ind. Both organizations also maintain offices at 1608 K Street NW, Washington, D.C. 20006.

JAMES C. WATKINS

BOYS AND GIRLS STATES

Boys and Girls States are American Legion and American Legion Auxiliary education programs. The aim of the programs is to enable boys and girls to participate in the practical functioning of local, county, and state governments.

Program. The training at Boys and Girls States is objective and practical, with city, county, and state governments operated by elective and appointive officials placed in office by the citizens of Boys and Girls States. The length of the program varies from six to 14 days, with the average participation being one week. The programs usually take place at a college or university campus or other educational institution.

Upon arrival, each boy or girl is assigned to a city, a county, and a mythical political party. Citizens of each city and county nominate members of their individual parties as candidates for various city and county offices. Elections are held, with the citizens conducting their own registration of voters and the actual balloting. Election boards serve at city, county, and state elections, according to the laws of each state.

Citizens of a state are instructed in the duties of public office. They learn the functions of each office (with its powers and limitations), set up their own government, have their own governor and staff of state officials, name appointive officers, establish the state supreme court and other courts, and organize the legislature and all other divisions of government.

Textbooks which explain the practical operation and functioning of state and local government are usually provided. Special lectures are given by experienced public officials and professional leaders. In many Boys and Girls States mock law schools are conducted, and citizen attorneys defend and prosecute. Each Boys and Girls State has its own newspaper, edited and printed by the participants. Counselors are qualified leaders and instructors, attorneys and judges, high school and college teachers, athletics instructors, and public officeholders.

Membership. The majority of delegates are high school juniors sponsored by an American Legion post or by an auxiliary unit. Some delegates are sponsored by various patriotic, civic, fraternal, or religious organizations. Support for the programs comes from the budgets of the legion and the auxiliary national organizations.

History. The first Boys State was conducted in 1935 by the American Legion Department of Illinois. The Legion Auxiliary of the District of Columbia initiated the first Girls State program in 1938. In 1970, Boys State programs were conducted in 48 states and the District of Columbia. Girls State programs were conducted in all 50 states, the District of Columbia, and the Panama Canal Zone.

The national headquarters of the American Legion is located at 700 N. Pennsylvania Street, Indianapolis, Ind. 46204; the auxiliary maintains its headquarters at 777 N. Meridian Street, Indianapolis, Ind. Both organizations have offices at 1608 K Street NW, Washington, D.C. 20006.

JAMES C. WATKINS

BOYS' CLUBS OF AMERICA

Boys' Clubs of America is a national nonprofit, nonsectarian organization of 890 Boys' Clubs serving over 875,000 boys. Boys' Clubs provide facilities and a program of educational-vocational activities, athletics, and character guidance. Staffed by college-trained, professional youth workers, the clubs are designed to prepare less-privileged youngsters for responsible, productive lives.

Program. Boys' Clubs emphasize what boys can achieve and should do rather than what they cannot achieve or should not do. A typical Boys' Club has a gymnasium, a library, craft and hobby shops, game rooms, and a kitchen. Many have swimming pools. Most clubs provide instruction in woodworking, electronics, automotive repairs, and the use of modern power tools. In photography laboratories members are taught to take and process photographs. Cooking classes, with an average enrollment of 11 boys, are conducted by chefs from local restaurants, who stress nutritional and hygienic concepts.

Personal hygiene and physical fitness activities include physical examinations and annual eye and dental clinics. Clubs operate swimming pools for recreational and educational purposes, and many clubs conduct community learn-to-swim campaigns. Club members from crowded tenements experience outdoor living in summer camps.

Club leaders emphasize activities that develop character and leadership qualities. They initiate community improvement programs such as cleanup, antivandalism, physical fitness, and get-out-the-vote campaigns; they also encourage members to work with the handicapped and to assist in charity fund drives. National Boys' Club Week, which is celebrated annually, pays tribute to the thousands of boys who participate in these programs. To represent them, clubs select a "Boy of the Year" on the basis of his service to home, school, church, community, and club. The national winner is announced by the president in a special White House ceremony. Hundreds of students are presently attending college under scholarships and grants from Boys' Clubs. Thousands of boys have received assistance through various scholarship programs.

Boys' Club workers undergo extensive training in colleges and universities which have four-year programs in club work and in other colleges which offer undergraduate work-study courses. Short courses are also given by the Personnel and Training Department of Boys' Clubs of America. Seminars and training institutes in techniques of youth work and administrative practices are conducted throughout the United States, and forums, workshops, and training courses are given by nationally known educators and civic and business leaders at annual conventions.

Organization. Boys' Clubs are located in 470 cities and towns in 46 states. Each club has its own board of directors and adheres to guidelines and standards established by the national board of directors of Boys' Clubs of America.

Membership. Any boy aged seven to 18 may join a Boys' Club. Membership fees range from 50 cents to $2 a year. Financial support is derived from Community Chest, United Fund, and special fund-raising projects.

History. The Boys' Club movement began in 1860, when a group of women in Hartford, Conn., recognizing the need to provide supervised after-school activities and leadership training for disadvantaged boys, founded the Dashaway Boys' Club. The idea spread to other communities and states, and in 1906 existing clubs formed the national organization. Boys' Clubs of America received a congressional charter in 1956.

Boys' Clubs of America has national offices at 771 First Avenue, New York, N.Y. 10017.

Paul V. McEntyre

CAMP FIRE GIRLS

Camp Fire Girls is a national youth organization which offers leisure-time education and recreation programs to all girls from second grade through high school. The aim of the organization is to assist girls in preparing for adult life through gradually more complex experiences.

Program. The four program levels of Camp Fire Girls are Blue Birds for girls of seven and eight; Camp Fire Girls for girls of nine, ten, and 11; Junior Hi Camp Fire Girls for girls of 12 and 13; and Horizon Club for senior high school girls. Blue Birds play games, sing, visit places of interest, learn simple handicrafts, explore nature,

and make new friends. Named for Maurice Maeterlinck's bird of happiness, Blue Birds "fly up" at a ceremony during which they become Camp Fire Girls.

The activities of the Camp Fire Girls center around the crafts of home, outdoors, creative arts, science, business, sports and games, and citizenship. Each craft has its own distinctive colored beads, which girls receive as marks of achievement. Camp Fire Girls may attain successive ranks of wood gatherer, fire maker, and trail seeker.

The program of Junior Hi Camp Fire Girls encourages girls to earn the title of group torch bearer. A girl may also become an individual torch bearer in any one of 25 specific subjects, such as aerospace and interior decoration.

Members of the Horizon Club participate in coeducational activities and explore career possibilities. They are trained for community service in hospitals, museums, homes for the aged, and schools for the handicapped. A three-year project adapted to physically handicapped children was tested in some metropolitan areas. In addition, special services were organized to meet the needs of low-income girls living in highly congested neighborhoods.

Other recent annual projects emphasized the creative arts. Art exhibits, including one in the Junior Division of the Metropolitan Museum of Art in New York City, were held across the United States. Camp Fire Girls was the first youth organization to sponsor a land and sea conference. The 20-day Horizon Club Conference Afloat to the Caribbean was attended by over 1,000 girls from 35 states. The Horizon Club Adventure '68, its second nationwide conference, was a 20-day venture which included exploration of land, sea, and sky. The Enchanted Lands Conference was held at Estes Park, Colo., in July 1968. Groups separated into "travelcades" of 30 girls each, traveled to 16 target areas, and completed needed conservation services. After the conference, participants returned home to work with local community groups and organizations.

Organization. The Camp Fire Girls has a national executive director and a 150-member policy-making body called the national council. Representatives chosen from the seven regional areas of the United States belong to the national council. The program is carried out by 374 chartered councils and 58 associations in more than 5,000 cities and towns. The president of the

United States is the honorary president of Camp Fire Girls, Inc.

Membership. With no specific membership qualifications, groups vary in size from eight to 20 girls. They are guided by adult volunteers and are sponsored by individuals and by civic, religious, fraternal, educational, and other organizations. Financial support is derived from membership in the United Fund and the Community Chest, donations, and membership dues.

History. Camp Fire Girls was founded in 1910. It was the first nonsectarian, nondenominational, education-recreation program for girls in the United States.

The national headquarters of Camp Fire Girls is located at 65 Worth Street, New York, N.Y. 10013.

Rosemary Kornfeld

DISTRIBUTIVE EDUCATION CLUBS OF AMERICA

Distributive Education Clubs of America is a national voluntary youth organization operating through the schools to attract young people to careers in marketing and distribution. DECA's three major goals are to assist state associations in their growth and development; to develop respect for education in marketing and distribution which will, in turn, contribute to occupational competence; and to promote understanding of the responsibilities of citizenship in a free and competitive enterprise system.

Program. The common interest of distributive education students is studying for a specific career. DECA programs offer students the opportunity to participate in planned school activities and to develop the responsibilities of citizenship. Members often receive state and national recognition for participation in DECA activities. Chapter activities are always school-centered and serve as teaching tools. They create interest in all phases of marketing management and distribution study, provide avenues of expression for individual talent, and assist in teaching poise in subject matter presentation.

Through creative marketing projects, DECA members have made numerous studies and surveys to aid the economic development of their communities. Many business firms employ distributive education (DE) students because of their interest in and related school study of that particular business. DE instruction and DECA activity emphasize competition and private enterprise.

DECA contributes to the employability of its members by encouraging and conducting competitive activities in such areas as advertising, sales demonstrations, job interviews, public speaking, display, marketing studies, training manuals, and management decision-making. A creative marketing project is designed to identify additional markets and/or employment possibilities for a given community. State and national leadership conferences have workshops on career development projects.

DECA chapters encourage members to practice parliamentary procedure and observe social amenities. Chapters sponsor good-grooming days for the entire student body. Many chapters engage in school improvement projects by providing equipment needed by the school and by representing the school in civic promotions.

DECA leaders encourage students to stay in school as well as to continue their education at postsecondary institutions. The national organization offers scholarships to needy students.

Organization. Each local chapter, which is composed of DE students, elects its own student officers; the DE teacher-coordinator serves as chapter adviser. All chapters within a state belong to a state association under the leadership of the state DECA adviser. Each state association elects its own student leaders. The national organization, composed of state associations, has a national executive director. Student delegates elected by each state in turn elect their own national leaders.

DECA is governed by a board of directors made up of 11 state supervisors of distributive education and an appointed representative of the U.S. Office of Education. DECA, Inc., is composed of the head state supervisors of distributive education of the states and territories of the United States. Three directors from the membership of DECA, Inc., are elected each year for three-year terms.

Membership. There are over 125,000 DECA members in 3,318 local chapters representing 50 state associations, Puerto Rico, and the District of Columbia. Over two million young people have been members of DECA.

DECA has its national headquarters at 200 Park Avenue, Falls Church, Va. 22046.

Harry A. Applegate

FOUR-H CLUBS

Four-H Clubs is an organization of rural, urban, and suburban young people who participate in a variety of projects concerned with farming, home-making, personal improvement, community service, and good citizenship. Club members strive for better family living, community progress, and world understanding.

Program. Four-H welcomes boys and girls from all economic and cultural backgrounds. The number of projects available ranges from one or two dozen in some states to about 100 in others. Some of the more popular projects are agricultural production and marketing, engineering, conservation, management, family living, and personal development. In recent years program emphasis has broadened from a how-to to a how-do approach, from quantity to quality production in agricultural projects, and from raising the crop or farm animal to developing the young person.

Television stations in many states offer a 4-H action series that teaches by videotape. Enrollees have workbooks to supplement the information provided by the program and receive homework assignments to prepare between lessons. Participation in 4-H can also be carried on through special interest groups without joining a club.

The International Farm Youth Exchange, established in 1948, has made it possible for young Americans to live for several months with host families in other countries and for young people of other lands to come to the United States to live and work with American families. When they return to their own countries, the young people share their experiences with youth groups, adult organizations, and individuals. Organizations similar to 4-H Clubs have been formed in about 80 overseas countries.

Organization. About 550,000 volunteer local leaders serve 4-H Clubs. Of these, about 400,000 are civic-minded adults; the others are older 4-H'ers who serve as junior leaders. Leaders are trained, counseled, and assisted by county extension agents, who supply educational information from resources of state land-grant universities and the U.S. Department of Agriculture. County, district, and state 4-H council groups are active in many areas to help plan and conduct various phases of club work.

Membership. Membership is open to any boy or girl from nine to 19 years of age, regardless of race or creed. There are no dues. Members run their own clubs, elect officers, plan and hold meetings, and select projects. Each club drafts its program to suit its members and their localities.

Meetings are usually held in homes, community centers, or schools. By 1970 nearly 4 million young people were participating in the 4-H program in all 50 states, the District of Columbia, Puerto Rico, the Virgin Islands, and Guam.

Government financial support is supplemented with funds contributed by civic groups, business, industry, agriculture, education, foundations, and other local, state, and national organizations.

History. The 4-H movement grew from a need in rural America in the early 1900's. Agricultural leaders discovered at that time that young people were more receptive than older people to the introduction of scientific methods on farms and in homes. Rural young people were encouraged to focus their learn-by-doing activities on improved agriculture. Corn, pig, tomato, and canning clubs were forerunners of 4-H Clubs. Between 1901 and 1905 interested leaders of these and other groups gradually set up patterns for organization and activity. In 1914, Congress passed the Smith-Lever Act, which provided for cooperative extension work in agriculture and home economics, including boys' and girls' club work. This law also established a system of federal funds to be matched by state and county funds as the basis of financial support for the cooperative educational program. In the past half century, about 30 million young people from all types of communities—urban and suburban as well as rural—have participated in the formerly all-farm youth program.

The national 4-H emblem, adopted in 1927, is a four-leaf clover with the letter *H* on each leaf. These letters denote the organization's emphasis on developing "Head, heart, hands, and health." The 4-H slogan is "learning by doing."

The 4-H national headquarters are in the Extension Service, U.S. Department of Agriculture, Washington, D.C. 20250.

FRANCES C. DICKSON

FUTURE BUSINESS LEADERS OF AMERICA–PHI BETA LAMBDA

Future Business Leaders of America–Phi Beta Lambda is a national organization for all secondary and postsecondary school students enrolled in business programs in public and nonpublic schools. The FBLA–PBL is designed to be an extension of the instructional program and thus an integral part of the business curriculum.

Program. The FBLA–PBL helps business students prepare for business and office occupations.

Members learn to engage in individual and group business enterprises; to carry out the responsibilities and duties of elective office; to work with representatives of other student organizations; and to compete honorably with their colleagues on the local, state, and national levels. The FBLA–PBL provides opportunities for participation in state and national leadership conferences, learning experiences through visits to business and industrial enterprises, and close contact with successful businessmen and businesswomen.

The FBLA–PBL emphasizes the development of both business and civic leadership. Its program brings students together in an effort to encourage vocational preparation; scholarship; school loyalty; community improvement; and worthwhile, desirable relationships with local, state, and national groups interested in the welfare of young people. The FBLA–PBL publishes *Tomorrow's Business Leader*, for student members in secondary and postsecondary schools.

Organization. The national organization of the FBLA–PBL includes local chapters of the FBLA in secondary schools; local chapters of Phi Beta Lambda in postsecondary schools, colleges, and universities; and state chapters, consisting of all local chapters within a particular state. There are local chapters of the FBLA–PBL in all the states and territories of the United States, as well as independents' schools in Germany, Japan, and the Canal Zone.

Organized state chapters function in 45 states. The services provided by the state organization include issuing a state news bulletin to local chapter officers and members; cooperating with the state department of education (or a college or university) in planning and conducting the annual state leadership conference; performing liaison functions on the state level with other youth and adult organizations; rendering advice and assistance to schools wishing to organize FBLA–PBL chapters; giving aid in the installation of new chapters; arranging an exchange of ideas for the successful operation of FBLA–PBL chapters through state-level conferences, workshops, and district meetings; offering competitive activities on the district and state levels; providing experience for members through officer and committee assignment responsibilities on district and state levels; selecting local and state chapter members to represent the state in national-level events and other leadership development activi-

ties; and assisting in the development of working materials for use in local chapter activities.

The national organization is governed by a ten-member board of directors. The board manages the business affairs of the FBLA–PBL and supervises the national organization's activities.

Membership. Membership in the FBLA–PBL is open to young men and women enrolled in business programs in secondary and postsecondary schools, colleges, and universities. Like most other youth organizations, it is financed by dues.

History. The first chapter of the FBLA for secondary students was organized in 1942 at Johnson City, Tenn. The first charter for a college chapter was granted the same year to Iowa State Teachers College (now the State College of Iowa). When the National Council for Business Education and the Department of Business Education of the National Education Association merged in 1946 to form the United Business Education Association (UBEA), sponsorship of the FBLA–PBL was assumed by the UBEA. In 1962 the UBEA changed its name to the National Business Education Association.

There are approximately 5,200 local chapters of the FBLA–PBL, with more than 100,000 members in the secondary division and over 15,000 in the postsecondary division. The FBLA–PBL became an independent nonprofit corporation in 1969.

The FBLA–PBL has its headquarters at 1201 16th Street NW, Washington, D.C. 20036.

O. J. BYRNSIDE, JR.

FUTURE FARMERS OF AMERICA

Future Farmers of America is an educational, nonprofit, nonpolitical youth organization. Its main objectives are to help develop qualities of leadership, character, scholarship, cooperation, and citizenship in its members. The FFA is an integral part of the high school vocational agriculture program and operates in cooperation with the Vocational and Technical Education Division of the U.S. Office of Education (USOE). State boards for vocational education and local high school departments of vocational agriculture also cooperate in the vocational agriculture and FFA programs.

Program. FFA activities supplement classroom study by encouraging the practical application of classroom instruction and by providing incentives for agricultural achievement. Advancement in the organization is based on individual achievement. Through the National FFA Foundation, incentive awards are provided for placement in agricultural production; crop production; dairy production; poultry production; livestock production; placement in sales and/or service; agricultural mechanics; agricultural electrification; placement in processing; ornamental horticulture; outdoor recreation; soil, water, and air management; fish and wildlife management; forest management; and home improvement. The awards are presented at local, state, and national levels for individual achievement. National awards are also provided for individual achievement in public speaking as well as for chapter achievement in safety and program development.

Nationally, the FFA operates the Future Farmers Supply Service, which provides FFA members with FFA jackets, jewelry, and other FFA materials. In addition, the FFA publishes its own bimonthly magazine, *National Future Farmer.*

A professional staff of four, headquartered at the National FFA Center in Alexandria, Va., plans and administers FFA programs from the national level.

A sound schedule of activities is a key to involving students in the FFA program. Local chapters sponsor educational tours, conduct safety and home improvement campaigns, organize recreational activities, and hold their own recognition banquets. Through a new community action program developed by the FFA in cooperation with the Farmers Home Administration, sponsored by Lilly Endowment, Inc., of Indianapolis, Ind., FFA members are becoming actively involved in helping make rural communities better places in which to live and work. Projects in the Building Our American Communities Program include community job and housing surveys, environmental clean-up campaigns, and landscaping and beautification projects in local parks, schools, and community facilities.

The annual FFA convention is the culmination of activities begun in local chapters. Regional and national awards are presented to students who have made outstanding achievements. Under the leadership of six national officers, more than 100 official student delegates representing 49 states discuss, conduct, and vote on business affecting the national organization.

Organization. Six student officers, including a president, secretary, and four regional vice-

presidents, are elected each year by the national convention delegates. The student officers meet three times a year with an adult board of directors, which includes five members of the Vocational and Technical Education Division of the USOE and four state supervisors of agricultural education. Although the adult board has the final authority, action on policy usually reflects the recommendations of student members. State associations and local chapters also elect officers annually in a method similar to the national organization.

Membership. All students enrolled in vocational agriculture are eligible to be FFA members. FFA members may remain in the organization for three years after graduation from high school or until age 21.

The National FFA Foundation, Inc., is sponsored by contributions from businesses, industries, organizations, and individuals who are interested in vocational agriculture and the FFA. The foundation is administered by a board of trustees representing the sponsoring organizations as well as state FFA associations, vocational agriculture teachers, and the Vocational and Technical Education Division of the USOE.

History. The FFA was organized in 1928 and was chartered by the U.S. Congress in 1950. It has approximately 430,000 active members in 8,200 local high school chapters located in 49 states, the Virgin Islands, and Puerto Rico. The organization carries out an active international program, cooperating with several nations in an agricultural work exchange program. The organization has also been instrumental in aiding the establishment of Future Farmer organizations in Japan, the Philippines, Vietnam, Korea, and other countries.

The Future Farmers of America, the Future Farmers Supply Service, and *National Future Farmer* magazine maintain their headquarters at the National FFA Center, Box 15160, Alexandria, Va. 22309.

A. DANIEL REUWEE

FUTURE HOMEMAKERS OF AMERICA

Future Homemakers of America is a nonprofit organization for home economics students in public and nonpublic junior and senior high schools. The FHA helps to channel the knowledge gained in classroom study into practical use through projects and group activities.

Program. The FHA's four-year national program of work provides guidelines to help individual chapters enrich the home economics programs in their schools. The objectives of the program are to help members recognize and develop their abilities and to stimulate members to participate actively in projects for family, community, and world improvement. The national FHA magazine, *Teen Times*, both stimulates interest in and gives direction to the FHA program.

FHA members work as volunteers, participating in local Head Start programs or working with the mentally retarded or the physically handicapped. Some chapters hold sessions to train students for baby-sitting. A Vermont chapter offered free baby-sitting service to enable parents to attend town meetings. Some chapters have adopted a foreign child, a student, or even an entire family. Some have corresponded with and sent packages to soldiers in Vietnam and to Peace Corps volunteers and have exchanged letters with overseas students. Others hold morals and manners clinics, study local government and history, visit and assist the elderly, conduct campaigns to keep potential dropouts in school, and work closely with members of their own families to bridge the generation gap.

An annual meeting is held in one of four geographic regions, with delegate attendance on a membership quota basis. State and district meetings are held yearly at the discretion of individual state associations. One week annually is designated as FHA Week and is observed with special activities by chapters throughout the United States.

Organization. Local chapters of the FHA may be certified in junior and senior high schools offering homemaking instruction. Home economics teachers serve as chapter advisers. The state supervisor of home economics education or a member of her staff serves as state adviser. The FHA membership annually elects a 12-member national executive council, which is responsible for directing the national program of work and planning and presiding over the annual meeting. The national advisory board, consisting of 18 professional members, advises the executive council and helps develop policy.

The U.S. Office of Education and the American Home Economics Association cosponsor the FHA.

Membership. Membership is open to any secondary school student of home economics. National membership is approximately 600,000 in 12,000 chapters in the United States, Puerto Rico, and American schools overseas. The FHA is supported entirely by membership dues.

History. The FHA was founded in Chicago in 1945. In 1965 the FHA merged with the New Homemakers of America, a similar organization of Negro home economics students in states which maintained separate school systems.

The FHA maintains headquarters at 2010 Massachusetts Avenue, NW, Washington, D.C. 20036.

PAT MOWER

FUTURE SCIENTISTS OF AMERICA

Future Scientists of America is a national organization of secondary school science clubs. The FSA aims to identify and to encourage young people with the potential to become scientists, engineers, and science teachers.

Program. FSA clubs are organized to give students an opportunity to meet and benefit from sharing scientific interests and abilities. Each club is a scientific community in miniature and is free to develop a program most suited to its own needs. The National Science Teachers Association (NSTA) offers guidance in planning club programs.

Clubs receive a charter plaque and a copy of *Sponsor's Guidebook*, which contains suggestions for organizing a club, planning meetings and activities, and preparing and presenting science papers. Members receive copies of *Centrifuge*, the FSA quarterly newsletter. Special mailings—such as *Award-Winning FSA Science Projects*, a collection of reports of student award-winning projects that have appeared in *The Science Teacher*, and *Graphic Communication in Science*—are sent to all active clubs from time to time.

Organization. FSA clubs are sponsored by the NSTA. All school science clubs are invited to affiliate with the FSA. The club affiliation fee is $8; annual dues are $5 thereafter.

Membership. The only requirement for student membership in the FSA is an interest in science.

The FSA has headquarters at 1201 16th Street NW, Washington, D.C. 20036.

DOROTHY K. CULBERT

GIRL SCOUTS OF THE U.S.A.

Girl Scouts of the U.S.A. is a voluntary nonsectarian organization for girls. It aims to meet the needs and interests of girls through an informal educational program of activities related to the arts, the home, and the outdoors.

Program. Girl Scout troops are organized according to four age levels. Brownies are seven and eight years old or in the second and third grades; Juniors are nine to 11 years old or in the fourth, fifth, and sixth grades; Cadettes are usually 12 to 14 years old or in the seventh, eighth, and ninth grades; and Seniors are usually 14 to 17 years old or in the ninth, tenth, 11th, and 12th grades. The educational program increases in complexity and broadens in scope at each age level; however, a girl may join a scout troop at any age.

Activities for Brownies are based on the three Brownie B's: Be a Discoverer; Be a Ready Helper; Be a Friendmaker. Brownies learn to get along in their group, to take care of themselves, and to help their families and communities.

Juniors have an opportunity to explore new fields of interest and develop new skills by working for proficiency badges. They may choose from almost 50 badges with such titles as active citizens, books, cook, cyclist, dabbler, folklore, health and safety, pets, water fun, and writer.

Cadette program activities include four challenges: social dependability, active citizenship, emergency preparedness, and the Girl Scout promises and laws. Each challenge requires advance preparation as well as action in a real-life or simulated situation. The 60 proficiency badges for Cadettes involve thought-provoking questions, which help a girl relate her interests and abilities to the pattern of her life.

Senior Girl Scouts are encouraged to concentrate their activities in one of eight major interest areas: arts, community action, homemaking, international friendship, mariner, mounted, trailblazer, and wing. If girls in a troop are attracted by several of these interests, they may form a Panorama troop. A Senior Scout may engage in one or more service aide projects, which are arranged in cooperation with libraries, hospitals, museums, and other institutions, organizations, or professions. Service aides function in 15 different areas, including animal care; aquatic safety; child care; aid to handicapped persons; and laboratory, office, program, and teacher aides.

Qualified Seniors Scouts are selected to attend nationwide conferences devoted to such subjects as service in the inner city, space, the arts, the home, inter-American culture, American Indian culture, and service to handicapped persons. Seniors may also participate in gatherings at four Girl Guide/Girl Scout world centers—in Switzerland, Mexico, India, and the United Kingdom; visits to Girl Guide camps abroad; and explorations of other countries. They may live abroad in private homes or hostels under arrangements between Girl Scouts of the U.S.A. and other member countries of the World Association of Girl Guides and Girl Scouts.

Membership. Membership in the Girl Scouts is open to all girls from seven through 17, regardless of race, creed, or national origin. Adult members serve as troop and camp leaders, program consultants, and members of local or national committees and boards of directors. Total membership is more than 3 million girls and 670,000 adults. The national organization receives the major portion of its income from membership dues and from the sale of official uniforms, equipment, accessories, and publications. Other sources of income include gifts, grants, bequests, and investments. Girls Scout councils depend for their income almost entirely on voluntary public contributions, primarily through federated giving.

History. Girl Scouts of the U.S.A. was founded in 1912, incorporated in 1915, and received a congressional charter in 1950. Girl Scouting developed from the British Girl Guides program and is continually adapted to meet the needs of girls in the United States.

Girls Scouts of the U.S.A. maintains its national headquarters at 830 Third Avenue, New York, N.Y. 10022.

NATALIE FLATOW

GIRLS CLUBS OF AMERICA

Girls Clubs of America, Inc., is a national youth organization established to foster the character development of all girls through a program of educational, vocational, health, social, and recreational activities. The basic aim of the Girls Club movement is to produce well-balanced, well-integrated girls who will become skilled and happy homemakers, good mothers, and responsible citizens of their country.

Program. The Girls Club program provides daily, clubhouse-centered after-school activities under professional and volunteer adult leadership. Local clubs vary greatly in size and staff, depending on the needs of the community and available financial support.

Supplementing the influence of school and

home, Girls Club activities are designed as an educational enrichment program and thus include cultural and historical trips and various forms of art participation and appreciation, depending on the resources available in each community. Activities, which are geared to the abilities of girls of different ages, also include cooking, sewing and homemaking arts, dramatics and music, arts and crafts, study hall and library, dancing and drill teams, leadership training, personal grooming, and sports and swimming.

A physical fitness program, sponsored jointly by the Reader's Digest Association and the GCA, was started in an effort to motivate girls to be physically fit in their youth and in their adult years. The Fit for Life program combines basic nutrition, self-motivated discipline, and exercise. Three institutes are conducted annually at college campuses in various parts of the United States. Several hundred handpicked Girls Club representatives attend these institutes and return to local clubs with sufficient experience and educational material to conduct courses at their own clubs.

During the summer months Girls Clubs programs operate daily on a morning and afternoon basis. In inner-city areas, when funds are available for additional staffing and enrichment programs, early evening sessions for teen-age girls or co-ed groups are also offered. The basic summer program for girls is similar to a day-camp program, since most clubhouses are located on grounds with sufficient space to hold outdoor sessions on camp crafts, outdoor cooking, and conservation. Some Girls Clubs maintain overnight campsites which are staffed throughout the summer months.

The GCA also maintains a national camp, called Iron Rail Camp, at Beverly, Mass. Girls Club members from all parts of the United States may attend this camp for two-week sessions throughout the summer. Most local clubs sponsor a campership fund-raising program to help girls attend either their own overnight camps or Iron Rail Camp.

The GCA annually sponsors a national awards program for members of its affiliated clubs as a means of encouraging interest and developing skills in cooking and sewing, in good citizenship, in scholarship, and in poster art. Local contests and regional competitions for local club winners take place in the GCA's nine regions. The awards program is supported and sponsored by individuals, foundations, and corporations. In addition to cash prizes, scholarships, and for the citizenship award winner a trip to Washington, D.C., the top winners receive expense-paid trips to the annual conference of the GCA.

In addition to sponsoring a program specifically for girls, local club operations frequently sponsor programs which benefit the community. Such community programs include adult education classes for mothers in homemaking, child care, and swimming and physical fitness; baby health clinics (usually sponsored in cooperation with city health departments or medical groups); nurseries for preschool children; swimming classes for non-Girls Club members in areas where swimming facilities are scarce; golden age clubs; and use of club facilities by community groups for meetings and activities.

Organization. Clubs accepted for membership must have a volunteer board of directors who accept financial responsibility for the club and a clubhouse suitable for a daily program of activities. The club must also serve a full range of girls from first grade through senior high school and employ at least one full-time qualified director.

The national organization for the GCA is managed by a national board of directors and officers elected by the national board. Through regional subcommittees and standing committees appointed by the national board and national staff members, the national organization provides help and advice to local groups trying to establish Girls Clubs programs and to clubs already established.

In addition to providing field service for local clubs, the national organization as a standards-setting agency issues program packets, basic reference handbooks on such subjects as administration and standard accounting, the quarterly *Newsletter*, and other publications as needed.

The national organization is also responsible for initial orientation and on-the-job training of Girls Club professional staff throughout the United States. An orientation course is conducted annually for new professionals. The GCA has also sponsored an annual college- or university-based seminar for Girls Club professionals. In 1970 this adult education program was expanded to include key volunteers on local, regional, and national levels.

An annual national conference for staff, board members, and program volunteers is held every spring. At these annual conferences local club leaders exchange program information and ideas and learn about new trends and research in the social sciences and education pertinent to youth programs.

Membership. Clubs serve girls of all races and religions and from all social and economic backgrounds. Approximately 68 percent of Girls Club members live in low-income neighborhoods. The GCA depends for major support of national operations upon gifts from foundations, business and industry, professional organizations, and philanthropic families and individuals. Local clubs receive support from the United Fund and other local civic organizations.

History. Although Girls Clubs of America was formally set up as a national organization in 1945, the movement actually started more than a century ago, when the first Girls Club was founded in Waterbury, Conn. Additional Girls Clubs were started in industrial towns of New England to serve as educational centers and homes away from home for farm girls who were employed in mills and factories.

In 1945 the GCA was formally established with 19 charter clubs. There are over 170 club operations in more than 25 states and in Canada, and additional clubs and extension clubs are being planned in approximately 50 cities throughout the United States. At the present time approximately 100,000 girls participate in Girls Clubs programs.

Girls Club of America has its headquarters at 133 East 62nd Street, New York, N.Y. 10021.

KATHERINE A. MAHON

INTERNATIONAL THESPIAN SOCIETY

The International Thespian Society is a nonprofit educational organization devoted to the advancement and improvement of theater arts in secondary schools. The society works with teachers and administrators to educate students in the performing arts and related subjects, to advance standards in all phases of theater arts, and to create an active and intelligent interest in theater.

Program. The society, which is nonsecret and nonsocial, is both a recognition and service organization. Students are granted membership for meritorious work in theater arts. Services include scholarships for students planning to teach theater;

royalty adjustments to schools presenting full-length dramatic productions on a minimum budget; library loans (over 10,000 play scripts and 1,000 theater books are available); free certificates of recognition for meritorious work achieved by individuals or groups; letters of recommendation for graduating seniors; and the opportunity to attend area, state, regional, and international theater arts conferences.

Theater arts conferences, held annually in most states and regions, are hosted by Thespian Troupes and/or universities and are open to all secondary schools. The programs may include workshops, play productions, guest speakers, talent shows, and banquets. Demonstration workshops conducted by Thespian Troupes, university professors, community theaters, and commercial theater personnel deal with lighting, staging, makeup, scenic design, directing, and acting. Cuttings and full-length presentations produced by secondary schools and universities include readers' theater, avant-garde productions, children's theater, the classics, original productions, musicals, comedies, and dramas.

Dramatics magazine, published monthly from October through May, is the official publication of the International Thespian Society. It is sent to directors, teachers, and students of theater arts. The editorial section includes feature articles relating to all aspects of theater; two series of articles in each issue relating to a specific area of study; supplementary illustrations, charts, and photographs; and a pictorial presentation of high school productions.

Organization. The affairs of the International Thespian Society are conducted by a nine-member board of trustees, who are elected from and by the regional directors. No member of the board of trustees is eligible for reelection after having served for six years. The officers of the International Thespian Society are the international director, assistant international director, executive secretary, executive treasurer, and editor of *Dramatics*. Officers are elected by the trustees.

Membership. The International Thespian Society has five membership classifications: student, sponsor, secondary school, honorary, and associate. Each unit of the society located in a secondary school is designated as a troupe under the direction of a troupe sponsor. The sponsor must be a regularly employed teacher or professional employee in the school in which the troupe is located. He must be officially appointed by the school administration and be responsible for the theater arts program.

The society has over 3,200 affiliated schools, with troupes located in all 50 states, Canada, the Canal Zone, Germany, Greece, Iran, Italy, and Okinawa. To retain an active status, each troupe is annually required to submit the names, addresses, year of graduation, and lifetime membership fees of at least six new initiates and to pay an assessment fee.

Students who are attending member secondary schools and who have met the qualifications established by the board of trustees may be initiated into the society upon payment of a $2 lifetime fee. The international office provides each troupe with a copy of the initiation ceremony and encourages its presentations at the local level. Each initiate's name is permanently recorded at the international office on the troupe's membership record. Honorary membership may be conferred upon an adult by a local troupe in recognition of extraordinary services rendered. Associate membership is open to individuals, schools other than secondary schools, and organizations whose primary purpose is the advancement and development of theater arts.

History. The International Thespian Society was organized in 1929 as the National Thespian Dramatic Honor Society for High Schools. The first official publication of the society was *High School Thespian*, which was published annually from 1929 through 1934. Starting in 1935, the magazine was published bimonthly during the school year. The title of the publication was changed to *Dramatics* in 1944.

The name of the society was officially changed to the National Thespian Society in 1950. In 1968 the society was incorporated under the name of the National Thespian Society. In January 1969 the society changed its name to the International Thespian Society.

The society's address is Box E, College Hill Station, Cincinnati, Ohio 45224.

RONALD L. LONGSTRETH

NATIONAL FORENSIC LEAGUE

The National Forensic League is a voluntary honor society for high school students and teachers. Its primary purpose is to interest students in public speaking and to hold their interest until they acquire a high degree of effectiveness as speakers.

Program. The NFL, which provides motivation to enter contests, sponsors one tournament and one congress annually in each of its 41 districts. It also sponsors a national speech tournament, in which the winners of district tournaments and state league tournaments compete for national honors.

The NFL believes in contests as one of the oldest and most effective education devices. It believes that overemphasis on winning can best be met by placing more stress on creditable participation. Superior work is emphasized, but those who do their best are also rewarded and encouraged to improve.

In the district and national tournaments the sweepstakes trophy is given not to the school winning the most places but to the school whose students participated in the greatest number of rounds. For the grand championship trophy the totals are carried forward from year to year, so that even a small school can gain this honor by consistent achievement.

To require students to diversify their speech performance, the NFL has established limits for the number of points which can be recorded in each of the several speaking divisions: 250 in debate; 200 in contests; and 100 for service projects. Achievement in NFL district and national tournaments is recorded beyond these limits in recognition of the superior competition encountered. The league offers its members advanced degrees for attaining totals of 75, 150, 250, and 500 points. Each degree adds a distinctive seal to the membership certificate and a special jewel to the key or pin. Students attaining the highest degree, the degree of distinction, are acknowledged in *Rostrum*, the NFL's monthly publication. Instructors also qualify for these advanced degrees and are awarded a diamond-set key upon coaching students to earn 15,000 points. About 40 instructors are honored annually.

Organization. The NFL is a nonprofit association of 1,100 secondary schools. More than 1,000 other schools hold affiliate membership while building their programs to meet NFL charter requirements. No qualified school is denied membership, but some must wait for a vacancy to develop. The league is governed by an executive council consisting of seven members, four of whom are elected by the general membership.

The executive secretary, a high school principal, and a superintendent of schools are elected by the council. Within each state or district a three-member committee is elected by the chapters to conduct the district tournament and student congress.

Membership. Membership in the NFL is available to both students and instructors who gain 25 NFL points according to an established schedule. Points are earned for participation in interscholastic speech contests, legislative assemblies, and community speaking projects. The instructors are credited with one-tenth the points earned by their students. The NFL is supported by the fees of its member schools and member students.

History. The NFL was established in 1925; in 1931 it began sponsoring a national speech tournament. During World War II it operated on a reduced basis but retained continuity of its program. Since the end of World War II, its biggest problem has been how to accept the increasing number of schools seeking membership and still retain the advantages inherent in a smaller organization. Although the NFL does not solicit new member schools, it endeavors to serve those who apply for membership.

The NFL maintains its headquarters at Smith Hall, Ripon, Wis. 54971.

Bruno E. Jacob

QUILL AND SCROLL

Quill and Scroll is an international honorary society for high school journalists. The society seeks to raise publications standards, promote research, and improve instruction in high school journalism.

Program. Through the Quill and Scroll Foundation, Edward J. Nell Memorial Scholarships of $500 each are granted annually to ten students selected from the more than 200 national winners of writing contests and a current-events quiz. Grants-in-aid to graduate students doing research in high school journalism are available through the foundation. The foundation publishes various handbooks for use by journalism advisers to keep them informed of research results. Other publications are issued as the need arises.

Quill and Scroll conducts an annual newspaper critical service, a national newspaper week contest, national writing contests, and a current-events quiz. It encourages participation in competition as a means of maintaining interest in the overall program of the society. *Quill and Scroll* magazine, for students and advisers, presents authoritative articles dealing with concrete problems of every phase of newspaper, magazine, and yearbook work.

The national organization has no requirements about the activities of local chapters. Each chapter may engage in such work and projects as will best serve the cause of journalism and school publications in its high school. A strong, active chapter can inspire publications staff members to greater efforts; attract students of high ability to publications work; undertake tasks necessary to the development of the journalism department; and secure greater recognition of journalism work by students, school officials, and the community.

Organization. The board of trustees of Quill and Scroll Corporation administers the affairs of the society. The Quill and Scroll Foundation, established in 1947, conducts research in high school journalism, cooperates with other organizations in pursuing special studies, and grants scholarships. Announcements of the work of the foundation and scholarship details are furnished to chapters at regular intervals.

Membership. Membership in the society may be secured only through a local chapter. When a charter is granted to a high school, publications advisers in the school automatically become Quill and Scroll members. Student members must be at least juniors; must rank scholastically in the upper third of their class, either for the year of their election or for the cumulative total of all their high school work; must have done superior work in some phase of journalism or school publication; must be recommended by their advisers or by a committee governing publications; and must be approved by the secretary-treasurer of the society.

There are no yearly membership dues. Each student pays an initiation fee, which entitles him to a regulation gold badge, an official membership card, and a one-year subscription to *Quill and Scroll* magazine.

History. Quill and Scroll was organized in 1926 in Iowa City, Iowa, by a group of 23 journalism advisers for the purpose of encouraging and rewarding individual achievement in journalism and related fields. The idea was first proposed by George H. Gallup, then an instructor at the University of Iowa. (Gallup has since become internationally prominent in public opinion research as a result of his founding the American Institute of Public Opinion and the famous Gallup Poll.)

Since its organization, Quill and Scroll has granted charters to approximately 10,000 high schools in the 50 states and in more than 20 foreign countries of the free world. More than 900,000 students have been accepted for individual membership.

Quill and Scroll maintains its headquarters at the School of Journalism, University of Iowa, Iowa City, Iowa 52240.

LESTER G. BENZ

RED CROSS YOUTH

Red Cross Youth is a national voluntary service organization for American youth. Through the American Red Cross, young people contribute their energies, talents, and enthusiasm in classrooms and in communities to help others.

Program. In elementary schools Red Cross programs are administered by a teacher who coordinates activities with other classroom teachers and receives technical guidance and program support from the local Red Cross chapter. The children produce arts and crafts to be distributed to patients in hospitals and nursing homes. Through the Friendship Box Program, students gather various small educational, recreational, and health items; prepare a collective letter to an unknown recipient; and place the items in small cartons provided by the Red Cross to be sent to Red Cross societies in other countries for distribution to children. Friendship boxes may also be filled for children in the United States. Courses in swimming are available for all ages; courses in lifesaving and first aid are provided for students 11 years of age and over. Home nursing, mother and baby care, and mother's aide courses are taught to those in upper elementary and secondary school grades. Additional safety and health education resources include illustrated guides for the use of teachers in elementary schools.

In high schools the emphasis shifts from formal classes to useful volunteer community service. Students help patients in hospitals and in nursing homes and work with the mentally and physically handicapped. Technical on-the-job training of volunteers is provided by the institutions at which they work.

Volunteers tutor young people requiring help to stay in school, and they aid in the educational and social development of the less advantaged.

Special efforts are made to involve young people from low-income urban and rural areas in both the planning and operation of Red Cross programs. Secondary school students acquire responsibility for group planning of service activities through participation in Red Cross Youth Councils and clubs. Red Cross chapters provide experiences—ranging from several days of formal group sessions to individualized task-oriented projects—which develop leadership potential.

Red Cross Youth publishes *American Red Cross Youth News*, which is distributed to elementary schools, and *American Red Cross Youth Journal*, which is distributed to junior and senior high schools. Each magazine contains articles, stories, and suggestions for volunteer service activities that can be adopted locally. A monthly braille edition featuring selections from the *News* and the *Journal* and an annual talking book edition of the *News* are also produced for distribution to schools and other institutions for the blind and visually handicapped.

Organization. A national Red Cross Youth staff in Washington, D.C., directs the implementation of approved policies, devises long-range plans, guides national programming, and coordinates the national activities of four area offices in the United States and two area offices abroad. Each area office is responsible for serving local chapters in its geographical jurisdiction and for assisting them in carrying out programs. The Red Cross has maintained close working relationships with various national, state, and local professional groups, including some governmental departments.

Membership. Since 1964, Red Cross programs and services have been available to all schools and colleges without the payment of fees or other financial requirements. Each student in an enrolled school or college who participates in Red Cross programs is considered a youth member of the American National Red Cross.

Students in local chapters may contribute to the support of the programs through contributions to Red Cross Youth Funds, if school and chapter policies permit. Contributions are used to finance programs for young people in the United States and throughout the world.

History. Red Cross Youth was founded in 1917. During World War I, Junior Red Cross members worked in food conservation drives, knitted scarves and sweaters for servicemen, helped feed Europe's hungry, and brightened the lives of children affected by war. The Children's Fund was created after the war, and American youngsters extended their assistance to children in war-ravaged countries. In 1919 they began filling Christmas boxes to be sent overseas. During the 1930's young Red Cross members collected food and clothing. During World War II millions of items were produced to aid servicemen on the battlefields and in hospitals. After the war, American youth helped children overseas. A formal international exchange program was established, and the number of youth-centered health and cheer programs for the homebound and hospitalized was increased.

In the mid-1960's the name Red Cross Youth was adopted as the overall title of American Red Cross programs for children and young adults.

Red Cross Youth has its office at the American National Red Cross, 18th and D Streets NW, Washington, D.C. 20006.

JOHN M. MANTHEI

VOCATIONAL INDUSTRIAL CLUBS OF AMERICA

Vocational Industrial Clubs of America is a national organization for trade, industrial, technical, and health education students in secondary and postsecondary school programs. Through club activities VICA aims to develop character, citizenship, and leadership.

Program. The VICA school program is cocurricular, complementing vocational instruction. Local club activities include safety campaigns, tours of industrial plants, career days, community service projects, study of parliamentary procedure, dances, and fund-raising campaigns. At the national level the VICA youth development program provides leadership development conferences, an individual achievement program, leadership development publications, and leadership awards and competitive activities. VICA sponsors competitive activities in such specific skill subjects as machine trades, bricklaying, welding, and cosmetology and in such general areas as safety, public speaking, parliamentary procedure, and job interview situations.

The VICA program functions through vocational trade, industrial, technical, and health education programs in the secondary schools, area vocational schools, and junior and community colleges. It is planned in conjunction with professional education organizations and is supported by the AFL–CIO, the U.S. Chamber of Commerce, and the National Association of Manufacturers. The annual national VICA leadership conference is on the approved list of national contests and activities of the National Association of Secondary School Principals.

Organization. Local VICA clubs affiliate through state or territorial associations, which, in turn, are granted charters by the Vocational Industrial Clubs of America, Inc., a nonprofit educational organization. VICA, Inc., is governed by an administrative board composed of representatives of state and territorial associations, the U.S. Office of Education, and the American Vocational Association. Ten national VICA officers are elected annually by student members of the high school division and ten by students of the postsecondary division. A national advisory council provides assistance and counsel to the administrative board. An executive director, appointed by the administrative board, is the administrative officer of the organization.

Membership. Any young man or woman enrolled as a full-time preparatory student in a vocational course in trade, industrial, technical, or health education in a secondary school, area vocational-technical school, or junior or community college is eligible for membership. Professional or associate membership is available to educators and other adults interested in VICA. The national VICA program is supported primarily by annual membership dues and by the Youth Development Foundation of VICA, Inc. The foundation solicits financial support from industry and labor for the development and administration of its programs.

History. The Future Craftsmen of America, established in the 1930's, was the forerunner of VICA. VICA was established at a meeting of trade and industrial youth and educators in 1965 in Nashville, Tenn. Initial financial support for VICA came from vocational industrial youth groups in 14 states, from the Future Farmers of America, and from the American Vocational Association. The first annual meeting in 1965 in Nashville was attended by more than 200 student advisers and representatives of labor and industry.

VICA has its national headquarters at 105 N. Virginia Avenue, Falls Church, Va. 22046.

LARRY JOHNSON

YOUNG MEN'S CHRISTIAN ASSOCIATION

The Young Men's Christian Association is an international membership organization concerned with the physical, educational, social, and religious needs of young men and boys. The Y stresses the Christian code of conduct, ecumenism, and community responsibility.

Program. The major programs of the YMCA are conducted through classes and club activities. A variety of adult education classes—including technical and vocational courses—are offered. Club activities include Hi-Y and Tri-Hi-Y groups for teen-agers, Gra-Y for grade-schoolers, and Indian Guides for fathers and sons. These groups emphasize the development of individual initiative and leadership qualities. In Y urban action projects throughout the United States, members have undertaken projects for the needy. As one of the six founding organizations of the United Service Organizations, the YMCA provides welfare, recreational, and religious programs for American servicemen.

YMCA buildings have gymnasiums and swimming pools, residence facilities for young men, and rooms for classes and club activities. They also have summer-camp and day-camp programs and facilities.

Organization. Each local YMCA is an autonomous corporation with its own board of directors and staff and is responsible to its community. Each YMCA is also a part of the national organization as a member-affiliate of the National Council of YMCA's, the legislative and policy-making national body. The National Council in turn is a member of the World Alliance, the YMCA international body. For administrative purposes, the American YMCA is structured into eight regions and two state organizations.

Membership. Membership in the YMCA is open to all boys and men, regardless of religious affiliation. In 1969 the YMCA in the United States had more than 5.5 million members in approximately 1,700 organized associations. Financial support for local associations is derived from membership dues, community chests, endowment funds, and sustaining memberships.

History. The YMCA was founded in 1844 in London by George Williams, a clerk in a dry-goods firm. The first meeting room was in a coffeehouse. The American YMCA was founded in 1851 in Boston by Thomas V. Sullivan, a retired sea captain. In 1852, YMCA's were formed in New York and Buffalo, N.Y.; Worcester and Springfield, Mass.; Portsmouth and Concord, N.H.; New London and Hartford, Conn.; Detroit;

Baltimore; Washington, D.C.; and New Orleans. By 1860 there were in the United States more than 200 YMCA's with 25,000 members.

The early concerns of YMCA leaders were with young men arriving in the cities. Revival meetings were the outstanding programs offered, and the associations sent out the first street workers to preach on street corners and around the wharves. They also sent out "gospel wagons" to dispense tracts and sermons in city neighborhoods.

Delegates from 15 associations met in New York City in 1861 and formed the United States Christian Commission, the first volunteer agency for spiritual and physical aid to American armed forces. During World War I the American YMCA provided religious services, recreational materials, entertainment programs, and canteens in home ports, on the front lines, and in cities overseas. Through the World Committee, the YMCA worked with prisoners of war on both sides of the conflict.

During World War II the YMCA, as part of its United Service Organization affiliation, worked with the armed services throughout the world. It also renewed its work with prisoners of war. In the postwar years the international associations undertook service to displaced persons by providing athletics programs, summer schools, entertainment, and children's camps. The YMCA also helped with the repatriation and resettlement of refugees from Europe.

The YMCA has its national headquarters at 291 Broadway, New York, N.Y. 10007.

JOE A. PISARRO

YOUNG MEN'S HEBREW ASSOCIATION AND YOUNG WOMEN'S HEBREW ASSOCIATION

The Young Men's Hebrew Association and Young Women's Hebrew Association are the original names of what are now called Jewish Community Centers. These centers are established by residents of a Jewish community to provide leisure-time activities. The aim is to strengthen Jewish family life, foster and enrich Jewish living in a democratic society, and provide shared experiences for all age groups.

Program. Center programs are multifaceted, flexible, and professionally directed. They provide courses in music, graphic arts, dance, drama, literature, and Jewish studies. Club activities stimulate personality development, leadership training, and participation in community affairs. Extensive programs for health and physical education, day and country camping, and outdoor recreational activities afford the opportunity for making decisions, acquiring new physical skills, and developing friendships.

The centers offer open forums, lectures, concerts, art and literary exhibits, dramatic productions, poetry recitals, and cultural festivals. Many centers maintain extensive libraries of Judaica. The 92nd Street YM–YWHA in New York City has residence facilities for approximately 400 young men and women. In 1969 the 92nd Street Y received an award from the New York State Council on the Arts for its long record of contribution to the arts.

Organization. The National Jewish Welfare Board (JWB) is the national association of Jewish Community Centers and YM–YWHA's. The center movement, served by the JWB, includes 447 centers, Y's, resident camps, and major branches in over 200 cities. The affiliated centers have a combined membership of 750,000 and aggregate local expenditures of over $40 million annually. They own facilities valued at $150 million and are staffed by more than 1,600 professional social workers and specialists in the arts, early childhood education, adult Jewish education, and health and physical education. The JWB functions through regional consultants, eight regional groups of centers and Y's, and a national staff and specialists at JWB headquarters.

The JWB provides a variety of program materials dealing with all aspects of center work, and it organizes and conducts regional and national conferences, institutes, seminars, and intercenter activities. It also recruits, orients, and places trained professional center workers and stimulates and administers local, regional, and national scholarships for graduate training of center workers. The JWB sponsors the Jewish Book Council of America and the National Jewish Music Council. The book council's *Jewish Book Annual* is a major source of information on Jewish literature. The music council encourages the commission of new Jewish music works and the presentation of Jewish vocal, instrumental, and orchestral compositions.

As the American member of the World Federation of YMHA's and Jewish Community Centers, the JWB performed a major role in the federation's sponsorship and establishment of the Jerusalem YMHA. It also encourages center work in 36 European, Latin American, Asian, and African countries. The JWB is governed by a national convention, which meets biennially. Between conventions, the board of directors carries on the organization's work.

The JWB represents the Jewish community in the United Service Organizations (USO), which serve the recreational and welfare needs of all military personnel. The JWB's regional consultants and national USO staff provide services to stateside USO clubs and councils and to small isolated Jewish communities serving Jews in nearby military installations.

Membership. Membership is open to all Jews three years of age or older. Most centers and Y's make membership available to all members of the community, regardless of race or religious affiliation. Members are grouped according to age, from youngsters in day nurseries to people over 60 in golden age clubs. Financial support is derived from membership dues, course and program fees, and funds from united fund-raising agencies.

History. The first YMHA was founded in 1854 in Baltimore, Md. By 1884 approximately 70 such agencies had been organized. In 1913 the National Council of Young Men's Hebrew and Kindred Societies was formed to unite the Y's in a national association. The National Jewish Welfare Board was founded in 1917 to meet the religious needs and improve the morale of Jews in the armed forces. In 1921 the two organizations merged, and the JWB became the national association for Jewish Community Centers and YM–YWHA's.

The JWB has its headquarters at 15 East 26th Street, New York, N.Y. 10010.

BERNARD POSTAL

YOUNG WOMEN'S CHRISTIAN ASSOCIATION

The Young Women's Christian Association is a a membership organization with a local, national, and international program of services for individual development and a goal of helping all women and girls make their full contribution to a society where justice and peace for all people shall prevail. The YWCA stresses improving the quality of education, with special emphasis on preparing girls to perform their multiple roles in society; providing opportunities for girls and women to continue their education; supplementing the academic work of high school and college students with involvement in community affairs; exploring the problems and needs of women students in urban settings; and motivating dropouts to return to school or prepare for gainful employment.

Program. The YWCA offers educational programs designed to meet specific needs. Literacy and tutoring classes have been initiated in local associations. YWCA projects, developed through government and foundation funds and grants, enable disadvantaged young women who are out of school and out of work to improve their employability potential or return to school.

The Jobs Corps-YWCA Extension Residence Program, operated by the YWCA's national board and financed by the Manpower Program of the Department of Labor, offers in some 20 community YWCA's living experience for girls completing the formal part of their Job Corps training and preparing to enter the work world. The program provides personal and social development as well as on-the-job training and job counseling.

Over 400,000 Y-Teens, girls of 12 to 17, are active in clubs and YWCA programs. Y-Teens are encouraged to develop their leadership potential, a quality that becomes an integral part of the total YWCA program and helps young people to have a sense of personal responsibility for their role in today's world.

The National Student YWCA attempts to meet the needs of university women and to deal with the escalating crisis in higher education. Utilizing students, staff, and nonstudent volunteers, local associations on over 300 campuses and in five regions have been struggling with issues related to the YWCA's Program for Action, with particular emphasis on raising consciousness about the nature of racism and developing strategies whereby students may most effectively become involved in social change in both the university and the community.

Thirteen networks on current issues keep students in touch with each other across the United States, and regional cluster conferences dealing with such issues as increasing women's self-perception, the nature of community service, and sexism-racism, offer more in-depth discussions and exchange of ideas.

The National Student YWCA also offers students opportunities for involvement in summer projects while earning summer wages and is developing plans for two national resource centers on political power and the concerns of black university women.

A typical YWCA usually has a large health,

physical education, and recreation program; classes in such subjects as cooking, sewing, shorthand, typing, sculpture, drama, and creative writing; and nurseries for the children of working mothers. A local YWCA may support a residence and serve as an informal employment agency.

Organization. The World YWCA, with headquarters in Geneva, provides a channel for the sharing of resources and the exchange of experience among its affiliated associations in 80 countries, including the United States. It helps them with the development of their leadership and program. It surveys new fields and promotes work to meet the needs therein. It acts in cooperation with world voluntary movements and with intergovernmental organizations in matters of common concern. It works for international understanding, for improved social and economic conditions, and for basic human rights for all people. In time of emergency it undertakes and sponsors international humanitarian, welfare, and relief work, irrespective of religious, social, political, national, or racial differences. It includes in its membership all women and girls who wish to participate.

The YWCA of the U.S.A. is composed of member associations: community YWCA's (including branches and centers, decentralized units), registered and accredited YWCA's, student associations, and USO-YWCA designations. Each local association governs itself and adopts an appropriate constitution in keeping with the requirements of affiliation with the national organization.

The national board of the YWCA of the U.S.A. unites the autonomous member associations into an effective, continuing national organization for furthering the purpose of the national association. The board administers triennial conventions for the development of a national program. At the April 1970 convention, a program for action for 1970–1973 based on one imperative, the elimination of racism, was adopted. It is this imperative that guides the association as it develops and expands programs to eliminate poverty; end war; build peace; reshape the quality of the environment; revolutionize society's expectations of women and their own self-perception; and involve youth intentionally in leadership and decision-making.

The national board acts as a clearinghouse for ideas from the community and student associations; it serves as a link between local YWCA's and the associations overseas; it represents associations of the United States in the World YWCA; and it publishes the organization's literature. Through its placement services and through assistance in training personnel, the National YWCA helps secure professional staffs for the local associations. Program aid is given through field visits, materials, and conferences for both staffs and volunteers.

Membership. Membership in the YWCA is open to any girl or woman 12 years of age or over, from any economic, racial, occupational, religious, or cultural group. All women of the campus community may join a student association. All dues-paying members 17 years old or older have voting privileges. Boys and men may become YWCA associates and take part in coeducational activities, especially in recreation, education, discussion, and community projects. There are over 2.5 million members in the YWCA of the U.S.A.

Community and student associations and smaller units derive most of their financial support from the United Way and the rest from membership dues and fees for community services. They in turn provide the national board with most of its income. The balance comes principally from earnings on investments and gifts from individuals, foundations, and corporations.

History. What is today the worldwide Young Women's Christian Association was founded in 1855 in London to provide homes for young workingwomen. The first YWCA residence was the North London Home, or General Female Training Institute. At the same time, the Prayer Union for Women and Girls was organized. By 1859 these two were merged under the name of Young Women's Christian Association. The movement spread rapidly. In 1858 the first U.S. group was organized in New York City; in 1866 the name Young Women's Christian Association appeared in Boston for the first time in America.

The YWCA has its headquarters at 600 Lexington Avenue, New York, N.Y. 10022.

EDITH M. LERRIGO

YUGOSLAVIA

The basis for all education in Yugoslavia is the 1958 General Law of Education, which stresses the socialist-communist orientation of education. According to this law, education is designed to enable the younger generations to contribute to the strengthening of the socialist system, to encourage the forming of superior citizens, and to foster the spirit of brotherhood, unity, equality, and patriotism.

By law, attendance is compulsory for Yugoslavs between the ages of seven and 15; the law may also be fulfilled by the completion of eight years of schooling. However, the law is not well enforced in isolated rural areas.

Structure. The 1958 law divides Yugoslav education into the categories of preprimary schools, primary schools, secondary schools, and institutions of higher education.

The language of instruction (Serbo-Croatian, Slovenian, or Macedonian) and the alphabet (Latin or Cyrillic) used in a particular school are those of the region. However, the dominant language—Serbo-Croatian—is also taught in the schools whose mother tongue is different; in such cases, the alphabet used in teaching Serbo-Croatian is that which is not used for the mother tongue.

Preprimary and primary schools. Preschool institutions, of which there are different types, generally accept children from the ages of three to six. At the age of seven the Yugoslav child is enrolled in an elementary school—an eight-year institution where it exists in its entirety. Although considerable progress has been made since the 1950's to expand educational opportunities in the country, a four-year primary education is still all that is available in some isolated regions. Such places, however, are becoming increasingly rare. Where the conditions do not as yet permit the organization of an eight-year program, complementary schools often have been formed. Complementary schools are extensions of the primary schools and may offer one, two, or even three years of additional work (that is, grades 5, 6, and 7).

Primary schools are also frequently found in the large cities. There, however, they form a part of the total school system of the community and are not considered terminal education. Graduates of these urban four-year schools ordinarily continue their education at either of two types of institutions; they may enroll in grade 5 of an *osmoletka* (a primary school having all eight grades) and there continue their studies to graduation, or they may enter an eight-year *gymnasium* (a secondary school containing grades 5 to 12). In either event all students take exactly the same comprehensive education courses, as the work in the junior course of the secondary school (the first four years) corresponds exactly to the material studied by pupils in the last four years of elementary school. Students completing the junior course of the *gymnasium* are given the same certificate as the graduates of the *osmoletka*, the "little baccalaureate" (*mala matura*).

Secondary schools. Several possibilities are open to students completing their eight-year elementary schooling. Some go to work immediately in agriculture or in industry, and some become apprentices in a craft or a trade. Some enroll in a vocational school. Many choose to complete the last four years of the *gymnasium*, a step which will admit them to the universities, the higher professional schools, and the art academies.

Higher education. Higher education is divided into three levels and lasts anywhere from three to six years, depending upon the particular curriculum. First-level studies, generally two years in length, train individuals for work of a practical nature and at the technician level. Second-level studies, again usually two years in duration, produce engineers, doctors, lawyers, and other professionals who have completed the requirements for specialized work. The third level of studies represents advanced training in a specific field and lasts from one to two years depending upon the faculty (that is, department) where the work is being taken. First-level and second-level studies may be combined into one program whose curriculum is usually four years in length (with the exception of forestry, which is three years in length, and medicine, which is five years in length). By law all university faculties must offer second-level work but may determine for themselves which of the other levels, if any, they will also offer. (Most faculties do offer work at more than one level and also have arrangements for part-time students.) Third-level studies culminate in a master's degree if the student's program is research-oriented; if the program is professionally oriented, the student receives a diploma which indicates that he has had further specialization as a practitioner in his chosen field. The doctor's degree is awarded to the graduate of second-level studies who has written and successfully defended a dissertation or to the graduate of third-level studies who can demonstrate, to the satisfaction of the faculty awarding the degree, that he has published papers clearly demonstrating his ability to do scholarly research in his chosen field. Usually some time must pass after he has completed the particular level of studies before he is awarded the doctorate. A thesis and its successful defense are required in both cases. Advanced research is generally carried out in specific research institutes, most of which are affiliated nominally or directly with an institution of higher learning.

Applicants to universities and professional schools generally must have successfully completed their secondary studies or the equivalent. Other applicants may be admitted if they can pass a special entrance examination.

Enrollments. In the mid-1960's more than 14,395 elementary schools enrolled approximately 3.1 million pupils; more than 345 *gymnasiums* enrolled more than 150,000 students; approximately 1,385 vocational schools enrolled more than 325,000 students; more than 95 teacher-training schools handled more than 25,000 students; more than 45 secondary art schools enrolled 5,000 students; and more than 1,220 schools (for adults, supplementary education, and special training) enrolled 93,000 students.

Administration. The National Federal Assembly is the supreme organ of government in Yugoslavia; its deputies are chosen from the six republics and two autonomous provinces. The assembly consists of five chambers; national policies relating to education are determined by the Chamber of Education and Culture. However, the Federal Executive Council, a group composed of at least ten deputies from the National Federal Assembly, has broad jurisdiction over the passing of legislation and decrees in many areas, including education. The actual administration of education at the national level rests with the Federal Secretariat for Education and Culture, which serves as the administrative arm of the Chamber of Education and Culture and the Federal Executive Council in carrying out decisions relating to education. The implementation of national laws and regulations, including those on education, is the responsibility of the republics, autonomous provinces, and smaller local bodies.

Each republic or province has its own assembly and executive council whose responsibilities are similar at their level to those of the National Federal Assembly and the National Executive Council. In addition, each republic and province has a council for education (or a council for education and culture), part of whose work concerns the development and improvement of education within its political jurisdiction. It is at the district and local (commune) level, however, that most of the educational policies are actually carried out. Both district and commune people's committees have the right to establish schools to meet their own needs. Once a school is established by such a body it usually remains that particular body's responsibility. A district people's committee, for example, must solve educational problems, draft necessary educational regulations, and generally finance and supervise the schools under its jurisdiction. A commune people's committee fulfills similar obligations toward its educational institutions.

The solution to problems specific to a school are usually worked out by the school board of the particular institution. A Yugoslav school board (*shkolski odbor*) is almost always the direct governing body for no more than one institution. Its membership, which numbers between seven and 21, is extremely complex in composition and includes representatives from the people's committee, the citizens of the district, certain economic, social, and professional groups, the council of teachers, and, sometimes, pupils from the upper grades. The director of the school serves as an ex officio member.

Each school also has a council of teachers (consisting of all of the teachers in the school), which meets in regular sessions convened by the director of the school. The council is governed by a constitution which delimits its activities and responsibilities. In addition, in the *gymnasiums* and in schools having grades 4 to 8, the pupils have their own organizations on a room, grade, and schoolwide basis.

School inspections. The work of each school is scrutinized by a well-developed system of inspections. This system operates at both the republic level and the local level. School inspections fulfill supervisory and counseling functions, with the latter function receiving increasing emphasis. The specific duties of district inspectors (or educational counselors, as they are now called) are to help teachers improve their teaching methods, to suggest ways of utilizing more effectively the required programs of study, and to make certain that all laws and regulations are being carried out. Furthermore, the district counselors evaluate the program of each school in relation to educational developments in the district as a whole. The inspector-counselors of each republic usually assist local school leaders in implementing broad educational policies.

School finance. The financing of the schools is basically the responsibility of each locality and republic. The federal government does not provide funds for the direct support of any school in the country, although it does provide assistance for the development of certain sections of the country; this assistance may include funds for education. Generally, then, the financial support of the schools, except for teachers' salaries, is the responsibility of their founders: the people's committee of the district, the municipality, the commune, or the social or economic organization. Since most often the commune is the political body which founds schools (especially elementary schools), the people's committee of the commune usually must pay for the schools' maintenance. This support covers expenses for new construction, school equipment and furniture, and educational materials. The pay of the teachers, however, is generally the responsibility of the district or the municipality.

Curricula. Curriculum development in Yugoslavia takes place at the republic level, and each republic's Ministry of Education is responsible for such development in its territory. In actual practice, however, the Federal Institute for the Study of School and Educational Problems issues a suggested guide which is adapted by the educational officers of each republic and applied to the regional situation.

The curriculum includes the broad areas of basic education, general technical training, and free activities. Basic education includes the study of the mother tongue (reading, writing, and speaking), mathematics, socialist morality, foreign languages, physical education, art, music, and domestic science. Topics relating to science and the social studies are covered in the first three grades in an area of study called getting acquainted with nature and society. In grade 4 this area is divided into two separate subareas known as getting acquainted with society (a type of social studies course) and getting acquainted with nature (a type of general science course). Foreign-language instruction is compulsory and begins in grade 5. In general, students choose English, French, German, or Russian; individual schools may offer only one or two of these languages. Beginning with grade 6, history and geography become separate subjects, and beginning with grade 7, physics, chemistry, and biology are taught separately.

General technical education—work in industrial and agricultural arts—is given to all pupils in every grade of the elementary school. During the first three years the fundamentals of this subject are provided through its integration in all the other areas of schoolwork, with no special time allotment being given to the program. Starting with the fourth grade, general technical education is given a block of time in the school curriculum.

In an attempt to expand the work of the school into other areas, the program of free activities (introduced into the curriculum after World War II) permits children to specialize in a particular activity or activities. These free activities are closely related to the Pioneer Organization (the national patriotic, socialist-communist organization in the schools), from which many of them stem. The exact activities included in the program vary from school to school, but a progressive school might have sections or interest groups in any or all of the following areas: photography, history, instrumental music, folklore, singing, school publications, sports and physical culture, the Izvidnitzi (a coeducational, paramilitary, and patriotic scout group), handicrafts, shop, nature study, mathematics, and agriculture. It might also have a chapter of the People's Youth, an organization for older pupils. Each teacher is usually assigned to work with a section according to his own interest and training.

Instructional methods. Yugoslav classroom instructional methods continue along traditional lines for the most part. These teaching techniques usually fall into three basic—although by no means mutually exclusive—categories:

(1) those involving demonstration and observation;
(2) those requiring a verbal presentation of some type;
(3) those using printed textual materials.

Of these three categories, verbal presentation appears to be widely used, especially its two variant forms of lecture and catechism. In addition to the above methods, pupil participation and field trips are widely used in general technical training and in the program of free activities.

Instructional materials. The most important instructional tool in Yugoslav schools continues to be the textbook. Textbooks must follow the course of study adopted by the republic and are selected for publication on the basis of open competitions for book manuscripts (announced in the republic's newspapers and school journals). Thus, all texts must be approved by the republic's Ministry of Education prior to publication and must bear its imprimatur on the front page. Such other teaching aids as television, radio, tapes, models, and experimental equipment are gradually becoming more widely available to the schools.

Teacher-training programs. Teachers are trained in different kinds of institutions in Yugoslavia depending upon their ultimate professional objectives and the grade level at which they plan to teach.

Prospective teachers for the first four grades of the elementary school usually receive their training in the normal schools for teachers; an eighth-grade diploma and a satisfactory mark in competitive examinations given by individual institutions of higher learning are required for admission. Teachers for the upper four elementary grades generally are trained in the higher teacher-training schools (which require three or four years of secondary education before a student may enroll in them). Prospective elementary school teachers who desire to specialize in the teaching of particular academic subjects usually receive their education at the appropriate faculty of the university. However, before these subject-matter specialists can teach in the elementary schools they must also have training in education. Teachers for the last four years of the secondary schools often have university training in their disciplines but no pedagogical training.

The total amount of time required for graduation from most teacher-training schools is six years; in some cases it is seven. Schools which have seven-year programs are termed pedagogical academies, and when the reorganization of the six-year schools is completed to include a seventh year, these schools will comprise the work of both the normal schools and the higher teacher-training schools.

The title by which a teacher is known depends upon the amount of education he has received. A teacher who has completed a three-year or four-year program has the title of *uchitel*; one who has graduated from a higher teacher-training institution or a pedagogical academy is given the title of *nastavnik*; and one who has completed the second-level program at a university is generally referred to as professor, even though he may be teaching elementary school. The title of professor is also used for the highest level of university staff members. Graduates of teacher-training schools are usually placed in their initial teaching position through their institutions, but experienced teachers may seek their own positions. The district people's committees and the republic's Ministry of Education usually serve as clearinghouses at their particular level for teacher vacancies.

BIBLIOGRAPHY

"Education in Yugoslavia" 1960 *Foreign Education Digest*, 25, no. 2:1–9.

GEORGEOFF, PETER JOHN 1964 "Yugoslav Youth and Student Organizations." *Comparative Education Review*, 8, no. 1:104–111.

GEORGEOFF, PETER JOHN 1967 "Patterns of Educational Administration and Supervision in Yugoslavia." *Political Scientist*, 3, no. 2:97–104.

ROUČEK, JOSEPH SLABEY 1957 "Tito's Educational Experiences and Experiments." *Educational Forum*, 21, no. 2 (part 1):193–201.

ROUČEK, JOSEPH SLABEY, AND KENNETH V. LOTTICH 1964 *Behind the Iron Curtain; The Soviet Satellite States: East European Nationalisms and Education.* Caldwell, Idaho, Caxton Printers.

"The Development of the School System in Yugoslavia" 1962 *Foreign Education Digest*, 26, no. 4:29–33.

U.S. OFFICE OF EDUCATION 1963 *Education in Yugoslavia and the New Reform: Legal Basis, Organization, Administration, and Program of the Secondary Schools.* Bulletin 1963, No. 20. Washington, D.C., Government Printing Office.

U.S. OFFICE OF EDUCATION 1962 "Yugoslavia." *Ministries of Education: Their Functions and Organizations.* By Kathryn G. Heath. Bulletin 1961, No. 21. Washington, D.C., Government Printing Office. Pages 633–639.

PETER JOHN GEORGEOFF

Z

ZAMBIA

Located in south-central Africa, Zambia (known as Northern Rhodesia until independence in 1964) was administered from 1899 to 1924 under royal charter by the British South Africa Company; was governed from 1924 to 1953 by the British Colonial Office; joined Southern Rhodesia (now Rhodesia) and Nyasaland (now Malawi) in the Federation of Rhodesia and Nyasaland from 1953 to 1963; and became the Republic of Zambia on October 24, 1964. About 98 percent of its population is composed of members of 73 African tribes; Europeans, mainly from Great Britain and South Africa, comprise 1 percent; and the remainder is made up of Asians and Eurafricans.

Organization and structure. During the federation period, European, Asian, and Eurafrican education for the three territories was under one federal ministry; each territory administered its own African schools. After independence and under the Education Act of 1966, the Zambian dual school system was amalgamated; the former federal schools (for Europeans, Asians, and Eurafricans) were designated fee-paying schools, and African schools were called non–fee-paying schools. The achievement of greater parity between fee-paying and non–fee-paying schools was attempted by reducing the non–fee-paying course from eight to seven years, by instituting common syllabi and academic standards, and by introducing English as the language of instruction in the first school year in non–fee-paying schools (four main vernaculars had previously been used as the languages of instruction in the African primary schools).

Primary education. The seven-year primary school consists of a four-year lower level (grades 1 through 4) for children between the ages of seven and 11, and a three-year upper level (grades 5 through 7) for children between the ages of 11 and 13. Study in primary schools leads to the primary school leaving certificate examination. In the late 1960's more than 600,000 pupils were enrolled annually in primary school.

Secondary education. The Zambian secondary school is divided into junior and senior levels. The junior level consists of a two-year general secondary course (forms 1 and 2, for students aged 14 to 16) leading to the junior secondary school leaving certificate examination and a three-year trade-training course (forms 1 through 3) leading to the trades test certificate examination. The senior secondary level consists of three courses: a three-year general secondary course (forms 3 through 5, for students between the ages of 16 and 18) leading to the Cambridge overseas school leaving certificate examination; a two-year teacher-training course (forms 3 and 4, for students aged 16 and 17) leading to the teachers' certificate examination for primary grades; and a three-year technical secondary course (forms 3 through 5, for students between the ages of 16 and 18) leading to the Cambridge overseas school leaving certificate examination. In the late 1960's more than 40,000 students were enrolled annually in secondary school programs.

Postsecondary and higher education. Postsecondary education includes a three-year teacher-training course leading to the teachers' certificate for secondary schools and a three-year technical training course leading to the technical certificate. Adult education is provided for more than 28,000 Zambians annually.

Admission to the University of Zambia, opened in March 1966, is made on the basis of the student's performance on the Cambridge overseas leaving certificate examination, ordinary level, in English and four other subjects. There are three-year courses at the university in the humanities, social sciences, and natural sciences; courses lead to the B.A. degree. A diploma in social work is offered, and a one-year postgraduate certificate of education course is also provided. The university also includes a five-year school of engineering and a seven-year school of medicine.

Administration and finance. The minister of education is responsible for most Zambian schools and adult education; excepted are education of the handicapped (which is under the Ministry of Labor and Social Development), mass literacy programs (which are under the Department of Community Development), and the training of youths not in school (which is controlled by the Ministry of Co-operatives, Youth, and Social Development). The permanent secretary of the Ministry of Education is assisted by undersecretaries, school inspectors, and a planning-unit staff. There is a chief education officer in each of the country's nine administrative regions; along with 75 percent of administrative and senior school personnel, the officers are Zambians. The three classes of schools include government schools, which are financially maintained and administered by the government through chief education officers; aided schools, which are financially maintained by the government but administered by the 16 missionary societies authorized to manage schools (all such schools are non–fee-paying—that is, mainly African—and comprise the bulk of the total school enrollment); and private schools, which are administered by private agencies, some of which charge tuition fees. The annual education budget represents about 23 percent of the national budget.

Trends and problems. A United Nations economic survey report published in 1964 indicated that in terms of high-level African manpower, Zambia is one of the least educated countries in Africa. According to the report, of those Zambians over 21, half the men and over four-fifths of the women had never been to school. According to the 1963 census, 75 percent of the males and 93 percent of the females over age 16 had less than four years of primary education; fewer than 14,000 Zambian Africans had received any secondary education. Of the 256,000 African males in wage-earning employment in Zambia at the time

of the government's 1963 census, fewer than 10,000 had been to secondary school; most of the labor force had a maximum of four years of schooling; and more than one-third were unschooled and illiterate. Many African leaders in Zambia attribute their country's educational shortcomings to economic discrimination during the ten-year federation period, charging that the bulk of income from Zambia's copper resources was drained off to benefit Southern Rhodesia's industries instead of going toward Zambian educational development.

To meet trained manpower needs, Zambia aimed, in its 1966–1970 National Development Plan, to provide every seven-year-old child with a place in a primary school, to allow all youths in urban areas to complete the full seven-year primary course, and to allow 75 percent of those in rural areas to complete the full seven-year primary course. On the secondary level the aim was for two-thirds of the junior secondary school students to proceed to the senior secondary school, leaving one-third to enter technical schools or employment. The aim was further to direct as many graduates as possible after form 5 to teacher-training colleges and to the University of Zambia. To meet this anticipated educational expansion, the recurrent expenditure on education was expected to rise to 7.5 percent of the gross domestic product by 1970.

Since independence, Zambia has been in the process of amalgamating the smaller, elite-oriented, mainly urban, compulsory school system for European, Asian, and Eurafrican pupils with the larger, mainly rural, noncompulsory African school system. It is apparently achieving this unity without sacrificing academic standards. An essential part of the strategy to accomplish this amalgamation has been to introduce English as the language of instruction for Africans from the first year of school; the English Medium Center (established in 1966) has been preparing teaching materials and methods to aid this transition. Zambia's expansion of secondary school places, its indigenous publishing of textbooks reflecting African interests and African countries, and its anticipated expansion under the 1966–1970 National Development Plan may help the nation achieve its educational goals ahead of schedule. The prize bestowed on Zambia by nature is copper, whose price fluctuates and which may be supplanted by new materials. So long as copper remains in demand, Zambia needs to invest in rural areas and in technical education to effect an agricultural and technical revolution.

BIBLIOGRAPHY

PARKER, FRANKLIN 1961 "Education in the Federation of Rhodesia and Nyasaland." *Journal of Negro Education*, 30, no. 3:286–293.

PARKER, FRANKLIN 1968 "Zambia: Education and National Development." Robert Murray Thomas, Lester B. Sands, and Dale L. Brubaker, eds., *Strategies for Curriculum Change: Cases From 13 Nations*. Scranton, Pa., International Textbook Company. Pages 228–250.

UNITED NATIONS. ECONOMIC COMMISSION FOR AFRICA AND FOOD AND AGRICULTURAL ORGANIZATION 1964 *Report of the UN/ECA/FAO Economic Survey Mission on the Economic Development of Zambia*. Lusaka, Government Printer.

FRANKLIN PARKER